THE
MILITARY
BALANCE
2010

published by

 Routledge
Taylor & Francis Group

for

The International Institute for Strategic Studies

ARUNDEL HOUSE | 13–15 ARUNDEL STREET | TEMPLE PLACE | LONDON | WC2R 3DX | UK

THE MILITARY BALANCE 2010

The International Institute for Strategic Studies

ARUNDEL HOUSE | 13–15 ARUNDEL STREET | TEMPLE PLACE | LONDON | WC2R 3DX | UK

DIRECTOR-GENERAL AND CHIEF EXECUTIVE **Dr John Chipman**
EDITOR **James Hackett**

DEFENCE ANALYSTS
GROUND FORCES **Nigel Adderley**
AEROSPACE **Wg Cdr Andrew Brookes**
MARITIME **Jason Alderwick**
DEFENCE ECONOMIST **Mark Stoker**
CONFLICT **Christopher Langton and Virginia Comolli**

EDITORIAL **Dr Ayse Abdullah, Sarah Johnstone, Dr Jeffrey Mazo, Carolyn West, Jessica Delaney**
DESIGN AND PRODUCTION **John Buck**
CARTOGRAPHER **Steven Bernard**
ADMINISTRATOR **Clara Catherall**
RESEARCH ASSISTANTS **Henry Boyd, Gary Li, Amy Tinley, Bernhard Klingen, Edward Allen, Edward Sherman, Zach Wolfraim, Oliver Hovorka**

This publication has been prepared by the Director-General and Chief Executive of the Institute and his Staff, who accept full responsibility for its contents. The views expressed herein do not, and indeed cannot, represent a consensus of views among the worldwide membership of the Institute as a whole.

FIRST PUBLISHED February 2010

© The International Institute for Strategic Studies 2010

ISBN 978-1-85743-557-3
ISSN 0459-7222

The *Military Balance* (ISSN 0459-7222) is published annually by Routledge Journals, an imprint of Taylor & Francis, 4 Park Square, Milton Park, Abingdon, Oxfordshire OX14 4RN, UK. The 2010 annual subscription rate is: UK£121 (individual rate), UK£248 (institution rate) UK£236 (online only); overseas US$202 (individual rate), US$437 (institution rate), US$414 (online only).

A subscription to the institution print edition, ISSN 0459-7222, includes free access for any number of concurrent users across a local area network to the online edition, ISSN 1479-9022.

Dollar rates apply to subscribers in all countries except the UK and the Republic of Ireland where the pound sterling price applies. All subscriptions are payable in advance and all rates include postage.

Journals are sent by air to the USA, Canada, Mexico, India, Japan and Australasia. Subscriptions are entered on an annual basis, i.e. January to December. Payment may be made by sterling cheque, dollar cheque, international money order, National Giro, or credit card (Amex, Visa, Mastercard).

Please send subscription orders to: USA/Canada: Taylor & Francis Inc., Journals Department, 325 Chestnut Street, 8th Floor, Philadelphia, PA 19106, USA. UK/Europe/Rest of World: Routledge Journals, T&F Customer Services, T&F Informa UK Ltd., Sheepen Place, Colchester, Essex, CO3 3LP, UK.

The print edition of this journal is printed on ANSI conforming acid-free paper by Bell & Bain, Glasgow, UK.

CONTENTS

Index of **TABLES**

Index of **MAPS**

Index of **FIGURES**

The Military Balance 2010
Editor's Foreword

Defence in a complex operating environment

The decision by US President Barack Obama to increase the deployment of US troops in Afghanistan by a further 30,000 marked the end of a period of uncertainty over the future of US strategy in that country. The move to bolster ISAF forces came on top of an earlier US 'surge' in 2009, as well as changes in senior military leadership designed to increase the tempo of counter-insurgency (COIN) operations. This strategy has 'the protection of the Afghan population' as its core objective with the accelerated training of Afghan national security forces as the key mission. It also aims to enable a phased drawdown of US forces from 2011.

The war remains contentious in the US, as well as in many other capitals of ISAF-contributing nations. The pace and volume of Afghan security-force training is increasing, enabled by the surge, though criticism remains over corruption and poor governance within Afghan institutions. Afghan and international casualties, meanwhile, continue to rise, with the issue of civilian casualties being of particular concern to US General Stanley McChrystal. Achievement of some success through the strategy will be crucial to maintain US congressional support, and thus funding for the overall effort. The definition of success is still subject to some debate, with generally accepted yardsticks focusing on increases in the training and retention of indigenous security forces. Continued US engagement is vital to maintain the wider international coalition, though some governments, pressed by domestic political constituencies and fear of 'mission creep', may adjust the form of their support. For others, the enhanced US engagement gave political and military backing that could allow them to renew and deepen their own contributions.

Ongoing military operations in Afghanistan, like those in Iraq, have forced a reassessment of the place held by COIN and stability operations in military planning; some doctrines are now drafted with these operations firmly in mind. But the 'transformational' military technologies so much discussed earlier in the decade within the context of the 'revolution in military affairs' (RMA) are not now necessarily secondary; rather, such technologies are now viewed by many as being a key component of, rather than comprising a 'framework' for, the application of military force. 'Information dominance' and advances in networking capacities remain important for militaries, but the lessons of recent combat operations have led to an appreciation of the limitations of such ideas in complex operating environments where combat is often undertaken at close quarters. Further, there is increasing appreciation of the need to better understand the operating environment – linguistically, historically, culturally and politically. Doing so could help establish the long-term relationships with host communities needed to generate trust and influence, foster the growth of local security and leadership capacity, and encourage effective civil-society organisations that can in turn assist in generating longer-term political maturity. The challenge is to take the RMA concept and mould it to the needs of COIN and other forms of twenty-first century warfare. In short, there is an acknowledgement that militaries should continually evolve rather than necessarily seek revolutionary capability enhancements; added to this is a need to accelerate and continually evaluate force-development processes.

Perceptions about organisational and doctrinal flexibility and leader education are changing. Militaries such as the US are beginning to give troops some flexibility in adjusting approaches to better suit uncertain conditions at the tactical, operational and strategic levels. Some responsibilities are being devolved onto troops at differing levels of command; the US Army uses the term 'decentralisation' in this context. While decentralisation may allow for greater flexibility of action within stabilisation and COIN operations, improved military education in the more traditional sense – in leadership training as well as more formal trade training – will remain essential for militaries requiring personnel to operate increasingly sophisticated equipment.

In the US, organisational depth, changes in the senior leadership and an increasingly influential and devolved 'lessons-learned' structure have aided a shift in thinking. Leaders are now saying that US forces should ready themselves for irregular warfare as well as 'high-end asymmetric threats' in an era characterised by uncertainty, complexity and persistent conflict. (How much the fundamental nature of conflict has actually changed has also been questioned.) For the US, these judgements are informed by a greater appreciation of the conflicts in which it is currently, or is likely to be, involved. Of course the potential for conflict with nations possessing considerable conventional-force capability as well as so-called 'asymmetric capabilities', remains a concern, as are the forces required for such eventualities. Some argue that maintaining conventional-force capabilities is not only critical for ensuring military effectiveness, but is also an essential component of conflict prevention. Others argue that a debate over developing either irregular or conventional-warfare capabilities is not useful because of a convergence of non-state and state-based capabilities, continuous shifts in the character of conflict such that wars resist clear categorisation, and the need for military forces to be able to employ a broad range of joint and combined-arms capabilities across the 'spectrum of conflict'. Militaries also have to consider emerging issues such as cyber warfare and the potential consequences of climate change.

Appraisals of the likely nature of future conflict and future adversaries, and the planning implications of this, may for the US lead to choices concerning the balance of capabilities within its armed forces. The Quadrennial Defense Review (QDR) process is expected to end in early 2010. Analysts believe that the defence department may in the QDR give emphasis to countering the challenge from hybrid threats or high-end asymmetric threats, and will increase moves to procure and rapidly field larger numbers of diverse, lower-specification platforms instead of the 'ever more baroque' platforms criticised by Secretary of Defense Robert Gates.

For other nations lacking the same organisational capacity, equipment or financial resources, similar assessments of future conflict may lead to choices over what type of militaries they want and are able to support, particularly given tight finances; in some cases this may lead to a reappraisal of the foreign- and security-policy aspirations that military forces are intended to support. In the United Kingdom, for instance, faced with a challenging fiscal environment, the upcoming defence review will likely be driven by consideration of these policy aspirations, but also by budget constraints: British ambitions and capabilities have reached a point of divergence and tough choices on both military plans and procurement need to be taken.

In other countries, even some that have participated in recent military operations, defence debates were animated by differing sets of issues. Australia's 2009 defence White Paper, for instance, was written amidst a widespread perception in analytical and policy circles that the distribution of power in the Asia-Pacific and Indian Ocean was in flux, with the document outlining significant capability improvements for the period to 2030. In Latin America, some of the aspirations in Brazil's 2008 national-defence strategy are related to that nation's place among the 'BRIC' group of emerging market economies. Meanwhile, China's most recent defence White Paper, issued in 2008, underlined the growing confidence of the People's Liberation Army, pointing out that China had reached a 'historic turning point' and was playing a major role in the international security order.

Many national defence developments are informed by a perception of the limited effectiveness of regional security institutions. This is the case in Southeast Asia and Australasia, where states have persisted with efforts to enhance military capacities, even in the face of a depressed global economy. Latin America is host to a number of military and security arrangements of which the most recent, the South American Defence Council, could do more to create a long-term agenda resistant to hijacking by sub-regional and single-issue concerns. African institutions remain weak, as do the military capabilities of African states. But some structural progress has been made with moves to establish regional standby forces, while instances of improved neighbourhood cooperation, such as that between Rwanda and the DRC over the capture of the rebel leader Laurent Nkunda, have been a positive development. NATO, meanwhile, remains the most successful security institution of the last 60 years, but its involvement in current conflicts is raising questions about the Alliance's institutional durability and future military direction. Such questions will be addressed in NATO's new strategic concept, due to be agreed in 2010. But for many of the nations committed to military operations under NATO's banner, economic realities may increasingly have a bearing on the shape of both their military contributions and their national military structures.

The transformation of the world's economic fortunes from steady growth to rapid contraction happened with extraordinary speed. In the fourth quarter of 2008, the global economy contracted at an annual rate of 6.25%, unemployment rates rose and budget deficits ballooned. The worst-affected countries were in the industrialised world, particularly those heavily dependent on exports: in 2009 the Japanese economy is estimated to have contracted by 5.4%, Germany's by 5.3% and the United States' by 3.4%. On the other hand, emerging economies – particularly in Asia – have withstood the financial turmoil better than expected. Economic stimulus measures and progress in stabilising financial institutions and markets succeeded in halting the slide by the end of the year. Tentative signs of recovery emerged, though the IMF said that the global economy would still contract by 1.1% in 2009, the first annual decline since the Second World War.

In terms of defence and security spending, the impact of the financial crisis has varied across regions and countries. Russia was hit hard by the recession, its economy contracting by some 7.5% in 2009. The government recorded a budget deficit for the first time in many years. As a result, a comprehensive re-equipment plan due to run from 2007–15 has effectively been abandoned and will be replaced with a new ten-year plan starting in 2011. In the US, where defence spending had almost doubled under the G.W. Bush administration, a budget deficit of 12.5% of GDP in 2009 marked the end of this phase of rising defence spending. Both Obama and Gates have signalled that fiscal realities will necessitate a dramatic reprioritisation within defence spending. In contrast to developments in advanced economies, both India and China have maintained their recent trend of double-digit increases in defence spending, with India boosting defence spending by 21% in 2009 following the Mumbai attacks. Other Asian states, such as Australia, Indonesia and Singapore, have also posted increases. In Europe, the introduction of stimulus packages contributed to an increase in budget deficits. Across the euro area, deficits in 2009 are estimated to have reached 6.2% of GDP compared to the target of 3% of GDP, and the UK is expected to have recorded a deficit of 11.6% of GDP.

When the time comes to redress these fiscal imbalances, discretionary spending will come under considerable pressure and defence is likely to suffer, particularly in those countries facing a looming demographic shift requiring greater expenditure on pensions and healthcare. The UK faces a challenge in reconciling its fiscal position with its large and growing future equipment plan. Among European members of NATO only Norway and Denmark are likely to increase their defence budgets in 2010, and over the medium term most other countries will do well to increase defence spending in line with inflation or match existing budget levels. Therefore, there will be financial pressure to step up pooling and multinational management of assets, role specialisation for niche capabilities and collective procurement of critical assets.

James Hackett
Editor, *The Military Balance*

The Military Balance 2010
Preface

The Military Balance is updated each year to provide an accurate assessment of the military forces and defence economics of 170 countries. Each edition contributes to the provision of a unique compilation of data and information enabling the reader to discern trends through the examination of editions back to the first edition in 1959. The data in the current edition are according to IISS assessments as at November 2009. Inclusion of a territory, country or state in *The Military Balance* does not imply legal recognition or indicate support for any government.

GENERAL ARRANGEMENT AND CONTENTS

The Editor's Foreword contains a general comment on defence matters and a summary of the book.

Part I of *The Military Balance* comprises the regional trends, military capabilities and defence economics data for countries grouped by region. Thus North America includes the US and Canada. Regional groupings are preceded by a short introduction describing the military issues facing the region. There is an essay on the defence industry in India. There are tables depicting aspects of defence activity including selected major training exercises, non-UN and UN multinational deployments, total US aircraft holdings, international defence expenditure, and the international arms trade.

Part II comprises reference material.

There are maps showing selected deployments in Iraq, Afghanistan, China's military regions and Mexico's military regions.

The loose Chart of Conflict is updated for 2009 to show data on recent and current armed conflicts, including fatalities and costs.

USING THE MILITARY BALANCE

The country entries in *The Military Balance* are an assessment of the personnel strengths and equipment holdings of the world's armed forces. Qualitative assessment is enabled by relating data, both quantitative and economic, to textual comment. The strengths of forces and the numbers of weapons held are based on the most accurate data available or, failing that, on the best estimate that can be made. In estimating a country's total capabilities, old equipment may be counted where it is considered that it may still be deployable.

The data presented each year reflect judgements based on information available to the IISS at the time the book is compiled. Where information differs from previous editions, this is mainly because of changes in national forces, but it is sometimes because the IISS has reassessed the evidence supporting past entries. An attempt is made to analyse the factors prompting these changes in the text that introduces each regional section, but care must be taken in constructing time-series comparisons from information given in successive editions.

In order to interpret the data in the country entries correctly, it is essential to read the explanatory notes beginning on page 8.

The large quantity of data in *The Military Balance* has been compressed into a portable volume by the extensive employment of abbreviations. An essential tool is therefore the alphabetical index of abbreviations for data sections, which starts on page 487.

ATTRIBUTION AND ACKNOWLEDGEMENTS

The International Institute for Strategic Studies owes no allegiance to any government, group of governments, or any political or other organisation. Its assessments are its own, based on the material available to it from a wide variety of sources. The cooperation of governments of all listed countries has been sought and, in many cases, received. However, some data in *The Military Balance* are estimates.

Care is taken to ensure that these data are as accurate and free from bias as possible. The Institute owes a considerable debt to a number of its own members, consultants and all those who help compile and check material. The Director-General and Chief Executive and staff of the Institute assume full responsibility for the data and judgements in this book. Comments and suggestions on the data and textual material contained within the book are always welcomed and should be communicated to the Editor of *The Military Balance* at: IISS, 13–15 Arundel Street, London WC2R 3DX, UK. Suggestions on the style and method of presentation are also much appreciated.

Readers may use data from *The Military Balance* without applying for permission from the Institute on condition that the IISS and *The Military Balance* are cited as the source in any published work. However, applications to reproduce portions of text, complete country entries, maps or complete tables from *The Military Balance* must be referred to the publishers. Prior to publication, applications should be addressed to: Taylor and Francis, 4 Park Square, Milton Park, Abingdon, Oxon, OX14 4RN, with a copy to the Editor of *The Military Balance*.

The Military Balance 2010
Explanatory Notes

ABBREVIATIONS AND DEFINITIONS

Abbreviations are used throughout to save space and avoid repetition. The abbreviations may be both singular or plural; for example, 'elm' means 'element' or 'elements'. The qualification 'some' means up to, while 'about' means the total could be higher than given. In financial data, '$' refers to US dollars unless otherwise stated; billion (bn) signifies 1,000 million (m). Footnotes particular to a country entry or table are indicated by letters, while those that apply throughout the book are marked by symbols (* for training aircraft counted by the IISS as combat-capable, and † where serviceability of equipment is in doubt). A list of abbreviations for the data sections appears in the reference section (page 487).

COUNTRY ENTRIES

Information on each country is shown in a standard format, although the differing availability of information and differences in nomenclature result in some variations. Country entries include economic, demographic and military data. Population aggregates are based on the most recent official census data or, in their absence, demographic statistics taken from the US Census Bureau. Data on ethnic and religious minorities are also provided in some country entries. Military data include manpower, length of conscript service where relevant, outline organisation, number of formations and units and an inventory of the major equipment of each service. This is followed, where applicable, by a description of the deployment of each service. Details of national forces stationed abroad and of foreign forces stationed within the given country are also detailed.

ARMS PROCUREMENTS AND DELIVERIES

Tables at the end of the regional texts show selected arms procurements (contracts and, in selected cases, contracts involved in major development programmes) and deliveries listed by country buyer, together with additional information including, if known, the country supplier, cost, prime contractor and the date on which the first delivery was due to be made. While every effort has been made to ensure accuracy, some transactions may not be fulfilled or may differ – for instance in quantity – from those reported. The information is arranged in the following order: land; sea and air.

GENERAL MILITARY DATA

Manpower

The 'Active' total comprises all servicemen and women on full-time duty (including conscripts and long-term assignments from the Reserves). When a gendarmerie or equivalent is under control of the MoD, they may be included in the active total. Under the heading 'Terms of Service', only the length of conscript service is shown; where service is voluntary there is no entry. 'Reserve' describes formations and units not fully manned or operational in peacetime, but which can be mobilised by recalling reservists in an emergency. Unless otherwise indicated, the 'Reserves' entry includes all reservists committed to rejoining the armed forces in an emergency, except when national reserve service obligations following conscription last almost a lifetime. *The Military Balance* bases its estimates of effective reservist strengths on the numbers available within five years of completing full-time service, unless there is good evidence that obligations are enforced for longer. Some countries have more than one category of 'Reserves', often kept at varying degrees of readiness. Where possible, these differences are denoted using the national descriptive title, but always under the heading of 'Reserves' to distinguish them from full-time active forces.

Other forces

Many countries maintain paramilitary forces whose training, organisation, equipment and control suggest they may be used to support or replace regular military forces. These are listed, and their roles described, after the military forces of each country. Their manpower is not normally included in the Armed Forces totals at the start of each entry. Home Guard units are counted as paramilitary. Where paramilitary groups are not on full-time active duty, '(R)' is added after the title to indicate that they have reserve status.

Units and formation strength

Company	100–200
Battalion	500–800
Brigade (Regiment)	3,000–5,000
Division	15,000–20,000
Corps (Army)	60,000–80,000

Non-state groups

In keeping with the last edition, *The Military Balance* lists within the book selected non-state groups which pose a militarily significant challenge to state and international security. For more information see the IISS Armed Conflict Database.

Equipment

Quantities are shown by function and type, and represent what are believed to be total holdings, including active and reserve operational and training units and 'in store' stocks. Inventory totals for missile systems – such as surface-to-surface missiles (SSM), surface-to-air missiles (SAM) and anti-tank guided weapons (ATGW) – relate to launchers and not to missiles. Stocks of equipment held in reserve and not assigned to either active or reserve units are listed as 'in store'. However, aircraft in excess of unit establishment holdings, held to allow for repair and modification or immediate replacement, are not shown 'in store'. This accounts for apparent disparities between unit strengths and aircraft inventory strengths.

Deployments

The Military Balance mainly lists permanent bases and operational deployments including peacekeeping operations, which are often discussed in the text for each regional section. Information in the country data files detail deployments of troops and military observers and, where available, the role and equipment of deployed units; tables 36 and 37 in the country-comparisons section constitute fuller listings of UN and non-UN deployments, including of police and civilian personnel. In these tables, deployments are detailed by mission, by region, and with the largest troop contributing country at the head of the list.

GROUND FORCES

The national designation is normally used for army formations. The term 'regiment' can be misleading. It

Principal Ground Equipment Definitions

The Military Balance uses the following definitions of equipment:

Main Battle Tank (MBT). An armoured, tracked combat vehicle, weighing at least 16.5 metric tonnes unladen, that may be armed with a turret-mounted gun of at least 75mm calibre. Any new-wheeled combat vehicles that meet the latter two criteria will be considered MBTs.

Armoured Combat Vehicle (ACV). A self-propelled vehicle with armoured protection and cross-country capability. ACVs include:

Armoured Infantry Fighting Vehicle (AIFV). An armoured combat vehicle designed and equipped to transport an infantry squad, armed with an integral/organic cannon of at least 20mm calibre. Variants of AIFVs are also included and indicated as such.

Armoured Personnel Carrier (APC). A lightly armoured combat vehicle, designed and equipped to transport an infantry squad and armed with integral/organic weapons of less than 20mm calibre. Variants of APCs converted for other uses (such as weapons platforms, command posts and communications vehicles) are included and indicated as such.

(Look-a-like. The term 'look-a-like' is used to describe a quantity of equipment, the precise role of which is unknown, but which has the basic appearance – and often employing the chassis – of a known equipment type.)

Artillery. A weapon with a calibre greater than 100mm for artillery pieces, and 60mm and above for mortars, capable of engaging ground targets by delivering primarily indirect fire. The definition also applies to guns, howitzers, gun/howitzers, multiple-rocket launchers.

Principal Naval Equipment Definitions

To aid comparison between fleets, the following definitions, which do not necessarily conform to national definitions, are used:

Submarines. All vessels equipped for military operations and designed to operate primarily below the surface. Those vessels with submarine-launched ballistic missiles are also listed separately under 'Strategic Nuclear Forces'.

Principal Surface Combatant. This term includes all surface ships with both 1,000 tonnes full-load displacement and a weapons system for purposes other than self-protection. All such ships are assumed to have an anti-surface-ship capability. They comprise aircraft carriers (defined below); cruisers (over 8,000 tonnes) and destroyers (less than 8,000 tonnes), both of which normally have an anti-air role and may also have an anti-submarine capability; and frigates (less than 8,000 tonnes), which normally have an anti-submarine role. Only ships with a flight deck that extends beyond two-thirds of the vessel's length are classified as aircraft carriers. Ships with shorter flight decks are shown as helicopter carriers.

Patrol and Coastal Combatants. These are ships and craft whose primary role is protecting a state's sea approaches and coastline. Included are corvettes (500–1,500 tonnes with an attack capability), missile craft (with permanently fitted missile-launcher ramps and control equipment) and torpedo craft (with anti-surface-ship torpedoes). Ships and craft that fall outside these definitions are classified as 'patrol' and divided into 'offshore' (over 500 tonnes), 'coastal' (75–500 tonnes), 'inshore' (less than 75 tonnes) and 'riverine'. The prefix 'fast' indicates that the ship's speed can be greater than 30 knots.

Mine Warfare. This term covers surface vessels configured primarily for mine laying or mine counter-measures (such as mine-hunters, minesweepers or dual-capable vessels). They are further classified into 'offshore', 'coastal', 'inshore' and 'riverine' with the same tonnage definitions as for 'patrol' vessels shown above.

Amphibious. This term includes ships specifically procured and employed to disembark troops and their equipment onto unprepared beachheads by such means as landing craft, helicopters or hovercraft, or directly supporting amphibious operations. The term 'Landing Ship' (as opposed to 'Landing Craft') refers to vessels capable of an ocean passage that can deliver their troops and equipment in a fit state to fight. Vessels with an amphibious capability but not assigned to amphibious duties are not included.

Support and Miscellaneous. This term covers auxiliary military ships. It covers four broad categories: 'underway support' (e.g. tankers and stores ships), 'maintenance and logistic' (e.g. sealift ships), 'special purposes' (e.g. intelligence-collection ships) and 'survey and research' ships.

Merchant Fleet. This category is included in a state's inventory when it can make a significant contribution to the state's military sealift capability.

Weapons Systems. Weapons are listed in the following order: land-attack missiles, anti-surface-ship missiles, surface-to-air missiles, guns, torpedo tubes, other anti-submarine weapons, and helicopters. Missiles with a range of less than 5km, and guns with a calibre of less than 76mm, are not included. Exceptions may be made in the case of some minor combatants with a primary gun armament of a lesser calibre.

Aircraft. All armed aircraft, including anti-submarine warfare and maritime-reconnaissance aircraft, are included as combat aircraft in naval inventories.

Organisations. Naval groupings such as fleets and squadrons frequently change and are often temporary organisations and are shown only where it is meaningful.

Principal Aviation Equipment Definitions

Different countries often use the same basic aircraft in different roles; the key to determining these roles lies mainly in aircrew training. In The Military Balance the following definitions are used as a guide:

Fixed Wing Aircraft

Fighter. This term is used to describe aircraft with the weapons, avionics and performance capacity for aerial combat. Multi-role aircraft are shown as fighter ground attack (FGA), fighter, reconnaissance, and so on, according to the role in which they are deployed.

Bomber. These aircraft are categorised according to their designed range and payload as follows:

Long-range. Capable of delivering a weapons payload of more than 10,000kg over an unrefuelled radius of action of over 5,000km;

Medium-range. Capable of delivering weapons of more than 10,000kg over an unrefuelled radius of action of between 1,000km and 5,000km;

Short-range. Capable of delivering a weapons payload of more than 10,000kg over an unrefuelled radius of action of less than 1,000km.

Some bombers with the radius of action described above, but designed to deliver a payload of less than 10,000kg, and which do not fall into the category of FGA, are described as light bombers.

Helicopters

Armed Helicopters. This term is used to cover helicopters equipped to deliver ordnance, including for anti-submarine warfare.

Attack Helicopters. These have an integrated fire-control and aiming system, designed to deliver anti-armour, air-to-surface or air-to-air weapons.

Combat Support. Helicopters equipped with area-suppression or self-defence weapons, but without an integrated fire-control and aiming system.

Assault. Armed helicopters designed to deliver troops to the battlefield.

Transport Helicopters. The term describes helicopters designed to transport personnel or cargo in support of military operations.

---

can mean essentially a brigade of all arms; a grouping of battalions of a single arm; or a battalion group. The sense intended is indicated in each case. Where there is no standard organisation, the intermediate levels of command are shown as headquarters (HQ), followed by the total numbers of units that could be allocated to them. Where a unit's title overstates its real capability, the title is given in inverted commas, with an estimate given in parentheses of the comparable unit size typical of countries with substantial armed forces. For guidelines for unit and formation strengths, see p. 9.

Military formations

The manpower strength, equipment holdings and organisation of formations such as brigades and divi-sions differ widely from country to country. Where possible, the normal composition of formations is given in parentheses. It should be noted that where both divisions and brigades are listed, only independent or separate brigades are counted and not those included in divisions.

NAVAL FORCES

Categorisation is based on operational role, weapon fit and displacement. Ship classes are identified by the name of the first ship of that class, except where a class is recognised by another name (such as *Udaloy*, *Petya*). Where the class is based on a foreign design or has been acquired from another country, the original class name is added in parentheses as is the country of origin. Each class is given an acronym. All such designators are included in the list of abbreviations. The term 'ship' refers to vessels with over 1,000 tonnes full-load displacement that are more than 60m in overall length; vessels of lesser displacement, but of 16m or more overall length, are termed 'craft'. Vessels of less than 16m overall length are not included. The term 'commissioning' of a ship is used to mean the ship has completed fitting out and initial sea trials, and has a naval crew; operational training may not have been completed, but otherwise the ship is available for service. 'Decommissioning' means that a ship has been removed from operational duty and the bulk of its naval crew transferred. Removing equipment and stores and dismantling weapons, however, may not have started. Where known, ships in long-term refit are shown as such.

AIR FORCES

The term 'combat aircraft' refers to aircraft normally equipped to deliver air-to-air or air-to-surface ordnance. The 'combat' totals include aircraft in operational conversion units whose main role is weapons training, and training aircraft of the same type as those in front-line squadrons that are assumed to be available for operations at short notice. Training aircraft considered to be combat capable are marked with an asterisk (*). Armed maritime aircraft are included in combat-aircraft totals. Operational groupings of air forces are shown where known. Squadron aircraft strengths vary with aircraft types and from country to country.

DEFENCE ECONOMICS

Country entries in Part I include defence expenditures, selected economic performance indicators and demographic aggregates. There are also international comparisons of defence expenditure and military manpower, giving expenditure figures for the past three years in per capita terms and as a % of GDP. The aim is to provide an accurate measure of military expenditure and the allocation of economic resources to defence. All country entries are subject to revision each year, as new information, particularly regarding defence expenditure, becomes available. The information is necessarily selective.

Individual country entries show economic performance over the past two years, and current demographic data. Where these data are unavailable, information from the last available year is provided. Where possible, official defence budgets for the current year and previous two years are shown, as well as an estimate of actual defence expenditures for those countries where true defence expenditure is thought to be considerably higher than official budget figures suggest. Estimates of actual defence expenditure, however, are only made for those countries where there are sufficient data to justify such a measurement. Therefore, there will be several countries listed in *The Military Balance* for which only an official defence budget figure is provided but where, in reality, true defence-related expenditure is almost certainly higher.

All financial data in the country entries are shown both in national currency and US dollars at current year, not constant, prices. US-dollar conversions are generally, but not invariably, calculated from the exchange rates listed in the entry. In some cases a US-dollar purchasing power parity (PPP) rate is used in preference to official or market exchange rates and this is indicated.

Definitions of terms

Despite efforts by NATO and the UN to develop a standardised definition of military expenditure, many countries prefer to use their own definitions (which are often not made public). In order to present a comprehensive picture, *The Military Balance* lists three different measures of military-related spending data.

- For most countries, an official defence budget figure is provided.
- For those countries where other military-related outlays, over and above the defence budget, are known, or can be reasonably estimated, an additional measurement referred to as defence expenditure is also provided. Defence expenditure figures will naturally be higher than official budget figures, depending on the range of additional factors included.
- For NATO countries, an official defence budget figure as well as a measure of defence expenditure (calculated using NATO's definition) is quoted.

NATO's definition of military expenditure, the most comprehensive, is defined as the cash outlays of central or federal governments to meet the costs of national armed forces. The term 'armed forces' includes strategic, land, naval, air, command, administration and support forces. It also includes other forces if these forces are trained, structured, and equipped to support defence forces and which are realistically deployable. Defence expenditures are reported in four categories: Operating Costs, Procurement and

Construction, Research and Development (R&D) and Other Expenditure. Operating Costs include salaries and pensions for military and civilian personnel; the cost of maintaining and training units, service organisations, headquarters and support elements; and the cost of servicing and repairing military equipment and infrastructure. Procurement and Construction expenditure covers national equipment and infrastructure spending, as well as common infrastructure programmes. R&D is defence expenditure up to the point at which new equipment can be put in service, regardless of whether new equipment is actually procured. Foreign Military Aid (FMA) contributions of more than US$1 million are also noted.

For many non-NATO countries the issue of transparency in reporting military budgets is fundamental. Not every UN member state reports defence budget data (even fewer real defence expenditures) to their electorates, the UN, the IMF or other multinational organisations. In the case of governments with a proven record of transparency, official figures generally conform to the standardised definition of defence budgeting, as adopted by the UN, and consistency problems are not usually a major issue. The IISS cites official defence budgets as reported by either national governments, the UN, the OSCE or the IMF.

For those countries where the official defence budget figure is considered to be an incomplete measure of total military-related spending, and appropriate additional data are available, the IISS will use data from a variety of sources to arrive at a more accurate estimate of true defence expenditure. The most frequent instances of budgetary manipulation or falsification typically involve equipment procurement, R&D, defence industrial investment, covert weapons programmes, pensions for retired military and civilian personnel, paramilitary forces and non-budgetary sources of revenue for the military arising from ownership of industrial, property and land assets.

The principal sources for national economic statistics cited in the country entries are the IMF, the Organisation for Economic Cooperation and Development (OECD), the World Bank and three regional banks (the Inter-American, Asian and African Development Banks). For some countries basic economic data are difficult to obtain. The Gross Domestic Product (GDP) figures are nominal (current) values at market prices. GDP growth is real, not nominal, growth, and inflation is the year-on-year change in consumer prices. Dollar exchange rates are annual averages for the year indicated except 2009 where the latest market rate is used.

Calculating exchange rates

Typically, but not invariably, the exchange rates shown in the country entries are also used to calculate GDP and defence budget and expenditure dollar conversions. Where they are not used, it is because the use of exchange rate dollar conversions can misrepresent both GDP and defence expenditure. For some countries, PPP rather than market exchange rates are sometimes used for dollar conversions of both GDP and defence expenditures. Where PPP is used, it is annotated accordingly.

The arguments for using PPP are strongest for Russia and China. Both the UN and IMF have issued caveats concerning the reliability of official economic statistics on transitional economies, particularly those of Russia, some Eastern European and Central Asian countries. Non-reporting, lags in the publication of current statistics and frequent revisions of recent data (not always accompanied by timely revision of previously published figures in the same series) pose transparency and consistency problems. Another problem arises with certain transitional economies whose productive capabilities are similar to those of developed economies, but where cost and price structures are often much lower than world levels.

Arms trade

The source for data on the global and regional arms trade is the US Congressional Research Service (CRS). It is accepted that these data may vary in some cases from national declarations of defence exports which is due in part to differences in the publication times of the various sets of data and national definitions of military-related equipment.

Chapter One
North America

THE UNITED STATES

Although incoming US President Barack Obama took office in January 2009, within weeks of his election victory in November 2008 he had indicated that Dr Robert Gates would continue to serve as defence secretary. Soon after the inauguration, Obama acceded to the recommendations of Gates, General David Petraeus and other key officials in revising the Iraq plan that had been central to his presidential campaign. Rather than remove all US combat forces within 16 months of the inauguration, Obama decided to take 19 months, to proceed slowly in drawing down troops throughout 2009, and to plan to retain the equivalent of five combat brigades in Iraq after the drawdown was complete. (Those brigades, called Advisory and Assistance Brigades, are modified versions of traditional combat formations with trainers and advisers, though retaining significant combat capability.)

Afghanistan has been a focus of some of the key defence debates in the new administration. On 27 March, the president unveiled a strategy that required roughly a doubling of US combat forces, agreeing with Pentagon recommendations to replace General David McKiernan (the original architect of the plan to bolster US forces as part of a transition to a more traditional counter-insurgency approach) with General Stanley McChrystal. McChrystal's 'Initial Assessment' on assuming command of the International Security Assistance Force (ISAF), made public in September 2009, served to sharpen the debate, with its stress on the need for additional resources (see Afghanistan, p. 343). In April, and continuing the attention on procurements noted in *The Military Balance 2009*, Gates announced several major changes in Pentagon policy. These included cuts or cancellations of some major weapons platforms such as the Army's Future Combat System (FCS), the F-22 aircraft, and several missile-defence systems, and at least modest increases in other programmes, notably the F-35 Joint Strike Fighter.

Doctrine and policy
The context for current decision-making has in some ways been set by Gates's actions since assuming office in December 2006. As of November 2009 the National Defense Strategy of August 2008 remained the most recent major US document on defence doctrine. Even when the next Quadrennial Defense Review (QDR) is completed and submitted (possibly in conjunction with the release of the 2011 budget request to Congress in February 2010), Gates's 2008 strategy will continue to have a powerful legacy. The National Defense Strategy emphasised the centrality of the counter-terrorist campaign, saying that 'for the foreseeable future, winning the Long War against violent extremist movements will be the central objective of the U.S.'. While some analysts reported that the document may have met resistance in some quarters of the military (with willingness to support large standing forces, and the purchase of systems such as mine-resistant ambush-protected vehicles (MRAPs) over longer, more-established programmes perhaps being less than wholehearted), Gates pushed back against such ideas. Nonetheless, when Gates delivered his statement on the defence budget in May 2009, after Obama's five-year budget plan for the military suggested capping future Pentagon budget growth at roughly the rate of inflation, there was minimal criticism from the uniformed services. This was a reflection of Gates's credibility, the fact that these proposals had already been aired in his April budget recommendation statement, the firm White House support that he clearly enjoyed and perhaps also his willingness to deal strongly with those deemed unsuccessful in post (see *The Military Balance 2009*, p. 13).

Gates's initial plan, prior to the QDR, to cut back on a number of weapons systems included many specifics. He proposed to halt further production of airborne laser aircraft, a key element of American missile-defence architecture. He would end procurement of the C-17 transport plane. He would end procurement of the DDG-1000 destroyer with the third vessel. He would defer development of a new bomber, while cancelling the so-called Transformational Satellite Communications programme as well the VH-71 presidential helicopter. Gates had already cancelled the FCS ground-vehicle programme.

But under his proposals Gates is not aiming to slash the defence budget, curtail modernisation or under-fund conventional capacities. According to Deputy Secretary of Defense William Lynn, the 'budget is about 10 percent for irregular warfare, about 50 percent for traditional, strategic and conventional conflict, and about 40 percent for capabilities that span the spectrum'. Funding for war efforts would remain robust. In addition, even after the planned cuts, missile-defence funding would remain roughly 50% larger than under President Ronald Reagan in inflation-adjusted terms, and the scope of some ground-based elements of the programme would be increased. Furthermore, Gates plans to prolong the DDG-51 destroyer programme and accelerate the F-35 programme. He plans to slow down aircraft-carrier production, resulting in an eventual reduction of the fleet from 11 to 10 carriers, but not until 2040. Total weapons-acquisition spending for the United States – that is, procurement plus research, development, testing and evaluation – will continue to be substantial, with annual price tags for these investment purposes remaining around US$200 billion. But while the administration may have hoped to limit budget growth over the next five years roughly to the rate of inflation, the measures proposed by Gates will not be sufficient to achieve this, so the QDR will have to find more savings or the defence-budget top line will have to increase. For 2010, at least, the effective real growth rate is closer to zero, since some of the apparent increase is due to bringing some functions that had been in supplemental appropriations during the Bush years back into the base budget (see Defence Economics, p. 21).

Developing strategy
While the higher priority for near-term operations in Iraq and Afghanistan than for hypothetical hegemonic competition undoubtedly plays a role in prompting these proposals, the QDR will further develop the conceptual framework behind the Obama administration's defence vision. Undersecretary for Defense Michèle Flournoy said in August 2009, after a discussion of existing strategic challenges and key trends, that the US must ready its forces for irregular warfare as well as 'high-end asymmetric threats'. Initial indications are that the Department of Defense (DoD) will give some emphasis in the QDR to countering the challenge from hybrid threats or high-end asymmetric threats, or enemies (both hostile states and non-state actors) that could employ a blend of irregular and asymmetric and futuristic techniques, perhaps in conjunction with more conventional military capabilities and operations (see p. 18). There are also moves towards examining capabilities based on a grounded projection of likely threats in the near future rather than focusing on 'leap-ahead' capabilities often associated with concepts of 'defence transformation' noted in previous defence plans. But these leap-ahead capabilities are still envisaged as an integral part of the overall force mix. As noted in *The Military Balance 2009* (p. 14), 'while the need for state-of-the art systems would not fade, [Gates has] wondered whether specialised, lower-cost, low-tech equipment suited to stability and counter-insurgency operations were also needed'. Another feature of Obama-administration thinking could perhaps be a move away from casting US defence strategy in terms of operational ambition, such as the ability to conduct two wars, one and a half wars, or other formulations. For the DoD, as Flournoy noted, 'the greatest priority, for the next few years, should be given to dealing with the emerging asymmetric challenges clustered at the middle and high end of the spectrum'. The QDR may result in a less catchy slogan to capture its core strategic essence than previous efforts, though perhaps what it will sacrifice in pithiness it will make up for by more accurately diagnosing the wide array of security challenges faced by the US and its allies.

Gates has stated that the US administration has to consider 'the right mix of weapons and platforms to deal with the span of threats we will likely face. The goal of our procurement should be to develop a portfolio – a mix of capabilities whose flexibility allows us to respond to a spectrum of contingencies'. The QDR 'will give a more rigorous analytical framework for dealing with a number of these issues'; this is one reason why Gates has delayed decisions on the 'follow-on manned bomber, the next generation cruiser, as well as overall maritime capabilities'. 'But where the trend of future conflict is clear, I have made specific recommendations.' These views inform his bid to reform the procurement process (see *The Military Balance 2009*, pp. 15–18), which has, according to some analysts, been shaped by his experience in having to procure many MRAP vehicles outside normal Pentagon procurement channels. In his April budget statement, Gates said that the challenges of contemporary battlefields and changing adversaries required 'an acquisition system that can perform with greater flexibility and agility' and 'the ability to streamline our requirements and acquisition execution procedures'. There needed to be a shift away from '99 percent "exquisite" service-centric programs' towards the '80 percent multi-service solution that can be produced on time, on budget and in significant numbers' (see *The Military Balance 2009*, pp. 14–15).

Military readiness

The US military is still under severe strain, notwithstanding all the resources that have been devoted to it, and the attention that Gates has devoted to personnel issues. US forces are substantially larger than those of America's allies, and the army, for instance, is expanding, but they are still suffering some personnel strains given the myriad burdens placed upon them, particularly continuing operations in Iraq and the war in Afghanistan. Despite contentions that US forces are near breaking point, data suggest that, though readiness is fragile and continues to exact a heavy toll on individuals (which may inform future decisions on force allocations and aggregate overseas deployments), it seems to be reasonably good across the force. The stress of continuous operations also, of course, takes its toll on equipment. Although the majority of equipment has not been deployed on operations, the amount that has, as well as the number of specialist platforms employed in particular theatres, means that equipment-reset tasks are of key and continuing importance (see Defence Economics, p. 21).

Personnel

Gates has argued that the US does not face an urgent readiness crisis. That is to say, US forces continue to perform impressively on the battlefield in Afghanistan, and Iraq, suggesting that they are tolerating current strain reasonably well, even at high levels of individual sacrifice. And America's residual airpower and naval power constitute potent deterrents against possible aggression or conflict in Korea, the Persian Gulf or the Taiwan Strait. But the greatest concern is that soldiers and marines will start leaving the force because of excessive deployments; the impact would be amplified if those in question were experienced NCOs and junior officers. The substantial funding allocated to personnel and family issues in the 2009 budget proposals are undoubtedly designed to forestall such trends (Gates noted '$9.2bn in improvements in childcare, spousal support, lodging, and education, some of which was previously funded in the bridge and supplemental budgets'), as are moves by Army Chief of Staff General George Casey to

address soldiers' deployment schedules. Currently, soldiers spend a year deployed and then a year and a half at home before their next rotation. According to Secretary of the Army John McHugh, Casey's plan is to reach a 1:2 ratio in the next few years and, ideally, a 1:3 ratio for the active force and 1:5 for the reserve force in the long term.

The Army's high-school graduation figure for new recruits for 2005 dipped to 83.5% and, according to analysis by the National Priorities Project, the figure continued to decline to just over 70% by 2007. The situation improved in 2008, with figures exceeding 80%, as tougher economic conditions combined with improved battlefield trends helped recruiting, and this upward trajectory continues. That was also the third straight year that the active-duty army met its recruiting goals – admittedly in part because of a worsened general economy, coupled with more bonuses and recruitment waivers on matters such as age and misdemeanour criminal records. In October 2009 Gates was able to report that the army had eliminated most waivers, and was on track to exceed 90% for the proportion of recruits with high-school diplomas for the year. Yet there are also disturbing trends. Suicide is a significant problem for the military, and a tragedy for many troops and their families. The suicide rate rose from 9.1 per 100,000 soldiers in 2001 to 17.3 per 100,000 soldiers in the US Army in 2006, although that was close to the age- and gender-adjusted average for the US population as a whole (for males, for example, the rate was 17.6 per 100,000), and on 30 January 2009 the *Washington Post* reported that the rate reached 20.2 per 100,000 in 2008. In one group of soldiers surveyed in 2008, among those who had been to Iraq on three or four separate tours, 27% displayed signs of post-traumatic stress disorders (after one and two tours the figures were 12% and 18.5% respectively). In mid-2009 the Army launched a study group in conjunction with the National Institute of Mental Health and four academic institutions in a bid to better understand the underlying causes of suicide. An early recommendation was reported to be an increase in the time troops spend at home relative to that deployed. But General Peter Chiarelli, the Army's vice chief of staff, noted that, 'unfortunately, in a growing segment of the Army's population, we've seen increased stress and anxiety manifest itself through high-risk behaviors'.

For US forces in general, the combat burden in the near term may lighten a little, though perhaps not dramatically. As of November 2009 it seemed likely that the combined Iraq–Afghanistan requirements for 2010 and 2011 would keep up to 15 brigade combat teams (BCTs, each 3,000–4,000 strong), plus many support units, engaged and deployed, in contrast to more than 20 at the height of the Iraq War surge, and 17 or 18 in 2003–06. These levels, coupled with an increase in military personnel and overall BCT numbers, mean US ground forces will likely settle into roughly a 1:2 ratio, matching General Casey's preference.

Training

Most soldiers and marines still have little time to do anything other than deploy to Iraq or Afghanistan, return, rest and then prepare to go back (see *The Military Balance 2009*, p. 15), and training other than for the current conflicts is necessarily being neglected. Indeed, recent efforts have been aimed at improving preparation for these current missions through improved coordination across agencies and other refinements of training and operations (as reflected, for example, in the US government's *Counterinsurgency Guide* released in January 2009). Over time, however, the ground forces will need to consider how to balance their development of different skills.

Other developments

The *Counterinsurgency Guide* is an attempt to devise a whole-of-government approach to an area of operations that had hitherto been addressed in scholarly literature or in single-service or departmental doctrines. The guide says it is the 'first serious U.S. effort at creating a national counterinsurgency framework in over 40 years' and is designed to prepare policymakers for the kinds of tasks they might have to carry out if the decision were taken to engage in a counter-insurgency. The guide is an example of the many doctrines being developed in the US military, some in reaction to the lessons that have been drawn from current operations and likely future contingencies. January 2009 also saw the release of a Capstone Concept for Joint Operations (CCJO), which discusses broad potential threats to US security through reference to the 'Joint Operating Environment 2008' and how US joint forces should operate in response to such threats. The CCJO 'envisions a future characterized fundamentally by uncertainty, complexity, rapid change, and persistent conflict', a theme which has also been echoed in the work that the US Army's Training and Doctrine Command has been

carrying out to produce a new Capstone Concept entitled 'Operational Adaptability – Operating Under Conditions of Complexity and Uncertainty in an Era of Persistent Conflict'. This Capstone Concept is intended to provide guidance to senior leaders as they seek to balance the current army so that it can prevail in current conflicts, while also shaping the army of 2016–18 so that it can address a 'combination of hybrid threats, adaptive enemies, and enemies in complex operating environments'. The document is intended to build on the 2005 Capstone Concept, which retained substantial focus on manoeuvre operations and network-enabled capacities, as well as the other documents noted above. In this document, assisting foreign security services is highlighted as a key requirement, while there is emphasis on the need to produce a force that can operate effectively under conditions of uncertainty, with the concept arguing that the way of improving this is to reinforce the importance of understanding situations in depth, decentralisation under the concept of mission command, and the ability to 'develop the situation through action'. The concept also emphasises the importance of leader development and education.

The army is also fielding concepts derived from the lessons of recent campaigns. One example is the Advisory and Assistance Brigade (AAB). These brigades, according to Gates, have 'three main functions: traditional strike capabilities, advisory roles, and the enablers and command and control to support both functions'. Some are already deployed in Iraq, after the Combined Arms Center dramatically reduced the doctrinal cycle, and developed and fielded the AAB doctrine in only a few months. (The intent is that they will comprise the entire US Army operation in Iraq by the end of 2010.) Much of the army's doctrine is now in 'wiki' format so those with recent operational experience can access and update the relevant manuals.

The Military Balance 2009 noted the on-going debate over aspects of the FCS programme, with General Chiarelli saying that the army needed to 'better explain the revolutionary potential' of the FCS ground-vehicle segment. As noted, this component, including eight manned FCS vehicles and the non-line-of-sight cannon, was cut in Gates's budget proposals. The army has adapted to this change by speeding the migration of FCS capacities to infantry soldiers, including tactical and urban unattended ground sensors, the non-line-of-sight-launch system, the Class I UAV, the small unmanned ground vehicle and network kits for the HMMWV. While the budget proposals speeded the deployment of FCS spin-outs to BCTs, much of the rest of the programme is transitioning to a BCT modernisation strategy, with Chiarelli keen to ensure that the FCS programme's network developments in particular are fielded. While the FCS ground-vehicle programme was cut, MRAPs have continued to arrive in large numbers in Afghanistan. In October 2009, the M-ATV, a mine-resistant all-terrain vehicle designed for operations in southern Afghanistan, arrived in Kandahar. According to the army, the M-ATV weighs around 25,000lbs (11,000kg), compared to the original MRAPs at around 60,000lbs (27,000kg). Gates has reiterated that he is committed to the army's ground-vehicle modernisation programme, 'but it has to be done in a way that reflects the lessons we've learned in the last few years about war in the 21st century, and that incorporates the [DoD's] nearly $30billion investment in MRAPs'.

The Military Balance 2009 (p. 16) also highlighted some of the debates under way over US Air Force modernisation programmes. The decision to end production of the F-22 and C-17 gained much attention, but the budget also proposed increasing procurement of the F-35 Joint Strike Fighter, with Gates saying in April that the US would purchase 513 F-35s over the five-year defence plan, with an eventual total of 2,443. The planned fielding of such a large number of advanced fighters led Gates to cast doubt on what some critics perceived as a looming fighter gap after the US retires some 230 aircraft as part of its modernisation programme. These aircraft, together with legacy platforms and growing numbers of UAVs, will, according to Gates, 'preserve American tactical air supremacy far into the future'. But there remains attention within the DoD (as noted above) on the possibility, raised by Gates in 2008, of employing larger fleets of lower-cost, lower-tech aircraft in situations where the US has air dominance. The MC-12 *Liberty*, a multi-mission turboprop containing advanced capacities for intelligence, surveillance and reconnaissance (ISR) duties and deployed to Iraq in June 2009, is perhaps a case in point and, according to a mid September speech by Gates, the air force is 'considering bringing online a fleet of light fighters and cargo aircraft – inexpensive, rugged platforms that can also be used to build local capacity in lift, reconnaissance, and close air support missions, and are also usable and affordable by local partners'. In the

same speech, he announced that source-selection authority was returning to the air force for the KC-X tanker (see *The Military Balance 2009*, p. 16), meaning that, while the procurement process for this aircraft has restarted, the air force will have to maintain its existing, and ageing, KC-135 fleet. Meanwhile, Global Strike Command, announced in October 2008, was activated in early August. Headquartered at Barksdale air base, the new command combines the air force's bombers and intercontinental ballistic missiles (ICBMs) under a single commander. 20th Air Force, with the ICBMs, came under the new command in December 2009, with the 8th Air Force (and the bombers) due to follow in April 2010. The new command was due to reach initial operating capacity in early August 2010.

The budget proposals to restrict the US Navy's DDG-1000 programme to three ships gained much attention, though the rising costs of the platform and dwindling projected buy were perhaps as responsible as questions over the future strategic value of the platform. The QDR will likely address some of the strategic assumptions underpinning naval programmes and employment strategies and will consist, in the words of Secretary of the Navy Ray Mabus, of 'a major examination of our strategy, [and] how we design and deploy our forces' – this coming two years after the navy released *A Cooperative Strategy for 21st Century Seapower*. Mabus also said that the navy will prepare for irregular warfare and hybrid campaigns as well as maintain conventional-warfare capacities. But Gates started the process, and indicated some of his preferences, with the DDG-1000 decision, the move to keep the DDG-51 programme (with its known costs and proven capabilities), accelerating LCS purchases, delaying the navy's CG-X cruiser programme, and delaying amphibious-ship and sea-basing programmes. In the latter two cases the objective behind delaying the programmes was to revisit overall requirements. Future threats were also a major factor behind the establishment of Fleet Cyber Command in October 2009. To be operated by a reconstituted 10th Fleet, this command will be a subordinate unit of the new US Cyber Command, announced by Gates in June, and which will itself report to US Strategic Command. Cyber Command is intended to better coordinate defence of the DoD's vast range of military networks (15,000 networks administered by 90,000 personnel; 7 million computers and IT devices used by about 3m employees).

Nuclear arms control, missile defence and global zero

The key military decisions of the Obama administration are not all being made by the Pentagon. On his first trip to Europe as president in April 2009, Obama gave a major speech in Prague committing himself to the vision of a nuclear-free world. Acknowledging that it might not happen in his lifetime, he nonetheless chose to demonstrate his resolve in pursuing the agenda. Precisely how this will happen remained to be seen, with the Pentagon's nuclear posture review (like the QDR) still incomplete. But, for the time being, Obama has restored some momentum to traditional US–Russian arms control, making offensive arms cuts a priority of his administration, adjusting the structure and deployment of the European missile-defence system planned for Poland and the Czech Republic by the Bush administration, and preparing for a possible effort to pursue ratification of the comprehensive nuclear test-ban treaty (CTBT) in the Senate in 2010. Meanwhile, the US and Russia announced an intention to work towards a legally binding agreement to replace the Strategic Arms Reduction Treaty (START I), which was due to expire on 5 December 2009. At the time of writing no agreement had been announced. US Secretary of State Hillary Clinton said in October that 'the nuclear status quo is neither desirable nor sustainable. It gives other countries the motivation or the excuse to pursue their own nuclear options.'

While pursuing the 67 votes needed for ratification of the CTBT, the administration will also have to finesse the issue of whether to plan on building a lower-yield replacement warhead for ageing American nuclear weapons. This is a matter on which Gates and Obama are believed to disagree, at least in part. Gates's view that some kind of replacement warhead will be necessary over the long term is on record, dating at least to an October 2008 speech just before the presidential election. He agrees with Obama that no such warhead should require testing, and seems to agree that it should not represent a meaningful upgrading or 'modernisation' of the arsenal with any new capabilities such as greater earth-penetration capacity.

Given that the existing warhead inventory is holding up better than many had expected, with plutonium pits or cores ageing less quickly than originally feared, no immediate production of new warheads would seem necessary, even if Gates's general view carries the day. The long-standing stockpile-stew-ardship programme, with an annual cost exceeding US$5bn, has focused on tracking trends in the arsenal to detect any early signs of problems. To date none have emerged that could not be redressed through straightforward methods such as component replacement within the warheads and refreshing tritium stocks in warheads as that element decays radioactively. But the administration has still to resolve its doctrinal position and establish a long-term plan.

Afghanistan

Obama's new Afghanistan strategy is the most important national-security concept of his first year in office. It emphasises classic counter-insurgency principles – protect the population, train and strengthen indigenous institutions – while following the 'clear, hold, build' concept of operations that was ultimately so successful in Iraq during the surge (see Afghanistan, pp. 343–8) In fact, Obama's thinking on Afghanistan is not radical. Gates was promising more US troops for the war in summer 2008, and General McKiernan, before being replaced by General McChrystal, was developing a new counter-insurgency-oriented strategy for Afghanistan even before election day. Obama increased the US military presence in Afghanistan to 68,000 uniformed personnel for an indefinite period, with the possibility of further modest increases thereafter. (The number reached 41,000 shortly after the policy was announced, with 15,000 assigned to ISAF and the other 26,000 part of the *Operation Enduring Freedom* mission; the total reached about 58,000 in June and just under 68,000 by the end of the summer.)

The United States is leading a strong NATO effort to reinforce the south and east of Afghanistan; more specifically, the United States will have what amounts to a '3+2+2' plan by late 2009: roughly three brigades in the east, two in the south, and two more dedicated to training Afghan security forces. The forces added during Obama's first year include a combat aviation brigade and a *Stryker* brigade for Kandahar province, a Marine Expeditionary Brigade (with associated airpower of its own) for Helmand province, and the fourth brigade of the 82nd airborne division to join the existing 48th National Guard Brigade with the Combined Security Transition Command-Afghanistan (CSTC-A) to train Afghan security forces. At most points prior to 2008, in contrast, there were virtually no US forces in southern Afghanistan, and only around 1,000 before the Obama plan was announced; it is also significant that the combat aviation brigade roughly quintuples the airpower available in the area of operations. In December, Obama announced a further 30,000 troops would deploy in 2010. The strategy has 'the protection of the Afghan population' as its core objective with the accelerated training of Afghan national security forces as its key mission. It also aims to enable a phased drawdown of US forces from 2011.

CANADA

Canada has continued to build capabilities and infrastructure consistent with the objectives of the Canada First defence strategy and the demands of current operations (see *The Military Balance 2009*, pp. 18–19, and *Strategic Survey 2009*, pp. 100–3). Internationally, meanwhile, Afghanistan remained the Canadian government's primary focus, with nearly 3,000 troops deployed in Afghanistan on *Operation Athena*, the majority in the Kandahar area. But, as noted in *Strategic Survey*, slow progress, high costs and waning domestic support forced the government to maintain its pledge to end Canada's combat mission in Afghanistan in 2011. Prime Minister Stephen Harper said that the government might propose maintaining some Canadian presence in Afghanistan after that date to focus primarily on reconstruction and development. This force might include helicopters, police and army trainers, a Provincial Reconstruction Team and CF-18 fighter aircraft.

Meanwhile, the defence department announced substantial procurement initiatives during 2009. In line with announcements in the Canada First strategy, Ottawa in August issued a contract for the purchase of 15 CH-47F *Chinook* helicopters with a value of approximately C$2.2bn including support and maintenance. The first is due for delivery in 2013. Earlier, in July, plans were announced for the procurement of the 'next generation' of Canadian land-combat vehicles. These projects, called the 'Family of Land Vehicles (FLCV) projects' were valued at around C$5bn. As part of the programme, the existing LAV III fleet would be upgraded and three new vehicle fleets procured (including 'Close Combat Vehicles, Tactical Armoured Patrol Vehicles and Force Mobility Enhancement Vehicles'). It was expected that specific contracts would be awarded by 2011. Infrastructure projects were also announced that would lead to major construction at the Gagetown and Trenton bases (including new maintenance facilities for Canada's C-17s at Trenton). Meanwhile, in July, a

new Combined Air Operations Centre was opened at 1 Canadian Air Division/Canadian NORAD HQ in Winnipeg. This facility was to provide 'operational level command and control of airspace' for the organisation's commander, and it was to be the 'focal point for planning, directing and assessing air and space operations'. As noted in *Strategic Survey 2009* (p. 101), 'securing Canada's arctic has become an increasingly important security objective of the Canadian government', particularly as the possibility of an ice-free Arctic grows, which would make the region more accessible to shipping. Canada has actively tried to assert its sovereignty in its northern territory with various procurement and infrastructure-development plans. However, the emerging positions of other nations indicates that 'Canada will likely face significant political obstacles in its efforts to assert its sovereignty in the region'.

DEFENCE ECONOMICS – UNITED STATES

Over the past year the US economy experienced the worst financial crisis since the Great Depression and plunged into a severe and protracted recession. In the second half of 2008, the collapse of investment bank Lehman Brothers and the forced rescue of US mortgage giants Fannie Mae and Freddie Mac signalled the start of a rapid deterioration in economic activity that saw GDP decline by 6.25% in the fourth quarter and a further 5.5% in the first quarter of 2009. In response to these shocks, US macroeconomic policy shifted to a war footing with the introduction of a broad range of emergency measures led by the Troubled Asset Relief Program (TARP) which provided an initial US$700bn of capital to stressed financial institutions. TARP was accompanied by a swift cut in interest rates to 0% and followed by a fiscal stimulus of more than 5% of GDP, support for the housing market, the introduction of quantitative easing and a host of other measures.

In February 2009, the authorities introduced a Financial Stability Plan that included further support to the housing market, up to US$1 trillion in consumer and business lending, a US$1tr Public–Private Investment Fund and a number of initiatives to improve financial stability, including stress tests to assess banks' resilience and a requirement for increased balance-sheet transparency. The combination of massive macroeconomic stimulus and financial-market intervention succeeded in stabilising financial and economic conditions and in the

Table 1 **US National Defense Budget Authority FY2007–2013**

(US$million)	2007	2008	2009 Base + Bridge	2009 Remaining Supplemental Request	2009 Total	2010 Request Base	2010 Request Overseas Contingency Operations	2010 Request Total
Military Personnel	130,756	139,033	129,805	16,658	146,463	141,079	13,586	154,665
Operations & Maintenance	240,252	256,223	240,072	32,412	272,484	186,334	90,561	276,895
Procurement	133,772	165,006	109,818	22,858	132,676	107,418	23,741	131,159
R,D,T & E	77,548	79,567	80,181	759	80,940	78,634	310	78,944
Military Construction	13,961	22,064	24,081	2,295	26,376	20,987	1,405	22,392
Family Housing	4,024	2,846	3,848	-	3,848	1,959	-	1,959
Other	934	9,976	114	847	961	1,282	397	1,679
Total Department of Defense	**602,247**	**674,715**	**587,919**	**75,829**	**663,748**	**537,693**	**130,000**	**667,693**
Department of Energy (defence-related)	17,189	16,636			22,899			17,671
Other (defence-related)	5,696	4,917			6,973			7,416
Total National Defense	**625,851**	**696,268**			**693,620**			**692,780**

third quarter of 2009 growth had returned, officially bringing the recession to an end. However, inventory restocking is a significant factor in this pick-up in activity and the economy at large remains weak, with unemployment in October 2009 rising above 10% of the workforce. In the medium term, the IMF believes that economic activity will remain subdued in the US as continuing financial strains weigh on investment, unemployment continues to rise, and growth in partner nations is modest.

The fiscal legacy of this crisis will be a high and rising debt that, according to the IMF, could become 'unsustainable without significant medium-term measures'. The government is projected to record a budget deficit of over 10% of GDP in both 2009 and 2010 and US national debt is forecast to jump

to nearly 110% of GDP by 2014. The debt situation created by the crisis would be troublesome enough without the additional fiscal challenge posed by the looming retirement of the 'baby boomer' generation, who began collecting Social Security and Medicare benefits in increasing numbers from 2008. The need to make significant budget adjustments in these circumstances is clear; however, under the George W. Bush presidency government expenditure on non-defence discretionary spending had already fallen near historic lows, suggesting that if any future reductions in overall debt levels are to be achieved then attention will shift to the current high level of defence spending.

Even before the onset of the economic slowdown, the future trajectory of US government finances in

Table 2 **US Defence Expenditure (Budget Authority)** as % of GDP

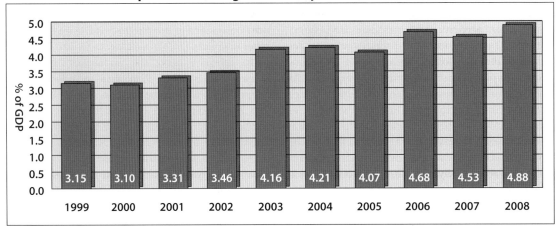

light of the forthcoming demographic 'shock' had already contributed to a debate about the appropriate level of defence spending. Between 2000 and 2009, the US defence budget rose by around 75% in real terms, and jumped from 3.1% to 4.9% of GDP. However, the Congressional Budget Office has regularly warned that future demographic developments suggest spending on discretionary programmes over the long term will come under sustained pressure. While much of the increase in defence spending can be attributed to additional spending on the wars in Iraq and Afghanistan, the Government Accountability Office has repeatedly criticised the DoD for its acquisition process, describing it as 'broken' and adding unnecessary billions to the cost of already-expensive military equipment. Senator Obama added to the debate during the 2008 presidential election campaign when he pledged to trim the defence budget of any excesses and promised a review of all existing programmes to root out waste. In January 2009, Gates gave a glimpse of his thinking when he told the Senate Armed Services Committee that painful choices between defence spending priorities were needed. He complained that, for too long, the Pentagon had emphasised long-term projects to develop near-perfect high-end weapons systems at the expense of being effective at the lower end of the spectrum, adding that he wanted to change this mindset and institutionalise a counter-insurgency focus in the acquisition process which would necessitate awkward decisions about existing programmes and processes. The problem of spiralling procurement costs has occurred at the same time as the decision by the Bush administration to substantially boost military end strength. Additional armed-forces personnel not only raise the immediate salary bill but lead to additional outlays on training, health care and housing and intensify the need for other maintenance and operational expenditure, putting pressure on investment accounts. In the past, a budget squeeze that pitted spending more on weapons programmes against additional outlays on personnel could be resolved by simply increasing defence spending, but in view of the government's dire fiscal position quite how far it would be able to go in that direction was debatable.

In April 2009, Gates laid out a vision for the US military taking into account that in the future the Pentagon will not be able to rely on unlimited resources with which to fight every kind of war. In short, he proposed a measured shift away from a historic emphasis on equipment programmes necessary for the US to fight conventional wars against peer competitors in favour of investment in the sort of equipment and capabilities necessary to fight insurgencies of the type in Iraq and Afghanistan. He made a number of bold proposals that were later confirmed in Obama's FY2010 defence budget request, including:

- Cancelling the VH-71 presidential helicopter.
- Postponing the plan to build a new long-range bomber until more is known about the 'operational requirements' for it.
- Cancelling the Transformational Satellite programme, and buying two additional extremely high frequency communications satellites instead.
- Capping the DDG 1000 programme at three ships, while restarting production of DDG 51 vessels and delaying the CG-X cruiser initiative.
- Cancelling the long-stalled CSAR-X search-and-rescue helicopter and cancelling a second airborne-laser aircraft.
- Cancelling the Future Combat System Manned Ground Vehicle programme.
- Cancelling the multiple-kill vehicle component of the missile-defence programme.
- Halting the procurement of any further F-22 or C-17s.
- Reducing the aircraft-carrier fleet to ten by 2040.
- Increasing purchases of the F-35 from 14 in FY2009 to 30 in FY2010.
- Increasing resources for intelligence, surveillance and reconnaissance assets.

In another affirmation that the defence budget could not continue growing at the pace of recent years, Gates also refused to align himself with the Joint Chiefs of Staff, who during the presidential election campaign had called for an additional US$450bn to be earmarked for defence during the next administration, noting instead that he expected the budget to grow by no more than the rate of inflation in coming years. Less noticeable among all the headline-programme adjustments was the action Gates took to deal with the informal 'unfunded requirements' process by which the services seek to increase their budgets outside of the formal budget-planning system. Every year, the Senate Armed Services Committee invites each service chief to submit a letter telling the committee what they wanted from the regular budget but did not receive. This opaque arrangement had grown

Table 3 **Budget Authority for Iraq, Afghanistan, and Other Global War on Terror Operations FY2001–FY2010 (US$bn)**

Operation and Source of Funding	FY01 & FY02	FY03	FY04	FY05	FY06	FY07	FY08	FY09	FY10 Pending Request	Cumulative Total FY01–FY10 incl. Request
Iraq										
Dept of Defense	0	50.0	56.4	83.4	98.1	126.8	138.3	90.6	61.9	705.5
Foreign Aid & Diplomatic Operations	0	3.0	19.5	2.0	3.2	3.2	1.9	3.0	2.3	37.9
VA Medical	0	0	0	0.2	0.4	0.9	0.9	1.2	1.2	4.7
Total Iraq	**0.0**	**53.0**	**75.9**	**85.5**	**101.7**	**130.8**	**141.1**	**94.8**	**65.4**	**748.2**
Afghanistan										
Dept of Defense	20.0	14.0	12.4	17.2	17.9	37.1	40.6	51.1	68.1	278.3
Foreign Aid & Diplomatic Operations	0.8	0.7	2.2	2.8	1.1	1.9	2.6	3.7	4.0	19.7
VA Medical	0	0	0	0	0	0.1	0.2	0.4	0.9	1.6
Total Afghanistan	**20.8**	**14.7**	**14.5**	**20.0**	**19.0**	**39.1**	**43.4**	**55.2**	**72.9**	**299.6**
Enhanced Security										
Dept of Defense	13.0	8.0	3.7	2.1	0.8	0.5	0.1	0.2	0.2	28.7
Total Enhanced Security	**13.0**	**8.0**	**3.7**	**2.1**	**0.8**	**0.5**	**0.1**	**0.2**	**0.2**	**28.7**
DOD Unallocated	0	5.5	0	0	0	0	0	0	0	5.5
Total All Missions	**33.8**	**81.2**	**94.1**	**107.6**	**212.4**	**170.4**	**184.4**	**150.4**	**138.6**	**1,082.4**

over time so that by 2008 the air force submitted a request for 'unfunded requirements' amounting to US$20bn. Whilst Gates did not ban this system outright, he asked for all correspondence to be first

Table 4 **DoD's War-Enacted Budget Authority FY2008 (US$bn)**

Regular Titles	2008
Military Operations	19.1
Operations & Maintenance	78.3
Defence Health	2.0
Other Defence Programmes	0.3
Procurement	44.8
R,D,T & E	1.6
Working Capital Funds	1.9
Military Construction	2.7
Subtotal: Regular Titles	**150.4**

Special Funds	
Iraqi Freedom Fund	3.8
Afghan Sy Forces Training Fund	2.8
Iraq Sy Forces Training Fund	3.0
Joint IED Defeat Fund	4.3
Strategic Reserve Readiness Fund	0
MRAP Account	16.8
Subtotal: Special Funds	**30.6**

DoD Total	**181.1**

reviewed by him, and revealingly in 2009 the air-force request dropped to less than US$2bn.

Despite these cost-saving initiatives, however, a deep imbalance remains in medium-term defence funding. In August 2009, the DoD confirmed Gates's suggestion that future budget growth would be limited when it instructed military planners to prepare for zero budget growth between FY2011 and FY2015. David Ochmanek, deputy assistant secretary for defense for force transformation and resources, went further when he revealed that work on the 2010 Quadrennial Defense Review had uncovered a deficit of US$60bn between the likely level of funding over the next four years and current spending commitments, even before the massive cost of withdrawing troops from Iraq and possibly Afghanistan was factored into the equation. The non-partisan Congressional Budget Office calculated that to balance its books the Pentagon would need its non-war-related spending over the next 18 years to average 6% more than the amount sought in the FY2010 budget request. Consequently, service chiefs were told to make further cuts over and above the 50 major programme adjustments announced by Gates in April. Given that there appears to be little 'low-hanging fruit' left, though, their room for manoeuvre is limited.

FY2010 National Defence Process

In May 2009, three months later than usual, the contents of Obama's first budget request to Congress were made public. True to his pledge during the election campaign, the FY2010 national-defence request included both a baseline budget proposal of US$587bn together with a further US$130bn to cover overseas contingency operations (OCOs). Under the Bush administration, OCOs had been funded by a separate supplemental appropriation, provoking criticism that total Pentagon funding was becoming less transparent. Once war costs are stripped out, the FY2010 request represents an increase in the base budget in real terms of around 2% over the previous year, which, as Gates made clear, will be the trend in coming years. In line with Gates's April statement, the request did not include funds for procurement of either F-22 or C-17 aircraft or the manned ground-vehicle portion of the FCS, but did include US$5.5bn for the procurement of 1,080 MRAP vehicles and US$2.2bn for an *Aegis*-class ship. Cancellation of the multiple-kill vehicle, airborne-laser and kinetic-energy interceptor resulted in a cut in the missile-defence budget request of US$1.4bn.

The shift in policy outlined by Gates and presented in Obama's budget request was broadly endorsed by both the House and Senate in their respective FY2010 National Defense Authorization bills, in which they acquiesced to most of the programme cuts outlined earlier in the year. Originally, both committees had rejected the call to cease production of the F-22 fighter and to discontinue development of an alternative engine for the F-35 Joint Strike Fighter, despite a warning from the administration that a bill containing either proposal would be vetoed by the president. However, on 23 July the Senate passed its version of the bill after adopting several amendments, including one that would, in effect, end production of the F-22 as the administration had requested. On 7 October a House–Senate conference committee finalised the FY2010 Defense Authorisation Bill which was duly sent to the president, who signed it into law on 28 October.

In signing the FY2010 Defense Authorization Act, Obama claimed partial victory in his battle against wasteful Pentagon spending, declaring that the bill eliminated 'tens of billions of dollars in waste' by cancelling the procurement of several unnecessary weapons systems. He also warned that the bill, although important in tackling waste, was only 'a first step' and that further cuts would be required if the US

Table 5 **US Agency for International Development: International Affairs Budget**

Budget Authority in US$m	FY2008 Actual	FY2009 Estimate	FY2010 Request
Economic Assistance for Europe, Eurasia and Central Asia	690	892	762
Economic Support Fund	5,362	7,017	6,504
International Military Education and Training	85	93	110
Foreign Military Financing	4,718	5,035	5,274
Global Health and Child Survival	6,498	7,189	7,595
Non-proliferation, Anti-terrorism, Demining	496	651	765
International Narcotics Control and Law Enforcement	724	556	1,202
International Disaster and Famine Assistance	956	1,463	1,947
Migration and Refugee Assistance	1,338	1,577	1,480
Total International Affairs (excluding supplementals)	**42,914**	**49,497**	**53,872**

was to 'build the 21st-centruy military we need'. The final authorisation act was very close to the original budget request submitted by Obama, with the exception that it included funds for C-17 transport aircraft and money for the alternative engine for the Joint Strike Fighter, both programmes that Obama and Gates had wanted to terminate.

Just how much weapons-programme reform is achieved in 2009, however, remains to be seen. Under the rather complex US legislative process, the Defense Authorization Act only shapes defence policies and programmes; actual funding limits are detailed in a separate Defense Appropriations Bill. As of November 2009, the House and Senate had both passed their own versions of the FY2010 Defense Appropriations Bill; however, there were major differences that needed to be resolved in the conference process, including:

- C-17 transport aircraft. The House wanted to spend US$674m to buy three; the Senate wanted to spend US$2.6bn to buy ten.
- The alternate Joint Strike Fighter engine. The House voted to spend US$560m on it whereas the Senate voted to spend nothing.
- Presidential helicopter. The House voted to spend US$485m to make five helicopters operational. The Senate called for starting a new programme altogether.
- DDG-51 destroyer. The Senate added US$1.7bn for an additional ship. The House wanted to buy just one.

Table 6 **Major US Research & Development FY2008–FY2010**

Classification	Designation	FY2008 Value ($m)	Estimate FY2009 Value ($m)	Request FY2010 Value ($m)
Joint				
UAV	*Global Hawk*	386	743	783
UAV	*Warrior*	103	62	85
Tpt	C-130	295	206	231
JTRS	Joint Tactical Radio System	831	843	876
	Missile Defense	9,605	9,372	8,186
	Joint Air to Ground Missile	51	118	127
	Small Diameter Bomb	158	145	197
Army				
	Warfighter Information Network	309	393	180
FCS	Future Combat System	3,302	3,380	2,635
Hel	AH-64 *Apache*	185	197	151
APC	*Stryker*	127	80	90
Navy				
EW	F/A-18G *Growler*	269	55	55
FGA	F-35 JSF	1,848	1,744	1,741
Hel	V-22	125	68	89
MPA	P-8A *Poseidon*	861	1,129	1,162
CVN	Carrier Replacement	85	147	173
DDG	DDG 1000	514	449	539
LCS	Littoral Combat Ship	309	368	360
SSN	*Virginia*	239	190	154
AEW	E-2 *Hawkeye*	785	482	364
Sat	MUOS	593	515	387
SAM	Standard	214	237	182
EFV	Amphibious vehicles	240	255	293
Air Force				
Bbr	B-2	278	364	415
Tpt	C-17	166	162	162
Tpt	C-5	174	127	95
FGA	F-22	607	605	569
FGA	F-15	114	198	311
FGA	F-16	77	127	141
FGA	F-35 JSF	1,939	1,734	1,858
Tkr	KC-X	30	23	439
Sat	AEHF	612	386	464
Sat	NAVSTAR GPS	556	789	867
Sat	NPOESS	331	287	396
Sat	SBIRS	583	542	512

- Kinetic Energy Interceptor. The House wanted US$80m to preserve the programme. The Senate, like the White House, wanted to cancel it.

Notwithstanding these unresolved matters, the bulk of the Appropriations Act is likely to mirror very closely the already passed Authorization Act.

So far as the FY2011 budget request is concerned, there is little reason to expect that it will reverse the new direction signposted by the president and his secretary of defense. The 2010 QDR, of course, will flesh out the Pentagon's broader programme for the next four years and is likely to contain further cuts to existing programmes and emphasise the allocation of additional funds to Gates's priority areas: helicopters, civil affairs, persistent ISR and intra-theatre lift. One vulnerable programme is the Marine Corps' Expeditionary Fighting Vehicle (EFV), which has been plagued by technical problems and has increased in cost from US$9bn in 2000 to US$13.7bn in 2009. In addition to cost overruns and delays, the vehicle's utility has come under question following the Marines' experience in Afghanistan – the EFV has a flat bottom, making it vulnerable to improvised explosive devices.

The cost of operations since 11 September 2001

With the enactment of the FY2009 Supplemental in June 2009, Congress has approved a total of about US$944bn for military operations, base security, reconstruction, foreign aid, embassy costs and veterans' health care for the three operations initiated since the 11 September 2001 attacks: *Operation Enduring Freedom* (Afghanistan and other counter-terrorist operations), *Operation Noble Eagle* (enhanced security at military bases), and *Operation Iraqi Freedom*.

For the first time since military operations began in 2001, funding for OCOs (previously the 'global war on terror') was included in the president's budget request. During his election campaign Obama had promised to end the practice of submitting separate supplemental requests to cover OCOs. In recent years there has been heated debate over the use of supplemental appropriations to fund OCOs, with criticism that such funds were increasingly being used to finance regular non-war activities. Historically, DoD financial regulations had defined the cost of OCO-type activities to include only incremental spending directly related to operations. But in October 2006 Deputy Secretary of Defense Gordon England appeared to have given

Table 7 **US National Defense Budget Function[1] and other selected budgets[2] 1992, 2000–2010**

(US$bn)	National Defense Budget Function		Department of Defense		Atomic Energy Defense Activities	Department of Homeland Security	Veterans Administration	Total Federal Government Outlays	Total Federal Budget Surplus/ Deficit
FY	BA	Outlay	BA	Outlay	BA	BA (Gross)	BA		
1992	295.1	298.3	282.1	286.9	10.6	n.a.	33.9	1,381	-290
2000	304.1	294.5	290.5	281.2	12.2	13.8	45.5	1,789	236
2001	335.5	305.5	319.4	290.9	13.0	16.4	47.6	1,863	128
2002	362.1	348.5	344.9	331.9	14.9	30.5	52.1	2,011	-157
2003	456.2	404.9	437.9	387.3	16.4	30.8	59.1	2,160	-377
2004	490.6	455.9	471.0	436.5	16.8	31.6	60.5	2,293	-412
2005	505.7	495.3	483.9	474.1	17.9	100.7	69.2	2,472	-318
2006	617.1	521.8	593.7	499.3	17.4	32.4	71.0	2,655	-248
2007	625.8	551.2	602.9	528.6	17.2	39.7	79.5	2,728	-160
2008	696.3	616.1	674.7	594.6	16.6	50.6	88.3	2,982	-458
2009 est.	693.6	690.3	663.7	664.9	22.9	45.3	97.4	3,997	-1,841
2010 est.	692.8	712.8	667.7	685.1	17.7	41.4	110.1	3,591	-1,258

Notes

FY = Fiscal Year (1 October–September)
[1] The National Defense Budget Function subsumes funding for the DoD, the Department of Energy Atomic Energy Defense Activities and some smaller support agencies (including Federal Emergency Management and Selective Service System). It does not include funding for International Security Assistance (under International Affairs), the Veterans Administration, the US Coast Guard (Department of Homeland Security), nor for the National Aeronautics and Space Administration (NASA). Funding for civil projects administered by the DoD is excluded from the figures cited here.
[2] Early in each calendar year, the US government presents its defence budget to Congress for the next fiscal year, which begins on 1 October. The government also presents its Future Years' Defense Program (FYDP), which covers the next fiscal year plus the following five. Until approved by Congress, the Budget is called the Budget Request; after approval, it becomes the Budget Authority.

the go-ahead for a broader interpretation of war costs when he issued new guidance to service chiefs that they could include requirements appropriate to the 'longer war on terror' in their supplemental requests, rather than limiting requests specifically to the annual costs incurred by operations in Iraq and Afghanistan. The effect of this change is illustrated by the subsequent jump in supplemental procurement requests, which rose from US$18bn in FY2005 to US$64bn in FY2008, and although some of this increase may reflect the cost of additional force protection and replacement of 'stressed' equipment, much may be in response to the new guidance. For example, requests for 'resetting' military equipment used in overseas operations became increasingly difficult to interpret. Resetting is usually limited to the replacement of war-worn equipment; however, the Pentagon's definition of reset has expanded significantly and now includes not only replacing battle losses (typically 10% of the total) and equipment repair (about half), but also recapitalisation that typically upgrades current equipment, and the repair and replacement of pre-positioned equipment stored overseas that has been tapped to meet war needs. Given that the army, in particular, had been planning to recapitalise equipment and modernise pre-positioned equipment stocks to match its new modular configuration, it is questionable whether these costs were indeed wartime requirements.

In addition to US$130bn for DoD activities, the FY2010 war request includes US$6.4bn for the State Department's foreign and diplomatic operations and US$2.1bn for Veterans Administration medical costs for *Operation Enduring Freedom* and *Operation Iraqi Freedom* veterans. On the face of it this would suggest that overall war funding is decreasing from a peak of US$185bn in FY2008, a consequence of the surge strategy in Iraq that year, to US$150bn in FY2009 and US$130bn in FY2010. However, given that the president has authorised a further 30,000 troops for Afghanistan, it seems certain that he will have to return to Congress with an additional supplemental request. In a January 2009 update, the Congressional Budget Office projected that additional war costs for FY2010 to FY2019 could range from US$388bn (if deployed troops fall to 30,000 by 2011) to US$867bn (if troop levels only fall to 75,000 by 2013), meaning that funding for Iraq, Afghanistan, and other OCOs could total US$1.3–1.8tr for 2001–19, depending on the scenario.

Canada CAN

Canadian Dollar $		2008	2009	2010
GDP	C$$	1.60tr	1.53tr	
	US$	1.51tr	1.47tr	
per capita	US$	45,504	44,104	
Growth	%	0.4	-2.5	
Inflation	%	2.4	0.1	
Def exp	C$$	21.0bn		
	US$	19.83bn		
Def bdgt	C$$	18.8bn	21.0bn	20.6bn
	US$	17.78bn	20.19bn	
US$1= C$$		1.06	1.04	

Population   33,487,208

Age	0 – 14	15 – 19	20 – 24	25 – 29	30 – 64	65 plus
Male	9%	3%	3%	3%	24%	6%
Female	9%	3%	3%	3%	24%	7%

Capabilities

ACTIVE 65,722 (Army 34,775 Navy 11,025 Air 19,922)

CIVILIAN 4,554 (Coast Guard 4,554)

RESERVE 33,967 (Army 23,153 (Rangers 4,303), Navy 4,167, Air 2,344)

Canadian Forces operations are organised with four joint operational commands. Canada Command (CANADA-COM) is responsible for all domestic and continental operations through six regional sub-commands. Canadian Expeditionary Force Command (CEFCOM) is responsible for all international operations. Canadian Special Operations Forces Command (CANSOFCOM) is responsible for generating all Special Forces operations and has forces permanently assigned to it. Canadian Operational Support Command (CANOSCOM) has responsibility for generation and employment of the operational-level support to CANADACOM and CEFCOM (and if required CANSOFCOM) for logistics, movements, general engineering, health services, communications, human resource management and military police support either through its permanently assigned forces or through augmented force generation. CANADACOM and CEFCOM normally have no permanently assigned forces allocated for operations but receive them from force generation commands; Maritime Command (MARCOM), Land Force Command (LFC) and Air Command (AIRCOM). Each of these commands have forces normally assigned to them for force generation by the Chief of Defence Staff (CDS) who has full command. Canadian Forces are expanding and the expected strength will be increasing to 70,000 Regular Force members and 30,000 Reserve Force members (less Rangers).

ORGANISATIONS BY SERVICE

Army (Land Forces) 34,775

FORCES BY ROLE

1 Task Force HQ

Comd   1 TF HQ; 3 bde gp HQ and sig sqn to form national or cadre of a multi-national TF HQ or a Land Component Command (LCC) of a joint operation

Mech Inf   1 (Canadian Mechanised) bde gp (1st CMBG) with 1 armd regt, (two *Leopard* 1C2 sqns and 1 armd recce sqn), 2 mech inf bn, 1 lt inf bn, 1 arty regt, 1 cbt engr regt; 2 bde gp (2nd CMBG and 5th CMBG) each with 1 armd recce regt , 2 mech inf bn, 1 lt inf bn, 1 arty regt, 1 cbt engr regt

AD   1 indep regt

Spt/Engr   1 indep regt

Cbt Spt   3 MP pl, 3 MI coy

Logistic   3 svc bn

Med   3 fd amb bn

EQUIPMENT BY TYPE

MBT 121: 20 *Leopard* 2 A6M on lease; 61 *Leopard* 1C2; 40 *Leopard* 2 A4

RECCE 201 LAV-25 *Coyote*

APC 1,142

  APC (T) 332: 64 Bv-206; 235 M-113; 33 M-577

  APC (W) 810: 635 LAV-III *Kodiak* (incl 33 RWS); 175 MILLAV *Bison* (incl 10 EW, 32 amb, 32 repair, 64 recovery)

    MRAP 78: 68 RG-31 *Nyala*; 5 *Cougar*; 5 *Buffalo*

ARTY 295

  TOWED 171 **105mm** 153: 27 C2 (M-101); 98 C3 (M-101); 28 LG1 MK II; **155mm** 18 M-777

  MOR 81mm 100

    SP 81mm 24 *Bison*

AT

  MSL 493

    SP 33 LAV-TOW

    MANPATS 460: 425 *Eryx*; 35 TOW-2A/ITAS

  RCL 84mm 1,075 *Carl Gustav*; M2/M3

  RL 66mm M-72 *LAW*

UAV • TACTICAL *Heron*; *Skylark*

AD

  SAM • SP 33 ADATS

    MANPAD *Starburst*

Land Reserve Organisations 23,153

Canadian Rangers 4,303 Reservists

The Canadian Rangers are a Reserve sub-component of the Canadian Forces, which provide a limited military presence in Canada's northern, coastal and isolated areas. It is a volunteer, part-time force.

Ranger   5 (patrol) gp (165 patrols)

Army	10 (bde gp) HQ
Armd Recce	18 regt
Inf	51 regt
Fd Arty	14 regt, 2 indep bty
Signals	6 regt, 16 indep sqn, 1 EW sqn
Engr	7 regt, 3 indep sqn

Cbt Engr	1 regt
MP	4 coy
Log	10 bn
Medical	14 coy, 4 dets
MI	4 coy

Navy (Maritime Command) 11,025

EQUIPMENT BY TYPE

SUBMARINES SSK 4

4 *Victoria* (ex-UK *Upholder*) each with 6 single 533mm TT each with Mk48 *Sea Arrow* HWT (1 hull currently operational)

PRINCIPAL SURFACE COMBATANTS 15

DESTROYERS • DDG 3 mod *Iroquois* each with 1 Mk 41 VLS with 29+ SM-2 MR SAM, 2 triple ASTT (6 eff.) each with Mk 46 LWT, 1 76mm gun, 2 CH-124 (SH-3) *Sea King* ASW hel

FRIGATES • FFG 12 *Halifax* with 2 quad (8 eff.) with 8 RGM-84 block II *Harpoon* tactical SSM, 2 octuple (16 eff.) Mk 48 *Sea Sparrow* with 16 RIM-7P *Sea Sparrow* SAM, 2 Mk 46 LWT, 2 twin 324mm ASTT (4 eff.) with 24 Mk 46 LWT, (capacity 1 CH-124 (SH-3) *Sea King* ASW hel)

PATROL AND COASTAL COMBATANTS 12

MCDV 12 *Kingston*

LOGISTICS AND SUPPORT 18

AOR 2 *Protecteur* each with 3 CH-124 (SH-3) *Sea King* ASW hel

YDT 8: 2 MCM support; 6 diving tender/spt less than 100 tonnes

TRG 8 *Orca*

FACILITIES

Bases Located at Esquimalt (Pacific), Halifax (Atlantic), Ottawa (National HQ), Quebec City (Naval Reserve HQ). Commanders for MARPAC and MARLANT directly or through their respective at-sea fleet commander, act as the MCC for the operational commands of CANADACOM and/or CEFCOM.

Reserves 4,167 reservists

HQ	1 HQ located at Quebec
Navy	24 div (tasks: crew 10 of the 12 MCDV; harbour defence; naval control of shipping)

Air Force (Air Command) 19,922 (plus 2,344 Primary Reservists integrated within total Air Force structure)

Flying hours 104,939 planned for the year

FORCES BY ROLE

1 CAN Air Division, HQ Winnipeg, is responsible for all CF air op readiness, combat air-spt, air tpt, SAR, MR and trg. This HQ is the ACC HQ for CANADACOM and CEFCOM. 1 CAN Air Div wgs directly support land forces (tac avn and UAV), maritime forces (maritime hel and long range MP), and Special Forces (hel) with OPCOM status. Other wgs undertake directly related air roles (AD, AT, SAR, trg) while remaining under direct 1 CAN Air Div control.

2 CAN Air Div is responsible for Air Force doctrine, initial training and education.

13 Wgs: 1 Wg (Kingston); 3 Wg (Bagotville); 4 Wg (Cold Lake); 5 Wg (Goose Bay); 8 Wg (Trenton); 9 Wg (Gander); 12 Wg (Shearwater); 14 Wg (Greenwood); 15 Wg (Moose Jaw); 16 Wg (Borden); 17 Wg (Winnipeg); 19 Wg (Comox); 22 Wg (North Bay). In addition, an Air Expeditionary Wg (AEW) at Bagotville (up to 550 personnel) will train and deploy together, and will comprise a cmd element, an ops support flt and a mission support flt.

FORCES BY ROLE

Strategic Surveillance	1 (NORAD Regional) HQ located at Winnipeg; 1 Sector HQ at North Bay with 10 North Warning System Long Range; 36 North Warning System Short Range; 4 Coastal; 2 Transportable (total of 52 Radar stn)
Ftr/FGA	3 sqn with CF-18AM/CF-18BM *Hornet* (1 sqn at Bagotville and 2 sqns at Cold Lake)
MP	3 sqn (2 sqn at Greenwood, 1 sqn at Comox) with CP-140 *Aurora**
Spec Ops	1 sqn with CH-146 *Griffon* (OPCON Canadian Special Operations Command)
ASW	3 sqn (2 sqn at Shearwater, 1 sqn at Victoria) with CH-124 *Sea King*
Tpt/SAR	1 tpt sqn with CC-177; 4 tpt/SAR sqns with CC-130E/H/CH-149; 1 tpt/SAR sqn with CC-115; 1 utl sqn with CC-138; 1 tpt sqn with CC-144 *Challenger*
Tkr/Tpt	1 sqn with KC-130H; 1 sqn with CC-150 / CC-150T (A-310 MRTT)
Hel	5 sqns (Edmonton, Borden, Valcartier, St Hubert, Cagetown) with CH-146 *Griffon*; 3 cbt spt sqns (Cold Lake, Bagotville, Goose Bay) with CH-146 *Griffon*
Trg	1 nav trg school in Winnipeg with CT-142 *Dash-8*; 1 SAR trg school in Comox (see also NATO Flt Trg Canada)
UAV	1 unit with CU-170 *Heron* UAV

EQUIPMENT BY TYPE

AIRCRAFT 97 combat capable

FGA 79: 61 CF-18AM *Hornet*; 18 CF-18BM *Hornet*

MP 18 CP-140 *Aurora**

TPT/TKR 7: 2 CC-150T (A-310MRTT); 5 KC-130H

TPT 47: 4 CC-177; 24 C-130E/H (16–E, 8–H, of which 3 grounded); 6 CC-115 *Buffalo*; 4 CC-138 (DHC-6) *Twin Otter*; 6 CC-144B *Challenger*; 3 CC-150 *Polaris*

TRG 4 CT-142 *Dash 8 Nav Trainer*

AIR DEMO 26 CT-144 *Tutor*

HELICOPTERS

SPT 6 CH-147 (CH-47D) *Chinook*

SAR 14 CH-149 *Cormorant*

ASW 28 CH-124 (SH-3) *Sea King*

UTL 85: 7 CH-139 *Jet Ranger*; 78 CH-146 *Griffon* (incl 10 spec ops)

UAV 5 CU-170 *Heron* (leased for 3 yrs)

RADARS 53

AD RADAR • NORTH WARNING SYSTEM 47: 11 Long Range; 36 Short Range

STRATEGIC 6: 4 Coastal; 2 Transportable

MSL

AAM AIM-7M *Sparrow*; AIM-9L *Sidewinder*; AIM-120C AMRAAM

ASM AGM-65 *Maverick*

BOMBS

Conventional: Mk 82; Mk 83; Mk 84

Laser-Guided: GBU-10/ GBU-12/ GBU-16 *Paveway II*; GBU-24 *Paveway III*

NATO Flight Training Canada

AIRCRAFT

TRG 45: 26 CT-156 *Harvard II(T-6A Texan II)*; 19 CT-155 *Hawk* (advanced wpns/tactics trg)

FACILITIES

Trg	1 pilot trg school in Moose Jaw with CT-155 *Hawk*, CT-156 *Harvard II*; 1 pilot trg school in Cold Lake with CT-155 *Hawk*

Contracted Flying Services – Southport

AIRCRAFT

TRG 34: 11 Grob G120A; 7 *King Air* C90B; 7 CT-139 *Jet Ranger*; 9 CT-146 *Outlaw*

FACILITIES

Trg	1 pilot trg school in Southport with Grob 120A, *Jet Ranger/Griffon* and *King Air*

Canadian Special Operations Forces Command 1,500

FORCES BY ROLE

Comd	1 HQ
SF	1 regt (Canadian Special Operations Regiment) located at CFB Petawawa
Counter-Terrorist	1 bn (JTF2) located at Dwyer Hill (CT, Surv, security advice and CP)
Special Ops Avn	1 sqn, with CH-146 *Griffon* located at CFB Petawawa
CBRN	Canadian Joint Incidence Response Unit (CJIRU) located at CFB Trenton

EQUIPMENT BY TYPE

RECCE 4 LAV *Bison* (NBC)

HEL • UTL CH-146 *Griffon*

Canadian Operational Support Command 2,000

Comd	1 HQ
Engr	1 engr support coy
Sigs	CAN Forces Joint Sig Regt (strategic and op signals and info management)
MP	1 (close protection) coy
Log	3 CAN support units; 4 Cdn movement units; 1 postal coy (1 supply, 1 postal, 1 movement unit); 1 CAN Material Support Gp (2x supply depots, 3 ammo depots)
Medical	1 (1 CAN Forces Field Hospital) bn

Canadian Coast Guard 4,554 (civilian)

Incl. Department of Fisheries and Oceans; all platforms are designated as non-combatant.

PATROL AND COASTAL COMBATANTS 60

PSO 4 Type-600

PCO 6: 1 *Tanu*; 2 *Louisbourg*; 1 *Quebecois*; 1 *Arrrow Post*; 1 *Gordon Reid*

PCI 9: 4 Type-400; 3 *Post Class*; 1 *Cumella Class*; 1 Type 200

PB 41: 10 Type 300-A; 31 Type-300B (SAR Lifeboats)

LOGISTICS AND SUPPORT 54

ACV 4 *Penac*

AGB 6

HEAVY ICEBREAKER 2: 1 *Gulf* class Type 1300; 1 *Terry Fox* class Type 1200

MEDIUM RIVER ICEBREAKER 4: 1 Modified R class+ Type 1200; 3 R class Type 1200

AGOR 10 (nearshore and offshore fishery vessels)

AGOS 7

Navaids 24 (incl specialist vessels)

Trg 3

HELICOPTERS

UTL 22: 14 Bo-105; 3 Bell 206L *Longranger*; 4 Bell 212; 1 Sikorsky 61

DEPLOYMENT

AFGHANISTAN

NATO • ISAF • *Operation Athena* 2,830; **Army:** 1 Inf BG with (1 lt inf bn HQ; 3 lt inf coy; 1 armd sqn; 1 armd recce sqn; 1 arty bty; 1 UAV flt; 1 cbt engr sqn); 1 MP coy; 20 *Leopard C2* MBT; some LAV III *Kodiak*; some LAV-25 *Coyote*; 6 M-777; 6 CH 147 *Chinook*; 8 CH-146 *Griffon*; CU-170 *Heron*

Operation Enduring Freedom – Afghanistan (Op Archer) 12

UN • UNAMA (*Operation Accius*) 2 obs

BOSNIA-HERZEGOVINA

NATO • NATO HQ Sarajevo (*Operation Bronze*) 8

OSCE • Bosnia and Herzegovina 2

CYPRUS

UN • UNFICYP (*Operation Snowgoose*) 1

DEMOCRATIC REPUBLIC OF CONGO

UN • MONUC (*Operation Crocodile*) 11 obs

EGYPT

MFO (*Operation Calumet*) 28

GERMANY

NATO (ACO) 287

HAITI

UN • MINUSTAH (*Operation Hamlet*) 5 obs

ISRAEL

USSC (*OperationProteus*) 9

MIDDLE EAST

UN • UNTSO (*Operation Jade*) 7 obs

SERBIA

NATO • KFOR • *Joint Enterprise* (*Operation Kobold*) 6

OSCE • Kosovo 2

SIERRA LEONE

IMATT (*Operation Sculpture*) 7

SUDAN
UN • UNMIS (*Operation Safari*) 8; 21 obs

SYRIA/ISRAEL
UN • UNDOF (*Operation Gladius*) 2

UNITED STATES
US CENTCOM (*Operation Foundation*) 3
US NORTHCOM / NORAD / NATO (ACT) 303

FOREIGN FORCES

United States Army 7; Navy 30; USAF 83; USMC 10

United States US

United States Dollar $		2008	2009	2010
GDP	US$	14.2tr	13.8tr	
per capita	US$	46,913	45,161	
Growth	%	0.4	-2.7	
Inflation	%	3.9	-0.4	
National Def Budget				
BA	US$	696.3bn	693.6bn	
Outlay	US$	551.2bn	690.3bn	
Request				
BA	US$			693.2 bn

Population   304,059,724

Age	0 – 14	15 – 19	20 – 24	25 – 29	30 – 64	65 plus
Male	11%	4%	4%	3%	23%	5%
Female	10%	3%	3%	3%	23%	7%

Capabilities

ACTIVE 1,580,255 (Army 662,232 Navy 335,822 Air 334,342 US Marine Corps 204,261 US Coast Guard 43,598)

CIVILIAN 11,035 (US Special Operations Command 3,376 US Coast Guard 7,659)

RESERVE 864,547 (Army 447,203 Navy 109,222 Air 191,038 Marine Corps Reserve 109,600 US Coast Guard 7,484)

ORGANISATIONS BY SERVICE

US Strategic Command

Combined Service   1 HQ located at Offutt AFB (NE)
Five missions   US nuclear deterrent; missile defence; global strike; info ops; ISR

US Navy
SUBMARINES • STRATEGIC • SSBN 14 *Ohio* (mod) SSBN 730 each with up to 24 UGM-133A *Trident* D-5 strategic SLBM

US Air Force • Air Combat Command
Bbr   6 sqn (incl 1 AFRC) at 2 AFB with 71 B-52H *Stratofortress* each with up to 20 AGM-86B nuclear ALCM and/or AGM-129A nuclear ACM; 2 sqn at 1 AFB with 19 B-2A *Spirit* each with up to 16 free-fall bombs (or up to 80 when fitted with Small Diameter Bombs); 4 B-52 test hvy bbr; 1 B-2 test hvy bbr

Air Force Space Command
Msl   9 sqn at 3 AFB with 500 LGM-30G *Minuteman III* (capacity 1-3 MIRV Mk12/Mk12A per missile)

Strategic Recce/Intelligence Collection (Satellites)
SPACE BASED SYSTEMS
   SATELLITES 63
      IMAGERY 6: 4 *Improved Crystal* (visible and infra-red imagery, resolution 6 inches); 2 *Lacrosse* (*Onyx* radar imaging satellite)
      ELINT/SIGINT 19: 3 *Mentor* (advanced *Orion*; 1 Advanced *Mentor*; 5 *Trumpe*t; 2 *Mercury*; 8 SBWASS (Space Based Wide Area Surveillance System); Naval Ocean Surveillance System
      ELECTRONIC OCEAN RECCE SATELLITE 6: 1 GFO (*Global Follow-On*); 5 DMSP-5
      SATELLITE TIMING AND RANGING 32: 12 NAVSTAR Block I/II/IIA; 20 NAVSTAR Block IIR (components of Global Positioning System (GPS))
   SENSORS • NUCLEAR DETONATION DETEC-TION 24: (detects and evaluates nuclear detonations. Sensors deployed in NAVSTAR satellites)

Strategic Defenses – Early Warning
North American Aerospace Defense Command (NORAD), a combined US–CAN org.
SPACE BASED SYSTEMS • SATELLITES 4 Defense Support Programme *DSP* (Infra-red surveillance and warning system. Detects missile launches, nuclear detonations, ac in afterburn, spacecraft and terrestrial infra-red events. Approved constellation: 4 operational satellites; 1 operational on-orbit spare)
   NORTH WARNING SYSTEM 15 North Warning System Long Range (range 200nm); 40 North Warning System Short Range (range 110–150km)
   OVER-THE-HORIZON-BACKSCATTER RADAR (OTH-B) 2: 1 AN/FPS-118 *OTH-B* (500–3,000nm) located at Mountain Home AFB (ID); 1 non-operational located at Maine (ME)
   STRATEGIC 2 Ballistic Missile Early Warning System *BMEWS* located at Thule, GL and Fylingdales Moor, UK; 1 (primary mission to track ICBM and SLBM; also used to track satellites) located at Clear (AK)
   SPACETRACK SYSTEM 11: 8 Spacetrack Radar located at Incirlik (TUR), Eglin (FL), Cavalier AFS (ND), Clear (AK), Thule (GL), Fylingdales Moor (UK), Beale AFB (CA), Cape Cod (MA); 3 Spacetrack Optical Trackers located at Socorro (NM), Maui (HI), Diego Garcia (BIOT)
   USN SPACE SURVEILLANCE SYSTEM *NAV SPASUR* 3 strategic transmitting stations; 6 strategic receiving sites in southeast US

PERIMETER ACQUISITION RADAR ATTACK CHARACTERISATION SYSTEM *PARCS* 1 at Cavalier AFS, (ND)

PAVE PAWS 3 at Beale AFB (CA), Cape Cod AFS (MA), Clear AFS (AK); 1 (phased array radar 5,500km range) located at Otis AFB (MA)

DETECTION AND TRACKING RADARS Kwajalein Atoll, Ascension Island, Antigua, Kaena Point (HI), MIT Lincoln Laboratory (MA)

GROUND BASED ELECTRO OPTICAL DEEP SPACE SURVEILLANCE SYSTEM *GEODSS* Socorro (NM), Maui (HI), Diego Garcia (BIOT)

STRATEGIC DEFENCES – MISSILE DEFENCES

SEA-BASED: *Aegis* engagement cruisers and destroyers in Pacific Fleet

LAND-BASED: 21 ground-based interceptors at Fort Greeley, (AK); 3 ground-based interceptors at Vandenburg, (CA).

US Army 553,044; 77,833 active ARNG; 31,355 active AR (total 662,232)

FORCES BY ROLE

The US Army continues its transition programme. The aim at present is to have an Active Component of 17 Heavy Brigade Combat Teams (HBCT), 20 Infantry BCT (IBCT) and 8 Stryker BCT (SBCT). The Reserve is planned to comprise 7 HBCT, 20 IBCT and 1 SBCT. The SBCT has 3 manoeuvre bn instead of 2, as in the HBCT and IBCT. The HBCT has 2 combined arms bn, an armed recce sqn, an armd fires bn, a Bde Support Bn (BSB) and a Bde Special Troops Bn (BSTB). The IBCT has 2 inf bn, a Reconnaissance, Surveillance and Target Acquisition (RSTA) squadron, a fires bn, a BSB and a BSTB. The SBCT has three Stryker infantry bn, an RSTA sqn, a fires bn, a BSB, and engr, sigs, MI and anti-armour coys. The army currently projects 18 division headquarters in the total force (10 Active and 8 ARNG). The army still plans to grow to include 73 BCTs (45 AC BCTs and 28 RC BCTs) and approximately 225 support brigades.

Comd	6 army HQ; 3 corps HQ 10 div HQ
Armd	15 HBCT (*each*: 2 (combined arms) armd / armd inf bn, 1 armd recce sqn, 1 SP arty bn, 1 BSTB, 1 BSB)
Armd Cav	1 heavy regt (3rd ACR) with 3 cav sqn (*each*: 3 cav tps, 1 tk coy, 1 arty bty), 1 air cav sqn with (3 atk tps, 1 lift coy), 1 chemical coy, 1 engr coy, 1 MI coy; 1 regt (11th ACR) – OPFOR
Armd Inf	2 bde (170th, 172nd) with (1 armd bn, 2 armd inf bn, 1 armd recce tp, 1 SP arty bty, 1 cbt engr bn, 1 BSB)
Mech Inf	6 SBCT (*each*: 1 HQ coy, 3 Stryker bn, 1 fd arty bn, 1 recce sqn, 1 AT coy, 1 engr coy, 1 sigs coy , 1 MI coy ,1 BSB)
Inf	10 IBCT (*each*: 2 inf bn, 1 recce sqn, 1 fd arty bn, 1 BSB, 1 BSTB)
Air Aslt	4 BCT (*each*: 2 air aslt bn, 1 RSTA bn, 1 arty bn, 1 BSB, 1 BSTB (1 MI coy, 1 engr coy, 1 sigs coy))
AB	6 BCT (*each*: 2 para bn, 1 recce bn, 1 arty bn, 1 BSB, 1 BSTB (1 MI coy, 1 engr coy, 1 sigs coy))
Arty	6 (Fires) bde (*each*: HQ coy, 1 MLRS bn, 1 UAV coy , 1 TA coy, 1 BSB bn)
Engr	5 bde
AD	5 bde with MIM-104 *Patriot*
Cbt Avn	11 CAB (5 heavy, 4 medium, 2 light) (*each*: 1 aslt hel bn, 2 atk hel bn, 1 avn spt bn, 1 gen spt avn bn); 1 (theatre avn) bde
Spt	13 (Sustainment) bde (*each*: 1 BSTB, 2 Cbt Spt bn, 1 Sigs coy)
Cbt Spt	2 (3rd bde late 2010) (Manoeuvre enhancement) bde (*each*: 1 spt bn, 1 sigs coy)
Surv	3 BfSB (*each*: 1 reconnaissance and surveillance sqn, 1 BSTB bn, 1 MI bn) forming
WMD / NBC / EOD	1 (CBRNE) comd (1 Chemical bde (2 chemical bn), 1 asymmetric warfare regt (initially under direct FORSCOM C2), 2 EOD gp (*each*: 2 EOD bn))
SF	*See US Special Operations Command*

Reserve Organisations

Army National Guard 358,391 reservists 77,833

Currently capable of manning 8 divs after mobilisation. Under the army's transformation process, the ARNG will assume an end-state structure consisting of 28 BCT (7 HBCT, 1 SBCT, 20 IBCT)

FORCES BY ROLE

Comd	8 div HQ
Armd	7 HBCT, 3 combined arms bn
Recce	3 RSTA sqn
Mech Inf	1 SBCT
Lt Inf	20 IBCT; 11 indep bn
SF	2 gp opcon USSOCOM (total: 3 SF bn)
Arty	7 Fires bde
Engr	4 bde
Avn	2 (heavy) cbt avn bde; 6 (air expeditionary) cbt avn bde (each: 1 aslt hel bn, 1 atk hel bn, 1 gen spt avn bn, 1 avn spt bn, 1 spt/sy hel bn (each: 3 spt/sy coy – to become 4)); 4 theatre avn bde
WMD	2 chemical bde; 1 EOD gp; 32 WMD-CST (Weapons of Mass Destruction Civil Support Teams)
AD	2 bde with MIM-104 *Patriot*; FIM-92A *Avenger*
Spt	9 spt bde, 17 regional spt gps
Surv	5 BfSB (*each*: 1 reconnaissance and surveillance sqn, 1 BSTB, 1 MI bn)
Cbt Spt	10 (Manoeuvre enhancement) bde (transforming)
Sigs	2 bde

Army Reserve 198,000 reservists (31,355 active)

Inf	5 div (exercise); 7 div (trg)
Avn	1 theatre avn bde with (air aslt hel, atk hel and gen spt avn bns)

Engr	4 bde
Sig	1 bde
Spt	8 spt bdè, 2 cbt spt bde
Civil Affairs	36 (coys) bn opcon USSOCOM; 12 (4 comd, 8 bde) HQ opcon USSOCOM
Psyops	2 gp opcon USSOCOM
Regional Spt	13 comd gps

Army Standby Reserve 700 reservists

Trained individuals for mobilisation

EQUIPMENT BY TYPE

MBT 5,850 M1-A1/M1-A2 *Abrams*

RECCE 96 Tpz-1 *Fuchs*

AIFV 6,452 M-2 *Bradley*/M-3 *Bradley*

APC 19,637

 APC (T) 3,943 M-113A2/M-113A3

 APC (W) 15,694: 2,744 *Stryker*

  MRAP 12,000; 950 M-ACV

ARTY 6,270+

 SP 155mm 1,594 M-109A1/M-109A2/M-109A6

 TOWED 1,780+: **105mm** 434 M-102; 416 M-119; **155mm** 697 M-198; 233+ M-777 (replacing M-198)

 MRL 227mm 830 MLRS (all ATACMS-capable)

 MOR 2,066: **81mm** 990 M-252; **120mm** 1,076 M-120/M-121

AT

 MSL 21,955

  SP 2,005: 1,379 HMMWV TOW; 626 M-901

  MANPATS 19,950: 950 *Javelin* (fire and forget); 19,000 M47 *Dragon*

 RL 84mm M136 (AT-4)

AMPHIBIOUS 124+

 LCU 45: 11 LCU-1600 (capacity either 2 M1-A1 *Abrams* MBT or 350 troops); 34 LCU-2000

 LC 79+: 6 *Frank Besson* (capacity 32 *Abrams* MBT); 73+ LCM-8 (capacity either 1 MBT or 200 troops)

AIRCRAFT

 RECCE 60: 2 O-2 *Skymaster*

 RC-12 49: 37 RC-12D *Guardrail*/RC-12H *Guardrail*/RC-12K *Guardrail*; 12 RC-12P *Guardrail*/RC-12Q *Guardrail*

 EW• ELINT 9: 3 *Dash-7* ARL-M (COMINT/ELINT); 3 *Dash-7* ARL-1 (IMINT); 3 *Dash-7* ARL-C (COMINT)

 TPT 168: 113 C-12 *Huron*; 2 C-20 *Gulfstream*; 42 C-23A *Sherpa*/C-23B *Sherpa*; 11 C-26 *Metro*

 UTL 28 UC-35 *Citation*

HELICOPTERS

 ATK 1,035: 697 AH-64 *Apache* (155 AH-64A ; 542 AH-64D); 338 OH-58D *Kiowa Warrior*

 OBS 247 OH-58A *Kiowa*/OH-58C *Kiowa*

 SAR 15 HH-60L *Black Hawk*

 ASLT 36 AH-6/MH-6 *Little Bird*

 SPEC OP 116: 6 MH-47E *Chinook*, 50 MH-47G *Chinook*; 60 MH-60K *Black Hawk*/MH-60L *Pave Hawk*

 SPT 372: 309 CH-47D *Chinook*, 63 CH-47F *Chinook*,

 UTL 1,902: 58 UH -72A *Lakota*; 951 UH-60A *Black Hawk*; 681 UH-60L *Black Hawk*; 108 UH-60M *Black Hawk*; 4 UH-60Q *Black Hawk*; 100 UH-1H *Iroquois* /UH-1V *Iroquois*

 TRG 154 TH-67 *Creek*

UAV • TACTICAL 4,034: 20 RQ-5A *Hunter*; 236 RQ-7A *Shadow*; 3 I-Gnat; 15 *Warrior*; 4 *Sky Warrior*; 3,756 RQ-11 *Raven*

AD• SAM 1,281+

 SP 798: 703 FIM-92A *Avenger* (veh-mounted *Stinger*); 95 M-6 *Linebacker* (4 *Stinger* plus 25mm gun)

 TOWED 483 MIM-104 *Patriot*

 MANPAD FIM-92A *Stinger*

RADAR • LAND 251: 98 AN/TPQ-36 *Firefinder* (arty); 56 AN/TPQ-37 *Firefinder* (arty); 60 AN/TRQ-32 *Teammate* (COMINT); 32 AN/TSQ-138 *Trailblazer* (COMINT); 5 AN/TSQ-138A *Trailblazer*

US Navy 329,390; 6,432 active reservists (total 335,822)

Comprises 2 Fleet Areas, Atlantic and Pacific. All combatants divided into 6 Fleets: 2nd – Atlantic, 3rd – Pacific, 4th – Caribbean, Central and South America, 5th – Indian Ocean, Persian Gulf, Red Sea, 6th – Mediterranean, 7th – W. Pacific; plus Military Sealift Command (MSC); Naval Reserve Force (NRF); for Naval Special Warfare Command, see US Special Operations Command element.

EQUIPMENT BY TYPE

SUBMARINES 71

 STRATEGIC • SSBN 14 *Ohio* (mod) SSBN 730 opcon US STRATCOM each with up to 24 UGM-133A *Trident* D-5 strategic SLBM

 TACTICAL 57

  SSGN 4 *Ohio* (mod), with total of 154 *Tomahawk* LAM

  SSN 53:

   22 *Los Angeles* each with 4 single 533mm TT each with Mk48 *Sea Arrow* HWT/UGM-84 *Harpoon* USGW

   23 *Los Angeles* imp, each with up to 12 *Tomahawk* LAM, 4 single 533mm TT each with Mk48 *Sea Arrow* HWT/UGM-84 *Harpoon* USGW

   3 *Seawolf*, each with 8 single 660mm TT each with up to 45 *Tomahawk* LAM/UGM-84C *Harpoon* USGW, Mk48 *Sea Arrow* HWT

   5 *Virginia* with SLCM *Tomahawk*, 4 single 533mm TT each with Mk48 ADCAP mod 6 HWT, 1 12 cell vertical launch system (12 eff.) (6th vessel expected ISD 2010; additional vessels in build)

PRINCIPAL SURFACE COMBATANTS 110

 AIRCRAFT CARRIERS 11

  CVN 11:

   1 *Enterprise* (typical capacity 55 F/A-18 *Hornet* FGA ac; 4 EA-6B *Prowler* ELINT EW ac; 4 E-2C *Hawkeye* AEW ac; 6 S-3B *Viking* ASW ac; 4 SH-60F *Seahawk* ASW hel; 2 HH-60H *Seahawk* SAR hel) with 3 Mk 29 *Sea Sparrow* octuple each with RIM-7M/RIM-7P, 2 Mk 49 RAM (may be fitted) with 21 RIM-116 RAM SAM

   10 *Nimitz* (typical capacity 55 F/A-18 *Hornet* FGA ac; 4 EA-6B *Prowler* ELINT EW ac; 4 E-2C *Hawkeye* AEW ac; 4 SH-60F *Seahawk* ASW hel; 2 HH-60H *Seahawk* SAR hel) each with 2–3 Mk 29 *Sea Sparrow* octuple each with RIM-7M/RIM-7P, 2 Mk 49 RAM with 42 RIM-116 RAM SAM

  CRUISERS • CG • 22 *Ticonderoga* Aegis Baseline 2/3/4 (CG-52-CG-74) each with, comd and control, 2 quad (8 eff.) each with RGM-84 *Harpoon* SSM, 2 61 cell Mk 41 VLS (122 eff.) each with SM-2 ER SAM/*Tomahawk* LAM, 2 127mm gun 2 SH-60B *Seahawk* ASW hel, (Extensive upgrade programme scheduled from 2006–2020, to include sensors and fire control systems, major weapons upgrade to include Evolved *Sea Sparrow* (ESSM), SM-3 / SM-2 capability and 2 MK 45 Mod 2 127mm gun)

DESTROYERS • DDG 56:

28 *Arleigh Burke* Flight I/II each with *Aegis* comd and control, 1 32 cell Mk 41 VLS (32 eff.) with ASROC tactical/ASSM SSM/SM-2 ER SAM/*Tomahawk* TLAM, 1 64 cell Mk 41 VLS (64 eff.) with ASROC/ASSM SSM/SM-2 ER SAM/*Tomahawk* TLAM, 2 quad (8 eff.) each with RGM-84 *Harpoon* SSM, 2 Mk 49 RAM with 42 RIM-116 RAM SAM, 2 triple ASTT (6 eff.) each with Mk 46 LWT, 1 127mm gun, 1 hel landing platform

28 *Arleigh Burke* Flight IIA each with *Aegis* comd and control, 1 32 cell Mk 41 VLS (32 eff.) with ASROC tactical/ASSM SSM/SM-2 ER SAM/*Tomahawk* TLAM, 1 64 cell Mk 41 VLS (64 eff.) with ASROC/ASSM SSM tactical/SM-2 ER SAM/*Tomahawk* TLAM, 2 quad (8 eff.) each with RGM-84 *Harpoon* SSM, 2 triple ASTT (6 eff.) each with Mk 46 LWT, 1 127mm gun, 2 SH-60B *Seahawk* ASW hel, (Ongoing build programme for 10 additional ships)

FRIGATES 21

FFG 21 *Oliver Hazard Perry* each with 2 triple 324mm ASTT (6 eff.) with 24 Mk 46 LWT, 1 76mm gun, (capacity 2 SH-60B *Seahawk* ASW hel)

LCS 2:

1 *Freedom* with RIM-116 RAM, MK-15 *Phalanx* CIWS, 1 57mm gun, (standard capacity either 2 MH-60R/S *Seahawk* hel or 1 MH-60 with 3 *Firescout* UAV) (1st of class undergoing trials)

1 *Independence* with RIM-116 RAM, MK-15 *Phalanx* CIWS, 1 57mm gun (standard capacity 1MH-60R/S *Seahawk* hel and 3 *Firescout* UAV) (1st of class undergoing trials)

PATROL AND COASTAL COMBATANTS 16

PFC 8 *Cyclone*

PCI 8

MINE WARFARE • MINE COUNTERMEASURES 9

MCM 9 *Avenger* (MCM-1) each with 1 SLQ-48 MCM system, 1 SQQ-32(V)3 Sonar (mine hunting)

ML (none dedicated)

COMMAND SHIPS • LCC 2:

2 *Blue Ridge* (capacity 3 LCPL; 2 LCVP; 700 troops; 1 med utl hel)

AMPHIBIOUS

PRINCIPAL AMPHIBIOUS SHIPS 31

LHD 8:

8 *Wasp* (capacity 5 AV-8B *Harrier II* FGA; 42 CH-46E *Sea Knight* spt hel; 6 SH-60B *Seahawk* ASW hel; 3 LCAC(L) ACV; 60 tanks; 1,890 troops) each with 2 Mk 29 *Sea Sparrow* octuple with 32 RIM-7M/RIM-7P, 2 Mk 49 RAM with 42 RIM-116 RAM SAM, (Additional platform in build)

LHA 2:

2 *Tarawa* (capacity 6 AV-8B *Harrier II* FGA ac; 12 CH-46E *Sea Knight* spt hel; 9 CH-53 *Sea Stallion* spt hel; 4 LCU; 100 tanks; 1,900 troops) each with 2 Mk 49 RAM with 42 RIM-116 RAM SAM

LPD 9:

4 *Austin* (capacity 6 CH-46E *Sea Knight* spt hel; 2 LCAC(L) ACV/LCU; 40 tanks; 788 troops)

5 *San Antonio* (capacity 1 CH-53E *Sea Stallion* hel or 2 CH-46 *Sea Knight* or 1 MV-22 *Osprey*; 2 LCAC(L); 14 AAAV; 720 troops) (additional 4 hulls in build; current programme totals 9 units)

LSD 12:

4 *Harpers Ferry* (capacity 2 LCAC(L) ACV; 40 tanks; 500 troops) each with 1–2 Mk 49 RAM with 21–42 RIM-116 RAM SAM, 1 hel landing platform (for 2 CH-35)

8 *Whidbey Island* (capacity 4 LCAC(L) ACV; 40 tanks; 500 troops) each with 2 Mk 49 RAM with 42 RIM-116 RAM SAM, 1 hel landing platform (for 2 CH-53)

AMPHIBIOUS CRAFT 269+

LCU 34 LCU-1600 (capacity either 2 M1-A1 *Abrams* MBT or 350 troops)

LCVP 8

LCPL 75

LCM 72

ACV 80 LCAC(L) (capacity either 1 MBT or 60 troops; (undergoing upgrade programme))

SF EQUIPMENT 6 DDS opcon USSOCOM

FACILITIES

Bases	1 opcon EUCOM located at Naples, ITA, 1 opcon EUCOM located at Soudha Bay, GRC, 1 opcon US Pacific Fleet located at Yokosuka, JPN, 1 opcon EUCOM located at Rota, ESP, 1 opcon US Pacific Fleet located at Sasebo, JPN
Naval airbases	1 opcon US Pacific Fleet (plus naval comms facility) located at Andersen AFB, 1 opcon US Pacific Fleet located at Diego Garcia (BIOT)
SEWS	1 opcon US Pacific Fleet located at Pine Gap, AUS
Comms facility	1 opcon US Pacific Fleet located at NW Cape, AUS
SIGINT stn	1 opcon US Pacific Fleet located at Pine Gap, AUS
Support facility	1 opcon EUCOM located at Ankara, TUR, 1 opcon EUCOM located at Izmir, TUR, 1 opcon US Pacific Fleet located at Diego Garcia, (BIOT), 1 opcon US Pacific Fleet located at Singapore, SGP

Combat Logistics Force

LOGISTICS AND SUPPORT

AOE 5: 4 *Sacramento* (capacity 2 CH-46E *Sea Knight* spt hel); 1 *Supply* (capacity 3 CH-46E *Sea Knight* spt hel)

Navy Reserve Surface Forces

PRINCIPAL SURFACE COMBATANTS

FFG 9 *Oliver Hazard Perry* in reserve each with 2 triple 324mm ASTT (6 eff.) with 24 Mk 46 LWT, 36 SM-1 MR SAM, 1 76mm gun, (capacity 2 SH-60B *Seahawk* ASW hel)

MINE WARFARE • MINE COUNTERMEASURES 15:

MCM 5 *Avenger* in reserve each with 1 SLQ-48 MCM system, 1 SQQ-32(V)3 Sonar (mine hunting)

MHC 10 *Osprey* in reserve each with 1 SLQ-48 MCM system, 1 SQQ-32(V)2 Sonar (mine hunting)

INSHORE UNDERSEA WARFARE 45 HDS/IBU/MIUW

Naval Reserve Forces 109,222 (total)

Selected Reserve 66,455

Individual Ready Reserve 42,767

Naval Inactive Fleet
Under a minimum of 60–90 days notice for reactivation
PRINCIPAL SURFACE COMBATANTS 22
  AIRCRAFT CARRIERS 6 CV
  BATTLESHIP 1 BB
  CRUISERS 3 CG
  DESTROYERS 12: 4 DD 8 DDG
AMPHIBIOUS
  LS 5 LKA
  CRAFT 5 LCT
LOGISTICS AND SUPPORT 7: 5 AG 2 AO

Military Sealift Command (MSC)

Naval Fleet Auxiliary Force
LOGISTICS AND SUPPORT 44
  AFH 4: 2 *Mars*; 2 *Sirius*
  AEH 5 *Kilauea*
  AS 1 *Emory S Land* (Additional vessel to transfer under MSC 2010)
  ARS 2 *Safeguard*
  AH 2 *Mercy*, with 1 hel landing platform
  ATF 4 *Powhatan*
  HSV 1
  T-AO 14 *Henry J. Kaiser*
  T-AOE RAS 4 *Supply* class
  T-AKEH 7 *Lewis* and *Clark* (5 additional vessels in build)

Maritime Prepositioning Program
LOGISTICS AND SUPPORT 32
  T-AK 6
  T-AKR 24:
    LMSR T-AKR 11: 3; 8 *Watson*
    T-AKRH 13
  T-AVB 2

Strategic Sealift Force
(At a minimum of 4 days readiness)
LOGISTICS AND SUPPORT 17:
  T-AOT 4 *Champion*
  T-AK 2 (breakbulk)
    T-AKR 11: 7 *Bob Hope*; 2 *Gordon*; 2 *Shughart*

Special Mission Ships
LOGISTICS AND SUPPORT 18:
  HSV 1
  T-AG 1 *Hayes*
  T-AGM 3 (additional vessel in build)
  T-ARC 1
  T-AGOS 5: 1 *Impeccable*; 4 *Victorious*
  T-AGS 7: 1 *John McDonnell*; 6 *Pathfinder*

US Maritime Administration Support • National Defense Reserve Fleet
LOGISTICS AND SUPPORT 18:
  T-ACS 3 *Keystone State*
  T-AK 14: 11 T-AK (breakbulk); 3 T-AK (heavy lift)
  T-AO 1

Ready Reserve Force
Ships at readiness up to a maximum of 30 days
LOGISTICS AND SUPPORT 49:
  T-ACS 6 *Keystone State*
  T-AK 6: 2 T-AK (breakbulk); 4 T-AK (heavy lift)
  T-AKR 34: 26 *Ro Ro*; 8 *Algol*
  T-AVB 2
  T-AOT 1

Augmentation Force • Active
Cargo handling   1 bn

Reserve
Cargo handling   12 bn

Naval Aviation 98,588
Operates from 11 carriers, 11 air wings (10 active 1 reserve). Average air wing comprises 7 sqns: 4 each with 12 F/A-18 (2 with F/A-18C, 1 with F/A18-E, 1 with F/A18-F), 1 with 6 SH-60, 1 with 4 EA-6B, 1 with 4 E-2C. (Numbers exclude Fleet Replacement Squadrons.)

FORCES BY ROLE

Air wing	10 wg
COMD	2 sqn with E-6B *Mercury*
FGA	10 sqn with F/A-18E *Super Hornet*; 10 sqn with F/A-18F *Super Hornet*; 14 sqn with F/A-18C *Hornet*; 1 sqn with F/A-18A+
ASW	9 sqn with SH-60B *Seahawk*; 7 sqn with HH-60H *Seahawk*; SH-60F *Seahawk*; 3 sqn with MH-60R *Seahawk*
ELINT	2 sqn with EP-3E *Aries II*
ELINT/ECM	12 sqn with EA-6B *Prowler*; 1 sqn with EA-18G *Growler*
MP	12 (land-based) sqn with P-3C *Orion**
AEW	12 sqn with total of E-2C *Hawkeye*
MCM	2 sqn with MH-53E *Sea Dragon*
Spt	9 sqn with MH-60S *Knight Hawk*
Tpt	2 sqn with C-2A *Greyhound*
Trg	1 (aggressor) sqn with F/A-18C *Hornet*/ F/A-18D *Hornet* / F/A-18E *Super Hornet*/ F/A-18F *Super Hornet*; 1 (aggressor) sqn with F/A-18B *Hornet*/F/A-18 C *Hornet* / F/A-18D *Hornet*; 1 sqn with F/A-18E/F *Super Hornet* 3 sqn with T-6A/B *Texan II*/T-39D/G/N *Sabreliner*; 5 sqn T-34C *Turbo Mentor*; 2 sqn with T-44A *Pegasus*; 4 sqn with T-45A/C *Goshawk*; 2 sqn with TH-57B *Sea Ranger*/TH-57C *Sea Ranger*

EQUIPMENT BY TYPE
AIRCRAFT 900 combat capable
  FGA 753: 33 F/A-18A *Hornet*; 24 F/A-18B *Hornet*; 268 F/A-18C *Hornet*; 41 F/A-18D *Hornet*; 171 F/A-18E *Super Hornet*; 216 F/A-18F *Super Hornet*
  ELINT 11 EP-3E *Aries II*
  ELINT/ECM 99: 92 EA-6B *Prowler*; 7 EA-18G *Growler*
  MP 147 P-3C *Orion**

AEW 66 E-2C *Hawkeye*
COMD 16 E-6B *Mercury*
TPT 64: 4 C-12C *Huron*; 35 C-2A *Greyhound*; 1 C-20A *Gulfstream III*; 2 C-20D *Gulfstream III*; 5 C-20G *Gulfstream IV*; 7 C-26D *Metro III*; 1 C-37; 1 CT-39G *Sabreliner*; 2 LC-130F *Hercules*; 1 LC-130R *Hercules*; 5 VP-3A *Orion*
UTL 32: 2 RC-12F *Huron*; 2 RC-12M *Huron*; 2 U-6A *Beaver*; 21 UC-12B *Huron*; 1 UC-35D *Citation Encore*; 4 UP-3A *Orion*
TRG 648: 47 T-6A *Texan II*; 2 T-6B *Texan II*; 270 T-34C *Turbo Mentor*; 9 T-38 *Talon*; 1 T-39D *Sabreliner*; 8 T-39G *Sabreliner*; 15 T-39N *Sabreliner*; 55 T-44A *Pegasus*; 74 T-45A *Goshawk*; 144 T-45C *Goshawk*; 21 TC-12B *Huron*; 2 TE-2C *Hawkeye*
TRIALS AND TEST 50: 5 EA-18G *Growler*; 1 NF/A-18A *Hornet*; 2 NF/A-18C *Hornet*; 3 NF/A-18D *Hornet*; 1 NP-3C *Orion*; 11 NP-3D *Orion*; 1 NT-34C *Mentor* test; 1 NU-1B *Otter* test; 2 QF-4N *Phantom II*; 16 QF-4S *Phantom II*; 2 X-26A test; 1 X-31A test; 1 YF-4J *Phantom II* (prototype, FGA); 1 YSH-60 *Seahawk* (prototype); 1 YSH-60B *Seahawk*; 1 YSH-60F *Seahawk*

HELICOPTERS
MCM 28 MH-53E *Sea Dragon*
OBS 3 OH-58A *Kiowa*
SAR 63: 23 HH-1N *Iroquois*; 4 HH-46D *Sea Knight*; 36 HH-60H *Seahawk*
ASW 220: 148 SH-60B *Seahawk*; 72 SH-60F *Seahawk*
SPT/SPEC OP 158: 35 MH-60R *Strike Hawk*; 123 MH-60S *Knight Hawk* (Multi Mission Support)
SPT 18: 9 CH-53D *Sea Stallion*; 9 CH-53E *Sea Stallion*
UTL 19: 1 UH-1N *Iroquois*; 4 UH-1Y *Iroquois*; 9 UH-46D *Sea Knight*; 3 UH-60L *Black Hawk*; 2 VH-3A *Sea King* (VIP)
TRG 132: 44 TH-57B *Sea Ranger*; 82 TH-57C *Sea Ranger*; 6 TH-6B in testing
TEST 3 N-SH-60B *Seahawk*

UAV 42+:
RECCE 2 RQ-4A *Global Hawk* (under evaluation and trials)
TAC 40+: 5 MQ-8B *Fire Scout* (under evaluation and trials); 35 RQ-2B *Pioneer*

MSL
ASM AGM-65A/F *Maverick*; AGM-84D *Harpoon*; AGM-84E SLAM/SLAM-ER; AGM-114B/K/M *Hellfire*; AGM-119A *Penguin 3*; AGM-88A HARM; AGM-154A JSOW
AAM AIM-7 *Sparrow*; AIM-9 *Sidewinder*; AIM-120 AMRAAM; RIM-116 RAM

BOMBS
Conventional: BLU-117/Mk 84 (2,000lb); BLU-110/Mk 83 (1,000lb); BLU-111/ Mk 82 (500lb); Mk 46; Mk 50; Mk 54
Laser-Guided: *Paveway* II; *Paveway* III (fits on Mk 82, Mk 83 or Mk 84)
INS/GPS guided: JDAM (GBU-31/32/38); Enhanced *Paveway* II

Naval Aviation Reserve

FORCES BY ROLE
FGA   1 sqn with F/A-18A+ *Hornet*

ASW   1 sqn with HH-60H *Seahawk*; 1 sqn with SH-60B
MR   2 sqn with P-3C *Orion*
AEW   1 sqn with E-2C *Hawkeye*
Spt   1 sqn with MH-60S *Knight Hawk*
ECM   1 sqn with EA-6B *Prowler*
Log spt 1 wg (3 log spt sqn with C-40A *Clipper*, 3 log spt sqn with C-20 A/D/G *Gulfstream*; C-37A / C-37B *Gulfstream*, 5 tactical tpt sqn with C-130T *Hercules*, 4 log spt sqn with C-9B *Skytrain II* / DC-9 *Skytrain*)
Trg   2 (aggressor) sqn with F-5E *Tiger II*/F-5F *Tiger II* / F-5N *Tiger II*; 1 (aggressor) sqn with F/A-18C *Hornet*

EQUIPMENT BY TYPE
AIRCRAFT 70 combat capable
FGA 24: 12 F/A-18A+ *Hornet*; 12 F/A-18C *Hornet*
MP 12 P-3C *Orion**
EW/ELINT 4 EA-6B *Prowler*
AEW 6 E-2C *Hawkeye*
TPT 44: 19 C-130T *Hercules*; 9 C-40A *Clipper*; 15 C-9B *Skytrain II*; 1 DC-9 *Skytrain*
UTL 16: 7 C-20 A/D/G *Gulfstream*; 1 C-37A *Gulfstream*; 3 C-37B *Gulfstream*; 5 UC-12B *Huron*
TRG 34 F-5E *Tiger II*/F-5F *Tiger II*/F-5N *Tiger II**
HELICOPTERS
MCM 8 MH-53E *Sea Stallion*
SAR 10 HH-60H *Rescue Hawk*
ASW 14: 6 SH-60B *Seahawk*; 8 MH-60S *Knight Hawk*

US Marine Corps 204,261 (incl 5,748 active reservists)

3 Marine Expeditionary Force (MEF), 3 Marine Expeditionary Brigade (MEB), 7 Marine Expeditionary Units (MEU) drawn from 3 div. An MEU usually consists of a battalion landing team (1 inf bn, 1 arty bty, 1 lt armd recce coy, 1 armd pl, 1 amph aslt pl, 1 cbt engr pl, 1 recce pl), an aviation combat element (1 medium lift sqn with attached atk hel, FGA ac and AD assets) and a composite log bn, with a combined total of about 2,200 men. Composition varies with mission requirements.

FORCES BY ROLE
Marine   1 div (1st) with (3 inf regt (*each:* 4 inf bn), 1 arty regt (4 arty bn), 1 armd bn, 2 (LAV-25) lt armd recce bn, 1 recce bn, 1 amph aslt bn, 1 cbt engr bn)
         1 div (2nd) with (3 inf regt (*each:* 4 inf bn) 1 arty regt (4 arty bn), 1 armd bn, 1 lt armd recce bn, 1 recce bn, 1 amph aslt bn, 1 cbt engr bn,)
         1 div (3rd) with (1 inf regt (3 inf bn), 1 arty regt (2 arty bn), 1 recce bn, 1 cbt spt bn (1 lt armd recce coy, 1 amph aslt coy, 1 cbt engr coy))
Spec Ops 3 MEF recce coy
Log   3 gp

EQUIPMENT BY TYPE
MBT 403 M1-A1 *Abrams*
RECCE 252 LAV-25 *Coyote* (25mm gun, plus 189 variants excluding 50 mor, 95 ATGW see below)

AAV 1,311 AAV-7A1 (all roles)
ARTY 1,867+
    TOWED 1,282+: **105mm**: 331 M-101A1; **155mm** 595 M-198; 356+ M-777(to replace M-198)
    MOR 81mm 585: 50 LAV-M; 535 M-252
AT
    MSL 2,299
      SP 95 LAV-TOW
      MANPATS 2,204: 1,121 *Predator*; 1,083 TOW
    RL 2,764: **83mm** 1,650 SMAW; **84mm** 1,114 AT-4
AD • SAM • MANPAD FIM-92A *Stinger*
UAV 1072: 972 3D Max *Dragon Eye*; 100 BQM-147 *Exdrone*; some RQ-11 *Raven*
RADAR • LAND 23 AN/TPQ-36 *Firefinder* (arty)

Marine Corps Aviation 34,700

3 active Marine Aircraft Wings (MAW) and 1 MCR MAW

Flying hours   365 hrs/year on tpt ac; 248 hrs/year on ac; 277 hrs/year on hel

FORCES BY ROLE

Ftr	2 sqn with F/A-18A *Hornet* / F/A-18A+ *Hornet*; 5 sqn with F/A-18C *Hornet*; 5 sqn (All Weather) with F/A-18D *Hornet*
FGA	7 sqn with AV-8B *Harrier II*
ECM	4 sqn with total of EA-6B *Prowler*
Tpt/CSAR	1 sqn with C-20G *Gulfstream IV*, C-9B *Nightingale*, UC-12B *Huron*/UC-12F *Huron*, UC-35C *Citation Ultra*/UC-35D *Citation Encore*, HH-1N *Iroquois*, HH-46E *Sea Knight*
Tkr	3 sqn with KC-130J *Hercules*
Atk hel	7 sqn with AH-1W *Cobra*, UH-1N *Iroquois*
Spt hel	6 sqn with MV-22B *Osprey*; 8 sqn with CH-46E *Sea Knight*; 3 sqn with CH-53D *Sea Stallion*; 7 sqn with CH-53E *Sea Stallion*
Trg	1 sqn with F/A-18B *Hornet*, F/A-18C *Hornet*, F/A18D *Hornet*; 1 sqn with AV-8B *Harrier II*, TAV-8B *Harrier*; 1 sqn with AH-1W *Cobra*, UH-1N *Iroquois*, HH-1N *Iroquois*; UH-1Y *Venom*; 1 sqn with MV-22A *Osprey*; 1 sqn with CH-46E *Sea Knight*; 1 sqn with CH-53E *Sea Stallion*
Test	1 sqn with V-22 *Osprey*
VIP	1 sqn with CH-46E *Sea Knight*; CH-53E *Sea Stallion*; VH-60N *Presidential Hawk*; VH-3D *Sea King*
AD	2 bn with FIM-92A *Avenger*; FIM-92A *Stinger* (can provide additional heavy calibre support weapons)
UAV	3 sqn with RQ-7B *Shadow*

EQUIPMENT BY TYPE

AC 371 combat capable
    FGA 354
      F/A-18 223: 44 F/A-18A/F/A-18 A+ *Hornet*; 2 F/A-18B *Hornet*; 83 F/A-18C *Hornet*; 94 F/A-18D *Hornet*; 131 AV-8B *Harrier II*
    EW 29 EA-6B *Prowler*
    TKR 34 KC-130J *Hercules*

TPT 3
    1 C-20G *Gulfstream IV*; 2 C-9B *Nightingale*
UTL 18
    11 UC-12B/F *Huron*; 7 UC-35C *Citation Ultra* / UC-35D *Citation Encore*
TRG 20
    3 T-34C *Turbo Mentor*; 17 TAV-8B *Harrier**
HELICOPTERS 145+ attack helicopters
    ATK 145+: 139 AH-1W *Cobra*; 6+ AH-1Z *Viper*
    SAR 9: 5 HH-1N *Iroquois*; 4 HH-46E *Sea Knight*
    SPT 323: CH-53 180: 35 CH-53D *Sea Stallion*; 145 CH-53E *Sea Stallion*; 135 CH-46E *Sea Knight*; 8 VH-60N *Presidential Hawk* (VIP tpt)
    UTL 96
      UH-1 85: 76 UH-1N *Iroquois*; 9 UH-1Y *Iroquois*; 11 VH-3D *Sea King* (VIP tpt)
    TILTROTOR 86+
      MV-22 82: 20 MV-22A *Osprey*: 62+ MV-22B *Osprey* (360 on order, deliveries continuing)
      V-22 *Osprey* 4
UAV • TACTICAL • 32 RQ-7B *Shadow*
AD
    SAM • SP some FIM-92A *Avenger*
      MANPAD some FIM-92A *Stinger*
MSL
    ASM AGM-65F IR *Maverick* / AGM-65E *Maverick*; AGM-84 *Harpoon*; AGM-114 *Hellfire*
    AAM AIM-9M *Sidewinder*; AGM-88A HARM; *AIM-7 Sparrow*; AIM-120 AMRAAM
BOMBS
    Conventional: CBU-59; CBU-99; MK-82 (500lb), MK-83 (1,000lb)
    Laser-Guided: GBU 10/12/16 *Paveway* II (fits on Mk82, Mk 83 or Mk 84)
    INS/GPS Guided: JDAM

Reserve Organisations

Marine Corps Reserve 109,600 (total)

FORCES BY ROLE

Marine	1 div (4th) with (3 inf regt (*each*: 3 Inf bn), 1 arty regt (4 arty bn), 1 (LAV-25) lt armd recce bn, 1 recce bn, 1 amph aslt bn, 1 cbt engr bn)
Spec Ops	2 MEF recce coy
Log	1 gp

Marine Corps Aviation Reserve 11,592 reservists

FORCES BY ROLE

Ftr	1 sqn with F/A-18A / F/A-18A+ *Hornet*
Tkr	2 sqn with KC-130T *Hercules*
Atk hel	1 sqn with AH-1W *Cobra*; 9 UH-1N *Iroquois*
Spt hel	2 sqn with CH-46E *Sea Knight*; 1 det with CH-53E *Sea Stallion*
Trg	1 sqn with F-5F *Tiger II* / F-5N *Tiger II*

EQUIPMENT BY TYPE

AIRCRAFT 27 combat capable
    FTR 13:1 F-5F *Tiger II*; 12 F-5N *Tiger II*
    FGA 14 F/A-18A/A+ *Hornet*
    TKR 28 KC-130T *Hercules*

UTL 7
   UC-12: 2 UC-12B *Huron* / UC-12F *Huron*
   UC-35: 5 UC-35C *Citation Ultra* / UC-35D *Citation Encore*
HELICOPTERS 18 attack helicopters
   ATK 18 AH-1W *Cobra*
   SPT 33
      27 CH-46E *Sea Knight*; 6 CH-53E *Sea Stallion*
   UTL 9 UH-1N *Iroquois*

Marine Stand-by Reserve 700 reservists

Trained individuals available for mobilisation

US Coast Guard 43,598 (military); 7,659 (civilian)

Two Area Commands: Pacific (Alameda, California) and Atlantic (Portsmouth, Virginia), supervising 9 districts (4 Pacific, 5 Atlantic). 2 (1 Atlantic, 1 Pacific) Maintenance and Logistics Command Atlantic (MLCA).
PATROL AND COASTAL COMBATANTS 160
   PSOH 42: 1 *Alex Haley*; 13 *Famous*; 12 *Hamilton*; 14 *Reliance*, 2 *Legend*
   PSO 1
   PFC 3 *Cyclone*
   PBC 114: 73 *Marine Protector*; 41 *Island*
LOGISTICS AND SUPPORT 92
   ABU 16 *Juniper*
   AGB 4: 1 *Mackinaw*; 1 *Healy*; 2 *Polar Icebreaker*
   Trg 2
   WLI 5
   WLIC 13
   WLM 14 *Keeper*
   WLR 18
   WTGB 9 *Bay Class*
   YTM 11

US Coast Guard Aviation

AIRCRAFT
   MP 61: 9 HU-25A *Guardian* (Additional 16 in reserve); 3 HU-25B (Additional 4 in store); 8 HU-25C (Additional 9 in store); 6 HU-25D; 6 HC-144A (CN-235-200; Additional ac on order)
   SAR 26: 21 MC-130H *Hercules* (Additional 5 in store)
   TPT 8: 6 C-130J *Hercules*; 1 C-37; 1 C-143A *Challenger*
HELICOPTERS
   SAR 144: 35 HH-60J *Jayhawk* (Additional 7 in store); 90 HH-65C (AS-366G1) *Dauphin II* (Additional 12 in store)
   UTL 8 MH-68A (A-109E) *Power*
UAV 3 (trials)

US Air Force (USAF) 334,342

Flying hours ftr 189, bbr 260, tkr 308, airlift 343
   Almost the entire USAF (plus active force ANG and AFR) is divided into 10 Aerospace Expeditionary Forces (AEF), each on call for 120 days every 20 months. At least 2 of the 10 AEFs are on call at any one time, each with 10,000–15,000 personnel, 90 multi-role ftr and bbr ac, 31 intra-theatre refuelling aircraft and 13 aircraft for ISR and EW missions.

Global Strike Command (GSC)

GSC (HQ at Barksdale AFB, LA) is bringing together USAF strategic nuclear forces under a single commander, and will provide combatant commanders with the forces to conduct strategic nuclear deterrence and global strike operations through ICBM, B-2 *Spirit* and B-52 *Stratofortress* operations. Due to reach initial operating capacity August 2010.

Air Combat Command (ACC) 96,000 active-duty members and civilians. (When mobilised, over 57,000 ANG and AFR personnel, with about 859 ac, are assigned to ACC)

ACC (Langley AFB, VA.), is the primary US provider of air combat forces. ACC operates ftr, bbr, recce, battle-management, and electronic-combat aircraft and in total, ACC and ACC-gained units fly more than 2,000 aircraft. It also provides C3I systems, and conducts global information operations. ACC numbered air forces (four are active-duty) provide the air component to CENTCOM, SOUTHCOM and NORTHCOM, with HQ ACC serving as the air component to Joint Forces Commands. ACC also augments forces to EUCOM, PACOM and STRATCOM, and the recently established AFRICOM.

ACC Organisation

First Air Force (Tyndall AFB, FLA.) provides surveillance and C2 for AD forces for CONUS in support of NORAD. It provides forces necessary for US national defence. Assigned units include the CONUS Regional Air Operations Centre, NORAD System Support Facility and the Southeast, Northeast and the Western Air Defence Sectors. Ten ANG ftr wg are assigned.
Eighth Air Force (Barksdale AFB, LA.) provides C2ISR; long-range attack; and information operations forces. It provides conventional forces to US Joint Forces Command and provides nuclear capable bombers, specified Global Strike assets, and C²ISR capabilities to US Strategic Command. Eighth Air Force also supports STRATCOM's Joint Force Headquarters - Information Operations and serves as the command element for air force-wide computer network operations.
Ninth Air Force (Shaw Air Force Base, SC) controls ACC fighter forces based on the US east coast, and serves as the air component for a 25-nation area within the CENTCOM AOR.
Tenth Air Force (NAS Joint Reserve Base, Fort Worth, TX.), directs more than 13,300 reservists and 900 civilians at 28 locations throughout the US. It currently commands Air Force Reserve Command units gained by five other major commands, including ACC.
Twelfth Air Force (Davis-Monthan AFB, AZ.) controls ACC's conventional ftr and bbr forces based in the western US and has warfighting responsibility for SOUTHCOM as well as US Southern Air Forces.
   Each numbered air force is composed of air wings; allocated to these air wings are role-specific squadrons.

FORCES BY ROLE

HQ (AF)	1 HQ located at Langley AFB (VA)
Bbr	4 sqn with B-1B *Lancer*; 5 sqn opcon US STRATCOM with B-52 *Stratofortress*; 2 sqn opcon US STRATCOM with B-2A *Spirit*
Ftr	5 sqn with F/A-22A *Raptor*; 15 sqn with F-16C /F-16D *Fighting Falcon*; 8 sqn with F-15E *Strike Eagle*; 6 sqn with F-15C/D *Eagle*
Attack/ FAC	5 sqn with A-10 *Thunderbolt II*/OA-10A *Thunderbolt II*
Recce	5 sqn with RC-135/OC-135; 2 sqn with U-2S/ TU-2S *Dragon Lady*; 2 sqn with MC-12W
EW	2 sqn with EC-130H *Compass Call Solo*; 1 sqn with EA-6B *Prowler* (personnel only – USN aircraft)
AEW	7 sqn with E-3B *Sentry*/E-3C *Sentry*); 1 sqn with E-4B
SAR	4 sqn with HC-130N *Hercules*/HC-130P *Hercules*/HH-60G *Pave Hawk*
Special Ops	2 sqn opcon USSOCOM with AC-130H/U *Spectre*; 3 sqn opcon USSOCOM with MC-130E/H *Combat Talon*; 1 sqn opcon USSOCOM with MC-130P *Combat Shadow*; 1 sqn opcon USSOCOM with MC-130P *Combat Shadow*/C-130 *Hercules*; 1 sqn opcon USSOCOM with MC-130W *Combat Spear*; 2 sqn opcon USSOCOM with U-28A; 2 sqn opcon USSOCOM with CV-22 *Osprey* (+2 sqn opcon USSOCOM personnel only); 1 sqn opcon USSOCOM with C-130E *Hercules*; An-26; UH-1N *Iroqouis*; Mi-8
Trg	3 (aggressor) sqn with F-16C/D *Fighting Falcon*; F-15C *Eagle*
UAV	4 sqn with MQ-1 *Predator*; 1 sqn opcon USSOCOM with MQ-1B *Predator*; 2 sqn with MQ-9 *Predator*; 1 sqn with RQ-4A *Global Hawk*

Air Mobility Command (AMC)

Provides strategic, tactical, special op airlift, aero medical evacuation, SAR and weather recce. 1 active air force (18th), 13 active air wgs and 1 air gp

FORCES BY ROLE

HQ (AF)	1 HQ located at Scott AFB (IL)
Strategic tpt	2 sqn with C-5 *Galaxy*; 13 sqn with C-17 *Globemaster* III
Tactical tpt	8 sqn with C-130E/H/J *Hercules*
Op spt tpt	8 sqn with C-12 *Huron*; C-20 *Gulfstream*; C-21 *Learjet*; C-32; C-37; C-40 *Clipper*; UH-1N *Huey*
VIP	1 wg with VC-25 *Air Force One*; C-20 *Gulfstream*; C-32; C-40
Tkr	10 sqn with KC-135 *Stratotanker* (+3 personnel only); 4 sqn with KC-10A *Extender DC-10*

Air Education and Training Command

2 active air forces (2nd and 19th), 10 active air wgs

FORCES BY ROLE

Air	7 sqn (AFR personnel) trained to fly ac
Flying trg	24 sqns with T-1 *Jayhawk*; T-38 *Talon*; T-43; T-6 *Texan II*
Mission trg	27 sqn with F/A-22A *Raptor*; F-16 *Fighting Falcon*; F-15 *Eagle*; A-10 *Thunderbolt II*; OA-10 *Thunderbolt II*; TU-2S; MC-130 *Hercules*; HC-130 *Hercules*; KC-135 *Stratotanker*; C-130 *Hercules*; C-135 *Stratolifter*; C-17 *Globemaster*; C-21 *Learjet*; C-5 *Galaxy*; CV-22 *Osprey*; HH-60 *Seahawk*; UH-1N *Huey*; 1 sqn with MQ-1 *Predator* and 1 sqn with MQ-9 *Reaper*
Trials and testing	Units with 2 B-1 *Lancer*; B-2 *Spirit*; B-52 *Stratofortress*; F-22 *Raptor*; F-117 *Nighthawk*; F-16 *Fighting Falcon*; F-15A *Eagle*/F-15B *Eagle*/F-15C *Eagle*/F-15D *Eagle*; A-10 *Thunderbolt* II; U-2; EC-130E *Commando Solo*; E-3B *Sentry*; AC-130 *Spectre*; KC-135 *Stratotanker*; C-135 *Stratolifter*; C-17 *Globemaster*; T-38C *Talon*; NC-130 *Hercules*; HH-60 *Seahawk*; UH-1N *Huey*

Reserve Organisations

Air National Guard 106,680 reservists

FORCES BY ROLE

Bbr	1 sqn B-2A *Spirit* (personnel only)
Ftr	1 sqn with F-22A *Raptor* (personnel only); 6 sqn with F-15 *Eagle* A/B/C/D
Recce	3 sqn with E-8C J-STARS (mixed active force and ANG personnel)
Attack/FAC	5 sqn with A-10 *Thunderbolt II*/OA-10 *Thunderbolt II*; 17 sqn with F-16C/D *Fighting Falcon*
Special Ops	1 sqn opcon USSOCOM with EC-130J *Commando Solo*
EW	RC-26 Metroliners distrib as single ac to 11 ANG air wgs
SAR	6 sqn with HC-130 *Hercules*/MC-130P *Combat Shadow*; HH-60G *Pavehawk*
Strategic tpt	3 sqn with C-5A *Galaxy*; 1 sqn with C-17 *Globemaster* (+1 sqn personnel only)
Tac tpt	19 sqn (+ 1 personnel only) with C-130E/ H/J *Hercules*; 1 sqn with C-38/C-40; 3 sqn with C-21 *Learjet*
Tkr	20 sqn with KC-135R *Stratotanker* (+2 sqn personnel only)
Mission trg	7 sqn with F-16 *Fighting Falcon*; F-15 *Eagle*; C-130 *Hercules*
UAV	1 sqn with MQ-1*Predator* (+ 1 sqn personnel only); 1 sqn with MQ-9 *Reaper* (personnel only)

Air Force Reserve Command 67,500 reservists

FORCES BY ROLE

Bbr	1 sqn opcon US STRATCOM with B-52H *Stratofortress*
Ftr	1 sqn with F-22A *Raptor* (personnel only); 2 sqn with F-16C/D *Fighting Falcon* (+3 sqn personnel only)

Attack/FAC	3 sqn with A-10 *Thunderbolt* II/OA-10 *Thunderbolt* II
Special Ops	2 sqn opcon USSOCOM with MC-130E *Combat Talon*; 1 sqn opcon USSOCOM with MC-130P *Combat Shadow* (personnel only)
SAR	3 sqn with HH-60G *Pavehawk*, HC-130P/N *Hercules*
Strategic tpt	3 sqn with C-5A/B *Galaxy* (+2 sqn personnel only); 1 sqn C-17 *Globemaster* (+9 sqn personnel only)
Tac tpt	10 sqn with C-130E/H/J *Hercules*; 1 (Aerial Spray) sqn with C-130H *Hercules*
VIP/Op Spt Tpt	1 sqn with C-9C *Nightingale*/C-40B/C
Tkr	6 sqn with KC-135R *Stratotanker* (+2 sqn personnel only); 4 sqn KC-10A *Extender* (personnel only);
Weather recce	1 sqn with WC-130H *Hercules*/WC-130J *Hercules*
Mission trg	1 sqn with F-15 *Eagle*/F-16 *Fighting Falcon*; A-10 *Thunderbolt* II; C-130 *Hercules*; 1 sqn with B-52H *Stratofortress*; 1 sqn with C-5A *Galaxy*
UAV	1 sqn with RQ-4A (personnel only), 1 sqn with MQ-1 (personnel only)

Civil Reserve Air Fleet

Commercial ac numbers fluctuate

AIRCRAFT • TPT 37 carriers and 1,376 aircraft enrolled, including 1,273 aircraft in the international segment (990 long-range and 283 short-range), plus 37 national, 50 aeromedical evacuation segments and 4 aircraft in the Alaskan segment.

Air Force Stand-by-Reserve 16,858 reservists

Trained individuals for mobilisation

EQUIPMENT BY TYPE

AIRCRAFT 2,708 (incl F-35A *Lightning* in test) combat capable

  LRSA 154 (145 Active Force; 9 Reserve): 64 B-1B *Lancer*; 19 B-2A *Spirit*; 62 B-52H *Stratofortress* (plus 9 Reserve; 18 in store)

  TAC 2,650 (1,793 Active Force; 135 Reserve; 722 Air National Guard): 139 F/A-22A *Raptor* (199 on order); 396 F-15A/B/C/D *Eagle* (plus 126 Air National Guard); 217 F-15E *Strike Eagle*; 738 F-16C/D *Fighting Falcon* (plus 69 Reserve; 473 Air National Guard); 143 A-10A *Thunderbolt* II (plus 46 Reserve; 84 Air National Guard); 70 OA-10A *Thunderbolt* II* (plus 6 Reserve; 18 Air National Guard); 8 AC130H* *Spectre* (SOC); 17 AC130U* *Spectre* (SOC); 14 EC130H *Compass Call*; 6 EC130J *Commando Solo* (SOC) (Air National Guard); 16 MC-130E/H *Combat Talon* I/II (SOC) (plus 14 Reserve); 23 MC-130P *Combat Shadow* (plus 4 Air National Guard); 12 MC-130W *Combat Spear*; 11 RC-26B *Metroliner* (Air National Guard)

  RECCE 106 (96 Active Force; 10 Reserve): 37 MC-12W (*King Air* 350ER); 5 TU-2S; 28 U-2S; 10 WC-130J *Hercules* (Reserve); 3 OC-135B *Open Skies*; 17 RC-135V/W *Rivet*

Joint; 2 RC-135U *Combat Sent*; 2 WC-135 *Constant Phoenix*; 2 E-9A

TRIALS & TEST 12 (all Active Force): 4 F-35A *Lightning*; 1 B-2 *Spirit*; 2 B-1B *Lancer*; 4 B-52 *Stratofortress*; 1 E-3 *Sentry*

COMD/AEW 54 (37 Active Force; 17 Air National Guard): 33 E-3B/C *Sentry*; 17 E-8C J-STARS (Air National Guard); 4 E-4B

TPT 844 (417 Active Force; 169 Reserve; 258 Air National Guard): 59 C-5A *Galaxy* (26 Reserve, 33 ANG); 47 C-5B *Galaxy* (incl 16 Reserve); 2 C-5C *Galaxy*; 3 C-5M *Galaxy*; 158 C-17A *Globemaster* III (plus 8 Reserve; 8 Air National Guard); 151 C-130E/H/J *Hercules* (plus 103 Reserve; 181 Air National Guard); 5 C-20B *Gulfstream* III; 2 C-20H *Gulfstream* III; 35 C-21 *Learjet* (plus 21 Air National Guard); 3 C-9C *Nightingale* (Reserve); 4 C-32A; 9 C-37A; 2 C-40 B/C (plus 3 Reserve, 2 Air National Guard); 2 VC-25A (Air Force One); 13 HC-130P/N *Hercules* (plus 10 Reserve, 13 Air National Guard)

TKR 512 (241 Active Force; 65 Reserve; 206 Air National Guard): 59 KC-10A *Extender* DC-10 (tkr/tpt); 182 KC-135 A/E/R/T *Stratotanker* (plus 65 Reserve, 206 Air National Guard)

TRG 1,141 (all Active Force): 179 T-1A *Jayhawk*; 405 T-6A *Texan* II1; 546 T-38A *Talon*; 11 T-43A

TILT-ROTOR 11: 3 CV-22 *Osprey* (testing); 8 CV-22A *Osprey* (SOC)

HELICOPTERS 167 (126 Active Force; 23 Reserve; 18 Air National Guard): 64 HH-60G *Pave Hawk* (plus 23 Reserve; 18 Air National Guard); 62 UH-1N *Huey* (TPT);

UAV 158 Large: 13 RQ-4A *Global Hawk*; Medium: 27 MQ-9 *Reaper*; 118 MQ-1 *Predator* (incl 7 ANG)

Small/micro UAV: 1 *Scan Eagle*; some RQ-11; some *Desert Hawk*; some Battlefield Air Targeting Micro Air Vehicles (BATMAV).

MSL 41,422+

  ASM 26,422+: 1,142 AGM-86B ALCM; 460 AGM-129A Advanced Cruise Missile; 400+ AGM-130A; 150+ AGM-142 *Popeye*; 17,000+ AGM-65A *Maverick*/AGM-65B *Maverick*/AGM-65D *Maverick*/AGM-65G *Maverick*; 70+ AGM-84B *Harpoon*; 700+ AGM-86C CALCM; 6,500+ AGM-88A HARM/AGM-88B HARM

  AAM 15,000+: 5,000+ AIM-120A AMRAAM/AIM-120B AMRAAM/AIM-120C AMRAAM; 3,000+ AIM-7M *Sparrow*; 7,000+ AIM-9M *Sidewinder*

BOMBS

  Conventional: BLU-109/Mk 84 (2,000lb); BLU-110/Mk 83 (1,000lb); BLU-111/Mk 82 (500lb)

  Laser-guided: *Paveway* II, *Paveway* III *(fits on Mk82, Mk83 or Mk84)*

  INS/GPS guided: JDAM (GBU 31/32/38); GBU-15 (with BLU-109 penetrating warhead or Mk 84); GBU-39B Small Diameter Bomb (250lb); *Enhanced Paveway* III

US Special Operations Command 31,496; 3,376 (civilian); 11,247 reservists (SOF) (total 46,119)

Commands all active, reserve, and National Guard Special Operations Forces (SOF) of all services based in CONUS

FORCES BY ROLE
Combined Service   1 HQ located at MacDill AFB (FL)

US Army

SF	5 gp (*each:* 3 SF bn)
Ranger	1 regt (3-4 Ranger bn)
Sigs	1 bn
Spt	1 sustainment bde
Avn	1 regt (160 SOAR) (4 avn bn)
Psyops	1 gp (5 psyops bn)
Civil Affairs	1 bn (5 civil affairs coy)

EQUIPMENT BY TYPE
UAV 57: 15 *Tern*; 14 *Mako*; 28 *Snowgoose*

Reserve Organisations

Army National Guard
SF   2 gp (*total:* 3 SF bn)

Army Reserve
Psyops   2 gp
Civil Affairs   12 (4 comd, 8 bde) HQ; 36 (coys) bn

US Navy Special Operations Forces 5,400
Naval Special Warfare Command (NSWC) is organised around eight SEAL Teams and two SEAL Delivery Vehicle (SDV) Teams. These components deploy SEAL Teams, SEAL Delivery Vehicle Teams, and Special Boat Teams worldwide to meet the training, exercise, contingency and wartime requirements of theatre commanders. Operationally up to two of the eight SEAL Teams are deployed at any given time.

FORCES BY ROLE
NSWC	1 comd; 8 SEAL team (48 pl);
	2 SDV team

EQUIPMENT BY TYPE
SF 6 DDS

Naval Reserve Force
Delivery veh	1 det
Naval Special Warfare	6 (Gp) det; 3 det; 1 det
Special Boat	2 unit; 2 sqn
HQ	1 (CINCSOC) det
SEAL	8 det

FACILITIES
Navy Special Warfare Command (NSWC), Coronado CA

US Marine Special Operations Command (MARSOC)
Marine Special Operations Command (MARSOC) is a component of USSOCOM and consists of four subordinate units: the 1st and 2nd Marine Special Operations Battalions; the Marine Special Operations Advisory Group; and the Marine Special Operations Support Group. MARSOC Headquarters, the 2nd Marine Special Operations Battalion, the Marine Special Operations School, and the Marine Special Operations Support Group are stationed at Camp Lejeune, NC. The 1st Marine Special Operations Battalion is stationed at Camp Pendleton, CA.

US Air Force
FORCES BY ROLE
Air Force Special Operations Command (AFSOC) includes about 13,000 active and reserve personnel. AFSOC is headquartered at Hurlburt Field, FL, along with the 720th Special Tactics Group, the 1st Special Operations Wing (SOW) and the USAF Special Operations School and Training Center. 27th SOW is located at Cannon Air Force Base, NM. 352nd Special Operations Group is at RAF Mildenhall, UK, and 353rd Special Operations Group, is at Kadena Air Base, Japan. Reserve AFSOC components include the 193rd SOW, ANG, stationed at Harrisburg, PA and the 919th Special Operations Wing, AFR, stationed at Duke Field, FL. AFSOC's three active-duty flying units have more than 100 fixed and rotary-wing aircraft. AFSOC plans to procure 50 CV-22s by 2017, and would like to increase its MC-130 fleet to 61 aircraft to accommodate the growth of army and marine corps special operations forces.

FORCES BY ROLE
Special Ops   2 sqn with AC-130H/U *Spectre*; 3 sqn with MC-130E/H *Combat Talon*; 1 sqn with MC-130P *Combat Shadow*; 1 sqn with MC-130P *Combat Shadow*/C-130 *Hercules*; 1 sqn with MC-130W *Combat Spear*; 2 sqn with U-28A; 2 sqn with CV-22 *Osprey* (+2 sqn personnel only); 1 sqn with C-130E *Hercules*; An-26; UH-1N *Iroqouis*; Mi-8; 1 sqn with MQ-1B *Predator*

Reserve Organisations

Air National Guard
Special Ops   1 sqn with EC-130J *Commando Solo*

Air Force Reserve
Special Ops   2 sqn with MC-130E *Combat Talon*; 1 sqn with MC-130P *Combat Shadow* (personnel only)

DEPLOYMENT

AFGHANISTAN
NATO • ISAF 34,800; 1 div HQ; 1 mech inf SBCT; 2 lt inf IBCT; 1 AB IBCT; 2 cbt avn bde; 1 USMC MEB with (1 RCT) US Central Command • *Operation Enduring Freedom – Afghanistan* 31,129; 1 AB IBCT (trg); 1 ARNG lt inf IBCT (trg)

EQUIPMENT BY TYPE (ISAF and OEF-A)
AH-64 *Apache*, OH-58 *Kiowa*, CH-47 *Chinook*, UH-60 *Black Hawk*, M119, M198, *Stryker*, 3,200 MRAP, M-ATV, F-15E *Strike Eagle*, A-10 *Thunderbolt II*, EC-130H *Compass Call*, C-130 *Hercules*, HH-60 *Pave Hawk*, MV-22B Osprey, AV-8B *Harrier*, KC-130J *Hercules*, AH-IW *Cobra*, CH-53 *Sea Stallion*, UH-IN *Iroquois*, RQ-7B *Shadow*, MQ-1 *Predator*, MQ-9 *Reaper*

ANTIGUA AND BARBUDA
US Strategic Command • 1 Detection and Tracking Radar located at Antigua Air Station

ARABIAN GULF AND INDIAN OCEAN
US Central Command • Navy • 5th Fleet • (5th Fleet's operating forces are rotationally deployed to the region from either the Pacific Fleet or Atlantic Fleet.);

EQUIPMENT BY TYPE
1 CVN; 1 CG; 2 DDG; 1 FFG; 1 LHD; 1 LPD; 1 LSD; 1 T-AOE

Maritime Security Operations • 1 CG; 3 DDG; 1 FFG; 4 MCM; 5 PFC; 6 PBC (Coast Guard); 1 T-AKEH; 2 T-AO;1 ATF

NATO • *Operation Ocean Shield* 1 DDG

ASCENSION ISLAND
US Strategic Command • 1 detection and tracking radar located at Ascension Auxiliary Air Field

ATLANTIC OCEAN
US Northern Command • US Navy • 2nd Fleet

EQUIPMENT BY TYPE
6 SSBN; 2 SSGN; 24 SSN; 6 CVN; 9 CG; 22 DDG; 17 FFG; 3 PFC; 6 MCM; 2 LHD; 1 LHA; 4 LPD; 4 LSD

AUSTRALIA
US Pacific Command • US Army 29; US Navy 21; USAF 63; USMC 25 • 1 SEWS located at Pine Gap; 1 comms facility located at Pine Gap; 1 SIGINT stn located at Pine Gap

BAHRAIN
US Central Command • US Army 18; US Navy 1,261; USAF 26; USMC 142; 1 HQ (5th Fleet)

BELGIUM
US European Command • US Army 685; US Navy 106; USAF 457; USMC 26

BOSNIA-HERZEGOVINA
OSCE • Bosnia and Herzegovina 10

BRITISH INDIAN OCEAN TERRITORY
US Strategic Command • US Navy 213; USAF 32 • 1 Spacetrack Optical Tracker located at Diego Garcia; 1 ground based electro optical deep space surveillance system (*GEODSS*) located at Diego Garcia

US Pacific Command
1 MPS sqn (MPS-2 with equipment for one MEB) located at Diego Garcia with 5 logistics and support ships
• 1 naval airbase located at Diego Garcia, 1 support facility located at Diego Garcia

CANADA
US Northern Command • US Army 7; US Navy 30; USAF 83; USMC 10

CENTRAL AFRICAN REPUBLIC/CHAD
UN • MINURCAT 2

COLOMBIA
US Southern Command • US Army 52; US Navy 4; USAF 9; USMC 19

CUBA
US Army 293; US Navy 482 located at Guantánamo Bay; USMC 127 located at Guantánamo Bay

DJIBOUTI
US Africa Command • US Army 190; US Navy 717; USAF 125; USMC 133 • 1 naval air base located at Djibouti

EGYPT
MFO 688; 1 inf bn; 1 spt bn

EL SALVADOR
US Southern Command • US Army 6; US Navy 1; USAF 2; USMC 12 • 1 Forward Operating Location (Military, DEA, USCG and Customs personnel)

GERMANY
US Africa Command • 1 HQ located at Stuttgart
US Africa Command • USAF • 1 HQ (17th Air Force) located at Ramstein AB; 100 pers.
US European Command • 1 Combined Service HQ (EUCOM) located at Stuttgart–Vaihingen
US European Command • US Army 38,537 (reducing; some deployed to Iraq)

FORCES BY ROLE
1 HQ (US Army Europe (USAREUR)) located at Heidelberg; 1 mech inf SBCT, 1 (hvy) cbt avn bde; 1 armd inf bde (plus 1 armd inf bde currently deployed to Iraq)

EQUIPMENT BY TYPE
M-1 *Abrams*; M-2/M-3 *Bradley*; *Stryker*, M109; MLRS; AH-64 *Apache*; CH-47 *Chinook* UH-60 *Black Hawk*

US European Command • US Navy 249
US European Command • USAF 14,856

FORCES BY ROLE
1 HQ (US Air Force Europe (USAFE)) located at Ramstein AB; 1 HQ (3rd Air Force) located at Ramstein AB; 1 ftr wg located at Spangdahlem AB with (2 ftr sqn with 21 F-16C *Fighting Falcon*; 1 atk/FAC sqn with 12 A-10 *Thunderbolt II*; 6 OA-10A *Thunderbolt II*); 1 airlift wg located at Ramstein AB, with 16 C-130E *Hercules*; 2 C-20 *Gulfstream*; 9 C-21 *Learjet*; 1 CT-43 Boeing 737

US European Command • USMC 318

GREECE
US European Command • US Army 11; US Navy 291; USAF 57; USMC 12 • 1 naval base located at Makri; 1 naval base located at Soudha Bay; 1 air base located at Iraklion

GREENLAND (DNK)
US Strategic Command • 1 ballistic missile early warning system (BMEWS) located at Thule; 1 Spacetrack Radar located at Thule

GUAM
US Pacific Command • US Army 40; US Navy 938; USAF 1,928; USMC 10 • 1 air base; 1 naval base

EQUIPMENT BY TYPE
3 SSN; 1 MPS sqn (MPS-3 with equipment for one MEB) with 4 Logistics and Support vessels

HAITI
UN • MINUSTAH 4

HONDURAS
US Southern Command • US Army 228; US Navy 2; USAF 183; USMC 8 • 1 avn bn with CH-47 *Chinook*; UH-60 *Black Hawk*

IRAQ

NATO • NTM-I 12

UN • UNAMI 2 obs

US Central Command • US Forces- Iraq 120,000

FORCES BY ROLE

1 corps HQ; 2 div HQ; 5 armd HBCT; 1 armd inf bde; 2 mech inf SBCT; 1 lt inf IBCT; 1 AB IBCT (AAB); 1 ARNG div HQ; 1 ARNG armd HBCT; 1 ARNG armd HBCT (LoC duties); 2 ARNG lt inf IBCT (LoC duties); 1 USMC MEF HQ

EQUIPMENT BY TYPE

M1 *Abrams*, M2 *Bradley*, M3 *Bradley*, *Stryker*, M109, M198, 9,341 MRAP, AH-64 *Apache*, OH-58 *Kiowa*, UH-60 *Black Hawk*, CH-47 *Chinook*, F-16D *Fighting Falcon*; A-10 *Thunderbolt II*; C-130 *Hercules*; C-17 *Globemaster III*; HH-60G *Pave Hawk*; RQ-1B *Predator*

ISRAEL

US Army 4; US Navy 3; USAF 15; USMC 24 • 1 AN/TPY-2 X-band radar located at Nevatim

ITALY

US European Command • **US Army 3,015** • 1 AB IBCT

US European Command • **US Navy 2,328**

1 HQ (US Navy Europe (USNAVEUR)) located at Naples; 1 HQ (6th Fleet) located at Gaeta

US European Command • **USAF 4,076**

1 ftr wg with 2 ftr sqn (with 21 F-16C *Fighting Falcon*/F-16D *Fighting Falcon*) located at Aviano; 1 MR sqn with 9 P-3C *Orion* located at Sigonella

US European Command • **USMC 55**

JAPAN

US Pacific Command • **US Army 2,548** • 1 HQ (9th Theater Army Area Command) located at Zama

US Pacific Command • **US Navy** • 7th Fleet 3,708 • 1 HQ (7th Fleet) located at Yokosuka; 1 base located at Sasebo; 1 base located at Yokosuka

EQUIPMENT BY TYPE

1 CVN; 2 CG; 8 DDG; 1 LCC; 2 MCM; 1 LHD; 2 LSD

US Pacific Command • **USAF** • 5th Air Force 12,758

FORCES BY ROLE

1 HQ (5th Air Force) located at Okinawa - Kadena AB; 1 ftr wg located at Okinawa – Kadena AB with (2 ftr sqn with total of 18 F-16 *Fighting Falcon* located at Misawa AB); 1 ftr wg located at Okinawa – Kadena AB with (1 AEW sqn with 2 E-3B *Sentry*, 1 SAR sqn with 8 HH-60G *Pave Hawk*, 2 ftr sqn with total of 24 F-15C *Eagle*/F-15D *Eagle*); 1 airlift wg located at Yokota AB with 10 C-130H *Hercules*; 2 C-12J; 1 Special Ops gp located at Okinawa – Kadena AB

US Pacific Command • **USMC 14,378**

FORCES BY ROLE

1 Marine div (3rd); 1 ftr sqn with 12 F/A-18D *Hornet*; 1 tkr sqn with 12 KC-130J *Hercules*; 2 spt hel sqn with 12 CH-46E *Sea Knight*; 1 spt hel sqn with 12 MV-22B *Osprey*; 3 spt hel sqn with 10 CH-53E *Sea Stallion*

KOREA, REPUBLIC OF

US Pacific Command • **US Army** • 8th Army 17,130

FORCES BY ROLE

1 HQ (8th Army) located at Seoul; 1 div HQ (2nd Inf) located at Tongduchon, 1 armd HBCT; 1 (hvy) cbt avn bde, 1 arty (fires) bde; 1 AD bde

EQUIPMENT BY TYPE

M-1 *Abrams*; M-2/M-3 *Bradley*; M-109; AH-64 *Apache* CH-47 *Chinook*; UH-60 *Black Hawk*; MLRS; MIM-104 *Patriot*/FIM-92A *Avenger*; 1 (APS) HBCT set

US Pacific Command • **US Navy 254**

US Pacific Command • **USAF** • 7th Air Force 7,857

FORCES BY ROLE

1 (AF) HQ (7th Air Force) located at Osan AB; 1 ftr wg located at Osan AB with (1 ftr sqn with 20 F-16C *Fighting Falcon*/F-16D *Fighting Falcon*, 1 ftr sqn with 12 A-10 *Thunderbolt II*, 12 OA-10 *Thunderbolt II*); 1 ftr wg located at Kunsan AB with (1 ftr sqn with total of 20 F-16C *Fighting Falcon*/F-16D *Fighting Falcon*); 1 Special Ops sqn

US Pacific Command • **USMC 133**

KUWAIT

US Central Command • Troops deployed as part of *Op Iraqi Freedom* • 2 AD bty eqpt with total of 16 PAC-3 *Patriot;* elm 1 (APS) HBCT set (Empty – equipment in use)

LIBERIA

UN • UNMIL 5; 4 obs

MARSHALL ISLANDS

US Strategic Command • 1 detection and tracking radar located at Kwajalein Atoll

MEDITERRANEAN SEA

US European Command • **US Navy** • 6th Fleet

EQUIPMENT BY TYPE

1 DDG; 1 LCC

NATO • *Operation Active Endeavour* • 1 FFG

MIDDLE EAST

UN • UNTSO 2 obs

MOLDOVA

OSCE • Moldova 1

NETHERLANDS

US European Command • **US Army 253; US Navy 23; USAF 237; USMC 15**

NETHERLANDS ANTILLES

US Southern Command • 1 Forward Operating Location located at Aruba

NORWAY

US European Command • **US Army 23; US Navy 4; USAF 39; USMC 10** • 1 (APS) SP 155mm arty bn set

PACIFIC OCEAN

US Pacific Command • **US Navy** • 3rd Fleet

EQUIPMENT BY TYPE

8 SSBN; 2 SSGN; 26 SSN; 3 CVN; 9 CG; 18 DDG; 10 FFG; 2 MCM; 4 LHD; 1 LHA; 4 LPD; 4 LSD

PHILIPPINES

US Pacific Command • **US Army 14; US Navy 5; USAF 10; USMC 82**

PORTUGAL

US European Command • US Army 28; US Navy 29 ; USAF 663; USMC 7 • 1 Support facility located at Lajes

QATAR

US Central Command • US Army 212; US Navy 3; USAF 181; USMC 36 • elm 1 (APS) HBCT set (Empty – equipment in use)

SAUDI ARABIA

US Central Command • US Army 144; US Navy 25; USAF 81; USMC 27;

OPM-SANG 500 (Combined Service)

SERBIA

NATO • KFOR • *Joint Enterprise* 1,475; 1 ARNG cbt spt bde
OSCE • Serbia 4
OSCE • Kosovo 11

SEYCHELLES

US Africa Command • some MQ-9 *Reaper* UAV

SIERRA LEONE

IMATT 3

SINGAPORE

US Pacific Command • US Army 8; US Navy 83; USAF 13; USMC 18 • 1 log spt sqn • 1 spt facility

SPAIN

US European Command • US Army 90; US Navy 689; USAF 350; USMC 145 • 1 air base located at Morón; 1 naval base located at Rota

TURKEY

US European Command • US Army 62; US Navy 8; USAF 1,514; USMC 16 • 1 air base located at Incirlik; 1 support facility located at Ankara; 1 support facility located at Izmir
US Strategic Command • 1 Spacetrack Radar located at Incirlik

UNITED ARAB EMIRATES

US Central Command • US Army 2; US Navy 1; USAF 84; USMC 17

UNITED KINGDOM

US European Command • US Army 345; US Navy 333; USAF 8,596; USMC 93

FORCES BY ROLE

1 ftr wg located at RAF Lakenheath with (1 ftr sqn with 24 F-15C *Eagle*/F-15D *Eagle*, 2 ftr sqn with 24 F-15E *Strike Eagle*); 1 tkr wg located at RAF Mildenhall, with 15 KC-135 *Stratotanker*; 1 special ops gp located at RAF Mildenhall with 5 MC-130H *Combat Talon II*; 5 MC-130P *Combat Shadow*; 1 C-130E *Hercules*

US Strategic Command • 1 ballistic missile early warning system (BMEWS) and 1 Spacetrack Radar located at Fylingdales Moor

FOREIGN FORCES

Canada 3 USCENTCOM; 303 NORTHCOM (NORAD)
Germany Air Force: 23 *Tornado* IDS Strike/FGA ac located at Holloman AFB (NM); 35 T-37B *Tweet* located at Sheppard AFB (TX); 40 T-38A *Talon* located at Sheppard AFB (TX); Missile trg located at Fort Bliss (TX); School located at Fort Bliss (TX) (GAF Air Defence); some (primary) trg sqn located at Goodyear (AZ) with Beech F-33 *Bonanza;* some (joint jet pilot) trg sqn located at Sheppard AFB (TX); 812 (flying trg) located at Goodyear AFB (AZ); Sheppard AFB (TX); Holloman AFB (NM); FAS Pensacola (FL); Fort Rucker (AL); Army: 1 (battle) Army gp (trg) (army trg area) with 35 *Leopard* 2; 26 *Marder* 1; 12 M-109A3G
Italy Air Force: 38
United Kingdom Army, Navy, Air Force ε700

Table 8 US Air Capability 2010

AIRCRAFT (fixed wing & rotary)	AIR FORCE				ARMY	MARITIME						Type Total
	Active Force	Air Force Reserve	Air National Guard	Air Force Total	US Army	Naval Aviation	Naval Aviation Reserve	Marine Corps Aviation	Marine Corps Aviation Reserve	Coast Guard	Store	
LRSA	145	9	0	154	0	0	0	0	0	0	18	172
B-1B *Lancer*	64			64								64
B-2A *Spirit*	19			19								19
B-52 *Stratofortress*	62	9		71							18	89
TAC	1793	135	722	2650	0	1010	74	383	27	48	13	4205
A-10 *Thunderbolt* II	143	46	84	273								273
AC-130H/U *Spectre* (SOC)	25			25								25
AV-8B *Harrier* II				0				131				131
EA-6B *Prowler* (EW)				0		92	4	29				125
EA-18G *Growler* (EW)				0		7						7
EC-130H *Compass Call*	14			14								14
EC-130J *Commando Solo* (SOC)			6	6								6
EP-3E *Aries II* (EW)				0		11						11
F-5E/F *Tiger* II				0			5		1			6
F-5N *Tiger* II				0			29		12			41
F/A-18A/A+ *Hornet*				0		33	12	44	14			103
F/A-18B *Hornet*				0		24		2				26
F/A-18C *Hornet*				0		268	12	83				363
F/A-18D *Hornet*				0		41		94				135
F/A-18E *Super Hornet*				0		171						171
F/A-18F *Super Hornet*				0		216						216
F-15A/B/C/D *Eagle*	396		126	522								522
F-15E *Strike Eagle*	217			217								217
F-16C/D *Fighting Falcon*	738	69	473	1280								1280
F/A-22A *Raptor*	139			139								139
HC-144A				0						6		6
HU-25A *Guardian*				0						25		25
HU-25B *Guardian*				0						3	4	7
HU-25C *Guardian*				0						8	9	17
HU-25D *Guardian*				0						6		6
MC-130E/H *Combat Talon* I/II (SOC)	16	14		30								30
MC-130P *Combat Shadow* (SOC)	23		4	27								27
MC-130W *Combat Spear*	12			12								12
OA-10 *Thunderbolt* II	70	6	18	94								94
P-3C *Orion*				0		147	12					159
RC-26B *Metroliner*			11	11								11
RECCE	96	10	0	106	60	4	0	0	0	0	0	170
Dash-7 ARL-C				0	3							3
Dash-7 ARL-I				0	3							3
Dash-7 ARL-M				0	3							3
E9-A	2			2								2
MC-12W	37			37								37
O-2 *Skymaster*				0	2							2
OC-135B *Open Skies*	3			3								3

Table 8 US Air Capability 2010

AIRCRAFT (fixed wing & rotary)	AIR FORCE Active Force	AIR FORCE Air Force Reserve	AIR FORCE Air National Guard	AIR FORCE Air Force Total	ARMY US Army	MARITIME Naval Aviation	MARITIME Naval Aviation Reserve	MARITIME Marine Corps Aviation	MARITIME Marine Corps Aviation Reserve	MARITIME Coast Guard	MARITIME Store	Type Total
RC-12D/H/K Guardrail				0	37							37
RC-12F Huron				0		2						2
RC-12M Huron				0		2						2
RC-12P/Q Guardrail				0	12							12
RC-135U Combat Sent	2			2								2
RC-135V/W Rivet Joint	17			17								17
U-2S	28			28								28
TU-2S	5			5								5
WC-130J Hercules		10		10								10
WC-135 Constant Phoenix	2			2								2
COMD / AEW	**37**	**0**	**17**	**54**	**0**	**82**	**6**	**0**	**0**	**0**	**0**	**142**
E-2C Hawkeye (AEW)				0		66	6					72
E-3B/C Sentry (AWACS)	33			33								33
E-4B	4			4								4
E-6B Mercury				0		16						16
E-8C Joint Stars			17	17								17
TPT	**417**	**169**	**258**	**844**	**196**	**92**	**60**	**21**	**7**	**29**	**5**	**1254**
C-2A Greyhound				0		35						35
C-5A Galaxy		26	33	59								59
C-5B Galaxy	31	16		47								47
C-5C Galaxy	2			2								2
C-5M Galaxy	3			3								3
C-9B/C Nightingale		3		3			15	2				20
C-12C/D/F/J/R Huron				0	113	4						117
C-17 Globemaster III	158	8	8	174								174
C-20A Gulfstream III				0		1	1					2
C-20B Gulfstream III	5			5	2							7
C-20D Gulfstream III				0		2	2					4
C-20G Gulfstream IV				0		5	4	1				10
C-20H Gulfstream III	2			2								2
C-21A Learjet	35		21	56								56
C-23A/B Sherpa				0	42							42
C-26 Metro				0	11							11
C-26D Metro III				0		7						7
C-32A (Air Force Two)	4			4								4
C-37A	9			9		1	1			1		12
C-37B				0			3					3
C-40A Clipper				0			9					9
C-40B/C	2	3	2	7								7
C-130E/H/J Hercules	151	103	181	435						6		441
C-130T Hercules				0			19					19
C-143A Challenger				0						1		1
CT-39G Sabreliner				0		1						1
DC-9				0			1					1

Table 8 **US Air Capability 2010**

AIRCRAFT (fixed wing & rotary)	AIR FORCE Active Force	Air Force Reserve	Air National Guard	Air Force Total	ARMY US Army	MARITIME Naval Aviation	Naval Aviation Reserve	Marine Corps Aviation	Marine Corps Aviation Reserve	Coast Guard	Store	Type Total
HC-130P/N *Hercules*	13	10	13	36								36
MC-130H *Hercules* (SAR)				0						21	5	26
LC-130F *Hercules*				0		2						2
LC-130R *Hercules*				0		1						1
U-6A *Beaver*				0		2						2
UC-12B/F *Huron* (UTL)				0		21	5	11	2			39
UC-35 *Citation* (UTL)				0	28							28
UC-35C/D *Citation Ultra/Citation Encore*				0		1		7	5			13
UP-3A *Orion*				0		4						4
VC-25A (Air Force One)	2			2								2
VP-3A *Orion*				0		5						5
TKR	**241**	**65**	**206**	**512**	**0**	**0**	**0**	**34**	**28**	**0**		**574**
KC-10A *Extender* (tkr/tpt)	59			59								59
KC-130J *Hercules*				0				34				34
KC-130R *Hercules*				0								0
KC-130T *Hercules*				0					28			28
KC-135 A/E/R/T *Stratotanker*	182	65	206	453								453
TRG	**1141**	**0**	**0**	**1141**	**0**	**648**	**0**	**20**	**0**	**0**		**1809**
T-1A *Jayhawk*	179			179								179
T-34C *Turbo Mentor*				0		270		3				273
T-38A *Talon*	546			546		9						555
T-39D *Sabreliner*				0		1						1
T-39G *Sabreliner*				0		8						8
T-39N *Sabreliner*				0		15						15
T-43A	11			11								11
T-44A *Pegasus*				0		55						55
T-45A *Goshawk*				0		74						74
T-45C *Goshawk*				0		144						144
T-6A *Texan* II	405			405		47						452
T-6B *Texan* II				0		2						2
TAV-8B *Harrier*				0				17				17
TC-12B *Huron*				0		21						21
TE-2C *Hawkeye*				0		2						2
TILT-ROTOR	**11**	**0**	**0**	**11**	**0**	**0**	**0**	**86**	**0**	**0**		**97**
CV-22 *Osprey* (being tested)	3			3								3
CV-22A *Osprey* (SOC)	8			8								8
MV-22A *Osprey*				0				20				20
MV-22B *Osprey*				0				62				62
V-22 *Osprey*				0				4				4
HELICOPTERS	**126**	**23**	**18**	**167**	**3877**	**644**	**32**	**573**	**60**	**133**	**19**	**5505**
AH-1W *Cobra*				0				139	18			157
AH-1Z *Viper*				0				6				6
AH-6/MH-6 *Little Bird*				0	36							36

Table 8 US Air Capability 2010

AIRCRAFT (fixed wing & rotary)	AIR FORCE				ARMY	MARITIME						Type Total
	Active Force	Air Force Reserve	Air National Guard	Air Force Total	US Army	Naval Aviation	Naval Aviation Reserve	Marine Corps Aviation	Marine Corps Aviation Reserve	Coast Guard	Store	
AH-64A/D *Apache*				0	697							697
CH-46E *Sea Knight*				0				135	27			162
CH-47D *Chinook*				0	309							309
CH-47F *Chinook*				0	63							63
CH-53D *Sea Stallion*				0		9		35				44
CH-53E *Sea Stallion*				0		9		145	6			160
HH-1N *Iroquois*				0		23		5				28
HH-46D/E *Sea Knight*				0		4		4				8
HH-60G *Pave Hawk*	64	23	18	105								105
HH-60H *Seahawk*				0		36	10					46
HH-60J *Jayhawk* (SAR)				0						35	7	42
HH-60L *Black Hawk*				0	15							15
HH-65C (AS-366G1) *Dauphin* II (SAR)				0						90	12	102
MH-47E *Chinook*				0	6							6
MH-47G *Chinook*				0	50							50
MH-53E *Sea Dragon*				0		28	8					36
MH-60K/L *Black Hawk*				0	60							60
MH-60R *Strike Hawk*				0		35						35
MH-60S *Knight Hawk*				0		123	8					131
MH-68A (A-109E) *Power* (UTL)				0						8		8
N-SH-60B (TEST)				0		3						3
OH-58A/C *Kiowa*				0	247	3						250
OH-58D *Kiowa Warrior*				0	338							338
SH-60B *Seahawk*				0		148	6					154
SH-60F *Seahawk*				0		72						72
TH-57B *Sea Ranger*				0		44						44
TH-57C *Sea Ranger*				0		82						82
TH-67 *Creek* (TRG)				0	154							154
TH-6B				0		6						6
UH-1H/V *Iroquois*				0	100							100
UH-1N *Huey* (tpt)	62			62								62
UH-1N *Iroquois*				0		1		76	9			86
UH-1Y *Iroquois*				0		4		9				13
UH-46D *Sea Knight*				0		9						9
UH-60A *Black Hawk*				0	951							951
UH-60L *Black Hawk*				0	681	3						684
UH-60M *Black Hawk*				0	108							108
UH-60Q *Black Hawk*				0	4							4
UH-72A *Lakota*				0	58							58
VH-3A *Sea King*				0		2						2
VH-3D *Sea King* (VIP tpt)				0				11				11
VH-60N *Presidential Hawk* (VIP tpt)				0				8				8

North America

Table 8 **US Air Capability 2010**

AIRCRAFT (fixed wing & rotary)	AIR FORCE Active Force	AIR FORCE Air Force Reserve	AIR FORCE Air National Guard	AIR FORCE Air Force Total	ARMY US Army	MARITIME Naval Aviation	MARITIME Naval Aviation Reserve	MARITIME Marine Corps Aviation	MARITIME Marine Corps Aviation Reserve	MARITIME Coast Guard	MARITIME Store	Type Total
UAV	151	0	7	158	4034	42	0	587	0	3	0	4824
I-Gnat				0	3							3
MQ-1 Predator	111		7	118								118
MQ-8B Fire Scout (trials)				0		5						5
MQ-9 Reaper	27			27								27
RQ-2B Pioneer				0		35						35
RQ-4A Global Hawk	13			13		2						15
RQ-5A Hunter				0	20							20
RQ-7A Shadow				0	236							236
RQ-7B Shadow				0				32				32
RQ-11B Raven				0	3756			555				4311
RQ-14 Dragon Eye (mini-UAV)				0								0
Warrior				0	15							15
Sky Warrior				0	4							4
TRIALS/TEST	12	0	0	12	0	50	0	0	0	0	0	62
B-52 Stratofortress	4			4								4
B-1B Lancer	2			2								2
B-2 Spirit	1			1								1
E-3 Sentry	1			1								1
EA-18G Growler				0		5						5
F-35A Lightning	4			4								4
NF/A-18A Hornet				0		1						1
NF/A-18C Hornet				0		2						2
NF/A-18D Hornet				0		3						3
NP-3C Orion				0		1						1
NP-3D Orion				0		11						11
NT-34C Mentor				0		1						1
NU-1B Otter				0		1						1
QF-4N Phantom II				0		2						2
QF-4S Phantom II				0		16						16
X-26A				0		2						2
X-31A				0		1						1
YF-4J Phantom II (prototype, FGA)				0		1						1
YSH-60				0		1						1
YSH-60B Seahawk (prototype)				0		1						1
YSH-60F Seahawk (prototype)				0		1						1
TOTAL AIRCRAFT				5484	256	1886	140	544	62	77	36	8485
TOTAL Combat Capable				2708	0	900	66	371	27	0	18	4090
TOTAL HELICOPTERS				167	3877	644	32	573	60	133	19	5505
TOTAL UAVs				158	4034	42	0	587	0	3	0	4824

Table 9 **Selected US Arms Orders**

Classification	Designation	FY2008 Value ($m)	Units	Estimate FY2009 Value ($m)	Units	Request FY2010 Value ($m)	Units
JOINT							
UAV	*Global Hawk*	573	5	710	5	667	5
UAV	*Predator*	299	24	377	38		
UAV	*Reaper*	374	20	444	24	489	24
UAV	*Warrior*	130	8	186	15	651	36
tpt	Joint Cargo Aircraft	156	4	263	7	319	8
Trg	JPATS	524	83	318	44	282	38
APC	MRAP	16,838	9,380	4,393	1,000	5,456	1,080
	Missile Defense	994		1,218		998	
	FCS	80		221		327	
AIR FORCE							
FGA	F-35 JSF	1,412	6	1,660	7	2,349	10
FGA	F-22	3,790	20	4,345	24	445	
FGA	F-16 Upgrades	383		371		244	
Bbr	B-2 Upgrades	102		347		699	
Tpt	C-17	3,826	15	880		690	
Tpt	C-130J	2,833	28	1,326	6	2,061	12
Tpt	C-5 Upgrades	345		574		772	
Tilt rotor	V-22	838	10	421	6	451	5
AAM	AMRAAM	190	133	203	133	291	196
Sat	Wideband GS	312	1	21		264	1
Sat	SBIR	399		1,793	2	500	1
Sat	AHEF	149		165		1,843	
Sat	GPS	248		134		60	
Launcher	EELV	1,091	4	1,350	2	1,295	5
	JDAM	124	4,312	190	7,049	201	7,452
ARMY							
Hel	Light Utility Helicopter	228	42	256	44	326	54
Hel	UH-60 *Blackhawk*	1,354	77	1,142	68	1,431	83
Hel	AH-64D			11		219	8
Hel	CH-47	1,386	47	1,290	50	1,052	39
MRL	HIMARS	263	2,070	309	2,652	354	3,306
ATGW	*Javelin*	278	1,320	377	1,320	289	1,334
MBT	*Abrams* modifications	2,361	260	1,384	111	471	22
AFV	*Stryker*	2,792	677	1,309	88	478	
Veh	HMMWV	2,796	17,012	1,676	10,995	1,532	10,214
Veh	FHTV	3,095		1,978		1,436	
Veh	FMTV	2,147	6,802	1,017	3,724	1,620	5,532
Veh	ASV	568	685	318	345	150	150
Tpt	JHSV	208	1	342	2	361	2
Comms	Warfighter INT	112	494	655		557	
NAVY and MARINES							
FGA	F/A-18 E/F	2,762	37	1,930	9	1,188	9
FGA	F-35 JSF	1,223	6	1,650	7	4,478	20
EW	E/A-18G *Growler*	1,525	21	1,594	22	1,632	22
Tilt-rotor	V-22	2,070	23	2,213	30	2,300	30
Hel	MH-60S	564	20	594	20	492	18
Hel	UH-1Y	416	15	636	20	835	30
Hel	MH-60R	1,143	28	1,260	31	1,025	24
AEW	E-2C *Hawkeye*	52		384	2	606	2
Tpt	C-130J	805	13	153	2		

Table 9 **Selected US Arms Orders**

Classification	Designation	FY2008 Value ($m)	Units	Estimate FY2009 Value ($m)	Units	Request FY2010 Value ($m)	Units
MPA	P-8 *Poseidon*			110		2,987	6
SLBM	*Trident*	1,044	12	1,085	24	1,135	24
TCM	*Tomahawk*	475	496	280	207	296	196
SAM	Standard	158	75	225	70	249	62
CVN	Carrier Replacement	3,145		3,915		1,223	
CVN	Refueling overhaul	295		613		1,775	
SSN	*Virginia* class	3,319	1	3,674	1	4,027	1
DDG	DDG 1000	2,906		1,504	1	1,084	
DDG	Aegis 51	47		199		2,241	1
FFG	Littoral Combat Ship			1,090	2	1,517	3
LPD	LDP-17	1,506	1	963	1	1,056	
Aux	T-AKE	720		962	2	940	2
UAV	TUAS	214		342	1	516	1

Table 10 **Selected arms procurements and deliveries, Canada**

Designation	Type	Quantity	Contract Value	Supplier Country	Prime Contractor	Order Date	First Delivery Due	Notes
LAV III	LAV Upgrade	550	CAN$1bn (US$859.7m)	Dom	General Dynamics (GDLS)	2009	2012	Focus on weapons and mobility systems. Part of FLCV upgrade and procurement project worth CAN$5bn
Halifax	FFG SLEP	12	CAN$3.1bn (US$2.9bn).	Dom	Halifax and Victoria Shipyards	2007	2010	SLEP: *Halifax*-class HCM/FELEX project. To be fitted with *Sea Giraffe* 150 HC surv radar. Final delivery due 2017
M777 Howitzer	Arty	25	_	US	BAE	2009	_	Acquired from US through FMS Programme. Total contract with BAE worth US$118m
150 HC 2D *Sea Giraffe*	Radar	12	US$23m	Dom	Saab	2009	2010	For *Halifax* FFG. Part of Frigate Equipment Life Extension Combat Systems Integration programme
C-130J *Super Hercules*	Tpt ac	17	US$1.4bn	US	Lockheed Martin	2007	2010	To replace current CC130 E. Final delivery due 2013
CH-148 *Cyclone*	Tpt hel	28	US$5bn	US	Sikorsky	2004	2010	(H-92 *Superhawk*). Incl US$1.8bn 20-year parts/training package. Deliveries delayed until Nov 2010. Final delivery due 2013
CH-47D *Chinook*	Tpt hel	6	CAN$292m	US	Boeing	2008	2008	Ex-US stock. For use in AFG until delivery of 16 CH-47F+. First hel delivered Nov 2008
CH-47F *Chinook*	Tpt hel	15	US$1.15bn	US	Boeing	2009	2013	For Army use
CP-140 (P-3) *Aurora*	MPA SLEP	10	US$156m	US	Lockheed Martin	2008	_	To extend service life by 15,000 flight hours over 20 to 25 years
Heron	UAV	2	CAN$95m	ISR	MDA	2008	2009	2 year lease. For use in AFG. Current contract will keep *Heron* in service until early 2011. Option for 3rd year
Scan Eagle	UAV	1	CAD14m	US	Boeing	2008	2009	For use in AFG

Chapter Two
Latin America and the Caribbean

There is now both a need and an opportunity for the nations of Latin America collectively to cater more effectively for the region's own security. The opportunity stems, in part, from a lack of appetite in the US for regional conflict management, while the need derives from the fact that there are increasingly numerous and complex threats to this security. Democratic decay, prospective state failure, transnational organised crime, terrorism and/or insurgency, the trafficking of illegal weapons, narcotics and people, resource competition, environmental degradation and the consequential disruption to social cohesion all pose serious threats to regional stability, and all these domestic and non-state problems impinge on regional relationships. As noted in recent editions of *The Military Balance*, nations in Latin America and the Caribbean have been trying to develop regional institutions to develop defence and security cooperation (see also 'South America: Framing Regional Security' by John Chipman and James Lockhart Smith, *Survival*, vol. 51, no. 6, December 2009–January 2010).

The Military Balance 2009 discussed how Central American states have organised more cooperation among their armed forces, as well as many other meetings, symposia and cooperation agreements (p. 53). Furthermore, the establishment of the Unión de Naciones Suramericanas (UNASUR) and the accompanying South American Defence Council (SADC) indicate that South America is now taking its own steps to address continental security. (UNASUR excludes Mexico, Central America and the Caribbean.) But gaps remain in the institutional architecture. In the Andean region, there is no systemic approach to the handling of transnational threats, despite past attempts to develop one within the Andean Community, while in the Southern Cone states, border and energy disputes regularly consume the détente achieved through careful diplomacy (Argentina and Chile's accommodation over their border notwithstanding). Although Brazil and Argentina put to one side their prior interest in nuclear weapons, Brazil is now interested in developing nuclear technology for submarine propulsion.

The SADC was off to a good start with the Santiago Declaration of March 2009, containing a four-part plan of action in the fields of defence policy, military cooperation, defence industries and training. Chipman and Lockhart Smith argue that the Council needs to do more to create a long-term agenda resistant to hijacking by sub-regional and single-issue concerns, such as enhancing defence transparency (through the publication and updating of White Papers), legal norms of transnational cooperation, information sharing on non-state actors, and harmonisation of participation in extra-regional security arrangements (such as the Proliferation Security Initiative).

Though regional security cooperation remains weak, limited military and security ties do exist bilaterally, through numerous other institutions in Central and South America, and with external actors. Mexico and Colombia have strengthened their military relationships with the United States, mainly through the Mérida Initiative and Plan Colombia. Venezuela has developed ties with China and Iran as well as with Russia, with whom it has been active in procurement discussions. Other members of the Bolivarian Alternative for the Americas (ALBA) – Ecuador, Bolivia, Nicaragua and Cuba – have also established or renewed military links with Russia. Many of the region's armed forces have transformed throughout the decade to address their national-security challenges with various degrees of success. However, with military expenditure increasing, the strategic purposes to which strengthened militaries might be put remain in many cases opaque.

Force transformation and modernisation
Mexico's war on organised crime has made headlines in recent years, with violence spilling over into the United States and Guatemala. As much as 90% of the cocaine in US markets travels through Mexico and is controlled by Mexican cartels. Mexican President Felipe Calderón has deployed 45,000 troops throughout the country and has scored major victories against the cartels. But the Mexican public has been increasingly affected by an unprecedented surge in violence. Calderón acknowledged that deploying the

army was an imperfect solution, but cast the move as temporary and one that would end when local forces were purged of corruption and the threat of violence from traffickers reduced. In the face of operations for which they were not ideally suited, the Mexican armed forces have undergone several transformations in force structure. Indeed, on 22 September 2009, the Mexican Senate promulgated a more ambitious initiative that would, if it proceeds, lead to the creation of a single defence ministry, replacing the current two-ministry structure (Ministry of National Defence for the army and air force and the Ministry of Marine for the navy).

The Mexican Army has adopted a new brigade structure, creating three light infantry brigades and consolidating the special forces into a single corps composed of 12 battalions. However, plans to create a 10,000-man anti-crime force dubbed the Federal Support Corps (see *The Military Balance 2008*, p. 55) have met with resistance from the Mexican Congress. Command and control functions have been redesigned and decentralised, allowing greater independence to each of the 12 Military Region commanders and establishing C⁴ units in every region, increasing the operational flexibility of regional commanders. These operations, moreover, have had a direct impact on equipment availability and procurement. During 2009, maintenance schedules were boosted and the army opted to acquire 2,200 4×4 pick-up trucks instead of 1,000 HMMWVs (humvees), since the former were seen as better suited to urban areas. Meanwhile, the Mexican Navy has created a maritime police-oriented marine infantry corps that has expanded to 32 battalions, as well as two amphibious-reaction brigades (each with six battalions), and special-forces groups. This reorganisation, dubbed the *Plan Sectorial 2007–2012*, began in 2007, and as of September 2009 the 32 infantry battalions were at 50% strength. They are due to be at full strength by 2012 at the latest. The navy is also restructuring. This will include a reorganisation and, it is reported, legal mandates regulating the use of force on public-security tasks, as well as enhanced cooperation with the army and air force. A new coastguard-type service will also function as part of the navy.

Meanwhile, two new locally built *Oaxaca*-class ocean-patrol vessels (OPVs), two *Polaris* II interceptor craft, eight CN-235MP *Persuader* surveillance aircraft, S4 unmanned aerial vehicles (UAVs) and AS565 *Panther* helicopters point to the navy's increasing role in interdiction activities. The navy has outlined plans to acquire five new exclusive economic zone patrol vessels, an amphibious logistics ship and two further locally built OPVs and a number of interceptor craft. The 'coastguard' is building 17 stations to increase search-and-rescue coverage and provide a clear maritime law-enforcement role; this will expand Mexico's naval presence into several areas where it was previously absent. The service will have two types of stations: six 'A' type stations, each with a self-righting motor-lifeboat, two *Defender* patrol boats and a helicopter, and 'B' types each with two *Defenders* and a helicopter. Six MD-902 helicopters have been put back into service and assigned to the coastguard role.

Moves to restructure Mexico's air force are driven by support to army activities. Reorganisation of the air force began in 2005 with the establishment of two northern air regions (replacing a single entity); this has led to a redeployment of operational units to balance coverage across the nation. New additions are due to include EC725, Bell 412 and UH-60 *Blackhawk* helicopters; intelligence, surveillance and reconnaissance assets; and C-295M transport aircraft. US assistance to the Mexican military through the Mérida Initiative (see *The Military Balance 2009*, p. 55) has so far been reported to include eight Bell 412 helicopters, non-intrusive detection equipment, four HH-60 medium helicopters and four CN-235MP *Persuader* surveillance aircraft, as well as a logistics, spare parts and training package. However, the bulk of the US assistance is increasingly earmarked for civilian law enforcement.

Much attention within **Central America** has focused on the removal from office by the military, and subsequent expulsion by court order, of the elected president of Honduras, Manuel Zelaya. Zelaya subsequently re-entered Honduras (residing in Brazil's embassy in Tegucigalpa) and at the time of writing, discussions between Zelaya and interim leader Roberto Micheletti to resolve the political crisis had broken down. On the sub-regional level, the armed forces of Guatemala, Honduras, El Salvador and Nicaragua form the Armed Forces Conference of Central America (CFAC), through which they have stood up a military humanitarian emergency-reaction unit (UHR) and plan to establish a peace-keeping battalion, the Unidad de Operaciones de Mantenimiento de Paz (UMOP) announced in June 2008. In general, CFAC forces demobilised considerably during the 1990s and national police forces were created to take over their internal security roles, though these police forces at times lack the equip-

Latin America and Caribbean

Map 1 **Mexico: military and air regions**

ment and training to fully address concerns ranging from drug cartels to gangs and arms smugglers. While attempts to considerably increase manpower levels and acquire modern hardware have failed due to lack of funding, the US has provided continued assistance through programmes such as US Southern Command's *Enduring Friendship,* which has provided a number of fast patrol boats and communication and radar equipment to local navies. To date, four boats each have been provided to Panama, the Dominican Republic, the Bahamas, Jamaica, Honduras and Nicaragua, while the programme for 2009 was due to include two boats to Belize, two more for the Bahamas, and scoping requirements for other nations. A larger US$300 million programme is aimed at upgrading air-interdiction and operational capability. Under this Regional Aircraft Modernization Program (RAMP), the US would share with partner nations the procurement costs of helicopter and airlift assets and establish long-term maintenance and training contracts. Although four air chiefs signed a non-binding agreement to move forward with RAMP, progress has so

far been mixed. Meanwhile, SOUTHCOM, which re-established the Fourth Fleet during 2008, with an HQ in Florida, retains inter-agency task forces at the Comalapa and Curacao Forward Operating Locations (FOLs). In September 2009 it returned the Manta FOL to Ecuador after its ten-year lease expired.

Colombia continues to be a major recipient of US assistance under Plan Colombia, which had provided US$6 billion in counter-narcotics funding since 2000. However, US$27m in funds have been frozen since 2007 on human-rights grounds and overall funding has recently fallen as the US Congress reduced the proportion of military spending. On 14 August 2009, the US and Colombia reached a provisional agreement *ad referendum* on a Defence Cooperation Agreement (DCA) covering issues (such as those concerning the presence of US military personnel) that have proved contentious with neighbouring governments. The agreement was signed on 30 October. Although the DCA does not permit the establishment of US bases in Colombia, it 'ensures continued US access to specific agreed Colombian facilities in order to undertake mutually agreed upon activities' in the country. Specifically, the agreement facilitates access to the Palanquero, Apiay and Malambo air bases, as well as two naval bases and two army sites. The personnel ceilings authorised by Congress in October 2004 (up to 800 military personnel and up to 600 civilian contractors) will be respected.

Under the government of President Alvaro Uribe, measures to combat the Revolutionary Armed Forces of Colombia (FARC) have borne fruit and the guerrillas have suffered a series of setbacks. As noted in the IISS *Strategic Survey 2009* (p. 114), plagued by deaths, captures and an unprecedented 3,000 desertions in 2008, the number of FARC personnel dropped from a reported high of 20,000 to 8,000. Although government operations, prosecuted under Uribe's 'Democratic Security Policy' (DSP), have hit FARC hard – which was perhaps reflected in the group's reconfigured 'Plan Rebirth' strategy – FARC stepped up urban bombing and extortion rackets, demonstrating that it retained an ability to inflict damage.

With doctrinal changes and the creation of specialised units under the DSP, Colombia's forces have transformed into a highly mobile and effective counter-insurgency force. The army has expanded by two full divisions, eight territorial brigades and 16 mobile (counter-guerrilla) brigades, and several other undermanned brigades have been strengthened. This translates into more than 60 counter-guerrilla battalions, six high-mountain battalions, four infantry battalions, two *Meteoro* battalions, 41 sniper platoons and four anti-explosives companies. Central rapid-reaction forces have been implemented in all of the divisions and army aviation has also been considerably expanded with *Blackhawk* and Mi-17 medium-lift helicopters.

Meanwhile, Colombia's navy has transformed into an efficient brown-water force, with an increased counter-insurgency focus. Ten new river support stations have been established. Meanwhile, a third river brigade has been created with two new battalions and the transfer of two existing marine infantry battalions from the first brigade. This river brigade thus contains three marine infantry battalions and a marine assault battalion. A new coastguard service with a network of 25 stations and 23 patrol vessels has also been stood up as part of the navy. Training is being conducted with some assistance from the US Coast Guard.

The Colombian air force has focused on a two-squadron multirole-fighter force backed up by a modified Boeing 767 tanker, plus significant close-air-support assets. It has signalled an intention to acquire other force multipliers such as airborne-early-warning aircraft, though this has yet to be funded. Helicopters and intelligence, surveillance and reconnaissance assets, such as Cessna 208B *Grand Caravan*, Beech *Super King Air* 350 and *Scan Eagle* UAVs, remain the acquisition focus.

Venezuela has sought to 'revolutionise' its armed forces through the implementation of a new doctrine giving the armed forces an active political role. Following President Hugo Chávez's victory in the February 2009 referendum on lifting term limits for elected officials, he used Venezuela's National Assembly to implement what he called his 'new geometry of power'. In March 2009, the legislature transferred control of ports, airports and highways to the federal government, depriving local government of tariff revenues. Chávez then sent the military to seize control of these facilities in the three states that had opposition governors.

Chávez had earlier removed the Ministry of Defence from the chain of command and created a new Strategic Operational Command controlling all services. Plans to replace the National Guard with a People's Militia were frustrated by internal opposition, and the militia was created as a separate service in September. Venezuela has also, as reported in *The Military Balance 2009* (p. 58), invested considerably in an ambitious modernisation programme, with much equipment purchased from Russia. A second programme, reported at US$2.2bn, was announced in September 2009, though its status is as yet uncertain. Announcements indicated that over 90 main battle tanks would form part of future deals, while an unspecified amount of *Smerch* multiple-launch rocket systems, Mi-28 combat helicopters, an array of air-defence systems possibly including S-300, *Kilo*-class submarines and five *Mirach* fast patrol craft were also reportedly discussed. Caracas has also reportedly expressed interest in Su-35 *Super Flanker* fighters, Il-76MD-90 strategic transports, Il-78MK *Midas* tankers, An-74 transports, BMP-3 and BMD-3 infantry fighting vehicles. Venezuela and Russia's public defence relationship saw bilateral exercises conducted in Caribbean waters and airspace in late 2008. These contacts had more symbolic than military importance, with Russian actions largely directed at the US, whose political engagement in Russia's near abroad, particularly Georgia, had angered Moscow. Transparency of the Venezuela–Russia relationship will be affected following the passing of the Ley de Protección Mutua de Información Clasificada (Classified Information Protection Law) by the Venezuelan Congress during late September, which announced that technical-military cooperation contracts with Russia will be secret.

Further south, there has been a complete overhaul of the command appointments and the general defence structure of the militaries of **Ecuador** and **Bolivia**. Ecuador's defence minister and army and air-force commanders were replaced a month after the 1 March 2008 incursion by Colombian forces pursuing FARC guerrillas. The old territorial defence commands have been replaced by a new Central Command that deploys task forces with specific missions, such as 'border sovereignty' on the Colombian border or 'energy sovereignty' to combat the illegal abstraction and smuggling of oil. The Ecuadorian transformation moves stem in large part from the March 2008 Colombian incursion. It is reported that funding has been secured for a procurement programme that would include close-air-support aircraft, radar systems, helicopters and UAVs. It has also sought to obtain second-hand fighters from South Africa and Venezuela to boost its air-defence capability.

In Bolivia, meanwhile, moves towards transformation resulted from the August–September 2008 secessionist crisis in the country's east. Bolivia has set up new regional joint commands that in some cases also involve the country's law-enforcement and customs agencies in an effort to leverage multi-agency assets. These comprise the Santa Cruz Joint Command made up of army, navy and air-force units in the cities of Camirí and Villamontes, the Amazonia Joint Command in the city of Puerto Rico, and the Joint Command South comprised of army, navy, air-force and national police units. This has been followed by a procurement programme including a mix of new and second-hand transport aircraft (such as two MA-60s, two C-212s and two DC-10s), two AS350B2 helicopters and a recent order for six new K-8 armed trainers from China. A US$100m programme to acquire weapons from Russia was announced in August.

Brazil has launched an ambitious military-modernisation programme as part of its new 'National Strategy of Defense' unveiled on 18 December 2008. This new policy has among its objectives the development of greater ability to monitor airspace, land and territorial waters; improvement of strategic mobility;

and strengthening 'three strategically important sectors: cybernetics, space and nuclear'. But, principally, Brazil is linking procurement to national development, actively promoting technology transfer and foreign direct investment in its defence industries. The document also reinforces the importance of mandatory military service, with the government apparently viewing this as of benefit to national and social cohesiveness. Those exempt from military service 'will be encouraged to render civilian services'. Meanwhile, the army is to redeploy from its current concentration in the south and southeast of the country towards the centre, from which it will be able to deploy to western and northern areas faster. Forces will be highly mobile and flexible, while a central force will act as a strategic reserve. The army is procuring *Leopard* 1 main battle tanks from Germany and subjecting them to a comprehensive upgrade, but its most important programme is the development of a next-generation family of vehicles, the VBTP-MR, to replace its large EE-9 and EE-11 *Urutu* fleet.

The navy has been tasked with increasing its presence in the mouth of the Amazon River and the Amazonia and Paraguay–Parana river basins, also with a view to the country's recently discovered offshore energy resources. The defence strategy continues by saying that 'to ensure the sea denial objective, Brazil will count on a powerful underwater naval force consisting of conventional and nuclear-propelled submarines', while the navy will furthermore 'dedicate special attention to the design and manufacturing of multi-purpose vessels that can also be used as aircraft carriers'. Its plans have so far included the local production of four submarines based on the *Scorpene*-class, development of an indigenous nuclear submarine, modernisation of its embarked air element through the upgrade of its A-4 *Skyhawk* fleet, acquisition of airborne-early-warning assets and S-70 *Seahawk* anti-submarine/anti-surface warfare helicopters (see Defence Economics, p. 59). The navy has been tasked with establishing, as near as possible to the mouth of the Amazon, 'a multi-purpose naval base that is comparable to the base at Rio de Janeiro'.

The air force is receiving ten P-3AM *Orion* anti-submarine warfare/maritime-patrol aircraft, upgraded by EADS CASA, and has launched a requirement for a smaller maritime-surveillance platform. Brazil is also in the process of selecting a new-generation fighter (FX2) which will see the acquisition of *Rafales*, *Gripen* NGs or F/A-18E/F *Super Hornets* plus technology transfers that will enable the local construction of fighters for a stated requirement of 120 aircraft to replace its AMX/F-5BR/*Mirage* 2000 fleet. A new tanker–transport is being procured in the form of the locally developed KC-390, while it is reported that 12 Mi-35M attack helicopters have been ordered from Russia. One of the most important administrative changes noted in Brazil's defence structure was the establishment of a centralised procurement office (the 'Secretariat of Defense Products') that will manage defence acquisitions. The first such contract is for 50 EC 725 medium-lift helicopters to be built at the local Helibras subsidiary of Eurocopter and delivered to all three branches of the armed forces.

The military forces of **Chile** have been transforming to a mobile and flexible all-professional force geared towards joint operations. The army is nearing the end of a modernisation process that began in 2002 and includes new equipment and a reorganisation of its force structure around seven brigades, comprising four armoured, one special-forces and two mountain-warfare units, while the navy has just finished a five-year re-equipment programme. A further significant change to Chile's defence structure will come if the much-discussed abolition of the Copper Law comes to pass. (See Defence Economics, below.)

Further east, **Argentina's** PEA 2025 modernisation programme was based on a re-organisation scheme that sought to transform the army into a more compact and mobile force, with better equipment, logistics support and training (see *The Military Balance 2008*, p. 56). The plan created a new Land Operations Command and made the brigade the main operational unit, subordinated in three (reduced from five) division-size corps. A new logistics agency has centralised procurement, but limited funding has led to progress only in a few projects. Meanwhile, upgrades to the *Patagon* light tank, *Gaucho* light vehicle, and TAM main battle tank have been either cancelled or postponed. Funding cuts during 2009 have restricted military fuel supplies, while training has reportedly been similarly affected. Meanwhile, two of Argentina's major defence industries were effectively re-nationalised during 2009. These included the AMC aircraft factory, which had been run since 1994 by Lockheed Martin, and the Tanador shipyards, which was privatised in the early 1990s. Both have been taken over by the Defence Ministry as part of a government strategy to revitalise national defence production.

DEFENCE ECONOMICS

The global financial crisis spread quickly to Latin America and the Caribbean, with equity markets and domestic currencies falling sharply. The region was hit by three converging factors: an increase in borrowing costs and consequent reduction in capital inflows; a sharp decline in commodity prices (particularly affecting such exporters of primary products as Chile, Brazil and Venezuela); and a reduction in exports and tourism. However, given that public and private balance sheets in the region were relatively strong when the crisis struck, together with the fact that most countries were less financially linked to advanced economies' banking systems, it is probable that the decline in growth may be less severe than in other regions of the world.

Although regional GDP is set to contract by 1.5% in 2009 (compared with growth of 4.2% the previous year) and fiscal balances will also deteriorate, the lasting impact of the financial crisis on defence spending is difficult to judge and is likely to vary markedly between countries. Chile, for example, which was approaching the end of a major procurement cycle, has already purchased the most expensive equipment it needed, whereas in Brazil repeated delays in recent years to several major procurement programmes means the government is faced with the task of acquiring big-ticket items at a time of economic difficulty. Given the fragile economic background several countries have opted to refurbish existing inventories rather than purchase new equipment; Colombia, for example, began upgrade to its fleet of Israeli *Kfir* fighters rather than procure new aircraft.

One trend that looks set to continue is the growth of Russian exports to the region. Past US arms restrictions have forced several nations to diversify their weapons suppliers and Russian exporters in particular have established a strong presence on the continent. Although countries such as Colombia and Mexico remain committed to US arms manufacturers, not least because the US provides a large portion of their defence funding in the role of counter-insurgency support, others, such as Venezuela and Peru, have taken advantage of generous Russian financing arrangements for the purchase of new equipment. In the last three years, Venezuela has spent over US$4bn on Russian equipment, and in December 2008 Peru signed a memorandum of understanding with Moscow covering the supply of defence equipment and training cooperation.

In March 2009, the 12 defence ministers of the South American Defence Council (SADC) – created to promote dialogue and coordination on regional security and defence issues – met for the first time. At an inaugural two-day meeting in Santiago, participants discussed proposals on how to increase transparency in military spending and equipment acquisitions. For many years, the lack of transparency in military expenditure has fostered mistrust in the region. Different countries include differing factors in their budgets and several derive additional military funding from a wide variety of opaque sources, including wealth taxes and the profits from commodity exports. It is thought that most countries, with the exception of Venezuela and Peru, indicated some willingness to increase transparency, although whether this will stretch as far as an Argentine proposal that all members adopt a standard defence-budget methodology remains to be seen.

As the region's biggest economy, **Brazil** has not been immune to the global economic downturn: growth of 5.1% in 2008 was followed by a 1.3% contraction in economic output in 2009. However, in their 2009 Article IV Consultation, the IMF praised the Brazilian government for its 'robust policy framework', suggested that the country was in a 'favourable position' to successfully weather the downturn, and forecast a return to positive growth of 2.5% in 2010. As in recent years, Venezuela's ongoing military-modernisation programme provided the background for another increase in Brazil's military budget. Between 2000 and 2004 military spending in Brazil was static and had fallen to 1.4% of GDP; since 2005,

however, the budget has increased by around 10% a year, and in 2009 it jumped to R51.3bn (US$29.7bn) or 1.7% of GDP. The government has rejected claims that its rising military budget is a reaction to developments elsewhere on the continent, saying instead – and not without reason – that the extra money is due to the urgent need to upgrade and replace parts of its ageing military inventory after years of underinvestment. Replacing the armed forces' old equipment, however, will continue to be a challenge, given that in 2009 only around US$2.3bn of the total budget was allocated to procurement, whereas US$22.4bn (75% of the budget) was spent on personnel-related issues.

Of the three services, the army is saddled with a particularly old, indeed in many cases obsolete, inventory. Acknowledging the dire state of much of the army's military equipment, the new national defence strategy, approved in December 2008, earmarked a sum of around US$70bn to upgrade the army's capabilities. The plan focused on two main areas: improving security in the Amazon region and the acquisition of new hardware. The army will be reorganised and modernised into units including a light infantry brigade based in Rio de Janeiro, a jungle infantry brigade based in Manaus and an airborne brigade based in Anapolis, while end strength will be increased by 59,000, with 22,000 troops based in the Amazon region. The re-equipment programme will focus on improving deterrence, flexibility, modularity and interoperability.

A second equipment programme, known as *Cobra*, will focus on procurement of the IVECO VBTP MR family of armoured vehicles (comprising 17 vari-

Table 11 **Latin America and the Caribbean Regional Defence Expenditure** as % of GDP

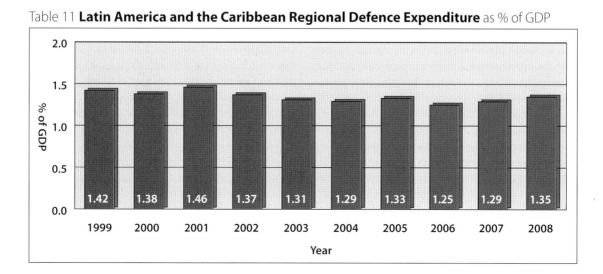

ants) as well as anti-tank weapons and unmanned aerial vehicles. In the short term, acquisitions will include 269 ex-German *Leopard* 1 main battle tanks and a dozen Russian Mi-35 *Hind* attack helicopters earmarked for use in counter-narcotics operations in the Amazon region. In the longer term, the army will receive up to 50 new EC-725 *Cougar* medium-lift helicopters, an acquisition that formed part of a major defence-cooperation agreement signed between Brazil and France.

The terms of that deal, signed in September 2009, were wide-ranging, covering not just procurement but defence technology transfer, offsets and other commercial benefits with a total value of over €10bn. In addition to the *Cougar* purchase, Brazil will buy four French conventional submarines (based on the *Scorpene* model), and French companies will provide technical assistance for the design and construction of the non-nuclear element of Brazil's first nuclear-powered submarine, as well as support the construction of a naval base and build a shipyard in Brazil where the submarines will be assembled. Similarly, the *Cougar* helicopters will also be assembled in Brazil by EADS subsidiary Helibras. The main outstanding requirement remains the choice of a platform to fulfil the long-running air-force FX2 fighter programme. Despite reports at the time that the French *Rafale* aircraft had been chosen for the role, by November 2009 there had been no confirmation that this was the case and SAAB remained particularly hopeful that its *Gripen* would in fact win the competition.

Development of the Brazilian Navy's submarine force was highlighted in the national defence strategy as the key component of sea denial (its strategic objective). In addition to outlining the navy's long-term aim of acquiring a large fleet of conventional and nuclear-powered submarines, the national defence strategy also included plans to rebalance the remaining fleet with the introduction of multi-purpose vessels able to address the objectives of sea control and force protection. It is envisaged that a mixture of offshore-patrol vessels, coastal- and river-patrol ships, multi-mission surface combatants and multi-purpose auxiliaries will be required. The first procurements under the programme were announced in June 2009, when the navy issued a request for information for the purchase of an initial three 1,800-tonne offshore-patrol vessels. The ships, which will need to be capable of hosting an 11-tonne helicopter and have a range of 6,000nm, will form the first element of a new second fleet operating from a base in or close to the Amazon River basin. As well as new offshore-patrol vessels, the navy announced that it would be acquiring an initial batch of 12 NAPA 500 patrol ships out of a total future requirement of 27.

Despite no final decision regarding the outcome of the FX2 programme, the air force moved ahead with its other priorities – airlift and tanker capabilities. In April 2009, Embraer signed a contract with the air force for the development of its new KC-390 medium-heavy tanker–transport aircraft. The company will invest around US$1.3bn in its development, and has a long term goal of capturing a third of the world market for military transport aircraft. The plane will have a similar cargo capability to the C-130 *Hercules* and the air force has indicated a requirement for 22 aircraft. To supplement the KC-390 fleet the air force also plans to acquire between six and 12 heavy-lift transport aircraft and is considering the relative merits of the Boeing C-17, Ilyushin Il-476 and Antonov An-70. In the more immediate term, it seems likely that the air force will procure an additional eight C-295 tactical transport aircraft (including four in search-and-rescue configuration) to supplement 12 acquired in 2005.

Although **Venezuela** has benefited from high oil prices in recent years, its economy was one of the worst hit in the region, and the IMF suggested that it would be the only country in South America where GDP would continue to decline into 2010. An equally pressing problem for the authorities is rampant inflation, which was projected to reach 36% in 2009. In light of the high rate of inflation, the nominal increase of 25% in the 2009 defence budget to US$4.2bn was less noteworthy than widely reported at the time. In addition to its allocation from the central budget, the Venezuelan military has historically also benefited from an arcane financial arrangement known as the Ley Paraguas or 'Umbrella Law', which has sometimes added up to US$500m to the annual military budget, although the status of this mechanism is currently unclear. Analysts also suggest that as much as US$3bn from the country's National Development Fund (Fonden), supposedly reserved for productive investment, education and health projects, has been diverted to the military in recent years. The true figure for defence spending is, therefore, likely to be higher than the official budget would indicate.

An additional factor that obscures the true level of military spending is the level of financial support offered by Russia. Between 2005 and 2007 Venezuela bought around US$4bn worth of Russian weapons systems, including 100,000 Kalashnikov rifles, more than 50 Mi-17B and Mi-35M combat helicopters, 12 *Tor M1* air-defence missile systems, Mi-26 heavy transport helicopters, 24 Su-30MKV multirole fighter aircraft and an extensive armaments package comprising beyond-visual-range air-to-air missiles, precision-guided air-to-surface weapons, spare parts and crew training programmes. In late 2008, following a visit by President Chávez to Moscow, it was revealed that Russia would extend a US$1bn credit line to enable the Venezuelan military to continue with its modernisation drive. It is thought that this loan was particularly aimed towards the supply of three *Kilo*-class submarines, a number of Ilyushin tanker and transport aircraft and an undisclosed number of T-72 main battle tanks and BMP-3 infantry fighting vehicles. New tanks and infantry fighting vehicles are urgently required as the army is about to be significantly enlarged with the number of armoured battalions doubled. In September 2009, Chávez announced that the terms of the Russian loan had been increased to US$2.2bn to cover the purchase of additional weapons systems, including a number of T-90 tanks, the S-300, *Buk* M2 and *Pechora* anti-aircraft missile systems and other military equipment.

Venezuela has also placed significant equipment orders with China and Spain in recent years. In 2005, China supplied the country with ten JYL-1 air-surveillance radars and in late 2008 announced a deal for the acquisition of 24 K-8 jet trainers. The K-8s will replace the air force's ageing VF-5D aircraft and the package consists of 24 airframes, a simulator and options on a further 12 units. This deal was quickly followed by the news in October 2008 that China had launched Venezuela's first communications satellite: the VENESAT-1 *Simón Bolívar*. Government officials revealed that the satellite programme was triggered following an unsuccessful coup against Chávez in 2002 to provide 'communications sovereignty' for the government.

Military-industrial relations with Spain centre around the delivery of eight new ships for the Venezuelan Navy. Construction of the ships, in two classes of four, was announced in 2005 in a deal reportedly worth €1.7bn (US$2.5bn), in which Spanish company Navantia would build the vessels and Thales Netherlands would supply the combat systems. Four 2,300-tonne POVZEE offshore-patrol vessels and four 1,500-tonne BVL coastal-patrol ships should all be delivered by 2011. In addition to procuring these new ships, the navy has also begun

a significant refit and upgrade programme for its *Capana*-class LSTs and is thought to be investigating the acquisition of a number of LPDs, each capable of carrying around 750 troops.

Following continuing tensions between Venezuela and **Colombia**, which deteriorated further after the announcement of the US-Colombian Defence Cooperation Agreement, Bogotá announced an 8.7% increase in defence spending for 2009 and revealed plans to further modernise its armed forces. Once spending on the National Police is taken into account, total military-related funding in 2009 amounts to pC19.2tr (US$6.5bn), or around 4% of GDP, making it the highest in the region by that measure. As elsewhere in Latin America, the Colombian armed forces are also known to benefit from additional funds derived, in their case, from both municipal government and revenues from their own security-related business activities. On top of this, the armed forces and national police also benefit from regular 'wealth taxes', the latest of which was intended to raise an extra pC8.6tr (US$1.5bn) between 2007 and 2010. The George W. Bush administration, moreover, in FY2009 requested US$68m in military equipment and training and US$329m under the Andean Counterdrug Program to be allocated to the Colombian government. In 2009 total military-related expenditure in Colombia thus probably exceeded US$10bn.

In light of the advanced age of much of its equipment – the navy's frigates are more than 20 years old and some of the army's artillery systems have been in service for nearly 50 years – the government has outlined a major equipment-modernisation programme valued at around US$4bn. Under the proposal all three services will be upgraded. The air force will receive 12 combat helicopters, nine transport aircraft, seven intelligence platforms, 25 *Legacy* FG primary trainers (to be built in Colombia from kits), and in a demonstration of the growing relationship between Israel and Colombia, Israel Aerospace Industries will upgrade Colombia's existing 11 *Kfir* fighter aircraft and provide a further 13 from Israeli stocks. Further trade between the two countries could see Colombia buying Israeli-made UAVs, *Spike* missiles and *Galil* assault rifles. The navy is scheduled to receive four *Nodriza*-class river-patrol boats, 131 patrol boats, three patrol aircraft and one CN-235 *Persuader* maritime-patrol aircraft. It will also upgrade its four *Almirante Padilla*-class frigates and two Type 209 submarines. Having already taken delivery of 40 *Blackhawk* helicopters, the army's Aviation Brigade will receive another 10 similar aircraft during 2009. Other confirmed orders include five Mi-17 helicopters, 20 105mm howitzers from France and 39 Cadillac Cage M1117 *Guardian* 4×4 armoured security vehicles.

The ambitious Núcleo Básico Eficaz (NBE) programme announced in 2007 to modernise **Peru's** armed forces is making slow progress. In December 2007, President Alan García announced that a new 10-year 'defence fund' amounting to US$1.3bn would be made available to the military on top of the regular allocation from the state budget to fulfil the plan. The additional funds were to be generated from higher hydrocarbon taxes, the sale of military property and austerity measures in other areas of government spending. During the first three years of the programme an initial US$650m would be made available, with the balance spread out over the following seven years. The air force is in a particularly parlous state, with only around 30% of its aircraft thought to be in a serviceable condition.

There has, however, been significant controversy over the funding of the NBE and the government has been unsuccessful in enacting proposed legislation which stipulates that 5% of the revenue from new mining and other national-resource projects be allocated to the military. Leaders of political organisations in the south of the country have threatened to 'take up arms' if the bill, which could provide an estimated US$300m per year to the armed forces, is approved. In the absence of such approval funding for the NBE has been piecemeal, with just US$126m allocated in 2009. Acquisitions confirmed thus far include two former US Navy *Newport*-class LSTs together with six *Sea King* helicopters and the purchase of Israeli and Russian anti-tank missiles. The army is also exploring the option of overhauling its fleet of T-55 tanks, while Russia and Peru have signed a memorandum of understanding that will allow the establishment of a joint helicopter-repair plant in Peru enabling the repair and modification of the armed forces' Mi-17 and Mi-26 helicopters.

Over the past year **Ecuador** continued to implement the emergency plan adopted after the Colombian air force bombed a FARC camp inside Ecuador in March 2008. In the immediate aftermath of the incident an initial US$500m general modernisation plan was proposed to cover the purchase of helicopters, UAVs, tanks, *Super Tucano* aircraft and patrol boats. A few months later the government provided further details, publishing a 10-year plan with a particular emphasis on boosting the army's military presence on the border with Colombia. During the first phase of this plan, the army will create a new rapid-reaction airmobile battalion supported by 15 medium-lift and 18 attack and reconnaissance helicopters. The second phase will see the acquisition of air-defence radars, airfield modernisation and new military infrastructure along the northern border.

Several acquisitions listed in the original programme have now moved ahead. In August 2008, Ecuador placed an order with Israel Aerospace Industries for the purchase of two *Heron* medium-altitude long-endurance UAVs, four *Searcher* tactical UAVs and a maritime-surveillance radar package. This was followed in October by the signing of a new defence-cooperation pact between Ecuador and China under which the Latin American nation will provide China with oil in return for Chinese-made military hardware. The first evidence of the new arrangement was revealed in early 2009 when the Ecuadorian Ministry of Defence announced that it had signed a US$60m contract for four air-defence radars from the China Electronics Technology Group Corporation that will fill a large air-defence vacuum over the northern border with Colombia. A second contract was forthcoming later in the year with the announcement that the Ecuadorian air force would replace its ageing BAE 748 transport aircraft with four XAC-MA60 aircraft from the China National Aero-Technology Import-Export Corporation (CATIC). The air force will also benefit from the delivery of 38 fighter aircraft and seven helicopters: 24 Embraer *Super Tucano* light attack aircraft; 14 ex-Chilean *Mirage* M50 combat aircraft; and seven *Dhruv* multirole advanced light helicopters. In purchasing the *Dhruv*, the Ecuadorian air force became the first overseas customer for India's indigenously developed helicopter. Deliveries of the 5.5-tonne aircraft will be completed in kit form by mid 2010 and will include medium-lift, tactical transport and search-and-rescue variants.

Chile saw GDP growth fall from 3.2% in 2008 to just 0.1% in 2009. The fall in metal prices that began in 2008 hit the world's largest copper exporter, but due to the government's prudent macroeconomic policy of recent years Chile's fiscal position remained positive.

Supported by this relatively healthy position, defence spending has increased at a steady rate in recent years. In 2009, the official budget of the Ministry of Defence was increased by a further 10% to pCH1.58tr (US$2.85bn). However, as noted in previous editions of *The Military Balance*, the Chilean armed forces also receive funds derived from other sources, including the military's own business interests and 10% of the value of the state mining company CODELCO's copper exports under the Copper Law, as well as funds from the social-security budget to cover the pensions of retired military personnel. Taking these additional sources of funding into account, the total national defence-related expenditure in 2009 could have been as high as US$5.9bn, of which the Copper Law may have provided at least US$500m. The law has come under increasing scrutiny in recent years as the high price of copper on international markets has boosted revenues dramatically. For many years the copper law had resulted in only a modest contribution of between US$100-200m going to the armed forces; however, as copper prices rose, payments to the military increased and several MPs expressed concern that a substantial part of defence funding was, as a result, undebated in the legislature. CODELCO's management, furthermore, made it clear that it would like to eliminate the mandatory payment and use the money for other projects and investments within the copper industry itself. Finally, in October 2009 (a year later than scheduled), the Chilean government sent a new draft law on Military Procurement Funding to parliament. Under the new system, the Copper Law will be abolished and in its place the armed forces will receive additional funds for procurement as part of the state budget. Equipment needs will be planned in periods of 12 years, subject to revision every four years, but projected spending levels will not be legally binding and the military is known to be concerned that no fixed 'floor' will be included. A separate Contingency Fund, comprising around US$2.8bn in unspent Copper Law surpluses, is also being created to provide for the replacement or refurbishment of military equipment specifically worn out or lost as the result of war, responses to international crises or disaster-relief operations.

Antigua and Barbuda ATG

East Caribbean Dollar EC$		2008	2009	2010
GDP	EC$	3.2bn		
	US$	1.2bn		
per capita	US$	14,022		
Growth	%	2.8	-6.5	
Inflation	%	5.3	-0.8	
Def bdgt	EC$	ε18m	21m	
	US$	ε6.7m	7.8m	
US$1=EC$		2.7	2.7	

Population   85,632

Age	0-14	15-19	20-24	25-29	30-64	65 plus
Male	14%	4%	4%	4%	23%	2%
Female	14%	4%	4%	4%	23%	3%

Capabilities

ACTIVE 170 (Army 125 Navy 45)
(all services form combined Antigua and Barbuda Defence Force)
RESERVE 75 (Joint 75)

ORGANISATIONS BY SERVICE

Army 125

Navy 45
EQUIPMENT BY TYPE
PATROL AND COASTAL COMBATANTS • PCI 3:
1 *Dauntless*; 1 Point; 1 *Swift*; (All vessels less than 100 tonnes)
FACILITIES
Base 1 located at St Johns

FOREIGN FORCES

United States US Strategic Command: 1 detection and tracking radar located at Antigua

Argentina ARG

Argentine Peso P		2008	2009	2010
GDP	P	1.03tr	1.05tr	
	US$	331bn	277bn	
per capita	US$	8,166	6,758	
Growth	%	6.8	-2.5	
Inflation	%	8.6	5.6	
Def bdgt	P	6.37bn	8.52bn	
	US$	2.03bn	2.22bn	
US$1=P		3.14	3.83	

Population   40,913584

Age	0-14	15-19	20-24	25-29	30-64	65 plus
Male	13%	4%	4%	4%	19%	4%
Female	12%	4%	4%	4%	19%	6%

Capabilities

ACTIVE 73,100 (Army 38,500 Navy 20,000 Air 14,600) **Paramilitary 31,240**

RESERVE none formally established or trained

ORGANISATIONS BY SERVICE

Army 38,500 (plus 7,000 civilians; 45,500 in total)
A strategic reserve is made up of armd, AB and mech bdes normally subordinate to corps level.
FORCES BY ROLE
Comd   3 corps HQ (mob def)
Mobile   1 Northeast force (1 jungle bde, 1 armd bde,
Defence   1 trg bde); 1 Northern force (1 AB bde (1 cdo coy), 1 mech inf bde, 1 mtn inf bde); 1 Patagonia and Southern Atlantic force (1 mtn inf bde, 1 armd bde, 3 mech inf bde)
Rapid   1 (rapid deployment) force (includes AB bde
Reaction   from corps level) (1 cdo coy)
Mot Cav   1 regt (presidential escort)
Mot Inf   1 bn (army HQ escort regt)
Arty   1 gp (bn)
ADA   2 gp
Engr   1 bn
Avn   1 gp

EQUIPMENT BY TYPE
MBT 213: 207 TAM, 6 TAM S21
LT TK 123: 112 SK-105A1 *Kuerassier*; 6 SK105A2 *Kuerassier*; 5 *Patagón*
RECCE 81: 47 AML-90; 34 M1025A2 *HMMWV*
AIFV 263 VCTP (incl variants); 114 M-113A2 (20mm cannon)
APC (T) 294: 70 M-113 A1-ACAV; 224 M-113A2
ARTY 1,103
  SP 155mm 37: 20 Mk F3; 17 VCA 155 *Palmaria*
  TOWED 179: **105mm** 70 M-56 (Oto Melara); **155mm** 109: 25 M-77 *CITEFA*/M-81 *CITEFA*; 84 SOFMA L-33

MRL **105mm** 4 SLAM *Pampero*
MOR 883: **81mm** 492; **120mm** 353 *Brandt*
  SP 38: 25 M-106A2; 13 TAM-VCTM
AT
  MSL • SP 3 HMMWV with total of 18 TOW-2A
  MANPATS msl
  RCL 150 M-1968
  RL 385+ **66mm** 385 M-72 *LAW*; **78mm** MARA
AIRCRAFT
  PTRL/SURV 10: 10 OV-1D *Mohawk* (6 with SLAR)
  TPT 16: 1 *Beech 80 Queen Air*; 1 CASA 212-200 *Aviocar*;
  2 DHC-6 *Twin Otter*; 3 G-222; 1 *Gaviao* 75A (Rockwell
  Sabreliner 75A); 3 SA-226 *Merlin IIIA*; 5 SA-226AT *Merlin
  IV/IVA*
  UTL 3 Cessna 207 *Stationair*
  TRG 5 T-41 *Mescalero*
  SURVEY 1 CE-500(survey) *Citation*
HELICOPTERS
  ARMED 6 UH-1H
  SAR 5 SA-315B
  SPT 3 AS-332B *Super Puma*
  UTL 30: 5 A-109; 1 Bell 212; 18 UH-1H *Iroquois*; 6 UH-
  1H-II *Huey II*
  TRG 8 UH-12E
AD
  SAM 6 RBS -70
  GUNS • TOWED 411: **20mm** 230 GAI-B01; **30mm** 21
  HS L81; **35mm** 12 GDF Oerlikon (*Skyguard* fire control);
  40mm 148: 24 L/60 training, 40 in store; 76 L/60; 8 L/70
  RADAR • AD RADAR 11: 5 Cardion AN/TPS-44; 6
  Skyguard
    LAND 18+: M-113 A1GE *Green Archer* (mor); 18
    RATRAS (veh, arty)

Navy 20,000 (plus 7,200 civilians; 27,200 in total)

Commands: Surface Fleet, Submarines, Naval Avn, Marines
FORCES BY ROLE
Navy Located at Mar del Plata (SS and HQ Atlantic),
    Ushuaio (HQ South), Puerto Belgrano (HQ Centre)

EQUIPMENT BY TYPE
SUBMARINES • TACTICAL • SSK 3:
  1 *Salta* (GER T-209/1200) with 8 single 533mm TT with
  14 Mk 37/SST-4
  2 *Santa Cruz* (GER TR-1700) each with 6 single 533mm
  TT with 22 SST-4 HWT
PRINCIPAL SURFACE COMBATANTS 14
  DESTROYERS • DDG 5:
  4 *Almirante Brown* (GER MEKO 360) each with 2 quad
  (8 eff.) with MM-40 *Exocet* tactical SSM, 2 B515 *ILAS-
  3* triple 324mm with 24 A244 LWT, 1 127mm gun,
  (capacity 1 AS-555 *Fennec* or *Alouette* III utl hel)
  1 *Hercules* (UK Type 42 - utilised as a fast troop
  transport ship), eq with 2 B515 *ILAS-3* triple 324mm
  each with A244 LWT, 1 114mm gun, (capacity 1 SH-
  3H *Sea King* utl hel)
  FRIGATES • FFG 9:
  3 *Drummond* (FRA A-69) each with 2 twin (4 eff.) with
  MM-38 *Exocet* tactical SSM, 2 Mk32 triple 324mm with
  A244 LWT, 1 100mm gun

6 *Espora* (GER MEKO 140) 2 twin (4 eff.) with MM-38
Exocet tactical SSM, 2 B515 *ILAS-3* triple 324mm with
A244 LWT, 1 76mm gun (capacity either 1 SA-319
Alouette III utl hel or 1 AS-555 *Fennec* utl hel)
PATROL AND COASTAL COMBATANTS 15
  PFT 2:
  1 *Interpida* (GER Lurssen 45m) with 2 single 533mm
  TT each with SST-4 HWT
  1 *Interpida* (GER Lurssen 45m) with 2 single each with
  1 MM-38 *Exocet* tactical SSM, 2 single 533mm TT with
  SST-4 HWT
  PCO 7:
  3 *Irigoyen* (US *Cherokee* AT)
  2 *Murature* (US *King*) (trg/river patrol) with 3 105mm
  gun
  1 *Sobral* (US *Sotoyomo* AT)
  1 *Teniente Olivieri* (ex-US oilfield tug)
  PCI 6: 4 *Baradero* less than 100 tonnes (Dabur); 2 Point
  less than 100 tonnes
AMPHIBIOUS 20: 4 **LCM**; 16 **LCVP**
LOGISTICS AND SUPPORT 12
  AORH 1 *Patagonia* (FRA *Durance*) with 1 SA-316 *Alouette
  III* utl hel
  AORL 1 *Ingeniero Julio Krause*
  AK 3 *Costa Sur*
  AGOR 1 *Commodoro Rivadavia*
  AGHS 1 *Puerto Deseado* (ice breaking capability, used
  for polar research)
  AGB 1 *Almirante Irizar*
  ABU 3 *Red*
  TRG 1 *Libertad*
FACILITIES

Bases	Located at Ushuaio (HQ Centre), Mar del Plata (SS and HQ Atlantic), Buenos Aires, Puerto Belgrano (HQ Centre), Zarate (river craft)
Naval airbases	Located at Trelew, Punta Indio
Construction and Repair Yard	Located at Rio Santiago

Naval Aviation 2,000

AIRCRAFT 23 combat capable
  STRIKE/FGA 2 *Super Etendard* (9 in store)
  ASW 5 S-2T *Tracker**
  MP 6 P-3B *Orion**
  TPT 4: 2 *Beech* 200F *Super King Air*; 2 F-28 *Fellowship*
  UTL 6: 5 BE-200F/BE-200M; 1 AU-23 *Turbo-Porter*
  TRG 10 T-34C *Turbo Mentor**
HELICOPTERS
  ASW/ASUW 4 ASH-3H *Sea King*
  UTL 13: 3 AS-555 *Fennec*; 6 SA-316B *Alouette III**; 4
  UH-3H *Sea King*
MSL
  ASM 21 AM-39 *Exocet*; AS-12 *Kegler*; AS-11 *Kilter*; AS-
  25K CITEFA *Martin Pescador*
  AAM R-550 *Magic*

Marines 2,500

FORCES BY ROLE

Spt/Amph	1 force (1 marine inf bn)

| Marine | 1 (fleet) force (1 arty bn, 1 AAV bn, 1 cdo gp, 1 ADA bn, 1 marine inf bn); 1 (fleet) force (2 marine inf bn, 2 navy det) |

EQUIPMENT BY TYPE
RECCE 52: 12 ERC-90F *Sagaie*; 40 M1097 HMMWV
APC (W) 24 *Panhard VCR*
AAV 17: 10 LARC-5; 7 LVTP-7
ARTY 100
   TOWED 105mm 18: 6 M-101; 12 Model 56 pack howitzer
   MOR 82: 70 **81mm**; 12 **120mm**
AT
   MSL • MANPATS 50 *Cobra*/RB-53 *Bantam*
   RCL 105mm 30 M-1974 FMK-1
   RL 89mm 60 M-20
AD
   SAM 6 RBS-70
   GUNS 30mm 10 HS-816; **35mm** GDF-001

Air Force 14,600 (plus 6,900 civilians, 21,500 in total)

4 Major Comds – Air Operations, Personnel, Air Regions, Logistics, 8 air bde

Air Operations Command

FORCES BY ROLE

Airspace Defence	1 sqn with *Mirage* EA/DA (*Mirage* III/E)
FGA/Ftr	5 (strategic air) sqn; 2 sqn with A-4AR/OA-4AR *Skyhawk*; 2 sqn with 14 IAI *Dagger Nesher* A/B; 1 sqn with *Mirage* 5 *Mara*; 2 (tac air) sqn with IA-58 *Pucara*
Tac Air	2 sqn with IA-58 *Pucara*, 6 *Tucano* (on loan for border surv/interdiction)
RECCE/Survey	1 sqn with *Learjet* 35A
SAR/Utl	3 sqn with Bell 212; *Hughes* 369*; MD-500*; SA-315B *Lama*; UH-1H *Iroquois*; UH-1N
Tpt/Tkr	1 sqn with B-707; 1 sqn with F-27 *Friendship*; 1 sqn with DHC-6 *Twin Otter*; 2 sqn with KC-130H *Hercules*; C-130B *Hercules*; C-130H *Hercules*; L-100-30; 1 (Pres) flt with B-757-23ER; S-70 *Black Hawk*; 1 sqn with F-28 *Fellowship*
Trg	Aviation school with B-45 *Mentor* (basic); EMB-312 *Tucano* (primary); Su-29AR; 3 MD-500

EQUIPMENT BY TYPE
AIRCRAFT 121 combat capable
   FTR 8 *Mirage* EA/DA (*Mirage* IIIE)
   FGA 89: 34 A-4AR/OA-4AR *Skyhawk*; 7 *Mirage* 5PA (*Mara*); 11 IAI *Dagger* A, 3 *Dagger* B; 34 IA-58 *Pucara*
   LEAD-IN FTR TRG 24: 18 AT-63*; 6 EMB-312* *Tucano* (on loan from Brazil)
   TKR 2 KC-130H *Hercules*

TPT 38: 1 B-757-23ER; 3 C-130B *Hercules*; 5 C-130H *Hercules*; 8 DHC-6 *Twin Otter*; 4 F-27 *Friendship*; 6 F-28 *Fellowship*; 1 L-100-30; 5 *Learjet* 35A; 1 *Learjet* LJ60; 4 *Saab* 340
TRG 43: 24 B-45 *Mentor*; 19 EMB-312 *Tucano*;
HELICOPTERS
   VIP 1 S-76
   UTL 28: 6 Bell 212; 15 *Hughes* 369*; 4 MD-500D*; 3 SA-315B *Lama*
   TRG 3 MD-500
MSL
   AAM 6 AIM-9L *Sidewinder*; 30+ R-550 *Magic*; 150+ *Shafrir IV*
AD
   GUNS 88: **20mm**: 86 Oerlikon/Rh-202 with 9 Elta EL/M-2106 radar; **35mm**: 2 Oerlikon GDF-001 with *Skyguard* radar
   RADAR 6: 5 AN/TPS-43; 1 BPS-1000

Paramilitary 31,240

Gendarmerie 18,000

Ministry of Interior
FORCES BY ROLE

| Region | 5 comd |
| Paramilitary | 16 bn |

EQUIPMENT BY TYPE
RECCE S52 *Shorland*
APC (W) 87: 47 *Grenadier*; 40 UR-416
ARTY • MOR 81mm
AIRCRAFT
   TPT 6: 3 PA-28-236 *Dakota*/PA-31P *Pressurized Navajo*; 3 PC-6 *Turbo-Porter*
   UTL 1 Cessna 206
HELICOPTERS
   SPT 8: 3 AS-350 *Ecureuil*,5 UH-1H
   UTL 3 MD-500C/MD-500D

Prefectura Naval (Coast Guard) 13,240

PATROL AND COASTAL COMBATANTS 32+:
   PCO 7: 1 *Mandubi*; 5 *Mantilla* (F30 *Halcón*); 1 *Delfin*
   PCI 20: 2 *Lynch* (US *Cape*); 18 *Mar del Plata* (Z-28)
   PCR 150+ (various all less than 100 tonnes)
AIRCRAFT
   TPT 5 CASA 212 *Aviocar*
HELICOPTERS
   SAR 1 AS-565MA
   SPT 1 AS-330L (SA-330L) *Puma*
   UTL 2 AS-365 *Dauphin 2*
   TRG 2 *Schweizer* 300C

DEPLOYMENT

CYPRUS
UN • UNFICYP 294; 2 inf coy; 1 avn unit; 2 Bell 212

HAITI
UN • MINUSTAH 560; 1 inf bn; 1 avn unit; 1 fd hospital

MIDDLE EAST
UN • UNTSO 6 obs

WESTERN SAHARA

UN • MINURSO 3 obs

Bahamas BHS

Bahamian Dollar B$		2008	2009	2010
GDP	B$	7.5bn		
	US$	7.5bn		
per capita	US$	24,612		
Growth	%	-1.7	-3.9	
Inflation	%	4.5	1.8	
Def bdgt	B$	49m	46m	
	US$	49m	46m	
US$1=B$		1.0	1.0	

Population   307,552

Age	0–14	15–19	20–24	25–29	30–64	65 plus
Male	14%	5%	4%	4%	19%	3%
Female	14%	5%	4%	4%	21%	4%

Capabilities

ACTIVE 860 (Royal Bahamian Defence Force 860)

ORGANISATIONS BY SERVICE

Royal Bahamian Defence Force 860

Marine 1 coy (Marines with internal and base sy duties)

EQUIPMENT BY TYPE

PATROL AND COASTAL COMBATANTS 13
  PCO 2 *Bahamas*
  PFC 1 *Protector*
  PCI 2: 1 *Challenger*; 1 *Keith Nelson* (all vessels less than 100 tonnes)
  PBF 4 *Boston Whaler* less than 100 tonnes
  PBI 4: 2 *Dauntless*; 2 *Sea-Ark* type (all vessels less than 100 tonnes)
AIRCRAFT
  TPT 4: 1 Cessna 404 *Titan*; 2 PA-31; 1 Beech A-350 *Super King Air*
  UTL 2: 1 Cessna 208 *Caravan*; 1 P-68 *Observer*
FACILITIES
Bases   Located at Coral Harbour, New Providence Island

FOREIGN FORCES

Guyana Navy: Base located at New Providence Island

Barbados BRB

Barbados Dollar B$		2008	2009	2010
GDP	B$	7.6bn	7.6bn	
	US$	3.8bn	3.8bn	
per capita	US$	13,404	13,353	
Growth	%	0.2	-3.0	
Inflation	%	8.1	3.5	
Def bdgt	B$	ε60m	ε65m	
	US$	30.0m	32.5m	
US$1=B$		2.0	2.0	

Population   284,589

Age	0–14	15–19	20–24	25–29	30–64	65 plus
Male	10%	4%	4%	4%	23%	3%
Female	10%	4%	4%	4%	25%	5%

Capabilities

ACTIVE 610 (Army 500 Navy 110)

RESERVE 430 (Joint 430)

ORGANISATIONS BY SERVICE

Army 500

Inf   1 bn (cadre)

Navy 110

FORCES BY ROLE

Navy 1 HQ located at HMBS Pelican, Spring Garden

EQUIPMENT BY TYPE

PATROL AND COASTAL COMBATANTS 9
  PC 3 *Damen Stan Patrol 4207*
  PCC 1 *Kebir*
  PCI 5: 2 *Dauntless* less than 100 tonnes; 3 *Guardian* less than 100 tonnes
FACILITIES
Base   located at HMBS Pelican, Spring Garden, secondary facilities St Ann's Fort, Bridgetown

Belize BLZ

Belize Dollar BZ$		2008	2009	2010
GDP	BZ$	2.0bn		
	US$	1.0bn		
per capita	US$	3,319		
Growth	%	3.8	1.0	
Inflation	%	6.4	2.7	
US$1=BZ$		2.0	1.92	

Population   307,899

Age	0–14	15–19	20–24	25–29	30–64	65 plus
Male	20%	6%	5%	4%	14%	2%
Female	20%	6%	5%	4%	14%	2%

Capabilities

ACTIVE ε1,050 (Army ε1,050)

RESERVE 700 (Joint 700)

ORGANISATIONS BY SERVICE

Army ε1,050
FORCES BY ROLE
Inf   3 bn (*each*: 3 inf coy)
Spt   1 gp

EQUIPMENT BY TYPE
MOR 81mm 6
RCL 84mm 8 *Carl Gustav*

Maritime Wing
PATROL AND COASTAL COMBATANTS • MISC
BOATS/CRAFT ε14 less than 100 tonnes

Air Wing
FORCES BY ROLE
MR/Tpt   sqn with BN-2A *Defender*; BN-2B *Defender*
Trg   unit with 1 Cessna 182 *Skylane*; 1 T67-200
          Firefly

EQUIPMENT BY TYPE
AIRCRAFT
    TPT 2: 1 BN-2A *Defender*; 1 BN-2B *Defender*
    TRG 2: 1 Cessna 182 *Skylane*; 1 T67-200 *Firefly*

Reserve
Inf   3 coy

FOREIGN FORCES

United Kingdom Army 30

Bolivia BOL

Bolivian Boliviano B		2008	2009	2010
GDP	B	120bn	130bn	
	US$	16.6bn	18.6bn	
per capita	US$	1,729	1,900	
Growth	%	6.1	2.8	
Inflation	%	14.3	4.3	
Def bdgt	B	1.80bn	1.70bn	
	US$	249m	243m	
US$1=B			7.23	7.00

Population   9,775,246

Age	0–14	15–19	20–24	25–29	30–64	65 plus
Male	18%	6%	5%	4%	14%	2%
Female	18%	6%	5%	4%	16%	3%

Capabilities

ACTIVE 46,100 (Army 34,800 Navy 4,800 Air 6,500)
Paramilitary 37,100

ORGANISATIONS BY SERVICE

Army 9,800; 25,000 conscript (total 34,800)
FORCES BY ROLE
HQ: 6 Military Regions, 10 Div org and composition varies

Armd	1 bn
Cav	1 (aslt) gp; 5 (horsed) gp
Mech Inf	2 regt
Inf/Presidential Guard	1 regt
Inf	21 bn
Mech Cav	1 regt
SF	3 regt
AB	2 regt (bn)
Mot Cav	1 gp
Mot Inf	3 regt
Arty	6 regt (bn)
ADA	1 regt
Engr	6 bn
Avn	2 coy

EQUIPMENT BY TYPE
LT TK 54: 36 SK-105A1 *Kuerassier*; 18 SK-105A2 *Kuerassier*
RECCE 24 EE-9 *Cascavel*
APC 115+
    APC (T) 91+: 4 4K-4FA-SB20 *Greif*; 50+ M-113, 37 M9 half-
    track
    APC (W) 61: 24 EE-11 *Urutu*; 22 MOWAG *Roland*; 15
    V-100 *Commando*
LT VEH 10: 10 *Koyak*
ARTY 311+
    TOWED 61: **105mm** 25 M-101A1; **122mm** 36 (M-30)
    M-1938
    MOR 250+: **60mm** M-224: **81mm** 250 M-29; Type-W87;
    107mm M-30; **120mm** M-120
AT • MSL• MANPATS 50+ HJ-8 (2 SP on *Koyak*)
    RCL **106mm** M-40A1; **90mm** M-67
    RL 200+: **66mm** M-72 *LAW*; **73mm** RPG-7V *Knout*; **89mm**
    200+ M-20
AIRCRAFT
    TPT 1 PA-34 *Seneca*
    UTL 1 Cessna 210 *Centurion*
AD • GUNS • TOWED 37mm 18 Type-65

Navy 4,800
FORCES BY ROLE
Organised into 6 naval districts with Naval HQ located at
Puerto Guayaramerín

EQUIPMENT BY TYPE
PATROL AND COASTAL COMBATANTS 54:
    PCR 1 Santa Cruz
    PBR 53

LOGISTICS AND SUPPORT 19:
  AH 2
  TPT 11 (river transports)
  SPT 6

FACILITIES

Bases Located at Riberalta, Tiquina, Puerto Busch, Puerto Guayaramerín, Puerto Villarroel, Trinidad, Puerto Suárez, Coral Harbour, Santa Cruz, Bermejo, Cochabamba, Puerto Villeroel

Marines 1,700 (incl 1,000 Naval Military Police)

Marine   6 inf bn (1 in each Naval District)
Mech inf 1 bn
MP   4 (naval MP) bn

Air Force 6,500 (incl conscripts)

FORCES BY ROLE

FGA   2 sqn with AT-33AN *Shooting Star*
Trg/COIN   1 sqn with PC-7 *Turbo Trainer*
SAR/   1 sqn with HB-315B *Lama*, AS-532AC
COMMS   *Cougar*
Tpt   1 sqn with Beech 90 *King Air*; 2 sqn with MA-60; DC-10; RC-130A/C-130B/C-130H *Hercules*; 1 sqn with F-27-400 *Friendship*; IAI-201 *Arava*; CV-440; CV-580; *Aerocommander* 690; Beech-1900; BAe-146-100
Liaison   3 sqn with Cessna 152; PA-32 *Saratoga*; PA-34 *Seneca*; Cessna 206; Cessna 210; Beech F-33 *Bonanza*
Survey   1 sqn with Cessna 402; *Learjet* 25B/25D (secondary VIP role); Cessna 206
Trg   3 sqn with Cessna 152; Cessna 172; T-25; T-34B Beech *Turbo Mentor*; A-122
Hel   1 (anti-drug) sqn with UH-1H *Huey*
AD   1 regt with Oerlikon; Type-65

EQUIPMENT BY TYPE

AIRCRAFT 33 combat capable
  FGA 15 AT-33AN *Shooting Star*
  Trg/COIN 18 PC-7 *Turbo Trainer**
  TPT 36: 2 MA-60; 1 DC-10; 3 Beech 90 *King Air*; 7 RC-130A/C-130B/C-130H *Hercules*; 1 Cessna 152; 1 Cessna 210; 1 CV-440; 1 CV-580; 3 F-27-400 *Friendship*; 1 Aero-Commander 690; 4 IAI-201 *Arava*; 2 Learjet 25B/ 25D (secondary VIP role); 1 PA-32 *Saratoga*; 3 PA-34 *Seneca*; 1 Beech-1900; 1 BAe-146-100; 3 C-212-100. (1 An-148 on order)
  UTL 21: 19 Cessna 206; 1 Cessna 212; 1 Cessna 402
  TRG 56: 1 Beech F-33 *Bonanza*; 9 Cessna 152; 2 Cessna 172; 28 A-122; 6 T-25; 10 T-34B Beech *Turbo Mentor*
HELICOPTERS
  ARMED HEL 15 UH-1H *Huey*
  UTL 4: 1 AS-532AC *Cougar*; 1 HB-315B *Lama*; 2 AS 350 B3. (5 Mi-17 on order)
AD•GUNS 18+: **20mm** *Oerlikon*; **37mm** 18 Type-65

Paramilitary 37,100+

National Police 31,100+
Frontier   27 unit
Paramilitary 9 bde; 2 (rapid action) regt

Narcotics Police 6,000+
FOE (700) - Special Operations Forces

DEPLOYMENT

CÔTE D'IVOIRE
UN • UNOCI 3 obs

DEMOCRATIC REPUBLIC OF CONGO
UN • MONUC 200; 7 obs; 2 inf coy

HAITI
UN • MINUSTAH 208; 1 mech inf coy

LIBERIA
UN • UNMIL 1; 2 obs

SUDAN
UN • UNAMID 1
UN • UNMIS 11 obs

Brazil BRZ

Brazilian Real R		2008	2009	2010
GDP	R	2.88tr	2.98tr	
	US$	1.57tr	1.72tr	
per capita	US$	8,040	8,670	
Growth	%	5.2	-0.7	
Inflation	%	5.7	4.8	
Def exp	R	39.89bn	48.0bn	
	US$	26.25bn	27.78bn	
Def bdgt	R	42.7bn	51.4bn	58.2bn
	US$	23.3bn	29.7bn	
US$1=R		1.83	1.73	

Population   198,739,269

Age	0–14	15–19	20–24	25–29	30–64	65 plus
Male	13%	5%	5%	5%	20%	2%
Female	13%	5%	5%	5%	20%	4%

Capabilities

ACTIVE 327,710 (Army 190,000 Navy 67,000 Air 70,710) Paramilitary 395,000

RESERVE 1,340,000
Terms of service 12 months (can be extended to 18)

ORGANISATIONS BY SERVICE

Army 120,000; 70,000 conscript (total 190,000)
FORCES BY ROLE
HQ: 7 Mil Comd, 12 Mil Regions; 7div (2 with Regional HQ)

Armd	2 bde (2 armd cav bn , 2 armd inf bn, 1 arty bn, 1 engr bn)
Mech Cav	4 bde (*each:* 1 armd cav bn, 1 arty bn, 2 mech cav bn)
SF	1 bde (1 SF bn, 1 cdo bn) with training centre (SF)
Mot Inf	8 bde (*total:* 29 mot inf bn)
Lt Inf	2 bde (total: 6 lt inf bn)
Jungle Inf	5 bde (total 15 bn)
Security	1 bde (total: 6 lt inf bn)
AB	1 bde (1 arty bn, 3 AB bn)
Arty	6 (med) gp
SP Arty	4 gp
ADA	1 bde
Engr	2 gp (*total:* 11 engr bn)
Hel	1 bde (4 hel bn (*each:* 2 hel sqn))

EQUIPMENT BY TYPE

MBT 219+: 128 *Leopard* 1 A1BE; 91 M-60A3/TTS; 220 *Leopard* 1 A5BR (to be delivered in 2010–11)
LT TK 152 M-41B/M-41C
RECCE 408: 408 EE-9 *Cascavel*
APC 807
  APC (T) 584 M-113
  APC (W) 223 EE-11 *Urutu*
ARTY 1,805
  SP 109: **105mm** 72 M-108/M-7; **155mm** 37 M-109A3
  TOWED 431
    105mm 336: 233 M-101/M-102; 40 L-118 *Light Gun*; 63 Model 56 pack howitzer
    155mm 95 M-114
  MRL 20+: **70mm** SBAT-70; 20 ASTROS II
  MOR 1,245: **81mm** 1,168: 453 Royal Ordnance L-16, 715 M936 AGR; **120mm** 77 M2
AT
  MSL • MANPATS 30: 18 *Eryx*; 12 *Milan*
  RCL 343: 106mm 194 M-40A1; **84mm** 149 *Carl Gustav*
  RL 84mm 540 AT-4
HELICOPTERS
  SPT 63: 19 AS-550U2 *Fennec* (armed); 8 AS-532 *Cougar*; 4 S-70A-36 *Black Hawk*; 32 AS-365 *Dauphin*
  TRG 16 AS-350 LI *Ecureuil*
AD
  MANPAD 53 SA-18 *Grouse* (*Igla*)
  GUNS 66: **35mm** 39 GDF-001 towed (some with *Super Fledermaus* radar); **40mm** 27 L/70 (some with BOFI)
  RADAR: 5 SABER M60

Navy 67,000 (incl 3,200+ conscript)

FORCES BY ROLE

Organised into 9 districts with HQ I Rio de Janeiro, HQ II Salvador, HQ III Natal, HQ IV Belém, HQ V Rio Grande, HQ VI Ladario, HQ VII Brasilia, HQ VIII Sao Paulo, HQ IX Manaus

EQUIPMENT BY TYPE

SUBMARINES • TACTICAL • SSK 5:
4 *Tupi* (GER T-209/1400) each with 8 single 533mm TT with MK 24 *Tigerfish* HWT
1 *Tikuna* with 8 single 533mm TT with MK 24 *Tigerfish* HWT (undergoing sea trials)

PRINCIPAL SURFACE COMBATANTS 16
  AIRCRAFT CARRIERS • CV 1:
1 *Sao Paulo* (FRA *Clemenceau*) (capacity 15–18 A-4 *Skyhawk* FGA ac; 4–6 SH-3D/SH-3A *Sea King* ASW hel; 3 AS-355F/AS-350BA *Ecureuil* spt hel; 2 AS-532 *Cougar* utl hel)
  FRIGATES 10
    FFG 9:
    3 *Greenhaigh* (UK *Broadsword*, 1 low readiness) 4 single with MM-38 *Exocet* tactical SSM, 2+ sextuple (12 eff.) with 32 *Sea Wolf* SAM), 6 single 324mm ASTT with Mk 46 LWT, 1 *Lynx* MK21A (*Super Lynx*) utl hel
    6 *Niteroi* each with 4 MM-40 *Exocet* tactical SSM, 1 *Albatros* Octuple with 24 *Aspide* SAM, 2 triple 324mm ASTT (6 eff.) with Mk 46 LWT, 1 2 tube *Bofors* 375mm (2 eff.), 1 115mm gun, 1 *Lynx* MK21A (*Super Lynx*) utl hel
    FF 1 *Para* (US *Garcia*) with 1 Mk 112 Octuple with tactical ASROC, 2 triple ASTT (6 eff.) with Mk 46 LWT, 2 127mm gun, 1 *Lynx* MK21A (*Super Lynx*) utl hel (low readiness, op. capability doubtful)
  CORVETTES • FSG 5:
    4 *Inhauma* each with 1 single with 4 MM-40 *Exocet* tactical SSM, 2 triple ASTT (6 eff.) each with Mk 46 LWT, 1 114mm gun, 1 *Lynx* MK21A (*Super Lynx*) utl hel
    1 *Barroso* with 2 single with 4 MM-40 *Exocet* tactical SSM, 2 triple ASTT (6 eff.) each with Mk 46 LWT, 1 114mm gun, 1 *Lynx* MK21A (*Super Lynx*) utl hel
PATROL AND COASTAL COMBATANTS 35:
  PCO 16: 12 *Grajau*; 2 *Imperial Marinheiro* with 1 76mm gun; 2 *Vigilante* (NAPA 500 additional vessels in build))
  PCC 10: 4 *Bracui* (UK *River*); 6 *Piratini* (US PGM)
  PCI 4 *Tracker* (Marine Police)
  PCR 5: 2 *Pedro Teixeira*; 3 *Roraima*
MINE WARFARE • MINE COUNTERMEASURES • MSC 6 *Aratu* (GER *Schutze*)
AMPHIBIOUS
  PRINCIPAL AMPHIBIOUS SHIPS • LSD 2:
    2 *Ceara* (US *Thomaston*) (capacity either 21 LCM or 6 LCU; 345 troops)
  LS • LST 1 *Mattoso Maia* (US *Newport*) (capacity 3 LCVP; 1 LCPL; 400 troops)
  LSLH 2: 1 *Garcia D'Avila* (UK *Sir Galahad*) (capacity 1 hel; 16 MBT; 340 troops); 1 *Almirante Saboia* (UK *Sir Bedivere*) (capacity 1 med hel; 18 MBT; 340 troops)
  CRAFT 46: 3 LCU; 35 LCVP; 8 **LCM**
LOGISTICS AND SUPPORT 39:
  AOR 2: 1 *Gastao Motta*; 1 *Marajo*
  ASR 1 *Felinto Perry* (NOR *Wildrake*)
  AG 2: 1 (troop carrier); 1 (river spt)
  AH 4: 2 *Oswaldo Cruz*; 1 *Dr Montegro*; 1 *Tenente Maximiano*
  AK 5
  AGOR 3: 1 *Ary Rongel* (Ice-strengthened hull, used for polar research); 1 *Cruzeiro do Sul* (research); 1 *Almirante Maximiano*
  AGHS 1 *Sirius*
  AGS 4: 1 *Antares*; 3 *Amorim Do Valle* (UK *Rover*)

ABU 6: 1 *Almirante Graca Aranah* (lighthouse tender); 5 *Comandante Varella*

ATF 5: 3 *Tritao*; 2 *Almirante Guihem*

TPT 2: 1 *Paraguassu*; 1 *Piraim* (river transports)

TRG 4

    AXL 3 *Nascimento*

    AXS 1

Naval Aviation 1,387

FORCES BY ROLE

FGA   1 sqn with 20 A-4 *Skyhawk*/A-4MB *Skyhawk*/ TA-4 *Skyhawk*; 3 TA-4MB *Skyhawk*

ASW   1 sqn with 4 SH-3G *Sea King*/SH-3H *Sea King*

Utl   1 sqn with 7 AS-332 *Super Puma*; 4 sqn with 18 AS-350 *Ecureuil* (armed); 8 AS-355 *Ecureuil* (armed)

Atk Hel 1 sqn with 12 Mk21A *Lynx*

Trg   1 sqn with 18 TH-57 *Sea Ranger*

EQUIPMENT BY TYPE

AIRCRAFT 23 combat capable

    FGA 20 A-4 *Skyhawk* FGA/A-4MB *Skyhawk* FGA/TA-4 *Skyhawk* trg*

    TRG 3 TA-4MB *Skyhawk**

HELICOPTERS

    ASW 16: 12 Mk21A *Lynx*; 4 SH-3G/SH-3H *Sea King*; (4 S-70B *Seahawk* on order)

    SPT 33: 7 AS-332 *Super Puma*; 18 AS-350 *Ecureuil* (armed); 8 AS-355 *Ecureuil* (armed); (16 EC-725 on order)

    TRG 18 TH-57 *Sea Ranger*

MSL • ASM: AM-39 *Exocet*; *Sea Skua*

Marines 15,520

FORCES BY ROLE

Amph   1 (Fleet Force) div (1 comd bn, 1 arty gp, 3 inf bn)

SF   1 bn

Marine 8+ (Regional) gp; 3 bn

Engr   1 bn

EQUIPMENT BY TYPE

LT TK 18 SK-105 *Kuerassier*

RECCE 6 EE-9 *Cascavel*

APC 35

    APC (T) 30 M-113

    APC (W) 12 *Piranha IIIC* (additional 18 on order)

AAV 25: 13 AAV-7A1; 12 LVTP-7

ARTY 49+

    TOWED 41: **105mm** 33: 18 L-118 Light Gun; 15 M-101; **155mm** 8 M-114

    MOR 18 **81mm**

AT

    MSL• MANPATS RB-56 *Bill*

    RCL 106mm 8 M-40A1

    RL 89mm M-20

AD • GUNS 40mm 6 L/70 (with BOFI)

Air Force 70,710

COMDABRA (aerospace defence), plus three general cmds – COMGAR (operations), COMGAP (logistics), COMGEP (personnel).

Brazilian air space is divided into 7 air regions, each of which is responsible for its designated air bases.

Air assets are divided among five designated air forces for operations (one temporarily deactivated).

I Air Force (HQ Natal) operates 3 avn gps (1º/5th, 2º/5th and 1º/11th GAV) and a Tactical Training Group (GITE) providing Air Combat Training for A-29A/B *Super Tucano* and A-27 *Tucano* aircraft. I Air Force also operates AT-26 *Xavante*, C-95 *Bandeirante* and UH-50 *Esquilo* helicopters.

II Air Force (HQ Rio de Janeiro) has some 240 aircraft organised into 3 Aviation Groups (7th, 8th and 10th GAVs). 7th GAV, responsible for Coastal Patrol, operates P-95A/B *Bandeirulhas* armed for ASV and ASW from 4 air bases. 8th and 10th GAVs, with H-60L *Blackhawk*, H-1H, *Super Puma* and *Esquilo* helicopters, are dedicated to SAR/utility, tpt ops and spec ops.

III Air Force (HQ Brasilia) 1st Air Defence Group is equipped with F-5EM/F-5BR *Tiger II*, AT-27 *Tucano* armed trainers and *Mirage* 2000B/C. The main light attack/armed recce force, with anti-narcotic and anti-terrorist roles, comprises 5 air groups with A-29 *Super Tucano*, AT-26 *Xavante* and A-1A/B; 6th GAV, with 5 EMB-145 AEW, 3 EMB-145RS and 5 R-95 electronic recce aircraft, is responsible for electronic surveillance, AEW and reconnaissance.

V Air Force (HQ Rio de Janeiro) operates some 160 air transport and flight refuelling aircraft from 5 air bases. Two tpt gps operate C-295M, ERJ-135/ERJ-145, EMB-190 transports, C/KC-130E/H *Hercules* tkr/tpts and KC-137 tankers.

FORCES BY ROLE

AD Ftr   1 gp with F-2000B/C, F-5EM, RC-95, R-99 and R-99A; 3 sqn with F-5EM/AT-27

FGA   2 sqn with A-1A/B; 4 sqn with A-29A/B; 1 sqn with AT-26; 3 sqn with A-27

Recce   1 sqn with A-1A/B; 1 sqn with RT-26

AWACS 1 sqn with R-99A/B

MP   4 sqn with P-95A/ P-95B

Tkr   1 sqn with KC-130, 1 sqn with KC-137

Tpt   1 sqn with VC-96, VC-1A, VC-99A/B, VU-35; 1 sqn with VC-97, VU-9; 2 sqn with C-97; CH/VH-55, 9 sqn with C-95A/B/C and R-95; 1 sqn with R-35A; 1 sqn with C-99, 3 sqn with C-130H/E, 2 sqn with C-98; 1 sqn with C-105A

Hel   4 sqn with H-1H; 1 sqn with H-34 (VIP) and EC-135; 2 sqn with H-50/H-55; 1 sqn with H-60L

Trg   1 sqn with T-25, 3 sqn with T-27 (incl. 1 air show sqn)

EQUIPMENT BY TYPE

AIRCRAFT 334 combat aircraft

    FTR 67: 12 F-2000 (*Mirage* 2000B/C); 49 F-5EM/FM; 6 F-5E

FGA 229: 40 A-1 (AMX); 50 A-29A *Super Tucano*; 75 A-29B *Super Tucano*; 10 AT-26A (*Impala* Mk.2); 2 AT-26B (*Impala* Mk.1); 28 AT-26 *Xavante*, 24 AT-27 *Tucano*
RECCE: 12: 4 RA-1 (AMX)*; 4 RT-26 *Xavante**; 4 RC-95
MP: 19: 10 P-95A *Bandeirulha* (EMB-111)*; 9 P-95B (EMB-111)*; 10 P-3AM *Orion* (delivery in progress)
ELINT 22: 4 EU-93A (Hawker 800XP); 3 R-99B (EMB-145S); 3 R-35A (Learjet 36); 2 EU-93 (HS-125), 1 EC-93 (HS-125), 9 EC-95 (EMB-110B *Bandeirante*)
AEW 5 R-99A (EMB-145RSA)
SAR 5: 4 SC-95B, 1 SC-130E
TKR 5: 2 KC-130H, 3 KC-137 (1 stored)
TKR/TPT 22 KC-390 (on order)
TPT 124: 1 VC-1A (Airbus ACJ); 2 VC-96 (B-737-200); 12 C-105 *Amazonas* (C-295M); 13 C-130H; 7 C-130E; 10 C-99A (ERJ-145); 2 VC-99C (ERJ-135BJ); 59 C-95A/B/C; 4 VC-97 *Brasilia*; 7 C-97 *Brasilia*; 8 VU-9 *Xingu*
UTL 58: 13 C-98 (Cessna 208B) *Caravan* I; 3 C-98A (Cessna 208-G1000); 13 U-7 (PA-34) *Séneca*; 6 L-42, 22 U-42 *Regente*; 3 U-19 *Ipanema*
TRG 110: 11 A-1B (AMX-T)*; 22 T-25A/C; 42 T-26 *Xavante*; 35 T-27 *Tucano* (6 on loan to Argentina)
HELICOPTERS
UTL 93: 32 H-50 (AS-350B); 8 H-55 (AS-355); 9 H-34 (AS-332M *Super Puma*); 32 H-1H; 10 H-60L *Blackhawk* (6 more on order); 2 EC-135 *Eurocopter*; (18 EC-725 *Super Cougar* on order)
MSL • AAM MAA-1 *Piranha*, *Python* III, Super 530F, *Magic* 2

Paramilitary 395,000 opcon Army

Public Security Forces 395,000

State police organisation technically under army control. However the military control is lessening with authority reverting to the individual states.

UAV 3 *Heron* deployed by Federal Police for Amazon and border patrols

DEPLOYMENT

CENTRAL AFRICAN REPUBLIC/CHAD
UN • MINURCAT 3 obs

CÔTE D'IVOIRE
UN • UNOCI 3; 4 obs

TIMOR LESTE
UN • UNMIT 4 obs

HAITI
UN • MINUSTAH 1,282; 1 inf bn; 1 engr coy

LIBERIA
UN • UNMIL 2

NEPAL
UN • UNMIN 6 obs

SUDAN
UN • UNMIS 2; 20 obs

WESTERN SAHARA
UN • MINURSO 10 obs

Chile CHL

Chilean Peso pCh		2008	2009	2010
GDP	pCh	88.5tr	88.5tr	
	US$	170bn	160bn	
per capita	US$	10,308	9,621	
Growth	%	3.2	-1.7	
Inflation	%	8.9	2.0	
Def exp[a]	pCh	2.73tr	2.90tr	
	US$	5.56bn	5.23bn	
Def bdgt	pCh	1.42tr	1.58tr	
	US$	2.73bn	2.85bn	
US$1=pCh		522	554	

[a] Including estimates for military pensions, paramilitary and Copper Fund

Population	16,601,707

Age	0–14	15–19	20–24	25–29	30–64	65 plus
Male	13%	4%	4%	4%	21%	3%
Female	12%	4%	4%	4%	21%	5%

Capabilities

ACTIVE 60,560 (Army 35,000 Navy 17,800 Air 7,760)
Paramilitary 41,500
Terms of service Army 1 year Navy and Air Force 22 months. Voluntary since 2005

RESERVE 40,000 (Army 40,000)

ORGANISATIONS BY SERVICE

Army 22,000; 13,000 conscript (total 35,000)
FORCES BY ROLE
6 military administrative regions. Currently being reorganised into 4 armoured, 2 motorised, 2 mountain and 1 special forces brigade.

Army	6 div (org, composition varies)
Composite	12 (reinforced) regt
Armd	2 bde (2 more being created)
Armd Cav	2 regt
Inf	10 regt
Spec Ops	1 bde (4 SF bn)
Arty	3 regt
Sigs	2 regt
Engr	2 regt
Avn	1 bde

EQUIPMENT BY TYPE
MBT 309: 140 *Leopard* 2 A4; 169 *Leopard* 1 (24 in store)
AIFV 309: 139 YPR-765; 170 *Marder*
APC 526
  APC (T) 342 M-113A1/A2
  APC (W) 184 Cardoen *Piranha*
ARTY 1,191
  SP 58: 105mm 21 M108; **155mm** 37: 24 M-109A3; 13 (AMX) Mk F3

TOWED 138: **105mm** 90 M-101 **155mm** 48 M-68
MRL 160mm 12 LAR-160
MOR 950:
  81mm 650: 300 M-29; 150 Soltam; 200 FAMAE; **120mm**
  170: 110 FAMAE; 60 Soltam M-65
  SP 130: **120mm** 130: 50 FAMAE (on *Piranha* 6x6); 80
  M-5L1A
AT
  MSL• MANPATS 99+ *Milan*; 99 *Spike*
  RCL 106mm M-40A1; **88mm** *Carl Gustav*
AIRCRAFT
  TPT 10: 1 Beech 90 *King Air*; 1 Beech 58 *Baron*; 5 CASA
  212 *Aviocar*; 2 CN-235; 1 CE-550 *Citation II*
  UTL 3 Cessna 208 *Caravan*
  TRG 6 Cessna R172K *Hawk XP*
HELICOPTERS
  SPT 17: 2 AS-332 *Super Puma*; 2 AS350B2; 6 AS-350B3
  Ecureuil; 1 AS-355F *Ecureuil II*; 6 SA-330 *Puma*
  UTL 18 MD-530F *Lifter* (armed)
AD
  SAM 24:
  MANPAD 24: 12 *Mistral*; 12 *Javelin*
  GUNS 68:
  SP 18: **20mm** 18 *Piranha*/TCM-20; **35mm** 30 *Gepard* being
  delivered
  TOWED 50: **20mm** 50 M-167 *Vulcan*

Navy 16,500; 1,300 conscript (total 17,800)

FORCES BY ROLE
Main Command: Fleet includes FF and SS flotilla; Naval
Aviation, Marines, Seals and Transport Units.
Navy 4 Naval Zones; 1st Naval Zone and main HQ
        located at Valparaiso (26S-36S); 2nd Naval Zone:
        at Talcahuano (36S-46S); 3rd Naval Zone at Punta
        Arenas (46S to Antarctica); 4th Naval Zone at
        Iquique (18S-26S)

EQUIPMENT BY TYPE
SUBMARINES • TACTICAL • SSK 4:
  2 *O'Higgins* (*Scorpene*) each with 6 single 533mm TT with
  18 A-184 *Black Shark* HWT & SUT
  2 *Thompson* (GER T-209/1300) each with 8 single 533mm
  TT with 14 SUT HWT
PRINCIPAL SURFACE COMBATANTS 8
  FRIGATES • FFG 8:
    1 *Williams* (UK Type 22) with 2x12 (24eff.) each with
    Sea Wolf naval SAM
    2 *Lattore* (NLD *Jacob Van Heemskerck* class) each with 2
    twin 324mm ASTT (4 eff.) each with Mk 46 LWT, 1 Mk
    13 GMLS with 40 SM-1 MR SAM, 2 Mk 141 *Harpoon*
    quad (8 eff.) with RGM-86C *Harpoon* tactical SSM
    2 *Almirante Riveros* (NLD *Karel Doorman class*) each
    with 2 quad (8 eff.) *Harpoon* SSM, 1 Mk 48 *Sea Sparrow*
    with 16 RIM-7P *Sea Sparrow* SAM, 4 single 324mm MK
    32 MOD 9 ASTT with MK 46 MOD 5 HWT, 1 76mm
    gun, (capacity 1 med hel)
    3 *Almirante Cochrane* (UK *Duke Class* Type 23*)* each
    with 2 twin 324mm ASTT (4 eff.) with *Sting Ray* LWT,
    2 Mk 141 *Harpoon* quad (8 eff.) with RGM-84C *Harpoon*
    tactical SSM, 1 32 canister *Sea Wolf* VLS with *Sea Wolf*
    SAM, 1 114mm gun, (capacity 1 NAS-332C *Cougar*)

PATROL AND COASTAL COMBATANTS 13
  PFM 7:
    3 *Casma* (ISR *Sa'ar* 4) each with 8 GI *Gabriel I* tactical
    SSM, 2 76mm gun
    4 *Tiger* (GER Type 148) each with 4 single with MM-40
    Exocet tactical SSM, 1 76mm gun
  PCO 6 *Ortiz* (*Taitao* class)
AMPHIBIOUS • LS 5
  LSM 2 *Elicura*
  LST 3: 2 *Maipo* (capacity 7 tanks; 140 troops) (FRA *Batral*);
  1 *Valdivia* (capacity 400 troops) (US *Newport*)
LOGISTICS AND SUPPORT 10:
  AOR 1 *Araucano*
  AS 1 (also used as general spt ship)
  AKSL 1
  AGOR 1 *Vidal Gormez*
  AGS 1 *Type 1200* (ice strengthened hull, ex-CAN)
  ATF 3: 2 *Veritas*; 1 *Smit Lloyd*
  TPT 1
  TRG • AXS 1
MSL
  SSM MM-38 *Exocet* tactical SSM
FACILITIES
Bases Located at Valparaiso, Talcahuano, Puerto Montt,
        Puerto Williams, Iquique, Punta Arenas

Naval Aviation 600

AIRCRAFT 17combat capable
  MP 6: 3 P-3A *Orion*; 3 CN-295MPA *Persuader* (5
  additional ac on order)
  TPT 13: 3 CASA 212A *Aviocar*; 8 Cessna O-2A
  *Skymaster**; 2 EMB-111 *Bandeirante**
  TRG 7 PC-7 *Turbo Trainer**
HELICOPTERS
  ASW 3 Bell 206 AS; 5 NAS-332C *Cougar**
  SAR 12: 7 HH-65 *Dauphin*, 5 Bo-105S
  UTL 6: 4 Bell 206 *JetRanger*; 2 Bell 412
MSL •ASM AM-39 *Exocet*

Marines 3,000

FORCES BY ROLE
Amph 1 bn
Marine 4 gp (*total*: 1 SSM bty (Excalibur Central Defence
        System), 2 trg bn, 4 inf bn, 4 ADA bty, 4 fd arty
        bty), 7 security det (one per naval zone)

EQUIPMENT BY TYPE
LT TK 16: 15 *Scorpion*; 1 *Sultan*
APC (W) 25 MOWAG *Roland*
ARTY 82
  TOWED 32: **105mm** 8 KH-178; **155mm** 24 G-5
  MOR 50 81mm
RCL 106mm ε30 M-40A1
AD • SAM
  SP 40 M1097 HMMWV *Avenger*
  MANPAD *Blowpipe*

Coast Guard

Integral part of the Navy
PATROL AND COASTAL COMBATANTS 61
  OPV 1 *Piloto Pardo* (OPV-80) (additional vessel in build)

PCC 18 *Alacalufe* (*Protector* WPB class)
PCI 37: 8 *Grumete Diaz* (*Dabor* class); 18 *Rodman*; 11 (LMP, LSR class)
MISC BOATS/CRAFT 5 *Defender* class (upto 10 vessels on order); 1 *Archangel* class (upto 18 vessels on order)

Air Force 7,300; 460 conscript (total 7,760)

Flying hours   100 hrs/year

FORCES BY ROLE

Ftr /FGA	1 sqn with F-5E *Tigre III*; F-5F *Tigre III*; 1 sqn with Block 50 F-16C/F-16D *Puma*; 1 sqn with F-16AM/F-16BM;
Recce	1 (photo) unit with Beech A-100 *King Air*; DHC-6-300 *Twin Otter*; Learjet 35A
AEW ELINT	B-707 *Phalcon* with tpt gp. Beech 99 *Petrel Alfa/Beta*
CCT	2 gps with A-37B *Dragonfly*; A-36CC *Halcon*; T-36BB; B-707 *Tanquero*
Tpt Liaison	3 gps with B-737-500 (VIP); B-737-300; B-767ER; C-130B *Hercules*; C-130H *Hercules*; CASA 212 *Aviocar*; DHC-6-100 *Twin Otter*; DHC-6-300; Gulfstream IV; Learjet 35A; PA-28-140 *Cherokee*; Beech 99A7; Cessna O-2A
Trg	1 gp with T-35A/B *Pillan*; CJ-1 *Citation*; Mirage IIIBE, T-36 *Halcon*, Bell 206A
Hel	3 gps with UH-1H; Bo-105CBS-4; Bell 412; S-70A-39 *Black Hawk*; Bell 206B (trg)
AD	1 regt (5 AD gp) with *Mygale*; *Mistral*; M-163 *Vulcan*/M-167 *Vulcan*; GDF-005; Oerlikon; *Crotale*

EQUIPMENT BY TYPE

AIRCRAFT 77 combat capable
  FTR 16: 13 F-5E *Tigre III*+; 3 F-5F *Tigre III*+
  FGA 59: 28 F-16 (6 Block 50 F-16C; 4 F-16D; 11 F-16AM; 7 F-16BM) (18 F-16AM on order); 13 A-37B *Dragonfly*; 9 A-36CC *Halcon*; 8 T-36BB
  RECCE 6: 1 Beech *King Air*; 2 Learjet 35A; 3 DHC-6-300
  AEW 1 B-707 (IAI *Phalcon*)
  ELINT 3 Beech 99 *Petrel Alfa*; 2 Beech 99 *Petrel Beta*
  TKR 1 B-707 *TanqueroSP*
  TPT 66: 1 B-737-300; 1 B-737-500; 1 B-767ER; 1 C-130B *Hercules*; 2 C-130H *Hercules*; 4 CASA 212 *Aviocar*; 5 DHC-6-100 *Twin Otter*; 8 DHC-6-300 *Twin Otter*; 1 Gulfstream IV; 31 PA-28-140 *Cherokee*; 3 Beech 99A; 6 Cessna 0-2A; 2 Learjet 35A
  TRG 44: 1 Mirage IIIBE; 38 T-35A/T-35B *Pillan*; 5 Cessna 525 *Citation CJ-1*; (12 EMB-324 *Super Tucano* on order)
HELICOPTERS
  UTL 23: 1 Bo-105CBS-4; 8 Bell 412 *Twin Huey* (delivery in progress); 10 UH-1H *Iroquois*; 1 S-70A-39 *Black Hawk*; 3 Bell 206B (trg); (5 Mi-17 on order)
AD
  SYSTEMS *Mygale*
  SAM *Mistral*
  SP 5 *Crotale*
  GUNS • TOWED 20mm M-163 *Vulcan* SP/M-167 *Vulcan*; 35mm GDF-005 Oerlikon

MSL • AAM AIM-9B *Sidewinder*/AIM-9J *Sidewinder*; Python III; *Shafrir*; BVR *Derby*

Paramilitary 41,500

Carabineros 41,500

Ministry of Defence

FORCES BY ROLE

13 Zones
Paramilitary   39 district; 174 comisaria

EQUIPMENT BY TYPE

APC (W) 20 MOWAG *Roland*
MOR 60mm; 81mm
AIRCRAFT
  TPT 10: 4 Cessna 182 *Skylane*; 1 Cessna 550 *Citation V*; 5 PA-31T *Navajo/Cheyenne II*
  UTL 5: 2 Cessna 206; 1 Cessna 208; 2 Cessna 210 *Centurion*
HELICOPTERS • UTL 18: 2 BK-117; 8 Bo-105; 2 Bell 206 *Jet Ranger*; 2 EC-135; 4 Agusta-Westland AW-109E

DEPLOYMENT

BOSNIA-HERZEGOVINA
EU • EUFOR • *Operation Althea* 21

HAITI
UN • MINUSTAH 500; 1 inf bn; 1 avn unit; elm 1 engr coy

INDIA/PAKISTAN
UN • UNMOGIP 2 obs

MIDDLE EAST
UN • UNTSO 4 obs

Colombia COL

Colombian Peso pC		2008	2009	2010
GDP	pC	479tr	495tr	
	US$	244bn	267bn	
per capita	US$	5,652	6,115	
Growth	%	2.5	-0.3	
Inflation	%	7.0	4.6	
Def exp [a]	pC	14.1tr	18.7tr	
	US$	9.54bn	10.07bn	
Def bdgt	pC	12.6tr	12.1tr	
	US$	6.41bn	6.51bn	
FMA	US$	55.0m	53m	66.3m
US$1=pC		1,967	1,856	

[a] including paramilitaries

Population   43,677,372

Age	0–14	15–19	20–24	25–29	30–64	65 plus
Male	16%	5%	4%	4%	19%	2%
Female	15%	5%	4%	4%	20%	3%

Capabilities

ACTIVE 285,220 (Army 237,466, Navy 34,620 Air 13,134) Paramilitary 144,097

RESERVE 61,900 (Army 54,700 Navy 4,800 Air 1,200 Joint 1,200)

ORGANISATIONS BY SERVICE

Army 237,466

FORCES BY ROLE

Mech   1 (1st) div with (1 bde (2nd) (2 mech inf bn, 1 COIN bn, 1 mtn inf bn, 1 engr bn, 1 MP bn, 1 cbt spt bn, 2 Gaula anti-kidnap gp);1 bde (10th) (1 mech inf bn, 1 (med) tk bn, 1 mech cav bn, 1 mtn inf bn, 2 fd arty bn, 2 engr bn, 1 cbt spt bn, 2 Gaula anti-kidnap gp); 1 EOD gp

COIN   1 div (2nd) with (1 bde (5th) (3 lt inf bn, 1 fd arty bn, 1 AD bn, 2 engr bn, 1 cbt spt bn, 1 Gaula anti-kidnap gp); 1 bde (18th) (1 airmob cav bn, 4 lt inf bn, 2 engr bn, 1 cbt spt bn);1 bde (30th) (1 cav recce bn, 2 lt inf bn, 1 COIN bn, 1 engr bn, 1 cbt spt bn))

Rapid   3 COIN mobile bde (*each:* 4 COIN bn, 1 cbt
Reaction   spt bn)1 div (4th) with (1 airmob bde (2 airmob inf bn, 1 lt inf bn, 1 COIN bn, 1 SF (anti-terrorist) bn, 1 airmob engr bn, 1 cbt spt bn, 1 Gaula anti-kidnap gp); 1 bde (16th) (1 mech cav recce bn, 1 lt inf bn, 3 COIN bn, 1 cbt spt bn, 1 Gaula anti-kidnap gp);1 (28th Jungle) bde (2 inf, 3 COIN, 2 marine (riverine) bn, 1 cbt spt bn); 1 bde (21st) with(3 x lt inf bn)

Lt Inf   1 div (3rd) with (1 bde (3rd) (1 cav recce bn, 3 lt inf bn, 1 mtn inf bn, 1 COIN bn, 1 Fd arty bn, 1 engr bn, 1 cbt spt bn, 1 MP bn, 1 Gaula anti-kidnap gp); 1 bde (8th) (2 lt inf bn, 1 COIN bn, 1 Fd arty bn, 1 engr bn, 1 Gaula anti-kidnap gp coy); 1 bde (29th) (1 mtn inf bn);
1 div (5th) with 1 bde (1st) (1 cav recce bn, 2 lt inf bn, 1 COIN bn, 1 fd arty bn, 2 engr bn, 1 cbt spt bn, 1 Gaula anti-kidnap gp); 1 bde (6th) (2 lt inf bn,1 mtn inf bn, 1 COIN bn, 1 cbt spt bn, 1 Gaula anti-kidnap gp); 1 bde (13th) (2 cav recce bn, 1 airmob inf bn, 2 lt inf bn, 1 mtn inf bn, 1 COIN bn, 1 Fd arty bn, 1 engr bn, 1 cbt spt bn, 2 MP bn);
1 div (6th) with 1 bde (12th) (2 lt inf bn, 1 mtn inf bn, 1 COIN bn, 1 engr bn, 1 cbt spt bn, 1 Gaula anti-kidnap gp); 1 (26th) jungle bde (1 lt jungle inf bn, 1 COIN bn, 1 cbt spt bn, 1 coast guard det); 1 (27th) bde (2 lt inf bn, 1 COIN bn, 2 engr bn, 1 cbt spt bn)

1 div (7th) with 1 bde (4th) (1 cav recce bn, 3 lt inf bn, 1 COIN bn, fd 1 arty bn, 2 engr bn, 1 cbt spt bn, 2 Gaula anti-kidnap gp, 1 SF (anti-terrorist) coy); 1 bde (11th) (1 airmob inf bn, 1 lt inf bn, 2 COIN bn, 1 engr bn, 1 cbt spt bn); 1 bde (14th) (3 lt inf bn, 2 COIN bn, 1 engr bn, 1 cbt spt bn); 1 bde (17th) (2 lt inf bn, 1 COIN bn, 1 engr bn, 1 cbt spt bn)

EOD   6 EOD gp (bn)

SF   2 SF gp (bn); 1 SF anti-terrorist bn

Spt/Logistic   1 bde (1 spt bn, 1 maint bn, 1 supply bn, 1 tpt bn, 1 medical bn, 1 logistic bn)

Avn   1 bde (1 hel bn (2 cbt hel sqn), 1 avn bn)

Counter-   1 indep bde (1 spt bn, 3 counter-narcotics bn)
Narcotics

EQUIPMENT BY TYPE

RECCE 176: 123 EE-9 *Cascavel*; 6 M-8 (anti-riot vehicle); 8 M-8 with 1 TOW; 39 M1117 *Guardian*

APC 194

  APC (T) 54 TPM-113 (M-113A1)

  APC (W) 140+: 80 BTR-80; 56 EE-11 *Urutu*; 4 RG-31 *Nyala*

ARTY 584

  TOWED 101: **105mm** 86 M-101; **155mm** 15 155/52 APU SBT-1

    MOR 521: **81mm** 125 M-1; **107mm** 148 M-2; **120mm** 210 *Brandt*, 38 HY12, AM50

AT

  MSL • **SP** 8+: 8 *TOW; Nimrod*

    MANPATS 10+: 10 TOW; *SPIKE-ER, APILAS*

  RCL 106mm 63 M-40A1

  RL 15+: **66mm** M-72 *LAW;* **73mm** RPG-22; **89mm** 15 M-20; **90mm** C-90C; **106mm** SR-106

AIRCRAFT

  EW • ELINT 2 B-200 *Super King Air*

  TPT 11: 2 CASA 212 *Aviocar* (Medevac); 1 CV-580; 2 PA-34 *Seneca*; 2 Rockwell *Turbo Commander 695A*; 1 Beechcraft C-90; 2 Beech 200 *Super King Air*; 1 An-32

  UTL 2 Cessna 208B *Grand Caravan*

  TRG 5 *Utva-75*

HELICOPTERS

  SPT 22: 8 Mi-17-1V *Hip*; 9 Mi-17-MD; 5 Mi-17-V5 *Hip*

  UTL 90: 30 UH-1H *Huey II*; 20 UH-1N *Twin Huey;* 35 UH-60L *Black Hawk*; 5 K-Max

AD

  SAM 15

    SP 5 M48 *Chaparral*

    TOWED 10: 3 *Skyguard/Sparrow*, 7 Eagle Eye

  GUNS 39+

    SP 12.7mm 18 M-8/M-55

    TOWED 21+: **35mm** GDF Oerlikon; **40mm** 21 M-1A1 (with 7 *Eagle Eye* radar)

Navy 34,620; (incl 7,200conscript)

FORCES BY ROLE

Navy 1 HQ (Tri-Service Unified Eastern Command HQ) located at Puerto Carreño

EQUIPMENT BY TYPE
SUBMARINES • TACTICAL 4
SSK 2 *Pijao* (GER T-209/1200) each with 8 single 533mm TT with 14 SUT HWT

SSI 2 *Intrepido* (ITA SX-506, SF delivery)

PRINCIPAL SURFACE COMBATANTS • CORVETTES
FSG 4 *Almirante Padilla* (undergoing modernisation programme) each with 2 quad (8 eff.) with MM-40 *Exocet* tactical SSM, 2 B515 *ILAS*-3 triple 324mm each with A244 LWT, 1 76mm gun, 1 Bo-105 / AS-555SN *Fennec* utl hel

PATROL AND COASTAL COMBATANTS 86
PSOH 1 *Reliance*

PFO 1 *Espartana* (ESP *Cormoran*)

PCO 3:
2 *Lazaga*
1 *Pedro de Heredia* (US tugs) with 1 76mm gun

PFC 1 *Quita sueno* (US *Asheville*) with 1 76mm gun

PCC 2 *Toledo*

PCI 10: 2 *Jaime Gomez*; 2 *Jose Maria Palas* (*Swiftships 105*); 2 *Castillo Y Rada* (*Swiftships 110*); 4 *Point*

PCR 68: 2 *Nodriza* (PAF-VII/VIII); 6 *Nodriza* (PAF-II) with B212 or B412 hel; 3 *Arauca*; 20 *Delfin*; 4 *Diligente*; 11 *Rio Magdalena*; 2 *Rotork*; 11 *Andromeda* (ex-*Pirahna*); 9 LPR-40 *Tenerife* (Further vessels on order)

AMPHIBIOUS 8:
LCM 1 LCM-8

LCU 7 *Morrosquillo* (LCU – 1466)

LOGISTICS AND SUPPORT 6:
AG 2 *Luneburg* (ex-GER, depot ship for patrol vessels)

AGOR 2 *Providencia*

AGS 1

ABU 1

FACILITIES
Bases Located at Puerto Leguízamo, Buenaventura, (Pacific) Málaga, (Main HQ) Catagena, Barrancabermeja, Puerto Carreño, Leticia, Puerto Orocue, Puerto Inirida

Naval Aviation 146
AIRCRAFT
MP 3: 2 CN-235MPA *Persuader* (Additional 2 ordered); 1 PA-31 *Navajo* (upgraded for ISR)

TPT 3: 1 C-212 (Medevac); 2 Cessna 208 *Caravan*,

UTL 5: 4 Cessna 206; 1 PA-31 *Navajo*

HELICOPTERS
ASW 2 AS-555SN *Fennec*

UTL 8: 2 Bo-105; 4 Bell 412; 1 Bell 212; 1 BK-117

Marines 14,000
FORCES BY ROLE
SF   1 bn; 2 (River) gp

Marine 1 bde (3 Marine bn, 2 COIN bn & 1 cmd & spt bn); 3 (River) bde (one with 3 marine inf bn; second with 3 marine inf bn, 3 assault inf bn & 1 cmd & spt bn; third with 4 marine inf bn)

EQUIPMENT BY TYPE
no hy equipment

APC (W) 8 BTR-80A (12 on order)

ARTY
MOR 97: 20 **81mm**; 77 *Commando* **60mm**

Air Force 13,134
6 Combat Air Commands (CACOM) plus. CACOM 7 (former Oriental Air Group) responsible for air ops in specific geographic area. Flts can be deployed or 'loaned' to a different CACOM

CACOM 1. (Capitán Germán Olano Air Base) operates 6 sqn (1 with *Kfir* C-7; 1 with *Mirage*-5COAM (maybe only 6 op), *Mirage*-5CODM (command post); 1 with AC-47T, Hughes 369; 1 with PA-31, 1 PA-42, UH-1H; 1 with T-37C) and is dedicated to air defence and combat training.

CACOM 2. (CT. Luis F. Gómez Niño Air Base) operates 4 sqn (1 with OV-10; 1 with EMB-312 *Tucano**; 1 with EMB-314 *Super Tucano**; 1 with MD500, UH-1H) and is dedicated to counter-insurgency and offensive operations.

CACOM 3. (Mayor General Alberto Pauwels Rodríguez Air Base) operates 2 sqn (1 with *Super Tucano*; 1 with Bell 212, C-95, *Queen Air*, T-41D*) and is dedicated to SAR and MP operations along the Caribbean Coast.

CACOM 4. (Teniente Coronel Luis Franciso Pinto Parra Air Base) operates 5 hel sqn (1 with Hughes 369; 1 with UH-1H, Hughes 369; 1 with Bell 206, Hughes 369; 2 trg sqn with Bell 206, Enstrom F-28F, UH-1F) and is dedicated to tactical support operations and training.

CACOM 5. (Brigadier General Arturo Lema Posada Air Base) operates 1 gp with AH-60L *Arpia* III*, UH-60 (CSAR); and is dedicated to SAR, tpt, and heavy hel support operations.

CACOM 6. (Capitán Ernesto Esguerra Cubides Air Base) operates 2 sqn with Schweizer SA-2-337, Cessna IV, Fairchild C-26B, Ce-208 and B-300 *Super King Air*; and is dedicated to counter-insurgency operations.

FORCES BY ROLE

Ftr/FGA/ Recce	1 sqn with *Kfir* C-10/12; 1 sqn with *Mirage*-5COAM, *Mirage*- 5CODM (used as command post); 1 sqn with AC-47T, *Hughes* 369; 1 sqn with A-37B/OA-37B; 1 sqn with OV-10; 1 sqn with EMB-312 *Tucano**; 1 sqn with EMB-314/A-29 *Super Tucano*
Elint/EW	2 sqn with Schweizer SA-2-337, Cessna IV, Fairchild C-26B, Ce-208, B-300 *Super King Air*
SAR/ MP	1 sqn with Bell 212, C-95, *Queen Air*, T-41D*
Tpt	1 sqn with C-130B, C-130H; 1 sqn with CN-235M, *Arava*, C-212, *King Air* C90, Do-328; 1 (Presidential) sqn with B-727, B-707 (tkr/tpt), B-737-700 (BBJ), B-767ER, C295-M, F-28, Bell 412, Bell 212
Hel	1 gp with AH-60L *Arpia* III*, UH-60 (CSAR); 1 sqn with MD500, UH-1H; 1 sqn with Hughes 369; 1 sqn with UH-1H, Hughes 369; 1 sqn with Bell 206, Hughes 369; 2 trg sqn with Bell 206, Enstrom F-28F, UH-1F
Trg	1 (primary trg) sqn with PA-31, PA-42, UH-1H; 1 sqn with T-37C; 1 (primary trg) sqn with T-41D*; 1 sqn basic trg with T-34

EQUIPMENT BY TYPE
AIRCRAFT 90 combat capable

FGA 31: 24 *Kfir* (10 C-2 (being upgraded to C-10), 10 C-12, 4 TC-7); 5 *Mirage*-5COAM; 2 *Mirage*-5CODM

CCT/TRG 59: 8 AC-47T; 10 A-37B/OA-37B *Dragonfly*; 25 A-29 *Super Tucano*; 4 T-37C; 12 EMB-312 *Tucano*

RECCE 11: 6 Schweizer SA-2-37; 2 B-300 *Super King Air*; 3 *Aero Commander*
SURVEILLANCE 9: 5 Ce-650 *Citation* IV, 4 C-26B,
ELINT 2 Ce-208 *Grand Caravan*
MEDEVAC 3: 2 Ce-208B; 1 *Super King Air* 350C
TKR 2: 1 KC-767, 1 B707
TPT 28: 1 B-737-700 (BBJ); 1 B-707 tkr/tpt; 1 B767ER; 4 C-130B *Hercules* (plus 3 in store); 3 C-130H *Hercules*; 1 *King Air* C90; 4 C-212; 3 CN-235M; 4 C-295M; 1 Ce-208; 1 Ce-550; 2 C-95 (EMB-110P1); 1 F-28T; 1 Arava
TRG 17: 9 T-34; 8 T-37B. (25 Lancair FG on order)
LIAISON 22: 2 B-300 *Super King Air* (Medevac); 1 Ce-185 Floatplane; 2 Ce-210; 2 Ce-337G/H; 1 Ce-401; 3 Ce-404; 2 PA-31 *Navajo*; 1 PA-31T *Navajo*; 1 PA-42 *Cheyenne*; 4 PA-34 *Seneca*; 1 PA-44 *Seminole*; 2 *Turbo Commander* 1000
HELICOPTERS
ATK 26: 1 MD-500MD *Defender*; 4 MD530MG *Escorpion*; 7 H369HM; 14 Sikorksy/Elbit AH-60L *Arpia* III
UTL 34: 16 UH-1H *Iroquois*; 8 H500C; 2 H500M; 2 UH-60Q; 6 UH-1H
TPT 37: 7 UH-1P *Huey* II; 12 Bell 212 *Twin Huey*; 2 Bell 412HP/SP; 8 UH-60A *Blackhawk*; 8 UH-60L ordered
TRG 15: 11 Bell 206B3; 2 H500C; 1 H500ME; 1 Bell 212
UAV 7 *Scan Eagle*
MSL•AAM *Python* III; R530

Paramilitary 144,097

National Police Force 136,097
AIRCRAFT
ELINT 3: 1 *Ce-* 208B, 2 C-26B
TPT 26: 1 *King* 300; 2 *King* 200; 5 *Caravan* 208; 2 DHC 6 *Twin Otter*; 1 *King Air* C-99; 4 C-26; 1 *Turbo Truck*; 3 Ayres 52R; 6 Air Tractor AT-802
TRG 3 Cessna C-152; 5 Cessna 206
HELICOPTERS
UTL 67: 7 Bell 206L *LongRanger*; 12 Bell 212; 3 Bell 206B; 1 Bell 412; 2 MD 500D; 1 MD-530F; 25 UH-1H-II *Huey* II; 7 UH-60L

Rural Militia 8,000

SELECTED NON-STATE GROUPS

Fuerzas Armadas Revolucionarias de Colombia (FARC) Est. strength: 8,000 Major equipments include: improvised mortars; improvised explosive devices; rocket propelled grenades; mines; reports of some riverine capability, reports of possible AT and MANPAD acquisition **Ejercito de Liberacion Nacional (ELN)** Est. strength: 3,000 Major equipments include: mines and IEDs; SALW **Bandas Criminales Emergente (BACRIM)** Est. strength: 3,500 Major equipments include: SALW

DEPLOYMENT

EGYPT
MFO 354; 1 inf bn

FOREIGN FORCES

United States US Southern Command: Army 52; Navy 4; USAF 9; USMC 19

Costa Rica CRI

Costa Rican Colon C		2008	2009	2010
GDP	C	15.6tr	16.7tr	
	US$	29.7bn	28.6bn	
per capita	US$	7,072	6,720	
Growth	%	2.6	-1.5	
Inflation	%	13.4	8.4	
Sy Bdgt[a]	C	82bn	105bn	113bn
	US$	156m	180m	
US$1=C		526	587	

[a] No armed forces. Paramilitary budget

Population   4,253,877

Age	0–14	15–19	20–24	25–29	30–64	65 plus
Male	15%	5%	5%	4%	19%	3%
Female	14%	5%	5%	4%	19%	3%

Capabilities
Paramilitary 9,800

ORGANISATIONS BY SERVICE

Paramilitary 9,800

Civil Guard 4,500
Police	1 (tac) *comisaria*
Provincial	6 *comisaria*
Spec Ops	1 unit
Paramilitary	7 (Urban) *comisaria* (reinforced coy)

Border Police 2,500
Sy 2 (Border) comd (8 *comisaria*)

Coast Guard Unit 400
EQUIPMENT BY TYPE
PATROL AND COASTAL COMBATANTS 20+
PFC 1 *Isla del Coco* (US *Swift* 32m)
PCC 1 *Astronauta* (US *Cape*)
PCI 8: 5 less than 100 tonnes; 3 *Point* less than 100 tonnes
MISC BOATS/CRAFT 10 (various)
FACILITIES
Bases Located at Golfito, Punta Arenas, Cuajiniquil, Quepos, Limbe, Moin

Air Surveillance Unit 400
AIRCRAFT
TPT 10: 1 DHC-7 *Caribou*; 2 PA-31 *Navajo*; 2 Cessna T210 *Centurion*; 1 PA-34 *Seneca* ; 4 Cessna U-206G *Stationair*
HELICOPTERS
UTL 2 MD-500E

Rural Guard 2,000
Ministry of Government and Police. Small arms only
Paramilitary 8 comd

Cuba CUB

Cuban Convertible Peso P		2008	2009	2010
GDP	P	62.0bn	66.0bn	
	US$	57.4bn	61.1bn	
per capita	US$	5,025	5,336	
Growth	%	4.3	1.0	
Inflation	%	3.4	4.3	
Def exp	US$	ε2.29bn		

Population   11,451,652

Age	0–14	15–19	20–24	25–29	30–64	65 plus
Male	10%	4%	3%	3%	25%	5%
Female	10%	4%	3%	3%	25%	6%

Capabilities

ACTIVE 49,000 (Army 38,000 Navy 3,000 Air 8,000)
Paramilitary 26,500

Terms of service 2 years

RESERVE 39,000 (Army 39,000) **Paramilitary 1,120,000**

Ready Reserves (serve 45 days per year) to fill out Active and Reserve units; see also Paramilitary.

ORGANISATIONS BY SERVICE

Army ε38,000

FORCES BY ROLE
3 Regional comd HQ, 3 army comd HQ

Army	1 (frontier) bde; 14 (reserve) bde
Armd	up to 5 bde
Mech Inf	9 bde (each: 1 armd regt, 1 arty regt, 1 ADA regt, 3 mech inf regt)
AB	1 bde
ADA	1 regt
SAM	1 bde

EQUIPMENT BY TYPE†
MBT ε900 T-34/T-54/T-55/T-62
LT TK PT-76
RECCE BRDM-1/BRDM-2
AIFV ε 50 BMP-1
APC • APC (W) ε500 BTR-152/BTR-40/BTR-50/BTR-60
ARTY 1,730+
   SP 40 2S1 *Carnation* **122mm**/2S3 **152mm**
   TOWED 500 **152mm** D-1 /**122mm** D-30 /**152mm** M-1937/ **122mm** M-30 /**130mm** M-46/ **76mm** ZIS-3 *M-1942*
   MRL SP 175 **140mm** BM-14/**122mm** BM-21
   MOR 1,000 **120mm** M-38 /**82mm** M-41/**120mm** M-43/**82mm** M-43
   STATIC 15 **122mm** 15 JS-2M (hy tk)
AT
   MSL • MANPATS AT-1 *Snapper*; AT-3 9K11 *Sagger*
   GUNS 700+: **100mm** 100 SU-100 SP; **85mm** D-44; **57mm** 600 M-1943

AD
   SAM 200 SA-13 *Gopher* SP/SA-14 *Gremlin*; SA-16 *Gimlet* MANPAD/SA-6 *Gainful* SP/SA-7 *Grail* MANPAD/SA-8 *Gecko* SP/SA-9 *Gaskin* SP (300–1,800 eff.)
   GUNS 400
      SP 57mm ZSU-57-2 SP/ **23mm** ZSU-23-4 SP/ **30mm** BTR-60P SP
      TOWED 100mm KS-19/M-1939 /**85mm** KS-12/**57mm** S-60 /**37mm** M-1939/**30mm** M-53/**23mm** ZU-23

Navy ε3,000

FORCES BY ROLE
Navy 1 (HQ Western Comd) located at Cabanas;
         1 (HQ Eastern Comd) located at Holquin

EQUIPMENT BY TYPE
PATROL AND COASTAL COMBATANTS 7
   PFM 6 *Osa* II† (FSU) each with 4 single each with SS-N-2B *Styx* tactical SSM (missiles removed to coastal defence units)
   PFC 1 *Pauk* II† (FSU) with 1 x4 manual with SA-N-5 *Grail* SAM, 4 single ASTT, 2 RBU 1200 (10 eff.), 1 76mm gun
MINE WARFARE AND MINE COUNTERMEASURES 5
   MSC 2 *Sonya*† (FSU)
   MHC 3 *Yevgenya*† (FSU)
LOGISTICS AND SUPPORT 1 **ABU**; 1 **TRG**

FACILITIES
Bases Located at Cabanas, Havana, Cienfuegos, Holquin, Nicaro, Punta Movida, Mariel

Coastal Defence
ARTY • TOWED 122mm M-1931/37; **130mm** M-46; **152mm** M-1937
MSL• SSM 2+: *Bandera* IV (reported); 2 SS-C-3 *Styx*

Naval Infantry 550+
Amph aslt 2 bn

Anti-aircraft Defence and Revolutionary Air Force ε8,000 (incl conscripts)

Air assets divided between Western Air Zone and Eastern Air Zone

Flying hours   50 hrs/year

FORCES BY ROLE

Ftr/ FGA	3 sqn with 2 MiG-29A *Fulcrum*, 1 MiG-29UB, 16 MiG-23ML *Flogger*/4 MiG-23MF/4 MiG-23UM, 4 MiG-21ML
Tpt	1 exec tpt sqn with 3 Yak-40 (VIP), 3 An-24, 2 Mi-8P
Hel	2 cbt hel sqn with 8 Mi-17, 4 Mi-35
Trg	2 tac trg sqns with 5 Zlin Z-142 (primary), 7 L-39C (basic), 7+ MiG-21UMr

EQUIPMENT BY TYPE
AIRCRAFT 45 combat capable (179 stored)
   FTR/FGA 31: 2 MiG-29 *Fulcrum*; 1 MiG-29UB; 16 MiG-23 ML *Flogger*; 4 MiG-23MF; 4 MiG-23UM; 4 MiG-21ML; (in store: 2 MiG-29; 20 MiG-23BN; 4 MiG-23MF; 6 MiG-23ML; 2 MiG-23UM; 70 MiG-21bis; 28 MiG-21PFM; 30 MiG-21F; 7 MiG-21UM; 4+ MiG-17; 6 MiG-15UTI)

TPT 12: 3 Yak-40; 3 An-24; 2 Il-76; 2 An-32; 1 An-30; 1 An-2; (in store: 18 An-26 *Curl*; 8 An-2 *Colt*)
TRG 59: 25 L-39 *Albatros*; 8 MiG-21U *Mongol A**; 4 MiG-23U *Flogger**; 2 MiG-29UB *Fulcrum**; 20 Z-326 *Trener Master*
HELICOPTERS
ATK 4 Mi-35 *Hind*
SPT 10: 2 Mi-8P *Hip*; 8 Mi-17; (in store: 8 Mi-35; 12 Mi-17; 5 Mi-14)
AD • SAM SA-3 *Goa*; SA-2 *Guideline* towed
MSL
ASM AS-7 *Kerry*
AAM AA-10 *Alamo*; AA-11 *Archer*; AA-2 *Atoll*; AA-7 *Apex*; AA-8 *Aphid*

FACILITIES
Surface To Air   13 with SA-3 *Goa* SAM; SA-2 *Guideline*
Missile Site   Towed SAM (active)

Paramilitary 26,500 active

State Security 20,000
Ministry of Interior

Border Guards 6,500
Ministry of Interior
PATROL AND COASTAL COMBATANTS 20
  PFI 20: 2 *Stenka* less than 100 tonnes (FSU); 18 *Zhuk*

Youth Labour Army 70,000 reservists

Civil Defence Force 50,000 reservists

Territorial Militia ε1,000,000 reservists

FOREIGN FORCES

United States Army: 293; Navy 482 (located at Guantánamo Bay); USMC 127 (located at Guantánamo Bay)

Dominican Republic DOM

Dominican Peso pRD		2008	2009	2010
GDP	pRD	1.59tr	1.59tr	
	US$	46.1bn	44.1bn	
per capita	US$	4,852	4,574	
Growth	%	5.3	0.5	
Inflation	%	10.6	0.9	
Def bdgt	pRD	9.6bn	11.4bn	
	US$	278m	318m	
US$1=pRD		34.6	36.0	

Population   9,650,054

Age	0–14	15–19	20–24	25–29	30–64	65 plus
Male	17%	5%	5%	4%	18%	3%
Female	16%	5%	4%	4%	17%	3%

Capabilities

ACTIVE 49,910 (Army 40,410 Navy 4,000 Air 5,500)
Paramilitary 15,000

ORGANISATIONS BY SERVICE

Army 15,000
FORCES BY ROLE
5 Defence Zones
Armd   1 bn
Air Cav   1 bde (1 cdo bn, 1 (6th) mtn regt, 1 sqn with 8 OH-58 *Kiowa*; 12UH-1H (op by Air Force), 4 R-22; 2 R-44 *Raven II*)
Inf   6 bde: 1st and 3rd (*each*: 3 inf bn); 2nd (4 inf bn, 1 mtn inf bn); 4th and 5th (*each*: 2 bn); 6th (1 inf bn) (*total*: 16 inf bn)
SF   3 bn
Arty   2 bn
Engr   1 bn
Presidential 1 regt
Guard
Security   1(MoD) bn

EQUIPMENT BY TYPE
LT TK 12 M-41B (76mm)
APC (W) 8 LAV-150 *Commando*
ARTY 104
  TOWED 105mm 16: 4 M-101; 12 *Reinosa* 105/26
  MOR 88: **81mm** 60 M-1; **107mm** 4 M-30; **120mm** 24 Expal Model L
AT
  RCL 106mm 20 M-40A1
  GUNS 37mm 20 M3
HEL
  OBS 8: 4 OH-58A *Kiowa*; 4 OH-58C *Kiowa*
  UTL 6: 4 R-22; 2 R-44

Navy 4,000
FORCES BY ROLE
Marine Sy 1 unit
Navy   1 HQ located at Santo Domingo
SEAL   1 unit

EQUIPMENT BY TYPE
PATROL AND COASTAL COMBATANTS 16
  PCO 4:
    2 *Balsam*
    2 *Tortuguero* (US ABU)
  PCI 8: 2 *Canopus*; 2 *Swift* (35mm); 4 *Bellatrix* (US Sewart Seacraft) All less than 100 tonnes
  PBR 4 *Damen Stan 1505*
AMPHIBIOUS 1 *Neyba* (US LCU 1675)
LOGISTICS AND SUPPORT 5:
  AG 2 *Draga Contencion*
  AT 3
FACILITIES
Bases Located at Santo Domingo, Las Calderas

Naval Aviation Unit
HELICOPTERS
SAR / UTL 2 Bell 206A-1 (CH 136)

Air Force 5,500
Flying hours   60 hrs/year

FORCES BY ROLE

CBT	1 sqn with *Super Tucano*
SAR/Medivac/Hel/ Liaison	1 sqn with Bell 430 (VIP); *Huey* II; UH-1H; Schweizer 333; CH-136 *Kiowa*
Tpt	1 sqn with CASA 212-400 *Aviocar*; Ce-206; PA-31 *Navajo*
Trg	1 sqn with T-35B *Pillan*
AD	1 bn with 20mm

EQUIPMENT BY TYPE
AIRCRAFT 8 combat capable
  CBT 8 EMB-314 *Super Tucano* (border patrol/ interdiction)
  TPT/MP 5: 3 CASA 212-400 *Aviocar*; 1 PA-31 *Navajo*; 1 Ce-206
  TRG 6 T-35B *Pillan*
HELICOPTERS
  UTL 34: 2 Bell 430 (VIP); 9 CH-136 *Kiowa*; 3 Schweizer 333; 8 *Huey* II; 12 UH-1H
AD • GUNS 20mm 4

Paramilitary 15,000

National Police 15,000

Ecuador ECU

Ecuadorian Sucre ES		2008	2009	2010
GDP	ES	1,386tr	1,307tr	
	US$	55.4bn	52.3bn	
per capita	US$	3,862	3,587	
Growth	%	6.5	-1.0	
Inflation	%	8.5	5.0	
Def bdgt	ES	27.6tr		
	US$	1.1bn		
US$1=ES		25,000	25,000	

Population   14,573,101

Age	0–14	15–19	20–24	25–29	30–64	65 plus
Male	17%	5%	5%	4%	16%	2%
Female	16%	5%	5%	4%	17%	3%

Capabilities

ACTIVE 57,983 (Army 46,500 Navy 7,283 Air 4,200)
Paramilitary 400
Terms of Service conscription 1 year, selective

RESERVE 118,000 (Joint 118,000)
Ages 18–55

ORGANISATIONS BY SERVICE

Army 46,500
FORCES BY ROLE
4 div (org, composition varies) (total: 1 armd bde, 1 SF bde, 1 arty bde, 1 engr bde, 1 avn bde, 3 jungle bde, 5 inf bde); 3 (hy mor) coy.

Armd cav	1 bde
Armd Recce	3 sqn
Mech Inf	2 bn
Inf	13 bn; 10 (jungle) bn
AB/SF	6 bn
Arty	1 bde
SP Arty	1 gp
MRL	1 gp
ADA	1 gp
Engr	3 bn
Avn	5 bn

EQUIPMENT BY TYPE
MBT 30 *Leopard* 1V from Chile being delivered
LT TK 24 AMX-13
RECCE 67: 25 AML-90; 10 EE-3 *Jararaca*; 32 EE-9 *Cascavel*;
APC 123
  APC (T) 95: 80 AMX-VCI; 15 M-113
  APC (W) 28: 18 EE-11 *Urutu*; 10 UR-416
ARTY 541+
  SP 155mm 5 (AMX) Mk F3
  TOWED 100: **105mm** 78: 30 M-101; 24 M-2A2; 24 Model 56 pack howitzer; **155mm** 22: 12 M-114; 10 M-198
  MRL 24: 18 122mm BM-21, 6 RM-70
  MOR 412+: **81mm** 400 M-29; **107mm** M-30 (4.2in); **160mm** 12 M-66 *Soltam*
AT
  RCL 404: **106mm** 24 M-40A1; **90mm** 380 M-67
AIRCRAFT
  TPT 12: 1 Beech 100 *King Air*; 2 CASA 212; 2 CN-235; 1 Cessna 500 *Citation I*; 1 DHC-5D *Buffalo*; 4 IAI-201 *Arava*; 1 PC-6 *Turbo-Porter*
  TRG 7: 2 MX-7-235 *Star Rocket*; 3 T-41D *Mescalero*; 2 CJ-6
HELICOPTERS
  ATK 18 SA-342 *Gazelle* (13 w/ HOT)
  SPT 21: 6 AS-332B *Super Puma*; 3 AS-350 *Ecureuil*; 9 Mi-17-1V *Hip*; 3 SA-330 *Puma* (in store)
  UTL 2 SA-315B *Lama*
AD
  SAM • MANPAD 185+: 75 *Blowpipe*; 20+ SA-7 *Grail*; 90 SA-18 *Grouse* (*Igla*)
  GUNS 240
    SP 44 M-163 *Vulcan*
    TOWED 196: **14.5mm** 128 ZPU-1/-2; **20mm** 38: 28 M-1935, 10 M-167 *Vulcan*; **40mm** 30 L/70/M1A1

Navy 7,283 (incl Naval Aviation, Marines and Coast Guard)
EQUIPMENT BY TYPE
SUBMARINES • TACTICAL • SSK 2:
2 *Shyri*† (GER T-209/1300, undergoing refit in Chile) each with 8 single 533mm TT with 14 SUT HWT

PRINCIPAL SURFACE COMBATANTS 8
FRIGATES • FFG 2:
1 *Presidente Eloy Alfaro*† (ex-UK *Leander* batch II) each with 4 single each with MM-40 *Exocet* tactical SSM, 3 twin (6 eff.) each with *Mistral* SAM, (capacity 1 Bell 206B *JetRanger II* utl hel)
1 *Condell* (mod UK *Leander*; under transfer from Chile) with 4 single with MM-40 *Exocet* tactical SSM, 2 triple ASTT (6 eff.) each with Mk 46 LWT, 2 x 114mm gun, (capacity 1 Bell 206B *JetRanger II* utl hel)
CORVETTES • FSG 6:
6 *Esmeraldas* (4†) each with 2 triple (6 eff.) each with MM-40 *Exocet* tactical SSM, 1 quad (4 eff.) with *Aspide* SAM, 2 B515 *ILAS-3* triple 324mm each with A244 LWT, 1 76mm gun, 1 hel landing platform (upgrade programme ongoing)
PATROL AND COASTAL COMBATANTS 3
PFM 3 *Quito* (GER Lurssen TNC-45 45m) each with 4 single with MM-38 *Exocet* tactical SSM, 1 76mm gun (upgrade programme ongoing)
AMPHIBIOUS • LS • LST 1:
1 *Hualcopo* (capacity 150 troops) (US LST-512-1152)
LOGISTICS AND SUPPORT 5:
AG 1
AWT 2
AGOS 1 *Orion*
ATF 1
FACILITIES

Bases   Located at Guayaquil (main base), Galápagos Islands
Naval airbase   Jaramijo

Naval Aviation 375
AIRCRAFT
MP 5: 1 CN-235-100; 1 CN-235-300M; MP 2 Beech 200T MP; 1 Beech 300 (CATPAS)
TPT 2: 1 Beech 200 *Super King Air*; 1 Beech 300 *Super King Air*;
TRG 6: 4 T-35B *Pillan*; 2 T-34C *Turbo Mentor*
HELICOPTERS
UTL 8: 2 Bell 230; 3 Bell 206B; 3 Bell 206A
UAV 6: 4 IAI *Searcher* Mk.2; 2 IAI *Heron*

Marines 2,160
Cdo   1 unit (no hy wpn/veh)
Marine 5 bn (on garrison duties)

EQUIPMENT BY TYPE
ARTY
MOR 32+ **60mm/81mm/120mm**
AD
SAM • MANPAD 64 *Mistral*/SA-18 *Grouse (Igla)*

Air Force 4,200

Operational Command
FORCES BY ROLE
Air   2 wg
Ftr   1 sqn with *Mirage* F-1JE (F-1E); *Mirage* F-1JB (F-1B)

FGA   3 sqn (1 with A-37B *Dragonfly*; 1 sqn with *Kfir* CE; *Kfir* C-2; *Kfir* TC-2; 1 sqn with BAC-167 *Strikemaster*); 2 sqn with *Super Tucano* (being delivered)
CCT   1 sqn with A-37B; BAC-167 *Strikemaster*

Military Air Transport Group
FORCES BY ROLE
SAR/Liaison   1 sqn with Bell 206B *JetRanger II*; SA-316B/SA-319 *Alouette III*; ALH
Tpt   4 sqn with B-727; C-130B *Hercules*, C-130H *Hercules*; DHC-6 *Twin Otter*; F-28 *Fellowship*; *Sabreliner* 40/60
Liaison   Beech E90 *King Air*; *Gaviao* 60; HS-748
TAME   1 mil controlled airline with Airbus A-320; EMB-170; EMB-190
Trg   units with Cessna 150; T-34C *Turbo Mentor*; T-41 *Mescalero*; MXP-650

EQUIPMENT BY TYPE
AIRCRAFT 60+ combat capable
FTR 15: 12 *Mirage* F-1JE; 1 F-1BJ. 3 *Mirage* 50 (2 50DV, 1 50EV) (3 more to come from Venezuela)
FGA 44+: 25+ A-37B *Dragonfly*; 7 *Kfir* CE, 4 C.2, 2 TC.2; 5 BAC-167 *Strikemaster*; 24 EMB-314 *Super Tucano* (being delivered)
TPT 27: 2 A320; 6 HS-748; 3 B-727; 1 Beech E-90 *King Air*; 4 C-130B; 1 C-130H; 2 EMB-170; 1 EMB-190; 3 DHC-6 *Twin Otter*; 1 F-28 *Fellowship*; 2 *Sabreliner* 40/60; 1 Legacy 600. (4 MA-60 on order)
TRG 37: 16 Ce-150; 15 T-34C; 1 MXP-650; 5 T-41
HEL 20: 4 SA-316B *Alouette III* / SA-319 *Alouette III* Utl Hel; 8 Bell 206B *Jet Ranger II*; 1 HB-315B *Gaviao*; 6 ALH *Dhruv*
MSL •AAM 60 *Python* III; 50 *Python* IV; R-550 *Magic*; Super 530; *Shafrir*
AD
SAM 7 M-48 *Chaparral*
SP 6 SA-8 *Gecko*
MANPAD 185+: 75 *Blowpipe*; SA-7; 20 *Igla*-1 (SA-16) *Gimlet*; 90 SA-18 *Grouse*
RADARS: 2 CFTC gap fillers; 2 CETC 2D
GUNS
SP 28 M-35 with **20mm**
TOWED 82: **23mm** 34: 34 ZU-23; **35mm** 30: 30 GDF-002 (twin); **37mm** 18: 18 Ch

Paramilitary
All police forces; 39,500

Police Air Service
2 B206B *Jet Ranger*, 1 R-22; 1 AS-350B *Ecureuil*

Coast Guard 500
PATROL AND COASTAL COMBATANTS 41+
PCC 11: 2 *Manta* (GER Lurssen 36m), 3 *Vigilante* (Protector), 4 *10 de Agosto*, 2 *Espada*
PCI 8: 1 PGM-71; 1 *Point*; 6 *Rio Puyango*
PBR 14: 2 *Río Esmeraldas*; 4 *Piraña*; 8 *Interceptor*
PBI 8 *Albatros*

DEPLOYMENT

CÔTE D'IVOIRE
UN • UNOCI 2 obs

HAITI
UN • MINUSTAH 67; elm 1 engr coy

LIBERIA
UN • UNMIL 1; 2 obs

SUDAN
UN • UNMIS 17 obs

El Salvador SLV

El Salvador Colon C		2008	2009	2010
GDP	C	192bn	194bn	
	US$	21.9bn	22.2bn	
per capita	US$	3,105	3,086	
Growth	%	2.5	-2.5	
Inflation	%	7.3	1.0	
Def bdgt	C	1.0bn	1.15bn	
	US$	115m	132m	
FMA	US$	5.6m	3.5m	4.8m
US$1=C		8.75	8.75	

Population   7,185,218

Age	0–14	15–19	20–24	25–29	30–64	65 plus
Male	19%	5%	5%	4%	14%	2%
Female	18%	5%	5%	4%	16%	3%

Capabilities

ACTIVE 15,500 (Army 13,850 Navy 700 Air 950)
Paramilitary 17,000
Terms of Service conscription 18 months voluntary

RESERVE 9,900 (Joint 9,900)

ORGANISATIONS BY SERVICE

Army 9,850; 4,000 conscript (total 13,850)
FORCES BY ROLE
6 Military Zones
Armd cav	1 regt (2 armd cav bn)
Inf	5 bde (*each:* 3 inf bn)
Spec Ops	1 gp (1 SF coy, 1 para bn, 1 (naval inf) coy
Arty	1 bde (1 AD bn, 2 fd arty bn)
Engr	1 comd (2 engr bn)
Sy	1 (special sy) bde (2 border gd bn, 2 MP bn)

EQUIPMENT BY TYPE
RECCE 5 AML-90; 4 (in store)
APC (W) 38: 30M-37B1 *Cashuat* (mod); 8 UR-416
ARTY 217+
    TOWED 105mm 54: 36 M-102; 18 M-56 (Yug)

MOR 163+: **81mm** 151 M-29; **120mm** 12+: M-74 in store; 12 UBM 52
AT
RCL 399: **106mm** 20 M-40A1 (incl 16 SP); **90mm** 379 M-67
RL **94mm** 791 LAW
AD
GUNS 35: **20mm** 31 M-55; 4 TCM-20

Navy 700 (incl some 90 Naval Inf and SF)
EQUIPMENT BY TYPE
PATROL AND COASTAL COMBATANTS 39
    PCC 3 *Camcraft* (30m)
    PCI 3 less than 100 tonnes
    MISC BOATS/CRAFT 33 *River Boats*
AMPHIBIOUS
    LCM 3
FACILITIES
Bases	Located at La Uníon
Minor Bases	Located at La Libertad, Acajutla, El Triunfo, Meanguera Is, Guija Lake

Naval Inf (SF Commandos) 90
SF 1 coy

Air Force 950 (incl 200 Air Defence)
Flying hours   90 hrs/year on A-37 *Dragonfly* FGA ac

FORCES BY ROLE
FGA/ Recce	sqn with A-37B *Dragonfly*; O-2A *Skymaster*; CM-170 *Magister*
Tpt	1 sqn with Bell 407; Bell 412 *Twin Huey*; MD-500; UH-1H *Iroquois* (incl 4 SAR); 1 sqn with Basler *Turbo-67*; IAI-201 *Arava*; SA-226T *Merlin IIIB*; Cessna 210 *Centurion*; C-47; Cessna 337G
Trg	sqn with *Rallye* 235GT; T-35 *Pillan*; T-41D *Mescalero*; TH-300
Hel	armed sqn with UH-1M *Iroquois*

EQUIPMENT BY TYPE
AIRCRAFT 19 combat capable
    FGA 5 A-37B *Dragonfly*
    RECCE 14: 10 O-2A O-2A/B *Skymaster**; 4 OA-37B *Dragonfly**
    TPT 10: 3 Basler *Turbo-67*; 2 C-47R *Skytrain*; 1 Cessna 337G *Skymaster*; 1 SA-226T *Merlin IIIB*; 3 IAI-201 *Arava*
    UTL 2 Cessna 210 *Centurion*
    TRG 11: 5 *Rallye* 235GT; 5 T-35 *Pillan*; 1 T-41D *Mescalero*
HELICOPTERS
    UTL 39 : 4 Bell 412 *Twin Huey*; 7 MD-500; 22 UH-1H *Iroquois* (incl 4 SAR); 5 UH-1M *Iroquois**; 1 Bell 407 (VIP tpt, gov owned)
    TRG 6 TH-300
MSL • AAM *Shafrir*

Paramilitary 17,000

National Civilian Police 17,000
Ministry of Public Security
PATROL AND COASTAL COMBATANTS •PBR 10
River Boats

AIRCRAFT • RECCE 1 O-2A *Skymaster*
HELICOPTERS • UTL 3: 1 MD-500D; 1 MD-520N; 1 UH-1H *Iroquois*

DEPLOYMENT

CÔTE D'IVOIRE
UN • UNOCI 3 obs

LEBANON
UN • UNIFIL 52; 1 inf pl

LIBERIA
UN • UNMIL 2 obs

SUDAN
UN • UNMIS 4 obs

WESTERN SAHARA
UN • MINURSO 3 obs

FOREIGN FORCES

United States US Southern Command: Army 6; Navy 1; USAF 2; USMC 12; 1 Forward Operating Location

Guatemala GUA

Guatemalan Quetzal q		2008	2009	2010
GDP	q	321bn	333bn	
	US$	42.5bn	40.0bn	
per capita	US$	3,266	3,011	
Growth	%	4.0	0.4	
Inflation	%	11.4	2.2	
Def bdgt	q	1.36bn	1.30bn	
	US$	179m	156m	
US$1=q		7.56	8.33	

Population	13,276,517					

Age	0–14	15 –19	20–24	25–29	30–64	65 plus
Male	21%	6%	5%	4%	13%	2%
Female	20%	6%	5%	4%	14%	2%

Capabilities

ACTIVE 15,212 (Army 13,444 Navy 897 Air 871) **Paramilitary 18,536**

RESERVE 63,863 (Navy 650 Air 900 Armed Forces 62,313)

(National Armed Forces are combined; the army provides log spt for navy and air force)

ORGANISATIONS BY SERVICE

Army 13,444
The cavalry regts have a strength of 118 personnel, 7 AFV. The arty gp is 3 bty of 4 guns.

FORCES BY ROLE
15 Military Zones

Armd	6 sqn
Cav	2 regt
Inf	1 (strategic) bde (2 inf bn, 1 SF pl, 1 recce sqn, 1 (lt) armd bn, 1 arty gp); 5 (regional) bde (*each*: 3 inf bn, 1 cav regt, 1 arty gp); 1 (frontier) det
SF	1 bde (1 trg bn, 1 SF bn)
AB	2 bn
Engr	2 bn
MP	1 bde (3 bn)
Sy	1 bn (Presidential Gd)
Trg	1 bn

EQUIPMENT BY TYPE
RECCE 7 M-8 in store
APC 52
    APC (T) 15: 10 M-113; 5 in store
    APC (W) 37: 30 *Armadillo*; 7 V-100 *Commando*
ARTY 161
    TOWED 105mm 76: 12 M-101; 8 M-102; 56 M-56
    MOR 85: 81mm 55 M-1; 107mm 12 M-30 in store; 120mm 18 ECIA
AT
    RCL 120+: 105mm 64 M-1974 FMK-1 (Arg); 106mm 56 M-40A1; 75mm M-20
    RL 89mm M-20 in store (3.5in)
AD• GUNS • TOWED 32: 20mm 16 GAI-D01; 16 M-55

Reserves
Inf ε19 bn

Navy 897
EQUIPMENT BY TYPE
PATROL AND COASTAL COMBATANTS 39+:
    PCI 10: 6 *Cutlass*; 1 *Kukulkan* (US *Broadsword* 32m); 2 *Sewart*; 1 *Dauntless;* (all vessels less than 100 tonnes)
    PCR 20
    PBI 9: 6 *Vigilante*; 3 BW-32
FACILITIES
Bases Located at Santo Tomás de Castilla, Puerto Quetzal

Marines 650 reservists
Marine 2 bn under strength

Air Force 871
2 Air Commands, 3 air bases – Guatemala City, Santa Elena Petén, Retalhuleu
FORCES BY ROLE
Serviceability of ac is less than 50%

FGA/Trg	1 sqn with A-37B *Dragonfly*; 1 sqn with PC-7 *Turbo Trainer*
Tpt	1 sqn with Basler *Turbo-67*; Beech 100 *King Air*; Beech 90 *King Air*; F-27 *Friendship*; IAI-201 *Arava*; PA-31 *Navajo*
Liaison	1 sqn with Cessna 310; Cessna 206

Trg   some sqn with Cessna R172K *Hawk XP*; T-35B
Hel   1 sqn with Bell 206 *Jet Ranger*; Bell 212
           (armed); Bell 412 *Twin Huey* (armed); UH-1H
           Iroquois

EQUIPMENT BY TYPE
AIRCRAFT 9 combat capable
   FGA 2 A-37B *Dragonfly*; 2 PC-7 *Turbo Trainer* (6 EMB-314
   Super Tucano on order)
   TPT 14: 4 Basler *Turbo-67*; 1 Beech 100 *King Air*; 1 Beech
   90 *King Air*; 1 Cessna 310; 2 F-27 *Friendship*; 4 IAI-201
   Arava; 1 PA-31 *Navajo*; 1 CE-208B
   UTL 2 Cessna 206
   TRG 15: 5 Cessna R172K *Hawk XP*; 5 PC-7 *Turbo Trainer**;
   4 T-35B *Pillan*
HELICOPTERS
   UTL 20: 9 Bell 206 *Jet Ranger*; 7 Bell 212 (armed); 1 Bell
   412 *Twin Huey* (armed); 3 UH-1H *Iroquois*

Tactical Security Group
Air Military Police
Armd 1 sqn
CCT   3 coy
AD   1 bty (army units for air-base sy)

Paramilitary 19,000 active (incl. Treasury Police)

National Police 16,500
Army   1 (integrated task force) unit (incl mil and
              treasury police)
SF   1 bn
Paramilitary 21 (departments) region
HELICOPTERS
   UTL 4 UH-1P *Huey* 2 (on lease 2008-2010)

Treasury Police 2,500

DEPLOYMENT

CÔTE D'IVOIRE
UN • UNOCI 5 obs

DEMOCRATIC REPUBLIC OF CONGO
UN • MONUC 150; 4 obs

HAITI
UN • MINUSTAH 118; 1 MP coy

LEBANON
UN • UNIFIL 2

NEPAL
UN • UNMIN 1 obs

SUDAN
UN • UNAMID 2
UN • UNMIS 1; 2 obs

Guyana GUY

Guyanese Dollar G$		2008	2009	2010
GDP	G$	236bn		
	US$	1.2bn		
per capita	US$	1,534		
Growth	%	3.0	2.0	
Inflation	%	8.1	2.9	
Def bdgt	G$	13.7bn		
	US$	67m		
US$1=G$			203	200

Population   752,940

Age	0–14	15–19	20–24	25–29	30–64	65 plus
Male	13%	5%	5%	5%	19%	2%
Female	13%	5%	5%	5%	20%	3%

Capabilities

ACTIVE 1,100 (Army 900 Navy 100 Air 100)
Paramilitary 1,500
Active numbers combined Guyana Defence Force

RESERVE 670 (Army 500 Navy 170)

ORGANISATIONS BY SERVICE

Army 900
FORCES BY ROLE
Inf   1 bn
SF   1 coy
Engr   1 coy
Spt   1 (spt wpn) coy
Presidential Guard 1 bn

EQUIPMENT BY TYPE
RECCE 9: 6 EE-9 *Cascavel* (reported); 3 S52 *Shorland*
ARTY 54
   TOWED 130mm 6 M-46†
   MOR 48: **81mm** 12 L16A1; **82mm** 18 M-43; **120mm** 18
   M-43

Navy 100
EQUIPMENT BY TYPE
PATROL AND COASTAL COMBATANTS 5
   PCC 1 *Orwell* (ex-UK)
   MISC BOATS/CRAFT 4
FACILITIES
Bases Located at Georgetown (HQ), Benab,
       Morawhanna

Air Force 100
FORCES BY ROLE
Tpt   unit with; 1 Y-12 1 Bell 412 *Twin Huey*; 1 *Rotorway*
       162F

EQUIPMENT BY TYPE
AIRCRAFT
TPT 1 Y-12
HELICOPTERS
UTL 2: 1 Bell 412 *Twin Huey*; 1 *Rotorway* 162F

Paramilitary 1,500+

Guyana People's Militia 1,500+

Haiti HTI

Haitian Gourde G		2008	2009	2010
GDP	G	272bn		
	US$	7.0bn		
per capita	US$	784		
Growth	%	1.2	2.0	
Inflation	%	14.5	3.5	
US$1=G		39.1	39.7	

Population   9,035,536

Age	0–14	15–19	20–24	25–29	30–64	65 plus
Male	21%	6%	5%	4%	11%	2%
Female	21%	6%	5%	4%	12%	2%

Capabilities

No active armed forces. On 1 June 2004, following a period of armed conflict, the United Nations established a multinational stabilisation mission in Haiti (MINUSTAH). The mission has an authorised strength of up to 6,700 military personnel and 2,066 civilian police. A National Police Force of some 2,000 pers remains operational.

FOREIGN FORCES

Argentina 560; 1 inf bn; 1 avn unit; 1 fd hospital
Bolivia 208; 1 mech inf coy
Brazil 1,282; 1 inf bn; 1 engr coy
Canada 5
Chile 500; 1 inf bn; 1 avn unit; elm 1 engr coy
Croatia 2
Ecuador 67; elm 1 engr coy
France 2
Guatemala 118; 1 MP coy
Jordan 727; 2 inf bn
Nepal 1,076; 2 inf bn
Paraguay 31
Peru 207; 1 inf coy
Philippines 157; 1 HQ coy
Sri Lanka 959; 1 inf bn
United States 4
Uruguay 1,146; 2 inf bn; 1 avn unit

Honduras HND

Honduran Lempira L		2008	2009	2010
GDP	L	270bn	276bn	
	US$	14.3bn	14.6bn	
per capita	US$	1,861	1,864	
Growth	%	4.0	-2.0	
Inflation	%	11.4	5.9	
Def bdgt	L	1.80bn	1.93bn	
	US$	95m	102m	
US$1=L		18.9	18.9	

Population   7,833,696

Age	0–14	15–19	20–24	25–29	30–64	65 plus
Male	21%	6%	5%	4%	13%	2%
Female	20%	6%	5%	4%	14%	2%

Capabilities

ACTIVE 12,000 (Army 8,300 Navy 1,400 Air 2,300)
Paramilitary 8,000

RESERVE 60,000 (Joint 60,000; Ex-servicemen registered)

ORGANISATIONS BY SERVICE

Army 8,300
FORCES BY ROLE
6 Military Zones

Armd cav	1 regt (1 lt tk sqn, 1 ADA bty, 1 arty bty, 1 recce sqn, 2 mech bn)
Inf	1 bde (3 inf bn); 3 bde (*each:* 1 arty bn, 3 inf bn)
Spec Ops	1 (special tac) gp (1 SF bn, 1 inf/AB bn)
Engr	1 bn
Presidential Guard	1 coy

EQUIPMENT BY TYPE
LT TK 12 *Scorpion*
RECCE 57: 13 RBY-1 *RAMTA*; 40 *Saladin*; 3 *Scimitar*; 1 *Sultan*
ARTY 118+
    TOWED 28: **105mm:** 24 M-102; **155mm:** 4 M-198
MOR 90+: **60mm**; **81mm**; **120mm** 60 FMK-2; **160mm** 30 M-66 *Soltam*
AT • RCL 170: **106mm** 50 M-40A1; **84mm** 120 *Carl Gustav*
AD • GUNS 48: **20mm** 24 M-55A2; 24 TCM-20

Reserves
Inf 1 bde

Navy 1,400
EQUIPMENT BY TYPE
PATROL AND COASTAL COMBATANTS 35
    PFC 3 *Guaymuras* (*Swift* 31m)

PFI 1 *Copan* less than 100 tonnes (US *Guardian* 32m)
PC 7: 6 *Swift* 21m; 1 *Swift* 26m
PBR 9: 5 various less than 100 tonnes; 4 BW-32
MISC BOATS/CRAFT 15 (river boats)
AMPHIBIOUS • **LCU** 1 *Punta Caxinas*

FACILITIES

Bases   Located at Puerto Cortés, Puerto Castilla,
        Amapala

Marines 830

Marine 3 indep coy

Air Force 2,300

FORCES BY ROLE

FGA   1 sqn with 8 A-37B *Dragonfly*; 1 sqn with 8
            F-5E *Tiger II*
Tpt   sqn with 1 C-130A *Hercules*; 2 C-47 *Skytrain*
Trg/COIN   some sqn with 2 Cessna 182 *Skylane*; 5
            T-41B/D; 9 EMB-312
Liaison   some sqn with 4 Cessna 185; 1 Cessna 401; 1
            PA-31 *Navajo*; 1 PA-32T *Saratoga*
Hel   2 sqn with 5 Bell 412SP *Twin Huey*; 2 Hughes
            500; 2 UH-1H *Iroquois*

EQUIPMENT BY TYPE

AIRCRAFT 16 combat capable
  FTR 8 F-5E *Tiger II*
  FGA 8 A-37B *Dragonfly*
  TPT 12: 1 C-130A *Hercules*; 2 C-47 *Skytrain*; 2 Cessna 182
  Skylane; 4 Cessna 185; 1 Cessna 401; 1 PA-31 *Navajo*; 1
  PA-32T *Saratoga*
  TRG 14: 5 T-41B/D; 9 EMB-312
HELICOPTERS
  UTL 9: 5 Bell 412SP *Twin Huey*; 2 Hughes 500; 2 UH-1H
  Iroquois
MSL • **AAM** *Shafrir*

Paramilitary 8,000

Public Security Forces 8,000

Ministry of Public Security and Defence
Region   11 comd

DEPLOYMENT

WESTERN SAHARA

UN • MINURSO 12 obs

FOREIGN FORCES

United States US Southern Command: Army: 228; Navy
2; USAF: 183; USMC 8; 1 avn bn with CH-47 *Chinook*; UH-
60 *Black Hawk*

Jamaica JAM

Jamaican Dollar J$		2008	2009	2010
GDP	J$	1.07tr	1.12tr	
	US$	14.8bn	12.7bn	
per capita	US$	5,275	4,486	
Growth	%	-1.0	-3.6	
Inflation	%	22.0	9.4	
Def bdgt	J$	ε7.0bn	ε8.0bn	
	US$	96m	90m	
US$1=J$		72.8	88.5	

Population   2,825,928

Age	0–14	15–19	20–24	25–29	30–64	65 plus
Male	17%	5%	5%	4%	15%	3%
Female	17%	5%	5%	4%	15%	4%

Capabilities

ACTIVE 2,830 (Army 2,500 Coast Guard 190 Air 140)
(combined Jamaican Defence Force)

RESERVE 953 (Army 877 Navy 60 Air 16)

ORGANISATIONS BY SERVICE

Army 2,500

FORCES BY ROLE

Inf   2 bn
Engr   1 regt (4 engr sqn)
Spt   1 bn

EQUIPMENT BY TYPE

APC (W) 4 LAV-150 *Commando*
MOR 81mm 12 L16A1

Reserves

Inf 1 bn

Coast Guard 190

EQUIPMENT BY TYPE

PATROL AND COASTAL COMBATANTS 18
  PFC 1 *Fort Charles* (US 34m)
  PFI 1 *Paul Bogle* less than 100 tonnes (US 31m)
  PCI 6: 4 *Dauntless*; 2 *Point* less than 100 tonnes
  PBF 3
  PB 7: 3 *Cornwall* (Damen Stan 4207); 4 (Nor-Tech 43)

FACILITIES

Bases   Located at Port Royal, Pedro Cays
Minor Base   Located at Discovery Bay

Air Wing 140

Plus National Reserve

FORCES BY ROLE

Tpt/MP   1 flt with 1 BN-2A *Defender*; 1 Cessna 210M
             Centurio; 2 DA-40-180FP *Diamond Star* (trg)

SAR/Tpt   2 flt with 4 AS-355N *Ecureuil*; 3 Bell 407; 3 Bell 412EP

EQUIPMENT BY TYPE
AIRCRAFT
   TPT 1 BN-2A *Defender*
   UTL 1 Cessna 210M *Centurion*
   TRG 2 DA-40-180FP *Diamond Star*
HELICOPTERS
   SPT 4 AS-355N *Ecureuil*
   UTL 6: 3 Bell 407; 3 Bell 412EP

DEPLOYMENT

SIERRA LEONE
IMATT 1

Mexico MEX

Mexican Peso NP		2008	2009	2010
GDP	NP	12.11tr	11.72tr	
	US$	1.09tr	888bn	
per capita	US$	9,922	7,985	
Growth	%	1.3	-7.3	
Inflation	%	5.1	5.4	
Def bdgt[a]	NP	48.2bn	58.2bn	58.4bn
	US$	4.34bn	4.41bn	
FMA (US)	US$	116m	39m	10m
US$1=NP		11.1	13.2	

[a] Excluding paramilitaries

Population   111,211,789

Age	0–14	15–19	20–24	25–29	30–64	65 plus
Male	16%	5%	4%	4%	17%	2%
Female	15%	5%	5%	4%	19%	3%

Capabilities

ACTIVE 267,506 (Army 200,000 Navy 55,961 Air 11,545) **Paramilitary 36,500**

Reserve 39,899 (Armed Forces 39,899)

ORGANISATIONS BY SERVICE

Army 200,000

12 regions (total: 46 army zones). The Mexican Armed Forces have reorganised into a brigade structure. The Army consists of one manoeurvre corps (1st), with three inf bde and one armd bde, one SF corps one AB corps and one MP corps. Command and control functions have been redesigned and decentralised, allowing greater independence to each of the 12 Military Region commanders and establishing C⁴ units in every region.

FORCES BY ROLE
Armd   1 (1st) corps (1 cbt engr bde (3 engr bn), 1 armd bde (2 armd recce bn, 2 lt armd recce bn, 1 (Canon) AT gp), 3 inf / rapid reaction bde (*each*: 3 inf bn, 1 arty regt, 1 (Canon) AT gp))

2 bde (*each*: 2 armd recce bn, 2 lt armd recce bn, 1 (Canon) AT gp)

Armd Recce	3 regt
Lt Armd Recce	2 regt
Mot Recce	24 regt
Inf	89 indep inf bn; 24 indep inf coy
Lt Inf	3 indep lt inf bde each (2 lt inf bn, 1 AT (Canon) gp)
Arty	6 indep regt
Para	1 bde (3 bn, 1 GANF SF gp,1 AT (Canon gp)
SF	3 bde (12 SF bn); 1 amph bde (5 SF bn)
Presidential Guard	1 SF gp, 1 mech inf bde (2 inf bn, 1 aslt bn) 1 cbt engr bn, 1 MP bde (3 bn, 1 special ops anti-riot coy) 1 mne bn (Navy)
MP	2 bde (3 MP bn)

EQUIPMENT BY TYPE
RECCE 237: 124 ERC-90F1 *Lynx* (4 trg); 40 M-8; 41 MAC-1; 32 VBL
APC 709
   APC (T) 475: 398 DNC-1 (mod AMX-VCI); 40 HWK-11; 34 M-5A1 half-track; 3 M-32 *Recovery Sherman*
   APC (W) 234: 95 BDX; 25 DN-4; 19 DN-5 *Toro*; 26 LAV-150 ST; 25 MOWAG *Roland*; 44 VCR (3 amb; 5 cmd post)
ARTY 1,390
   TOWED 123: **105mm** 123: 40 M-101; 40 M-56; 16 M-2A1, 14 M-3; 13 NORINCO M-90
   MOR 1,267: **81mm** 400 M-I, 400 *Brandt*, 300 SB
   120mm 167: 75 *Brandt*; 60 M-65; 32 RT61
AT
   MSL • SP 8 *Milan* (VBL)
   RL 1,187+
   SP 106mm M40A1
   64mm RPG-18 *Fly* **82mm** B-300 **73mm** RPG-16; **106mm** M40A1
   GUNS 37mm 30 M3
AD
   GUNS 80
   TOWED 12.7mm 40 M-55; **20mm** 40 GAI-B01

Navy 55,961

Two Fleet Commands: Gulf (6 zones), Pacific (11 zones)

FORCES BY ROLE

Navy 1 HQ located at Acapulco; 1 HQ (exercise) located at Vera Cruz

EQUIPMENT BY TYPE
PRINCIPAL SURFACE COMBATANTS 6
   FRIGATES • FF 6:
   2 *Bravo* (US *Bronstein*) each with 1 Mk 112 octuple (8 eff.) with tactical ASROC, 2 triple ASTT (6 eff.) with Mk 46 LWT, 1 hel landing platform
   4 *Allende* (US *Knox*) each with 1 Mk 112 octuple with ASROC/RGM-84C *Harpoon* SSM, 1 Mk 29 GMLS with *Sea Sparrow* SAM, 2 twin TT (4 eff.) with Mk 46 LWT, 1 127mm gun, capacity 1 MD-902 utl hel)
PATROL AND COASTAL COMBATANTS 189
   PSOH 21:
   3 *Sierra* (capacity 1 MD-902 *Explorer*)

4 *Oaxaca* each with 1 AS-565 MB *Panther* utl hel (2 additional hulls in build)

4 *Durango* with 1 57mm gun, each with 1 Bo-105 utl hel

4 *Holzinger* (capacity 1 MD-902 *Explorer*)

6 *Uribe* (ESP *Halcon*) each with 1 Bo-105 utl hel

PFM 2 *Huracan* (Il *Aliya*) with *Phalanx* CIWS and 4 *Gabriel* SSM

PCO 10 *Leandro Valle* (US *Auk* MSF) (being withdrawn from service from 2009 to be replaced with 4 additional *Oaxaca* class)

PCC 25: 20 *Azteca*; 3 *Cabo* (US *Cape Higgon*); 1 *Democrata*; 1 *Caribe*

PCI 6: 4 *Isla* less than 100 tonnes (US *Halter*); 2 *Punta* less than 100 tonnes (US *Point*)

PCR 48 (Modified *Stridsbat 90*) less than 100 tonnes

PBF 77+ all less than 100 tonnes; 48 *Polaris* (SWE CB90); 4 *Polaris II* (SWE IC 16M; 16 additional vessels under construction); 6 *Acuario*; 2 *Acuario B*; 17 *Defender*

AMPHIBIOUS • LS • LST 3: 2 *Papaloapan* (US *Newport*); 1 *Panuco* (ex US LST-1152)

LOGISTICS AND SUPPORT 19:

AG 1 *Manzanillo* (troop transport ship, also deployed as SAR and disaster relief ship)

AK 3

AGOR 3: 2 *Robert D. Conrad*; 1 *Humboldt*

AGS 4

ATF 4

TRG 4: 1 *Manuel Azuela*; 2 *Huasteco* (also serve as troop transport, supply and hospital ships); **AXS** 1

FACILITIES

Bases   Located at Vera Cruz, Tampico, Chetumal, Ciudad del Carmen, Yukalpetén, Lerna, Frontera, Coatzacoalcos, Isla Mujéres, Acapulco, Ensenada, La Paz, Guaymas, Mayport (FL), US, Salina Cruz, Puerto Madero, Lazaro Cádenas, Puerto Vallarta,

Naval Aviation 1,250

FORCES BY ROLE

AEW   1 sqn with 3 E-2C; 2 Rockwell *Sabreliner* 60

MR   1 sqn with 8 CASA 212PM *Aviocar**; 1 sqn with 7 L-90 *Redigo*; 5 sqn with 4 Beech F-33C *Bonanza*; 1 Cessna 404 *Titan*; 12 MX-7 *Star Rocket*; 6 Lancair IV-P; 4 Beech 55 *Baron*; (8 CN-235MPA *Persuader* on order)

Tpt   1 sqn with 6 AN-32B *Cline*; 1 VIP sqn with 1 DHC-8 *Dash 8*; 2 Beech 90 *King Air*; 5 Rockwell *Turbo Commander* 1000; 3 Learjet 24; (1 G-IV on order)

Hel   5 sqn with 20 Mi-17 (Mi-8MT) *Hip H*/Mi-8 *Hip* (8 armed); 2 sqn with 2 PZL Mi-2 *Hoplite*; 2 AS-555 *Fennec*; 4 AS-565MB; 6 MD 902 *Explorer* (stored); 2 sqn with 11 Bo-105 CBS-5

EQUIPMENT BY TYPE

AIRCRAFT 7 combat capable*

RECCE 14: 7 CASA 212PM *Aviocar** 7 L-90TP *Redigo*

MR 8 CN-235 (all ac on order)

AEW 3 E-2C *Hawkeye*;

TPT 30: 6 AN-32B *Cline*; 1 DHC-8 *Dash 8*; 2 Rockwell *Sabreliner* 60; 3 Learjet 24; 5 Rockwell *Turbo Commander*

1000; 2 Beech 90 *King Air*; 1 Cessna 404 *Titan*; 4 Beech 55 *Baron*; 6 Lancair IV-P

TRG 28: 4 Beech F-33C *Bonanza*; 8 Z-242L; 7 L-90 *Redigo*; 9 MX-7 *Star Rocket*

HELICOPTERS

RECCE 10: 6 MD-902 *Explorer* (SAR role); 4 AS-565MB *Panther*

SPT 23: 2 PZL Mi-2 *Hoplite*; 21 Mi-17 (Mi-8MT) *Hip H*/Mi-8 *Hip* spt hel

UTL 20: 2 AS-555 *Fennec*; 11 Bo-105 CBS-5; 4 MD-500E; 2 R-22 *Mariner*; 1 R-44

FACILITIES

Trg School   1 with 8 Z-242L; 1 R-44; 4 MD-500E; 4 *Schweizer* 300C

Marines 19,328

FORCES BY ROLE

Inf	3 bn
Amphibious Reaction Force	2 bde
AB	1 bn
SF	2 coy
Presidential Guard	1 bn

EQUIPMENT BY TYPE

APC (W) 29: 3 BTR-60 (APC-60); 26 BTR-70 (APC-70)

ARTY 122

TOWED 105mm 16 M-56

MRL 122mm 6 Firos-25

MOR 60mm/81mm 100

RCL 106mm M-40A1

AD • SAM • MANPAD 5+ SA-18 *Grouse (Igla)*

Air Force 11,545

FORCES BY ROLE

Ftr/CCT   1 sqn with F-5E/F-5F *Tiger II*; 4 sqn with PC-7, PC-9M

Surv/Recce   1 sqn with EMB-145 *Erieye* (AEW), EMB-145RS (Remote Sensing), SA-2-37B, C-26B

Anti-narc Spraying   sqn with Cessna T206H; Bell 206

Tpt   1 sqn with C-130E; C-130K; L-100-20; B-727; 1 sqn with An-32B, PC-6B, IAI-201/202 *Arava*; 1 Presidential gp with B-757, B-737; Gulfstream III; Learjet 35; *Turbo Commander*; As-332 *Super Puma*; EC225; 1 VIP tpt gp with S-70; Cessna 500 *Citation*; Beech-200

Liaison   6 sqn with Ce-182S; 1 sqn with Ce-206

Hel   1 sqn with MD-530F; 1 sqn with S-70A-24 *Black Hawk*, S-65 *Yas'ur* 2000, B-412, SA-330S; 1 sqn with Mi-8T; Mi-17; Mi-26T; 3 sqn with Bell 212, Bell 206B; 1 sqn with Bell 206B; Bell 206L

Trg   5 sqn with PT-17; SF-260EU; Beech F-33C *Bonanza*; PC-7

UAV   unit with *Hermes* 450 (delivery 2009); *Skylark* Mk.I

EQUIPMENT BY TYPE

AIRCRAFT 78 combat capable

FTR 10: 8 F-5E *Tiger II*; 2 F-5F *Tiger II*
COIN/TRG 66: 64 PC-7, 2 PC-9M*
RECCE 8: 2 EMB-145RS; 2 SA-2-37A; 4 C-26B
AEW 1 EMB-145AEW *Erieye*
TPT 38: 3 B-727; 2 B-737; 1 B-757; 1 Beech 200; 2 C-130
E; 4 C-130K; 1 L-100-20; 1 Cessna 500 *Citation*; 11 IAI-
201/202 *Arava*; ; 3 An-32B; 4 PC-6B; 1 Rockwell *Turbo
Commander* 680; 2 Gulfstream III; 2 Learjet 35
UTL 73: 3 Cessna 206; 62 Cessna 182; 8 Cessna T206H
TRG 61: 32 Beech F-33C *Bonanza*; 26 SF-260EU; 3 PT-17;
HELICOPTERS
CBT 20 MD-530MF
SPT 142 : 21 Mi-17; 8 Mi-8T; 1 Mi-26T; 4 S-65C *Yas'ur
2000*; 6 S-70A-24 *Black Hawk*; 2 SA-330S; 4 AS332L; 14
Bell 206B *JetRanger II*; 7 Bell 206L; 16 Bell 212; 9 Bell
412EP (8 more on order); 4 AS332L (VIP), 2 EC225 (VIP);
44 Bell 206. (6 EC725 on order for delivery 2011)
MSL • AAM AIM-9J *Sidewinder*
UAV TUAV 2 *Hermes* 450
Mini-UAV 2 *Skylark* Mk.I

Paramilitary 36,500

Federal Preventive Police 14,000

Public Security Secretariat
AIRCRAFT
    TPT 17: 2 An-32B *Cline*; 1 CN-235M; 5 Cessna 182
    Skylane; 1 Cessna 404 *Titan*; 1 Gulfstream II; 1 Learjet 24;
    1 Rockwell *Sabreliner* 60; 5 Rockwell *Turbo Commander*
    5
    UTL 1 Cessna 210 *Centurion*
HELICOPTERS
    SPT 15: 2 AS-350B *Ecureuil*; 4 Mi-17 *Hip*; 1 SA-330C
    Puma; 1 SA-330F *Puma*; 7 UH-60L *Blackhawk* (4 more
    on order)
    UTL 23: 1 AS-555 *Fennec*; 14 Bell 206 *Jet Ranger*; 1 Bell
    212; 5 EC-120; 2 MD-530F *Lifter*
    TRG 7 Bell 206B
UAV 8
    TUAV 2 S4 *Ehécatl*
    Mini-UAV 6: 2 E1 *Gavilán*, 4 *Orbier*

Federal Ministerial Police 4,500

HELICOPTERS
Anti-narcotics 44: 7 Bell 212; 26 Bell UH-1H; 11
Schweizer 333

Rural Defense Militia 18,000

Inf	13 units
Horsed Cav	13 units

NON-STATE GROUPS

Mexican military and security forces are engaged
in operations against a number of drug trafficking
organisations; all use SALW, while the capture of MANPATS
has been reported: **Sinaloa Cartel; Gulf Cartel; Beltran
Leyva Organisation**; Tijuana Cartel; Juarez Cartel; Los
Zetas – Est strength: 500 Major equipments include: n.k.
La Familia Michoacana Cartel Est strength: 4,000 Major
equipments include:.n.k.

Nicaragua NIC

Nicaraguan Gold Cordoba Co		2008	2009	2010
GDP	Co	123bn	129bn	
	US$	6.4bn	6.3bn	
per capita	US$	1,101	1,063	
Growth	%	3.2	-1.0	
Inflation	%	19.9	4.3	
Def bdgt	Co	809m	837m	
	US$	41m	40m	
US$1=Co		19.3	20.6	

Population	5,891,199

Age	0–14	15–19	20–24	25–29	30–64	65 plus
Male	19%	6%	5%	4%	14%	1%
Female	18%	6%	5%	4%	15%	2%

Capabilities

ACTIVE 12,000 (Army 10,000 Navy 800 Air 1,200)
Terms of service voluntary, 18–36 months

ORGANISATIONS BY SERVICE

Army ε10,000
FORCES BY ROLE

Region	1 (Comandos Regionales Militares (CRM)) comd (3 inf bn); 5 (CRM) comd (*each*: 2 inf bn)
Comd	1 HQ (1 sy bn, 1 inf bn, 1 sigs bn, 1 int unit, 1 SF bde (3 SF bn))
Inf	2 det (*total*: 2 inf bn)
Mech	1 (lt) bde (1 tk bn, 1 mech inf bn, 1 recce bn, 1 AT gp, 1 fd arty gp (2 fd arty bn))
SF	1 bde (3 SF bn)
Engr	1 bn
Tpt	1 regt (1 (APC) army bn)

EQUIPMENT BY TYPE
MBT 127: 62 T-55; 65 in store
LT TK 10 PT-76 in store
RECCE 20 BRDM-2
APC (W) 166: 102 BTR-152 in store; 64 BTR-60
ARTY 800
    TOWED 42: **122mm** 12 D-30; **152mm** 30 D-20 in store
    MRL 151: **107mm** 33 Type-63; **122mm** 118: 18 BM-21; 100
    GRAD 1P (BM-21P) (single-tube rocket launcher, man
    portable)
    MOR 607: **82mm** 579; **120mm** 24 M-43; **160mm** 4 M-160
    in store
AT
    MSL
        SP 12 BRDM-2 *Sagger*
        MANPATS AT-3 9K11 *Sagger*
    RCL **82mm** B-10
    RL **73mm** RPG-16/RPG-7 *Knout*
    GUNS 461: **100mm** 24 M-1944; **57mm** 264 ZIS-2 *M-1943*;
    90 in store; **76mm** 83 ZIS-3

AD • SAM • MANPAD 200+ SA-14 *Gremlin*/SA-16 *Gimlet*/ SA-7 *Grail*

Navy ε800

EQUIPMENT BY TYPE
PATROL AND COASTAL COMBATANTS 24
PFI 5: 3 *Dabur* less than 100 tonnes; 2 *Zhuk*† less than 100 tonnes (FSU)
PBR 19 Assault Craft

FACILITIES
Bases Located at Corinto, Puerto Cabezzas, El Bluff

Air Force 1,200

FORCES BY ROLE
Tpt   sqn with An-2 *Colt*; An-26 *Curl*; Cessna 404 *Titan* (VIP)
Trg/Utl some sqn with T-41D *Mescalero*
ADA   1 gp with ZU-23; C3-*Morigla* M1
Hel   some sqn with Mi-17 (Mi-8MT) *Hip H* (VIP/tpt/ armed)

EQUIPMENT BY TYPE
AIRCRAFT
TPT 6: 1 An-2 *Colt*; 4 An-26 *Curl*; 1 Cessna 404 *Titan* (VIP)
TRG 1 T-41D *Mescalero*
HELICOPTERS
SPT 16: 1 Mi-17 (Mi-8MT) *Hip H* (VIP); 3 (tpt/armed); 12† (tpt/armed). 2 Mi-17 on order
AD • GUNS 36: 18 ZU-23; 18 C3-*Morigla* M1
MSL • ASM AT-2 *Swatter*

Panama PAN

Panamanian Balboa B		2008	2009	2010
GDP	B	23.2bn	23.5bn	
	US$	23.2bn	23.5bn	
per capita	US$	7,010	6,993	
Growth	%	9.2	1.8	
Inflation	%	8.8	2.3	
Def bdgt	B	226m	269m	
	US$	226m	269m	
US$1=B		1.0	1.0	

Population   3,360,474

Age	0–14	15–19	20–24	25–29	30–64	65 plus
Male	16%	5%	4%	4%	19%	3%
Female	15%	5%	4%	4%	18%	3%

Capabilities
Paramilitary 12,000

ORGANISATIONS BY SERVICE

Paramilitary 12,000

National Police Force 11,000
No hy mil eqpt, small arms only
Police   18 coy
SF   1 unit (reported)
Paramilitary   8 coy
Presidential Guard   1 bn under strength
MP   1 bn

National Maritime Service ε600

FORCES BY ROLE
Air Wing 1 HQ located at Amador

EQUIPMENT BY TYPE
PATROL AND COASTAL COMBATANTS 45
PCO 1 *Independencia* (US *Balsam* class)
PCC 5: 2 *Panquiaco* (UK Vosper 31.5m); 3 (various)
PCI 10: 3 *Chiriqui* less than 100 tonnes (US); 1 *Negrita* less than 100 tonnes (US); 5 *Tres De Noviembre* less than 100 tonnes (US *Point*); 1 US MSB Class (MSB 5)
PBR 29: 4(Nor-Tech 43); 25 various

FACILITIES
Bases Located at Amador, Balboa, Colón

National Air Service 400

FORCES BY ROLE
Tpt   sqn with BN-2B *Islander*; CASA 212M *Aviocar*; PA-34 *Seneca*; Presidential flt with Gulfstream II; S-76C
Trg   unit with T-35D *Pillan,* Cessna 152/172
Hel   sqn with Bell 205; Bell 212; UH-1H *Iroquois*

EQUIPMENT BY TYPE
AIRCRAFT
TPT 9: 1 BN-2B *Islander*; 5 CASA 212M *Aviocar*; 1 Gulfstream II; 2 PA-34 *Seneca*
TRG 6 T-35D *Pillan;* 1 Cessna 152, 1 Cessna 172
HELICOPTERS
TPT 2 S-76C
UTL 21: 2 Bell 205; 6 Bell 212; 13 UH-1H *Iroquois*

Paraguay PRY

Paraguayan Guarani Pg		2008	2009	2010
GDP	Pg	69.7tr	69.2tr	
	US$	16.0bn	14.1bn	
per capita	US$	2,339	2,020	
Growth	%	5.5	-4.5	
Inflation	%	10.2	2.8	
Def bdgt	Pg	576bn	625bn	
	US$	132m	127m	
US$1=Pg		4,363	4,900	

Population   6,995,655

Age	0–14	15–19	20–24	25–29	30–64	65 plus
Male	19%	5%	4%	4%	16%	2%
Female	19%	5%	4%	4%	15%	3%

Capabilities

ACTIVE 10,650 (Army 7,600 Navy 1,950 Air 1,100)
Paramilitary 14,800
Terms of service 12 months Navy 2 years

RESERVE 164,500 (Joint 164,500)

ORGANISATIONS BY SERVICE

Army 6,100; 1,500 conscript (total 7,600)

The infantry regiments, each of which forms the major peace-time element of the six infantry 'divisions' have a strength of little more than 500. The three cavalry 'divisions' each have two regiments with a strength of approximately 750.

FORCES BY ROLE
3 corps HQ

Army	3 corps (*each:* 2 inf div, 1 cav div, 1 arty gp); 6 inf div in total; 20 (frontier) det
Armd Cav	3 regt
Cav	3 div (*each:* 2 (horse) regt)
Inf	6 regt (bn)
Arty	2 gp (bn); 1 gp divided between 2 of the corps
ADA	1 gp
Engr	6 bn
Presidential Guard	1 unit (1 inf bn, 1 SF bn, 1 arty bty, 1 MP bn, 1 (lt) armd sqn)

EQUIPMENT BY TYPE
MBT 5 M4A3 *Sherman*
LT TK 12 M-3A1 *Stuart*
RECCE 30 EE-9 *Cascavel*
APC (T) 20 M-9 half-track
APC (W) 10 EE-11 *Urutu*
ARTY 115
  TOWED 105mm 35: 15 M-101; **75mm** 20 1935
  MOR 81mm 80
AT
  RCL 75mm M-20
  RL 66mm M-72 *LAW*
AD • GUNS 19:
  SP 20mm 3 M-9
  TOWED 16: **40mm** 10 M-1A1, 6 L/60

Reserves
Cav 4 regt
Inf 14 regt

Navy 1,100; 850 conscript (total 1,950)

EQUIPMENT BY TYPE
PATROL AND COASTAL COMBATANTS 28
  PCR 8: 2 (ROC); 1 *Capitan Cabral*; 2 *Capitan Ortiz* less than 100 tonnes (ROC *Hai Ou*); 1 *Itapu*; 2 *Nanawa*†
  MISC BOATS/CRAFT 20
AMPHIBIOUS 2 LCT
LOGISTICS AND SUPPORT 3: 2 **AKSL** (also serve as river transport); 1 **TRG**

FACILITIES
Bases   Located at Asunción (Puerto Sajonia), Bahía Negra, Cuidad Del Este

Naval Aviation 100

FORCES BY ROLE

Utl	1 sqn with 2 HB-350 *Esquilo*; 1 OH-13 *Sioux*
Liaison	1 sqn with 2 Cessna 310; 1 Cessna 210 *Centurion*; 2 Cessna 150; 1 Cessna 410

EQUIPMENT BY TYPE
AIRCRAFT
  UTL 4: 2 Cessna 310; 1 Cessna 210 *Centurion*; 1 Cessna 410
  TRG 2 Cessna 150
HELICOPTERS
  SPT 2 HB-350 *Esquilo*
  UTL 1 OH-13 *Sioux*

Marines 700; 200 conscript (total 900)

Marine 3 bn under strength

Air Force 900; 200 conscript (total 1,100)

FORCES BY ROLE

Tac	some sqn with EMB-312 *Tucano*
SAR/Liaison	some sqn with 2 Cessna 402B; 1 PA-32R *Saratoga*; 3 Cessna U-206 *Stationair*; 2 PZL-104 *Wilga 80*; I Beech 33 *Debonair*; 2 Beech A36 *Bonanza*; 1 Cessna 210 *Centurion*; 1 EMB-720D *Minuano*; 1 EMB-721C *Sertanejo*; 1 EMB-810C *Seneca*
Tpt	some sqn with 1 C-47 *Skytrain*; 5 CASA 212 *Aviocar*; 1 DHC-6 *Twin Otter*
Trg	some sqn with 3 T-35A *Pillan*; 4 T-35B *Pillan*; 6 Neiva T-25 *Universal*
Hel	some sqn with 3 HB-350 *Esquilo*; 7 UH-1H *Iroquois*

EQUIPMENT BY TYPE
AIRCRAFT 3 combat capable
  COIN: 3 EMB-312 *Tucano*
  TPT 20: 1 B-707; 1 Beech 55 *Baron* (army co-op); 1 C-47 *Skytrain*; 5 CASA 212 *Aviocar*; 1 Cessna 310 (army co-op); 2 Cessna 402B; 1 DHC-6 *Twin Otter*; 1 PA-32R *Saratoga*; 1 Beech 33 *Debonair*; 2 Beech A36 *Bonanza*; 1 Cessna 210 *Centurion*; 1 EMB-720D *Minuano*; 1 EMB-721C *Sertanejo*; 1 EMB-810C *Seneca*;
  UTL 6: 1 Cessna 206 (army co-op); 3 Cessna U-206 *Stationair* 2 PZL-104 *Wilga 80*
  TRG 13: 3 T-35A *Pillan*; 4 T-35B *Pillan*; 6 Neiva T-25 *Universal*
HELICOPTERS
  SPT 3 HB-350 *Esquilo*
  UTL 7 UH-1H *Iroquois*

Paramilitary 14,800

Special Police Service 10,800; 4,000 conscript (total 14,800)

DEPLOYMENT

AFGHANISTAN
UN • UNAMA 1 obs

CÔTE D'IVOIRE
UN • UNOCI 2; 8 obs

DEMOCRATIC REPUBLIC OF CONGO
UN • MONUC 17 obs

HAITI
UN • MINUSTAH 31

LIBERIA
UN • UNMIL 1; 2 obs

NEPAL
UN • UNMIN 6 obs

SUDAN
UN • UNMIS 9 obs

WESTERN SAHARA
UN • MINURSO 5 obs

Peru PER

Peruvian Nuevo Sol NS		2008	2009
GDP	NS	373bn	395bn
	US$	127bn	138bn
per capita	US$	4,378	4,674
Growth	%	9.8	1.5
Inflation	%	5.8	3.2
Def bdgt	NS	4.15bn	4.51bn
	US$	1.42bn	1.57bn
US$1=NS		2.92	2.86

Population   29,546,963

Age	0–14	15–19	20–24	25–29	30–64	65 plus
Male	16%	5%	4%	4%	18%	2%
Female	15%	5%	4%	4%	18%	3%

Capabilities

ACTIVE 114,000 (Army 74,000 Navy 23,000 Air 17,000) Paramilitary 77,000

RESERVE 188,000 (Army 188,000) Paramilitary 7,000

ORGANISATIONS BY SERVICE

Army 74,000
FORCES BY ROLE
4 Military Regions
North Region
Cav   1 bde (1st) (4 mech bn, 1 arty gp)

Inf   1 bde (1st reinforced) (1 tk bn, 3 inf bn, 1 arty gp); 2 bde (7th & 32nd) (each: 3 inf bn, 1 arty gp)

Jungle 1 bde (6th) (4 jungle bn, 1 arty gp, 1 engr bn)
Inf

Central Region
Inf   1 bde (1st) (4 mech bn, 1 arty gp); 2 bde (2nd & 31st) (each: 3 mot inf bn, 1 arty gp); 1 bde (8th) (3 mot inf bn, 1 arty gp, 1 AD bn)

SF   1 bde (1st) (4 SF bn, 1 airmob arty gp); 1 bde (3rd) (3 cdo bn, 1 airmob arty gp, 1 AD gp)

Arty   1 gp (regional troops)

Avn   1 bde (1 atk hel / recce hel bn, 1 avn bn, 2 aslt hel / tpt hel bn)

Trg   1 armd bde (18th) (1 armd bn, 2 tk bn, 1 armd inf bn, 1 engr bn, 1 SP fd arty gp)

South Region
Armd   1 bde (3rd) (3 mech inf bn, 1 mot inf bn, 1 arty gp, 1 AD gp, 1 engr bn); 1 bde (3rd) (2 tk bn, 1 armd inf bn, 1 arty gp, 1 AD gp, 1 engr bn)

SF   1 gp (regional troops)

Mtn Inf 1 bde (4th) (1 armd regt, 3 mot inf bn, 1 arty gp); 1 bde (5th) (1 armd regt, 2 mot inf bn, 3 jungle coy, 1 arty gp)

Arty   1 gp (regional troops)

AD   1 gp (regional troops)

Engr   1 bn (regional troops)

Eastern Region
Jungle 1 bde (5th) (1 SF gp, 3 jungle bn, 3 jungle coy, 1
Inf   jungle arty gp, 1 AD gp, 1 jungle engr bn)

EQUIPMENT BY TYPE
MBT 240: 165 T-55; 75†
LT TK 96 AMX-13
RECCE 95: 30 BRDM-2; 15 Fiat 6616; 50 M-9A1
APC 299
   APC (T) 120 M-113A1
   APC (W) 179: 150 UR-416; 25 Fiat 6614; 4 *Repontec*
ARTY 998
   SP • 155mm 12 M-109A2
   TOWED 290
      105mm 152: 44 M-101; 24 M-2A1; 60 M-56; 24 Model 56 pack howitzer; **122mm**; 36 D-30; **130mm** 36 M-46; **155mm** 66: 36 M-114, 30 Model 50
   MRL • 122mm 22 BM-21 *Grad*
   MOR 674+: **81mm/107mm** 350; **120mm** 300+ *Brandt/ Expal Model L*
      SP 107mm 24 M-106A1
AT • MSL • MANPATS 838: 350 AT-3 9K11 *Sagger* / HJ-73C, 244 *Kornet*, 244 SPIKE-ER
   RCL 106mm M-40A1
AIRCRAFT
   TPT 9: 2 An-28 *Cash*; 3 AN-32B *Cline*; 1 Beech 350 *Super King Air*; 2 PA-31T *Navajo/Cheyenne II*; 1 PA-34 *Seneca*
   UTL 8: 3 Cessna U-206 *Stationair*; 1 Cessna 208 *Caravan I*; 4 IL-103
HELICOPTERS
   SPT 34: 14 Mi-17 (Mi-8MT) *Hip H*; 8 in store; PZL Mi-2 *Hoplite* 9; Mi-26T 1; 2 in store
   UTL 2 A-109K2;
   TRG 5 Enstrom F-28F

AD

SAM • MANPAD 298+: 70 SA-14 *Gremlin*; 128 SA-16
Gimlet; 100+ SA-7 *Grail*
GUNS 165
    SP 23mm 35 ZSU-23-4
    TOWED 23mm 130: 80 ZU-23-2; 50 ZU-23;

Navy 23,000 (incl 1,000 Coast Guard)

Commands: Pacific, Lake Titicaca, Amazon River

EQUIPMENT BY TYPE
SUBMARINES • TACTICAL • SSK 6:
4 *Angamos* (GER T-209/1200) each with 6 single 533mm
TT with A-185 HWT
2 *Angamos* in refit/reserve (GER T-209/1200) each with 6
single 533mm TT with A-185 HWT
PRINCIPAL SURFACE COMBATANTS 9
CRUISERS • CG 1 *Almirante Grau* (NLD *De Ruyter*) with
8 single each with Mk 2 Otomat SSM, 4 twin 152mm gun
(8 eff.)
FRIGATES • FFG 8 *Carvajal* (mod ITA *Lupo*) each with 8
single each with Mk 2 Otomat SSM, 1+ *Albatros* octuple
with *Aspide* SAM, 2 triple ASTT (6 eff.) with A244 LWT,
1 127mm gun, with 1 AB-212 (Bell 212) Utl/SH-3D *Sea
King* ASW
PATROL AND COASTAL COMBATANTS 14
PFM 6 *Velarde* (FRA PR-72 64m) each with 4 single each
with MM-38 *Exocet* tactical SSM, 1 76mm gun
PCR 5:
    2 *Amazonas* each with 1 76mm gun
    2 *Maranon* each with 2 76mm gun
    1 *Huallaga* with 40mm gun, (Additional vessel in
    build)
MISC BOATS/CRAFT 3 craft (for lake patrol)
AMPHIBIOUS • LS • LST 4 *Paita* (capacity 395 troops)
(US *Terrebonne Parish*)
LOGISTICS AND SUPPORT 11:
AOR 1 *Mollendo*
AOT 2
ARS 1 *Guardian Rios*
AH 1
AGS 4: 1 *Carrasco*; 2 (coastal survey vessels); 1 (river
survey vessel for the upper Amazon)
TRG • AXS 1
TRV 1

FACILITIES
Bases Located at Callao (Ocean), Puerto Maldonaldo
     (*River*), Iquitos (*River*), Talara (Ocean), Puno (Lake),
     Paita (Ocean), San Lorenzo Island (Ocean)

Naval Aviation ε800

FORCES BY ROLE
MR   2 sqn with 5 Beech 200T *Maritime Patrol*; 3
         SH-3D *Sea King*; 3 AB-212 (Bell 212); 1 F-27
         Friendship
Tpt   1 flt with 2 AN-32B *Cline*
Liaison 1 sqn with 4 Mi-8 *Hip*; 5 Bell 206B *JetRanger II*
Trg   1 sqn with 5 T-34C *Turbo Mentor*; 5 Enstrom
        F28F

EQUIPMENT BY TYPE
AIRCRAFT
MP 5 Beech 200T *Maritime Patrol*
TPT 2 An-32B *Cline*
ELINT 1 F-27 *Friendship*
TRG 5 T-34C *Turbo Mentor*
HELICOPTERS
ASW 3 SH-3D *Sea King*
SPT 4 Mi-8 *Hip*
UTL 8: 3 AB-212 (Bell 212); 5 Bell 206B *Jet Ranger II*
TRG 5 Enstrom F28F
MSL • ASM AM-39 *Exocet*

Marines 4,000

FORCES BY ROLE
Inf   1 (jungle) bn; 2 (indep) bn; 1 gp
Cdo   1 gp
Marine 1 bde (1 arty gp, 1 spec ops gp, 1 recce bn,
         1 (amph veh) amph bn, 2 inf bn)

EQUIPMENT BY TYPE
APC (W) 35+: 20 BMR-600; V-100 *Commando*; 15 V-200
Chaimite
ARTY 18+
    TOWED 122mm D-30
    MOR 18+: **81mm**; **120mm** ε18
    RCL 84mm *Carl Gustav*; **106mm** M-40A1
AD • GUNS 20mm SP (twin)

Air Force 17,000

FORCES BY ROLE
Air Force divided into five regions – North, Lima, South,
Central and Amazon.
Ftr   1 sqn with MiG-29C *Fulcrum*; MiG-29SE
         Fulcrum; MiG-29UB *Fulcrum*
FGA   1 sqn with M-2000P (M-2000E) *Mirage*;
         M-2000DP (M-2000ED) *Mirage*; 1 sqn with
         A-37B *Dragonfly*; 3 sqn with Su-25A *Frogfoot
         A*†; Su-25UB *Frogfoot B*†*
RECCE 1 (photo-survey) unit with *Learjet* 36A; C-26B
Tpt   3 gp; 7 sqn with An-32 *Cline*; B-737; DC-8-62F;
         DHC-6 *Twin Otter*; FH-227; L-100-20; PC-6
         Turbo-Porter; Y-12(II); 1 (Presidential) flt with
         F-28 *Fellowship*, *Falcon* 20F
Tkr   KC-707-323C
Liaison 1 sqn with PA-31T *Navajo/Cheyenne II*; UH-1D
         Iroquois
Atk Hel/ 1 sqn with Mi-24 *Hind*/Mi-25 *Hind D*; Mi-17TM
Aslt Hel *Hip H*;
Spt Hel 3 sqn with Mi-17 *Hip H*; BO-105C; Bell 206 *Jet
         Ranger*; AB-212 (Bell 212); Bell 412 *Twin Huey*;
         Schweizer 300C
Trg   drug interdiction sqn with EMB-312 *Tucano*;
         MB-339A; T-41A/T-41D *Mescalero*; Z-242
AD   6 bn with SA-3 *Goa*

EQUIPMENT BY TYPE
AIRCRAFT 70 combat capable
    FTR 18: 15 MiG-29C *Fulcrum*; 3 MiG-29SE *Fulcrum*

FGA 42: 10 A-37B *Dragonfly*; 2 M-2000DP (M-2000ED) *Mirage*; 10 M-2000P (M-2000E) *Mirage*; 10 Su-25A *Frogfoot A*†; 10 MB-339A

RECCE 6: 2 Learjet 36A; 4 C-26B

TKR 1 KC-707-323C

TPT 35: 6 An-32 *Cline*; 1 B-737; 2 DC-8-62F; 5 DHC-6 *Twin Otter*; 1 *Falcon* 20F; 5 L-100-20; 1 PA-31T *Navajo/Cheyenne II*; 8 PC-6 *Turbo-Porter*; 2 Y-12(II) (incl 4 in stiore)

TRG 50: 19 EMB-312 *Tucano*; 2 MiG-29UB *Fulcrum**; 6 T-41A *Mescalero*/T-41D *Mescalero*; 15 Z-242; 8 Su-25UB *Frogfoot B*†*

HELICOPTERS

ATK 16 Mi-24 *Hind*/Mi-25 *Hind D*

SPT 23: 10 Mi-17TM *Hip H*; 5 MI-8; 13 Mi-17 (Mi-8MT) *Hip H*

UTL 33: 14 AB-212 (Bell 212); 10 Bo-105C; 8 Bell 206 *JetRanger*; 1 Bell 412 *Twin Huey*

TRG 6 Schweizer 300C

AD

SAM 100+: SA-3 *Goa*; 100+ *Javelin*

MSL

ASM AS-30

AAM AA-2 *Atoll*; AA-8 *Aphid*; AA-10 *Alamo*; AA-12 *Adder*; R-550 *Magic*

Paramilitary • National Police 77,000 (100,000 reported)

APC (W) 100 MOWAG *Roland*

General Police 43,000

Security Police 21,000

Technical Police 13,000

Coast Guard 1,000

Personnel included as part of Navy

PATROL AND COASTAL COMBATANTS 21

PCC 5 *Rio Nepena*

PCI 16: 3 *Dauntless* less than 100 tonnes; 13 various

AIRCRAFT

TPT 2 F-27 *Friendship*

Rondas Campesinas ε7,000 gp

Peasant self-defence force. Perhaps 7,000 rondas 'gp', up to pl strength, some with small arms. Deployed mainly in emergency zone.

SELECTED NON-STATE GROUPS

Sendero Luminoso Est strength: 500 Major equipments include: mines and IEDs, SALW

DEPLOYMENT

CÔTE D'IVOIRE

UN • UNOCI 3 obs

CYPRUS

UN • UNFICYP 2

DEMOCRATIC REPUBLIC OF CONGO

UN • MONUC 7 obs

HAITI

UN • MINUSTAH 207; 1 inf coy

LIBERIA

UN • UNMIL 2; 2 obs

SUDAN

UN • UNMIS 13 obs

Suriname SUR

Suriname Dollar gld		2008	2009	2010
GDP	gld	6.39tr		
	US$	2.3bn		
per capita	US$	4,906		
Growth	%	6.0	1.5	
Inflation	%	14.6	7.5	
Def bdgt	gld	85bn	107bn	134bn
	US$	31m	39m	
US$1=gld		2,740	2,740	

Population 481,267

Age	0–14	15–19	20–24	25–29	30–64	65 plus
Male	15%	5%	5%	4%	19%	3%
Female	14%	5%	4%	4%	19%	3%

Capabilities

ACTIVE 1,840 (Army 1,400 Navy 240 Air 200)

(All services form part of the army)

ORGANISATIONS BY SERVICE

Army 1,400

FORCES BY ROLE

Mech Cav 1 sqn

Inf 1 bn (4 inf coy)

MP 1 bn (coy)

EQUIPMENT BY TYPE

RECCE 6 EE-9 *Cascavel*

APC (W) 15 EE-11 *Urutu*

MOR 81mm 6

RCL 106mm: M-40A1

Navy ε240

EQUIPMENT BY TYPE

PATROL AND COASTAL COMBATANTS 8

PCI 3 *Rodman*† less than 100 tonnes

PBR 5

FACILITIES

Base Located at Paramaribo

Air Force ε200

FORCES BY ROLE

MP 2 CASA 212-400 *Aviocar**

Trg/Tpt 1 sqn with 1 BN-2 *Defender**; 1 PC-7 *Turbo Trainer**

Liaison 1 Cessna U-206 *Stationair*; 1 Cessna 182

EQUIPMENT BY TYPE

AIRCRAFT 4 combat capable

MP 2 CASA 212-400 *Aviocar**

TPT 1 BN-2 *Defender**

UTL 1 Cessna U-206 *Stationair*; 1 Cessna 182

TRG 1 PC-7 *Turbo Trainer**

Trinidad and Tobago TTO

Trinidad and Tobago Dollar TT$		2008	2009	2010
GDP	TT$	152bn	174bn	
	US$	24.2bn	27.6bn	
per capita	US$	19,657	22,420	
Growth	%	2.3	-0.8	
Inflation	%	12.1	7.2	
Def bdgt	TT$	ε900m	ε1.0bn	
	US$	ε143m	ε158m	
US$1=TT$		6.28	6.31	

Population   1,229,953

Age	0–14	15–19	20–24	25–29	30–64	65 plus
Male	11%	5%	6%	4%	22%	4%
Female	10%	5%	5%	4%	20%	5%

Capabilities

ACTIVE 4,063(Army 3,000 Coast Guard 1,063)

(All services form the Trinidad and Tobago Defence Force)

ORGANISATIONS BY SERVICE

Army ε3,000

FORCES BY ROLE

Inf 4 bn

SF 1 unit

Spt 1 bn

EQUIPMENT BY TYPE

MOR 6: **81mm** L16A1

AT

RCL 84mm ε24 *Carl Gustav*

RL 82mm 13 B-300

Coast Guard 1063

FORCES BY ROLE

Marine 1 HQ located at Staubles Bay

EQUIPMENT BY TYPE

PATROL AND COASTAL COMBATANTS 25

PCO 1 *Nelson* (UK *Island*)

PFC 2 *Barracuda* (SWE *Karlskrona* 40m) non-operational

PCI 11: 4 *Plymouth* less than 100 tonnes; 4 *Point* less than 100 tonnes; 2 *Wasp* less than 100 tonnes; 1 (Austal-30M) (additional 5 vessels on order)

MISC BOATS/CRAFT 11: 1 Aux Vessels; 10 boats

FACILITIES

Bases Located at Staubles Bay, Hart's Cut, Point Fortin, Tobago, Galeota

Air Wing 50

AIRCRAFT

TPT 5: 2 C-26 *Metro*; 1 Cessna 310; 2 PA-31 *Navajo*

ANTI-CRIME UNIT 4: 1 Sikorsky S-76 *Sprit*; 1 AS-355F *Ecureuil* 2; 1 Aeros-40B *SkyDragon*; 1 Westinghouse *Skyship* 600

National Helicopter Services Ltd 7: 4 Bo-105 (1 dedicated to support police); 3 S-76

Uruguay URY

Uruguayan Peso pU		2008	2009	2010
GDP	pU	674bn	722bn	
	US$	32.2bn	34.9bn	
per capita	US$	9,273	9,982	
Growth	%	8.9	0.6	
Inflation	%	7.9	7.5	
Def bdgt	pU	5.44bn	7.73bn	
	US$	260m	373m	
US$1=pU		20.9	20.7	

Population   3,494,382

Age	0–14	15–19	20–24	25–29	30–64	65 plus
Male	12%	4%	4%	4%	20%	5%
Female	11%	4%	4%	4%	21%	8%

Capabilities

ACTIVE 24,621 (Army 16,234 Navy 5,403 Air 2,984) **Paramilitary 920**

ORGANISATIONS BY SERVICE

Army 16,234

Uruguayan units are sub-standard size, mostly around 30%. Div are at most bde size, while bn are of reinforced coy strength. Regts are also coy size, some bn size, with the largest formation being the Armd Cav Regt '2 Regimento Tte. Gral Pablo Galarza de Caballeria Blindado No2' with 21 M-41A1UR and 16 M-113 A1. Each tank regt (sqn size) has only 7 TI-67, while 5 of the 6 Mech Cav Regts have only 6 M-64/-93 on strength.

FORCES BY ROLE

4 Military Regions/div HQ

Armd	2 (Nos 5, 8) cav bdo regt
Armd Inf	1 (No2) armd cav regt
Mech Inf	5 (Nos 4,6,7,10) cav mech regt ; 8 mech inf
Mot Inf	1 bn
Inf	5 Inf bn
Para	1 bn

SF	1 trg centre
Arty	1 Strategic Reserve regt; 5 Field Arty gp
Engr	1 (1st) bde (2 engr bn)
Cbt engr	4 bn
AD	1 gp

EQUIPMENT BY TYPE
MBT 15 TI-67
LT TK 38: 16 M-24 *Chaffee*; 22 M-41A1UR
RECCE 110: 15 EE-9 *Cascavel*; 48 GAZ-39371 *Vodnik*; 47 OT-93;
AIFV 18 BMP-1
APC 133:
 APC (T) 29: 24 M-113A1UR; 3 M-93 (MT-LB); 2 PTS
 APC (W) 94: 54 *Condor*; 40 MOWAG *Piranha*
ARTY 185
 SP 122mm 6 2S1 *Carnation*
 TOWED 44: **105mm** 36: 28 M-101A1; 8 M-102; **155mm** 8 M-114A1
 MOR 135: **81mm** 91: 35 M1, 56 LN; **120mm** 44 SL
AT
 MSL • MANPATS 15 *Milan*
 RCL 69: **106mm** 69 M-40A1
UAV • TACTICAL 1 *Charrua*
AD • GUNS • TOWED 14: **20mm** 14: 6 M-167 *Vulcan*; 8TCM-20 (w/ Elta M-2016 radar)

Navy 5,403 (incl 1,800 Prefectura Naval Coast Guard)

FORCES BY ROLE
Navy HQ located at Montevideo

EQUIPMENT BY TYPE
PRINCIPAL SURFACE COMBATANTS • FRIGATES
FFG 2:
 2 *Uruguay* (PRT *Joao Belo*) with 2 triple 550mm ASTT (6 eff.) each with L3 HWT, 2 single, 2 100mm gun
PATROL AND COASTAL COMBATANTS 25
 PCC 2 (FRA *Vigilante* 42m)
 PCI 3: 2 *Colonia* less than 100 tonnes (US *Cape*); 1 *Paysandu* less than 100 tonnes
 PBR 20: 4 *UPF-Class*; 16 *Vigilante 27'*
MINE WARFARE • MINE COUNTERMEASURES
MSC 3 *Temerario* (*Kondor* II)
AMPHIBIOUS 4: 2 LCVP; 2 LCM
LOGISTICS AND SUPPORT 7:
 ARS 1 *Vanguardia*
 AR 1 *Artigas* (GER, *Freiburg*, general spt ship) with HB-355 med hel
 AG 1 *Maldonado*
 AGHS 2: 1 *Helgoland*; 1 *Trieste*
 ABU 1 *Sirius*
 TRG • AXS 1

FACILITIES
Bases	Located at Montevideo (main base), Fray Bentos, Rio Negro (river)
Naval airbases	Located at La Paloma, Laguna del Sauce

Naval Aviation 211
FORCES BY ROLE
ASW	flt with 1 Beech 200T *Maritime Patrol**; 2 BAe *Jetstream* MK2
Utl / SAR	1 sqn with 1 *Wessex* MK60/HC2; 6 Bo-105 M; 1 *Esquilo* AS 350 B2
Trg/Liaison	flt with 2 T-34C *Turbo Mentor*

EQUIPMENT BY TYPE
AIRCRAFT 5 combat capable
 ASW / MP 3: 2 BAe *Jetstream* MK2; 1 Beech 200T *Maritime Patrol**
 TRG 2 T-34C *Turbo Mentor*
HELICOPTERS
 UTL 8: 1 *Wessex* HC2/MK60; 6 Bo-105 M; 1 *Esquilo* AS 350 B2

Naval Infantry 450
Marine 1 bn (under strength)

Coast Guard 1,800
Prefectura Naval (PNN) is part of the Navy
PATROL AND COASTAL COMBATANTS 14
 PCC 2
 MISC BOATS/CRAFT 12: 9 Type-44; 3 Type-PS

Air Force 2,984
Flying hours   120 hrs/year

FORCES BY ROLE
FGA	1 sqn with A-37B *Dragonfly*, 1 sqn with IA-58B *Pucará*
Tpt	1 sqn with C–130B *Hércules*; EMB–110C *Bandeirante*; EMB–120 *Brasilia*; CASA C-212 *Aviocar*
Liaison	sqn Cessna 206H; T– 41D; L–21 *Piper*
Survey	1 flt with EMB–110 *Bandeirante*
Trg	some sqn with PC- 7U *Turbo Trainer*; SF–260 EU; UB 58 *Baron*
Hel	1 sqn with AS–365 *Dauphin*; Bell 212; UH–1H *Iroquois*

EQUIPMENT BY TYPE
FGA 16: 11 A–37B *Dragonfly*; 5 IA–58 B *Pucará*
TPT 8: 2 C–130B *Hércules*; 3 CASA C–212 *Aviocar*; 2 EMB–110C *Bandeirante*; 1 EMB-120 *Brasilia*
SURVEY 1 EMB–110 *Bandeirante*
LIAISON 16: 4 T–41D; 11 Cessna 206H; 1 L–21 *Piper*
TRG 19: 5 PC-7U *Turbo Trainer*; 12 SF–260 EU; 2 UB-58 *Baron*
HELICOPTERS • UTL 11: 1 AS–365 *Dauphin*; 4 Bell 212; 6 UH–1H *Iroquois*

Paramilitary 920

Guardia de Coraceros 368 (under Interior Ministry)

Guardia de Granaderos 450

DEPLOYMENT

AFGHANISTAN
UN • UNAMA 1 obs

CÔTE D'IVOIRE
UN • UNOCI 2 obs

DEMOCRATIC REPUBLIC OF CONGO
UN • MONUC 1,324; 47 obs; 1 inf bn; 1 engr coy; 3 mne coy; 1 air spt unit

EGYPT
MFO 58; 1 engr/tpt unit

HAITI
UN • MINUSTAH 1,146; 2 inf bn; 1 avn unit

INDIA/PAKISTAN
UN • UNMOGIP 2 obs

NEPAL
UN • UNMIN 3 obs

WESTERN SAHARA
UN • MINURSO 3 obs

Venezuela VEN

Venezuelan Bolivar Bs		2008	2009	2010
GDP	Bs	696tr	759bn	
	US$	321bn	355bn	
per capita	US$	12,136	13,228	
Growth	%	4.8	-2.0	
Inflation	%	30.4	29.5	
Def exp	Bs	5.51bn	7.12bn	
	US$	3.32bn	3.2bn	
Def bdgt	Bs	7.12bn	8.97bn	
	US$	3.31bn	4.19bn	
US$1=Bs		2.14	2.14	

Population 26,814,843

Age	0–14	15–19	20–24	25–29	30–64	65 plus
Male	15%	5%	5%	5%	18%	2%
Female	14%	5%	5%	4%	19%	3%

Capabilities

ACTIVE 115,000 (Army 63,000 Navy 17,500 Air 11,500 National Guard 23,000)
Terms of service 30 months selective, varies by region for all services

RESERVE 8,000 (Army 8,000)

ORGANISATIONS BY SERVICE

Army ε63,000

FORCES BY ROLE
Armd   1 div (4th) (1 armd bde, 1 Lt armd bde, 1 mot cav bde, 1 AD bty)

Mot Cav   1 div (9th) (1 mot cav bde, 1 ranger bde, 1 sec and spt bde)

Inf   1 div (1st) (1 armd unit, 1 SF unit, 2 inf bde, 1 arty unit, 1 AAA bty, 1 spt unit); 1 div (2nd) (2 inf bde, 2 ranger bde (*each*: 2 ranger bn), 1 AD Bty, 1 special dev and security bde); 1 div (3rd) (1 inf bde, 1 ranger bde (2 ranger bn), 1 comms regt, 1 MP bde)

lt Inf   1 div (5th) (2 jungle inf bde each (3 jungle inf bn, 1 hy mor bty), 1 engr bn, 1 cav sqn)

AD   1 bty with 8 *Tor* M1 (18 more to be delivered)

AB   1 para bde

Cbt Engr   1 corps (3 regt)

Avn   1 comd (1 ac bn, 1 armd hel bn, 1 reccce bn)

Logistics 1 Log Comd (2 regt)

EQUIPMENT BY TYPE
MBT 81 AMX-30V
LT TK 109: 31AMX-13; 78 *Scorpion* 90
RECCE 431: 42 *Dragoon* 300 LFV2; 79 V-100/-150; 310 UR-53AR50 *Tiuna*
APC 91
   APC (T) 45: 25 AMX-VCI; 12 VCI-PC; 8 VACI-TB
   APC (W) 46: 36 *Dragoon* 300; 10 TPz-1 *Fuchs*
ARTY 370
   SP 155mm 12 (AMX) Mk F3
   TOWED 92: **105mm** 80: 40 M-101; 40 Model 56 pack howitzer; **155mm** 12 M-114
   MRL 160mm 20 LAR SP (LAR-160)
   MOR 246+: **81mm** 165; **120mm** 60 *Brandt*
    SP 21+: **81mm** 21 *Dragoon* 300PM; AMX-VTT
AT
   MSL • MANPATS 24 IMI MAPATS
   RCL 106mm 175 M-40A1
   RL 84mm AT-4
   GUNS 76mm 75 M-18 *Hellcat*
AD
   SAM 8 *Tor* M1
   MANPAD RBS-70; *Mistral*
   GUNS
    SP 40mm 6+ AMX-13 *Rafaga*
    TOWED 40mm M-1; L/70
AIRCRAFT
   TPT 17: 4 IAI-102/201/202 *Arava*; 1 Beech C90 *King Air*; 12 M28 *Skytruck*
   UTL 8: 2 Cessna 206; 2 Cessna 207 *Stationair*; 1 Cessna 172; 3 Cessna 182 *Skylane*
   TRG 1 C-90 *King Air*
HELICOPTERS
   ATK 10 Mi-35M2
   SPT 37: 18 Mi-17-1V; 2 AS-61D; 10 Bell 412EP; 2 Bell 412SP; 4 UH-1H in store; 1 Bell 205A-1 in store
   TPT 3 Mi-26T2
   UTL 4: 3 Bell 206B *Jet Ranger*, 1 Bell 206L-3 *Longranger II*
RADAR • LAND RASIT (veh, arty)
MSL • ASM AS-11 *Kilter*

Reserve Organisations

Reserves 8,000 reservists

Armd   1 bn
Inf   4 bn
Ranger 1 bn
Arty   1 bn
Engr   2 regt

Navy ε14,300; ε3,200 conscript (total 17,500)

Naval Commands: Fleet, Marines, Naval Aviation, Coast
Guard, Fluvial (River Forces)

FORCES BY ROLE

Navy 1 HQ (HQ *Arauca River*) located at El Amparo;
      1 HQ (HQ Fluvial Forces) located at Ciudad
      Bolivar; 1 HQ located at Caracas

EQUIPMENT BY TYPE

SUBMARINES • TACTICAL • SSK 2:
  2 *Sabalo* (GER T-209/1300) each with 8 single 533mm TT
  with 14 SST-4 HWT

PRINCIPAL SURFACE COMBATANTS • FRIGATES
  FFG 6 *Mariscal Sucre* (ITA mod *Lupo*) each with 8 single
  with Mk 2 Otomat SSM, 1 *Albatros* Octuple with 8 *Aspide*
  SAM, 2 triple ASTT (6 eff.) with A244 LWT, 1 127mm
  gun, 1 AB-212 (Bell 212) utl hels,

PATROL AND COASTAL COMBATANTS 8:
  PSOH 2 *Guaicamacuti* each with 1 76 mm gun, 1 AB-212
  hel (2 additional vessels in build); 1 *Guaicaipuro* each with
  1 76mm gun , 1 AB-212 hel (expected ISD 2010 additional
  3 vessels in build)
  PFM 3 *Federación* (UK Vosper 57m) each with 2 single
  each with Mk 2 Otomat SSM
  PCO 3 *Constitucion* (UK Vosper 37m) each with 1 76mm
  gun

AMPHIBIOUS 8
  LST 4 *Capana* (capacity 12 tanks; 200 troops) (FSU
  Alligator)
  CRAFT 4: 1 LCM-8; 2 *Margarita* **LCU** (river comd); 1 **LCVP**

LOGISTICS AND SUPPORT 6
  AORH 1
  AGOR 1 *Punta Brava*
  AGHS 2
  ATF 1
  TRG • AXS 1

FACILITIES

Bases   Located at Puerto Caballo (SS, FF, amph
              and service sqn), Caracas, Punto Fijo
              (patrol sqn)
Minor Bases   Located at Maracaibo (Coast Guard),
              Ciudad Bolivar, El Amparo, La Guaira
              (Coast Guard)
Naval airbases Located at Turiamo, Puerto Hierro,
              La Orchila

Naval Aviation 500

FORCES BY ROLE

ASW 1 sqn with 7 AB-212 (Bell 212)
MP   flt with 3 CASA 212-200 MPA

Spt   Sqn with 4 Bell 412EP *Twin Huey*; 6 Mi-17V-5
      Hip
Tpt   1 sqn with 1 Beech 200 *Super King Air*; 4 CASA 212
      Aviocar; 1 Rockwell *Turbo Commander* 980C
Trg   1 sqn with 2 Cessna 310Q; 2 Cessna 402;
      1 Cessna 210 *Centurion,* 1 Bell 206B *Jet Ranger II*; 1
      Bell TH-57A *Sea Ranger*

EQUIPMENT BY TYPE

AIRCRAFT 10 combat capable
  MP 3 CASA 212-200 MPA*
  TPT 11: 1 Beech 200 *Super King Air*; 1 Beech C90 *King
  Air;* 4 CASA 212 *Aviocar*; 2 Cessna 310Q; 2 Cessna 402;
  1 Rockwell *Turbo Commander* 980C
  UTL 1 Cessna 210 *Centurion*

HELICOPTERS
  ASW 7 AB-212 ASW (Bell 212)*
  UTL 11: 1 Bell 206B *Jet Ranger II* (trg)**;** 4 Bell 412EP *Twin
  Huey;* Bell TH-5 7A *Sea Ranger*; 6 Mi-17V-5 *Hip*

Marines ε7,000

FORCES BY ROLE

HQ   1 div HQ
Amph   1 (amph veh) bn
Inf   2 (river) bn; 6 bn
Arty   1 bn (1 AD bn, 3 fd arty bty)
Marine   1 (river) bde; 2 (landing) bde
Engr   1 BCT; 4 bn

EQUIPMENT BY TYPE

APC (W) 32 EE-11 *Urutu*
AAV 11 LVTP-7 (to be mod to -7A1)
ARTY • TOWED 105mm 18 M-56
  MOR 120mm 12 *Brandt*
AD • GUNS • SP 40mm 6 M-42
AD • SAM RBS-70
AT•AT-4 Skip
  RCL 84mm M3 *Carl Gustav*; **106mm** M-40A1

Coast Guard 1,000

EQUIPMENT BY TYPE

PRINCIPAL SURFACE COMBATANTS •
CORVETTES • FS 2:
  2 *Almirante Clemente* each with 2 triple ASTT (6 eff.), 2
  76mm gun

PATROL AND COASTAL COMBATANTS 43
  PCI 20: 12 *Gavion* less than 100 tonnes; 4 *Petrel* (USCG
  Point class); 2 *Manaure*; 2 *Guaicapuro*
  PCR 23: 3 *Terepaima* (*Cougar*); 7 *Polaris* I; 2 *Protector*; 6
  Courage; 5 *Interceptor*

LOGISTICS AND SUPPORT 2 *Los Tanques* (salvage
ship)

FACILITIES

Minor Base 1 (operates under Naval Comd and
            Control, but organisationally separate)
            located at La Guaira

Air Force 11,500

Flying hours   155 hrs/year

FORCES BY ROLE

Ftr/FGA	2 gp with Su-30MKV; 1 gp with CF-5; 2 gp with F-16A/B *Fighting Falcon*
COIN	1 gp with OV-10A/E *Bronco**; AT-27*
ECM	1 sqn with *Falcon* 20DC, C-26B
Tpt	3 gp and Presidential flt with A-319CJ, B-737; Gulfstream III/Gulfstream IV; *Learjet* 24D; B-707; C-130H *Hercules*; G-222; HS-748
Liaison	Beech 200 *Super King Air*; Beech 65 *Queen Air*; Beech 80 *Queen Air*; Ce-182/206/208; Shorts 360; Cessna 500 *Citation I*; CE-550 *Citation II*; Cessna 182 *Skylane*
Hel	sqns with AS-332B *Super Puma*; AS-532 *Cougar*, UH-1B/H/N: Bell 212/ 412
Trg	1 gp with 15 EMB-312 *Tucano**; 12 SF-260EV;
AD	1 bty Tor-M1 (3 bty planned); *Barak*

EQUIPMENT BY TYPE

AIRCRAFT 81 combat capable

FTR/FGA 55: 24 Su-30MKV; 7 VF-5, 3 NF-5B; 17 F-16A *Fighting Falcon*; 4 F-16B *Fighting Falcon*

LIFT: 18 K-8 being delivered 2010

COIN 8 OV-10A/E *Bronco**

EW 4: 2 *Falcon* 20DC; 2 C-26B,

TPT 53: 1 A-319CJ; 2 B-707; 1 B-737; 5 Beech 200 *Super King Air*; 2 Beech 65 *Queen Air*; 5 Beech 80 *Queen Air*; 6 C-130H *Hercules*; 10 Ce-182N *Skylane*; 6 Ce-206 *Stationair*; 4 Ce-208B *Caravan*; 1 Ce-500 *Citation I*; 3 CE-550 *Citation II*; 1 Cessna *551*; 1 G-222; 1 Learjet 24D; 2 Shorts 360 *Sherpa*; 1 SD-330 ; 1 *Falcon* 50 (VIP)

TRG 30: 18 EMB-312 *Tucano**; 12 SF-260E

HELICOPTERS

CSAR 2 AS-532 *Cougar*

TPT 26: 8 Mi-17VS; 2 Mi-172 (VIP); 6 AS-332B *Super Puma*; 10 AS-532 *Cougar* (incl 2 VIP)

UTL 14 3 UH-1B, 9 UH-1H, 2 Bell 412SP

AD

SAM 14+: 4 *Tor*-M1 (further 8 on order); 10+ *Barak*

  MANPAD 200 *Igla*-S; ADAMS; *Mistral*

GUNS

  TOWED 228+: **20mm**: 114 TCM-20; **35mm**; **40mm** 114 L/70

RADARS • LAND *Flycatcher*

MSL ASM AM-39 *Exocet*; KH-29T (AS-14 *Karen*); Kh-31 A/P (AS-17 *Krypton*); KH-59M (AS-18 *Kent*)

  AAM AIM-9L *Sidewinder*; AIM-9P *Sidewinder*; R73E (AA-11 *Archer*); R-77 (AA-12 *Adder*); *Python* 4; R530

National Guard (Fuerzas Armadas de Cooperacion) 23,000

(Internal sy, customs) 8 regional comd

APC (W) 44: 24 Fiat 6614; 20 UR-416

MOR 50 **81mm**

PATROL AND COASTAL COMBATANTS • MISC

BOATS/CRAFT 52 boats/craft

AIRCRAFT

TPT 13: 1 Beech 200C *Super King Air*; 1 Beech 55 *Baron*; 2 Beech 80 *Queen Air*; 1 Beech 90 *King Air*; 2 Cessna 185; 4 IAI-201 *Arava*; 2 Cessna 402C

UTL/TRG 22: 5 Cessna U-206 *Stationair*; 11 M-28 *Skytruck*; 3 Cessna 152 *Aerobat*; 1 PZL 106 *Kruk*; 2 PLZ M-26 *Isquierka*

HELICOPTERS • UTL 48+: 4 A-109; 1 AB-212 (Bell 212); 12 Bell 206B/L *Jet Ranger*; 6 Mi-17; 10 Bell 412; AS-350B; 9 AS-355F *Ecureuil*; 1 Enstrom F-28C; 5 F-280C

Table 12 **Selected arms procurements and deliveries, Latin America and the Caribbean**

Designation	Type	Quantity	Contract Value	Supplier Country	Prime Contractor	Order Date	First Delivery Due	Notes
Argentina (ARG)								
OPV 80	OPV	Up to 5	US$125m	Dom / GER	Astillero Rio Santiago	2009	2010	Based on Fassmer OPV 80 design. Patrulleros de Alta Mar (PAM) programme
Brazil (BRZ)								
Leopard 1A5	MBT	270	€8m	GER	_	2006	2008	Ex-GER. 220 tk, plus 20 for spares and 30 in trg or engr role. First delivered October 2009
Piranha IIIC	APC	18	_	CHE	Mowag	2008	2010	For marines. Ambulance, APC and CP versions
_	SSK	4	_	FRA	DCNS	2009	2015	To be built by Itaguaí Construções Navais (JV between DCNS and Odebrecht)
_	SSN	1	_	Dom	DCNS	2009		Contract covers work on the non-nuclear segments of the submarine
NAPA 500 (*Vigilante* 400 CL 54)	PCO	up to 27	_	FRA/ Dom	INACE/ CMN/ 2nd batch: EISA	2006	2009	Delivery in progress. Call for tender for 3rd batch due in early 2010
P-3A *Orion*	MPA Upgrade	8	US$401m	ESP	EADS CASA	2005	_	Upgrade to P-3AM. Option on a 9th ac. First ac upgraded by Apr 2009
EC725 *Super Cougar*	Tpt Hel	51	US$2bn	Dom	EADS Brazil	2008	2010	To be manufactured in BRZ by Helibras
KC-390	Tkr/tpt	22	US$3bn	Dom	Embraer	2009	_	To replace C-130. Each ac due to have capacity to carry up to 80-tps, total load of 90 tonnes. ISD due 2015
UH-60L *Black Hawk*	Hel	10	US$60.4m	US	Sikorsky	2009	2010	For Air Force SAR. Part of FMS programme
Mi-35M	Hel	12	US$150-300m	RUS	Rosboron-export	2008	2009	Contract value incl spares and trg. Delivery status unclear
Embraer 190	Tpt ac	2	_	Dom	Embraer	2008	2009	VIP config. To replace 2 B737-200 (VC-96). First ac delivered in Sept 2009
Chile (CHL)								
Satellite	Sat	1	US$72m	FRA/GER	EADS	2008	2010	Role incl border surv and military uses. Financed by military
Piloto Pardo	OPV	4	_	Dom/GER	ASMAR	_	2008	First in service
F-16	FGA	18	US$270m	NLD	_	2008	2010	Ex-NLD stock. To replace Northrop F-5E *Tiger* II (*Tigre* III)
C-295	MPA	3	US$120m	ESP	EADS CASA	2007	–	For navy. Cost incl ASM and torp. Option for a further 5 MPA
EMB-314 *Super Tucano*	Trg ac	12	US$120m	Dom	Embraer	2008	2009	First due to be delivered end-2009
Bell 412	Hel	12	_	US	Bell	2007	_	4 rotor blade version. Delivery status unclear
Colombia (COL)								
M117 *Guardian*	ACV	39	US$35m	US	Textron	2009	2009	Further requirement for 30 APC. Delivery status unclear
OPV 80	OPV	1	_	Dom	Cotecmar shipyard	2008	_	Based on Fassmer design
PAF-P	PCR	2	_	Dom	Cotecmar shipyard	_	2009	*Alexander Pérez* (ARC 614) and *Cristian Reyes Holguín* (ARC 615)
PAF-L	PCR	10	_	Dom	Cotecmar shipyard	_	2010	In development
Kfir C10	FGA	24	_	ISR	IAI	2008	2009	Ex ISR stock, upgraded from C7 to C10 by IAI. First delivery mid-2009

Table 12 **Selected arms procurements and deliveries, Latin America and the Caribbean**

Designation	Type	Quantity	Contract Value	Supplier Country	Prime Contractor	Order Date	First Delivery Due	Notes
EMB-314 *Super Tucano*	Trg/light atk ac	12	US$110m–130m	BRZ	Embraer	2008	–	Delivery status unclear
767-200ER	MRTT	1	US$50–65m	ISR	IAI	2008	2009	To be converted by IAI for VIP and tkr purposes
UH-1N	Hel	6	–	US	–	–	2009	Refurbished ex-US stock
Dominican Republic (DOM)								
EMB-314 *Super Tucano*	Light atk ac	8	US$94m	BRZ	Embraer	2008	2009	Incl trg, spares and log spt for five years
Ecuador (ECU)								
Leopard 1V	MBT	30	–	CHL	–	2009	2009	Ex-CHL stock. To replace 90 AMX-13
Shyri (Type 209/1300)	SSK SLEP	2	US$120m	CHL	ASMAR/DCNS	2008	2012	SLEP. To extend service life by 20 years
Super Tucano	FGA	24	–	BRZ	Embraer	2009		For air force. Deliveries ongoing
XAC MA-60	Tpt ac	4	US$60m	PRC	CATIC	2009	–	For air force. To replace BAE 748-SRS-2A
Dhruv multirole advanced light helicopter	Hel	7	US$50.7m	IND	HAL	2008	2009	For air force. Final delivery June 2009. One in VIP config
Heron, Searcher	UAV	6	US$23m	ISR	IAI	2008	2009	2 *Heron*, 4 *Searcher*, plus radar, control stations, spares and trg
Mexico (MEX)								
CN-235 *Persuader*	MPA	2	–	US	–	2008	–	In connection with the Mérida Initiative
CN-235 *Persuader*	MPA	2	–	–	EADS CASA	2008	2010	Option for 2 more
CN-235 *Persuader*	MPA	1	$60m	US	EADS North America	2009	–	
S4 *Ehecatl* (S4E)	UAV	3	US$3m	Dom	Hydra Technologies	2009	–	For navy. Primary anti-narcotics role & secondary SAR role.
EC725 *Super Cougar*	Spt hel	6	–	–	Eurocopter	2009		For tpt and civil sy missions
Peru (PER)								
Newport-class	LST	2	–	US	–	2009	–	Ex-US stock. USS *Fresno* (LST 1182) and USS *Racine* (LST 1191)
Clavero-Class	PCI	2	–	Dom	Sima	–	2008	First of class (CF-16) launched Jun 2008
UH-3H *Sea King*	Hel	6	US$6m	US	–	2009	–	Ex-US stock. Likely to be for SAR
Trinidad and Tobago (TTO)								
–	PSOH	3	GBP150m (US$296m)	UK	VT Group	2007	2010	Two 90m vessels (under construction). Second to be delivered in 2010
–	PFC	6	TTD390.8m (US$62.4m)	AUS/NZL	Austal	2008	2010	–
AW-139	Utl hel	4	US$348m	UK	Augusta Westland	2009	–	For Air Guard. Contract incl trg & log spt for five years
Uruguay (URY)								
Cougar 6x6	APC	40	US$3.7m	CAN	FAMAE	2007	2008	Ex-CAN stock (US$1.3m) . First batch of 4 delivered Dec 2008. Final delivery due mid-2009

Table 12 **Selected arms procurements and deliveries, Latin America and the Caribbean**

Designation	Type	Quantity	Contract Value	Supplier Country	Prime Contractor	Order Date	First Delivery Due	Notes
3-D *Lanza*	Radar	2	US$25m	ESP	Indra	2007	2008	3-year contract. One fixed, one portable. Final delivery due end-2008
IA 58 *Pucará*	FGA	3	_	COL	_	2008	_	Ex-COL stock. For spares
Venezuela (VEN)								
VENSAT-1 *Simón Bolívar*	Comms sat	1	US$406m	PRC	_	2003	2008	Launched Nov 2008. VEN due to take ctrl Jan 2009. Contract value incl cost of two ground-control stations
Tor-M1	AD	3 bty	Undisclosed	RUS	Rosoboron-export	2006	2007	First bty delivered Dec 2007. Delivery status of others unknown
BVL type	PBC	4	See notes	ESP	Navantia	2005	2008	€1.2bn (US$1.5bn) incl 4 FS. To replace 6 *Constitution*-class PCF. First vessel launched Oct 2008. Final delivery due 2011
POV	FS	4	See notes	ESP	Navantia	2005	2010	US$2.2bn incl 4 *Buque de Vigilancia de Litoral* coastal patrol ships. Final delivery due 2011
Project 636 (Imp *Kilo*)	SSK	1	_	RUS	_	2008	_	*Varshavyanka* (Original procurement plan of 3 SSK reduced for financial reasons)
JL-8 *Nanchang* (K-8 *Karokorum*)	Ftr/trg	24	est US$380	PRC	Hongdu	2008	2010	To be used primarily for counter-narcotics
Mi-17V5	Hel	14	See Notes	RUS	Rosoboron-export	2006	2008	Part of US$484m order with 2 Mi-35M and 2 Mi-26T (delivered). Reports suggest possible order of 20 further Mi-17-V5. Civil or military use is unclear
T-72 and T-90	MBT	up to 100	US$500m	RUS	_	2009	_	Delivery status unclear

Chapter Three
Europe

NATO

Towards a new strategic concept

NATO's 60th anniversary summit in Strasbourg, France, and Kehl, Germany, launched the process to develop the Alliance's new strategic concept, which is to be approved at a summit in 2010. At the 2009 summit, held on 3–4 April, NATO leaders adopted a 'Declaration on Alliance Security' drafted by outgoing Secretary-General Jaap de Hoop Scheffer, which served as the official tasking document. Mindful of member governments' insistence that the declaration should not pre-empt the new strategic concept itself, the document reassured members that Article V collective-defence commitments were not in competition with non-Article V missions and reaffirmed the need for unity of purpose and a willingness to share operational risks and responsibilities.

To assist the concept-development process, NATO appointed a group of 12 experts chaired by former US Secretary of State Madeleine Albright. Jeroen van der Veer, a former CEO of Royal Dutch Shell, was appointed vice-chair. While the group brings together experienced and qualified individuals, none of its members has direct military experience. The group began work on 4 September 2009 and is expected to consult widely on all aspects of the strategic concept, even though it is not clear what kind of product it will produce nor how any report could affect the deliberations of the allied heads of state and government.

The strategic concept has to codify decisions and practices established through a string of ministerial and summit communiqués since the last concept in 1999, while also fulfilling a public-diplomacy function in explaining the Alliance to electorates in NATO member states and audiences further afield. Most importantly, the strategic concept needs to provide direction for NATO by identifying threats to allied security and specifying how the Alliance should deal with them. As the concept-development process unfolds, it is clear that several fault-lines exist among allies. Some governments insist that a core purpose of the new strategy should be to forge a renewed consensus about NATO's fundamental role and mission, particularly in light of the Alliance's enlarge-ment, with the new strategic concept building on the 1999 version. Others take the view that the international environment has changed tremendously since 1999, and suggest that a more revolutionary approach is required.

The August 2008 war between Russia and Georgia sharpened debate about whether NATO was striking the right balance between collective defence and crisis-response operations, such as the mission in Afghanistan. How expeditionary should NATO be? The 2009 Summit Declaration asserted that NATO's Article V commitment remained its most important task and that the transformation agenda, which was largely designed to increase the usability of forces, would strengthen the ability of allies to conduct both territorial-defence and crisis-response operations outside allied territory. The debate underlined the need for greater clarity about NATO's core meaning and purpose in the contemporary security context. Admiral Giampaolo Di Paola, chairman of NATO's Military Committee, recently insisted that the strategic concept, while primarily a political document, had to give clear guidance on the meaning of NATO's collective-defence obligations in today's context, including on such issues as what would constitute 'armed aggression' against a member state. This is particularly important when one considers that piracy, terrorism, insurgency and cyber attacks play an increasing role in many threat assessments. In part, it will be the responsibility of the group of experts, working with new NATO Secretary-General Anders Fogh Rasmussen, who took over on 1 August 2009, to strike a balance acceptable to all NATO members.

The Strasbourg–Kehl Summit Declaration confirmed that further enlargement of NATO was seen as less urgent than before. Albania and Croatia were welcomed as new members but Macedonia could not be admitted due to an ongoing dispute with Greece about the country's name. Following the war in Georgia, leaders deferred the issue of membership for Georgia and Ukraine by confirming their readiness in principle to admit the two countries but stipulating that both would have to tackle a significant reform agenda first, and that doing so successfully would require political stability. Hence, NATO validated the view that any enlargement should be in the Alliance's interest and was not an end in itself. Bosnia-Herzegovina's application to join NATO's Membership Action Plan on 2 October 2009 highlighted the greater feasibility of further NATO enlargement in the western Balkans.

The 2008 war between Russia and Georgia was also a severe setback for NATO–Russia relations. In response to the conflict, NATO suspended normal cooperation through the NATO–Russia Council (NRC), and Moscow responded by freezing military exchanges. (In 2007, relations had suffered as a result of Russia's suspension of its participation in the Conventional Forces in Europe (CFE) Treaty. One lesson from the conflict was that cooperation between NATO and Russia – the NRC had, for instance, created a network of meetings and exchanges – had little influence on mutual perceptions and interests. East European allies depicted this as a strategic failure. Nonetheless, in light of the offer of the US administration of President Barack Obama to 'reset' US–Russian relations, NATO foreign ministers decided on 5 March 2009 to resume formal NRC meetings. A first meeting at ambassadorial level was held on 27 May, and the atmosphere was reported as constructive. Success in this effort will be determined by progress toward defining a pragmatic agenda for cooperation on such issues as Afghanistan, arms control, terrorism and narcotics trafficking. In this context, Rasmussen suggested that NATO and Russia conduct a joint review of contemporary security challenges so that a conception of common threats could be developed and deepened.

France formally reintegrated into NATO's military structure at the anniversary summit, reversing President Charles de Gaulle's 1966 withdrawal. President Nicolas Sarkozy's decision was based on the realisation that France could only wield influence commensurate with its budgetary, operational and political importance if it had a full seat at the table. Even before the decision was made, a slow process of de facto involvement of French officers in the integrated structures had begun during the 1990s, leading to some 250 French officers serving in various NATO commands by early 2009. Now France needs to fill some 1,250 posts. The two most visible appointments have been those of General Stéphane Abrial to head Allied Command Transformation and General Philippe Stoltz to head NATO's Joint Forces Command in Lisbon.

Practically speaking, the impact of France's decision will be moderate. It will have little effect, for example, on France's force structure or general defence posture, since all important decisions in this regard were set out in the 2008 White Paper (see *The Military Balance 2009*, p. 104). And France had long been a major contributor to NATO operations before it decided to fully reintegrate into the Alliance's command structure. But the move was welcomed, not least for its symbolic importance. France's awkward position in NATO had fostered suspicion that it would seek to weaken the Alliance; Sarkozy's decision removes a major political irritant.

EUROPEAN UNION

Sweden took over the EU presidency from the Czech Republic on 1 July 2009 and quickly defined an ambitious agenda for the security and defence portfolio. Harmonisation and transparency issues in the European defence market, more flexibility in the use of EU battlegroups, an interoperable civil–military maritime-surveillance capability for the EU maritime domain, and general civil–military capability development for the European Security and Defence Policy (ESDP) were all singled out as priorities.

EU battlegroups in particular have received much attention. Since 2005, the European Union has had rapid-response battlegroups on standby for operations under the EU flag and, from January 2007 onwards, two have been on call at all times. So far, however, no battlegroup has actually been deployed in an operation, even though EU member states have invested significantly to build their capabilities and in spite of calls for deployments in several instances, such as the 2008 Darfur crisis, which caused security problems in neighbouring Chad and Central African Republic. Stockholm has launched an initiative aimed at fostering conditions that would enable the EU to make use of the tool it has created by seeking greater flexibility in its application. The Swedish proposals have generated much interest among EU members, as well as concerns. Several members do not want to dilute the idea of rapid response as the *raison d'être* for battlegroups, even though they understand that too dogmatic an interpretation will inevitably block deployment. One possible solution is that states contributing to a specific battlegroup should be allowed to state their willingness to undertake certain types of operations beyond the core concept. This would delegate power to the governments involved

Table 13 **EU Battlegroups**

Year	Semester*	Lead nation	Contributing nations
2005	1	UK	UK
	1	France	France
	2	Italy	Italy
2006	1	Germany	France, Germany
	1	Spain	Greece, Italy, Portugal, Spain
	2	France	Belgium, France, Germany,
2007	1	Germany	Finland, Germany, Netherlands
	1	France	Belgium, France
	2	Italy	Hungary, Italy, Slovenia
	2	Greece	Bulgaria, Cyprus, Greece, Romania
2008	1	Sweden	Estonia, Finland, Ireland, Norway, Sweden
	1	Spain	France, Germany, Portugal, Spain
	2	Germany	Belgium, France, Germany, Luxembourg, Spain
	2	UK	UK
2009	1	Italy	Greece, Italy, Portugal, Spain
	1	Greece	Bulgaria, Cyprus, Greece, Romania
	2	Czech Republic	Czech Republic, Slovakia
	2	Belgium	Belgium, France, Luxembourg
2010	1	Poland	Germany, Latvia, Lithuania, Poland, Slovakia
	1	UK	Netherlands, UK
	2	Italy	Italy, Romania, Turkey
	2	Spain	France, Portugal, Spain
2011	1	Netherlands	Austria, Finland, Germany, Lithuania, Netherlands
	1	Sweden	Estonia, Finland, Ireland, Norway, Sweden
	2	Greece	Bulgaria, Cyprus, Greece, Romania
	2	Not yet determined	France, Italy, Portugal and Spain, or France alone
2012	1	Vacant	Vacant
	1	Vacant	Vacant
	2	Italy	Hungary, Italy, Slovenia
	2	Germany	Austria, Croatia, Czech Republic, Former Yugoslav Republic of Macedonia, Germany
2013	1	Poland	France, Germany, Poland
	1	Vacant	Vacant
	2	UK	Sweden, UK
	2	Belgium	Belgium (tbc)

*1 = January–June; 2 = July–December

and would enable them to surpass the lowest common denominator of involvement if desired.

Spain, due to take over the EU presidency for six months on 1 January 2010, indicated that it would attempt to make ESDP a priority as well, though with a different emphasis. Given that in 2010 the time-frames for both the EU's civilian and military head-line goals come to an end, it was expected that Spain might seek to lead discussion on follow-on planning. Furthermore, it was reported that Spain would try to establish a defence ministers' formation of the EU Council of Ministers. Hitherto, defence ministers have only met in informal meetings, with defence matters being addressed in the General Affairs and External Relations Council run by foreign ministers.

Domestic debates and operational demands
Afghanistan remained a thorny operational challenge for NATO in 2009, with security and stability in the country still lacking. Operations continued to be hampered by an inability to hold territory and by the absence of a truly common and comprehensive approach among allies and the international community at large (see Afghanistan, p. 343). Elusive success means that a number of problems are resurfacing which threaten to undermine NATO's political and

military cohesion. Questions about burden-sharing are increasing once more as the International Security Assistance Force (ISAF) becomes visibly Americanised. The increase in US troops during 2009 has found no European equivalent. As of 1 October 2009, ISAF had a total strength of over 67,000, including around 32,000 American troops, a number that was set to rise even higher. Persistent caveats, interoperability problems and capability shortfalls suggested that not all allies were willing or able to make the same kind of contribution in qualitative terms. Rasmussen repeated an oft-heard mantra when he said in October that 'the Alliance is about sharing security, but that doesn't just mean sharing the benefits. It also means sharing the costs and the risks.'

A general problem for NATO is that the absence of clearly identifiable progress in Afghanistan, and rising casualty figures among allied forces, have begun to undermine the domestic sustainability of the deployment. For example, the Dutch parliament voted in early October 2009 that the country's military commitment should end in 2010. While this decision is not binding for the Dutch government, it is difficult to see how it could be ignored.

Even countries like the **United Kingdom**, where overseas deployments have traditionally been relatively uncontroversial, were not spared an intensifying, and some might say 'overdue', defence debate. By early 2010, the UK may have increased its deployment to Helmand province to some 9,500 troops. An increase of 700, first announced as temporary because of the Afghan elections in August 2009, was later made permanent, and plans for a further boost of 500 were mooted in autumn 2009, though certain conditions were laid down for this deployment. Furthermore, a battlegroup previously based in Kabul was due to be committed to Helmand. The issues of troop deployments and equipment remained high on the political agenda throughout the year. As the UK moved into an election year, debate over the country's overall defence priorities grew, especially as the strain on government finances grew more apparent. Some questioned whether the UK would have to downscale its global ambitions in light of the available resources for defence. While there was cross-party consensus that security challenges and risks to the UK would not diminish in the foreseeable future, no major political party foresaw a budget increase for defence, and all hinted at necessary, though unspecified, cuts. British ambitions and capabilities have reached a point of

divergence, and whichever party wins the election, the government is likely to commission a defence review in which the overall level of ambition is reassessed and substantive decisions taken regarding procurement programmes and processes. As of late 2009, the process was under way for the generation of a Green Paper that will inform a later defence review. Given that the last paper was produced in 1998, some have also argued that this review process should be placed on a more regular footing, with Bernard Gray's report arguing that reviews should take place 'in the first session of a new parliament' (see Defence Economics, p. 109).

General elections on 27 September 2009 in **Germany** saw the formation of a centre-right governing coalition led by incumbent Chancellor Angela Merkel. With the Social Democrats (SPD) losing support to a degree unprecedented in post-war Germany, Merkel was able to end the grand-coalition arrangement and join forces with her preferred partner, the Free Democrats (FDP), under the leadership of Guido Westerwelle. The change of government is unlikely to have a major impact on Germany's operational commitments, and the extension of the country's Afghanistan mandate in December 2009 was expected to be approved with a significant majority in parliament. However, the structural underfunding of the German defence budget and the lack of financial room for manoeuvre made it likely that the new government would conduct a review of the armed forces' structure in 2010 to align it with resources and procurement priorities.

A significant increase in piracy off the Horn of Africa prompted increasing involvement of European navies in an effort to combat this phenomenon through both the EU and NATO. In March 2009 NATO launched *Operation Allied Protector*, a maritime mission to counter piracy and armed robbery off the Horn of Africa, involving vessels from NATO's Standing Maritime Group 1, which in turn was replaced by *Operation Ocean Shield* in August 2009.

The EU began its anti-piracy activities on 19 September 2008 when it set up a military coordination cell, EUNAVCO, in the secretariat of the EU Council to organise a response to incidents of piracy and to protect maritime trade. EUNAVCO was to mobilise EU member states and organise escort slots. Its duties were taken over by *Operation Atalanta*, the first EU naval operation, which was launched in December 2008. In June 2009 the EU Council extended *Atalanta*'s mandate by another year to December 2010. Personnel in *Atalanta* can arrest, detain and transfer individuals who are suspected of involvement in acts of piracy or armed robbery at sea. They can further seize the vessels and goods involved. Since March 2009, the EU has been cooperating with Kenya, which prosecutes detained individuals on the basis of a bilateral agreement. While EU member states can also prosecute suspected pirates, the precise legal situation varies between member states. This has an impact on national approaches. The Spanish defence minister, for instance, has actively encouraged Spanish vessels to use private security contractors given the limited operational and legal capacity of the Spanish armed forces to address piracy beyond their contribution to multinational efforts. Overall, the EU's naval mission was relatively successful in tackling legal questions of arrest and prosecution of suspects, and demonstrated the widening range of the Union's – albeit still modest – capacity to mobilise capabilities for challenging missions.

Meanwhile, the EU completed its mission in Chad and the Central African Republic (EUFOR TCHAD/RCA) and handed over responsibility to MINURCAT, the UN mission, in March 2009. EUFOR had carried out some 3,000 short-range and 440 long-range patrols. EU leaders estimated that an improved security situation had enabled some 10,000 displaced persons to return to their villages. Furthermore, cooperation with the UN appeared to have matured compared with earlier such attempts in the Democratic Republic of the Congo. EUFOR helped strengthen MINURCAT by providing escorts for convoys and securing sites. In contrast to previous practice, under which contingents from EU member states left the theatre after EU operational duties were completed, a significant number of troops transitioned into the UN force to provide continuity and improve capability.

The EU's civilian monitoring mission to Georgia, EUMM Georgia, launched in October 2008, was extended by the EU Council in July 2009 by one year to September 2010. Its task was to monitor implementation of the ceasefire agreement between Georgia and Russia, particularly the withdrawal of Russian forces to the positions held prior to the outbreak of hostilities. EUMM Georgia also monitored the deployment of Georgian police and observed whether all parties were complying with human-rights obligations. At the time of writing, EUMM Georgia had still not gained access to Abkhazia and South Ossetia, limiting its impact. In Kosovo, the delayed civilian EU rule-of-law mission, EULEX, finally reached full opera-

tional capability on 6 April 2009. By July 2009, EULEX consisted of some 1,710 international staff plus 925 local staff. Mandated until 14 June 2010, its main objectives were to assist and support the authorities in Kosovo, which declared independence from Serbia in February 2008, in the areas of police, judiciary and customs. Meanwhile, NATO continued its KFOR military mission in Kosovo. The EU also began preparatory work for a possible transition of the 2,000-strong *Operation Althea* in Bosnia into a capacity-building and training mission. However, EU leaders said such a move would depend on political circumstances on the ground. While initial planning steps for such a transition have been taken, several member states, including the United Kingdom, have cautioned that the situation in Bosnia remains fragile.

Capability gaps

On 11 December 2008, the EU Council adopted a 'Declaration on Strengthening Capabilities' which reflected the desire of the then-French EU presidency to reinvigorate this topic. Despite ESDP reaching its tenth anniversary in 2009, the core capability shortfalls identified in 1999–2000 in strategic and tactical lift, intelligence and reconnaissance, and force protection in large part remained. The declaration was noteworthy in that it set out in relatively clear terms the EU's level of ambition for civilian and military crisis-management missions: the EU, in implementing the military and civilian Headline Goal 2010 obligations, should be able to simultaneously conduct two major stabilisation and reconstruction operations involving up to 10,000 troops plus a civilian contingent for at least two years; two rapid-response operations using EU battlegroups; an evacuation operation lasting fewer than ten days; a maritime- or air-surveillance/interdiction operation; a civil–military humanitarian-assistance operation lasting up to 90 days; and around one dozen civilian missions, including one major operation involving up to 3,000 personnel for several years. Notably absent from this list of scenarios is an operation dealing with the separation of parties by force. Even though such an operation falls within the EU's ambitions, persistent capability shortfalls seem to have precluded its inclusion.

The declaration prioritised improvements in civilian capabilities, given expectations for increasing demand in this field. On the military side, the declaration asked member states to embrace innovative methods for capabilities development, including the pooling and multinational management of assets;

Table 14 **Innovative Methods for Capability Development**

Method	Possible Definition	Example
Sharing of capabilities	Joint use of national capabilities without a specific mechanism for use	European Carrier Group Initiative (ECGI; declaration of intent signed 10 November 2008)
Pooling of capabilities	Delegation of nationally owned resources to a multinational structure for use	Movement Coordination Centre Europe (MCC-E), Eindhoven
Role and task sharing	States rely on other states or a multinational structure for certain capabilities. Options include the sharing of niche capabilities, such as CBRN or medical aircraft, or the sharing of rare and costly capabilities, such as satellite-based reconnaissance	European Air Transport Fleet (EATF; declaration of intent signed 10 November 2008)
Pooling through acquisition of enabling capabilities	Capabilities funded by national governments but held and operated by multinational structures	Airborne Warning and Control System (AWACS); Strategic Airlift Capability (SAC)

role specialisation for rare and costly niche capabilities; and the collective procurement of critical capabilities. Pursuing such a course is increasingly understood to be one of the few remaining options for significantly improving available capabilities. The need for such innovative collaboration will have to be balanced with governments' desire to maintain national security and defence priorities, since such methods invariably increase mutual interdependence among participating countries.

It is notable that 2008 saw a flurry of capability-related initiatives driven by groups of EU member states rather than the Union as a whole. On 10 November 2008, a declaration of intent to establish a European Air Transport Fleet (EATF) was signed by 12 EU member states (Belgium, Czech Republic, France, Germany, Greece, Italy, Luxembourg, the Netherlands, Portugal, Romania, Slovakia and Spain). The goal was the pooling of services and aircraft such as the C-130 *Hercules* and the planned A-400M airlifter. From 2014 to 2017, member states were to make aircraft available; purchase, provide and exchange flying hours; and pool support functions, all with the aim of increasing availability, generating economies of scale, and making more effective use of assets. Belgium, France, Germany and Luxembourg later signed a separate declaration of intent to set up a multinational unit for the A-400M, though the Airbus-managed project to build the aircraft encountered further delays. On the same day, Belgium, France, Germany, Greece, Italy, the Netherlands, Portugal, Spain and the UK signed a declaration of intent to enable the generation of a combined European maritime-strike capability. Called the European Carrier Group Interoperability Initiative, the declaration aimed to increase interoperability among European navies and associated air groups so that participating countries would find it easier to

contribute assets into a composite carrier strike group in support of EU and NATO commitments.

A separate airlift effort was also under way within NATO. Ten members (Bulgaria, Estonia, Hungary, Lithuania, the Netherlands, Norway, Poland, Romania, Slovenia and the United States), as well as Finland and Sweden, signed a Strategic Airlift Capability (SAC) agreement on 1 October 2008. This activated the NATO Airlift Management Organisation, which has acquired three C-17s that are flown and maintained by international crews. The aircraft were delivered between July and October 2009, are based in Hungary and can be employed on NATO, EU and UN operations. The SAC Heavy Airlift Wing began flying operational missions in late summer 2009, delivering materiel to troops in both Kosovo and Afghanistan (see Table 19 NATO/EU Transport and Air Refuelling Capability, p. 210).

Tactical-helicopter transport capability has consistently ranked as one of the most pressing force-generation problems for NATO and the EU. According to European Defence Agency (EDA) figures, only 6–7% of helicopters in the inventories of European armed forces were deployed on crisis-management operations. Thus, the problem was one of availability. Both aircraft and crews were often unable to fly in demanding operational environments such as deserts and mountainous areas. The EDA was to focus on the problem with a three-pronged initiative. For crews, the short-term ambition was to establish a Helicopter Tactics Training Programme to be launched in 2010. In the medium term, the agency aimed to focus on upgrade programmes for helicopters, particularly the Mi- range of Soviet-era models in the inventories of most Central and East European forces. For the long term, the EDA sought to lead the development of a Future Transport Helicopter able to lift up to 13 tonnes with a range of 1,000km.

NATO EUROPE – DEFENCE ECONOMICS

Economic activity in much of developed Europe had already begun to contract before the catastrophic September 2008 financial blowout, and despite initial perceptions that relatively healthy household balance sheets would enable European economies to escape a full-blown recession it was not long before the consequences of the shock to the world's financial systems led to a severe downturn. Regional GDP, which grew by an anaemic 0.5% in 2008, contracted by a massive 4.8% in 2009 as consumer and business confidence plunged. Countries particularly badly hit included Iceland (which had to seek IMF support following the total collapse of its overextended financial sector), Spain and the United Kingdom, which suffered the combined effects of the end of twin bubbles in real estate and financial-services.

Initially it had seemed that problems in Europe would be limited to a few banks, and therefore the macroeconomic implications were not considered great. As such, immediate fiscal- and monetary-policy responses were limited. Once it became clear, however, that the close links between Europe's major financial institutions, together with their high leverage, were having a severe impact on regional economic activity, remedial policies were introduced. The European Economic Recovery Plan called for discretionary fiscal measures to be taken mostly at the national level to provide a stimulus of 1.5% of EU GDP. A number of countries, including Germany, Spain and the UK, introduced even larger discretionary rescue packages. As a result of these initiatives, public finances have deteriorated sharply, with the OECD calculating that combined EU budget deficits in 2009 would reach 5.6% of GDP, rising to 7% of GDP in 2010, compared with a deficit limit of 3% of GDP that is a cornerstone of the Stability and Growth Pact governing membership of the single European currency.

In its October 2009 World Economic Outlook report, the IMF suggested that during the second half of the year the pace of decline in economic activity in Europe was moderating due to rising exports, a turn in the inventory cycle and continued support from stimulus programmes, and that the region had emerged from recession. While noting that upside potential had appeared in several economies, it warned that the recovery could be more sluggish than expected if conditions in the financial and corporate sectors were to worsen or unemploy-

ment were to rise faster than anticipated. The report also stressed the importance of a suitable fiscal exit strategy: withdrawal of support too early could forestall a fledgling recovery, whereas leaving policy loose for too long could usher in a rise in inflation as output gaps diminished.

The parlous condition of government spending across Europe quickly had a negative impact on defence spending, and that trend looks set to continue, at least over the medium term. Of the 24 European members of NATO for which 2010 budgets were available, only Norway and Denmark proposed higher real terms budgets compared to the previous year. The biggest cuts were in the Czech Republic (down 12%) and Romania (down 17.4%). The fact that most countries held spending at broadly the same nominal level in 2010 is probably misleading as many will likely be forced to trim discretionary spending over the coming years in order to deal with deficits.

As the worst-hit of the advanced European economies the **United Kingdom** will have a particularly difficult task reconciling its defence ambitions with available financial resources. The recession in the UK has been particularly severe because of the country's large financial sector, high household indebtedness and strong cross-border links. Economic growth has turned sharply negative; house prices have fallen by more than 20% from their peak; and unemployment has increased as banks have concentrated on reducing leverage, causing credit availability to fall dramatically. The government reacted to the crisis with a wide range of measures to both stabilise the financial system and support demand, but as a consequence will run up fiscal deficits of around 13% of GDP in 2009 and 2010. National debt is set to double over the next five years to nearly 100% of GDP.

Even before the implications of the financial crisis on the UK's public finances became clear, tensions between military activity and the defence budget were apparent. The cost of running two overseas operations in Iraq and Afghanistan, coupled with a comprehensive equipment plan that suffers from repeated delays and cost overruns, was putting increasing strain on a budget that was rising by only a point or two above inflation each year. In March 2008, the House of Commons Defence Committee acknowledged the situation, warning that the Ministry of Defence (MoD) would need to take 'difficult decisions' in order to compile a realistic and affordable equipment programme, and that this would mean 'cutting whole equipment programmes, rather than just delaying orders or making cuts in the number of platforms ordered'. That summer, it was announced that the ministry had abandoned plans to increase the fleet of Type-45 air-defence ships from six to eight, despite the navy's insistence that a fleet of eight ships would be essential for undertaking simultaneous carrier-task-group and amphibious-task-group operations. According to Defence Secretary Bob Ainsworth, the cancellation was the result of a lack of financing: he admitted that the ministry did 'not have unlimited resources'. Soon after, it was also announced that the navy's flagship aircraft-carrier programme and Military Afloat Reach and Sustainability replacement programme would be delayed; the *Future Lynx* helicopter programme would be cut from 70 to 62 aircraft; the *Nimrod* maritime-surveillance aircraft programme would be cut to nine from 12 (compared with 21 originally); the *Soothsayer* programme would be axed; and the army would terminate the utility variant of the Future Rapid Effects System (FRES) programme. In commenting on the decision to cancel this element of FRES, the Defence Committee labelled the programme a fiasco that had wasted ministry and industry 'time and money', noting that around £130m (US$210m) had so far been invested in the vehicle.

The MoD's equipment-management problems were further exposed by the National Audit Office (NAO) in their Major Projects Report published in December 2008. The report suggested that a lack of realism in project planning had helped cause cost overruns of £205m (US$331m) and delays of 96 months in 20 of the armed forces' largest programmes during 2008. It went on to calculate that the total forecasted cost of the 20 projects had risen to £28bn (US$45bn), an increase of £3bn (US$4.8bn) over the budgeted costs when the main investment decisions were taken. In commenting on these findings, the NAO reiterated previous criticisms that acquisition planning was often driven by the available budget, encouraging defence companies to submit bids that would never actually be realised, and accused the MoD of failing to recognise the complexities and key inter-dependencies in several of its major programmes.

Criticism of the ministry's way of procuring military equipment came to a head in October 2009 with the publication of Bernard Gray's independent review of the acquisition process. In a sharply worded analysis, the review attacked civil servants, senior members of the armed forces, politicians and industry executives for failing to manage a range of procurement projects or recognise the spending constraints faced by the UK. The study supported comments made by the NAO, revealing that on average defence programmes are five years late into service and cost an extra £300m (US$484m), effectively cutting £900m–2.2bn (US$1.5bn–3.5bn) from the annual MoD budget. Gray concluded that the current equipment programme 'is unaffordable on any likely projection of future budgets'. In particular, he highlighted a 'toxic set of incentives' in the procurement process that had led to the habitual

Table 15 **NATO Ex-US Defence Expenditure** as % of GDP

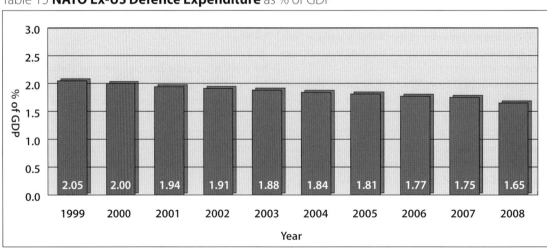

Year	1999	2000	2001	2002	2003	2004	2005	2006	2007	2008
% of GDP	2.05	2.00	1.94	1.91	1.88	1.84	1.81	1.77	1.75	1.65

underestimation of programme costs and a preference for delaying rather than cancelling individual projects, resulting in vast cost overruns. According to Gray, this approach had caused a massive procurement 'bow wave' that was permanently situated beyond the ten-year financial-planning horizon used by the department, creating an illusion about the size and scope of Britain's armed forces but ignoring the 'cold fact' that the appropriate budget to fulfil these ambitions did not exist. To remedy the situation, the report made the case that a fresh Strategic Defence Review should automatically occur in the first session of any new parliament, and suggested that UK Defence Equipment and Support (DE&S, the procurement arm of the defence ministry) should, at the very least, begin to operate as either a commercial trading fund or, more ambitiously, be slimmed down into a government-owned, contractor-operated (Go–Co) entity that would be able to take full advantage of private-sector management expertise together with enterprise-wide management information and financial-control tools. Commenting on the report, Lord Drayson, minister for strategic defence acquisition reform, commended Gray for coming up with a 'strong package of measures' and said that his department would accept most of the recommendations. The notion that DE&S would become 'Go–Co', however, was quickly scotched by Defence Secretary Ainsworth, who said that 'having the DE&S as fully part of defence ensures a close working relationship with the military'.

In addition to the financial difficulties associated with the UK's defence-equipment programmes, the impact of overseas operations on the core defence budget has become a growing problem. When combat operations in Iraq and Afghanistan began, government ministers stressed that all war costs would be fully funded by Treasury reserves. With the missions now entering their ninth year, however, and costs to date exceeding £15bn (US$24bn), the Treasury has changed its attitude towards the purchase of Urgent Operational Requirements (UORs), the process by which the vast majority of equipment used in Iraq and Afghanistan is acquired, with the result that the core budget is now part-funding UOR procurement. In 2007, it was decided that the MoD would bear half the cost of any spending on UORs that exceeded pre-agreed limits, though this was later changed to cover all additional spending. In November 2008, another measure was introduced that further complicated the acquisition process: under the new initiative, the

Treasury will decide whether an acquisition should be classified as a 'true UOR' – that is, specific to unique threats in Iraq and Afghanistan – or whether the equipment would enhance the armed services' core capabilities over the long term, in which case the ministry will be required to pay for it entirely from its own budget. Of the £700m (US$1.1bn) package of new armoured vehicles destined for Afghanistan announced in late 2008, for example, the Treasury has determined that £120m (US$194m) represents a boost to core capabilities and is thus payable from the central defence budget.

In July 2009, the government conceded that with so many new factors now influencing the defence debate, the 1998 Strategic Defence Review (SDR) was largely out of date and would be replaced by a new SDR to be published in 2010, after the next general election. Senior defence figures have since argued that the new review should be driven by policy, not finances, but the reality is that the financial background against which it will be conducted will be crucial. It has been calculated, for example, that if defence spending falls in line with the government's general reduction in outlays the defence budget could fall by 11% in real terms by 2016; however, if health and education, hitherto the Labour government's favoured areas of expenditure, receive a reprieve from this fate and see their budgets frozen at current levels, other government departments could face cuts of up to 14%. Either way, the likelihood of anything other than a cut in defence funding seems highly improbable, and the SDR will have to reflect this. What this will mean for future pay, procurement and operational spending is not clear, other than that SDR planners will be paying attention to where savings could be made. In terms of procurement, the scope for savings on major procurement projects may be relatively limited, given an overhang of outstanding contractual commitments amounting to some £18bn (US$29bn), the cancellation of which would incur steep financial penalties. Moreover, with the British commitment to Afghanistan remaining a government priority, it is difficult to see where particularly significant savings in operational outlays could be realised. The possibility of saving significant sums in personnel costs is complicated by the fact that the remuneration of the armed forces is based on recommendations from the Armed Forces Pay Review Body and therefore out of the government's direct control. As noted by Defence Secretary Ainsworth in commenting on the forthcoming SDR, 'we cannot exclude major shifts in the way we use our defence spending to refocus our priorities … There will be tough choices ahead.'

Following the publication of its 2008 defence White Paper, in 2009 the **French** government laid out a more detailed funding schedule in its new six-year military budget plan covering the period 2009–14. The White Paper, which was published before the full impact of the global recession had become clear, included a commitment to provide a total of €377bn (US$563bn) for the military between 2009 and 2020, stipulating that the defence budget would be frozen at current levels in real terms until 2012, after which it would increase by 1% above inflation each year until 2020. The document laid out plans to cut 54,000 military personnel and channel these savings into procurement accounts, particularly in such areas as space and intelligence, at the expense of more traditional platforms such as warships and aircraft. Because of these new spending priorities, the Ministry of Defence is having to negotiate stretch-outs and cuts in the delivery of big-ticket items, including new FREMM multi-mission frigates, *Rafale* fighter aircraft and *Tiger* combat helicopters. The White Paper included a reduction in the number of FREMM frigates from 17 to 11, and the delivery schedule was stretched from one vessel every eight months to one every 12–14 months. At the time the White Paper was published Defence Minister Hervé Morin had warned that the 2009–14 six-year plan would include a range of equipment cuts and delays, saying that total investment would need to increase by over 40% in order to pay for all the planned programmes. He warned that such an outcome is 'impossible … priorities will need to be defined and choices made'.

Before announcing the new 2009–14 budget plan, the government was forced to address the growing recession and implemented a €26bn (US$39bn) economic stimulus package, including a €1.4bn (US$2.1bn) allocation to defence, which included funds for research programmes. The government also withdrew over 2,000 troops from Côte d'Ivoire and Chad in an effort to reduce the military's annual overseas deployment outlays of around €1bn (US$1.5bn). When it was finally published in July 2009, the six-year Loi de Programmation Militaire (LPM) included a number of changes, both quantitative and qualitative, to the plans originally laid out in the 2008 White Paper. In particular, the White Paper had called for an annual target of €18bn (US$27bn) to be spent on equipment for a six-year total of €108bn (US$161bn); however, the LPM included only €102bn (US$152bn) for equipment, a reduction of €1bn (US$1.5bn) a year during the course of the programme. This suggests that if the government is to keep its long-term ambitions on target the money lost in this cycle will need to be added to the next LPM covering 2015–20. In recognition of the increased wear and tear on equipment deployed in Afghanistan, there is provision for an additional €1.5bn (US$2.2bn), making a total of €3bn (US$4.5bn), to be spent specifically on maintenance of operational equipment, though whether this amount, when spread out over six years, will be sufficient is questionable. It is intended that the air force should consist of 300 fighter aircraft, though the LPM only projects a total of 195 by 2020 (118 *Rafales* and 77 *Mirage* 2000Ds).

In October 2009, the government revealed the growing pressure on its finances when it published the defence budget for 2010. Having indicated in both the White Paper and LPM that the budget would increase by the rate of inflation each year until 2012, 2010 funding was essentially unchanged at €32.1bn (US$47.9bn). In defending the budget, Defence Minister Morin pointed out that equipment spending would amount to €17bn (US$25bn) in 2010, in line with LPM forecasts, and that he was expecting a second tranche of €700m (US$1.04bn) from the government's stimulus programme to be added to the budget during the year. Among equipment set for delivery in 2010 was France's fourth *Le Triomphant*-class nuclear-powered, ballistic-missile submarine, equipped with the country's new 9,000km-range M-51 nuclear missile, 11 *Rafale* combat aircraft and seven *Tiger* attack helicopters.

Germany also responded to the global recession with a significant stimulus package that, like France's, allocated funds to the defence sector. Out of the country's €50bn (US$74bn) economic package, the Ministry of Defence was provided with €500m (US$746m) to accelerate a number of procurement plans that would specifically benefit lower- and mid-level companies in the supply chain. Half the money was directed towards new and additional capabilities for current and future operations (*Dingo* 2 vehicles, mortar combat systems, mine-hunting drones and night-vision equipment for the *Tornado* fleet), while the other half was earmarked for improving the armed forces' barracks and infrastructure.

It is not yet clear what priority the new government will give to defence funding. The previous four-year

Grand Coalition government incrementally raised defence spending from €27.9bn (US$41.6bn) in 2006 to €31.2bn (US$46.6bn) in 2009 following several years when the budget had been left unchanged. Given that the Bundeswehr is in the midst of a transformation from a territorial-defensive force to an international-intervention force, it seems unlikely that the budget will fall below €30bn (US$44.8bn), a level that appears to have become politically symbolic. Indeed, figures published at the same time as the 2010 defence budget show that the outgoing government intended to hold spending constant in coming years, averaging €31bn (US$46.3bn) per year to 2013, with procurement outlays fixed at around €5.5bn (US$8.2bn) per year.

The 2010 defence budget of €31.14bn (US$46.5bn) was virtually unchanged from the previous year, although with personnel costs increasing by around €1bn (US$1.5bn) a year and funds for overseas operations also on the increase it would seem that a static budget over the medium term would have a negative impact on some procurement programmes. The *Bundeswehrplan 2009* (the Ministry of Defence's medium-term investment plan) indicated that the next phase of equipment priorities for the German armed forces would be strategic transport, theatre and global reconnaissance, command and control systems and strategic air defence. However, even at the time of publication it was acknowledged that there would be insufficient funds to fulfil all the proposed programmes and that legacy systems currently in service would have to undergo life-extension upgrades that, in the long run, would increase outlays on essential maintenance, further straining the investment budget.

Despite the fact that procurement spending in 2009 reached €5.27bn (US$7.87bn), higher than originally budgeted, there were varying degrees of progress made on the Defence Ministry's major equipment programmes. Following months of negotiations, the four-nation Eurofighter partnership finally signed a contract to begin production of the Tranche 3 model. With talks having stalled over financing the contract, the German government had written to its Spanish, Italian and UK counterparts suggesting that the Tranche 3 procurement be split into A and B phases to aid funding. This proposal was accepted by the manufacturing partnership and in June 2009 Germany signed up for the purchase of 31 Tranche 3A models, bringing its total fleet of *Typhoon* aircraft to 143. However, with the defence budget likely to

shrink in real terms over the next few years, the fate of Germany's remaining 37 Tranche 3B units appears uncertain, as does the procurement of the A400M and MALE unmanned aerial vehicles, two other major air-force programmes that will come under scrutiny in a structural review of the Bundeswehr likely to be completed next year following the appointment of a new chief of defence staff and three new chiefs of staff of the major services. Important programmes that did get the go-ahead in 2009 include a €3.1bn (US$4.6bn) order for 405 *Puma* armoured infantry fighting vehicles (to be delivered between 2010 and 2020 to replace the ageing *Marder* 1 vehicles), the new Mortar Combat System (replacing the 40-year-old 120mm towed mortar system) and a replacement for the *Pinguin* unmanned underwater vehicle.

Following a series of setbacks, the tri-nation Medium Air Defence System (MEADS) alliance between Germany, Italy and the US appeared to receive a boost in 2009 with the successful completion of its subsystem-design reviews, paving the way for potential production of the system's major components, although the eventual fielding of a completed system is still far from certain. In 2005, the Bundestag approved the acquisition of 17 MEADS systems to replace Germany's HAWK air-defence systems, and allocated €800m (US$1.2bn) to the project. However, in 2008 it appeared as if funding problems might derail the project when the German defence secretary warned parliament that the defence industry had underestimated the technological complexity and financial expenditure necessary to successfully complete the system. As a result, the NATO MEADS Management Agency and US Department of Defense implemented a review of cost estimates for the project and warned of an 18-month delay. A year later it was reported that the US was considering sweeping changes to the programme that its two partners said were incompatible with the original common trilateral goals. Specifically, the US Army, which funds 58% of the project, indicated it wanted to push ahead with its own Integrated Battlefield Control System rather than the commonly designed MEADS BM4CI control system, causing the German Ministry of Defence to warn that such a fundamental change would threaten the existence of the entire programme. An independent study group was appointed to examine this possibility and concluded that MEADS should keep its own battle-management system but also incorporate functionalities required by the US Army.

With the successful completion of the design-review process, the decision on moving forward with the system now depends on final approval from the US Office of the Secretary of Defense.

With the **Italian** government facing a budget deficit of over 5% of GDP (and an outstanding national debt of 110% of GDP), defence spending fell by 4.5% in 2009, and preliminary indications suggest that the budget will be unchanged in 2010. However, the opaque nature of data on Italy's military spending obscures the true picture of defence expenditure. For example, a law passed in 2008 stipulates that all international missions be funded by money provided by the government outside of the official defence budget. Total spending on such operations in the first six months of 2009 was more than €700m (US$1.04bn), with the largest outlays going to operations in Afghanistan (€242m/US$361m), Lebanon (€192m/US$287m) and the Balkans (€114m/US$170m). Italian forces are also deployed in other operations including *Active Endeavour*, the NATO training mission in Iraq, and EU-led operations in Georgia and off the Somali coast.

In addition to the arrangements for funding overseas missions, the Italian armed forces also receive extra budgetary funds for procurement and research and development. In 2009, spending on defence procurement and R&D broke down as follows: ministry of defence procurement was officially €2.66bn (US$3.97bn), including €324m (US$484m) for infrastructure and €179m (US$267m) on radio frequencies for Wi-Max Internet services, plus €224m (US$334m) for R&D; added to that were €888m (US$1.3bn) for procurement and another €400m (US$597m) for R&D provided by the Ministry of Economic Development (MED). Critics of the system argue that because money provided by the MED is only ever made available for the purchase of domestic equipment, around 40% of the armed forces' investment budget is not subject to open tenders. Furthermore, getting funds from the MED can be a terribly inefficient process: the CEO of Finmeccanica has noted that his company had to complete a 37-step process before it could proceed with the air force's procurement of M-346 jet trainers.

Not only are there inefficiencies in the budgeting process, but the internal breakdown of the defence budget has remained unbalanced following the withdrawal of conscription, which saw a dramatic increase in personnel costs. The Ministry of Defence has a target that 50% of its budget be allocated to personnel costs, with 25% allocated to procurement and another 25% to running and operational outlays. However, in 2009 personnel expenditure accounted for 67% of the budget, procurement 20% and running costs just 13%. In light of this imbalance, the government has called for proposals from an inter-ministerial commission on the future make-up of the Italian armed forces. In particular it is thought that the commission will examine the possibility of further force reductions (announced manpower cuts will already bring down the total number of personnel in the armed forces to 141,000 in 2012) to address the current spending imbalance. Given that the planned cuts will come from the lower ranks and mostly from personnel on short-term contracts, leaving the armed forces with less than one-third of its personnel as regular soldiers and more than two-thirds as officers and NCOs, any further cuts would be particularly hard on the army.

In terms of equipment, the most significant procurement announced during 2009 was the army's €900m (US$1.3bn) contract to acquire 16 new *Chinook* helicopters. The aircraft will be operated by the Army Aviation 1st Antares Regiment and will replace an ageing fleet of 40 CH-47Cs that have been in service since 1973. Deliveries will run from 2013 to 2017 and the aircraft will be jointly built by AgustaWestland and Boeing. (The production agreement also includes a licensing agreement that will enable AgustaWestland to produce, market and sell the CH-47F *Chinook* to other European countries.) In the longer term both the air force and navy are likely to suffer under a constrained funding environment. The reduction in the operational budget is bringing further rationalisation to the Italian air force as more air bases are disbanded and the number of aircraft is cut – since 1999 nine air bases and three combat bases have been scrapped, and there are plans to reduce the number of aircraft from 390 to 310. Meanwhile, ambitions to acquire a Maritime Multirole Aircraft and Airborne Early Warning aircraft look likely to be thwarted.

The navy is also likely to have to compromise on a challenging future procurement programme. After the navy had taken delivery of two new-generation, air-independent propulsion equipped submarines, Fincantieri announced a follow-on order for a further two boats due to be delivered in 2015 and 2016. At the same time, the navy is set to receive up to ten 6,000-tonne FREMM ASW and general-purpose frigates. To date, however, only six of the vessels have been ordered, and there is currently no contract for the four land-attack variants. (It may be that Italy will follow in the footsteps of France, which, due to budgetary restrictions, has already had to entirely eliminate the land-attack model from its programme.) Other major surface-combatant requirements looming in the future include a successor to Italy's fleet of 12 mine-countermeasures vessels, a double-hulled replacement for the ageing *Stromboli* class of replenishment tankers and a new LHD-type vessel to replace the *San Giorgio* class of amphibious-assault ships. Without a rebalancing of the defence budget to reduce personnel costs and increase investment funds there are likely to be casualties in the procurement plans of all three services.

In June 2009, **Denmark** released a new five-year defence plan covering the period 2010–14. During the previous five years, the armed forces had received an average of DKR21.5bn (US$4.3bn) a year, and this will rise to an average of just over DKR22bn (US$4.4bn) a year, around half the amount requested by the Ministry of Defence. Each year the budget will include DKR140m (US$27.8m) to create a secure computer network-operations capacity, a maximum of DKR1bn (US$198m) for participation in international missions, and around DKR400m (US$79m) for 'one-off expenditures'. Over the next five years, the armed forces will become smaller but stronger with the goal of being able to deploy 2,000 personnel on operations outside the country, though with pressure on the budget there will be a number of cutbacks. Among the reductions will be a cut in the number of operational *Leopard* 2 main battle tanks to 34, and in the number of F-16 aircraft from 48 to 30. The army will decommission its long-range fire-support system of M109 howitzers and cut its long-range anti-tank missile units. The navy will cut its number of maritime-response ships for permanent surveillance of Danish waters from four to three and reduce the air force's *Fennec* helicopter personnel and equipment, ending the international capability of that fleet. In terms of new equipment, the biggest project will be the future fighter to replace the current fleet of F-16s, while the Danish army will receive new armoured vehicles, communications equipment and personnel-protection suites for infantry troops. The navy is scheduled to take delivery of new maritime helicopters, weapons systems, small vessels and auxiliary ships.

Several countries in Eastern Europe that had boosted military spending in the run-up to joining NATO have already indicated that their economic problems will reverse this trend, opening up the likelihood of greater defence cooperation between them in order to eke out any available economies of scale. **Lithuania** cut its 2009 budget by 9% and then by a further 36% in 2010. As a result of such dramatic cuts the Ministry of Defence has been forced to cancel its plan to reintroduce national military conscription (resurrected in reaction to the 2008 Russia–Georgia war); withdraw forces from overseas missions such as Kosovo; impose salary reductions for officers; cut training schedules; and defer payments, though some procurement programmes have been unaffected. Programmes that will still proceed include the delivery of a final C-27J transporter, a third StanFlex 300 patrol ship, two ex-Royal Navy minehunters, off-road trucks and rifles. However, as funding for these items will wipe out the chance of any further purchases in the medium term, Lithuania has stepped up its consultations with its Baltic neighbours and Poland in an effort to pool resources for joint procurements to drive down operating costs.

In **Latvia**, the government was forced to approach the IMF for emergency financing in return for implementing an austerity budget. The reduction in state spending resulted in a 21% cut in the 2009 defence budget and a temporary pause in the 12-year, long-term defence plan implemented in 2001, designed to produce a professional, highly competent force providing niche capabilities in the areas of medical response, military police and engineering support. In order to continue with its commitment in Afghanistan, Latvia will end its participation in NATO- and EU-led military missions in Kosovo and Bosnia-Herzegovina. Likewise, despite events in Georgia and a series of Russian cyber attacks on the government's computer network, **Estonia** has also been forced to cut its defence budget with resulting cuts in both salaries and procurement.

Having only just approved a new four-year armed-forces development for 2009–12 and a longer-term z60bn (US$20.8bn) investment plan to run to 2018, the economic crisis resulted in the **Polish** government cutting the 2009 budget from z24.5bn (US$8.5bn) to z22.6bn (US$8bn). This meant that even though there is a statutory commitment to hold spending at 1.95% of GDP, it fell to 1.85% of GDP in 2009. As a result of the move, the Ministry of Defence scrapped the planned acquisition of two multirole tanker transports, reduced its purchase of *Rosomak* 8×8s to 48, cancelled its participation in NATO's Alliance Ground Surveillance programme, and withdrew from international operations in Lebanon, Syria and Chad. By late 2009, however, following public criticism of the Defence Ministry by Polish Land Forces Commander General Waldemar Skrzypczak over the delayed delivery of equipment to Polish forces in Afghanistan, the prime minister released around z1bn (US$350m) for urgent equipment needs. Among the items being procured are five new helicopters (probably Mi-17 transports), 60 mine-resistant, ambush-protected vehicles and two mid-range unmanned aerial vehicles.

NON-NATO EUROPE – DEFENCE ECONOMICS

With few exceptions, most countries in non-NATO Europe have experienced the full force of the global recession. Among the advanced economies, Ireland was the most high-profile victim, but other countries, including Austria, Finland, Sweden and Switzerland, all experienced significant economic contraction as the consequences of the banking crisis proved to be more serious than first expected. However, it was among the **Commonwealth of Independent States** (CIS) countries that some of the most dramatic reversals of economic fortune occurred. Countries such as Ukraine, Belarus, Armenia and Moldova were badly hit as three major shocks appeared simultaneously: the financial crisis itself, which greatly curtailed access to external funding; slumping demand from advanced economies; and the related fall in

commodity prices, notably for energy. Commenting on developments, the IMF suggested that although many CIS economies were better positioned to weather the crisis than they were in the aftermath of Russia's 1998 debt default, the economic fallout would nonetheless be severe and that CIS growth in 2009 would be the lowest among all emerging regions. Indeed, such were the problems experienced by Belarus, Armenia and Ukraine in accessing external financing that they were eventually forced to turn to the IMF for financial assistance.

Although the government's fiscal position deteriorated during 2009, **Sweden** pushed on with its long-standing military-reorganisation programme, driven by events elsewhere in the region that appear to have halted the decline in military spending. The armed forces 'New Defence' plan was first revealed in 1999 and outlined the most extensive reform programme in the history of the country's military. Central to the plan was a switch by Sweden's armed forces from a traditional structure geared toward territorial defence to a force comprising smaller, more flexible units capable of undertaking overseas peacekeeping missions with allied nations, primarily under a UN mandate. This has resulted in significantly reduced personnel levels and cuts in defence expenditure. In 2000, defence spending amounted to 2.0% of GDP, but by 2008, in line with the New Defence programme, Sweden had reduced its defence budget to just 1.4% of national output. This dramatic cut in the defence outlay has led to clashes between the government and Ministry of Defence, which has regularly claimed that it is increasingly

Table 16 **Non-NATO Europe Regional Defence Expenditure** as % of GDP

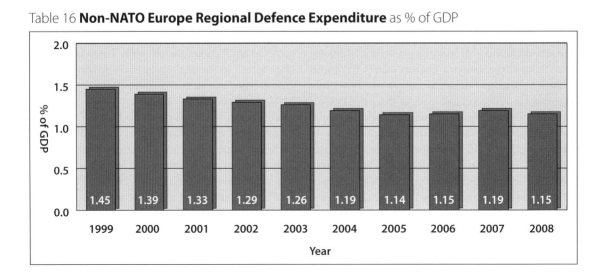

underfunded. In 2008, defence chief General Haken Syren suggested that the shortfall in the budget was so severe that recruitment efforts needed to be curtailed, air-force flight times reduced and land-forces exercises cancelled. In response, Defence Minister Sten Tolgfors complained that such measures had the appearance of emergency cuts and urged the armed forces to achieve ever-greater efficiency savings to make up for shortfalls.

In January 2009, General Syren presented the armed forces' proposals for the next phase of the transformation project, covering the period 2010–14. Anticipating further demands for force reductions and budget cuts from the government, 'Vision 2014' included plans to reduce the army by a third, cut land forces to eight battalions and halve the number of tanks while freezing the budget at no less than SEK39bn (US$5.6bn) annually through 2014. At first it appeared that the government was receptive to the document and that, despite claims to the contrary made during the Georgia crisis in 2008, another round of military downsizing was in the offing. However, in an abrupt reversal of its previous declarations, in March 2009 the government presented its own proposal to parliament which called for, among other surprises, a halt in its plans to further shrink the army and a new focus on strengthening the country's rapid-response components. Citing the Georgia crisis as a driver, the government explained that its plan was to develop a 'totally new approach to defence policy' that would 'remove the division between a national operational organisation and an international force'. The proposal also revoked plans calling for the closure of bases and a reduction in the tank inventory, and outlined initiatives to strengthen capacities in areas that had been ignored over recent years, such as the Baltic Sea and the island of Gotland, which will receive additional air, sea and land assets including a unit of *Leopard* 2 tanks. A Rapid Mobilisation and Deployment Reserve Force, consisting of four battalions, will be created, boosting the number of deployable mobile battalions at the military's disposal from three to eight, while the Home Guard will be fixed at 22,000 personnel, of which 17,000 will receive improved training and equipment and be under a service obligation even in peacetime. Greater emphasis was placed on deployability, and in future the entire 50,000-strong force will be available within one week 'to serve where and when necessary', compared to a year at present. Contrary to previous suggestions,

most of the armed forces' major weapons systems will be retained: the number of *Gripen* C/D aircraft will be fixed at 100; the number of all MBT, artillery and air-defence units will be unchanged; new helicopters and protected vehicles will be procured; and the navy will retain its submarines and fleet of seven corvettes (including five *Visby*-class ships).

Not surprisingly, the 2008 Georgia crisis also had an impact on military thinking in **Finland**. Before the crisis erupted, it seemed likely that financial limitations would force Finland to develop smaller but better-equipped and -trained armed forces. However, in a direct response to events in Georgia, the Finnish government boosted the 2009 defence budget by 16% and indicated that it would be willing to carry on raising the budget in future years. Details of the proposed funding plans were laid out in the 2009 Finnish Defence and Security Policy document, which suggested that spending should be increased by 2% a year in real terms from 2011. In addition, the policy included the provision that future defence budgets could be increased further if currency fluctuations and other 'unanticipated changes' negatively impacted on the armed forces' spending power. Personnel strength was fixed at 15,000 for the foreseeable future and annual crisis-management appropriations were increased to €150m (US$224m) a year. Opposition parties, however, were unhappy with these provisions and argued that the armed forces should implement a new wave of cost-cutting measures rather than rely on increased state funding. The government eventually won the day and in a June vote the new policy was adopted, thus providing the Ministry of Defence with approximately US$600m in new funds during the period 2011–14.

With the extra funds now secure the ministry will be able to pursue the wide range of weapons-systems and materiel-procurement objectives outlined in the White Paper. These include developing up to three so-called readiness brigades; creating two mechanised battlegroups, a helicopter battalion and a special-forces battalion; and establishing five regional battlegroups, six main air-force bases and three fighter squadrons. Listed among the White Paper's other defence-development programmes is the creation of two missile fast-attack craft squadrons, two mine-countermeasure squadrons and two coastal infantry battalions.

In contrast to developments in Scandinavia, the **Austrian** armed forces seem likely to be adversely affected by the country's fiscal difficulties. In April

2009, the military leadership signed a letter to the defence minister complaining about the national defence budget, which at only 0.7% of GDP is the lowest in Europe by this measure. The letter pointed out that regular promises to increase the budget to at least 1% of GDP have been ignored, leaving the military with a shortfall of around €300m (US$448m) a year. The letter also criticised the country's acquisition of Eurofighter *Typhoon*, claiming that promises made in 2002 when the procurement was agreed that the core defence budget would not be affected had been broken. At the time of the deal the Ministry of Defence was told that if *Typhoon* operating costs exceeded €50m (US$75m) a year it would be compensated. In 2008 total spending on the *Typhoon*s reached €276m (US$412m), but despite his protestations the defence minister was unable to secure extra funds for the military and was forced to announce the postponement of a number of key procurement programmes. The most immediate casualty was the €200m (US$298.5m) programme to acquire 145 *Dingo* armoured patrol vehicles; also 'postponed to later budgets' were the replacement of Austria's 40-year-old Saab jet trainers and the upgrading of 23 Agusta-Bell 212 helicopters. In announcing the delays, the minister said they would release around €70m (US$104.5m) for the renovation and construction of new barracks.

Albania ALB

Albanian Lek		2008	2009	2010
GDP	lek	1.12tr		
	US$	13.4bn		
per capita	US$	3,694		
Growth	%	6.8	0.7	
Inflation	%	3.4	1.7	
Def bdgt	lek	21.3bn	23.6bn	
	US$	254m	254m	
FMA (US)	US$	2.1m	2.1m	5.0m
US$1=lek		83.9	92.7	

Population	3,639,453

Age	0 – 14	15 – 19	20 – 24	25 – 29	30 – 64	65 plus
Male	14%	5%	4%	4%	20%	4%
Female	13%	5%	4%	4%	19%	4%

Capabilities

ACTIVE 14,295 (Joint Force Comd 8,150, Support Command 4,300 , TRADOC 1,000, MoD and General Staff 795) **Paramilitary** 500

Terms of service conscription 12 months

The Albanian Armed Forces (AAF) is a joint, primarily land-oriented force centred on light infantry capabilities supported by naval and air units.

ORGANISATIONS BY SERVICE

Joint Forces Command (JFC)

Land Element

FORCES BY ROLE

Joint Forces Command (JFC) consists of the Rapid Reaction Brigade, Commando Regiment, Area Support Brigade, Air Brigade, Naval Brigade, Logistics Battalion and Communications Battalion. JFC units maintain the readiness to conduct and support international peace support and humanitarian operations, and multipurpose tasks in support of Albanian crisis management. The armed forces are being re-constituted. Restructuring is now planned to be completed by 2010

FORCES BY ROLE

Rapid Reaction	1 lt inf bde
Cdo	1 regt
Arty	1 bn
Spt	1 bde
Sigs	1 bn
Logistics	1 bn

EQUIPMENT BY TYPE
MBT 3
APC (T) 6 Type 5310
ARTY
TOWED 18 **152 mm**

MOR 81: **82mm** 81
AD
GUNS 42 **37mm** M-1939 /S 60

Navy Element

FORCES BY ROLE

The Albanian Navy Brigade, under the command of JFC, is organised into two naval flotillas with additional hydrographic, logistics, auxiliary and training support services. The first Flotilla is located in Durrës with the other located in Vlorë.

EQUIPMENT BY TYPE
PATROL AND COASTAL COMBATANTS 27
PFC 1 *Shanghai* II† (PRC)
PFI 2 Po-2† (FSU)
PB 12: 1 *Patrol Type 4207* (Damen Stan – 3 additional vessels in build) 3 Mk3 *Sea Spectre*; 8 V-4000; (Coast Guard use)
PBR 12: 7 Type 2010; 1 Type 303; 4 Type 227; (for Coast Guard use)
MINE WARFARE • MINE COUNTERMEASURES 1
MSO 1 T-43
LOGISTICS AND SUPPORT 5: 1 **LCT** 4 **AG**
FACILITIES
Base   1 located at Durrës (HQ), 1 located at Vlorë

Air Element

The Air Brigade, under JFC command, is organised in one Helicopter Base (Farka) and two Reserve Air Bases (Gjadër & Kucova), an Active Air Base (Rinas), Air Defense Battalion (Marikaj), Air Surveillance Operation Centre (ASOC - Rinas), Aircraft Maintenance Centre (Kucove) and Meteorological Service Centre (Laprak). Pilots and other aircraft crew aim to fly at least 10–15 hrs/year.

EQUIPMENT BY TYPE
HELICOPTERS 16
RECCE 7 AB-206C
UTL 3 AB-205; 5 Bo-105; 1 A-109

Support Command (SC)

SC consists of the Logistics Brigade, GS Support Regiment, Infrastructure Regiment, Personnel and Recruiting Centre, Military Hospital, Systems Development Centre and Military Police Battalion.

FORCES BY ROLE

Med	1 hosp
Security	1 MP bn
Logistics	1 bde (1 GS Spt Regt (tpt, EOD,maint)

Training and Doctrine Command (TRADOC)

TRADOC consists of the Defense Academy, Military University, NCO Academy, Basic Training Brigade, the consolidated Troops School, Centre for Defense Analysis and Training Support Centre.

Paramilitary ε500

DEPLOYMENT

Legal provisions for foreign deployment:
Constitution: Codified constitution (1998)
Decision on deployment of troops abroad: By the parliament upon proposal by the president (Art.171 II)

AFGHANISTAN
NATO • ISAF 250; 1 inf coy

BOSNIA-HERZEGOVINA
EU • EUFOR • *Operation Althea* 13

CENTRAL AFRICAN REPUBLIC/CHAD
EU • EUFOR Tchad/RCA 63; 1 HQ coy

FOREIGN FORCES

Italy 1 (HQ Tirana); 29 DIA

Belgium BEL

Euro €		2008	2009	2010
GDP	€	344bn	321bn	
	US$	506bn	479bn	
per capita	US$	48,624	46,000	
Growth	%	1.0	-3.2	
Inflation	%	4.5	0.3	
Def exp[a]	€	3.77bn		
	US$	5.55bn		
Def bdgt	€	2.85bn	2.84bn	2.87bn
	US$	4.20bn	4.23bn	
US$1=€		0.68	0.67	

[a] including military pensions

Population	10,414,336

Age	0–14	15–19	20–24	25–29	30–64	65 plus
Male	9%	3%	3%	3%	24%	7%
Female	8%	3%	3%	3%	24%	9%

Capabilities

ACTIVE 38,452 (Army 14,013 Navy 1,605 Air 7,203 Medical Service 1,912 Joint Service 13,719)

RESERVE 2,040

ORGANISATIONS BY SERVICE

Land Component 14,013
FORCES BY ROLE
1 Comd HQ (COMOPSLAND)

Comd	1 Comd HQ (COMOPSLAND); 2 bde HQ
Rapid Reaction	1 regt (1 cdo bn, 2 para bn
Mech	2 bde (1st and 7th) (2 mech inf regt, 1 tk bn, 1 fd arty regt, 1 recce regt);
Recce/Psyops	1 unit (CIMIC)

SF	1 gp
AD	1 regt (2 SAM bty with *Mistral*)
Engr	2 bn
MP	1 Coy (1 pl dedicated to EUROCORPS)
Logistic	6 bn
EOD	1 unit
Info Ops	1 gp
CIS	5 gp

FACILITIES
Trg Centre 1 (para); 1 (cdo)

EQUIPMENT BY TYPE
MBT 40 *Leopard* 1A5
AIFV 30: 24 YPR-765(25mm); 6 *Piranha III-C* DF30
APC 226
  APC (T) 47 M-113 (spt)
  APC (W) 179: 48 *Pandur* (45 obs 3 spt); 86 *Dingo*; 45 *Piranha III -C*
ARTY 179
  TOWED 105mm 24 LG1 MK II
  MOR 73: **81mm** 43; **120mm** 30
AT • MSL • MANPATS 82 *Milan*
AD
SAM 18 *Mistral*
RADARS 9 M-113 Land (battlefield surveillance)

Reserves 2,040

Territorial Support Units
Army 11 unit

Navy Component 1,605
EQUIPMENT BY TYPE
PRINCIPAL SURFACE COMBATANTS 2
FRIGATES
  FFG 2 *Karel Doorman* each with 2 quad (8 eff.) *Harpoon* SSM, 1 16 cell Mk 48 VLS with 16 RIM-7P *Sea Sparrow* SAM, 4 single 324mm MK 32 MOD 9 ASTT with 4 MK 46 MOD 5 HWT, 1 76mm gun, (capacity 1 med hel)
PATROL AND COASTAL COMBATANTS
PCR 10
MINE WARFARE • MINE COUNTERMEASURES 6
  MHC 6 *Aster* (Tripartite – *Flower* class)
LOGISTICS AND SUPPORT 8: 1 *Stern* **AG**; 1 *Belgica* **AGOR**; 4 **AT**; 1 *Godetia* **Spt** (log spt/comd, with hel platform); **TRG** 1 YDT
FACILITIES
Base   Located at Zeebrugge

Naval Aviation
HELICOPTERS
UTL 3 SA-316B *Alouette III* (part of the Air Component); (NH-90 on order)

Air Component 7,203
Flying hours   165 hrs/yr on cbt ac. 500 hrs/yr on tpt ac. 200 hrs/yr for trg purposes

FACILITIES
Air bases   Located at Coxijde, Kleine-Brogel, Florennes, Bierset, Beauvechain, Melsbroek

FORCES BY ROLE

AD/FGA/ Recce	2 (Tac) wg with F-16 MLU *Fighting Falcon* (4 ADX/FBX sqn, 1 AD/FGA/trg unit)
SAR	1 unit *Sea King* MK48
Tpt	1 wg with A-310-222; C-130H *Hercules*; ERJ-135 LR; ERJ-145 LR; *Falcon* 20 (VIP); *Falcon* 900B
Trg	1 wg (1 trg sqn with SF-260D/SF-260M, 1 FRA/BEL trg unit with *Alpha Jet*)
Hel	1 wg with A-109 (obs); SA-318 *Alouette II*
UAV	1 sqn with B-*Hunter*

EQUIPMENT BY TYPE

AIRCRAFT 60 combat capable
  FGA 60 F-16 MLU *Fighting Falcon* (Mid-Life Update*)*
  TPT 20: 2 A-310-222; 11 C-130H *Hercules*; 2 ERJ-135 LR; 2 ERJ-145 LR; 2 *Falcon* 20 (VIP); 1 *Falcon* 900B
  TRG 60: 28 *Alpha Jet*; 32 SF-260D/M
HELICOPTERS
  SAR 4 *Sea King* MK48
  UTL 29: 26 A-109 (obs); 3 SA-318 *Alouette II*
UAV 18 B-*Hunter* systems
SAM 24 *Mistral*
MSL
  AAM AIM-120B AMRAAM; AIM-9M/N *Sidewinder*
BOMBS
  Conventional: Mk 84, Mk 82, BLU 109 II; GBU-24 *Paveway* III
  INS/GPS guided: GBU-31 JDAM
  Laser-Guided: GBU-10/ GBU-12 *Paveway*
PODS Infra-red/TV: 6 LANTIRN, 7 *Sniper*

DEPLOYMENT

Legal provisions for foreign deployment:
Constitution: Codified constitution (1831)
Specific legislation: 'Loi relatif à la mise en oeuvre des forces armées, à la mise en condition, ainsi qu'aux périodes et positions dans lesquelles le militaire peut se trouver' (1994)
Decision on deployment of troops abroad: By the monarch, the government and the minister of defence (1994 law, Art. 3, § 1)

AFGHANISTAN
NATO • ISAF 530; **Air Component:** 6 F-16 *Fighting Falcon*

ARABIAN GULF AND INDIAN OCEAN
EU • *Operation Atalanta* 1 FFG

BOSNIA- HERZEGOVINA
OSCE • Bosnia and Herzegovina 1

DEMOCRATIC REPUBLIC OF CONGO
EU • EUSEC RD Congo 6
UN • MONUC 22; 6 obs; 1 C-130

FRANCE
NATO • **Air Component** • TRG: 29 *Alpha Jet* located at Cazeaux/Tours

LEBANON
UN • UNIFIL 229; **Land Component**: 1 engr coy

MIDDLE EAST
UN • UNTSO 2 obs

SERBIA
NATO • KFOR • *Joint Enterprise* 219; 1 mech inf coy

SUDAN
UN • UNMIS 4 obs

FOREIGN FORCES
NATO HQ, Brussels; HQ SHAPE, Mons
United States Army 685; Navy 106; USAF 457; USMC 26

Bulgaria BLG

Bulgarian Lev L		2008	2009	2010
GDP	L	66.7bn	67.6bn	
	US$	50.2bn	51.2bn	
per capita	US$	6,905	7,108	
Growth	%	6.0	-6.5	
Inflation	%	12.2	2.7	
Def exp	L	1.74bn		
	US$	1.31bn		
Def bdgt	L	1.55bn	1.46bn	1.49bn
	US$	1.16bn	1.11bn	
FMA (US)	US$	6.5m	7.4m	13.2m
US$1=L		1.33	1.32	

Population   7,204,687

Ethnic groups: Turkish 9%; Macedonian 3%; Romany 3%

Age	0–14	15–19	20–24	25–29	30–64	65 plus
Male	7%	3%	4%	4%	23%	8%
Female	7%	3%	3%	4%	25%	10%

Capabilities

ACTIVE 34,975 (Army 16,268 Navy 3,471 Air 6,706 **Central Staff 8,530) Paramilitary 34,000**
Terms of service 9 months

RESERVE 302,500 (Army 250,500 Navy 7,500 Air 45,000)

ORGANISATIONS BY SERVICE

Army 16,268
Forces are being reduced in number.

FORCES BY ROLE

Mil District	1 corps HQ
Armd	1 bde
Armd Recce	1 regt
Mech Inf	2 bde
Lt Inf	1 bde
SF	1 bde
Arty	1 arty bde

MRL   1 bde
Engr   1 regt
NBC   1 regt

EQUIPMENT BY TYPE
MBT 362: 362 T-72
AIFV 185: 90 BMP-1; 95 BMP-2 / BMP-3
APC 1,393
   APC (T) 1,297: 508 MT-LB; 789 look-a-likes
   APC (W) 96 BTR-60
ARTY 817
   SP • 122mm 329 2S1 *Carnation*
   TOWED 152: **122mm** 20 (M-30) M-1938; **152mm** 132 D-20
   MRL 122mm 124 BM-21
   MOR 120mm 212 2S11 SP *Tundzha*
AT
   MSL SP: 24 BRDM-2
   MANPATS 436: 200 AT-3 9K11 *Sagger* in store; 236 AT-4 9K111 *Spigot* / AT-5 9K113 *Spandrel*
   GUNS 276: **100mm** 126 MT-12; **85mm** 150 D-44 in store
AD
   SAM • SP 24 SA-8 *Gecko*
   MANPAD SA-7 *Grail*
   GUNS 400 **100mm** KS-19 towed/**57mm** S-60 towed/**23mm** ZSU-23-4 SP/ZU-23 towed
RADARS • LAND GS-13 *Long Eye* (veh); SNAR-1 *Long Trough* (arty); SNAR-10 *Big Fred* (veh, arty); SNAR-2/-6 *Pork Trough* (arty); *Small Fred* / *Small Yawn* (veh, arty)

Army Reserve 250,500 reservists

Army   4 bde

Navy 3,471

EQUIPMENT BY TYPE
SUBMARINES • TACTICAL
   SSK 1 *Slava*† (FSU *Romeo*) with 8 single 533mm TT with 14 SAET-60 HWT
PRINCIPAL SURFACE COMBATANTS 4
   FRIGATES 4
     FFG 1 *Drazki* (BEL *Weilingen*) with 2 twin (4 eff.) with MM-38 *Exocet* SSM, 1 MK29 *Sea Sparrow* octuple with RIM-7P *Sea Sparrow* SAM, 2 ASTT with total of 2 L5 HWT, 1 MLE 54 *Creusot-Loire* 375mm (6 eff.), 1 100mm gun
     FF 1 *Smeli* (FSU *Koni*) with 1 twin (2 eff.) with 2 SA-N-4 *Gecko* SAM, 2 RBU 6000 *Smerch 2* (24 eff.), 2 twin 76mm gun (4 eff.)
     FS 2 *Pauk* each with 1 SA-N-5 *Grail* SAM, 4 single 406mm TT, 2 RBU 1200 (10 eff.)
PATROL AND COASTAL COMBATANTS 19
   PFM 7:
     1 *Tarantul* II with 2 twin (4 eff.) with 4 SS-N-2C *Styx* tactical SSM, 2 quad (8 eff.) with 8 SA-N-5 *Grail* SAM, 1 76mm gun
     6 *Osa* I/II † each with 4 SS-N-2A *Styx*/SS-N-2B *Styx*
   PFI 9 *Zhuk* less than 100 tonnes
   PBI 3 *Nesebar* (BEL *Neustadt*)
MINE COUNTERMEASURES 17
   MHC 1 (Tripartite - BEL *Flower* class)
   MSC 8: 4 *Sonya*; 4 *Vanya*

   MSI 8: 6 *Olya*, less than 100 tonnes; 2 *Yevgenya*, less than 100 tonnes
AMPHIBIOUS 8
   LSM 2 *Polnochny* A (FSU) (capacity 6 MBT; 180 troops)
   CRAFT • LCU 6 *Vydra*
LOGISTICS AND SUPPORT 14: 1 **AORL**; 1 **AOL**; 1 **ARS**; 5 **ATS**; 3 **AGS**; 1 **YDG**; 2 **YDT**
FACILITIES
Bases   Located at Atya, Balchik, Vidin, Sozopol, Burgas, Varna

Naval Aviation
HELICOPTERS
   ASW 6 Mi-14 *Haze* (3 operational) to be replaced by 6 AS-565MB *Panther* 2010–2011

Coastal Arty
FORCES BY ROLE
Arty 2 regt; 20 bty

EQUIPMENT BY TYPE
MSL • TACTICAL • SSM: SS-C-1B *Sepal*; SS-C-3 *Styx*
GUN • 130mm 4 SM-4-1

Naval Guard
Gd 3 coy

Air Force 6,706

Flying hours   30 to 40 hrs/yr

FORCES BY ROLE
1 AD Cmd,1 Tactical Aviation Cmd

Ftr/Recce 3rd Fighter Air Base (Graf Ignatievo). 1 sqn with MiG-29A/UB *Fulcrum*; 1 sqn with MiG-21bis/UM *Fishbed*

FGA 22nd Attack Air Base (Bezmer). 2 sqn with Su-25K/UBK *Frogfoot* (5 upgraded to NATO compatibility)

Tpt 16th Tpt Air Base (Sofia) with CJ-27; An-2 *Colt*; An-26 *Curl*; L-410 UVP; TU-134B *Crusty*; PC-12M

Trg Air Trg Base (Dolna Milropolia) with L-39ZA *Albatros* (advanced); PC-9M (basic)

Hel 24th Hel Air Base (Krumovo) with Mi-24D/V *Hind D*; AS 532AL *Cougar*; Mi-17 *Hip*; Bell 206 *JetRanger*

EQUIPMENT BY TYPE
AIRCRAFT 62 combat capable
   FTR 38: 20 MiG-29 *Fulcrum* A/UB; 18 MiG-21bis/UM *Fishbed*
   FGA 24 Su-25K/UBK *Frogfoot*
   TPT 17: 1 An-2 *Colt*; 3 An-26 *Curl*; 3 C-27J; 1 AN-30 *Clank*; 7 L-410UVP/L-410UVP-E; 1 TU-134B *Crusty*; 1 PC-12M
   TRG 12: 6 L-39ZA *Albatros*; 6 PC-9M (basic)
HELICOPTERS
   ATK 18 Mi-24D/V *Hind D** (12 being upgraded to NATO standard)
   SPT 23: 11 AS 532AL *Cougar*; 12 Mi-17 *Hip* (6 to be upgraded to NATO standard)

UTL: 6 Bell 206 *JetRanger*
UAV *Yastreb*-2S
AD
  SAM SA-10 *Grumble* (quad) SP/SA-2 *Guideline* towed/
  SA-3 *Goa*/SA-5 *Gammon* static (20 sites, 110 launchers)
MSL
  AAM AA-11 *Archer*; AA-2 *Atoll*; AA-7 *Apex*; AA-10
  Alamo
  ASM AS-14 *Kedge*; AS-7 *Kerry*; AS-10 *Karen*
FACILITIES
Air base   1 (ftr/recce), 1 (FGA)
Hel base   1 (hel)
School   2 with L-39ZA *Albatros* trg ac (advanced);
           PC-9M (basic trg)

Paramilitary 34,000

Border Guards 12,000
Ministry of Interior
FORCES BY ROLE
Paramilitary   12 regt

EQUIPMENT BY TYPE
PATROL AND COASTAL COMBATANTS ε50
  PCI ε12 **PB** 2 (FSU, under 100 tonnes)
  MISC BOATS/CRAFT: ε38 various craft all under 100
  tonnes

Railway and Construction Troops 18,000

Security Police 4,000

DEPLOYMENT
Legal provisions for foreign deployment:
Constitution: Codified constitution (1991)
Decision on deployment of troops abroad: By the
president upon request from the Council of Ministers and
upon approval by the National Assembly (Art. 84 XI)

AFGHANISTAN
NATO • ISAF 460; 1 mech inf coy

ARMENIA/AZERBAIJAN
OSCE • Minsk Conference 1

BOSNIA-HERZEGOVINA
EU • EUFOR • *Operation Althea* 119; 1 inf coy
OSCE • Bosnia and Herzegovina 1

IRAQ
NATO • NTM-I 2

LIBERIA
UN • UNMIL 2 obs

MOLDOVA
OSCE • Moldova 1

SERBIA
NATO • KFOR • *Joint Enterprise* 47; 1 engr pl
OSCE • Kosovo 3

Croatia CRO

Croatian Kuna k		2008	2009	2010
GDP	k	342bn	331bn	
	US$	69.4bn	67.4bn	
per capita	US$	15,445	15,016	
Growth	%	2.4	-5.2	
Inflation	%	6.1	2.8	
Def bdgt	k	5.37bn	5.04bn	
	US$	1.09bn	1.02bn	
US$1=k		4.93	4.91	

Population	4,489,409

Age	0 – 14	15 – 19	20 – 24	25 – 29	30 – 64	65 plus
Male	9%	3%	4%	3%	23%	6%
Female	8%	3%	3%	3%	24%	10%

Capabilities

ACTIVE 18,600 (Army 11,390 Navy 1,850 Air 3,500
Joint 1,860) **Paramilitary 3,000**
The armed forces of Croatia are subject to arms limitations
established under the Dayton Peace Accord. An agreement
signed by BIH, its two entities, CRO and FRY on 14 June
1996, established ceilings for holdings of the armed forces
of the parties. *Terms of service* 6 months.

RESERVE 21,000 (Army 18,500 Navy 250 Air 2,250)

ORGANISATIONS BY SERVICE

Joint 1,860 (General Staff)

Army 11,390
FORCES BY ROLE
Armd	1 bde
Inf	1 bde
SF	1 bn
MRL	1 regt
AT	1 regt
ADA	1 regt
Engr	1 regt
Gd	3 regt (org varies)
MP	1 regt

EQUIPMENT BY TYPE
MBT 261: 72 M-84; 3 T-72M; 186 T55; 30 decommissioning
AIFV 103: 103 M80; 1 decommissioning
APC 38
  APC (T) 16 BTR-50
  APC (W) 22: 9 BOV-VP; 13 LOV OP
ARTY 1,436
  SP 122mm 8 2S1 *Carnation*
  TOWED 416: **105mm** 165: 89 M-2A1; 29
  decommissioning; 47 M-56H1 decommissioning;
  122mm 95: 53 D-30; 42 *M-1938* decommissioning;

130mm 78: 44 M-46; 34 M-46H1 **152mm** 41: 20 D-20; 18 M-84; 3 M 84H; **155mm** 18 M-1H1; **203mm** 19 M-2
MRL 222
  SP 42: **122mm** 39: 1 SVLR M 96 *Typhoon*, 7 M91*Vulkan* 31 BM-21 *Grad*; **128mm** 2 LOV RAK M91 R24; **262mm** 1 M-87 *Orkan*
  MOR 790: **82mm** 475: 339 LMB M96; 136 decommissioning; **120mm** 315: 310M-75; 5 UBM 52
AT • MSL 567
  SP 43 POLO BOV 83
  MANPATS 560+: 418 AT-3 9K11 *Malyjutka (Sagger)*; 81 AT-4 9K111 *Fagot (Spigot)*; 23 AT-7 9K115 *Metis (Saxhorn)*; 38 9K113 *Konkurs* M1; *Milan* (reported)
  RL 73mm RPG-22 *Net*/RPG-7 *Knout*; **90mm** M-79
  GUNS 100mm 133 T-12
AD • GUNS 463
  SP 62: **20mm** 45: 44 BOV-3 SP; 1 decommissioning; **30mm** 17 BOV-3
  MANPADS 619: 539 9K32M Strella 2M (SA-7 *Grail*); 80 9K38 *Igla* (**SA-18** *Grouse*)
  TOWED 401: **20mm** 390: 177 M55; 213 decommissioning; **40mm** 11

Navy 1,600; 250 conscript (total 1,850)
Navy Central Command located at Split, with two naval districts; NAVSOUTH and NAVNORTH
FORCES BY ROLE
Navy 1 HQ located at Split

EQUIPMENT BY TYPE
SUBMARINES • TACTICAL • SDV 2 *Mala*
PRINCIPAL SURFACE COMBATANTS • CORVETTES
• **FSG** 2 *Kralj* each with 2–4 twin (8 eff.) with RBS-15B tactical SSM
PATROL AND COASTAL COMBATANTS 7
  PFM 3:
  2 *Helsinki Class* each with 4 twin (8 eff.) with RBS-15M SSM, 2 *Sadral* sextuple with *Mistral* SAM and 1 57mm gun
  1 *Koncar* with 2 twin (4 eff.) with RBS-15B tactical SSM
  PCC 4 *Mirna*
MINE WARFARE • MINE COUNTERMEASURES 1
MHI 1 *Korcula*
AMPHIBIOUS
  LCT 2
  LCVP 4
LOGISTICS AND SUPPORT 3:
  AGS 1 *Moma* (FSU, trg); **ASR** 1; **AKL** 1;
FACILITIES
Bases   Located at Split, Pula, Sibenik, Dubrovnik, Ploce
Minor Bases   Located at Lastovo, Vis

Coastal Defence
FORCES BY ROLE
SSM 3 bty with RBS-15K

Arty 21+ bty

EQUIPMENT BY TYPE
MSL • TACTICAL • SSM RBS-15K

Marines
Inf 2 indep coy

Air Force and Air Defence 3,500
Flying hours   50 hrs/year
FORCES BY ROLE
Two air bases
Ftr/FGA   2 mixed sqns with MiG-21bis/MiG-21 UMD *Fishbed*
Tpt   1 tpt ac sqn, 2 tpt hel sqn
Firefighting 1 sqn
Trg   1 trg ac sqn, 1 trg hel sqn

EQUIPMENT BY TYPE
AIRCRAFT 12 combat capable
  FTR 12: 8 MiG-21bis; 4 MiG-21UMD *Fishbed*
  TPT 2 An-32 *Cline*
  Firefighting 5: 1 AT-802F; 4 Canadair CL-415
  UTL/TRG 24: 20 PC-9M; 4 UTVA-75 being replaced by 5 Zlin Z242L (basic trg)
HELICOPTERS
  SPT 24: 10 Mi-171Sh; 11 Mi-8MTV; 3 Mi-8T
  UTL 8 Bell 206B *JetRanger II*
AD • RADAR 8: 5 FPS-117; 3 S-600
AD • SAM
  SP SA-10 *Grumble* (quad); SA-9 *Gaskin*
  MANPAD SA-14 *Gremlin*; SA-16 *Gimlet*
MSL • AAM AA-2 *Atoll*; AA-8 *Aphid*

Paramilitary 3,000

Police 3,000 armed

DEPLOYMENT
Legal provisions for foreign deployment:
Constitution: Codified constitution (2004)
Decision on deployment of troops abroad: By the parliament (Art. 7 II); simplified procedure for humanitarian aid and military exercises

AFGHANISTAN
NATO • ISAF 290

BOSNIA-HERZEGOVINA
OSCE • Bosnia and Herzegovina 1

CENTRAL AFRICAN REPUBLIC/CHAD
UN • MINURCAT 17

CYPRUS
UN • UNFICYP 4

HAITI
UN • MINUSTAH 2

INDIA/PAKISTAN
UN • UNMOGIP 8 obs

LEBANON
UN • UNIFIL 1

LIBERIA
UN • UNMIL 3

SERBIA
NATO • KFOR • *Joint Enterprise* 20
OSCE • Serbia 1
OSCE • Kosovo 7

SUDAN
UN • UNMIS 5

SYRIA/ISRAEL
UN • UNDOF 94; 1 inf coy

WESTERN SAHARA
UN • MINURSO 7 obs

Czech Republic CZE

Czech Koruna Kc		2008	2009	2010
GDP	Kc	3.69tr	3.59tr	
	US$	216bn	205bn	
per capita	US$	21,147	20,122	
Growth	%	2.7	-4.3	
Inflation	%	6.3	1.6	
Def exp	Kc	54.1bn		
	US$	3.16bn		
Def bdgt	Kc	54.2bn	55.9bn	49.3bn
	US$	3.16bn	3.19bn	
FMA (US)	US$	2.8m	3.0m	7.0m
US$1=Kc		17.1	17.5	

Population   10,211,904

Ethnic groups: Slovak 3%; Polish 0.6%; German 0.5%

Age	0–14	15–19	20–24	25–29	30–64	65 plus
Male	8%	3%	3%	4%	25%	6%
Female	7%	3%	3%	4%	25%	8%

Capabilities

ACTIVE 17,932(Army 12,656, Air 5,276)
Paramilitary 3,100

CIVILIAN 7,888 (Army 1,013, Air 815 MOD Staff 6,060)

The armed forces are being reorganised with full operational capability planned for 2010–12. The military forces are Joint Forces, composed of Army, Air Force and Joint Forces Support Units.

ORGANISATIONS BY SERVICE

Army 12,656 military, 1,013 civilian (total 13,669)

FORCES BY ROLE

Rapid Reaction	1 bde (4ᵗʰ) (2 mech bn, 1 AB bn, 1 mot inf bn)
Mech	1 bde (7ᵗʰ)(1 armd bn, 2 mech inf bn, 1 mot inf bn)
SF	1 gp
Arty	1 bde (13ᵗʰ) (2 arty bn)
Recce	1 bn
Presidential Guard	1 bde (Subordinate to Ministry of Interior) (2 Gd bn (*each*: 3 Gd coy), 1 Presidential Sy coy)

EQUIPMENT BY TYPE

MBT 175: 175 T-72CZ
AIFV 525: 257 BMP-1; 175 BMP-2; 76 BPzV; 17 *Pandur II* (of 72)
APC 78:
   APC (T) 29 OT-90
   APC (W) 49: 43 OT-64; 6 *Dingo* 2
LAV 19: IVECO DV LMV *Panther*
ARTY 257
   SP 152mm 105: 48 M-77 *Dana*; 7 trg; 50 in store
   MRL 122mm 59: 16 RM-70; 3 trg; 40 in store
   MOR 120mm 93: 85 M-1982; 8 SPM-85
AT• MSL 671
   SP 496: 3 9P133 BRDM-2 *Sagger*; 21 9P148 BRDM-2 *Spandrel*; 472 9S428
   MANPATS 175 9P135 (AT-4 9K111) *Spigot*
RADARS • LAND 3 ARTHUR

Active Reserve

FORCES BY ROLE

Territorial Def	14 comd
Inf	14 coy (1 per territorial comd) (*each*: 1 logistic pl, 3 inf pl, 1 cbt spt pl)
Armd	1 armd coy

Air Force 5,276 military, 815 civilian (total 6,091)

The principal task is to secure the integrity of the Czech Republic's airspace. This mission is fulfilled within NATO Integrated Extended Air Defence System (NATINEADS) and, if necessary, by means of the Czech national reinforced air defence system. In addition, the Air Force provides close air support for the Army, and performs tasks associated with the transportation of troops and material.

Flying hours   100hrs/yr combat ac 150 for tpt ac
5 Air bases

FORCES BY ROLE

Integrated with Jt Forces

Ftr/FGA	1 sqn JAS 39C/ JAS 39D *Gripen*
FGA	1 sqn with L-159 ALCA (Lead-in ftr trg); 1 sqn L-39ZA
Tpt	2 sqn with Airbus A-319CJ; Tu-154M *Careless*; An-26 *Curl*; CL-601 *Challenger*; L-410 *Turbolet*; Yak-40 *Codling*
Trg	1 Aviation Trg Centre with L-39C; Z-142C; L-410 *Turbolet*; EW-97 *Eurostar*
Hel	1 sqn with Mi-24/Mi-35 *Hind**; 1 sqn with Mi-17/ 171 Sh; 1 sqn with Mi-8/17, PZL W-3A SOKOL
AD	1 (msl) bde

EQUIPMENT BY TYPE

AIRCRAFT 48 combat capable
  FTR/FGA 14: 12 JAS 39C; 2 JAS 39D *Gripen*
  FGA 24: 20 L-159 ALCA; 4 L-159T (trg)
  TPT 18: 2 Airbus A-319CJ; 5 An-26 *Curl*; 1 CL-601 *Challenger*; 8 L-410 *Turbolet*; 2 Yak-40 *Codling*
  TRG 29: 10 L-39ZA*; 8 L-39C *Albatros*; 8 Z-142C; 2 L-410 *Turbolet*; 1 EW-97 *Eurostar*
HELICOPTERS
  ATK 24: 18 Mi-35; 6 Mi-24 *Hind**
  SPT 41: 27 Mi-17/171 Sh; 4 MI-8; 10 PZL W3A (SOKOL)
  UAV 2 *Sojka* 3
AD • SAM SA-13 *Gopher*; SA-6 *Gainful*; RBS-70; (SA-7 *Grail* available for trg RBS-70 gunners)
MSL • AAM AIM-9M *Sidewinder*; AIM-120 AMRAAM
BOMBS
  Conventional: GBU Mk 82; Mk 84
  Laser-guided: GBU *Paveway*

Joint Forces Support Units

CBRN	1 CBRN bde (2 CBRN bn, 1 CBRN warning centre)
Engr rescue	1 bde (3 engr bn, 2 engr rescue coy)
CIMIC/Psyops	1 (103rd) Centre with (1coy (1 CIMIC pl, 1 PSYOPS pl)
Logistics	1 bde (1 spt bn; 1 supply bn)
EW	1 Centre

Paramilitary 3,100

Border Guards 3,000

Internal Security Forces 100

DEPLOYMENT

Legal provisions for foreign deployment:
Constitution: Codified constitution (1992)
Decision on deployment of troops abroad: By the parliament (Art. 39, 43) or by the government (Art. 43)

AFGHANISTAN
NATO • ISAF 480; **Army**: 19 IVECO DV LMV *Panther* Operation Enduring Freedom – Afghanistan up to 100
UN • UNAMA 1 obs

ARMENIA/AZERBAIJAN
OSCE • Minsk Conference 1

BOSNIA-HERZEGOVINA
OSCE • Bosnia and Herzegovina 1

DEMOCRATIC REPUBLIC OF CONGO
UN • MONUC 2 obs

SERBIA
NATO • KFOR • Joint Enterprise 393; **Army**: 1 inf coy

Denmark DNK

Danish Krone kr		2008	2009	2010
GDP	kr	1.73tr	1.69tr	
	US$	341bn	337bn	
per capita	US$	62,112	61,286	
Growth	%	-1.2	-2.4	
Inflation	%	3.3	1.3	
Def exp	kr	22.7bn		
	US$	4.46bn		
Def bdgt	kr	22.7bn	23.1bn	24.9bn
	US$	4.46bn	4.58bn	
US$1=kr		5.09	5.04	

Population   5,500,510

Age	0–14	15–19	20–24	25–29	30–64	65 plus
Male	10%	3%	3%	3%	25%	6%
Female	9%	3%	3%	3%	24%	8%

Capabilities

ACTIVE 26,585 (Army 10,570 Navy 3,498 Air 3,446 Joint 9,071 (incl civilians))
Terms of service 4–12 months

Home Guard 53,507 (Army) 40,800 (Navy) 4,500 (Air Force) 5,307 (Service Corps) 2,900

ORGANISATIONS BY SERVICE

Army 8,236; 2,130 conscript 204 civilian (total 10,570)

FORCES BY ROLE

Army	1 (op) comd
Mech Inf	1 div (1 mech inf bde with (1 tk bn, 2 mech inf bn, 1 SP arty bn, 1 engr coy, 1 MP coy; (1 bde (lower readiness, exclusively a trg bde and consists of 9 different trg units. The bde can, if necessary, be transformed to a composition equivalent to the 1st bde)
Recce	1 bn
SF	1 unit
Engr	1 bn
AD	1 bn

EQUIPMENT BY TYPE

MBT 167: 65 *Leopard* 2 A4/2A5; 102 *Leopard* 1A5 (in store awaiting disposal)
RECCE 117: 32 *Eagle* 1 (MOWAG); 85 *Eagle IV*
APC 487
  APC (T) 401: 372 M-113 (incl variants and incl 80 in store awaiting disposal); 29 CV9030 Mk II (another 16 due)
  APC (W) 86 *Piranha* III (incl variants)
ARTY 69
  SP 155mm 24 M-109

MRL 227mm 12 MLRS (in store awaiting disposal)
MOR • SP 81mm 33 M-125A2
AT
MSL • SP 21 TOW on M113 (in store awaiting disposal)
MANPATS 20 TOW
RCL 84mm 349 *Carl Gustav*
RL 84mm 4,200 AT-4
AD • SAM • MANPAD FIM-92A *Stinger*
RADAR • LAND ARTHUR

Navy 2,992; 306 civilian; 200 conscript (total 3,498)

EQUIPMENT BY TYPE
PATROL AND COASTAL COMBATANTS 49
PSOH 4 *Thetis* each with 2 twin (4 eff.) with *Stinger*, 1 76mm gun, 1 *Super Lynx* MK 90B
PFM 4 *Flyvefisken* (capacity 60 mines) each with 2 Mk 141 *Harpoon* quad (8 eff.) with RGM-84C *Harpoon*/RGM-84L *Harpoon* tactical SSM, 1 6 cell Mk 48 VLS with 6 *Sea Sparrow* SAM, 2 single 533mm TT, 1 76mm gun
PFT 2 *Flyvefisken* (Patrol fit) each with 1 Mk 48 *Sea Sparrow* VLS with *Sea Sparrow* SAM, 2 single 533mm TT, 1 76mm gun
PCC 9: 1 *Agdlek*; 2 *Knud Rasmussen*; 6 *Diana*
PCI 30 in reserve (Home Guard)
MINE WARFARE 14
MINE COUNTERMEASURES • MHC 4 *Flyvefisken* each with 1 76mm gun
MCMV 4 MSF MK-I
MHD 6 *Sav*
LOGISTICS AND SUPPORT 21:
MRV 6 *Holm*-class (Multi Role – MCM, Survey and general training)
AE 1 *Sleipner*
AG 2 *Absalon* (flexible-support-ships) each with 2 octuple VLS with 16 RGM-84 Block 2 *Harpoon* 2 SSM tactical, 4 twin (4 eff.) with *Stinger* SAM, 3 12 cell Mk 56 VLS with 36 RIM-162B *Sea Sparrow* naval SAM, 1 127mm gun (capacity 2 LCP, 7 MBT or 40 vehicles; 130 troops)
AGB 3; **ABU** 2 (primarily used for MARPOL duties); **AK** 4 *Ro/Ro*; **Tpt** 2; **RY** 1

FACILITIES
Bases   Located at Korsøer and Frederikshavn
Naval airbases Located at Karup, Jutland

Naval Aviation
HELICOPTERS • ASW 8 *Super Lynx* MK90B

Air Force 3,189 plus,145 conscript 112 civilian (total 3,446)
Three air bases
Flying hours   165 hrs/yr

Tactical Air Comd
FORCES BY ROLE
Ftr/FGA   2 sqn with F-16AM/F-16BM *Fighting Falcon*
SAR /Spt 1 sqn with S-61A *Sea King*; EH-101 *Merlin*; 1 sqn with AS-550 *Fennec* (obs)

Tpt   1 sqn with C-130J-30 *Hercules*; CL-604 *Challenger* (MR/VIP)
Trg   1 flying school with SAAB T-17

EQUIPMENT BY TYPE
AIRCRAFT 48 combat capable
FTR: 48 F-16AM/F-16BM *Fighting Falcon*
TPT 7: 4 C-130J-30 *Hercules*; 3 CL-604 *Challenger*
TRG 28 SAAB T-17
HELICOPTERS
ASW 21: 7 S-61A *Sea King* (being phased out); 14 EH-101 *Merlin*
UTL 12 AS-550 *Fennec*
MSL
ASM AGM-65 *Maverick*
AAM AIM-120A AMRAAM; AIM-9L/X *Sidewinder*
BOMBS
INS/GPS-guided: GBU-31 JDAM; EGBU-12/GBU-24 *Paveway* LGB

Control and Air Defence Group
1 Control and Reporting Centre, 1 Mobile Control and Reporting Centre. 4 Radar sites. No SAM.

Reserves
Home Guard (Army) 40,800 reservists (to age 50)
Army 5 (local def) region (*each:* up to 2 mot inf bn); 2 regt cbt gp (*each:* 1 arty bn, 3 mot inf bn)

Home Guard (Navy) 4,500 reservists (to age 50) organised into 30 Home Guard units
EQUIPMENT BY TYPE
PATROL AND COASTAL COMBATANTS 32
PC 32: 18 MHV800; 6 MHV900; 6 MHV90; 2 MHV70

Home Guard (Air Force) 5,307 reservists (to age 50)

Home Guard (Service Corps) 2,900 reservists

DEPLOYMENT
Legal provisions for foreign deployment:
Constitution: Codified constitution (1849)
Decision on deployment of troops abroad: On approval by the parliament (Art. 19 II)

AFGHANISTAN
NATO • ISAF 690; 1 mech BG with (2 mech inf coy; 1 tk pl; 1 hel det); 1 fd hospital; 4 *Leopard* 2A5
UN • UNAMA 1 obs

DEMOCRATIC REPUBLIC OF CONGO
UN • MONUC 2 obs

INDIA/PAKISTAN
UN • UNMOGIP 1 obs

IRAQ
Army 27 (sy forces)
NATO • NTM-I 10
UN • UNAMI 2 obs

LIBERIA
UN • UNMIL 2 obs

MIDDLE EAST
UN • UNTSO 11 obs

SERBIA
NATO • KFOR • *Joint Enterprise* 242: 1 inf gp (1 scout sqn, 1 inf coy)
UN • UNMIK 1 obs

SUDAN
UN • UNMIS 4; 8 obs

Estonia EST

Estonian Kroon kn		2008	2009	2010
GDP	kn	248bn	214bn	
	US$	23.2bn	20.2bn	
per capita	US$	17,725	15,528	
Growth	%	-3.6	-14.0	
Inflation	%	10.2	0.0	
Def exp	kn	4.81bn		
	US$	450m		
Def bdgt	kn	4.59bn	4.05bn	4.10bn
	US$	429m	382m	
FMA (US)	US$	1.5m	1.5m	3.0m
US$1=kn		10.7	10.6	

Population   1,299,371

Ethnic groups: Russian 26%; Ukrainian 2%; Belarussian 1%

Age	0–14	15–19	20–24	25–29	30–64	65 plus
Male	8%	4%	4%	3%	21%	6%
Female	8%	4%	4%	3%	24%	11%

Capabilities

ACTIVE 4750 (Army 4,200 Navy 300 Air 250)

Defence League 10,766

RESERVE 25,000 (Joint 25,000)

Terms of service 8 months, officers and some specialists 11 months.

ORGANISATIONS BY SERVICE

Army 2,200; 2,000 conscript (total 4,200)
FORCES BY ROLE
4 Def region. All units except Scouts bn are reserve based
Inf   1(1ˢᵗ) Bde (2 inf bn (Kalef, Scouts bn), CSS bn); 3 bn (Kuperjanov, Viru, Guards bn)
Recce 1 bn
Arty 1 bn
AD   1 bn
Engr 1 bn

Defence League 10,766
15 Districts

EQUIPMENT BY TYPE
APC (W) 88: 7 *Mamba*; 58 XA-180 *Sisu*; 20 BTR-80; 2 BTR-70; 1 BTR-60
ARTY 335
   TOWED 104:
      105mm 38 M 61-37; **122mm** 42 H63; **155mm** 24 FH-70
   MOR 230:
      81mm 51: 41 B455; 10 NM95; **120mm** 179: 14 2B11; 165 41D
AT
   MANPAT *Milan*
   RCL 160
      106mm: 30 M-40A1; **90mm** 130 PV-1110
AD
   MANPAD SAM *Mistral*
FACILITIES
Centre 1 (peace ops)

Navy 300 (inclusive of a platoon size conscript unit)
LVA, EST and LTU have set up a joint Naval unit BALTRON with bases at Liepaja, Riga, Ventspils (LVA), Tallinn (EST), Klaipeda (LTU).
EQUIPMENT BY TYPE
PRINCIPAL SURFACE COMBATANTS • CORVETTES
• **FS** 1 *Admiral Pitka* with 1 76mm gun
MINE WARFARE • MINE COUNTERMEASURES 4
   MHC 3 *Admiral Cowan* (UK *Sandown*)
   ML 1 Tasuja (DNK *Lindormen*)
FACILITIES
Bases Located at Tallinn, Miinisadam

Air Force 250
Flying hours   120 hrs/year
1 air base
FORCES BY ROLE
Recce   1 surv wg
EQUIPMENT BY TYPE
AIRCRAFT
   TPT 2 An-2 *Colt*
HELICOPTERS • UTL 4 R-44

DEPLOYMENT

Legal provisions for foreign deployment:
Constitution: Codified constitution (1992)
Decision on deployment of troops abroad: By parliament (Art. 128). Also, International Military Cooperation Act stipulates conditions for deployment abroad; parliament decides deployment, unless otherwise provided for by international agreement.

AFGHANISTAN
NATO • ISAF (RC S UKTF Helmand) 150; 1 mech inf coy with 14 XA-180 *Sisu*; 1 mor det with 3 81mm

BOSNIA-HERZEGOVINA
EU • EUFOR • *Operation Althea* 2

IRAQ
NATO • NTM-I 3

MIDDLE EAST
UN • UNTSO 1 obs

MOLDOVA
OSCE • Moldova 2

NATO AOR
NATO • NRF 1 EOD team; 1 MCM

SERBIA
NATO • KFOR • 31; 1 inf pl
OSCE • Serbia 2

France FRA

Euro €		2008	2009	2010
GDP	€	1.94tr	1.92tr	
	US$	2.86tr	2.87tr	
per capita	US$	44,698	44,669	
Growth	%	0.3	-2.4	
Inflation	%	3.2	0.3	
Def exp[a]	€	45.6bn		
	US$	67.1bn		
Def bdgt	€	30.38bn	32.02bn	32.10bn
	US$	44.6bn	47.8bn	
US$1=€		0.68	0.67	

[a] including military pensions

Population   64,420,073

Age	0–14	15–19	20–24	25–29	30–64	65 plus
Male	9%	3%	3%	3%	23%	7%
Female	9%	3%	3%	3%	23%	9%

Capabilities

**ACTIVE 352,771 (Army 134,000 Navy 43,995 Air
57,600 Central Staff 5,200 Service de Santé 8,600
Gendarmerie 103,376)**

**CIVILIAN 46,390 (Army 25,000 Navy 10,265 Air
8,400 Gendarmerie 1,925)**

**RESERVE 70,300 (Army 18,000 Navy 6,000 Air 5,800
Gendarmerie 40,000)**

ORGANISATIONS BY SERVICE

Strategic Nuclear Forces

Navy 2,200
SUBMARINES • STRATEGIC • SSBN 3
3 *Le Triomphant* S 616 each with 16 M-45 SLBM each
with 6 TN-75 nuclear warheads, 4 single 533mm TT

each with up to 18 F17 Mod 2 HWT/SM-39 *Exocet*
tactical USGW (additional vessel expected ISD 2010)
AIRCRAFT • STRIKE/FGA 24 *Super Etendard*

Air Force 1,800

Air Strategic Forces Command

Strike	3 sqn with M-2000N *Mirage* each with 1 ASMP/ASMP-A missile, 2 *Magic* 2 missiles; (for conv missions – MK82 and GBU)
Tkr	1 sqn with C-135FR; KC-135 *Stratotanker*

EQUIPMENT BY TYPE
AIRCRAFT 60 combat capable
 FGA 60 M-2000N *Mirage*
 TKR 14: 11 C-135FR; 3 KC-135 *Stratotanker*

Gendarmerie 41

Army 134,000; 25,000 (civilian)
FORCES BY ROLE
regt normally bn size

Army	4 (task force) HQ; 1 (land) comd HQ; 5 region HQ
Armd	1 bde (FRA/GER bde 2,500 personnel) (1 mech inf regt, 1 armd cav regt); 2 bde *each* (2 armd regt, 2 armd inf regt, 1 SP arty regt, 1 engr regt)
Lt Armd	2 bde with (1 armd cav regt, 2 mech (APC) inf regt, 1 SP arty regt, 1 engr regt)
Mech Inf	2 bde (*each:* 1 armd cav regt, 1 armd inf regt, 1 mech inf regt, 1 SP arty regt, 1 engr regt)
Mtn Inf	1 bde (1 armd cav regt, 3 mech inf regt, 1 arty regt, 1 engr regt)
AB	1 bde (1 armd cav regt, 4 para regt, 1 arty regt, 1 engr regt, 1 spt regt)
Avn	1 bde (4th) (3 cbt, 1 cbt and tpt regt)
Arty/AD	1 bde (3 SAM regt (1 with *I-HAWK MIM-23B*), 2 MLRS regt)
Engr	1 bde (5 engr regt, 1 CBRN regt)
Sigs	1 bde (7 sigs regt, 1 spt regt)
EW/Int	1 bde (1 recce cav regt, 2 UAV regt, 1 EW regt, 1 int bn)

Foreign Legion 7,700

Armd Cav	1 regt (incl in lt armd bde above)
Mech Inf	1 regt (incl in lt armd bde above)
Lt inf	1 regt (Guyana)
Para	1 regt (incl in AB bde above)
Spt	1 regt
Trg	1 Inf regt

Marines 18,100

Marine	14 regt (France); 4 regt (Africa); 15 regt (French overseas possessions)

Special Operation Forces 2,300

FORCES BY ROLE

HQ   1 comd

Para   2 regt

Avn   3 cbt hel; 3 tpt hel sqn

FACILITIES

Training Centre   3

Reserves 18,500

Reservists form:

99 UIR (Reserve Intervention Units) of about 105 to 115 troops, for 'Proterre' (combined land projection forces) battalions.

18 USR (Reserve Specialised Units), of about 85 troops, in specialised regiments.

EQUIPMENT BY TYPE

MBT 637: 400 *Leclerc*; 237 AMX-30

RECCE 1,802: 335 AMX-10RC; 187 ERC-90F4 *Sagaie*; 1,280 VBL M-ll

AIFV 709+: 100+ VBCI; 609 AMX-10P/PC

APC (W) 3,894: 3,806 VAB; 61 VAB BOA; 27 VAB NBC

ARTY 598

  SP 155mm 90: 74 AU-F-1; 16 CAESAR

  TOWED 155mm 98 TR-F-1

  MRL 227mm 61 MLRS

  MOR 120mm 349 RT-F1

AT • MSL

  SP 399: 99 VAB HOT ; 112 VAB *Milan*; 188 VAB *Eryx*;

  MANPATS 553 *Milan*

  RL 84mm AT-4

AIRCRAFT

  TPT 17: 5 PC-6 *Turbo-Porter*; 12 TBM-700

HELICOPTERS 298 attack helicopters

  ATK 298: 25 AS-665 *Tiger*; 272 SA-342M *Gazelle* (all variants)

  RECCE 25: 4 AS-532UL *Cougar Horizon*; 21 AS-532UL *Cougar*

  Spt 8 EC 725AP;

SPT 106: 106 SA-330 *Puma*

UAV 50: 35 CL-289 (AN/USD-502); 15 *SDTI/Sperwer*

AD • SAM 455+

  TOWED 26+ MIM-23B; *I-HAWK* MIM-23B

  MANPAD 882 *Mistral*

RADAR • LAND 74: 10 *Cobra*; 64 RASIT/ RATAC

Gendarmerie 103,376, 1,925 civilians. 40,000 reservist

3,193 (Headquarters); 4,092 (Administration); 2,051 (Maritime Air (personnel drawn from other departments)); 16,754 (Mobile); 4,999 (Republican Guard, Air Tpt, Arsenals); 5,444 (Schools); 63,162 (Territorial); 1,925 (civilians); 3,640 (Overseas); 41 opcon Strategic Nuclear Forces

EQUIPMENT BY TYPE

LT TK 28 VBC-90

APC (W) 153 VBRG-170

ARTY MOR 157+ **60mm**; **81mm**

PATROL AND COASTAL COMBATANTS 41

  PCO 1 *Fulmar*

  PCC 1 *Patra*

PCR 1 *Stellis*

PCI 38 (all less than 100 tonnes)

HELICOPTERS

  UTL 35: 20 EC 135; 15 EC 145

Navy 43,995; 10,265 (civilian); 2,200 opcon Strategic Nuclear Forces (total 46,195 plus 10,265 civilians)

FORCES BY ROLE

Navy 1 HQ opcon HRF (N) located at Toulon; 1 HQ opcon ALFOST located at Brest

EQUIPMENT BY TYPE

SUBMARINES 9

  STRATEGIC • SSBN 3:

    3 *Le Triomphant* S 616 opcon Strategic Nuclear Forces each with 16 M-45 SLBM with 6 TN-75 nuclear warheads, 4 single 533mm TT with up to 18 F17 Mod 2 HWT/SM-39 *Exocet* tactical USGW (additional vessel expected ISD 2010)

  TACTICAL • SSN 6:

    6 *Rubis* each with 4 single 533mm TT with F-17 HWT/SM-39 *Exocet* tactical USGW

PRINCIPAL SURFACE COMBATANTS 33

  AIRCRAFT CARRIERS 2:

    CVN 1 *Charles de Gaulle* with 4 octuple VLS each with *Aster* 15 SAM, 2 *Sadral* sextuple with *Mistral* SAM (capacity 20 *Super Etendard* ftr/FGA ac; 12 *Rafale* M ftr; 3 E-2C *Hawkeye* AEW ac; 2 SA-360 *Dauphin* SAR hel; 3 SA-321 *Super Frelon* SAR hel)

    CVH 1 *Jeanne d'Arc* with 2 triple (6 eff.) each with MM-38 *Exocet* tactical SSM, (capacity 8 SA-319B *Alouette III* ASW hel), 2 100mm gun

  DESTROYERS • DDG 11:

    2 *Cassard* each, with 2 quad (8 eff.) with 8 MM-40 *Exocet* tactical SSM, 1 Mk 13 GMLS with 40 SM-1 MR SAM, 2 single ASTT with L5 HWT, 1 100mm gun, each with 1 AS-565SA *Panther* ASW hel

    7 *Georges Leygues* each with 1 Mk 46 LWT, 8 MM-40 *Exocet* tactical SSM, 1 octuple (8 eff.) with 26 *Crotale* SAM, 2 single ASTT each with L5 HWT, 1 100mm gun, each with 2 *Lynx* utl hel

    2 *Forbin* each with 1 48-cell VLS with *Aster* 15 SAM / *Aster* 30 SAM, 2 *Sadral* sextuple each with *Mistral* SAM, 2 twin TT (4 eff.) with MU-90, 2 76mm, each with 1 NH90 TTH utl hel, (vessels undergoing acceptance trials expected ISD 2010)

    2 *Tourville* each with 6 single with MM-38 *Exocet* tactical SSM, 1 octuple (8 eff.) with 26 *Crotale* SAM, 2 single ASTT with Mk 46 LWT/MU-90, 2 100mm gun, each with 2 *Lynx* Mk4 (*Lynx* MK3) ASW hel

  FRIGATES 20

    FFH 11:

      6 *Floreal* each with, 2 single with 2 MM-38 *Exocet* tactical SSM, 1 100mm gun, each with 1 AS-565SA *Panther* ASW hel

      5 *La Fayette* (space for fitting 2 x 8 cell VLS launchers for *Aster* 15/30), 2 quad (8 eff.) with 8 MM-40 *Exocet* tactical SSM, 1 octuple (8 eff.) with *Crotale* SAM, 1 100mm gun, (capacity either 1 AS-565SA *Panther* ASW hel or 1 SA-321 *Super Frelon* SAR hel)

FF 9 *D'Estienne d'Orves* each with 4 MM-40 *Exocet* tactical SSM, 4 single ASTT, 1 100mm gun

PATROL AND COASTAL COMBATANTS 25

PCO 25: 1 *Arago*; 1 *Grebe*; 1 *Sterne*; 1 *Albatros*; 10 *L'Audacieuse*; 3 *Flamant*; 8 *Leopard* (TRG)

MINE WARFARE • MINE COUNTERMEASURES 21

MCCS 1 *Loire*

MCM SPT 7: 3 *Antares*; 4 *Vulcain*

MHC 13 *Eridan*

AMPHIBIOUS

PRINCIPAL AMPHIBIOUS SHIPS 8

LHD 2 *Mistral* (capacity mixed air group of up to 16 NH-90 or SA-330 *Puma* utl hel or AS-532 *Cougar* utl hel or AS-665 *Tiger* atk hel; 2 LCAC or 4 LCM; 60 AVs; 450 troops)

LPD 2 *Foudre* (capacity 4 AS-532 *Cougar*; either 2 *Edic* LCT or 10 LCM; 22 tanks; 470 troops)

LS • LST 4 *Batral* (capacity 12 trucks; 140 troops)

CRAFT 19: 4 **LCT**; 15 **LCM**

LOGISTICS AND SUPPORT 42:

AORH 4 *Durance* (capacity either 1 SA-319 *Alouette III* utl hel or 1 AS-365 *Dauphin*; 2 utl hel or 1 *Lynx* utl hel)

AF 3

AG 1

AGOR 2

AGI 1 *Dupuy de Lome*

AGM 1

AGS 3

YDT 2

YTM 25

FACILITIES

Bases	1 (HQ) located at Toulon, 1 (HQ) located at Brest, 1 located at Cherbourg , 1 located at Lorient, 1 (HQ) located at Papeete (Tahiti), 1 located at Dzaoudzi (Mayotte), 1 (HQ) located at Port-des-Galets (La Réunion), 1 located at Fort de France (Martinique), 1 located at Nouméa (New Caladonia), 1 located at Cayenne, Gf
Naval air bases	Located at Nîmes-Garons, Landivisiau, Lann-Bihoue, Hyères

Naval Aviation 6,400

Flying hours	180 to 220 hrs/yr on *Super Etendard* strike/FGA ac

FORCES BY ROLE

Nuclear Strike	43 *Super Etendard* (incl Strategic Nuclear Forces)
Ftr	1 sqn with 13 *Rafale* M *F3*; 2 *Rafale* M *F2*
ASW	1 sqn with 31 *Lynx* Mk4 (*Lynx* MK3); 1 sqn with 16 AS-565SA *Panther*
MR	1 sqn with 10 N-262 *Fregate*
MP	2 sqn with 27 *Atlantique* 2*
AEW	1 sqn with 3 E-2C *Hawkeye*
SAR	1 sqn with 9 AS-365F *Dauphin 2*; 1 sqn with 8 SA-321 *Super Frelon*
Trg	1 sqn with 13 SA-319B *Alouette III*; 12 SA-316B *Alouette*; 1 unit with N-262 *Fregate*; 1 unit with 8 CAP 10; 9 *Rallye* MS-880*

EQUIPMENT BY TYPE

AIRCRAFT 87 combat capable

FTR 9 *Rafale* M F1 (in store); 13 *Rafale* M F3; 2 *Rafale* M F2

STRIKE/FGA 43 *Super Etendard* (incl Strategic Nuclear Forces)

MP 36: 27 *Atlantique* 2*; 4 *Falcon* 50M; 5 *Falcon* 200 *Gardian*

AEW 3 E-2C *Hawkeye*

TPT 21: 11 EMB-121 *Xingu*; 10 N-262 *Fregate*

TRG 23: 8 CAP 10; 6 *Falcon* 10 MER; 9 *Rallye* MS-880*

HELICOPTERS

SAR 8 SA-321 *Super Frelon*

ASW 70: 16 AS-565SA *Panther*; 27 *Lynx* Mk4 (*Lynx* MK3); 27 SA-319B *Alouette III*

UTL 9 AS-365 *Dauphin 2*

MSL

ASM AM-39 *Exocet*; ASMP

AAM AS 30 *Laser*; MICA; R-550 *Magic 2*

Marines 2,500

Commando Units

Recce	1 gp
Aslt	3 gp
Atk Swimmer	1 gp
Raiding	1 gp
Spt	1 gp

Fusiliers-Marin 1,600

Force Protection	9 units - 14 (Naval Base) gp

Public Service Force

Naval personnel performing general coast guard, fishery protection, SAR, anti-pollution and traffic surveillance duties. Command exercised through Maritime Prefectures (Premar): Manche (Cherbourg), Atlantique (Brest), Méditerranée (Toulon)

Ships incl in naval patrol and coastal totals

PATROL AND COASTAL COMBATANTS 5

PSO 1 *Albatros*

PCC 4: 3 *Flamant*; 1 *Sterne*

AIRCRAFT • TPT 4 N-262 *Fregate*

HELICOPTERS • UTL 4 AS-365 *Dauphin 2*

Reserves 6,000 reservists

Territorial Command • Atlantic

CECLANT

Navy 1 HQ located at Brest

Indian Ocean

ALINDIEN

Navy 1 (afloat) HQ located at Toulon

Mediterranean

CECMED

Navy 1 HQ located at Toulon

Europe (NATO)

North Sea/Channel

COMAR CHERBOURG
Navy 1 HQ located at Cherbourg

Pacific Ocean

ALPACI
Navy 1 HQ located at Papeete, PF

Air Force 57,600; 8,400 (civilian); 5,800 reservists;

Flying hours 180 hrs/year

Air Forces Command 17,000

Combat Brigade

FORCES BY ROLE

Multi-role	2 AD sqn (St Dizier) plus test and evaluation at Mont-de-Marsan with *Rafale* F2-B/F2-C/F3)
Ftr	2 sqn with M-2000C *Mirage* and M-2000B *Mirage* (Cambrai and Orange), 1 sqn with M-2000-5 *Mirage* (Dijon)
FGA	3 sqn with M-2000D *Mirage* (Nancy), 1 composite sqn with *Mirage* 2000-C/*Mirage* 2000-D (Djibouti)
Recce	2 sqn with F-1CR *Mirage* (Reims)
EW	1 flt with C-160G *Gabriel* (ESM) (Metz)
OCU	1 sqn equipped with *Mirage* 2000B; 1 sqn with *Mirage* Fl-B (Colmar)

EQUIPMENT BY TYPE

AIRCRAFT 277 combat capable

MULTI-ROLE 51: 24 *Rafale* F2-B; 7 *Rafale* F2-C; 12 *Rafale* F3-B; 8 *Rafale* F3-C

FTR 74: 22 M-2000-5 *Mirage*; 52 M-2000C *Mirage*

FGA 88: 66 M-2000D *Mirage*; 22 F-1CT *Mirage*

RECCE 39 F-1CR *Mirage**

EW • ELINT 2 C-160G *Gabriel* (ESM)

TRG 25: 8 F-1B *Mirage**; 17 M-2000B *Mirage**

MSL

AAM MICA; R-550 *Magic* 2; *Super* 530D;

ASM AS-30L; SCALP; *Apache*

BOMBS

Laser-guided: GBU-12 *Paveway* II

Air Mobility Brigade

FORCES BY ROLE

Tpt	heavy sqn with A-310-300; A-319; A-340-200 (on lease)
Tkr/tac tpt	6 sqn with C-130H *Hercules*; C-130H-30; C-160 *Transall*; Transall C-160NG
SAR/trg/tpt/ utl	7 light sqn with CN-235M; DHC-6 *Twin Otter*; *Mystère* 20 (*Falcon* 20); *Falcon* 50 (VIP); *Falcon* 900 (VIP); TBM-700; EC 725 *Caracal*; AS-555 *Fennec*
OCU	1 sqn with SA-330 *Puma*; AS-555 *Fennec*; 1 unit with C-160 *Transall*
Hel	5 sqn with AS-332 *Super Puma*; SA-330 *Puma*; AS-532 *Cougar* (tpt/VIP); AS-555 *Fennec*

EQUIPMENT BY TYPE

AIRCRAFT

TPT 106: 3 A-310-300; 2 A-319 (VIP); 2 A-340-200 (on lease); 5 C-130H; 9 C-130H-30; 42 C-160 *Transall*; 20 CN-235M; 5 DHC-6 *Twin Otter*; 4 *Falcon* 50 (VIP); 2 *Falcon* 900 (VIP); 12 TBM-700; *Mystère* 20

TPT/TKR 15 *Transall* C-160NG

HELICOPTERS

CSAR 6 EC 725 *Caracal*

SPT 36: 7 AS-332 *Super Puma*; 29 SA-330 *Puma*

UTL 45: 3 AS-532 *Cougar* (tpt/VIP); 42 AS-555 *Fennec*

Air Space Control Brigade

FORCES BY ROLE

Air Space	1 Surveillance & Control sqn with E-3F *Sentry*; 1 *Helios*-2a satellite obs sqn (Creil)
AD	8 sqn with *Crotale* 3000, *Crotale* upgraded & *Crotale* NG; 20mm 76T2; *Mistral*
Radar	5 (Control)

EQUIPMENT BY TYPE

SPACE BASED SYSTEMS • SATELLITES

2 IMAGERY 1 *Helios*-2a (Creil)

AIRCRAFT

AEW 4 E-3F *Sentry*

AD SYSTEMS STRIDA (Control)

SAM *Crotale* 3000; *Crotale* upgraded and *Crotale* NG; SATCP

GUNS 20mm 76T2

LAUNCHER *Mistral*

Security and Intervention Brigade

34 protection units

33 fire fighting and rescue sections

3 intervention paratroop commandos

Air Training Command

Over 6,000 personnel

FORCES BY ROLE

Trg some sqn with EMB-121 *Xingu*; *Alpha Jet*; CAP 10; EMB-312 *Tucano*; TB-30 *Epsilon*; Grob G120A-F

EQUIPMENT BY TYPE

AIRCRAFT

TPT 23 EMB-121 *Xingu*

TRG 164: 91 *Alpha Jet*; 25 EMB-312 *Tucano*; 25 TB-30 *Epsilon* (incl many in storage); 18 Grob G120A-F; 5 CAP 10

Reserves 5,800 reservists

DEPLOYMENT

Legal provisions for foreign deployment:

Constitution: Codified constitution (1958)

Specific legislation: 'Order of 7 January 1959'

Decision on deployment of troops abroad: De jure: by the minister of defence, under authority of the PM and on agreement in council of ministers ('Order of 7 January 1959', Art. 16, Art.20-1 of constitution)

AFGHANISTAN

NATO • ISAF 3,095 (*Operation Pamir*): 1 bde HQ; 1 (Marine) inf BG; 1 (Foreign Legion) inf BG (*GTIA Kapisa*); 1 3 AMX 10 RC; 113 VAB APC; 57 VBL; 6 *Mirage* 2000D/SEM; 1 cbt hel bn (3 AS-665 *TigerAH*, 2 AS-532 *Cougar*, 3 EC-725 CSAR hel; 3 *Gazelle* AHl)

Operation Enduring Freedom - Afghanistan (Operation Epidote) 35

ARABIAN GULF AND INDIAN OCEAN

EU • *Operation Atalanta* 3 FFH; 1 SSN; 1 *Atlantique* Maritime Security Operations 1 FFG; 1 AORH

BOSNIA-HERZEGOVINA

EU • EUFOR • *Operation Althea* (*Operation Astrée*) 4 **OSCE** • Bosnia and Herzegovina 7

CENTRAL AFRICAN REPUBLIC

Operation Boali 240; 1 inf coy; 1 spt det

CENTRAL AFRICAN REPUBLIC/CHAD

UN • MINURCAT 308; elm 1 inf coy; 1 engr coy; 1 log bn; 1 tpt coy

CHAD

Operation Epervier 1,200; **Army:** 1 mech inf BG with (elm 1 mech inf regt; elm 1 armd cav regt) **Air Force:** 1 avn gp with 6 F-1CR/F-1CT *Mirage*, 1 C-135, 3 C-160 *Transall*; 1 hel det with 3 SA-330 *Puma*

CÔTE D'IVOIRE

Operation Licorne 900; **Army:** 1 (Marine) mech inf BG with (elm 1 mech inf regt; elm 1 armd cav regt); 1 hel unit ; 1 Gendarmerie sqn **Air Force** 1 C-160 *Transall*, 1 CN-235 **UN** • UNOCI 8; 2 obs

DEMOCRATIC REPUBLIC OF CONGO

UN • MONUC 5 obs

DJIBOUTI

Army 1,690; 1 (Foreign Legion) BG with (1 engr coy, 1 arty bty, 2 recce sqn, 2 inf coy); 1 (Marine) combined arms regt with (1 engr coy, 1 arty bty, 2 recce sqn, 2 inf coy) **Navy:** 1 LCT

Air Force: 1 Air unit with 10 M-2000C/D *Mirage*; 1 C-160 *Transall*; 3 SA-342 *Gazelle*; 7 SA-330 *Puma*; 1 AS-555 *Fennec*; 1 SA-319 *Alouette III*

EGYPT

MFO 18; **Air Force:** 1 CN-235M

FRENCH GUIANA

Army 1,435 1 (Foreign Legion) inf regt; 1 (Marine) inf regt; 1 SMA regt

Navy 150**;** 2 PCO

Air Force 1 tpt unit; 4 SA-330 *Puma*; 3 AS-555 *Fennec* **Gendarmerie** 3 coy; 1 AS-350 *Ecureuil*

FRENCH POLYNESIA

Army 640 (incl Centre d'Expérimentation du Pacifique); 1 (Marine) inf regt; 3 SMA coy

Navy 710; 1 HQ located at Papeete; 1 FFH with 1 AS-565SA *Panther* ASW hel; 4 PCO; 2 LST; 1 AOT; 3 *Gardian* **Air Force** 1 tpt unit; 2 CN-235M; 1 AS-332 *Super Puma*; 1 AS-555 *Fennec*

FRENCH WEST INDIES

Army 775; 2 (Marine) inf regt; 2 SMA regt **Navy** 450; 1 FFH; 1 PCO; 1 LST: 1 naval base located at Fort de France (Martinique)

Air Force 1 tpt unit; 3 CN-235M; 2 SA-330 *Puma*; 1 AS-555SN *Fennec*

Gendarmerie 4 coy; 2 AS-350 *Ecureuil*

GABON

Army 775; 1 recce pl with ERC-90F1 *Lynx*; 1 (Marine) inf bn; 3 SA-330 *Puma* **Air Force** 2 C-160 *Transall*; 1 AS-555 *Fennec*

GERMANY

Army 2,800 (incl elm Eurocorps and FRA/GER bde (2,500)); 1 (FRA/GER) army bde (1 army HQ, 1 armd cav regt, 1 mech inf regt)

HAITI

UN • MINUSTAH 2

INDIAN OCEAN

Army 1,000 (incl La Réunion and TAAF); 1 (Marine) para regt; 1 (Foreign Legion) inf det; 1 SMA regt **Navy** 1 base located at Dzaoudzi (Mayotte), 1 HQ located at Port-des-Galets (La Réunion); 1 FFH with 2 AS-555 *Fennec* utl hel; 1 PSO; 2 PCO; 1 LST

Air Force 1 tpt unit; 2 C-160 *Transall*; 1 spt hel; 2 AS-555 *Fennec*

Gendarmerie 5 coy; 1 SA-319 *Alouette III*

KYRGYZSTAN

NATO • ISAF 1 C-135 tkr

LEBANON

UN • UNIFIL 1,585; **Army** 1 armd inf bn; 1 armd sqn; 1 arty tp; 1 engr coy; 13 *Leclerc*; 35 AMX-1; 4 155mm *Grande Cadence de Tir*; 6 *Mistral*; 2 *Cobra* radar

LIBERIA

UN • UNMIL 1

MIDDLE EAST

UN • UNTSO 2 obs

MOLDOVA

OSCE • Moldova 1

NEW CALEDONIA

Army 935; 1 (Marine) mech inf regt; 2 SMA coy; 6 ERC-90F1 *Lynx*

Navy 510; 1 base with 2 *Gardian* located at Nouméa **Air Force** some air det; 1 tpt unit; 3 CASA 235 MPA; 5 SA-330 *Puma*; 2 AS-555 *Fennec*

Gendarmerie 4 coy; 2 AS-350 *Ecureuil*

SENEGAL

Army 575; 1 (Marine) mech inf bn; 1 recce sqn with ERC-90F1 *Lynx*

Navy 230; 1 LCT; 1 *Atlantique*

Air Force 1 C-160 *Transall*; 1 AS-555 *Fennec*

SERBIA

NATO • KFOR • *Joint Enterprise* 1,294; Army: 1 armd inf BG with (elm 1 armd regt, elm 1 armd inf regt); 1 Gendarmerie regt; some spt units (incl atk hel)

OSCE • Serbia 1
OSCE • Kosovo 14

TAJIKISTAN
NATO • ISAF 160; 1 C-130 *Hercules*; 2 C-160 *Transall*

UAE
3 *Mirage* 2000-5, 1 KC-135F at al-Dhafra (To operate alongside UAE *Mirage*-9s); naval and army contingent

WESTERN SAHARA
UN • MINURSO 13 obs

FOREIGN FORCES

Belgium Air Force: 29 *Alpha Jet* trg ac located at Cazaux/Tours
Germany Army: 209 (GER elm Eurocorps)
Singapore Air Force: 200; 1 trg sqn with 4 A-4SU *Super Skyhawk*; 10 TA-4SU *Super Skyhawk*

Germany GER

Euro €		2008	2009	2010
GDP	€	2.48tr	2.28tr	
	US$	3.65tr	3.40tr	
per capita	US$	44,420	41,352	
Growth	%	1.2	-5.3	
Inflation	%	2.9	0.3	
Def exp [a]	€	31.9bn		
	US$	46.9bn		
Def bdgt	€	29.5bn	31.1bn	31.1bn
	US$	43.3bn	46.5bn	
US$1=€		0.68	0.67	

[a] including military pensions

Population	82,329,758					
Age	0–14	15–19	20–24	25–29	30–64	65 plus
Male	7%	3%	3%	3%	25%	8%
Female	7%	3%	3%	3%	24%	10%

Capabilities

ACTIVE 250,613 (Army 163,962 Navy 24,407 Air 62,244)
Terms of service 9 months; 10–23 months voluntary. *Reserves:* junior ranks to age 45; NCOs and officers to 60.

RESERVE 161,812 (Army 144,548 Navy 3,304 Air 13,960)

ORGANISATIONS BY SERVICE

Army 116,739; 47,223 conscript (total 163,962)

Germany contributes to all multinational Corps HQs in Europe and is the Framework Nation for European Corps, (Strasbourg), the German-Netherlands Corps (Münster) and the Multinational Corps Northeast (Szczecin).

German transformation is due to be complete in 2010 and is proceeding on schedule. Three force categories constitute the core of transformation: Response Forces (RF), Stabilisation Forces (StF) and support forces. These force categories will be specifically trained and equipped for their respective missions. Their overall capability will be enhanced as required from the Army, Air Force, Navy, Joint Support Service and Central Medical Service. The Army forces consists of five divisional headquarters, three of them are deployable, and a total of twelve brigades. Forces are tailored to form Response Forces (1st Armd Div/GER/FRA Bde), 1 bde Special Forces, 1 air mobile div and four stabilisation brigades. The Response Forces brigades are structured to fight in a divisional context supported by the capabilities of the divisional troops. The stabilisation brigades would normally deploy under the command of the Air Mobile Div HQ and receive any additional capability from its Army Support Arms bde. The Special Operations Division Headquarters is designed to provide a multinational special forces headquarters at command level. Its airborne brigades are generally capable of concurrently conducting operations against irregular forces and military evacuation operations. The Joint Support Service assists the individual services in terms of logistics, command support and protection. Its assets include psyops capabilities, logistic follow on support, communication systems and EW-capabilities. Medical support is provided by the Joint Medical Service.

FORCES BY ROLE

Armd   1 div (1st) (RF) with (2 armd bde each (1–2 armd bn, 1–2 armd inf bn, 1 SP arty bn, 1 armd recce coy); spt (armd recce, UAV, MRL, engr, AD regt, NBC units))

Mech   1 (13) div (StF) with 2 bde each (1 armd, 2 armd inf , 1 recce, 1 engr, 1 sig, 1 log bn); 1 div (10) (StF) with 1 bde (1 armd, 2 armd inf, 1 recce, 1 engr, 1 sig,1 log bn), 1 bde (3 mtn inf bn, 1 recce, 1 engr, 1 sig,1 log bn)

Spec Ops 1 div (RF) SF comd, 2 (31, 26) airborne bde each (2 para bn, 1 recce coy, 1 UAV unit, 1 engr coy), 1 SF bde)

Air Mob   1 div (RF) 1 air manoeuvre bde (1 atk hel bn, 1 spt hel bn, 1 air mob inf regt) 1 air tpt bde (2 med tpt (CH-53) hel regt, 1 lt tpt (NH-90) regt (in future)), 1 spt bde (arty, AD, NBC)

Inf   I lt inf bn (GER/FRA Bde)

Arty   1 bn (GER/FRA Bde)

Engr   1 cbt engr coy (GER/FRA Bde)

Trg   1 BG with (35 *Leopard* 2; 26 *Marder* 1; 12 M-109A3G)

EQUIPMENT BY TYPE

MBT 1,385: 1,001 *Leopard* 2 (350 to be upgraded to A6) 384 *Leopard* 1 / A3 / A5 / 1A 4 in store
RECCE 288: 212 *Fennek* (incl 24 engr recce, 10 fires spt); 76 Tpz-1 *Fuchs* (NBC)
AIFV 2,044: 1,911 *Marder* 1 A2 / 1 A3; *5 Puma* (test); 133 *Wiesel* (with 20mm gun)

APC 2,307
  APC (T) 1,161: 200 Bv-206; 961 M-113 (inc 109 arty obs and other variants)
  APC (W) 1,146: 397 APV-2 *Dingo II*; 749 TPz-1 *Fuchs* (incl variants)
ARTY 1201
  SP • 155mm 693: 512 M-109A3G; 181 PzH 2000
  TOWED 77
    105mm 10: 10 M-101
    155mm 67: 67 FH-70
  MRL • 227mm 130: 130 MLRS
  MOR • 120mm 301: 301 *Tampella*
AT • MSL 1,165
  SP 82 *Wiesel* (TOW)
  MANPATS 1,083 *Milan*
AMPHIBIOUS 13 LCM (river engr)
HELICOPTERS 159
  ATK 159 Bo-105 M, Bo-105 (PAH-1) (with HOT)
  RECCE 2 Bo-105M
  SPT 93 CH-53G *Stallion*
  UTL 107: 14 EC 135; 93 UH-1D *Iroquois*
UAV 11: 6 KZO; 5 *Luna* X-2000
UAV MICRO 154: 115 *Aladin*; 39 *MIKADO*
AD
  SAM 289+
    SP SAM 170: 50 ASRAD *Ozelot*; 120 *Roland*
    TOWED 28 PAC-3 *Patriot*
    MANPAD: some FIM-92A *Stinger*
    SPAAGM 91 *Gepard*
  GUNS
    TOWED 20mm • 1,155: 1,155 Rh 202
RADARS 106+: 12 *Cobra*; 65 RASIT (veh, arty); 41 RATAC (veh, arty)

Navy 20,449; 3,958 conscript (total 24,407)

Previous Type Comds have been merged into two Flotillas. Flotilla I combines SS, MCM, PBF and SF whilst Flotilla II comprises 2 FF and Aux squadrons.

EQUIPMENT BY TYPE
SUBMARINES • TACTICAL • SSK 12:
  8 Type 206A each with 8x1 533mm ASTT each with DM2 HWT
  4 Type 212A (2 further vessels on order) each with 6 single 533mm TT with 12 A4 *Seehecht* DM2 HWT
PRINCIPAL SURFACE COMBATANTS 18
  FRIGATES 15
    FFGHM 3:
      3 *Sachsen* each with 2 Mk 141 *Harpoon* quad (8 eff.) each with RGM-84F tactical SSM, 1 32 cell Mk 41 VLS (32 eff.) with 24 SM-2 MR SAM, 32 RIM-162B *Sea Sparrow* SAM, 2 Mk 49 RAM with 21 RIM-116 *RAM* SAM; (capacity either 2 NH-90 utl hel or 2 *Lynx* utl hel)
    FFG 12:
      4 *Brandenburg* each with 2 twin (4 eff.) with MM-38 *Exocet* tactical SSM, 2 Mk 49 RAM with 21 RIM-116 *RAM* SAM, 1 Mk 41 VLS with 16 RIM-7M/RIM-7P, 4 x1 324mm ASTT with Mk 46 LWT, 1 76mm gun, (capacity either 2 MK88 *Sea Lynx* ASW hel or 2 *Sea Lynx* MK88A ASW)

      8 *Bremen* each with 2 Mk 141 *Harpoon* quad (8 eff.) with RGM-84A *Harpoon*/RGM-84C *Harpoon* tactical SSM, 1 Mk 29 *Sea Sparrow* octuple with 16 RIM-7M/RIM-7P, 2 Mk 49 RAM with 21 RIM-116 RAM SAM, 2 twin 324mm ASTT (4 eff.) with Mk 46 LWT, 1 76mm gun, (capacity either 2 MK88 *Sea Lynx* ASW hel or 2 *Sea Lynx* MK88A ASW)
  CORVETTES 3
    FS 3 *Braunschweig* (K130) (further two of class expected 2009-2010)
PATROL AND COASTAL COMBATANTS • PFM 10
  10 *Gepard* each with 2 twin (4 eff.) with MM-38 *Exocet* tactical SSM, 1 Mk 49 RAM with 21 RIM-116 *RAM* SAM, 1 76mm gun
MINE WARFARE • MINE COUNTERMEASURES 37:
  MHC 14: 9 *Frankenthal*; 5 *Kulmbach*
  MSC 5 *Ensdorf*
  MSD 18 *Seehund*
AMPHIBIOUS • LC 3
  LCM 1
  LCU 2 Type 521
LOGISTICS AND SUPPORT 31
  AO 2 *Walchensee* Type 703
  AOT 2 *Spessart* Type 704
  AFH 2 *Berlin* Type 702 (capacity either 2 NH-90 utl hel or 2 *Sea King* MK41 SAR hel; 2 RAMs)
  AE (AMMO) 1 *Westerwald* Type 760
  AG 6: 3 *Schwedeneck* Type 748; 3 *Stollergrund* Type 745
  AGOR 1 *Planet* Type 751
  AGI 3 *Oste* Type 423
  AT 5
  Trg 1
  SPT 6 *Elbe* Type 404 (2 specified for PFM support; 1 specified for SSK support; 3 specified for MHC/MSC support)
  Trial Ship 2
FACILITIES
Bases Located at Olpenitz, Wilhelmshaven, Glücksburg (Maritime HQ), Warnemünde, Eckernförde, Kiel

Naval Aviation 2,227
AIRCRAFT
  MP 9: 1 *Atlantic*; 8 AP-3C *Orion*
  TPT 2 Do-228 (2 pollution control)
HELICOPTERS
  SAR 21 *Sea King* MK41 (SAR)
  ASW 22 *Sea Lynx* MK88A (ASW/ASuW)
MSL • TACTICAL • ASM *Sea Skua*

Air Force 50,270; 11,974 conscript (total 62,244)
Flying hours   150 hrs/year

Air Force Command
FORCES BY ROLE

Air	1st, 2nd and 4th Air Divs
Ftr	1 wg (2 sqn with F-4F *Phantom II*); 2 wg with EF-2000 *Eurofighter*
FGA	2 wg (4 FGA sqn with *Tornado* IDS); 1 wg (2 FGA sqn with *Tornado* ECR* plus IDS)

Recce	1 wg (2 recce sqn with *Tornado* IDS (recce))
Radar	3 (tac air control) gp
SAM	3 wg (each 2 SAM gp) with MIM-104 *Patriot*
Trg	sqns with 35 T-37B *Tweet*; 40 T-38A *Talon*

EQUIPMENT BY TYPE

AIRCRAFT 303 combat capable
FTR 114: 38 EF-2000 *Eurofighter*; 76 F-4F *Phantom II*
STRIKE/FGA: 156 *Tornado* IDS (incl 42 recce); another 64 in store
SEAD 33 *Tornado* ECR*
TRG 75: 35 T-37B *Tweet*; 40 T-38A *Talon*
AD • SAM • TOWED MIM-104 *Patriot*
MSL
    ASM KEPD 350
    ASSM *Kormoran* 2
    ARM AGM-88B HARM
    AAM AIM-9L/Li *Sidewinder*; LFK AIM-2000 *Iris*-T (being introduced); AIM 120A/B AMRAAM
BOMBS
    LGB: GBU-24 *Paveway* III

Transport Command

FORCES BY ROLE

| Tkr/tpt | 1 (special air mission) wg with 7 A-310 (4 MRTT, 3 MRT); 6 CL-601 *Challenger*; 3 AS-532U2 *Cougar II* (VIP) |
| Tpt | 3 wg (*total*: 4 tpt sqn with 80 UH-1D (76 SAR, tpt, liaison, 4 VIP)(1 OCU); 3 tpt sqn with 83 C-160 *Transall* (1 OCU)) |

EQUIPMENT BY TYPE

AIRCRAFT • TPT 96: 7 A-310 (incl tpt/tkr); 83 C-160 *Transall*; 6 CL-601 *Challenger* (VIP)
HELICOPTERS • UTL 83: 3 AS-532U2 *Cougar II* (VIP); 80 UH-1D *Iroquois* (76 SAR, tpt, liaison, 4 VIP)

Training

OCU	1 with 23 *Tornado* IDS
Missile trg	Located at Fort Bliss (TX), US
NATO joint pilot trg	Sheppard AFB (TX) with T-6 *Texan* TII, 40 T-38A

DEPLOYMENT

Legal provisions for foreign deployment:
Constitution: Codified constitution ('Basic Law', 1949)
Specific legislation: 'Parlamentsbeteiligungsgesetz' (2005)
Decision on deployment of troops abroad: a) By parliament: in general and in the case of military intervention; b) by government: in urgent cases of threat or emergency (parliamentary consent a posteriori), or for preparatory measures or humanitarian interventions; c) simplified procedure for 'missions of low intensity' or if the government seeks an extension of parliamentary approval (§§ 1–5 of the 2005 law)

AFGHANISTAN

NATO • ISAF 4,365 (PRTs in Kunduz and Fayzabad; QRF in RC-N.) **Army:** 1 bde HQ; 1 air mob inf regt; *Marder*; AIFV; TPz-1 *Fuchs*; *Fennek*; 100 *Dingo* II; LUNA UAV **Air Force:** 6 *Tornado* ECR (SEAD); CH-53 spt hel; C-160 tpt ac
UN • UNAMA 1 obs

ARABIAN GULF AND INDIAN OCEAN

EU • Operation Atalanta 2 FFG
Maritime Security Operations 1 FFG

BOSNIA-HERZEGOVINA

EU • EUFOR • Operation Althea 129; 28 SPz-2 *Luchs*; TPz-1 *Fuchs*; 3 CH-53 *Sea Stallion*; 2 UH-1D
OSCE • Bosnia and Herzegovina 3

DEMOCRATIC REPUBLIC OF CONGO

EU • EUSEC RD Congo 3

FRANCE

Army 209 (GER elm Eurocorps)

ITALY

Navy: 3 MP ac (in ELMAS/Sardinia)

LEBANON

UN •UNIFIL 459; Navy:2 PC; 1 SPT

LITHUANIA

NATO • Baltic Air Policing 100; 6 F-4F *Phantom II*

MEDITERRANEAN SEA

NATO • Operation Active Endeavour 1 AOT

MOLDOVA

OSCE • Moldova 1

POLAND

Army 67 (GER elm Corps HQ (multinational))

SERBIA

NATO • KFOR • Joint Enterprise 2,486; **Army:** 1 inf bn HQ; 3 inf coy; elm 1 hel bn; elm 1 recce coy; elm 1 engr coy; 1 sigs bn; 1 CIMIC coy; elm 1 log unit; elm 1 MP coy; 1 med unit; 26 *Leopard* C2; 17 SPz-2 *Luchs*; 25 *Marder* 1; 54 TPz-1 *Fuchs*; 10 M-109A3G; 6 *Wiesel* (TOW); 3 CH-53 *Sea Stallion*; **Air Force** 3 UH-1D *Iroquois*
OSCE • Serbia 3
OSCE • Kosovo 16

SUDAN

UN • UNMIS 5; 26 obs
UN • UNAMID 7

UNITED STATES

Army: 1 (battle) army gp (trg) (army trg area) with 35 *Leopard* 2; 26 *Marder* 1; 12 M-109A3G **Air Force:** 812 (flying trg) located at Goodyear AFB (AZ); Sheppard AFB (TX) with 35 T-37 *Tweet* trg ac and 40 T-38 *Talon* trg ac; Holloman AFB (NM) with 23 *Tornado* IDS; NAS Pensacola (FL); Fort Rucker (AL)
NATO • Air Force • Missile trg located at Fort Bliss (TX) Primary trg sqn located at Goodyear AFB (AZ), Joint jet pilot trg sqn located at Sheppard AFB (TX); some Beech F-33 *Bonanza*

UZBEKISTAN

NATO • ISAF 104: C-160 *Transall* tpt ac

FOREIGN FORCES

Canada NATO 287

France Army: 1 (FRA/GER) army bde (1 army HQ, 1 armd cav rgt, 1 mech inf regt); 2,800 (incl elm Eurocorps and FRA/GER bde (2,500))

Netherlands Air Force: 300

United Kingdom Army 22,000; 1 army corps HQ (multinational); 1 armd div **Royal Navy** 30; **Air Force** 320

United States US Africa Command: **Army**; 1 HQ located at Stuttgart **USAF**; 1 HQ (17th Air Force) located at Ramstein AB. US European Command: 1 combined service HQ (EUCOM) located at Stuttgart-Vaihingen **Army** 38,537; 1 HQ (US Army Europe (USAREUR) located at Heidelberg; 1 mech inf SBCT; 1 armd inf bde; 1 (hvy) cbt avn bde (1 armd inf bde deployed to Iraq); 1 (APS) armd HBCT eqpt. set (transforming); some M-1 *Abrams*; some M-2/M-3 *Bradley*; some *Stryker*; some M-109; some MLRS; some AH-64 *Apache*; some CH-47 *Chinook*; some UH-60 *Black Hawk* **Navy** 249 **USAF** 14,856; 1 HQ (US Airforce Europe (USAFE)) located at Ramstein AB; 1 HQ (3rd Air Force) located at Ramstein AB; 1 ftr wg located at Spangdahlem AB with (1 atk/FAC sqn with 12 A-10 *Thunderbolt II*; 6 OA-10 *Thunderbolt II*, 2 ftr sqn each with 21 F-16C *Fighting Falcon*); 1 airlift wg located at Ramstein AB with 16 C-130E *Hercules*; 2 C-20 Gulfstream; 9 C-21 Learjet; 1 CT-43 *Boeing 737*; **USMC** 318

Greece GRC

Euro €		2008	2009	2010
GDP	€	242bn	261bn	
	US$	356bn	390bn	
per capita	US$	33,189	36,280	
Growth	%	2.9	-0.8	
Inflation	%	4.2	1.3	
Def exp[a]	€	6.89bn		
	US$	10.1bn		
Def bdgt	€	4.16bn	4.32bn	
	US$	6.11bn	6.45bn	
US$1=€		0.68	0.67	

[a] including military pensions and procurement

Population   10,737,428

Age	0–14	15–19	20–24	25–29	30–64	65 plus
Male	7%	3%	3%	4%	24%	8%
Female	7%	3%	3%	4%	24%	10%

Capabilities

ACTIVE 156,600 (Army 93,500 Navy 20,000 Air 31,500 Joint 11,600) **Paramilitary 4,000**

Terms of service: Conscripts in all services up to 12 months

RESERVE 237,500 (Army 198,000 Navy 8,000 Air 31,500)

ORGANISATIONS BY SERVICE

Army 93,500; ε35,530 conscript

FORCES BY ROLE

Field army to re-org. Units are manned at 3 different levels – Cat A 85% fully ready, Cat B 60% ready in 24 hours, Cat C 20% ready in 48 hours (requiring reserve mobilisation). There are 3 military regions

Comd	1 HQ; 4 corps HQ (incl NDC-GR)
Armd	1 div HQ; 4 bde (*each*: 1 mech inf bn, 1 SP arty bn, 2 armd bn)
Recce	5 bn
Mech Inf	3 div HQ; 7 bde (*each*: 1 armd bn, 1 SP arty bn, 2 mech bn)
Inf	1 div HQ ; 5 bde (*each*: 1 armd bn, 1 arty regt, 3 inf regt)
SF	1 comd (1 (cdo) amph bde; 1 cdo para bde)
Marine	1 bde
Fd Arty	1 bde (8 regt (incl 2 bn MLRS))
Air Mob	1 bde
AD	3 bn (2 I-*HAWK*, 1 *TOR* M1)
Avn	1 bde (1 avn regt (2 atk hel bn), 1 spt hel bn, 3 avn bn)
Log	2 div (4 bde)

EQUIPMENT BY TYPE

MBT 1,688: 170 *Leopard* 2A6HEL; 180 *Leopard* 2 A4; 511 *Leopard* 1; 324 M-60A1 / M-60A3; 503 M-48A5
RECCE 242 VBL
AIFV 377 BMP-1
APC (T) 2,105: 432 *Leonidas* Mk1/*Leonidas* Mk2; 1,673 M-113A1/M-113A2
ARTY 3,163
  SP 348: **155mm** 221: 197 M-109A1B/M-109A2/M-109A3GEA1/M-109A5; 24 PzH 2000; **203mm** 127 M-110A2
  TOWED 412: **105mm** 283: 265 M-101; 18 M-56; **155mm** 129 M-114
  MRL 151: **122mm** 115 RM-70 *Dana*; **227mm** 36 MLRS (incl ATACMS)
  MOR 2,252: **81mm** 1,632; **107mm** 620 M-30 (incl 231 SP)
AT
  MSL 1,108
    SP 362: 320 M-901; 42 *Milan* HMMWV
    MANPATS 746: 196 9P163 *Kornet-E*; 262 9K111 AT-4 *Spigot*; 248 *Milan*; 40 TOW
  RCL 4,090:
    SP 106mm 746 M-40A1
    MANPAT 3,344: **84mm** 2,000 *Carl Gustav*; **90mm** 1,344 EM-67
AIRCRAFT
  TPT 3: 1 C-12C *Huron*; 2 C-12R/AP *Huron*
  UTL 38 U-17A
HELICOPTERS
  ATK 32: 20 AH-64A *Apache*; 12 AH-64D *Apache*
  SPT 15 CH-47D *Chinook*
  UTL 114: 14 AB-206 (Bell 206) *JetRanger*; 100 UH-1H *Iroquois*
UAV 12-18 *Sperwer*

Europe (NATO)

AD
  SAM 1,722
    SP 113: 21 SA-15 *Gauntlet* (TOR-M1); 38 SA-8B *Gecko*;
    54 ASRAD HMMWV
    TOWED 42 *I-HAWK MIM-23B*
    MANPAD 1,567 FIM-92A *Stinger*
  GUNS
    TOWED 683: **20mm** 160 Rh 202; **23mm** 523 ZU-23-2
  RADAR • LAND 76: 3 ARTHUR, 5 AN/TPQ-36 *Firefinder*
  (arty, mor); 8 AN/TPQ-37(V)3; 40 BOR-A; 20 MARGOT

National Guard 34,500 reservists

Internal security role

Inf	1 div
Para	1 regt
Fd Arty	8 bn
ADA	4 bn
Avn	1 bn

Navy 16,000; 4,000 conscript; (total 20,000)

EQUIPMENT BY TYPE
SUBMARINES • TACTICAL • SSK 8:
  8 *Glavkos* (GER T-209/1100) each with 8 single 533mm TT
  each with UGM-84C *Harpoon* tactical USGW, SUT HWT
  2 *Papanikolis* (*Poseidon* class) (GER T-214) (two more in
  build); 3rd in trials all vessels under contractual dispute)
  with 8 single 533mm TT each with UGM-84C *Harpoon*
  tactical USGW, SUT HWT
PRINCIPAL SURFACE COMBATANTS 17
  FRIGATES • FFG 14:
    4 Standard Class Batch I (*Elli* class*)* (NLD *Kortenaer*
    Batch 2) each with 2 Mk 141 *Harpoon* quad (8 eff.) each
    with RGM-84A *Harpoon*/RGM-84C *Harpoon* tactical
    SSM, 1 Mk 29 *Sea Sparrow* octuple with 16 RIM-7M/
    RIM-7P *Sea Sparrow* SAM, 2 twin ASTT (4 eff.) each
    with Mk 46 LWT, 1 76mm gun, (capacity 2 AB-212 (Bell
    212) utl hel)
    2 Standard Class Batch II (*Elli* class*)* (NLD *Kortenaer*
    Batch 2) each with 2 Mk 141 *Harpoon* quad (8 eff.) each
    with RGM-84A *Harpoon*/RGM-84C *Harpoon* tactical
    SSM, 1 Mk 29 *Sea Sparrow* octuple with 16 RIM-7M/
    RIM-7P *Sea Sparrow* SAM, 2 twin ASTT (4 eff.) each
    with Mk 46 LWT, 2 76mm gun, (capacity 2 AB-212 (Bell
    212) utl hel)
    4 Standard Class Batch III (*Elli* class*)* (NLD *Kortenaer*
    Batch 2) each with 2 Mk 141 *Harpoon* quad (8 eff.) each
    with RGM-84A *Harpoon*/RGM-84C *Harpoon* tactical
    SSM, 1 Mk 29 *Sea Sparrow* octuple with 16 RIM-7M/
    RIM-7P *Sea Sparrow* SAM, 2 twin ASTT (4 eff.) each
    with Mk 46 LWT, 1 76mm gun, (capacity 2 AB-212 (Bell
    212) utl hel)
    4 *Hydra* (GER MEKO 200) each with 2 quad (8 eff.) each
    with RGM-84G *Harpoon* tactical SSM, 1 16 cell Mk 48
    MOD5 VLS with 16 RIM-7M *Sea Sparrow* SAM, 2 triple
    ASTT (6 eff.) each with Mk 46 LWT, 1 127mm gun,
    (capacity 1 S-70B *Seahawk* ASW hel)
  CORVETTES • FS 3:
    3 *Doxa* (GER *Thetis*) each with 2 triple 324mm ASTT (6
    eff.) each with Mk 46 LWT, 2 twin 40mm gun (4 eff.)

PATROL AND COASTAL COMBATANTS 40
  PFM 20:
    5 *Kavaloudis* (FRA *La Combattante* II, III, IIIB) each with
    6 RB 12 *Penguin* tactical SSM, 2 single 533mm TT each
    with SST-4 HWT, 2 76mm gun
    4 *Laskos* (FRA *La Combattante* II, III, IIIB) each with 4
    MM-38 *Exocet* tactical SSM, 2 single 533mm TT each
    with SST-4 HWT, 2 76mm gun
    2 *Votsis* (FRA *La Combattante*) each with 2 Mk-141
    Harpoon twin each with RGM-84C *Harpoon* tactical
    SSM, 1 76mm gun
    4 *Votsis* (FRA *La Combattante* IIA) each with 4 MM-38
    Exocet tactical SSM, 1 76mm gun
    5 *Roussen* (*Super Vita*) with 8 MM-40 *Exocet* tactical
    ASSM, (2 additional vessels in build)
  PFT 4 *Andromeda* (NOR *Nasty*) each with 4 single 533mm
  TT each with SST-4 HWT
  PC 2 *Stamou* with 4 single SS 12M tactical SSM
  PCO 8: 2 *Armatolos* (DNK *Osprey*); 2 *Pirpolitis*; 4 *Machitis*
  PCC 2 *Tolmi*
  PCI 4
MINE COUNTERMEASURES 11
    MHC 4: 2 *Evropi* (UK *Hunt*); 2 *Evniki* (US *Osprey*)
    MSC 7 *Alkyon* (US MSC-294)
AMPHIBIOUS
  LS • LST 5:
    5 *Chios* (capacity 4 LCVP; 300 troops) each with 1 hel
    landing platform (for med hel)
  CRAFT 52: 2 LCT; 4 LCU; 31 LCVP; 4 LCM; 7 LCA
    ACV 4 *Kefallinia* (*Zubr*) (capacity either 3 MBT or 10
    APC (T); 230 troops)
LOGISTICS AND SUPPORT 23:
  AORH 1 AE *Etna*
  AOT 6: 2; 4 (small)
  AE 2 (ex-GER *Luneburg*)
  AWT 6
  AGHS 3
  TPT 2
  TRG 1
  YTL 2
FACILITIES
Bases Located at Salamis, Patras, Soudha Bay

Naval Aviation

FORCES BY ROLE
ASW	1 Division with 11 S-70B *Seahawk*; 8 AB-212 (Bell 212) ASW; 2 SA-319 *Alouette III*
MP	2 sqn with 6 P-3B *Orion*; 2 CL-415GR (CL-415)

EQUIPMENT BY TYPE
AIRCRAFT
  MARITIME PATROL 6 P-3B *Orion*
  SPT 2 CL-415GR (CL-415)
HELICOPTERS 11 attack helicopters
  ASW 11 S-70B *Seahawk*
  UTL 10: 8 AB-212 (Bell 212); 2 SA-319 *Alouette III*
MSL
  ASM AGM-119 *Penguin*
  ASSM MM-40 *Exocet*

Air Force 31,500 (incl 11,000 conscripts)

Tactical Air Force

FORCES BY ROLE

AD/FGA   4 sqn with F-16CG/DG Block 30, *Fighting Falcon*; 3 sqn with F-16CG/DG Block 52+ *Fighting Falcon*; 1 sqn with M-2000-5 Mk 2 *Mirage*; 2 sqn with M-2000E/BGM *Mirage*; 2 sqn with F-4E *Phantom II*; 2 sqn with A/TA-7E/H *Corsair II*

Recce   1 sqn with RF-4E *Phantom II*

AEW   1 sqn with EMB-145H *Erieye*

EQUIPMENT BY TYPE

AIRCRAFT 242 combat capable

  FTR 25 M-2000-5 Mk 2 *Mirage* (20 -5EG, 5 -5BG)

  FGA 198: 20 M-2000EG/BG *Mirage*; 70 F-16CG/DG Block 30 *Fighting Falcon*: 30 F-16 C/D Block 52+ *Fighting Falcon* (20 F-16C/10 F-16D); 35 F-4E *Phantom II*; 43 A/TA-7E/H *Corsair II*

  RECCE 19 RF-4E *Phantom II**

  AEW 4 EMB-145H *Erieye*

MSL

  AAM AIM 120B/C AMRAAM; AIM-7E/F *Sparrow*; AIM-9L/AIM-9P *Sidewinder*; MICA; R-550 *Magic 2*; Super 530; IRIS-T

  ASM AGM-65A/B/G *Maverick*; SCALP EG

  ASSM AM 39 *Exocet*

  ARM AGM-88 HARM

BOMBS

  Conventional: GBU-8B HOBOS

  Laser-guided: GBU-12/ GBU-16 *Paveway* II; GBU-24 *Paveway* III

Air Defence

FORCES BY ROLE

SAM   6 sqn/bty PAC-3 *Patriot* with 36 launchers [MIM-104 (A/B SOJC/D GEM)]; 2 sqn/bty with S-300 PMU-1 with 12 launchers; 12 bty *Skyguard* with *Sparrow* RIM-7/GUNS; 9 *Crotale* NG/GR; 4 SA-15 *Gauntlet* (TOR-M1)

EQUIPMENT BY TYPE

  AD

    SAM TOWED 61+: 36 PAC-3 *Patriot*; 12 S-300 PMU-1; 9 *Crotale* NG/GR; 4 SA-15 *Gauntlet* (TOR-M1); some *Skyguard/Sparrow*

    GUNS 35+ 35mm

Air Support Command

FORCES BY ROLE

CSAR   1 sqn with S-332 *Super Puma*

Tpt   3 sqn with C-130B *Hercules*; C-130H *Hercules*; YS-11-200; C-47 *Skytrain*; Do-28; 1 sqn with C-27J *Spartan* (8 AT and 4 AAR); 1 sqn with EMB-135; *Gulfstream* V

Hel   1 sqn with AS-332 *Super Puma* (SAR); AB-205A (Bell 205A) (SAR); AB-212 (Bell 212) (VIP, tpt); Bell 47G (liaison)

EQUIPMENT BY TYPE

AIRCRAFT • TPT 39: 5 C-130B *Hercules*; 10 C-130H *Hercules*; 12 C-27J *Spartan* (8 AT and 4 AAR) – being delivered; 2 C-47 *Skytrain*; 6 Do-28; 2 EMB-135; 1 *Gulfstream* V; 1 YS-11-200

HELICOPTERS

  SPT 10 AS-332 *Super Puma*

  UTL 17: 4 AB-212 (Bell 212) (VIP, tpt); 13 AB-205A (Bell 205A) (SAR),

  TRG 7 Bell 47G (liaison)

Air Training Command

FORCES BY ROLE

Trg   5 sqn with T-2C/E *Buckeye*; T-41 D; T-6A/B *Texan II*

EQUIPMENT BY TYPE

AIRCRAFT • TRG 104: 40 T-2C/E *Buckeye*; 19 T-41D; 20 T-6A *Texan II*; 25 T-6B *Texan II*

Paramilitary • Coast Guard and Customs 4,000

PATROL AND COASTAL COMBATANTS 90: 4 PCO; 1 PFC; 7 PCC; 39 PBC; 39 PBI

AIRCRAFT • UTL 4

2 Cessna 172RG *Cutlass*

2 TB-20 *Trinidad*

DEPLOYMENT

Legal provisions for foreign deployment:

Constitution: Codified constitution (1975/1986/2001)

Specific legislation: 'Law 2295/95' (1995))

Decision on deployment of troops abroad: By the Government Council on Foreign Affairs and Defence

AFGHANISTAN

NATO • ISAF 145; **Army:** 1 engr coy **Air Force**: 1 C-130

ARABIAN GULF AND INDIAN OCEAN

EU • *Operation Atalanta* 1 FFG; 1 AP-3C *Orion*

NATO • *Operation Ocean Shield* 1 FFG

BOSNIA-HERZEGOVINA

EU • EUFOR • *Operation Althea* 44

OSCE • Bosnia and Herzegovina 4

CYPRUS

Army 950 (ELDYK army); ε200 (officers/NCO seconded to Greek-Cypriot National Guard) (total 1,150)

1 mech bde (1 armd bn, 2 mech inf bn, 1 arty bn); 61 M-48A5 MOLF MBT; 80 *Leonidas* APC; 12 M-114 arty; 6 M-107 arty; 6 M-110A2 arty

LEBANON

UN • UNIFIL 45; 1 PB

SERBIA

OSCE • Serbia 1

NATO • KFOR • *Joint Enterprise* 588; 1 mech inf bn

OSCE • Kosovo 5

SUDAN

UN • UNMIS 1; 2 obs

WESTERN SAHARA

UN • MINURSO 1 obs

FOREIGN FORCES

United States US European Command: **Army** 11; **Navy:** 291; **USAF** 57; **USMC** 12; 1 naval base located at Makri; 1 naval base located at Soudha Bay; 1 air base located at Iraklion

Hungary HUN

Hungarian Forint f		2008	2009	2010
GDP	f	26.2tr	25.5tr	
	US$	153bn	139bn	
per capita	US$	15,374	14,082	
Growth	%	0.6	-6.7	
Inflation	%	6.0	4.5	
Def exp	f	321bn		
	US$	1.86bn		
Def bdgt	f	354bn	340bn	367bn
	US$	2.06bn	1.86bn	
FMA (US)	US$	1.0m	1.0m	1.0m
US$1=f		172	183	

Population   9,905,596

Ethnic groups: Romany 4%; German 3%; Serb 2%; Romanian 1%; Slovak 1%

Age	0–14	15–19	20–24	25–29	30–64	65 plus
Male	8%	3%	3%	4%	23%	6%
Female	8%	3%	3%	4%	25%	9%

Capabilities

ACTIVE 29,450 (Army 10,936, Air 5,664 Joint 12,850) **Paramilitary 12,000**

RESERVE 44,000 (Army 35,200 Air 8,800)

Terms of service HDF has a voluntarily (contracted soldier) system.

ORGANISATIONS BY SERVICE

Hungary's armed forces have reorganised into a joint force.

Joint Component 12,850

FORCES BY ROLE

Comd	1 (HDF) HQ (Sig regt)
CS	1 Bde
EOD	1 Riverine ptrl bn

Land Component 10,936 (incl riverine element)

FORCES BY ROLE

Armd	1 bn
Lt inf	2 bde (*total:* 4 mech inf, 1 lt inf, 1 mixed bn)
SOF	1 bn ; 1 AB/air asslt bn
Engr	1 bde (1 engr, 1 CBRN bn)
Log	1 regt
Sigs	1 regt

EQUIPMENT BY TYPE

MBT 30 T-72
AIFV 164 BTR-80A
APC (W) 164 BTR-80
ARTY 219+
    SP **122mm** 153+ 2S1 *Carnation* in store awaiting disposal
    TOWED **152mm** 16 D-20
    MOR **81mm** 50
AT • MSL • MANPATS 130: 30 AT-4 9K111 *Spigot*; 100 AT-5 9K113 *Spandrel*
PATROL AND COASTAL COMBATANTS • PBR 2
FACILITIES
Training Centre 2

Air Component 5,664

Flying hours	50 hrs/yr1 hel base (Szolnok), 2 air bases (Kecskemet, Papa)

FORCES BY ROLE

Comd	1 Comd and Air Surv rgt
Multirole	1 tac ftr sqn with JAS-39 *Gripen*: 1 tac ftr sqn with MiG-29B/MiG-29UB *Fulcrum*)
Tpt	1 tpt hel bn with Mi-/17 *Hip*; 1 tac airlift sqn with An-26 *Curl*.
Trg	1 trg sqn with L-39ZO; Yak-52
Atk hel	1 (cbt) bn with Mi-24 *Hind*
AD	1 AD rgt with 9 *Mistral* bty; 3 SA-6 *Gainful* bty
NATO AT	NATO Hy Airlift Wg with 3 C-17A *Globemaster* based at Papa

EQUIPMENT BY TYPE

AIRCRAFT 27 combat capable
    MULTIROLE 14 JAS-39 *Gripen* (12 -C, 2 -D)
    FTR 11 MiG-29B *Fulcrum*
    TPT 5 An-26 *Curl*
    TRG 18: 7 L-39ZO *Albatros*; 2 MiG-29UB *Fulcrum**; 9 Yak-52
HELICOPTERS
    ATK 12 Mi-24 *Hind*
    SPT 17: 10 Mi-8 *Hip*; 7 Mi-17 (Mi-8MT) *Hip*
AD • SAM 61
    SP 16 SA-6 *Gainful*
    MANPAD 45 *Mistral*
    RADAR: 3 RAT-31DL, 6 P-18: 6 SZT-68U; 14 P-37
MSL
    AAM AIM 120C AMRAAM on order; 84 AA-10 *Alamo*; 210 AA-11 *Archer*; 60 AIM-9 *Sidewinder*
    ASM 20 AGM-65 *Maverick*; 150 AT-2 *Swatter*; 80 AT-6

Paramilitary 12,000

Border Guards 12,000 (to reduce)

Ministry of Interior

FORCES BY ROLE

Paramilitary   1 (Budapest) district (7 Rapid Reaction coy); 11 (regt/district) regt

EQUIPMENT BY TYPE
APC (W) 68 BTR-80

DEPLOYMENT

Legal provisions for foreign deployment:
Constitution: Codified constitution (1949)
Decision on deployment of troops abroad: By gov in case of NATO/EU operations (Art. 40/C para 1). Otherwise, by parliament (Art. 19, para 3 point j)

AFGHANISTAN
NATO • ISAF 360; **Land Component**: 1 lt inf coy

ARMENIA/AZERBAIJAN
OSCE • Minsk Conference 1

BOSNIA-HERZEGOVINA
EU • EUFOR • *Operation Althea* 160; **Land Component**: 1 inf coy
OSCE • Bosnia and Herzegovina 2

CYPRUS
UN • UNFICYP 84; **Land Component**: elm 1 inf coy

EGYPT
MFO 38 1 MP unit

IRAQ
NATO • NTM-I 4

LEBANON
UN • UNIFIL 4

SERBIA
NATO • KFOR • *Joint Enterprise* 243: **Land Component**: 1 mot inf coy
OSCE • Serbia 1
OSCE • Kosovo 4

WESTERN SAHARA
UN • MINURSO 7 obs

Iceland ISL

Icelandic Krona K		2008	2009	2010
GDP	K	1.46tr	1.58tr	
	US$	16.8bn	12.8bn	
per capita	US$	55,325	41,704	
Growth	%	1.3	-8.5	
Inflation	%	12.7	10.8	
Sy Bdgt [a]	K	ε3.87bn		
	US$	ε44.5m		
US$1=K		87	124	

[a] Iceland has no armed forces. Budget is mainly for coast guard.

Population	306,694					
Age	0–14	15–19	20–24	25–29	30–64	65 plus
Male	11%	4%	4%	4%	22%	5%
Female	11%	4%	4%	4%	22%	6%

Capabilities

ACTIVE NIL Paramilitary 130

ORGANISATIONS BY SERVICE

Paramilitary

Iceland Coast Guard 130

EQUIPMENT BY TYPE
PATROL AND COASTAL COMBATANTS • PCOH: 3: 2 *Aegir*; 1 *Odinn*
LOGISTICS AND SUPPORT • RESEARCH CRAFT 1 *Baldur*
AIRCRAFT • TPT 1 *Dash* 8-300
HELICOPTERS
  SPT 1 AS-322L1 *Super Puma*
  UTL 1 AS-365N *Dauphin 2*
FACILITIES
Base   Located at Reykjavik

FOREIGN FORCES

NATO • Iceland Air Policing: Aircraft and personnel from various NATO members on a rotating basis.

Italy ITA

Euro €		2008	2009	2010
GDP	€	1.56tr	1.51tr	
	US$	2.30bn	2.26bn	
per capita	US$	39,683	39,000	
Growth	%	-1.0	-5.1	
Inflation	%	3.6	1.1	
Def exp [a]	€	21.03		
	US$	30.9bn		
Def bdgt	€	16.4bn	15.4bn	15.5bn
	US$	24.1bn	23.0bn	
US$1=€		0.68	0.67	

[a] including military pensions

Population	58,126,212					
Age	0–14	15–19	20–24	25–29	30–64	65 plus
Male	7%	2%	3%	3%	25%	8%
Female	7%	2%	3%	3%	25%	10%

Capabilities

ACTIVE 293,202 (Army 108,300, Navy 34,000, Air 42,935 Carabinieri 107,967) **Paramilitary 142,933**

Terms of service all professional

RESERVES 41, 867 (Army 38,284 Navy 3,234)

ORGANISATIONS BY SERVICE

Army 108,300
FORCES BY ROLE
Comd   1 comd HQ (COMFOTER)

Rapid Reaction	1 NATO HQ (NRDC-IT) with: 1 Sigs bde , 1 spt regt (IT-HRF(L), rotational; currently comprises 1 (*Sassari*) light mech bde; 1 (*Aosta*) mech bde; 1 (*Friuli*) air mob bde; 1 (*Julia*) mnt bde)
Mech	1 (*Mantova*) div (1st FOD) with: 1 (*Ariete*) armd bde with (3 tk , 2 mech inf, 1 arty, 1 engr regt, 1 log bn); 1 (*Pozzuolo del Friuli*) cav bde with (3 cav, 1 amph, 1 arty regt); 1 (*Folgore*) AB bde with (1 SF, SF RSTA, 3 para, 1 cbt engr regt); 1 (*Friuli*) air mob bde with (1 cav, 1 airmob, 2 aviation regt). 1 (*Acqui*) div (2nd FOD) with: 1 (*Pinerolo*) mech bde with (1 tk, 3 mech inf, 1 SP arty, 1 cbt engr regt); 1 (*Granatieri*) mech bde with (1 cav, 2 mech inf, 1 SP arty regt); 1 (*Garibaldi*) Bersaglieri bde with (1 tk, 1 cav, 2 heavy mech inf , 1 SP arty, 1 cbt engr regt); 1 (*Aosta*) mech bde with (1 cav, 3 mech inf, 1 SP arty, 1 cbt engr regt); 1 (*Sassari*) light mech bde with (2 mech inf, 1 cbt engr regt).
Mtn Inf	1 Mtn HQ 1 (*Tridentina*) mtn div with: 1 (*Taurinense*) mtn bde with 3 mtn inf (2nd, 3rd, 4th), 1 cav (3rd *Nizza Cavalleria*), 1 arty, 1 mtn cbt engr regt, 1 spt bn; 1 (*Julia*) mtn bde with (3 mtn inf (5th, 7th, 8th), 1 arty, 1 mtn cbt engr regt, 1 spt bn) 1 (6th) mtn inf trg regt
SF	1 (4th *Alpini*)
EW	1 CIS/EW comd HQ (1 EW/RISTA bde with (1 RISTA , 1 EW, 1 HUMINT bn, 2 Sigs bde)
Spt	1 LAND FORCES Spt Comd
Arty	1 arty bde (1 hy arty regt, 1 NBC regt, 2 arty regt, 1 psyops regt)
AD	1 AD bde (2 (*HAWK*) SAM regt, 2 SHORAD regt, 1 training and simulation center
Engr	1 engr bde (3 engr, 1 CIMIC regt)
Avn	1 Army Aviation HQ; 1 avn bde (1 avn bn, 3 avn regt)
Log	1 log div (4 manoeuvre log regt, 4 tpt regt)

EQUIPMENT BY TYPE
MBT 320: 200 C1 *Ariete*; 120 *Leopard* 1A5
RECCE 300 B-1 *Centauro*
AIFV 254: 200 VCC-80 *Dardo*; 54 VBM 8x8 *Freccia*
APC
 APC (T) 1,752: 241 Bv-206; 384 M-113 (incl variants); 1,127 VCC-1 *Camillino*/VCC-2
 APC (W) 617: 57 Fiat 6614; 560 *Puma*
AAV 16: 14 LVTP-7; 1 AAVC-7; 1 AAVR-7
ARTY 931
 SP 155mm 164: 124 M-109L; 40 PzH 2000

TOWED 155mm 164 FH-70
MRL 227mm 22 MLRS
MOR 581: **81mm** 253; **120mm** 183 *BRANDT*; 145 RT-F1;
AT
 MSL • MANPATS 1,327: 32 *SPIKE*; 1,000 *Milan*; 295 I-TOW
 RCL 80mm 482 *Folgore*
 RL 110mm 2,000 Pzf 3 *Panzerfaust* 3
AIRCRAFT
 TPT 6: 3 ACTL-1 (Do-228); 3 P-180
HELICOPTERS
 ATK 60 A-129 ESS *Mangusta*
 SPT 21 CH-47C *Chinook*
 UTL 148: 60 AB-205; 43 AB-206 *JetRanger*; 18 AB-212; 22 AB-412 (Bell 412) *Twin Huey*; 5 TTH NH-90
AD
 SAM 132
  TOWED 68: 36 MIM-23 *HAWK*; 32 *Skyguard/Aspide*
  MANPAD 64 FIM-92A *Stinger*
 GUNS • SP 25mm 64 SIDAM

Navy 34,000

FORCES BY ROLE

Fleet	1 Fleet Commander CINCNAV with 6 subordinate operational commands
Navy	COMFORAL (Front – Line Forces located at Taranto), COMFORPAT (Patrol Forces located at Augusta), COMFORDRAG (MCM Forces located at La Spezia), COMFORSUB (Submarine Forces located at Taranto), COMFORAER (Naval Aviation Forces located at Rome), COMFORSBARC (Amphibious/ Landing Forces located at Brindisi).
Maritime	1 High Readiness Forces HQ

EQUIPMENT BY TYPE
SUBMARINES • TACTICAL • SSK 6:
 4 *Pelosi* (imp *Sauro*, 3rd and 4th series) each with 6 single 533mm TT each with 12 Type A-184 HWT / DM2A4 HWT
 2 *Salvatore Todaro* (Type U212A) with 6 single 533mm TT each with 12 Type A-184 HWT / DM2A4 HWT
PRINCIPAL SURFACE COMBATANTS 26
 AIRCRAFT CARRIERS • CVS 2:
  1 *G. Garibaldi* with 1 single 533mm ASTT with Mk 46 LWT, 2 *Albatros* octuple with (16 eff.) *Aspide* SAM, 4 twin (8 eff.) with up to 4 Mk 2 *Otomat* SSM, (capacity mixed air group of either 15 AV-8B *Harrier II*; 17 SH-3D *Sea King* or EH101 *Merlin*),(LHA role under development)
  1 *Cavour* with 1 32-cell VLS with Aster 15 Naval SAM 2 76mm gun, (capacity 8 AV-8B *Harrier II*; 12 EH101 *Merlin*)
 DESTROYERS • DDG 4:
  2 *Andrea Doria* each with 1 48-cell VLS with *Aster* 15 SAM /*Aster* 30 SAM, 2 twin TT (4 eff.) with MU-90, 3 76mm, (capacity either 1 EH101 spt hel or 1 NH90 TTH utl hel) (Undergoing trials, 2nd vessel ISD expected 2010)

2 *Luigi Durand de la Penne* (ex-*Animoso*) each with 2 quad (8 eff.) with 8 *Milas* AS/Mk 2 *Otomat* SSM, 1 Mk 13 GMLS with 40 SM-1 MR SAM, 2 triple 324mm ASTT (6 eff.) each with Mk 46 LWT, 1 *Albatros* octuple with 16 *Aspide* SAM, 1 127mm gun, (capacity 1 AB-212 (Bell 212) utl hel)

FRIGATES • FFG 12:

4 *Artigliere* each with 8 single each with 1 Mk 2 *Otomat* SSM, 1 *Albatros* octuple with 8 *Aspide* SAM, 1 127mm gun, (capacity 1 AB-212 (Bell 212) utl hel)

8 *Maestrale* each with 4 single with 4 Mk 2 *Otomat* SSM, 1 *Albatros* octuple with 16 *Aspide* SAM, 2 triple 324mm ASTT (6 eff.) each with Mk 46 LWT, 2 single 533mm ASTT each with A-184 *Black Shark* HWT, 1 127mm gun, (capacity 2 AB-212 (Bell 212) utl hel)

CORVETTES • FS 8 *Minerva* (4 fitted) with 1 *Albatros* octuple (8 eff.) with *Aspide* SAM, 1 76mm gun

PATROL AND COASTAL COMBATANTS 14

PSOH 10:

4 *Cassiopea* each with 1 76mm gun, with 1 AB-212 (Bell 212) utl hel

6 *Comandante Cigala Fuligosi* 4 with 1 76mm gun, (capacity 1 AB-212 (Bell 212) or 1 NH-90 utl hel)

PCO 4 *Esploratore*

MINE WARFARE • MINE COUNTERMEASURES 12

MHC 12: 8 *Gaeta*; 4 *Lerici*

AMPHIBIOUS

PRINCIPAL AMPHIBIOUS SHIPS • LPD 3

2 *San Giorgio* each with 1 76mm gun (capacity 3-5 hel EH101 ASW hel; NH-90; SH3-D; AB-212; 1 CH-47 *Chinook* spt hel; 3 LCM 2 LCVP; 30 trucks; 36 APC (T); 350 troops)

1 *San Giusto* with 1 76mm gun, (capacity 4 EH101 *Merlin* ASW hel; 1 CH-47 *Chinook* spt hel; 3 LCM 2 LCVP; 30 trucks; 36 APC (T); 350 troops)

CRAFT 26: 17 **LCVP**; 9 (+4 in build) **LCM**

LOGISTICS AND SUPPORT 87

AORH 3: 1 *Etna* (capacity 1 EH-101 or 1 NH-90); 2 *Stromboli* (capacity 1 EH-101 or 1 NH-90)

AOT 4

ARS 1

AKSL 6

AWT 3

AG 2

AGI 1

AGS 3: 1; 2 (coastal)

ABU 5

ATS 7

AT 9 (coastal)

TRG 9: 7 AXS; 2

YDT 2

YTL 32

FACILITIES

Bases Located at La Spezia (HQ), Taranto (HQ), Brindisi, Augusta

Naval Aviation 2,200

FORCES BY ROLE

FGA   Fixed wing strike unit with AV-8B *Harrier II*

ASW   5 sqn with AB-212AS (Bell 212 ASW/ASUW); EH-101; SH-3D *Sea King*; EH-101

Aslt hel   some sqn with SH-3D *Sea King*; AB-212 (Bell 212)

Trg   Flight with TAV-8B *Harrier*

EQUIPMENT BY TYPE

AIRCRAFT 17 combat capable

FGA 15 AV-8B *Harrier II*

TRG 2 TAV-8B *Harrier*

HELICOPTERS 41 attack helicopters

ASW 41: 25 AB212 ASW/ASuW; 8 EH-101 ASW; 8 SH-3D ASW/ASuW *Sea King*

SPT 20: 8 EH-101 ASH; 8 SH-3D ASH *Sea King*; 4 EH-101 EW

UTL 6 AB-212ASH (Bell 212)

MSL

ASM AGM-65 *Maverick*; some *Marte* Mk 2

AAM AIM-120 *AMRAAM*; AIM-9L *Sidewinder*

Marines 2,000

FORCES BY ROLE

Op   1 San Marco regt (1,300 Marine)

Log 1 regt

LC   1 gp

EQUIPMENT BY TYPE

APC (T) 40 VCC-2

AAV 18 AAV-7

ARTY • MOR 12: **81mm** 8 *Brandt*; **120mm** 4 *Brandt*

AT • MSL • MANPATS 6 *Milan*

AD • SAM • MANPAD FIM-92A *Stinger*

Special Forces Command

FORCES BY ROLE

Diving   1 op

Navy SF   1 op

SF   1 comd

FACILITIES

Centre   1 (Research)

School   1

Air Force 42,935

4 Commands – Air Sqn Cmd (air defence, attack, recce, mobility, support, force protection, EW ops); Training; Logistics; Operations (national and international exercises)

FORCES BY ROLE

Ftr   2 sqn with F-2000A *Typhoon*; 3 sqn with F-16A/ F-16B *Fighting Falcon* on lease

FGA   2 sqn with *Tornado* IDS; 3 sqn with AMX *Ghibli* (50% of 1 sqn devoted to recce)

ECR/SEAD   1 sqn with *Tornado* ECR*

MR   1 sqn opcon Navy with BR 1150 *Atlantic**

EW/Tpt/Tkr   1 sqn with G-222VS, B-767MRTT

CSAR   4 sqn with HH-3F *Pelican**

SAR   1 det with AB-212

Spt   1 sqn with AB-212 ICO

Cal/Tpt	1 sqn with P-180; P-166-DL3
Tpt	2 sqn with C-130J *Hercules*; 1 sqn with C-27J
Liaison	2 sqn (VIP tpt) with A-319CJ; *Falcon 50*; *Falcon 900EX*; *Falcon 900 Easy*; SH-3D *Sea King*.
Trg	1 sqn with F-2000 *Typhoon*; 1 sqn with MB-339A (aerobatic team); 1 sqn with NH-500D; 1 sqn with *Tornado*; 1 sqn with AMX-T *Ghibli*; 1 sqn with MB-339A; 1 sqn with MB-339CD*; 1 sqn with SF-260EA
AD	7 bty with *Spada* towed SAM
UAV	1 sqn with RQ-1B *Predator*

EQUIPMENT BY TYPE
AIRCRAFT 245 combat capable
  FTR 52: 27 F-2000A Tranche 1 *Typhoon* (9 -T, 18 -S); 25 F-16A/4 F-16B *Fighting Falcon* on lease to 2010
  STRIKE/FGA 138: 70 *Tornado* IDS; 68 AMX *Ghibli*
  ECR/SEAD 16 *Tornado* ECR*
  MP 10 BR 1150 *Atlantic**
  TPT 91: 3 A-319CJ; 1 B-767MRTT; 21 C-130J *Hercules*; 9 C-27J; 9 G-222; 2 *Falcon 50* (VIP); 3 *Falcon 900EX* (VIP); 2 *Falcon 900 Easy*; 6 P-166-DL3; 15 P-180; 20 SIAI-208 20 (liaison)
  TRG 134: 23 AMX-T *Ghibli*; 52 MB-339A (18 aero team, 34 trg); 29 MB-339CD*; 30 SF-260M
HELICOPTERS
  SAR 25 HH-3F *Pelican* (of which 6*)
  UTL 34: 32 AB-212 (of which 29 SAR); 2 SH-3D *Sea King* (liaison/VIP)
  TRG 50 NH-500D
UAV • RECCE 6 RQ-1B *Predator*.
AD • SAM
  TOWED *Spada*
MSL
  AAM AIM 120 AMRAAM; *Sidewinder*; IRIS-T
  ARM AGM-88 HARM
  ASM SCALP EG *Storm Shadow*
BOMBS
  Laser-guided/GPS: Enhanced *Paveway* II; Enhanced *Paveway* III

Carabinieri 107,967

The Carabinieri are organisationally under the MoD. They are a separate service in the Italian Armed Forces as well as a police force with judicial competence. As a military force they carry out military police and security tasks in support of the armed forces in Italy and abroad. As a national police force they report to the Minister of the Interior and are tasked with the maintainance of public order and law enforcement, as well as criminal investigations, counter terrorism and counter organised crime. The Carabinieri Territorial Command Structure is based on 5 Inter-Regional Commands; 5 Regional Commands; 102 Provincial Commands; and one Group Command. In addition there are 17 Territorial Depts; 18 Group Comd; 538 Company Comd; 44 Lieutenancy Comd; 4,624 Station Comd.

Mobile and Specialised Branch

Comd	1 HQ
Spec Ops	1 gp (ROS)
Mobile	1 div (1 Mobile bde (1st)(1 Horsed Cav regt, 11 Mobile bn); 1 Mobile bde(2nd) (1 (1st) AB regt, 1 (Special Intervention) GIS gp, 2 (7th,13th)Mobile regt))
Specialised	1 div (1 Ministry of Foreign Affairs Carabinieri HQ; 9 Carabinieri HQ (spt to Civil Ministries))
Hel	1 gp

EQUIPMENT BY TYPE
RECCE 18 Fiat 6616
APC 37
  APC (T) 25: 10 VCC-1 *Camillino*; 15 VCC-2
  APC (W) 12 *Puma*
AC: 1 Piaggio P180 Avant II
HELICOPTERS 86: 32 A-109; 21 AB-206 (Bell 206) *JetRanger*; 33 AB-412 (Bell 412)

Training

FORCES BY ROLE
Trg   1 HQ

FACILITIES

School	5
Center of Excellence	1

Paramilitary 142,933

Customs

(Servizio Navale Guardia Di Finanza)
PATROL AND COASTAL COMBATANTS 101:
  PCO 3 *Antonio Zara*
  PFC 26 *Corrubia*
  PCC 28: 2 *Mazzei*; 26 *Bigliani*
  PCI 42 *Meatini*
LOGISTICS AND SUPPORT • TRG 2

Coast Guard 11,266

(Guardia Costiera – Capitanerie Di Porto)
PATROL AND COASTAL COMBATANTS 96:
  PSO 6 *Saettia*
  PCO 1
  PFC 4
  PCC 9
  PCI 76 less than 100 tonnes
LOGISTICS AND SUPPORT • TRG 1 (ex-US *Bannock*)
AIRCRAFT
  MP 2 ATR-42 MP *Surveyor*
  TPT 14 P-166-DL3
HELICOPTERS • UTL 12 AB-412SP *Griffin*

DEPLOYMENT

Legal provisions for foreign deployment:
Constitution: Codified constitution (1949)
Decision on deployment of troops abroad: By the government upon approval by the parliament

AFGHANISTAN
NATO • ISAF 2,795; **Army:** 1 AB bde HQ; 3 para regt; some AIFV *Dardo*; 6 A-129 *Mangusta*; 4 CH-47; **Air Force:** some C-130

ALBANIA
NATO 1 (HQ Tirana)
Delegazione Italiana Esperti (DIA) 29

ARABIAN GULF AND INDIAN OCEAN
NATO • *Operation Ocean Shield* 1 FFG

BOSNIA-HERZEGOVINA
EU • EUFOR • *Operation Althea* 300
NATO • NATO HQ Sarajevo 7

CANADA
Air Force 12 (flying trg)

DEMOCRATIC REPUBLIC OF CONGO
EU • EUSEC RD Congo 4

EGYPT
MFO 78; 1 coastal patrol unit

INDIA/PAKISTAN
UN • UNMOGIP 7 obs

IRAQ
NATO • NTM-I Training Mission 91

LEBANON
UN • UNIFIL 2,576; 3 inf bn; 1 avn unit; 1 MP coy; 1 FF

MALTA
Air Force 37; 2 AB-212 (Bell 212)
Armed Forces
12 MIATM cbt spt (Missione Italiana d'Assistenza Tecnico Militare)

MIDDLE EAST
UN • UNTSO 8 obs

MOLDOVA
OSCE • Moldova 1

SERBIA
OSCE • Serbia 3
NATO • KFOR • *Joint Enterprise* 1,892; 1 mech inf BG; 1 engr unit; 1 hel unit; 1 sigs unit; 1 CSS unit OSCE • Kosovo 14

SUDAN
UN • UNAMID 1

UNITED STATES
Air Force 38 (flying trg)

WESTERN SAHARA
UN • MINURSO 4 obs

FOREIGN FORCES
Germany 3 MP ac (in ELMAS/Sardinia)
United States US European Command: **Army** 3,015; 1 AB IBCT; some M-119; some M-198; **Navy** 2,328; 1 HQ (US Navy Europe (USNAVEUR)) located at Naples; 1 HQ (6th Fleet) located at Gaeta **USAF** 4,076; 1 ftr wg with (2 ftr sqn with 21 F-16C *Fighting Falcon*/F-16D *Fighting Falcon* located at Aviano); 1 MR Sqn eq. with 9 P-3C *Orion* located at Sigonella **USMC** 55

Latvia LVA

Latvian Lat L		2008	2009	2010
GDP	L	16.2bn	13.9bn	
	US$	33.8bn	29.0bn	
per capita	US$	15,031	12,977	
Growth	%	-4.6	-18.0	
Inflation	%	15.9	3.1	
Def exp	L	260m		
	US$	542m		
Def bdgt	L	260m	172m	134m
	US$	542m	358m	
FMA (US)	US$	1.5m	1.5m	3.0m
US$1=L		0.48	0.48	

Population   2,231,503

Age	0–14	15–19	20–24	25–29	30–64	65 plus
Male	7%	4%	4%	3%	22%	6%
Female	7%	4%	4%	3%	25%	11%

Capabilities

ACTIVE 5,745 (Army 1,058 Navy 587 Air 319 Joint Staff 3,202 National Guard 579)

RESERVE 10,866 (Army Volunteer Reservist 10,866)

ORGANISATIONS BY SERVICE

Joint 3,202
FORCES BY ROLE
Comd   1 Joint HQ (1 Staff bn)
            1 log HQ (1 Tpt bn, 1 log bn)
            1 Trg and Doctrine Comd
SF   1 Ranger bn, 1 cbt diver unit, 1 anti-terrorist unit
Security 1 MP unit

Army 1,058
FORCES BY ROLE
Inf   1 bde (2 inf bn)

National Guard 579; 10,866 part-time (11,445 in total)
Inf   14 bn
Fd Arty   1 bn
AD   1 bn
Engr   1 bn
NBC   1 bn

EQUIPMENT BY TYPE
MBT 3 T-55 (trg)
RECCE 2 BRDM-2
ARTY 121
   TOWED 100mm 26 K-53
   MOR 95: **71mm** 40; **82mm** 5; **120mm** 50

AT
 RL 73mm RPG-7 *Knout*; **84mm** AT-4; **90mm**
  GUNS 143: **76mm** 3; **90mm** 140
AD
 SAM • MANPAD 5 *Strela* 2M (SA-7) *Grail*
 GUNS • TOWED 52: **14.5mm** 2 ZPU-4; **20mm** 10 FK-20;
 23mm 16 GSH-23; **30mm** 2: 1; 1 AK-230; **40mm** 22 L/70

Navy 587 (incl Coast Guard)
1 Naval HQ commands a Naval Forces Flotilla separated into two squadrons: an MCM squadron and a Patrol Boat squadron. LVA, EST and LTU have set up a joint Naval unit* BALTRON with bases at Liepaja, Riga, Ventspils (LVA), Tallinn (EST), Klaipeda (LTU).*Each nation contributes 1–2 MCMVs

EQUIPMENT BY TYPE
PATROL AND COASTAL COMBATANTS 12
 PCO 1 *Valpas* (Coast Guard)
 PFB 4 *Storm* with 1 L-70 40mm gun, 1 TAK-76 76mm gun
 PB 7: 5 KBV 236; 1 *Lokki Class*; 1 *Astra* (All for Coast Guard duties)
MINE WARFARE • MINE COUNTERMEASURES 5
 MHC 5: 1 *Lindau*; 4 *Imanta* (NLD *Alkmaar*)
LOGISTICS AND SUPPORT 3
 AG 1 *Vidar*
 SPT 1 *Varonis* (C3 and support ship, ex-*Buyskes*)
 YDT 1
FACILITIES
Bases Located at Liepaja, Daugavgriva (Riga – Coast Guard)

Air Force 319
Main tasks are air space control and defence, maritime and land SAR and air transportation.

FORCES BY ROLE
Comd   1 AF HQ
Surv   1 sqn
Spt   1 sqn
AD   1 bn
AIRCRAFT
 TPT 3: 2 An-2 *Colt*; 1 L-410 *Turbolet*
HELICOPTERS • SPT 6: 4 Mi-17; 2 PZL Mi-2

Paramilitary 11,034

 National Guard 551 (full time); 10,483 (part-time) (total 11,034)

DEPLOYMENT
Legal provisions for foreign deployment:
Constitution: Codified constitution (1922)
Specific legislation: 'Law on Participation of the National Armed Forces of Latvia in International Operations' (1995) (Annex of 21 Jan 2009 allows Latvian armed forces to take part in quick response units formed by NATO/EU)
Decision on deployment of troops abroad: a) By parliament (Section 5 I of the 1995 'Law on Participation', in combination with Art. 73 of constitution); b) by cabinet, if deployment is for rescue or humanitarian operations (Section 5 II of the 1995 law) or for military exercises (Section 9 of the 1995 law)

AFGHANISTAN
NATO • ISAF 175

MOLDOVA
OSCE • Moldova 1

Lithuania LTU

Lithuanian Litas L		2008	2009	2010
GDP	L	111bn	99bn	
	US$	47.2bn	42.5bn	
per capita	US$	13,249	11,951	
Growth	%	3.0	-18.5	
Inflation	%	11.1	3.5	
Def exp	L	1.28bn		
	US$	547m		
Def bdgt	L	1.28bn	1.16bn	741m
	US$	545m	501m	
FMA (US)	US$	1.5m	1.7m	3.3m
US$1=L		2.35	2.33	

Population   3,555,179

Ethnic groups: Lithuanian 84.6%; Polish 6.3%; Russian 5.1%; Belarussian 1.1%

Age	0–14	15–19	20–24	25–29	30–64	65 plus
Male	8%	4%	4%	4%	22%	5%
Female	8%	4%	4%	3%	24%	9%

Capabilities

ACTIVE 8,850 (Army 7,190 Navy 470 Air 950)
Paramilitary 14,600
Terms of service 12 months.

RESERVE 6,700 (Army 6,700)

ORGANISATIONS BY SERVICE

Army 2,590; 4,600 active reserves (total 7,190)
FORCES BY ROLE
1 mil region
Reaction 1 bde (Iron Wolf) (2 mech inf bn, 2 mot inf bn, 1
Force   arty bn)
Engr   1 bn
Security 1 MP bn
Trg   1 regt

EQUIPMENT BY TYPE
RECCE 10 BRDM-2
APC (T) 187 M-113A1, Bv 206
ARTY 133
 TOWED 105mm 72 M-101
 MOR 120mm 61 M-43
AT • MSL 28

SP 10 M1025A2 HMMWV with *Javelin*
MANPATS 18 *Javelin*
RCL 84mm 273 *Carl Gustav*
AD SAM *Stinger*

Reserves

National Defence Voluntary Forces 4,600 active reservists

Territorial Def   5 regt; 36 bn (total: 150 def coy)
Trg   1 bn
Avn   1 sqn

Special Operation Force

SF   1 gp (1 CT unit; 1 Jaeger bn, 1 cbt diver unit)

Navy 350; 120 conscript (total 470)

LVA, EST and LTU established a joint naval unit BALTRON with bases at Liepaja, Riga, Ventpils (LVA), Tallinn (EST), Klaipeda (LTU), HQ at Tallinn

EQUIPMENT BY TYPE
PRINCIPAL SURFACE COMBATANTS • FRIGATES
•**FFL** 1 *Grisha* III (†) with 2 twin 533mm ASTT (4 eff.), 1 twin (2 eff.), 2 RBU 6000 *Smerch 2* (24 eff.)
PATROL AND COASTAL COMBATANTS 7
　PB 2 *Standard Flex 300* (DNK *Flyvefisken*) (Patrol fit) with 1 76mm gun, (1 additional vessel due on transfer from DNK)
　PFB 2 *Storm*
　PBR 3 (Harbour Security Provision)
MINE WARFARE • MINE COUNTERMEASURES
MHC 2 *Suduvis* (Lindau)
LOGISTICS AND SUPPORT 2
AG 1 *Vidar*
SPT 1 (Used for SAR)

FACILITIES
Base   Located at Klaipeda

Air Force 950

Flying hours   120 hrs/year

FORCES BY ROLE

Air base, Airspace Surveillance and Control Command (ASSCC), AD btn, armament and equipment repair depot

EQUIPMENT BY TYPE
AIRCRAFT
　TPT 5: 3 C-27J *Spartan*; 2 L-410 *Turbolet*
　TRG 2 L-39ZA *Albatros*
HELICOPTERS • SPT: 9 Mi-8 *Hip* (tpt/SAR)
AD • RBS-70 AD system

Joint Logistics Support Command 850

FORCES BY ROLE
Log   1 spt bn (forward); 1 spt bn (main)

Joint Training and Doctrine Command (TRADOC) 670 Conscripts 480 (Total 1,350)

Facilities 3 (Each service has a training school)

Recce   1 trg centre
Engr   1 trg centre
Trg   1 regt

Paramilitary 14,600

Riflemen Union 9,600

State Border Guard Service 5,000
Ministry of Internal Affairs

Coast Guard 540
PATROL AND COASTAL COMBATANTS • PCC 3
AMPHIBIOUS • LC • ACV 1 UCAC

DEPLOYMENT

Legal provisions for foreign deployment:
Constitution: Codified constitution (1992)
Decision on deployment of troops abroad: By parliament (Art. 67, 138, 142)

AFGHANISTAN
NATO • ISAF 250

BOSNIA-HERZEGOVINA
EU • EUFOR • *Operation Althea* 1

IRAQ
NATO • NTM-I 4

SERBIA
NATO • KFOR • *Joint Guardian* 36
OSCE • Kosovo 1

FOREIGN FORCES

Germany NATO Baltic Air Policing 100; 6 F-4F *Phantom II*

Luxembourg LUX

Euro €		2008	2009	2010
GDP	€	36.7bn	34.8bn	
	US$	54.0bn	51.9bn	
per capita	US$	111,049	105,618	
Growth	%	0.7	-4.8	
Inflation	%	4.0	-0.3	
Def exp	€	158m		
	US$	232m		
Def bdgt	€	120m		
	US$	176m		
US$1=€		0.68	0.67	

Population   491,775
Foreign citizens: ε124,000

Age	0–14	15–19	20–24	25–29	30–64	65 plus
Male	10%	3%	3%	3%	24%	6%
Female	9%	3%	3%	3%	24%	8%

Capabilities

ACTIVE 900 (Army 900) Paramilitary 612

ORGANISATIONS BY SERVICE

Army 900

FORCES BY ROLE

Recce 2 coy (1 to *Eurocorps*/BEL div, 1 to NATO pool of deployable forces)

Lt inf 1 bn

EQUIPMENT BY TYPE

ARTY • **MOR 81mm** 6

AT • **MSL• MANPATS** 6 TOW

  RL 66mm M-72 *LAW*

Air Force

FORCES BY ROLE

None, but for legal purposes NATO's E-3A AEW ac have LUX registration

Air   1 sqn with 17 E-3A *Sentry* (NATO standard); 3 B-707 (trg)

EQUIPMENT BY TYPE

AIRCRAFT

  AEW 17 E-3A *Sentry* (NATO standard)

  TPT 3 B-707 (trg)

Paramilitary 612

  Gendarmerie 612

DEPLOYMENT

Legal provisions for foreign deployment:

Constitution: Codified constitution (1868)

Specific legislation: 'Loi du 27 juillet 1992 relatif à la participation du Grand-Duché de Luxembourg à des opérations pour le maintien de la paix (OMP) dans le cadre d'organisations internationales'

Decision on deployment of troops abroad: By government after formal consultation of relevant parliamentary committees and the Council of State (Art. 1–2 of the 1992 law)

AFGHANISTAN

NATO • ISAF 8

BOSNIA-HERZEGOVINA

EU • EUFOR • *Operation Althea* 1

LEBANON

UN • UNIFIL 3

SERBIA

NATO • KFOR • *Joint Enterprise* 23

Netherlands NLD

Euro €		2008	2009	2010
GDP	€	594bn	576bn	
	US$	874bn	860bn	
per capita	US$	52,479	51,430	
Growth	%	2.0	-4.2	
Inflation	%	2.2	1.4	
Def exp	€	8.34bn		
	US$	12.2bn		
Def bdgt	€	8.09bn	8.73bn	8.55bn
	US$	11.9bn	13.0bn	
US$1=€		0.68	0.67	

Population   16,715,999

Age	0–14	15–19	20–24	25–29	30–64	65 plus
Male	9%	3%	3%	3%	25%	6%
Female	9%	3%	3%	3%	25%	7%

Capabilities

ACTIVE 46,882 (Army 21,825; Navy 9,420; Air 9,559; Military Constabulary 6,078)

RESERVE 3,339 (Army 2,778 Air 397, Military Constabulary 63)

Soldiers/sailors to age 35, NCOs to 40, officers to 45

ORGANISATIONS BY SERVICE

Army 21,825

FORCES BY ROLE

1 (GER/NLD) Corps HQ; 1   Land Operations Support Command (LOSC), (EOD, Engr, CS and Logistic Sp elements)

Mech   2 bde (13, 43) (*each:* 2 armd inf bn, 1 tk bn, 1 armd recce sqn, 1 SP arty bn (2 bty), 1 engr bn, 1 maint coy, 1 medical coy)

Air Asslt   1 bde (11) (3 air asst inf bn, 1 mor, 1 AD , 1 engr, 1 med, 1 supply, 1 maint coy)

SF   5 coy (1 counter-terrorist, 1 mtn , 1 amph, 1 para unit)

EOD   46 EOD teams

Engr   1 gp (3 engr bn) (2 in mech bde above 1 in spt comd)

CS   1 Bde (101) with (1 AD comd (3 bty); 1 ISTAR bn (2 armd recce sqn, 1 EW coy, 1 UAV bty, 1 arty bty); 1 CIS bn; 1 engr bn

Logistic Sp   1 bde (3 maint coy, 2 tpt / supply bn, 1 med bn)

EQUIPMENT BY TYPE

MBT60: 44 *Leopard* 2A6 (16 in store)

RECCE (W) 148 *Fennek*

AIFV 224 YPR-765; CV9035 (deliveries (184) from 2009)

APC • APC (W) 70: 70 XA-188 *Sisu*

LFV 67 *Bushmaster* IMV

ARTY 357:

  SP 155mm 169: 43 PzH 2000; 126 M109A2/90 in store

MOR 43: **81mm** 27 L16/M1
TOWED 120mm 16 *Brandt*
AT
  ATGW 168
    SP 96 *Fennek* MRAT
    MANPATS 906+: 72 MR *Spike (Gill)*
  RL 834 Pzf
PATROL AND COASTAL COMBATANTS 6: 3 **PBR**; 3 **PCC**
LOGISTICS AND SUPPORT 1 tpt (tk)
UAV 43: 30 *Sperwer*; 5 *Aladin*; 8 MALE
AD
  SAM
    SP 18 *Fennek* with FIM-92A *Stinger* 18 MB with FIM-92A *Stinger*
    MANPAD 18 FIM-92A *Stinger*
  GUNS• SP35mm 60 *Gepard* (in store for sale)
RADAR • LAND 6 AN/TPQ-36 *Firefinder* (arty, mor); WALS; *SQUIRE*

Reserves 2,778 reservists

National Command

Cadre bde and corps tps completed by call-up of reservists (incl Territorial Comd)

Inf 5 bn (Could be mob for territorial defence).

Navy 9,420 (incl 2,654 Marines)

EQUIPMENT BY TYPE
SUBMARINES • TACTICAL • SSK 4:
  4 *Walrus* each with 4 single 533mm TT with Mk48 *Sea Arrow* HWT/UGM-84C *Harpoon* tactical USGW (equipped for *Harpoon* but not embarked)
PRINCIPAL SURFACE COMBATANTS 6
  DESTROYERS • DDG 4:
    4 *Zeven Provinciën* each with 2 Mk 141 *Harpoon* quad (8 eff.) with RGM-84F *Harpoon* tactical SSM, 1 40 cell Mk 41 VLS (40 eff.) with 32 SM-2 MR SAM, 32 enhanced *Sea Sparrow* SAM (quad pack), 2 twin ASTT (4 eff.) each with Mk 46 LWT, 1 Otobreda 127mm gun, (capacity 1 *Lynx* MK86 ASW hel)
  FRIGATES • FFG 2:
    2 *Karel Doorman* each with 2 Mk 141 *Harpoon* quad (8 eff.) with RGM-84A *Harpoon*/RGM-84C *Harpoon*, 1 Mk 48 VLS with 16 RIM-7P *Sea Sparrow* SAM, 2 twin 324mm ASTT (4 eff.) with Mk 46 LWT 1 76mm gun, (capacity 1 *Lynx* ASW hel)
MINE WARFARE • MINE COUNTERMEASURES • MHC 10 *Alkmaar* (tripartite)
AMPHIBIOUS
  PRINCIPAL AMPHIBIOUS SHIPS • LPD 2:
    1 *Rotterdam* (capacity either 6 *Lynx* utl hel or 4 NH-90 utl hel; either 6 LCVP or 4 LCU or 4 LCM; either 170 APC (T) or 33 MBT; 600 troops)
    1 *Johan de Witt* (capacity 6 NH-90 utl hel or 4 EH101 *Merlin*; either 4 LCVP or 2 LCU or 2 LCM; either 170 APC (T) or 33 MBT; 610 troops)
  CRAFT 17: 5 **LCU**; 12 **LCVP**
LOGISTICS AND SUPPORT 15
  AORH 1 *Amsterdam* with capacity for 4 *Lynx* or 2 NH-90
  AOL 1 *Zuiderkruis* with capacity for 2 *Lynx* or NH-90
  AORL 1 *Patria*

TRG 2
SPT 1 *Pelikaan*
TRV 1 *Mercuur*
YDT 4
YFS 4
FACILITIES
Bases   Located at Den Helder, Willemstad (Dutch Antilles)
Naval airbase Located at De Kooy (hel)

Naval Aviation (part of NLD Air Force Defence Helicopter Command)

HELICOPTERS 21: 14 ac in use; 7 (extended maintenance)
ASW/SAR 14 SH-14D *Lynx** (ASW/SAR); SH-14D *Lynx** to be replaced by 12 NH-90 NFH and 8 NH-90 TNFH first hel expected 2009)

Marines 3,100

FORCES BY ROLE
Marine   2 infantry bn (1 cadre); 1 bn (integrated with UK 3 Cdo Bde to form UK/NLD Amphibious Landing Force)
CS   1 amphibious support bn (1 recce coy, 2 mor coy, 1 AD plt, SF, 2 amphibious beach units, 1 Maritime Joint Effect Battery, 1 AD plt)
CSS   1 bn (2 CSS units, 1 Sea Based Support Group, 2 medical facility)

EQUIPMENT BY TYPE
ATV 74 BVS-10 *Viking*
ATV/S 153 BV-206D
APC (W) 20 XA-188 *Sisu (Patria)*
ARTY • MOR 32: **81mm** 18; **120mm** 14 *Brandt*
AT • MSL • MANPATS • MRAT *Gill*
  RL 84mm SRAT *Pantserfaust* III Dynarange 2000
AD • SAM • MANPAD FIM-92A *Stinger*

Air Force 9,559

Flying hours   180 hrs/year

FORCES BY ROLE
Comd   1 logistics HQ; 1 Tac Air HQ; 1 Education HQ
Ftr/FGA/Recce   5 (multi role) sqn with F-16 MLU AM/15 F-16 MLU BM *Fighting Falcon*
SAR   1 sqn with AB-412SP *Griffin*; 3 SH-14D *Lynx* at readiness for SAR
Tpt   1 sqn with KDC-10/ DC-10; C-130H/C-130H-30 *Hercules*; Fokker 50; *Gulfstream* IV
Trg   1 sqn with PC-7 *Turbo Trainer*
Hel   1 sqn with CH-47D *Chinook*; 1 sqn with AS-532U2 *Cougar II*; SA-316 *Alouette III*; 1 sqn with AH-64D *Apache*;
AD   4 sqn (*total*: 7 AD Team. 4 AD bty with MIM-104 *Patriot* (TMD capable))
Multi-national Strat Airlift   NLD participation in Euro Air Tpt Coord centre in Eindhoven, NLD. Participation in Strategic Airlift Interim Solution (SALIS) with An-124 hy flt transport in full-time lease, based in Leipzig, Germany. Participation in Heavy Airlift Wg (HAW) with 3 C-17 ac based Papa, Hungary

EQUIPMENT BY TYPE

AIRCRAFT 87 combat capable
FGA 87 F-16 MLU AM/F-16 MLU BM *Fighting Falcon*
TKR 2 KDC-10
TPT 8: 1 DC-10; 2 C-130H; 4 C-130H-30 *Hercules*; 1 *Gulfstream* IV
TRG 13 PC-7 *Turbo Trainer*

HELICOPTERS
ATK 29 AH-64D *Apache*
ASW/SAR 21: SH-14D *Lynx* (to be replaced by 12 NH-90 NFH and 8 NH-90 TNFH, starting 2010)
SPT 11 CH-47D *Chinook*
UTL 24: 3 AB-412SP *Griffin*; 17 AS-532U2 *Cougar II*; 4 SA-316 *Alouette III*

AD • SAM
TOWED 32 MIM-104 *Patriot* (TMD capable with 136 PAC-3 msl, of which 32 delivered)
MANPAD 284 FIM-92A *Stinger*

MSL
AAM AIM-120B AMRAAM; AIM-9L/M/N *Sidewinder*
ASM AGM-114K *Hellfire*; AGM-65D/G *Maverick*

BOMBS
Conventional Mk 82; Mk 84
Laser-guided GBU-10/ GBU-12 *Paveway* II; GBU-24 *Paveway* III (all supported by LANTIRN)

FACILITIES
Air Bases 5: 2 F-16, 1 land hel, 1 maritime hel, 1 trg

Royal Military Constabulary 6,078

Subordinate to the Ministry of Defence, but performs most of its work under the authority of other ministries.

FORCES BY ROLE

Paramilitary 6 district (*total:* 60 Paramilitary 'bde')

EQUIPMENT BY TYPE

AIFV 24 YPR-765

DEPLOYMENT

Legal provisions for foreign deployment:
Constitution: Codified constitution (1815)
Decision on deployment of troops abroad: By the government (Art. 98)

AFGHANISTAN

NATO • ISAF 2,160; **Army**: 1 air aslt bde HQ; 1 armd inf BG; some YPR-765; 12 *Fennek*; 3 Pzh SP; some *Sperwer* UAV **Navy**: 1 Marine inf coy; some BVS-10 Viking **Air Force**: 4-8 F-16 *Fighting Falcon*; 5 AH-64D *Apache*; 5 AS-332U2 *Cougar*; 1 C-130; 1 KDC-10

ARABIAN GULF AND INDIAN OCEAN

EU • *Operation Atalanta* 1 FFG

BOSNIA-HERZEGOVINA

EU • EUFOR • *Operation Althea* 73
OSCE • Bosnia and Herzegovina 1

BURUNDI

UN • BINUB 1 obs

CURAÇAO

Navy Base located at Willemstad

DEMOCRATIC REPUBLIC OF CONGO

EU • EUSEC RD Congo 3

GERMANY

Air Force 300

IRAQ

NATO • NTM-I 7

MIDDLE EAST

UN • UNTSO 12 obs

NETHERLANDS ANTILLES

(NLD, Aruba and the Netherlands Antilles operate a Coast Guard Force to combat org crime and drug smuggling. Comd by Netherlands Commander Caribbean. HQ Curaçao, bases Aruba and St. Maarten.)
Navy 20; 1 FFG **Marines** 1 (cbt) amph det; 1 coy at Aruba; 1 base located at Willemstad

SERBIA

NATO • KFOR • *Joint Enterprise* 8
OSCE • Serbia 3
OSCE • Kosovo 3

SUDAN

UN • UNMIS 2; 12 obs
UN • UNAMID 1

FOREIGN FORCES

United Kingdom Air Force 120
United States US European Command: **Army** 253; **Navy** 23; **USAF:** 237; **USMC** 15

Norway NOR

Norwegian Kroner kr		2008	2009	2010
GDP	kr	2.54tr	2.44tr	
	US$	452bn	435bn	
per capita	US$	97,271	93,335	
Growth	%	2.1	-1.9	
Inflation	%	3.6	2.5	
Def exp	kr	33.1bn		
	US$	5.86bn		
Def bdgt	kr	31.5bn	33.5bn	34.9bn
	US$	5.59bn	5.94bn	
US$1=kr		5.64	5.63	

Population	4,660,539

Age	0–14	15–19	20–24	25–29	30–64	65 plus
Male	10%	3%	3%	3%	24%	6%
Female	10%	3%	3%	3%	23%	7%

Capabilities

ACTIVE 24,025 (Army 7,900 Navy 3,550 Air 2,500, Home Guard 475, Central Support 9,600)
Terms of service: conscription with maximum 18 months of duty. Conscripts initially serve 12 months at the age

of 19 to 21, and then up to 4-5 refresher training periods until the age of 35, 44, 55 or 60 depending on rank and function. Numbers above includes conscripts during initial service.

RESERVE 45,250 (Army 270 Navy 320 Home Guard 44,250 Central Support, Adm. and Com. 350)

Reserves: readiness varies from a few hours to several days; obligation to age of 44, (conscripts remain with fd army units to age of 35, officers to 55, regulars to 60)

ORGANISATIONS BY SERVICE

Army 3,500; 4,400 conscript (total 7,900)

The Norwegian Army consists of one mechanised brigade – Brigade North – one border guard battalion, one guard infantry battalion (His Majesty the King's Guard), one special operations regiment and one joint logistic/support centre. Brigade North trains new personnel of all categories, provides units for international operations, and is a low readiness brigade. At any time around 1/3 of the brigade will be trained and ready to conduct operations across the whole spectrum of operations. The Brigade has also one high readiness mechanised battalion (Telemark Battalion) with combat support and combat service support units on high readiness. Other organisational elements are the Training and Doctrine Command, the Army Special Operations Command and the Army Military Academy.

Joint Command is exercised from The Norwegian National Joint Headquarters.

FORCES BY ROLE

Army	1 HQ
Mech Inf	1 bde (2 mech inf, 1 lt inf, 1 arty, 1 engr 1 CIS, 1 ISTAR (EW, MI, LR recce, UAV), 1 CSS, 1 medical bn and MP coy)
SF	SOF Comd (1 regt)
Inf	1 bn (His Majesty the King's Guards)
Border Guard	1 lt recce bn (HQ and garrison coy, border control coy, training coy)

EQUIPMENT BY TYPE

MBT 72: 52 *Leopard* 2A4; 20 *Leopard* 1A5NO (for trg only)
AIFV 104 CV9030N
APC 390
  APC (T) 315 M-113 (incl variants)
  APC (W) 75 XA-186 *Sisu*/XA-200 *Sisu*
ARTY 316
  SP 155mm 54 M-109A3GN
  MOR 262:
  SP 36: 81mm 24 M-106A1; 12 M-125A2
  81mm 226 L-16
AT
  MANPATS 514: 424 *Eryx*; 90 *Javelin*
  RCL 84mm 2,517 *Carl Gustav*
  RL 66mm M-72 *LAW*
  Radar wpn loc: 12 ARTHUR

FACILITIES

Bases: Finnmark, Tromso, Østerdalen and Oslo.

Navy 2,100; 1,450 conscripts (total 3,550 reserves)

Joint Command – Norwegian National Joint Headquarters. The Royal Norwegian Navy is organised into three elements under the command of the Chief of Staff of the Navy; the naval units 'Kysteskadren', the schools 'Sjoforsvarets Skoler' and the coast guard 'Kystvakten'.

FORCES BY ROLE

Navy	1 HQ (CNORTG)
Naval Units	Surface, Underwater, Mine Warfare and Coast Guard
SF	1 Sqn
ISTAR	1 coy (Coastal Rangers)
EOD	1 plt

EQUIPMENT BY TYPE

SUBMARINES • TACTICAL • SSK 6 *Ula* each with 8 single 533mm TT each with A3 *Seal* DM2 HWT
PRINCIPAL SURFACE COMBATANTS • FRIGATES 3
  FFGHM 3 *Fridjof Nansen* with 2 quad (8 eff.) with total of 8 NSM ASSM (under acquisition), 1 MK41 VLS with 32 enhanced *Sea Sparrow* SAM, 2 twin (4 eff.) with total of 4 *Sting Ray* LWT, 1 76mm; (additional 2 vessels under construction); (capacity NH-90 TTH hel – operated by the RoNAF – to be delivered from 2012)
PATROL AND COASTAL COMBATANTS • PFM 6
  6 *Skjold* each with 8 NSM ASSM; 1 twin (2 eff.) with Mistral Naval SAM; 1 76mm gun (3 units full op by 2009, 2 units expected ISD 2010, 1 unit expected ISD 2011)
MINE WARFARE 6
  MINE COUNTERMEASURES • MSC 3 *Alta* **MHC** 3 *Oksoy*
AMPHIBIOUS • CRAFT 20
  LCP 20 S90N
LOGISTICS AND SUPPORT 17
  ATS 1 *Valkyrien*
  AGI 1 *Marjata*
  AGS 5
  RY 1 *Norge*
  TRG 2 *Hessa*
  YDT 7

FACILITIES

Bases Located at Bergen, Ramsund and Trondenes and Sortland (Coast Guard)

Coast Guard

PATROL AND COASTAL COMBATANTS 13
  PSOH 10: 1 *Svalbard*; 3 *Nordkapp* each with 6 single (fitted for but not embarked) with RB 12 *Penguin* tactical SSM, with 1 *Lynx* utl hel (SAR/recce); 5 *Nornen* Class; 1 *Harstad*; 1 *Barentshav* Class (expected ISD 2009; 2 additional vessels in build)
  PCO 3 (leased from commercial contractors)
HELICOPTERS • ASW/ SAR 6 *Lynx* MK86; 8 NH-90 TTH (to be delivered from 2010); (Air Force-manned)

Air Force 1,650; 850 conscript (total 2,500)

Joint Command – Norwegian National HQ

Flying hours   180 hrs/year

FORCES BY ROLE

FGA   3 sqn with F-16AM/F-16BM*Fighting Falcon*
MR   1 sqn with P-3C *Orion**; P-3N *Orion* (pilot trg)
SAR   1 sqn with *Sea King* MK43B
EW/CAL 1 sqn with DA-20 *Jet Falcon* 20C (EW, Flight
               Inspection Service)
Tpt   1 sqn with C-130J *Hercules*
Trg   1 sqn with MFI-15 SAAB *Safari*
Hel   2 sqn with Bell 412SP; 1 sqn with *Lynx* MK86
SAM   1 reinforced bty with NASAMS II

EQUIPMENT BY TYPE

AIRCRAFT 52 combat capable
  FTR 57 F-16AM/F-16BM *Fighting Falcon*
  MP 6: 4 P-3C *Orion**; 2 P-3N *Orion* (pilot trg)
  TPT 2 C-130J (second pair in 2010)
  EW 3 DA-20 *Jet Falcon*
  TRG 15 MFI-15 SAAB *Safari*
HELICOPTERS
  SAR 12 *Sea King* MK43B (SAR)
  UTL 18 Bell 412SP (12 tpt, 6 mainly support to SF)
  ASW/SAR 6 *Lynx* Mk86 (to be replaced by 8 NH-90TTH
  from 2012 onwards)
AD
  SAM
    TOWED NASAMS
  MSL
    AAM AIM-120B AMRAAM; AIM-9L *Sidewinder;*
    AIM-2000 *IRIS T*
BOMBS
  Laser-guided: EGBU-12 *Paveway* II
  INS/GPS guided: JDAM
  FACILITIES
  Bases: Rygge, Bodo, Ørland, Bardufoss, Gardemoen,
  Andoeya

Central Support, Administration and Command 8,600; 1,000 conscripts (total 9,600)

Central Support, Administration and Command includes
military personnel in all joint elements including, among
others, the Ministry of Defence, the NJHQ, the Norwegian
Defence Logistics Organisation (NDLO), the Norwegian
Armed Forces Medical Services, the Defence Command
and Staff College, the CIS and intelligence communities.
Several of these elements do not provide forces as such,
but others do, and they are responsible for logistics and CIS
in support of all forces in Norway and abroad

Home Guard 475 (total 475 – with 46,000 reserves)

The Home Guard is a separate organisation, but closely
cooperates with all services. The Home Guard can be
mobilised on very short notice for local security operations.
The main body of the Home Guard are land forces, but it
also includes smaller elements for naval and air operations
support. The Home Guard relies on recruitment and
basic training conducted in the services, while basic
officer training is partly done within the Home Guard
organisation. The Home Guard has its own tactics and
weapons centre.

Land Home Guard 42,650 with reserves

11 Home Guard Districts with mobile Rapid Reaction
Forces (5,000 troops in total) as well as reinforcements
and follow-on forces (37,150 troops in total). The
reinforcements and follow-on forces are organised in
company size 'Home Guard Areas', mainly intended for
local security operations

Naval Home Guard 1,900 with reserves

Consisting of Rapid Reaction Forces with a total of 500
troops, and 17 'Naval Home Guard Areas' with a total of
1,250 troops. From 2010, the Naval Home Guard will be
equipped with 2 vessels of the *Reine* class and 12 smaller
vessels, deployed along the Norwegian coastline. In
addition, a number of civilian vessels can be requisitioned
as required.

Air Home Guard 1,450 with reserves

Provides force protection and security detachments for
air bases.

DEPLOYMENT

Legal provisions for foreign deployment:
Constitution: Codified constitution (1814)
Decision on deployment of troops abroad: By royal
prerogative exercised by the government (Art. 25, 26)

AFGHANISTAN
NATO • ISAF 480; Army: 1 mech inf coy; 1 spt coy
UN • UNAMA 2 obs

ARABIAN GULF AND INDIAN OCEAN
EU • *Operation Atalanta* 1 FFG

BOSNIA-HERZEGOVINA
NATO • NATO HQ Sarajevo 2

CENTRAL AFRICAN REPUBLIC/CHAD
UN • MINURCAT 177; 1 med coy

DEMOCRATIC REPUBLIC OF CONGO
UN • MONUC 1 obs

EGYPT
MFO 6

MIDDLE EAST
UN • UNTSO 11 obs

SERBIA
NATO • KFOR • *Joint Enterprise* 6
OSCE • Serbia 3
UN • UNMIK 1

SUDAN
UN • UNMIS 7; 14 obs

FOREIGN FORCES

United States US European Command: **Army** 23; **Navy** 4;
USAF 39; **USMC** 10; 1 (APS) 155mm SP Arty eqpt. set;
NATO Joint Warfare Centre (JWC)/ACT situated
Stavanger; E-3A Fwd Op Location at Ørland airbase

Poland POL

Polish Zloty z		2008	2009	2010
GDP	z	1.27tr	1.33tr	
	US$	525bn	465bn	
per capita	US$	13,644	12,072	
Growth	%	4.9	1.0	
Inflation	%	4.2	3.5	
Def exp	z	24.5bn		
	US$	10.1bn		
Def bdgt	z	22.5bn	24.8bn	25.4bn
	US$	9.36bn	8.63bn	
FMA (US)	US$	27.0m	27.0m	47.0m
US$1=z		2.41	2.88	

Population 38,482,919

Ethnic groups: German 1.3%; Ukrainian 0.6%; Belarussian 0.5%

Age	0–14	15–19	20–24	25–29	30–64	65 plus
Male	8%	4%	4%	4%	23%	5%
Female	8%	4%	4%	4%	23%	8%

Capabilities

ACTIVE 100,000 (Army 46,400, Navy 8,000, Air 17,500, Joint 28,100)

ORGANISATIONS BY SERVICE

Land Forces Command 46,400

Land Forces Command directly controls airmobile bdes and their avn. Transition to lighter forces is continuing but is hampered by lack of funds. The military police are directly under the Minister of National Defence and are transforming with 15% (1,540 personnel) forming special units of bn size to enable support to counter-terrorism, VIP protection and NATO operations.

FORCES BY ROLE

Comd	1 (2ⁿᵈ) mech corps HQ; MNC NE Corps HQ (Polish contribution)
Armd	1 armd cav div (11th) (2 armd cav, 1 mech bde, 1 recce bn, 1 arty, 2 AD regt 1 engr bn)
Mech	1 div (1st) (1 armd ,1 mech, 1 mtn bde, 1 recce bn, 1 arty, 1 AD regt, 1 engr bn); 1 div (12th) (2 mech, 1 coastal bde, 1 arty, 2 AD regt , 1 engr bn); 1 div (16th) (1 armd, 2 mech bde , 1 recce bn, 1 arty, 1 AD regt, 1 AT regt, 1 engr bn)
Airmob	1 aslt bde (6th) (2 aslt, 1 para bn), 1 air cav bde (25th) (2 spt hel bn, 2 air cav bn, 1 casevac unit)
Recce	2 regt
Arty	2 bde
Engr	2 bde, 1 regt
Chem	1 regt, 1 bn
Avn	1 cbt regt (49th) with (3 atk sqn with Mi-24, 1 recce sqn with Mi-2) 1 cbt regt (56th) (1 atk sqn with Mi-24V, 2 recce sqn with Mi-2, 1 spt sqn with Mi-2)

EQUIPMENT BY TYPE

MBT 946: 128 *Leopard* 2 2A4; 232 PT-91 *Twardy*; 586 T-72 MBT/T-72M1D/T-72M1

RECCE 376 BRDM-2

AIFV 1508:

AIFV (T) 1,297 BMP-1

APC (W) 239 *Rosomak (Patria)*

MRAP 40 *Cougar*

ARTY 1,081

  SP 608: **122mm** 522 2S1 *Carnation*; **152mm** 86 M-77 *Dana*

  MRL 122mm 236: 205 BM-21; 30 RM-70 *Dana* 1 WR-40 *Langusta*

  MOR 237: **98mm** 99 M-98; **120mm** 138 M-120

AT • MSL • MANPATS 327: 129 AT-3 9K11 *Sagger*; 77 AT-4 9K111 *Spigot*; 18 AT-5 9K113 *Spandrel*; 7 AT-7 9K115 *Saxhorn*; 96 *Spike* LR

HELICOPTERS

  ATK 53: 31 Mi-24D *Hind D*; 22 PZL Mi-2URP *Hoplite*

  SPT 91: 37 PZL W-3A *Sokol*/PZL W-3W *Sokol*; 17 Mi-8T *Hip* spt/Mi-8U *Hip* trg; 24 PZL Mi-2 *Hoplite*; 13 Mi-17T *Hip* spt/Mi-17U *Hip H* trg

UAV Micro 15

AD

  SAM 971

    SP 144: 80 GROM *Poprad*; 64 OSA-AK

    MANPAD 582: 246 *SA-7*, 336 GROM

  GUNS 441

    SP 23mm 37: 36 ZSU-23-4; 1 SPAAG

    TOWED 23mm 404 ZU-23-2

RADAR • LAND SNAR-10 *Big Fred* (veh, arty)

Navy 8,000

Comd	Navy HQ 1 Surface Combatant Flotilla 1 Coastal Defence Flotilla 1 Naval Aviation bde (3 Naval Sqn)

EQUIPMENT BY TYPE

SUBMARINES • TACTICAL 5

  SSK 5:

    4 *Sokol* (Type-207) each with 8 single 533mm TT

    1 *Orzel* (ex-*Kilo*) with 6 single 533mm TT with 12 T-53/T-65 HWT

PRINCIPAL SURFACE COMBATANTS 8

  FRIGATES 3

    FFG 2 *Pulaski* (US *Oliver Hazard Perry* class) each with 1 Mk 13 GMLS with 36 SM-1 MR SAM, 4 RGM-84D/F *Harpoon* tactical SSM, 2 triple 3x 324mm ASTT (6 eff.) each with 24 A244 LWT, 1 76mm gun, (capacity 2 SH-2G *Super Seasprite* ASW hel)

    FF 1 *Kaszub* with 2 twin 533mm ASTT (4 eff.) with SET-53 HWT, 1 quad (4 eff.) with SA-N-5 *Grail* SAM, 2 RBU 6000 *Smerch* 2 (24 eff.), 1 76mm gun

  CORVETTES • FSG 5:

    2 *Tarantul* each with 2 twin (4 eff.) with 4 SS-N-2C *Styx* tactical SSM, 1x4 manual with SA-N-5 *Grail* SAM, 1 76mm gun

3 *Orkan* (GDR *Sassnitz*. Refit programme in progress) each with 2 quad (8 eff.) with RBS-15M tactical SSM, 1 x4 manual with SA-N-5 *Grail* SAM, 1 76mm gun

MINE WARFARE • MINE COUNTERMEASURES 20
MSC 13 *Goplo*
MHC 7: 3 *Krogulec*; 4 *Mamry*

AMPHIBIOUS 8
LS • LSM 5 *Lublin* (capacity 9 tanks; 135 troops)
CRAFT • LCU 3 *Deba* (capacity 50 troops)

LOGISTICS AND SUPPORT 33
AORL 1
AOL1
MRV 1 Project 890
ARS 4
AGI 2 *Moma*
AGS 8: 2; 6 (coastal)
ATF 3
TRG 6: 1 AXS
YDG 2
YTM 5

FACILITIES
Bases Located at Kolobrzeg, Gdynia (HQ), Swinoujscie, Hel Peninsula (Spt), Gdynia-Babie Doly

Naval Aviation 1,300

FORCES BY ROLE
ASW / 1 sqn with MI-14PL *Haze A*; MI-14PS *Haze C*;
SAR   PZL W-3RM *Anakonda*; PZL MI-2; SH-2G *Super Seasprite*
Tpt /Utl 1 sqn with An-28B1R; An-28E 1 sqn with An-28TD; PZL W-3T; PZL W-3RM; Mi-17; PZL MI-2

EQUIPMENT BY TYPE
AIRCRAFT
TPT 2 An-28TD
UTL 10: 8 An-28B1R; 2 An-28E
HELICOPTERS
ASW 10: 6 MI-14PL; 4 SH-2G *Super Seasprite*
SAR 10: 3 Mi-14PS *Haze C*; 7 PZL W-3RM *Anakonda*
SPT 6: 2 PZL W-3T *Sokol*; 2 Mi-17 (Mi-8MT) *Hip H*; 2 PZL MI-2

Air Force 17,500
Flying hours   160 to 200 hrs/year

2 tac air wg: 1st (5 sqn, 4 air bases); 2nd (3 sqn, 2 air bases)
1 tpt air wg: 3rd (4 sqn, 4 air bases)
1 spec air tpt: 36th
2 rocket AD bdes (1st and 3rd), 2 rocket AD regt (61st ,78th)
4 Control and Reporting Centres

FORCES BY ROLE
Multi-role 3 sqn with F-16C/D Block 52+
Ftr   2 sqn with MiG-29 *Fulcrum* A/UB
FGA/Recce 3 sqn with Su-22M-4 *Fitter*
Tpt   4 sqn with C-130E; C-295M; PZL M-28 *Bryza*. 1 regt with Tu-154M; Yak-40
Trg   trg units with PZL-130; TS-11; An-28
Hel   2 sqn with PZL W-3 *Sokol*; Mi-2; Mi-8MT; Bell 412 *Twin Huey*; PZL SW-4 (trg)

SAM   2 bde with SA-3 *Goa*; 1 indep regt with SA-3/ SA-5; 1 indep regt with SA-4

EQUIPMENT BY TYPE
AIRCRAFT 128 combat capable
Multi Role 48: 36 F-16C, 12 F-16D *Fighting Falcon*
FTR 26 MiG-29A *Fulcrum*
FGA 48 Su-22M-4 *Fitter*
TPT 39: 5 C-130E *Hercules*; 2 An-28 *Cash*; 11 CASA C-295M; 15 M-28 *Bryza TD*; 2 Tu-154 *Careless*; 4 Yak-40 *Codling*.
TRG 94: 54 PZL TS-11; 34 PZL-130; 6 MiG-29UB *Fulcrum**
HELICOPTERS
SPT 66: 17 PZL W-3 *Sokol*; 11 Mi-8MT *Hip*; 38 PZL Mi-2
UTL 1 Bell 412 *Twin Huey*
TRG 11 PZL SW-4
AD • SAM 90 SA-3 *Goa*
SP 78; 60 SA-3, 14 SA-4
STATIC 12 SA-5
MSL
AAM AA-8 *Aphid*; AA-11 *Archer*, AIM-9 *Sidewinder*, AIM 120C AMRAAM
ASM AS-7 *Kerry*; AGM-65J/G *Maverick*

Paramilitary 21,400

Border Guards 14,100
Ministry of Interior and Administration

Maritime Border Guard
PATROL AND COASTAL COMBATANTS 19: 1 **PSO**; 2 **PCO**; 1 **PCC**; 2 **PCI**; 7 **PBF**; 6 **PB**

Prevention Units of Police 6,300; 1,000 conscript (total 7,300)
OPP–Ministry of Interior

DEPLOYMENT
Legal provisions for foreign deployment:
Constitution: Codified constitution (1997)
Decision on deployment of troops abroad: a) By president on request of prime minister in cases of direct threat (Art. 136);
b) in general, specified by ratified international agreement or statute (both must be passed by parliament, Art. 117)

AFGHANISTAN
NATO • ISAF 1,910; **Army**; 1 mtn inf bde HQ with (1 mtn inf BG); 1 air cav bde HQ with (elm 2 hel bn); 35 *Rosomak*; 68 other IFV; 6 Mi-24 *Hind*; 4 Mi-17 *Hip*

ARMENIA/AZERBAIJAN
OSCE • Minsk Conference 1

BOSNIA-HERZEGOVINA
EU • EUFOR • *Operation Althea* 188; **Army**: 1 inf coy

CENTRAL AFRICAN REPUBLIC/CHAD
UN • MINURCAT 311; elm 1 inf bn

CÔTE D'IVOIRE
UN • UNOCI 4 obs

DEMOCRATIC REPUBLIC OF CONGO
UN • MONUC 2 obs

IRAQ
NATO • NTM-I 3

LEBANON
UN • UNIFIL 461; **Army:** 1 inf coy; 1 log bn

LIBERIA
UN • UNMIL 2 obs

MOLDOVA
OSCE • Moldova 2

SERBIA
NATO • KFOR • *Joint Enterprise* 226; **Army:** elm 1 inf bn
OSCE • Kosovo 2
UN • UNMIK 1 obs

SUDAN
UN • UNMIS 2 obs

SYRIA/ISRAEL
UN • UNDOF 333; 1 inf bn

WESTERN SAHARA
UN • MINURSO 1 obs

FOREIGN FORCES

Germany Army: 67 (GER elm Corps HQ (multinational))

Portugal PRT

Euro €		2008	2009	2010
GDP	€	166bn	161bn	
	US$	244bn	240bn	
per capita	US$	22,846	22,441	
Growth	%	0.0	-3.0	
Inflation	%	2.7	-0.2	
Def exp[a]	€	2.53bn		
	US$	3.72bn		
Def bdgt	€	1.79bn	1.82bn	1.97bn
	US$	2.63bn	2.72bn	
US$1=€		0.68	0.67	

[a] including military pensions

Population   10,707,924

Age	0–14	15–19	20–24	25–29	30–64	65 plus
Male	9%	3%	4%	4%	22%	7%
Female	8%	3%	3%	4%	24%	10%

Capabilities

ACTIVE 43,330 (Army 26,700 Navy10,540 Air 7,100)
Paramilitary 47,700

RESERVE 210,900 (Army 210,000 Navy 900)
Reserve obligation to age 35

ORGANISATIONS BY SERVICE

Army 26,700
5 Territorial Comd (2 mil region, 1 mil district, 2 mil zone)
FORCES BY ROLE
Rapid Reaction	1 bde (1 (RI 3) Inf bn, 1 AT coy, 1 recce sqn, 1 AD bty, 1 engr coy, 1 fd arty bn, 2 (RI 10 and 15) para bn)
Mech inf	1 bde (1 (RC4) tk regt, 2 (1st and 2nd) mech inf bn)
Lt inf	1 (intervention) bde (1 (RC 6) cav regt, 1 (RE3) engr bn, 1 (RAAA 1) AD bn, 1 (RA4) fd arty bn, 3 (RI13,14 and 19) inf bn)
Spec Ops	1 unit
Cdo	1 bn
MP	1 regt
Garrison	2 (Madeira and Azores) gp (Madeira 2 inf bn (RG 1 and RG 2), Azores 1 Inf bn (RG 3) 1 AD unit)

Reserves 210,000 reservists
Territorial Def   3 bde (on mob)

EQUIPMENT BY TYPE
MBT 225: 38 *Leopard* 2A6; 86 M-60A3; 8 M-60A4, 7 M-60; 86 M-48A5
RECCE 40: 15 V-150 *Chaimite*; 25 ULTRAV M-11
APC 353
  APC (T) 280: 240 M-113; 40 M-577 A2
  APC (W) 161: 73 V-200 *Chaimite*; 88 *Pandur II* (32 due in 2010)
ARTY 350+
  SP 155mm 20: 6 M-109A2; 14 M-109A5
  TOWED 135: **105mm** 97: 21 L-119; 52 M-101; 24 M-56; **155mm** 38 M-114A1
  COASTAL 21: **150mm** 9; **152mm** 6; **234mm** 6 (inactive)
  MOR 174+: **81mm** (incl 21 SP); **107mm** 76 M-30 (incl 14 SP); **120mm** 98 *Tampella*
AT
  MSL • MANPATS 118: 68 *Milan* (incl 6 ULTRAV-11); 50 TOW (incl 18 M-113, 4 M-901)
  RCL 402: **106mm** 128 M-40; **84mm** 162 *Carl Gustav*; **90mm** 112
AD
  SAM • MANPAD 52: 37 *Chaparral*; 15 FIM-92A *Stinger*
  GUNS • TOWED 93: **20mm** 31 Rh 202; **40mm** 62 L/60

Navy 9,110; (total 10,540) incl Marines
EQUIPMENT BY TYPE
SUBMARINES • TACTICAL • SSK 1 *Albacora* with 12 single 550mm TT (8 bow, 4 stern) each with 12 E14/E15 HWT
PRINCIPAL SURFACE COMBATANTS • FRIGATES 12
FFG 5
  3 *Vasco Da Gama* each with 2 Mk 141 *Harpoon* quad (8 eff.) with RGM-84C *Harpoon* tactical SSM, 2 Mk 36 triple 324mm ASTT with Mk 46 LWT, 1 Mk 29 *Sea Sparrow* octuple with RIM-7M *Sea Sparrow* SAM,

1 100mm gun, (capacity 2 *Lynx* MK95 (*Super Lynx*) utl hel)

2 *Karel Dorman class (ex*-NLD*)* each with 2 Mk 141 *Harpoon* quad (8 eff.) with RGM-84C *Harpoon* tactical SSM, 2 Mk 32 twin ASTT with Mk 46 LWT, 1 Mk 48 VLS (8 eff.) with RIM-7M *Sea Sparrow* SAM, 1 76mm gun, (capacity for 1 SH-14D hel)

CORVETTES • FSH 7

3 *Baptista de Andrade* each with 1 100mm gun, 1 hel landing platform

4 *Joao Coutinho* each with 2 76mm gun, 1 hel landing platform

PATROL AND COASTAL COMBATANTS 18

PSOH 2 *Viana do Castelo* (expected ISD 2010)

PCO 4 *Cacine*

PCI 9: 5 *Argos*; 4 *Centauro*

PCR 3: 2 *Albatroz*; 1 *Rio Minho*

AMPHIBIOUS • CRAFT 1 LCU

LOGISTICS AND SUPPORT 10:

AORLH 1 *Bérrio* (ex UK *Rover*) with 1 hel landing platform (for medium hel)

AGS 4

ABU 2

TRG 3 AXS

FACILITIES

Base   Located at Lisbon

Naval airbase   Located at Montijo

Support bases   Leca da Palmeira (North), Portimao (South), Funchal (Madiera), Ponta Delgada (Azores)

Marines 1,430

FORCES BY ROLE

Police   1 det

Lt inf   2 bn

Spec Ops   1 det

Fire spt   1 coy

EQUIPMENT BY TYPE

APC 20 *Pandur* II (due 2010)

ARTY •MOR 15 120mm

Naval Aviation

HELICOPTERS • UTL 5 *Lynx* MK95 (*Super Lynx*)

Air Force 7,100

Flying hours   180 hrs/year on F-16 *Fighting Falcon*

FORCES BY ROLE

Air   1 (op) COFA comd; 5 (op) gp

FGA   1 sqn with F-16A/B *Fighting Falcon*; 1 sqn with F-16 MLU *Fighting Falcon*

Surv   1 sqn with CASA 212 *Aviocar*

MR   1 sqn with P-3P/C *Orion**

CSAR/SAR/   1 sqn with with EH-101 *Merlin*; SA-330S

Fishery   *Puma*

Protection

Tpt   1 sqn with CASA 212 *Aviocar* (to be replaced by 12 CN-295M); 1 sqn with *Falcon* 50; 1 sqn with C-130H *Hercules*

Liaison/utl 1 sqn with FTB337 *Skymaster* (Cessna *337*)

Trg   1 sqn with TB-30 *Epsilon*; 1 sqn with SA-316 *Alouette III*; 1 sqn with *Alpha Jet*

EQUIPMENT BY TYPE

AIRCRAFT 25 combat capable

FTR 19: 16 F-16A/3 F-16B *Fighting Falcon* (21 F-16 MLU by 2010)

MP 6 P-3P *Orion**

RECCE 2 CASA 212B *Aviocar* (survey)

TPT 45: 6 C-130H *Hercules* (tpt/SAR); 24 CASA 212A *Aviocar* (tpt/SAR, Nav/ECM trg, fisheries protection). First of 12 C-295; 12 FTB337 *Skymaster* (Cessna 337) 12 (being phased out); 3 *Falcon* 50 (tpt/VIP)

TRG 41: 25 *Alpha Jet* (FGA/trg); 16 TB-30 *Epsilon*

HELICOPTERS

SPT 12 EH-101 *Merlin* (6 SAR, 4 CSAR, 2 fishery protection); 4 SA-330S *Puma* (SAR)

UTL 18 SA-316 *Alouette III* (trg, utl)

UAV 34 *Armor X7*

MSL

AAM AIM-120 AMRAAM; AIM-9J/ AIM-9L/ AIM-9P *Sidewinder*; AIM-7M *Sparrow*

ASM AGM-65A *Maverick*; AGM-84A *Harpoon*

BOMBS

Laser-guided: *Paveway* II

Paramilitary 47,700

National Republican Guard 26,100

APC (W): some *Commando* Mk III (*Bravia*)

HELICOPTERS • UTL 7 SA-315 *Lama*

Public Security Police 21,600

DEPLOYMENT

Legal provisions for foreign deployment:

Constitution: Codified constitution (1976)

Decision on deployment of troops abroad: By government

AFGHANISTAN

NATO • ISAF 145

UN • UNAMA 1

ANGOLA

Navy 11 (Technical military cooperation)

BOSNIA-HERZEGOVINA

EU • EUFOR • *Operation Althea* 51

OSCE • Bosnia and Herzegovina 1

CENTRAL AFRICAN REPUBLIC/CHAD

UN • MINURCAT 1 obs

IRAQ

NATO • NTM-I 8

LEBANON

UN • UNIFIL 146; 1 engr coy

MEDITERRANEAN SEA

NATO • *Active Endeavour* 1 FFG

MOZAMBIQUE

Navy 7

SÃO TOME AND PRINCIPÉ
Navy 1
Air Force 5; 1 CASA 212 *Aviocar*

SERBIA
NATO • KFOR • *Joint Enterprise* 295; **Army**: 1 inf bn (KTM)
OSCE • Kosovo 5

TIMOR LESTE
UN • UNMIT 3 obs

FOREIGN FORCES

United States US European Command: **Army** 28; **Navy** 29; **USAF** 663; **USMC** 7; 1 Support facility located at Lajes

Romania ROM

Lei		2008	2009	2010
GDP	lei	493bn	521bn	
	US$	196bn	180bn	
per capita	US$	8,829	8,087	
Growth	%	7.1	-8.5	
Inflation	%	7.8	5.5	
Def exp	lei	7.54bn		
	US$	3.0bn		
Def bdgt	lei	8.34bn	9.83bn	8.12bn
	US$	3.32bn	3.39bn	
FMA (US)	US$	11.1m	12.0m	16.5m
US$1=lei		2.51	2.90	

Population   22,215,421

Ethnic groups: Hungarian 9%

Age	0–14	15–19	20–24	25–29	30–64	65 plus
Male	8%	4%	4%	4%	22%	6%
Female	8%	4%	4%	4%	23%	9%

Capabilities

ACTIVE 73,350 (Army 43,000 Navy 7,150 Air 9,700 Joint 13,500) **Paramilitary 79,900**

RESERVE 45,000 (Joint 45,000)

ORGANISATIONS BY SERVICE

Army 43,000

FORCES BY ROLE
Readiness is reported as 70–90% for NATO designated forces and 40–70% for the 7 bde for generation and regeneration)

HQ	2 Div
Mech Inf	5 bde (1 NATO designated (2 regt))
Inf	1 bde (NATO designated (1 regt))
Mtn Inf	1 bde (NATO designated (1 regt))
Arty	1 bde; 1 regt
AD	2 regt
Engr	1 bde
Log	2 bde

EQUIPMENT BY TYPE
MBT 299: 164 T-55; 42 TR-580; 93 TR-85 M1
AIFV 26 MLI-84
APC 1,069
  APC (T) 75 MLVM
  APC (W 994: 31 *Piranha III*; 69 B33 TAB *Zimbru*; 375 TAB-71; 155 TAB-77; 364 TABC-79;
  TYPE VARIANTS 505 APC
ARTY 838
  SP 122mm 24: 6 2S1 *Carnation;* 18 Model 89
  TOWED 390: **122mm** 42 (M-30) M-1938 (A-19); **152mm** 348: 245 M-1981 Model 81; 103 gun/howitzer M1985
  MRL 122mm 140 APR-40
  MOR 120mm 274 M-1982
AT
  MSL 138: 12 9P122 *BRDM-2 Sagger*; 78 9P133 BRDM-2 *Sagger*; 48 9P148 BRDM-2 *Spandrel*
  GUNS 100mm 233: 208 M1977 Gun 77; 25 SU-100 SP
AD • GUNS 60
  SP 35mm 18 *Gepard*
  TOWED 42: **35mm** 24 GDF-203; **37mm** 18
RADARS • LAND 8 SNAR-10 *Big Fred*)

Navy 7,150

Navy HQ with 1 Naval Operational Component, 1 Fleet Command, 1 Frigate Flotilla, 1 Riverine Flotilla (Danube based)

EQUIPMENT BY TYPE
PRINCIPAL SURFACE COMBATANTS 7
  FRIGATES • FFG 3:
    2 *Regele Ferdinand* (ex UK Type-22), each with 1 76mm gun (capacity 1 IAR-330 (SA-330) *Puma*), (platforms undergoing upgrades)
    1 *Marasesti* with 4 twin (8 eff.) with SS-N-2C *Styx* tactical SSM, each with SA-N-5 *Grail* SAM, 2 triple 533mm ASTT (6 eff.) with Russian 53–65 ASW, 2 RBU 6000 *Smerch 2* (24 eff.), 2 x2 76mm gun (4 eff.), (capacity 2 IAR-316 (SA-316) *Alouette III* utl hel)
  CORVETTES • FS 4:
    2 *Tetal* I each with 2 twin 533mm ASTT (4 eff.) with Russian 53-65 ASW, 2 RBU 2500 *Smerch 1* (32 eff.), 2 twin 76mm gun (4 eff.)
    2 *Tetal* II each with 2 twin 533mm ASTT (4 eff.), 2 RBU 6000 *Smerch 2* (24 eff.), 1 76mm gun, (capacity 1 IAR-316 (SA-316) *Alouette III* utl hel)
PATROL AND COASTAL COMBATANTS 17
  PSO 3 *Zborul* each with 2 twin (4 eff.) with SS-N-2C *Styx* tactical SSM, 1 76mm gun
  PCR 14:
    5 *Brutar* each with 1 BM-21 MRL RL, 1 100mm gun
    3 *Kogalniceanu* each with 2 100mm gun
    6 VD 141 (ex MSI now used for river patrol)
MINE WARFARE 11
  MINE COUNTERMEASURES 10
    MSO 4 *Musca*

MSI 6 VD 141 (used for River MCM)
MINELAYERS • ML 1 *Cosar* with up to 100 mines
LOGISTICS AND SUPPORT 10: 3 **AOL**; 2 **AE**; 1 **AGOR**; 1 **AGS**; 2 **AGF**; 1 **AXS**

FACILITIES

Base Located at Tulcea, Braila (Danube), Mangalia, Constanta (coast)

Naval Infantry

FORCES BY ROLE
Naval inf 1 bn

EQUIPMENT BY TYPE
APC (W) 16: 13 ABC-79M; 3 TABC-79M

Air Force 9,700

Flying hours 120 hrs/year

FACILITIES
Air bases 3 combat air bases with *Lancer* and *Puma*.
1 Tpt air base
1 Trg air base

FORCES BY ROLE

HQ (AF)	1 AF HQ: 1 (op) air ops centre, 1 AD bde, 1 engr regt
Ftr	2 sqn with MiG-21 *Lancer* C
FGA	4 sqn with MiG-21 *Lancer* A/*Lancer* B
Tpt/survey/ spt hel	1 tpt ac sqn with An-24 *Coke*, An-26 *Curl*,1 An-30 *Clank*; C-130 B/H *Hercules*, C-27J *Spartan*; 2 multi-role hel sqns with IAR-330 *Puma* SOCAT; 1 tpt hel with IAR-330 (SA-330) *Puma*
Trg	1 sqn with IAR-99 *Soim*; 1 sqn with IAK-52; 1 sqn with 12 An-2; 1 sqn with IAR-316B (*Alouette III*)

EQUIPMENT BY TYPE
AIRCRAFT 49 combat capable
  FTR 20 MiG-21 *Lancer* C
  FGA 29 MiG-21 *Lancer* A/B
  TPT 12: 1 C-130H; 4 C-130B *Hercules*; 2 C-27J *Spartan* (5 more on order); 4 An-26 *Curl*; 1 An-30 *Clank*
  TRG 43: 10 IAR-99; 11 IAR-99 *Soim*; 12 IAK-52; 10 An-2
HELICOPTERS
  SPT 58: 23 IAR-330 *Puma* SOCAT; 35 IAR-330 (SA-330) *Puma*
  UTL 6 IAR-316B (SA-316B) *Alouette III*
AD • SAM 6 SA-2 *Guideline*; 8 HAWK PIP III
MSL
  AAM R-550 *Magic* 2; *Python* 3; AA-8 *Aphid*; AA-11 *Archer*; AA-2 *Atoll*
  ASM SPIKE-ER

Paramilitary 79,900

Border Guards 22,900 (incl conscripts)
Ministry of Interior

Gendarmerie ε57,000
Ministry of Interior

DEPLOYMENT

Legal provisions for foreign deployment:
Constitution: Codified constitution (1991)
Decision on deployment of troops abroad: By parliament (Art. 62); or b) by president upon parliamentary approval (Art. 92)

AFGHANISTAN
NATO • ISAF 990; **Army**: 1 mtn inf bde HQ; 1 inf bn; some TAB-77; some TABC-79; some *Piranha* IIIC
Operation Enduring Freedom 37
UN • UNAMA 1 obs

BOSNIA-HERZEGOVINA
EU • EUFOR • *Operation Althea* 56
OSCE • Bosnia and Herzegovina 1

CÔTE D'IVOIRE
UN • UNOCI 7 obs

DEMOCRATIC REPUBLIC OF CONGO
UN • MONUC 22 obs

IRAQ
NATO • NTM-I 3

LIBERIA
UN • UNMIL 2 obs

NEPAL
UN • UNMIN 7 obs

SERBIA
NATO • KFOR • *Joint Enterprise* 145 ; 1 AB coy
OSCE • Kosovo 4
UN • UNMIK 2 obs

SUDAN
UN • UNMIS 1; 10 obs

Slovakia SVK

Slovak Koruna Ks		2008	2009	2010
GDP	Ks	2.02tr	61.0bn	
	US$	95bn	91bn	
per capita	US$	17,453	16,666	
Growth	%	6.4	-4.7	
Inflation	%	4.6	1.5	
Def exp	Ks	31.4bn		
	US$	1.47bn		
Def bdgt	Ks	31.2bn	980m	986m
	US$	1.46bn	1.46bn	
FMA (US)	US$	1.0m	1.0m	1.5m
US$1=Ks /€ from 2009		21.3	0.67	

Population 5,463,046

Ethnic groups: Hungarian 11%; Romany ε5%; Czech 1%

Age	0–14	15–19	20–24	25–29	30–64	65 plus
Male	9%	4%	4%	4%	23%	5%
Female	8%	4%	4%	4%	24%	7%

Capabilities

ACTIVE 16,531 (Army 7,322 Air 4,190 Cental Staff 1,462 Support and Training 3,557)

Terms of service 6 months

ORGANISATIONS BY SERVICE

Army 7,322

1 Land Forces Comd HQ

FORCES BY ROLE

Mech inf	1 bde (1st)(3 mech inf bn (11th, 12th 13th), 1 log spt bn); 1 bde (2nd) (2 mech inf bn (21st 22nd), 1 tk bn, 1 mixed SP arty bn ,1 log spt bn)
Recce	1 (5th Special) regt
Arty	1 MBL bn
Engr	1 bn
NBC	1 bn

EQUIPMENT BY TYPE
MBT 245 T-72M
AIFV 383: 292 BMP-1; 91 BMP-2
APC 132:
  APC (T) 108 OT-90
  APC (W) 24: 17 OT-64; 7 *Tatrapan* (6x6)
ARTY 340
  SP 193:**122mm** 1 2S1 *Carnation*; 45 in store; **152mm** 131: 119 M-77 *Dana*; 12 in store; **155mm** 16 M-2000 *Zuzana*
  TOWED 122mm 51 D-30
  MRL 84: **122mm** 59 RM-70; **122/227mm** 25 RM-70/85 MODULAR
  MOR 120mm 12: 8 M-1982; 4 PRAM SPM
AT
  MANPATS 425: AT-3 9K11 *Sagger*/AT-5 9K113 *Spandrel*
  SP 9S428 with Malyutka *Sagger* on BMP-1; 9P135 *Fago*t on BMP-2; 9P148 with *Spandrel* on BRDM
AD
  SAM • TOWED SA-13 *Gopher*
  SP 48 SA-13 *Gopher*
  MANPADS SA-16 *Gimlet*; SA-7 *Grail*
  RADAR • LAND SNAR-10 *Big Fred* (veh, arty)

Air Force 4,190

Flying hours	90 hrs/yr for MiG-29 pilots (NATO Integrated AD System); 140 hrs/yr for Mi-8/17 crews (reserved for EU & NATO), min 20hrs/yr for remainder
Air Bases	Sliac tac wg; Presov hel wg; Kuchyna tpt wg

FORCES BY ROLE

Ftr	1 wg with MiG-29/UB/ SD/AS *Fulcrum*
Trg	L-39 *Albatros*
Hel	1 wg with Mi-24D *Hind D*/Mi-24V *Hind E**; Mi-8 *Hip*; Mi-17 (Mi-8MT) *Hip H*; PZL MI-2 *Hoplite*
AD	1 bde with SA-10B *Grumble*; SA-6 *Gainful*; SA-7 *Grail*

EQUIPMENT BY TYPE
AIRCRAFT 22 combat capable

FTR 22 MiG-29 /MiG-29 UB *Fulcrum* (12 MiG-29SD/AS modernised to NATO standard)
TRG 15 L-39 *Albatross*
HELICOPTERS
  ATK 16 Mi-24D *Hind D*/Mi-24V *Hind E*
  SPT 21: 14 Mi-17 *Hip H*; 1 Mi-8 *Hip*; 6 PZL MI-2 *Hoplite*
AD • SAM
  SP SA-10B *Grumble*; SA-6 *Gainful*
  MANPAD SA-7 *Grail*
MSL
  AAM AA-8 *Aphid*; AA-11 *Archer*; AA-10 *Alamo*
  ASM S5K/S5KO (57mm rockets); S8KP/S8KOM (80mm rockets)

DEPLOYMENT

Legal provisions for foreign deployment:
Constitution: Codified constitution (1992)
Decision on deployment of troops abroad: By the parliament (Art. 86)

AFGHANISTAN
NATO • ISAF 245

BOSNIA-HERZEGOVINA
EU • EUFOR • *Operation Althea* 32
OSCE • Bosnia and Herzegovina 2

CYPRUS
UN • UNFICYP 196; elm 1 inf coy; 1 engr pl

MIDDLE EAST
UN • UNTSO 2 obs

SERBIA
NATO • KFOR • *Joint Enterprise* 145; **Army**: 1 inf coy
OSCE • Serbia 1
OSCE • Kosovo 1

Slovenia SVN

Slovenian Tolar t		2008	2009	2010
GDP	t/€	37bn	35.4bn	
	US$	54bn	53bn	
per capita	US$	27,100	26,343	
Growth	%	3.5	-4.7	
Inflation	%	5.9	0.5	
Def exp	t	567m		
	US$	834m		
Def bdgt	t	546m	589m	
	US$	802m	879m	
US$1=€		0.68	0.67	

Population 2,005,692

Ethnic groups: Croat 2.8%; Serb 2.4%

Age	0–14	15–19	20–24	25–29	30–64	65 plus
Male	7%	3%	4%	4%	25%	6%
Female	7%	3%	3%	4%	25%	9%

Capabilities

ACTIVE 7,200 (Army 7,200) Paramilitary 4,500

RESERVE 3,800 (Army 3,800)

ORGANISATIONS BY SERVICE

Army 7,200
1 Force Comd
FORCES BY ROLE
Inf	1 bde (3 mot inf bn, 1 arty bn, 1 recce coy, 1 log bn)
SF	1 unit
ISTAR	1 bn
Sigs	1 bn
Engr	1 bn
CBRN	1 bn
MP	1 bn

EQUIPMENT BY TYPE
MBT 70: 40 M-84; 30 T-55S1
APC (W) 124: 85 *Valuk* (*Pandur*); 39 *Patria*
ARTY 140
  TOWED • 155mm 18 TN-90
  MOR 116: **82mm** 60; **120mm** 56: 8 M-52; 16 M-74; 32 MN-9
AT • MSL • SP 24: 12 BOV-3 AT-3 9K11 *Sagger*; 12 BOV-3 AT-4 9K111 *Spigot*
MANPATS AT-3 9K11 *Sagger*; AT-4 9K111*Spigot*

Reserves
Mtn Inf	1 bn (6 Coy)
Tk	1 bn

Army Maritime Element 47
FORCES BY ROLE
Maritime 1 bn (part of Sp Comd)
EQUIPMENT BY TYPE
PATROL AND COASTAL COMBATANTS • PB 1 *Super Dvora* MKII
FACILITIES
Base   Located at Koper

Air Element 530
FORCES BY ROLE
1 fixed wg sqn; 1 rotary wg sqn; 1 AD bn; 1 airspace control bn; 1 avn school; 1 air maintenance coy; 1 mil ATC coy. All at Cerklje air base except airspace control bn at Brnik air base.
EQUIPMENT BY TYPE
AIRCRAFT 9 combat capable
  TPT 3: 1 L-410 *Turbolet*; 2 PC-6 *Turbo-Porter*
  TRG 11: 2 PC-9; 9 PC-9M*
HELICOPTERS
  UTL 12: 4 AS 532AL *Cougar*; 8 Bell 412 *Twin Huey* (some armed)
  TRG 4 AB-206 (Bell 206) *Jet Ranger*

AD
  SAM 138
    SP 6 *Roland* II
    MANPAD 132: 36 SA-16 *Gimlet*; 96 SA-18 *Grouse* (*Igla*)

Paramilitary 4,500

Police 4,500 (armed); 5,000 reservists (total 9,500)
HELICOPTERS • UTL 5: 1 A-109; 2 AB-206 (Bell 206) *Jet Ranger*; 1 AB-212 (Bell 212); 1 Bell 412 *Twin Huey*

DEPLOYMENT
Legal provisions for foreign deployment:
Constitution: Codified constitution (1991)
Decision on deployment of troops abroad: By government (Art. 84 of Defence Act)

AFGHANISTAN
NATO • ISAF 130

BOSNIA-HERZEGOVINA
EU • EUFOR • *Operation Althea* 26
OSCE • Bosnia and Herzegovina 1

LEBANON
UN • UNIFIL 14

MIDDLE EAST
UN • UNTSO 2 obs

SERBIA
NATO • KFOR • *Joint Enterprise* 389; **Army**: 1 inf bn HQ; 2 mot inf coy; 1 engr gp
OSCE • Serbia 1
OSCE • Kosovo 1

Spain ESP

Euro €		2008	2009	2010
GDP	€	1.09tr	1.03tr	
	US$	1.61tr	1.54tr	
per capita	US$	39,769	38,082	
Growth	%	0.9	-3.8	
Inflation	%	4.1	-0.1	
Def exp[a]	€	13.1bn		
	US$	19.2bn		
Def bdgt	€	8.14bn	7.84bn	
	US$	11.9bn	11.7bn	
US$1=€		0.68	0.67	

[a] including military pensions plus extra budgetary expenditure

Population	40,525,000					
Age	0–14	15–19	20–24	25–29	30–64	65 plus
Male	7%	3%	3%	4%	24%	7%
Female	7%	3%	3%	4%	24%	9%

Capabilities

ACTIVE 128,013 (Army 79,736 Navy 17,943 Air 21,606 Joint 8,728) **Paramilitary 80,210**

RESERVE 319,000 (Army 265,000 Navy 9,000 Air 45,000)

ORGANISATIONS BY SERVICE

Army 79,736

The Army Force is organised in Land Forces High Readiness HQ, Land Force, Operational Logistic Force and the Canary Islands Command. The principal deployable elements are the Heavy Forces (FUP) consisting of 2 mech bde and 1 Armoured bde, and the Light Forces (FUL) consisting of 1 Cavalry, 1 Legion, 1 AB and 2 light bde. The Land Forces High Readiness HQ Spain provides one NATO Rapid Deployment Corps HQ (NRDC-SP).

FORCES BY ROLE

Infantry regiments usually comprise 2 bn. Spain deploys its main battle tanks within its armd/mech inf formations, and its armd cav regt

Comd	1 corps HQ (CGTAD) (1 HQ bn, 1 shell bn); 2 div HQ (coordinative role)
Armd	1 bde (12th) (1 HQ bn, 1 armd inf regt, 1 mech inf bn, 1 SP arty bn, 1 recce bn, 1 engr bn, 1 logistic bn, 1 sig coy)
Armd Cav	1 bde (2nd) (1 engr bn, 1 HQ bn, 1 armd cav regt, 1 fd arty regt, 1 logistic bn, 3 light armd cav regt, 1 lt cav rgt, 1 sig coy)
Mech Inf	2 bde (10th and 11th) (each: 1 HQ bn, 1 mech inf regt, 1 armd inf bn, 1 recce bn, 1 SP arty bn, 1 engr bn, 1 logistic bn, 1 sig coy)
Air Mob	1 bde (7th) (1 HQ bn, 1 inf regt, 1 inf bn, 1 fd arty bn, 1 engr unit, 1 logistic bn, 1sig coy)
Mtn Inf	1 comd (1st) (1 engr unit, 1 HQ bn, 1 logistic bn, 1 fd arty bn, 2 mtn inf regt, 1 mtn inf bn)
Lt inf	1 bde (La Legion) (1 HQ bn, 1 inf regt, 1 inf bn, 1 recce bn, 1 fd arty bn, 1 engr unit, 1 logistic bn, 1 sig coy); 1 bde (5th) (1 HQ bn, 2 lt inf regt, 1 armd inf bn, 1 fd arty bn, 1 engr unit, 1 logistic bn, 1 sig coy)
SF	1 comd (1 HQ bn, 3 Spec Ops bn, 1 sig coy)
AB	1 bde (6th) (1 HQ bn, 1 para bn, 1 air aslt bn, 1 air mob bn, 1 fd arty bn, 1 engr bn, 1 logistic bn, 1 sig coy)
Fd Arty	1 comd (3 fd arty regt)
Coastal Arty	1 comd (1 sig unit, 1 coastal arty regt)
ADA	1 comd (5 ADA regt, 1 sig unit)
Engr	1 comd (1 NBC regt, 1 engr bridging regt, 1 engr regt, 1 railway regt)
Sig / EW	1 bde (2 EW regt, 2 sig regt)
Avn	1 comd (FAMET) (1 avn bde HQ, 1 atk hel bn, 2 spt hel bn, 1 tpt hel bn, 1 logistic unit (1 spt coy, 1 supply coy), 1 sig bn)
Logistic	2 div (each: 3 logistic regt)
Medical	1 bde (1 logistic unit, 1 field hospital unit, 3 medical regt)
Territorial	1 (Canary Islands) comd (lt inf bde (1 HQ bn, 3 lt inf bn, 1 fd arty regt, 1 AD regt, 1 engr bn, 1 logistic bn, 1 spt hel bn, 1 sig coy)); 1 (Balearic Islands) comd (1 HQ bn, 1 inf regt, 1fd arty regt, 1engr bn, 1 logistic bn, 1 lt inf div HQ); 2 (Ceuta and Melilla) comd (each: 1 HQ bn, 1 Inf regt, 1 Inf bn, 1 cav regt, 1 arty regt, 1 engr bn, 1 logistic bn, 1 sig coy, 1 lt inf div HQ)

EQUIPMENT BY TYPE

MBT 498: 108 *Leopard* 2A4; 206 *Leopard* 2A5E; 184 M-60A3TTS

RECCE 312: 84 B-1 *Centauro*; 228 VEC-3562 *BMR-VEC*

AIFV 144 *Pizarro* (incl 22 comd)

APC 1,465

  APC (T) 966 M-113 (incl variants)

  APC (W) 499: BMR-600 / BMR-600M1

ARTY 1,959

  SP 130: **105mm** 34 M-108; **155mm** 96 M-109A5

  TOWED 296

    105mm 226: 56 L-118 light gun; 170 Model 56 pack howitzer; **155mm** 70: 52 M-114; 18 SBT-1

  COASTAL 50:

    155mm 8 SBT 52; **305mm** 3; **381mm** 3; **6in** 36

  MRL 140mm 14 *Teruel*

  MOR 1,469:

    SP 556: **81mm** 446; **120mm** 110 SP

    81mm 594; **120mm** 319

AT

  MSL

    SP 174: 106 *Milan*; 68 TOW

    MANPATS 482: 52 *Spike LR*; *Spike* (of 260 being delivered); 298 *Milan*; 132 TOW

  RCL 106mm 507

HEL

  ATK 6 AS-665 *Tiger*

  OBS 9 OH-58 *Kiowa*

  SPT 17 HT-17D (CH-47D) *Chinook*

    HU-21 (AS-332) *Super Puma*

  UTL 103: 26 BO-105; 6 HU.18 (Bell 212); 15 AS-532UC *Cougar*; 16 AS-532UL *Cougar*; 20 HU-10B (UH-1H) *Iroquois*

  UAV 4 *Pasi*

AD

  SAM 256

    SP 18: 16 *Roland*; 2 *Spada*

    TOWED 58: 36 I *HAWK* Phase III MIM-23B; 6 *Skyguard/Aspide*; 8 NASAMS; 8 Pac *Patriot* 2

    MANPAD 180 *Mistral*

  GUNS • TOWED 267: **20mm** 175 GAI-B01; **35mm** 92 GDF-002

RADAR

  AIRBORNE *Sentinel* RMK1

  LAND ARTHUR; 2 AN/TPQ-36 *Firefinder*

Reserves 265,000 reservists

Cadre units

Railway	1 regt

Armd Cav 1 bde
Inf 3 bde

Navy 17,943 (incl Naval Aviation and Marines)

FORCES BY ROLE

Navy 1 comd HQ located at Madrid
   1 Strike Group
   2 Frigate Squadrons
   1 Submarine Flotilla
   1 MCM Flotilla
   1 Naval Aviation Flotilla

EQUIPMENT BY TYPE

SUBMARINES • TACTICAL • SSK 4:
   4 *Galerna* each with 4 single 533mm TT each with 20 F17 Mod 2/L5
PRINCIPAL SURFACE COMBATANTS 12
   AIRCRAFT CARRIERS • CVS 1 *Principe de Asturias* (capacity 10 AV-8B *Harrier II* FGA ac /AV-8B *Harrier II Plus* FGA ac; 8 SH-3 *Sea King* ASW hel; 2 HU-18 (Bell 212) utl hel
   FRIGATES • FFG 11:
   4 *Alvaro de Bazan* each with 2 twin 324mm ASTT (4 eff.) with 24 Mk 46 LWT, 2 Mk 141 *Harpoon* quad (8 eff.) each with RGM-84F tactical SSM, 1 48 cell Mk 41 VLS (LAM capable) with 32 SM-2 MR SAM, 64 RIM-162B *Sea Sparrow* SAM (quad packs), 1 127mm gun; Baseline 5 Aegis C2, (capacity 1 SH-60B *Seahawk* ASW hel)
   1 *Baleares* (limited operational role only; planned for decommissioning) with 2 Mk 141 *Harpoon* quad (8 eff.) each with RGM-84C *Harpoon* tactical SSM, 1 Mk 112 octuple (8 eff.) with 16 tactical ASROC, 1 Mk 22 GMLS with 16 SM-1 MR SAM, 2 twin ASTT (4 eff.) each with Mk 46 LWT, 1 127mm gun
   6 *Santa Maria* each with 2 Mk32 triple 324mm each with 6 Mk 46 LWT, 1 Mk 13 GMLS with 32 SM-1 MR SAM, 8 RGM-84C *Harpoon* tactical SSM, 1 76mm gun (capacity 2 SH-60B *Seahawk* ASW hel)
MINE WARFARE • MINE COUNTERMEASURES 7
   MCCS 1 *Diana*
   MHO 6 *Segura*
AMPHIBIOUS
   PRINCIPAL AMPHIBIOUS SHIPS 4
   LHD 1 *Juan Carlos I* (capacity 4 LCM; 42 APC; 46 MBT; 700 troops; able to operate as alternate platform for CVS aviation group) (expected ISD 2011)
   LPD 2 *Galicia* (capacity 6 AB-212 or 4 SH-3D *Sea King*; 4 LCM or 6 LCVP; 130 APC or 33 MBT; 450 troops)
   LS • LST 1 *Pizarro* (2nd of class in reserve)
   CRAFT 20 LCM
LOGISTICS AND SUPPORT 3
   AORH 2: 1 *Patino*; 1 *Cantabria* (expected ISD '09)
   AO 1 *Marques de la Ensenada*

FACILITIES

Bases | Located at El Ferrol, Rota (Fleet HQ), Cartagena (ALMART HQ, Maritime Action), Las Palmas (Canary Islands), Mahon (Menorca), Porto Pi (Mallorca)
Naval Air Stations | Located at Mahón (Menorca), Porto Pi (Mallorca)

Navy – Maritime Action Force

FORCES BY ROLE

Navy Canary Islands Maritime Command (Cadiz) Maritime Action Units Command (Ferrol) Maritime Action Command, Balear Islands Maritime Area

PATROL AND COASTAL COMBATANTS 32
   PSOH 11: 4 *Descubierta*; 4 *Serviola*; 3 *Alboran*
   PSO 11: 1 *Chilreu*; 9 *Anaga*, 1 *Buquesde Accion Maritime* (*BAM* - 1st of 4 vessels on order)
   PFC 2 *Barcelo*
   PCC 6: 4 *Conejera* 2 *Toralla*
   PBR 2
LOGISTICS AND SUPPORT 27:
   AWT 2
   AGOR 2 (with ice strengthened hull, for polar research duties in Antarctica)
   AGHS 2
   AGS 2
   ATF 2
   AT 2
   AK 3
   YDT 1
   TRG 11: 1 **AX**; 5 **AXL**; 5 **AXS**

Naval Aviation 814

Flying hours 150 hrs/year on AV-8B *Harrier II* FGA ac; 200 hrs/year on hel

FORCES BY ROLE

COMD/tpt | 1 sqn with HU-18 (Bell 212)
FGA | 1 sqn with AV-8B *Harrier II Plus*; AV-8B *Harrier II*
ASW | 1 sqn with SH-3D *Sea King*; 1 sqn with SH-60B *Seahawk*
EW | 1 sqn with SH-3D *Sea King* (AEW)
Liaison | 1 sqn with CE-550 *Citation II*
Trg | 1 flt with 1 TAV-8B *Harrier* on lease (USMC); 1 sqn with Hughes 500MD

EQUIPMENT BY TYPE

AIRCRAFT 16 combat capable
   FGA 16: 12 AV-8B *Harrier II Plus*; 4 AV-8B *Harrier II*
   TPT 3 CE-550 *Citation II*
   TRG 1 TAV-8B *Harrier* on lease (USMC)
   MP 7 P-3 *Orion*
HELICOPTERS
   ASW 24: 3 SH-3D *Sea King* (AEW); 9 SH-3; 12 SH-60B *Seahawk*
   UTL 18: 8 HU-18 (Bell 212); 10 Hughes 500MD
MSL
   ASM AGM-119 *Penguin*, AGM-65G *Maverick*
   AAM AIM-120 *AMRAAM*, AIM-9L *Sidewinder*

Marines 5,300

FORCES BY ROLE

Marine | 1 bde (2,500) (1 mech inf bn, 2 inf bn, 1 arty bn, 1 log bn, 1 spec ops unit)
Marine Garrison | 5 gp

EQUIPMENT BY TYPE

MBT 16 M-60A3TTS

APC (W) 18 *Piranha*
AAV 19: 16 AAV-7A1/AAVP-7A1; 2 AAVC-7A1; 1 AAVR-7A1
ARTY 18
   SP 155mm 6 M-109A2
   TOWED 105mm 12 M-56 (pack)
AT • MSL • MANPATS 24 TOW-2
   RL 90mm C-90C
AD • SAM • MANPAD 12 *Mistral*

Air Force 21,606 (plus 6,006 civilian; 27,612 in total)

The Spanish Air Force is organised in 3 commands – General Air Command, Combat Air Command and Canary Islands Air Command

Flying hours 120 hrs/year on hel/tpt ac; 180 hrs/year on FGA/ftr

FORCES BY ROLE

Ftr/OCU	2 sqn with EF *Typhoon*; 1 EF *Typhoon* OCU; 2 sqn with F-1CE (F-1C) *Mirage*/F-1EDA/ *Mirage* F-1EE (F-1E)
FGA	5 sqn with EF-18A (F/A-18A)/EF-18B (F/A-18B) *Hornet*; EF-18 MLU
MP	1 sqn with P-3A *Orion**; P-3B *Orion** (MR)
EW	3 sqn with B-707; CASA 212 *Aviocar*; *Falcon* 20 (EW)
SAR	1 sqn with F-27 *Friendship* (SAR), HU-21 (AS-332) *Super Puma*; 1 sqn with CN-235 (maritime surv/SAR); 1 sqn with CASA 212 *Aviocar*, HU-21 (AS-332) *Super Puma*; 1 sqn with CASA 212 *Aviocar*, AS-330 (SA-330) *Puma*
Spt	1 sqn with CASA 212 *Aviocar*; Cessna 550 *Citation V* (recce); Canadair CL-215
Tkr/tpt	1 sqn with KC-130H *Hercules*; 1 sqn with Boeing 707
Tpt	1 sqn with CN-235 (12 tpt, 2 VIP); 1 sqn with C-130H/C-130H-30 *Hercules*; 1 sqn with CASA 212 *Aviocar*; 1 sqn with A-310, *Falcon* 900; 1 sqn with Beechcraft C90 *King Air* (VIP), HU-21 (AS-332) *Super Puma*; 1 sqn with Boeing 707
Tkr	1 sqn with A-310; B-707
OCU	1 sqn with EF-18A (F/A-18A)/EF-18B (F/A-18B) *Hornet*
Lead-in trg	2 sqn with F-5B *Freedom Fighter*
Trg	2 sqn with CASA C-101 *Aviojet*; 1 sqn with CASA 212 *Aviocar*; 1 sqn with Beech F-33C *Bonanza* (trg); 2 sqn with EC-120 *Colibri*; S-76C; 1 sqn with E-26 (T-35) *Pillan*

EQUIPMENT BY TYPE

AIRCRAFT 179 combat capable
FTR 81: 18 EF *Typhoon* Tranche 1 (10 C.16/8 CE.16) (87 *Typhoon* on order); 43 F-1CE (F-1C) *Mirage*/F-1EDA *Mirage* F-1EE (F-1E)/*Mirage* F-1EE (F-1E); 20 F-5B *Freedom Fighter* (lead-in ftr trg)
FGA 88 EF-18A (F/A-18A)/EF-18B (F/A-18B) *Hornet* (67 being given MLU)
MP 13: 2 P-3A *Orion**; 5 P-3B *Orion** (MR); 6 CN-235 maritime surv/SAR

TKR 7: 5 KC-130H *Hercules*, 2 Boeing 707
TPT 107: 2 A-310; 4 B-707 (incl EW & tkr); 6 C-130H /C-130H-30 *Hercules*; 57 CASA 212 *Aviocar*; 7 CASA C-295 (9 on order to replace some CASA 212); 14 CN-235 (12 tpt, 2 VIP); 2 Cessna 550 *Citation V* (recce); 3 F-27 *Friendship* (SAR); 4 *Falcon*; 20 (2 EW, 2 NAVAID); 5 *Falcon* 900 (VIP); 1 Beechcraft C90 *King Air*
SPT/Firefighting 16: 15 Canadair CL-215; 1 CL-415
TRG 105: 46 CASA C-101 *Aviojet*; 22 Beech F-33C *Bonanza* (trg); 37 E-26 (T-35) *Pillan*
HELICOPTERS
SPT 17: 5 AS-330 (SA-330) *Puma*; 12 HU-21 (AS-332) *Super Puma*
UTL 25: 15 EC-120 *Colibri*; 2 AS-532 (VIP); 8 S-76C
AD
SAM *Mistral*; R-530
TOWED *Skyguard/Aspide*
MSL
AAM AIM-120B/C AMRAAM; AIM-9L/ AIM-9M/ AIM-9N/ AIM-9P *Sidewinder*; AIM-7F/M *Sparrow*, R-530
ARM AGM-88A HARM;
ASM AGM-65A/G *Maverick*; AGM-84C/D *Harpoon*; *Taurus* KEPD 350
BOMBS
Conventional: Mk 82; Mk 83; Mk 84; BLU-109; BPG-2000; BR-250; BR-500;
BME-330B/AP; CBU-100 (anti-tank)
Laser-guided: GBU-10/16 *Paveway* II; GBU-24 *Paveway* III

General Air Command (Torrejon)

3 Wg

Spt	1 sqn with CASA 212 *Aviocar*; Cessna 550 *Citation V*; 1 sqn with Canadair CL-215/CL-415; 1 sqn with CASA 212 *Aviocar*; HU-21 (AS-332) *Super Puma* (SAR)
Tpt	1 sqn with A-310; B-707 (tkr/tpt); 1 sqn with HU-21 (AS-332) *Super Puma* (tpt); 1 sqn with *Falcon* 900; 1sqn with A-310, Beechcraft C90 *King Air*
Trg	1 sqn with CASA C-101 *Aviojet*; 1 sqn with E-24 (Beech F-33) *Bonanza*; 1 sqn with CASA 212 *Aviocar*

Combat Air Command (Torrejon)

6 Wg

Ftr	7 sqn with EF-18 (F/A-18) *Hornet*; 1 sqn with *Typhoon*; 2 sqn with F-1CE (F-1C)/ F-1BE (F-1B) *Mirage*
Spt	1 sqn with CASA 212 *Aviocar*; AS-330 (SA-330) *Puma*; 1 sqn with B-707, CASA 212 *Aviocar*, Falcon 20 (EW)
MR	1 sqn with P-3A/P-3B *Orion*
Tpt	1 sqn with CASA 212 *Aviocar*; 1 sqn with KC-130H *Hercules* (tkr/tpt); C-130H *Hercules*; 2 sqn with CN-235; 1 sqn with CASA C-295; 1 sqn with B-707 (tkr/tpt)
OCU	1 sqn with EF-18 (F/A-18) *Hornet*

Lead-in trg 2 sqn with F-5B *Freedom Fighter*

Trg   2 sqn with EC-120B *Colibri*; S-76C; 1 sqn with E-26 (T-35) *Pillan*; 1 sqn with CASA C-101 *Aviojet*; 1 sqn with CASA 212 *Aviocar*

Canary Island Air Command (Gando)

1 Wg

FGA   1 sqn with EF-18 (F/A-18) *Hornet*

SAR   1 sqn with F-27 *Friendship*; HU-21 (AS-332) *Super Puma*

Tpt   1 detachment with 2 CN-235

Logistic Support Air Command (Madrid)

Trials and 1 sqn with F-5A *Freedom Fighter* test; F-1
Testing   *Mirage* test; EF-18 (F/A-18) *Hornet* test; CASA 212 *Aviocar* test; CASA C-101 *Aviojet* test

Emergencies Military Unit (UME)

FORCES BY ROLE

HQ   1 (div)

Air   1 gp with Firefighting planes belonging to the Air Force
1 emergency hel bn belonging to the Army Aviation (FAMET)

Emergency 5 bn
Intervention

Paramilitary 80,210

Guardia Civil 79,950

9 regions, 56 Rural Comds

FORCES BY ROLE

Inf   17 (Tercios) regt

Spec Op   10 (rural) gp

Sy   6 (traffic) gp; 1 (Special) bn

EQUIPMENT BY TYPE

APC (W) 18 BLR

HELICOPTERS

    ARMED 26 Bo-105ATH

    UTL 12: 8 BK-117; 4 EC135P2

Guardia Civil Del Mar 760

PATROL AND COASTAL COMBATANTS 53

    PCC 15

    PCI 1

    PBF 22

    PB 15

DEPLOYMENT

Legal provisions for foreign deployment:
Constitution: Codified constitution (1978)
Specific legislation: 'Ley Orgánica de la Defensa Nacional' (2005)
Decision on deployment of troops abroad: a) By the government (Art. 6 of the 'Defence Law'); b) parliamentary approval is required for military operations 'which are not directly related to the defence of Spain or national interests' (Art. 17 of the 'Defence Law')

AFGHANISTAN
NATO • ISAF 1,000; 1 inf bn

ARABIAN GULF AND INDIAN OCEAN
EU • *Operation Atalanta* 1 FFG; 1 P-3A Orion

BOSNIA-HERZEGOVINA
EU • EUFOR • *Operation Althea* 316; **Army**: 1 inf bn HQ; 1 inf coy; 1 recce pl
OSCE • Bosnia and Herzegovina 4

DEMOCRATIC REPUBLIC OF CONGO
UN • MONUC 2 obs

LEBANON
UN • UNIFIL 1,045; 1 inf bn; 1 avn coy

SERBIA
OSCE • Kosovo 10
UN • UNMIK 1 obs

FOREIGN FORCES

United States US European Command **Army** 90; **Navy** 689; **USAF** 350; USMC 145; 1 air base located at Morón; 1 naval base located at Rota

Turkey TUR

New Turkish Lira L		2008	2009	2010
GDP	L	950bn	960bn	
	US$	731bn	658bn	
per capita	US$	9,642	8,561	
Growth	%	0.9	-6.5	
Inflation	%	10.4	6.3	
Def exp [a]	L	17.6bn		
	US$	13.5bn		
Def bdgt	L	13.3bn	14.5bn	
	US$	10.2bn	9.9bn	
FMA (US)	US$	6.8m	1.0m	5.0m
US$1=L		1.30	1.46	

[a] including coast guard and gendarmerie

Population   76,805,524
Ethnic groups: Kurds ε20%

Age	0–14	15–19	20–24	25–29	30–64	65 plus
Male	13%	5%	5%	5%	20%	3%
Female	13%	5%	5%	5%	19%	4%

Capabilities

ACTIVE 510,600 (Army 402,000 Navy 48,600 Air 60,000) **Paramilitary 102,200**

Terms of service 15 months. Reserve service to age of 41 for all services. Active figure reducing

RESERVE 378,700 (Army 258,700 Navy 55,000 Air 65,000) **Paramilitary 50,000**

ORGANISATIONS BY SERVICE

Army ε77,000; ε325,000 conscript (total 402,000)

FORCES BY ROLE

4 Army HQ; 10 corps HQ

Armd	17 bde
Mech inf	15 bde
Inf	2 div; 11 bde
Trg/inf	4 bde
SF	1 comd HQ with (4 cdo bde)
Cbt hel	1 bn
Avn	4 regt; 3 bn (*total:* 1 tpt bn, 2 trg bn)
Trg/arty	4 bde

EQUIPMENT BY TYPE

MBT 4,503: 298 *Leopard* 2A4; 170 *Leopard* 1A4; 227 *Leopard* 1A3; 274 M-60A1; 658 M-60A3; 2,876 M-48A5 T1/M-48A5 T2 (1,300 to be stored)

RECCE 250+: ε250 *Akrep*; ARSV *Cobra*

AIFV 650

APC (T) 3,643: 830 AAPC; 2,813 M-113/M-113 A1/M-113A2

ARTY 7,450+

  SP 868+: **105mm** 391: 26 M-108T; 365 M-52T; **155mm** 222 M-44T1; TU SpH Storm (K-9) *Thunder*; **175mm** 36 M-107; **203mm** 219 M-110A2

  TOWED 685+: **105mm** M-101A1; **155mm** 523: 517 M-114A1/M-114A2; 6 *Panter*; **203mm** 162 M-115

  MRL 84+: **70mm** 24; **107mm** 48; **122mm** T-122; **227mm** 12 MLRS (incl ATACMS)

  MOR 5,813+

    SP 1,443+: **81mm**; **107mm** 1,264 M-30; **120mm** 179

    TOWED 4,370: **81mm** 3,792; **120mm** 578

AT

  MSL 1,283

  SP 365 *TOW*

  MANPATS 998: 80 *Kornet*; 186 *Cobra*; ε340 *Eryx*; 392 *Milan*

  RCL 3,869: **106mm** 2,329 M-40A1; **57mm** 923 M-18; **75mm** 617

  RL 66mm M-72 *LAW*

AIRCRAFT

  TPT 7: 4 Beech 200 *Super King Air*; 3 Cessna 421

  UTL 98 U-17B

  TRG 63: 34 7GCBC *Citabria*; 25 T-41D *Mescalero*; 4 T-42A *Cochise*

HELICOPTERS

  ATK 37 AH-1P *Cobra*/AH-1W *Cobra*

  OBS 3 OH-58B *Kiowa*

  SPT 50 S-70B *Black Hawk*

  UTL 162: 2 AB-212 (Bell 212); 10 AS-532UL *Cougar*; 12 AB-204B (Bell 204B); 64 AB-205A (Bell 205A); 20 Bell 206 *JetRanger*; ε45 UH-1H *Iroquois*; 9 Bell 412 *Twin Huey*

  TRG 28 Hughes 300C

UAV 215+: AN/USD-501 *Midge*; *Falcon* 600/*Firebee*; CL-89; 19 *Bayraktar*

  RECCE • TAC 196 *Gnat* 750 *Harpy*

AD

  SAM SP 148: 70 *Altigan* PMADS octuple *Stinger*, 78 *Zipkin* PMADS quad *Stinger* lnchr

  MANPAD 935: 789 FIM-43 *Redeye* (being withdrawn); 146 FIM-92A *Stinger*

  GUNS 1,664

    SP 40mm 262 M42A1

    TOWED 1,402: **20mm** 439 GAI-D01; **35mm** 120 GDF-001/GDF-003; **40mm** 843: 803 L/60/L/70; 40 T-1

RADAR • LAND AN/TPQ-36 *Firefinder*

Navy 14,100; 34,500 conscript (total 48,600 inclusive Coast Guard 2,200 and Marines 3,100)

FORCES BY ROLE

HQ 1 (Ankara) Naval Forces Command HQ (1 (Altinovayalova) Training HQ, 1 (Gölcük) Fleet HQ HQ, 1 (Istanbul) Northern Sea Area HQ, 1 (Izmir) Southern Sea Area HQ)

EQUIPMENT BY TYPE

SUBMARINES • TACTICAL 14

  SSK 14:

    6 *Atilay* (GER Type 209/1200) each with 8 single 533mm ASTT each with 14 SST-4 HWT

    8 *Preveze/Gur* (GER Type 209/1400) each with 8 single 533mm ASTT with UGM-84 *Harpoon* tactical USGW, *Tigerfish* HWT

PRINCIPAL SURFACE COMBATANTS • FRIGATES 23

  FFG 23:

    2 *Barbaros* (mod GER MEKO 200 F244, F245) each with 2 Mk 141 *Harpoon* quad (8 eff.) with RGM-84C *Harpoon* tactical SSM, 1 Mk 29 *Sea Sparrow* octuple with 24 *Aspide* SAM, 2 Mk32 triple 324mm TT with Mk 46 LWT, 1 127mm gun, 1 AB-212 utl hel

    2 *Barbaros* (mod GER MEKO 200 F246, F247) each with 2 Mk 141 *Harpoon* quad (8 eff.) with RGM-84C *Harpoon* tactical SSM, 1 8 cell Mk 41 VLS with 24 *Aspide* SAM, 2 Mk32 triple 324mm ASTT with Mk 46 LWT, 1 127mm gun, 1 AB-212 utl hel

    6 *Burak* (FRA *d'Estienne d'Orves*) each with 2 single each with 4 MM-38 *Exocet* tactical SSM, 1 twin Manual with SIMBAD twin, 4 single ASTT each with 4 L5 HWT, 1 100mm gun

    8 *Gaziantep* (ex-US *Oliver Hazard Perry*-class) each with 1 Mk 13 GMLS with 36 SM-1 MR SAM, 4+ RGM-84C *Harpoon* tactical SSM, 2 Mk32 triple 324mm each with 24 Mk 46 LWT, 1 76mm gun, (capacity 1 S-70B *Seahawk* ASW hel)

    1 *Muavenet* (ex-US *Knox*-class) with 1 Mk16 Mk 112 octuple with ASROC/RGM-84C *Harpoon* SSM (from ASROC launcher), 2 twin 324mm ASTT (4 eff.) each with 22+ Mk 46 LWT, 1 127mm gun, (capacity 1 AB-212 (Bell 212) utl hel)

    4 *Yavuz* (GER MEKO 200 F244, F245) each with 2 Mk 141 *Harpoon* quad (8 eff.) with RGM-84C *Harpoon* tactical SSM, 1 Mk 29 *Sea Sparrow* octuple with 24 *Aspide* SAM, 2 Mk32 triple 324mm each with Mk 46 LWT, 1 127mm gun, 1 AB-212 (Bell 212) utl hel

PATROL AND COASTAL COMBATANTS 43

  PSO 8: 1 *Trabzon*; 6 *Karamursel* (GER *Vegesack*); 1 *Hisar*

PFM 25:

8 *Dogan* (GER *Lurssen*-57) each with 1 76mm gun, 2 quad (8 eff.) with RGM-84A *Harpoon*/RGM-84C *Harpoon*

8 *Kartal* (GER *Jaguar*) each with 4 single each with RB 12 *Penguin* tactical SSM, 2 single 533mm TT

7 *Kilic* each with 2 Mk 141 *Harpoon* quad (8 eff.) each with 1 RGM-84C *Harpoon* tactical SSM, 1 76mm gun (2 additional vessels in build)

2 *Yildiz* each with 1 76mm gun, 2 quad (8 eff.) each with RGM-84A *Harpoon*/RGM-84C *Harpoon*

PCO 6 *Turk*

PCC 4 PGM-71

MINE WARFARE • MINE COUNTERMEASURES 22

MCM 6 spt (tenders)

MHC 7: 5 *Edineik* (FRA *Circe*); 4 *Aydin* (additional vessels on order)

MSC 5 *Silifke* (US *Adjutant*)

MSI 4 *Foca* (US *Cape*)

AMPHIBIOUS

LS 5

LST 5:

2 *Ertugrul* (capacity 18 tanks; 400 troops) (US *Terrebonne Parish*)

1 *Osman Gazi* (capacity 4 LCVP; 17 tanks; 980 troops;)

2 *Sarucabey* (capacity 11 tanks; 600 troops)

CRAFT 41: 24 **LCT**; 17 **LCM**

LOGISTICS AND SUPPORT 49:

AORH 2

AORL 1

AOT 2

AOL 1

AF 2

ASR 1

ARS 1

AWT 13: 11; 2 (harbour)

ABU 2

ATF 3

TPT 1

TRV 3

YTM 17

FACILITIES

Bases Located at Gölcük, Erdek, Canakkale, Eregli, Bartin, Izmir, Istanbul, Foka, Aksaz, Antalya, Mersin, Iskanderun

Marines 3,100

Arty   1 bn (18 guns)

Marine 1 HQ; 1 regt; 3 bn

Naval Aviation

FORCES BY ROLE

ASW some sqn with AB-204AS (Bell 204AS); AB-212 (Bell 212); S-70B *Seahawk*

Trg   1 sqn with CN-235; ATR-72

EQUIPMENT BY TYPE

AIRCRAFT • MP •ASW 7: 6 CN-235; 1 *Alenia* ATR-72 (additional ac on order)

HELICOPTERS

ASW 10: 3 AB-204AS (Bell 204AS); 7 S-70B *Seahawk*

UTL 11 AB-212 (Bell 212)*

Naval Forces Command

HQ Located at Ankara

Fleet

HQ Located at Gölcük

Northern Sea Area

HQ Located at Istanbul

Southern Sea Area

HQ Located at Izmir

Training

HQ Located at Altinovayalova

Air Force 60,000

2 tac air forces (divided between east and west)

Flying hours   180 hrs/year

FORCES BY ROLE

Ftr   3 sqn with F-16C *Fighting Falcon*/F-16D *Fighting Falcon*; 2 sqn with F-4E *Phantom II*; 2 sqn with F-5A *Freedom Fighter*/F-5B *Freedom Fighter*

FGA   5 sqn with F-16C *Fighting Falcon*/F-16D *Fighting Falcon*; 2 sqn with F-4E *Phantom II*

Recce 2 sqn with RF-4E *Phantom II*

AEW   Sqn forming with B-737 AEW&C

SAR   sqn with 20 AS-532 *Cougar* (14 SAR/6 CSAR)

Tpt   1 (VIP) sqn with C-20 *Gulfstream*; CN-235; UC-35 *Citation*; 2 sqn with CN-235; 1 sqn with C-160 *Transall*; 1 sqn with 13 C-130B *Hercules*/C-130E *Hercules*

Tkr   sqn with 7 KC-135R *Stratotanker*

Liaison 10 base flt with CN-235 (sometimes); UH-1H *Iroquois*

OCU   1 sqn with F-4E *Phantom II*; 1 sqn with F-16C *Fighting Falcon*/F-16D *Fighting Falcon*; 1 sqn with F-5A *Freedom Fighter*/F-5B *Freedom Fighter*

Trg   1 sqn with T-37B *Tweet*/T-37C *Tweet*; T-38A *Talon*; 1 sqn with 40 SF-260D; 1 sqn with 28 T-41 *Mescalero*

SAM   4 sqn with 92 MIM-14 *Nike Hercules*; 2 sqn with 86 *Rapier*; 8 (firing) unit with MIM-23 *HAWK*

EQUIPMENT BY TYPE

AIRCRAFT 426 combat capable

FTR 87 F-5A/F-5B *Freedom Fighter*; (48 being upgraded as lead-in trainers)

FGA 339: 213 F-16C/D *Fighting Falcon* (all being upgraded to Block 50 standard (further 30 F-16 Block 52+ on order); 126 F-4E *Phantom II* (79 FGA, 47 ftr (52 upgraded to *Phantom* 2020))

RECCE 35 RF-4E *Phantom II* (recce)

AEW 1 B-737 AEW&C (first of 4)

TKR 7 KC-135R *Stratotanker*

TPT 77: 13 C-130B *Hercules*/C-130E *Hercules*; 16 *Transall* C-160D; some C-20 *Gulfstream*; 46 CN-235 (tpt/EW); 2 UC-35 *Citation* (VIP)

TRG 198: 40 SF-260D (trg); 60 T-37B *Tweet*/T-37C *Tweet*; 70 T-38A *Talon*; 28 T-41 *Mescalero*

HELICOPTERS

UTL 20 UH-1H *Iroquois* (tpt, liaison, base flt, trg schools); 20 AS-532 (14 SAR/6 CSAR)

UAV 18 *Gnat* 750; 10 *Heron*

AD

SAM 178+: 86 *Rapier*
  TOWED: MIM-23 *HAWK*
  STATIC 92 MIM-14 *Nike Hercules*

MSL

AAM AIM-120A/B AMRAAM; AIM-9S *Sidewinder*; AIM-7E *Sparrow, Shafrir* 2

ARM AGM-88A HARM

ASM AGM-65A/G *Maverick; Popeye* I

BOMBS

Conventional BLU-107; GBU-8B HOBOS (GBU-15)

Infra-Red 40 AN/AAQ 14 LANTIRN; 40 AN/AAQ 13 LANTIRN

Laser-guided *Paveway* I; *Paveway* II

Paramilitary

Gendarmerie/National Guard 100,000; 50,000 reservists (total 150,000)

Ministry of Interior; Ministry of Defence in war

FORCES BY ROLE

Army   1 (Border) div; 2 bde

Cdo   1 bde

EQUIPMENT BY TYPE

RECCE *Akrep*

APC (W) 560: 535 BTR-60/BTR-80; 25 *Condor*

AIRCRAFT

  RECCE • OBS Cessna O-1E *Bird Dog*

  TPT 2 Do-28D

HELICOPTERS

  SPT 33: 14 S-70A *Black Hawk*; 19 Mi-17 (Mi-8MT) *Hip H*

  UTL 23: 1 AB-212 (Bell 212); 8 AB-204B (Bell 204B); 6 AB-205A (Bell 205A); 8 AB-206A (Bell 206A) *JetRanger*

Coast Guard 800 (Coast Guard Regular element); 1,050 (from Navy); 1,400 conscript (total 3,250)

PATROL AND COASTAL COMBATANTS 88:

  PSO 30
  PFC 17
  PCC 8
  PBF 19
  PBI 14

AIRCRAFT

  TPT 3 CN-235 (MP)

HELICOPTERS

  UTL 8 AB-412EP (SAR)

SELECTED NON-STATE GROUPS

Partiya Karkeren Kurdistan (PKK) Reportedly active in Turkey's Southeast and from bases across the Iraqi border. Est strength 3,000. Major equipments include: mines and IEDs, mortars, SALW

DEPLOYMENT

Legal provisions for foreign deployment:

Constitution: Codified constitution (1985)

Decision on deployment of troops abroad: a) In general, by parliament (Art. 92); b) in cases of sudden aggression and if parliament is unable to convene, by president (Art. 92, 104b)

AFGHANISTAN

NATO • ISAF 720; 1 inf bn

ARABIAN GULF AND INDIAN OCEAN

Maritime Security Operations 1 FFG

NATO • *Operation Ocean Shield* 1 FFG

BOSNIA-HERZEGOVINA

EU • EUFOR • *Operation Althea* 273; **Army**: 1 inf coy

OSCE • Bosnia and Herzegovina 1

CYPRUS (NORTHERN)

Army ε36,000

1 army corps HQ; some air det; 1 armd bde; 1 indep mech inf bde; 2 inf div; 1 cdo regt; 1 arty bde; 1 avn comd; 8 M-48A2 training; 441 M-48A5T1/M-48A5T2; 361 AAPC (incl variants); 266 M-113 (incl variants); (towed arty) 102: **105mm** 72 M-101A1; **155mm** 18 M-114A2; **203mm** 12 M-115; (SP) **155mm** 90 M-44T; (MRL) **122mm** 6 T-122; (MOR) 450: **81mm** 175; **107mm** 148 M-30; **120mm** 127 HY-12; (AT MSL) 114: 66 *Milan*; 48 TOW; (RCL) **106mm** 192 M-40A1; **90mm** M-67; **RL 66mm** M-72 *LAW*; (AD towed) **20mm** Rh 202; **35mm** GDF 16 GDF-003; **40mm** 48 M-1; 3 U-17 utl ac; 1 AS-532UL *Cougar*; 3 UH-1H *Iroquois* utl hel; 1 **PCI** less than 100 tonnes

IRAQ

NATO • NTM-I 2

LEBANON

UN • UNIFIL 366; 1 engr coy; 2 PB

SERBIA

NATO • KFOR • *Joint Enterprise* 509; **Army**: 1 inf bn HQ; 2 inf coy; 1 log coy; elm 1 hel bn; elm 1 recce coy; elm 1 engr coy; elm 1 MP coy **Marines**: 1 coy **Gendarmerie**: 1 pl

OSCE • Serbia 2

OSCE • Kosovo 10

UN • UNMIK 1 obs

SUDAN

UN • UNMIS 3

UN • UNAMID 1

FOREIGN FORCES

Israel Air Force: up to 1 ftr det (occasional) located at Akinci with F-16 *Fighting Falcon* (current status uncertain)

United States US European Command: **Army** 62; **Navy** 8; **USAF** 1,514; **USMC** 16; 1 support facility located at Izmir; 1 support facility located at Ankara; 1 air base located at Incirlik • US Strategic Command: 1 Spacetrack Radar located at Incirlik

United Kingdom UK

British Pound £		2008	2009	2010
GDP	£	1.44tr	1.40tr	
	US$	2.67tr	2.26tr	
per capita	US$	43,817	37,000	
Growth	%	0.7	-4.4	
Inflation	%	3.6	1.9	
Def exp[b]	£	32.8bn		
	US$	60.7bn		
Def bdgt[a]	£	38.5bn	38.7bn	36.7bn
	US$	71.4bn	62.4bn	
US$1=£		0.54	0.62	

[a] Resource Accounting and Budgeting terms
[b] NATO definition

Population 61,113,205

Religious groups: Northern Ireland 1,685,267; Protestant and other Christian 53.1%; Roman Catholic 43.8%

Age	0–14	15–19	20–24	25–29	30–64	65 plus
Male	9%	3%	3%	3%	24%	7%
Female	9%	3%	3%	3%	23%	8%

Capabilities

ACTIVE 175,690 (Army 100,290 Navy 35,650 Air 39,750)

RESERVE 199,280 (Army 134,180 Navy 22,200 Air 42,900)
Includes both trained and those currently under training within the Regular Forces.

ORGANISATIONS BY SERVICE

Strategic Forces 1,000

Armed Forces
RADAR • STRATEGIC 1 Ballistic Missile Early Warning System *BMEWS* located at Fylingdales Moor

Royal Navy
SUBMARINES • STRATEGIC • SSBN 4:
4 *Vanguard* each with 4 533mm TT each with *Spearfish* HWT, up to 16 UGM-133A *Trident D-5* SLBM (Each boat will not deploy with more than 48 warheads, but each missile could carry up to 12 MIRV, some *Trident D-5* capable of being configured for sub-strategic role)
MSL • STRATEGIC 48 SLBM (Fewer than 160 declared operational warheads)

Army 96,790; 3,500 (Gurkhas) (total 100,290)
Regt normally bn size
FORCES BY ROLE
1 Land Comd HQ, 1 Corps HQ, 3 deployable div HQ, 8 deployable bde HQ and 1 tri-service Joint Hel Comd. The UK Field Army has a capability to form 46 battlegroups drawing on 5 armd regts, 5 armd recce regts, 6 SP arty regts, 9 armd inf bn, 3 mech inf bn and 20 lt inf bn. Within Joint Hel Comd is 16 Air Aslt Bde with 2 para bn and 2 air aslt bn. The two operational divisions have become a mix of force types having armoured as well as light infantry units in their structure. Additional spt is provided from theatre troops. For army units within 3 Cdo Bde, who now have an additional army infantry bn, see the Naval section.

Comd	1 (ARRC) Corps HQ , 1 (6th) div HQ
Armd	1 div (1st) with (2 armd bde (7th and 20th) (*each:* 1 armd regt, 2 armd inf bn, 1 lt inf bn), (1 bde (4th) (1 armd regt, 1 armd inf regt, 1 mech regt, 2 lt inf bn); (1 lt inf bde (52nd) 2 lt inf bn, 1 Gurkha bn) 3 armd recce regt; 1 cbt spt gp (3 SP arty regt; 1 AD regt; 3 cbt engr; 1 engr regt))
Mech	1 div (3rd) with (1 mech bde (1st) (1 armd regt, 1 armd inf regt, 1 mech inf regt, 1 lt inf bn); 1 mech bde (12th) (1 armd regt, 1 armd inf bn, 1 mech inf bn,); 1 mech bde (19th) (1 armd inf regt, 3 lt inf bn); 1 mech bde (11th) (3 lt inf bn); 2 recce regt; 1 cbt spt gp (2 SP arty regt; 1 arty regt; 1 AD regt; 2 cbt engr regt; 2 engr regt))
Air Aslt	1 bde (16th) (2 para bn, 2 air aslt bn, 1 arty bn, 1 engr regt)
Lt Inf	4 bn
Arty	1 bde HQ; 1 regt (trg); 1 MLRS regt, 1 STA regt, 1 UAV regt
SF	1 (SAS) regt, 1 SF spt gp, 1 recce and surveillance regt
Gurkha	1 bn (1 more in 52nd Bde above)
Engr	1 bde (2 EOD regt, 1 Air Spt)
Atk Hel	2 regt
Spt Hel	3 regt, 4 indep flt
Flying Trg	1 regt
NBC	1 (joint) regt (army/RAF)
Log	2 bde
AD	1 bde HQ; (OPCOM Air), 1 regt with *Rapier* C

Home Service Forces • Gibraltar 200 reservists; 150 active reservists (total 350)

Reserves

Territorial Army 37,260 reservists
The Territorial Army has been reorganised to enable the regular army to receive relevant manpower support from their associated territorial unit.

Armd	2 regt
Armd Recce	2 regt

Inf	13 bn
SF	2 regt (SAS)
AB	1 bn
Obs	1 regt
Arty	3 lt regt, 1 UAV regt
MLRS	1 regt
Engr	5 regt, 1 EOD regt, 1 sqn, 1 geo sqn , 1 cdo sqn
Avn	2 regt
AD	1 regt

EQUIPMENT BY TYPE

MBT 386 CR2 *Challenger 2*

RECCE 475: 137 *Sabre*; 327 *Scimitar*; 11 Tpz-1 *Fuchs*

AIFV 575 MCV-80 *Warrior*

APC 2,718

   APC (T) 1,883: 380 *Bulldog* Mk 3 (106 up-armoured for Iraq); 771 AFV 432; 597 FV 103 *Spartan*; 135 FV4333 *Stormer*

   APC (W) 835: 649 AT105 *Saxon (only Northern Ireland)*; 186 *Mastiff*

   TYPE VARIANTS 1,675 AIFV/APC

CPV 100 *Jackal*

ARTY 877

   SP 155mm 178 AS-90 *Braveheart*

   TOWED 105mm 166 L-118 Light gun/L-119

   MRL 227mm 63 MLRS; GMLRS

   MOR 470: **81mm SP** 110; **81mm** 360

AT • MSL 800+

   SP 60 *Swingfire* (FV 102 *Striker*)

   MANPATS 740 *Milan*; TOW

   RL 94mm LAW-80

AC • RECCE 3 BN-2T-4S *Defender* (4th on order); 1 Beechcraft *King Air* 350ER (3 more on order)

HELICOPTERS

   ATK 66 AH-64D *Apache*

   OBS 133 SA-341 *Gazelle*

   ASLT 99: 77 *Lynx* AH MK7*; 22 *Lynx* AH MK9

UAV • TACTICAL *Hermes* 450; *Desert Hawk*; *Buster*; *Watchkeeper* (Test)

AD • SAM 339+

   SP 135 HVM

   TOWED 57+ *Rapier* FSC

   MANPAD 147 *Starstreak* (LML)

RADAR • LAND 157: 4-7 *Cobra*; 150 MSTAR

PATROL AND COASTAL COMBATANTS • MISC BOATS/CRAFT 4 workboats

AMPHIBIOUS 4 LCVP

LOGISTICS AND SUPPORT 6 RCL

Royal Navy 34,650; incl 420 active reservists

The Royal Navy has undergone major changes to its organisational structure since 2002.

Administratively, the Fleet and Personnel/Training Headquarters are now placed within a unified structure based at Whale Island, Portsmouth. This new Fleet Headquarters has three main roles: Force Generation, Force Deployment and Resource Management.

Operationally, Full Command is held by Commander in Chief FLEET with operational command and control delegated for all Units not involved in operations to Commander Operations, a 2 star based at Northwood, London. The 2002 review created permanent Battle Staffs allowing for operations to be commanded by either one of two 2 star Commanders or two subordinate 1 star Commanders, depending on the scale of the operation. RN and RM units are also frequently assigned to UK Joint Rapid Reaction Force (JRRF), under the operational command of the Permanent Joint Headquarters (PJHQ). In addition the RN may declare units to various national, NATO, EU or UN commands and groups not listed here.

Below the Fleet HQ, RN surface and sub-surface units are structured administratively into three Flotillas based in Portsmouth, Devonport and Faslane. Aircraft are split between two Typed Air Stations at Culdrose and Yeovilton with a SAR detachment at Prestwick Airport, Scotland. Royal Marines remain under 3 Cdo Bde with a 1 star RM commander, RM Units are located at Arbroath, Plymouth, Taunton and Chivenor.

EQUIPMENT BY TYPE

SUBMARINES 12

   STRATEGIC • SSBN 4:

   4 *Vanguard*, opcon Strategic Forces, each with 4 533mm TT each with *Spearfish* HWT, up to 16 UGM-133A *Trident* D-5 SLBM (Each boat will not deploy with more than 48 warheads, but each missile could carry up to 12 MIRV, some *Trident* D-5 capable of being configured for sub strategic role)

   TACTICAL • SSN 8:

   1 *Swiftsure* each with 5 single 533mm TT each with *Spearfish* HWT/ 5 UGM–84 *Harpoon* tactical USGW

   7 *Trafalgar* each with 5 single 533mm TT each with *Spearfish* HWT/12 *Tomahawk* tactical LAM/5 UGM 84 *Harpoon* tactical USGW

   1 *Astute* each with 6 single 533mm TT with *Spearfish* HWT/UGM-84 *Harpoon* tactical USGW/*Tomahawk* tactical LAM (Total load at 38 weapons) (First of class undergoing initial sea trials.) Additional vessels in build.

PRINCIPAL SURFACE COMBATANTS 25

   AIRCRAFT CARRIERS • CV 2:

   2 *Invincible* with either 3 single MK 15 *Phalanx-1B* or *Goalkeeper* CIWS, (capacity 'tailored air group' 8–12 *Harrier* GR9A; 4 *Merlin* HM MK1 ASW hel; 4 *Sea King* ASAC MK7 AEW hel)

   DESTROYERS • DDGH 6

   2 Type-42 Batch 2 each with 1 twin (2 eff.) with 22 *Sea Dart* SAM, 2 single MK 15 *Phalanx* CIWS, 1 114mm gun, (capacity 1 *Lynx* utl hel), (1 decommissioning late '09; 2 additional units at extended readiness)

   4 Type-42 Batch 3 each with 1 twin (2 eff.) with 22 *Sea Dart* SAM, 2 single MK 15 *Phalanx-1B* CIWS, 1 114mm gun, (capacity 1 *Lynx* utl hel)

   1 *Daring* (Type-45) (capacity either 1 *Lynx* MKS ASW hel or 1 *Merlin* HM MK1 ASW hel) (First of class undergoing sea trials, ISD expected '10, additional vessels in build)

   FRIGATES • FFG 17

   4 *Cornwall* (Type-22 Batch 3) each with 2 Mk 141 *Harpoon* quad (8 eff.) each with RGM-84C *Harpoon*

tactical SSM, 2 sextuple (12 eff.) each with 1 *Sea Wolf* SAM, 1 *Goalkeeper* CIWS, 1 114mm gun, (capacity 2 *Lynx* utl hel)

13 *Norfolk* (Type-23) each with 2 twin 324mm ASTT (4 eff.) each with *Sting Ray* LWT, 2 Mk 141 *Harpoon* quad (8 eff.) each with 1 RGM-84C *Harpoon* tactical SSM, 1 32 canister *Sea Wolf* VLS with *Sea Wolf* SAM, 1 114mm gun, (capacity either 2 *Lynx* utl hel or 1 *Merlin* HM MK1 ASW hel)

PATROL AND COASTAL COMBATANTS 23
  PSOH 1 *River* (mod)
  PSO 3 *River*
  PCI 16 *Archer* (trg)
  PBF 2 *Scimitar*
  ICE PATROL 1 *Endurance*
MINE WARFARE • MINE COUNTERMEASURES 16
  MCC 8 *Hunt* (incl 4 mod *Hunt*)
  MHO 8 *Sandown*
AMPHIBIOUS
  PRINCIPAL AMPHIBIOUS SHIPS 7
  LPD 2 *Albion* (capacity 2 med hel; 4 LCVP; 6 MBT; 300 troops)
  LPH 1 *Ocean* (capacity 18 hel; 4 LCU or 2 LCAC; 4 LCVP; 800 troops)
  LSD 4 *Bay* (capacity 4 LCU; 2 LCVP; 1 LCU; 24 CR2 *Challenger* 2 MBT; 350 troops) (RFA manned)
  CRAFT 47: 13 **LCU**; 34 **LCVP**
LOGISTICS AND SUPPORT 5
  AGHS 3: 1 *Scott*; 2 *Echo*
  AGS 2: 1 *Roebuck*; 1 *Gleaner* (inshore/coastal)

FORCES BY ROLE

Navy/Marine 1 party located at Diego Garcia, BIOT

FACILITIES

Bases	Located at Portsmouth (Fleet HQ), Faslane, Devonport, Gibraltar
Naval airbases	Located at Prestwick, Culdrose, Yeovilton

Royal Fleet Auxiliary

Support and Miscellaneous vessels are mostly manned and maintained by the Royal Fleet Auxiliary (RFA), a civilian fleet owned by the UK MoD, which has approximately 2,500 personnel with type comd under CINCFLEET.

LOGISTICS AND SUPPORT 12
  AORH 4: 2 *Wave Knight*; 2 *Fort Victoria*
  AOR 2 *Leaf*
  AORLH 2 *Rover*
  AFH 2 Fort *Grange*
  AR 1 *Diligence*
  AG 1 *Argus* (Aviation trg ship with secondary role as Primarily Casualty Receiving Ship)
  RoRo 6 (Not RFA manned)

Naval Aviation (Fleet Air Arm) 5,520

FORCES BY ROLE

FGA	1 sqn (Joint Force Harrier) with 13 *Harrier* GR9A; 1 T10 *Harrier*

ASW/ASUW	4 sqn with *Merlin* HM MK1
ASW/Atk hel	1 sqn with *Lynx* MK3 / *Lynx* MK8; *Lynx* MK3 (in indep flt)
AEW	3 sqn with *Sea King* AEW MK7
SAR	1 sqn and detached flt with *Sea King* HAS MK5 utl
Spt	3 sqn with *Sea King* HC MK4; some (Fleet) sqn with Beech 55 *Baron* (civil registration); Cessna 441 *Conquest* (civil registration); *Falcon* 20 (civil registration); *Grob* 115 (op under contract); 1 sqn with *Lynx* AH MK7 (incl in Royal Marines entry)
Trg	1 (operational evaluation) sqn with *Merlin* HM MK1*; *Sea King* HC MK4; 1 sqn with *Jetstream* T MK2/TMK3; 1 sqn with *Lynx* MK3

EQUIPMENT BY TYPE
AIRCRAFT 13 combat capable
  FGA 13 *Harrier* GR8/9A
  TPT 21: 1 Beech 55 *Baron* (civil registration); 1 Cessna 441 *Conquest* (civil registration); 19 *Falcon* 20 (civil registration)
  TRG 29: 5 Grob 115 (op under contract); 2 *Harrier* T10; 12 *Hawk* T MK1 (spt); 10 *Jetstream* T MK2/T MK3
HELICOPTERS 119 atk hel
  ATK 6 *Lynx* AH MK7 (incl in Royal Marines entry)
  ASW/ASuW 113: 71 *Lynx* MK3/*Lynx* MK8; 42 *Merlin* HM MK1
  UTL/SAR 15 *Sea King* HAS MK5 Utility
  AEW 13 *Sea King* AEW MK7
  SPT 37 *Sea King* HC MK4 (for RM)
MSL
  ASM *Sea Skua*
  AAM AIM-9 *Sidewinder*, AIM-120C *AMRAAM*

Royal Marines Command 6,840 (excl Army elements)

FORCES BY ROLE

LCA	3 sqn opcon Royal Navy; 1 sqn (539 Aslt Sqn RM)
Sy	1 Fleet Protection Group, opcon Royal Navy
Navy	Naval Parties. Various Royal Marines det opcon to RN
SF	4 sqn
Cdo	1 (declared to NATO) bde (3 cdo regt, 1 lt inf bn (army) 1 cdo arty regt (army))
Cdo AD arty	1 bty (army)
Cdo engr	2 sqn (1 army, 1 TA)
Logistic	1 bn
Cdo lt hel	2 sqn opcon Royal Navy

EQUIPMENT BY TYPE
APC (T) 150 BvS-10 *Viking*
MOR 81mm
AMPHIBIOUS 28
  ACV 4 *Griffon* 2000 TDX (M)

LC 24 RRC
HELICOPTERS
ATK/SPT 43: 6 *Lynx* AH MK7; 37 *Sea King* HC MK4
AD • SAM • SP HVM
RADAR • LAND 4 MAMBA (*Arthur*)

Air Force 39,750; 140 active reservists (total 39, 890)

Air Command operates from a fully integrated HQ at High Wycombe. Its role is to provide a fully operational and flexible combat air force, comprising more than 500 aircraft and 42 stations or units, and it supports operations in the Gulf region and Afghanistan as well as maintaining an RAF presence in Cyprus, Gibraltar, Ascension Island and the Falkland Islands.

Air Comd operations are delegated to two operational groups. No 1 Group, the Air Combat Group, controls the combat fast jet aircraft (*Typhoon*, *Tornado* and *Harrier*), and has eight airfields in the UK plus RAF Unit Goose Bay in Canada. No 2 Group, the Combat Support Group, controls Air Transport and Air-to-Air Refuelling (AT/AAR); ISTAR and Force Protection assets. No 22 (Training) Gp recruits RAF personnel and provides trained specialist personnel to the RAF and other two Services.

RAF Expeditionary Air Wings, designed to generate a structure better able to deploy units of agile, scaleable, interoperable and capable air power, operate from RAF Main Operating Bases as follows:

RAF Waddington – No 34 EAW (ISTAR); RAF Lyneham – No 38 EAW (Air Transport); RAF Coningsby – No 121 EAW (Multi Role); RAF Cottesmore – No 122 EAW (Fighter /Ground Attack); RAF Leuchars – No 125 EAW (Fighter); RAF Leeming – No 135 EAW (Fighter); RAF Marham – No 138 EAW (Fighter/Ground Attack); RAF Lossiemouth – No 140 EAW (Fighter/Ground Attack); RAF Kinloss – No 325 EAW (Maritime Patrol & Surveillance). The deployable elements of each station form the core of each EAW, reinforced by assigned Capability-based Module Readiness System (CMRS) personnel and elements of the Air Combat Support Units (ACSUs). EAWs enable the RAF to train as cohesive air power units capable of transitioning quickly from peacetime postures and deploying swiftly on operations.

Flying hours   210/yr on fast jets; 290 on tpt ac; 240 on support hels; 90 on *Sea King*

FORCES BY ROLE

Ftr	1 sqn with *Tornado* F-3
FGA	5 sqn with *Tornado* GR4; 2 sqn with *Tornado* GR4A
Multirole	4 sqn (incl 1 Op Eval Unit) with *Typhoon*
Off support	2 sqn with *Harrier* GR7/ GR7A/GR9/ T10/T12;
ELINT	1 sqn with *Nimrod* R1
MR	2 sqn with *Nimrod* MR2*
ISTAR	2 sqn with E-3D *Sentry*; 1 sqn with *Sentinel* RMK1/ 4 Beechcraft *King Air* 350 *Shadow* R1; 1 sqn with *Predator* A/B UAV
SAR	2 sqn with *Sea King* HAR-3A/*Sea King* HAR-3
Tkr/tpt	1 sqn with *Tristar* C2; *Tristar* K1; *Tristar* KC1; 1 sqn with VC-10C1K; VC-10K3/VC-10K4
Tpt	4 sqn with C-130K/C-130J *Hercules*; 1 (comms) sqn with BAe-125; BAe-146; AS-355 *Squirrel*; 2 BN-2A *Islander* CC2; 3; 1 sqn with 4 C-17 *Globemaster*
OCU	5 sqn with *Typhoon*, *Tornado* F-3; *Tornado* GR4; *Harrier* GR7/T10; *Nimrod* MR2
CAL	1 sqn with *Hawk* T MK1A/*Hawk* T MK1W/ *Hawk* T MK1
Trg	Units (including postgraduate training on 203(R) sqn) with *Sea King* HAR-3; Beech 200 *Super King Air*; *Dominie* T1; Grob 115E *Tutor*; *Hawk* T MK1A/*Hawk* T MK1W/*Hawk* T MK1; *Tucano* T MK1 (Shorts 312); T67M/M260 *Firefly*; *Sea King* HAR-3A
Hel	3 sqn with CH-47 *Chinook*; 2 sqn with *Merlin* HC MK3; 2 sqn with SA-330 *Puma*; 1 sqn *Griffin*; 3 sqn with *Sea King* HAR-3

EQUIPMENT BY TYPE
AIRCRAFT 287 combat capable
  FTR 40: 28 *Typhoon* (13 F2, 15 T1/1A); 12 *Tornado* F-3
  MULTI-ROLE 30 *Typhoon* (28 FGR4, 2 T3)
  STRIKE/FGA 168: 113 *Tornado* GR4; 55 *Harrier* GR7/ GR7A/GR9/GR9A
  RECCE 29: 24 *Tornado* GR4A*
  ISTAR 9: 5 *Sentinel* RMK1; 4 Beechcraft *King Air* 350 *Shadow* R1
  MP 11 *Nimrod* MR2*
  ELINT 3 *Nimrod* R1
  AEW 7 E-3D *Sentry*
  TPT 66: 6 C-17A *Globemaster*; 19 C1/C3 (3 C-130K; 16 C-130K-30 *Hercules*); 24 C4/C5 (14 C-130J-30; 10 C-130J *Hercules*); 6 BAe-125 CC-3 5; 2 BAe-146 MKII; 7 Beech 200 *Super King Air* on lease; 2 BN-2A *Islander* CC2/3
  TPT/TKR 25: 3 *Tristar* C2 (pax); 2 *Tristar* K1 (tkr/pax); 4 *Tristar* KC1 (tkr/pax/cgo); 10 VC-10C1K (tkr/cgo); 4 VC-10K3; 2 VC-10K4
  TRG 375: 38 *Firefly* M260 T67M; 9 *Dominie* T1; 101 Grob 115E *Tutor*; 117 *Hawk* T MK1/1A/1W; 6 *Hawk* 128 (28 on order); 95 *Tucano* T1; 9 *Harrier* T10/T12*
HELICOPTERS
  SPT 131: 40 CH-47 HC2/2A *Chinook*; 1 CH-47 HC3 *Chinook* in test; 28 HC MK3 *Merlin*; 34 SA-330 *Puma* HC1; 25 *Sea King* HAR-3A; 4 Bell 412EP *Griffin* HAR-2
  TRG 43: 31 AS-355 *Squirrel*; 12 Bell 412EP *Griffin* HT1
UAV • RECCE/ATK 3 MQ-9 *Predator* B
MSL
  AAM AIM-120B/AIM-120 C5 AMRAAM; AIM-132 ASRAAM; *Skyflash*; AIM-9L / AIM-9L/I *Sidewinder*
  ARM ALARM
  ASM *Brimstone*; *Storm Shadow*; AGM-65G2 *Maverick*
  ASSM AGM-84D *Harpoon*; *Stingray*
BOMBS
  Conventional Mk 82; CRV-7; BL/IBL/RBL755 (to be withdrawn from service by end- 2009);
  Laser-Guided/GPS: *Paveway* II; GBU-10 *Paveway* III; Enhanced *Paveway* II/III; GBU-24 *Paveway* IV

Royal Air Force Regiment

FORCES BY ROLE

Air   3 (tactical Survival To Operate (STO)) sqn + HQ; 7 (fd) sqn

Trg   1 (joint) unit (with army) with *Rapier* C

Tri-Service Defence Hel School

HELICOPTERS : 28 AS-350 *Ecureuil*; 7 *Griffin* HT1

Volunteer Reserve Air Forces

(Royal Auxiliary Air Force/RAF Reserve)

Air   1 (air movements) sqn; 2 (intelligence) sqn; 5 (field) sqn; 1 (HQ augmentation) sqn; 1 (C-130 Reserve Aircrew) flt

Medical   1 sqn

DEPLOYMENT

Legal provisions for foreign deployment:
Constitution: Uncodified constitution which includes constitutional statutes, case law, international treaties and unwritten conventions
Decision on deployment of troops abroad: By the government

AFGHANISTAN

NATO • ISAF 9,000 (UK forms 5 BG covering Helmand Province. Ground forces are supported by an air gp of fixed and rotary wing ac.)
Army: 1 div HQ (6th); 1 lt inf bde HQ (11th) with (5 lt inf bn; 1 armd recce regt; 1 fd arty regt; 1 engr regt); 1 GMLRS tp; 1 UAV bty; 1 EOD tp; 1 spt bn; 1 theatre log spt gp; 1 medical bn; 29 *Warrior*; 130 *Mastiff*; 12 L-118; 4 GMLRS; 8 AH-64D *Apache*; 5 *Lynx*; some *Hermes 450*; some *Predator* B; some *Desert Hawk*
Royal Navy: 55 *Viking*; 6 *Sea King* HC Mk4
Air Force: 8 *Tornado* GR4; 4 C-130 *Hercules*; 8 CH-47 *Chinook*; 6 HC Mk3 *Merlin*; 4 Beechcraft *King Air* 350 *Shadow* R1
UN • UNAMA 1 obs

ARMENIA/AZERBAIJAN

OSCE • Minsk Conference 1

ASCENSION ISLAND

Air Force 23

ATLANTIC (NORTH)

Atlantic Patrol Task (N) Maritime force 1 DD / FF; 1 AO

ATLANTIC (SOUTH)

Atlantic Patrol Task (S) Maritime force 1 DD / FF; 1 OPV (Falkland Islands Patrol Ship, Ice Patrol (rotational six months)); 1 AO

ARABIAN GULF AND INDIAN OCEAN

Maritime Security Operations 4 FFG; 1 MCC; 4 MHO; 2 LSD; 1 AORH
NATO • *Operation Ocean Shield* 1 FFG

BAHRAIN

Air Force 1 BAe-125, 1 BAe-146

BELIZE

Army 30

BOSNIA-HERZEGOVINA

EU • EUFOR • *Operation Althea* 9
OSCE • Bosnia and Herzegovina 1

BRITISH INDIAN OCEAN TERRITORY

Royal Navy 40
1 Navy/Marine party located at Diego Garcia

BRUNEI

Army 550; 1 Gurkha bn; 1 jungle trg centre; 1 hel flt with 3 hel

CANADA

Army 500; 2 trg units
Air Force 57

CYPRUS

Army 1,678; 2 inf bn; 1 hel flt
Navy 42
Air Force 1,071; 1 SAR sqn with 4 Bell 412 *Twin Huey*; 1 radar (on det)
UN • UNFICYP 257; 1 inf coy

DEMOCRATIC REPUBLIC OF CONGO

UN • MONUC 6 obs

FALKLAND ISLANDS

Army 420; 1 AD det with *Rapier* FSC
Navy 420
Air Force 680; 1 ftr flt with 4 E-F *Typhoon* FGR.4; 1 SAR sqn with *Sea King* HAR-3A/*Sea King* HAR-3; 1 tkr/tpt flt with C-130 *Hercules*; VC-10 K3/4

GERMANY

Army 22,000; 1 army corps HQ, 1 armd div
Navy 30
Air Force 320

GIBRALTAR

Army 270 (incl 175 pers of Gibraltar regt)
Air Force 70 some (periodic) AEW det

IRAQ

Royal Navy: 75; 1 Navy Transition Team Navy / Cdo team (training the Iraqi Riverine Patrol Service .
Air Force: *Puma*
NATO • NTM-I 15
UN • UNAMI 1 obs

KENYA

Army trg team 52

KUWAIT

Army 35
Air Force 6 EH101 *Merlin*

MOLDOVA

OSCE • Moldova 1

NATO MARITIME AOR

NATO • SNMCMG-1 • 1 MCM /MCMV

NEPAL
Army 280 (Gurkha trg org)

NETHERLANDS
Air Force 120

OMAN
Army 40
Navy 20
Air Force 20: 1 *Sentinel*; *Nimrod* MR2; 1 *Tristar* tkr

QATAR
Air Force 4 C-130J

SERBIA
NATO • KFOR • *Joint Enterprise* 8
OSCE • Serbia 3
OSCE • Kosovo 4

SIERRA LEONE
IMATT 63 (incl trg team, tri-service HQ and spt)

SUDAN
UN • UNAMID 1
UN • UNMIS 2

UNITED STATES
Army/Navy/Air Force ε700

FOREIGN FORCES

United States US European Command: **Army** 345; **Navy** 333; **USAF** 8,596; 1 ftr wg located at RAF Lakenheath with (1 Ftr sqn with 24 F-15C *Eagle*/F-15D *Eagle*, 2 Ftr sqn with 24 F-15E *Strike Eagle*); 1 tkr wg located at RAF Mildenhall with 15 KC-135 *Stratotanker*; 1 Special Ops gp located at Mildenhall with 5 MC-130H *Combat Talon II*; 5 MC-130P *Combat Shadow*; 1 C-130E *Hercules*; **USMC** 93 • US Strategic Command: 1 Ballistic Missile Early Warning System (*BMEWS*) located at Fylingdales Moor; 1 Spacetrack radar located at Fylingdales Moor;

Europe (NATO)

Armenia ARM

Armenian Dram d		2008	2009	2010
GDP	d	3.64tr		
	US$	11.9bn		
per capita	US$	4,014		
Growth	%	6.8	-15.6	
Inflation	%	9.0	3.0	
Def bdgt	d	121bn	144bn	163bn
	US$	395m	376m	
FMA (US)	US$	3.0m	3.0m	3.0m
US$1=d		306	385	

Population   2,967,000

Age	0 – 14	15 – 19	20 – 24	25 – 29	30 – 64	65 plus
Male	12%	5%	5%	4%	17%	4%
Female	11%	5%	5%	4%	22%	6%

Capabilities

ACTIVE 46,684 (Army 43,772, Air/AD Aviation Forces (Joint) 1,044, other Air Defence Forces 1,868) **Paramilitary 4,748**

Terms of service conscription 24 months. Reserves some mob reported, possibly 210,000 with military service within 15 years.

ORGANISATIONS BY SERVICE

Army 16,803; 26,969 conscripts (total 43,772)

5 Army Corps HQ

FORCES BY ROLE

Army	1 (1st) corps HQ (1 indep tk bn, 1 maint bn, 1 indep recce bn, 2 indep MR regt); 1 (2nd) corps HQ (1 indep arty bn, 1 indep tk bn, 1 indep recce bn, 1 indep rifle regt, 2 indep MR regt); 1 (3rd) corps HQ (1 indep sigs bn, 1 indep rifle regt, 1 indep arty bn, 1 indep tk bn, 1 indep recce bn, 1 indep rocket bn, 1 maint bn, 4 indep MR regt); 1 (4th) corps HQ (1 indep sigs bn, 1 indep SP arty bn, 4 indep MR regt); 1(5th) corps HQ (with 2 fortified areas) (1 indep MR regt, 1 indep rifle regt);
MR	1 bde (trg)
SF	1 regt
Arty	1 bde; 1 SP regt
AT	1 regt
Engr	1 regt with Demining centre
AD	1 SAM bde;(2 regt; 1 (Radiotech) regt)

EQUIPMENT BY TYPE
MBT 110: 102 T-72; 8 T-54
AIFV 104: 80 BMP-1; 7 BMP-1K; 5 BMP-2; 12 BRM-1K
APC (W) 136: 11 BTR-60; 100 look-a-like; 21 BTR-70; 4 BTR-80

ARTY 239
SP 38: **122mm** 10 2S1 *Carnation*; **152mm** 28 2S3
TOWED 131: **122mm** 69 D-30; **152mm** 62: 26 2A36; 2 D-1; 34 D-20
MRL 51: **122mm** 47 BM-21; **273mm** 4 WM-80
MOR **120mm** 19 M-120
AT • **MSL** 22
SP 13 9P149 MT-LB *Spiral*
MANPATS 9 AT-5 9K113 *Spandrel*
AD • **SAM**
SP SA-4; SA-6
TOWED SA-2; SA-3

Air and Air Defence Aviation Forces 1,044

AD/Air   1 (Joint) comd; 2 air bases, 1 avn sqn

EQUIPMENT BY TYPE
AIRCRAFT 16 combat capable
FTR 1 MiG-25 *Foxbat*
FGA 15 Su-25 *Frogfoot*
TPT 2 Il-76 *Candid*
TRG 4 L-39 *Albatros*
HELICOPTERS
ATK 8 Mi-24P *Hind**
RECCE 2 Mi-24K
CBT SPT 14: 2 Mi-24R; 10 Mi-8MT; 2 Mi-9
TPT 9 PZL MI-2
GUNS
SP ZSU-23-4
TOWED **23mm** ZU-23-2
RADAR • **LAND** 6 SNAR-10

Paramilitary 4,748

Ministry of Internal Affairs

FORCES BY ROLE
Paramilitary   4 bn

EQUIPMENT BY TYPE
AIFV 55: 5 BMD-1; 44 BMP-1; 1 BMP-1K; 5 BRM-1K
APC (W) 24 BTR-152/BTR-60/BTR-70

Border Troops
Ministry of National Security
AIFV 43: 5 BMD-1; 35 BMP-1; 3 BRM-1K
APC (W) 23: 5 BTR-60; 18 BTR-70

DEPLOYMENT

Legal provisions for foreign deployment:
Constitution: Codified constitution (1995, amended 2005)
Specific legislation: 'Law on Defence of the Republic of Armenia'
Decision on deployment of troops abroad: by the president, in accordance with 'Law on Defence of the Republic of Armenia' (Article 5 (2) (1). Also, under Art.55 (13) of constitution, president can call for use of armed forces (and National Assembly shall be convened). (Also Art.81 (3) of constitution.)

SERBIA
NATO • KFOR • *Joint Enterprise* 70

OSCE • Kosovo 1

FOREIGN FORCES

Deployment in Armenia and Azerbaijan unless stated
Bulgaria OSCE 1
Czech Republic OSCE 1
Hungary OSCE 1
Kazakhstan OSCE 1
Poland OSCE 1
United Kingdom OSCE 1
Russia 3,214 (Gyumri, Armenia): 1 MR bde; 74 MBT; 201 ACV; 84 arty; (8 mor; 8 MRL 68 SP/towed)
Military Air Forces (Yerevan, Armenia): 1 ftr sqn with 18 MiG-29 *Fulcrum*; 2 SAM bty with S-300V; 1 SAM bty with SA-6

Austria AUT

Euro €		2008	2009	2010
GDP	€	282bn	281bn	
	US$	415bn	419bn	
per capita	US$	50,450	51,083	
Growth	%	2.0	-3.8	
Inflation	%	3.1	0.5	
Def exp	€	2.17bn		
	US$	3.19bn		
Def budget	€	2.03bn	2.11bn	2.12bn
	US$	2.99bn	3.14bn	
US$1=€		0.68	0.67	

Population   8,210,281

Age	0 – 14	15 – 19	20 – 24	25 – 29	30 – 64	65 plus
Male	8%	3%	3%	3%	25%	6%
Female	8%	3%	3%	3%	25%	10%

Capabilities

ACTIVE 27,300 (Army 13,600; Air 2,300; Spt 11,400)

CIVILIAN 9,400 (Joint 9,400)

RESERVE 195,000 (Joint structured 35,000, 160,000 Joint unstructured)
Air Service forms part of the army. Some 66,000 reservists a year undergo refresher trg in tranches.
Terms of service 6 months recruit trg, 30 days reservist refresher trg for volunteers; 90–120 days additional for officers, NCOs and specialists.

ORGANISATIONS BY SERVICE

Joint Command – Land Forces 6,700; 6,900 conscript (total 13,600)

Joint Forces Command is located in Graz and Salzburg. Special Forces Task Groups are a separate command directly under the control of the Chief of Defence staff.

FORCES BY ROLE
Mech Inf   2 bde (3rd and 4th) (1 tk bn, 1 mech inf bn, 1 inf bn, 1 SP arty, 1recce bn, 1 engr bn, 1 spt bn)
Inf   1 bde (6th) (3 inf bn, 1 engr bn); 1 bde (7th) (3 inf,1 Arty, 1 recce , 1 engr bn)

EQUIPMENT BY TYPE
MBT 114 *Leopard* 2 A4
LT TK 119: 48 SK-105 *Kuerassier*; 71 in store
AIFV 112 *Ulan*
APC 458
　APC (T) 367: 261 4K4E *Saurer*/4K4F *Saurer* (incl look-a-likes); 106 in store
　APC (W) 91: 71 *Pandur*; 20 APCV-2 *Dingo II*
ARTY 684
　SP 155mm 189 M-109A2/M-109A3/M-109A5ÖE
　TOWED 105: **105mm** 85 IFH (deactivated); **155mm** 20 M-1A2 (deactivated)
　MRL 128mm 16 M-51 (deactivated)
　MOR 374: **107mm** 133; **120mm** 241: 158 M-43; 83 in store
AT • MSL 461
　SP 89 RJPz-(HOT) *Jaguar 1* in store
　MANPATS 372: 307 RB-56 *Bill*; 65 in store
　RCL 1,420: **106mm** 374 M-40A1 in store; **84mm** 1,046 *Carl Gustav*
AD • GUNS 469: **20mm** 56; 413 in store

Joint Command - Air Force 2,300 (1,400 regulars, 900 conscripts)
The Air Force is part of Joint Forces Cmd and consists of 2 bde; Air Support Cmd and Airspace Surveillance Cmd
Flying hours 120 hrs/year on hel/tpt ac; 110 hrs/year on FGA/ftr

FORCES BY ROLE
Ftr   1 wg (2 ftr sqn with EF-2000A *Typhoon* 1 trg sqn with Saab 105Öe*)
Tpt   1 sqn with C-130K *Hercules*
Hel   1 wg with (2 sqn with SA-319 *Alouette* III); 2 sqn with AB-212 (Bell 212)
Spt   1 wg with (1 recce sqn PC-6B *Turbo Porter*; 1 hel sqn with OH-58B *Kiowa*; 1 hel sqn with S-70A *Black Hawk*)
Trg   Trg units with PC-7 *Turbo Trainer*
AD   2 bn
Air surv   1 radar bn, some local radar stns

EQUIPMENT BY TYPE
AIRCRAFT 37 combat capable
　FTR 15 EF-2000A *Typhoon* (Tranche 1, Block 5)
　TPT 11: 3 C-130K *Hercules*; 8 PC-6B *Turbo Porter*
　TRG 34: 12 PC-7 *Turbo Trainer*; 22 Saab 105Öe*
HELICOPTERS
　OBS 11 OH-58B *Kiowa*
　SPT 9 S-70A *Black Hawk*
　UTL 47: 23 AB-212 (Bell 212); 24 SA-319 *Alouette III*
AD
　SAM 36 *Mistral*
　GUNS: 53 x **35mm** Z-FIAK system
MSL • AAM AIM-9P3 *Sidewinder* and IRIS-T

Support (11,400)

Spt forces are formed into three Commands - Joint Services Support Command (repair, supply Military Police and units), C3I Command and The Agencies and Academies Command. The Agencies include Intelligence, Security, Defence Technology, Medical and Personnel whilst the Academies comprise training elements and schools including The National Defence and NCO Academies.

DEPLOYMENT

Legal provisions for foreign deployment:
Constitution: Includes 'Federal Constitutional Law' (1/1930)
Specific legislation: 'Bundesverfassungsgesetz über Kooperation und Solidarität bei der Entsendung von Einheiten und Einzelpersonen in das Ausland' (KSE-BVG, 1997)
Decision on deployment of troops abroad: By government on authorisation of the National Council's Main Committee; simplified procedure for humanitarian and rescue tasks (Art. 23f IV of the 'Federal Constitutional Law'; § 2 of the KSE-BVG)

AFGHANISTAN
NATO • ISAF 4

BOSNIA-HERZEGOVINA
EU • EUFOR • *Operation Althea* 96
OSCE • Bosnia and Herzegovina 3

CENTRAL AFRICAN REPUBLIC/CHAD
UN • MINURCAT 131; elm 1 tpt coy

CYPRUS
UN • UNFICYP 4 obs

DEMOCRATIC REPUBLIC OF CONGO
EU • EU SEC RD Congo 1

MIDDLE EAST
UN • UNTSO 7 obs

NEPAL
UN • UNMIN 2 obs

SERBIA
NATO • KFOR • *Joint Enterprise* 447; 1 inf bn HQ, 2 inf coy, elm 1 hel bn, elm 1 recce coy, elm 1 engr coy, elm 1 MP coy, elm 1 log unit
OSCE • Kosovo 15

SYRIA/ISRAEL
UN • UNDOF 378; 1 inf bn

WESTERN SAHARA
UN • MINURSO 2 obs

Azerbaijan AZE

Azerbaijani Manat m		2008	2009	2010
GDP	m	40bn	41bn	
	US$	49bn	51bn	
per capita	US$	5,995	6,190	
Growth	%	11.6	7.5	
Inflation	%	20.8	2.2	
Def bdgt	m	1.30bn	1.20bn	
	US$	1.58bn	1.50bn	
FMA (US)	US$	2.9m	3.0m	4.0m
US$1=m		0.81	0.80	

Population   8,238,672

Age	0 – 14	15 – 19	20 – 24	25 – 29	30 – 64	65 plus
Male	14%	5%	5%	4%	18%	3%
Female	13%	5%	4%	4%	20%	5%

Capabilities

ACTIVE 66,940 (Army 56,840 Navy 2,200 Air 7,900)
Paramilitary 15,000
Terms of service 17 months, but can be extended for ground forces.

RESERVE 300,000
Reserves some mobilisation reported, 300,000 with military service within 15 years

ORGANISATIONS BY SERVICE

Army 56,840
5 Army Corps HQ
FORCES BY ROLE
MR   23 bde
Arty 1 bde
MRL   1 bde
AT   1 regt
EQUIPMENT BY TYPE
MBT 320: 220 T-72; 100 T-55
AIFV 127: 20 BMD-1; 44 BMP-1; 41 BMP-2; 1 BMP-3; 21 BRM-1
APC 469
  APC (T) 404: 11 BTR-D; 393 MT-LB
  APC (W) 65: 25 BTR-60; 28 BTR-70; 12 BTR-80A
ARTY 282
  SP 122mm 12 2S1 *Carnation*
  TOWED 132: **203mm** 3 2S7; **152mm** 3-6 2S3 **122mm** 80 D-30; **152mm** 52: 22 2A36; 30 D-20
  GUN/MOR 120mm 26 2S9 *NONA*
  MRL 65: **300mm** 12 9A52 *Smerch*; **122mm** 53 BM-21
  MOR 120mm 47 PM-38
AT • MSL • MANPATS ε250 AT-3 9K11 *Sagger*/AT-4 9K111 *Spigot*/AT-5 9K113 *Spandrel*/AT-7 9K115 *Saxhorn*
AD • SAM • SP ε40 SA-13 *Gopher*/SA-4 *Ganef*/SA-8 *Gecko* (80–240 eff.)

MSL • SSM ε4 SS-21 *Scarab (Tochka)*
RADAR • LAND SNAR-1 *Long Trough*/SNAR-2/-6 *Pork Trough* (arty); *Small Fred/Small Yawn*/SNAR-10 *Big Fred* (veh, arty); GS-13 *Long Eye* (veh)
UAV 6: 3 *Orbiter*; 3 *Aerostar*

Navy 2,200

EQUIPMENT BY TYPE
PRINCIPAL SURFACE COMBATANTS
FS 1 Petya *II* with 2 RBU 6000 *Smerch 2* (24 eff.), 4 76mm gun
PATROL AND COASTAL COMBATANTS 5
PSO 1 *Luga* (*Woodnik 2* Class) (additional trg role)
PCO 2 *Petrushka*
PCC 1 *Turk*; 1 *Point*
PCI 1 *Zhuk*
MINE WARFARE • MINE COUNTERMEASURES 2
MSI 2 *Yevgenya*
AMPHIBIOUS 4
LSM 3: 2 *Polnochny A* (capacity 6 MBT; 180 troops); 1 *Polynochny B* (capacity 6 MBT; 180 troops)
LCU 1 *Vydra†* (capacity either 3 AMX-30 MBT or 200 troops)
LOGISTICS AND SUPPORT • ARS 1
FACILITIES
Base Located at Baku

Air Force and Air Defence 7,900

FORCES BY ROLE
Ftr 1 sqn with MiG-25 PD *Foxbat*; MiG-25PU *Foxbat*
FGA 1 regt with MiG-21 *Fishbed*; Su-25 *Frogfoot*; Su-24 *Fencer*; Su-17 *Fitter*; Su-25UB *Frogfoot B*
Tpt 1 sqn with An-12 *Cub*; Yak-40 *Codling*
Trg L-29 *Delfin*; L-39 *Albatros*; Su-17U *Fitter*
Hel 1 regt with Mi-24 *Hind**; Mi-8 *Hip*; PZL Mi-2 *Hoplite*

EQUIPMENT BY TYPE
AIRCRAFT 57 combat capable
FTR 37: 23 MiG-25PD *Foxbat* (+9 in store); 4 MiG-21 *Fishbed* (+1 in store)
FGA 15: 6 Su-25 *Frogfoot*; 5 Su-24 *Fencer*; 4 Su-17 *Fitter*
TPT 4: 1 An-12 *Cub*; 3 Yak-40 *Codling*
TRG 46: 28 L-29 *Delfin*; 12 L-39 *Albatros*; 3 MiG-25PU *Foxbat**; 1 Su-17U *Fitter*; 2 Su-25UB *Frogfoot B**
HELICOPTERS
ATK 15 Mi-24 *Hind**
SPT 20: 13 Mi-8 *Hip*; 7 PZL Mi-2 *Hoplite*
UAV 4 *Aerostar*
AD • SAM 100 SA-2 *Guideline* towed/S-125 *Neva* (SA-3 *Goa*)/S-200 *Vega* (SA-5 *Gammon)* static

Paramilitary ε15,000

Border Guard ε5,000
Ministry of Internal Affairs
AIFV 168 BMP-1/BMP-2
APC (W) 19 BTR-60/BTR-70/BTR-80
PATROL AND COASTAL COMBATANTS 4

PFI 2 *Stenka*
PCI 2 (ex-US)

Militia 10,000+
Ministry of Internal Affairs
APC (W) 7 BTR-60/BTR-70/BTR-80

DEPLOYMENT

Legal provisions for foreign deployment:
Constitution: Codified constitution (1995)
Decision on deployment of troops abroad: By parliament upon proposal by president (Art. 109, No. 28)

AFGHANISTAN
NATO • ISAF 90

SERBIA
OSCE • Kosovo 3

FOREIGN FORCES

OSCE numbers represents total deployment in Armenia and Azerbaijan unless stated
Bulgaria OSCE 1
Czech Republic OSCE 1
Hungary OSCE 1
Kazakhstan OSCE 1
Poland OSCE 1
United Kingdom OSCE 1

Belarus BLR

Belarusian Ruble r		2008	2009	2010
GDP	r	128tr		
	US$	60bn		
per capita	US$	6,227		
Growth	%	10.0	-1.2	
Inflation	%	14.8	13.0	
Def bdgt	r	1.44tr	1.67tr	
	US$	674m	611m	
US$1=r		2,136	2,743	

Population 9,648,533

Age	0 – 14	15 – 19	20 – 24	25 – 29	30 – 64	65 plus
Male	8%	4%	4%	4%	22%	5%
Female	8%	4%	4%	4%	24%	10%

Capabilities

ACTIVE 72,940 (Army 29,600 Air 18,170 Joint 25,170) **Paramilitary 110,000**
Terms of service 9–12 months

RESERVE 289,500 (Joint 289,500 with mil service within last 5 years)

ORGANISATIONS BY SERVICE

Joint 25,170 (Centrally controlled units and MoD staff)

Army 29,600

FORCES BY ROLE

MoD Comd Tps

SF	1 bde
SSM	2 bde
Sigs	2 bde

Ground Forces

Arty	1 gp (5 bde)
Cbt Engr	1 bde
Engr Bridging	1 bde
NBC	1 regt
Mob	1 bde

North Western Op Comd

Mech	1 indep bde
Mob	2 bde
Arty	2 regt
MRL	1 regt
SAM	1 bde

Western Op Comd

Mech	1 indep bde
Mob	2 bde
Arty	2 regt
MRL	1 regt
Engr	1 regt
SAM	1 bde

EQUIPMENT BY TYPE

MBT 1,586: 92 T-80; 1,465 T-72; 29 T-55

AIFV 1,588: 154 BMD-1; 109 BMP-1; 1,164 BMP-2; 161 BRM

APC 916

　APC (T) 88: 22 BTR-D; 66 MT-LB

　APC (W) 828: 188 BTR-60; 446 BTR-70; 194 BTR-80

ARTY 1,499

　SP 578: **122mm** 246 2S1 *Carnation*; **152mm** 296: 13 2S19 *Farm*; 163 2S3; 120 2S5; **203mm** 36 2S7

　TOWED 452: **122mm** 202 D-30; **152mm** 250: 50 2A36; 136 2A65; 58 D-20; 6 M-1943

　GUN/MOR 120mm 54 2S9 *NONA*

　MRL 338: **122mm** 213: 5 9P138; 208 BM-21; **132mm** 1 BM-13; **220mm** 84 9P140 *Uragan*; **300mm** 40 9A52 *Smerch*

　MOR 120mm 77 2S12

AT • MSL • MANPATS 480 AT-4 9K11 *Spigot*/AT-5 9K111 *Spandrel*/AT-6 9K114 *Spiral*/AT-7 9K115 *Saxhorn* (some SP)

AD • SAM • SP 350 SA-11 *Gadfly*/SA-12A *Gladiator*/SA-12B *Giant (Twin)*/SA-13 *Gopher*/SA-8 *Gecko* (700–2,100 eff.)

RADAR • LAND GS-13 *Long Eye*/SNAR-1 *Long Trough*/SNAR-2/-6 *Pork Trough* (arty); some *Small Fred*/*Small Yawn*/SNAR-10 *Big Fred* (veh, arty)

MSL • TACTICAL • SSM 96: 36 FROG/SS-21 *Scarab (Tochka)*; 60 *Scud*

Air Force and Air Defence Forces 18,170

Flying hours　15 hrs/year

FORCES BY ROLE

Ftr	2 bases with Su-27P *Flanker-B*/Su-27UB *Flanker C*; MiG-29S *Fulcrum C*/MiG-29UB *Fulcrum*
FGA/recce	4 sqn with Su-24MK *Fencer D*/Su-24MR *Fencer-E*; Su-25 *Frogfoot*/Su-25UB *Frogfoot B*
Tpt	1 base with An-12 *Cub*; An-24 *Coke*; 6 An-26 *Curl*; IL-76 *Candid*; Tu-134 *Crusty*
Trg	sqns with L-39 *Albatros*
Atk hel	sqns with Mi-24 *Hind*
Spt hel	some (combat) sqn with Mi-24K *Hind G2*; Mi-6 *Hook*; Mi-24R *Hind G1*; Mi-8 *Hip*; Mi-26 *Halo*

EQUIPMENT BY TYPE

AIRCRAFT 175 combat capable

　FTR/FGA 175: 23 Su-27P *Flanker-B* FTR/Su-27UB *Flanker C*; 35 Su-24MK *Fencer D* FGA/Su-24MR *Fencer-E* recce; 41 MiG-29S *Fulcrum C* FTR/MiG-29UB *Fulcrum* MiG-29U; 76 Su-25 *Frogfoot* FGA/Su-25UB *Frogfoot B*

　TPT 27: 3 An-12 *Cub*; 1 An-24 *Coke*; 6 An-26 *Curl*; 4 Il-76 *Candid*; (+12 Il-76 civil available for mil use); 1 Tu-134 *Crusty*

　TRG L-39 *Albatros*

HELICOPTERS

　ATK 50 Mi-24 *Hind*

　RECCE 8 Mi-24K *Hind G2*

　SPT 180: 14 Mi-26 *Halo*; 29 Mi-6 *Hook*; 8 Mi-24R *Hind G1*; 125 Mi-8 *Hip*; 4 Mi-24R *Hind G1*

MSL

　ASM AS-10 *Karen*; AS-11 *Kilter*; AS-14 *Kedge*

　ARM AS-11 *Kilter*

　AAM AA-10 *Alamo*; AA-11 *Archer*; AA-7 *Apex*; AA-8 *Aphid*

Air Defence

AD data from Uzal Baranovichi EW radar

1 AD bde (2 bn) with SAM/AAA units, ECM/ECCM units

AD • SAM 175 SA-10 *Grumble* (quad) SP/SA-3 *Goa*/SA-5 *Gammon* static (175–700 eff.). First S-300PS delivered to replace SA-3

Paramilitary 110,000

Border Guards 12,000

Ministry of Interior

Militia 87,000

Ministry of Interior

Ministry of Interior Troops 11,000

DEPLOYMENT

BOSNIA-HERZEGOINVA
OSCE • Bosnia and Herzegoinva 1

SERBIA
OSCE • Kosovo 2

FOREIGN FORCES

Russia: Military Air Forces: 4 SAM units with SA-10 *Grumble* (quad)

Bosnia–Herzegovina BIH

Convertible Mark		2008	2009	2010
GDP	mark	25bn	24bn	
	US$	18.6bn	18.3bn	
per capita	US$	4,046	3,957	
Growth	%	5.5	-3.0	
Inflation	%	7.4	0.9	
Def bdgt	mark	324m	371m	474m
	US$	244m	281m	
FMA (US	US$	3.3m	3.6m	6.0m
US$1=mark		1.33	1.32	

Population   4,613,414

Age	0 – 14	15 – 19	20 – 24	25 – 29	30 – 64	65 plus
Male	10%	4%	4%	4%	25%	5%
Female	9%	4%	4%	4%	24%	6%

Capabilities

ACTIVE 11,099 (Joint Operational Command 144 State Joint Staff 243 AFBiH 9,910, AF/AD 802)

Bosnia-Herzegovina established a single State level army in a major reform process from 2003 – 2006. The State Forces now consist of three mixed infantry brigades, one tactical support brigade, and an air force /air defence brigade and a minor reserve component (about 50% of the standing forces) consisting of former professional soldiers.

ORGANISATIONS BY SERVICE

State Joint Staff 243; State Joint Operational Command 144 ; AF/AD 802

AFBiH 9,910

FORCES BY ROLE

Op	1 comd
Inf	3 bde
Cbt Spt	1 comd, 1 bde
Trg	1 comd
Log	1 comd, 4 bn

EQUIPMENT BY TYPE
Due to ongoing restructuring, inconsistencies may exist.
MBT 325: 71 M-84; 50 AMX-30; 45 M-60A3; 142 T-55; 12 T-54, 5 T-34
Lt tk 2 PT-76
AIFV 134: 25 AMX-10P; 109 M-80
APC 142
  APC (T) 80 M-113A2
  APC (W) 62: 21 BOV; 3 BTR-70; 30 OT-60, 1 BTR-50; 1 BDRM; 60 T-60 PB
ARTY 1,757
  SP 122mm 24 2S1 *Carnation*
  TOWED 730: **105mm** 161: 36 L-118 Light Gun; 24 M-2A1; 101 M-56 **122mm** 268 D-30 **130mm** 74: 61 M-46; 13 M-82; **152mm** 30: 13 D-20; 17 M-84 **155mm** 197: 119 M-114A2; 78 M-1
  MRL 154: **107mm** 28 VLR Type-63; **122mm** 43: 1 BM-21; 5 GRAD; 36 GRAD/APRA 40; 1 KACUSA; **128mm** 78: 22 M-63; 21 M-77; 35 M-91; **262mm** 5 SVLR
  MOR 849: **82mm** 81 MB M-69; 220 MB M60; 1 MB M 1937 **120mm** 547: 22 M-74; 450 M-75; 25 UB M-52; 11 HADID; 16 KROM ; 23 MB-120
AT • MSL
  SP 45: 2 M-92 *Lovac Tenkova*; 3 POLO 9P122; 9 POLO 9P133; 31 POLO M-83
  MANPATS 691: 508 AT-3 9K11 *Sagger*; 5 Polk *Milan*; 76 9K111 *Fagot*/AT-4 *Spigot*; 51 HJ-8; 51 *Red Arrow*
  GUNS 100mm 45mm T12/T12
AD • SAM
  SP 27: 1 SA-13 *Gopher Stela* 10M3; 20 SA-6 *Gainful*; 6 SA-9 *Gaskin*
  MANPAD SA-14 *Gremlin*; SA-16 *Gimlet*
  GUNS 760
  SP 136: **20mm** 9 BOV-3 SPAAG; **30mm** 121 M-53/M59; **57mm** 6 ZSU 57/2
  TOWED 624: **20mm** 505: 32 M-55A2, 4 M38, 1 M55 A2B1, 293 M55 A3/A4, 175 M75 **23mm 30**: 29 ZU-23, 1 GSh -23 **30mm** 33 M5 **37mm** 7 Type 55 **40mm** 49: 31 L 60, 16 L 70, 2 M 12

Air Wing

FORCES BY ROLE
Avn	1 avn regt

EQUIPMENT BY TYPE
AC 19 combat capable
  FGA 13: 6 J-21 (J-1) *Jastreb*; 7 J-22 *Orao* 1
  RECCE 2 IJ-21 (RJ-1) *Jastreb*
  TRG 4: 1 N-62 *Super Galeb G-4**; 3 NJ-21 *Jastreb* TJ-1*
HEL 45
  ATK 13: 7 HN-45 *GAMA* SA-341/SA-342 *Gazelle*; 5 H-45; 1 HN-42
  SPT 16: 11 Mi-8; 4 Mi-8 MTV; 1 Mi-17 (Mi-8MT) *Hip H*
  UTL 16: 1 Mi-34 *Hermit*; 15 UH-1H *Iroquois*

DEPLOYMENT

Legal provisions for foreign deployment:
Constitution: Codified constitution within Dayton Peace Agreement (1995)

Specific legislation: 'Defence Law of Bosnia and Herzegovina (2003)
Decision on deployment of troops abroad: By the members of the Presidency (2003 'Defence Law' Art. 9, 13)

AFGHANISTAN
NATO • ISAF 10

DEMOCRATIC REPUBLIC OF CONGO
UN • MONUC 5 obs

SERBIA
OSCE • Serbia 2
OSCE • Kosovo 7

FOREIGN FORCES

Part of EUFOR – *Operation Althea* unless otherwise stated.
Albania 13
Austria 96; 2 S-70A *Blackhawk* hel; (3 *Allouette III* 2010) • OSCE 3
Belarus OSCE 1
Belgium OSCE 1
Bulgaria 119 • OSCE 1
Canada NATO HQ Sarajevo (*Op Bronze*) 6 • OSCE 2
Chile 21
Croatia OSCE 1
Czech Republic OSCE 1
Estonia 2
Finland 4 • OSCE 1
France 4 • OSCE 7
Germany 129 • OSCE 3
Greece 44 • OSCE 4
Hungary 160; 1 inf coy • OSCE 2
Ireland 43 • OSCE 5
Italy 300 • NATO HQ Sarajevo 7 • OSCE 7
Kyrgyzstan OSCE 1
Latvia 2
Lithuania 1
Luxembourg 1
Macedonia, Former Yugoslav Republic of 12
Netherlands 73 • OSCE 1
Norway NATO HQ Sarajevo 2
Poland 188; 1 inf coy
Portugal 51 • OSCE 1
Romania 56 • OSCE 1
Russia OSCE 3
Slovakia 32 • OSCE 2
Slovenia 25 • OSCE 1
Spain 304; (1 inf bn HQ; 1 inf coy; 1 recce pl) • OSCE 4
Sweden OSCE 3
Switzerland 25
Tajikistan OSCE 1
Turkey 246; 1 inf coy • OSCE 1
United Kingdom 9• OSCE 1
United States • OSCE 11

Cyprus CYP

Cypriot Pound C£		2008	2009	2010
GDP	C£	16.9bn		
	US$	24.9bn		
per capita	US$	23,296		
Growth	%	3.6	-0.5	
Inflation	%	4.6	0.4	
Def bdgt	C£	365m	377m	
	US$	536m	562m	
US$1=C£		0.68	0.67	

Population   1,084,748

Age	0 – 14	15 – 19	20 – 24	25 – 29	30 – 64	65 plus
Male	11%	4%	4%	3%	22%	5%
Female	10%	4%	4%	3%	22%	6%

Capabilities

ACTIVE 10,050 (National Guard 10,050)
Paramilitary 750
Terms of service conscription, 24 months, then reserve to age 50 (officers 60)

RESERVE 50,000 (National Guard 50,000)

ORGANISATIONS BY SERVICE

National Guard 950 regular; 9,100 conscript (total 10,050)

FORCES BY ROLE

Home Guard	1 comd HQ
Armd	1 bde (3 armd bn)
Mech Inf	2 div each (3 inf bn); 1 bde (4th) (2 inf regt)
SF	1 comd (regt) (1 SF bn)
Lt Inf	1 (3rd) bde (2 inf regt)
Arty	1 comd (8 arty bn)
Spt	1 (svc) bde

EQUIPMENT BY TYPE
MBT 147: 41 T-80U; 54 AMX-30G; 52 AMX-30 B2
RECCE 139: 15 EE-3 *Jararaca*; 124 EE-9 *Cascavel*
AIFV 43 BMP-3
APC 294
  APC (T) 168: 168 *Leonidas*
  APC (W) 126 VAB (incl variants)
ARTY 526+
  SP 155mm 24: 12 Mk F3; 12 *Zuzana*
  TOWED 104: **100mm** 20 M-1944; **105mm** 72 M-56; **155mm** 12 TR-F-1
  MRL 22: **122mm** 4 BM-21; **128mm** 18 M-63 *Plamen*
  MOR 376+: **81mm** 240+: 70+ M-1/M-29 in store; 170 E-44; **107mm** 20 M-2/M-30; **120mm** 116 RT61
AT • MSL • MANPATS 115: 70 HOT; 45 *Milan*
  RCL 153: **106mm** 144 M-40A1; **90mm** 9 EM-67
  RL 1,850+: **66mm** M-72 *LAW*; **73mm** 850 RPG-7 *Knout*; **112mm** 1,000 APILAS

AD • SAM 48
  SP 6 SA-15 *Gauntlet*; *Mistral*
  STATIC 12 *Aspide*
  MANPAD 30 *Mistral*
  GUNS • TOWED 60: **20mm** 36 M-55; **35mm** 24 GDF-003
(with *Skyguard*)

Maritime Wing
FORCES BY ROLE
SSM 1 (coastal defence) bty with 24 MM-40 *Exocet*

EQUIPMENT BY TYPE
PATROL AND COASTAL COMBATANTS 6
  PCC 6: 1 *Kyrenia* (GRC *Dilos*); 2 *Rodman* 55; 1 *Salamis*;
  2 *Cantieri Vittoria*
MSL • TACTICAL • SSM 24 MM-40 *Exocet*

Air Wing
AIRCRAFT
  TPT 1 BN-2 *Islander*
  TRG 1 PC-9
HELICOPTERS
  ATK 15: 11 Mi-35P *Hind*; 4 SA-342 *Gazelle* (with HOT)
  UTL 2 Bell 206C L-3 *Long Ranger*

Paramilitary 750+

Armed Police 500+
FORCES BY ROLE
Mech 1 (rapid-reaction) unit

EQUIPMENT BY TYPE
APC (W) 2 VAB VTT
AIRCRAFT • TPT 1 BN-2A *Defender*
HELICOPTERS • UTL 2 Bell 412 SP

Maritime Police 250
PATROL AND COASTAL COMBATANTS 10
  PCC 7: 5 *SAB-12*; 2 *Cantieri Vittoria*
  PFI 3: 2 *Evagoras*; 1 *Shaldag*

DEPLOYMENT
Legal provisions for foreign deployment:
Constitution: Codified constitution (1960)
Decision on deployment of troops abroad: By parliament, but president has the right of final veto (Art. 50)

LEBANON
UN • UNIFIL 2

FOREIGN FORCES
Argentina UNFICYP 294; 2 inf coy; 1 avn unit
Austria UNFICYP 4
Canada UNFICYP 1
Croatia UNFICYP 4
Greece Army: 950; ε200 (officers/NCO seconded to Greek-Cypriot National Guard)
Hungary UNFICYP 84; elm 1 inf coy
Peru UNFICYP 2
Slovakia UNFICYP 196; elm 1 inf coy; 1 engr pl

United Kingdom Army 1,678; 2 inf bn; 1 hel flt; Navy 42; Air Force 1,071; 1 hel sqn with 4 Bell 412 *Twin Huey* • UNFICYP 257: 1 inf coy

TERRITORY WHERE THE GOVERNMENT DOES NOT EXERCISE EFFECTIVE CONTROL

Data presented here represent the de facto situation on the island. This does not imply international recognition as a sovereign state.

Capabilities
ACTIVE 5,000 (Army 5,000) **Paramilitary 150**
Terms of service conscription, 24 months, then reserve to age 50.

RESERVE 26,000 (first line 11,000 second line 10,000 third line 5,000)

ORGANISATIONS BY SERVICE

Army ε5,000
FORCES BY ROLE
Inf 7 bn

EQUIPMENT BY TYPE
ARTY
  MOR 73 **120mm**
AT
  MSL • MANPATS 6 *Milan*
  RCL 36 **106mm**

Paramilitary

Armed Police ε150
SF 1 (Police) unit

Coast Guard
PATROL AND COASTAL COMBATANTS 6
  PCC 5: 2 SG45/SG46; 1 *Rauf Denktash*; 2 US Mk 5
  PCI 1

FOREIGN FORCES
TURKEY
Army ε36,000
  1 army corps HQ, some air det, 1 armd bde, 1 indep mech inf bde, 2 inf div, 1 cdo regt, 1 arty bde, 1 avn comd
EQUIPMENT BY TYPE
  MBT 8 M-48A2 MBT
  TRG 441 M-48A5T1/M-48A5T2
  APC (T) 627: 361 AAPC (T) (incl variants); 266 M-113 (T) (incl variants)
  ARTY
    SP 155mm 90 M-44T
    TOWED 102; **105mm** 72 M-101A1; **155mm** 18 M-114A2; **203mm** 12 M-115
    MRL 122mm 6 T-122

MOR 450: **81mm** 175; **107mm** 148 M-30; **120mm** 127 HY-12

AT

MSL • MANPATS 114: 66 *Milan*; 48 TOW

RCL 106mm 192 M-40A1; **90mm** M-67

RL 66mm M-72 *LAW*

AD • GUNS

TOWED 20mm Rh 202; **35mm** 16 GDF-003; **40mm** 48 M-1

AC 3 U-17 Utl

HEL 4: 1 AS-532UL *Cougar* utl; 3 UH-1H *Iroquois* utl

PATROL AND COASTAL COMBATANTS 1 **PCI** less than 100 tonnes

Finland FIN

Euro €		2008	2009	2010
GDP	€	186bn	173bn	
	US$	274bn	258bn	
per capita	US$	52,153	49,180	
Growth	%	1.0	-6.4	
Inflation	%	3.9	1.0	
Def exp	€	2.47bn		
	US$	3.63bn		
Def bdgt	€	2.42bn	2.82bn	2.72bn
	US$	3.55bn	4.21bn	
US$1=€		0.68	0.67	

Population   5,250,275

Age	0 – 14	15 – 19	20 – 24	25 – 29	30 – 64	65 plus
Male	9%	3%	3%	3%	24%	6%
Female	9%	3%	3%	3%	24%	10%

Capabilities

ACTIVE 22,600 (Army 16,000 Navy 3,800 Air 2,750) **Paramilitary 2,950**

General Conscription terms of Service 6-9-12 months (12 months for officers NCOs and soldiers with special duties. 25,000 reservists a year do refresher training: total obligation 40 days (75 for NCOs, 100 for officers) between conscript service and age 50 (NCOs and officers to age 60).
Reserve total reducing to 340,000.

CIVILIAN 4,600 (Army 3,000 Navy 500 Air 1,100)

RESERVE 350,000 (Army 280,000 Navy 32,000 Air 38,000) **Paramilitary 11,500**

ORGANISATIONS BY SERVICE

Army 5,000; 11,000 conscript (total 16,000); civilian 3,000

FORCES BY ROLE

Has no peacetime structure. Recent re-organisation has involved the replacement of the previous commands

with seven military provinces. Finland's army maintains a mobilisation strength of about 300,000. In support of this requirement two cycles, each for about 15,000 conscripts and 17,000 reservists, take place each year. After conscript training, reservist commitment is to the age of 60. Reservists are usually assigned to units within their local geographical area. All service appointments or deployments outside Finnish borders are voluntary for all members of the armed services. All brigades are reserve based. Any 'Reaction Forces' are regular elements and volunteers under contract.

Comd	1 Army HQ; 4 Military Commands
Rapid Reaction	1 regt (Utti) (SF gp, Ab gp, hel Sqn)
Armd	1 bde with (3 composite armd bn, 1 armd recce coy, 1 AT coy, 1 fd arty regt, 1 sigs bn, 1 AD bn, 1 log bn, 1 engr bn,)
Jaeger	3 bde with (3 Jaeger bn, 1 AT coy, 1 HQ coy, 1 sigs coy, 1 AD bn, 1 engr bn, 1 fd arty regt, 1 log coy, 1 Recce coy); 2 regts
Arty	1 bde
Engr	1 Bde
AD	2 regt
Sig	1 regt

EQUIPMENT BY TYPE

MBT 100 *Leopard* 2 A4

AIFV 212: 110 BMP-2; 102 CV90

APC 990

APC (T) 300: 16 MT-LBU; 98 MT-LBV; 186 BMP 1TJ/BTR-50 YV1

APC (W) 690 XA-180 *Sisu*/XA-185 *Sisu*; XA-203 *Sisu*

ARTY 1,136

SP 90: **122mm** 72 PsH 74 (2S1) *Carnation* **152mm** 18 Telak 91 (2S5)

TOWED 354: **122mm** 84 H 63 (D-30); **130mm** 36 K 54; **152mm** 180 H 88-38/H 88–40; **155mm** 54 K 83/K 98

MRL 82: **22mm:** 24 Rahlt; 36 RM7U 227mm 22 M270

MOR 120mm 610 KRH 92

AT

MSL 100 Spike; **TOW** 2

HEL

SPT 17: 2 Mi-8 *Hip*; 8 NH-90; 7 Hughes 500 D/E

Utl 7 Hughes 500 D/E

UAV • TACTICAL 6 *Ranger*

AD • SAM

SP 36 +: 16 ITO 05 (*ASRAD*); 20 ITO 90 (*Crotale* NG); ITO 96 (SA-11) *Gadfly*

MANPAD: 86 (SA-16) *Gimlet*; ITO 86M (SA-18) *Grouse* (*Igla*); ITO 05; 128 RBS 70

GUNS 23mm; 30mm; 35mm; 57mm

Reserve Organisations

60,000 in manoeuvre forces and 220,000 in territorial forces

Jaeger	2 bde
Inf	6 bde; 29 bn/ BG; 170 coy
CS/CSS	engr, AD, sigs, log

Navy 2,000; 1,850 conscript (total 3,850); civilian 500

FORCES BY ROLE

Naval Command HQ located at Turku; with two subordinate Naval Commands; 1 Naval bde; 3 Spt elm (Naval Materiel Cmd, Naval Academy, Naval Research Institute)

EQUIPMENT BY TYPE

PATROL AND COASTAL COMBATANTS 8

PFM 8:

4 *Hamina* each with 2 twin (4 eff.) with 4 15SF (RBS-15M) RBS-15 SSM, 1 *Sadral* sextuple with *Mistral* SAM

4 *Rauma* each with 2 single with 2 15SF (RBS-15M) RBS-15 SSM, 2 twin (4 eff.) with 4 15SF (RBS-15M) RBS-15 SSM, 1 *Sadral* sextuple with *Mistral* SAM

MINE WARFARE 19

MINE COUNTERMEASURES • **MSI** 13: 7 *Kiiski*; 6 *Kuha*

MINELAYERS • **ML** 6:

2 *Hameenmaa* each with 1 *Sadral* octuple with *Umkhonto* SAM, 2 RBU 1200 (10 eff.), up to 150–200 mine (undergoing upgrade programme)

3 *Pansio* each with 50 mine

1 *Pohjanmaa* with up to 100–150 mine

AMPHIBIOUS

LCU 7: 2 *Kala*; 3 *Kampela*; 2 *Lohi*

LCP 66: 36 *Jurmo*; 30 *Meriuisko*

LOGISTICS AND SUPPORT 30:

AGOR 1 *Aranda* (Ministry of Trade Control)

AKSL 15: 6 *Hauki*; 4 *Hila*; 5 *Valas*

AGB 9: 2 *Karhuj*; 2 *Urho*; 2 *Tarmo*; 2 *Fennica*; 1 *Botnica* (Board of Navigation control)

AGS 1 *Prisma* (Maritime Administration)

TRG 3 *Fabian Wrede*

TRIAL 1

FACILITIES

Base   Located at Upinniemi (Helsinki) and Turku

Coastal Defence

ARTY •**COASTAL** 118: **130mm** 102: 30 K-53tk (static); 72 K-54 RT; **100mm** 16 (TK) tank turrets

MSL • **TACTICAL** • **SSM** 4 RBS-15K

Air Force 2,000; 750 conscript (total 2,750); civilian 1,100

3 Air Comds: Satakunta (West), Karelia (East), Lapland (North). Each Air Comd assigned to one of the 3 AD areas into which FIN is divided. 3 ftr wings, one in each AD area.

Flying hours   90-140 hrs/year

FORCES BY ROLE

FGA	3 wg with 55 F/A-18C *Hornet*; 8 F/A-18D *Hornet*
Advanced AD/ Attack Trg/Recce	3 sqn with 47 *Hawk* MK50/*Hawk* MK51A; 18 MK66 *Hawk*; 1 F-27 *Maritime Enforcer* (ESM/Elint)
Tpt	1 sqn with 2 C-295M
Liaison	4 sqn with 5 PA-31-350 *Piper Chieftain*; 8 L-90 *Redigo*
Survey	1 sqn with 3 *Learjet* 35A (survey, ECM trg, target-towing)
Trg	Trg unit with 28 L-70 *Vinka*

EQUIPMENT BY TYPE

AIRCRAFT 63 combat capable

FGA 63: 55 F/A-18C *Hornet*; 8 F/A-18D *Hornet*

ASW 1 F-27 *Maritime Enforcer* (ESM/Elint)

TPT 13: 2 C-295M; 3 *Learjet* 35A; 3 (survey; ECM trg; tgt-tow); 5 PA-31-350 *Piper Chieftain*

TRG 101: 47 *Hawk* MK50/*Hawk* MK51A; 18 MK66 *Hawk*; 28 L-70 *Vinka*; 8 L-90 *Redigo*

MSL • **AAM** AIM-120 *AMRAAM*; AIM-9 *Sidewinder*

Paramilitary

Border Guard 2,950

Ministry of Interior. 4 Border Guard Districts and 2 Coast Guard Districts

FORCES BY ROLE

Land	4 Border Guard Districts
Coast Guard	6 (offshore patrol) sqn with 7 OPV; 7 ACV; 60 PB
Air	1 (patrol) sqn with 2 Do-228 (maritime surv); 3 AS-332 *Super Puma*; 3 AB-206L (Bell 206L) *LongRanger*; 4 AB-412 (Bell 412) *Twin Huey*; 1 AB-412EP (Bell 412EP) *Twin Huey*

EQUIPMENT BY TYPE

PATROL AND COASTAL COMBATANTS 74

OPV 7

PB 60

ACV 7

AIRCRAFT • **TPT** 2 Do-228 (MP)

HELICOPTERS

SPT 3 AS-332 *Super Puma*

UTL 8: 4 AB-412 (Bell 412) *Twin Huey*; 1 AB-412EP (Bell 412EP) *Twin Huey*; 3 AB-206L (Bell 206L)

Reserve 11,500 reservists on mobilisation

DEPLOYMENT

Legal provisions for foreign deployment:
Constitution: Codified constitution (2000)
Specific legislation: 'Act on Peace Support Operations' (2000)
Decision on deployment of troops abroad: By president upon proposal by government (Art. 129 of constitution) and after formal consultation of parliamentary Foreign Affairs Committee ('Act on Peace Support Operations', Ch. 1, Section 2)

AFGHANISTAN

NATO • ISAF 165

BOSNIA-HERZEGOVINA

EU • EUFOR • *Operation Althea* 4
OSCE • Bosnia and Herzegovina 1

CENTRAL AFRICAN REPUBLIC/CHAD

UN • MINURCAT 74; elm 1 inf bn

INDIA/PAKISTAN
UN • UNMOGIP 5 obs

LIBERIA
UN • UNMIL 2

MIDDLE EAST
UN • UNTSO 15 obs

MOLDOVA
OSCE • Moldova 1

SERBIA
NATO • KFOR • *Joint Enterprise* 405; 1 inf coy; 1 int/surv/recce coy; 1 log coy
OSCE • Kosovo 2

SUDAN
UN • UNMIS 1

Georgia GEO

Georgian Lari		2008	2009	2010
GDP	lari	19.0bn		
	US$	12.8bn		
per capita	US$	2,754		
Growth	%	2.1	-4.0	
Inflation	%	10.0	1.2	
Def bdgt	lari	1,545m	897m	750m
	US$	1.03bn	537m	
FMA (US)	US$	9.0m	11.0m	16.0m
US$1=lari		1.49	1.67	

Population   4,615,807

Age	0 – 14	15 – 19	20 – 24	25 – 29	30 – 64	65 plus
Male	10%	4%	4%	3%	21%	6%
Female	9%	4%	4%	3%	23%	9%

Capabilities

ACTIVE 21,150 (Army 17,767 Navy 495 Air 1,310 National Guard 1,578) **Paramilitary 11,700**

Terms of service conscription, 18 months

ORGANISATIONS BY SERVICE

Army 14,000; 3,767 conscript (total 17,767)

FORCES BY ROLE
Although forces and manpower remain largely intact much equipment as well as important bases were destroyed in the August 2008 war.
1 Land Forces HQ

Inf	5 bde
SF	1 bde
Marine Inf	2 bn (1 cadre)
Arty	2 bde

EQUIPMENT BY TYPE
Considerable amounts of equipment have been destroyed and or removed.
MBT 66: 41 T-72; 2 T-55 (23 in store)
AIFV 66: 19 BMP-1 (9 in store); 32 BMP-2 (5 in store); 1 BRM-1K
APC 46
  APC (T) 8 MT-LB
  APC (W) 38: 17 BTR-70 (1 in store); 15 BTR-80 (5 in store)
ARTY 185
  SP 35: **152mm** 12 2S3 (1 in store); 20 DANA; 1 2S19 (in store); **203mm** 1 2S7
  TOWED 69: **122mm** 56: 53 D-30; 3 M-30(in store); **152mm** 13: 3 2A36; 10 2A65
  MRL 18: **122mm** 12 BM-21; 6 RM70
  MOR 63: **120mm** 1 M-120 (17 in store); 7 2B11 (7 in store); 21 M75 (10 in store)
AT ε50
  MSL ε10
  GUNS ε40
AD • SAM • SP SA-13 *Gopher*

Navy 495

Significant damage sustained to Navy and Coast Guard units during the August 2008 war. It is probable that all surviving units will be merged under one force structure.

FORCES BY ROLE
Navy 1 HQ located at Tbilisi

EQUIPMENT BY TYPE
PATROL AND COASTAL COMBATANTS 4
  PCC 4: 2 *Dilos*; 1 *Turk*; 1 *Akhneta*
AMPHIBIOUS 1 LCU

FACILITIES
Bases Located at Tbilisi, Poti

Air Force 1,310 (incl 290 conscript)

1 avn base, 1 hel air base
AIRCRAFT 11 combat capable
  FGA 10: 3 Su-25 *Frogfoot*; 7 Su-25K *Frogfoot A*
  TPT 9: 6 An-2 *Colt*; 1 Tu-134A *Crusty* (VIP); 2 Yak-40 *Codling*
  TRG 10: 9 L-29 *Delfin*; 1 Su-25UB *Frogfoot B*
HELICOPTERS
  SPT 16 Mi-8T *Hip*
  UTL 7 UH-1H *Iroquois*
AD • SAM 1-2 bn *Buk*-MI (SA-11), 8 *Osa*-AK (SA-8B) (two bty), 6-10 *Osa*-AKM updated SAM systems.

National Guard 1,578 active reservists opcon Army

MRR   1 bde (plus trg centre)

Paramilitary 11,700

Border Guard 5,400

Coast Guard
PATROL AND COASTAL COMBATANTS 11
PCI 11: 7 *Zhuk*; 2 *Point*; 2 *Dauntless* (all less than 100 tonnes)

Ministry of Interior Troops 6,300

DEPLOYMENT
Legal provisions for foreign deployment of armed forces:
Constitution: Codified constitution (1995)
Decision on deployment of troops abroad: By the presidency upon parliamentary approval (Art. 100)

AFGHANISTAN
NATO • ISAF 1

SERBIA
OSCE • Serbia 1
OSCE • Kosovo 4

TERRITORY WHERE THE GOVERNMENT DOES NOT EXERCISE EFFECTIVE CONTROL
Following the August 2008 war between Russia and Georgia, the areas of Abkhazia and South Ossetia declared themselves independent. Data presented here represent the de facto situation and does not imply international recognition as sovereign states.

FOREIGN FORCES
Russia Army ε3,400; 2 MR bde; at locations incl Gudauta (Abkhazia), Djava and Tskhinvali (S. Ossetia)

Ireland IRL

Euro €		2008	2009	2010
GDP	€	181bn		
	US$	266bn		
per capita	US$	64,044		
Growth	%	-3.0	-7.5	
Inflation	%	3.1	-1.6	
Def bdgt	€	1,000m	1,031m	
	US$	1.47bn	1.53bn	
US$1=€		068	0.67	

Population   4,203,200

Age	0 – 14	15 – 19	20 – 24	25 – 29	30 – 64	65 plus
Male	11%	4%	4%	4%	22%	5%
Female	10%	4%	4%	4%	22%	6%

Capabilities

ACTIVE 10,460 (Army 8,500 Navy 1,110 Air 850)

RESERVE 14,875 (Army 14,500 Navy 300 Air 75)

ORGANISATIONS BY SERVICE

Army ε8,500
FORCES BY ROLE
Armd Recce   1 sqn
Inf   3 bde (*each:* 3 inf bn, 1 cav recce sqn, 1 fd arty regt (2 fd arty bty), 1 fd engr coy, 1 log bn)
Ranger   1 coy
AD   1 regt (1 AD bty)
Constr Engr   1 coy

EQUIPMENT BY TYPE
LT TK 14 *Scorpion*
RECCE 52: 15 *Piranha* IIIH; 18 AML-20; 19 AML-90
APC (W) 67: 65 *Piranha* III; 2 XA-180 *Sisu*
ARTY 495
 TOWED 24: **105mm** 24 L-118 Light Gun
 MOR 471: **81mm** 400; **120mm** 71
AT
 MSL • MANPATS 57: 36 *Javelin*; 21 *Milan*
 RCL 84mm 444 *Carl Gustav*
 RL 84mm AT-4
AD
 SAM • MANPAD 7 RBS-70
 GUNS • TOWED 40mm 32 L/70 each with 8 *Flycatcher*

Reserves 14,500 reservists
The Reserve consists of two levels. Of these the 'Integrated' Reserve would provide nine rifle companies (one per regular infantry battalion, three cavalry troops (one per regular squadron) and three field batteries (one per regular field artillery regiment) on mobilisation. The three reserve brigades form the 'Non-Integrated' Reserve and unlike the regular infantry battalions their component battalions have a variable number of rifle companies, five having four companies each, three having three and one having only two.
Cav   3 tps (integrated)
Inf   3 bde (non integrated) (*each:* 1 fd arty regt (2 fd arty bty), 1 fd engr coy, 1 cav recce sqn,1 log bn)
Inf   9 coy (integrated); 9 inf bn (non integrated 31 coy)
SF   1 coy (2 asslt pl, 1spt pl
Arty   3 bty (integrated)
Log   1 bn
AD   3 bty

Navy 1,110
EQUIPMENT BY TYPE
PATROL AND COASTAL COMBATANTS 8
 PSOH 1 *Eithne* with 1 hel landing platform
 PSO 7: 3 *Emer*; 2 *Orla* (UK *Peacock*) each with 1 76mm gun; 2 *Roisin* each with 1 76mm gun
FACILITIES
Bases   Located at Cork, Haulbowline

Air Corps 850

FORCES BY ROLE

Air   2 ops wg; 2 spt wg; 1 comms and info sqn; 1 air corps college

EQUIPMENT BY TYPE

AIRCRAFT

  MP 2 CASA 235 MPA

  Police Support 1 BN *Defender* 4000

  TPT 3: 1 Beech 200 *Super King Air*; 1 Gulfstream GIV; 1 Learjet 45 (VIP)

  UTL 5 Cessna FR-172H

  TRG 8 PC-9M

HELICOPTERS:

  UTL 10: 2 EC135 P2 (incl trg/medevac); 6 AW139; 1 EC135 T2 ; 1 AS 355N (police support)

DEPLOYMENT

Legal provisions for foreign deployment:

Constitution: Codified constitution (1937)

Specific legislation: 'Defence (Amendment) Act' 2006

Decision on deployment of troops abroad: a) By parliament; b) by government if scenario for deployment corresponds with conditions laid out in Art.3 of 2006 'Defence (Amendment) Act' which exempts from parliamentary approval deployments for purposes of participation in exercises abroad; monitoring, observation, advisory or reconnaissance missions; and 'humanitarian operations 'in response to actual or potential disasters or emergencies.

AFGHANISTAN

NATO • ISAF 7

BOSNIA-HERZEGOVINA

EU • EUFOR • *Operation Althea* 43

OSCE • Bosnia and Herzegovina 5

CENTRAL AFRICAN REPUBLIC/CHAD

UN • MINURCAT 427; elm 1 inf bn

CÔTE D'IVOIRE

UN • UNOCI 2 obs

DEMOCRATIC REPUBLIC OF CONGO

UN • MONUC 3 obs

LEBANON

UN • UNIFIL 8

MIDDLE EAST

UN • UNTSO 12 obs

SERBIA

NATO • KFOR • *Joint Enterprise* 233; 1 mech inf coy; 1 log coy

OSCE • Serbia 2

OSCE • Kosovo 7

WESTERN SAHARA

UN • MINURSO 3 obs

Macedonia, Former Yugoslav Republic FYROM

Macedonian Denar d		2008	2009	2010
GDP	d	390bn	379bn	
	US$	9.3bn	9.1bn	
per capita	US$	4,526	4,387	
Growth	%	4.9	-2.5	
Inflation	%	8.5	-0.5	
Def bdgt	d	8.02bn	7.0bn	7.3bn
	US$	191m	167m	
FMA (US)	US$	2.8m	2.8m	6.0m
US$1=d		41.8	41.8	

Population   2,066,718

Age	0 – 14	15 – 19	20 – 24	25 – 29	30 – 64	65 plus
Male	11%	4%	4%	4%	22%	5%
Female	10%	4%	4%	4%	22%	6%

Capabilities

ACTIVE 8,000

RESERVE 4,850

ORGANISATIONS BY SERVICE

Joint Operational Command 8,000

Army

FORCES BY ROLE

2 Corps HQ (cadre)

Tk   1 bn

Inf   2 bde

SF   1 (Special Purpose unit 1 SF bn, 1 Ranger bn)

Arty   1 (mixed) regt

Security   1 MP bn

AD   1 coy

Sig   1 bn

NBC   1 coy

Logistic Support Command

Log   3 bn

Engr   1 bn (1 active coy0

EQUIPMENT BY TYPE

MBT 31: 31 T-72A

RECCE 51: 10 BRDM-2; 41 M-1114 HMMWV

AIFV 11: 10 BMP-2; 1 BMP-2K

APC 201

  APC (T) 47: 9 *Leonidas*; 28 M-113A; 10 MT-LB

  APC (W) 154: 58 BTR-70; 12 BTR-80; 84 TM-170 *Hermelin*

ARTY 879

TOWED 70: **105mm** 14 M-56; **122mm** 56 M-30 M-1938

MRL 17: **122mm** 6 BM-21; **128mm** 11

MOR 39: **120mm** 39
AT • MSL • MANPATS 12 *Milan*
RCL 57mm; **82mm** M60A
AD
  SAM 13: 8 SA-13 *Gopher*
  MANPAD 5 SA-16 *Gimlet*
  Guns 40mm 36 L20

Reserves
Inf   1 bde

Marine Wing
PATROL AND COASTAL COMBATANTS
PCR 4

Air Wing
Air Wg is directly under Joint Operational Cmd
FORCES BY ROLE
VIP   1 VIP sqn with An-2
Atk hel   1 sqn with Mi-24V *Hind E*; Mi-24K *Hind G2*
Trg   1 trg sqn with Z-242; 1 trg sqn with UH-1H
          Iroquois
Atk Hel   1 AH sqn with Mi-24
Tpt hel   1 sqn with Mi-8/Mi-17

EQUIPMENT BY TYPE
AIRCRAFT
TPT: 1 An-2
TRG 3 Zlin-242
HELICOPTERS
ATK 12 Mi-24V *Hind E*; 2 Mi-24K *Hind G2* (being
modernised by Elbit)
SPT 6: 2 Mi-17; 4 Mi-8MTV (being modernised by Elbit)
TRG 2 UH-1H *Iroquois*

Paramilitary

Police 7,600 (some 5,000 armed)
incl 2 SF units
APC BTR APC (W)/M-113A APC (T)
HELICOPTERS • UTL 3: 1 AB-212 (Bell 212); 1 AB-206B
(Bell 206B) *JetRanger II*; 1 Bell 412EP *Twin Huey*

DEPLOYMENT

Legal provisions for foreign deployment of armed
forces:
Constitution: Codified constitution (1991)
Specific legislation: 'Defence Law' (2005)
Decision on deployment of troops abroad: a) by the
government is deployment is for humanitarian missions or
military exercises; b) by the parliament if for peacekeeping
operations ('Defence Law', Art. 41)

AFGHANISTAN
NATO • ISAF 165

BOSNIA-HERZEGOVINA
EU • EUFOR • *Operation Althea* 12

LEBANON
UN • UNIFIL 1

SERBIA
OSCE • Kosovo 3

Malta MLT

Maltese Lira ML		2008	2009	2010
GDP	ML	5.6bn		
	US$	8.2bn		
per capita	US$	20,408		
Growth	%	2.1	-2.1	
Inflation	%	4.7	2.1	
Def bdgt	ML	33.4m	36.1m	37.8m
	US$	50m	54m	
US$1=ML		0.68	0.67	

Population   405,165

Age	0 – 14	15 – 19	20 – 24	25 – 29	30 – 64	65 plus
Male	9%	4%	4%	4%	23%	6%
Female	8%	3%	3%	3%	24%	8%

Capabilities

ACTIVE 1,954 (Armed Forces of Malta 1,954)

RESERVE 167 (Emergency Volunteer Reserve Force
120 Individual Reserve 47)

ORGANISATIONS BY SERVICE

Armed Forces of Malta 1,954
FORCES BY ROLE
Inf   1 regt (No1) with (1 HQ coy, 3 inf coy, 1 spt
          coy)
Logistic 1 regt (No 3) with (1 HQ coy, 1 elec & mech sqn,
          1 ammo & explosives coy, 1 engr sqn) 1 regt (No
          4) with (1 HQ coy, 1 C^{3}I coy, 1 catering coy, 1
          security coy (Revenue Security Corps), 1 band)

Maritime Squadron
The AFM maritime element is organised into 5 Divisions:
Offshore Patrol; Inshore Patrol; Rapid Deployment and
Training; Marine Engineering and Logistics.
EQUIPMENT BY TYPE
PATROL AND COASTAL COMBATANTS 9
  OPV 1 *Diciotti*
  PCI 4: 2 *Bremse*; 2 *Swift*
  PBC 2 *Marine Protector*
  PB 2 *Cantieri Vittoria*

Air Wing
1 Base Party. 1 Flt Ops Div; 1 Maint Div; 1 Integrated Logs
Div; 1 Rescue Section
EQUIPMENT BY TYPE
AIRCRAFT
  TPT/MP 2 BN-2B *Islander*
  TRG 5 *Bulldog* T MK1

HELICOPTERS
SAR/UTL 7: 5 *Alouette* III SA-316B (2 utl, 3 SAR/utl); 2 Nardi-Hughes 500M
TRG 1 Bell 47G2

DEPLOYMENT

Legal provisions for foreign deployment:
Constitution: Codified constitution (1964)
Decision on deployment of troops abroad: The constitution does not regulate any responsibilities and mechanisms with regard to the use of armed forces abroad.

SERBIA
OSCE • Kosovo 1

FOREIGN FORCES

Italy 12 cbt spt MIATM (Missione Italiana d'Assistenza Tecnico Militare); Air Force: 37; 2 Bell 212 utl hel

Moldova MDA

Moldovan Leu L		2008	2009	2010
GDP	L	62.8bn	57.0bn	
	US$	6.2bn	5.1bn	
per capita	US$	1,410	1,188	
Growth	%	7.2	-9.0	
Inflation	%	12.7	1.4	
Def bdgt	L	223m	250m	
	US$	22m	22m	
US$1=L		10.3	11.1	

Population   4,320,748

Age	0 – 14	15 – 19	20 – 24	25 – 29	30 – 64	65 plus
Male	10%	5%	4%	4%	20%	4%
Female	10%	5%	4%	4%	23%	6%

Capabilities

ACTIVE 5,998 (Army 5,148 Air 850) **Paramilitary 2,379**
Terms of service 12 months

RESERVE 66,000 (Joint 66,000)

ORGANISATIONS BY SERVICE

Army 3,167; 1,981 conscript (total 5,148)
FORCES BY ROLE

Mot Inf	3 bde (1st, 2nd and 3rd)
SF	1 bn
Arty	1 bde
Engr	1 bn
Gd	1 (MOD) indep unit
Peacekeeping	1 bn (22nd)

EQUIPMENT BY TYPE
AIFV 44 BMD-1
APC 164
   APC (T) 64: 9 BTR-D; 55 MT-LB
   APC (W) 100: 11 BTR-80; 89 TAB-71
ARTY 148
   TOWED 69: **122mm** 17 (M-30) *M-1938*; **152mm** 52: 21 2A36; 31 D-20
   GUN/MOR • **SP 120mm** 9 2S9 *Anona*
   MRL 220mm 11 9P140 *Uragan*
   MOR 59: **82mm** 52; **120mm** 7 M-120
AT
   MSL • **MANPATS** 117: 71 AT-4 9K111 *Spigot*; 19 AT-5 9K113 *Spandrel*; 27 AT-6 9K114 *Spiral*
   RCL 73mm 138+ SPG-9
   GUNS 100mm 36 MT-12
AD • **GUNS** • **TOWED** 37: **23mm** 26 ZU-23; **57mm** 11 S-60
RADAR • **LAND** 1+: 1 L219/200 *PARK-1* (arty); GS-13 *Long Eye*/SNAR-1 *Long Trough* (arty); *Small Fred/Small Yawn*/SNAR-10 *Big Fred*/SNAR-2/-6 *Pork Trough* (veh, arty)

Air Force 850 (incl 360 conscripts)
1 Air Force base, 1 AD regt
FORCES BY ROLE

Trg/Tpt	2 sqn with An-2; Yak-18; An-26; An-72; Mi-8 PS *Hip*
SAM	1 regt with SA-3 *Goa*

EQUIPMENT BY TYPE
AIRCRAFT • **TPT** 6: 2 An-2; 1 Yak-18; 1 An-26; 2 An-72
HELICOPTERS • **SPT** 6: 5 Mi-8 MTV1, 1 Mi-8 PS *Hip*
AD • **SAM** 12 SA-3 *Goa*

Paramilitary 2,379
Ministry of Interior

OPON 900 (riot police)
Ministry of Interior

DEPLOYMENT

Legal provisions for foreign deployment:
Constitution: Codified constitution (1994)
Decision on deployment of troops abroad: By the parliament (Art. 66)

CÔTE D'IVOIRE
UN • UNOCI 3 obs

LIBERIA
UN • UNMIL 2 obs

SERBIA
OSCE • Serbia 2
OSCE • Kosovo 2

SUDAN
UN • UNMIS 2 obs

FOREIGN FORCES
Bulgaria OSCE 1
Estonia OSCE 2

Finland OSCE 1
France OSCE 1
Germany OSCE 1
Italy OSCE 1
Latvia OSCE 1
Poland OSCE 2
Tajikistan OSCE 1
Russia ε1,500 (including ε500 peacekeepers) Military Air Forces 7 Mi-24 *Hind* / Mi-8 *Hip* spt hel
Ukraine 10 mil obs (Joint Peacekeeping Force)
United Kingdom OSCE 1
United States OSCE 1

Montenegro MNE

Euro €		2008	2009	2010
GDP	€	2.1bn		
	US$	3.1bn		
per capita	US$	4,554		
Growth	%	7.5	-4.0	
Inflation	%	9.2	3.4	
Def bdgt	€	48.6m	40.8m	26.5m
	US$	71m	61m	
US$1=€		0.68	0.67	

Population	672,180

Capabilities

ACTIVE 3,127 (Army 2,500 Navy 401 Air Force 226)
Paramilitary 10,100

ORGANISATIONS BY SERVICE

Army ε2,500

FORCES BY ROLE
Comd   1 op comd
Mot inf   2 bde (2 inf regt (2 inf bn))
Lt Inf   1 Bde
SF   1 unit (forming)
Log   1 centre
Arty   1 coastal bn
Security   1 MP bn

EQUIPMENT BY TYPE
APC 8
  APC (W) 8 BOV-VP M-86
ARTY 138
  SP 18: **130mm** 18 M46
  TOWED 12: **122mm** 12 D-30
  MRL **122mm** 18 M63 *Plamen*/M 94 *Plamen* (SP)
  MOR 90: **82mm** 47; **120mm** 43
AT
  SP 10 M83
  MSL • MANPATS 117: 71 AT-4 9K111 *Spigot*; 19 AT-5 9K113 *Spandrel*; 27 AT-6 9K114 *Spiral*
  GUNS **100mm** 36 MT-12

Navy 401

A new armed forces organisational structure is under development (1 Naval Cmd HQ with 4 Operational Naval Units (Patrol Boat; Coastal Surveillance; Maritime Detachment and SAR) with additional Sig, Log and Trg units with a separate Coast Guard Element). Many listed units are in the process of decommissioning or sale.

EQUIPMENT BY TYPE
SUBMARINES • TACTICAL • SDV 2 † (*Mala*)
PRINCIPAL SURFACE COMBATANTS • FRIGATES
FFG 1 *Kotor* with 4 single each with 1 SS-N-2C *Styx* tactical SSM, 1 twin (2 eff.) with SA-N-4 *Gecko* SAM, 2 RBU 6000 *Smerch* 2 (24 eff.); (weapons systems removed; 2nd vessel planned for reactivation)
PATROL AND COASTAL COMBATANTS 4
  PFM 2 *Rade Koncar*
  PB 2 *Mirna* (Type140) (Police units)
MINE WARFARE • MINE COUNTERMEASURES 2
  MHC 2 *Sirius*
AMPHIBIOUS 11
  LCT 1 *Silba* (capacity either 6 medium tk or 7 APCs or 4 towed 130mm or 300 troops) with 1 quad (4 eff.) with SA-N-5 *Grail* SAM, up to 94 mine
  LCU 10: 3 (Type 21); 7 (Type 22)
LOGISTICS AND SUPPORT 3
AOTL 1; **TPT** 1 *Lubin* (PO-91); **AXS** 1

FACILITIES
Bases   Located at Kumbor, Novi Sad (river comd), Bar, Tivat

Air Force 226

Golubovci (Podgorica) air base under army command.
AC 18: 1 mixed sqn with 15 G-4 *Super Galeb* (of which 7-8 serviceable); 3 UTVA-75 (basic trg).
HEL 16: 1 sqn with separate army support, tpt and utlity flts. 15 SA 341/SA 342L *Gazelle* (7-8 serviceable) and 1 Mi-8T (stored awaiting overhaul)

Paramilitary ε10,100

Montenegrin Ministry of Interior Personnel ε6,000

Special Police Units ε4,100

DEPLOYMENT

LIBERIA
UN • UNMIL 2 obs

SERBIA
OSCE • Kosovo 1

Serbia SER

Serbian Dinar d		2008	2009	2010
GDP	d	2.73tr	2.99tr	
	US$	49.2bn	47.4bn	
per capita	US$	6,633	6,426	
Growth	%	5.4	-4.0	
Inflation	%	11.7	9.9	
Def bdgt	d	57.5bn	67.1bn	70.7bn
	US$	1.03bn	1.06bn	
US$1=d		55.7	63.1	

Population   7,379,339

Age	0 – 14	15 – 19	20 – 24	25 – 29	30 – 64	65 plus
Male	9%	4%	4%	4%	22%	6%
Female	9%	4%	4%	4%	23%	8%

Capabilities

ACTIVE 29,125 (Army 12,260, Air Force and Air Defence 4,262, Training Command 6,212, MoD 6,391)

RESERVE 50,171

Terms of service 6 months

ORGANISATIONS BY SERVICE

Army 10,460 conscripts 1,800 (12,260 in total)

Reconstruction continues

FORCES BY ROLE

Comd	1 Land Forces HQ
Mech	4 bde (3 (2nd 3rd and 4th) mech bde (*each:* 1 MRL bn, 1 SP arty bn, 1 AD bn, 1 inf bn, 2 mech inf bn, 1 tk bn); 1 (1st) Mech bde (1 AD bn, 2 Mech Inf bn, 1 Inf bn, 1 SP arty bn, 1 MRL bn, 1 engr bn))
Gd	1 bde (ceremonial, 2 MP bn, 1 anti terrorist bn)
SF	1 bde with (1 anti terrorist, 1 cdo, 1 para bn)
Engr	4 bn
Sig	1 bn
Arty	7 bn, 1 (mixed) bde (3 arty bn, 1MRL bn)
Riverine	2 det (under review), 2 pontoon br bn
NBC	1 bn

EQUIPMENT BY TYPE

MBT 212: 199 M-84; 13 T-72
RECCE 46: 46 BRDM-2
AIFV 323 M-80
APC 39 BOV VP M-86
ARTY 515
   SP 122mm 67 2S1 *Carnation*
   TOWED 204: **122mm** 78 D-30; **130mm** 18 M-46; **152mm** 36 M-84; **155mm** 72: 66 M-1; 6 M-65
   MRL 81: **128mm** 78: 18 M-63 *Plamen*; 60 M-77 *Organj*; **262mm** 3 *Orkan*
   MOR 163: **82mm** 106 M-69; **120mm** 57: M-74/ M-75

AT • MSL
   SP 48 BOV-1 (M-83) AT-3 9K11 *Sagger*
   MANPATS 168: 99 AT-3 9K11 *Sagger*; 69 AT-4 9K111 *Fagot (Spigot)*
   RCL 6: **90mm** 6 M-79;
AD • SAM 156
   SP 77 SA-6 *Gainful*; 12 *S-1M* (SA-9 *Gaskin*); 5 *SAVA S10M*;
   MANPADS 62: 8 S-2M (SA-7 *Strela*-2); 54 SA-16 *Šilo*
GUNS 36
   TOWED 40mm: 36 L70 Bofors

Reserve Organisations

Territorial brigades 8.

Air Force and Air Defence 3,785 (plus 477 conscipts) Total 4,262

Comprises a Cmd HQ, 2 air bases (Batajnica near Belgrade and Ladevci, central Serbia), 1 SAM bde; 1 centre for early warning and reporting, 1 comms bn and 1 eng bn.

Flying hours: Ftr – 40 per yr

FORCES BY ROLE

Ftr	1 sqn with MiG-29 *Fulcrum* and /MiG-21bis
FGA	1 sqn with J-22 *Orao 1* and N-62 G-4 *Super Galeb*
Recce	2 flts with IJ-22 *Orao 1**; MiG-21R *Fishbed H**
Tpt	2 sqns (1 tpt and 1 hel) with An-26, Jak-40, Do-28, An-2, Mi-8, Mi-17, Mi-24
Trg	1 sqn with UTVA 75 (basic trg), H-62 G-4 *Super Galeb* (adv trg/light atk), Ho-42-45 SA-341/342 *Gazelle*
Cbt hel	1 sqn with Hn-42/45 and Mi-24
SAM	1 bde (4 bn) with SA-3 (Neva); SA-6 *Kub*, SA-7/16 MANPAD
EW	2 bns for early warning and reporting

EQUIPMENT BY TYPE

AIRCRAFT 83 combat capable
   FTR 29: 3 MiG-29B *Fulcrum*; 1 MiG-29UB *Fulcrum*; 20 MiG-21bis *Fishbed L & N*; 5 MiG-21UM *Mongol B*
   FGA 42: 22 J-22 *Orao 1*; 20 N-62 G-4 *Super Galeb*
   RECCE 12: 10 I J-22R *Orao 1**; 2 MiG-21R *Fishbed H**
   TPT 8: 4 An-26 *Curl*; 1 An-2; 1 Do-28 *Skyservant*; 2 JAK-40
   TRG 8 UTVA-75
HELICOPTERS
   SPT 65: 9 HT-40, 16 Ho-42/45, 2 Hi-42, 34 HN-42/45, 2 Mi-24, 2 Mi-17
AD • SAM 6 SA-3; 9 SA-6
MANPADS 156 SA-7/16
GUNS 24 40mm L-70 Bofors
MSL
AAM: 20 AA-8 (R-60R; R-60MK); AA-10 (R-27R1) and AA-11 (R-73) are time expired
ASM AGM-65 *Maverick*, A-77 *Thunder*

DEPLOYMENT

Legal provisions for foreign deployment:
Constitution: Codified constitution (2006)

Decision on deployment of troops abroad: By parliament (Art. 140)

CÔTE D'IVOIRE
UN • UNOCI 3 obs

DEMOCRATIC REPUBLIC OF CONGO
UN • MONUC 6 (Air Medical Evacuation Team)

LIBERIA
UN • UNMIL 4 obs

FOREIGN FORCES
All OSCE.
Bosnia-Herzegovina 2
Croatia 1
Estonia 2
France 1
Georgia 1
Germany 3
Greece 1
Hungary 1
Ireland 2
Italy 3
Moldova 2
Netherlands 3
Norway 3
Slovakia 1
Slovenia 1
Sweden 4
Turkey 2
Ukraine 1
United Kingdom 3
United States 4

TERRITORY WHERE THE GOVERNMENT DOES NOT EXERCISE EFFECTIVE CONTROL

Data presented here represent the *de facto* situation in Kosovo. This does not imply international recognition as a sovereign state. In February 2008 Kosovo declared itself independent. Serbia remains opposed to this, and while Kosovo has not been admitted to the United Nations, a number of states have recognised Kosovo's self-declared status.

FOREIGN FORCES

All under Kosovo Force (KFOR) comd. unless otherwise specified. KFOR has been deployed in Kosovo since 1999.
Armenia 70 • OSCE (Kosovo) 1
Austria 447; 1 inf bn HQ; 2 inf coy; elm 1 hel bn; elm 1 recce coy; elm 1 engr coy; elm 1 MP coy; elm 1 log unit• OSCE (Kosovo) 15
Azerbaijan OSCE (Kosovo) 3
Belarus OSCE (Kosovo) 2
Belgium 219; 1 mech inf coy
Bosnia-Herzegovina OSCE (Kosovo) 7

Bulgaria 47; elm 1 engr coy • OSCE (Kosovo) 3
Canada 6 • OSCE (Kosovo) 2
Chile UNMIK 1 obs
Croatia 20 • OSCE (Kosovo) 7
Czech Republic 393; 1 inf coy
Denmark 242; 1 inf gp (1 scout sqn, 1 inf coy) • UNMIK 1 obs
Estonia 31; 1 inf pl
Finland 405; 1 inf coy; 1 int/surv/recce coy; 1 log coy • OSCE (Kosovo) 2
France 1,294; 1 armd inf BG; 1 Gendarmerie regt; some spt unit (incl atk hel) • OSCE (Kosovo) 14
Georgia OSCE (Kosovo) 4
Germany 2,486; 1 inf bn HQ; 3 inf coy; elm 1 hel bn; elm 1 recce coy; elm 1 engr coy; 1 sigs bn; 1 CIMIC coy; elm 1 log unit; elm 1 MP coy; 1 med unit; 26 C2 *Leopard* MBT; 17 SPz-2 *Luchs* recce; 25 *Marder* 1 AIFV; 21 APC (T); 54 TPz-1 *Fuchs* APC (W); 10 M-109A3G 155mm SP; 6 *Wiesel* (TOW) msl; 3 CH-53G *Stallion* spt hel; 9 UH-1D *Iroquois* utl hel • OSCE (Kosovo) 16
Greece 588; 2 mech inf bn • OSCE (Kosovo) 5
Hungary 243; 1 mot inf coy • OSCE (Kosovo) 4
Ireland 233; 1 mech inf coy; 1 log coy • UNMIK 4 obs • OSCE (Kosovo) 7
Italy 1,819; 1 mech inf BG; 1 engr unit;1 hel unit; 1 sigs unit; 1 CSS unit; • OSCE (Kosovo) 14
Lithuania 36 • OSCE (Kosovo) 1
Luxembourg 23
Macedonia, Former Yugoslav Republic of OSCE (Kosovo) 3
Malta OSCE (Kosovo) 1
Moldova OSCE (Kosovo) 2
Montenegro OSCE (Kosovo) 1
Morocco 222; 1 inf det
Netherlands 8 • OSCE (Kosovo) 3
Norway 6 • UNMIK 1 obs
Pakistan UNMIK 1 obs
Poland 226; elm 1 inf bn • UNMIK 1 obs • OSCE (Kosovo) 2
Portugal 295; 1 inf bn (KTM) • UNMIK 2 obs • OSCE (Kosovo) 5
Romania 145 • UNMIK 2 obs • OSCE (Kosovo) 4
Russia UNMIK 1 obs • OSCE (Kosovo) 2
Slovakia 145; 1 inf coy • OSCE (Kosovo) 1
Slovenia 389; 1 inf bn HQ; 2 mot inf coy; 1 engr gp
Spain UNMIK 1 obs • OSCE (Kosovo) 10
Sweden 245; 1 inf coy • OSCE (Kosovo) 2
Switzerland 207; 1 inf coy; 1 spt coy; elm 1 hel bn; elm 1 MP coy; elm 1 log unit
Turkey 509; 1 inf bn HQ; 2 inf coy; 1 marine coy; 1 log coy; 1 Gendarmerie pl; elm 1 hel bn; elm 1 recce coy; elm 1 engr coy; elm 1 MP coy • UNMIK 1 obs • OSCE (Kosovo) 10
Ukraine 180 • UNMIK 1 obs • OSCE (Kosovo) 2
United Kingdom 8; • OSCE (Kosovo) 4
United States 1,475; 1 ARNG cbt spt bde• OSCE (Kosovo) 11
Uzbekistan OSCE (Kosovo) 2

Sweden SWE

Swedish Krona Skr		2008	2009	2010
GDP	Skr	3.15tr	2.99tr	
	US$	479bn	429bn	
per capita	US$	52,945	47,367	
Growth	%	-0.2	-4.8	
Inflation	%	3.3	2.2	
Def bdgt[a]	Skr	39.9bn	39.2bn	39.4bn
	US$	6.06bn	5.61bn	
US$1=Skr		6.59	6.97	

[a] Excluding Civil Defence

Population   9,059,651

Age	0 – 14	15 – 19	20 – 24	25 – 29	30 – 64	65 plus
Male	9%	3%	3%	3%	24%	7%
Female	8%	3%	3%	3%	23%	10%

Capabilities

ACTIVE 13,050 (Army 5,900 Navy 2,850 Air 4,300)
Paramilitary 800 Voluntary Auxiliary Organisations 42,000

Terms of service: Army, Navy, Air Force 10–11 months

RESERVE 200,000

ORGANISATIONS BY SERVICE

Army 4,400; 1,500 conscript (total 5,900)

FORCES BY ROLE
1 Joint Forces Comd, 22 Training Detachments whose main task is to provide support to the Home Guard and other voluntary defence organisations; the Military Districts were disbanded in 2005. The army has been transformed to provide brigade sized task forces depending on the operational requirement. Sweden provided the majority of forces to the EU Nordic Battlegroup.

Army	1 Div HQ (on mobilisation); 2 Bde Hq
Armd	3 regt
Cav	1 regt
Mech	8 bn
Arty	2 bn
AD	3 bn
Engr	3 bn
Log	2 bn
Home Guard	60 bn

EQUIPMENT BY TYPE
MBT 280: 120 Strv-122 (*Leopard 2*); 160 Strv-121 (*Leopard* 2A4)
AIFV 336 Strv 9040 (CV 9040)
APC 687
  APC (T) 519: 137 Pbv 401A (56 Ambulance version 4020); 332 Pbv 302; 50 Bv S 10 *Viking*
  APC (W) 168 XA-180 *Sisu*/XA-203 *Sisu*
ARTY 280
  SP 24 *Archer* (being delivered)

TOWED 155mm 49 FH-77B
MOR 120mm 207
AT • MSL • MANPATS RB-55; RB-56 *Bill*
  RCL 84mm *Carl Gustav*
  RL 84mm AT-4
AIRCRAFT
  UAV • TACTICAL 3 *Sperwer*
AD • SAM
  SP 16 RBS-70
  TOWED RBS-90
  MANPAD RBS-70
  GUNS • SP 40mm 30 Strv 90LV
RADAR • LAND ARTHUR (arty); M-113 A1GE *Green Archer* (mor)

Navy 1,800; 400 (Coastal Defence); 650 conscript; (total 2,850)

FORCES BY ROLE
Maritime forces restructured

Navy	2 Surface flotillas
Maritime	1 Surveillance and info bn
Amph	1 Amph bde (1 Amph bn)
SS	1 Submarine flotilla
Log	1 bn

EQUIPMENT BY TYPE
SUBMARINES • TACTICAL • SSK4:
  2 *Gotland* (AIP fitted) each with 2 x1 400mm TT with 6 Tp 432/Tp 451, 4 single 533mm TT with 12 Tp 613/Tp 62
  2 *Sodermanland* (AIP fitted) each with 6 single 533mm TT with 12 Tp 613/Tp 62, 6 Tp 432/Tp 451
  SSI 1 *Spiggen II* midget submarine
PRINCIPAL SURFACE COMBATANTS • CORVETTES
  FSG 5 *Visby* with 8 RBS-15 SSM, 4 single ASTT each with Tp 45 LWT, Saab 601 mortar, 1 Bofors 57mm, 1 hel landing plaform (for med hel); (1st of class assuming interim operational role 2008; additional vessels ISDs expected by 2010)
PATROL AND COASTAL COMBATANTS 14
  PFM 2:
    2 *Stockholm* each with 4 single ASTT (may not be fitted) each with Tp 431 LWT, 4 twin (8 eff.) each with RBS-15M tactical SSM, 4 Saab 601 mortars
  PCR 12 *Tapper*
MINE WARFARE 22
  MINE COUNTERMEASURES 17
    MCMV 4: 3 *Styrso*; 1 *Uto*
    MHC 7: 2 *Landsort*; 5 *Koster*
    MSD 6: 5 *Sam*; 1 *Sokaren*
  MINELAYERS 5
    ML(I) 2
    MLC 3
AMPHIBIOUS
  LCM 17 *Trossbat*
  LCU 23
  LCPL 145 *Combatboat*
LOGISTICS AND SUPPORT 30:
  ARS 1 *Furusund* (former ML)
  AG 6: 2; 1 *Carlskrona* with 1 hel landing platform (former ML); 1 *Trosso* (Spt ship for corvettes and patrol vessels

but can also be used as HQ ship); 2 *Arkosund* (former ML); 2 (various)

AK 1 *Visborg*
AKSL 1
AGI 1
AGS 2
Trg 3: 2 **AXS**; 1 *Gassten*
TPT 1
TRV 2
YDT 1
YTM 2
YTL 9

FACILITIES

Bases   Located Karlskrona, naval det at Muskö

Support base   Located at Göteborg

Coastal Defence 600

FORCES BY ROLE

Amph   1 bde; 1 bn

EQUIPMENT BY TYPE

APC (W) 3+ *Piranha*
ARTY • MOR 81mm; **120mm** 70
AD • SAM RBS-70
MSL • SSM 96: 6 RBS-15KA; 90 RBS-17 *Hellfire*
GUNS 24+: **40mm** L-70; **75mm**; **105mm**; **120mm** 24 CD-80 *Karin* (mobile)

Air Force 3,800; 500 conscript (total 4,300)

Flying hours   110 to 140 hrs/year

Units: F 7, Skaraborg Wing in Såtenäs; F 17, Blekinge Wing in Ronneby; F 21, Norrbotten Wing in Luleå; Helicopter Wing in Linköping (also operates in Luleå, Såtenäs and Ronneby; Air Combat School (LSS) in Uppsala

FORCES BY ROLE

COMD   1 HQ (2 air base bn)

Ftr/FGA/Recce 4 sqn with JAS 39 A/B (C/D) *Gripen*:

SIGINT   1 sqn with S-102B (Gulfstream IV SRA-4)

AEW   1 sqn with S-100B *Argus*

Tpt   1 sqn with C-130E *Hercules*/Tp-84 (C-130H) *Hercules*

Trg   1 trg school with SK-60

AD   1 (fighter control and air surv) bn

EQUIPMENT BY TYPE

AIRCRAFT 165 combat capable
   MULTIROLE 165: 82 JAS 39A/14 39B *Gripen* (31 JAS A/B to be updated to C/D standard); 56 JAS 39C/13 39D *Gripen* (By 2012, will have reduced to 75 JAS 39C and 25 JAS 39D)
   EW • ELINT 2 S-102B (Gulfstream IV SRA-4)
   AEW 2 S-100B *Argus*
   TPT 16: 8 C-130E *Hercules*/Tp-84 (C-130H) *Hercules* (7 tpt, 1 tkr); 1 Tp-100A (VIP); 2 Tp-102A (Gulfstream IV); 5 Tp-100A (Saab 340)
   TRG 80 SK-60
MSL
   ASM RB-15F; RB-75 (AGM-65) *Maverick*
   AAM RB-99 (AIM-120B) *AMRAAM*; RB-74 (AIM-9L) *Sidewinder*; RB-71 (*Sky Flash*)
BOMB BK-39

Armed Forces Hel Wing (included in Air Force figures)

FORCES BY ROLE

Hel   1 bn with 1 HKP-14 (NH 90); 8 HKP-10 (AS-332) *Super Puma* (SAR); 14 HKP-4 (Boeing Vertol 107) (ASW/tpt/SAR); 19 HKP-15 (A-109M); 17 HKP-9A (Bo-105CB) (trg)

EQUIPMENT BY TYPE

HELICOPTERS
   SPT 11: 3 HKP-14 (NH 90); 8 HKP-10 (AS-332) *Super Puma* (SAR)
   UTL 36: 19 HKP-15 (A-109M); 17 HKP-9A (Bo-105CB) (trg)

Paramilitary 800

Coast Guard 800

PATROL AND COASTAL COMBATANTS 28
   PSOH 1 *KBV-001*(2 Additional vessels in build expected ISD 2010)
   PSO 2 *KBV-181* (fishery protection)
   PCO 2 *KBV-201*
   PCC 2 *KBV-101*
   PCI 20
LOGISTICS AND SUPPORT 12 **AG** (MARPOL-CRAFT)

Air Arm

AIRCRAFT • HP/SAR 3 DASH 8Q-300

DEPLOYMENT

Legal provisions for foreign deployment:
Constitution: Constitution consists of four fundamental laws; the most important is 'The Instrument of Government' (1974)
Decision on deployment of troops abroad: By the government upon parliamentary approval (Ch. 10, Art. 9)

AFGHANISTAN
NATO • ISAF 430
UN • UNAMA 1

BOSNIA-HERZEGOVINA
OSCE • Bosnia and Herzegovina 3

DEMOCRATIC REPUBLIC OF CONGO
UN • MONUC 4 obs

INDIA/PAKISTAN
UN • UNMOGIP 5 obs

KOREA, REPUBLIC OF
NNSC • 5 obs

MIDDLE EAST
UN • UNTSO 7 obs

NEPAL
UN • UNMIN 2 obs

SERBIA
NATO • KFOR 245; 1 inf coy
OSCE • Serbia 4
OSCE • Kosovo2

SUDAN
UN • UNMIS 2; 1 obs

Switzerland CHE

Swiss Franc fr		2008	2009	2010
GDP	fr	532bn	528bn	
	US$	493bn	518bn	
per capita	US$	64,973	68,071	
Growth	%	1.7	-2.0	
Inflation	%	2.4	-0.4	
Def bdgt	fr	4.45bn	4.51bn	4.90bn
	US$	4,12bn	4.42bn	
US$1=fr		1.08	1.02	

Population	7,604,467					

Age	0 – 14	15 – 19	20 – 24	25 – 29	30 – 64	65 plus
Male	9%	3%	3%	3%	25%	6%
Female	8%	3%	3%	3%	25%	9%

Capabilities

ACTIVE 22,059 (Joint 4,059, 18,000 conscript)

RESERVE 174,071 (Army 123,720, Air 27,151, Armed Forces Logistic Organisation 10,800 Command Support Organisation 12,400)

Civil Defence 80,000

Terms of service 18 weeks compulsory recruit trg at age 19–20 (19,000 (2006)), followed by 7 refresher trg courses (3 weeks each) over a 10-year period between ages 20–30. (189,000 continuation trg (2006))

ORGANISATIONS BY SERVICE

Joint 4,059 active; 18,000 conscript; 197,272 on mobilisation; (total 22,059 – 197,272)

Armed Forces Logistic Organisation 10,800 on mobilisation

Log 1 bde

Command Support Organisation 12,400 on mobilisation

Spt 1 (comd) bde

Land Forces (Army) 123,720

With the exception of military security all units are non-active. Re-organisation is due to be completed by end 2010 and is reflected below.

FORCES BY ROLE
4 Territorial Regions

Comd   4 regional ((1st and 4th, with (1 sig bn, 2 (disaster relief) engr bn); 2nd and 3rd, with (1 sigs bn, 1 (disaster relief) engr bn, 1 engr bn))

Armd   1 bde (1st) (3 tk bn, 1 recce bn, 1 mech inf bn, 1 sigs bn, 1 sp arty bn, 1 engr bn);
1 bde (11th) (2 tk bn, 1 mech inf bn, 1 armd recce bn, 1 ISTAR bn, 1 SP arty bn, 1 armd engr bn, 1 sigs bn)

Armd/Arty 1 trg unit
Inf   1 trg unit;
2 bde (2nd and 5th) (4 inf bn, 1 recce bn, 1 SP arty bn, 1 sigs bn);
1 bde (4th) to be dissolved 2010 (4 inf bn, 1 arty bn, 1 armd recce bn, 1 armd engr bn, 1 sigs bn

Mtn Inf   1 bde (9th) (5 mtn inf bn , 1 SP Arty bn, 1 sigs bn,);
1 bde (12th) (3 mtn inf bn, 2 inf bn 1 fortress arty bn, 1 sigs bn);
1 bde (10th (2 armd bn, 2 mtn inf bn, 2 (mt) rifle bn, 1 armd recce bn, 1 SP arty bn, 2 sigs bn)

Engr Rescue 1 bde (trg)
Sigs   1 bde (trg)
Supply   1 bde (trg)
Sy   1 bde

EQUIPMENT BY TYPE
MBT 353 Pz-87 *Leo* (*Leopard 2*)
RECCE 329: 154 *Eagle I*; 175 *Eagle II*
AIFV 154 CV9030
   APC (W) 407 *Piranha*
AIFV/APC look-a-likes 538: M-113/*Piranha* II (8x8)/*Piranha* IIIC (8x8)/CV 9030 CP
ARTY 884
   SP 155mm 348 M-109/U
   MOR434: **SP 120mm** 132 M-64
   81mm 302 M-113 with M-72/91
AT
   MSL
    SP 110 TOW-2 SP Mowag *Piranha*
    MANPATS 3,393 M47 *Dragon*
   RL 67mm 10,958 PZF 44 *Panzerfaust*
AD • SAM • MANPAD FIM-92A *Stinger*
UAV • TACTICAL *Ranger*
PATROL AND COASTAL COMBATANTS
   PBR 11 *Aquarius*

Air Force 27,151 (incl air defence units and military airfield guard units)

Flying hours   200–250 hrs/year

FORCES BY ROLE

Ftr   3 sqn with 26 F/A-18C/ 7 F/A-18D *Hornet*; 3 sqn with 42 *Tiger II/F-5E*, 12 F-5F *Tiger II/F-5F*

Tpt   1 sqn with 15 PC-6 *Turbo-Porter*; 1*Falcon-50*; 1 Cessna XL *Citation*; 1 DHC-6 *Twin Otter*; 1 Beech 350 *Super King Air*; 1 *Beechcraft* 1900D; 1 PC-12 and 1 PC-6 owned by amarsuisse

Trg   1 sqn with 33 PC-7 *Turbo Trainer*; 6 PC-21; 1 sqn with 11 PC-9 (tgt towing)

Hel   6 sqn with 15 AS-332 *Super Puma*; 12 AS-532 *Cougar*; 18 SA-316 *Alouette III*; 16 EC-635

UAV   1 bn with 4 Systems ADS 95 *Ranger*

EQUIPMENT BY TYPE
AIRCRAFT 87 combat capable
   FTR 54: 42 F-5E *Tiger II*; 12 F-5F *Tiger II*
   FGA 33: 26 F/A-18C *Hornet*; 7 F/A-18D *Hornet*

TPT 20: 15 PC-6 *Turbo-Porter*; 1 *Falcon*-50; 1 Cessna *XL Citation*; 1 DHC-6 *Twin Otter*; 1 Beech 350 *Super King Air*; 1 *Beechcraft* 1900D; 1 PC-12 and 1 PC-6 (owned by armasuisse, civil registration)
TRG 50: 33 PC-7 *Turbo Trainer*; 6 PC-21; 11 PC-9 (tgt towing)
HELICOPTERS
SPT 15 AS-332 *Super Puma*
UTL 44: 12 AS-532 *Cougar*; 16 SA-316 *Alouette III*; 16 EC635
UAV • RECCE 4 Systems ADS 95 *Ranger*
MSL • AAM AIM-120B *AMRAAM*; AIM-9P/X *Sidewinder*

Ground Based Air Defence (GBAD)

FORCES BY ROLE
ADA GBAD assets can be used to form AD clusters to be deployed independently as task forces within Swiss territory. Equipment includes a number of *Rapier* guided missile systems, *Stinger* MANPADS and 35mm AA guns 63/90 backed up by the *Skyguard* fire control system

EQUIPMENT BY TYPE
AD • SAM • TOWED *Rapier*
  MANPAD FIM-92A *Stinger*
  GUNS 35mm
  RADARS • AD RADARS *Skyguard*

Civil Defence 80,000

(not part of armed forces)

DEPLOYMENT

Legal provisions for foreign deployment:
Constitution: Codified constitution (1999)
Decision on deployment of troops abroad:
Peace promotion (66, 66a, 66b Swiss Mil Law): UN.OSCE mandate. Decision by govt; if over 100 tps deployed or op over 3 weeks Fed Assembly must agree first, except in emergency.
Support service abroad (69, 60 Swiss Mil Law): Decision by govt; if over 2,000 tps or op over 3 weeks Fed Assembly must agree in next official session

BOSNIA-HERZEGOVINA
EU • EUFOR • *Operation Althea* 25

BURUNDI
UN • BINUB 1 mil advisor

DEMOCRATIC REPUBLIC OF CONGO
UN • MONUC 3 obs

KOREA, REPUBLIC OF
NNSC • 5 officers

MIDDLE EAST
UN • UNTSO 10 obs

NEPAL
UN • UNMIN 3 monitors

SERBIA
NATO • KFOR • *Joint Enterprise* 207 (military volunteers); 1 inf coy; 1 spt coy; elm 1 hel bn; elm 1 MP coy; elm 1 log unit; 2 hel

Ukraine UKR

Ukrainian Hryvnia h		2008	2009	2010
GDP	h	949bn	892bn	
	US$	180bn	108bn	
per capita	US$	3,923	2,369	
Growth	%	2.1	-14.0	
Inflation	%	25.3	16.3	
Def bdgt	hª	9.49bn	11.65bn	
	US$	1.80bn	1.41bn	
FMA (US)	US$	6.0m	7.0m	16.0m
US$1=h		5.26	8.24	

ª = excluding military pensions

Population   45,700,395

Ethnic groups: Ukrainian 77.8%; Russian 17.3%; Belarussian 0.6%; Moldovan 0.5%; Crimean Tatar 0.5%

Age	0 – 14	15 – 19	20 – 24	25 – 29	30 – 64	65 plus
Male	8%	4%	4%	4%	21%	5%
Female	8%	4%	4%	4%	25%	10%

Capabilities

ACTIVE 129,925 (Army 70,753 Navy 13,932 Air 45,240) **Paramilitary 84,900**
Terms of Service Army, Air Force 18 months, Navy 2 years

RESERVE 1,000,000 (Joint 1,000,000)
mil service within 5 years

ORGANISATIONS BY SERVICE

Ground Forces (Army) 70,753

FORCES BY ROLE
The three army mechanised corps are now under command of Army HQ and the territorial commands will be disbanded. Transformation of the army is due to be completed by 2015. The proposed structure is: a Joint Rapid Reaction Force; a Main Defence Force; and Strategic Reserve. Some units will become subordinate to Army HQ namely a msl bde, SF and a NBC protection group. The resulting 3 corps (div) formation organisation is:

Comd   1 (ground forces) comd (1 AM bde, 1 SSM bde, 2 SF regts, 1 Presidential Guard regt, 1 engr regt); 1 (MoD) gp (1 engr bde, 1 sy bde)
6 Corps   1 tk bde, 3 mech bde, 1 AB bde, 1 arty bde, 1 MRL regt, 1 AD regt
8 Corps   1 tk bde, 2 mech bde, 1 AM bde, 1 arty bde, 1 AD regt
13 Corps   3 mech bde, 1 mech regt, 1 AM regt, 1 arty bde, 1 MRL regt, 1 AD regt

FORCES BY ROLE:
Tk   2 bde
Mech   8 bde, 1 regt
AB   1 bde

Air Mob	2 bde, 1 regt
Arty	3 bde, 2 MRL regt
AD	3 regt
SF	2 regt
SSM	1 bde

Northern Op Comd

To be disbanded

Southern Op Comd Administrative

From Western Comd the 6th and 13th Corps will form. The likely composition for the 6th is 2 mech bde (3), 1 tank bde (1), 1 air mob bde (1) and arty bde . The 13th bde in scheduled to be composed of 1 light inf bde (0), 2 mech inf bde (3) and 1 arty bde (1). Present number of bde shown in ()

Western Op Comd Administrative

EQUIPMENT BY TYPE
MBT 2,988: 10 T-84-120 *Oplot* (development complete) 167 T-80; 1,032 T-72; 1,667 T-64; 112 T-55
RECCE 600+ BRDM-2
AIFV 3,028: BMD 138: 60 BMD-1; 78 BMD-2; 994 BMP-1; 1,434 BMP-2; 4 BMP-3; 458 BRM-1K
APC 1,432
  APC (T) 44 BTR-D
  APC (W) 1,398: up to 10 BTR 4; 136 BTR-60; 857 BTR-70; 395 BTR-80
ARTY 3,351
  SP 1,226: **122mm** 600 2S1 *Carnation*; **152mm** 527: 40 2S19 *Farm*; 463 2S3; 24 2S5; **203mm** 99 2S7
  TOWED 1,065: **122mm** 371: 369 D-30; 2 (M-30) *M-1938*; **152mm** 694: 287 2A36; 185 2A65; 215 D-20; 7 ML-70
  GUN/MOR 120mm 69:
    SP 67 2S9 *Anona*
    TOWED 2 2B16 *NONA-K*
  MRL 554: **122mm** 335: 20 9P138; 315 BM-21; **132mm** 2 BM-13; **220mm** 137 9P140 *Uragan*; **300mm** 80 9A52 *Smerch*
  MOR 120mm 437: 318 2S12; 119 PM-38
AT • MSL • MANPATS AT-4 9K111 *Spigot*/AT-5 9K113 *Spandrel*/AT-6 9K114 *Spiral*
  GUNS 100mm ε500 MT-12/T-12
HELICOPTERS
  ATK 139 Mi-24 *Hind*
  SPT 38 Mi-8 *Hip*
AD • SAM • SP 435: 60 SA-11 *Gadfly*; ε150 SA-13 *Gopher*; 100 SA-4 *Ganef*; 125 SA-8 *Gecko*
  GUNS 470:
    SP 30mm 70 2S6
    TOWED 57mm ε400 S-60
RADAR • LAND *Small Fred/Small Yawn/SNAR-10 Big Fred* (arty)
MSL • SSM 212: 50 FROG; 90 SS-21 *Scarab* (*Tochka*); 72 *Scud*-B

Navy 11,932; 2,000 conscript (total 13,932 incl. Naval Aviation and Naval Infantry)

After intergovernmental agreement in 1997, the Russian Federation Fleet currently leases bases in Sevastopol and Karantinnaya Bays and also shares facilities jointly with Ukr warships at Streletskaya Bay. The overall serviceability of the fleet is assessed as low.

EQUIPMENT BY TYPE
SUBMARINES • TACTICAL • SSK 1 *Foxtrot* (T-641)†
PRINCIPAL SURFACE COMBATANTS 4
  FRIGATES 1
    FF 1 *Hetman Sagaidachny* (RUS *Krivak* III) with 1 Twin (2 eff.) with 20 SA-N-4 *Gecko* SAM, 2 quad 533mm ASTT (8 eff.) each with T-53 HWT, 1 100mm gun, (capacity 1 Ka-27 *Helix* ASW hel)
  CORVETTES • FS 3 *Grisha* (II/V) each with 1 twin (2 eff.) with 20 SA-N-4 *Gecko* SAM, up to 2 RBU 6000 *Smerch* 2 (24 eff.), 2 twin 533mm ASTT (4 eff.) each with SAET-60 HWT, 1 76mm gun
PATROL AND COASTAL COMBATANTS 5
  PFM 1 *Tarantul II*
  PHM 2 *Matka* each with 2 single with 2 SS-N-2C *Styx*/ SS-N-2D *Styx*, 1 76mm gun
  PFT 1 *Pauk* I with 1 quad with 4 SA-N-5 *Grail* SAM, 4 Single 406mm TT, 1 76mm gun
  PCI 1 *Zhuk*
MINE WARFARE • MINE COUNTERMEASURES 4
  MHC 1 *Yevgenya*
  MSC 1 *Sonya*
  MSO 2 *Natya*
AMPHIBIOUS
  LS 2:
    LSM 1 *Polnochny* C (capacity 6 MBT; 180 troops)
    LST 1 *Ropucha* with 4 quad (16 eff.) each with SA-N-5 *Grail* SAM, 2 57mm twin gun (4 eff.), 92 mine, (capacity either 10 MBT or 190 troops; either 24 APC (T) or 170 troops)
  CRAFT ACV 1 *Pomornik* (*Zubr*) each with 2 quad (8 eff.) each with SA-N-5 *Grail* SAM, (capacity 230 troops; either 3 MBT or 10 APC (T))
LOGISTICS AND SUPPORT 36
  AGF 1 *Bambuk*
  AR 1 *Amur* (can also act as a comd. ship or as a spt ship for surface ships and submarines)
  AWT 1
  AGS 2: 1 *Moma* (mod); 1 *Biya*
  ABU 1
  TRG • 3 AXL
  YDG 1
  YDT 20: 8 *Yelva*; 12
  YTM 6

FACILITIES

Bases	Located at Sevastopol, Kerch, Donuzlav, Chernomorskoye, Odessa, Ochakov
Construction and Repair Yards	Located at Nikolaev, Balaklava

Naval Aviation ε2,500

AIRCRAFT 10 combat capable
  ASW 10 Be-12 *Mail**
  TPT 16: 5 An-12 *Cub*; 1 An-24 *Coke*; 8 An-26 *Curl*; 1 Il-18 *Coot*; 1 Tu-134 *Crusty*
HELICOPTERS
  ASW 72: 28 Ka-25 *Hormone*; 2 Ka-27E *Helix*; 42 Mi-14 *Haze*
  SPT 5: 5 Mi-6 *Hook*

Naval Infantry 3,000

Naval inf 1 bde

Air Forces 45,240

Air   3 air cmd – West, South, Centre plus Task Force 'Crimea'. Flying hours 40-50hrs/yr

FORCES BY ROLE

Ftr   5 bde with MiG-29 *Fulcrum*; Su-27 *Flanker*

FGA/Bbr   2 bde with Su-24M *Fencer*; Su-25 *Frogfoot*

Recce   2 sqn with Su-24MR *Fencer**

Tpt   3 bde with An-24; An-26; An-30; Tu-134 *Crusty*; Il-76 *Candid*

Spt hel   sqns with Mi-8; Mi-9; PZL Mi-2 *Hoplite*

Trg   sqns with L-39 *Albatros*

EQUIPMENT BY TYPE

AIRCRAFT 211 combat capable
  FTR 116: 80 MiG-29 *Fulcrum*; 36 Su-27 *Flanker*
  FGA 72: 36 Su-25 *Frogfoot*; 36 Su-24 *Fencer*
  RECCE 23 Su-24MR*
  TPT 49: 3 An-24 *Coke*; 21 An-26 *Curl*; 3 An-30; 2 Tu-134 *Crusty*; 20 Il-76 *Candid*
  TRG 39 L-39 *Albatros*
HELICOPTERS • SPT 38: 4 Mi-9; 31 Mi-8 *Hip*; 3 PZL Mi-2 *Hoplite*
AD • SAM 825 SA-10 *Grumble* (quad)/SA-11 *Gadfly*/SA-12A *Gladiator* SA-2 *Guideline* (towed)/ SA-3 *Goa* (towed)/ SA-5 *Gammon* (static)/SA-6 *Gainful*
MSL
  ASM: AS-10 *Karen*; AS-11 *Kilter*; AS-12 *Kegler*; AS-13 *Kingbolt*; AS-14 *Kedge*; AS-15 *Kent*; AS-9 *Kyle*
  ARM: AS-11 *Kilter*; AS-12 *Kegler*
  AAM: AA-10 *Alamo*; AA-7 *Apex*; AA-8 *Aphid*; AA-9 *Amos*

Paramilitary

MVS ε39,900 active

(Ministry of Internal Affairs)

FORCES BY ROLE

Mil Region   4 tps

MP   1 (Internal Security) tps

Border Guard 45,000 active

Maritime Border Guard

The Maritime Border Guard is an independent subdivision of the State Comission for Border Guards and is not part of the navy.

FORCES BY ROLE

Air Wing   1 (gunship) sqn

Air   3 sqn

MCM   1 sqn

Paramilitary 2 (river) bde; 1 (aux ship) gp; 4 (cutter) bde

Trg   1 div

EQUIPMENT BY TYPE

PATROL AND COASTAL COMBATANTS 45
  PFT 3 *Pauk* I each with 4 SA-N-5 *Grail* SAM, 4 single 406mm TT, 1 76mm gun

  PHT 3 *Muravey* each with 2 single 406mm TT, 1 76mm gun
  PFC 10 *Stenka* each with 4 single 406mm TT, 4 30mm gun
  PCC 1
  PCI 16 *Zhuk*
  PBR 12
  LOGISTICS AND SUPPORT
    AGF 1
  AIRCRAFT • TPT: An-24 *Coke*; An-26 *Curl*; An-72 *Coaler*; An-8 *Camp*
  HELICOPTERS • ASW: Ka-27 *Helix A*

Civil Defence Troops 9,500+ (civilian)

(Ministry of Emergency Situations) Army
4 indep bde; 4 indep regt

DEPLOYMENT

Legal provisions for foreign deployment:
Constitution: Codified constitution (1996)
Specific legislation: 'On the procedures to deploy Armed Forces of Ukraine units abroad' (1518-III, March 2000).
Decision on deployment of troops abroad: Parliament authorised to approve decision to provide military assistance, deploy troops abroad and allow foreign military presence in Ukraine (Art. 85, para 23); Also, in accordance with Art. 7 of the specific legislation (above), president is authorised to take a decision to deploy troops abroad and at the same time to submit a draft law to the Parliament of Ukraine for approval

AFGHANISTAN
NATO • ISAF 10

DEMOCRATIC REPUBLIC OF CONGO
UN • MONUC 13 obs

IRAQ
NATO • NTM-I 9

LIBERIA
UN • UNMIL 302; 1 obs; 2 avn unit

MOLDOVA
10 mil obs

SERBIA
NATO • KFOR • *Joint Enterprise* 180; elm 1 inf bn
OSCE • Serbia 1
OSCE • Kosovo 2
UN • UNMIK 1 obs

SUDAN
UN • UNMIS 11 obs

FOREIGN FORCES

Russia ε13,000 Navy 1 Fleet HQ located at Sevastopol; 1 indep naval inf regt; 102 AIFV/APC (T)/APC (W); 24 arty; Strategic Deterrent Forces *Dnepr* Radar Stn located at Sevastopol and Mukachevo

Table 17 **Selected arms procurements and deliveries, NATO Europe**

Designation	Type	Quantity	Contract Value	Supplier Country	Prime Contractor	Order Date	First Delivery Due	Notes
Belgium (BEL)								
Piranha IIIC	APC	242	€700m (US$844m)	CHE	Mowag	2006	2010	First batch (138 veh) due by 2010. Second (81) and third batches (23) due 2010-2015. Option on further 104
Dingo II	APC	220	€170m	GER	KMW	2005	2005	Option on further 132. Deliveries ongoing
A-400M	Tpt ac	7	–	Int'l	Airbus	2003	2010	In development. Official unit cost US$80m. First delivery delayed
NH-90	Hel	8	–	Int'l	EADS	2007	–	4 TTH, 4 NFH. Option on further 2
Bulgaria (BLG)								
Flower-class	MHC	1	See notes	BEL	–	2008	2009	Ex BEL stock. €54m (US$85m) incl 2 Wielingen-class FF. Delivery complete
Gowind	FS	2	€800m (US$1.25bn)	FRA	DCNS	2008	2012	Option on a further 2
C-27J Spartan	Tpt ac	5	US$133m	ITA	Alenia	2006	2007	To replace An-26. First ac delivered Nov 2007. Remaining deliveries at one per year
AS-532 Cougar	Hel	12	See notes	Int'l	Eurocopter	2005	2006	For air force. AUR360m (US$460m) incl 6 AS-565. Deliveries ongoing. Option on 7 more
AS-565 Panther	Hel	6	See notes	Int'l	Eurocopter	2005	2010	For navy. AUR360m (US$460m) incl 12 AS-532
Czech Republic (CZE)								
Pandur II 8x8	APC	107	US$828m	AUT	General Dynamics	2008	2009	To replace OT-64 SKOT. 72 in IFV and APC; 16 recce, 11 CP, 4 ARV and 4 armoured ambulance variants. Final delivery due 2013
Dingo II	APC	15	CZK 499m (€ 20.1)	GER	KMW	2007	2008	For use in AFG. Final delivery was due by Nov 2008
C-295M	Tpt ac	4	CZK3.5 bn (US$167m)	ESP	EADS CASA	2009	2009	For army. Contract value incl. an aircraft exchange. Final delivery due 2011
Denmark (DNK)								
CV9035 MkIII	AIFV	45	DKK1.68bn (US$273m)	SWE	BAE	2005	2007	Offset deal concluded 2009. 16 to be delivered
Patrol Frigates	FFG	3	DKK4.3bn (US$471m)	NLD	–	2006	2012	Projekt Patruljeskib
EH101 Merlin	Hel	6	–	Int'l	Agusta Westland	2007	2009	To replace 6 EH101 sold to UK
Estonia (EST)								
Ground Master 403	Radar	2	–	–	Thales-Raytheon	2009	2012	Acquisition part of agreement with FIN. Air surv for W. and SE. EST
L-410 Turbolet	Tpt / MPA	1	–	CZE/ SWE	LET	2007	–	Equipped with MSS 6000 maritime surv system
France (FRA)								
Syracuse 3	Sat	3	€2.3 bn (US$2.9 bn)	Dom	Alcatel Alenia Space	2000	2003	Second launched 2006. Third due for launch 2010

Table 17 **Selected arms procurements and deliveries, NATO Europe**

Designation	Type	Quantity	Contract Value	Supplier Country	Prime Contractor	Order Date	First Delivery Due	Notes
Spirale	Sat	–	–	Dom	Thales Alenia Space	2004	–	Demonstrator for future space-based early warning system. Launched early 2009
M51	SLBM	–	over €3bn	Dom	EADS	2004	2010	To replace M-45. Development phase from 2000-04. Final delivery due 2014
VBCI 8x8	IFV	630	–	Dom	Nexter	2000	2008	To replace AMX10P. Total requirement of 630 (520 VCIs, 110 VPCs), further 332 ordered in 2009. Final delivery due 2015
Petits Véhicules Protégé (PVP)	LAV	232	€28m (US$36m)	Dom	Panhard	2009	2009	2009 plan suggests additional contracts to provide total of 1,544 PVP by 2015
CAESAR 155mm	Arty	72	€300m (US$362m)	Dom	Nextar	2004	2008	Final delivery due 2011
Mistral - class	LHD	1	€420m (US$554m)	Dom	STX France Cruise	2009	–	–
FREMM (*Aquitaine*-class)	FFG	11	US$23.6bn	Dom / ITA	DCNS	2002	2012	Multi mission FFG. First-of-class FNS *Aquitaine* scheduled for commissioning 2012. Further 3 ordered in Oct 2009 (2 anti-air warfare, 1 ASW). Final delivery due 2022
Barracuda	SSN	6	€8bn (US$10.5bn)	Dom	DCNS	2006	2016	One SSN to be delivered every two years until 2027. First to enter service 2017
Le Triomphant (*Le Terrible*)	SSBN	1	–	Dom	DCNS	2000	2010	4th of class. 3 already in service
ESPADON	MCM Demon-strator	–	–	Dom	DCNS, ECA, Thales	2009	–	Autonomous Underwater Vehicles (AUVs) for naval mine clearance
SCALP	NLACM	250	€910m (US$1.2bn)	Int'l	MDBA	2007	2013	To be deployed on new SSN and FFG
Rafale F3	FGA	120	–	Dom	Dassault	1984	2006	First delivery Sept 2009. Final delivery due 2011
A-400M	Tpt ac	50	See notes	Int'l	Airbus	2003	2009	In development. Official unit cost US$80m. First deliveries delayed
Eagle 1 / SIDM	UAV	–	See notes	Int'l	EADS	2001	2009	In development. Total programme cost: US$1.4 bn
AS-665 *Tiger*	Hel	80	–	Dom/GER	Eurocopter	1999	2005	40 HAD, 40 HAP variant. 18 HAP delivered by Jan 2009
AGM-114 *Hellfire* II	ASM	–	–	US	Lockheed Martin	2007	–	For 40 *Tiger*. Final delivery due 2012. Msl no. and contract value undisclosed; projected requirement of 680
NH-90 TTH	Hel	34	See notes	Int'l	NH Industries	2007	2012	For army avn. 12 ordered 2007 with option for a further 56. 22 more ordered Jan 2009. €1.8bn if all options taken
NH-90 NFH	Hel	27	–	Int'l	NH Industries	2000	2009	For navy. Final delivery due 2019
EC725 *Cougar*	Hel	14	unknown	Int'l	Eurocopter	2009	2010	Final delivery due 2012 (6 air force; 8 army - delivered)
EGBU-12 *Enhanced Paveway II*	LGB	–	US$ 22m	US	Raytheon	2008	–	For *Mirage* 2000D

Europe (Non-NATO)

Table 17 **Selected arms procurements and deliveries, NATO Europe**

Designation	Type	Quantity	Contract Value	Supplier Country	Prime Contractor	Order Date	First Delivery Due	Notes
Germany (GER)								
Phase 2 of SATCOMBw programme	Sat	2	€938.7m (US$1.1bn)	Dom	Astrium	2006	2008	2 comms sat, tac and strat ground stations plus network control sys. System expected to be in operation by the end of 2010
IRIS-T SLS	SAM	–	€123m (US$166m)	Dom	Diehl BGT	2007	2012	Surface-launched variant of infra-red guided IRIS-T AAM. ISD from 2012. Secondary msl for army MEADS
Puma	AIFV	405	€3.1 bn (US$4.3 bn)	Dom	PSM	2007	2010	To replace *Marder* 1A3/A4/A5 AIFVs. Some to be fitted with *Spike* twin LR ATGW launcher. Final delivery 2020
Bv-206S	AFV	81	€67m	Dom	Rhein-metall	2005	2006	Delivered 2009
Dingo 2	APC	98	€73.6m	Dom	KMW	2008	2008	50 in standard ptrl veh config and 48 in battle damage repair veh config
Mungo NC Recce	AFV	25	–	Dom	KMW	2009	–	–
Boxer (8x8)	APC	272	€1.5bn (US$2.1bn)	Dom/NLD	ARTEC GmbH	2006	2009	135 APC, 65 CP variants, 72 ambulances. First delivery Sept 2009
Fennek	ARSV	202	–	Dom / NLD	ARGE Fennek	2001	2003	178 in recce role and 24 in cbt engr role. Deliveries ongoing
Fennek	ARSV	20	US$94m	Dom / NLD	ARGE Fennek	2007	2009	Joint fire support role.Second batch ordered in 08/09 (US$48m), to be delivered late 2011
Wiesel 2	LAV	8	€61.5m	Dom	Rhein-metall	2009	–	For use in Afg. 120mm mortar. Option on further 2 C2 veh
Spike LR	GMLS	311	€35m (US$49m)	Dom	Eurospike	2009	–	For Puma AIFV. Option for further 1,160 for est €120m
Skyshield 35 / NBS	C-RAM	2	€136m	Dom	Rhein-metall	2009	2011	In devt, original contract from 2007. Each consists of six *Skyshield* 35 mm wpn, two sensor units and C2 centre
K130 (*Braun-schweig*-class)	FS	5	–	Dom	TMS	2001	2008	*Erfurt*, *Oldenburg*, and *Ludwigshafen* in trials in mid-2009
Berlin-class (Type 72)	CSS	1	€245m US$330m	Dom	ARGE shipbuilding	2008	2013	–
Type 212A	SSK	2	–	Dom	HDW	2006	–	Due to enter service from 2012
Eurofighter (*Typhoon*)	FGA	79	–	Int'l	Eurofighter GmbH	2004	2008	Tranche 2. Tranche 3 order (68 ac) due to be signed 2009
A-400M	Tpt ac	60	See notes	Int'l	Airbus	2003	2010	In development. Official unit cost US$80m. First deliveries delayed
A319 / Bombardier *Global 5000*	VIP tpt ac	6	US$270m	Dom	Airbus	2007	2010	2 A319 due 2010, 4 *Global 5000* to be delivered 2011. To replace Bombardier *Challenger* 601 fleet
AS-665 Tiger (UHT variant)	Hel	80	US$2.6bn	Dom	Eurocopter	1984	2005	20 delivered by Sep 2008. Deliveries ongoing to trials and test
NH-90 TTH	Hel	80	–	NLD	NH Industries	2000	2007	50 for army, 30 for air force. Deliveries in progress to trials and test
NH-90 TTH	Hel	42	–	NLD	NH Industries	2007	–	30 for army air corps and 12 for air force
Eurohawk	UAV	5	€430m (US$559m)	Int'l	EADS/ Northrop Grumman	2007	2010	Final delivery due 2015

Table 17 **Selected arms procurements and deliveries, NATO Europe**

Designation	Type	Quantity	Contract Value	Supplier Country	Prime Contractor	Order Date	First Delivery Due	Notes
Greece (GRC)								
Katsonis-class Type 214	SSK	4	_	GER	TMS/ HDW	2000	2005	Reportedly subject to contractual dispute
Elli-class (S Type)	FFG MLU	6	_	Dom	Hellenic Shipyards	2005	2006	MLU to extend service life to 2020. 4 vessels delivered by Jan 2009. Final vessel due 2010
Roussen/Super Vita	PFM	5	€630m (US$800m)	Dom	Elefsis/ VT	2003	2007	First three delivered by October 2008. Deliveries ongoing
Roussen/Super Vita	PFM	2	€299m (US$405m)	Dom	Elefsis/ VT	2008	2010	Further order to bring total to 7
F-16 Block 52+	FGA	30	US$1.99bn	US	Lockheed Martin	2005	2009	20 F-16C and 10 F-15D. Option on further 10. First 4 delivered May 2009. Final delivery due March 2011
AH-64A *Apache*	Atk hel Upgrade	20	_	US	_	2008	2012	Upgrade to D standard to commence 2010; 4 to have *Longbow* radar
NH-90 TTH	Hel	20	€657m	NLD	EADS	2002	2005	16 tac tpt variants and 4 Special Op variants. Option on further 14. Delivery status unclear
Hungary (HUN)								
Cougar	MRAP	3	US$1.3m	US	Force Protection	2009	_	Contract value incl spares and trg
Iceland (ISL)								
Thor	PCO	1	€30m (US$39.6m)	CHL	ASMAR	2006	2009	For coast guard. To replace *Odinn* PCO
Italy (ITA)								
PzH 2000	How	70	_	GER	OTO Melara/ KMW	1999	2004	40 delivered. Final delivery 2010
FREMM	FFG	6	€1,628m (US$2,361m)	Dom /FRA	Orizzonte Sistemi Navali	2002	2010	Requirement of 10 Multi-Mission FFG. Batch 1 (2 vessels) in production. Batch 2 (4 vessels) had funding confirmed Mar 2008 - deliveries due 2014 - 2017
Todaro-class (Type 212A)	SS	2	€915m (US$1.34 bn)	Dom	Fincantieri	2008	2015	Second batch - option exercised from 1996 contract. With AIP
Eurofighter (*Typhoon*)	FGA	121	_	Int'l	Eurofighter GmbH	1985	2004	Tranche 1 ordered 1998 (29 ac). Tranche 2 ordered 2004 (46 ac). Tranche 3 order (46 ac) due to be signed 2009
KC-767	MRTT	4	_	US	Boeing	_	2008	First delivery delayed.
ATR-42MP	MPA	1	_	Dom	Alenia	2008	2010	For MSO
ATR-72MP	MPA	4	€360-400m	Dom	Alenia Aeronautica	2009	2012	To be fitted with long-range surv suite. Final delivery due 2014
M-346 *Master*	Trg ac	6	€220m	Dom	Alenia Aeronautica	2009	2010	Part of agreement for 15. First due for delivery end-2010
CH-47F *Chinook*	Tpt Hel	16	€900m	US	Agusta Westland	2009	2013	For army. Final delivery due 2017
NH-90 TTH	Hel	116	_	NLD	Agusta-Westland	1987	2007	60 for army; 56 for navy. 5 delivered to army. Remaining delivery status unclear

Europe (Non-NATO)

Table 17 **Selected arms procurements and deliveries, NATO Europe**

Designation	Type	Quantity	Contract Value	Supplier Country	Prime Contractor	Order Date	First Delivery Due	Notes
AW139	SAR Hel	2	–	–	Agusta-Westland	2008	2009	Likely to replace current fleet of Agusta-Bell 412HP hel. Delivery due late 2009.
Lithuania (LTU)								
Flyvefisken-class (Standard Flex 300)	PB	3	–	DNK	–	2006	2008	Ex-DNK stock. 2 delivered by end-2009
Hunt-class	MCMV	2	€55m	UK	Thales	2008	2010	Ex-UK stock. Former HMS *Cottesmore* and HMS *Dulverton*
C-27J *Spartan*	Tpt ac	3	€75m (US$98.9 m)	ITA	Alenia Aeronautica	2006	2006	Final ac delivered Oct 2009
Luxembourg (LUX)								
Dingo 2	ASRV	48	–	GER	Thales/ KMW	2008	2010	To meet Protected Recce Vehicle requirement and be deployed in AFG
A-400M	Tpt ac	1	See notes	Int'l	Airbus	2003	2010	In development. Official unit cost US$80m. First deliveries delayed
Netherlands (NLD)								
Bushmaster	LACV	9	Appox US$9m	AUS	Thales Australia	2009	2009	Fitted with IED detection aids. First delivery due Apr 2009
Bushmaster	LACV	14	–	AUS	Thales Australia	2009	–	Extra 14 ordered
CV90	AIFV	184	€749m (US$981m	SWE	Hagglunds	2004	2007	CV9035NL version. 150 in IFV role and 34 in CP role. Final delivery due 2011
PzH 2000	How	57	US$420m	GER	KMW	2000	2004	Deliveries ongoing
Holland-class	OPV	4	€365m	Dom	Schelde and Thales	2007	2011	*Holland, Zeeland, Groningen, Friesland*
Walrus-class	SSG SLEP	4	€50-150m (US$77-232m)	Dom	–	2011 - see notes	2018	Incl combat systems and nav upgrades. Pre-SLEP programme to commence 2008
C-130H *Hercules*	Tpt ac	2	€54m (US$65m)	US	–	2005	2008	Ex-USN EC-130Q ac refurbished to C-130H standard. First ac flight tested June 2009
NH90	Hel	20	–	Int'l	NH Industries	1987	2007	Final 4 due 2013
Ch-47F *Chinook*	Tpt Hel	6	US$335m	US	Boeing	2007	2009	Final delivery due 2010
Enhanced *Paveway* II	LGB	200	–	US	Raytheon	2008	–	For upgraded F-16AMs. EGBU-12 (GBU-49/B) 500 lb
Norway (NOR)								
Fridtjof Nansen	FFG	5	–	ESP	Navantia	2000	2006	Final vessel launched Feb 2009 and due for commissioning 2010
Sting Ray Mod 1	AS Torp	–	GBP99m (US$144m)	UK	BAE	2009	2010	For *Fridtjof Nansen*-class, NH90 ASW hel and P-3 *Orion*
Naval Strike Missile (NSM)	SSM	–	NOK2.2746bn (US$466m)	Dom	KDA	2007	–	Final delivery due 2014. For 5 *Fridtjof Nansen*-class FF and 6 *Skjold*-class fast strike craft
Oksoy class/ *Alta* class	MCMV	2	–	FRA	Thales	2007	–	Sonar upgrade involving the delivery of 6 TSM2022 MK3 N hull mounted sonars

Table 17 **Selected arms procurements and deliveries, NATO Europe**

Europe (Non-NATO)

Designation	Type	Quantity	Contract Value	Supplier Country	Prime Contractor	Order Date	First Delivery Due	Notes
C-130J-30 *Hercules*	Tpt ac	4	NOK3.7bn US$608m	US	Lockheed Martin	2007	2008	Final delivery due 2010
P-3 *Orion*	MPA SLEP	6	US$95m	US	Lockheed Martin	2007	2009	SLEP. Final delivery due Mar 2010
Poland (POL)								
AMV XC-360P	APC	690	US$ 1.7bn	FIN	Patria	2003	2004	Final delivery due 2014
Spike-LR	ATGW	264	PLN1.487bn (US$512m)	FRA	Rafael/ ZM Mesko	2003	2004	264 launchers and 2,675 msl. Manuf under licence
BM-21 launchers	MRL	36	PLN97m (US$ 43.9m)	Dom	Centrum Produkcji Wojskowej	2008	2010	Upgrade to WR-40 *Langusta* MRL standard
Project 621-*Gawron*	FSG	2	Zl 77m (US$24.8m)	Dom	SMW	2004	2008	Based on Ge MEKO A100. Project suspended Sept 2009
RBS 15 Mk 3	ASSM	36	PLN560m (US$178m)	SWE	ZM Mesko	2006	2009	For *Orkan*-class and *Gawron*-class. Incl, spares, spt, trg and simulator. Final delivery due 2012
Naval Strike Missile (NSM)	ASSM	12	NOK800m (US$115m)	NOR	Kongsberg Defence & Aerospace	2008	2012	Contact value incl 6 firing veh
C-130 E *Hercules*	Tpt ac	5	US$98.4m	US	SAIC	2006	2007	Refurbished ex-US stock. Deliveries delayed. First ac delivered Mar 2009
M-28B/PT *Bryza*	Tpt ac	8	PLN399m	US	Polskie Zaklady Lotnicze	2008	2010	For air force. Order reduced from 12 to 8 in 2009 due to budget cuts. Final delivery due 2013
M28B-1R/bis (*Bryza*-1R/bis)	ASW/MPA	3/4	–	Dom	PZL	–	2008	First delivered 2008. Remainder expected by 2010
PZL SW-4	Hel	24	PLN112m (US$37.8)	Dom	PZL-Świdnik	2006	2007	Incl trg simulator. Final deliveries due late 2009
Portugal (PRT)								
Pandur II 8x8	APC	260	€344.3m (US$415m)	AUT	Steyr Daimler Puch Spezial- fahrzeug GmbH	2005	2006	240 for army in 11 config. 20 for marines in 4 config. Final delivery due 2010
Viana do Castelo (NPO2000)	PSOH	10		Dom	ENVC	2002	2006	2 Pollution Control Vessels, 8 PSOH. First delivery expected early 2010. Final delivery due 2015
Type 209PN	SS	2	€800m (US$958m)	GER	TKMS	2004	2009	To replace 3 *Albacora*-class SS. *Tridente* launched Jul 2008, delivery due end 2009; *Arpao* launched June 2009 at Kiel, delivery due 2011
C-295M	Tpt ac	12	€270m (US$326m)	Int'l	EADS CASA	2006	2008	To replace C212. 7 ac in troop/cargo tpt role, 2 in maritime surv role and 3 in *Persuader* config. Final delivery due 2010
Romania (ROM)								
MICA (VL MICA)	SAM	–	–	FRA	MBDA	2009	–	Launch customer for land-based version
C-27J	Tpt ac	7	€220m (US$293m)	ITA	Alenia	2006	2007	To replace An-26. Incl log and trg spt. 1st aircraft received July 2009. Remaining 6 due from 2010

Table 17 **Selected arms procurements and deliveries, NATO Europe**

Designation	Type	Quantity	Contract Value	Supplier Country	Prime Contractor	Order Date	First Delivery Due	Notes
Slovakia (SVK)								
C-27J *Spartan*	Tpt ac	2 to 3	€120m (US$167m)	ITA	Alenia Aeronautica	2008	–	Procurement suspended until 2011 due to budget cuts
Mi-17	Hel	4	–	Dom	LOTN	2004	2008	Upgrade to SAR role. Final hel delivered 2009
Slovenia (SVN)								
Patria 8x8	APC	135	SIT66.61bn (US$365.9m)	FIN	Patria	2007	2007	First veh accepted June 2009. Final delivery due 2013
Spain (ESP)								
Paz satellite	Sat	2	€160m	Dom	Hidesat/ EADS CASA	2008	2012	–
National Advanced Surface-to-Air Missile System (NASAMS)	SAM	4	–	Dom/US	Raytheon	2003	–	Four units each with 3D radar, ctrl unit and 2 six-round truck-mounted launchers. Successfully tested 2008. In devt
Leopard 2E	MBT	239	€1.94bn (US$2.34bn)	Dom/GER	General Dynamics SBS	1998	2003	ESP version of 2A6. Incl 16 ARV and 4 trg tk. Final deliveries due 2009
Pizarro	AIFV	212	€707m (US$853m)	Dom	General Dynamics SBS	2003	2005	In five variants. Final deliveries due 2010
RG-31 Mk 5E	APC	100	€75m (US$118m)	RSA	GDSBS	2008	2009	85 in APC role, 10 ambulance and 5 CP versions. Delivery ongoing
ARTHUR	Radar	–	€69m	SWE	SAAB Microwave	2006	2007	Contract incl 4 remote control units, trg sys and log spt. First delivery April 2009
SBT (V07)	How	70	€181m (US$216m)	Dom	General Dynamics	2005	–	4 155/52 APU SBT (V07) how, plus design and production of 66 how (SIAC). Also retrofit of 12 APU SBT how from V06 to V07 version and 82 towing vehicles
Spike-LR	ATGW	See notes	US$424.5m	US	General Dynamics SBS	2007	2007	260 launchers, 2,600 msl and spt svcs. Deliveries ongoing
Alvaro de Bazan F-100	FFG	1	€71.5m (US$105.4m)	Dom	Navantia	2005	2012	*Roger de Lauria*. Option for one more FFG. Weapons to incl MK 41 Baseline VII. F105 keel laid 20 Feb 2009, delivery due summer 2012
Aegis	BMS	1	US$117m	US	Lockheed Martin	2007	2012	For *Roger de Lauria* F-100
Buques de Accion Maritima (BAM)	PCO	4	€1.1 bn (US$1.4bn)	Dom	Navantia	2005	2009	To be named *Meteoro, Rayo, Relámpago* and *Tornado*. Deliveries delayed by over 1 year. First keel layed March 2009. First delivery scheduled end 2010. Addl vessels ordered 2009
Strategic Projection Ship	LHD	1	–	Dom	Navantia	2003	2010	*Juan Carlos I*. Capacity 6 NH90 or 4 CH-47. Delivery scheduled for early 2010
S-80A	SSK with AIP	4	–	Dom	Navantia	2003	2013	First vessel, S-81, due for delivery Dec 2013

Table 17 **Selected arms procurements and deliveries, NATO Europe**

Designation	Type	Quantity	Contract Value	Supplier Country	Prime Contractor	Order Date	First Delivery Due	Notes
Eurofighter (*Typhoon*)	FGA	87	–	Int'l	Eurofighter GmbH	1994	2004	Tranche 2 ordered 2004 (33 ac). Tranche 3 order (34 ac) due to be signed 2009
AV-8B *Harrier* II	FGA upgrade	4	€11.5m (US$17.8m)	Dom	EADS	2008	2011	Upgrade: To AV-8B *Harrier* II Plus standard
A-400M	Tpt ac	27	See notes	Int'l	Airbus	2003	2010	In development. Official unit cost US$80m. First deliveries delayed
CN-235 S300	MPA ac	2	–	Int'l	EADS CASA	2007	2008	For Guardia Civil maritime patrol duties
AS 532AL *Cougar*	Hel	5	€116m (US$171m)	Int'l	Eurocopter	2008	–	3 for army air wing. 2 for Emergencies Military Unit
NH-90 TTH	Hel	45	–	Int'l	NH Industries	2007	2010	–
AS-665 *Tiger* (HAD)	Hel	24	€1.4bn	FRA	Eurocopter	2003	2007	First 3 hel delivered May 2007, second 3 by 2008. Final delivery due 2011
Turkey (TUR)								
Gokturk (recce & surv sat)	Sat	1	€ 270m (US$380m)	ITA	Telespazio	2009	–	Thales Alenia Space responsible for Sat. Dom companies involved in design and development stage & supply of subsystems
M60 A1/ *Sabra* Mk III	MBT Upgrade	170	US$688m	ISR	IMI	2002	2006	Final deliveries due 2010
Altay	MBT	250	See notes	Dom/ROK	Otokar	2007	–	4 initial prototypes by 2014 for approx US$500m. To be followed by an order for 250 units following testing
Firtina 155mm/52-cal	How	–	–	ROK/ Dom	Samsung	2001	2003	ROK Techwin K9 *Thunder*. Total requirement of 300. Deliveries ongoing
U-214	SSK	6	US$3.5bn	GER	HDW, TKMS and MFI	2009	2015	To be built at Golcuk shipyard
Ada-class	FSG	8	–	Dom	Istanbul Naval Shipyard	1996	2011	First of class, TCG *Heybeliada* launched 2008, ISD 2011. Part of *Milgem* project which incl requirement for 4 F-100 class FFG
Coast Guard SAR project	PC/SAR	4	€352.5m	Dom	RMK Marine	2007	2011	Based on *Sirio*-class PCO design. For Coast Guard. Final delivery due 2011
56m PB	PB	16	€402m (US$545m)	Dom	Dearsan	2007	2010	Final delivery due 2015
F-16C/D Block 50	FGA	30	US$1.78bn	US/Dom	Lockheed Martin	2009	2011	14 F-16C and 16 F-16D variants. Final assembly in TUR. Final delivery due 2014
F-16C/D	FGA Upgrade	216	US$635m	US	Lockheed Martin/ TAI	2006	–	Upgrade. 216 modernisation kits, flight testing, training, technical spt and sustainment activities
A-400M	Tpt ac	10	See notes	Int'l	Airbus	2003	2012	In development. Official unit cost US$80m. First deliveries delayed
B-737	AEW&C	4	US$1bn	US	Boeing	2002	2009	*Peace Eagle* programme. Option for further 2. Delivery delayed
ATR-72	MPA	10	US$210m	ITA	Alenia Aeronautica	2005	2010	First five deliveries by 2010. Final delivery due 2012
KT-1 *Woong-Bee*	Trg ac	40	US$500m	Dom / ROK	KAI / TAI	2007	2009	To replace T-37 trg ac. Option for 15 further ac
S-70B *Seahawk*	Hel	17	–	US	Sikorsky	2006	2009	Delivery status unclear

Table 17 **Selected arms procurements and deliveries, NATO Europe**

Designation	Type	Quantity	Contract Value	Supplier Country	Prime Contractor	Order Date	First Delivery Due	Notes
Mangusta A129/T129	Hel	30	US$2.7bn	Int'l	Turkish Aerospace Industries	2007	2013	In development. Option for further 20 hel. Quoted contract value is for 50 hel. To be armed with Cirit long-range ATGW
Heron	UAV	10	US$183m	ISR	'Israel UAV Partnership'	2005	–	Navy to receive 2, army 4 and navy 4. 2 delivered undergoing further upgrades
AGM-84H SLAM-ER	ASM	48	US$79.1m	US	McDonnell Douglas	2007	2008	Incl 3 SLAM-ER instrumented recoverable air test vehicles and 59 msl containers. Final delivery due 2011
T129	Hel	51	US$3bn	Dom	TAI/ Aselsan/ Agusta Westland	2008	_	Option on further 41. Serial production planned for 2013

United Kingdom (UK)

Designation	Type	Quantity	Contract Value	Supplier Country	Prime Contractor	Order Date	First Delivery Due	Notes
Surveillance and Target Acquisition (STA) equipment	SURV	_	UK£150m (US$246m)	Dom	UK Thales	2009	2010	Part of Future Integrated Soldier Technology programme
Cougar	MRAP	157	US$94m	US	Force Protection	2008	_	To be converted to Ridgback by NP Aerospace
BvS10 Viking Mk II	APC	24	US$38m	_	BAE Systems	2009	2010	Upgrade to replace vehicles damaged on ops. 22 troop carriers, 2 comd vehicles. Delivery due early 2010
Warthog (formerly Bronco)	APC	115	US$233m	SGP / Dom	ST Kinetics / Thales	2008	2009	To replace BvS 10 Vikings. Final deliveries due late 2010
Jackal 2	Recce	110	GBP74m	Dom	Supacat	2009	2009	Babcock Marine to manufacture. Contract value incl 70 Coyote. Deliveries ongoing
Coyote	Recce	70	GBP74m	Dom	Supacat	2009	2009	6x6 derivative of Jackal. Babcock Marine to undertake manufacture. Contract value incl 110 Jackal 2
Shadow R1 (King Air 350ER)	ISTAR	4	_	US	Raytheon	2007	_	Purchased and operated by AAC but with RAF personnel
2400TD	LC ACV	4	UK£3.26m (US$6.5m)	Dom	Griffon Hovercraft	2008	_	To replace 2000TD. Trials scheduled for late 2009
Future Carrier (Queen Elizabeth Class)	CV	2	UK£3.9bn (US$8bn)	Dom	BAE Systems	2007	2014	In devt. Several spt contracts signed 2008. HMS Queen Elizabeth (2014) and HMS Prince of Wales (2016). Delivery delayed by at least one year due to cost savings. Construction began July 2009
Type-45 Daring	DDG	6	See notes	Dom	VT Group / BAE Systems	2001	2008	Initial budget projection: UK£5.47bn. Overall cost now expected to be UK£6.46bn (US$12.7bn). First of class ISD due 2010
Astute	SSN	4	See notes	Dom	BAE	1994	2008	First vessel launched Jun 2007, but commissioning delayed. 4th UK£200m (US$303.8m) vessel, Audacious, ordered 2008. To be fitted with Tomahawk Block IV SLCM

Table 17 **Selected arms procurements and deliveries, NATO Europe**

Designation	Type	Quantity	Contract Value	Supplier Country	Prime Contractor	Order Date	First Delivery Due	Notes
F 35B *Joint Strike Fighter* (STOVL)	FGA	3	US$600m	US	Lockheed Martin	2009	_	In development. Contractual commitment to purchase 3 STOVL ac. Requirement for 138 F35A and F35B variants
Eurofighter (*Typhoon*)	FGA	232	_	Int'l	Eurofighter GmbH	1984	2003	Tranche 3 order (88 ac) signed 2009. Orders likely to be reduced around 160
A-400M	Tpt ac	25	See notes	Int'l	Airbus	2003	2010	In development. Official unit cost US$80m. First deliveries delayed
A330-200	Tpt/Tkr ac	14	UK£13bn (US$26 bn)	Int'l	AirTanker consortium	2008	2011	First ac arrived at Getafe facility July 2009 for avionics and aerial refuelling fitting. Due Oct 2011
Hawk Mk 128/ T.2	Trg ac	28	UK£450m	Dom	BAE	2006	2008	First delivery July 2009
Nimrod MRA4	MPA	12	UK£2.8bn	Dom	BAE	1996	2009	Cost now forecast to be UK£3.5bn, though production contract worth UK£1.1bn for 12 ac. Delayed by 80 months
Future Lynx/ AW159 Lynx Wildcat	Hel	62	UK£1bn (US$1.8bn)	ITA / UK	Agusta Westland	2006	2014	34 for Army, 28 for Navy. Option for a further 10 hel, 5 for Army and 5 for Navy. Final delivery due 2015
Chinook HC.3	Spt hel	8	GBP62m (US$124m)	US	Boeing	2007	2009	Conversion to HC.2/2A standard. First to be delivered in late 2009, remainder early 2010
Hermes 450	UAV	–	US$110m	Int'l	Thales	2007	2010	Contract incl trg, log spt and management services
Chinook HC.2/2A	Hel Upgrade	48	US$656m	Dom	Honeywell/ Thales	2009	_	Upgrade with T55-L-714 engines and Thales TopDeck cockpits for op requirements
SA 330E *Puma* HC.1	Tpt Hel Upgrade	28	US$479m	Dom	Eurocopter	2009	2011	Life-extension programme. First 14 acs due to be in service by late 2012, final delivery due 12/04. Option on two more acs

Table 18 **Selected arms procurements and deliveries, Non-NATO Europe**

Designation	Type	Quantity	Contract Value	Supplier Country	Prime Contractor	Order Date	First Delivery Due	Notes
Azerbaijan (AZE)								
BTR-80	APC	70	US$20m (est)	RUS	Rosoboron-export	2007	2009	Delivery status unclear
Belarus (BLR)								
S-400 *Triumf* (*Growler*)	AD/SAM	_	_	RUS	Rosoboron-export	2009		Delivery status unclear
Croatia (CRO)								
Patria 8x8	APC	84	€112m	Dom / FIN	Patria	2007	2012	Original order for 126 reduced to 84
Cyprus (CYP)								
Mi-35P *Hind-F*	Atk hel Upgrade	11	US$26m	RUS	Mil	2007	–	Upgrade: airframe and engine refurb
Finland (FIN)								
Norwegian Advanced Surface-to-Air Missile System (NASAMS)	AD	unknown	NOK3bn (US$458m)	Dom/US	Kongsberg/ Raytheon	2009	2009	To replace Buk-M1 (SA-11 *Gadfly*). Delivery status unclear
2010 Project vessel	MCM	3	€244.8m (US$315m)	ITA/GER	Intermarine	2006	2010	Final delivery due 2012. First vessel, *Katanpaa*, launched at La Spezia June 2009
F/A-18C *Hornet*	FGA Upgrade	10	US$30 m	US	Boeing	2008	2009	AN/AAQ-28 *Litening* ATP upgrade. Block 2 pods for MLU 2 programme
PC-12 NG	Liaison ac	6	€22.5m (US$29.6m)	CHE	Pilatus	2009	2010	To replace Piper PA-31-350 *Chieftain*
Hawk Mk 51 / 51A	Trg ac	30/45	€20m (US$26.3m)	US	Patria	2007	2010	Avionics upgrade. 30 ac receive level 1 upgrade, a further 15 ac to receive level 2 upgrade. First delivered June 2009
NH-90 TTH	Hel	20	€370m	NLD	NH Industries	2001	2004	Due to delays, 6 due by end 2008, 6 in 2009 and final 8 in 2010. First delivered Mar 2008
RBS 70	MANPAD	–	SEK600m (US$85.5m)	SWE	Saab Bofors Dynamics	2006	2008	Final delivery due 2010
Ireland (IRL)								
RG32M	MRAP	27	_	UK / RSA	BAE	2008	2010	_
AW-139	Hel	4	€49m (US$59m)	ITA / UK	Augusta-Westland	2006	2008	Incl option for further 2
Malta (MLT)								
21.2m PCI	PCI	4	US$12m	AUS	Austal	2009	2009	First two ships launched. Final delivery due Nov 2009
Sweden (SWE)								
RG32M	MRAP	60	€18m (US$24m)	UK / RSA	BAE	2008	2010	_

Table 18 **Selected arms procurements and deliveries, Non-NATO Europe**

Designation	Type	Quantity	Contract Value	Supplier Country	Prime Contractor	Order Date	First Delivery Due	Notes
Armoured Modular Vehicle (AMV)	APC	113	€240m (US$338m)	FIN	Patria	2009	2011	Further 113 req. Was subject to contractual dispute
AMOS 120mm	Mor	2	SKR30m (approx US$4m)	Int'l	_	2006	2011	Two prototypes to be mounted on Vv90 tracked chassis
Koster	MCV MLU	5	US$133m	Dom	Kockums	2007	2009	MLU. HMS *Koster* and *Vinga* re-commissioned Mar 2009, *Ulvön*, *Kullen* and *Ven* ISD due 2010
Visby	FSGH	5	_	Dom	Kockums	1995	2005	First vessel ltd op role 2008; add'l vessels ISD expected by 2010
CB 90H	LCA Upgrade	145	_	Dom	_	2008	_	Upgrade from 90H to 90HS
JAS 39A/B *Gripen*	FGA Upgrade	31	SEK3.9bn (US$611m)	Dom	SAAB	2007	2012	Upgrade: 18 to become JAS 39Cs and 13 to become JAS 39D two-seaters
NH-90	Hel	18	_	Int'l	Eurocopter	2001	2007	13 TTT/SAR hel and 5 ASW variants. Option for 7 further hel. Deliveries ongoing
Switzerland (CHE)								
Piranha I	APC	160	_	Dom	Mowag	2006	2008	Re-role of *Piranha* I tank hunter APC to protected comd vehicles. Final delivery due 2010
Piranha IIIC	NBC Recce	12	See notes	Dom	Mowag	2008	2010	CHF260m (€167m) incl 232 DURO IIIP. Final delivery due 2012
DURO IIIP	APC/NBC lab	232	See notes	Dom	Mowag	2008	2010	CHF260m (€167m) incl 12 Piranha IIIC. 220 personnel veh and 12 NBC labs. Final delivery due 2012
EC135	Hel	2	_	Int'l	EADS	2006	2008	Final delivery due 2010
EC635	Tpt/trg hel	18	_	Int'l	EADS	2006	2008	3 delivered by Aug 2008. Final delivery due 2010
Ukraine (UKR)								
An-70	Tpt ac	5	_	RF	Antonov	1991	2008	Limited serial production started. First delivery due 2010

Table 19 **NATO/EU Transport and Air Refuelling Capability**

Aircraft Type	NATO/EU Country	Holding	Type Total	North America Country	Holding	Type Total
A-310 MRTT/CC150T**	Germany	4	4	Canada	2	2
A-310/CC150	Belgium	2	10	Canada	3	3
	France	3				
	Germany	3				
	Spain	2				
A-319	Czech Republic	2	7			
	Italy	3				
	France	2				
A-340	France	2	2			
An-124	NATO	2	2			
An-2	Bulgaria	1	5			
	Estonia	2				
	Latvia	2				
An-26	Bulgaria	3	17			
	Czech Republic	5				
	Hungary	5				
	Romania	4				
An-28	Poland	14	14			
An-32	Croatia	2	2			
B-707 300(KC)*	Spain	2	2			
B-767 MRTT**	Italy	1	1			
C-130	Austria	3	163	Canada	21	481
	Belgium	11		United States	460	
	Denmark	4				
	France	14				
	Greece	15				
	Italy	22				
	Netherlands	6				
	Norway	2				
	Poland	5				
	Portugal	6				
	Romania	5				
	Spain	7				
	Sweden	7				
	Turkey	13				
	UK	43				
C-160	France	42	141			
	Germany	83				
	Turkey	16				
C-160NG**	France	15	15			

Aircraft Type	NATO/EU Country	Holding	Type Total	North America Country	Holding	Type Total
C-17	NATO	3	9	Canada	4	178
	UK	6		United States	174	
C-27J	Bulgaria	3	29			
	Greece	12				
	Italy	9				
	Lithuania	3				
	Romania	2				
C-5				United States	111	111
CASA 212	Portugal	24	81			
	Spain	57				
CASA C-295	Poland	11	19			
	Portugal	1				
	Spain	7				
CC-115				Canada	6	6
CL-601	Czech Republic	1	7			
	Germany	6				
CN-235	France	20	80			
	Spain	14				
	Turkey	46				
DC-10	Netherlands	1	1			
ERJ-135 LR	Belgium	2	4			
	Greece	2				
ERJ-145 LR	Belgium	2	2			
G-222	Italy	9	9			
KC-10A**				United States	59	59
KC-130*	Spain	5	6	Canada	5	67
	Sweden	1		United States	62	
KC-135R*	Turkey	7	7	United States	453	453
KDC-10	Netherlands	2	2			
M-28	Poland	15	15			
Tristar C2	UK	3	3			
Tristar** K1/KC1	UK	6	6			
Tu-134B	Bulgaria	1	1			
Tu-154	Poland	2	2			
VC-10**	UK	10	10			
VC-10 K3/K4	UK	6	6			
Grand Totals			684			1360

* Tkr

** Tkr tpt

Chapter Four
Russia

New defence reforms underway

In September 2008, Russian President Dmitry Medvedev launched an ambitious attempt to reform and modernise the Russian armed forces. The concept document was publicly presented on 14 October at the meeting of the Collegium of the Ministry of Defence (MoD), and was entitled 'The Future Outlook of the Russian Federation Armed Forces and Priorities for its Creation for the period of 2009–2020' (*Perspektivny oblik Vooruzhennykh Sil RF i pervoocherednye mery po ego formirovaniu na 2009–2020 gody*).

Over the past 15 years, there have been a series of attempts to implement 'defence reform' in the Russian armed forces, so the change in terminology to 'Future Outlook' is itself of note. With these attempts at reform having been neither comprehensively implemented nor properly resourced, the term has become associated with reorganisations driven by particular service interests – such as the Strategic Rocket Forces (SRF) or the army – that have had little qualitative impact on the overall readiness of the armed forces or personnel welfare. The last such reform, initiated by former Defence Minister Sergei Ivanov, and officially 'completed' in 2004, led to some improvements, such as the creation of a limited number of permanent-readiness units and the recruitment of an equally small number of professional (contract) soldiers. Though it did not fundamentally change the structure of the Russian armed forces, it arguably paved the way for more systemic reform by subordinating the General Staff to the MoD.

Army General Nikolai Makarov, appointed on 3 June 2008 as Russian chief of the General Staff, has said the current moves are the most radical changes within the Russian armed forces in the past 200 years. Some analysts have said that, if successful, Defence Minister Anatoly Serdyukov's plans could create in the next decade fundamentally different armed forces for Russia: no longer would Russia have a mass-mobilisation army but a much smaller force suited for local or regional conflicts, and better able to support Russian foreign-policy objectives. But this strategy has also provoked resistance within the military and political class, and its success might be chal-lenged by a shortage of resources and lack of political consensus on the armed forces' key missions.

Motivating factors

It is widely held that these changes were a response to the lessons learned in the brief August 2008 war with Georgia, though the aftermath of this campaign also provided an opportunity for Serdyukov to enact previously held plans. Russia's victory was mainly due to its numerical superiority, the basic military skills of its ground troops and the assistance received from highly motivated South Ossetian para-militaries familiar with the difficult mountainous terrain. Analysis of Russia's performance during the campaign (see *The Military Balance 2009*, pp. 210–12) highlighted fundamental shortcomings in force composition, training, command and control, equipment and doctrine. This poor performance increased doubt that the military could be seen as a reliable instrument to support Russian foreign- and security-policy objectives, and also reinforced the perception that the armed forces could not in the future guarantee reliable conventional defence capabilities. But the plan also resulted from consideration of a number of other factors.

Negative demographic trends mean that the number of conscript-age males is declining. According to Makarov, in 2012 this number will be only half of the 2001 figure. Secondly, the Russian armed forces' inventory remains stocked with ageing Soviet equipment, and there is currently limited capacity to finance and produce substantial numbers of modernised or replacement systems, particularly if the mobilisation-centric doctrine remains. The so-called 'reserve units', little more than storage sites for equipment to be used by reservists in case of mobilisation, have even more outdated capabilities, with little operational value. Thirdly, a confluence of personnel issues was seen as hindering force effectiveness. Corruption, crime and peacetime casualties within the Russian army had by 2008 grown substantially, with the total number of crimes committed by the military reported at 20,425. Over 500 officers were prosecuted for corruption, including 117 senior commanding officers and 20 generals. A further 604 servicemen died as a result of non-combat losses, with 231 committing suicide, often as a result of bullying. While the number of non-combat deaths and suicides had fallen in other para-military services, such as Interior Forces and Border Guards, it had increased by over 35% in the armed forces.

Fourthly, a number of reforms since the mid 1990s – conceived and implemented by the military and often influenced by personal or service interests – were conducted with no clear methodology for measuring success and with little transparency for the wider political and civilian constituencies that were formally tasked with oversight of the military. This resulted in increased political competition across the services, a lack of 'joint' military thought and a delegitimisation of the role of civilian oversight of, and participation in, defence-reform plans. Soviet-era thinking persisted in the military, sustained by an unreformed military-education system, a lack of meaningful interaction with other modern militaries and an inability to assess Russia's real military capabilities beyond broad judgements primarily relying on inventory numbers. With the 'victory' in Chechnya and military support for then President Vladimir Putin, there was also a lack of political will within Russia's leadership to push the military towards real modernisation, but the aftermath of the Georgia campaign galvanised public support, and political will, for reform.

Some changes were in fact announced earlier in 2008, such as the intention to replace warrant officers and midshipmen with professional NCOs. Conscript service was also reduced to one year in early 2008, and some MoD positions also transitioned to civilian staffs. But the August war provided a political window of opportunity for Serduykov's reform plans. Indeed, it has become apparent that the Russian MoD has been actively studying Western experience and ideas, though they are implementing the conclusions drawn from it in a distinctly Russian manner.

The reform programme detailed a set of aspirations for the development of Russia's armed forces:

All ground forces to become fully manned, permanent-readiness units
Ground-force units would be outfitted with modern equipment, undergo regular training and be ready for deployment at short notice within their region of responsibility. Serduykov's plan noted the adoption of a number of measures necessary to implement this goal. Firstly, overall personnel strength was to drop to 1 million by 2012. The number of officers, mean-

while, was to fall from 355,000 to 150,000. Generals were to be reduced from 1,107 to 886; colonels from 25,665 to 9,114; majors from 99,550 to 25,000; and captains from 90,000 to 40,000. (It was also planned that from 2008–11, 120,000 warrant officers and midshipmen would be made redundant, with 20,000 retained in the navy.) The number of lieutenants was to increase from 50,000 to 60,000, and new professional NCOs were to be recruited and trained at special training establishments. Indeed, all NCOs were to be professional, while the number of contract soldiers was to be increased. Three-year contracts are now being offered to private soldiers and NCOs. All brigades in the North Caucasus Military District were to be manned with professionals, and in other parts of Russia on a mixed professional–conscript basis. All 'cadre units' (units only to be fully manned – with reservists – during wartime) were to be closed down or transformed into 'logistical bases' for equipment storage, while logistics itself was to be reorganised and mostly 'civilianised' on the basis of public–private partnerships with private, commercial companies involved in providing services for the military.

Improving command effectiveness
The 'new look' programme also envisaged a change in the levels of command, from a four-tier structure (military district (MD), army, division, regiment) to a three-tier structure (MD, operational command, brigade). Military districts were to have command responsibility over all forces within their geographic territory, in a bid to reinforce 'joint' command. According to Makarov, each MD should have sufficient capacity to manage local conflict within its zone of responsibility without requiring the involvement of forces from another. Meanwhile, the operational commands should be able to carry out missions in different regions; Makarov said that from 2009 many exercises for permanent-readiness units would be conducted in other parts of the country.

The number of ground-force units was also slated to be reduced from 1,890 to 172, while the air force was to drop from 240 units to 120 and the navy from 240 to 123. If these totals were reached, ground forces would comprise 36% of the total force, up from the current 30%. One of the changes that prompted much analysis concerned the move from divisional formations to brigades. The plan was that, by 1 December 2009, ground-force divisions were to transform into brigades capable of independent operations, causing

23 motor-rifle and tank divisions, missile and artillery regiments, engineering units, air-defence, communication and support units to transform into 39 ground-force brigades, 21 missile and artillery brigades, seven army air-defence brigades, 12 communications brigades and two electronic-warfare brigades. In most cases each permanent-readiness division was due to be transformed into two brigades. One division would remain in the Far East; 17 independent regiments would also remain. (During an assessment of units published in November 2009, 60% of brigades received a 'satisfactory' rating, with 30% 'good'; four brigades were deemed 'unsatisfactory'; and only four were rated 'excellent', all of them naval units.)

Other forces were also to undergo change. While the SRF would retain its divisional structure, the number of missile divisions would be reduced from 12 to eight. (Space forces would be reduced from seven to six divisions.) The SRF was due to see 35 units eliminated in 2009, including two missile regiments, with ten units restructured. The percentage of contract NCOs was planned to increase to 100% in 2016 from the current 25%.

Airborne divisions were initially to be transformed into eight airborne brigades acting as essentially rapid-response forces in each military district, but this plan was abandoned in June 2009 after the appointment of Lieutenant-General Vladimir Shamanov as the commander of the VdV (Russian Airborne Troops). A new Airborne Brigade is due to be established in the Moscow MD and a separate parachute regiment in the Leningrad MD. The airborne forces average 37% contract or professional servicemen: in the Tula Division the proportion is 9% (the division is mostly manned by conscripts, many of whom later join as contract soldiers and move to other divisions); 60% in the Ulyanovsk Brigade; 37% in the Novorossyisk Division; 40% in the Pskov Division; and 49% in the Ivanov Division. Contract airborne troops receive a salary of R22–32,000 (US$746–1,085) per month.

By 2012 all air divisions and regiments in the air force are expected to be disbanded, with the formation of 55 air bases distributed throughout four strategic commands. These will each be assigned a category, depending on the number of squadrons and the quantity of tasks assigned. First-category bases will handle large-scale operations; second-category bases will fulfil tasks currently handled by aviation regiments; and third-category bases will include separate squadrons. The former Command of Special Air Defence Forces around Moscow will be incorporated into the air force and will become the basis of a new Air-Space Command within the force.

Introducing modern weapons and equipment

In March 2009, Serdyukov said that only 10% of all weapons and equipment in the contemporary Russian armed forces were 'modern'. If enacted, the 'new look' programme would increase the share of modern weapons in inventories to 30% by 2015 and 70% by 2020. Large-scale modernisation is due to start in 2011, but remains an ambitious target given the slow pace of domestic procurement coupled with the impact of the financial crisis (see Defence Economics, p. 216). It has been asserted that modernisation will focus on the comprehensive rearmament of entire units rather than the procurement of specific items of weapons and equipment. Meanwhile, authorities are for the first time considering the procurement of foreign-produced equipment: Russia signed a contract with an Israeli company to supply UAVs, and entered into talks with Paris to procure a *Mistral*-class amphibious-assault ship (Landing Helicopter Dock – LHD), and jointly build three more under licence in Russian shipyards.

Improving military education and career management

It is envisaged that by 2013 the current 65 military-education establishments will be reduced to ten 'educational centres' incorporating existing military schools and universities. Problems in attracting sufficient recruits led to the opening of a new NCO training centre on 1 December 2009 at the Ryazan Higher Airborne (VdV) School. The centre is meant to prepare junior command personnel and features a more ambitious training programme conducted over two years and ten months. (Under the plans, these NCOs will be paid the same monthly salary as active generals: R35,000.) Meanwhile, more selective admissions criteria are being applied at the General Staff Academy. As a result, in 2009 only 16 officers were admitted to the Senior General Staff Academy course, a significant reduction compared with previous years; most entrants were from the Interior Ministry or other security structures.

Dealing with redundancies and conditions for serving personnel

Although around 205,000 officer positions will be officially abolished in the proposed reorganisation, the actual number of redundancies will be much less. Taking into account existing vacancies, planned retirements and the elimination of two-year officer service, the actual number of officers made redundant in the next three years is more likely to be around 117,500. As part of the manpower-reduction process, each officer and contract serviceman is being assessed as to his competencies and likely place in the future forces. In some cases, these evaluations may recommend the dismissal of an officer on the basis of non-fulfilment of contract; that individual would thus leave without the benefits and compensation which are legally guaranteed to any retiring officer (whether on the basis of reaching the retirement age or as a result of premature retirement from the armed forces). But a key obstacle to these plans is the requirement that officers leaving the forces should be provided with housing. According to MoD statistics, almost half of the officers to be made redundant have no housing; significant financial resources will be required within the next three years to provide the amount of housing needed to meet the planned reduction targets.

If one aim of the reform process is to attract more and better junior offices and professional servicemen, adjustments will have to be made in the forces' salary levels. Currently, a platoon commander receives R23,500 (US$797) per month, while a contract soldier receives R11–13,000 (US$373–441). Serdyukov has promised that from 1 January 2012 remuneration for all servicemen will increase by a factor of three, though it remains to be seen how this increase will be funded.

Challenges in implementation

Critics of the proposed reforms were vocal and more visible within the public debate, including in parliament and the press. While there were some efforts to explain the process to interested groups in Russia, as well as the general population (and also perhaps the international community), these public-outreach measures remained limited. Serdyukov established a Public Council tasked with providing public input and also public oversight over the activities of the MoD and its reform strategies, though it is unclear to what extent this council is able to provide advice and expert support in order to modify the reform plans.

The main criticism is that these plans were drawn up without a clear decision on the underlying strategic basis for them. In Russia, this strategic rationale is usually provided by the military doctrine, but no new doctrine was adopted before the current changes started. There is thus a lack of clarity and

consensus within Russian society and the political elite about what kind of armed forces Russia needs and why it needs them. In other words, there is no general agreement about what the key threats to Russia are likely to be in the short, medium and long terms, and what the key tasks of the armed forces will be in light of these threats. The chief of the Russian General Staff responded to this criticism by stating that there was no time to shape this consensus and to develop such documents. In his view, the lack of comprehensive reforms since the end of the Soviet Union had resulted in such deterioration of the armed forces that urgent measures were needed to prevent an even deeper crisis. Still, the drafting process for a new defence doctrine began in 2009, and this document was due to be presented to the president before January 2010. In October 2009, Nikolai Patrushev, secretary of the National Security Council, said that several points in the new doctrine would be the same as in the 2003 document, such as an emphasis on regional wars and armed conflicts instead of large-scale conflict. But he also said that the document would provide for the use of nuclear weapons to deter attacks on Russia and in local conflicts in which Russia is attacked, and also in cases of preemption against a potential aggressor. These discussions have caused some disquiet abroad, as did the 9 November decree giving the president the right to operationally deploy Russian armed forces abroad without parliamentary permission. (In August 2008 no such permission was even sought before the deployment.) The amendment specified scenarios in which such a 'simplified' decision-making procedure is applicable: an attack against Russian forces stationed abroad; defence against or prevention of an attack on another state that has requested Russian support; protection of Russian citizens abroad from attack; and anti-piracy operations and the provision of maritime security.

The financial crisis may have an impact on the progress of modernisation. Russia has experienced a large budget deficit for the first time in almost a decade (see Defence Economics, p. 216). While the budgets of other 'force ministries' – the Interior Ministry, Federal Security Service and Ministry of Emergencies – have been reduced by 15%, President Medvedev said he would reduce the MoD's budget by only 9% and keep unchanged the amounts originally allocated for social programmes for servicemen and for the implementation of the State Defence Order. It is difficult to predict whether the Russian government will be able to keep meeting the increasing need for funds to support both the professionalisation of the armed forces and the ambitious social programmes. Added to this, the scale of the proposed modernisation programme will require significant funds in the next decade, and defence will be competing with other sectors for modernisation and diversification.

The success of the plans largely depends on the ability of the Russian defence industry to deliver on its promises of rapid modernisation and re-equipment. So far, domestic procurement plans have been relatively unsuccessful, particularly those related to the development and serial production of key new platforms. Future challenges for modernisation concern the poor state of Russian defence-industry and defence-science R&D; continuing high inflation in machine-building and the defence industry (which limits the purchasing power of allocated resources); and an acute shortage of specialist workers who will be required to enable mass production of major new platforms for the armed forces. In his annual speech to parliament, in an apparent attempt to put pressure on the defence industry, President Medvedev discussed the contents of the 2010 State Defence Order, saying 'In the next year we need to provide the Armed Forces with more than 30 ballistic land- and sea-based missiles, 5 *Iskander* missile systems, about 300 modern armoured vehicles, 30 helicopters, 28 combat aircraft, 3 nuclear-powered submarines, 1 corvette-class battleship and 11 spacecraft. All this simply has to be done'. (He also set a deadline to replace analogue with digital communications systems by 2012, with priority to the North Caucasus MD.) But analysts have raised questions over the viability of Moscow's shopping list. It remains unclear whether industry can deliver 30 ballistic missiles of the types desired: *Topol* missiles will continue to be supplied, but the *Bulava* programme is still experiencing problems, with a number of unsuccessful tests this year. This has implications for the *Borey*-class submarines due to receive *Bulava* missiles.

Elements of the current reforms have been poorly explained to, and are poorly understood by, many within their key constituency: the armed forces. There is abundant confusion about impending redundancies, relocation and changes in the requirements for serving officers, and protests have taken place in units that were directed to change location quickly without guarantees that social infrastructure would

be ready on arrival. Many officers resigned or were pushed out when they expressed disagreement with the proposals. The perception also exists that many mid-level officers are being made redundant because they lack necessary qualifications and have been deemed unsuitable for retraining. As a consequence, morale within the armed forces has suffered, although in the long run the current changes should benefit young officers, who may enjoy new equipment and better living conditions. But the risk is still that many able officers will leave, at a time when difficulties in recruiting and retaining younger officers and qualified NCOs continue.

If the proposed reductions in professional officers, elimination of all two-year 'conscripted' officers and removal of all warrant officers are implemented, there is concern over whether the armed forces' numbers might actually drop below 1 million; some experts believe that in 2010–12 manning could fall to around 800,000. If sufficient funding is not provided to attract more officers, NCOs and contract soldiers there is a possibility that the numbers could fall even further. Moreover, the quality of conscripts remains low: according to MoD data, only 68% are deemed suitable for service; others require basic physical and educational training before they can fulfil their duties, while the dwindling recruitment pool has led to the drafting of not only those with criminal convictions but also some with prison records. The recruitment of contract soldiers and NCOs also remains problematic. In 2009, the first months of recruitment for NCO training courses showed that many candidates did not meet educational requirements, while some analysts say it will be increasingly difficult to fill professional NCO positions given falling interest in the forces. It is not known whether the MoD has a clear strategy for increasing retention levels among current contract soldiers.

Although the proposed reforms are directed at improving the armed forces' overall readiness levels, it remains unclear how quickly these can be improved, and it is likely that several years will pass before the 'new look' programme will deliver a new level of readiness. In mid-to-late 2009 the *Kazkaz 2009* and *West 2009* exercises were designed to test the impact of the reforms on readiness levels, with emphasis on interoperability and force mobility. On 17 November, Makarov told an expanded session of the MoD board that the response time involved after issuing the order to deploy had been reduced from 24 hours to one hour.

Implications

These proposals mark a significant point of discontinuity from Soviet traditions in terms of the structure of the armed forces, command and control, and recruitment and training. If successful, the Russian armed forces will likely be better suited to operate on the modern battlefield and to be more effective in fighting local and regional conflicts. At the same time, the transformation will signify the end of the mass-mobilisation army. However, the success of this transformation will ultimately depend not on organisational restructuring but on the ability of the state and of military leaders to attract and retain sufficient talent into the army, to provide them with necessary training, to delegate authority to NCOs and to implement the ambitious re-armament and modernisation programme.

RUSSIA – DEFENCE ECONOMICS

After a decade of uninterrupted economic growth, Russia has been severely affected by the world financial crisis and the decline in global energy prices. Although GDP growth measured a respectable 5.6% in 2008, the first half of 2009 saw an extraordinary double-digit contraction in the Russian economy and the return of a large budget deficit. During the eight years of Vladimir Putin's presidency from 2000 to 2008, Russia enjoyed robust growth, accumulated very large foreign-currency reserves and ran large budget surpluses. As the decline in the economy deepened, however, it exposed Putin's reluctance to embrace economic reforms and emphasised the government's still-high dependence on revenues from oil and gas. As the global recession worsened and oil prices fell, the Russian economy contracted by 10.2% in the first five months of 2009, the rouble fell by 35% and at one stage the Russian stock market plummeted by 75%.

For the first time in many years, Russia is set to record a budget deficit in 2009, expected to be around 5% of GDP. In the short term, the government will be able to cover the deficit from its healthy reserves and the return on its investments. But the dire state of Russia's finances revealed the economy's overwhelming dependence on the export of hydrocarbons and other commodities. At first the government was slow to react to the global financial crisis, arguing that it was a US phenomenon and that Russia would remain largely unaffected. By early 2009, however, President Medvedev was forced to concede that his country's emerging economic problems had Russia-specific characteristics. By mid 2009 therefore the government had introduced a range of policy responses including the distribution of funds to support the banking system and high-tech companies; cuts in oil-export duties and corporate and personnel taxes; greater provision of social support; and increased investment in infrastructure projects. Even so, the World Bank estimated that in 2009 unemployment would reach 13% (the highest rate since Putin became president) and that 17% of the population would be living below the poverty level.

During the 1990s, Russia endured a series of crippling budget deficits, but beginning in 2000 a convergence of positive factors helped turn the government's fiscal position around. In 1997 the consolidated budget deficit measured 6.5% of GDP, but in 2006 a surplus of 8.3% was achieved, thanks not only to hydrocarbon revenues but government initiatives that included eliminating tax loopholes, more rigorous enforcement of tax laws and tight management of government expenditure. In 2006, with the 2007 Duma elections looming, spending restraints were weakened as the government increased spending on civil servants' salaries, education, health, housing and defence. Fearing that the government's hard-won budget discipline would further deteriorate in the run-up to the elections (and partly, it was suggested, to tie the hands of his successor), Putin introduced a shift in fiscal policy in July 2007 when for the first time he submitted a three-year budget, which included substantial future increases in national defence expenditure, indicative of the growing priority afforded to Russian's armed forces.

Since the economic crisis of 1998, Russian defence spending has been on an upward path, more than doubling in real terms by 2007. And budgets presented before the current economic downturn had called for spending to increase further from R820 billion in 2007 to R1,400bn in 2010. Although current economic circumstances have resulted in a revision to this target it seems that the long-term upward trajectory in defence spending will continue, albeit at a slower rate than originally envisaged. For example, in 2005 the government passed legislation outlining the 'State Programme of Armament 2007–2015' (*Gosuardstvennyi Programm Vooruzheniya*, GPV) which earmarked R5 trillion (US$169bn) for military procurement during the nine-year period. In 2007, only 10% of Russia's military inventory was classified as 'modern', and the goal of the GPV was to raise this figure to 30% by 2015 and ultimately to 70% by 2020.

While the programme contained a laundry list of new weapons systems, its primary focus was the improvement of Russia's strategic nuclear forces, which were slated to receive 34 new silo-launched and 66 mobile-launched *Topol*-M missile systems, while the navy would acquire SSBN submarines among 31 new vessels. The plan also provided for the modernisation of 159 long-range aviation platforms including Tu-160, Tu-95 and Tu-22 aircraft, many of which are thought to be in storage. However, the GPV was built on the premise that the economy would grow at an average rate of almost 6.5% to 2020, and it now seems highly unlikely that it will be implemented in full. Indeed, to date all of post-communist Russia's long-term GPVs have had to be abandoned when it was found that they had been based on unrealistic expectations regarding economic growth and the cost of new weapons systems. In March 2009, Medvedev indicated that the existing GPV was effectively dead and announced that work was under way on a draft of a new GPV to cover the period 2011–20 and based on a new economic forecast provided by the Ministry of Economic Development (Minekon). Given the depth of the economic crisis it seems unlikely that the economy will return to strong growth for some time, meaning the new version of the GPV is bound to be more modest that its predecessor. In terms of total national defence spending, the government appears to have decided that a level of about 2.5% of GDP is sustainable, and although the defence budget will jump to nearly 3% of GDP in 2009, this should be seen as a reflection of the contracting economy rather than a deliberate change in policy.

The 2009 and 2010 defence budgets

In August 2008, before the economic crisis was fully apparent, Minekon produced a background report on which the 2009 budget was based. The report itself was based on the rather optimistic assumption that oil prices would average US$95 a barrel during 2009 and that this would create growth of around 7%. Given these assumption, the 2009 national defence budget was set at R1,336bn (US$45.3bn). However, shortly after the budget became law, Minekon revised its forecast, and in the end the defence budget was reduced by 9% to R1,211bn (US$41bn). In spite of the cut, however, both Medvedev and now Prime Minister Putin signalled that spending on equipment programmes and social benefits would be maintained as originally planned and that savings would have to be found from elsewhere within the budget. Unfortunately, in recent years a number of changes to the way state budgets are presented have made the collection and analysis of precise military-spending data more difficult. In 2005, chapters in the federal budget were revised and the chapter on 'National Defence' was broadened to include certain military-related expenditures that had hitherto been part of separate ministries. Then, in 2006, details of the state defence order and other aspects of national defence spending were classified. In 2007, the government adopted its three-year budget framework, only to confuse matters further when, in response to the uncertainty generated by the economic crisis, it reverted to an annual budget for 2009.

At the height of the crisis in March 2009, Medvedev said that plans to modernise the country's armed

Table 20 **Estimated Russian Defence Expenditure** as % of GDP

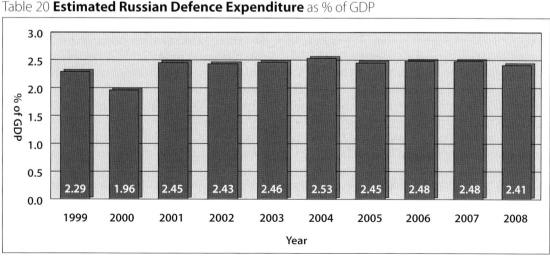

Year	1999	2000	2001	2002	2003	2004	2005	2006	2007	2008
% of GDP	2.29	1.96	2.45	2.43	2.46	2.53	2.45	2.48	2.48	2.41

forces would remain on track, claiming that 'despite the current financial difficulties, Russia has never had more favourable conditions to create modern and highly efficient armed forces'. He reinforced this view later in the year when he confirmed that procurement and housing benefits would be ring-fenced. Whether the Ministry of Defence is able to honour these pledges remains to be seen, but the statements are consistent with the prioritisation of spending on the Russian armed forces, also reflected in the support given to the country's defence industries since the start of the crisis. The economic crisis came at an awkward time for the Russian defence industry, which was two years into a major modernisation programme intended to help it to meet the twin challenges of domestic rearmament and a hefty export order book. Before the crisis struck, Boris Alyoshin, president of the Russian League of Assistance to Defence Enterprises, had already suggested that the 'entire work pattern of the Russian defence industry is obsolete' and forecast that retooling and modernising the industry would cost around US$5bn a year. In November 2008, former Defence Minister Sergei Ivanov revealed that the country's defence firms had been 'crippled' by the global financial crisis and were facing a 'dire cash shortage'. With the commercial sector unwilling to lend money to Russia's already heavily subsidised and largely loss-making defence companies the government was forced to step in with a rescue package. Totalling US$5.4bn, the measures included US$1.8bn to subsidise interest payments on loans, US$3.6bn of state guarantees for loans, the exchange of equity for support and the prevention of bankruptcies. Many observers, long critical of the inefficient and corrupt nature of Russia's defence-industrial base, suggested that the problems of dated management practices and a lack of entrepreneurship were unlikely to be helped by even greater state intervention. In light of the new, harsher financial climate, former Deputy Defence Minister for Financial and Economic Matters Lyubov Kudelina revealed that the defence ministry had drastically cut research and development spending on any projects that would not result in new arms for 2009–10, and later reports indicated that 300 projects had been halted.

The scale of the problems facing many defence companies was illustrated in August 2009 when Putin announced that plans by the United Aircraft Corporation (UAC) to pay off its debts had failed due to the economic downturn. UAC and its subsidiaries owe around US$3.7bn to creditors and had planned to settle the debt through the sale of 'unprofitable assets, refinancing or floating shares'. Putin criticised the company for, among other things, selling aircraft at a loss, and went on to warn the aviation sector in general that the state would not 'cover losses indefinitely, pull you out of debt and correct management mistakes'. He instructed the government to draft a financial rehabilitation programme for the aircraft-manufacturing industry.

By a stroke of good fortune, the Defence Ministry had finalised a 2009–11 state defence order (*Gosudarstvennyi Oboronnyi Zakaz* (GOZ)) in late August 2008, before the full effects of the financial crisis were apparent, and both the president and prime minister promised to uphold that part of the budget, if not for the entire period then certainly for 2009. Although the precise content of GOZ is never revealed, details do appear from time to time, usually in interviews or speeches by leading defence figures. The 2009 GOZ is thought to include 14 new ICBMs, seven new space launchers, six satellites, 24 MiG-29SMT aircraft originally exported to Algeria but later returned as defective, two Su-34 aircraft, 63 T-90 tanks, 31 new and modernised helicopters and over 300 armoured vehicles. Details for 2010 and 2011 are sparse, but it seems likely that the army will receive new *Buk*-M3 and *Tor*-M2 air-defence systems and *Iskander*-M theatre ballistic missiles, and the navy is expecting to take delivery of *Bulava* submarine-launched ballistic missiles. This programme, however, is years behind schedule and previous delivery dates have come and gone without orders being filled.

Delays in the delivery of the *Bulava* missiles have come against a backdrop of broader problems within Russia's shipbuilding industry. In March 2007, then President Putin created the United Shipbuilding Company (USC) with the intention of consolidating the entire Russian shipbuilding sector, including design bureaus, maintenance docks and major shipyards, into a single state-owned enterprise within three years. However, in July 2009 a report by the *Independent Military Review* alleged that the Russian navy was facing an 'irreversible collapse' due to the poor state of the shipbuilding industry, which it characterised as 'incapable of producing warships in either the quantity or at the level of quality' required by the navy. The situation was later acknowledged by the commander in chief of the Russian navy, Admiral Vladimir Vysotsky, who declared that he didn't want to waste billions of roubles repairing ageing ships that only had ten years of service life remaining, and that he was therefore open-minded about the prospect of acquiring new ships from overseas manufacturers. In that respect Russian industry officials have held talks with both DCNS of France and Thales of the UK that might lay the groundwork for a set of cooperative arrangements. The first project could result in Russia taking delivery of up to four *Mistral*-class amphibious-assault ships.

As part of the new GPV, the air force has revealed its preferred future structure and equipment needs. According to the commander of the Russian air force, Alexander Zelin, the backbone of the service will consist of a strategic aviation force comprising Tu-95C and Tu-160 bombers, as well as Tu-22M3 long-range bombers and IL-78 aerial tankers. The aircraft will be equipped with new systems that will also allow them to use conventional unguided bombs, and optimised to improve operational ranges. In addition to the fifth-generation fighter being jointly developed with India, the air force will also receive modernised Su-27SM and MiG-29SMT aircraft, Su-35S and MiG-35C fighters, and will replace its ageing Su-24 bombers with the more advanced Su-34. Of the 300 transport planes currently in service, the An-12s, An-22s and An-26s will be decommissioned and replaced by lighter IL-112B aircraft and a new medium-lift, 20-tonne-capacity fleet also being jointly developed with India. Existing An-124 and IL-76 platforms will be retained and upgraded. As for helicopters, the existing fleet of Mi-24 attack aircraft will be completely replaced with new-generation Mi-28 *Night Hunter* and Ka-52 *Alligator* attack helicopters. The first orders for a number of these aircraft were placed during the 2009 Moscow Aviation and Space Salon air show with the signing of a major contract between Sukhoi and the Russian government. Under the deal, Russia's Vnesheconombank will lend Sukhoi $110 million to start production of the Su-35, an aircraft originally conceived for export sales only but which, due to delays in the development of Russia's fifth-generation fighter, is now needed by the Russian air force itself. The total deal includes 48 Su-35s, 12 Su-27SMs and four Su-30MK2 aircraft that were originally intended for China.

Details about the 2010 defence budget remain sparse and, as in 2009, figures for only one year rather than three are available. According to the 2010 federal budget, spending on national defence will increase modestly compared with 2009, rising by 3.5% to R1,253bn (US$42.5bn), but with inflation hovering around 10% this represents an actual cut and is signif-

Table 21 **Draft Russian National Defence Expenditure (Rm)**

A: Chapter 2 'National Defence'	2008	2009	2010
Armed Forces of the Russian Federation	771.7	894.6	945.9
Mobilisation of external forces	4.6	3.6	2.6
Mobilisation of the economy	4.7	4.6	4.9
Collective peacekeeping	0.3	0.6	11.1
Military nuclear programmes	17.1	19.1	18.8
International treaty obligations	2.7	4.8	4.4
Applied R&D	129.7	162.9	137.9
Other	110.1	121.7	127.5
Sub-total: Chapter 2 'National Defence'	1,040.9	1,211.9	1,253.2

B: Additional military-related expenditure	2008	2009	2010
Internal troops	54.7	58.2	65.4
Security organs of the State	147.7	178.9	205.6
Border troops	64.9	79.9	77.6
Subsidies to closed towns	n.a.	n.a.	n.a.
Ministry of emergencies	49.9	57.2	60.2
Military pensions	212.0	223.2	240.8
Sub-total: Additional military-related expenditure	529.2	597.4	649.6
Total Defence-related Expenditure (A+B)	1,570.1	1,809.3	1,902.8
as % of GDP	3.76	4.46	4.07
as % of total outlays	20.7	18.2	19.2

icantly less than the figure of R1,391 (US$47.2bn) proposed in the three-year budget of 2008. To date only 54% of national defence spending is declassified; the limited details available about the 2010 State Defence Order are noted on p. 215.

Arms exports

In the immediate aftermath of the collapse of the Soviet Union, Russian arms manufacturers saw both exports and domestic orders plummet. In the last decade, however, Russian manufacturers have successfully forged new relationships and exports have boomed, often bringing in higher revenue than weapons delivered to the Russian armed forces themselves. Among the largest customers for Russian arms are China and India, which together have accounted for around 70% of arms exports in recent years. In 1993 Russia and India signed a Treaty of Friendship and Cooperation which included a defence-cooperation accord aimed at ensuring a continued supply of Russian arms and spare parts for India's military and the promotion of joint production of defence equipment. Since then, India has bought a wide range of equipment from Russia including T-90 tanks, multiple-launch rocket systems, howitzers, diesel-submarine upgrades, *BrahMos* anti-ship missiles and Su-30MKI fighter aircraft specifically designed for the Indian air force and built under licence by Hindustan Aeronautics Ltd. In 2009, the two countries were expected to finalise details of a new India–Russia Long-Term Inter-Governmental Agreement for Military Technical Cooperation, and work is continuing on a range of joint ventures including a fifth-generation fighter aircraft and a new multi-role transport aircraft. Meanwhile, China, Russia's other main trade partner, has imported over US$16bn of Russian equipment since 2001, averaging US$1bn a year in weapons imports since 1992, including Su-27 and Su-30 fighter aircraft, *Sovremenny*-class destroyers and *Kilo*-class diesel-electric submarines.

In recent years, however, as China and India have attempted to produce more of their own military equipment, the economic value of these two relationships to Russia has begun to wane. In 2005, China decided not to import additional Su-30s, leading Russian officials to express concern that Indian and Chinese demand for weapons systems would decline in the next five to ten years. The signing of a historic nuclear-cooperation agreement between India and the US will open the Indian market to US firms. China's position is less clear: the Western embargo on selling military equipment to Beijing makes Russia the only major advanced military power willing to sell equipment to the People's Liberation Army, but it seems unlikely that trade will increase from current levels. Indeed, in 2008 China accounted for only 18% of total Russian defence exports compared with some 50% earlier in the decade.

The most notable new market for Russian exports is Latin America. Contracts with Venezuela, Mexico, Peru, Colombia and Brazil have been signed, and future deals are currently being negotiated with Bolivia, Uruguay and Ecuador. In 2007, Venezuela emerged as Russia's second-largest export market when it agreed to purchase a substantial package of weapons including 24 Su-30MKV fighter aircraft, nine Mi-17 transport helicopters, five Mi-35 attack helicopters, two Mi-26 heavy-lift helicopters and 100,000 assault rifles. Since then the relationship has deepened, and in 2008 Moscow agreed to provide a US$1bn credit facility to the Venezuelan government for the purchase of Russian defence equip-

ment. In 2009 this facility was increased to a total of US$2.2bn. In the short term the facility will cover the delivery of around 100 T-72 main battle tanks and *Smerch* multiple-launch rocket systems from Russia, though in the longer term it is thought the credit arrangement is linked to an eventual acquisition by Venezuela of a multilayered air-defence system that would include *Tor*-M1 short- to medium-range air-defence batteries as well as S-300, *Buk*-M2 and *Pechora* units. Russia's strategy of using loans to facilitate weapons sales has been extended to a number of other countries, most notably Indonesia, where a US$1bn facility is in place. Moscow has also adopted other financial arrangements in an effort to boost weapons sales. Part of its deal with Venezuela, for example, includes access to Venezuelan oil fields by Russian companies, and as part of its multi-year weapons deal signed with Algeria in 2006, Russia agreed to write off around US$5bn in Algerian debt in return for access to Algerian oil and gas fields by LUKOIL and Gazprom.

In the Middle East, Russian firms are hoping that the imminent delivery of *Pantsir* air-defence systems to the UAE will revive regional interest in Russian military technology first sparked in 2000 when then President Putin cancelled an agreement with the US to restrict Russia's arms and nuclear sales to Iran, and later boosted by the Algerian deal. The most likely catalyst for an increase in trade would come if Russian firms could make inroads into the Saudi Arabian defence market, the largest in the region. In February 2009, Russia's state arms-export agency, Rosoboronexport, announced that it had secured a deal with an unnamed Middle Eastern country, widely believed to be Saudi Arabia. It is thought that a prospective US$2bn deal is currently being discussed that would see Saudi Arabia buy a variety of equipment including 30 Mi-35 attack helicopters, 120 Mi-17 transport helicopters, 150 T-90 tanks and 250 BMP-3 infantry fighting vehicles. Reports also suggest that Russia is hoping to sell its advanced S-400 air-defence systems to Riyadh, though whether this is an attempt by Saudi Arabia to convince Moscow not to sell the same weapons to Iran is unclear. Given that there are no overwhelming practical reasons for Saudi Arabia to embark on such an extensive procurement drive, any agreed contracts between the two countries could be interpreted as an attempt by Riyadh to achieve some leverage over Russia regarding its relationship with Tehran. Elsewhere in the region, Libya is emerging as a likely purchaser of significant quantities of Russian military equipment. At the 2009 Libyan Aviation Exhibition the two countries announced the completion of five contracts that follow on from a US$2.5bn agreement for military equipment and support services first outlined in mid 2008. According to Rosoboronexport, contracts so far agreed cover the modernisation of T-72 tanks and the supply of spare parts and maintenance equipment for a range of naval and ground-force systems. Future contracts are expected to include Su-35 and Su-30 fighter aircraft, Yak-130 combat-training planes, Mi-17 and Mi-35 helicopters and air-defence systems such as the S-300PMU2 and *Tor*-M1.

Estimating Russian military expenditure

As ever, estimating the real scale of Russian military spending is fraught with difficulty, not least because of recent changes in the presentation of budget data. Taken at face value, the official national-defence allocation for 2008, R1,041bn, corresponded to 2.49% of GDP; however, as indicated in Table 21, this figure excludes funds made available for other military-related expenditures such as pensions and paramilitary forces, not to mention the rising level of subsidies provided to the defence-industrial sector for which figures are unavailable. Including these additional budget allocations brings overall defence-related expenditure for 2008 to around R1,570bn, or 3.76% of that year's GDP.

Using the prevailing market exchange rate for 2008, Russia's stated defence expenditure was worth US$41.9bn, or US$63.3bn with the additional expenditures factored in. However, when assessing macroeconomic data from countries in transition, the market exchange rate does not usually reflect the actual purchasing power of the domestic currency, and economists therefore use an alternative methodology to make currency conversions, known as Purchasing Power Parity (PPP). For example, in 2008 Russia's GDP measured US$1,680bn when converted at market exchange rates; however, the World Bank has also calculated that, in PPP terms, Russia's 2008 GDP was equivalent to US$2,288bn. If this crude methodology is applied to military spending, then total defence-related expenditure in 2008 would jump to the equivalent of US$86bn.

Note: Although PPP rates can be a useful tool for comparing macroeconomic data, such as GDP, of countries at different stages of development, because there is no specific PPP rate to apply to the military sector, its use in this context should be treated with caution. In addition, there is no definitive guide as to which elements of military spending should be calculated using available PPP rates.

Russia

Russia RUS

Russian Rouble r		2008	2009	2010
GDP	r	41.66tr	40.51tr	
	US$	1.68tr	1.37tr	
per capita	US$	11,941	9,806	
Growth	%	5.6	-7.5	
Inflation	%	14.0	12.3	
Def exp	US$ᵃ	86bn		
Def bdgt	r	1.00tr	1.21tr	1.25tr
	US$	40.48bn	41.05bn	
US$1=r		24.8	29.5	

ᵃ PPP estimate

Population   140,041,247

Ethnic groups: Tatar 4%; Ukrainian 3%; Chuvash 1%; Bashkir 1%; Belarussian 1%; Moldovan 1%; Other 8%;

Age	0–14	15–19	20–24	25–29	30–64	65 plus
Male	7%	4%	4%	4%	22%	4%
Female	7%	4%	4%	4%	25%	10%

Capabilities

ACTIVE 1,027,000 (Army 360,000 Airborne 35,000 Navy 142,000 Air 160,000 Strategic Deterrent Forces 80,000 Command and Support 250,000) **Paramilitary 449,000**

(Estimated 170,000 in the permanent readiness units)
Terms of service: 12 months conscription.

RESERVE 20,000,000 (all arms)

Some 2,000,000 with service within last 5 years; Reserve obligation to age 50.

ORGANISATIONS BY SERVICE

Strategic Deterrent Forces ε80,000 (includes personnel assigned from the Navy and Air Force)

Navy
SUBMARINES • STRATEGIC • SSBN 14
5 *Delta* III (1†) (3 based in Pacific Fleet, 2 based in Northern Fleet) (80 msl) each with 16 RSM-50 (SS-N-18) *Stingray* strategic SLBM;
4 *Delta* IV (3 based in Northern Fleet and 1 based in Pacific Fleet), (64 msl) each with 16 RSM-54 (SS-N-23) *Skiff* strategic SLBM;
2 *Delta* IV in refit in Northern Fleet (32 msl) each with 16 RSM-52 (SS-N-23) *Skiff* strategic SLBM;
2 *Typhoon* based in Northern Fleet (40 msl) each with 40 RSM-52 (SS-N-20) *Sturgeon* strategic SLBM; 1 *Typhoon*† in reserve based in Northern Fleet with capacity for 20 RSM-52 (SS-N-20) *Sturgeon* strategic SLBM and 1+ *Bulava* (SS-N-30) strategic SLBM (trials / testing);
1 *Yury Dolgoruky* (limited OC undergoing sea trials; 2 additional units in build)

Strategic Rocket Force Troops
3 Rocket Armies operating silo and mobile launchers with 430 missiles and 1,605 nuclear warheads organised in 12 divs (reducing to 8). Launcher gps normally with 10 silos (6 for SS-18) and one control centre
MSL • STRATEGIC 430
  ICBM 385: 68 RS-20 (SS-18) *Satan* (mostly mod 4/5, 10 MIRV per msl); 180 RS12M (SS-25) *Sickle* (mobile single warhead); 72 RS18 (SS-19) *Stiletto* (mostly mod 3, 6 MIRV per msl.); 50 *Topol*-M (SS-27) silo-based/15 *Topol* M (SS-27) road mobile single warhead (5 regts); 1 regt RS-24 (MIRV)

Long-Range Aviation Command • 37th Air Army
FORCES BY ROLE
Bbr   2 heavy div with 4 regt at 3 air bases operating 79 bbr carrying up to 856 LRCM

EQUIPMENT BY TYPE
AIRCRAFT • LRSA 79: 16 Tu-160 *Blackjack* each with up to 12 KH-55SM/RKV-500B (AS-15B *Kent*) nuclear ALCM; 32 Tu-95MS6 (*Bear* H-6) each with up to 6 Kh-55/RKV-500A (AS-15A *Kent*) nuclear ALCM; 31 Tu-95MS16 (*Bear* H-16) each with up to 16 Kh-55/RKV-500A (AS-15A *Kent*) nuclear ALCM
Test ac 10: 5 Tu-95, 5 Tu-160

Warning Forces 3rd Space and Missile Defence Army
ICBM/SLBM launch-detection capability. 5 operationalsatellites
RADAR (9 stations) 1 ABM engagement system located at Sofrino (Moscow). Russia leases ground-based radar stations in Baranovichi (Belarus); Balkhash (Kazakhstan); Gaballa (Azerbaijan). It also has radars on its own territory at Lekhtusi, (St. Petersburg); Armavir, (southern Russia); Olenegorsk (northwest Arctic); Pechora (northwest Urals); Mishelevka (east Siberia).
MISSILE DEFENCE 2,064: 32 SH-11 *Gorgon;* 68 SH-08 *Gazelle;* 1,900 S-300PMU/SA-10 *Grumble;* 64 S-400 *Growler/*SA-21 *Triumf;*

Space Forces 40,000
Formations and units withdrawn from Strategic Missile and Air Defence Forces to detect missile attack on the RF and its allies, to implement BMD, and to be responsible for military/dual-use spacecraft launch and control.

Army ε205,000 (incl 35,000 AB); ε190,000 conscript (total 395,000)
6 Mil Districts. Transformation continues with large manpower reductions in senior and middle officer ranks, replacing and transferring the warrant officer class' responsibilities to NCOs. There has been a rationalisation of structures and equipment to reflect existing organisations and equipment. The first priority was, from January to June, to reorganise 39 bdes. The second to reorganise by December, combat support organisations.
FORCES BY ROLE
Comd   7 Army HQ

Tk	4 bde (each: 3 tk bn, 1 MR (BMP-2) bn, 1 armd recce bn, 1 arty regt, 1 SAM regt, 1 EW, 1 NBC, 1 engr coy)
MR	34 bde each (3 MR , 1 tk bn, 1 recce bn, 1 arty regt, 1 AT bn, 1 SAM regt, 1 EW, 1 NBC, 1 engr coy); 1 (coastal) bde; 1 trg regt
SF	9 (Spetsnaz) bde ; 1 SF Recce regt;
Air Aslt	2 bde (Ground Forces)
AB	4 (VdV) div (each: 2 para/air aslt regt, 1 arty regt); 1 (VdV) indep bde
Arty	1 div; 10 arty bde
SSM	10 bde each with 18 SS-21 *Scarab* (*Tochka*) (replacement by *Iskander*-M began during 2005 with 12 per bde)
MGA	1 div
AD	12 bde

EQUIPMENT BY TYPE

MBT 23,000: 250–300 T-90; 4,500 T-80/T-80UD/T-80UM/T-80U; 9,500 T-72L/T-72M; 3,000 T-72; 4,000 T-64A/T-64B; 150 T-62, 350 in store; 1,200 T-55

LT TK 150 PT-76

RECCE 2,000+ BRDM-2

AIFV 15,180+: 1,500+ BMD-1/BMD-2/BMD-3; 8,100 BMP-1; 4,600 BMP-2; 280 BMP-3; 700 BRM-1K; BTR-80A

APC 9,900+

  APC (T) 5,000: 700 BTR-D; 3,300 MT-LB; 1,000 BTR 50

  APC (W) 4,900+: 4,900 BTR-60/BTR-70/BTR-80; BTR-90

ARTY 26,121+

  SP 6,010: **122mm** 2,780 2S1 *Carnation*; **152mm** 3,100: 550 2S19 *Farm*; 1,600 2S3; 950 2S5; **203mm** 130 2S7

  TOWED 12,765: **122mm** 8,350: 4,600 D-30; 3,750 M-30 *M-1938*; **130mm** 650 M-46; **152mm** 3,725: 1,100 2A36; 750 2A65; 1,075 D-20; 700 M-1943; 100 ML-20 M-1937; **203mm** 40 B-4M

  GUN/MOR 820+

    SP 120mm 820: 30 2S23 *NONA-SVK*; 790 2S9 *NONA-S*
    TOWED 120mm 2B16 *NONA-K*

  MRL 3,976+: **122mm** 2,970: 2,500 BM-21; 50 BM-16; 420 9P138; **132mm** BM-13; **140mm** BM-14; **220mm** 900 9P140 *Uragan*; **300mm** 106 9A52 *Smerch*

  MOR 2,550

    SP 240mm 430 2S4
    TOWED 2,120: **120mm** 1,820: 920 2S12; 900 PM-38; **160mm** 300 M-160

AT

  MSL • MANPATS AT-2 3K11 *Swatter*; AT-3 9K11 *Sagger*; AT-4 9K111 *Spigot*; AT-5 9K113 *Spandrel*; AT-6 9K114 *Spiral*; AT-7 9K115 *Saxhorn*; AT-9 9M114M1 *Ataka*; AT-10 9K116 *Stabber*

  RCL 73mm SPG-9; **82mm** B-10

  RL 64mm RPG-18 *Fly*; **73mm** RPG-16/RPG-22 *Net*/RPG-26/RPG-7 *Knout*; **105mm** RPG-27/RPG-29

  GUNS 526+

    SP 57mm ASU-57; **85mm** ASU-85; D-44/SD44
    TOWED 526 **100mm** T-12A/M-55; T-12

AD

  SAM 2,465+

    SP 2,465+: 220 SA-4 A/B *Ganef* (twin) (Army/Front wpn – most in store); 225 SA-6 *Gainful* (div wpn); 550 SA-8 *Gecko* (div wpn); 350 SA-11 *Gadfly* (replacing SA-4/-6); 800 SA-9 *Gaskin*/SA-13 *Gopher* (regt wpn); 200 SA-12A (S-300V) *Gladiator*/SA-12B *Giant* (twin); 120 SA-15 *Gauntlet* (replacing SA-6/SA-8); SA-19 *Grison* (8 SAM, plus twin 30mm gun); SA-20 (S-400) *Triumph*

    MANPAD SA-7 *Grail* (being replaced by -16/-18); SA-14 *Gremlin*; 9K310 (SA-16) *Gimlet*; SA-18 *Grouse (Igla)*

  GUNS

    SP 23mm ZSU-23-4; **30mm** 2S6; **57mm** ZSU-57-2
    TOWED 23mm ZU-23; **57mm** S-60; **85mm** M-1939 *KS-12*; **100mm** KS-19; **130mm** KS-30

  UAV BLA-06; BLA-07; Tu-134 *Reys*; Tu-243 *Reys*/Tu-243 *Reys-D*; Tu-300 *Korshun*; *Pchela*-1; *Pchela*-2

  MSL • SSM ε200+: 200 SS-21 *Scarab* (*Tochka*); SS-26 *Iskander* (*Stone*); FROG in store; *Scud* in store

FACILITIES

Bases	2 (each 1 MR bde; subord. to North Caucasus MD) located in Abkhazia/ South Ossetia, 1 located in Tajikistan, 1 located in Armenia
Training centres	6 (District (each = bde; 1 per MD)), 1 (AB (bde))

Reserves

Cadre formations, on mobilisation form

MR	11 div

Navy 142,000

FORCES BY ROLE

4 major Fleet Organisations (Northern Fleet, Pacific Fleet, Baltic Fleet, Black Sea) and Caspian Sea Flotilla

Northern Fleet

FORCES BY ROLE

1 Navy HQ located at Severomorsk

FACILITIES

Bases   Located at Severomorsk and Kola Peninsula

EQUIPMENT BY TYPE

  SUBMARINES 42

    STRATEGIC 12: 8 SSBN; 4 in reserve
    TACTICAL 22: 12 SSN; 3 SSGN; 7 SSK
    SUPPORT 8: 4 SSAN (other roles); 4 in reserve (other roles)

  PRINCIPAL SURFACE COMBATANTS 10: 1 **CV**; 2 **CGN** (1 in reserve); 1 **CG**; 7 **DDG** (1 in reserve)

  PATROL AND COASTAL COMBATANTS 12: **FF** 8; **FS** 4

  MINE WARFARE 10 **MCMV**

  AMPHIBIOUS 5

  LOGISTICS AND SUPPORT 20+

Naval Aviation

EQUIPMENT BY TYPE

  AIRCRAFT

    BBR 39 Tu-22M *Backfire C*
    FTR 20 Su-27 *Flanker*
    FGA 10 Su-25 *Frogfoot*
    ASW 32: 14 Il-38 *May*; 18 Tu-142 *BearF/J*

TPT 27: 2 An-12 *Cub* (MR/EW); 25 An-12 *Cub*/An-24 *Coke*/An-26 *Curl*

HELICOPTERS
ASW 20 Ka-27 *Helix A*
ASLT 10 Ka-29 *Helix B*
SPT 15 Mi-8 *Hip*

Naval Infantry

Naval inf   1 regt with 74 MBT; 209 ACV; 44 arty

Coastal Defence

Coastal def   1 bde with 360 MT-LB; 134 arty
SAM   1 regt

Pacific Fleet

FORCES BY ROLE
Fleet HQ located at Vladivostok

FACILITIES
Bases located at Fokino, Magadan, Petropavlovsk-Kamchatsky, Sovetskya Gavan, Viliuchinsk and Vladivostok

EQUIPMENT BY TYPE
SUBMARINES 23
    STRATEGIC • SSBN 4: 3 and 1 in reserve
    TACTICAL 20: 4 SSN/SSGN and 7 in reserve; SSK 6 and 3 in reserve
PRINCIPAL SURFACE COMBATANTS 15: 1 CG; 5 DDG 3 in reserve; 9 FFG/FF
PATROL AND COASTAL COMBATANTS 16 PFM
MINE WARFARE 9 MCMV
AMPHIBIOUS 4
LOGISTICS AND SUPPORT 15+

Naval Aviation

EQUIPMENT BY TYPE
AIRCRAFT
    BBR 17 Tu-22M *Backfire C*
    FTR 30 MiG-31 *Foxhound A*
    ASW 29: 15 Il-38 *May*; 14 Tu-142 *Bear* F/J
    TPT 10 An-12 *Cub* (MR/EW); An-26 *Curl*
HELICOPTERS
    ASW 31 Ka-28 (Ka-27) *Helix*
    ASLT 6 Ka-29 *Helix*
    SPT 26 Mi-8 *Hip* (TPT)

Naval Infantry

Inf   1 div HQ (Pacific Fleet) (1 arty bn, 1 tk bn, 3 inf bn)

Coastal Defence

Coastal Def   1 bde

Black Sea Fleet

The RUS Fleet is leasing bases in Sevastopol and Karantinnaya Bay, and is based, jointly with UKR warships, at Streletskaya Bay. The Fleet's overall serviceability is assessed as medium.

FORCES BY ROLE
1 Navy HQ located at Sevastopol, UKR

FACILITIES
Bases located at Sevastopol, Novorossiysk and Temryuk

EQUIPMENT BY TYPE
SUBMARINES • TACTICAL SSK 2:1 (1 *Tango* in reserve)
PRINCIPAL SURFACE COMBATANTS 11: 2 CG; 1 DDG; 8 FFG/FS
PATROL AND COASTAL COMBATANTS 10: 7 PFM; 3 PHM
MINE WARFARE • MINE COUNTERMEASURES MCMV 7
AMPHIBIOUS 7: 4 *Ropucha*; 3 *Alligator*
LOGISTICS AND SUPPORT 6+

Naval Aviation

EQUIPMENT BY TYPE
AIRCRAFT
    FGA 18 Su-24 *Fencer*
    ASW 14 Be-12 *Mail*
    TPT 4 An-12 *Cub* (MR/EW); An-26
HELICOPTERS
    ASW 33 Ka-28 (Ka-27) *Helix*
    SPT 9: 1 Mi-8 *Hip* (TPT); 8 (MR/EW)

Naval Infantry

Naval inf   1 regt with 59 ACV; 14 arty

Baltic Fleet

FORCES BY ROLE
1 Navy HQ located at Kaliningrad

FACILITIES
Bases located at Kronstadt and Baltiysk

EQUIPMENT BY TYPE
SUBMARINES • TACTICAL SSK 2: 1 (and 1 in reserve)
PRINCIPAL SURFACE COMBATANTS 5: 2 DDG; 3 FFG
PATROL AND COASTAL COMBATANTS 22: 12 PFM; 10 FF
MINE WARFARE • MINE COUNTERMEASURES MCMV 11: 10 (and 1 in reserve)
AMPHIBIOUS 4 *Ropucha*
LOGISTICS AND SUPPORT 8+

Naval Aviation

EQUIPMENT BY TYPE
AIRCRAFT
    FTR 24 Su-27 *Flanker*
    FGA 29 Su-24 *Fencer*
    TPT 14: 12 An-12 *Cub*/An-24 *Coke*/An-26 *Curl*; 2 An-12 *Cub* (MR/EW)
HELICOPTERS
    ATK 11 Mi-24 *Hind*
    ASW 12 Ka-28 (Ka-27) *Helix*
    ASLT 8 Ka-29 *Helix*
    SPT 17 Mi-8 *Hip* (TPT)

Naval Infantry

Naval inf   1 bde with 26 MBT; 220 ACV; 52 MRL

Coastal Defence

FORCES BY ROLE
Arty   2 regt with 133 arty

SSM 1 regt with 8 SS-C-1B *Sepal*

AD 1 regt with 28 Su-27 *Flanker* (Baltic Fleet)

EQUIPMENT BY TYPE
AD 50 SAM

Caspian Sea Flotilla
The Caspian Sea Flotilla has been divided between AZE (about 25%), RUS, KAZ, and TKM.

FACILITIES
Base located at Astrakhan, Kaspiysk and Makhachkala

EQUIPMENT BY TYPE
PRINCIPAL SURFACE COMBATANTS • FRIGATES FFG 1

PATROL AND COASTAL COMBATANTS 6: 3 PFM; 3 PHM

MINE WARFARE • MINE COUNTERMEASURES 9: 5 MSC; 4 MSI

AMPHIBIOUS 6

LOGISTICS AND SUPPORT 5+

Naval Infantry
Naval inf 1 bde

NAVY EQUIPMENT BY TYPE
SUBMARINES 66

STRATEGIC 14

SSBN 14:

5 *Delta* III (1†) (3 based in Pacific Fleet, 2 based in Northern Fleet) (80 msl) each with 16 RSM-50 (SS-N-18) *Stingray* strategic SLBM

4 *Delta* IV (3 based in Northern Fleet and 1 based in Pacific Fleet), (64 msl) each with 16 RSM-54 (SS-N-23) *Skiff* strategic SLBM

2 *Delta* IV in refit in Northern Fleet (32 msl) each with 16 RSM-52 (SS-N-23) *Skiff* strategic SLBM

2 *Typhoon* based in Northern Fleet (40 msl) each with 40 RSM-52 (SS-N-20) *Sturgeon* strategic SLBM; 1 *Typhoon*† in reserve based in Northern Fleet with capacity for 20 RSM-52 (SS-N-20) *Sturgeon* strategic SLBM and 1+ *Bulava* (SS-N-30) strategic SLBM (trials / testing)

1 *Yury Dolgoruky* (limited OC undergoing sea trials; 2 additional units in build)

TACTICAL 52

SSGN 7:

5 *Oscar* II each with 2 single 650mm TT each with T-65 HWT, 4 single 553mm TT with 24 SS-N-19 *Shipwreck* tactical USGW

2 *Oscar* II (1 in reserve, 1 in refit), with 2 single 650mm TT each with T-65 HWT, 1 VLS with 24 SS-N-19 *Shipwreck* tactical USGW

SSN 17:

2 *Akula* II each with 4 single 533mm TT each with SS-N-21 *Sampson* tactical SLCM, 4 single 650mm TT each with single 650mm TT

5 *Akula* I each with 4 single 533mm TT each with SS-N-21 *Sampson* tactical SLCM, 4 single 650mm TT each with T-65 HWT; 3 *Akula* I in reserve (+RUS *Nerpa* undergoing trials for lease agreement with IND)

2 *Sierra* II with 4 single 533mm TT each with, SS-N-21 *Sampson* tactical SLCM, 4 single 650mm TT each with T-65 HWT/T-53 HWT

1 *Sierra* I in reserve†

4 *Victor* III (1 in reserve) each with 4 single 533mm TT each with SS-N-21 *Sampson* tactical SLCM, T-65 HWT

SSK 20:

15 *Kilo* each with 6 single 533mm TT each with T-53 HWT; 4 *Kilo* in reserve

1 *Lada* (Undergoing sea trials, expected ISD 2010) with 6 single 533mm TT, (2 additional vessels in build, planned for export)

SUPPORT • SSAN 8: 1 *Delta Stretch*; 1 *Losharik*; 2 *Paltus*; 3 *Uniform*; 1 *X-Ray*

PRINCIPAL SURFACE COMBATANTS 57

AIRCRAFT CARRIERS • CV 1 *Kuznetsov* (capacity 18 Su-33 *Flanker D* FGA ac; 4 Su-25 *Frogfoot* ac, 15 Ka-27 *Helix* ASW hel, 2 Ka-31 *Helix* AEW hel,) with 1 12 cell VLS (12 eff.) with SS-N-19 *Shipwreck* tactical SSM, 4 sextuple VLS (24 eff.) each with 8 SA-N-9 *Gauntlet* SAM

CRUISERS 5

CGN 1 *Kirov* with 10 twin VLS (20 eff.) each with SS-N-19 *Shipwreck* tactical SSM, 2 twin (4 eff.) each with 20 SA-N-4 *Gecko* SAM, 12 single VLS each with SA-N-6 *Grumble* SAM, 10 single 533mm ASTT, 1 single ASTT with 1 SS-N-15 *Starfish* ASW, 1 twin 130mm gun (2 eff.), (capacity 3 Ka-27 *Helix* ASW hel) (2nd *Kirov* undergoing extensive refit currently non operational)

CG 4:

1 *Kara*, with 2 quad (8 eff.) each with SS-N-14 *Silex* tactical SSM, 2 twin (4 eff.) each with 36 SA-N-3 *Goblet* SAM, 2 (4 eff.) each with 20 SA-N-4 *Gecko* SAM, 2 quad (4 eff.) ASTT (10 eff.), (capacity 1 Ka-27 *Helix* ASW hel)

3 *Slava* each with 8 twin (16 eff.) each with SS-N-12 *Sandbox* tactical SSM, 8 octuple VLS each with 8 SA-N-6 *Grumble* SAM, 8 single 533mm ASTT, 1 twin 130mm gun (2 eff.), (capacity 1 Ka-27 *Helix* ASW hel)

DESTROYERS • DDG 14:

1 *Kashin* (mod) with 2 quad (8 eff.) each with SS-N-25 *Switchblade* tactical SSM, 2 twin (4 eff.) each with SA-N-1 *Goa* SAM, 5 single 533mm ASTT, 2 76mm gun

5 *Sovremenny* (additional 2 in reserve) each with 2 quad (8 eff.) each with SS-N-22 *Sunburn* tactical SSM, 2 twin (4 eff.) each with 22 SA-N-7 SAM, 2 twin 533mm TT (4 eff.), 2 twin 130mm gun (4 eff.), (capacity 1 Ka-27 *Helix* ASW hel)

7 *Udaloy* each with 2 quad (8 eff.) each with SS-N-14 *Silex* tactical SSM, 8 octuple VLS each with SA-N-9 *Gauntlet* SAM, 2 quad 533mm ASTT (8 eff.), 2 100mm gun, (capacity 2 Ka-27 *Helix* ASW hel)

1 *Udaloy* II with 2 quad (8 eff.) each with SS-N-22 *Sunburn* tactical SSM, 8 octuple VLS each with SA-N-9 *Gauntlet* SAM, 8 SA-N-11 *Grisson* SAM, 10 single 533mm ASTT, 2 CADS-N-1 CIWS (4 eff.), 2 100mm gun, (capacity 2 Ka-27 *Helix* ASW hel)

FRIGATES 14

FFG 7:

1 *Gepard* with 2 quad (8 eff.) each with SS-N-25 *Switchblade* tactical SSM, 1 twin (2 eff.) with SA-N-4

Gecko SAM, 2 1 30mm CIWS, 1 76mm gun, (2nd vessel on trials expected ISD 2010)

2 *Krivak* I each with 1 quad (4 eff.) with SS-N-14 *Silex* tactical SSM, 1 twin (2 eff.) with 20 SA-N-4 *Gecko* SAM, 2 quad 533mm ASTT (8 eff.), 2 x12 RL (24 eff.), 2 100mm gun, 2 x2 76mm gun (4 eff.), (capacity 1 Ka-27 *Helix* ASW hel)

2 *Krivak* II each with 1 quad (4 eff.) with SS-N-14 *Silex* tactical SSM, 2 twin (4 eff.) each with 10 SA-N-4 *Gecko* SAM, 2 quad 533mm ASTT (8 eff.), 2 x12 RL (24 eff.), 2 100mm gun

2 *Neustrashimy* with 4 octuple (32 eff.) each with SA-N-9 *Gauntlet* SAM, 6 single 533mm ASTT, 1 RBU 12000 (10 eff.), 1 100mm gun, (capacity 1 Ka-27 *Helix* ASW) (3rd in build)

FF 7 *Parchim* II each with 2 quad (8 eff.) each with SA-N-5 *Grail* SAM, 2 twin 533mm ASTT (4 eff.), 2 RBU 6000 *Smerch* 2 (24 eff.), 1 76mm gun

CORVETTES 23:

1 *Steregushchiy* with 2 quad (8eff.) with SA-N-11 *Grisson* SAM , 1 100mm gun,(4 units in build)

3 *Grisha* III with 1 twin (2 eff.) with 20 SA-N-4 *Gecko* SAM, 2 twin 533mm ASTT (4 eff.), 2 RBU 6000 *Smerch* 2 (24 eff.)

19 *Grisha* V each with 1 twin (2 eff.) with 20 SA-N-4 *Gecko* SAM, 2 twin 533mm ASTT (4 eff.), 1 RBU 6000 *Smerch* 2 (12 eff.), 1 76mm gun

1 *Scorpion* with 2 quad (8 eff.) with SS-N-26 *Yakhont* SSM, 1 100mm gun, (ISD expected 2011)

PATROL AND COASTAL COMBATANTS 75

PFM 37

13 *Nanuchka* III each with 2 triple (6 eff.) each with 1 SS-N-9 *Siren* tactical SSM, 1 twin (2 eff.) eq. with SA-N-4 *Gecko*, 1 76mm gun

1 *Nanuchka* IV with 2 triple (6 eff.) each with SS-N-9 *Siren* tactical SSM, 1 twin (2 eff.) eq. with SA-N-4 *Gecko*, 1 76mm gun

4 *Tarantul* II each with 2 twin (4 eff.) each with SS-N-2C *Styx*/SS-N-2D *Styx* tactical SSM

18 *Tarantul* III each with 2 twin (4 eff.) each with SS-N-22 *Sunburn* tactical SSM

1 *Astrakhan* Project 21630 (First of 5–7 on order)

PHM 11:

2 *Dergach* each with 2 quad (8 eff.) each with SS-N-22 *Sunburn* tactical SSM, 1 twin (2 eff.) with 1 SA-N-4 *Gecko* SAM, 1 76mm gun

9 *Matka* each with 2 single each with SS-N-2C *Styx* tactical SSM/SS-N-2D *Styx* tactical SSM

PHT 6:

1 *Mukha* with 2 quad 406mm TT (8 eff.)

5 *Turya* each with 4 single 533mm ASTT

PFC 21:

1 *Pauk* each with 4 single 533mm ASTT, 2 RBU 1200 (10 eff.)

20 ε *Stenka*

MINE WARFARE • MINE COUNTERMEASURES 37

MCO 2 *Gorya*
MSO 9 *Natya*
MSC 22 *Sonya*
MHC 4 *Lida*
AMPHIBIOUS: 42+

PRINCIPAL AMPHIBIOUS SHIPS • LPD

1 *Ivan Rogov* (capacity 4–5 Ka-28 (Ka-27) *Helix* ASW hel; 6 ACV or 6 LCM; 20 tanks; 520 troops)

LS 22

LSM 3:

3 *Polnochny*† B (capacity 6 MBT; 180 troops); (3 in reserve)

LST 19:

1 Ivan Green (Mod – *Alligator*) (capacity 1 Ka-29 Helix B; 13 MBT; 300 troops), (expected ISD 2010)

4 *Alligator* (capacity 20 tanks; 300 troops)

14 *Ropucha* II and I (capacity either 10 MBT and 190 troops or 24 APC (T) and 170 troops)

CRAFT 19+

LCM 6 *Ondatra*

LCU 3 *Serna* (capacity 100 troops)

ACV 10:

3 *Aist* (capacity 4 lt tank)

3 *Lebed*

2 *Orlan*

2 *Pomornik* (*Zubr*) (capacity 230 troops; either 3 MBT or 10 APC (T))

LOGISTICS AND SUPPORT 105+

A significant element of the RUS Auxiliary and Support Fleet (Estimated at 370+ vessels) is either no longer active, at extended readiness or awaiting disposal - the following is a considered and revised assessment of significant RUS operationally active logistics and support elements:

AOR 5 *Chilikin*

AOL 9: 2 *Dubna*; 2 *Uda*; 5 *Altay mod*

AORL 2 *Olekma*

AS 1 *Malina* (Project 2020)

ARS 9 *Goryn*

AR 4 *Amur*

ARC 7: 4 *Emba*; 3 *Klasma*

AG 2 *Amga* (msl spt ship)

ATS 10: 5 *Katun*; 2 *Neftegaz*; 3 *Ingul*

AH 3 *Ob* †

AGOR 4: 2 *Akademik Krylov*; 2 *Vinograd*

AGI 11: 1 *Balzam*; 3 *Moma*; 7 *Vishnya*

AGM 1 *Marshal Nedelin*

AGS(I) 24: 3 *Biya*; 19 *Finik*; 2 *Moma*

AGB 4 *Dobrynya Mikitich*

ABU 6: 2 *Kashtan*; 4 *Sura*

ATF 1 *Sorum*

TRG • AXL 2 *Smolny*

Naval Aviation ε35,000

4 Fleet Air Forces, each organised in air div; each with 2–3 regt with an HQ elm and 2 sqn of 9–10 ac each; configured recce, ASW, tpt/utl org in indep regt or sqn

Flying hours   ε40 hrs/year

FORCES BY ROLE

Bbr	sqns with Tu-22M *Backfire C*
Ftr/FGA	sqn with Su-27 *Flanker*; 10 Su-25 *Frogfoot*; 58 Su-24 *Fencer*; 30 MiG-31 *Foxhound*
ASW	sqns with Ka-27 *Helix*; Mi-14 *Haze-A*; sqn with Be-12 *Mail*; Il-38 *May*; Tu-142 *Bear*
MR/EW	sqns with An-12 *Cub*; Il-20 RT *Coot-A*; Mi-8 *Hip* J

Tpt   sqns with An-12 *Cub*/An-24 *Coke*/An-26 *Curl*

ATK hel   sqns with Mi-24 *Hind*

Aslt hel   sqns Ka-29 *Helix*; 26 Mi-8 *Hip*

Tpt hel   sqns with Ka-25 PS *Hormone* C, Ka-27 PS
              Helixe D; Mi-6 *Hook*; Mi-14 PS *Haze* C

EQUIPMENT BY TYPE

AIRCRAFT 259 combat capable

  BBR 56 Tu-22M *Backfire* C

  FTR 79: 49 Su-27 *Flanker*; 30 MiG-31 *Foxhound*

  FGA 52: 5 Su-25 *Frogfoot*; 47 Su-24 *Fencer*

  ASW 27 Tu-142 *Bear* F/J*

  MP 44: 15 Be-12 *Mail**; 29 Il-38 *May**

  EW • ELINT 2 Il-20 RT *Coot-A*; 5 An-12 *Cub*

  TPT 37: 37 An-12 *Cub*/An-24 *Coke*/An-26 *Curl*

HELICOPTERS

  ATK 11 Mi-24 *Hind*

  ASW 105: 70 Ka-27 *Helix*; 20 Mi-14 *Haze*-A

  EW 8 Mi-8 *HipJ*

  ASLT 28 Ka-29 *Helix*

  SAR 62: 22 Ka-25 PS *Hormone* C/Ka-27 PS *Hormone*-D;
  40 Mi-14 PS *Haze* C

  SPT 36: 26 Mi-8 *Hip*; 10 Mi-6 *Hook*

MSL • TACTICAL

  ASM AS-10 *Karen*; AS-11 *Kilter*; AS-12 *Kegler*; AS-4
  Kitchen; AS-7 *Kerry*; KH-59 (AS-13) *Kingbolt*

Coastal Defence • Naval Infantry (Marines) 9,500

FORCES BY ROLE

Naval inf   3 indep bde (*total:* 1 AT bn, 1 arty bn, 1
              MRL bn, 1 tk bn, 4 naval inf bn); 1 indep
              bn; 3 regt; 1 indep regt;

Inf   1 div HQ (Pacific Fleet) (3 inf bn, 1 tk bn, 1
              arty bn)

SF   3 (fleet) bde (1 op, 2 cadre) (*each:* 1 para bn,
              1 spt elm, 2–3 underwater bn)

EQUIPMENT BY TYPE

MBT 160 T-55M/T-72/T-80

RECCE 60 BRDM-2 each with AT-3 9K11 *Sagger*

AIFV 150+: ε150 BMP-2; BMP-3; BRM-1K

APC 750+

  APC (T) 250 MT-LB

  APC (W) 500+ BTR-60/BTR-70/BTR-80

ARTY 367

  SP 113: **122mm** 95 2S1 *Carnation*; **152mm** 18 2S3

  TOWED 122mm 45 D-30

  GUN/MOR 113

    SP 120mm 95: 20 2S23 *NONA-SVK*; 75 2S9 SP
    NONA-S

    TOWED 120mm 18 2B16 *NONA-K*

  MRL 122mm 96 9P138

  AT • MSL • MANPATS 72 AT-3 9K11 *Sagger*/AT-5
  9K113 *Spandrel*

  GUNS 100mm T-12

  AD • SAM 320

    SP 70: 20 SA-8 *Gecko*; 50 SA-9 *Gaskin*/SA-13 *Gopher*
    (200 eff.)

    MANPAD 250 SA-7 *Grail*

    GUNS 23mm 60 ZSU-23-4

Coastal Defence Troops 2,000

FORCES BY ROLE

(All units reserve status)

Coastal Def   2 bde

Arty   2 regt

AD   1 regt with 28 Su-27 *Flanker*

SAM   2 regt

EQUIPMENT BY TYPE

MBT 350 T-64

AIFV 450 BMP

APC 320

  APC (T) 40 MT-LB

  APC (W) 280 BTR-60/BTR-70/BTR-80

ARTY 364

  SP 152mm 48 2S5

  TOWED 280: **122mm** 140 D-30; **152mm** 140: 50 2A36;
  50 2A65; 40 D-20

  MRL 122mm 36 BM-21

AIRCRAFT • FTR 28 Su-27 *Flanker*

AD • SAM 50

Military Air Forces 160,000 reducing to 148,000 (incl conscripts)

4,000+ ac, 833 in reserve

HQ at Balashikha, near Moscow. The Military Air Forces comprise Long Range Aviation (LRA), Military Transport Aviation Comd (VTA), 5 Tactical/Air Defence Armies comprising 49 air regts. Tactical/Air Defence roles include air defence, interdiction, recce and tactical air spt. LRA (2 div) and VTA (9 regt) are subordinated to central Air Force comd. A joint CIS Unified Air Defence System covers RUS, ARM, BLR, GEO, KAZ, KGZ, TJK, TKM, UKR and UZB.

The Russian Air Force is embarking on a period that will see significant restructuring, both in terms of general organization as well as air base and unit structure.

Long-Range Aviation Command • 37th Air Army

Flying hours: 80-100 hrs/yr

FORCES BY ROLE

Bbr   2 heavy bbr div; 4 heavy regt (non-strategic); 4
              heavy regt (START accountable) with 116 Tu-
              22M-3/MR *Backfire* C

Tkr   1 base with 20 Il-78 *Midas*/Il-78M *Midas*

Trg   1 hvy bbr trg centre with 4 Tu-22M-3, 4 Tu-95MS,
              30 Tu-134 *Crusty*

EQUIPMENT BY TYPE

AIRCRAFT 116 combat capable

  BBR 116 Tu-22M-3/Tu-22MR *Backfire* C

  TKR 20 IL-78 *Midas* /Il-78M *Midas*

  TPT 30 Tu-134 *Crusty*

Tactical Aviation

Flying hours   25 to 40 hrs/year

FORCES BY ROLE

Bbr/FGA   7 regt with Su-25A/SM *Frogfoot*; 1 regt with
              Su-34P *Fullback*; 1 bbr div plus 13 FGA regt
              with Su-24/Su-24M2 *Fencer*; Su-25

Ftr   9 regt with MiG-31 *Foxhound*; 9 regt with MiG-29 *Fulcrum* (24 being upgraded); 6 regt with Su-27 *Flanker* (incl Su-27SM); trg units with MiG-25 *Foxbat*

Recce   4 regt with MiG-25R *Foxbat*; 5 regt with Su-24MR *Fencer*

AEW   1 base with A-50 *Mainstay*/A-50U *Mainstay*

ECM   some sqn with Mi-8(ECM) *Hip J*

Trg   2 op conversion centres

SAM   35 regt with 1,900+ S-300 (SA-10) *Grumble* (quad) (7,600 eff.). First SA-20/S-400 (*Triumph*) bn op Elektrostal in Moscow region.

EQUIPMENT BY TYPE

AIRCRAFT 1,743 combat capable

BBR/FGA 807: 241 Su-25A/SM *Frogfoot*; 550 Su-24 *Fencer* (up to 7 upgraded to Su-24M2); 16 Su-34P *Fullback* (Su-27IB)

FTR 725: 188 MiG-31 *Foxhound*; 226 MiG-29 *Fulcrum* (24 being upgraded); 281 Su-27 (18 upgraded to 27SM) incl 40 Su-27SMK *Flanker*; 30 MiG-25 *Foxbat*;

RECCE 119: 40 MiG-25R *Foxbat**; 79 Su-24MR *Fencer**

AEW 20 A-50 *Mainstay* AEW/A-50U *Mainstay*

TRG 92: 40 MiG-29 *Fulcrum**; 21 Su-27 Flanker*; 15 Su-25 *Frogfoot*;* 16 Su-24 *Fencer** (instructor trg)

HELICOPTERS 60 Mi-8(ECM) *Hip J*

UAV *Pchela*-1T; *Albatross†*; *Expert†*

AD • SAM • SP 1,900+ S-300 (SA-10) *Grumble* (quad) / S-400 (SA-20) *Triumph*

MSL • ARM AS-11 *Kilter*; AS-12 *Kegler*; AS-17 *Krypton*

ASM AS-14 *Kedge*; AS-15 *Kent*; AS-16 *Kickback*; AS-4 *Kitchen*; AS-7 *Kerry*

AAM R-27T (AA-10) *Alamo*; R-60T (AA-8) *Aphid*; R-73M1 (AA-11) *Archer*

BOMBS

Laser-guided KAB-500; KAB-1500L

TV-guided KH-59 (AS-13 *Kingbolt*); KAB-500KR; KAB-1500KR; KAB-500OD

INS/GPS/GLONASS guided KH-101; KH-555

Military Transport Aviation Command• 61st Air Army

Flying hours   60 hrs/year

FORCES BY ROLE

Air   9 regt incl. 5 indep regt; 1 div with 12 An-124 *Condor*; 21 An-22 *Cock* (Under MoD control); 210 Il-76 *Candid*

Civilian Fleet   Some sqn (medium and long-range passenger)

EQUIPMENT BY TYPE

AIRCRAFT • TPT 293+: 50 An-12 *Cub*; 12 An-124 *Condor*; 21 An-22 *Cock* (Under MoD control); 210 Il-76M/MD/MF *Candid*

Army Aviation Helicopters

Under VVS control. Units organic to army formations.

Flying hours   55 hrs/year

FORCES BY ROLE

Atk hel   20 regt/sqn with 8 Ka-50 *Hokum*; ε620 Mi-24 *Hind*; 7 Mi-28N *Havoc* (300 by 2010)

Tpt/ECM   mixed regts with 35 Mi-26 *Halo* (hy); 8 Mi-6 *Hook*; ε600 MI-17 (Mi-8MT) *Hip H*/ Mi-8 *Hip*

EQUIPMENT BY TYPE

HELICOPTERS

ATK 635: 8 Ka-50 *Hokum*; 620 Mi-24 *Hind* D/V/P; 7 Mi-28N *Havoc* (300 by 2015)

TPT/ECM ε643: 35 Mi-26 *Halo* (hy); 8 Mi-6 *Hook*; ε600 Mi-17 (Mi-8MT) *Hip H*/Mi-8 *Hip* Spt

Air Force Aviation Training Schools

EQUIPMENT BY TYPE

AIRCRAFT 980+

FTR MiG-29 *Fulcrum*; Su-27 *Flanker*; MiG-23 *Flogger*

FGA Su-25 *Frogfoot*

TPT Tu-134 *Crusty*

TRG 336 L-39 *Albatros*

FACILITIES

Aviation Institute   5 sqn regt with MiG-29 *Fulcrum*; Su-27 *Flanker*; MiG-23 *Flogger*; Su-25 *Frogfoot*; Tu-134 *Crusty* tpt; L-39 *Albatros* trg ac

Kaliningrad Special Region 10,500 (Ground and Airborne); 1,100 (Naval Infantry) (total 11,600)

These forces operated under the Ground and Coastal Defence Forces of the Baltic Fleet. Probably no MR (trg) regt end 2009.

Army

FORCES BY ROLE

MR   1 bde; 1 indep regt (trg) (disbanded by end 2009/early 2010)

SSM   1 bde with 12-18 SS-21 *Tochka* (*Scarab*)

Arty   1 bde

Hel   1 indep regt

AD   1 bde

FACILITIES

Bases   Located at Baltiysk and Kronstadt

EQUIPMENT BY TYPE

MBT 811

ACV 1,239: 865; 374 look-a-like

ARTY 345 ARTY/MOR/MRL

Navy • Baltic Fleet – see main Navy section

Russian Military Districts

Leningrad MD 28,700 (Ground and Airborne); 1,300 (Naval Infantry – subordinate to Northern Fleet) (total 30,000)

Combined Service 1 HQ located at St Petersburg

Army

FORCES BY ROLE

MR   2 indep bde, 1 coastal bde

SF   1 (Spetsnaz) bde

AB   1 (VdV) div (2-3 air aslt regt, 1 arty regt)

Arty	1 bde,
SSM	1 bde with 12-18 SS-21 *Tochka* (*Scarab*)
AD	1 bde

Reserve

MR	1 bde

FACILITIES

Training Centre   1 located at Sertolovo (District)

EQUIPMENT BY TYPE

MBT 300
ACV 2,350: 100; 2,250 look-a-like
ARTY 690 MOR/MRL

Navy • Northern Fleet – see main Navy section

Military Air Force

6th Air Force and AD Army

FORCES BY ROLE

PVO	2 corps
Bbr	1 div with 56 Su-24M *Fencer*
Ftr	1 div with 30 MiG-31 *Foxhound*; 55 Su-27 *Flanker*
Recce	1 regt with 20 Su-24MR *Fencer*; 28 MiG-25R/U *Foxbat*; some MiG-31
AEW/AWACS	A-50 *Mainstay*
Tpt	Sqns with An-12, An-24, An-26, Tu-134
Cbt spt	57 Mi-8 *Hip* (incl ECM), some Mi-8PPA, 38 Mi-24, 4 Mi-6

AD • SAM 525 incl S-300V

Moscow MD 86,200 (Ground and Airborne)

Combined Service   1 HQ located at Moscow

Army

FORCES BY ROLE

Comd	1(20th) Army HQ
Tk	2 Bde
MR	3 bde
SF	1 (Spetsnaz) bde; 1 AB recce regt
AB	2 div (each: 2 para regt, 1 arty regt)
Arty	1 div HQ (3 arty bde)
SSM	2 bde each with 12-18 SS-21 *Scarab* (*Tochka*) (may reduce to 1 bde)
AD	2 bde

Reserve

MR	1 bde

EQUIPMENT BY TYPE

MBT 2,500
ACV 3,100: 2,100; 1,000 look-a-like
ARTY 1,300 ARTY/MOR/MRL

Military Air Force

Moscow Air Defence and Air Army has 1 corps. Due to have additional AD regt (2 bn) equipped with S-400 SAM system.

FORCES BY ROLE

PVO Air	1 (32 PVO) corps 1 16th Air Army
Ftr	regts with 41 MiG-31 *Foxhound*, 45 MiG-29 *Fulcrum*; 30 Su-27
FGA	regts with 52 Su-25 *Frogfoot*, 80 Su-24 *Fencer*
Recce	regt with 55 Su-24MR
Tpt	regt with An-12, An-24, An-26, An-30, Tu-134
Cbt Spt	sqns with 98 Mi-8/ Mi-8PPA/sMV (incl 46 Mi-8(ECM)
Utl	sqns with Mi-8
Trg	30 MiG-29, 18 Su-27, 1 Su-25
UAV	*Pchela*-1T at Combat Training Centre, Egor'evsk, Moscow

EQUIPMENT BY TYPE

AD • SAM 600

Volga-Ural MD 55,000 (Ground and Airborne)

Combined Service   1 HQ located at Yekaterinburg

Army

1 Army HQ

FORCES BY ROLE

Comd	1 (2nd) Army HQ
Tk	1 bde
MR	4 bde; 3 bde (Tajikistan)
SF	2 (Spetsnaz) bde (may reduce to 1 bde)
AB	1 (VdV) bde
Arty	1 bde
SSM	1 bde each with 12-18 SS-21 *Tochka* (*Scarab*)
AD	1 bde

FACILITIES

Training Centre   1 located at Kamshlov (district)

EQUIPMENT BY TYPE

MBT 3,000
ACV 2,300
ARTY 2,700 ARTY/MOR/MRL

Navy • Caspian Sea Flotilla see main Navy section

Military Air Force

5th AF and AD Army has no ac subordinated, incl storage bases

EQUIPMENT BY TYPE

AIRCRAFT •
FTR 34 MiG-31
FGA Su-25 *Frogfoot*
TPT An-12; An-26
COMMS Mi-14
HELICOPTERS • SPT: Mi-6, 25 Mi-8 *Hip* (comms); Mi-24, 24 Mi-26
TRG MiG-25U, MiG-29, Su-25, Su-27; 300 L-39 *Albatros*, Mi-2 *Hoplite*

North Caucasus MD 88,600 (Ground And Airborne); ε1,400 (Naval infantry) (total 90,000)

including Trans-Caucasus Group of Forces (GRVZ)
Combined Service   1 HQ located at Rostov-on-Don

Army

FORCES BY ROLE

Army	1 (58th) Army HQ
MR	8 bdes; 1 bde (Armenia); 1 bde (South Ossetia (manning may reduce to 1,700 FSB)); 1 bde (Abkhazia); 2 Mtn bde
SF	2 (Spetsnaz) bde
Air Aslt	1 bde (ground forces)
AB	1 (VdV) div (2 air asslt regt,1 arty regt)
Arty	2 bde
SSM	1 bde each with 12-18 SS-21 *Tochka* (*Scarab*)
AD	2 bde

EQUIPMENT BY TYPE
MBT 800
ACV 2,000
ARTY 900 ARTY/MOR/MRL

Navy • Black Sea Fleet – see main Navy section

Military Air Force
6th AF and AD Army

FORCES BY ROLE
390 cbt ac

Bbr	1 div with 62 Su-24 *Fencer* (some 32 likely to be retired)
Ftr	1 corps (4 regt with 105 MiG-29 *Fulcrum*; 59 Su-27 *Flanker*)
FGA	1 div with 98 Su-25 *Frogfoot*; 36 L-39
Recce	1 regt with 30 Su-24MR *Fencer*
ECM	1 sqn with 52 Mi-8(ECM) *Hip J*
Tpt	Sqns with An-12, An-24, An-26, Tu-134
Cbt Spt	regts with 58 Mi-8PPA/SMV, 75 Mi-24, 40 Mi-28N *Night Hunter*
Utl	4 Mi-6, 10 Mi-26
Trg	tac aviation regt

Siberian MD 52,000 (Ground and Airborne)
Combined Service   1 HQ located at Chita

Army

FORCES BY ROLE

Army	2 (36th and 41st) Army HQ (may reduce to 1 HQ)
Tk	1 bde
MR	4 bde
SF	1 (Spetsnaz) bde
Air Aslt	1 bde (ground forces)
Arty	2 arty bde
SSM	2 bde each with 12-18 SS-21 *Tochka* (*Scarab*)
AD	2 bde

Reserve
MR   6 Bde

FACILITIES
Training Centre 1 located at Peschanka (district)

EQUIPMENT BY TYPE
MBT 4,000
ACV 6,300
ARTY 2,600 MOR/MRL

Military Air Force
14th AF and AD Army (HQ Novosibirsk)
200 cbt ac

FGA/bbr	some sqn with 30 Su-25 *Frogfoot*; 56 Su-24M *Fencer*
Ftr	some sqn with 39 MiG-31 *Foxhound*; 46 MiG-29 *Fulcrum*
Recce	some sqn with 29 Su-24MR *Fencer-E*; MiG-25R/MiG-25U
Tpt	sqns with An-12, An-26
Cbt Spt	sqns with Mi-8PPA/sMV; Mi-24
Utl/Comms	sqns with Mi-8

AD • SAM S-300O

Far Eastern MD 72,500 (Ground and Airborne); 2,500 (Naval infantry) (total 75,000)
Incl Pacific Fleet and Joint Command of Troops and Forces in the Russian Northeast (comd of Pacific Fleet)
Joint Forces Command 1 HQ located at Petropavlovsk
Combined Service   1 HQ located at Khabarovsk

Army

FORCES BY ROLE

Army	2 (5th and 35th) Army HQ (may reduce to 1 HQ)
MR	6 bde
SF	2 bde (SF may reduce to 1 bde)
Arty	3 bde
SSM	2 bde each with 12-18 SS-21 *Scarab* (*Tochka*)
MGA	1 div
AD	3 bde

Reserve
MR   6 Bde

FACILITIES
Training Centre 1 located at Khabarovsk (district)

EQUIPMENT BY TYPE
MBT 3,000
ACV 6,000
ARTY 4,100 MOR/MRL

Navy • Pacific Fleet – see main Navy section

Military Air Force
11th AF and AD Army (HQ Khabarovsk)

FGA/bbr	1 regt with 23 Su-27SM; 97 Su-24M *Fencer*
Ftr	sqn with 26 MiG-31 *Foxhound*; ≤100Su-27 *Flanker*;
Recce	sqns with 51 Su-24MR *Fencer*
Tpt	regts with An-12, An-26
Cbt Spt	regts with Mi-8PPA/sMV
Comms	sqns with Mi-8; Mi-24, Ka-50
UAV	1 sqn with *Pchela*-1 (Arseniev, Primorskyy)

AD • SAM S-300P

Paramilitary 449,000

Federal Border Guard Service ε160,000 active

Directly subordinate to the President; now reportedly all contract-based personnel

FORCES BY ROLE
10 regional directorates
Frontier 7 gp

EQUIPMENT BY TYPE
AIFV/APC (W) 1,000 BMP/BTR
ARTY • SP 90: **122mm** 2S1 *Carnation*; **120mm** 2S12; **120mm** 2S9 *Anona*
PRINCIPAL SURFACE COMBATANTS 14
  FRIGATES 13
    FFG 7 *Krivak III* each with 1 twin (2 eff.) with SA-N-4 *Gecko* naval SAM, 2 quad 533mm TT (8 eff.), 2 RBU 6000 *Smerch 2* (24 eff.), (capacity 1 Ka-27 *Helix A* ASW hel; 1 100mm)
    FFL 6: 3 *Grisha* II; 3 *Grisha* III
  CORVETTES • FS 1 *Grisha* V
PATROL AND COASTAL COMBATANTS 180
  PFM 22:
    2 *Pauk II* each with 1 quad (4 eff.) with SA-N-5 *Grail* naval SAM, 2 twin 533mm TT (4 eff.), 2 RBU 1200 (10 eff.), 1 76mm
    20 *Svetlyak* each with 1 quad (4 eff.) with SA-N-5 *Grail* naval SAM, 2 single 406mm TT, 1 76mm
  PFT 17 *Pauk I* each with 1 quad (4 eff.) with SA-N-5 *Grail* naval SAM, 4 single 406mm TT, 1 76mm
  PHT 3 *Muravey*
  PSO 12: 8 *Alpinist*; 4 *Komandor*
  PFC 15 *Stenka*
  PCC 36: 9 *Mirazh*; 27 *Type 1496*
  PCI 12 *Zhuk*
  PCR 32: 3 *Ogonek*; 7 *Piyavka*; 15 *Shmel*; 5 *Vosh*; 2 *Yaz*
  PBF 31: 1 *A-125*; 1 *Mangust*; 1 *Mustang* (Project 18623); 15 *Saygak*; 12 *Sobol*; 1 *Sokzhoi*
LOGISTICS AND SUPPORT 24: 1 AO
  AK 10 *Neon Antonov*
  AKSL 6 *Kanin*
  AGS 2 *Yug* (primarily used as patrol ships)
  AGB 5 *Ivan Susanin* (primarily used as patrol ships)
AIRCRAFT • TPT ε86: 70 An-24 *Coke*/An-26 *Curl*/An-72 *Coaler*/Il-76 *Candid*/Tu-134 *Crusty*/Yak-40 *Codling*; 16 SM-92
HELICOPTERS: ε200 Ka-28 (Ka-27) *Helix* ASW/Mi-24 *Hind* Atk/Mi-26 *Halo* Spt/Mi-8 *Hip* Spt

Interior Troops 200,000 active

FORCES BY ROLE
7 Regional Commands: Central, Urals, North Caucasus, Volga, Eastern, North-Western and Siberian
Paramilitary   5 (special purpose) indep div (ODON) (*each*: 2–5 paramilitary regt); 6 div; 65 regt (bn – incl special motorised units); 10 (special designation) indep bde (OBRON) (*each*: 1 mor bn, 3 mech bn); 19 indep bde
Avn   gp

EQUIPMENT BY TYPE
MBT 9
AIFV/APC (W) 1,650 BMP-1 /BMP-2/BTR-80
ARTY 35
  TOWED 122mm 20 D-30
  MOR 120mm 15 PM-38
HELICOPTERS • ATK 4 Mi-24 *Hind*

Federal Security Service ε4,000 active (armed)

Cdo unit (incl Alfa and Vympel units)

Federal Protection Service ε10,000–30,000 active

Org include elm of ground forces (mech inf bde and AB regt)

Mech inf	1 bde
AB	1 regt
Presidential Guard	1 regt

Federal Communications and Information Agency ε55,000 active

MOD • Railway Troops ε50,000
Paramilitary   4 (rly) corps; 28 (rly) bde

Special Construction Troops 50,000

SELECTED NON-STATE GROUPS

Security forces are active in the North Caucasus against a number of rebel groups operating in Chechnya, Daghestan, Kabardino-Balkaria, North Ossetia and Ingushetia. The strength of these groups varies (Chechen rebels are believed to number between 2-3,000), and equipments include mines and IEDs, mortars, SALW

DEPLOYMENT

ARABIAN GULF AND INDIAN OCEAN
Maritime Security Operations 1 DDG; 1 AOE; 1 ATF

ARMENIA
Army 3,214; 1 MR bde; 74 MBT; 330 AIFV; 14 APC (T)/APC (W); 68 SP/towed arty; 8 mor; 8 MRL; 1 base
Military Air Forces • Tactical Aviation
1 AD sqn with 18 MiG-29 *Fulcrum*; 2 SAM bty with S-300V (SA-12A) *Gladiator*; 1 SAM bty with SA-6 *Gainful*

Air Base located at Yerevan

BELARUS
Strategic Deterrent Forces • Warning Forces
1 radar station located at Baranovichi (*Volga* system; leased)
1 Naval Communications site

BOSNIA-HERZEGOVINA
OSCE • Bosnia and Herzegovina 3

CÔTE D'IVOIRE
UN • UNOCI 7 obs

CENTRAL AFRICAN REPUBLIC/CHAD
UN • MINURCAT 117; 1 hel det with 4 Mi-8MT

DEMOCRATIC REPUBLIC OF CONGO
UN • MONUC 28 obs

GEORGIA
Army ε3,400; Abkhazia 1 MR bde; South Ossetia 1 MR bde; **Military Air Forces** • Tactical Aviation; atk hel

KAZAKHSTAN
Strategic Deterrent Forces • Warning Forces
1 radar station located at Balkhash, (*Dnepr* system; leased)

KYRGYZSTAN
Military Air Forces ε500; some Su-27 *Flanker*; 5+: 5 Su-25 *Frogfoot*; some Su-24 *Fencer* FGA; Army Aviation Helicopters; some Mi-8 *Hip* spt hel

LIBERIA
UN • UNMIL 4 obs

MIDDLE EAST
UN • UNTSO 5 obs

MOLDOVA/TRANSDNESTR
Army ε1,500 (including ε500 peacekeepers)
FORCES BY ROLE
2 MR bn (subord to Moscow MD)
EQUIPMENT BY TYPE
ACV 100

Military Air Forces 7 Mi-24 *Hind* atk hel; MI-8 *Hip* Spt Hel

SERBIA
OSCE • Kosovo 2
UN • UNMIK 1 obs

SUDAN
UN • UNMIS 122; 12 obs; 1 avn unit
Military Air Forces 1 hel det

SYRIA
Army and Navy 150
1 naval facility under renovation at Tartus

TAJIKISTAN
Army 5,500; 1 mil base (201st - subord Volga-Ural MD) with (3 MR bde); 54 MBT; 350 ACV; 190 Mor/MRL; 4 Mi-8 *Hip*
Military Air Forces 5 Su-25 *Frogfoot* FGA

UKRAINE
Navy • Coastal Defence • 13,000 including Naval Infantry (Marines) 1,100; Arty: 24; AIFV /APC (T) / APC (W): 102
Navy Black Sea Fleet; 1 Fleet HQ located at Sevastopol: Strategic Deterrent Forces. Warning Forces; 2 radar stations located at Sevastopol (*Dnepr* System, leased) and Mukachevo (*Dnepr* system, leased).

WESTERN SAHARA
UN • MINURSO 15 obs

Table 22 **Selected arms procurements and deliveries, Russia**

Designation	Type	Quantity	Contract Value	Supplier Country	Prime Contractor	Order Date	First Delivery Due	Notes
Bulava 30 (SS-NX-30)	SLBM	_	_	Dom	_	_	2009	In development, production due to commence 2009. First test 2005. For *Borey*-class SSBN
T-72 and T-80	MBT	180	_	Dom	_	2006	2007	Some to be modernised. Number may be subject to change
BTR-80 and BTR-90	APC	100	_	Dom	_	2005	2006	Delivery status unclear
Buk-M2 (SA-17 'Grizzly')	SAM	_	_	Dom	_	_	_	To replace *Buk*-M1-2 systems in service with army AD
Tor-M2E (SA-15 'Gauntlet')	SAM	_	_	Dom	Almaz-Antey	_	2010	Bty formations. First AD regts due to be re-equipped by 2010–11
S-400 *Triumf* (SA-21 *Growler*)	AD	18 bn	_	Dom	_	_	2007	Two bn deployed by Mar 2009. Delivery status unclear
Project 22350 / *Admiral Gorshkov*	FFG	1	US$400m	Dom	Severnaya Verf Shipyard	2005	2009	Navy estimates need for up to 20 vessels by 2015. Delayed. First launch due 2011
Project 20380 / *Steregushchiy*-class	FS	4	_	Dom	Severnaya Verf Shipyard	_	2009	Second vessel (*Stoiky*) due 2010. Up to 20 planned. First vessel delivered
Agat-class (*Natya* III) / Project 266M	MSC	1		Dom		2000	2008	*Vitse-Admiral Zakharin*. Launched Jan 2008
Dyugon	LCU	1	R200m (US$69m)	Dom	Volga Shipyard	2005	2007	Laid down 2006. Delivery status unclear
Project 955 *Borey*	SSBN	4	_	Dom	Sevmash Shipyard	1996	2006	Lead SSBN, *Yuri Dolgoruky* launched Feb 2008. ISD due 2010. 2nd launch due 2009. 3rd vessel ordered 2006 and due 2011. Fourth vessel began construction 2009. Possible order of 8–10
Project 885 *Yasen*	SSN	6	_	Dom	Sevmash Shipyard	1993	2010	Construction of second vessel began July 2009. First of class, *Severodvinsk*, expected to be launched Dec 2009 and delivered late 2010. Delayed for financial reasons
Typhoon (Akula)-class	SSBN SLBM Upgrade	1	_	Dom	_	1994	_	*Dmitriy Donskoy* modernised for testing of new *Bulava* 30 (SS-NX-30) SLBM and will remain in service until *Borey*-class SSBN are operational
Seliger	Research Ship	2	_	Dom	Yantar Shipyard	2009	2011	Laid down July 2009. Second vessel due to be laid down 2010
Su-34 *Fullback*	FGA	24	US$864m	Dom	Sukhoi	2006	2006	Delivered in batches; 2 in 2006, 7 in 2007, 10 in 2008 and 5 in 2009–10. First 2 delivered Dec 2006
Su-35S *Flanker*	Multi-role ac	48	US$2.5bn	Dom	Sukhoi	2009	2015	Upgrade with new avionics, longer range radar and more powerful engines (air force)
Su-27SM, Su-30M2		16 (12 Su-27, 4 Su-30)	US$2.5bn	Dom	Sukhoi	2009	2015	Combined with above deal in contract worth US$2.5bn (air force)
Medium Transport Aircraft (MTA)	Tpt ac	50	_	Dom/IND	Irkut/HAL	2007	2014	In development. RUS obliged to order at least 50 under deal signed with India in 2007
Tu-160 *Blackjack*	Bbr	30	_	Dom	UAC	2007	2012	Upgrade of 15 current Tu-160s, plus 15 new bbr

Russia

Table 22 **Selected arms procurements and deliveries, Russia**

Designation	Type	Quantity	Contract Value	Supplier Country	Prime Contractor	Order Date	First Delivery Due	Notes
Yak-130 AJT (Advanced Jet Trainer)	Trg ac	200	_	Dom	Yakolev	2005	2015	To replace current L-39. Purchase to begin 2009 following flight testing
Mi-28N *Night Hunter*	Hel	8	_	Dom	Rostvertol	2005	2009	Plans for 45 to 67 Mi-28N. Delivery status unclear
Ka-52 *Hokum-B*	Atk/recce hel	30	_	Dom	Progress	2008	2009	Twin-seat version of Ka-50 *Black Shark* For air force. Final delivery 2012. Delivery status unclear
Searcher II	UAV	US$50m	_	ISR	IAI	2009	_	Contract incl *I-View 150* and *Bird-Eye 400*

Chapter Five

Middle East and North Africa

IRAQ

In mid November 2008, after a year of intense negotiations, the United States and the Iraqi government signed a Status of Forces Agreement and a Strategic Framework Agreement, in a bid to formalise relations between the two sovereign states for the first time since the 2003 invasion and subsequent regime change. These agreements set out an unambiguous timetable for Iraq's security forces to take sole responsibility for law and order across the whole country. At the end of June 2009, US forces withdrew from all of Iraq's cities, towns and villages, and by December 2009, the US military's role in Iraq will have evolved into an assistance, training and advisory mission. By August 2010, the US troop presence is due to fall from the current 120,000 to 50,000. Under Article 24 of the new US–Iraq treaty, 'all US forces are to be withdrawn from all Iraqi territory, water and airspace' by the end of December 2011.

Iraqi security forces

With such a rigid timetable for the complete removal of all US combat troops, Iraq's future stability lies in the hands of its own army and police force. This is a daunting responsibility for a military force less than seven years old. In May 2003, the US occupation authority disbanded the old Iraqi army, thereby hastening Iraq's descent into an insurgency and civil war that lasted until at least 2007. Realising its error, the US quickly attempted to build a new and effective Iraqi military force.

As of April 2009, Iraq's security forces employed around 600,000 personnel, spread between the interior and defence ministries, as well as the Iraqi National Counter-Terrorism Force. Officially, their command and control is centred on the Iraqi Joint Forces Command, which reports to the National Operations Centre in Baghdad. However, since his appointment in 2006 Prime Minister Nuri al-Maliki has subverted the formal chain of command, tying senior army commanders and paramilitary units to him personally. This has been achieved, firstly, through the creation of the Office of the Commander in Chief (see *The Military Balance 2008*, pp. 228–9).

Maliki has used this platform to appoint and promote senior officers loyal to him. Secondly, Maliki has used a number of operational commands to bring both the army and the police force together under one regional organisation and appointed a favoured general to run each centre. To date, command centres have been created in Baghdad, Basra, Diyala, Karbala and Samarra, allowing the prime minister to control the security forces in five of Iraq's most important provinces. In addition, in April 2007, as control of Iraq's special forces was handed from the US to the Iraqi government, a Counter-terrorism Bureau was set up to manage special forces at ministerial level, effectively placing them under the direct control of the prime minister.

Lack of autonomous capacity

The main focus of American attempts to reconstitute an indigenous security force has been the Iraqi army. Iraq currently has 13 infantry divisions and one mechanised division. Its ground force includes 185 fully trained battalions and over 55 brigades. Although all military operations are now conducted in conjunction with the Iraqi army, the US Department of Defense has indicated that the Iraqi military only takes the lead in areas of the country where the security threat is low. In terms of operational readiness, the US military estimates that the vast majority of Iraq's security forces are at 'level two', which means they are capable of conducting counter-insurgency operations only with US assistance, or 'level three', which means they can operate only in conjunction with US forces. There are several reasons for this continued lack of autonomous capacity: the relatively short time since this army was created; poor levels of education among rank-and-file soldiers (25% of soldiers do not meet the army's own educational standards and 15% are illiterate); and a shortage of junior and non-commissioned officers capable of leading troops into battle.

The Iraqi army is still dependent upon the US military for close air support and communications, intelligence, surveillance and logistical infrastructure. These technical shortcomings could be overcome through extended investment and training, but US military trainers and advisers are concerned that the investment already made in hardware and training may not be sustainable. Over the last few years the Iraqi army and national police have taken delivery of more than 5,000 'humvees', the all-purpose vehicle that has become the workhorse of the security services. An investigation by the special inspector general for Iraq reconstruction into how these vehicles were used concluded that in spite of a US$682 million investment in maintenance infrastructure, 'the Iraqi Army's ability to conduct maintenance operations and operate a supply system is questionable'. Reports suggest that the Iraqi army has failed to develop the logistics needed to re-equip and repair its humvees, leading army commanders in the field to cannibalise other vehicles instead of sending them in for repair, for fear that they might not be returned.

Obstacles to security-force development

Beyond the problems of personnel, training and logistics, there are three further major impediments to the development of Iraq's security forces. The first is the ongoing influence of Ba'athist ideology and operating procedures. The speed with which the Iraqi army was reconstituted after 2003 meant that up to 70% of the new officer corps had served in the former Iraqi army. This led US Colonel Timothy Reese, who was in July 2009 chief of the Baghdad Operations Command Advisory Team, to claim that a Ba'athist–Soviet military culture remained entrenched and 'will not change'. This culture, he argued, led to the neglect and mistreatment of enlisted men, a lack of initiative, and the extreme centralisation of command and control.

The second obstacle is corruption. In the aftermath of the devastating truck bombings in Baghdad on 19 August 2009 which left 95 dead and 500 injured, reports pointed to corrupt military officers taking bribes to let truck bombs through the security cordon which surrounds the centre of Baghdad. According to Reese, 'corruption among officers is widespread' with 'cronyism and nepotism rampant in the assignment and promotion system'. In 2008, Iraq's own government anti-corruption watchdog, the Commission on Public Integrity, opened 736 cases into corruption involving the Ministry of Interior which controls both the national and local police. US and Iraqi authorities have attempted to limit corruption in the security forces by conducting personnel audits of both the army and police to purge them of 'ghost employees', fictitious policemen and soldiers whose wages are stolen by senior officers. Reports suggest that up to

25% of the Ministry of Defence's payroll is stolen in this way.

Sectarian and religious divisions among rank-and-file and mid-level officers represent the final weakness constraining Iraqi security forces' ability to operate effectively. Given that Iraq was mired in civil conflict until at least the end of 2007, it is hardly surprising that sectarian tensions still exist. The worst excesses, which in 2005–06 saw the national police and some units of the army repeatedly accused of ethnic cleansing and sectarian murder, have now stopped. However, Major General (retd) Najim Abed al-Jabouri, an officer in the former Iraqi Air Defense forces, who has also held the posts of police chief and mayor of Tal Afar in Ninevah Province, argued in August 2009 that the politicisation of the Iraqi security services by ethno-sectarian parties posed the largest obstacle to their becoming a genuinely professional and truly national force. Al-Jabouri argued that Iraqi army divisions in five of Iraq's provinces – Kut, Diwanya, Salahadeen, Anbar and Diyala – have been weakened by the malign influence of various political parties. Reese agreed, pointing to the Iraqi army's inability to stand up to the Shia political parties as a major source of its weakness.

But in spite of the many factors impeding the ability of the security services to operate effectively, progress has undoubtedly been made. As noted above, both the army and national police are no longer active players in sectarian violence. And the Iraqi army, alongside its US counterpart, has played a major role in reducing the violence that dominated the country in 2006–07. In order for the security forces to progress further, sustained investment by Baghdad will be needed over the next decade, in spite of fluctuating oil prices. Over the same period, the US and NATO will need to conduct training missions to increase the skills and infrastructure of the armed forces, and also to limit the politicisation of the army and especially the national police.

International troop presence

At the end of 2009, NATO's training mission in Iraq currently consisted of up to 200 personnel from 14 nations, with teams within Iraqi Training and Doctrine Command, the Iraqi Military Academy at Ar-Rustamiyah and Iraqi Ground Forces Command, among other locations. The UK Royal Navy's contribution to the international naval training team represents the last substantial British military presence in Iraq, following its withdrawal of personnel and equip-

Map 2 **Iraq**

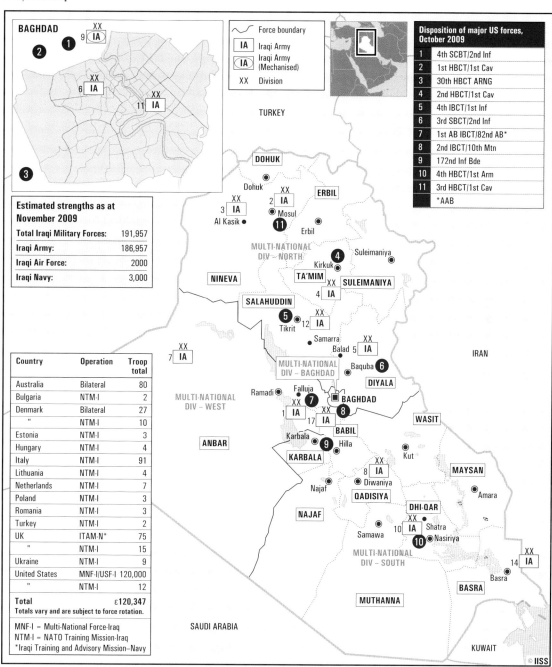

BAGHDAD

Disposition of major US forces, October 2009	
1	4th SCBT/2nd Inf
2	1st HBCT/1st Cav
3	30th HBCT ARNG
4	2nd HBCT/1st Cav
5	4th IBCT/1st Inf
6	3rd SBCT/2nd Inf
7	1st AB IBCT/82nd AB*
8	2nd IBCT/10th Mtn
9	172nd Inf Bde
10	4th HBCT/1st Arm
11	3rd HBCT/1st Cav
	*AAB

Force boundary
IA Iraqi Army
IA Iraqi Army (Mechanised)
XX Division

Estimated strengths as at November 2009

Total Iraqi Military Forces:	191,957
Iraqi Army:	186,957
Iraqi Air Force:	2000
Iraqi Navy:	3,000

Country	Operation	Troop total
Australia	Bilateral	80
Bulgaria	NTM-I	2
Denmark	Bilateral	27
"	NTM-I	10
Estonia	NTM-I	3
Hungary	NTM-I	4
Italy	NTM-I	91
Lithuania	NTM-I	4
Netherlands	NTM-I	7
Poland	NTM-I	3
Romania	NTM-I	3
Turkey	NTM-I	2
UK	ITAM-N*	75
"	NTM-I	15
Ukraine	NTM-I	9
United States	MNF-I/USF-I	120,000
"	NTM-I	12
Total		**ε120,347**

Totals vary and are subject to force rotation.

MNF-I = Multi-National Force-Iraq
NTM-I = NATO Training Mission-Iraq
*Iraqi Training and Advisory Mission–Navy

TURKEY

DOHUK

Dohuk

ERBIL

Al Kasik

Mosul

Erbil

MULTI-NATIONAL DIV – NORTH

NINEVA

Kirkuk

TA'MIM

SULEIMANIYA

Suleimaniya

SALAHUDDIN

Tikrit

Samarra

Balad

IRAN

MULTI-NATIONAL DIV – BAGHDAD

Baquba

DIYALA

Ramadi

Falluja

MULTI-NATIONAL DIV – WEST

BAGHDAD

ANBAR

Karbala

BABIL

Hilla

Kut

WASIT

KARBALA

Diwaniya

MAYSAN

Najaf

QADISIYA

Amara

NAJAF

DHI-QAR

Samawa

Shatra

Nasiriya

MULTI-NATIONAL DIV – SOUTH

Basra

MUTHANNA

BASRA

SAUDI ARABIA

KUWAIT

© IISS

Middle East and North Africa

ment in mid 2009. This Iraqi Training and Advisory Mission (Navy) (Umm Qasr) is reported to consist of around 100 UK and US personnel. Following the Iraqi parliament's delayed sanctioning of an agreement between London and Baghdad regulating the presence of the UK contingent, British personnel had to relocate to Kuwait and Bahrain, only returning to Iraq in mid October. Their mission is to train, mentor and equip the personnel of the Iraqi navy and marines. On 30 April, coinciding with the flag-lowering ceremony for British forces in Basra, Iraqi naval forces took over responsibility for the protection of the Khawr al-Amaya and Basra oil terminals, as well as the ports of Umm Qasr and al-Zubair, though they remain dependent on the presence of foreign militaries' frigates and destroyers. The Iraqi navy, meanwhile, which has a number of officers in training in the UK in addition to their Iraq-based training, has seen its inventory increase in line with these heightened responsibilities. It took delivery of a series of small boats for riverine and inshore duties, while a patrol boat procured from Italy (the first of four on order) was due to come into service at the end of 2009.

ISRAEL, GAZA AND IRAN

The June 2008 ceasefire between **Israel** and Hamas held for a number of months despite rocket attacks by mainly non-Hamas militants, but by November the rate of fire had increased. The first armed clash between an Israel Defense Forces (IDF) raiding party and Hamas forces occurred on 4 November. Dozens of rockets and mortars were fired in retaliation and additional IDF incursions to close border tunnels effectively annulled the ceasefire, which had been due to expire on 19 December. Around 330 rockets and mortar rounds had been fired during the six-month ceasefire; in the week after the deadline passed, almost half that number were launched into southern Israel.

As detailed in *Strategic Survey 2009* (pp. 236–9), Israel initiated an aerial assault on Gaza on 27 December 2008 with the aim of reducing rocket attacks and 'restoring Israeli deterrence'. *Operation Cast Lead* was a broad bombing campaign and ground invasion aimed to knock out as much of Hamas's command-and-control facilities as possible. A ground invasion began on 3 January 2009, proceeded from the northern part of Gaza and surrounded Gaza City within a few days. During the campaign, rocket and mortar fire persisted, but decreased in intensity as Israel's forces tightened their grip. After firing some 600 rockets into Israel and losing 1,200 to IDF attacks, Hamas was only left with about 1,200 by the time of a renewed ceasefire on 17 January (though rocket fire and Israeli military strikes carried on until the spring). The two-week offensive caused substantial damage to Gaza's infrastructure – extending to 14,000 homes, 68 government buildings and 31 NGO offices. At least 1,300 Palestinians and 13 Israelis were reported killed. The large difference in fatalities stemmed from the IDF's use of heavy firepower, which kept Israeli casualties low, but led to many casualties on the Palestinian side. There was a strong international reaction to the campaign and the post-conflict humanitarian situation in Gaza. Perhaps partly in response to the international reaction, but more directly to a domestic debate arising out of the critical testimony of some soldiers who had fought in *Cast Lead,* the IDF carried out internal investigations relating to its conduct during the campaign. A number of commanders gave interviews focusing on rules of engagement and IDF actions on the ground in Gaza, while IDF Chief of the General Staff Lieutenant-General Gabi Ashkenazi repudiated soldiers' critical testimonies. (In October 2009, a report by Judge Richard Goldstone alleging possible war crimes by both sides during the conflict was endorsed by the UN Human Rights Council. Given its contents, the report was subject to much critical attention.)

As noted in previous editions of *The Military Balance*, Israel's air force is engaged in a project to move some of its bases and units to the south of the country. A number of squadrons moved to the Nevatim air base in the Negev in August 2008, and elements of the last squadron to leave Lod air base in central Israel flew south in January 2009. Lod was subsequently closed. The move to the Negev locations gives more flexibility in terms of infrastructure, but the Israeli government is also promoting the moves in terms of developing and settling the south. Meanwhile, the IDF has stated that it has learnt lessons both from the 2006 conflict in Lebanon (*The Military Balance 2006* (p. 233) noted the establishment of the Winograd Commission to investigate the conflict) as well as *Cast Lead*. Reports during 2009 point to efforts to develop inter-service cooperation, while in the wake of the successful missile attack on the INS *Hanit* during the conflict in Lebanon, the navy conducted a review of its missile-boat operations, aiming to improve operational procedures as well as issues concerning crew training and morale.

Iran's nuclear activities continue to be of great concern to the international community. Israel, in particular, considers a nuclear-armed Iran an existential threat and refuses to rule out the possibility of a pre-emptive or preventive strike against Iran's nuclear infrastructure. But while Iran in early 2009 had already produced enough low-enriched uranium for one nuclear weapon if further enriched, it had not yet crossed the line of weaponisation that would present an imminent threat. Many other problems make a military option difficult for Israel. Even if Iran's major nuclear sites at Isfahan, Natanz and Arak could be successfully destroyed through air attacks or missile launches, this might not be enough if Iran has redundant secret facilities. Indeed, the unmasking of Iran's hitherto secret enrichment facility outside Qom, in September, (although known to Western governments before Iran was effectively forced into admitting its existence) increased the sense of uncertainty over whether unknown sites would remain after any attack. While Israel has GBU-28 'bunker-buster' bombs, in 2008 it was denied a shipment of the smaller and more accurate GBU-39. Other problems with any potential strike include the route, which would involve flying over Israel's Arab neighbours, as well as surmounting Iran's air defences (that is, if an air strike is the preferred option; the deployment of Israeli naval assets to the Red Sea in mid 2009 was perhaps designed to create uncertainty over the means of any possible action). Were such an operation to be mounted, one of the key questions would concern the definition of mission success. 'There is no military option that does anything more than buy time', US Defense Secretary Robert Gates said in September. 'The estimates are one to three years or so.' Such questions would have to be considered in conjunction with the potential risks of Iranian retaliation, as well as the doubtless deleterious regional and international impact of such a strike.

Iran's expanding missile capabilities also provoked concern. As noted in *Strategic Survey 2009* (p. 221), Iran has already fielded a *Shahab*-3 missile with the one-tonne payload capacity and 1.2m airframe diameter necessary to carry a nuclear warhead. Its 1,300km range encompasses Israel, Turkey and Saudi Arabia. The *Shahab*-3 also formed the first stage of the two-stage rocket Iran used to launch its first satellite into low-earth orbit in February 2009. Perhaps more worrying was the November 2008 test firing of a new medium-range ballistic missile, the solid-fuelled *Sajjil*. Though its range and payload are similar to the *Shahab*, the faster launch time of a solid-fuelled rocket of this type reduces vulnerability to pre-emptive strikes. Iran also reported successful firings of *Shahab* and *Sajjil* missiles at the end of the *Great Prophet IV* exercise conducted by the Iranian Revolutionary Guard Corps (IRGC) in September 2009.

But Tehran must also contend with home-grown security threats: six commanders of the IRGC (including the deputy commander of the IRGC ground forces) were killed in an 18 October attack in Sistan-Baluchistan Province, which killed 43 in total. The Jundullah terrorist group, which has promoted a brand of Sunni radicalism in the tribal region through abductions and executions of police and military officers, claimed responsibility. Earlier in the year, the Basij paramilitary force, which is effectively under IRGC control, was heavily employed against demon-strators during protests over the announced victory, in the presidential election, of Mahmoud Ahmadinejad.

OTHER DEVELOPMENTS

Concerns about Iran's missile-development programme also prompted moves to develop ballistic-missile defence within the Gulf region. Speaking at the IISS *Manama Dialogue* in December 2008, US defence secretary Gates observed that since 2007 there had been 'significant changes in air and missile defence throughout the Middle East. Several GCC nations are in the process of acquiring, or have expressed interest in, shared early warning, near real-time information on air and missile attacks that would allow maximum time for a nation to defend itself. Additionally, all GCC countries have expressed a desire to obtain, or are already obtaining, active defence systems.' In September 2009 Gates elaborated on this, saying that the US was working, on a bilateral and multilateral basis, to establish regional missile defence; he then noted existing *Patriot* systems in the region, as well as *Aegis* ships. The US did, he continued, have 'strong bilateral relationships in developing missile defense with several of the countries in the Gulf'. As an illustration of moves in this direction, in late 2008 Raytheon and Lockheed Martin were awarded contracts to deliver *Patriot* GEM-T and PAC-3 missiles and associated systems to the United Arab Emirates (Saudi Arabia and Kuwait already field *Patriot* variants among their air-defence systems, while in 2008 the UAE also requested to purchase Terminal High Altitude Air Defense systems from the US.) President Barack Obama's 17 September 2009 decision to substitute a mobile, adaptable ship- and land-based missile shield for President George W. Bush's plan to deploy silo-housed missile interceptors in Poland and an advanced tracking radar in the Czech Republic will provide additional protection to US forces and friends in the Middle East against an Iranian missile threat.

In October, **Saudi Arabia's** Royal Saudi Air Force was reported to have commenced flying operations with the first of its Eurofighter *Typhoon* Tranche 2 purchases. The final purchase number is 72 (see Defence economics, p. 240 and *The Military Balance* 2009, p. 235) and in order to provide support services for this *Project Salam* deal, the *Salam Support Solution* was agreed, which will include training for both pilots and support technicians. BAE Systems will operate this through a 'full availability service contract'. In mid 2009, Saudi Arabia also signed a contract for three more A330 multi-role tanker transport (MRTT) aircraft with EADS. A contract for an initial three aircraft was signed in 2008, with the first aircraft due for delivery in 2011. (In 2008, the MRTT was also selected by the **UAE**.) In late May 2009, France opened a military base in the UAE, comprising port and support facilities in Abu Dhabi, an aviation detachment at al-Dhafra and a ground component. In opening the base, reference was made to an earlier bilateral agreement between France and the UAE, as well as the 2008 French defence White Paper's emphasis of the strategic importance to France of the Gulf. There will also be hopes that this presence could lead to further ties through the sale of defence-related equipment. In late 2009, military forces from **Yemen** were engaged in further fighting in the north of the country against Houthi rebels. A conflict that has been going on for a number of years (in an area of the country that has long been insecure) intensified with government forces pushing into areas of Sa'ada and Amran governorates. It was reported that rebel forces had suffered substantial losses, though they also inflicted losses on the Yemeni armed forces' ground and air arms (Sana'a claimed that aircraft crashes were a result of technical failure). It was further reported that incursions by rebels into Saudi Arabia prompted military actions by Saudi forces (including air strikes).

MIDDLE EAST AND NORTH AFRICA – DEFENCE ECONOMICS

The global financial crisis, together with the dramatic halving of oil prices during 2008 and 2009, hit the Middle East hard. Across the region, growth is projected to decline from 6% in 2008 to 2.5% in 2009, affecting both oil-producing and non-oil-producing countries alike. The biggest casualty is likely to be the UAE where the flight of external funds (which had entered the country on speculation of a currency revaluation) has contributed to a large contraction in liquidity, a sizeable fall in overheated property and equity prices, and substantial pressure on the banking system. Unsurprisingly, dwindling surpluses in oil-producing countries will result in worsening fiscal balances as revenues decline and governments use recent windfall gains to sustain domestic demand by maintaining ongoing investment projects.

However, despite the precipitous fall in oil prices, the continued threat from Iran and the re-integration of a fragile Iraq into the regional equation is unlikely to lead to anything but a temporary pause in the region's widespread military-modernisation programmes. Indeed, available figures show that in most countries defence budgets in 2009 actually increased, even if only modestly. Ongoing trends include a focus on air assets, missiles and anti-missile defensive technologies, the upgrade and modernisation of significant offshore assets and the growing presence of Russia as a weapons supplier.

Following something of a spending spree over the past two years, the collapse in oil prices put a brake on **Saudi Arabia's** activity in the international defence market in 2009. Over the past two decades there has been a noticeable correlation between increasing defence spending and rising oil revenues, although the reverse is not the case, suggesting that the authorities have established a floor below which spending will not fall. During the 1990s, therefore, when oil prices were low but defence spending remained high, the Kingdom built up debt and, although it has enjoyed a significant boom from the recent spike in oil prices, previous budget deficits together with anticipated future expenditure have to some extent reduced the government's cushion against the current downturn. Economic growth measured 4.6% in 2008 but the economy is expected to contract by around 1% in 2009.

As is common across the Middle East, Saudi Arabia's economy is ill prepared for a looming demographic shock whereby demand for jobs from an increasingly young population is now far outstripping supply. In the recent past, increased public-sector employment has helped to cushion the impact, however, it is calculated that Saudi Arabia will need to generate in the order of 3.5m new jobs over the coming decade in order to meet the challenge. With this in mind, the authorities have embarked on a so-called 'Saudiisation' policy in an effort to diversify the economy and create new jobs. The policy has been applied in all sectors including defence: the procurement of new weapons systems and the associated offset requirements are now viewed not only in practical terms, particularly in relation to advances being made by Iran, but as an important means of developing the indigenous defence industry. However, progress in this regard has been hampered by the lack of defence-research institutions, as well as the small pool of technicians and engineers in the country. Saudi Military Industries, which is owned by King Abdullah, has revealed that it is often forced to recruit key staff from Russia and the UK owing to a shortage of suitable local candidates.

The policy of Saudiisation has figured prominently in the Kingdom's most recent procurement decisions, of which the largest is the purchase of 72 Eurofighter *Typhoon* fighter aircraft. The massive deal, known as *Project Salam*, signalled the start of an enhanced strategic alliance between the UK and Saudi Arabia and was a significant boost to UK–Saudi defence-industrial cooperation. European Eurofighter partner nations will supply the major components of the aircraft, which will be built by a new joint venture company between BAE Systems and Alsalam Aircraft Company at a new plant being constructed within Saudi Arabia. In addition to building the new aircraft, Saudi Arabia will take responsibility for the long-term maintenance and support of the *Typhoon* and estimates that in total the programme will create around 15,000 new jobs. BAE Systems has acknowledged that its role in Saudi Arabia is changing as it turns its focus to in-country manufacturing and through-life support that will include the development of the appropriate infrastructure and the ongoing training of Saudi nationals.

For many years, US and European defence companies have enjoyed a virtual monopoly on lucrative defence contracts with the Saudi Arabian armed forces, but over the past two years Riyadh has sought to diversify its arms suppliers. In particular, the Saudi government is thought to be less willing to enter into contracts with US companies via the traditional foreign-military-sales (FMS) process, preferring instead to focus on direct government-to-manufacturer arrangements. While most new contracts are

still likely to be awarded to the country's traditional trading partners, Russia has emerged as a potential alternative weapons supplier. In 2008, the two countries signed a military cooperation agreement and in 2009 a top delegation from the Kremlin and Rosoboronexport (Russia's state-owned arms-export monopoly) visited Saudi Arabia and met with King Abdullah. Current discussions cover an initial deal that could amount to US$2bn and is thought to include up to 150 helicopters (30 Mi-35 aircraft and 120 Mi-17s of various modifications), over 150 T-90S main battle tanks (MBTs), 250 BMP-3 infantry-combat vehicles and air-defence missile systems. Future deals may feature S-400 air-defence systems and Mi-28 combat helicopters.

This new-found relationship between Riyadh and Moscow is something of a blow to France, which had been hoping to clinch several deals of its own. Having failed to persuade the Saudi armed forces to buy its *Rafale* fighter aircraft, the emerging deal with Russia may well put a stop to France's broader ambitions to sell its own mix of domestically produced helicopters to the Kingdom. French attention is now likely to shift towards laying the groundwork for a potential sale of some of its recently ordered FREMM frigates. Originally, the French navy had intended to procure 17 of the multi-mission vessels, but the 2008 White Paper indicated that there were likely to be insufficient funds to achieve this, raising the prospect that any surplus vessels would be offered for sale overseas. Meanwhile, there was success in the Kingdom for European defence company EADS, which achieved some notable new sales in 2009: three additional A330 multi-role tanker transports

Table 23 **Middle East and North Africa Regional Defence Expenditure** as % of GDP

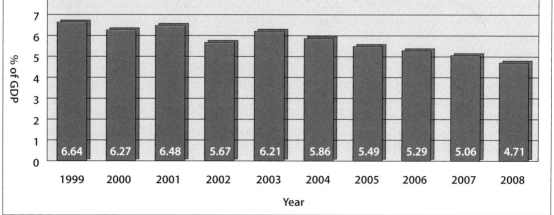

Year	1999	2000	2001	2002	2003	2004	2005	2006	2007	2008
% of GDP	6.64	6.27	6.48	5.67	6.21	5.86	5.49	5.29	5.06	4.71

for the Saudi Air Force, bringing to the total order to six; and a US$1.5bn contract to provide phase one of the massive border-surveillance programme, which includes the supply of 225 ground and surveillance radar systems, a comprehensive 'C4I system', buried radio-detection sensors and the construction of a double-lined concertina-shaped wired fence along the entire length of the Saudi desert border. Phase two will feature the acquisition of ground-based naval and airborne equipment.

In addition to orders for the three primary services and the border surveillance programme, there has been a noticeable increase in resources allocated to the Saudi Arabian National Guard. In 2006, a massive US$10bn FMS package was agreed with the US, which covered the delivery of 724 light-armoured vehicles, 58 new M1A1 MBTs and the upgrading of 315 M1A2 MBTs.

Despite efforts over the years to diversify its economy, the **United Arab Emirates** still relies on the energy sector for around 40% of its GDP. In 2001 oil revenues amounted to US$21bn, but as the price of crude oil rose, revenues hit US$100bn in 2009, helping to fund the significant growth in defence spending. Although transparency is a major problem in the UAE, figures published by the IMF suggest that combined spending on defence from both the federal budget and Abu Dhabi amounted to around US$15bn in 2009. In common with Saudi Arabia, the UAE has embarked on a major drive towards greater self sufficiency, as illustrated by several procurement contracts awarded during the 2009 International Defence Exhibition and Conference (IDEX) held in Abu Dhabi. The UAE placed a series of major new equipment orders that included provisions for joint ventures specifically drafted with the intention of transferring knowledge and technology to an increasingly well-educated and sophisticated domestic employment pool upon which an indigenous industrial capability is being built. At the forefront of this drive has been Emirates Advanced Investments, which was incorporated in 2005, and signed multiple agreements with Thales, EADS and ITT Defense during IDEX 2009. The Baynunah Group announced a new joint venture with MBDA Missile Systems and the partly government-owned Injazat Data Systems signed a memorandum of agreement with Northrop Grumman.

France's close military cooperation with the UAE and its growing commitment to security in the region was made significantly more visible in May 2009 when President Nicolas Sarkozy followed up on a 2008 bilateral agreement and officially opened a major new permanent military base in Abu Dhabi, capable of housing up to 500 French military personnel. The base is indicative of a broader intention among GCC member states to diversify both their equipment suppliers and training expertise beyond a traditional reliance on the US. As well as providing support for anti-piracy missions off the coast of Somalia, the new base will provide a multi-service support facility for French operations in the region and includes an air base, a naval facility at Mina Zayed port and an army camp. A further illustration of the bilateral defence relationship will come when the UAE air force confirms its selection of the Dassault *Rafale* to replace its *Mirage* fleet. At the 2009 Paris air show, UAE state media announced that the country had delivered specific technical requirements for the aircraft to the French government, which are thought to include: Thales Reco-NG reconnaissance pods; *Damocles* XF targeting pods (providing an independent laser-guided weapon capability); and MBDA *Exocet* AM 39 anti-ship missiles. The UAE is also considering funding the development of a more powerful engine for its aircraft that would allow its *Rafale* fleet to carry up to three SCALP EG/*Storm Shadow* cruise missiles, two under-wing fuel tanks and four MICA anti-aircraft missiles.

As well as cementing new industrial relationships, IDEX 2009 was also notable for the number of equipment contracts announced by the UAE government. The air force will receive a major enhancement to its airlift capabilities with the procurement of strategic and tactical transport aircraft. The finance house Al Waha Capital will manage the purchase of four C-17s (US$1.2bn) and 12 C-130J aircraft (US$1.6bn) that, according to IDEX, Chairman Major-General Obaid al Ketbi, will allow the UAE to 'actively participate in rescue and humanitarian missions worldwide'. Deliveries of the aircraft are expected to begin within four years and once complete will make the UAE the largest regional customer for both platforms. Another major announcement was the US$1bn selection of 48 *Alenia* Aermacchi M-346 planes as an advanced trainer and close air-support aircraft for the air force.

However, the most expensive defence contracts announced by the UAE in the last two years came just before IDEX when the government confirmed it would install a comprehensive new air-defence system specifically targeted to counter Iran's growing military reach. The most substantial part of the US$10bn package will see the UAE become the first foreign country to take delivery of the US-designed Terminal High Altitude Air Defense ballistic-missile defence system, capable of destroying incoming ballistic missiles at a range of 200m. The programme also provides funds for the deployment of 10 *Patriot* PAC-3 fire units, plus 200 missiles and a wide array of technical assistance, logistics support, and through-life support and training.

In common with other Gulf states possessing significant offshore assets, the UAE is in the process of upgrading its maritime capabilities and announced further procurement plans during 2009. In future, the UAE's naval forces will be centred around six 72m *Baynunah*-class multi-mission corvettes supplemented by a number of smaller craft. During IDEX 2009, the navy announced that it would be procuring 12 new missile-armed fast craft that will be built to a modified *Ghannatha* design. The new vessels, to be built by Abu Dhabi Ship Building (ADSB) at a cost of US$200m, will be a stretched version of the existing *Ghannatha* and will be fitted with box launchers for four MBDA *Marte* Mk 2/N surface-to-surface guided missiles. A second contract will see the navy's 12 existing *Ghannatha* fast troop carriers split into two separate sub-classes: six will be modified as mortar platforms; the remainder will continue as troop carriers but with additional armament. In a separate development, ADSB will work with the Turkish shipbuilder Yonca Onuk to build a total of 34 16m fast-interceptor vessels based on the latter's MRTP16 design. Surveillance capabilities will be boosted by the conversion of four Bombardier *Dash* 8 airlines into maritime-patrol configuration and a single 88m Italian-built corvette that, as well as patrolling, will include facilities for an embarked helicopter and an organic anti-submarine warfare capability.

In **Israel,** tensions between the government and armed forces over the appropriate level of military spending persist. Following the 2006 conflict in Lebanon, the Israeli defence establishment had complained that the poor performance of the Israeli Defense Forces (IDF) during that conflict was a direct result of years of under-funding, which had resulted in a serious lack of manpower, training and equipment, and requested an immediate increase in the defence budget of NIS7bn. In response to this accusation, the Finance Ministry set up the Brodet Committee, to conduct a comprehensive review of Israeli defence-funding mechanisms and to propose a new framework for the future. In its final report, the Brodet Committee suggested that funding levels were not the primary reason for the IDF's poor performance during the Lebanese war, concluding that current funds were adequate and that future defence budgets only needed to be increased by around 2% annually. Much to the irritation and disappointment of the IDF, the government accepted these findings. The following year, the IDF received better news when it emerged that the Israeli government had been successful in negotiating an increase in the amount of military aid it receives each year from the US. Under the revised initiative, the US agreed to a ten-year US$30bn Foreign Military Financing (FMF) package, representing a 25% increase over the previous ten years. Annual payments will increase by US$150m a year, rising from US$2.4bn in 2007 to US$3.1bn in 2011 and each year thereafter.

In 2009, with defence financing still generating conflict between the government and IDF, and the Israeli economy suffering from the global slowdown, the Likud-led government settled on a two-year budget deal that included cuts of just NIS1.5bn during FY09 and FY10. The government had originally outlined a two-year defence budget that included cuts of some NIS6bn; however, this was rejected by the coalition Labor Party and, in view of the government's shaky position, a compromise was agreed. However, with most government departments seeing cuts of around 6% in 2009 the final agreement that defence spending would only be cut by 2% is something of a coup for Labor leader Ehud Barak, who had threatened to resign if more drastic cuts were implemented. It was also agreed that external consultants would be brought into the Ministry of Defense to help design an ambitious ten-year NIS30bn efficiency programme.

The combination of the Brodet review, together with the completion of FMF negotiations and several enquiries into the conflict with Hizbullah, finally resulted in a new five-year plan to cover the period 2008–12. Known as 'Tefen 2012', the plan highlighted four main threat scenarios: conventional war with Syria, missile attack by Iran, instability in neighbouring moderate countries and asymmetric terror and rocket attacks. Under the plan, nine core capabilities must be either maintained or upgraded:

- Modern MBTs
- Precision-strike capability (including the *Joint Strike Fighter* (JSF) aircraft

- Upgraded F-15s and HALE unmanned aerial vehicles (UAVs) for air superiority
- Long-reach capabilities, including aerial refuelling tankers
- Intelligence superiority
- The *Tsayad* digital command-and-control programme
- Naval supremacy
- Anti-missile defence systems
- Expanded emergency-munition stocks

Prior to the publication of Tefen 2012, the IDF had intended to downsize its ground forces. However, the 2006 conflict with Hizbullah prompted a re-think and new priorities were placed on manpower, readiness and training instead. In terms of new equipment, the army will receive hundreds of new *Namer* infantry fighting vehicles (based on the domestic *Merkava* main-battle-tank platform), hundreds of *Stryker* 8×8 medium-armoured vehicles, additional *Merkava*-4 tanks and dozens of tactical UAVs. With a renewed focus on ground forces, the air force, traditionally the highest priority in terms of procurement funding, has been forced to limit its requirements over the next five years. The most high-profile adjustment to air-force procurement plans is a reduction in the number of JSF aircraft, down from an original expectation of 100 units to just 25 in the current five-year plan. And in a further bid to keep costs in check, the air force has

had to defer its requirement to integrate indigenous munitions and an additional fuel tank to its first batch of the multi-role aircraft. The air force's request for an additional squadron of AH-64D *Apache* attack helicopters has also been limited to just six, while there are no funds for new tanker aircraft, only the upgrade of existing KC-707s.

Under Tefen 2012, the Israeli Navy was allocated US$250m for the acquisition of the first of two 2–3,000-tonne multi-purpose missile vessels, with the most likely option out of an original field of five contenders being the US Littoral Combat Ship (LCS). However, in light of the spiralling cost of the LCS programme, the Israeli Navy has abandoned its plans and is looking at other alternatives. A proposal by Northrop Gruman to build an expanded version of the navy's *Sa'ar*-5 corvette has also been rejected and the most probable solution now appears to be the acquisition of a stretched version of Germany's MEKO A-100 corvette equipped with phased array radars and a vertical-launch system capable of extending the IDF's air-defence capabilities. The plan may well meet strong resistance from Israel's other services as the construction of LCS vessels would have been funded by US FMF, whereas building the ships outside of the US will require scarce resources from the domestic local currency budget.

Algeria ALG

Algerian Dinar D		2008	2009	2010
GDP	D	11.0tr	11.6tr	
	US$	171bn	161bn	
per capita	US$	5,067	4,714	
Growth	%	3.0	2.2	
Inflation	%	4.3	4.6	
Def bdgt	D	334bn	383bn	
	US$	5.17bn	5.30bn	
US$1=D		64.5	72.3	

Population 34,178,188

Age	0–14	15–19	20–24	25–29	30–64	65 plus
Male	15%	6%	6%	5%	17%	2%
Female	14%	6%	6%	5%	17%	2%

Capabilities

ACTIVE 147,000 (Army 127,000 Navy 6,000 Air 14,000) Paramilitary 187,200

Terms of service Conscription in army only,18 months (6 months basic, 12 months wth regular army often involving civil projects)

RESERVE 150,000 (Army 150,000) to age 50

ORGANISATIONS BY SERVICE

Army 47,000; ε80,000 conscript (total 127,000)

FORCES BY ROLE

6 Mil Regions; re-org into div structure on hold

Armd	2 div (each: 3 tk regt, 1 mech regt); 1 indep bde
Mech	3 div (each: 1 tk regt, 3 mech regt)
Mech Inf/Mot Inf	5 indep bde
AB/SF	1 (Rapid Reaction) div with (5 (18th SF, and 1st, 4th, 5th 12th) para regt)
Arty	7 regt
AD	5 bn
Engr	4 indep bn

EQUIPMENT BY TYPE

MBT 1,082: 187 T-90S; 325 T-72; 300 T-62; 270 T-54/T-55
RECCE 90: 26 BRDM-2; 64 BRDM-2 (upgrade) each with AT-5 9M113 Kornet E
AIFV 1,040: 100 BMP-3; 260 BMP-2 (upgrade) each with AT-5 9M113 Kornet E; 680 BMP-1
APC (W) 750: 300 BTR-60; 150 BTR-80; 150 OT-64; 50 M-3 Panhard; 100 TH 390 Fahd
ARTY 1,019
  SP 170: **122mm** 140 2S1 Carnation; **152mm** 30 2S3
  TOWED 375: **122mm** 160 D-30; 25 D-74; 100 M-1931/37; 60 M-30 M-1938; **130mm** 10 M-46; **152mm** 20 ML-20 M-1937
  MRL 144: **122mm** 48 BM-21; **140mm** 48 BM-14/16; **240mm** 30 BM-24; **300mm** 18 9A52 Smerch

MOR 330: **82mm** 150 M-37; **120mm** 120 M-1943; **160mm** 60 M-1943
AT
  MSL • MANPATS 200+: 200 Milan; Kornet-E being delivered; Metis-M1 being delivered; AT-3 9K11 Sagger; AT-4 9K111 Spigot; AT-5 9K113 Spandrel
  RCL 180: **107mm** 60 B-11; **82mm** 120 B-10
  GUNS 300: **57mm** 160 ZIS-2 M-1943; **85mm** 80 D-44: **100mm** 50 SU-100 SP (in store); 10 T-12
AD • SAM 288+
  SP 68: ε48 SA-8 Gecko; ε20 SA-9 Gaskin
  MANPAD 220+: ε220 SA-7A Grail/SA-7B Grail; SA-14 Gremlin/SA-16 Gimlet;
  GUNS ε875
  SP ε225 ZSU-23-4
  TOWED ε650: **14.5mm** 100: 60 ZPU-2; 40 ZPU-4; **20mm** 100; **23mm** 100 ZU-23; **37mm** ε100 M-1939; **57mm** 70 S-60; **85mm** 20 M-1939 KS-12; **100mm** 150 KS-19; **130mm** 10 KS-30

Navy ε6,000 (incl 500 officers)

EQUIPMENT BY TYPE

SUBMARINES • TACTICAL • SSK 2 Kilo (FSU) each with 6 single 533mm TT with 18 Test-71ME HWT (1 in refit); (two additional vessels in build)
PRINCIPAL SURFACE COMBATANTS 9
  FRIGATES • FF 3 Mourad Rais (FSU Koni) each with 1 twin (2 eff.) with 20 SA-N-4 Gecko SAM, 2 RBU 6000 Smerch 2 (24 eff.), 4 76mm gun (undergoing modernisation programme)
  CORVETTES 6
    FSG 3:
      2 Rais Hamidou (FSU Nanuchka II) each with 4 single each with 1 SS-N-2C Styx tactical SSM, 1 twin (2 eff.) with 20 SA-N-4 Gecko SAM
      1 Rais Hamidou (FSU Nanuchka II) with 4 quad (16 eff.) with 16 SS-N-25 Switchblade tactical SSM, 1 twin (2 eff.) with 20 SA-N-4 Gecko SAM
    FS 3 Djebel Chenona each with 2 twin (4 eff.) CSS-N-8 Saccade tactical SSM, 1 76mm gun
PATROL AND COASTAL COMBATANTS 20
  PFM 9 Osa II each with 4 single each with 1 SS-N-2B Styx tactical SSM (3†)
  PFC 11 Kebir
AMPHIBIOUS • LS 3
  LSM 1 Polnochny B (capacity 6 MBT; 180 troops)
  LST 2 Kalaat beni Hammad (capacity 7 tanks; 240 troops) each with 1 med hel landing platform
LOGISTICS AND SUPPORT 10
  TRG 8: 1 Daxin; **AXL** 7 EL Mouderrib
  SPT 1
  TRV 1 Poluchat (Used for SAR)

FACILITIES

Bases Located at Mers el Kebir, Algiers, Annaba, Jijel

Coast Guard ε500

PATROL AND COASTAL COMBATANTS 16
  PCC 11: 4 Baglietto; 7 El Mouderrib (PRC Chui-E)
  PCI 4 El Mounkid less than 100 tonnes
  PB 1 (Ocea FPB-98); (additional vessels on order)
LOGISTICS AND SUPPORT 1 **SPT**

Air Force 14,000

Flying hours   150 hrs/year

FORCES BY ROLE

Ftr	2 sqn with MiG-25 *Foxbat*; 4 sqn with MiG-29C *Fulcrum*/MiG-29UB *Fulcrum*; 2 sqn with MiG-23MF/MS/U *Flogger*
FGA	1 sqn with Su-30MKA; 2 sqn each with Su-24M *Fencer*/Su-24MK *Fencer D*; 2 sqn with MiG-23BN *Flogger*; 1 sqn with MiG-29UBT
Recce	1 sqn with Su-24E *Fencer*; 1 sqn with MiG-25R *Foxbat*
MR	2 sqn with Beech 200T *Maritime Patrol*
Tpt	2 sqn with C-130H *Hercules*; C-130H-30 *Hercules*; Gulfstream IV-SP; Gulfstream V; Il-76MD *Candid B*; Il-76TD *Candid*; L-100-30; 2 (VIP) sqn with F-27 *Friendship*; *Falcon* 900
Tkr	1 sqn with Il-78 *Midas*
Atk hel	4 sqn with Mi-24 *Hind*
Tpt hel	7 sqn with AS-355 *Ecureuil*; Mi-17/Mi-8 *Hip*; Mi-171
Trg	2 sqn with Z-142; 1 sqn with Yak-130; 2 sqn 36 L-39ZA; L-39C *Albatros*; hel sqn with 28 PZL Mi-2 *Hoplite*
AD	3 bde with 725 100mm/130mm/85mm
SAM	3 regt with ε140 SA-2 *Guideline*/SA-3 *Goa*/SA-6 *Gainful*/SA-8 *Gecko* (140–840 eff.)

EQUIPMENT BY TYPE

AIRCRAFT 197 combat capable

FTR 55: 12 MiG-25 *Foxbat*; 25 MiG-29C *Fulcrum*/MiG-29UB *Fulcrum*; 18 MiG-23MF/MS/U *Flogger*

FGA 134: 28 Su-30MKA; 34 MiG-29SMT/ UBT; 34 Su-24M/Su-24MK *Fencer D*; 38 MiG-23BN *Flogger*

RECCE 14: 6 Beech 1900D (electronic surveillance); 4 MiG-25R *Foxbat**; 4 Su-24E *Fencer**

MP 6 Beech 200T *Maritime Patrol* (additional units on order)

TKR 6 Il-78 *Midas*

TPT 39: 9 C-130H; 8 C-130H-30 *Hercules*; 3 F-27 *Friendship*; 3 *Falcon* 900; 4 Gulfstream IV-SP; 1 Gulfstream V; 3 Il-76MD *Candid B*; 6 Il-76TD *Candid*; 2 L-100-30

TRG 99: 16 Yak-130; 36 L-39ZA *Albatros*; 7 L-39C; 40 Z-142

HELICOPTERS

ATK 33 Mi-24 *Hind*

SPT 114: 8 AS-355 *Ecureuil*; 42 Mi-171; 64 Mi-17 (Mi-8MT) *Hip H*/Mi-8 *Hip*

TRG 28 PZL Mi-2 *Hoplite*

AD

SAM ε140 SA-2 *Guideline* Towed/SA-3 *Goa*/SA-6 *Gainful* SP/SA-8 *Gecko* SP (140–840 eff.)

GUNS 725 **100mm/130mm/85mm**

MSL

ASM AS-10 *Karen*; AS-12 *Kegler*; AS-14 *Kedge*; AS-17 *Krypton*; AS-7 *Kerry*

AAM AA-10 *Alamo*; A-11 *Archer*; AA-2 *Atoll*; AA-6 *Acrid*; AA-7 *Apex*; AA-8 *Aphid*

Paramilitary ε187,200

Gendarmerie 20,000
Ministry of Defence

FORCES BY ROLE
Army 6 region

EQUIPMENT BY TYPE
RECCE AML-60/110 M-3 *Panhard* APC (W)
APC (W) 100 TH 390 *Fahd*
HELICOPTERS • SPT PZL Mi-2 *Hoplite*

National Security Forces 16,000
Directorate of National Security. Small arms

Republican Guard 1,200
RECCE AML-60
APC (T) M-3

Legitimate Defence Groups ε150,000
Self-defence militia, communal guards (60,000)

SELECTED NON-STATE GROUPS

Al-Qaeda in the Islamic Maghreb/Groupe Salafiste pour la Predication et le Combat (GSPC) Est strength: 500 (GSPC) Major equipments include: mines and IEDs; mortars; SALW

DEPLOYMENT

DEMOCRATIC REPUBLIC OF CONGO
UN • MONUC 5 obs

Bahrain BHR

Bahraini Dinar D		2008	2009	2010
GDP	D	7.6bn	7.7bn	
	US$	20bn	20bn	
per capita	US$	27,810	27,446	
Growth	%	6.1	3.0	
Inflation	%	3.5	3.0	
Def bdgt	D	210m	265m	279m
	US$	552m	697m	
FMA (US)	US$	3.9m	8m	19.5m
US$1=D		0.38	0.38	

Population   728,709

Ethnic groups: Nationals 64%; Asian 13%; other Arab 10%; Iranian 8%; European 1%)

Age	0–14	15–19	20–24	25–29	30–64	65 plus
Male	14%	4%	4%	4%	28%	2%
Female	14%	4%	4%	3%	17%	2%

Capabilities

ACTIVE 8,200 (Army 6,000 Navy 700 Air 1,500)
Paramilitary 11,260

ORGANISATIONS BY SERVICE

Army 6,000

FORCES BY ROLE

Armd 1 bde under strength (2 armd bn, 1 recce bn)

Inf 1 bde (2 mech inf bn, 1 mot inf bn)

SF 1 bn

Arty 1 bde (1 lt arty bty, 1 hy arty bty, 1 MRL bty, 2 med arty bty)

Gd 1 (Amiri) bn

AD 1 bn (1 ADA bty, 2 SAM bty)

EQUIPMENT BY TYPE

MBT 180 M-60A3

RECCE 46: 22 AML-90; *Ferret* 8 (in store); 8 S52 *Shorland*; 8 *Saladin* (in store)

AIFV 25 YPR-765 (with 25mm)

APC 325+

APC (T) 205 M-113A2

APC (W) 120+: 10+ AT105 *Saxon*; 110 M-3 *Panhard*

ARTY 92

   SP 33: **155mm** 20 M109A5; **203mm** 13 M-110

   TOWED 26: **105mm** 8 L-118 Light Gun; **155mm** 18 M-198

   MRL 227mm 9 MLRS (with 30 ATACMS)

   MOR 24: **SP 120mm** 12

   81mm 12

AT • MSL • MANPATS 60 *Javelin*

   RCL 31: **106mm** 25 M-40A1; **120mm** 6 MOBAT

AD • SAM 93

   SP 7 *Crotale*

   TOWED 8 I-HAWK *MIM-23B*

   MANPAD 78: 18 FIM-92A *Stinger*; 60 RBS-70

   GUNS 27: **35mm** 15 Oerlikon; **40mm** 12 L/70

Navy 700

EQUIPMENT BY TYPE

PRINCIPAL SURFACE COMBATANTS 3

   FRIGATES • FFG 1 *Sabah* (US *Oliver Hazard Perry*) with SM-1 MR SAM, 4+ RGM-84C *Harpoon* tactical SSM, 2 triple ASTT (6 eff.), 1 76mm gun, (capacity either 1 Bo-105 utl hel or 2 SH-2G *Super Seasprite* ASW hel)

   CORVETTES • FSG 2 *Al Manama* (GER Lurssen 62m with hel deck) each with 2 twin (4 eff.) each with MM-40 *Exocet* tactical SSM, 1 76mm gun, (capacity 1 Bo-105 utl hel)

PATROL AND COASTAL COMBATANTS 8

   PFM 4 *Ahmed el Fateh* (GER Lurssen 45m) each with 2 twin (4 eff.) each with MM-40 *Exocet* tactical SSM, 1 76mm gun

   PFC 2 *Al Riffa* (GER Lurssen 38m)

   PCI 2 *Al Jarim* all less than 100 tonnes (US *Swift* FPB-20)

AMPHIBIOUS • CRAFT 5

   LCU 5: 1 *Loadmaster*; 4 LCU (additional vessels in build)

LOGISTICS AND SUPPORT • SPT 1 *Ajeera*

FACILITIES

Base Mina Salman

Naval Aviation

EQUIPMENT BY TYPE

HELICOPTERS • SPT 2 Bo-105 utl hel

Air Force 1,500

FORCES BY ROLE

Ftr 2 sqn with F-16C/F-16D *Fighting Falcon*

FGA 1 sqn with F-5E/F-5F *Tiger II*

Tpt some sqn with B-727; Gulfstream II; Gulfstream III (VIP); RJ-85

VIP 1 unit with S-70A *Black Hawk*; Bo-105; UH-60L *Black Hawk*

Trg some sqn with T67M *Firefly*, Hawk Mk-129

Hel 3 sqn with AH-1E *Cobra*; TAH-1P *Cobra**; 1 sqn with AB-212 (Bell 212)

EQUIPMENT BY TYPE

AIRCRAFT 33 combat capable

   FTR 12: 8 F-5E *Tiger II*; 4 F-5F *Tiger II*

   FGA 21: 17 F-16C *Fighting Falcon*; 4 F-16D *Fighting Falcon*

   TPT 4: 1 B-727; 1 Gulfstream II; 1 Gulfstream III (VIP); 1 RJ-85

   TRG 9: 3 T67M *Firefly*; 6 Hawk Mk-129

HELICOPTERS

   ATK 22 AH-1E *Cobra*

   SPT 3 S-70A *Black Hawk*

   UTL 16: 12 AB-212 (Bell 212); 3 Bo-105; 1 UH-60L *Black Hawk*

   TRG 6 TAH-1P *Cobra**

MSL

   ASM AGM-65D/G *Maverick*

   ARM AS-12 *Kegler*

   AAM AIM-7 *Sparrow*, AIM-9P *Sidewinder*

MSL some TOW

Paramilitary ε11,260

Police 9,000

Ministry of Interior

HELICOPTERS • UTL 5: 1 Bo-105; 2 Bell 412 *Twin Huey*; 2 Hughes 500

National Guard ε2,000

Paramilitary 3 bn

Coast Guard ε260

Ministry of Interior

PATROL AND COASTAL COMBATANTS 24:

   7 **PCC**; 17 **PBI** (less than 100 tonnes)

LOGISTICS AND SUPPORT 1 **SPT**

FOREIGN FORCES

United Kingdom Air Force 1 BAe-125 CC-3; 1 BAe-146 MKII

United States US Central Commmand: Army 18; Navy 1,261; USAF 26; USMC 142; 1 HQ (5th Fleet)

Egypt EGY

Egyptian Pound E£		2008	2009	2010
GDP	E£	865bn	1,028bn	
	US$	157bn	186bn	
per capita	US$	2,035	2,370	
Growth	%	7.2	4.7	
Inflation	%	11.7	16.2	
Def exp	E£	ε25.1bn		
	US$	ε4.56bn		
Def bdgt	E£	ε18.0bn		
	US$	ε3.27bn		
FMA (US)	US$	1.28bn	1.30bn	1.30bn
US$1=E£		5.50	5.50	

Population   78,866,635

Age	0–14	15–19	20–24	25–29	30–64	65 plus
Male	17%	5%	5%	4%	17%	2%
Female	16%	5%	5%	4%	17%	3%

Capabilities

ACTIVE 468,500 (Army 340,000 Navy 18,500 Air 30,000 Air Defence Command 80,000) **Paramilitary 397,000**

Terms of service 12 months-3 years (followed by refresher training over a period of up to 9 years)

RESERVE 479,000 (Army 375,000 Navy 14,000 Air 20,000 Air Defence 70,000)

ORGANISATIONS BY SERVICE

Army 90,000–120,000; 190,000–220,000 conscript (total 280,000–340,000)

FORCES BY ROLE

Armd   4 div (each: 2 armd bde, 1 mech bde, 1 arty bde); 1 (Republican Guard) bde; 4 indep bde

Mech Inf 7 div (each: 1 arty bde, 1 armd bde, 2 mech inf bde); 4 indep bde

Air Mob 2 bde

Inf   1 div, 2 indep bde

Cdo   1 HQ (5 cdo gp, 1 Counter-Terrorist unit (Unit 777 (Thunderbolt Force (El Saiqa)), str 300.)

Para   1 bde

Arty   15 indep bde

SSM   1 bde with 9 FROG-7; 1 bde with 9 Scud-B

EQUIPMENT BY TYPE

MBT 3,723: 973 M1A1 Abrams; 300 M-60A1; 850 M-60A3; 500 T-62 in store; 260 Ramses II (mod T-54/55); 840 T-54/T-55 in store

RECCE 412: 300 BRDM-2; 112 Commando Scout

AIFV 610: 220 BMP-1 (in store); 390 YPR-765 (with 25mm)

APC 4,160

APC (T) 2,600 M-113A2 (incl variants); 500 BTR-50/OT-62 (most in store)

APC (W) 1,560: 250 BMP-600P; 250 BTR-60; 410 Fahd-30/TH 390 Fahd; 650 Walid

ARTY 4,480

SP 492: **122mm** 124 SP 122; **155mm** 368: 164 M-109A2; 204 M-109A5

TOWED 962: **122mm** 526: 190 D-30M; 36 M-1931/37; 300 M-30 M-1938; **130mm** 420 M-46; **155mm** 16 GH-52

MRL 498: **122mm** 356: 96 BM-11; 60 BM-21; 50 Sakr-10; 50 Sakr-18; 100 Sakr-36; **130mm** 36 Kooryong; **140mm** 32 BM-14; **227mm** 26 MLRS; **240mm** 48 BM-24 in store

MOR 2,528

  SP 100: **107mm** 65 M-106A1; 35 M-106A2; **81mm** 50 M-125A2; **82mm** 500; **120mm** 1,848: 1,800 M-1943; 48 Brandt; **160mm** 30 M-160

AT • MSL 2,362

  SP 262: 52 M-901, 210 YPR 765 PRAT

  MANPATS 2,100: 1,200 AT-3 Sagger (incl BRDM-2); 200 Milan; 700 TOW-2

  RCL 107mm 520 B-11

UAV R4E-50 Skyeye

AD • SAM 2,096+

  SP 96: 50 FIM-92A Avenger; 26 M-54 Chaparral; 20 SA-9 Gaskin

  MANPAD 2,000+: 2,000 Ayn al-Saqr/SA-7 Grail; FIM-92A Stinger

  GUNS 705+

  SP 205: **23mm** 165: 45 Sinai-23; 120 ZSU-23-4; **57mm** 40 ZSU-57-2

  TOWED 500+: **14.5mm** 300 ZPU-4; **23mm** 200 ZU-23-2; **57mm** S-60

RADAR • LAND AN/TPQ-36 Firefinder; AN/TPQ-37 Firefinder (arty/mor)

MSL • TACTICAL • SSM 42+: 9 FROG-7; 24 Sakr-80; some (trials); 9 Scud-B

Central Zone

Mil Region 1 zone HQ located at Cairo

Eastern Zone

Mil Region 1 zone HQ located at Ismailiya
Armd   1 div
Mech Inf   2 div

Northern Zone

Mil Region 1 zone HQ located at Alexandria
Armd   1 div
Mech Inf   2 div

Southern Zone

Mil Region 1 zone HQ located at Aswan
Armd Cav   1 div
Mech Inf   2 div

Western Zone

Mil Region 1 zone HQ located at Mersa Matruh
Armd   1 div
Mech Inf   2 div

Navy ε8,500 (incl 2,000 Coast Guard); 10,000 conscript (total 18,500)

Two Fleets: Mediterranean and Red Sea. Naval Organisation: 1 Submarine Bde, 1 Destroyer Bde, 1 Patrol Bde, 1 Fast Attack Bde and 1 Special Ops Bde.

FORCES BY ROLE

Navy 1 HQ located at Alexandria; 1 HQ located at Safaqa

EQUIPMENT BY TYPE

SUBMARINES • TACTICAL • SSK 4 *Romeo*† each with 8 single 533mm TT with UGM-84C *Harpoon* tactical USGW
PRINCIPAL SURFACE COMBATANTS 10
  FRIGATES • FFG 10:
    2 *Abu Qir* (ESP *Descubierta*) each with 2 Mk 141 *Harpoon* quad (8 eff.) each with RGM-84C *Harpoon* tactical SSM, 2 triple ASTT (6 eff.) each with *Sting Ray* LWT, 1 twin tube *Bofors* mortar 375mm (2 eff.), 1 76mm gun
    2 *Damyat* (US *Knox*) each with 1 Mk16 Mk 112 octuple with 8 RGM-84C *Harpoon* tactical SSM, tactical ASROC, 2 twin 324mm TT (4 eff.), 1 127mm gun, (capacity 1 SH-2G *Super Seasprite* ASW hel)
    4 *Mubarak* (US *Oliver Hazard Perry*) each with 1 Mk 13 GMLS with 4 RGM-84C *Harpoon* tactical SSM, 36 SM-1 MP SAM, 1 76mm gun, (capacity 2 SH-2G *Super Seasprite* ASW hel)
    2 *Najim Al Zaffer* (PRC *Jianghu* I) each with 2 twin (4 eff.) each with HY-2 (CSS-N-2) *Silkworm* tactical SSM, 2 RBU 1200 (10 eff.)
PATROL AND COASTAL COMBATANTS 41
  PFM 23:
    5 *Tiger* class each with 2 single each with Otomat tactical SSM
    4 *Hegu* (*Komar* type) (PRC) each with 2 single each with 1 SY-1 tactical SSM
    5 *October* (FSU Komar) each with 2 single each with 1 SY-1 tactical SSM
    3 *Osa* I (FSU) each with 4 single each with 1 SS-N-2A *Styx* tactical SSM
    6 *Ramadan* each with 4 single each with 1 Otomat tactical SSM
  PFC 18:
    5 *Hainan* (PRC) each with 2 triple 324mm TT (6 eff.), 4 x1 RL
    3 *Hainan*† in reserve (PRC) each with 2 triple (6 eff.) 324mm TT (6 eff.), 4 single RL
    4 *Shanghai* II (PRC)
    4 *Shershen* each with 1+ SA-N-5 *Grail* SAM (manual aiming), 1 12 tube BM-24 MPL (12 eff.)
    2 *Shershen* (FSU) each with 4 single 533mm TT, 1 8 tube BM-21 MRL (8 eff.)
MINE WARFARE • MINE COUNTERMEASURES 14
  MSO 3 *Assiout* (FSU T-43 class)
  MSC 4 *Aswan* (FSU *Yurka*)
  MHC 5: 2 *Osprey*; 3 *Dat Assawari*
  MHI 2 *Safaga* (US Swiftships)
AMPHIBIOUS 12
  LS • LSM 3 *Polnochny* A (capacity 6 MBT; 180 troops) (FSU)
  CRAFT • LCU 9 *Vydra* (capacity either 3 AMX-30 MBT or 100 troops)
LOGISTICS AND SUPPORT 20:

AOT 7 *Toplivo*
AE 1 *Halaib* (*Westerwald*-class)
AR 1 *Shaledin* (*Luneberg*-class)
ATF 4
TRG 3: 1 *El Fateh*† training (UK 'Z' class); 1 *Tariq*† (UK FF); 1 *El Horriya* (also used as the Presidential yacht)
TRV 2 *Poluchat*
YDT 2

FACILITIES

Bases Alexandria, Port Said, Mersa Matruh, Port Tewfig, Safaqa, Hurghada, Suez, Al Ghardaqah

Coastal Defence

Army tps, Navy control
MSL • TACTICAL • SSM SSC-2b *Samlet*
LNCHR 3:
  3 twin each with 1 Mk 2 Otomat SSM
GUN 100mm; **130mm** SM-4-1; **152mm**

Naval Aviation

All aircraft armed and operated by Air Force
AIRCRAFT • TPT • BEECH 1900: 4 Beech 1900C (Maritime Surveillance)
HELICOPTERS
  ATK 5 SA-342 *Gazelle*
  ASW 15: 10 SH-2G *Super Seasprite* each with Mk 46 LWT; 4 *Sea King* MK47
UAV 2 *Camcopter* 5.1

Coast Guard 2,000

PATROL AND COASTAL COMBATANTS 80+
  PCC 50: 5 *Nisr*; 9 *Swiftships*; 21 *Timsah*; 9 *Type83*; 6+ *Swift Protector Class* (Additional vessels on order)
  PCI 12 *Sea Spectre MKIII*;
  PFI 6 *Crestitalia* less than 100 tonnes
  PBI 12 (various)

Air Force 30,000 (incl 10,000 conscript)

FORCES BY ROLE

Ftr	2 sqn with *Mirage* 5D/E; 2 sqn with F-16A *Fighting Falcon*; 1 sqn with M-2000C *Mirage*; 7 sqn with F-16C *Fighting Falcon*; 6 sqn with MiG-21 *Fishbed*
FGA	2 sqn with F-4E *Phantom II*; 2 sqn with J-6 (MiG-19S) *Farmer B*; 1 sqn with *Alpha Jet**; 1 sqn with *Mirage* 5E2
ASW/Hel	2 sqn with SH-2G *Super Seasprite**; *Sea King* MK47*; SA-342L *Gazelle** (Navy use)
Tac/Hel/ Tpt	sqns with CH-47C *Chinook*; CH-47D *Chinook* (medium); *Commando* (of which 3 VIP); Mi-6 *Hook*; S-70 *Black Hawk* (VIP, light); Mi-8 *Hip*; AS-61; UH-60A *Black Hawk*; UH-60L *Black Hawk* (VIP); UH-12E
Recce	2 sqn with MiG-21R *Fishbed H**; *Mirage* 5SDR (*Mirage* 5R)*
MP	1 sqn with Beech 1900C
EW	1 sqn with Beech 1900 (ELINT); C-130H *Hercules* (ELINT); *Commando* 2E (ECM)
AEW	1 sqn with E-2C *Hawkeye*

Tpt   1 regt with B-707-366C; B-737-100; Beech 200 *Super King Air*; C-130H *Hercules*; DHC-5D *Buffalo*; *Falcon* 20; Gulfstream III; Gulfstream IV, An-74TK-200A; Gulfstream G-45P

Atk hel   6 sqn with AH-64A *Apache*; SA-342K *Gazelle* (44 with HOT, 30 with 20mm)

Trg   sqns with F-16B *Fighting Falcon**; F-16D *Fighting Falcon**; DHC-5 *Buffalo*; *Alpha Jet*; EMB-312 *Tucano*; *Gomhouria*; Grob 115EG; L-29 *Delfin*; L-39 *Albatros*; L-59E *Albatros**; M-2000B *Mirage**; MiG-21U *Mongol A**; JJ-6 (MiG-19UTI) *Farmer*; K-8*

UAV   sqn with 20 R4E-50 *Skyeye*; 29 Teledyne-Ryan 324 *Scarab*

EQUIPMENT BY TYPE

AIRCRAFT 461 combat capable

FTR 165: 26 F-16A *Fighting Falcon*; 12 F-16B *Fighting Falcon*; 74 J-7 (MiG-21F) *Fishbed C*; 53 *Mirage* 5D/E

FGA 238: 18 M-2000C *Mirage*; 113 F-16C/ 6 F-16D *Fighting Falcon*; 16 *Mirage* 5E2; 29 F-4E *Phantom II*; 44 J-6 (MiG-19S) *Farmer B*; 12 *Alpha Jet*

RECCE 20: 14 MiG-21R *Fishbed H**; 6 *Mirage* 5SDR (*Mirage* 5R)*

AEW 6 E-2C *Hawkeye*

TPT 59: 3 An-74TK-200A (first of 6); 3 B-707-366C; 1 B-737-100; 1 Beech 1900 (ELINT); 4 Beech 1900C; 1 Beech 200 *Super King Air*; 2 C-130H *Hercules* (ELINT); 22 C-130H (tpt); 4 DHC-5; 5 DHC-5D *Buffalo*; 3 *Falcon* 20; 3 Gulfstream III; 3 Gulfstream IV; 4 Gulfstream G-45P

TRG 322: 24 *Alpha Jet*; 34 EMB-312 *Tucano*; 36 *Gomhouria*; 74 Grob 115EG; 80 K-8; 26 L-29 *Delfin*; 10 L-39 *Albatros*; 35 L-59E *Albatros**; 3 M-2000B *Mirage**

HELICOPTERS

ELINT 4 *Commando* 2E (ECM)

ATK 105: 35 AH-64A *Apache*; 65 SA-342K *Gazelle* (44 with HOT, 30 with 20mm); 5 SA-342L *Gazelle** (Navy use)

ASW 15: 10 SH-2G *Super Seasprite**; 5 *Sea King* MK47*

SPT 100: 3 CH-47C *Chinook*; 16 CH-47D *Chinook* (Medium); 25 *Commando* (of which 3 VIP); 12 Mi-6 *Hook*; 4 S-70 *Black Hawk* (VIP, light); 40 Mi-8 *Hip*

UTL 9: 2 AS-61; 2 UH-60A *Black Hawk*; 5 UH-60L *Black Hawk* (VIP)

TRG 17 UH-12E

UAV 49: 20 R4E-50 *Skyeye*; 29 Teledyne-Ryan 324 *Scarab*

MSL

ASM 245+: 80 AGM-65A *Maverick*; 123 AGM-65D *Maverick*; 12 AGM-65F *Maverick*; 30 AGM-65G *Maverick*; AGM-119 *Hellfire*; AGM-84 *Harpoon*; AM-39 *Exocet*; AS-30L HOT

ARM *Armat*; AS-12 *Kegler*

AAM AA-2 *Atoll*; AIM-7E *Sparrow*/AIM-7F *Sparrow*/ AIM-7M *Sparrow*; AIM-9F *Sidewinder*/AIM-9L *Sidewinder*/AIM-9P *Sidewinder*; R-550 *Magic*; R530

Air Defence Command 30,000; 50,000 conscript; 70,000 reservists (total 150,000)

FORCES BY ROLE

AD 5 div (geographically based) (*total:* 12 SAM bty with M-48 *Chaparral*, 12 radar bn, 12 ADA bde (*total:* 100 ADA bn), 12 SAM bty with I-HAWK MIM-23B, 14 SAM bty with *Crotale*, 18 SAM bn with *Skyguard*, 110 SAM bn with *Pechora* (SA-3A) *Goa*/SA-3 *Goa*; SA-6 *Gainful*; SA-2 *Guideline*)

EQUIPMENT BY TYPE

AD

SYSTEMS 72+: *Amoun* each with RIM-7F *Sea Sparrow* SAM, 36+ quad SAM (144 eff.), *Skyguard* towed SAM, 36+ twin 35mm guns (72 eff.)

SAM 702+

SP 130+: 24+ *Crotale*; 50+ M-48 *Chaparral*; 56+ SA-6 *Gainful*

TOWED 572+: 78+ I-HAWK *MIM-23B*; SA-2 *Guideline* 282+ *Skyguard*; 212+ *Pechora* (SA-3A) *Goa*/SA-3 *Goa*

GUNS 1,566+

SP • 23mm 266+: 36+ *Sinai*-23 (SPAAG) each with *Ayn al-Saqr* MANPAD, Dassault 6SD-20S land; 230 ZSU-23-4

TOWED 57mm 600 S-60; **85mm** 400 M-1939 *KS-12*; **100mm** 300 KS-19

Paramilitary ε397,000 active

Central Security Forces 325,000

Ministry of Interior; Includes conscripts
APC (W) 100+: 100 *Hussar*; *Walid*

National Guard 60,000

Lt wpns only

FORCES BY ROLE

Paramilitary 8 (cadre status) bde (*each:* 3 paramilitary bn)

EQUIPMENT BY TYPE

APC (W) 250 *Walid*

Border Guard Forces 12,000

Ministry of Interior; lt wpns only
18 (Border Guard) regt

DEPLOYMENT

CENTRAL AFRICAN REPUBLIC/CHAD

UN • MINURCAT 1; 2 obs

CÔTE D'IVOIRE

UN • UNOCI 1

DEMOCRATIC REPUBLIC OF CONGO

UN • MONUC 26 obs

LIBERIA

UN • UNMIL 5 obs

NEPAL

UN • UNMIN 5 obs

SUDAN

UN • UNMIS 1235 troops; 20 obs; 1 inf coy; 1 engr coy; 1 med coy; 1 demining coy

UN • UNAMID 2420; 12 obs; 1 inf bn; 1 engr coy; 1 sigs coy; 1 tpt coy

WESTERN SAHARA
UN • MINURSO 21 obs

FOREIGN FORCES

Australia MFO (*Operation Mazurka*) 25
Canada MFO 28
Colombia MFO 354; 1 inf bn
Fiji MFO 338; 1 inf bn
France MFO 18; 1 CN-235M
Hungary MFO 38 1 MP unit
Italy MFO 78; 1 coastal ptl unit
New Zealand MFO 26 1 trg unit; 1 tpt unit
Norway MFO 6 (staff)
United States MFO 688; 1 inf bn; 1 spt bn (1 EOD coy, 1 medical coy, 1 spt hel coy)
Uruguay MFO 58 1 engr/tpt unit

Iran IRN

Iranian Rial r		2008	2009	2010
GDP	r	3,181tr	3,563tr	
	US$	337bn	359bn	
per capita	US$	5,122	5,418	
Growth	%	2.5	1.5	
Inflation	%	26.0	12.0	
Def bdgt[a]	r	90.4tr		
	US$	9.59bn		
US$1=r		9,428	9,900	

[a] Excluding any defence industry funding

Population   66,429,284

Ethnic groups: Persian 51%; Azeri 24%; Gilaki/Mazandarani 8%; Kurdish 7%; Arab 3%; Lur 2%; Baloch 2%; Turkman 2%

Age	0–14	15–19	20–24	25–29	30–64	65 plus
Male	14%	6%	7%	5%	17%	2%
Female	13%	6%	6%	5%	16%	2%

Capabilities

ACTIVE 523,000 (Army 350,000 Islamic Revolutionary Guard Corps 125,000 Navy 18,000 Air 30,000) **Paramilitary 40,000**

Armed Forces General Staff coordinates two parallel organisations: Regular Armed Forces and Revolutionary Guard Corps

RESERVE 350,000 (Army 350,000, ex-service volunteers)

ORGANISATIONS BY SERVICE

Army 130,000; 220,000 conscript (total 350,000)

FORCES BY ROLE
5 Corps–Level Regional HQ

Armd	4 div each (2 armd, 1 mech bde , 1 recce, 1 SP arty bn); 1 indep bde
Mech Inf	2 div each (1 armd, 2-3 mech inf bde , 1 recce bn, 1 SP arty, 1 arty bn)
Inf	4 div each (3-4 inf ,1 arty bde); 1 indep bde
SF	1 bde
Cdo	1 div; 3 bde
AB	1 div
Arty	6 gp
Avn	some gp

EQUIPMENT BY TYPE
Totals incl those held by Islamic Revolutionary Guard Corps Ground Forces. Some equipment serviceability in doubt

MBT 1,613+: ε100 *Zulfiqar*; 480 T-72; 150 M-60A1; 75+ T-62; 100 *Chieftain* Mk3/Mk5; 540 T-54/T-55/Type-59; 168 M-47/M-48
LT TK 80+: 80 *Scorpion*; *Towsan*
RECCE 35 EE-9 *Cascavel*
AIFV 610: 210 BMP-1; 400 BMP-2
APC 640
  APC (T) 340: 140 *Boragh*; 200 M-113
  APC (W) 300 BTR-50/BTR-60
ARTY 8,196+
  SP 310+ : **122mm** 60+: 60 2S1 *Carnation*; *Thunder* 1; **155mm** 180+: 180 M-109; *Thunder* 2; **170mm** 10 M-1978; **175mm** 30 M-107; **203mm** 30 M-110
  TOWED 2,010+: **105mm** 130 M-101A1; **122mm** 640: 540 D-30; 100 Type-54 (M-30) M-1938; **130mm** 985 M-46; **152mm** 30 D-20; **155mm** 205: 120 GHN-45; 70 M-114; 15 Type 88 WAC-21; **203mm** 20 M-115
  MRL 876+: **107mm** 700+: 700 Type-63; *Fadjr* 1; HASEB; **122mm** 157: 7 BM-11; 100 BM-21; 50 *Arash/Hadid/Noor*; **240mm** 19: ε10 *Fadjr* 3; 9 M-1985; **333mm** *Fadjr* 5
  MOR 5,000: **60mm**; **81mm**; **82mm**; **107mm** M-30; **120mm** M-65
AT
  MSL • MANPATS 75 AT-3 9K11 *Sagger*/AT-4 9K111 *Spigot*/AT-5 9K113 *Spandrel/Saeqhe* 1/*Saeqhe* 2/*Toophan*/TOW (some AT-3 SP), *Toophan* (TOW)
  RCL 200+: **75mm** M-20; **82mm** B-10; **106mm** ε200 M-40; **107mm** B-11
  RL 73mm RPG-7 *Knout*
AIRCRAFT TPT 17: 10 Cessna 185; 2 F-27 *Friendship*; 1 *Falcon* 20; 4 Rockwell *Turbo Commander* 690
HELICOPTERS
  ATK 50 AH-1J *Cobra*
  SPT 45: 20 CH-47C *Chinook*; 25 Mi-17 (Mi-8MT) *Hip H*/Mi-8 *Hip*
  UTL 128: 68 AB-205A (Bell 205A); 10 AB-206 (Bell 206) *JetRanger*; 50 Bell 214
UAV • TACTICAL *Mohajer II / Mohajer III / Mohajer IV*
AD • SAM
  SP HQ-7 (reported); 10 *Pantsyr* S-1E (SA-22 *Greyhound*)
  MANPAD SA-14 *Gremlin*/SA-16 *Gimlet*/SA-7 *Grail*; *Misaq* (QW-1)
  GUNS 1,700
  SP 23mm ZSU-23-4; **57mm** ZSU-57-2

TOWED 14.5mm ZPU-2; ZPU-4; **23mm** ZU-23; **35mm**; **37mm** M-1939; **57mm** S-60
MSL • TACTICAL • SSM ε30 CSS-8 (175 msl)); 12+ *Scud*-B/*Scud*-C (Up to 18 launchers/launch vehicles (300 msl)); *Shahin-1/Shahin-2; Nazeat; Oghab*

Islamic Revolutionary Guard Corps 125,000+

Islamic Revolutionary Guard Corps Ground Forces 100,000+

Controls Basij paramilitary forces

Lightly manned in peacetime. Primary role: internal security; secondary role: external defence, in conjunction with regular armed forces.

Inf   Up to 15 div (Some divs are designated as armd or mech but all are predominantly infantry); some indep bde
AB   1 indep bde

Islamic Revolutionary Guard Corps Naval Forces 20,000+ (incl 5,000 Marines)

FORCES BY ROLE

Navy some (coast-defence) elm (*total:* some SSM bty with HY-2 (CSS-C-3) *Seersucker*, some arty bty)

EQUIPMENT BY TYPE
PATROL AND COASTAL COMBATANTS 50+
  PFM 10 *Thondor* (PRC *Houdong)* each with C-802 (CSS-N-8) *Saccade* tactical SSM
  PB 40+ Boghammar Marin (SWE) each with AT (ATGW), RCL, gun (machine guns)
MSL • TACTICAL • SSM HY-2 (CSS-C-3) *Seersucker*

FACILITIES
Bases Located at Bandar-e Abbas, Khorramshahr, with 40+ Boghammar Marin PB (SWE) each with AT (ATGW), RCL, gun (machine guns) bases located at Larak, Abu Musa, Al Farsiyah, Halul (oil platform), Sirri

Islamic Revolutionary Guard Corps Marines 5,000+

Marine 1 bde

Islamic Revolutionary Guard Corps Air Force

Controls Iran's strategic missile force.

FORCES BY ROLE

Msl ε1 bde *Shahab*-1/2 with 12–18 launchers; ε1 bn with up to 12 launchers with *Shahab*-3 strategic IRBM; some *Ghadr*-1; *Sajjil* (in devt)

EQUIPMENT BY TYPE
LAUNCHER 24: 12–18 for *Shahab*-1/2; up to 12 launchers with *Shahab*-3 IRBM; some for *Ghadr*-1; *Sajjil* (in devt)

Navy 18,000

FORCES BY ROLE

Navy 1 HQ located at Bandar-e Abbas

EQUIPMENT BY TYPE
SUBMARINES • TACTICAL • SSK 3 *Kilo* (RUS Type 877) each with 6 single 533mm TT

SSC 4 *Ghadir* (fitted with facility to operate SDV) (additional vessels in build)
SDV 3+ *Al Sabehat* (SF insertion and mine laying capacity)
PRINCIPAL SURFACE COMBATANTS 6
  FRIGATES • FFG 4:
  4 *Alvand* (UK Vosper Mk 5) each with 3 twin (6 eff.) each with CSS-N-4 *Sardine* tactical SSM, 1 single RL, 1 114mm gun
  CORVETTES • FS 2 *Bayandor* (US PF-103) each with 2 76mm gun
PATROL AND COASTAL COMBATANTS 146+
  PFM 13 *Kaman* (FRA *Combattante II*) each with 2–4 CSS-N-4 *Sardine* tactical SSM
  PCC 5: 3 *Parvin*; 2 *Kaivan*
  PCI 9 *China Cat* each with 2 twin (4 eff.) FL-10 SSM / C-701 *Kowsar* tactical SSM (less than 100 tonnes)
  PFI 42: 11 *Peykaap II* (IPS-16 mod) each with 2 twin (4eff.) FL-10 SSM / C-701 *Kowsar* tactical SSM; 15 *Peykaap I* (IPS 16); 6 (semi-submersible craft); 10 (various); (All vessels less than 100 tonnes)
  PBI 40
  PB 37
MINE WARFARE • MINE COUNTERMEASURES 5
  MSC 3: 2 Type-292; 1 *Shahrokh* (in Caspian Sea as trg ship)
  MSI 2 *Riazi* (US *Cape*)
AMPHIBIOUS
  LS 13
    LSM 3 *Iran Hormuz 24* (capacity 9 tanks; 140 troops) (ROK)
    LST 7:
      3 *Hejaz* (mine laying capacity)
      4 *Hengam* each with up to 1 hel (capacity 9 tanks; 225 troops)
    LSL 3 *Fouque*
  CRAFT 8
    UCAC 8: 7 *Wellington*; 1 *Iran*
LOGISTICS AND SUPPORT 26
  AORH 3: 2 *Bandar Abbas*; 1 *Kharg*
  AWT 4 *Kangan*
  SPT 19: 6 *Delvar*; 12 *Hendijan*; 1 *Hamzah*
FACILITIES
Bases Located at Bandar-e Abbas, Bushehr, Kharg Island, Bandar-e Anzelli, Bandar-e Khomeini, Bandar-e Mahshahr, Chah Bahar, Jask

Marines 2,600

Marine 2 bde

Naval Aviation 2,600

AIRCRAFT
  MP 3 P-3F *Orion*
  EW • ELINT 3 Da-20 *Falcon*
  TPT 13: 5 Do-228; 4 F-27 *Friendship*; 4 Rockwell *Turbo Commander* 680
HELICOPTERS
  ASW ε10 SH-3D *Sea King*
  MCM 3 RH-53D *Sea Stallion*
  UTL 17: 5 AB-205A (Bell 205A); 2 AB-206 (Bell 206) *JetRanger*; 10 AB-212 (Bell 212)

Air Force 30,000 (incl 12,000 Air Defence)

FORCES BY ROLE

Serviceability probably about 60% for US ac types and about 80% for PRC/Russian ac. Includes Islamic Revolutionary Guard Corps Air Force equipment.

Ftr	2 sqn with F-14 *Tomcat*; 1 sqn with F-7M *Airguard*; 2 sqn with MiG-29A *Fulcrum A*/MiG-29UB *Fulcrum*
FGA	1 sqn with F-1E *Mirage*; Su-25K *Frogfoot A*; Su-24MK *Fencer D*; 4 sqn with F-4D/F-4E *Phantom II*; 4 sqn with F-5E/F-5F *Tiger II*
Recce	1 (det) sqn with RF-4E *Phantom II**
MP	1 sqn with P-3MP *Orion**
Tkr/tpt	1 sqn with B-707; B-747
Tpt	5 sqn with Y-7 (An-24) *Coke*; B-727; B-747F; C-130E *Hercules*/C-130H *Hercules*; F-27 *Friendship*; *Falcon* 20; Il-76 *Candid*; *Jetstar*; PC-6B *Turbo Porter*; Rockwell *Turbo Commander* 680; Y-12; *Iran-140*
Trg	trg units with F-5B *Freedom Fighter**; TB-200 *Tobago*; TB-21 *Trinidad*; Beech F-33A *Bonanza*/Beech F-33C *Bonanza*; EMB-312 *Tucano*; JJ-7 *Mongol A**; MFI-17 *Mushshak*; PC-7 *Turbo Trainer*
Hel	sqn with CH-47 *Chinook*; *Shabaviz* 2-75; *Shabaviz* 2061; AB-206A (Bell 206A) *JetRanger*; AB-214C
SAM	16 bn each with ε150 I-HAWK MIM-23B; 5 sqn with FM-80 (*Crotale*); total of 30 *Rapier*; 15 *Tigercat*; 45 SA-2 *Guideline*; 10 SA-5 *Gammon*; FIM-92A *Stinger*; SA-7 *Grail;* 29 Tor-M1 systems (reported delivered early 2007)

EQUIPMENT BY TYPE

AIRCRAFT 312 combat capable
  FTR 133: 44 F-14 *Tomcat*; 35 MiG-29A/UB/U *Fulcrum*; 10 F-1E *Mirage*; 20 F-5B *Freedom Fighter*; 24 F-7M *Airguard* (6 *Azarakhsh* reported)
  FGA 168+: 13 Su-25K *Frogfoot A/T/UBK*; 30 Su-24MK *Fencer D*; 65 F-4D *Phantom II*/F-4E *Phantom II*; 60+ F-5E *Tiger II*/F-5F *Tiger II*. (3 *Saegheh* reported)
  RECCE: 6+ RF-4E *Phantom II**
  MP 5 P-3MP *Orion**
  TPT 104: 3 B-707; 1 B-727; 4 B-747F; 19 C-130E *Hercules*/C-130H *Hercules*; 10 F-27 *Friendship*; 1 *Falcon* 20; 12 Il-76 *Candid*; 5 Iran-140 *Faraz* (45 projected); 1 *Jetstar*; 10 PC-6B *Turbo Porter*; 3 Rockwell *Turbo Commander* 680; 9 Y-12; 14 Y-7 (An-24) *Coke*; 1 B-747; 11 An-72
  UTL 12: 4 TB-200 *Tobago*; 8 TB-21 *Trinidad*
  TRG 169: 25 Beech F-33A *Bonanza*/Beech F-33C *Bonanza*; 23 EMB-312 *Tucano*; 15 JJ-7 *Mongol A*; 25 MFI-17 *Mushshak*; 45 PC-7 *Turbo Trainer*; 9 T-33; 12 *Parastu*; 15 PC-6
HELICOPTERS
  SPT 2+ CH-47 *Chinook*; *Shabaviz* 2-75 (indigenous versions in production); *Shabaviz* 2061
  UTL 32: 2 AB-206A (Bell 206A) *JetRanger*; 30 AB-214C
  AD • SAM 279+: FM-80 (*Crotale*); 30 *Rapier*; 15 *Tigercat*; ε 150+ I-HAWK MIM-23B; 45 SA-2 *Guideline*; 10 SA-5 *Gammon*; 29 SA-15m *Gauntlet* (Tor-M1) (reported)
  MANPAD FIM-92A *Stinger*; SA-7 *Grail*
  GUNS • TOWED 23mm ZU-23; **37mm** Oerlikon
MSL
  ASM up to 3,000 AGM-65A *Maverick*/AS-10 *Karen*/AS-11 *Kilter*/AS-14 *Kedge*/C-801K (CSS-N-4) *Sardine* ALCM

  AAM AA-10 *Alamo*; AA-11 *Archer*; AA-8 *Aphid*; AIM-54 *Phoenix*; AIM-7 *Sparrow*; AIM-9 *Sidewinder*; PL-2A; PL-7

Paramilitary 40,000-60,000

Law-Enforcement Forces 40,000 – 60,000 (border and security troops); 450,000 on mobilisation (incl conscripts)

Part of armed forces in wartime
PATROL AND COASTAL COMBATANTS 130
  MISC BOATS/CRAFT 40 harbour craft
  PCI ε 90
AIRCRAFT • TPT: 2 *Iran*-140; some Cessna 185/Cessna 310
HELICOPTERS • UTL ε24 AB-205 (Bell 205)/AB-206 (Bell 206) *JetRanger*

Basij Resistance Force up to ε1,000,000 on mobilisation

Paramilitary militia, with claimed membership of 12.6 million, including women and children; perhaps 1 million combat capable; in the process of closer integration with Islamic Revolutionary Guard Corps Ground Forces.
Militia 2,500 bn (claimed); some (full time)

DEPLOYMENT

ARABIAN GULF AND INDIAN OCEAN
Navy: 1 FFG; 1 AORH

SUDAN
UN • UNMIS 2 obs

Iraq IRQ

Iraqi Dinar D		2008	2009	2010
GDP	US$	84.1bn	76.0bn	
per capita	US$	3,000	2,627	
Growth	%	9.5	4.3	
Inflation	%	2.7	6.9	
US$1=D		1,193	1,150	

Population	28,945,569

Ethnic and religious groups: Arab 75–80% (of which Shi'a Muslim 55%, Sunni Muslim 45%) Kurdish 20–25%

Age	0–14	15–19	20–24	25–29	30–64	65 plus
Male	20%	6%	5%	4%	14%	1%
Female	20%	6%	5%	4%	13%	2%

Capabilities

ACTIVE 578,269 (Army 186,957 Navy 2,000 Air 3,000 Ministry of Interior 386,312)

ORGANISATIONS BY SERVICE

Military Forces ε191,957

Figures for Iraqi security forces reflect ongoing changes in organisation and manpower.

Army ε186,957

FORCES BY ROLE

Armd   1 div with (3 armd bde, 1 lt mech bde)
Mot Inf 8 div (each: 4 mot inf bde); 2 div (each: 3 mot
         inf bde); 2 (Presidential) bde; 1 (Baghdad)
         indep bde
Inf   1 div with (1 mech inf bde, 2 inf bde, 1 air mob
         inf bde); 1 div with (3 inf bde)
Lt Inf   1 div with (4 lt inf bde)

SOF   2 bde

EQUIPMENT BY TYPE

MBT 149+: 77+ T-72; 72 T-55
RECCE 53 EE-9 Cascavel; 18 BRDM 2
AIFV 434 BMP-1
APC 1,479
  APC (T) 383: 100 FV 103 Spartan; 233 M-113 A1; 50
  M-113A2
  APC (W) 1,123: 98 BTR-80; 600 DZIK-3; 425 LAV
  Cougar
ARTY
  Mor 4 M-252

Navy ε2,000

Iraqi Coastal Defence Force (ICDF)

EQUIPMENT BY TYPE

PATROL AND COASTAL COMBATANTS 38+:
  PCC 1 Saettia (ITA Diciotti – additional 3 vessels in
  build))
  PC 7: 5 27m (PRC-built Predator); 2 Type-200
  PBR 30: 4 Type-2010; 16 (US Defender class); 10+ (RIB
  various)

FACILITIES

Base Located at Umm Qasr

Iraqi Air Force ε3,000

FORCES BY ROLE

Recce   1 sqn at Basra with SB7 L -360 Seeker; 1 sqn at
         Kirkuk with SB7L-360 Seeker (infrastructure
         patrols); Cessna 208B Grand Caravan (day-
         night surveillance, Hellfire msl, live downlink
         capability)
Tpt   1 sqn at New al-Muthanna with C-130E
         Hercules; Beech King Air 350 (VIP tpt/trainer)
Tpt/utl 4 sqn at Taji with Bell 206-B3 JetRanger; UH-1H
         Huey II; Mi-17 2 PZL W-3W
Trg   1 flying trg school Kirkuk with Cessna 172

EQUIPMENT BY TYPE

AIRCRAFT
  ATK/RECCE 6 Cessna AC-208B Combat Caravan
  RECCE 10: 2 SB7L-360 Seeker; 8 SAMA CH2000
  TPT 14: 3 C-130E Hercules; 6 Beech King Air 350; 5
  Comp Air 7SL
  TRG 8 Cessna 172
HELICOPTERS
  SPT 20: 18 Mi-17; 2 PZL W-3WA
  UTL 38: 10 Bell 206-B3 JetRanger; 16 UH-1H Huey II; 10
  OH-58; 2 Sokol

MSL
  ASM AGM-114 Hellfire

Ministry of Interior Forces ε386,312 (Includes Civil Intervention Force, Emergency Response Unit, Border Enforcement (39,294) and Dignitary Protection)

Iraqi Police Service ε305,713 (including Highway Patrol)

National Police ε41,305

SELECTED NON-STATE GROUPS

Al-Qaeda in Iraq (AQI) Est strength: n.k. Major equipments include: mines and IEDs, mortars, SALW Islamic Army in Iraq Est strength: 4,000 Major equipments include: mines and IEDs, mortars, SALW Islamic State of Iraq Est strength: n.k. Major equipments include: mines and IEDs, mortars, SALW Partiya Karkeren Kurdistan (PKK) Reportedly active in Turkey's Southeast and from bases across the Iraqi border. Est strength 3,000. Major equipments include: mines and IEDs, mortars, SALW

FOREIGN FORCES

Australia 80; 1 sy det with ASLAV • UNAMI 2 obs
Bulgaria NTM-I 2
Denmark 27 (sy forces) • NTM-I 10 • UNAMI 2 obs
Estonia NTM-I 3
Fiji UNAMI 221; 3 sy unit
Hungary NTM-I 4
Italy NTM-I 91
Jordan UNAMI 2 obs
Lithuania NTM-I 4
Nepal UNAMI 2 obs
Netherlands NTM-I 7
New Zealand UNAMI 1 obs
Poland NTM-I 3
Romania NTM-I 3
Turkey NTM-I 2
Ukraine NTM-I 9
United Kingdom 75; Navy: 1 Navy Transition Team (Navy / Cdo team training the Iraqi Riverine Patrol Service (IRPS)) Air Force: Puma SH
NTM-I 15 • UNAMI 1 obs
United States 120,000 Army: 1 corps HQ; 2 div HQ; 5 armd HBCT; 1 armd inf bde; 2 mech inf Stryker BCT; 1 lt inf IBCT; 1 AB IBCT (AAB); 1 ARNG div HQ; 1 ARNG armd HBCT; 1 ARNG HBCT (LoC duties); 2 ARNG lt inf IBCT (LoC duties); some M1 Abrams; some M2/M3 Bradley; some Stryker; some M109; some M198; 9,341 MRAP; some AH-64 Apache; some OH-58 Kiowa; some UH-60 Black Hawk; some CH-47 Chinook USMC: 1 MEF HQ; 1 FSSG regt. Air Force: some F-16D Fighting Falcon; some A-10 Thunderbolt II; some C-130 Hercules; some C-17 Globemaster; Some HH-60G Pave Hawk; some RQ-1B Predator • NTM-I 12 • UNAMI 2 obs

Israel ISR

New Israeli Shekel NS		2008	2009	2010
GDP	NS	714bn	741bn	
	US$	199bn	198bn	
per capita	US$	28,042	27,390	
Growth	%	4.0	-0.1	
Inflation	%	4.6	3.6	
Def exp	NS	52.8bn	48.5bn	
	US$	14.77bn	12.96bn	
Def bdgt	NS	34.7bn	36.5bn	37.8bn
	US$	9.70bn	9.78bn	
FMA (US)	US$	2.38bn	2.55bn	2.77bn
US$1=NS		3.58	3.74	

Population   7,233,701

Ethnic and religious groups: Jewish 76%; Arab 20%; others 4%.
(Muslim 17%; Christian 2%; Druze 2%)

Age	0–14	15–19	20–24	25–29	30–64	65 plus
Male	14%	4%	4%	4%	20%	4%
Female	13%	4%	4%	4%	20%	6%

Capabilities

ACTIVE 176,500 (Army 133,000 Navy 9,500 Air 34,000) **Paramilitary 8,050**

RESERVE 565,000 (Army 500,000 Navy 10,000 Air 55,000)

Terms of service officers 48 months, other ranks 36 months, women 24 months (Jews and Druze only; Christians, Circassians and Muslims may volunteer). Annual trg as cbt reservists to age 41 (some specialists to age 54) for men, 24 (or marriage) for women

ORGANISATIONS BY SERVICE

Strategic Forces

Israel is widely believed to have a nuclear capability – delivery means include ac, *Jericho* 1 and *Jericho* 2 (IRBM and SRBM)

MSL • STRATEGIC
 IRBM: *Jericho* 2
 SRBM: *Jericho* 1
WARHEADS up to 200 nuclear warheads

Strategic Defences

17 batteries MIM-23B Improved HAWK
6 batteries MIM-104 *Patriot*
3 batteries (24 launchers) *Arrow/Arrow* 2 ATBM with *Green Pine* radar and *Citrus Tree* command post. Launchers sited Hadera and Palmachim (N and C Israel)
1 US EUCOM AN/TPY-2 X-band radar at Nevatim, SE of Beersheba

Army 26,000; 107,000 conscript; 500,000+ on mobilisation; (total 133,000–633,000)

Organisation and structure of formations may vary according to op situations. Equipment includes that required for reserve forces on mobilisation.

FORCES BY ROLE
3 regional commands each with 2 regular div; 1-2 regional/territorial div; 2 regular bde

Armd   2 div; 15 bde
Inf   4 div; 12 bde
Para   8 bde
Arty   4 regt
SP arty   8 regt

EQUIPMENT BY TYPE
MBT 3,501: 441 *Merkava* Mk1; 455 *Merkava* MkII; 454 *Merkava* MkIII; 175 *Merkava* MkIV; 111 *Magach-7*; 261 Ti-67 (T-55 mod); 711 M-60/M-60A1/M-60A3; 206 *Centurion*; 126 T-54/T-55/T-62S; 561 M-48A5
RECCE 408: ε400 RBY-1 RAMTA; ε8 Tpz-1 *Fuchs*
APC 10,419+
 APC (T) 10,418+: up to 45 *Namer*; 276 *Achzarit* (modified T-55 chassis); 6,131 M-113A1/M-113A2; 180 M-2 (some in store); 3,386 M-3 half-track (some in store); ε400 *Nagmachon* (*Centurion* chassis); *Nakpadon*
 APC (W) 46: 34 BTR-152; 6 BTR-40; 6 *Puma* (*Centurion*)
ARTY 5,432
 SP 620: **155mm** 548: 148 L-33; 350 M-109A1; 50 M-50; **175mm** 36 M-107; **203mm** 36 M-110
 TOWED 456: **105mm** 70 M-101A1; **122mm** 5 D-30; **130mm** 100 M-46; **155mm** 281: 50 M-114A1 in reserve; 100 M-46; 50 M-68/M-71; 81 M-839P/M-845P
 MRL 224: **122mm** 58 BM-21; **160mm** 50 LAR-160; **227mm** 60 MLRS; **240mm** 36 BM-24; **290mm** 20 LAR-290
 MOR 4,132: **52mm** 2,000; **81mm** 1,358; **120mm** 652 (towed); **160mm** 122: 104 M-43 in reserve; 18 M-66 *Soltam*
AT
 MSL • MANPATS 1,225+: 900 M47 *Dragon*; AT-3 9K11 *Sagger*; 25 IMI MAPATS; *Gil/Spike*; 300 TOW-2A/TOW-2B (incl *Ramta* (M-113) SP)
 RCL 106mm 250 M-40A1
 RL 82mm B-300
AD • SAM 1,270
 SP 20 *Machbet*
 MANPAD 1,250: 1,000 FIM-43 *Redeye*; 250 FIM-92A *Stinger*
RADAR • LAND AN/PPS-15 (arty); AN/TPQ-37 *Firefinder* (arty); EL/M-2140 (veh)
MSL 107
 STRATEGIC ε100 *Jericho* 1 SRBM/*Jericho* 2 IRBM
 TACTICAL • SSM 7 *Lance* (in store)

Navy 7,000; 2,500 conscript; 10,000 on mobilisation (total 9,500–19,500)

EQUIPMENT BY TYPE
SUBMARINES • TACTICAL • SSK 3 *Dolphin* (GER Type-212 variant) each with 6 single 533mm TT each with 5 UGM-84C *Harpoon* tactical USGW, 16 HWT, 4 single 650mm TT
PRINCIPAL SURFACE COMBATANTS • CORVETTES
 FSG 3 *Eilat* (*Sa'ar* 5) each with 2 Mk 140 *Harpoon* quad (8 eff.) each with RGM-84C *Harpoon* tactical SSM, 2 32 cell VLS (64 eff.) each with up to 64 *Barak* SAM, 2 triple (6 eff.)

TT each with Mk 46 LWT, 1 76mm gun, (capacity either 1 AS-565SA *Panther* ASW hel or 1 AS-366G *Dauphin II* SAR hel)

PATROL AND COASTAL COMBATANTS 61
PFM 10:
8 *Hetz* (*Sa'ar* 4.5) each with 6 single each with 1 GII *Gabriel II* tactical SSM, 2 Mk 140 twin each with RGM-84C *Harpoon* tactical SSM, 1 32 Cell/Mk 56 (1-32 eff.) with *Barak* SAM, 1 76mm gun
2 *Reshef* (*Sa'ar* 4) each with 4–6 single each with 1 GII *Gabriel II* tactical SSM, 1 Mk 140 twin with RGM-84C *Harpoon* tactical SSM, 1 76mm gun
PFI 40:
15 *Dabur* less than 100 tonnes each with 2 single 324mm TT each with Mk 46 LWT
13 *Super Dvora* MKI and II less than 100 tonnes (SSM, and TT may be fitted) each with 2 single 324mm TT each with Mk 46 LWT
8 *Super Dvora* MK III
4 *Shaldag* (Additional vessel in build*)*
PBF 11: 8 *Tzir'a*; 3 *Stingray*
MISC BOATS/CRAFT • SPECIAL WARFARE SUPPORT CRAFT: 1 *Katler*
AMPHIBIOUS • CRAFT 2:
LCT 1 *Ashdod*
LCM 1 US type
LOGISTICS AND SUPPORT 3:
AG 2 (ex German Type T45)
Trial 1

FACILITIES
Bases   Located at Haifa, Atlit (Naval Commandos), Eilat, Ashdod

Naval Aviation
AC • TPT 2 C-130
HELICOPTERS • ASW 7 AS-565SA *Panther*; 2 SA-366 G *Dauphin*
SAR/UTL 17 Bell 212

Naval Commandos ε300

Air Force 34,000
Responsible for Air and Space Coordination

FORCES BY ROLE
Ftr/FGA   2 sqn with F-15A/F-15B *Eagle*; F-15C/F-15D *Eagle*; 1 sqn with F-15I *Ra'am*; 8 sqn with F-16A/F-16B *Fighting Falcon*; F-16C/F-16D *Fighting Falcon*; 4 sqn with F-16I *Sufa*; 3 sqn with A-4N *Skyhawk*/F-4 *Phantom II/Kfir* C-7 in reserve
ASW   sqn with AS-565SA *Panther* (missions flown by IAF but with non-rated aircrew)
MP   1 sqn with IAI-1124 *Seascan*
EW   sqns with RC-12D *Guardrail*; Beech 200CT *Super King Air*; EC-130H *Hercules* (ELINT); Do-28; EC/RC-707 (ELINT/ECM) being replaced by Gulfstream G-550 *Shavit*; IAI-202 *Arava*
AEW   1 sqn with *Phalcon* B-707 (being replaced with Gulfstream G550 *Eitam*)
Tpt   1 sqn with C-47 *Skytrain*
Tpt/tkr   1 sqn with B-707

Tkr   1 sqn with KC-130H *Hercules*
Liaison   1 sqn with BN-2 *Islander*; Beech 80 *Queen Air*; Cessna U-206 *Stationair*
Atk hel   4 sqn with AH-1E *Cobra*; AH-1F *Cobra*; AH-64A *Apache*; AH-64D *Apache*
Tpt hel   6 sqn with CH-53D *Sea Stallion*; S-70A *Black Hawk*; Bell 206 *JetRanger*; Bell 212; UH-60A *Black Hawk*; UH-60L *Black Hawk*
Trg   Trg units with Beech 80 *Queen Air*; T-6A (replacing CM-170 *Magister*); Grob 120; TA-4H *Skyhawk**; TA-4J *Skyhawk**
UAV   1 sqn with 22+ *Searcher I/II* (being replaced by MALE (Medium Altitude Long Endurance) *Shoval*; *Delilah*; *Firebee*; *Harpy*; RQ-5A *Hunter*; *Samson*; *Scout*; Silver Arrow *Hermes* 450;
SAM   2 bty each with 9 *Arrow* II; 3 bty each with 16 PAC-2; 17 bty with MIM-23 *HAWK*; 5 bty with MIM-104 *Patriot*; 35 M-163 *Vulcan*

EQUIPMENT BY TYPE
AIRCRAFT 461 combat capable
FTR 168: 90 F-16A *Fighting Falcon*; 16 F-16B *Fighting Falcon*; 27 F-15A *Eagle*; 7 F-15B *Eagle*; 17 F-15C *Eagle*; 11 F-15D *Eagle*
FGA 267: 25 F-15I *Ra'am*; 39 A-4N *Skyhawk*; 52 F-16C *Fighting Falcon*; 49 F-16D *Fighting Falcon*; 102 F-16I *Sufa*; [200+ A-4N *Skyhawk*/F-4 *Phantom II/Kfir* C-7 (in reserve)]
AEW 4: 3 *Phalcon* B-707; 1 Gulfstream G550 *Eitam* (2 more on order)
RECCE 6 RC-12D *Guardrail*
ELINT 11: 3 B-707 (ELINT/ECM); 3 Gulfstream G-500 *Shavit*; 2 EC-130H *Hercules* AEW; 3 B-707 *Phalcon*
MP 3 IAI-1124 *Seascan*
TPT/TKR 9: 4 B-707; 5 KC-130H *Hercules*
TPT 42: 5 C-130 *Hercules*; 2 BN-2 *Islander*; 4 Beech 200CT *Super King Air*; 12 Beech 80 *Queen Air*; 1 C-47 *Skytrain*; 9 IAI-202 *Arava*
TRG 107: 20 T-6A; 17 Grob 120; 10 TA-4H *Skyhawk**; 16 TA-4J *Skyhawk**; 22 A-26 *Bonanza* (*Hofit*); 22 TB-21 (*Pashosh*)
HELICOPTERS
ATK 81: 33 AH-1E/AH-1F *Cobra*; 30 AH-64A *Apache*; 18 *Sarat* (AH-64D) *Apache*
ASW 7 AS-565SA *Panther* (missions flown by IAF but with non-rated aircrew)
SPT 87: 38 CH-53D *Sea Stallion*; 49 S-70A *Black Hawk*
UTL 113: 34 Bell 206 *JetRanger*; 55 Bell 212; 10 UH-60A *Black Hawk*; 14 UH-60L *Black Hawk*
UAV 48+: 4 *Heron* II (*Shoval*); *Harpy*; RQ-5A *Hunter*; *Samson*; *Scout*; 22 *Searcher* MK II (22+ in store); Siver Arrow *Hermes* 450
AD
SAM • TOWED 48+: 48 PAC-2; MIM-104 *Patriot*; MIM-23 HAWK
GUNS 920
SP 165 **20mm** 105 M-163 Machbet *Vulcan*; **23mm** 60 ZSU-23-4
TOWED 755 **23mm** 150 ZU-23; **20mm/37mm** 455 M-167 *Vulcan* towed 20mm/M-1939 towed 37mm/TCM-20 towed 20mm; **40mm** 150 L/70

MSL
ASM AGM-114 *Hellfire*; AGM-45 *Shrike*; AGM-62B *Walleye*; AGM-65 *Maverick*; AGM-78D *Standard*; *Popeye* I tactical ASM/*Popeye* II
AAM AIM-120 *AMRAAM*; AIM-7 *Sparrow*; AIM-9 *Sidewinder*; *Python* III; *Python* IV; *Shafrir*
BOMB • PGM • JDAM GBU-31

Airfield Defence 3,000 active; 15,000 reservists (total 18,000)

Regional/Territorial Forces
Can be mobilised in 72hrs
Inf 11 (territorial/regional) bde

Reserve Organisations

Reserves ε380,000 reservists
Armd   8 div (*total:* 15 armd bde, 6 arty regt, 4 inf bde, 6 mech inf bde)
Air Mob 1 div (3 air mob bde, 1 para bde)

Paramilitary ε8,050

Border Police ε8,000

Coast Guard ε50
PATROL AND COASTAL COMBATANTS 4
  PC 3; **PCR** 1 (US)

DEPLOYMENT

TURKEY
Air Force up to 1 ftr det (occasional) located at Akinci, TUR, with F-16 *Fighting Falcon* (current status uncertain)

FOREIGN FORCES
UNTSO unless specified. Figures represent total numbers for mission in Israel, Syria, Lebanon
Argentina 6 obs
Australia 11 obs
Austria 7 obs
Belgium 2 obs
Canada 7 obs • 9 (*Operation Proteus*) USSC
Chile 4 obs
China 4 obs
Denmark 11 obs
Estonia 1 obs
Finland 15 obs
France 2 obs
Ireland 12 obs
Italy 8 obs
Nepal 3 obs
Netherlands 12 obs
New Zealand 7 obs
Norway 11 obs
Russia 5 obs
Slovakia 2 obs
Slovenia 2 obs

Sweden 7 obs
Switzerland 10 obs
United States 2 obs • Army 4; Navy 3; USAF 15; USMC 24; 1 AN/TPY-2 X-band radar located at Nevatim with 120 pers

Jordan JOR

Jordanian Dinar D		2008	2009	2010
GDP	D	14.2bn	14.9bn	
	US$	20.0bn	21.0bn	
per capita	US$	3,261	3,347	
Growth	%	7.9	3.0	
Inflation	%	14.9	0.2	
Def bdgt	D	1.51bn	1.64bn	1.77bn
	US$	2.12bn	2.31bn	
FMA (US)	US$	348m	335m	300m
US$1=D		0.71	0.71	

Population   6,269,285
Ethnic groups: Palestinian ε50-60%

Age	0–14	15–19	20–24	25–29	30–64	65 plus
Male	18%	5%	5%	5%	18%	2%
Female	17%	5%	5%	4%	15%	2%

Capabilities

ACTIVE 100,500 (Army 88,000 Navy 500 Air 12,000)
Paramilitary 10,000

RESERVE 65,000 (Army 60,000 Joint 5,000)

ORGANISATIONS BY SERVICE

Army 88,000
Jordan has re-organised from a divisional structure to 4 commands, a strategic reserve and a special operations command. The strategic reserve still has a divisional structure and special operations command is responsible for counter terrorism and unconventional operations. The Royal Guard also comes under this command.

FORCES BY ROLE
Armd   1 comd (Southern) (1 armd bde, 1 inf bde); 1 div (strategic reserve) (3 armd, 1 arty, 1 AD bde)
Mech   1 comd (Northern) (2 mech bde, 1 inf bde, 1 arty bde, 1 AD bde,); 1 comd (Eastern) (2 mech bde, 1 AD bde, 1 arty bde); 1 comd (Central) (1 mech bde, 1 lt inf bde, 1 AD bde, 1 arty bde)
Spec Ops 1 bde (2 ab bn, 1 ab arty bn, 1 psyops unit; 2 SF bn)

EQUIPMENT BY TYPE
MBT 1,182: 390 CR1 *Challenger 1* (*Al Hussein*); 274 FV4030/2 *Khalid*; 88 M-60 *Phoenix*; 115 M-60A1/M-60A3 (in store); 292 *Tariq* (*Centurion* – in store); 23 M-47/M-48A5 (in store)
LT TK 39 *Scorpion* (used as recce; in store)
RECCE 103 *Scimitar*

AIFV 303: 31 BMP-2: 259 *Ratel*-20; 13 YPR-765
APC • APC (T) 1,391: 1,072 M-113A1; 276 M-113A2 MK-1J; 3 YPR-765; 40 *Spartan*
ARTY 1,232
  SP 359: **105mm** 4 M-52; **155mm** 273: 253 M-109A1/M-109A2; 20 M-44; **203mm** 82 M-110A2
  TOWED 94: **105mm** 54: 36 M-102; 18 MOBAT; **155mm** 36: 18 M-1/M-59; 18 M-114; **203mm** 4 M-115
  MOR 779:
  SP 81mm 130
  TOWED 649: **81mm** 359; **107mm** 60 M-30; **120mm** 230 Brandt
AT • MSL 765
  SP 115: 70 M-901; 45 YPR-765 with *Milan*
  MANPATS 650: 30 *Javelin* (110 msl); 310 M47 *Dragon*; 310 TOW/TOW-2A
  RL 4,800+: **73mm** RPG-26; **94mm** 2,500 LAW-80; **112mm** 2,300 APILAS
AD • SAM 992+
  SP 152: 92 SA-13 *Gopher*; 60 SA-8 *Gecko*
  MANPAD 840+: 250 FIM-43 *Redeye*; 300 SA-14 *Gremlin*; 240 SA-16 *Gimlet*; 50 SA-7B2 *Grail*; SA-18 *Grouse* (*Igla*)
  GUNS • SP 395: **20mm** 139 M-163 *Vulcan*; **23mm** 40 ZSU-23-4; **40mm** 216 M-42 (not all op)
RADAR • LAND 7 AN/TPQ-36 *Firefinder*/AN/TPQ-37 *Firefinder* (arty, mor)

Navy ε500

EQUIPMENT BY TYPE
PATROL AND COASTAL COMBATANTS 13
  PFI 3 *Al Hussein* less than 100 tonnes (UK Vosper 30m)
  PB 10: 2 *Al Hashim* (*Rotork*); 4 *Faysal*; 4 *Abduhlla* (US *Dauntless*)

FACILITIES
Bases Located at Aqaba

Air Force 12,000

Flying hours   180 hrs/year

FORCES BY ROLE
Ftr   1 sqn with F-1CJ (F-1C) *Mirage*/*Mirage* F-1BJ (F-1B); 1 sqn with F-16A *Fighting Falcon*; F-16B *Fighting Falcon*;

FGA/Recce 1 sqn with *Mirage* F-1EJ (F-1E); 1 sqn with F-16AM/BM *Fighting Falcon*; 3 sqn with F-5E *Tiger II*/F-5F *Tiger II*

Surv   sqn with RU-38A *Twin Condor*

Tpt   1 sqn with C-130H *Hercules*; CASA 212A *Aviocar*; CL-604 *Challenger*; CN-235; TB-20 *Trinidad*

VIP   1 (Royal) flt with A-340-211; Gulfstream IV; L-1011 *Tristar*; S-70A *Black Hawk*

Atk hel 2 sqn with AH-1F *Cobra* with TOW tactical ASM

Tpt hel 2 sqn with AS-332M *Super Puma*; Bo-105 (operated on behalf of the police); EC-635 (utl/SAR); UH-1H *Iroquois*; 1 hel sqn dedicated to SF

Trg   3 sqn with *Bulldog* 103 (being replaced by T-67M); CASA C-101 *Aviojet*; Hughes 500D

UAV   2 bde (*total:* 14 AD bty with 80 I-HAWK MIM-1 unit with *Seeker* SB7L

AD   1 cmd (5–6 bty with PAC-2 *Patriot*; 5 bty with I-HAWK MIM-2BB Phase III; 6 bty with *Skyguard*/*Aspide*)

EQUIPMENT BY TYPE
AIRCRAFT 102 combat capable
  FTR 50: 20 F-16A/4 F-16B *Fighting Falcon*; 11 F-16C/D *Fighting Falcon*; 15 F-1CJ (F-1C) *Mirage* FTR/*Mirage* F-1BJ (F-1B)
  FGA 52: 8 F-16AM/4 F-16BM *Fighting Falcon*; 15 *Mirage* F-1FJ (F-1E); 25 F-5E *Tiger II*/F-5F *Tiger II*
  MP 2 RU-38A *Twin Condor*
  TPT 18: 1 A-340-211; 4 C-130H *Hercules*; 2 CASA 212A *Aviocar*; 2 CL-604 *Challenger*; 2 CN-235; 2 Gulfstream IV; 1 L-1011 *Tristar*; 2 Il-76; 2 CN-295
  UTL 2 TB-20 *Trinidad*
  TRG 27: 15 *Bulldog* 103 (being replaced by 16 T-67M *Firefly*); 10 CASA C-101 *Aviojet*; 2 TB-20 *Socata*
HELICOPTERS
  ATK 25 AH-1F *Cobra* each with TOW tactical ASM
  SPT 26: 12 AS-332M *Super Puma*; 14 S-70A *Black Hawk*
    UTL 60: 3 Bo-105 (operated on behalf of the police); 13 EC-635 (ult/SAR); 8 Hughes 500D; 36 UH-1H *Iroquois*; 5 BK-117
UAV 6 *Seeker* SB7L
AD • SAM 80+: 40 PAC-2 *Patriot*; 24 I-HAWK MIM-23B Phase III
MSL
  ASM AGM-65D *Maverick*
  AAM AIM-7 *Sparrow*; AIM-9 *Sidewinder*; R-550 *Magic*; R530; AIM-120C AMRAAM

Paramilitary 10,000 active

Public Security Directorate ε10,000 active
Ministry of Interior
FORCES BY ROLE
Sy 1 (Police Public) bde
EQUIPMENT BY TYPE
LT TK: *Scorpion*
APC (W) 55+: 25+ EE-11 *Urutu*; 30 FV603 *Saracen*

Reserve Organisations 60,000 reservists
Armd   1 (Royal) div (1 arty bde, 1 AD bde, 3 armd bde)

Civil Militia 'People's Army' ε35,000 reservists
Men 16–65, women 16–45

DEPLOYMENT

AFGHANISTAN
NATO • ISAF 7

CÔTE D'IVOIRE
UN • UNOCI 1,057; 7 obs ; 1 inf bn ; 1 SF coy

DEMOCRATIC REPUBLIC OF CONGO
UN • MONUC 65; 24 obs; 1 fd hospital

HAITI
UN • MINUSTAH 727; 2 inf bn

IRAQ
UN • UNAMI 2 obs

LIBERIA
UN • UNMIL 119; 4 obs; 1 fd hospital

NEPAL
UN • UNMIN 4 obs

SUDAN
UN • UNAMID 12; 4 obs
UN • UNMIS 5; 10 obs

WESTERN SAHARA
UN • MINURSO 2 obs

Kuwait KWT

Kuwaiti Dinar D		2008	2009	2010
GDP	D	40.4bn	34.7bn	
	US$	155bn	123bn	
per capita	US$	59,837	46,027	
Growth	%	6.5	-1.5	
Inflation	%	10.5	4.6	
Def bdgt	D	1.77bn	1.86bn	
	US$	6.81bn	6.65bn	
US$1=D		0.26	0.28	

Population   2,692,285

Ethnic groups: Nationals 35%; other Arab 35%; South Asian 9%; Iranian 4%; other 17%

Age	0–14	15–19	20–24	25–29	30–64	65 plus
Male	14%	4%	7%	9%	25%	2%
Female	13%	4%	5%	5%	11%	1%

Capabilities

ACTIVE 15,500 (Army 11,000 Navy 2,000 Air 2,500)
Paramilitary 7,100
Terms of service voluntary

RESERVE 23,700 (Joint 23,700)
Terms of service obligation to age 40; 1 month annual trg

ORGANISATIONS BY SERVICE

Army 11,000
FORCES BY ROLE

Army	1 (reserve) bde
Armd	3 bde
Mech/Recce	1 bde
Mech Inf	2 bde
SF	1 unit (forming)

Cdo	1 bn
Arty	1 bde
Engr	1 bde
Gd	1 (Amiri) bde
AD	1 comd (AD bty, 4 (HAWK Phase III),AD bty, 5 (*Patriot* PAC-2) AD bty, 6 (*Amoun* (*Skyguard/Aspide*)) AD bty)

EQUIPMENT BY TYPE
MBT 368: 218 M1-A2 *Abrams*; 75 M-84; 75 in store
AIFV up to 450: up to 76 BMP-2; up to 120 BMP-3; 254 *Desert Warrior* (incl variants)
APC 321
 APC (T) 270: 230 M-113A2; 40 M-577
 APC (W) 51: 40 TH 390 *Fahd* in store; 11 TPz-1 *Fuchs*
ARTY 218
 SP 155mm 113: 18 AU-F-1 in store; 23 M-109A3; 18 (AMX) Mk F3; 54 PLZ45
 MRL 300mm 27 9A52 *Smerch*
 MOR 78: **81mm** 60; **107mm** 6 M-30; **120mm** ε12 RT-F1
AT • MSL 118+
 SP 74: 66 HMMWV TOW; 8 M-901
 MANPATS 44+: 44 TOW-2; M47 *Dragon*
 RCL 84mm ε200 *Carl Gustav*
AD • SAM 60+
 STATIC/SHELTER 12 *Aspide*
 MANPAD 48 *Starburst; Stinger*
 GUNS • TOWED 35mm 12+ Oerlikon

Navy ε2,000 (incl 500 Coast Guard)
EQUIPMENT BY TYPE
PATROL AND COASTAL COMBATANTS 10
 PFM 10:
  1 *Al Sanbouk* (GER Lurssen TNC-45) with 2 twin (4 eff.) each with MM-40 *Exocet* tactical SSM
  1 *Istiqlal* (GER Lurssen FPB-57) with 2 twin (4 eff.) each with MM-40 *Exocet* tactical SSM
  8 *Um Almaradim* (FRA P-37 BRL) each with 2 twin (4 eff.) each with *Sea Skua* tactical SSM, 1 sextuple (6 eff.) (launcher only)
AMPHIBIOUS 2 LCM
LOGISTICS AND SUPPORT • SPT 1 *Sawahil*
FACILITIES
Base   Located at Ras al Qalaya

Air Force 2,500
Flying hours   210 hrs/year
FORCES BY ROLE

Ftr/FGA	2 sqn with F/A-18C/18D *Hornet*
CCT	1 sqn with *Hawk* MK64; *Tucano* T MK52 (Shorts 312);
Tpt	2 sqn with B-737; DC-9; L-100-30; AS-332 *Super Puma* (tpt/SAR/atk); SA-330 *Puma*
Trg/atk hel	1 sqn with SA-342 *Gazelle* each with HOT tactical ASM
Atk hel	1 sqn with AH-64D *Apache*
Trg	trg unit with *Hawk* MK64*; *Tucano* T MK52 (Shorts 312)

AD   1 comd (5-6 SAM bty with 40 PAC-2 *Patriot*;
            5 SAM bty with 24 MIM-23B *I HAWK Phase
            III*; 6 SAM bty with 12 *Skyguard/Aspide*)

EQUIPMENT BY TYPE
AIRCRAFT 50 combat capable
FGA 39: 31 F/A-18C *Hornet*; 8 F/A-18D *Hornet*
TPT 5: 1 B-737-200; 1 DC-9; 3 L-100-30
TRG 19: 11 *Hawk* MK64*; 8 *Tucano* T MK52
HELICOPTERS
ATK 12 AH-64D *Apache*
ASLT 13 SA-342 *Gazelle** each with HOT tactical ASM
SPT 103: 5 AS-332 *Super Puma* (tpt/SAR/attack); 5 SA-330 *Puma*
MSL
ASM AGM-65G *Maverick*; AGM-84A *Harpoon*; AGM-114K *Hellfire*
AAM AIM-7F *Sparrow*, AIM-9L *Sidewinder*; *Magic* 1
SAM 40 PAC-2 *Patriot*; 24 MIM-23B *I HAWK Phase III*; 12 *Skyguard/Aspide*

Paramilitary ε7,100 active

National Guard ε6,600 active
FORCES BY ROLE
Armd   1 (armd car) bn
SF   1 bn
Paramilitary 3 (national guard) bn
MP   1 bn

EQUIPMENT BY TYPE
RECCE 20 VBL
APC (W) 92: 70 *Pandur*; 22 S600 (incl variants)

Coast Guard 500
PATROL AND COASTAL COMBATANTS 58+
  PCC 10: 3 *Al Shaheed*; 4 *Inttisar* (Aust 31.5m); 3 *Kassir* (Aust 22m)
  PB 10 *Subahi*
  PBR 38+
AMPHIBIOUS • CRAFT 3 LCU

FOREIGN FORCES
United Kingdom Army 35 Air Force 6 *Merlin* SH
United States United States Central Command: 2 AD bty with total of 16 PAC-3 *Patriot*; elm 1 (APS) HBCT eqpt. set (equipment in use)

Lebanon LBN

Lebanese Pound LP		2008	2009	2010
GDP	LP	41.8tr	46.3tr	
	US$	27.7bn	30.7bn	
per capita	US$	6,983	7,642	
Growth	%	8.5	7.0	
Inflation	%	11.0	2.5	
Def bdgt	LP	1.13tr	1.37tr	
	US$	751m	911m	
FMA (US)	US$	7m	90m	100m
US$1=LP		1,510	1,510	

Population   4,017,095

Ethnic and religious groups: Christian 30%; Druze 6%; Armenian 4%, excl ε300,000 Syrians and ε350,000 Palestinian refugees

Age	0–14	15–19	20–24	25–29	30–64	65 plus
Male	14%	4%	5%	6%	17%	3%
Female	13%	4%	5%	5%	20%	4%

Capabilities

ACTIVE 59,100 (Army 57,000 Navy 1,100 Air 1,000)
Paramilitary 20,000
The usual number of Lebanese troops in peacetime is around 59,100. It can increase to 291,735 if there is a recall of conscripts.

ORGANISATIONS BY SERVICE

Army 57,000
FORCES BY ROLE
Region	5 comd (Beirut, Bekaa Valley, Mount Lebanon, North, South)
Armd	2 regt
Mech inf	5 bde
Mot Inf	6 bde
Mne cdo	1 regt
SF	5 regt
Cdo	1 regt
AB	1 regt
Arty	2 regt
Security	5 intervention , 2 border sy regt
Presidential Guard	1 bde
MP	1 indep bde
Engr	1 indep regt
Logistics	1 indep bde
Medical	1 indep regt

EQUIPMENT BY TYPE
MBT 326: 233 T-54/T-55; 93 M-48A1/M-48A5
RECCE 54 AML
APC 1,240
  APC (T) 1,240: 1,164 M-113A1/M-113A2; 1 M-3VTT; 75 VAB VCT
LT VEH 379 M998 HMMVW

ARTY 516

TOWED 160: **105mm** 21: 13 M-101A1; 8 M-101;
122mm 56: 24 D-30; 32 M-30 M-1938;
130mm 16 M-46; **155mm** 67: 18 M-114A1; 35 M-198;
14 Model-50

MRL 122mm 22 BM-21

MOR 334: **81mm** 134; **82mm** 112; **120mm** 88 Brandt

AT

MSL • MANPATS 38: 26 *Milan*; 12 TOW

RCL 106mm 113 M-40A1

RL 73mm 3,263: 13 M-50; 3,250 RPG-7 *Knout*;
90mm 8 M-69

AD

SAM • MANPAD 84 SA-7A *Grail*/SA-7B *Grail*

GUNS 81

TOWED 20mm 23; **23mm** 58 ZU-23

UAV • TACTICAL 8 *Mohajer IV*

Navy 1,100

EQUIPMENT BY TYPE

PATROL AND COASTAL COMBATANTS 25+

PCI 7: 5 *Attacker*; 2 *Tracker* (UK all units under 100 tonnes)

PB 3: 1 *Tabarja* (GER *Bergen*); 1 *Naquora* (GER *Bremen*); 1 (GER *Aamchat*)

PBR 15

AMPHIBIOUS • LS • LST 2 *Sour* (capacity 8 APC; 96 troops) (FRA *Edic*)

FACILITIES

Bases   Located at Jounieh, Beirut

Air Force 1,000

3 air bases

FORCES BY ROLE

FGA	1 sqn with Hawker *Hunter* Mk9, Mk 6, T66 at Rayak; 1 Cessna *Caravan* at Beirut
Atk hel	1 sqn with SA-342L *Gazelle* at Rayak
Utl hel	2 sqn with UH-1H at Beirut; 1 sqn with UH-1H at Rayak; 1 sqn with UH-1H at Koleyate; 1 AW139 VIP hel at Beirut; 3 S-61N (fire fighting) hel at Beirut
Trg hel	1 trg sqn with R-44 *Raven* II at Rayak

EQUIPMENT BY TYPE

AIRCRAFT

FGA 7: 6 Hawker *Hunter* MK 9, MK6, T66 (3 serviceable); 1 Cessna *Caravan*

TRG 3 *Bulldog* (could be refurbished)

HELICOPTERS

ATK 8 SA-342L *Gazelle* (plus 5 grounded – could be refurbished)

VIP 1 AW-139

UTL 19: 12 UH-1H *Huey* (+ 11 unserviceable); 4 R-44 *Raven* II (basic trg); 7 Bell 212 unserviceable (6 could be refurbished); 5 *Puma* SA-330 all grounded (3 could be refurbished) (10 expected from UAE): 5 SA-316 *Alouette III* unserviceable (3 could be refurbished); 1 SA-318 *Alouette II* unserviceable (could be refurbished); 3 S-61N (fire fighting)

Paramilitary ε20,000 active

Internal Security Force ε20,000

Ministry of Interior

FORCES BY ROLE

Police	1 (Judicial) unit
Regional	1 coy
Paramilitary	1 (Beirut Gendarmerie) coy

EQUIPMENT BY TYPE

APC (W) 60 V-200 *Chaimite*

Customs

PATROL AND COASTAL COMBATANTS 7

PCI 7: 5 *Aztec*; 2 *Tracker* (All vessels less than 100 tonnes)

NON-STATE GROUPS

Hizbullah In the wake of the Doha agreement, Lebanon's cabinet includes representatives from all major parties, including supporters of Hizbullah. The organisation maintains its military force outside state structures.Est strength: 2,000 Major equipments incl: *Katyusha* 122mm rockets; *Fadjr* 3/5 rockets; *Zelzal* 2 rockets; mortars; ATGW; C-802 ASM; SALW

FOREIGN FORCES

Unless specified, figures refer to UNTSO and represent total numbers for the mission in Israel, Syria, Lebanon.

Argentina 6 obs

Australia 11 obs

Austria 7 obs

Belgium 2 obs • UNIFIL 229 Army: 1 engr coy

Brunei UNIFIL 7

Canada (*Op Jade*) 7 obs

Chile 4 obs

China, People's Republic of 4 obs • UNIFIL 344; 1 engr coy; 1 fd hospital

Croatia UNIFIL 1

Cyprus UNIFIL 2

Denmark 11 obs

El Salvador UNIFIL 52; 1 inf pl

Estonia 1 obs

Finland 15 obs

France 2 obs • UNIFIL 1,585: Army: 1 armd inf bn; 1 armd sqn; 1 arty tp; 1 engr coy; 13 *Leclerc* MBT ; 35 AMX-10P AIFV; 4 AUF1 155mm SP; 6 *Mistral* MANPAD SAM; 2 *Cobra*

Germany UNIFIL 459: Navy: 2 PC; 1 SPT

Ghana UNIFIL 874; 1 inf bn

Greece UNIFIL 45: Navy: 1 PB

Guatemala UNIFIL 2

Hungary UNIFIL 4

India UNIFIL 898; 1 inf bn; 1 fd hospital

Indonesia UNIFIL 1,248; 1 inf bn; 1 FS

Ireland 12 obs • UNIFIL 8;

Italy 8 obs • UNIFIL 2,576: Army: 3 inf bn; 1 avn unit; 1

MP coy Navy: 1 FF
Korea, Republic of UNIFIL 367; 1 inf bn
Luxembourg UNIFIL 3
Macedonia, Former Yugoslav Republic of UNIFIL 1
Malaysia Army: UNIFIL 742; 1 inf bn
Nepal 3 obs • UNIFIL 868; 1 mech inf bn
Netherlands 12 obs
New Zealand 7 obs • UNIFIL 1
Norway 11 obs • UNIFIL 5
Poland UNIFIL 461; 1 inf coy; 1 log bn
Portugal UNIFIL 146; 1 engr coy
Qatar UNIFIL 3
Russia 5 obs
Sierra Leone UNIFIL 2
Slovakia 2 obs
Slovenia 2 obs • UNIFIL 14
Spain UNIFIL 1,045: Army: 1 inf bn; 1 avn coy
Sweden 7 obs
Switzerland 10 obs
Tanzania UNIFIL 72; 1 MP coy
Turkey UNIFIL 366: Army: 1 engr coy; Navy: 2 PB
United States 2 obs

Libya LBY

Libyan Dinar D		2008	2009	2010
GDP	D	82bn	45bn	
	US$	65.5bn	37.2bn	
per capita	US$	10,590	5,880	
Growth	%	3.4	1.8	
Inflation	%	10.4	5.0	
Def exp	D	ε1.0bn		
	US$	ε800m		
US$1=D		1.25	1.21	

Population	6,324,357					

Age	0–14	15–19	20–24	25–29	30–64	65 plus
Male	17%	5%	5%	5%	16%	2%
Female	17%	5%	5%	5%	15%	2%

Capabilities

ACTIVE 76,000 (Army 50,000 Navy 8,000 Air 18,000)
Terms of service selective conscription, 1–2 years

RESERVE ε40,000 (People's Militia)

ORGANISATIONS BY SERVICE

Army 25,000; ε25,000 conscript (total 50,000)

FORCES BY ROLE
11 Border Def and 4 Sy Zones
Army	1 (elite) bde (regime sy force)
Tk	10 bn
Mech inf	10 bn
Inf	18 bn
Cdo/para	6 bn
Arty	22 bn
SSM	4 bde
ADA	7 bn

EQUIPMENT BY TYPE
MBT 2,205: 180 T-90S; 200 T-72; 115 in store; 100 T-62; 70 in store; 500 T-55; 1,040 T-54/T-55 in store
RECCE 120: 50 BRDM-2; 70 EE-9 *Cascavel*
AIFV 1,000+: 1,000 BMP-1; BMD
APC 945
  APC (T) 778: 28 M-113; 750 BTR-50/BTR-60
  APC (W) 167: 100 EE-11 *Urutu*; 67 OT-62/OT-64
ARTY 2,421+
  SP 444: **122mm** 130 2S1 *Carnation*; **152mm** 140: 60 2S3; 80 M-77 *Dana*; **155mm** 174: 14 M-109; 160 VCA 155 *Palmaria*
  TOWED 647+: **105mm** 42+ M-101; **122mm** 250: 190 D-30; 60 D-74; **130mm** 330 M-46; **152mm** 25 M-1937
  MRL 830: **107mm** ε300 Type-63; **122mm** 530: ε200 BM-11; ε230 BM-21; ε100 RM-70 *Dana*
  MOR 500: **82mm** 428; **120mm** ε48 M-43; **160mm** ε24 M-160
AT • MSL 3,000
  SP 40 9P122 BRDM-2 *Sagger*
  MANPATS 2,960: 620 AT-3 9K11 *Sagger*; 1,940 AT-3 9K11 *Sagger*/ AT-4 9K111 *Spigot* / AT-5 9K113 *Spandrel*; 400 *Milan*
  RCL 620: **106mm** 220 M-40A1; **84mm** 400 *Carl Gustav*
  RL 73mm 2,300 RPG-7 *Knout*
AD • SAM • SP 424+: 24 *Crotale* (quad); 400 SA-7 *Grail*; SA-13 *Gopher*; SA-9 *Gaskin*
  GUNS 490
    SP 23mm 250 ZSU-23-4
    TOWED 240: **14.5mm** 100 ZPU-2; **30mm** M-53/59; **40mm** 50 L/70; **57mm** 90 S-60
RADAR • LAND RASIT (veh, arty)
MSL • TACTICAL • SSM 45 FROG-7

Navy 8,000 (incl Coast Guard)

EQUIPMENT BY TYPE
SUBMARINES • TACTICAL • SSK 2 *Kyhber†* (FSU *Foxtrot*)
PRINCIPAL SURFACE COMBATANTS 3
  FRIGATES • FFG 2 *Al Hani†* (FSU *Koni*) with 2 twin (4 eff.) each with SS-N-2C *Styx* tactical SSM, 2 twin 406mm ASTT (4 eff.) each with USET-95 Type 40 LWT, 1 RBU 6000 *Smerch* 2 (12 eff.)
  CORVETTES • FSG 1 *Tariq Ibin Ziyad* (FSU *Nanuchka* II) with 4 single each with 1 SS-N-2C *Styx* tactical SSM
PATROL AND COASTAL COMBATANTS 14
  PFM 10:
  4 *Al Zuara* (FSU *Osa* II) each with 4 single each with 1 SS-N-2C *Styx* tactical SSM
  6 *Sharaba* (FRA *Combattante* II) each with 4 single each with 1 Mk 2 Otomat SSM, 1 76mm gun
  PBC 4 *PV-30LS* (constabulary duties, additional units to follow)
MINE WARFARE • MINE COUNTERMEASURES •
MSO 4 *Ras al Gelais* (FSU *Natya*)

AMPHIBIOUS 4
  LS 1
    LST 1 *Ibn Harissa* (capacity 1 SA-316B *Alouette III* utl hel; 11 MBT; 240 troops); (2nd vessel undergoing reactivation)
  CRAFT 3† LCT
LOGISTICS AND SUPPORT 12:
  ARS 1
  TPT 10 *El Temsah*
  YDT 1
FACILITIES
Bases   Located at Tripoli, Benghazi, Tobruk, Khums
Minor bases Located at Derna, Zuwurah, Misonhah

Coastal Defence
FORCES BY ROLE
Msl 1 bty with SS-C-3 *Styx*

EQUIPMENT BY TYPE
MSL • TACTICAL • SSM: some SS-C-3 *Styx*

Naval Aviation
HELICOPTERS • SAR 7 SA-321 *Super Frelon* (air force assets)

Air Force 18,000
Flying hours   85 hrs/year
FORCES BY ROLE
Bbr   1 sqn with Tu-22 *Blinder*
Ftr   9+ sqn with *Mirage* F-1ED (F-1E); MiG-25 *Foxbat*; MiG-23 *Flogger*; MiG-21 *Fishbed*; *Mirage* F-1BD (F-1B); MiG-25U *Foxbat*
FGA   7 sqn with Su-24MK *Fencer D*; *Mirage* F-1AD (F-1A); MiG-23BN *Flogger H*; Su-17M-2 *Fitter D*/Su-20 (Su-17M) *Fitter C*; MiG-23U *Flogger*
Recce   2 sqn with MiG-25R *Foxbat*; *Mirage* 5DP30
Tpt   7 sqn with An-124 *Condor*; An-26 *Curl*; C-130H *Hercules*; G-222; Il-76 *Candid*; L-100-20; L-100-30; L-410 *Turbolet*
Atk hel sqns with Mi-25 *Hind D*; Mi-35 *Hind*
Tpt hel sqns with CH-47C *Chinook* (hy); Mi-17 (Mi-8MT) *Hip H*/Mi-8 *Hip* (med); AB-206 (Bell 206) *Jet Ranger* (lt); SA-316 *Alouette III*
Trg   sqns with Tu-22 *Blinder*; G-2 *Galeb*; L-39ZO *Albatros*; SF-260WL *Warrior*; PZL Mi-2 *Hoplite*

EQUIPMENT BY TYPE
(many non-operational, many ac in store)
AIRCRAFT 374 combat capable
  BBR 7 Tu-22 *Blinder*
  FTR 229: 15 *Mirage* F-1ED (F-1E); 94 MiG-25 *Foxbat*; 75 MiG-23 *Flogger*; 45 MiG-21 *Fishbed*
  FGA 113: 6 Su-24MK *Fencer D*; 14 *Mirage* F-1AD (F-1A); 40 MiG-23BN *Flogger H*; 53 Su-17M-2 *Fitter D*/Su-20 (Su-17M) *Fitter C*
  RECCE 7 MiG-25R *Foxbat*
  TPT 85+: 2 An-124 *Condor*; 23 An-26 *Curl*; 15 C-130H *Hercules*; G-222; 25 Il-76 *Candid*; 2 L-100-20; 3 L-100-30; 15 L-410 *Turbolet*

  TRG 250: 90 G-2 *Galeb*; 115 L-39ZO *Albatros*; 15 MiG-23U *Flogger**; 3 MiG-25U *Foxbat**; 4 *Mirage* 5DP30*; 3 *Mirage* F-1BD (F-1B)*; 20 SF-260WL *Warrior*
HELICOPTERS
  ATK 35: 23 Mi-25 *Hind D*; 12 Mi-35 *Hind*
  SPT 85: 4 CH-47C *Chinook* (hy); 35 Mi-17 (Mi-8MT) *Hip H*/Mi-8 *Hip* (med); 46 PZL Mi-2 *Hoplite*
  UTL 16: 5 AB-206 (Bell 206) *Jet Ranger* (lt); 11 SA-316 *Alouette III* (lt)
MSL
  ASM AS-11 *Kilter*; AS-7 *Kerry*; AS-9 *Kyle*; AT-2 *Swatter*
  ARM AS-11 *Kilter*
  AAM AA-2 *Atoll*; AA-6 *Acrid*; AA-7 *Apex*; AA-8 *Aphid*; R-550 *Magic*; R530

Air Defence Command
Senezh AD comd and control system
FORCES BY ROLE
AD 5 region (with ε3 AD bde each with 20–24 SA-6 *Gainful*/SA-8 *Gecko* 2–3 AD bde each with 12 SA-3 *Goa*, 5–6 AD bde each with 18 SA-2 *Guideline*); 4 bde with SA-5A *Gammon* (*each*: 1 radar coy, 2 AD bn with 6 launcher, 4+ ADA bn with guns)

EQUIPMENT BY TYPE
AD
  SAM 216+:
    SP 72 SA-6 *Gainful*/SA-8 *Gecko* (216–432 eff.)
    TOWED 144: 108 SA-2 *Guideline*
    STATIC SA-5A *Gammon*; 36 SA-3 *Goa*
  GUNS some

DEPLOYMENT
PHILIPPINES
Army 6 obs (Awaiting potential IMT reactivation)

Mauritania MRT

Mauritanian Ouguiya OM		2008	2009	2010
GDP	OM	724bn		
	US$	3.0bn		
per capita	US$	967		
Growth	%	2.2	2.3	
Inflation	%	7.3	4.9	
Def bdgt	OM	ε5.0bn		
	US$	ε20m		
US$1=OM			245	260

Population   3,129,486

Age	0–14	15–19	20–24	25–29	30–64	65 plus
Male	23%	5%	4%	4%	12%	1%
Female	23%	5%	4%	4%	13%	1%

Capabilities
ACTIVE 15,870 (Army 15,000 Navy 620 Air 250)
Paramilitary 5,000
Terms of service conscription 24 months authorised

ORGANISATIONS BY SERVICE

Army 15,000

FORCES BY ROLE

6 Mil Regions

Army	2 (camel corps) bn
Armd	1 bn (T-54/55 MBT)
Armd recce	1 sqn
Inf	8 (garrison) bn
Mot inf	7 bn
Cdo/para	1 bn
Arty	3 bn
ADA	4 bty
Engr	1 coy
Gd	1 bn

EQUIPMENT BY TYPE

MBT 35 T-54/T-55

RECCE 70: 20 AML-60; 40 AML-90; 10 *Saladin*

APC
  APC (W) 25: 5 FV603 *Saracen*; ε20 M-3 *Panhard*

ARTY 194
  TOWED 80: **105mm** 36 HM-2/M-101A1; **122mm** 44: 20 D-30; 24 D-74
  MOR 114: **60mm** 24; **81mm** 60; **120mm** 30 *Brandt*

AT • MSL • MANPATS 24 *Milan*
  RCL 114: **75mm** ε24 M-20; **106mm** ε90 M-40A1
  RL 73mm ε48 RPG-7 *Knout*

AD • SAM 104
  SP ε4 SA-9 *Gaskin* (reported)
  MANPAD ε100 SA-7 *Grail*
  GUNS • TOWED 82: **14.5mm** 28: 16 ZPU-2; 12 ZPU-4; **23mm** 20 ZU-23-2; **37mm** 10 M-1939; **57mm** 12 S-60; **100mm** 12 KS-19

Navy ε620

EQUIPMENT BY TYPE

PATROL AND COASTAL COMBATANTS 12
  PSO 1 *Voum-Legleita*
  PCO 3: 1 *Abourbekr Ben Amer* (FRA OPV 54); 1 *N'Madi* (UK *Jura*, fishery protection); 1 *Arguin*
  PCC 1 *El Nasr* (FRA *Patra*)
  PCI 4 *Mandovi* less than 100 tonnes
  PCR 1 *Huangpu*
  PBC 2 *Conjera*

FACILITIES

Bases   Located at Nouadhibou, Nouakchott

Air Force 250

FORCES BY ROLE

MP	sqn with Cessna 337 *Skymaster*
Tpt	sqn with PA-31T *Navajo/Cheyenne II*; Y-12(II)
COIN	sqn with FTB-337 *Milirole*; BN-2 *Defender*; Basler Turbo-67

EQUIPMENT BY TYPE

AIRCRAFT

RECCE 2 FTB-337 *Milirole*
TPT 12: 5 BN-2 *Defender*; 1 Basler Turbo-67; 2 Cessna 337 *Skymaster*; 2 PA-31T *Navajo/Cheyenne II*; 2 Y-12(II)
TRG 4 SF-260E

Paramilitary ε5,000 active

Gendarmerie ε3,000

Ministry of Interior

Regional 6 coy

National Guard 2,000

Ministry of Interior

Aux 1,000

Customs

PATROL AND COASTAL COMBATANTS •
PB 1 *Dah Ould Bah* (FRA *Amgram* 14)

Morocco MOR

Moroccan Dirham D		2008	2009	2010
GDP	D	663bn	734bn	
	US$	85.5bn	95.2bn	
per capita	US$	2,765	3,043	
Growth	%	5.6	5.0	
Inflation	%	3.9	2.8	
Def bdgt	D	23.1bn	24.6bn	
	US$	2.97bn	3.19bn	
FMA (US)	US$	3.6m	3.6m	9m
US$1=D		7.75	7.71	

Population	31,285,174					

Age	0–14	15–19	20–24	25–29	30–64	65 plus
Male	16%	5%	5%	4%	16%	2%
Female	16%	5%	5%	4%	17%	3%

Capabilities

ACTIVE 195,800 (Army 175,000 Navy 7,800 Air 13,000) Paramilitary 50,000

Terms of service conscription 18 months authorised; most enlisted personnel are volunteers

RESERVE 150,000 (Army 150,000)

Terms of service obligation to age 50

ORGANISATIONS BY SERVICE

Army ε75,000; 100,000 conscript (total 175,000)

FORCES BY ROLE

2 Comd (Northern Zone, Southern Zone)

Sy	1 light bde
Armd	12 indep bn
Mech/Mot Inf	8 regt (*each*: 2-3 mech inf bn)

Mech Inf	3 bde
Inf	35 indep bn
Mot Inf	3 (camel corps) indep bn
Mtn Inf	1 indep bn
Cdo	4 indep unit
Para	2 bde
AB	2 indep bn
Arty	11 indep bn
Engr	7 indep bn
AD	1 indep bn

Royal Guard 1,500

Army	1 bn
Cav	1 sqn

EQUIPMENT BY TYPE

MBT 580: 40 T-72, 220 M-60A1; 120 M-60A3; ε200 M-48A5 in store

LT TK 116: 5 AMX-13; 111 SK-105 *Kuerassier*

RECCE 384: 38 AML-60-7; 190 AML-90; 80 AMX-10RC; 40 EBR-75; 16 *Eland*; 20 M1114 *HMMWV*

AIFV 70: 10 AMX-10P; 30 MK III-20 *Ratel*-20; 30 MK III-90 *Ratel*-90

APC 765

  APC (T) 400 M-113A1/A2

  APC (W) 365: 45 VAB VCI; 320 VAB VTT

ARTY 2,141

  SP 282: **105mm** 5 Mk 61; **155mm** 217: 84 M-109A1/M-109A1B; 43 M-109A2; 90 (AMX) Mk F3; **203mm** 60 M-110

  TOWED 118: **105mm** 50: 30 L-118 Light Gun; 20 M-101; **130mm** 18 M-46; **155mm** 50: 30 FH-70; 20 M-114

  MRL 35 BM-21

  MOR 1,706

    SP 56: **106mm** 32-36 M-106A2; **120mm** 20 (VAB APC)

    TOWED 1,650: **81mm** 1,100 Expal model LN; **120mm** 550 *Brandt*

AT • MSL 790

  SP 80 M-901

  MANPATS 710: 40 AT-3 9K11 *Sagger*; 440 M47 *Dragon*; 80 *Milan*; 150 TOW

  RCL 106mm 350 M-40A1

  RL 700: **66mm** 500 M-72 LAW; **89mm** 200 M-20

  GUNS 36

    SP 100mm 8 SU-100

    TOWED 90mm 28 M-56

UAV R4E-50 *Skyeye*

AD • SAM 119

  SP 49: 12 2K22M *Tunguska* SPAAGM; 37 M-48 *Chaparral*

  MANPAD 70 SA-7 *Grail*

  GUNS 407

    SP 60 M-163 *Vulcan*

    TOWED 347: **14.5mm** 200: 150-180 ZPU-2; 20 ZPU-4; **20mm** 40 M-167 *Vulcan*; **23mm** 75-90 ZU-23-2; **100mm** 17 KS-19

RADAR • LAND: RASIT (veh, arty)

Navy 7,800 (incl 1,500 Marines)

EQUIPMENT BY TYPE

PRINCIPAL SURFACE COMBATANTS • FRIGATES • FFG 3:

  1 *Lt Col Errhamani* (ESP *Descubierto*) with 2 twin (4 eff.) each with MM-38 *Exocet* tactical SSM, 1 *Albatros* octuple with 24 *Aspide* SAM, 2 triple ASTT (6 eff.) each with Mk 46 LWT, 1 76mm gun (capacity 1 AS-565SA *Panther*),

  2 *Mohammed V* (FRA *Floreal*) each with 2 single each with MM-38 *Exocet* SSM, 1 76mm gun, (capacity 1 AS-565SA *Panther*)

PATROL AND COASTAL COMBATANTS 27

  PFM 4 *Cdt El Khattabi* (ESP *Lazaga* 58m) each with 4 single each with MM-40 *Exocet* tactical SSM, 1 76mm gun

  PCC 17:

    4 *El Hahiq* (DNK *Osprey* 55, incl 2 with customs)

    6 *LV Rabhi* (ESP 58m B-200D)

    2 *Okba* (FRA PR-72) each with 1 76mm gun

    5 *Rais Bargach* (under control of fisheries dept)

  PFI 6 *El Wacil* (FRA P-32, under 100 tonnes, incl 4 with customs)

AMPHIBIOUS

  LS 4:

    LSM 3 *Ben Aicha* (FRA *Champlain* BATRAL) (capacity 7 tanks; 140 troops)

    LST 1 *Sidi Mohammed Ben Abdallah* (US *Newport*) (capacity 3 LCVP; 400 troops)

  CRAFT • LCT 1 *Edic* (capacity 8 APCs; 96 troops)

LOGISTICS AND SUPPORT 4:

  AK 2; **AGOR** 1 (US lease); 1 **YDT**

FACILITIES

Bases Located at Casablanca, Agadir, Al Hoceima, Dakhla, Tangier

Marines 1,500

Naval inf	2 bn

Naval Aviation

HELICOPTERS • ASW/ASUW 3 AS-565SA *Panther*

Air Force 13,000

Flying hours	100 hrs/year on F-1 *Mirage*/F-5A *Freedom Fighter Tiger*

FORCES BY ROLE

Ftr	1 sqn with F-1CH (F-1C) *Mirage*
FGA	1 sqn with F-5A/F-5B *Freedom Fighter*; 2 sqn with F-5E/F-5F *Tiger II*; 2 sqn with *Mirage* F-1EH (F-1E)
Recce	sqn with OV-10 *Bronco**; C-130H *Hercules* (with side-looking radar)
EW	sqn with C-130 *Hercules* (ELINT); *Falcon* 20 (ELINT)
Tpt	sqn with Beech 100 *King Air*; Beech 200 *Super King Air*; C-130H *Hercules*; CN-235; Do-28; *Falcon* 20; *Falcon* 50 (VIP); Gulfstream II (VIP)
Tkr	sqn with KC-130H *Hercules* (tpt/tkr); B-707
Liaison	sqn with Beech 200 *Super King Air*
Atk hel	sqn with SA-342 *Gazelle* (with HOT, 12 with cannon)

Tpt hel   sqn with CH-47D *Chinook* (hy); SA-330 *Puma* (med); AB-205A (Bell 205A); AB-206 (Bell 206) *Jet Ranger* (lt); AB-212 (Bell 212) (lt); UH-60 *Black Hawk*

Trg   sqn with AS-202 *Bravo*; *Alpha Jet**; CAP 10; T-34C *Turbo Mentor*; T-37B *Tweet* (being replaced by K-8); CAP-231

EQUIPMENT BY TYPE
AIRCRAFT 89 combat capable
  FTR 66: 8 F-5A *Freedom Fighter*; 2 F-5B *Freedom Fighter*; 20 F-5E *Tiger II*; 3 F-5F *Tiger II*; 19 F-1CH (F-1C) *Mirage*; 14 *Mirage* F-1EH (F-1E). 24 F-16 Block 52 on order (18 F-16C, 6 F-16D)
  FAC 4 OV-10 *Bronco**
  TKR 2 KC-130H *Hercules* (tpt/tkr)
  TPT 44: 1 B-707; 4 Beech 100 *King Air*; 5 Beech 200 *Super King Air*; 2 C-130 (ELINT); 15 C-130H *Hercules*; 2 C-130H (with side-looking radar); 6 CN-235; 2 Do-28; 2 *Falcon* 20; 2 (ELINT); 1 *Falcon* 50 (VIP); 2 Gulfstream II (VIP)
  TRG 51: 7 AS-202 *Bravo*; 19 *Alpha Jet**; 2 CAP 10; 9 T-34C *Turbo Mentor*; 14 T-37B *Tweet* (being replaced by K-8)
  TRIALS AND TEST 4 CAP-231
HELICOPTERS
  ASLT 19 SA-342 *Gazelle* (7 with HOT, 12 with cannon)
  SPT 32: 8 CH-47D *Chinook* (hy); 24 SA-330 *Puma* (med)
  UTL 41: 11 AB-206 (Bell 206) *Jet Ranger* (lt); 3 AB-212 (Bell 212) (lt); 25 AB-205A (Bell 205A); 2 UH-60 *Black Hawk*
MSL
  ASM AGM-62B *Walleye* (For F-5E); HOT
  AAM AIM-9B/D/J *Sidewinder*; R-550 *Magic*, R530

Paramilitary 50,000 active

Gendarmerie Royale 20,000
FORCES BY ROLE
Coast Guard   1 unit
Para   1 sqn
Paramilitary   1 bde; 4 (mobile) gp
Avn   1 (air) sqn

EQUIPMENT BY TYPE
PATROL AND COASTAL COMBATANTS • MISC BOATS/CRAFT 18 boats
AIRCRAFT • TRG 2 *Rallye* 235 *Guerrier*
HELICOPTERS
  SAR 2 SA-360 *Dauphin*
  ASLT 6 SA-342K *Gazelle*
  SPT 6 SA-330 *Puma*
  UTL 8: 3 SA-315B *Lama*; 2 SA-316 *Alouette III*; 3 SA-318 *Alouette II*

Force Auxiliaire 30,000 (incl 5,000 Mobile Intervention Corps)

Customs/Coast Guard
PATROL AND COASTAL COMBATANTS 44
  PCI 4 *Erraid*
  PBF 15
  PB 18
  MISC BOATS/CRAFT 7 SAR craft

DEPLOYMENT

CÔTE D'IVOIRE
UN • UNOCI 726; 1inf bn

DEMOCRATIC REPUBLIC OF CONGO
UN • MONUC 831; 5 obs; 1 mech inf bn; 1 fd hospital

SERBIA
NATO • KFOR • *Joint Enterprise* 222; **Army**: 1 inf det

Oman OMN

Omani Rial R		2008	2009	2010
GDP	R	20.8bn	20.6bn	
	US$	54.7bn	54.2bn	
per capita	US$	16,529	15,860	
Growth	%	7.8	4.1	
Inflation	%	12.6	3.3	
Def bdgt	R	1.77bn	1.54bn	
	US$	4.67bn	4.06bn	
FMA (US)	US$	4.7m	7.0m	16.6m
US$1=R		0.38	0.38	

Population   3,418,085

Expatriates: 27%

Age	0–14	15–19	20–24	25–29	30–64	65 plus
Male	22%	5%	4%	4%	20%	1%
Female	21%	4%	4%	3%	10%	1%

Capabilities

ACTIVE 42,600 (Army 25,000 Navy 4,200 Air 5,000 Foreign Forces 2,000 Royal Household 6,400) **Paramilitary 4,400**

ORGANISATIONS BY SERVICE

Army 25,000
FORCES BY ROLE
(Regt are bn size)
Armd   1 bde HQ; 2 regt (*each*: 3 tk sqn)
Armd Recce   1 regt (3 armd recce sqn)
Inf   2 bde HQ; 8 regt
Rifle   1 indep coy (Musandam Security Force)
AB   1 regt
Inf Recce   1 regt (3 recce coy)
Med Arty   1 regt (2 med arty bty)
Fd Arty   2 regt
ADA   1 regt (2 ADA bty)
Fd Engr   1 regt (3 fd engr sqn)

EQUIPMENT BY TYPE
MBT 117: 38 CR2 *Challenger 2*; 6 M-60A1; 73 M-60A3
LT TK 37 *Scorpion*
RECCE 137: 13 *Sultan*; 124 VBL

APC 206

   APC (T) 16: 6 FV 103 *Spartan*; 10 FV4333 *Stormer*
   APC (W) 190: 175 *Piranha* (incl variants); 15 AT-105 *Saxon*

ARTY 233

   SP 155mm 24 G-6
   TOWED 108: **105mm** 42 ROF lt; **122mm** 30 D-30; **130mm** 24: 12 M-46; 12 Type-59-I; **155mm** 12 FH-70
   MOR 101: **81mm** 69; **107mm** 20 M-30; **120mm** 12 Brandt

AT • MSL 88

   SP 8 VBL (TOW)
   MANPATS 80: 30 *Javelin;* 32 *Milan*; 18 TOW/TOW-2A
   RL 73mm RPG-7 *Knout*; **94mm** LAW-80

AD • SAM 74+

   SP 20: up to 12 *Pantsyr* S1E SPAAGM; 8 *Mistral* 2
   MANPAD 54: 20 *Javelin*; 34 SA-7 *Grail*
   GUNS 26: **23mm** 4 ZU-23-2; **35mm** 10 GDF-005 (with *Skyguard*); **40mm** 12 L/60 (Towed)

Navy 4,200

EQUIPMENT BY TYPE

PRINCIPAL SURFACE COMBATANTS • CORVETTES
• **FSG** 2 *Qahir Al Amwaj* each with 2 quad (8 eff.) each with MM-40 *Exocet* tactical SSM, 2 triple 324mm TT (6 eff.) (to be fitted) each with MM-40 *Exocet* tactical SSM, 1 octuple (8 eff.) with 16 *Crotale* SAM, 1 76mm gun, with hel landing platform for *Super Lynx* type hel

PATROL AND COASTAL COMBATANTS 11

   PFM 4: 1 *Dhofar* with 2 triple (6 eff.) (not fitted); 3 *Dhofar* each with 2 quad (8 eff.) with MM-40 *Exocet* SSM tactical
   PCC 3 *Al Bushra* (FRA P-400) each with 4 single 406mm TT, 1 76mm gun
   PCI 4 *Seeb* (UK Vosper 25m, under 100 tonnes)

AMPHIBIOUS

   LS • LST 1 *Nasr el Bahr* (with hel deck) (capacity 7 tanks; 240 troops)
   CRAFT 4: 1 LCU; 3 **LCM**

LOGISTICS AND SUPPORT 8

   AK 1 *Al Sultana*
   AGHS 1
   T-AP 2 *Shinas* (Commercial Tpt - Auxiliary military role only) (capacity 56 veh; 200 tps)
   RY 2: 1 *Al Said;* 1 (Royal Dhow)
   TRG 1 *Al Mabrukah* (with hel deck, also used in OPV role)
   SPT 1 (Royal Yacht spt)

FACILITIES

Bases Located at Muaskar al Murtafaia (Seeb), Alwi, Main HQ located at Widam A'Sahil, Ghanam Island, Musandam, Salalah

Air Force 5,000

FORCES BY ROLE

FGA	1 sqn with Block 50 F-16C *Fighting Falcon*/F-16D *Fighting Falcon*; 2 sqn with *Jaguar* OS/ *Jaguar* OB
Ftr/FGA	1 sqn with *Hawk* Mk103; *Hawk* Mk203
Tpt	1 sqn with C-130H *Hercules*; 1 sqn with SC.7 3M *Skyvan* (7 radar-equipped, for MP); 1 sqn with BAC-111
Tpt Hel	2 (med) sqn with AB-205 (Bell 205) *Jet Ranger*; AB-212 (Bell 212); *Lynx* Mk 300 *Super Lynx* (maritime/SAR)
Trg	1 sqn with AS-202-18 *Bravo*; MFI-17B *Mushshak*; PC-9*; SF-25 *Falke*; AB-206 hel
AD	2 sqn with 40 *Rapier*; 6 *Blindfire*; S713 *Martello*

EQUIPMENT BY TYPE

AIRCRAFT 64 combat capable

   FTR/FGA 52: 12 F-16C/D (8 –C, 4 –D) Block 50 *Fighting Falcon*; 24 *Jaguar* (20 OS (single seat), 4 OB (dual seat)); 4 *Hawk* Mk103; 12 *Hawk* Mk203
   TPT 16: 3 BAC-111; 3 C-130H *Hercules* (1 C-130J-30 on order for delivery 2012); 10 SC.7 3M *Skyvan* (7 radar-equipped, for MP)
   TRG 26: 4 AS-202-18 *Bravo*; 8 MFI-17B *Mushshak*; 12 PC-9*; 2 SF-25

HELICOPTERS • UTL 41: 19 AB-205 (Bell 205) to be replaced by 20 NH-90; 3 AB-206 (Bell 206) *Jet Ranger* (basic rig); 3 AB-212 (Bell 212); 16 *Lynx* Mk 300 *Super Lynx* (maritime/SAR)

AD • SAM 40 *Rapier*

RADAR • LAND 6+: 6 *Blindfire*; S713 *Martello*

MSL

   AAM AIM-9LM *Sidewinder*; AIM-120C AMRAAM
   ASM 20 AGM-84D *Harpoon*; AGM-65 *Maverick*

Royal Household 6,400

(incl HQ staff)

SF 2 regt (1,000 men)

Royal Guard bde 5,000

LT TK 9 VBC-90
APC (W) 73: ε50 Type-92; 14 VAB VCI; 9 VAB VDAA
ARTY • MRL 122mm 6 Type-90A
AT • MSL • MANPATS *Milan*
AD • SAM • MANPAD 14 *Javelin*
GUNS • 20mm • SP 9: 9 VAB VDAA

Royal Yacht Squadron 150

PATROL AND COASTAL COMBATANTS • MISC BOATS/CRAFT • DHOW 1 *Zinat Al Bihaar*
LOGISTICS AND SUPPORT 2
   RY 1 (with hel deck)
   TPT 1 *Fulk Al Salamah* (also veh tpt) with up to 2 AS-332C *Super Puma* spt hel

Royal Flight 250

AIRCRAFT • TPT 5: 2 B-747SP; 1 DC-8-73CF; 2 Gulfstream IV
HELICOPTERS • SPT 6: 3 AS-330 (SA-330) *Puma*; 2 AS-332F *Super Puma*; 1 AS-332L *Super Puma*

Paramilitary 4,400 active

Tribal Home Guard 4,000

org in teams of est 100

Police Coast Guard 400

PATROL AND COASTAL COMBATANTS 52
  PCI 5: 3 CG 29 less than 100 tonnes; 1 CG 27 less than 100 tonnes; 1 *P-1903 Type*
  PB 22
  PBF 20
  PBI 5

Police Air Wing

AIRCRAFT • TPT 4: 1 BN-2T *Turbine Islander*; 2 CN-235M; 1 Do-228
HELICOPTERS • UTL 5: 2 Bell 205A; 3 AB-214ST

FOREIGN FORCES

United Kingdom Army 40; Navy 20; Air Force 20; 1 *Tristar* tkr; 1 *Nimrod* MR2; 1 *Sentinel*

Palestinian Autonomous Areas of Gaza and Jericho PA

New Israeli Shekel NS		2008*	2009*	2010
GDP	US$	6.5bn		
per capita	US$	1,663		
Growth	%	2.3		
Inflation	%	9.9		

*definitive economic data unavailable

Population   4,013,123

Capabilities

ACTIVE 0 Paramilitary 56,000

Personnel strength figures for the various Palestinian groups are not known

ORGANISATIONS BY SERVICE

There is very little data concerning the status of the organisations mentioned below. The Cairo and Washington agreements recognised several organisations under the Palestinian Directorate of Police Force. Some have little or no military significance and it is difficult to estimate the size of the total forces that do. Following internal fighting in June 2007, the Gaza Strip is under the *de facto* control of Hamas, while the West Bank is controlled by the emergency Palestinian Authority administration.

Paramilitary

National Forces ε56,000 (reported)

GENERAL SECURITY
Presidential security 3,000
SF 1,200
Police 9,000
Preventative Security n.k.
Civil Defence 1,000

AD • SAM • MANPAD SA-7 *Grail*; *Stinger* reported

The **Al-Aqsa Brigades** profess loyalty to the Fatah group which dominates the Palestinian Authority. It is believed that this group has access to equipments including mines and IEDs as well as SALW. The strength of this group is not known.

Hamas maintain a security apparatus in the Gaza Strip that, though degraded in the aftermath of *Operation Cast Lead* (the military operation by Israeli forces in late 2008 and early 2009) still ensures that Hamas remain in control in the Gaza Strip. Hamas groupings include internal security groupings such as the **Executive Force** (Est strength: 10–12,000; Major equipments include: artillery rockets, mortars, SALW) and the **al-Qassam Brigades** (Est strength: 10,000; Major equipments include: mines and IEDs, artillery rockets, mortars, SALW)

Qatar QTR

Qatari Riyal R		2008	2009	2010
GDP	R	365bn	328bn	
	US$	100bn	90bn	
per capita	US$	121,576	108,138	
Growth	%	16.4	11.5	
Inflation	%	15.0	0.0	
Def bdgt	R	6.39bn		
	US$	1.75bn		
US$1=R		3.64	3.64	

Population   883,285

Ethnic groups: Nationals 25%; Expatriates 75% of which Indian 18%; Iranian 10%; Pakistani 18%

Age	0–14	15–19	20–24	25–29	30–64	65 plus
Male	12%	4%	4%	5%	37%	3%
Female	12%	4%	3%	3%	12%	1%

Capabilities

ACTIVE 11,800 (Army 8,500 Navy 1,800 Air 1,500)

ORGANISATIONS BY SERVICE

Army 8,500
FORCES BY ROLE

Tk	1 bde (1 tk bn, 1 mech inf bn, 1 mor sqn, 1 AT bn)
Mech inf	3 bn
SF	1 coy
Fd arty	1 bn
Royal Guard	1 bde (3 inf regt)

EQUIPMENT BY TYPE
MBT 30 AMX-30
RECCE 68: 12 AMX-10RC; 20 EE-9 *Cascavel*; 12 *Ferret*; 8 V-150 *Chaimite*; 16 VBL
AIFV 40 AMX-10P
APC 226
  APC (T) 30 AMX-VCI
  APC (W) 196: 36 *Piranha* II; 160 VAB

ARTY 89
   SP 155mm 28 (AMX) Mk F3
   TOWED 155mm 12 G-5
   MRL 4 ASTROS II
   MOR 45
      SP • 81mm 4: 4 VAB VPM 81
      81mm 26: 26 L16
      120mm 15: 15 *Brandt*
AT • MSL 148
   SP 24 VAB VCAC HOT
   MANPATS 124: 24 HOT; 100 *Milan*
   RCL 84mm ε40 *Carl Gustav*

Navy 1,800 (incl Marine Police)

FORCES BY ROLE
Navy 1 HQ located at Doha

EQUIPMENT BY TYPE
PATROL AND COASTAL COMBATANTS 21
   PFM 7:
      4 *Barzan* (UK *Vita*) each with 2 quad (8 eff.) each with
      MM-40 *Exocet* tactical SSM, 1 sextuple (6 eff.) with
      Mistral SAM, 1 76mm gun
      3 *Damsah* (FRA *Combattante* III) each with 2 quad (8 eff.)
      each with MM-40 *Exocet* tactical SSM, 1 76mm gun
   PB 14+ (11 operated by Marine Police)
AMPHIBIOUS
   CRAFT • LCT 1 *Rabha* (capacity 3 MBT; 110 troops)
FACILITIES
Bases Located at Doha, Halul Island

Coastal Defence

FORCES BY ROLE
Navy 1 bty with 3 quad (12 eff.) each with MM-40
      Exocet tactical SSM

EQUIPMENT BY TYPE
LAUNCHER 3 quad each with MM-40 *Exocet* SSM

Air Force 1,500

FORCES BY ROLE

Ftr/FGA	1 sqn with *Alpha Jet*; 1 sqn with M-2000ED *Mirage*; M-2000D *Mirage*
Tpt	1 sqn with A-340; B-707; B-727; *Falcon* 900
Atk hel	1 sqn with *Commando* MK 3 (*Exocet*); SA-342L *Gazelle* (with HOT)
Tpt hel	sqn with *Commando* MK 2A; *Commando* MK 2C; SA-341 *Gazelle*

EQUIPMENT BY TYPE
AIRCRAFT 18 combat capable
   FGA 12: 9 M-2000ED *Mirage*; 3 M-2000D *Mirage*
   TPT 8: 2 C-17A *Globemaster*; 1 A-340; 2 B-707; 1 B-727; 2 *Falcon* 900
   TRG 6 *Alpha Jet**
HELICOPTERS
   ASUW 8 *Commando* MK 3
   ATK 11 SA-342L *Gazelle**
   SPT 24: 18 AW-139 being delivered; 3 *Commando* MK 2A; 1 *Commando* MK 2C; 2 SA-341 *Gazelle*

AD • SAM 75: 24 *Mistral*
   SP 9 *Roland* II
   MANPAD 42: 10 *Blowpipe*; 12 FIM-92A *Stinger*; 20 SA-7 *Grail*
MSL
   ASM AM-39 *Exocet*; *Apache*; HOT
   AAM MICA; R-550 *Magic*

DEPLOYMENT

LEBANON
UN • UNIFIL 3

FOREIGN FORCES

United Kingdom Air Force: 4 C-130J
United States US Central Command: Army 212; Navy 3; USAF 181; USMC 36; elm 1 (APS) HBCT set (equipment in use)

Saudi Arabia SAU

Saudi Riyal R		2008	2009	2010
GDP	R	1.75tr	1.54tr	
	US$	468bn	410bn	
per capita	US$	16,647	14,316	
Growth	%	4.4	-0.9	
Inflation	%	9.9	4.5	
Def bdgt[a]	R	143bn	154bn	
	US$	38.2bn	41.2bn	
US$1=R		3.75	3.75	

[a] Defence and security budget

Population 28,686,633

Ethnic groups: Nationals 73% of which Bedouin up to 10%, Shi'a 6%, Expatriates 27% of which Asians 20%, Arabs 6%, Africans 1%, Europeans <1%

Age	0–14	15–19	20–24	25–29	30–64	65 plus
Male	19%	5%	6%	6%	17%	1%
Female	19%	5%	4%	4%	12%	1%

Capabilities

ACTIVE 233,500 (Army 75,000 Navy 13,500 Air 20,000 Air Defence 16,000 Industrial Security Force 9,000 National Guard 100,000) **Paramilitary 15,500**

ORGANISATIONS BY SERVICE

Army 75,000
FORCES BY ROLE

Armd	3 bde (*each:* 3 tk bn ,1 mech bn, 1 fd arty bn, 1 recce bn, 1 AD bn, 1 AT bn)
Mech	5 bde (*each:* 1 tk bn, 3 mech bn, 1 fd arty bn, 1 AD bn, 1 spt bn,)
AB	1 bde (2 AB bn, 3 SF coy)

Arty   1 bde (5 fd arty bn, 2 (SP) MRL bn, 1 (SP) msl bn)

Avn   1 comd (1 atk hel bde, 1 hel bde)

Royal Guard 1 regt (3 lt inf bn)

EQUIPMENT BY TYPE

MBT 910: 115 M1-A2 *Abrams*; 200 in store; 145 AMX-30 in store; 450 M-60A3

RECCE 300 AML-60/AML-90

AIFV 780: 380 AMX-10P; 400 M-2 *Bradley* each with 2 TOW msl, 1 30mm gun

APC 2,240

    APC (T) 1,650 M-113A1/M-113A2/M-113A3 (incl variants)

    APC (W) 190: ε40 AF-40-8-1 *Al-Fahd* (in store); 150 M-3 *Panhard*

ARTY 855

    SP 155mm 170: 60 AU-F-1; 110 M-109A1B/M-109A2

    TOWED 225: **105mm** 100 M-101/M-102 in store; **155mm** 117: 40 FH-70 in store; 50 M-114; 27 M-198 in store; **203mm** 8 M-115 in store

    MRL 60 ASTROS II

    MOR 400:

      SP 220: **81mm** 70; **107mm** 150 M-30

      TOWED 180: **81mm/107mm** M-30 70; **120mm** 110 Brandt

AT • MSL 2,240+

    SP 290+: 90+ AMX-10P (HOT); 200 VCC-1 *ITOW*

    MANPATS 1950: 1,000 M47 *Dragon*; 950 TOW-2A

    RCL 450: **84mm** 300 *Carl Gustav*; **106mm** 50 M-40A1; **90mm** 100 M-67

    RL 112mm ε200 APILAS

HELICOPTERS

    ATK 12 AH-64 *Apache*

    SPT 27: 12 S-70A-1 *Desert Hawk*; 15 Bell 406 CS *Combat Scout*

    UTL 28: 6 AS-365N *Dauphin 2* (medevac); 22 UH-60A *Black Hawk* (4 medevac)

AD • SAM 1,000+

    SP *Crotale*

    MANPAD 1,000: 500 FIM-43 *Redeye*; 500 FIM-92A *Stinger*

RADAR • LAND AN/TPQ-36 *Firefinder*/AN/TPQ-37 *Firefinder* (arty, mor)

MSL • TACTICAL • SSM 10+ CSS-2 (40 msl)

Navy 13,500

FORCES BY ROLE

Navy 1 HQ (Eastern Fleet) located at Jubail; 1 HQ (Western Fleet) located at Jeddah; 1 HQ (Naval Forces) located at Riyadh

EQUIPMENT BY TYPE

PRINCIPAL SURFACE COMBATANTS 11

    FRIGATES • FFG 7:

      3 *Al Riyadh* with 1 octuple (8 eff.) with MM-40 *Exocet* block II SSM, 2 x 8 cell VLS each with *Aster* 15 SAM, 1 x 76mm gun, 4 x 533mm TT each with F17P HWT each with 1 hel landing platform (plus hangar for med-sized hel)

      4 *Madina* (FRA F-2000) each with 2 quad (8 eff.) each with Mk 2 Otomat SSM, 1 octuple (8 eff.) with 26 *Crotale* SAM, 4 x1 533mm ASTT each with F17P HWT, 1 100mm gun, (capacity 1 AS-365F *Dauphin 2* utl hel)

CORVETTES • FSG 4 *Badr* (US *Tacoma*) each with 2 Mk 140 *Harpoon* quad (8 eff.) each with RGM-84C *Harpoon* tactical SSM, 2 triple ASTT (6 eff.) each with Mk 46 LWT, 1 76mm gun

PATROL AND COASTAL COMBATANTS 65

    PFM 9 *Al Siddiq* (US 58m) each with 2 Mk 140 twin each with RGM-84C *Harpoon* tactical SSM, 1 76mm gun

    PCI 17 (US *Halter Marine*, under 100 tonnes)

    PBI 39 (FRA *Simonneau*)

MINE WARFARE • MINE COUNTERMEASURES 7

    MCC 4 *Addriyah* (US MSC-322)

    MHO 3 *Al Jawf* (UK *Sandown*)

AMPHIBIOUS 8

    LCU 4 (capacity 120 troops)

    LCM 4 (capacity 80 troops)

LOGISTICS AND SUPPORT 5

    AORH 2 *Boraida* (mod FRA *Durance*) (capacity either 2 AS-365F *Dauphin 2* utl hel or 1 AS-332C *Super Puma* spt hel)

    RY 3

FACILITIES

Bases HQ (Eastern Fleet) located at Jubail; (HQ Western Fleet) Jeddah; (HQ Naval Forces) Riyadh; Dammam; Al Wajh; Ras al Mishab; Ras al Ghar

Naval Aviation

HELICOPTERS

    ASLT 15 AS-565* each with AS-15TT tactical ASM

    SPT 25: 12 AS-532B *Super Puma*/AS-332F *Super Puma* each with AM-39 *Exocet* tactical ASM; 13 Bell 406 CS *Combat Scout*

    UTL 6 AS-365N *Dauphin 2*

Marines 3,000

FORCES BY ROLE

Inf 1 regt (2 Inf bn)

EQUIPMENT BY TYPE

APC (W) 140 BMP-600P

Air Force 20,000

FORCES BY ROLE

Ftr   1 sqn with *Tornado* ADV; 1 sqn with F-15S *Eagle*; 4 sqn with F-15C; F-15D *Eagle*

FGA 1 sqn with *Typhoon* Tranche 2; 3 sqn with *Tornado* IDS (incl IDS recce); 1 sqn with F-5B *Freedom Fighter*/F-5F *Tiger II*/RF-5E *Tigereye*; 2 sqn with F-15S *Eagle*

AEW 1 sqn with E-3A *Sentry*

Tpt   3 sqn with C-130E *Hercules*; C-130H *Hercules*; C-130H-30 *Hercules*; CN-235; L-100-30HS (hospital ac)

Tkr   sqn with KC-130H *Hercules* (tkr/tpt); KE-3A

OCU 2 sqn with F-5B *Freedom Fighter**

Trg   3 sqn with *Hawk* MK65 (incl aerobatic team); *Hawk* MK65A; 1 sqn with *Jetstream* MK31; sqn with MFI-17 *Mushshak*; 1 sqn with Cessna 172; 2 sqn with PC-9

Hel   2 sqn with AS-532 *Cougar* (CSAR); AB-205 (Bell 205); AB-206A (Bell 206A) *JetRanger*; AB-212 (Bell 212); AB-412 (Bell 412) *Twin Huey* (SAR)

EQUIPMENT BY TYPE
AIRCRAFT 280 combat capable
FTR 121: 66 F-15C *Eagle*; 18 F-15D *Eagle*; 15 Tornado ADV; 22 F-5B/F-5F *Tiger II*/RF-5E *Tigereye**
STRIKE/FGA 159: 4 *Typhoon* Tranche 2 (72 on order); 70 F-15S *Eagle*; 85 Tornado IDS (incl 10 IDS recce)
AEW 5 E-3A *Sentry*
TKR 15: 8 KC-130H *Hercules* (tkr/tpt); 7 KE-3A
TPT 45: 7 C-130E *Hercules*; 29 C-130H; 2 C-130H-30 *Hercules*; 4 CN-235; 3 L-100-30HS (hospital ac)
UTL 13 Cessna 172
TRG 123: 25 *Hawk* MK65 (incl aerobatic team); 18 *Hawk* MK65A; 14 F-5B; 1 *Jetstream* MK31; 20 MFI-17 *Mushshak*; 45 PC-9
HELICOPTERS
UTL 78: 22 AB-205 (Bell 205); 17 AB-212 (Bell 212); 16 AB-412 (Bell 412) *Twin Huey* (SAR); 10 AS-532 *Cougar* (CSAR); 13 AB-206A (Bell 206A) *JetRanger*
MSL
ASM AGM-65 *Maverick*; Sea Eagle
ARM ALARM
AAM AIM-7 *Sparrow*; AIM-7M *Sparrow*/AIM-9J *Sidewinder*/AIM-9L *Sidewinder*/AIM-9P *Sidewinder*; *Sky Flash*; AIM-120 AMRAAM

Royal Flt
AIRCRAFT • TPT 16: 1 B-737-200; 2 B-747SP; 4 BAe-125-800; 1 Cessna 310; 2 Gulfstream III, 2 *Learjet* 35; 4 VC-130H
HELICOPTERS
SPT 1 S-70 *Black Hawk*
UTL 3+: AB-212 (Bell 212); 3 AS-61

Air Defence Forces 16,000
FORCES BY ROLE
SAM   16 bty with total of 96 PAC-2; 17 bty with total of 73 *Shahine*; with 50 AMX-30SA; 16 bty with total of 128 MIM-23B *I-HAWK*; 73 units (static defence) with total of 68 *Crotale* / *Shahine*

EQUIPMENT BY TYPE
AD • SAM 1,805
SP 581: 40 *Crotale*; 400 FIM-92A *Avenger*; 73 *Shahine*; 68 *Crotale*/*Shahine*
TOWED 224: 128 I-HAWK MIM-23B; 96 PAC-2
MANPAD 500 FIM-43 *Redeye*
NAVAL 500 *Mistral*
GUNS 1,220
SP 942: **20mm** 92 M-163 *Vulcan*; **30mm** 850 AMX-30SA;
TOWED 278: **35mm** 128 GDF *Oerlikon*; **40mm** 150 L/70 in store
RADARS • AD RADAR 80: 17 AN/FPS-117; 28 AN/TPS-43; AN/TPS-59; 35 AN/TPS-63; AN/TPS-70

Industrial Security Force 9,000+
The force is part of a new security system that will incorporate surveillance and crisis management.

National Guard 75,000 active; 25,000 (tribal levies) (total 100,000)
FORCES BY ROLE
Cav   1 (ceremonial) sqn
Mech Inf   3 bde (*each:* 4 army bn (all arms))
Inf   5 bde (*each:* 1 Arty bn, 1 Supply bn, 3 (combined arms) bn)

EQUIPMENT BY TYPE
RECCE 450 LAV-25 *Coyote*
AIFV 1,117 IFV-25
APC • APC (W) 2,220: 1,120 *Piranha II*; 290 V-150 *Commando*; 810 in store
ARTY • TOWED 90: **105mm** 50 M-102; **155mm** 40 M-198
  MOR 81mm
AT • MSL • MANPATS 116+: 116 TOW-2A (2,000 msl); M47 *Dragon*
RCL • 106mm M-40A1
AD • GUNS • TOWED 160: **20mm** 30 M-167 *Vulcan*; **90mm** 130 (M-2)

Paramilitary 15,500+ active

Border Guard 10,500
FORCES BY ROLE
Subordinate to Ministry of Interior. HQ in Riyadh. 9 subordinate regional commands

Mobile Defence some (long-range patrol/spt) units
MP   some units
Border Def   2 (patrol) units
Def   12 (infrastructure) units; 18 (harbour) units
Coastal Def some units

EQUIPMENT BY TYPE
HEL 6 attack helicopters
ASW/ASUW 6 AS-332F *Super Puma* with total of 12 AM-39 *Exocet* ASM tactical
SPT 6 AS-332B *Super Puma*

Coast Guard 4,500
EQUIPMENT BY TYPE
PATROL AND COASTAL COMBATANTS ε 262 (except Al-Jouf, all units less than 100 tonnes)
PFI 4 *Al Jouf*
PBF 2 *Seaguard*
PB 6 *StanPatrol2606*
PBI ε250: 39 *Simonneau 51* Type; 211 other
AMPHIBIOUS • CRAFT 13: 8 UCAC; 5 LCAC
LOGISTICS AND SUPPORT 4: 1 **Trg**; 3 **AO** (small)
FACILITIES
Base   Located at Azizam

General Civil Defence Administration Units
HELICOPTERS • SPT 10 Boeing Vertol 107

Special Security Force 500
APC (W): UR-416

DEPLOYMENT

ARABIAN GULF AND INDIAN OCEAN

Maritime Security Operations 2 FFG

FOREIGN FORCES

United States US Central Command: Army 144; Navy 25; USAF 81; USMC 27; OPM-SANG 500

Syria SYR

Syrian Pound S£		2008	2009	2010
GDP	S£	2.36tr	2.45tr	
	US$	51.4bn	53.3bn	
per capita	US$	2,411	2,448	
Growth	%	45.2	3.0	
Inflation	%	15.2	7.5	
Def bdgt	S£	89.3bn	86.2bn	
	US$	1.94bn	1.87bn	
US$1=S£		46.0	46.0	

Population   21,762,978

Age	0–14	15–19	20–24	25–29	30–64	65 plus
Male	19%	6%	5%	4%	14%	2%
Female	18%	6%	5%	4%	14%	2%

Capabilities

ACTIVE 325,000 (Army 220,000 Navy 5,000 Air 40,000 Air Defence 60,000) **Paramilitary 108,000**

RESERVE 314,000 (Army 280,000 Navy 4,000 Air 10,000 Air Defence 20,000)

Terms of service conscription, 30 months

ORGANISATIONS BY SERVICE

Army 220,000 (incl conscripts)

FORCES BY ROLE

3 Corps HQ

Armd	7 div (*each:* 3 armd; 1 mech; 1 arty bde)
Tk	1 indep regt
Mech	3 div (under strength) (*each:* 1 armd, 2 mech, 1 arty bde)
Inf	4 indep bde
SF	1 div (10 SF gp)
Arty	2 indep bde
AT	2 indep bde
SSM	1 (Coastal Def) bde with SS-C-1B *Sepal* and SS-C-3 *Styx*; 1 bde (3 SSM bn with FROG-7); 1 bde (3 SSM bn with SS-21); 1 bde (3 SSM bn with *Scud*-B/-C)
Border Guard	1 indep bde
Security	1 div (Republican Guard) (3 armd, 1 mech, 1 arty bde)

Reserves

Armd	1 div HQ; 4 bde; 2 regt
Inf	31 regt
Arty	3 regt

EQUIPMENT BY TYPE

MBT 4,950: 1,500–1,700 T-72 T-72M; 1,000 T-62K/T-62M; 2,250 T-55/T-55MV (some in store)
RECCE 590 BRDM-2
AIFV up to 2,450 BMP-1/BMP-2/BMP-3
APC (W) 1,500: 500 BTR-152; 1,000 BTR-50/BTR-60/BTR-70
ARTY up to 3,440+
  SP 500+: **122mm** 450+: 400 2S1 *Carnation* (*Gvosdik*); 50+ D-30 (mounted on T34/85 chassis); **152mm** 50 2S3 (*Akatsiya*)
  TOWED 2,030: **122mm** 1,150: 500 D-30; 150 (M-30) M1938; 500 in store (no given designation); **130mm** 700-800 M-46; **152mm** 70 D-20/ML-20 M1937; **180mm** 10 S23
  MRL up to 500: **107mm** up to 200 Type-63; **122mm** up to 300 BM-21 (*Grad*)
  MOR 410+: **82mm**; **120mm** circa 400 M-1943; **160mm** M-160 (hundreds); **240mm** up to 10 M-240
AT • MSL 2,600
  SP 410 9P133 BRDM-2 *Sagger*
  MANPATS 2190+: 150 AT-4 9K111 *Spigot*; 40 AT-5 9K113 *Spandrel*; AT-7 9K115 *Saxhorn*; 800 AT-10 9K116 *Stabber*; 1,000 AT-14 9M133 *Kornet*; 200 *Milan*
  RL **73mm** RPG-7 *Knout*; **105mm** RPG-29
AD • SAM 4,184+
  SP 84: 14 SA-8 *Gecko*; 20 SA-9 *Gaskin*; 20 SA-11 *Gadfly*; 30 SA-13 *Gopher*
  MANPAD 4,100+: 4,000+ SA-7 *Grail*/SA-18 *Grouse* (*Igla*); 100 SA-14 *Gremlin*
  GUNS 1,225+
  SP ZSU-23-4
  TOWED **23mm** 600 ZU-23; **37mm** M-1939; **57mm** 600 S-60; **100mm** 25 KS-19
MSL • TACTICAL • SSM 94+: 18 *Scud*-B/*Scud*-C/*Scud*-D; 30 look-a-like; 18 FROG-7; 18+ SS-21 *Tochka* (*Scarab*); 4 SS-C-1B *Sepal*; 6 SS-C-3 *Styx* (ɛ850 SSM msl total)

Navy 5,000

EQUIPMENT BY TYPE

PRINCIPAL SURFACE COMBATANTS • FRIGATES •
FF 2 *Petya* III each with 1 triple 533mm ASTT (3 eff.) with SAET-60 HWT, 4 RBU 2500 *Smerch* 1 (64 eff.)†, 2 76mm twin gun
PATROL AND COASTAL COMBATANTS 21:
  PFM 10 *Osa* I/II each with 4 single each with 1 SS-N-2C *Styx* tactical SSM
  PFI 11: 8 *Zhuk* less than 100 tonnes; ɛ3 *Tir* each with 2 single with C-802 (CSS-N-8) *Saccade* tactical SSM
MINE WARFARE • MINE COUNTERMEASURES 5:
  MSC 1 *Natya*
  MSI 3 *Yevgenya*
  MSO 1 T-43 (FSU)

AMPHIBIOUS • LS • LSM 3 *Polnochny* B (capacity 6 MBT; 180 troops)
LOGISTICS AND SUPPORT 3: 2 **AGOR**; 1 **TRG**
FACILITIES

Bases   Located at Latakia, Tartus, Minet el-Baida

Naval Aviation

HELICOPTER 13 atk hel
ASW 13: 2 Ka-28 (Ka-27PL) *Helix A* (air force manpower); 11 Mi-14 *Haze*

Air Force 40,000 (incl 10,000 reserves); 60,000 Air Defence (incl 20,000 reserves) (total 100,000)

Flying hours   15 to 25 hrs/year on FGA/ftr; 70 hrs/year; 50 hrs/year on MBB-223 *Flamingo* trg ac

FORCES BY ROLE

Ftr   4 sqn with MiG-25 *Foxbat*; 4 sqn with MiG-23 MLD *Flogger*; 3 sqn with MiG-29A *Fulcrum A*

FGA   2 sqn with MiG-23BN *Flogger H*; 1 sqn with Su-24 *Fencer*; 5 sqn with Su-22 (Su-17M-2) *Fitter D*; 7 sqn with MiG-21 *Fishbed*;

Recce   4 sqn with MiG-21H *Fishbed*/MiG-21J *Fishbed**; MiG-25R *Foxbat**

Tpt   sqn with An-24 *Coke*; An-26 *Curl*; *Falcon* 20; *Falcon* 900; Il-76 *Candid*; Yak-40 *Codling*; Mi-17 (Mi-8MT) *Hip H*/Mi-8 *Hip*; PZL Mi-2 *Hoplite*

Atk hel 3 sqns with Mi-25 *Hind D*; SA-342L *Gazelle*

Trg   PA-31 *Navajo*; L-39 *Albatros*; MBB-223 *Flamingo* (basic); MFI-17 *Mushshak*; MiG-21U *Mongol A**; MiG-23UM*; MiG-25U *Foxbat**

EQUIPMENT BY TYPE
AIRCRAFT 555 combat capable
  FTR 150+: 40+ MiG-29A *Fulcrum*; 30 MiG-25 *Foxbat*; 80 MiG-23MLD *Flogger*
  FGA 289: 20 Su-24 *Fencer*; 60 MiG-23BN *Flogger H*; 159 MiG-21H; 50 Su-22 (Su-17M-2) *Fitter D*
  RECCE 48: 8 MiG-25R *Foxbat**; 40 MiG-21 H/J*
  TPT 22: 1 An-24 *Coke*; 6 An-26 *Curl*; 2 *Falcon* 20; 1 *Falcon* 900; 4 Il-76 *Candid*; 2 PA-31 *Navajo*; 6 Yak-40 *Codling*
  TRG 139: 70 L-39 *Albatros* (40 armed*); 35 MBB-223 *Flamingo* (basic); 6 MFI-17 *Mushshak*; 20 MiG-21U *Mongol A**; 6 MiG-23UM*; 2 MiG-25U *Foxbat**
HELICOPTERS
  ATK 71: 36 Mi-25 *Hind D*; 35 SA-342L *Gazelle*
  SPT 120: 100 Mi-17 (Mi-8MT) *Hip H*/Mi-8 *Hip*; 20 PZL Mi-2 *Hoplite*
MSL
  ASM AS-7 *Kerry*; HOT
  AAM AA-10 *Alamo*; AA-2 *Atoll*; AA-6 *Acrid*; AA-7 *Apex*; AA-8 *Aphid*

Air Defence Command 60,000

FORCES BY ROLE

AD   2 div (*total*: 25 AD bde (*total*: 150 SAM bty with total of 148 SA-3 *Goa*; 195 SA-6 *Gainful*; 320 SA-2 *Guideline*, some ADA bty with total of 4,000 SA-7A *Grail*/SA-7B *Grail*))

SAM   2 regt (*each*: 2 SAM bn (*each*: 2 SAM bty with total of 44 SA-5 *Gammon*))

EQUIPMENT BY TYPE
AD • SAM 4,707
  SP 195 SA-6 *Gainful*
  TOWED 468: 320 SA-2 *Guideline*; 148 SA-3 *Goa*
  STATIC/SHELTER 44 SA-5 *Gammon*
  MANPAD 4,000 SA-7A *Grail*/SA-7B *Grail*

Paramilitary ε108,000

Gendarmerie 8,000
Ministry of Interior

Workers' Militia ε100,000
People's Army (Ba'ath Party)

FOREIGN FORCES

UNTSO unless specified. Figures represent total numbers for mission in Israel, Syria and Lebanon.
Argentina 6 obs
Australia 11 obs
Austria 7 obs • UNDOF 378; 1 inf bn
Belgium 2 obs
Canada 7 obs • UNDOF 2
Chile 4 obs
China, People's Republic of 4 obs
Croatia UNDOF 94; 1 inf coy
Denmark 11 obs
Estonia 1 obs
Finland 15 obs
France 2 obs
Ireland 12 obs
Italy 8 obs
India UNDOF 195; elm 1 log bn
Japan UNDOF 31; elm 1 log bn
Nepal 3 obs
Netherlands 12 obs
New Zealand 7 obs
Norway 11 obs
Philippines UNDOF 12
Poland UNDOF 333; 1 inf bn
Russia 5 obs • Army/Navy 150, naval facility reportedly under renovation at Tartus
Slovakia 2 obs
Slovenia 2 obs
Sweden 7 obs
Switzerland 10 obs
United States 2 obs

Tunisia TUN

Tunisian Dinar D		2008	2009	2010
GDP	D	51bn	51bn	
	US$	41.6bn	39.9bn	
per capita	US$	4,000	3,800	
Growth	%	4.6	3.0	
Inflation	%	5.1	3.5	
Def bdgt	D	657m		
	US$	534m		
FMA (US)	US$	8.3m	12m	15m
US$1=D		1.23	1.29	

Population   10,486,339

Age	0–14	15–19	20–24	25–29	30–64	65 plus
Male	13%	5%	5%	5%	19%	3%
Female	12%	5%	5%	5%	19%	3%

Capabilities

ACTIVE 35,800 (Army 27,000 Navy 4,800 Air 4,000)
Paramilitary 12,000

Terms of service 12 months selective

ORGANISATIONS BY SERVICE

Army 5,000; 22,000 conscript (total 27,000)

FORCES BY ROLE

Mech   3 bde (*each*: 1 armd regt, 2 mech inf regt, 1 arty regt,
1 AD regt)
SF   1 (Sahara) bde; 1 bde
Engr   1 regt

EQUIPMENT BY TYPE

MBT 84: 30 M-60A1; 54 M-60A3
LT TK 48 SK-105 *Kuerassier*
RECCE 60: 40 AML-90; 20 *Saladin*
APC 268
  APC (T) 140 M-113A1/M-113A2
  APC (W) 128: 18 EE-11 *Urutu*; 110 Fiat 6614
ARTY 276
  TOWED 115: **105mm** 48 M-101A1/M-101A2; **155mm** 67:
  12 M-114A1; 55 M-198
  MOR 161: **81mm** 95; **107mm** 48 (some SP); **120mm** 18
  Brandt
AT • MSL 590
  SP 35 M-901 ITV TOW
  MANPATS 555: 500 *Milan*; 55 TOW
  RL **89mm** 600: 300 LRAC; 300 M-20
AD • SAM 86
  SP 26 M-48 *Chaparral*
  MANPAD 60 RBS-70
  GUNS 127
  SP **40mm** 12 M-42
  TOWED 115: **20mm** 100 M-55; **37mm** 15 Type-55 (M-1939)/Type-65
RADAR • LAND RASIT (veh, arty)

Navy ε4,800

EQUIPMENT BY TYPE
PATROL AND COASTAL COMBATANTS 25
  PFM 12:
    3 *Bizerte* (FRA P-48) each with 8 SS 12M tactical SSM
    3 *La Galite* (FRA *Combattante* III) each with 2 Mk 140
    Harpoon quad (8 eff.) each with MM-40 *Exocet* tactical
    SSM, 1 76mm gun
    6 *Albatros* (GER Type 143B) with 2 x 76mm gun, 2
    twin launcher (4 eff.) for MM-38 *Exocet* SSM, 2 single
    533mm TT
  PCC 3 *Utique* (mod PRC *Haizhui* II)
  PCI 10 (less than 100 tonnes)
LOGISTICS AND SUPPORT 6:
  AWT 1
  AGS 1
  ABU 3
  TRG 1 *Salambo* (US *Conrad*, survey)
FACILITIES
Bases   Located at Bizerte, Sfax, Kelibia

Air Force 4,000

FORCES BY ROLE

FGA   1 sqn with F-5E/F-5F *Tiger* II
CCT   1 sqn with MB-326K; MB-326L
Tpt   1 sqn with C-130B *Hercules*; C-130E *Hercules*;
          C-130H *Hercules*; Falcon 20; G-222; L-410 *Turbolet*
Liaison   1 sqn with S-208A
Tpt/utl   2 sqn with AS-350B *Ecureuil*; AS-365 *Dauphin* 2;
hel   AB-205 (Bell 205); SA-313; SA-316 *Alouette* III; UH-
          1H *Iroquois*; UH-1N *Iroquois*; 1 sqn with HH-3E
Trg   2 sqn with L-59 *Albatros**; MB-326B; SF-260

EQUIPMENT BY TYPE

AIRCRAFT 27 combat capable
  FTR 12 F-5E *Tiger* II/F-5F *Tiger* II
  FGA 3 MB-326K
  TPT 20: 8 C-130B *Hercules*; 1 C-130E *Hercules*; 2 C-130H
  Hercules; 1 *Falcon* 20; 5 G-222; 3 L-410 *Turbolet*
  UTL 2 S-208A
  TRG 33: 12 L-59 *Albatros**; 4 MB-326B; 3 MB-326L; 14
  SF-260
HELICOPTERS
  SPT 6 AS-350B *Ecureuil*
  UTL 37: 15 AB-205 (Bell 205); 11 HH-3; 1 AS-365
  Dauphin 2; 6 SA-313; 3 SA-316 *Alouette* III; 10 UH-1H
  Iroquois; 2 UH-1N *Iroquois*
MSL • AAM AIM-9J *Sidewinder*

Paramilitary 12,000

National Guard 12,000

Ministry of Interior
PATROL AND COASTAL COMBATANTS 30
  PCC 6 *Kondor* I (GDR)
  PCI 24: 5 *Bremse* (GDR); 4 *Gabes*; 4 *Rodman*; 2 *Socomena*;
  All units less than 100 tonnes
HELICOPTERS • UTL 8 SA-318 *Alouette* II/SA-319
Alouette III

DEPLOYMENT

CENTRAL AFRICAN REPUBLIC/CHAD
UN • MINURCAT 3; 1 obs

CÔTE D'IVOIRE
UN • UNOCI 4; 7 obs

DEMOCRATIC REPUBLIC OF CONGO
UN • MONUC 461; 26 obs; 1 mech inf bn

United Arab Emirates UAE

Emirati Dirham D		2008	2009	2010
GDP	D	991bn	902bn	
	US$	270bn	245bn	
per capita	US$	58,430	51,220	
Growth	%	7.4	-0.2	
Inflation	%	12.9	2.5	
Def bdgt[a]	D	50.4bn	56.8bn	
	US$	13.73bn	15.47bn	
US$1=D		3.67	3.67	

[a] Excludes possible extra-budgetary procurement funding

Population   4,798,491

Ethnic groups: Nationals 24%; Expatriates 76% of which Indian 30%, Pakistani 20%; other Arab 12%; other Asian 10%; UK 2%; other European 1%

Age	0–14	15–19	20–24	25–29	30–64	65 plus
Male	13%	6%	5%	4%	29%	3%
Female	12%	5%	5%	3%	14%	1%

Capabilities

ACTIVE 51,000 (Army 44,000 Navy 2,500 Air 4,500)
The Union Defence Force and the armed forces of the UAE (Abu Dhabi, Dubai, Ras al-Khaimah, Fujairah, Ajman, Umm al-Qawayn and Sharjah) were formally merged in 1976 and headquartered in Abu Dhabi. Dubai still maintains independent forces, as do other Emirates to a lesser degree.

ORGANISATIONS BY SERVICE

Army 44,000 (incl Dubai 15,000)
FORCES BY ROLE
GHQ Abu Dhabi
Armd	2 bde
Mech Inf	3 bde
Inf	2 bde
Arty	1 bde (3 arty regt)
Royal Guard	1 bde

Dubai Independent Forces
Mech inf 2 bde

EQUIPMENT BY TYPE
MBT 471: 390 *Leclerc*; 36 OF-40 Mk2 (*Lion*); 45 AMX-30

LT TK 76 *Scorpion*
RECCE 129: 49 AML-90; 20 *Ferret* in store; 20 *Saladin* in store; 24 VBL; 16 TPz-1 *Fuchs* (NBC)
AIFV 430: 15 AMX-10P; 415 BMP-3
APC 892
  APC (T) 136 APC (incl 53 engr plus other variants)
  APC (W) 756: 90 BTR-3U *Guardian*; 120 EE-11 *Urutu*; 370 M-3 *Panhard*; 80 VCR (incl variants); 20 VAB; 76 RG-31 *Nyala*
ARV 46
ARTY 541+
  SP 155mm 221: 78 G-6; 125 M-109A3; 18 Mk F3
  TOWED 93: **105mm** 73 ROF lt; **130mm** 20 Type-59-I
  MRL 72+: **70mm** 18 LAU-97; **122mm** 48+: 48 Firos-25 (est 24 op); Type-90 (reported); **300mm** 6 9A52 *Smerch*
  MOR 155: **81mm** 134: 20 Brandt; 114 L16; **120mm** 21 Brandt
AT • **MSL** 305+
  SP 20 HOT
  MANPATS 285+: 30 HOT; 230 *Milan*; 25 TOW; *Vigilant* in store
  RCL 262: **84mm** 250 *Carl Gustav*; **106mm** 12 M-40
AD • **SAM** • **MANPAD** 40+: 20+ *Blowpipe*; 20 *Mistral*
  GUNS 62
  SP 20mm 42 M3 VDAA
  TOWED 30mm 20 GCF-BM2
MSL • **TACTICAL** • **SSM** 6 *Scud*-B (up to 20 msl)

Navy ε2,500
EQUIPMENT BY TYPE
PRINCIPAL SURFACE COMBATANTS 4
  FRIGATES • **FFG** 2 *Abu Dhabi* †(NLD *Kortenaer*) each with 2 Mk 141 *Harpoon* quad (8 eff.) (no weapons embarked) each with RGM-84A *Harpoon* tactical SSM, 1 Mk 29 *Sea Sparrow* octuple with 24 RIM-7F/M *Sea Sparrow* SAM, 2 Twin 324mm TT (4 eff.) each with A244/Mk 46, 1 76mm gun, each with 2 AS-565SA *Panthe* ASW/ASUW hel
  CORVETTES • **FSG** 2 *Muray Jib* (GER Lurssen 62m) each with 1 SA-316 *Alouette III* utl hel, 2 quad (8 eff.) each with MM-40 *Exocet* tactical SSM
PATROL AND COASTAL COMBATANTS 14
  PFM 8:
    6 *Ban Yas* (GER Lurssen TNC-45) each with 2 twin (4 eff.) each with MM-40 *Exocet* tactical SSM, 1 76mm gun
    2 *Mubarraz* (GER Lurssen 45m) each with 2 twin (4 eff.) each with MM-40 *Exocet* tactical SSM, 1 76mm gun
  PCC 6 *Ardhana* (UK Vosper 33m)
MINE WARFARE • **MINE COUNTERMEASURES** •
MHC 2 *Al Murjan* (*Frankenthal Class* Type 332)
AMPHIBIOUS • **CRAFT** 28
  LCP 16: 12 (capacity 40 troops); 4 (Fast Supply Vessel multi-purpose)
  LCU 5: 3 *Al Feyi* (capacity 56 troops); 2 (capacity 40 troops and additional vehicles)
  LCT 7
LOGISTICS AND SUPPORT 3: 1 **YDT**; 2 **YTM**

FACILITIES

Bases   Located at Mina Sakr (Sharjah), Mina Rashid, Khor Fakkan, Mina Zayed (Dubai), Dalma, Abu Dhabi (Main base), Mina Khalid, Mina Jabal (Ras al-Khaimah)

Naval Aviation

AIRCRAFT • TPT 2 *Learjet 35A*
HELICOPTERS
    ASW/ASUW 14: 7 AS-332F *Super Puma* (5 in ASUW role); 7 AS-565 *Panther*
    UTL 4 SA-316 *Alouette III*

Air Force 4,500

Incl Police Air Wing
Flying hours   110 hrs/year

FORCES BY ROLE

FGA   3 sqn with F-16E/F-16F *Falcon* Block 60; 3 sqn with *Mirage* 2000-9DAD/2000-9RADe; 1 sqn with *Mirage* M-2000DAD; 1 sqn with *Hawk* MK63A/*Hawk* MK63C/*Hawk* MK63; 1 sqn with *Hawk* MK102
Recce   1 sqn with M-2000 RAD *Mirage**
SAR   1 sqn with A-109K2; AB-139
Tpt   3 sqn with An-124 *Condor*; Beech 350 *Super King Air*; C-130H *Hercules*; C-130H-30 *Hercules*; CASA 235M-100; DHC-6-300 *Twin Otter*; IL-76 *Candid* on lease; L-100-30
OCU   *Hawk* MK61*
Trg   sqn with Grob 115TA; PC-7 *Turbo Trainer*
Atk hel   2 sqn with AH-64A/D *Apache*; AS-550C3 *Fennec*; SA-342K *Gazelle* (eq. with HOT) ASM
Tpt hel   1 sqn with IAR-330 SOCAT *Puma*/SA-330 *Puma*; CH-47C *Chinook* (SF); AB-139 (VIP); AS-365F *Dauphin 2* (VIP); Bell 206 *JetRanger* trg; Bell 214; Bell 407; Bell 412 *Twin Huey*

EQUIPMENT BY TYPE

AIRCRAFT 184 combat capable
    FGA 155: 55 F-16E Block 60 *Desert Eagle*; 25 F-16F Block 60 (13 to remain in US for trg); 18 *Mirage* 2000-9DAD; 44 *Mirage* 2000-9RAD; 13 *Hawk* MK102
    RECCE 7 *Mirage* 2000 RAD*
    TPT 23: 1 An-124 *Condor*; 2 Beech 350 *Super King Air*; 4 C-130H; 2 C-130H-30 *Hercules*; 7 CASA 235M-100; 1 DHC-6-300 *Twin Otter*; 4 Il-76 *Candid* on lease; 2 L-100-30. 4 C-17 and 12 C-130J reportedly on order
    TRG 64: 5 *Hawk* MK61*; 17 *Hawk* MK63 A/*Hawk* MK63C*; 12 Grob 115TA; 30 PC-7 *Turbo Trainer*
HELICOPTERS
    ATK 40+: 30 AH-64A *Apache* (being upgraded to AH-64D standard); AS-550C3 *Fennec*; 10 SA-342K *Gazelle*
    SPT 27: 12 CH-47C *Chinook* (SF); 15 IAR-330 SOCAT *Puma* aslt/SA-330 *Puma* spt
    UTL 40: 3 A-109K2; 8 AB-139 (incl 2 VIP); 4 AS-365F *Dauphin 2* (VIP); 9 Bell 206 *JetRanger* trg; 3 Bell 214; 1 Bell 407; 9 Bell 412 *Twin Huey*
MSL
    ASM AGM-65G *Maverick*; AGM-114 *Hellfire*; AS-15

Kent; *Black Shaheen*; *Hydra-70*; PGM-1 *Hakeem 1*; PGM-2 *Hakeem 2*; HOT
AAM AIM-9L *Sidewinder*; MICA; R-550 *Magic*; AIM-120 AMRAAM

Air Defence

FORCES BY ROLE

AD   2 bde (*each*: 3 bn with I-*HAWK* MIM-23B)
SAM   3 short-range bn with *Crotale*; *Mistral*; *Rapier*; RB-70; *Javelin*; SA-18 *Grouse* (*Igla*)

EQUIPMENT BY TYPE

AD • SAM
    SP *Crotale*; RB-70
    TOWED I-*HAWK* MIM-23B; *Rapier*
    MANPAD *Javelin*; SA-18 *Grouse* (*Igla*)
    NAVAL *Mistral*

Paramilitary • Coast Guard

Ministry of Interior
PATROL AND COASTAL COMBATANTS 95+
    PCC 7: 2 *Protector*; 5 (US Camcraft '77)
    PBF 9
    PB 25: 16 (US Camcraft '65); 9 (ITA *Baglietto*)
    PBI 54 (Seaspray Assault)

DEPLOYMENT

AFGHANISTAN
NATO • ISAF 25

FOREIGN FORCES

France 3 *Mirage* 2000-5, 1 KC-135F at al Dhafra (To operate alongside UAE *Mirage* 2000-9s); naval and army contingent
United States US Central Command: Army 2; Navy 1; USAF 84; USMC 17

Yemen, Republic of YEM

Yemeni Rial R		2008	2009	2010
GDP	R	4.67tr	4.70tr	
	US$	23.5bn	22.9bn	
per capita	US$	1,058	1,000	
Growth	%	3.5	4.2	
Inflation	%	19.0	8.4	
Def bdgt	R	297bn	318bn	448bn
	US$	1.49bn	1.55bn	
FMA (US)	US$	3.9m	2.8m	10m
US$1=R		199	205	

Population   22,858,238

Ethnic groups: Majority Arab, some African and South Asian

Age	0–14	15–19	20–24	25–29	30–64	65 plus
Male	24%	6%	5%	4%	11%	1%
Female	23%	6%	5%	4%	11%	1%

Capabilities

ACTIVE 66,700 (Army 60,000 Navy 1,700 Air Force 3,000, Air Defence 2,000) Paramilitary 71,200

Terms of service conscription, 2 years

ORGANISATIONS BY SERVICE

Army 60,000 (incl conscripts)

FORCES BY ROLE

Armd	8 bde
Mech	6 bde
Inf	16 bde
SF	1 bde
Cdo/AB	2 bde
Arty	3 bde
SSM	1 bde
Gd/Central Guard	1 force
AD	2 bn

EQUIPMENT BY TYPE

MBT 790: 50 M-60A1; 60 T-72; 200 T-62; 450 T-54/T-55; 30 T-34

RECCE 145: 80 AML-90; 15 LAV; 50 BRDM-2

AIFV 200: 100 BMP-1; 100 BMP-2

APC 728

  APC (T) 60 M-113A

  APC (W) 668: 60 BTR-40; 100 BTR-60; 20 BTR-152; 470 BTR-40/BTR-60/BTR-152 in store; 18 YLAV *Cougar*

ARTY 1,167

  SP 122mm 25 2S1 *Carnation*

  TOWED 310: **105mm** 25 M-101A1; **122mm** 200: 130 D-30; 30 M-1931/37; 40 M-30 M-1938; **130mm** 60 M-46; **152mm** 10 D-20; **155mm** 15 M-114

  COASTAL 130mm 36 SM-4-1

  MRL 294: **122mm** 280 BM-21 (150 op); **140mm** 14 BM-14

  MOR 502: **81mm** 200; **82mm** 90 M-43; **107mm** 12; **120mm** 100; **160mm** ε100

AT • MSL • MANPATS 71: 35 AT-3 9K11 *Sagger*; 24 M47 *Dragon*; 12 TOW

  RCL 75mm M-20; **82mm** B-10; **107mm** B-11

  RL 66mm M-72 LAW; **73mm** RPG-7 *Knout*

  GUNS 50+

    SP 100mm 30 SU-100

    TOWED 20+: **85mm** D-44; **100mm** 20 M-1944

AD • SAM ε800

  SP SA-9 *Gaskin*; SA-13 *Gopher*

  MANPAD SA-7 *Grail*; SA-14 *Gremlin*

  GUNS 530

    SP 70: **20mm** 20 M-163 *Vulcan*; **23mm** 50 ZSU-23-4

    TOWED 460: **20mm** 50 M-167 *Vulcan*; **23mm** 100 ZU-23-2;

    37mm 150 M-1939; **57mm** 120 S-60; **85mm** 40 M-1939 KS-12

MSL • TACTICAL • SSM 28: 12 FROG-7; 10 SS-21 *Scarab (Tochka)*; 6 *Scud*-B (ε33 msl)

Navy 1,700

EQUIPMENT BY TYPE

PATROL AND COASTAL COMBATANTS 20

  PFM 4:

    3 *Huangfen*† each with 4 single fitted, for YJ-1 (CSS-N-4) *Sardine* tactical SSM

    1 *Tarantul*† with 2 twin (4 eff.) fitted, for SS-N-2C *Styx* tactical SSM

  PB 10 *Austal*

  PBF 6 *Baklan*

MINE WARFARE • MINE COUNTERMEASURES 6

  MHC 5 *Yevgeny* † (FSU)

  MSO 1 *Natya* (FSU)

AMPHIBIOUS

  LS • LSM 1 NS-722 (capacity 5 MBT; 110 troops)

  CRAFT 5:

    LCU 3 *Deba*

    LCM 2 *Ondatra* (FSU)

FACILITIES

Bases	Located at Aden, Hodeida
Minor Bases	These have naval spt eqpt. located at Socotra, Al-Mukalla, Perim Island

Air Force 3,000

FORCES BY ROLE

Ftr	3 sqn with F-5E *Tiger II*; MiG-29SMT/MiG-29UBT *Fulcrum*; MiG-21 *Fishbed*;
FGA	1 sqn with Su-20 (Su-17M) *Fitter C*/Su-22 (Su-17M-2) *Fitter D*
Tpt	1 sqn with An-12 *Cub*; An-26 *Curl*; C-130H *Hercules*; Il-14 *Crate*; Il-76 *Candid*
Trg	1 trg school with F-5B *Freedom Fighter*†*; L-39C; MiG-21U *Mongol A**; Yak-11; Z-242
Hel	1 sqn with Mi-35 *Hind* (attack); AB-47 (Bell 47); Mi-8 *Hip*; Bell 212

EQUIPMENT BY TYPE

AIRCRAFT 79 combat capable

  FTR 43: 16 MiG-29SMT *Fulcrum*; 2 MiG-29UBT; 10 F-5E *Tiger II*; 15 MiG-21 *Fishbed*

  FGA 30 Su-20 (Su-17M) *Fitter C* Su-17 FGA/Su-22 (Su-17M-2) *Fitter D*

  TPT 18: 2 An-12 *Cub*; 6 An-26 *Curl*; 3 C-130H *Hercules*; 4 Il-14 *Crate* 4; 3 Il-76 *Candid*

  TRG 44: 12 L-39C; 4 MiG-21U *Mongol A**; 2 F-5B *Freedom Fighter*†*; 14 Yak-11 *Moose*; 12 Z-242

HELICOPTERS

  ATK 8 Mi-35 *Hind*

  SPT 10: 1 AB-47 (Bell 47); 9 Mi-8 *Hip*

  UTL 2 Bell 212

Air Defence 2,000

AD • SAM:

  SP SA-6 *Gainful*; SA-9 *Gaskin*; SA-13 *Gopher*

  TOWED SA-2 *Guideline*; SA-3 *Goa*

  MANPAD SA-7 *Grail*; SA-14 *Gremlin*

MSL • AAM AA-2 *Atoll*; AIM-9 *Sidewinder*

Paramilitary 71,200+

Ministry of the Interior Forces 50,000

Tribal Levies 20,000+

Yemeni Coast Guard Authority ε1,200
PATROL AND COASTAL COMBATANTS 29
   PCI 5 *Interceptor* (French)
   PB 8: 4 *Defender* (US); 4 *Archangel* (US)
   PBI 16

SELECTED NON-STATE GROUPS

Government forces were active in 2009 in military operations against al-Houthi rebels in the mountainous areas north of Sa'ada. The rebel groups are believed to use a mixture of equipments, including SALW, mines and IEDs. Their strength is unknown.

DEPLOYMENT

CENTRAL AFRICAN REPUBLIC/CHAD
UN • MINURCAT 2

COTE D'IVOIRE
UN • UNOCI 1; 8 obs

DEMOCRATIC REPUBLIC OF CONGO
UN • MONUC 5 obs

LIBERIA
UN • UNMIL 1

SUDAN
UN • UNAMID 14; 12 obs
UN • UNMIS 2; 21 obs

WESTERN SAHARA
UN • MINURSO 10 obs

Table 24 **Selected arms procurements and deliveries, Middle East and North Africa**

Designation	Type	Quantity	Contract Value	Supplier Country	Prime Contractor	Order Date	First Delivery Due	Notes
Algeria (ALG)								
T-90S	MBT	300	US$1bn	RUS	Rosoboron-export	2006	–	Delivery may be delayed due to order suspension in 2008
T-72	MBT Upgrade	250	US$200m	RUS	Rosoboron-export	2006	–	Upgrade. Delivery may be delayed due to order suspension in 2008
BMP-2	IFV	400	US$200m	RUS	Rosoboron-export	2006	–	Upgrade. Delivery may be delayed due to order suspension in 2008
S-300PMU-2	AD	8	US$1bn	RUS	Rosoboron-export	2006	–	8 bty. Delivery may be delayed due to order suspension in 2008
Tunguska-M1 (SA-19) ADGMS	AD	24	US$500m	RUS	Rosoboron-export	2006	–	Option for 30 further systems. Delivery may be delayed due to order suspension in 2008
Kornet- E (AT-14)	ATGW	216	US$50m	RUS	Rosoboron-export	2006	–	Delivery may be delayed due to order suspension in 2008
Metis- M1 (AT-13)	ATGW	–	US$50m	RUS	Rosoboron-export	2006	–	Delivery may be delayed due to order suspension in 2008
FPB 98	PCF	21	€135m (US$198m)	FRA	OCEA	2008	2009	Final delivery due 2012
SU-30 MKA	FGA	28	US$1.5bn	RUS	NPK Irkut	2006	2010	Deliveries ongoing
Yak-130	Trg	16	US$200m	RUS	Rosoboron-export	2006	2009	Incl simulator. First delivery due 2010
AW101 Merlin/ AW139	Hel	100	est US$5bn	UK/Dom	Agusta Westland	2009	2010	Follow-on deal from 2007 supply of 6 AW101 *Merlin* and 4 *Super Lynx Mk 130*
Bahrain (BHR)								
M113A2	APC Upgrade	–	–	TUR	FNSS	2007	–	Refit with MKEK 81-mm mortars
Landing Craft	LC	4	–	UAE	ADSB	2008	–	Two 42m landing craft and two 16m Fast Landing Craft
Mk5 Special Ops Craft	PCF	2	–	US	USMI	–	2009	Two 25m, 57-ton tactical SOC. Delivery due late 2009
Egypt (EGY)								
M1-A1 *Abrams*	MBT	125	US$349m	US	General Dynamics	2007	2009	Co-production with Cairo plant. Final delivery due July 2011
Ambassador Mk III	PFM	3	US$393m	US	VT Halter Marine	2008	2012	Phase II of the Fast Missile Craft (FMC) project
RAM Mk49	GMLS	3	US$24.75m	US	Raytheon	2005	2009	Upgrade for Fast Missile Craft. Mk49 RAM launchers and RAM Block 1A msl. Delivery status unclear
E-2C	AEW&C Upgrade	1	US$38m	US	Northrop Grumman	2008	–	Refurbishment and upgrade to *Hawkeye* 2000 (HE2K) standard
S-125 *Pechora* (SA-3 *Goa*)	SAM	30	–	RUS	Oboron-itelniye Sistemy	1999	–	Upgrade to *Pechora*-2M. 30 bty to be ugraded in 3 stages. 1st stage completed 2006. 2nd stage ongoing
Iran (IRN)								
T-72	MBT Upgrade	–	See notes	RUS	Rosoboron-export	2005	–	Upgrade. Part of US$1.5bn procurement deal
S-300 (SA-10 *Grumble*/SA-20 *Gargoyle*)	SAM/AD	–	US$800m	RUS	–	2007	2008	RUS claims contract signed but no systems delivered by Mar 2009. Numbers, cost and exact type subject to confirmation
Su-24	FGA Upgrade	30	See notes	RUS	Rosoboron-export	2005	–	Upgrade. Part of US$1.5bn procurement deal
MiG-29	Ftr	–	See notes	RUS	Rosoboron-export	2005	–	Upgrade. Part of US$1.5bn procurement deal
Iraq (IRQ)								
M1 *Abrams*	MBT	140	US$1.4bn	US	General Dynamics	2009	2010	M1A1 SA config. 140 further M1 may be ordered

Table 24 **Selected arms procurements and deliveries, Middle East and North Africa**

Designation	Type	Quantity	Contract Value	Supplier Country	Prime Contractor	Order Date	First Delivery Due	Notes
M88A2	ARV	8	US$31.5m	US		2009	2010	
Defender-class	PBF	26	–	US	SAFE Boats	2008	2008	Part of 26-15-4-2 acquisition programme. Deliveries ongoing
Saettia-class	PB	4	US$110m	ITA	Fincantieri	2008	2009	Based on Diciotti class . Part of 26-15-4-2 acquisition programme. Final delivery due December 2009
35PB 1208E-1455	PC	9	US$181m	US	Swiftship	2009	2012	35 m PC for Navy. Up to 15 may be procured
C-130J Super Hercules	Tpt ac	4	US$292.8m	US	Lockheed Martin	2009	–	For air force. FMS contract, ISD 2011
C-130J-30	Tpt ac	2	US$140.3m	US	Lockheed Martin	2009	–	For air force. ISD 2011
King Air 350 ER	Tpt ac/ ISTAR	6	US$10.5m	US	Hawker Beechcraft	2008	2010	5 Extended Range (ER) ISR ac; 1 lt tpt ac; plus spares and spt
Hawker Beechcraft T-6A Texan II	Trg ac	7	US$170.4m	US	Hawker Beechcraft	2009	–	For air force. Signed Aug 2009, incl spt and log.
Hawker Beechcraft T-6A Texan II	Trg ac	8	US$86.6m	US	Hawker Beechcraft	2009	–	For air force. Signed 17 Aug, lower value as no spt etc needed for follow-on procurement.
EC 635	Hel	24	€360m (US$490m)	FRA	Eurocopter	2009	–	Cost incl trg and maintenance
Mi-17CT	Hel	22	US$80.6m	RUS	Aeronautical Radio Incorporated	2009	–	Prime contractor Aeronautical Radio Incorporated; Mi-17s to be supplied by Mil/ Kazan
Bell 407	Hel	24	US$60.3m	US	Bell	2009	–	For air force. FMS contract
Israel (ISR)								
Merkava Mk IV	MBT	up to 400	–	Dom	–	2001	2004	Estimated 50-60 tk per year over four year. Delivery status unclear
Arrow 2	ATBM/ BMD	–	Undisclosed	Dom/US	IAI	2008	–	Number and cost undisclosed. In trials by 2009
Dolphin (Type 800) class	SSK	2	€1bn (US$1.21bn)	GER	HDW	2006	2012	With Air-Independent Propulsion (AIP) system
Super Dvora MKIII	PFI	4	–	Dom	IAI/Ramta	2005	–	Phase II of navy patrol fleet modernisation programme
Shaldag MkII	PFI	3	–	Dom	IAI/Ramta	2005	–	Phase II of navy patrol fleet modernisation programme
F-16I Sufa	FGA	102	–	US	Lockheed Martin	2001	2006	Deliveries ongoing
Skylark I-LE	UAV	100		Dom	Elbit Systems	2008	–	Part of Sky Rider programme
AIM-120C-7	AAM	200	US$171m	US	Raytheon	2007	–	
Joint Direct Attack Munitions (JDAM)	ASM	5,000	–	US	Boeing	2004	–	Deliveries ongoing
Jordan (JOR)								
IL-76MF (Candid)	Tpt ac	2	–	RUS	Rosoboron-export	2005	2007	2 delivered. Option for further 2 ac
F-16A/B Block 15	Ftr Upgrade	17	US$87m	TUR	Lockheed Martin	2005	2007	MLU. Deliveries ongoing
Kuwait (KWT)								
Aspide	AD Upgrade	–	€65m (US$87.3m)	Int'l	MBDA	2007	–	Upgrade to Spada 2000 config. To be completed over 3 years
MK V	PFB	12	US$175m	US	USMI	2006	2007	First vessel delivered May 2008. Final delivery due 2009. Derlivery status unclear
MK V	PFB	10	US$61m	US	USMI	2009	–	For Navy. Final del due 2013

Table 24 **Selected arms procurements and deliveries, Middle East and North Africa**

Designation	Type	Quantity	Contract Value	Supplier Country	Prime Contractor	Order Date	First Delivery Due	Notes
Lebanon (LBN)								
MiG-29 *Fulcrum*	FGA	10	Free transfer	RUS	–	2008	2009	To be modernised 'to export standards.' Delivery status unclear
Libya (LBY)								
T-72	MBT Upgrade	–	–	RUS	–	2009	–	Reportedly part of a cancellation of a US$4.5 billion debt to RF. More than 145. Upgrade of previously supplied MBTs. Upgrade may also include T-62, T-55, and T-54 fleet
T-90S	MBT	48	–	RUS	–	2008	–	Part of a cancellation of a US$4.5 billion debt to RUS
Morocco (MOR)								
FREMM	FF	1	€470m (US$676m)	FRA/ITA	DCNS	2008	2012	–
SIGMA	FFH	3	€600m (US$875m)	NLD	Schelde	2008	2011	(Ship Integrated Geometrical Modularity Approach) Final delivery due 2012
F-16C/D Block 52	FGA	24	US$233.6m	US	Lockheed Martin	2008	–	Incl mission equipment and spt package
C-27J	Tpt ac	4	€130m (US$166m)	ITA	Alenia Aeronautica	2008	2010	Deliveries due 2010-11
Oman (OMN)								
Project *Khareef*	PSOH	3	GBP400m (US$785m)	UK	VT Ship-building	2007	2010	First vessel launched July 2009
A320	Tpt ac	2	–	FRA/ITA	EADS	2007	–	
C-130J-30 *Hercules*	Tpt ac	1	–	US	Lockheed Martin	2009	2012	
NH-90 TTH	Hel	20	–	NLD	EADS	2003	2008	First flight May 2007
Qatar (QTR)								
C-130J-30 *Hercules*	Tpt ac	4	US$393.6m	US	Lockheed Martin	2008	2011	Contract value incl additional packages.
AW139	Tpt hel	18	€260m (US$413m)	ITA	Agusta-Westland	2008	2010	For air force
Saudi Arabia (SAU)								
M113	APC Upgrade	300	US$200m	TUR	FNSS	2007	2008	Upgrade. Follow-on contract could lead to upgrade of entire fleet of 2,000 M113. Delivery status unclear
Eurofighter (*Typhoon*)	FGA	72	GBP4.43bn (US$8.9bn)	Int'l	Eurofighter	2005	2008	Project Salam. Forty-eight ac to be assembled in SAU. First delivered June 2009
A330 MRTT	Tkr	6	US$600m	FRA	EADS	2008	2011	3 more purchased July 2009 for undisclosed fee. First delivery expected 2011
E-3A *Sentry*	AWACS Upgrade	5	US$16m	US	Data Link Solutions	2006	–	Comms upgrade. Link 16 MIDS
UH-60L *Black Hawk*	Hel	–	US$286 m	US	Sikorsky	2008	2010	Number undisclosed
AIM-9X *Sidewinder*	AAM	250	US$164m	US	Raytheon	2009	–	For F-15. Number and value undisclosed. FMS request was for 250 AIM-9X *Sidewinder* short-range AAM, 84 AIM-9X captive air trg msl 12 AIM-9X dummy air trg msl
AN/AAQ-33 *Sniper*	ATP	–	–	US	Lockheed Martin	2009	–	FMS contract. Part of US$100m contract to replace LANTIRN pods used by RSAF F-15S
Syria (SYR)								
Buk-M2	SAM	–	US$200m	RUS	Rosoboron-export	2007	2008	Delivery status unclear
96K6 *Pantsyr*-S1E (SA-22 *Greyhound*)	AD	50	US$730m	RUS	Rosoboron-export	–	2007	Delivery status unclear

Table 24 **Selected arms procurements and deliveries, Middle East and North Africa**

Designation	Type	Quantity	Contract Value	Supplier Country	Prime Contractor	Order Date	First Delivery Due	Notes
9M133 *Kornet/* 9M131*Metis* 2	Msl	–	US$73m	RUS	Rosoboron-export	2003	–	Several thousand msl
United Arab Emirates (UAE)								
Fuchs 2 NBC-RS	APC	32	€160m (US$205m)	GER	Rheinmetall	2005	2007	16 NBC recce vehicles, 8 BW detection vehicles, 8 mobile CP vehicles. Deliveries ongoing
Patria 8x8	APC	–	–	FIN	Patria	2008	–	Contract value and number of units not declared
Nimr 4x4	HMTV	500	US$41m	Dom	Advanced Industries of Arabia	2005	2005	High mobility tactical vehicles. Delivery status unclear
Patriot Advanced Capability (PAC) 3	AD System	10 fire units, 172 msl	US$3.3bn	US	Raytheon	2008	2009	To replace *HAWK*. Incl 172 Lockheed Martin PAC-3 msl and 42 launcher mod packs, plus some GEM-T msl. Final delivery due 2012
96K6 *Pantsir-S1E*	AD	50	US$734m	RUS	Rosoboron-export	2000	2004	To be mounted on MAN SX 45 8x8 trucks. First 4 delivered March 2009. Final delivery due 2012
Agrab (Scorpion) 120mm MMS	Mor	48	AED390m (US$106m)	UK/SGP RSA/Dom	IGG	2007	2008	Delivery status unclear
Javelin	MANPAT	100	(US$135m)	US	Raytheon/ Lockheed Martin	2008	2009	1,000 msl
Baynunah	FSG	6	AED3bn (US$820m)	Dom/FRA	ADSB	2003	2006	First of class built in FRA, others to be built in UAE. First in-service date due 2009. First launched June 2009
Commandante Class	ASW FS	2	AED430m (US$117m)	ITA	Fincantieri	2009	2011	
Abu Dahbi Class	FS	1	–	ITA	Fincantieri	2009	2011	
Project *Al Saber*	PB	12	AED127m (US$34.6m)	Dom	ADSB	2008	–	For Coast Guard
C-130 J-30 *Hercules*	Tpt ac	12	AED5.9bn	US	Lockheed Martin	2009	2013	–
A330 MRTT	Tkr ac	3	–	Int'l	EADS	2008	2011	Order for 3 more possible
AB-139	Hel	8	UK£83m (US$143m)	US/ITA	Agusta-Westland	2005	2005	6 SAR, 2 VIP. Delivery status unclear
AH-64D *Apache Longbow*	Hel Upgrade	30		US	Boeing	2007	–	Upgrade from AH-64A to D standard
Yemen, Republic of (YEM)								
T-72 and T-80	MBT	–	–	RUS	Rosoboron-export	2009		
MiG-29 SMT *Fulcrum*	FGA	32	US$1.3bn	RUS	Rosoboron-export	2006	–	
MiG-29	FGA	66	US$1bn	RUS	Rosoboron-export	2006	2007	Incl repair contract in first quarter of 2007. Delivery status unclear

Chapter Six
Sub-Saharan Africa

The strategic importance of sub-Saharan Africa is rising gradually. Its oil and gas reserves, though insufficient to dislodge broad dependence on Middle East supplies, are substantial enough to warrant global concern about potential sources of their insecurity or inaccessibility, which include the activities of militia groups like the Movement for the Emancipation of the Niger Delta (MEND) in Nigeria, internal political instability in key oil-producing countries and competing major-power customers. These include, in particular, the United States and China; the latter's geostrategic priorities are exemplified by its increasingly close bilateral security and economic relationship with Angola (sub-Saharan Africa's second-largest oil producer after Nigeria, which sells 44% of its exported oil to the United States). China is now sub-Saharan Africa's third largest trading partner after the United States and the EU, and gaining. Beijing also has a growing foreign-assistance programme on the continent (see Defence Economics, p. 289 and the IISS *Adelphi* book *China's African Challenges*). Meanwhile, Somalia is becoming an increasingly popular destination for aspiring jihadists in search of training, with similar fears expressed for Yemen and the Maghreb.

Despite the ambitious agenda of the African Union (AU) and its active efforts to enhance its diplomatic and military capabilities, African nations still lack the capacity to deal with many of the difficult and substantial political and security challenges their continent faces, although there are encouraging signs on the structural level, such as the establishment of the African Standby Force (ASF). The continent is host to half of the United Nations' global peacekeeping operations. One promising development, however, has been heightened cross-border military cooperation. The Democratic Republic of the Congo (DRC) restored full diplomatic ties with Rwanda and Uganda in the summer of 2009; their rapprochement had already facilitated Rwanda's capture of renegade militia leader Laurent Nkunda in January 2009. Also, with help from the Central African Republic (CAR), Ugandan forces pursued Lord's Resistance Army (LRA) rebels into Congolese and CAR territory leading to their effective expulsion from northern Uganda. Then, from December 2008 to March 2009, Congolese, south Sudanese and Ugandan forces pressed an offensive against the LRA. While the LRA is a diminished force, starting in May 2009 it set about raiding villages in northeast Congo, southern Sudan and the CAR, burning property, taking hostages, and stealing crops and livestock.

SUDAN

The January 2005 Comprehensive Peace Agreement (CPA) has become increasingly fragile. As detailed in *The Military Balance 2009*, pp. 277–8, the Sudan People's Liberation Army/Movement (SPLA/M) withdrew from the agreement in October 2007, though the gravest threat to the CPA arose a month later when clashes began in the disputed oil-rich Abyei region. 50,000 people were displaced by May 2008, and hundreds were killed, with UN Mission in Sudan (UNMIS) forces unable to protect civilians against a 16,000-strong force of Khartoum-backed militias.

In July 2009, after a judgement by the Permanent Court of Arbitration in The Hague, the North was awarded the Bamboo and Heglig oilfields, the railway town of Meiram and a strip of grazing land, while the South was allowed to retain the high-production Diffra oilfield and more grazing area than the North preferred. The ruling brings greater legal certainty and an ostensibly equitable compromise, but tension could still arise over: the SPLA/M's loss of the Heglig, Bamboo and other oilfields (especially given that the Diffra field's output is falling); the government's loss of grazing areas; the northern Misseriya nomads' protests over a possible restriction of grazing rights; and the theoretical bar on those living near Meiram from voting in the referendum on independence in 2011. The only mandated security forces in Abyei are Joint Integrated Units (JIUs) composed of government and SPLA/M military forces, and Joint Integrated Police Units. But in July 2009 the UN Secretary-General's Special Representative for Sudan, Ashraf

Qazi, indicated that ongoing insecurity as well as tensions among JIUs themselves meant that UNMIS must have full freedom of movement in the Abyei region. The greatest source of uncertainty in North–South relations in Sudan remains whether the South will vote for independence in 2011 and, if so, whether Khartoum will acquiesce. If not, it remains to be seen how the outside powers – in particular, the US, which as the principal broker of the CPA has a substantial stake in it – will respond.

The other major area of crisis in Sudan is Darfur, where conflict continued among armed opposition factions, the Sudanese armed forces, government-backed militias and ethnic groups, displacing some 2.7 million people. Between January and mid May 2009, violence uprooted another 137,000. Although the security situation marginally improved in 2009, it remained poor overall. In August, the UN–AU Mission in Darfur (UNAMID) received 124 additional police officers from Tanzania, the Philippines and Cameroon. This increase, to at that time over 2,000 police officers, enabled UNAMID to increase police patrols throughout Darfur. Meanwhile, the military component also increased modestly during the year, including new contributions from Tanzania and Burkina Faso, as well as additions from Senegal and South Africa. However, at time of writing, UNAMID's total military and police forces stood at around 75% of their mandated strength of 26,000.

Insecurity in Sudan has continued to affect the security of neighbouring Chad, where about 250,000 of 500,000 refugees and internally displaced persons are from Darfur and the CAR. The European Union peacekeeping force (EUFOR), which deployed around 3,300 troops in eastern Chad and northern CAR to protect displaced civilians and assist in operations in support of UNAMID, ended its mission in March 2009 and transferred operational responsibility to a strengthened UN Mission in the CAR and Chad (MINURCAT). But MINURCAT is underfunded, and attacks by rebels seeking to overthrow Chad's government have challenged the force's mandated political neutrality.

THE AFRICAN STANDBY FORCE

As noted in recent editions of *The Military Balance*, the ASF is the AU's prescribed instrument for eventually meeting the military demands of the continent, with five regional brigades planned of roughly 6,500 soldiers in each. The 'Policy Framework for the Establishment of the ASF' sets out six scenarios as contingency-planning guidelines for the five regional brigades:

- **Scenario one**: AU/regional military advice to a political mission.
- **Scenario two**: AU/regional observer mission co-deployed with UN mission.
- **Scenario three**: Stand-alone AU/regional observer mission.
- **Scenario four**: AU/regional peacekeeping force for preventive deployment missions and those mandated under Chapter VI of the UN Charter.
- **Scenario five**: AU peacekeeping force for complex multidimensional peacekeeping mission, including low-level spoilers (a feature of many current conflicts).
- **Scenario six**: AU intervention – e.g. genocide situations where the international community does not act promptly.

For the ASF, 2010 is an important year. According to the AU's African Peace and Security Architecture (APSA) roadmap of 2005, by then the ASF must be ready to implement all of the conflict and missions scenarios, but especially scenario six. The roadmap set out a phased implementation plan for the ASF to build capacity as follows:

- **Phase 1 (completed by 30 June 2006):**
  - **AU:** Expanded planning elements for management of a political mission and co-deployed AU observer mission, deployable within 30 days (scenarios one and two). Establish military observers and civilian police standby rosters.
  - **Regions:** Planning elements, brigade headquarters, regional standby arrangements; Chapter VI operation and preventive deployment, deployable within 30 days (scenario four). (Implementation of these arrangements did not always go according to plan and the regional forces selectively implemented according to practicality. Nonetheless, these elements do exist in all the brigades in one form or another).

- **Phase 2 (to be completed by 30 June 2010):**
  - **AU:** Ability to manage complex missions. Development of civilian roster.

○ **Regions:** Deployment of mission HQ for Chapter VI and preventive deployment within 30 days.

The focus of the regional brigades in the first half of 2010 will be in ensuring that they are operationally ready for deployment if needed to execute any of the six scenarios above.

The five regional brigades planned and held various exercises during 2009 in anticipation of the AU's *Exercise Amani Africa,* planned for 2010, and which will test their readiness to implement the conflict and missions scenarios. The West Africa ASF has already completed two exercises, while the East Africa ASF is planning one for late 2009 or early 2010. The East and West Africa ASF exercises are supported by European and US funding, equipment and advisers.

The South African Development Community Standby Brigade (SADCBRIG) recently held *Exercise Golfinho* in South Africa. The September 2009 field-training exercise, involving 7,000 troops from 12 countries, was preceded by a map exercise in Angola in January 2009 and a command post exercise in Mozambique in April 2009. In an effort to prove its own operational competence, the SADC made a deliberate decision not to draw on external support for the planning and execution of *Exercise Golfinho,* which was instead a locally driven exercise from the scenario-generation stage onwards.

Tackling the two most difficult situations – a scenario-six intervention mandated by Chapter VII of the UN Charter and a scenario-five multidimensional peacekeeping operation – *Golfinho* involved the joint deployment of military police and civilian components. It also tested force interoperability; meanwhile the issue of strategic lift was overcome by using multiple modes of transport (air, road, rail and sea) to assemble the force. Portuguese-, French- and English-speaking troops were dispersed throughout the formations, with each of the battalions composed of as many countries as possible (other regional standby forces have tried this tactic with mixed success). SADCBRIG deemed the exercise a success saying that all objectives were met, lessons were learned and shortcomings were identified. After the exercise, SADCBRIG declared that it could deploy to anywhere in Africa or even beyond, provided that the strategic lift is available and logistical support can be sustained. Indeed, the biggest challenge for the APSA is not how to intervene in complex emergencies, but how to equip, fund and sustain such interventions.

The situation faced by the AU Mission in Somalia (AMISOM) is an example of the type of contingency that the ASF brigades should be able to address, and exposes the amount of work that remains to be done by the regional brigades before their 2010 readiness deadline. Since its establishment in June 2002, AMISOM has consisted of a lead nation assisted by other contributing nations; in contrast to the ASF concept. The AU has learned lessons from these deployments and hopes to address them through a serious of regional-level exercises culminating in *Exercise Amani*. But unlike the SADCBRIG *Exercise Golfinho,* the AU is already using international support to plan and execute *Amani Africa*.

TERRORISM IN SUB-SAHARAN AFRICA

Following counter-terrorism operations by US and Pakistani forces in Afghanistan and Pakistan, as well as similar efforts by Saudi Arabia, there has been some movement of al-Qaeda operatives into Yemen, where al-Qaeda in the Arabian Peninsula appears to have relocated. Yemen's security forces are facing substantial difficulties in combating the threats posed by insurgents, as well as al-Qaeda, but if they can respond effectively, jihadist migration could shift towards Somalia.

Though some Somali Islamists seem to harbour relatively little rancour for the internationally recognised and essentially secular Transitional Federal Government (TFG) – particularly after the TFG's change of leadership – the administration remains beleaguered (see IISS *Strategic Survey 2009*, p. 279). The TFG was reformed through greater Islamist representation but, nonetheless, militant Islamism has intensified with the rise of the rejectionist terrorist groups al-Shabaab (the youth), which is tied to al-Qaeda, and Hizbul Islam. In addition to staging terrorist operations against the TFG throughout Somalia, al-Shabaab retaliated against a September 2009 US military operation in Somalia that killed Saleh Ali Saleh Nabhan – one of the most-wanted al-Qaeda members in Africa, linked to the 1998 embassy bombings in Tanzania and Kenya, and the 2002 hotel attack in Kenya – by attacking AU peacekeepers in Mogadishu, and has recruited operatives from the Somali diaspora in North America. Meanwhile, the activity of al-Qaeda in the Islamic Maghreb (AQIM) continued in 2009. The group has focused mainly on Algerian security forces, with one attack in summer 2009 killing about 30; in May they also killed a British hostage.

SOMALIA

Ethiopia's expeditious US-backed suppression in 2006–07 of the grassroots Islamic Courts Union and support of the TFG tamped down the terrorist threat in the short term, but after the withdrawal of most of Ethiopia's forces in early 2009, the Islamists, with broad but clandestine support from Eritrea, have re-emerged. In May and September 2009, the AU and the Inter-governmental Authority for Development called for UN sanctions against Eritrea. Meanwhile, Ethiopia dispatched perhaps hundreds of troops, reportedly with tacit US approval, to thwart Islamist takeovers of Somali towns near the Ethiopian border – in particular, Beledweyne, which in August 2009 had been overrun by Hizbul Islam militiamen – but denied any intent to re-occupy the country. In any case, an Ethiopian re-occupation would risk repeating the counter-productive dynamic that fuelled the rejuvenation of the Somali Islamist movement. At the same time, even at its full strength of 8,000 troops, the AMISOM peacekeeping force appears to have little chance of controlling a factionalised, heavily armed Somali population. The deployment as of September 2009 of about 5,000 Ugandan and Burundian soldiers has improved AMISOM's efforts to protect the TFG and in September 2009 it was given a more muscular mandate for peace enforcement, but it remains too small and underequipped to be truly effective.

Meanwhile, burgeoning and increasingly bold attacks over the last two years by Somali pirates in the Indian Ocean and the Gulf of Aden on commercial vessels carrying vital cargo such as oil, food and weapons – enabled by the absence of the rule of law on the ground – have transformed Somali piracy from a mere nuisance into something approaching a strategic challenge. In October 2008 NATO launched *Operation Ocean Shield*, assigning warships from a standing naval group for close protection and deterrence patrols, and in December 2008 the EU launched *Operation Atalanta*, the EU's first naval mission, designed to combat piracy and escort ships for the World Food Programme. Then, in January 2009, US Navy maritime surface and air assets assigned to US Central Command (CENTCOM) assumed the main elements of the new Combined Task Force 151, patrolling the Gulf of Aden and the Indian Ocean, and tasked with an anti-piracy brief (the existing CTF-150 was created primarily for counter-terrorism purposes). Other national navies (including those of India, Japan, Malaysia and Russia) commercially

affected by Somali piracy have also engaged in patrols.

Despite the often dramatic and successful interdictions that have taken place, even modern blue-water navies cannot identify and target all of the small pirate vessels operating in vast expanses of water. Thus, the deterrent effect of this surge has been ambiguous at best. By September 2009, the number of Somali pirate attacks had outstripped the total for 2008. As well as maritime assets, the contributing nations have also deployed surveillance assets in the form of helicopters and fixed-wing aircraft while in autumn 2009, in a bid to boost surveillance coverage, the US added the high-altitude, high-speed *Reaper* unmanned aerial vehicle (with over 14 hours' loiter time and a range of 3,000 nautical miles) to its anti-piracy arsenal. Meanwhile, ties have been forged with the nascent coastguard forces in the area: NATO has started to develop relations with the coastguard operating out of Puntland; and the EU has expressed interest in training coastguards in Somalia itself. A greater appreciation has also been made of Somaliland's coastguard forces.

Piracy is unlikely to abate appreciably until young Somali men are provided with viable economic alternatives, and until Somalia has state security forces willing and able to counter those who choose piracy anyway. Persistent political instability in Somalia also poses significant threats to Western interests: it is a source of and inspiration for transnational jihadist terrorism, and the potential site for a proxy war between Ethiopia and Eritrea. A narrow set of counter-terrorism measures, consisting of military containment in addition to covert support for pro-Western factions, has not substantially mitigated these threats. Given the political liabilities that intervention in a Muslim country would entail, and the disenchanting US experience of 1992–94, any overt major-power military involvement would be very unlikely even if the resources were available. By default, outside diplomatic engagement is needed.

OTHER DEVELOPMENTS

Established in the wake of 'Africa's great war', which drew in the **Democratic Republic of the Congo**'s eight neighbouring countries, the UN Organisation Mission in the DRC (MONUC) is still the largest peacekeeping force in the world, with almost 19,000 uniformed personnel – nearly its full authorised strength – and an annual budget of US$1.35 billion. Notwithstanding the adoption of a new constitution (in

December 2005) and the democratic election of Joseph Kabila as president (in October 2006), rebel activity – particularly in the eastern part of the country – has prevented sustainable peace and stability from taking hold. But heightened cooperation between the DRC and Rwanda led to a joint operation in January 2009, which included MONUC and was aimed at disarming Rwandan Hutu fighters in the DRC. The operation left the fighters' command weakened and culminated in the arrest of Laurent Nkunda, the maverick general who claimed to be protecting the Tutsi minority from the Hutu rebels. However, the heightened military activity increased insecurity, with further reports of internal displacement and rape, with some abuses allegedly committed by Congolese national forces. Accordingly, MONUC's near-term focus is likely to be on improving its population-protection capabilities as part of an overall emphasis on peacekeeping and security-sector reform in the east, while concentrating on development in the less problematic western part of the country. The DRC government's intention, announced in September 2009, that MONUC should withdraw by 2011 appears unrealistic.

Nigeria's autumn 2008 offensive against MEND – the largest of several linked militant groups angered by the government's perceived unfair distribution of oil wealth in the Niger Delta – resulted in reduced rebel activity against oil-producing entities in summer 2009, despite threatening rhetoric from the rebels. On 15 July, Nigerian President Umaru Yar'Adua declared a 60-day amnesty, also promising to improve the lives of poor Nigerians living in the region. By late September 2009, of the estimated 12–15,000 rebels only a few hundred had handed in their weapons – far short of the 8–10,000 that the government had hoped would relent – with MEND leaders declaring that the government could not be trusted. In early October, while the government declared the amnesty a 'monumental success', stating that some 8,299 militants had relinquished their weapons and citing MEND leader Government Ekpemupolo's agreement to give up his militia's weapons, other MEND leaders vowed to resume attacks as a 90-day ceasefire of their own expired on 15 October.

Analysts have pointed to possible acquisitions, by Nigeria, of several military systems that could assist in prosecuting operations against militia groups, with reported purchases including two *Shaldag* MK-2 armed patrol boats, as well as air and sea unmanned vehicles and an accompanying surveillance system. Further deals reportedly include 20 troop-carrying catamarans designed for the kind of riverine operations that counter-insurgency efforts in the Niger Delta could require, two 38-metre *Manta*-class patrol boats, another four 17m *Mantas* and 35 armed fast-patrol boats. The Nigerian air force also bought from Russia at least 15 Mi-24, Mi-34, and Mi-35 helicopter gunships and support transport helicopters. Insofar as these purchases signify a broadly coercive government approach to security problems, they could be a portent of rising tensions throughout the country. The government's repression of Boko Haram, an Islamist extremist group in the north, and especially the death of its leader, Sheikh Muhammad Yusuf, in May 2009 while in police custody, served to alienate many moderate Muslims who had previously supported the government.

In August 2009, the Eritrea–Ethiopia Claims Commission, housed at the Permanent Court of Arbitration in The Hague, awarded **Ethiopia** US$174m and **Eritrea** a little more than US$161m for damages occurring during the 1998–2000 war, meaning that Eritrea owes Ethiopia about US$12.5m. Eritrea said it would 'abide' by the decision, while Ethiopia said its damages award was insufficient. The border between the two countries, however, is still in dispute and tens of thousands of troops remain deployed along its length, though each side appears to favour diplomacy over war as a means of resolving the issue. The AU is keenly aware of the importance of the dispute, which its chairman Muammar Gadhafi characterised as a 'time bomb' at the AU special summit in August 2009.

Tensions over the border conflict between **Eritrea** and **Djibouti** – in which about 35 soldiers were killed and dozens more wounded in June 2008 – have continued. In January 2009, the UN Security Council passed Resolution 1862, demanding that Eritrea withdraw its troops from the border, but Asmara has been reluctant to do so. Djibouti, which is 60% ethnic Somali, hosts US and French military bases and supports their efforts to combat terrorism and extremism in the region, but the Djiboutian government perceives a slowly rising threat from al-Shabaab, the Somali militant Islamist group that has demonstrated some transnational ambitions. In addition, the Front pour la Restauration de l'Unité et de la Démocratie, an ethnic Afar insurgency that was believed to have been subdued by virtue of a 2001 peace treaty, appears dissatisfied with the treaty's implementation and engaged government troops in September 2009.

Notable security developments took place in three West African countries. In **Côte d'Ivoire**, after many postponements, elections were scheduled for 29 November 2009. It is hoped that they will consolidate the process of political reconciliation and mark the end of the civil war. During the run-up to the election, the government was seeking to disarm 18,500 combatants and integrate 5,000 rebels into the national army. In July 2009, the UN Security Council extended the mandate of UN Operations in Côte d'Ivoire until 31 January 2010. As improvements continued in **Liberia**'s stability and governance, in September 2009 the UN Security Council, while extending the mandate of the UN Mission in Liberia (UNMIL) to 30 September 2010, endorsed the continuation of a phased withdrawal involving 2,029 troops, which would bring the UNMIL deployment down to 8,202 soldiers. In **Guinea-Bissau**, President João Bernardo Vieira and army chief Batista Tagme Na Waie were assassinated in March 2009 and replaced by interim head of state Raimundo Pereira. Following a general election in June, on 26 July Malam Bacai Sanha won a presidential run-off with 63% of the vote, vowing at his inauguration to continue to combat government corruption and the country's burgeoning narco-trafficking industry. While many European observers regarded the assassinations as evidence of the failure of the EU's security-sector reform mission aimed at downsizing and restructuring the country's security forces, others were encouraged by the relatively smooth electoral process and saw new opportunities for reform. In May, the EU mission was extended six months beyond its initial expiry date of 31 May 2009 'to further explore the capacity and the commitment of the new government to carry forward the reform process and to assess the willingness of the international community to support it'.

UNITED STATES' STRATEGIC POSTURE

The US has two main priorities in its treatment of Africa's strategic importance: counter-terrorism and energy security. Regional stability, democratic development, fighting HIV/AIDS, economic reform, good governance and humanitarian assistance are considered as subsidiary objectives that can also serve these two core interests. Fortunately, these priorities complement those of individual African nations, which are: conflict resolution/peacekeeping; sustainable development; debt relief; improved terms of trade; increased foreign direct investment; health and education; and good governance

US agencies are also aware of the need to adopt a non-traditional security paradigm that embraces the following elements: the integration of Africa into a global security community; a developmental approach to security; cooperative security arrangements; diplomatic efforts towards resolving long-standing conflicts; and maximum use of American 'soft power'.

Africa Command (AFRICOM), the new US combatant command, was officially inaugurated in October 2008. With its headquarters in Stuttgart, Germany, its physical presence on the African continent will be relatively small. But its budget, about US$310m in FY2009, is rising incrementally. The Obama administration's proposed FY2010 budget requests some US$300m for AFRICOM's operation and maintenance, another US$263m to provide additional personnel, airlift and communications support, and a total of US$451m to replace or upgrade facilities at long-term CENTCOM and AFRICOM locations. While African governments and populations remain worried about American hegemony and the 'militarisation' of US Africa policy, AFRICOM's stated priorities are couched in interagency terms, stressing war prevention over war fighting, long-term capacity building, and African ownership and responsibility, with an emphasis on creating stability on the continent.

One of AFRICOM's principal instruments remains the US Navy's Africa Partnership Station (APS), consisting mainly of several US Navy ships, which completed its first six-month tour of Gulf of Guinea ports in April 2008 (see *The Military Balance 2009*, p. 280). Eventually, as bilateral security cooperation in other regions of Africa grows and the APS concept and its implementation are refined in the Gulf of Guinea, wider continental deployment may be considered. In 2008–09, the APS did make port visits and conduct limited operations in southern Africa and East Africa. At present, AFRICOM has one principal military ground asset in the form of the 2,300-strong Combined Joint Task Force–Horn of Africa (CJTF–HOA), also under US Navy command, based at Camp Lemonier in Djibouti. US Air Forces Africa (based in Germany) have meanwhile developed programmes to bolster air safety on the continent, with a team at one stage evaluating Nigeria's mainly non-airworthy C-130s for possible repair. The US and its partners also provide considerable training, technical and financial support to cooperative governments in East Africa and the Horn (under the East Africa Counterterrorism Initiative) and predominantly Muslim Chad, Mali, Mauritania and Niger in north-central Africa (under the Trans-Sahara Counterterrorism Initiative), as well as helping to coordinate the AU's nascent ASF training and exercises – as exemplified by AFRICOM's 29-nation *Africa Endeavor* inter-operability programme and its bi-annual *Natural Fire* humanitarian relief joint exercise in East Africa.

Although it has operational capabilities, AFRICOM's primary function so far has been diplomatic, from the APS to CJTF-HOA's civil-affairs programmes in East Africa and the Horn, and to efforts to build the command and training infrastructure required to support the ASF and mount multilateral military efforts. Indications of a stronger Bureau of African Affairs under new US Assistant Secretary of State Johnnie Carson also suggest marginally greater prospective US engagement in Africa. But President Obama's July 2009 speech in Ghana did hedge against an extensive American commitment with its message that 'Africa's future is up to Africans'.

SUB-SAHARAN AFRICA – DEFENCE ECONOMICS

Following an eight-year period during which sub-Saharan Africa had enjoyed its best phase of economic growth since the early 1970s, three negative factors converged during 2009 that resulted in GDP growth falling to just 2% compared to 5.2% in 2008 and 6.2% in 2007. The main shock to buffet the continent was the significant deterioration in external demand resulting from the global slowdown. Secondly, the sharp fall in commodity prices (of around 50%) had a particularly negative impact on resource-rich countries in the region (Angola and Equatorial Guinea). And lastly, poor global credit conditions led to a significant decline in Foreign Direct Investment (FDI) and portfolio flows to emerging and frontier markets (Ghana, Kenya, Nigeria and South Africa). Not surprisingly, in the face of dramatically reduced commodity-based revenues the overall fiscal position of many countries, notably Angola, Republic of Congo, Equatorial Guinea and Nigeria, deteriorated significantly and in its 2009 Finance and Development Report the IMF warned that the emergence of budget deficits poses an immediate threat to the macroeconomic stability that years of economic reform have helped to establish.

The history of growth in Africa over the last 30 years has been characterised by episodic growth phases followed by prolonged decline, usually as a result of commodity booms and busts, but for the first time in many years the region's current economic difficulties are largely the result of external factors. Highlighting the sudden deterioration in sub-Saharan economies, the African Development Bank has calculated that to return to pre-crisis growth rates the region would need US$50bn to finance the gap between investments and savings. Furthermore, to meet the Millennium Development Goals that financing gap widens to US$117bn.

Though the IMF suggested that regional growth may pick up during 2010, it also notes that the risks to this forecast are firmly tilted to the downside, identifying the main danger as a deeper and more protracted global slump which would lead to lower export demand for African goods, falling revenues from tourism and a continued deterioration in FDI and portfolio flows.

China's enormous political and economic influence in the region continues to grow and it has quickly become one of Africa's most important trading partners, foreign investors and providers of foreign aid. Trade between the two has grown by more than 30% a year during the last decade and in 2008 reached over US$100bn, a level that had not been expected to occur until 2010. This means that China is now the region's third-largest trading partner behind the EU and US. However, the trading relationship continues to be unequally distributed throughout the continent – in 2008, for example, Angola accounted for 25% of Sino-African trade, while in the same year 16 countries (including Uganda, Tanzania and Ethiopia) actually experienced a drop in exports. To date, the bulk of Sino-African trade has centred on energy products, with crude oil being by far the most important commodity. The involvement of China's national oil companies continues to grow with new exploration projects such as the investment in Sudan's Unity oilfields. The importance of other commodities such as wood, cotton and iron is also growing steadily. For instance, in 2008 China and the DRC closed a large deal covering copper and cobalt extraction.

Most of the arrangements between the two blocs are structured as basic resources-for-infrastructure agreements: in return for African commodities, China makes significant investments in large infrastructure projects such as the repair of transport links and the construction of schools, hospitals, hydroelectric dams and prestigious government buildings. However, while such deals remain central to bilateral business relationships, activities in other sectors are rapidly emerging: most notably in agriculture, telecommunications, IT and satellite broadcasting, as well as financial services. The Industrial and Commercial Bank of China, for example, holds a 20% stake in South Africa's Standard Bank, which operates in 18 sub-Saharan countries.

While the global recession will undoubtedly dent Sino-African economic growth, its longer-term impact is likely to be muted. Even under normal circumstances, the growth in bilateral trade was unlikely to have been sustainable and a slower pace of growth would surely have emerged. That said, economic relations between the two are now robust and in the medium term Chinese demand for African resources will receive a boost from Beijing's strong fiscal stimulus package, while China's relative liquidity is likely to increase the importance of Chinese institutions as providers of loans to African governments.

The **South African** economy, for several years an engine of growth in the region, has been particularly badly hit by the global recession. Despite buoyant investment associated with the 2010 World Cup, the economy contracted by 0.9% in 2009 as significant capital outflows led to a sharp adjustment in asset prices and economic activity in general, while

the loss of tax revenue resulted in a deteriorating government budget position. That said, having reduced total debt from 36% of GDP in 2004 to just 28% of GDP in 2008 the government retains some fiscal flexibility.

Despite the challenging economic environment, the government announced an increase in the headline defence budget for 2009 of 15.4%, up from R27.7bn in 2008 to R32bn in 2009 (later trimmed to R31.3bn). However, with inflation running at over 10%, the real-terms increase in defence spending is much more modest. In recent years inflation has taken a heavy toll on successively higher defence outlays, which has prompted calls for the defence budget to be fixed at a certain level of national income, particularly in light of the increasing domestic and international responsibilities being assumed by the South African National Defence Force (SANDF). In recent years SANDF personnel have been deployed on peacekeeping and reconstruction tasks in Burundi, Côte d'Ivoire, the DRC, Ethiopia, Eritrea, Nepal and Sudan, while other contingents have undertaken election-support duties in Comoros, the DRC, Madagascar and Lesotho.

In consideration of the increasing roles undertaken by the SANDF and the negative impact of inflation on the budget, in March 2009 the parliamentary Joint Standing Committee (JSC) on defence warned that on present budget trends the country's armed forces were in a 'downward spiral' and could become 'inadequate to fulfil their constitutional mandate'. In a scathing report the committee said that the SANDF had arrived at a 'cross-roads' at

Table 25 **Sub-Saharan Africa Regional Defence Expenditure** as % of GDP

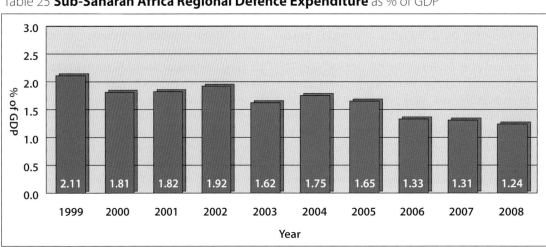

Table 26 **South African Defence Budget by Programme, 2005–2011**

Rand m	2005	2006	2007	Revised 2008	Budget 2009	Revised Budget 2009	Budget 2010	Budget 2011
Administration	1,869	2,012	2,153	2,459	2,860	2,880	3,142	3,505
Landward Defence	5,603	6,422	7,128	7,062	8,749	8,909	9,502	9,988
Air Defence	7,924	7,261	7,314	8,021	10,272	9,056	8,885	9,402
Maritime Defence	3,019	2,643	2,396	1,874	1,968	2,011	2,102	2,145
Military Health Support	1,557	1,705	1,877	2,148	2,440	2,482	2,605	2,791
Defence Intelligence	219	353	461	512	589	599	612	646
Joint Support	1,710	1,911	2,266	4,036	3,341	3,460	3,676	3,960
Force Employment	1,605	1,508	1,581	1,783	1,801	1,924	1,862	1,978
Total	**23,510**	**23,817**	**25,180**	**27,899**	**32,024**	**31,325**	**32,389**	**34,418**

which it must be decided whether the force would remain 'finance-driven' or 'mandate-driven' and called for an increase in the budget from the current level of 1.2% of GDP to 1.7% over the next four years. The committee's report had been preceded by the Department of Defence's Annual Report 2008 which said that for the SANDF to 'largely attain' its Credible Force Design (CFD) by 2025 and fully realise it by 2031, a 30% increase in the defence budget would need to be achieved by 2011.

Both reports pointed to severe strain within the South African Army (SAA) in particular, with the JSC noting that the service must have increased funding as a 'matter of urgency'. In the past decade the army has lost out in budget terms to the air force and navy, which have enjoyed the bulk of procurement funds under the Strategic Defence Procurement Programme (SDPP). The result is that the army is now considered too small to sustain its current deployments and lacks the funding to train its personnel properly, or maintain and procure vital equipment.

As illustrated in Table 27, now that annual payments towards the SDPP – four MEKO-class A-200 frigates, three diesel-electric submarines, 30 utility helicopters, 24 *Hawk* trainers and 26 *Gripen* fighter aircraft – have fallen dramatically from their peak in 2002 there is greater potential to increase the funding of the SAA. Under plans outlined in Defence Update 2007, the country's landward forces budget is set to grow to enable the SAA to become more flexible and mobile, creating 'the backbone of South Africa's peace and stability initiative on the continent'.

The first priority will be light and motorised forces, intelligence and engineering elements used mainly in support of international commitments, and concomitant air and maritime inter- or intra-theatre lift. This was to be provided by eight Airbus A400M transport aircraft and two strategic support ships capable of carrying about 12 helicopters and 800 soldiers, plus their equipment and vehicles. Second-tier priorities include mechanised infantry, artillery, armour and other conventional elements of the SANDF's landward capability. However, in November 2009, the government announced that it was terminating its contract with Airbus Military for the A400M, saying the decision was 'due to extensive cost escalation and a failure on the part of the supplier to deliver the aircraft within the stipulated timeframe'. This leaves the armed forces with a fleet of aging C-130 and C-160 transport platforms which the chief of joint operations has indicated is inadequate, owing to the long lines of communication experienced by the deployment of forces across the continent. It has been suggested that the air force may now turn its attention to the acquisition of C-295, as a short-term stop-gap.

Without significant additional resources, the DoD has indicated that it will probably have to scale back its ambitions and will only be able to partially fulfil its CFD targets. As such, the emphasis would shift to those programmes that are deemed critical to the fulfilment of South Africa's international UN and AU peace missions, humanitarian and disaster assistance, and contributions to the ASF. Under this scenario important force elements would be motorised infantry battalions, airborne and other rapid-entry forces, engineering, tactical intelligence, logistics support and military health capabilities. There would be little or no money for mechanised elements and these platforms would, therefore, have

Sub-Saharan Africa

Table 27 **South Africa's Strategic Armaments Package – Quantities and Costs (Rm)**

	Cost of 4 MEKO frigates	Cost of 3 Type-209 submarines	Cost of 30 A109 utility helicopters	Cost of 28 *Gripen* aircraft	Cost of 24 *Hawk* trainer aircraft	Total cost
2000	1,643	126	154	228	750	2,901
2001	1,846	755	316	446	861	4,223
2002	1,895	1,528	434	1,104	1,381	6,342
2003	2,100	1,461	213	713	1,376	5,864
2004	1,188	1,303	106	1,460	445	4,502
2005	599	1,254	235	3,199	1,045	6,331
2006	378	820	447	2,599	293	4,537
2007	–	753	201	2,794	767	4,515
2008	41	23	176	3,457	185	3,882
2009	–	130	169	1,447	98	1,843
2010	–	–	–	1,323	–	1,323
2011	–	–	–	1,136	–	1,136
Total	9,690	8,152	2,451	19,908	7,200	47,401

to be retained in 'survival mode with life extension programmes'.

In July 2009, new Defence Minister Lindiwe Sisulu used her first budget speech to acknowledge the impact that the recession was having on the government's finances and the pressure that this may place on defence spending, but argued that the economic environment should not be used as an excuse to erode the defence budget, as was the case in the 1990s. In light of possible budget restraints she singled out efficiency gains as a major goal, noting that the strained relationship between the DoD and SANDF was detrimental in this regard. Her speech also included a commitment to review South Africa's 'outdated defence policy', which she said would take account of the new challenges facing the country and continent. She noted that previous defence policies had been deliberately designed in a way that did not intimidate South Africa's neighbours, but now left a force that was lacking the strength and capabilities required for the regional security role that had emerged.

It remains to be seen whether Sisulu and other interested parties can garner sufficient support in the Cabinet to obtain the necessary funding to recover from this 'downward spiral'. However, regardless of the trajectory of future defence spending, the composition of the spending itself will need to be addressed. Despite efforts by the DoD and individual service branches, personnel costs will have risen from 30% of the budget in 2004 to 38% of spending by 2011. But in spite of higher

salaries and improved benefits, the SANDF is still failing to attract enough people into the force. The air force, for example, has experienced a steady drain of experienced staff, meaning that there is a shortage of individuals to train and mentor newer members. In 2008, the SAAF had only 38% of its target strength in fighter pilots and 60% in technicians; the helicopter force had 72% of its necessary pilots and 68% technicians; and the transport force had 68% of its target pilot quota and 59% of technicians. Equally troublesome are the rising costs of operational and training activities due to improvements in air- and naval-base infrastructure to accommodate the platforms procured by the SDPP, as well as the costs of deploying around 4,000 personnel abroad.

With the budget being squeezed by rising personnel, training, maintenance and operational costs, the fate of a number of procurement programmes is uncertain. One immediate concern is *Project Vistula*, a R3.2bn programme to acquire more than 1,200 tactical logistical vehicles that was meant to have been completed between 2008 and 2011. Another army programme that has yet to get the go-ahead is *Project Sapula*, a new family of armoured personnel carriers to replace the 30-year old *Casspir* and *Mamba* vehicles, while funding for the ground-based air-defence system (GBADS) also appears to have dried up. The first phase of the new GBADS involves the deployment of multiple batteries of *Starstreak* surface-to-air missiles (SAMs), which will be followed by the development of mobile anti-aircraft and SAM batteries to protect restructured army formations.

Given the constrained budget environment, the navy has decided against exercising its option to acquire a fifth *Valour*-class (MEKO A-200) frigate, opting instead to focus on the acquisition of six new 85m offshore patrol vessels (OPVs) to contribute to a more balanced surface fleet. Options are thought to include procuring three fully equipped OPVs with some out-of-area capability, together with three vessels equipped mainly for inshore operations, or alternatively three smaller 55m inshore patrol vessels that would enable junior officers to assume command earlier than normal. Whatever the final configuration, the vessels are intended primarily for littoral patrol, surveillance, counter-smuggling and fisheries protection, with the potential to undertake mine countermeasures, surveys and general support functions. As for construction, it is likely that the vessels will be built locally, although a wider concept being explored is the development of a core OPV design which could be built in a number of African countries, with each nation equipping and arming the ships to meet its own particular requirements.

Angola ANG

New Angolan Kwanza AOA		2008	2009	2010
GDP	AOA	5.95tr	6.65tr	
	US$	79.4bn	77.7bn	
per capita	US$	6,335	6,074	
Growth	%	132.2	0.2	
Inflation	%	12.1	14.0	
Def bdgt	AOA	181bn	237bn	
	US$	2.43bn	2.77bn	
USD1=AOA		75.0	85.6	

Population   12,799,293

Ethnic groups: Ovimbundu 37%; Kimbundu 25%; Bakongo 13%

Age	0–14	15–19	20–24	25–29	30–64	65 plus
Male	22%	5%	4%	4%	14%	1%
Female	22%	5%	4%	4%	13%	2%

Capabilities

ACTIVE 107,000 (Army 100,000 Navy 1,000 Air 6,000) **Paramilitary 10,000**

ORGANISATIONS BY SERVICE

Army 100,000

FORCES BY ROLE

Armd/Inf   42 regt (dets/gps – strength varies)

Inf   16 indep bde

EQUIPMENT BY TYPE †

MBT 300+: ε200 T-54/T-55; 50 T-62; 50 T-72; T-80/T-84 (reported)

RECCE 600 BRDM-2

AIFV 250+ : 250 BMP-1/BMP-2; BMD-3

APC (W) ε170 BTR-152/BTR-60/BTR-80

ARTY 1,408+

    SP 16+: **122mm** 2S1 *Carnation*; **152mm** 4 2S3; **203mm** 12 2S7

    TOWED 552: **122mm** 500 D-30; **130mm** 48 M-46; **152mm** 4 D-20

    MRL 90+: **122mm** 90: 50 BM-21; 40 RM-70 *Dana*; **240mm** BM-24

    MOR 750: **82mm** 250; **120mm** 500

AT • MSL • MANPATS AT-3 9K11 *Sagger*

    RCL 500: 400 **82mm** B-10/**107mm** B-11 †; **106mm** 100†

    RL 73mm RPG-7 *Knout*†

    GUNS • SP 100mm SU-100†

AD • SAM • MANPAD 500 SA-7 *Grail*/SA-14 *Gremlin*/SA-16 *Gimlet*

    GUNS • TOWED 450+: **14.5mm** ZPU-4; **23mm** ZU-23-2; **37mm** M-1939; **57mm** S-60

Navy ε1,000

FORCES BY ROLE

Navy 1 HQ located at Luanda

EQUIPMENT BY TYPE

PATROL AND COASTAL COMBATANTS 9

PCI 7: 4 *Mandume*†; 3 *Patrulheiro*†

PBI 2 *Namacurra*

FACILITIES

Base   Located at Luanda

Coastal Defence

MSL • TACTICAL • SSM SS-C-1B *Sepal* (at Luanda base)

Air Force/Air Defence 6,000

FORCES BY ROLE

Ftr	sqn with MiG-21bis /MiG-21MF *Fishbed*; Su-27 *Flanker*; 2 sqn with MiG-23ML *Flogger*
FGA	sqn with MiG-23 *Flogger*; Su-25 *Frogfoot*; Su-24 *Fencer*; SU-22 (Su-17M-2) *Fitter D*
MP	sqn with F-27 MK 200MPA; CASA 212 *Aviocar*
Tpt	sqn with EMB-135BJ *Legacy* 600 (VIP); An-12 *Cub*; An-24 *Coke*; An-26 *Curl*; An-32 *Cline*; An-72 *Coaler*; C-130 *Hercules*; CASA 212 *Aviocar*; IL-62 *Classic*; IL-76TD *Candid*; PC-6B *Turbo Porter*; PC-7 *Turbo Trainer*/PC-9*
Atk hel	sqn with Mi-24 *Hind*/Mi-35 *Hind*; SA-342M *Gazelle* (HOT)
Trg	sqn with EMB-312 *Tucano*; L-29 *Delfin*
Hel	units with Bell 212; AS-565; Mi-17 (Mi-8MT) *Hip H*/Mi-8 *Hip*; IAR-316 (SA-316) *Alouette III* (incl trg)
SAM	5 bn; 10 bty each with 12 SA-3 *Goa*; 10 SA-13 *Gopher*†; 25 SA-6 *Gainful*; 15 SA-8 *Gecko*; 20 SA-9 *Gaskin*; 40 SA-2 *Guideline*

EQUIPMENT BY TYPE

AIRCRAFT 85 combat capable

    FTR ε34: up to 14 Su-27 *Flanker*; 20 MiG-21bis /MiG-21MF *Fishbed*; 18 MiG-23ML *Flogger*

    FGA 42: 8 Su-25 *Frogfoot*; 12 Su-24 *Fencer*; 8 MiG-23BN *Flogger*; 14 Su-22 (Su-17M-2) *Fitter D*

    MP 8: 1 F-27 MK 200MPA; 7 CASA 212 *Aviocar*

    TPT 44: 1 EMB-135BJ *Legacy* 600 (VIP); 6 An-12 *Cub*; 2 An-24 *Coke*; 12 An-26 *Curl*; 3 An-32 *Cline*; 8 An-72 *Coaler*; 1 C-130 *Hercules*; 5 CASA 212 *Aviocar*; 1 IL-62 *Classic*; 1 IL-76TD *Candid*; 4 PC-6B *Turbo Porter*

    TRG 25: 9 PC-7 *Turbo Trainer*/PC-9*; 8 EMB-312 *Tucano*; 6 L-29 *Delfin*; 2 L-39C *Albatros*

HELICOPTERS

    ATK 16: 14 Mi-24 *Hind*/Mi-35 *Hind*; 2 SA-342M *Gazelle* (HOT)

    SPT 27 Mi-17 (Mi-8MT) *Hip H*/Mi-8 *Hip*

    UTL 26: 8 Bell 212; 10 IAR-316 (SA-316) *Alouette III* (incl trg); 8 AS-565

AD • SAM 122

    SP 70: 10 SA-13 *Gopher*†; 25 SA-6 *Gainful*; 15 SA-8 *Gecko*; 20 SA-9 *Gaskin*

    TOWED 52: 40 SA-2 *Guideline*; 12 SA-3 *Goa*

MSL

    ASM AS-9 *Kyle*; AT-2 *Swatter*; HOT

    AAM AA-2 *Atoll*; AA-6 *Acrid*; AA-7 *Apex*; AA-8 *Aphid*

Paramilitary 10,000

Rapid-Reaction Police 10,000

FOREIGN FORCES

Portugal Navy: 11 (Technical Military Cooperation)

Benin BEN

CFA Franc BCEAO fr		2008	2009	2010
GDP	fr	3.06tr	3.20tr	
	US$	6.9bn	7.2bn	
per capita	US$	805	820	
Growth	%	5.1	3.8	
Inflation	%	8.0	4.0	
Def bdgt	fr	ε30bn	ε35bn	
	US$	ε67m	ε79m	
US$1=fr		447	444	

Population	8,791,832

Age	0–14	15–19	20–24	25–29	30–64	65 plus
Male	24%	6%	5%	4%	11%	1%
Female	23%	5%	5%	4%	12%	1%

Capabilities

ACTIVE 4,750 (Army 4,300 Navy 200 Air 250)
Paramilitary 2,500
Terms of service conscription (selective), 18 months

ORGANISATIONS BY SERVICE

Army 4,300
FORCES BY ROLE

Armd   1 sqn
Inf   3 bn
Cdo/AB 1 bn
Arty   1 bty
Engr   1 bn

EQUIPMENT BY TYPE
LT TK 18 PT-76 (op status uncertain)
RECCE 31: 14 BRDM-2; 7 M-8; 10 VBL
APC (W): 22 M-113
ARTY 16+
    TOWED 105mm 16: 12 L-118 Light Gun; 4 M-101
    MOR 81mm
AT • **RL 73mm** RPG-7 *Knout*; **89mm** LRAC

Navy ε200
EQUIPMENT BY TYPE
PATROL AND COASTAL COMBATANTS • **PB** 2 *Matelot Brice Kpomasse* (ex-PRC)
FACILITIES
Naval airbase   Located at Cotonou

Air Force 250
no cbt ac
AIRCRAFT
    TPT 11: 2 An-26 *Curl*†; 1 B-707-320† (VIP); 2 C-47 *Skytrain*†; 1 DHC-6 Twin *Otter*†; 2 Do-128 *Skyservant*†; 1 F-28 *Fellowship*† (VIP); 1 HS-748†; 1 Rockwell *Commander* 500B†
HELICOPTERS
    SPT 1 AS-350B *Ecureuil*†
    UTL 5: 4 A-109BA; 1 SE 3130 *Alouette II*†

Paramilitary 2,500

Gendarmerie 2,500
4 (mobile) coy

DEPLOYMENT

CÔTE D'IVOIRE
UN • UNOCI 428; 8 obs; 1 inf bn

DEMOCRATIC REPUBLIC OF CONGO
UN • MONUC 749; 10 obs; 1 inf bn

LIBERIA
UN • UNMIL 1; 2 obs

SUDAN
UN • UNMIS 4 obs

Botswana BWA

Botswana Pula P		2008	2009	2010
GDP	P	91bn	79bn	
	US$	13.4bn	12.1bn	
per capita	US$	6,850	6,076	
Growth	%	2.9	-10.3	
Inflation	%	12.6	8.4	
Def bdgt	P	ε2.0bn		
	US$	ε293m		
US$1=P		6.82	6.58	

Population	1,990,876

Age	0–14	15–19	20–24	25–29	30–64	65 plus
Male	20%	7%	6%	4%	11%	1%
Female	19%	7%	6%	5%	12%	2%

Capabilities

ACTIVE 9,000 (Army 8,500 Air 500) **Paramilitary 1,500**

ORGANISATIONS BY SERVICE

Army 8,500
FORCES BY ROLE
Armd 1 bde (under strength)

Inf   2 bde (*total:* 1 cdo unit, 1 armd recce regt, 1 engr regt, 2 ADA regt, 4 inf bn)

Arty   1 bde

AD   1 bde (under strength)

EQUIPMENT BY TYPE

LT TK 55: ε30 SK-105 *Kuerassier*; 25 *Scorpion*

RECCE 72+: RAM-V-1; ε8 RAM-V-2; 64 VBL

APC 156

　APC (T) 6 FV 103 *Spartan*

　APC (W) 150: 50 BTR-60; 50 LAV-150 *Commando* (some with 90mm gun); 50 MOWAG *Piranha* III

ARTY 46

　TOWED 30: 105mm 18: 12 L-118 Light Gun; 6 Model 56 pack howitzer; 155mm 12 Soltam

　MOR 16: 81mm 10; 120mm 6 M-43

AT • MSL 6+

　SP V-150 TOW

　MANPATS 6 TOW

　RCL 84mm 30 *Carl Gustav*

　RL 73mm RPG-7 *Knout*

AD • SAM • MANPAD 27: 5 *Javelin*; 10 SA-16 *Gimlet*; 12 SA-7 *Grail*

　GUNS • TOWED 20mm 7 M-167 *Vulcan*

Air Wing 500

FORCES BY ROLE

Ftr/FGA   1 sqn with F-5A *Freedom Fighter*; F-5D *Tiger II*

Tpt   2 sqn with BN-2 *Defender**; Beech 200 *Super King Air* (VIP); C-130B *Hercules*; CASA 212 *Aviocar*; CN-235; *Gulfstream* IV

Recce   1 sqn with O-2 *Skymaster*

Trg   1 sqn with PC-7 *Turbo Trainer**

Hel   1 sqn with AS-350B *Ecureuil*; Bell 412 *Twin Huey*; Bell 412EP *Twin Huey* (VIP); Bell 412SP *Twin Huey*

EQUIPMENT BY TYPE

AIRCRAFT 31 combat capable

　FTR 15: 10 F-5A *Freedom Fighter*; 5 F-5D *Tiger II*

　RECCE 5 O-2 *Skymaster*

　TPT 19: 10 BN-2 *Defender**; 1 Beech 200 *Super King Air* (VIP); 3 C-130B *Hercules*; 2 CASA 212 *Aviocar*; 2 CN-235; 1 *Gulfstream* IV

　TRG 6 PC-7 *Turbo Trainer**

HELICOPTERS

　SPT 8 AS-350B *Ecureuil*

　UTL 7: 1 Bell 412 *Twin Huey*; 1 Bell 412EP *Twin Huey* (VIP); 5 Bell 412SP *Twin Huey*

Paramilitary 1,500

Police Mobile Unit 1,500 (org in territorial coy)

Burkina Faso BFA

CFA Franc BCEAO fr		2008	2009	2010
GDP	fr	4.13tr		
	US$	9.3bn		
per capita	US$	606		
Growth	%	5.0	3.5	
Inflation	%	10.7	3.8	
Def bdgt	fr	ε50bn	ε55bn	
	US$	ε111m	ε123m	
US$1=fr		447	444	

Population   15,746,232

Age	0–14	15–19	20–24	25–29	30–64	65 plus
Male	24%	6%	5%	4%	11%	1%
Female	23%	5%	5%	4%	12%	1%

Capabilities

ACTIVE 11,200 (Army 6,400 Air 600 Gendarmerie 4,200) Paramilitary 250

ORGANISATIONS BY SERVICE

Army 6,400

FORCES BY ROLE

3 Mil Regions

Tk   1 bn (2 tk pl)

Inf   5 regt HQ (*each:* 3 inf bn (*each:* 1 inf coy (5 inf pl)))

AB   1 regt HQ (1 AB bn, 2 AB coy)

Arty   1 bn (2 arty tps)

Engr   1 bn

EQUIPMENT BY TYPE

RECCE 83: 19 AML-60/AML-90; 24 EE-9 *Cascavel*; 30 *Ferret*; 2 M-20; 8 M-8

APC (W) 13 M-3 *Panhard*

ARTY 18+

　TOWED 14: 105mm 8 M-101; 122mm 6

　MRL 107mm ε4 Type-63

　MOR 81mm Brandt

AT

　RCL 75mm Type-52 (M-20); 84mm *Carl Gustav*

　RL 89mm LRAC; M-20

AD • SAM • MANPAD SA-7 *Grail*

　GUNS • TOWED 42: 14.5mm 30 ZPU; 20mm 12 TCM-20

Air Force 600

FORCES BY ROLE

Tpt   sqn with B-727 (VIP); Beech 200 *Super King Air*; CN-235; HS-748; N-262 *Fregate*; Rockwell *Commander* 500B

Liaison   sqn with Cessna 172; AS-350 *Ecureuil*; Mi-17 (Mi-8MT) *Hip* H/Mi-8 *Hip*; SA-316B *Alouette* III

Trg   sqn with SF-260W *Warrior*/SF-260WL *Warrior**

EQUIPMENT BY TYPE

AIRCRAFT
TPT 8: 1 B-727 (VIP); 1 Beech 200 *Super King Air*; 1 HS-748; 1 N-262 *Fregate*; 1 Rockwell *Commander* 500B; 1 Cessna 172 *Skyhawk*; 1 Cessna 337; 1 CN-235
TRG SF-260WL *Warrior**

HELICOPTERS
ATK 2 Mi-35
SPT 4: 1 AS-350 *Ecureuil*; 3 Mi-17 (Mi-8MT) *Hip H*/Mi-8 *Hip* spt hel
UTL 1 SA-316B *Alouette III*

Gendarmerie 4,200

Paramilitary 250

People's Militia (R) 45,000 reservists (trained)

Security Company 250

DEPLOYMENT

DEMOCRATIC REPUBLIC OF CONGO
UN • MONUC 2 obs

SUDAN
UN • UNAMID 279; 6 obs: elm 1 inf bn

Burundi BDI

Burundi Franc fr		2008	2009	2010
GDP	fr	1.31tr		
	US$	1.11bn		
per capita	US$	121		
Growth	%	4.5	3.2	
Inflation	%	24.3	12.9	
Def bdgt	fr	98.3bn	101bn	
	US$	83m	82m	
US$1=fr		1,185	1,230	

Population 9,511,330
Ethnic groups: Hutu 85%; Tutsi 14%

Age	0–14	15–19	20–24	25–29	30–64	65 plus
Male	23%	6%	5%	4%	10%	1%
Female	23%	6%	5%	3%	11%	2%

Capabilities

ACTIVE 20,000 (Army 20,000) **Paramilitary 31,050**
In line with the Pretoria Peace Accord signed in October 2003 rebels from the FDD and government forces are now being integrated into a new National Defence Force with significant troop reductions expected.

ORGANISATIONS BY SERVICE

Army 20,000

FORCES BY ROLE
Lt armd 2 bn (sqn)
Inf 7 bn; some indep coy
Arty 1 bn
Engr 1 bn
AD 1 bn

EQUIPMENT BY TYPE
RECCE 55: 6 AML-60; 12 AML-90; 30 BRDM-2; 7 S52 *Shorland*
APC (W) 57: 10 BTR 80; 20 BTR-40; 9 M-3 *Panhard*; 12 RG-31 *Nyala*; 6 *Walid*
ARTY 120
  TOWED 122mm 18 D-30
  MRL 122mm 12 BM-21
  MOR 90: **82mm** 15 M-43; **120mm** ε75
AT
  MSL • MANPATS *Milan* (reported)
  RCL 75mm 60 Type-52 (M-20)
  RL 83mm RL-83 *Blindicide*
AD • SAM • MANPAD ε30 SA-7 *Grail*
  GUNS • TOWED 150+: **14.5mm** 15 ZPU-4; 135+ **23mm** ZU-23/**37mm** Type-55 (M-1939)

Reserves
Army 10 (reported) bn

Air Wing 200
AIRCRAFT 2 combat capable
  TPT 4: 2 DC-3; 2 Cessna 150L†
  TRG 2 SF-260TP/SF-260W *Warrior**
HELICOPTERS
  ATK 2 Mi-24 *Hind**
  SPT 4 Mi-8 *Hip* (non-op); 2 SA342L *Gazelle*
  UTL 3 SA-316B *Alouette III*

Paramilitary 31,050

Marine Police 50
16 territorial districts
PATROL AND COASTAL COMBATANTS 7
  PHT 3 *Huchuan*†
  Misc Boats/Craft 4
AMPHIBIOUS 1 LCT
LOGISTICS AND SUPPORT 1 SPT

General Administration of State Security ε1,000

Local Defence Militia ε30,000

DEPLOYMENT

SOMALIA
AU • AMISOM 2,550; 3 inf bn

SUDAN
UN • UNAMID 4; 7 obs

FOREIGN FORCES

All forces part of BINUB unless otherwise stated.

Bangladesh 1 obs
Niger 1 obs
Pakistan 1 obs
Senegal 1 obs
South Africa *Operation Curriculum* (AUSTF) 417
Switzerland 1 obs

Cameroon CMR

CFA Franc BEAC fr		2008	2009	2010
GDP	fr	10.6tr	10.7tr	
	US$	23.9bn	24.1bn	
per capita	US$	1,296	1,279	
Growth	%	2.9	1.6	
Inflation	%	5.3	2.9	
Def bdgt	fr	137bn		
	US$	306m		
US$1=fr			447	444

Population   18,879,301

Age	0–14	15–19	20–24	25–29	30–64	65 plus
Male	21%	6%	5%	4%	13%	1%
Female	21%	6%	5%	4%	13%	2%

Capabilities

ACTIVE 14,100 (Army 12,500 Navy 1,300 Air 300)
Paramilitary 9,000

ORGANISATIONS BY SERVICE

Army 12,500

FORCES BY ROLE
3 Mil Regions

Armd Recce	1 bn
Inf	3 bn (under comd of Mil Regions); 5 bn; 1 bn (trg)
Cdo/AB	1 bn
Arty	1 bn (5 arty bty)
Engr	1 bn
Presidential Guard	1 bn
AD	1 bn (6 AD bty)

EQUIPMENT BY TYPE
RECCE 65: 31 AML-90; 6 AMX-10RC; 15 *Ferret*; 8 M-8; 5 VBL
AIFV 22: 8 LAV-150 *Commando* with 20mm gun; 14 LAV-150 *Commando* with 90mm gun
APC 33
   APC (T) 12 M-3 half-track
   APC (W) 21 LAV-150 *Commando*
ARTY 112+
   SP 18 ATMOS 2000

TOWED 58: **75mm** 6 M-116 pack; **105mm** 20 M-101; **130mm** 24: 12 Model 1982 gun 82 (reported); 12 Type-59 (M-46); **155mm** 8 I1
MRL 122mm 20 BM-21
MOR 16+: **81mm** (some SP); **120mm** 16 Brandt
AT • MSL 49
   SP 24 TOW (on jeeps)
   MANPATS 25 *Milan*
   RCL 53: **106mm** 40 M-40A2; **75mm** 13 Type-52 (M-20)
   RL 89mm LRAC
AD • GUNS • TOWED 54: **14.5mm** 18 Type-58 (ZPU-2); **35mm** 18 GDF-002; **37mm** 18 Type-63

Navy ε1,300

FORCES BY ROLE
Navy 1 HQ located at Douala

EQUIPMENT BY TYPE
PATROL AND COASTAL COMBATANTS 11
   PCO 2: 1 *Bakassi* (FRA P-48); 1 *L'Audacieux* (FRA P-48)
   PCI 1 *Quartier*
   PCR 2 *Swift*-38
   PB 6: 2 *Rodman* 101; 4 *Rodman* 46
AMPHIBIOUS • LCU 2 (93 ft)
FACILITIES
Bases   Located at Douala, Limbe, Kribi

Air Force 300-400

FORCES BY ROLE

Air	1 composite sqn; 1 Presidential Fleet
FGA	sqn with MB-326K; *Alpha Jet*†; CM-170 *Magister*
MP	sqn with Do-128D-6 *Turbo SkyServant*
Tpt	sqn with B-707; C-130H-30 *Hercules*; DHC-4 *Caribou*; DHC-5D *Buffalo*; *Gulfstream* III; IAI-201 *Arava*; PA-23 *Aztec*
Atk hel	sqn with Mi-24 *Hind*; SA-342 *Gazelle* (with HOT)
Spt hel	sqn with AS-332 *Super Puma*; AS-365 *Dauphin* 2; Bell 206 *Jet Ranger*; SA-318 *Alouette II*; SA-319 *Alouette III*; SE 3130 *Alouette II*; Bell 206 L-3

EQUIPMENT BY TYPE
AIRCRAFT 15 combat capable
   FGA 15: 6 MB-326K *Impala I/Impala II*; 4 *Alpha Jet*†; 5 CM-170 *Magister*
   TPT 13: 1 B-707; 3 C-130H-30 *Hercules*; 1 DHC-4 *Caribou*; 4 DHC-5D *Buffalo*; 2 Do-128D-6 *Turbo SkyServant*; 1 *Gulfstream* III; 1 IAI-201 *Arava*
   UTL 2: 2 PA-23 *Aztec*
HELICOPTERS
   ATK 7: 3 Mi-24 *Hind*; 4 SA-342 *Gazelle* (with HOT)
   SPT 1 AS-332 *Super Puma*
   UTL 12: 1 AS-365 *Dauphin* 2; 3 Bell 206 *Jet Ranger*; 2 Bell 206L-3 *Long Ranger*; 1 SA-318 *Alouette II*; 2 SA-319 *Alouette III*; 3 SE 3130 *Alouette II*

Paramilitary 9,000

Gendarmerie 9,000

Regional Spt 3 gp

DEPLOYMENT

CENTRAL AFRICAN REPUBLIC
ECCAS • MICOPAX 120

DEMOCRATIC REPUBLIC OF CONGO
UN • MONUC 5 obs

Cape Verde CPV

Cape Verde Escudo E		2008	2009	2010
GDP	E	129bn		
	US$	1.72bn		
per capita	US$	4,017		
Growth	%	6.0	3.5	
Inflation	%	6.8	1.5	
Def bdgt	E	663m		
	US$	8.8m		
US$1=E		75.2	75.2	

Population   429,474

Age	0–14	15–19	20–24	25–29	30–64	65 plus
Male	20%	6%	5%	3%	12%	3%
Female	19%	6%	5%	3%	14%	4%

Capabilities

ACTIVE 1,200 (Army 1,000 Coast Guard 100 Air 100)
Terms of service conscription (selective)

ORGANISATIONS BY SERVICE

Army 1,000
FORCES BY ROLE
Inf 2 bn (gp)

EQUIPMENT BY TYPE
RECCE 10 BRDM-2
ARTY 42
  TOWED 24: **75mm** 12; **76mm** 12
  MOR 18: **82mm** 12; **120mm** 6 M-1943
AT • RL **73mm** RPG-7 *Knout*; **89mm** (3.5in)
AD • SAM • MANPAD 50 SA-7 *Grail*
  GUNS • TOWED 30: **14.5mm** 18 ZPU-1; **23mm** 12 ZU-23

Coast Guard ε100
PATROL AND COASTAL COMBATANTS 3
  PCC 1 *Kondor I*
  PCI 2: 1 *Espadarte*; 1 *Tainha* (PRC-27m) all less than 100 tonnes

Air Force up to 100
FORCES BY ROLE
MR 1 sqn with Do-228; EMB-110

EQUIPMENT BY TYPE
AIRCRAFT • **TPT** 4: 1 Do-228; 1 EMB-110; 2 An-26 *Curl*†

Central African Republic CAR

CFA Franc BEAC fr		2008	2009	2010
GDP	fr	946bn		
	US$	2.1bn		
per capita	US$	476		
Growth	%	2.2	2.4	
Inflation	%	9.3	4.6	
Def bdgt	fr	ε9bn	ε10bn	
	US$	ε20m	ε22m	
US$1=fr		447	444	

Population   4,511,488

Age	0–14	15–19	20–24	25–29	30–64	65 plus
Male	21%	6%	5%	4%	12%	2%
Female	21%	6%	5%	4%	13%	2%

Capabilities

ACTIVE 3,150 (Army 2,000 Air 150 Gendarmerie 1,000)
Terms of service conscription (selective), 2 years; reserve obligation thereafter, term n.k.

ORGANISATIONS BY SERVICE

Joint
Combined Service 1 (Intervention and spt) bn

Army ε2,000
FORCES BY ROLE
HQ/Spt   1 regt
Army   1 (combined arms) regt (1 mech bn, 1 inf bn)
Territorial Def 1 regt (bn) (2 territorial bn (intervention))

EQUIPMENT BY TYPE
MBT 3 T-55†
RECCE 9: 8 *Ferret*†; 1 BRDM-2
AIFV 18 *Ratel*
APC (W) 39+: 4 BTR-152†; 25+ TPK 4.20 VSC *ACMAT*†; 10+ VAB†
ARTY • **MOR** 12+: **81mm**††; **120mm** 12 M-1943†
AT • RCL **106mm** 14 M-40†
  RL **73mm** RPG-7 *Knout*††; **89mm** LRAC†
PATROL AND COASTAL COMBATANTS 9 PCR† less than 100 tonnes

Air Force 150
FORCES BY ROLE
no cbt ac, no armed hel
Tpt   sqn with C-130; Cessna 337 *Skymaster*; *Mystère* 20 (*Falcon* 20)
Liaison sqn with AL-60;
Hel   sqn with AS-350 *Ecureuil*; SE 3130 *Alouette II*; Mi-8 *Hip*

Sub-Saharan Africa

EQUIPMENT BY TYPE

AIRCRAFT • TPT 9: 1 C-130; 6 AL-60; 1 Cessna 337 *Skymaster*; 1 *Mystère* 20 (*Falcon* 20)

HELICOPTERS

SPT 1 AS-350 *Ecureuil*; 2 Mi-8 *Hip*

UTL 1 SE 3130 *Alouette II*

Paramilitary

Gendarmerie ε1,000

3 Regional legions, 8 bde

FOREIGN FORCES

All forces part of MINURCAT unless otherwise stated. MINURCAT numbers represent total forces deployed in the Central African Republic and Chad unless stated.

Albania 63; 1 HQ coy

Austria 131; elm 1 tpt coy

Bangladesh 5; 2 obs

Brazil 3 obs

Cameroon MICOPAX 120

Chad MICOPAX 121

Congo MICOPAX 60

Croatia 17

Democratic Republic of Congo 1

Egypt 1; 2 obs

Ethiopia 13

Equatorial Guinea MICOPAX 60

Finland 74; elm 1 inf bn

France 308; elm 1 inf coy; 1 engr coy; 1 log bn; elm 1 tpt coy • *Operation Boali* 240; 1 inf coy; 1 spt det

Gabon 1 obs • MICOPAX 139

Ghana 219; 1 obs; 1 mech inf bn

Ireland 427; elm 1 inf bn

Kenya 4

Malawi 5

Mongolia 1

Namibia 4

Nepal 302; 1 obs; 1 inf bn; 1 MP pl

Nigeria 15; 2 obs

Norway 177; 1 med coy

Pakistan 5

Poland 311; elm 1 inf bn

Russia 117; 1 avn bn

Rwanda 1 obs

Senegal 13; 1 obs

South Africa *Operation Vimbezela* 54

Togo 457; 1 HQ coy; elm 1 inf coy

United States 2

Yemen, Republic of 2

Chad CHA

CFA Franc BEAC fr		2008	2009	2010
GDP	fr	3.64tr		
	US$	8.1bn		
per capita	US$	806		
Growth	%	-0.2	1.6	
Inflation	%	8.3	6.5	
Def bdgt	fr	64.8bn	67.1bn	63.7bn
	US$	145m	151m	
US$1=fr		447	444	

Population   10,329,208

Age	0–14	15–19	20–24	25–29	30–64	65 plus
Male	24%	5%	4%	4%	10%	1%
Female	24%	5%	4%	4%	12%	2%

Capabilities

ACTIVE 25,350 (Army 17,000–20,000 Air 350 Republican Guard 5,000) **Paramilitary 9,500**

Terms of service conscription authorised

ORGANISATIONS BY SERVICE

Army ε17,000–20,000 (being re-organised)

FORCES BY ROLE

7 Mil Regions

Armd 1 bn

Inf   7 bn

Arty   1 bn

Engr   1 bn

EQUIPMENT BY TYPE

MBT 60 T-55

RECCE 256: 132 AML-60/AML-90; ε100 BRDM-2; 20 EE-9 *Cascavel*; 4 ERC-90F *Sagaie*

AIFV 89: 80 BMP-1; 9 LAV-150 *Commando* (with 90mm gun)

APC (W) 52: 24 BTR-8; 8 BTR-3E; ε20 BTR-60

ARTY 7+

SP 122mm 2 2S1 *Carnation*

TOWED 105mm 5 M-2

MOR 81mm some; **120mm** AM-50

AT • MSL • MANPATS *Eryx*; *Milan*

RCL 106mm M-40A1

RL 112mm APILAS; **73mm** RPG-7 *Knout*; **89mm** LRAC

AD • GUNS • TOWED 14.5mm ZPU-1/ZPU-2/ZPU-4; **23mm** ZU-23

Air Force 350

FORCES BY ROLE†

COIN   Unit with Su-25 *Frogfoot*; PC-7; PC-9; SF-260M *Warrior*

Tpt   sqn with An-26 *Curl*; C-130 *Hercules*; Mi-17 (Mi-8MT) *Hip H*; Presidential Flt with Beech 1900, 1 DC-9-87

Hel   sqn with Mi-24V *Hind*; SA-316 *Alouette III**

EQUIPMENT BY TYPE

AIRCRAFT 6 combat capable
  FGA: 3 Su-25 *Frogfoot*
  TRG 4: 1 SF-260M *Warrior**; 2 PC-7 (only 1*); 1 PC-9 *Turbo Trainer**
  TPT 5: 1 Beech 1900, 1 DC-9-87; 2 An-26 *Curl*; 1 C-130H *Hercules*;
HELICOPTERS
  ATK 7 Mi-24V *Hind*
  SPT 8: 2 Mi-171 *Hip-H*; 6 Mi-17 (Mi-8MT) *Hip-H*
  UTL 2 SA-316 *Alouette III**

Paramilitary 9,500 active

Republican Guard 5,000

Gendarmerie 4,500

DEPLOYMENT

CENTRAL AFRICAN REPUBLIC

ECCAS • MICOPAX 121

CÔTE D'IVOIRE

UN • UNOCI 1; 1 obs

FOREIGN FORCES

All forces part of MINURCAT unless otherwise stated. MINURCAT numbers represent total forces deployed in the Central African Republic and Chad unless stated.

Albania 63; 1 HQ coy
Austria 131; elm 1 tpt coy
Bangladesh 5; 2 obs
Brazil 3 obs
Croatia 17
Democratic Republic of Congo 1
Egypt 1; 2 obs
Ethiopia 13
Finland 74; elm 1 inf bn
France 308; elm 1 inf coy; 1 engr coy; 1 log bn; elm 1 tpt coy • *Operation Epervier* 1,200; 1 mech inf BG with (elm 1 mech inf regt, elm 1 armd cav regt); 1 avn gp with 6 F-1CR *Mirage*/F-1CT *Mirage*; 1 C-135 *Stratolifter*; 3 C-160 *Transall*; 1 hel det with 3 SA 330 *Puma*
Gabon 1 obs
Ghana 219; 1 obs; 1 mech inf bn
Ireland 427; elm 1 inf bn
Kenya 4
Malawi 5
Mongolia 1
Namibia 4
Nepal 302; 1 obs; 1 inf bn; 1 MP pl
Nigeria 15; 2 obs
Norway 177; 1 med coy
Pakistan 5
Poland 311; elm 1 inf bn
Russia 117; 1 avn bn
Rwanda 1 obs
Senegal 13; 1 obs

Togo 457; 1 HQ coy; elm 1 inf coy
United States 2
Yemen, Republic of 2

Congo COG

CFA Franc BEAC fr		2008	2009	2010
GDP	fr	5.61tr	5.13tr	
	US$	12.6bn	11.6bn	
per capita	US$	3,214	2,880	
Growth	%	5.6	7.4	
Inflation	%	6.0	6.9	
Def bdgt	fr	ε50bn		
	US$	ε112m		
US$1=fr		447	444	

Population   4,012,809

Capabilities

ACTIVE 10,000 (Army 8,000 Navy 800 Air 1,200)
Paramilitary 2,000

ORGANISATIONS BY SERVICE

Army 8,000

FORCES BY ROLE

Armd	2 bn
Inf	1 bn; 2 bn (gp) (*each*: 1 lt tk tp, 1 (76mm gun) arty bty)
Cdo/AB	1 bn
Arty	1 gp (how, MRL)
Engr	1 bn

EQUIPMENT BY TYPE†

MBT 40+: 25 T-54/T-55; 15 Type-59; T-34 in store
LT TK 13: 3 PT-76; 10 Type-62
RECCE 25 BRDM-1/BRDM-2
APC (W) 68+: 20 BTR-152; 30 BTR-60; 18 *Mamba*; M-3 *Panhard*
ARTY 66+
  SP 122mm 3 2S1 *Carnation*
  TOWED 25+: **76mm** ZIS-3 *M-1942*; **100mm** 10 M-1944; **122mm** 10 D-30; **130mm** 5 M-46; **152mm** D-20
  MRL 10+: **122mm** 10 BM-21; **122mm** BM-14/**140mm** BM-16
  MOR 28+: **82mm**; **120mm** 28 M-43
AT • RCL 57mm M-18
  RL 73mm RPG-7 *Knout*
  GUNS 57mm 5 ZIS-2 *M-1943*
AD • GUNS 28+
  SP 23mm ZSU-23-4
  TOWED 14.5mm ZPU-2/ZPU-4; **37mm** 28 M-1939; **57mm** S-60; **100mm** KS-19

Navy ε800

EQUIPMENT BY TYPE

PATROL AND COASTAL COMBATANTS 3+

PFI 3 *Zhuk*†
MISC BOATS/CRAFT: various river boats

FACILITIES

Base   Located at Pointe Noire

Air Force 1,200†

FORCES BY ROLE

FGA   sqn with MiG-21 *Fishbed* (non-op)

Tpt   sqn with An-24 *Coke*; An-26 *Curl*;
       B-727; N-2501 *Noratlas*

Trg   sqn with L-39 *Albatros*

Hel   sqn with Mi-8 *Hip*; AS-365 *Dauphin 2*;
       SA-316 *Alouette III*; SA-318 *Alouette II*; Mi-24 *Hind*

EQUIPMENT BY TYPE†

AIRCRAFT no combat-capable ac

  FTR 12 MiG-21 *Fishbed* (non-op)

  TPT 9: 1 An-12BK; 5 An-24 *Coke*; 1 An-26 *Curl*; 1 B-727; 1
  N-2501 *Noratlas*

  TRG 4 L-39 *Albatros*

HELICOPTERS†

  ATK 2 Mi-24 *Hind* (in store)

  SPT 3 Mi-8 *Hip* (in store)

  UTL 3: 1 AS-365 *Dauphin 2*; 1 SA-316 *Alouette III*; 1 SA-
  318 *Alouette II*

MSL AAM AA-2 *Atoll*

Paramilitary 2,000 active

Gendarmerie 2,000

Paramilitary   20 coy

Presidential Guard some

Paramilitary   1 bn

DEPLOYMENT

CENTRAL AFRICAN REPUBLIC

ECCAS • MICOPAX 60

Côte D'Ivoire CIV

CFA Franc BCEAO fr		2008	2009	2010
GDP	fr	10.3tr	10.8tr	
	US$	23.1bn	24.4bn	
per capita	US$	1,146	1,183	
Growth	%	2.3	3.7	
Inflation	%	6.3	5.9	
Def bdgt	fr	ε150bn	ε160bn	
	US$	ε335m	ε360m	
US$1=fr		447	444	

Population   20,617,068

Age	0–14	15–19	20–24	25–29	30–64	65 plus
Male	20%	6%	5%	4%	14%	1%
Female	21%	6%	5%	4%	13%	1%

Capabilities

ACTIVE 17,050 (Army 6,500 Navy 900 Air 700
Presidential Guard 1,350 Gendarmerie 7,600)
Paramilitary 1,500

RESERVE 10,000 (Joint 10,000)

ORGANISATIONS BY SERVICE

Army 6,500

FORCES BY ROLE

4 Mil Regions

Armd   1 bn

Inf   3 bn

AB   1 gp

Arty   1 bn

ADA   1 coy

Engr   1 coy

EQUIPMENT BY TYPE

MBT 10 T-55

LT TK 5 AMX-13

RECCE 34: 15 AML-60/AML-90; 13 BRDM-2; 6 ERC-90F4
Sagaie

AIFV 10 BMP-1/BMP-2

APC (W) 41: 12 M-3 *Panhard*; 10 *Mamba*; 13 VAB; 6 BTR-
80

ARTY 36+

  TOWED 4+: **105mm** 4 M-1950; **122mm** (reported)

  MRL 122mm 6 BM-21

  MOR 26+: **81mm**; **82mm** 10 M-37; **120mm** 16 AM-50

AT • MSL • MANPATS AT-14 9M133 *Kornet* (reported);
AT-5 9K113 *Spandrel* (reported)

  RCL 106mm ε12 M-40A1

  RL 73mm RPG-7 *Knout*; **89mm** LRAC

AD • SAM • MANPAD SA-7 *Grail* (reported)

  GUNS 21+

    SP 20mm 6 M3 VDAA

    TOWED 15+: **20mm** 10; **23mm** ZU-23-2; **40mm** 5 L/60

AIRCRAFT • TPT 1 An-12†

Navy ε900

EQUIPMENT BY TYPE

PATROL AND COASTAL COMBATANTS 3

  PCC 1 *Intrepide* (FRA *Patria*)

  PBR 2 *Rodman* (fishery protection duties)

AMPHIBIOUS • 2 LCM

FACILITIES

Base   Located at Locodjo (Abidjan)

Air Force 700

Largely non combat capable

EQUIPMENT BY TYPE

HELICOPTERS

ATK 1 Mi-24 (possible)

SPT 2 IAR-330L (SA-330L) *Puma*†

Paramilitary 10,450

Presidential Guard 1,350

Gendarmerie 7,600
APC (W): some VAB
PATROL AND COASTAL COMBATANTS 4 PB

Militia 1,500

Armed Forces 10,000 reservists

FOREIGN FORCES

All forces part of UNOCI unless otherwise stated.
Bangladesh 2,082; 15 obs; 2 inf bn; 1 engr coy; 1 sigs coy; 1 fd hospital
Benin 428; 8 obs; 1 inf bn
Bolivia 3 obs
Brazil 3; 4 obs
Chad 1; 1 obs
China, People's Republic of 7 obs
Ecuador 2 obs
Egypt 1
El Salvador 3 obs
Ethiopia 2 obs
France 8; 2 obs • *Operation Licorne* 900; **Army:** 1 (Marine) mech inf BG with (elm 1 mech inf regt, elm 1 armd cav regt); 1 hel unit; 1 Gendarme sqn **Air Force:** 1 C-160 *Transall*; 1 CN-235
Gambia 3 obs
Ghana 542; 6 obs; 1 inf bn; 1 avn unit; 1 fd hospital
Guatemala 5 obs
Guinea 3 obs
India 8 obs
Ireland 2 obs
Jordan 1,057; 7 obs; 1 inf bn; 1 SF coy
Korea, Republic of 2 obs
Moldova 3 obs
Morocco 726; 1 inf bn
Namibia 2 obs
Nepal 1; 3 obs
Niger 386; 6 obs; 1 inf bn
Nigeria 7 obs
Pakistan 1,137; 12 obs; 1 inf bn; 1 engr coy; 1 tpt coy
Paraguay 2; 8 obs
Peru 3 obs
Philippines 3; 4 obs
Poland 4 obs
Romania 7 obs
Russia 7 obs
Senegal 327; 9 obs; 1 inf bn
Serbia 3 obs
Tanzania 2; 1 obs
Togo 313; 7 obs; 1 inf bn
Tunisia 4; 7 obs
Uganda 2; 3 obs
Uruguay 2 obs
Yemen, Republic of 1; 8 obs
Zambia 2 obs
Zimbabwe 1 obs

Democratic Republic of Congo
DRC

Congolese Franc fr		2008	2009	2010
GDP	fr	6.31tr		
	US$	11.3bn		
per capita	US$	170		
Growth	%	6.2	2.7	
Inflation	%	18.0	39.2	
Def bdgt	fr	94.1bn		
	US$	168m		
US$1=fr			559	866

Population   68,692,542

Capabilities

ACTIVE 139,251–151,251 (Central Staffs: ε14,000, Army 110–120,000 Republican Guard 6–8,000 Navy 6,703 Air 2,548)

ORGANISATIONS BY SERVICE

Army (Forces du Terre) ε110–120,000
FORCES BY ROLE

Mech Inf	1 bde
Inf	17 bde (integrated)
Cdo	2 regt

EQUIPMENT BY TYPE†
MBT 49: 12–17 Type-59 †; 32 T-55
LT TK 40: 10 PT-76; 30 Type-62† (reportedly being refurbished)
RECCE up to 52: up to 17 AML-60; 14 AML-90; 19 EE-9 *Cascavel*; 2 RAM-V-2
AIFV 20 BMP-1
APC 138:
  APC (T) 3 BTR-50
  APC (W) 135: 30-70 BTR-60PB; 58 M-3 *Panhard*†; 7 TH 390 *Fahd*
ARTY 540+
  SP 122mm 6 2S1 *Carnation*
  TOWED 149: **75mm** 30 M-116 pack; **122mm** 77 (M-30) M-1938/D-30/Type-60; **130mm** 42 Type-59 (M-46)/Type-59 I
  MRL 57: **107mm** 12 Type-63; **122mm** 24 BM-21; **128mm** 6 M-51; **130mm** 3 Type-82; **132mm** 12
  MOR 328+: **81mm** 100; **82mm** 200; **107mm** M-30; **120mm** 28: 18; 10 Brandt
AT • RCL 36+: **57mm** M-18; **73mm** 10; **75mm** 10 M-20; **106mm** 16 M-40A1
  GUNS 85mm 10 Type-56 (D-44)
AD • SAM • MANPAD 20 SA-7 *Grail*

GUNS • TOWED 114: **14.5mm** 12 ZPU-4; **37mm** 52 M-1939; **40mm** ε50 L/60† (probably out of service)

Republican Guard circa 6–8,000

FORCES BY ROLE

Armd	1 regt
Republican Guard	3 bde

Navy 6,703 (incl. infantry and marines)

EQUIPMENT BY TYPE
PATROL AND COASTAL COMBATANTS 3
    PFC 1 *Shanghai* II Type-062 (2 additional vessels †)
    PCI 2 *Swiftships*†; 20 various (all under 50ft)
FACILITIES
Bases Located at Kinshasa (*River*), Boma (*River*), Lake Tanganyika, Matadi (*Coastal*)

Air Force 2,548

AIRCRAFT 5 combat capable
    FTR 2 MiG-23 *Flogger*
    FGA 3 Su-25 *Frogfoot*
    TPT 1 An-26 *Curl*
HELICOPTERS
    ATK 4 Mi-24/35 *Hind*
    SPT 36: 1 Mi-26 *Halo* (non op); 35 Mi-8 *Hip* (very few serviceable)

Paramilitary • National Police Force

incl Rapid Intervention Police (National and Provincial forces)

People's Defence Force

SELECTED NON-STATE GROUPS

Coalition of Congolese Patriots (PARECO) Est strength n.k. Major equipments include: SALW • **Democratic Liberation Forces of Rwanda (FDLR)** Est strength 3,000 Major equipments include: SALW • **Mai-Mai** Est strength n.k.Major equipments include: SALW • **Mouvement de Liberation Congolais (MLC)** Est strength 18,000 Major equipments include: SALW • **National Congress for the Defence of the People (CNDP/ANC)** Est strength n.k.Major equipments include: SALW • **Patriotic Resistance Front in Ituri (FRPI)** Est strength n.k. Major equipments include: SALW • **Rassemblement Congolais pour la Democratie (RCD)** Est strength 20,000 Major equipments include: SALW • **Lord's Resistance Army** Est strength: 1,500 Major equipments include: mines and IEDs, SALW

DEPLOYMENT

CENTRAL AFRICAN REPUBLIC/CHAD
UN • MINURCAT 1

FOREIGN FORCES

All part of MONUC unless otherwise specified.
Algeria 5 obs
Austria EU SEC RD Congo 1
Bangladesh 1,520; 26 obs; 1 mech inf bn; 2 avn unit

Belgium 22; 6 obs; EU SEC RD Congo 6
Benin 749; 10 obs; 1 inf bn
Bolivia 200; 7 obs; 2 inf coy
Bosnia and Herzegovina 5 obs
Burkina Faso 2 obs
Cameroon 5 obs
Canada (*Operation Crocodile*) 11 obs
China, People's Republic of 218; 15 obs; 1 engr coy; 1 fd hospital
Czech Republic 2 obs
Denmark 2 obs
Egypt 26 obs
France 5 obs
Germany EU SEC RD Congo 3
Ghana 462; 23 obs; 1 mech inf bn
Guatemala 150; 4 obs
India 4,249; 52 obs; 3 mech inf bn; 1 inf bn; 2 avn unit; 1 atk hel unit; 1 fd hospital
Indonesia 174; 16 obs; 1 engr coy
Ireland 3 obs
Italy EU SEC RD Congo 4
Jordan 65; 24 obs; 1 fd hospital
Kenya 23 obs
Malawi 111; 19 obs; 1CSS coy
Malaysia 17 obs
Mali 19 obs
Mongolia 2 obs
Morocco 831; 5obs; 1 mech inf bn; 1 fd hospital
Mozambique 2 obs
Nepal 1,030; 24 obs; 1 mech inf bn; 1engr coy
Netherlands EU SEC RD Congo 3
Niger 11 obs
Nigeria 22 obs
Norway 1 obs
Pakistan 3,589; 51 obs; 4 mech inf bn; 1 inf bn
Paraguay 17 obs
Peru 7 obs
Poland 2 obs
Romania 22 obs
Russia 28 obs
Senegal 460; 23 obs; 1 inf bn
Serbia 6
South Africa (*Operation Mistral*) 1,205; 17 obs; 1 inf bn; 1 engr coy; 1 avn unit (air med evacuation team, air base control det) • *Operation Teutonic* 17
Spain 2 obs
Sri Lanka 2 obs
Sweden 4 obs
Switzerland 3 obs
Tunisia 461; 26 obs; 1 mech inf bn
Ukraine 13 obs
United Kingdom 6 obs
Uruguay 1,324; 47 obs; 1 inf bn; 1 engr coy; 3 mne coy; 1 air spt unit
Yemen, Republic of 5 obs
Zambia 23 obs

Djibouti DJB

Djiboutian Franc fr		2008	2009	2010
GDP	fr	186bn		
	US$	1.04bn		
per capita	US$	1,473		
Growth	%	5.9	5.1	
Inflation	%	12.0	5.5	
Def bdgt	fr	2.72bn	2.34bn	1.72bn
	US$	15m	13m	
FMA (US)	US$	1.9m	2.0m	2.5m
US$1=fr		178	174	

Population   724,622

Ethnic groups: Somali 60%; Afar 35%

Age	0–14	15–19	20–24	25–29	30–64	65 plus
Male	22%	5%	5%	4%	14%	2%
Female	22%	5%	5%	4%	12%	2%

Capabilities

ACTIVE 10,450 (Army 8,000 Navy 200 Air 250
Gendarmerie 2,000) National Security Force 2,500

ORGANISATIONS BY SERVICE

Army ε8,000

FORCES BY ROLE

MOD and Army HQs, 4 military districts (Tadjourah, Dikhil, Ali-Sabieh and Obock)

Rep Guard	1 regt (1 sy sqn, 1 spt sqn (arty, armd and motorcycle pls), 1 close prot sqn, 1 ceremonial sqn,1 comd and spt sqn; incl CT and cdo role)
Armd	1 regt (3 armd sqns, 1 *Ratel* sqn, 1 anti-smuggling coy)
Inf	4 joint regts (3–4 coys, comd and spt coy, training camp(s), 1 rapid reaction regt (4 coys, comd and spt coy, 1 hvy spt sect; incl CT and cdo / abn role)
Arty	1 regt
Engr	1 demining coy, 1 plant coy
Comd	1 HQ regt, 1 comms comd, 1 CIS sect
Spt	1 log sp regt

EQUIPMENT BY TYPE
RECCE 39: 4 AML-60†; 15 VBL; 16-20 *Ratel*
APC (W) 20: 8 BTR -80; 12 BTR-60†
ARTY 96
   TOWED 122mm 6 D-30
   MOR 45: **81mm** 25; **120mm** 20 Brandt
AT
  RCL 106mm 16 M-40A1
  RL 73mm RPG-7 *Knout*; **89mm** LRAC
AD • GUNS 15+
  SP 20mm 5 M-693 (SP
  TOWED 10: **23mm** 5 ZU-23; **40mm** 5 L/70

Navy ε200

EQUIPMENT BY TYPE
PATROL AND COASTAL COMBATANTS 8
  PCI 2: 1 *Sawari* less than 100 tonnes; 1 *Plascoa*
  PB 6: 4 (USCG); 2 *Battalion-17*
FACILITIES
Base   Located at Djibouti

Air Force 250

FORCES BY ROLE

Tpt	some sqn with An-28 *Cash*; L-410UVP *Turbolet*; Cessna U-206G *Stationair*; Cessna 208 *Caravan I*
Hel	some sqn with AS-355F *Ecureuil II*; Mi-17 (Mi-8MT) *Hip H*; Mi-24 (atk)
Trg	unit with EMB-314 *Super Tucano*

EQUIPMENT BY TYPE
AIRCRAFT
  TPT 4: 1 An-28 *Cash*; 1 Cessna 402 (in store); 2 L-410UVP *Turbolet*
  UTL 2: 1 Cessna U-206G *Stationair*; 1 Cessna 208 *Caravan I*
  TRG Some EMB-314 *Super Tucano*
HELICOPTERS • ATK 2 Mi-24 *Hind*
SPT 3: 1 AS-355F *Ecureuil II*; 1 Mi-8 in store; 1 Mi-17 (Mi-8MT) *Hip H*;

Gendarmerie 2,000 +

Ministry of Defence
FORCES BY ROLE
Paramilitary   1 bn

EQUIPMENT BY TYPE
  PATROL AND COASTAL COMBATANTS 1 PB

Paramilitary ε2,500

National Security Force ε2,500

Ministry of Interior

DEPLOYMENT

WESTERN SAHARA
UN • MINURSO 2 obs

FOREIGN FORCES

France 1,690 Army; 1 (Foreign Legion) BG with (1 engr coy, 1 arty bty, 2 recce sqn, 2 inf coy); 1 (Marine) combined arms regt with (1 engr coy, 1 arty bty, 2 recce sqn, 2 inf coy) Navy; 1 LCT Air Force; 1 air sqn with 10 M-2000C/D *Mirage*; 1 C-160 *Transall*; 3 SA-342 *Gazelle*; 7 SA-330 *Puma*; 1 AS-555 *Fennec*; 1 SA-319 *Alouette III*

United States US Africa Command: Army 190; Navy 717; USAF 125; USMC: 133; 1 naval air base

Equatorial Guinea EQG

CFA Franc BEAC fr		2008	2009	2010
GDP	fr	7.70tr	5.92tr	
	US$	17.2bn	13.3bn	
per capita	US$	27,947	21,067	
Growth	%	11.3	-5.4	
Inflation	%	5.9	4.1	
Def bdgt	fr	ε5bn		
	US$	ε11m		
US$1=fr		447	444	

Population   633,441

Age	0–14	15–19	20–24	25–29	30–64	65 plus
Male	21%	5%	5%	4%	12%	2%
Female	21%	5%	5%	4%	14%	2%

Capabilities

ACTIVE 1,320 (Army 1,100 Navy 120 Air 100)

ORGANISATIONS BY SERVICE

Army 1,100
FORCES BY ROLE
Inf   3 bn

EQUIPMENT BY TYPE
RECCE 6 BRDM-2
AIFV 20 BMP-1
APC (W) 10 BTR-152

Navy ε120
EQUIPMENT BY TYPE†
PATROL AND COASTAL COMBATANTS 5
  PC 1 *Daphne*
  PCI 2 *Zhuk*
  PBR 2
FACILITIES
Bases Located at Bata, Malabo (Santa Isabel)

Air Force 100
EQUIPMENT BY TYPE
AIRCRAFT 4 Combat Capable
FGA 2 Su-25 *Frogfoot*,
TPT 1 Dassault 900 *Falcon* (VIP); 1 Cessna 337 *Skymaster*
TRG 4: 2 Su-25UB *Frogfoot**; 2 L-39C
HELICOPTERS
ATK 3 Mi-24 *Hind*
SPT 1 Mi-17 (Mi-8MT) *Hip-H*
UTL 2 SA-316 *Alouette III*

Paramilitary

Guardia Civil some
  2 coy

Coast Guard
PATROL AND COASTAL COMBATANTS PCI 1†

DEPLOYMENT

CENTRAL AFRICAN REPUBLIC
ECCAS • MICOPAX 60

Eritrea ERI

Eritrean Nakfa ERN		2008	2009	2010
GDP	ERN	24bn		
	US$	1.57bn		
per capita	US$	285		
Growth	%	1.0	0.3	
Inflation	%	12.6	14.0	
Def bdgt	ERN	n.a.		
	US$	n.a.		
USD1=ERN		15.3	15.0	

Population   5,647,168

Ethnic groups: Tigrinya 50%; Tigre and Kunama 40%; Afar; Saho 3%

Age	0–14	15–19	20–24	25–29	30–64	65 plus
Male	22%	5%	5%	4%	12%	2%
Female	22%	5%	5%	4%	12%	2%

Capabilities

ACTIVE 201,750 (Army 200,000 Navy 1,400 Air 350)
Terms of service 16 months (4 month mil trg)

RESERVE 120,000 (Army ε120,000)

ORGANISATIONS BY SERVICE

Army ε200,000
FORCES BY ROLE
Army 4 corps
Mech 1 bde
Inf   19 div
Cdo   1 div

Reserve Organisations
Reserve ε 120,000 reported reservists
Inf   1 div

EQUIPMENT BY TYPE
MBT 270 T-54/T-55
RECCE 40 BRDM-1/BRDM-2
AIFV 15 BMP-1
APC • APC (W) 25 BTR-152 APC (W) / BTR-60 APC (W)
ARTY 204+
  SP 25: **122mm** 32 2S1 *Carnation*; **152mm** 13 2S5
  TOWED 19+: **122mm** D-30; **130mm** 19 M-46
  MRL 44: **122mm** 35 BM-21; **220mm** 9 BM-27/9P140
  Uragan

MOR **120mm/160mm** 100+
AT
    MSL • MANPATS 200 AT-3 9K11 *Sagger*/AT-5 9K113 *Spandrel*
    RL 73mm RPG-7 *Knout*
    GUNS 85mm D-44
AD • SAM • MANPAD SA-7 *Grail*
    GUNS 70+
        SP 23mm ZSU-23-4
        TOWED 23mm ZU-23

Navy 1,400

FORCES BY ROLE

Navy 1 HQ located at Massawa

EQUIPMENT BY TYPE

PATROL AND COASTAL COMBATANTS 13
    PFM 1 *Osa* II† with 4 single each with SS-N-2B *Styx* tactical SSM
    PFI 4 *Super Dvora* less than 100 tonnes
    PCI 3 *Swiftships*
    PBF 5 *Battalion-17*
AMPHIBIOUS
    LS • LST 2: 1 *Chamo*† (Ministry of Transport); 1 *Ashdod*†
FACILITIES
Bases   Located at Massawa, Assab, Dahlak

Air Force ε350

FORCES BY ROLE

Ftr/FGA	sqn with MiG-29 *Fulcrum*; Su-27 *Flanker*; MiG-23 *Flogger*†; MiG-21 *Fishbed*†; MiG-29UB *Fulcrum*; Su-27UBK *Flanker*
Tpt	sqn with IAI-1125 *Astra*; Y-12(II)
Trg	sqn with L-90 *Redigo*; MB-339CE*
Hel	sqn with Mi-24-4 *Hind*; Mi-17 (Mi-8MT) *Hip H*/Mi-8 *Hip*

EQUIPMENT BY TYPE

AIRCRAFT 31 combat capable
    FTR 23: 8 MiG-29 *Fulcrum*; 8 Su-27 *Flanker*; 4 MiG-23 *Flogger*†; 3 MiG-21 *Fishbed*†
    TPT 4: 1 IAI-1125 *Astra*; 3 Y-12(II)
    TRG 16: 8 L-90 *Redigo*; 4 MB-339CE*; 2 MiG-29UB *Fulcrum** ; 2 Su-27UBK *Flanker*
HELICOPTERS
    ATK 1 Mi-24-4 *Hind*
    SPT 8: 4 Mi-17 (Mi-8MT) *Hip H*/Mi-8 *Hip*; 4 Agusta-Bell 412

Ethiopia ETH

Ethiopian Birr EB		2008	2009	2010
GDP	EB	285bn	355bn	
	US$	29.8bn	28.2bn	
per capita	US$	362	331	
Growth	%	11.6	7.5	
Inflation	%	25.3	36.4	
Def bdgt	EB	3.5bn	4.0bn	
	US$	366m	317m	
FMA (US)	US$	0.8m	0.8m	3.0m
US$1=EB		9.5	12.6	

Population   85,237,338

Ethnic groups: Oromo 40%; Amhara and Tigrean 32%; Sidamo 9%; Shankella 6%; Somali 6%; Afar 4%

Age	0–14	15–19	20–24	25–29	30–64	65 plus
Male	22%	6%	5%	4%	13%	1%
Female	22%	6%	5%	4%	13%	1%

Capabilities

ACTIVE 138,000 (Army 135,000 Air 3,000)

ORGANISATIONS BY SERVICE

Army 135,000

FORCES BY ROLE

4 Mil Regional Commands (Northern, Western, Central, and Eastern) each acting as corps HQ and one functional (Support) Command; strategic reserve of 4 divs and 6 specialist bdes centred on Addis Ababa.

Army 4 corps HQ (*each*: 1 mech div, 4-6 inf div)

EQUIPMENT BY TYPE

MBT 246+ T-54/T-55/T-62
RECCE/AIFV/APC (W) ε450 BRDM/BMP/BTR-60/BTR-152/Type 89
ARTY 460+
    SP 10+: **122mm** 2S1 *Carnation*; **152mm** 10 2S19 *Farm*
    TOWED 400+: **76mm** ZIS-3 *M-1942*; **122mm** ε400 D-30/(M-30) *M-1938*; **130mm** M-46
    MRL 122mm ε50 BM-21
    MOR 81mm M-1/M-29; **82mm** M-1937; **120mm** M-1944
AT • MSL • MANPATS AT-3 9K11 *Sagger*; AT-4 9K111 *Spigot*
    RCL 82mm B-10; **107mm** B-11
    GUNS 85mm εD-44
AD • SAM ε370
    TOWED SA-2 *Guideline*/SA-3 *Goa*
    MANPAD SA-7 *Grail*
    GUNS
        SP 23mm ZSU-23-4
        TOWED 23mm ZU-23; **37mm** M-1939; **57mm** S-60

Air Force 3,000

FORCES BY ROLE

FGA	sqns with Su-27 *Flanker*; MiG-21MF *Fishbed J*; Su-25T *Frogfoot*; MiG-23BN *Flogger H*; Su-25UB *Frogfoot B*

Sub-Saharan Africa

Tpt   sqns with AN-12 *Cub*; C-130B *Hercules*; DHC-6
      Twin Otter; Y-12; YAK-40 *Codling* (VIP); Mi-6 *Hook*

Atk hel   sqn with Mi-24/Mi-35 *Hind*; Mi-14 *Haze*

Spt hel   sqn with Mi-17 (Mi-8MT) *Hip H*/Mi-8 *Hip*

Trg   sqn with L-39 *Albatros*; SF-260

EQUIPMENT BY TYPE

AIRCRAFT 42 combat capable
  FTR 26: 11 Su-27 *Flanker*; 15 MiG-21MF *Fishbed J*
  FGA 14: 2 Su-25T *Frogfoot*; 12 MiG-23BN *Flogger H*
  TPT 17: 9 An-12 *Cub*; 3 C-130B *Hercules*; 2 DHC-6 *Twin Otter*; 2 Y-12; 1 YAK-40 *Codling* (VIP)
  TRG 18: 12 L-39 *Albatros*; 4 SF-260; 2 Su-25UB *Frogfoot B**
HELICOPTERS
  ATK 20: 15 Mi-24 *Hind*; 3 Mi-35 *Hind*; 2 Mi-14 *Haze*
  SPT 12 Mi-17 (Mi-8MT) *Hip H*/Mi-8 *Hip*
  UTL 18: 10 Mi-6 *Hook*; 8 SA316 *Alouette III*

DEPLOYMENT

CENTRAL AFRICAN REPUBLIC/CHAD
UN • MINURCAT 13

COTE D'IVOIRE
UN • UNOCI 2 obs

LIBERIA
UN • UNMIL 872; 12 obs; 1 inf bn

SUDAN
UN • UNAMID 1,763; 9 obs; 1 inf bn; 1 recce coy; 1 tpt coy

Gabon GAB

CFA Franc BEAC fr		2008	2009	2010
GDP	fr	6.72tr	5.39tr	
	US$	15.0bn	12.2bn	
per capita	US$	10,121	8,026	
Growth	%	2.3	-1.0	
Inflation	%	5.1	2.6	
Def bdgt	fr	ε60bn		
	US$	ε134m		
US$1=fr		447	444	

Population	1,514,993					

Age	0–14	15–19	20–24	25–29	30–64	65 plus
Male	21%	6%	4%	3%	13%	2%
Female	21%	6%	4%	4%	13%	2%

Capabilities

ACTIVE 4,700 (Army 3,200 Navy 500 Air 1,000)
Paramilitary 2,000

ORGANISATIONS BY SERVICE

Army 3,200

FORCES BY ROLE

Inf	8 coy
Cdo/AB	1 coy
Engr	1 coy
Presidential Guard	1 (bn) gp (under direct presidential control) (1 ADA bty, 1 arty bty, 1 armd/recce coy, 3 inf coy)

EQUIPMENT BY TYPE

RECCE 70: 24 AML-60/AML-90; 12 EE-3 *Jararaca*; 14 EE-9 *Cascavel*; 6 ERC-90F4 *Sagaie*; 14 VBL
AIFV 12 EE-11 *Urutu* (with 20mm gun)
APC (W) 28+: 9 LAV-150 *Commando*; 6 Type-92 (reported); 12 VXB-170; M-3 *Panhard*; 1 *Pandur* (Testing)
ARTY 51
  TOWED 105mm 4 M-101
  MRL 140mm 8 Teruel
  MOR 39: **81mm** 35; **120mm** 4 Brandt
AT • MSL • MANPATS 4 *Milan*
  RCL 106mm M-40A1
  RL 89mm LRAC
AD • GUNS 41
  SP 20mm 4 ERC-20
  TOWED 37: **23mm** 24 ZU-23-2; **37mm** 10 M-1939; **40mm** 3 L/70

Navy ε500

FORCES BY ROLE
Navy 1 HQ located at Port Gentil

EQUIPMENT BY TYPE
PATROL AND COASTAL COMBATANTS 9
  PFM 1 *Patra*
  PCO 2 *General Ba'Oumar* (FRA P-400)
  PB 6 *Rodman* (all less than 100 tonnes)
AMPHIBIOUS
  LS • LST 1 *President Omar Bongo* (FRA *Batral*) (capacity 1 LCVP; 7 MBT; 140 troops) with 1 hel landing platform for a medium sized hel
  CRAFT 1 LCM

FACILITIES
Base   Located at Port Gentil

Air Force 1,000

FORCES BY ROLE

FGA   1 sqn with *Mirage* 5G/5DG; *Mirage* 5E2; *Mirage* F1-AZ

MP   1 sqn with EMB-111*

CCT   1 (Presidential Guard) sqn with CM-170 *Magister*; T-34 *Turbo Mentor*

Tpt   1 (Presidential Guard) sqn with ATR-42F; EMB-110 *Bandeirante*; *Falcon* 900; AS-332 *Super Puma*; sqn with C-130H *Hercules*; CN-235; EMB-110 *Bandeirante*; YS-11A

Hel   1 sqn with SA-342 *Gazelle**; SA-330C *Puma*/SA-330H *Puma*; SA-316 *Alouette III*/SA-319 *Alouette III*; AB-412 (Bell 412) *Twin Huey*

EQUIPMENT BY TYPE
AIRCRAFT 14 combat capable
FGA 13: 3 *Mirage* 5G/DG (*Mirage* 5); 4 *Mirage* 5E2; 6 *Mirage* F1-AZ
RECCE 1 EMB-111*
TPT 8 1 ATR-42F; 3 C-130H *Hercules*; 1 CN-235; 2 EMB-110 *Bandeirante*; 1 *Falcon* 900
UTL 2 YS-11A
TRG 7: 4 CM-170 *Magister*; 3 T-34 *Turbo Mentor*
HELICOPTERS
ATK 5 SA-342 *Gazelle**
SPT 4: 1 AS-332 *Super Puma*; 3 SA-330C *Puma*/SA-330H *Puma*
UTL 5: 3 SA-316 *Alouette III*/SA-319 *Alouette III*; 2 AB-412 (Bell 412) *Twin Huey*

Paramilitary 2,000

Gendarmerie 2,000
FORCES BY ROLE
Armd   2 sqn
Paramilitary 3 bde; 11 coy
Avn   1 unit with 2 AS-350 *Ecureuil*; 1 AS-355 *Ecureuil*

EQUIPMENT BY TYPE
HELICOPTERS • SPT 3: 2 AS-350 *Ecureuil*; 1 AS-355 *Ecureuil*

DEPLOYMENT

CENTRAL AFRICAN REPUBLIC/CHAD
UN • MINURCAT 1 obs
ECCAS • MICOPAX 139

FOREIGN FORCES
France Army 775; 1 recce pl with ERC-90F1 *Lynx*; 1 (Marine) inf bn; 3 SA-330 *Puma* Air Force: 2 C-160 *Transall*; 1 AS-555 *Fennec*

Gambia GAM

Gambian Dalasi D		2008	2009	2010
GDP	D	17.5bn		
	US$	735m		
per capita	US$	425		
Growth	%	6.1	3.6	
Inflation	%	4.5	6.5	
Def bdgt	D	380m	189m	
	US$	16m	7m	
US$1=D		23.8	26.7	

Population   1,778,081

Age	0–14	15–19	20–24	25–29	30–64	65 plus
Male	22%	5%	4%	4%	13%	1%
Female	22%	5%	4%	4%	13%	1%

Capabilities

ACTIVE 800 (Army 800)

ORGANISATIONS BY SERVICE

Gambian National Army 800
Inf   2 bn
Engr   1 sqn
Presidential Guard 1 coy

Marine Unit ε70
EQUIPMENT BY TYPE
PATROL AND COASTAL COMBATANTS 3 PCI less than 100 tonnes
FACILITIES
Base   Located at Banjul

Air Wing
EQUIPMENT BY TYPE
AIRCRAFT
FGA 1 Su-25 *Frogfoot*
TPT 1 Il-62M (VIP)
UTL 2 AT-802A
FACILITIES
Base   Located at Banjul (Yundum Int'l Airport)
FACILITIES
Banjul-Yundum Int'l Airport

DEPLOYMENT

CÔTE D'IVOIRE
UN • UNOCI 3 obs

LIBERIA
UN • UNMIL 2 obs

SUDAN
UN • UNAMID 201; 1 obs; 1 inf coy

Ghana GHA

Ghanaian Cedi C		2008	2009	2010
GDP	C	17.6bn	21.6bn	
	US$	15.2bn	15.0bn	
per capita	US$	647	628	
Growth	%	7.3	4.5	
Inflation	%	16.8	18.5	
Def bdgt	C	122m	381m	
	US$	105m	264m	
US$1=C		1.16	1.44	

Population   23,887,812

Age	0–14	15–19	20–24	25–29	30–64	65 plus
Male	20%	6%	5%	4%	14%	2%
Female	19%	6%	5%	4%	14%	2%

Sub-Saharan Africa

Capabilities

ACTIVE 15,500 (Army 11,500 Navy 2000 Air 2.000)

ORGANISATIONS BY SERVICE

Army 11,500

FORCES BY ROLE
2 Comd HQ

Army	6 inf bn
Recce	1 regt (3 recce sqn)
AB/SF	2 coy
Arty	1 regt (1 arty bty, 2 mor bty)
Fd engr	1 regt (bn)
Trg	1 bn

EQUIPMENT BY TYPE
RECCE 3 EE-9 *Cascavel*
AIFV 39: 24 *Ratel* FSC-90; 15 *Ratel*-20
APC (W) 50 *Piranha*
ARTY 84
  TOWED 122mm 6 D-30
  MOR 78: 81mm 50; **120mm** 28 *Tampella*
AT • RCL 84mm 50 *Carl Gustav*
AD • SAM • MANPAD SA-7 *Grail*
  GUNS • TOWED 8+: **14.5mm** 4+: 4 ZPU-2; ZPU-4;
  23mm 4 ZU-23-2

Navy 2,000

FORCES BY ROLE
Navy Naval HQ located at Accra; 1 (Western) HQ located
  at Sekondi; 1 (Eastern) HQ located at Tema

EQUIPMENT BY TYPE
PATROL AND COASTAL COMBATANTS 7
  PFC 2 *Achimota* (GER Lurssen 57m)
  PCO 4: 2 *Anzole* (US); 2 *Dzata* (GER Lurssen 45m)
  PBI 1(US)
FACILITIES
Bases Located at Sekondi, Tema

Air Force 2,000

Main base Accra. Tpt element at Takoradi

FORCES BY ROLE

Light attack	1 sqn with KA-8 *Karakorum*; MB-326K/L-39ZO/ MB-339A
Tpt	1 sqn with *Defender*; F-27 *Friendship*; Cessna 172; F-28 *Fellowship* (VIP)
Trg	Flying school with Cessna 172
Hel	1 sqn with Mi-171V; A-109A; AB-212 (Bell 212); SA-319 *Alouette III*

EQUIPMENT BY TYPE†
AIRCRAFT 11 combat capable
  FGA 5: 3 MB-326K; 2 MB-339A
  TPT 6: 1 *Defender*; 4 F-27 *Friendship*; 1 F-28 *Fellowship*
  (VIP)
  TRG 9: 2 L-39ZO*; 3 Cessna 172; 4 KA-8 *Karakorum*

HELICOPTERS
  SPT 4: 4 Mi-171V
  UTL 5: 1 AB-212 (Bell 212) ; 2 A-109A; 2 SA-319 *Alouette III*

DEPLOYMENT

CENTRAL AFRICAN REPUBLIC/CHAD
UN • MINURCAT 219; 1 obs; 1 mech inf bn

CÔTE D'IVOIRE
UN • UNOCI 542; 6 obs; 1 inf bn; 1 avn unit; 1 fd hospital

DEMOCRATIC REPUBLIC OF CONGO
UN • MONUC 462; 23 obs; 1 mech inf bn

LEBANON
UN • UNIFIL 874; 1 inf bn

LIBERIA
UN • UNMIL 707; 8 obs; 1 inf bn

SUDAN
UN • UNAMID 10; 3 obs

WESTERN SAHARA
UN • MINURSO 17 obs

Guinea GUI

Guinean Franc fr		2008	2009	2010
GDP	fr	24.0tr		
	US$	4.9bn		
per capita	US$	495		
Growth	%	4.9	0.0	
Inflation	%	18.4	4.9	
Def bdgt	fr	ε250bn	ε275bn	
	US$	ε50m	ε55m	
US$1=fr		4,950	5,020	

Population   10,057,975

Age	0–14	15–19	20–24	25–29	30–64	65 plus
Male	22%	5%	4%	4%	13%	1%
Female	22%	5%	4%	4%	13%	2%

Capabilities

ACTIVE 12,300 (Army 8,500 Navy 400 Air 800
Gendarmerie 1,000 Republican Guard 1,600)
Paramilitary 7,000
Terms of service conscription, 2 years

ORGANISATIONS BY SERVICE

Army 8,500

FORCES BY ROLE

Armd	1 bn
Inf	5 bn
SF	1 bn

Ranger 1 bn
Cdo 1 bn
Arty 1 bn
Engr 1 bn
AD 1 bn

EQUIPMENT BY TYPE

MBT 38: 8 T-54; 30 T-34
LT TK 15 PT-76
RECCE 27: 2 AML-90; 25 BRDM-1/BRDM-2
APC (W) 40: 16 BTR-40; 10 BTR-50; 8 BTR-60; 6 BTR-152
ARTY 47+
    TOWED 24: **122mm** 12 M-1931/37; **130 mm** 12 M-46
    MRL 220mm 3 BM-27/9P140 *Uragan*
    MOR 20+: **82mm** M-43; **120mm** 20 M-1943/M-38
AT • MSL • MANPATS AT-3 9K11 *Sagger* ; AT-5 9M113
Spandrel
    RCL 82mm B-10
    RL 73mm RPG-7 *Knout*
    GUNS 6+: **57mm** ZIS-2 *M-1943*; **85mm** 6 D-44
AD • SAM • MANPAD SA-7 *Grail*
    GUNS • TOWED 24+: **30mm** M-53 (twin); **37mm** 8
    M-1939; **57mm** 12 Type-59 (S-60); **100mm** 4 KS-19

Navy ε400

EQUIPMENT BY TYPE
PATROL AND COASTAL COMBATANTS • PCI 2
Swiftships† less than 100 tonnes

FACILITIES
Bases   Located at Conakry, Kakanda

Air Force 800

FORCES BY ROLE

FGA   sqn with MiG-21 *Fishbed*; MiG-17F *Fresco C*
Tpt   sqn with An-24 *Coke*; AN-14
Trg   sqn with MiG-15UTI *Midget*
Hel   sqn with Mi-24 *Hind*; SA-342K *Gazelle*; SA-330 *Puma*;
    Mi-8 *Hip*

EQUIPMENT BY TYPE†

AIRCRAFT 7 combat capable (none currently operational)
  FTR 7: 3 MiG-21 *Fishbed*: 4 MiG-17F *Fresco C*
  TPT 1 An-24 *Coke*
  UTL 4 An-14
  TRG 2 MiG-15UTI *Midget*
HELICOPTERS
  ATK 5: 4 Mi-24 *Hind*; 1 SA-342K *Gazelle*;
  SPT 3: 1 SA-330 *Puma†*; 2 Mi-8 *Hip*
MSL
  AAM: AA-2 *Atoll*

Paramilitary 2,600 active

Gendarmerie 1,000

Republican Guard 1,600

People's Militia 7,000

DEPLOYMENT

CÔTE D'IVOIRE
UN • UNOCI 3 obs

SUDAN
UN • UNMIS 6 obs

WESTERN SAHARA
UN • MINURSO 3 obs

Guinea Bissau GNB

CFA Franc BCEAO fr		2008	2009	2010
GDP	fr	214bn		
	US$	479m		
per capita	US$	318		
Growth	%	3.3	1.9	
Inflation	%	10.4	0.4	
Def exp	fr	ε8bn	ε9bn	
	US$	ε18m	ε20m	
US$1=fr		447	444	

Population   1,533,964

Age	0–14	15–19	20–24	25–29	30–64	65 plus
Male	21%	5%	5%	4%	13%	1%
Female	21%	5%	5%	4%	13%	2%

Capabilities

ACTIVE ε6,458 (Army ε4,000 (numbers reducing)
Navy 350 Air 100 Gendarmerie 2,000)
Terms of service conscription (selective).
Manpower and eqpt totals should be treated with caution.
Recent governments have envisaged reducing the armed
forces. In April 2008, a census of the armed forces ended
with ID cards issued to 4,458 active personnel (senior and
mid-level officers totalled 2,473). The EU has been leading
SSR moves. A number of draft laws to restructure the
armed services and police have been produced.

ORGANISATIONS BY SERVICE

Army ε4,000 (numbers reducing)

FORCES BY ROLE

Armd   1 bn (sqn)
Recce   1 coy
Inf   5 bn
Arty   1 bn
Engr   1 coy

EQUIPMENT BY TYPE

MBT 10 T-34
LT TK 15 PT-76
RECCE 10 BRDM-2
APC (W) 55: 35 BTR-40/BTR-60; 20 Type-56 (BTR-152)
ARTY 26+

TOWED 122mm 18 D-30/*M-1938*
MOR 8+: **82mm** M-43; **120mm** 8 M-1943
AT
  RCL 75mm Type-52 (M-20); **82mm** B-10
  RL 89mm M-20
  GUNS 85mm 8 D-44
AD • SAM • MANPAD SA-7 *Grail*
  GUNS • TOWED 34: **23mm** 18 ZU-23; **37mm** 6 M-1939;
  57mm 10 S-60

Navy ε350

EQUIPMENT BY TYPE
PATROL AND COASTAL COMBATANTS 2
  PCI 2 *Alfeite* †
FACILITIES
Base   Located at Bissau

Air Force 100

FORCES BY ROLE
Ftr/FGA   sqn with MiG-17 *Fresco*
Hel   sqn with SA-318 *Gazelle*;
          SA-319 *Alouette III*

EQUIPMENT BY TYPE
AIRCRAFT 2 cbt capable
FTR 2 MiG-17 *Fresco* †
HELICOPTERS • UTL 3: 1 *Gazelle*; 2 SA-319 *Alouette* III

Paramilitary 2,000 active

Gendarmerie 2,000

Kenya KEN

Kenyan Shilling sh		2008	2009	2010
GDP	sh	2.36tr	2.90tr	
	US$	34.3bn	38.6bn	
per capita	US$	903	990	
Growth	%	1.7	2.5	
Inflation	%	13.1	12.0	
Def bdgt	sh	50.8bn	52.3bn	
	US$	735m	696m	
US$1=sh			69.1	75.1

Population   39,002.772

Ethnic groups: Kikuyu ε22–32%

Age	0–14	15–19	20–24	25–29	30–64	65 plus
Male	21%	6%	6%	5%	12%	1%
Female	21%	6%	5%	4%	12%	1%

Capabilities

ACTIVE 24,120 (Army 20,000 Navy 1,620 Air 2,500)
Paramilitary 5,000
(incl HQ staff)

ORGANISATIONS BY SERVICE

Army 20,000
FORCES BY ROLE
Armd   1 bde (3 armd bn)
Air Cav 1 indep bn
Inf   1 bde (2 inf bn); 1 bde (3 inf bn); 1 indep bn
AB   1 bn
Arty   1 bde (2 arty bn)
ADA   1 bn
Engr   1 bde (2 engr bn)

EQUIPMENT BY TYPE
MBT 188: 110 T-72 (reported); 78 Vickers Mk 3
RECCE 92: 72 AML-60/AML-90; 12 *Ferret*; 8 S52 *Shorland*
APC (W) 94: 10 M-3 *Panhard* in store; 52 UR-416; 32 Type-92
(reported)
ARTY 115
  TOWED 105mm 48: 8 Model 56 pack howitzer; 40 lt
  Gun
  MRL 122mm 11 BM-21 (reported)
  MOR 62: **81mm** 50; **120mm** 12 Brandt
AT • MSL • MANPATS 54: 40 *Milan*; 14 *Swingfire*
  RCL 84mm 80 *Carl Gustav*
AD • GUNS • TOWED 94: **20mm** 81: 11 Oerlikon; ε70
TCM-20; **40mm** 13 L/70

Navy 1,620 (incl 120 marines)
EQUIPMENT BY TYPE
PATROL AND COASTAL COMBATANTS 11
  PFM 2 *Nyayo* each with 2 twin (4 eff.) each with 1
  Otomat tactical SSM, 1 76mm gun
  PCO 2 *Shujaa* each with 1 76mm gun
  PCI 1 *Mamba*
  PBF 6: 1 *Archangel*; 5 *Defender*
AMPHIBIOUS LCM 2 *Galana*
LOGISTICS AND SUPPORT 1 AT *Tug*
FACILITIES
Base   Located at Mombasa

Air Force 2,500
FORCES BY ROLE
FGA   sqns with F-5E *Tiger II*/F-5F *Tiger II*
Tpt   sqn with DHC-5D *Buffalo*†; DHC-8 *Dash 8*†;
        Fokker 70† (VIP); PA-31 *Navajo*†;
        Y-12(II)†
Atk hel sqn with Hughes 500MD *Scout Defender*† (with
        TOW); Hughes 500ME†; Hughes 500M†
Spt hel sqn with SA-330 *Puma*†;
Trg   sqn with up to *Bulldog* 103/*Bulldog* 127†; EMB-
        312 *Tucano*†*; *Hawk* MK52†*; Hughes 500D†

EQUIPMENT BY TYPE†
AIRCRAFT 42 combat capable
  FTR 22 F-5E *Tiger II*/F-5F *Tiger II*
  TPT 30: 4 DHC-5D *Buffalo*†; 3 DHC-8 *Dash 8*†; 6 Do-
  28D-2† in store; 1 Fokker 70† (VIP); 1 PA-31 *Navajo*†; 10
  Y-12(II)†

TRG up to 25: up to 5 *Bulldog* 103/*Bulldog* 127†; 12 EMB-312 *Tucano*†*; 8 *Hawk* MK52†*

HELICOPTERS
ATK 11 Hughes 500MD *Scout Defender*† (with TOW)
ASLT 8 Hughes 500ME†
SPT 11 SA-330 *Puma*†;
UTL 17: 2 Hughes 500D†; 15 Hughes 500M†

MSL
ASM AGM-65 *Maverick* (TOW)
AAM AIM-9 *Sidewinder*

Paramilitary 5,000

Police General Service Unit 5,000

PATROL AND COASTAL COMBATANTS 17
PCI 5 less than 100 tonnes (2 Lake Victoria)
MISC BOATS/CRAFT 12 boats

Air Wing

AIRCRAFT • TPT 7 *Cessna*
HELICOPTERS
UTL 1 Bell 206L *Long Ranger*
TRG 2 Bell 47G

DEPLOYMENT

CENTRAL AFRICAN REPUBLIC/CHAD
UN • MINURCAT 4

DEMOCRATIC REPUBLIC OF CONGO
UN • MONUC 23 obs

SUDAN
UN • UNMIS 726, 4 obs; 1 inf bn; 1 de-mining coy
UN • UNAMID 84; 2 obs; 1 MP coy

FOREIGN FORCES

United Kingdom Army 52

Lesotho LSO

Lesotho Loti M		2008	2009	2010
GDP	M	14.1bn	17.7bn	
	US$	1.71bn	2.40bn	
per capita	US$	802	1,129	
Growth	%	3.5	-1.0	
Inflation	%	10.7	7.7	
Def bdgt	M	ε300m		
	US$	ε36m		
US$1=M		8.26	7.36	

Population   2,130,819

Age	0–14	15–19	20–24	25–29	30–64	65 plus
Male	19%	6%	5%	4%	12%	2%
Female	18%	6%	5%	4%	14%	3%

Capabilities

ACTIVE 2,000 (Army 2,000)

ORGANISATIONS BY SERVICE

Army ε2,000

FORCES BY ROLE
Recce 1 coy
Inf   7 coy
Arty   1 bty under strength (with 2 x 105 guns)
Avn   1 sqn
Spt   1 coy (with 81mm mor)

EQUIPMENT BY TYPE
RECCE 22: 4 AML-90; 10 RBY-1 *RAMTA*; 8 S52 *Shorland*
ARTY 12
    TOWED 105mm 2
    MOR 81mm 10
AT • RCL 106mm 6 M-40

Air Wing 110
AIRCRAFT
    MP 1 CASA 212-400 *Aviocar* (tpt, VIP tpt, casevac)
    TPT 3: 2 CASA 212-300 *Aviocar*; 1 GA-8 *Airvan* 1
HELICOPTERS
    UTL 6: 3 Bo-105LSA-3 (tpt, trg); 2 Bell 412 (SP); 1 Bell 412EP *Twin Huey* (tpt, VIP tpt, SAR)

Liberia LBR

Liberian Dollar L$		2008	2009	2010
GDP	US$	1.6bn	1.6bn	
per capita	US$	480	465	
Growth	%	7.1	4.9	
Inflation	%	17.5	7.3	
Def bdgt	L$	n.a.	n.a.	
	US$	n.a.	n.a.	
FMA (US)	US$	0.3m	1.5m	9.0m
US$1=L$		63	70	

Population   3,441,790
Ethnic groups: Americo-Liberians 5%

Age	0–14	15–19	20–24	25–29	30–64	65 plus
Male	21%	6%	5%	4%	13%	1%
Female	21%	6%	5%	4%	13%	1%

Capabilities

ACTIVE 2,400 (Armed Forces 2,400)

ORGANISATIONS BY SERVICE

Armed Forces 2,400
Armed Forces expected to be formed by 2010 and will include General Staff at MOD HQ an Army force, comprising 1 (23rd) Inf Bde

FORCES BY ROLE

Inf   1 inf bde (2 inf bn, 1 engr coy, 1 MP coy) (All
           non operational)
Trg   1 unit (forming, non operational)

FACILITIES

Bases   3 (Barclay Training Camp, Sandee S. Ware and
           Edward B. Kessely military barracks)

FOREIGN FORCES

All under UNMIL comd unless otherwise specified

Bangladesh 2,340; 11 obs; 2 inf bn; 2 engr coy; 1 sigs pl; 2
log coy; 1 MP unit
Benin 1; 2 obs
Bolivia 1; 2 obs
Brazil 2
Bulgaria 2 obs
China, People's Republic of 564; 2 obs; 1 engr coy; 1 tpt
coy; 1 fd hospital
Croatia 3
Denmark 2 obs
Ecuador 1; 2 obs
Egypt 5 obs
El Salvador 2 obs
Ethiopia 872; 12 obs; 1 inf bn
Finland 2
France 1
Gambia 2 obs
Ghana 707; 8 obs; 1 inf bn
Indonesia 2 obs
Jordan 119; 4 obs; 1 fd hospital
Korea, Republic of 1; 1 obs
Kyrgyzstan 2 obs
Malaysia 6 obs
Mali 2 obs
Moldova 2 obs
Mongolia 250; 1 inf coy
Montenegro 2 obs
Namibia 3; 1 obs
Nepal 18; 2 obs
Niger 2 obs
Nigeria 1,626; 13 obs; 1 inf bn; 3 sigs pl
Pakistan 3,072; 9 obs; 1 mech inf bn; 2 inf bn; 3 engr coy; 1
fd hospital
Paraguay 1; 2 obs
Peru 2; 2 obs
Philippines 136; 2 obs; 1 inf coy
Poland 2 obs
Romania 2 obs
Russia 4 obs
Senegal 2; 1 obs
Serbia 4 obs
Togo 1; 2 obs
Ukraine 302; 1 obs; 2 avn unit
United States 5; 4 obs;
Yemen, Republic of 1
Zambia 3 obs
Zimbabwe 2 obs

Madagascar MDG

Malagsy Ariary fr		2008	2009	2010
GDP	fr	16.13tr		
	US$	9.4bn		
per capita	US$	471		
Growth	%	7.1	-0.4	
Inflation	%	9.4	9.9	
Def bdgt	fr	176bn		
	US$	103m		
US$1=fr		1,708	2,013	

Population   20,653,556

Age	0–14	15–19	20–24	25–29	30–64	65 plus
Male	22%	5%	4%	4%	12%	1%
Female	22%	5%	4%	4%	13%	2%

Capabilities

ACTIVE 13,500 (Army 12,500 Navy 500 Air 500)
Paramilitary 8,100
Terms of service conscription (incl for civil purposes) 18 months

ORGANISATIONS BY SERVICE

Army 12,500+

FORCES BY ROLE
Army 2 (gp) bn
Engr 1 regt

EQUIPMENT BY TYPE
LT TK 12 PT-76
RECCE 73: ε35 BRDM-2; 10 *Ferret*; ε20 M-3A1; 8 M-8
APC (T) ε30 M-3A1 half-track
ARTY 25+
    TOWED 17: **105mm** 5 M-101; **122mm** 12 D-30
    MOR 8+ : **82mm**M-37; **120mm** 8 M-43
AT • RCL 106mm M-40A1
    RL 89mm LRAC
AD • GUNS • TOWED 70: **14.5mm** 50 ZPU-4; **37mm** 20
Type-55 (M-1939)

Navy 500 (incl some 100 Marines)

EQUIPMENT BY TYPE
PATROL AND COASTAL COMBATANTS 6
PB 6 (USCG)
AMPHIBIOUS • LCT 1 (FRA *Edic*)
LOGISTICS AND SUPPORT 1 tpt/trg†
FACILITIES
Bases Located at Diégo Suarez, Tamatave, Fort Dauphin,
       Tuléar, Majunga

Air Force 500

FORCES BY ROLE
Tpt   sqn with An-26 *Curl*; BN-2 *Islander*; CASA 212
           Aviocar; Yak-40 *Codling* (VIP)

Liaison sqn with Cessna 310; Cessna 337 *Skymaster*; PA-23 *Aztec*

Trg   sqn with Cessna 172

Hel   sqn with Mi-8 *Hip*

EQUIPMENT BY TYPE

AIRCRAFT

TPT 11: 1 An-26 *Curl*; 1 BN-2 *Islander*; 2 CASA 212 *Aviocar*; 1 Cessna 310; 2 Cessna 337 *Skymaster*; 4 Yak-40 *Codling* (VIP)

UTL 5: 4 Cessna 172; 1 PA-23 *Aztec*

HELICOPTERS • SPT 5 Mi-8 *Hip*

Paramilitary 8,100

Gendarmerie 8,100

PATROL AND COASTAL COMBATANTS 5 PCI less than 100 tonnes

Malawi MWI

Malawian Kwacha K		2008	2009	2010
GDP	K	401bn	463bn	
	US$	2.9bn	3.3bn	
per capita	US$	196	220	
Growth	%	9.7	5.9	
Inflation	%	8.7	8.6	
Def bdgt	K	ε6bn		
	US$	ε43m		
US$1=K		140	140	

Population   15,028,757

Age	0–14	15–19	20–24	25–29	30–64	65 plus
Male	23%	6%	5%	4%	11%	1%
Female	23%	6%	5%	4%	11%	2%

Capabilities

ACTIVE 5,300 (Army 5,300) **Paramilitary** 1,500

ORGANISATIONS BY SERVICE

Army 5,300

FORCES BY ROLE

Inf   3 bn

Para   1 indep bn

Spt   1 (general) bn (1+ marine coy 1 armd recce sqn, 1 engr unit, 2 lt arty bty)

EQUIPMENT BY TYPE

Less than 20% serviceability

RECCE 41: 13 *Eland*; 20 FV721 *Fox*; 8 *Ferret*

ARTY 17

TOWED 105mm 9 lt

MOR 81mm 8 L16

AD • SAM • MANPAD 15 *Blowpipe*

GUNS • TOWED 14.5mm 40 ZPU-4

Maritime Wing 220

EQUIPMENT BY TYPE

PATROL AND COASTAL COMBATANTS 15

PCI 3: 1 *Kasungu†* less than 100 tonnes; 2 *Namacurra* less than 100 tonnes

PBR 12 (†various)

AMPHIBIOUS 1 LCU

FACILITIES

Base Located at Monkey Bay (Lake Nyasa)

Air Wing 200

FORCES BY ROLE

Tpt   1 sqn with Basler *Turbo-67*; Do-228; Hawker 800

Tpt hel sqn with AS-332 *Super Puma* (VIP); AS-350L *Ecureuil*; SA-330F *Puma*

EQUIPMENT BY TYPE

AIRCRAFT • TPT 7: 2 Basler *Turbo-67*; 4 Do-228; 1 Hawker 800

HELICOPTERS • SPT 3: 1 AS-332 *Super Puma* (VIP); 1 AS-350L *Ecureuil*; 1 SA-330F *Puma*

Paramilitary 1,500

Mobile Police Force 1,500

RECCE 8 S52 *Shorland*

AIRCRAFT 4

MP 3 BN-2T *Defender* (border patrol)

TPT 1 SC.7 3M *Skyvan*

HELICOPTERS • UTL 2 AS-365 *Dauphin 2*

DEPLOYMENT

CENTRAL AFRICAN REPUBLIC/CHAD

UN • MINURCAT 5

DEMOCRATIC REPUBLIC OF CONGO

UN • MONUC 111; 19 obs; 1 CSS coy

SUDAN

UN • UNAMID 5; 6 obs

Mali MLI

CFA Franc BCEAO fr		2008	2009	2010
GDP	fr	3.27tr		
	US$	7.3bn		
per capita	US$	559		
Growth	%	5.1	4.1	
Inflation	%	9.1	2.5	
Def bdgt	fr	ε70bn	ε80bn	
	US$	ε156m	ε180m	
US$1=fr		447	444	

Population   13,443,225

Ethnic groups: Tuareg 6-10%

Age	0–14	15–19	20–24	25–29	30–64	65 plus
Male	24%	6%	5%	4%	9%	1%
Female	24%	5%	4%	4%	12%	2%

Capabilities

ACTIVE 7,350 (Army 7,350) **Paramilitary 4,800 Militia 3,000**

ORGANISATIONS BY SERVICE

Army ε7,350

FORCES BY ROLE

Tk   2 bn
Inf   4 bn
SF   1 bn
AB   1 bn
Arty   2 bn
AD   2 bty
Engr   1 bn
SAM   1 bty

EQUIPMENT BY TYPE†

MBT 33: 12 T-54/T-55; 21 T-34
LT TK 18 Type-62
RECCE 55 BRDM-2
APC (W) 64: 24 BTR-60; 30 BTR-40; 10 BTR-152
ARTY 46+
   TOWED 14+: **100mm** 6 M-1944; **122mm** 8 D-30; **130mm** M-46 (reported)
   MRL 122mm 2 BM-21
   MOR 30+: **82mm** M-43; **120mm** 30 M-43
AT • MSL • MANPATS AT-3 9K11 *Sagger*
   RL 73mm RPG-7 *Knout*
   GUNS 85mm 6 D-44
AD • SAM 12+
   TOWED 12+ SA-3 *Goa*
   MANPAD SA-7 *Grail*
   GUNS • TOWED 12: **37mm** 6 M-1939; **57mm** 6 S-60

Navy 50

EQUIPMENT BY TYPE

PATROL AND COASTAL COMBATANTS 3 PCR†
less than 100 tonnes

FACILITIES

Bases Located at Bamako, Mopti, Segou, Timbuktu

Air Force 400

FORCES BY ROLE

Ftr   1 sqn with MiG-21 *Fishbed*
Tpt   regt with An-24 *Coke*; An-26 *Curl*; An-2 *Colt*
Trg   sqn with L-29 *Delfin*; Yak-11 *Moose*; Yak-18 *Max*; MiG-21UM *Mongol*
Hel   sqn with AS-350 *Ecureuil*; Mi-8 *Hip*; Z-9 (AS-365N) *Dauphin* 2

EQUIPMENT BY TYPE

AIRCRAFT 13 combat capable
   FTR 13 MiG-21 *Fishbed*
   TPT 5: 2 An-24 *Coke*; 1 An-26 *Curl*; 2 An-2 *Colt*
   TRG 13: 6 L-29 *Delfin*; 4 Yak-11 *Moose*; 2 Yak-18 *Max*; 1 MiG-21UM *Mongol*

HELICOPTERS
   ATK 2 Mi-2424D *Hind*
   SPT 2: 1 AS-350 *Ecureuil*; 1 Mi-8 *Hip*
   UTL 2 Z-9 (AS-365N) *Dauphin* 2

Paramilitary 4,800 active

Gendarmerie 1,800
Paramilitary 8 coy

Republican Guard 2,000

National Police 1,000

Militia 3,000

DEPLOYMENT

DEMOCRATIC REPUBLIC OF CONGO
UN • MONUC 19 obs

LIBERIA
UN • UNMIL 2; 2 obs

SUDAN
UN • UNMIS 3 obs
UN • UNAMID 7; 9 obs

Mauritius MUS

Mauritian Rupee R		2008	2009	2010
GDP	R	265bn	273bn	
	US$	9.3bn	9.0bn	
per capita	US$	7,323	6,970	
Growth	%	6.6	2.1	
Inflation	%	8.8	6.4	
Def bdgt	R	1.03bn	1.24bn	
	US$	36m	41m	
US$1=R		28.4	30.5	

Population   1,284,264

Age	0–14	15–19	20–24	25–29	30–64	65 plus
Male	12%	4%	4%	4%	22%	3%
Female	12%	4%	4%	4%	22%	4%

Capabilities

ACTIVE NIL Paramilitary 2,000

ORGANISATIONS BY SERVICE

Paramilitary 2,000

Special Mobile Force ε1,500

FORCES BY ROLE

Rifle   6 coy
Paramilitary 2 (mob) coy
Engr   1 coy
Spt   1 pl

EQUIPMENT BY TYPE
RECCE BRDM-2; *Ferret*
AIFV 2 VAB with 20mm gun
APC (W) 16: 7 *Tactica*; 9 VAB
ARTY • MOR 81mm 2
AT • RL 89mm 4 LRAC

Coast Guard ε500
PATROL AND COASTAL COMBATANTS 27
PSOH 1 *Vigilant* (capacity 1 hel) (CAN *Guardian* design)
PCC 1 SDB-MK3
PCI 3: 2 *Zhuk*; less than 100 tonnes (FSU); 1 P-2000
PBI 22: 16; 6 *Tornado Viking*
AIRCRAFT • MP 3: 1 BN-2T *Defender*; 2 Do-228-101

Police Air Wing
HELICOPTERS • UTL 4 SA-316 *Alouette III*; 1 AS-355

Mozambique MOZ

Mozambique Metical M		2008	2009	2010
GDP	M	220bn	263bn	
	US$	9.2bn	9.0bn	
per capita	US$	431	417	
Growth	%	6.8	4.3	
Inflation	%	10.1	3.5	
Def bdgt	M	1.83bn	2.01bn	
	US$	76m	70m	
US$1=M			24	29

Population   21,669,278

Age	0–14	15–19	20–24	25–29	30–64	65 plus
Male	22%	5%	4%	4%	13%	1%
Female	21%	5%	4%	4%	14%	2%

Capabilities

ACTIVE 11,200 (Army 10,000 Navy 200 Air 1,000)
Terms of service conscription, 2 years

ORGANISATIONS BY SERVICE

Army ε9,000–10,000
FORCES BY ROLE
Inf   7 bn
SF   3 bn
Arty   2–3 bty
Engr   2 bn
Log   1 bn

EQUIPMENT BY TYPE†
Equipment at estimated 10% or less serviceability
MBT 60+ T-54
RECCE 30 BRDM-1/BRDM-2
AIFV 40 BMP-1
APC (W) 271: 160 BTR-60; 100 BTR-152; 11 *Casspir*

ARTY 126
TOWED 62; 100mm 20 M-1944; 105mm 12 M-101; 122mm 12 D-30; 130mm 6 M-46; 152mm 12 D-1
MRL 122mm 12 BM-21
MOR 52: 82mm 40 M-43; 120mm 12 M-43
AT • MSL • MANPATS 290: 20 AT-3 9K11 *Sagger*; 120 in store; 12 AT-4 9K111 *Spigot*; 138 in store
RCL 75mm; 82mm B-10; 107mm 24 B-12
GUNS 85mm 18: 6 D-48; 12 Type-56 (D-44)
AD • SAM • MANPAD 250: 20 SA-7 *Grail*; 230 in store
GUNS 330+
SP 57mm 20 ZSU-57-2
TOWED 310+: 20mm M-55; 23mm 120 ZU-23-2; 37mm 100: 90 M-1939; 10 in store; 57mm 90: 60 S-60; 30 in store

Navy ε200
Bases   Located at Pemba - Metangula (Lake Malawi), Nacala, Beira, Maputo

EQUIPMENT BY TYPE
PATROL AND COASTAL COMBATANTS 5
PBI 2 *Namacurra*
PBR 3

Air Force 1,000
FORCES BY ROLE
(incl AD units)
FGA   MiG-21bis *Fishbed L & N* (non-operational)
Tpt   1 sqn with An-26 *Curl*; CASA 212 *Aviocar*; PA-32 *Cherokee* (non-operational)
Trg   sqn with Cessna 182 *Skylane*; Z-326 *Trener Master*
Hel   sqn with Mi-24 *Hind*†*; Mi-8 *Hip* (non-operational)
SAM   bty with SA-3 *Goa* (non-operational); SA-2 *Guideline*†

EQUIPMENT BY TYPE
AIRCRAFT none combat capable
FTR some MiG-21bis *Fishbed L & N* (non-operational)
TPT 5: 2 An-26 *Curl*; 2 CASA 212 *Aviocar*; 1 Cessna 182 *Skylane*
TRG 11: 4 PA-32 *Cherokee* (non-operational); 7 Z-326 *Trener Master*
HELICOPTERS
ATK 2 Mi-24 *Hind*†*
SPT 2 Mi-8 *Hip* (non-operational)
AD • SAM 10+ SA-3 *Goa* (non-operational)
TOWED: SA-2 *Guideline*†

DEPLOYMENT

DEMOCRATIC REPUBLIC OF CONGO
UN • MONUC 2 obs

SUDAN
UN • UNAMID 7 obs

FOREIGN FORCES
Portugal Navy: 7

Namibia NAM

Namibian Dollar N$		2008	2009	2010
GDP	N$	73bn	87bn	
	US$	8.8bn	11.8bn	
per capita	US$	4,225	5,619	
Growth	%	2.9	-0.7	
Inflation	%	7.1	9.1	
Def bdgt	N$	2.37bn	2.24bn	
	US$	287m	305m	
US$1=N$		8.26	7.36	

Population   2,108,665

Age	0–14	15–19	20–24	25–29	30–64	65 plus
Male	20%	6%	5%	4%	13%	2%
Female	19%	6%	5%	4%	14%	2%

Capabilities

ACTIVE 9,200 (Army 9,000 Navy 200) **Paramilitary 6,000**

ORGANISATIONS BY SERVICE

Army 9,000

The MOD plans to build new military bases including at Luiperdsvallei outside Windheek, Osana near Okahandja, Keetmanshoop and Karibib

FORCES BY ROLE

Inf	6 bn
AT	1 regt
Cbt Spt	1 bde (1 arty regt)
Presidential Guard	1 bn
AD	1 regt

EQUIPMENT BY TYPE
MBT T-54/T-55†; T-34†
RECCE 12 BRDM-2
APC (W) 60:10 BTR-60; 20 *Casspir*; 30 *Wolf Turbo 2*
ARTY 69
   TOWED 40mm 24 G2
   MRL 122mm 5 BM-21
   MOR 40: **81mm**; **82mm**
AT • RCL 82mm B-10
   GUNS 12+: **57mm**; **76mm** 12 ZIS-3
AD • SAM • MANPAD 74 SA-7 *Grail*
   GUNS 65
     SP 23mm 15 *Zumlac*
     TOWED 14.5mm 50 ZPU-4

Navy ε200

Fishery protection, part of the Ministry of Fisheries

EQUIPMENT BY TYPE
PATROL AND COASTAL COMBATANTS 9
   PCO 3
   PCC 2: 1 *Oryx*; 1 *Brendan Simbwaye* with 1 40mm gun

PBI 4: 2 Ex *Namacurra*; 2 *Tracker II* (additional vessels on order)
AIRCRAFT • UTL 1 F406 *Caravan II*
hel 1
FACILITIES
Base   Located at Walvis Bay

Paramilitary 6,000

Police Force • Special Field Force 6,000 (incl Border Guard and Special Reserve Force)

Air Force

FORCES BY ROLE

FGA   sqn with MiG-23 *Flogger* (reported); F-7NM (J-7); FT-7NG (J-7)
Surv   sqn with Cessna 337 *Skymaster*/O-2A *Skymaster*
Tpt   sqn with An-26 *Curl*; *Falcon* 900; Learjet 36; 2 Y-12
Trg   sqn with K-8
Hel   sqn with Mi-25 *Hind D*; Mi-17 (Mi-8MT) *Hip H*; SA-319 *Alouette III*

EQUIPMENT BY TYPE
AIRCRAFT 24 combat capable
   FTR 10: 2 MiG-23 *Flogger* (reported); 8 F-7NM (J-7)
   TPT 11: 2 An-26 *Curl*; 1 *Falcon* 900; 1 Learjet 36; 2 Y-12, 5 Cessna 337 *Skymaster* tpt/O-2A *Skymaster*
   TRG 14: 12 K-8 *Karakorum**; 2 FT-7NG (J-7)*
HELICOPTERS
   ATK 2 Mi-25 *Hind D*
   SPT 2 Mi-17 (Mi-8MT) *Hip H*
   UTL 2 SA-319 *Alouette III*

DEPLOYMENT

CENTRAL AFRICAN REPUBLIC/CHAD
UN • MINURCAT 4

CÔTE D'IVOIRE
UN • UNOCI 2 obs

LIBERIA
UN • UNMIL 3; 1 obs

SUDAN
UN • UNMIS 7 obs
UN • UNAMID 12; 5 obs

Niger NER

CFA Franc BCEAO fr		2008	2009	2010
GDP	fr	2.39tr		
	US$	5.4bn		
per capita	US$	364		
Growth	%	9.5	1.0	
Inflation	%	11.3	4.8	
Def bdgt	fr	ε26bn	ε30bn	
	US$	ε58m	ε67m	
US$1=fr			447	444

Population   15,306,252

Ethnic groups: Tuareg 8-10%

Age	0–14	15–19	20–24	25–29	30–64	65 plus
Male	24%	6%	4%	4%	11%	1%
Female	23%	5%	4%	4%	13%	1%

Capabilities

ACTIVE 5,300 (Army 5,200 Air 100) Paramilitary 5,400

Terms of service selective conscription (2 year)

ORGANISATIONS BY SERVICE

Army 5,200

FORCES BY ROLE

3 Mil Districts

Armd recce	4 sqn
Inf	7 coy
AB	2 coy
Engr	1 coy
AD	1 coy

EQUIPMENT BY TYPE

RECCE 132: 35 AML-20/AML-60; 90 AML-90; 7 VBL

APC (W) 22 M-3 *Panhard*

ARTY • MOR 40: **81mm** 19 Brandt; **82mm** 17; **120mm** 4 Brandt

AT • RCL 14: **75mm** 6 M-20; **106mm** 8 M-40

   RL 89mm 36 LRAC

AD • GUNS 39

   SP 10 M3 VDAA

   TOWED 20mm 29

Air Force 100

FORCES BY ROLE

Tpt	sqn with An-26 *Curl*; B-737-200 (VIP); C-130H *Hercules*; Do-28
Hel	sqn with Mi-24 *Hind*; Mi-17 *Hip H*
Liaison	sqn with Cessna 337D *Skymaster*

EQUIPMENT BY TYPE

AIRCRAFT

   SURV 2 DA42 MPP

TPT 6: 1 An-26 *Curl*; 1 B-737-200 (VIP); 1 C-130H *Hercules*; 2 Cessna 337D *Skymaster*; 1 Do-28

HELICOPTERS

   ATK 2 Mi-24 *Hind*

   SPT 2 Mi-17 *Hip H*

Paramilitary 5,400

Gendarmerie 1,400

Republican Guard 2,500

National Police 1,500

DEPLOYMENT

BURUNDI

UN • BINUB 1 obs

CÔTE D'IVOIRE

UN • UNOCI 386; 6 obs; 1 inf bn

DEMOCRATIC REPUBLIC OF CONGO

UN • MONUC 11 obs

LIBERIA

UN • UNMIL 2 obs

Nigeria NGA

Nigerian Naira N		2008	2009	2010
GDP	N	23.8tr	20.2tr	
	US$	202bn	135bn	
per capita	US$	1,382	909	
Growth	%	6.0	2.9	
Inflation	%	11.6	12.0	
Def bdgt	N	158bn	223bn	
	US$	1.33bn	1.49bn	
FMA (US)	US$	1.3m	1.3m	1.3m
US$1=N		117	149	

Population   149,220,000

Ethnic groups: North (Hausa and Fulani) South-west (Yoruba) South-east (Ibo); these tribes make up ε65% of population

Age	0–14	15–19	20–24	25–29	30–64	65 plus
Male	21%	5%	5%	4%	14%	1%
Female	21%	5%	5%	4%	13%	2%

Capabilities

ACTIVE 80,000 (Army 62,000 Navy 8,000 Air 10,000) **Paramilitary 82,000**

Reserves planned, none org

ORGANISATIONS BY SERVICE

Army 62,000

FORCES BY ROLE

Army	1 (comp) div (2 mot inf bde, 1 AB bn, 1 amph bde, 1 engr bde, 1 arty bde, 1 recce bde)
Armd	1 div (1 recce bn, 1 engr bde, 1 arty bde, 2 armd bde)
Mech	2 div (*each*: 1 engr bn, 1 mot inf bde, 1 mech bde, 1 recce bn, 1 arty bde)
Presidential Guard	1 bde (2 Gd bn)
AD	1 regt

EQUIPMENT BY TYPE

MBT 276: 176 Vickers Mk 3; 100 T-55†
LT TK 157 *Scorpion*
RECCE 452: 90 AML-60; 40 AML-90; 70 EE-9 *Cascavel*; 50 FV721 *Fox*; 20 *Saladin* Mk2; 72 VBL (reported); 110 *Cobra*
APC 484+
  APC (T) 317: 250 4K-7FA *Steyr*; 67 MT-LB
  APC (W) 167+: 10 FV603 *Saracen*; 110 *Piranha*; 47 BTR-3U; EE-11 *Urutu* (reported)
ARTY 506
  SP 155mm 39 VCA 155 *Palmaria*
  TOWED 112: **105mm** 50 M-56; **122mm** 31 D-30/D-74; **130mm** 7 M-46; **155mm** 24 FH-77B in store
  MRL 122mm 25 APR-21
  MOR 330+: **81mm** 200; **82mm** 100; **120mm** 30+
AT • MSL • MANPATS *Swingfire*
  RCL 84mm *Carl Gustav*; **106mm** M-40A1
AD • SAM 164
  SP 16 *Roland*
  MANPAD 148: 48 *Blowpipe*; ε100 SA-7 *Grail*
  GUNS 90+
  SP 30 ZSU-23-4
  TOWED 60+: **20mm** 60+; **23mm** ZU-23; **40mm** L/70
RADAR • LAND: some RASIT (veh, arty)

Navy 8,000 (incl Coast Guard)

FORCES BY ROLE

Navy Western Comd HQ located at Apapa; Eastern Comd HQ located at Calabar; Naval Bases at Warri, Port Harcourt, Naval Trg school at Sapele, Delta State.

EQUIPMENT BY TYPE

PRINCIPAL SURFACE COMBATANTS 2
  FRIGATES • FFG 1 *Aradu* (GER MEKO 360) with 8 single each with 1 Otomat tactical SSM, 1 *Albatros* octuple with 24 *Aspide* SAM, 2 STWS 1B triple 324mm with 18 A244 LWT, 1 127mm gun, (capacity 1 Lynx MK 89 SAR hel)
  CORVETTES • FS 1 *Enymiri* (UK Vosper Mk 9) each with 1 x 3 Seacat Systems (3 eff.) with *Seacat* SAM, 1 2 tube Bofors 375mm (2 eff.), 1 76mm gun
PATROL AND COASTAL COMBATANTS 27
  PFM 1 *Ayam* (FRA *Combattante*) each with 2 twin (4 eff.) each with 1 MM-38 *Exocet* tactical SSM, 1 76mm gun (Additional 2 vessels†)
  PCO 6: 2 *Manta* (Suncraft 38m; 4 additional vessels on order); 4 *Balsam* (buoy tenders (US))
  PCC 5: 1 *Ekpe* (GER Lurssen 57m (Additional 2 vessels †)) with 1 76mm gun; 4 *Manta* (ST Marine 17m)

PBF 15 *Defender*
MINE WARFARE • MINE COUNTERMEASURES •
MCC 2 *Ohue* (mod ITA *Lerici*)
AMPHIBIOUS • LS • LST 1 *Ambe* (capacity 5 tanks; 220 troops) (GER)
LOGISTICS AND SUPPORT 5:
  1 **AGHS**; 3 **YTL**; 1 **TRG**

FACILITIES

Bases Located at Lagos, Apapa, Calabar

Naval Aviation

HELICOPTERS

  SAR 4: 2 AB-139 (AW-139); 2 *Lynx* MK 89† non-operational
  UTL 3 A-109E *Power*†

Air Force 10,000

FORCES BY ROLE†

Very limited op capability

Ftr/FGA	1 sqn with *Jaguar* S(N)† (non-operational); *Jaguar* B(N)†; 1 sqn with *Alpha Jet*; 1 sqn with MiG-21bis/MiG-21FR†; MiG-21MF†; MiG-21U†*; F-7NI (J-7); FT-NI (JJ-7)
Tpt	2 sqn with C-130H *Hercules*; C-130H-30 *Hercules*; Do-128D-6 *Turbo SkyServant*; Do-228-200 (incl 2 VIP); G-222; Presidential flt with *Gulfstream* II/*Gulfstream* IV; B-727; BAe-125-1000; *Falcon* 900
Trg	sqns with MB-339A* (all being upgraded); L-39MS *Albatros*†*; *Air Beetle*†; Hughes 300
Hel	sqns with Mi-24/Mi-35 *Hind*†; Bo-105D†; AS-332 *Super Puma*; SA-330 *Puma*; Mi-34 *Hermit* (trg);

EQUIPMENT BY TYPE

AIRCRAFT 87 combat capable
  FTR 26: 5 MiG-21MF *Fishbed* J†; 12 MiG-21bis *Fishbed* L/N/MiG-21 FTR/MiG-21FR *Fishbed* (Recce)†; 9 F-7NI (J-7) being delivered
  FGA 36: 24 L-39MS *Albatros*†; 12 Jaguar B(N)† non-operational
  TPT 53: 2 *Gulfstream* II/*Gulfstream* IV; 1 B-727; 1 BAe-125-1000; 5 C-130H *Hercules*; 3 C-130H-30 *Hercules*; 17 Do-128D-6 *Turbo SkyServant*; 16 Do-228-200 (incl 2 VIP); 2 *Falcon* 900; 6 G-222†
  TRG 83: 58 *Air Beetle*† (up to 20 awaiting repair); 6 *Alpha Jet* (FGA/trg)*; 3 *Jaguar* B(N)†*; 12 MB-339AN* (all being upgraded); 1 MiG-21U *Mongol A*†*; 3 FT-NI (JJ-7*) being delivered
HELICOPTERS
  ATK 9: 5 Mi-35 *Hind*; 4 Mi-24 *Hind* (2 -24P, 2 -24V)
  SPT 13: 7 AS-332 *Super Puma*; 2 SA-330 *Puma*; 4 Mi-171 *Hip*
  UTL 5 Bo–105D†
  TRG 18: 13 Hughes 300; 5 Mi-34 *Hermit*†
MSL • AAM AA-2 *Atoll*; PL-9C

Paramilitary ε82,000

Coast Guard

Port Security Police ε2,000

PATROL AND COASTAL COMBATANTS • MISC
BOATS/CRAFT 60+ boats
AMPHIBIOUS 5+ ACV

Security and Civil Defence Corps • Police 80,000

APC (W) 70+: 70+ AT105 Saxon†; UR-416
AIRCRAFT • TPT 4: 1 Cessna 500 Citation I; 2 PA-31
Navajo; 1 PA-31-350 Navajo Chieftain
HELICOPTERS • UTL 4: 2 AB-212 (Bell 212); 2 AB-222 (Bell 222)

SELECTED NON-STATE GROUPS

Movement for the Emancipation of the Niger Delta
(MEND) According to some assessments an umbrella
group Est strength: n.k. Major equipments include: mines
and IEDs, SALW, small surface vessels • Egbesu Boys of
Africa – Ijaw Est strength: 1,000 Major equipments include:
SALW • Federated Niger Delta Ijaw Communities Est
strength: 3,000 Major equipments include: SALW • Niger
Delta People's Volunteer Force Est strength: n.k.Major
equipments include: SALW • Niger Delta Vigilantes
Est strength: n.k. Major equipments include: SALW •
Niger Delta Volunteer Force Est strength: 3,000 Major
equipments include: SALW

DEPLOYMENT

CENTRAL AFRICAN REPUBLIC/CHAD
UN • MINURCAT 15; 2 obs

CÔTE D'IVOIRE
UN • UNOCI 7 obs

DEMOCRATIC REPUBLIC OF CONGO
UN • MONUC 22 obs

LIBERIA
UN • UNMIL 1,626; 13 obs; 1 inf bn; 3 sigs pl

NEPAL
UN • UNMIN 5 obs

SIERRA LEONE
IMATT 1

SUDAN
UN • UNMIS 2; 9 obs
UN • UNAMID 3,331; 8 obs; 4 inf bn

WESTERN SAHARA
UN • MINURSO 9 obs

Rwanda RWA

Rwandan Franc fr		2008	2009	2010
GDP	fr	2.11tr		
	US$	3.9bn		
per capita	US$	371		
Growth	%	11.2	5.3	
Inflation	%	15.4	11.5	
Def bdgt	fr	38.8bn	43.4bn	
	US$	71m	76m	
US$1=fr		546	569	

Population   10,746,311

Ethnic groups: Hutu 80%; Tutsi 19%

Age	0–14	15–19	20–24	25–29	30–64	65 plus
Male	21%	6%	5%	4%	12%	1%
Female	21%	6%	5%	4%	13%	2%

Capabilities

ACTIVE 33,000 (Army 32,000 Air 1,000) Paramilitary
2,000

ORGANISATIONS BY SERVICE

Army 32,000

FORCES BY ROLE
Army 4 div (each: 3 Army bde)

EQUIPMENT BY TYPE
MBT 24 T-54/T-55
RECCE 106: ε90 AML-60/AML-90/AML-245; 16 VBL
AIFV 35+: BMP; 15 Ratel-90; 20 Ratel-60
APC (W) 56+: 36 RG-31 Nyala; BTR; Buffalo (M-3 Panhard);
20 Type-92 (reported)
ARTY 155+
   TOWED 35+: 105mm 29 Type-54 (D-1); 122mm 6 D-30;
   152mm†
   MRL 122mm 5 RM-70 Dana
   MOR 115: 81mm; 82mm; 120mm
AD • SAM • MANPAD SA-7 Grail
   GUNS ε150: 14.5mm; 23mm; 37mm

Air Force ε1,000

FORCES BY ROLE
Tpt   sqn with An-2 Colt; An-8 Camp;
      B-707; BN-2A Islander
Trg   sqn with L-39 Albatros
Hel   sqn with Mi-24V Hind E; Mi-17MD (Mi-8MTV5) Hip
      H

EQUIPMENT BY TYPE
AIRCRAFT
   TPT 5+: An-2 Colt; 2–3 An-8 Camp; 1 B-707; 1 BN-2A
   Islander
   TRG L-39 Albatros

HELICOPTERS
ATK 5–7 Mi-24V *Hind E*
SPT 8–12 Mi-17MD (Mi-8MTV5) *Hip H*

Paramilitary

Local Defence Forces ε2,000

DEPLOYMENT

CENTRAL AFRICAN REPUBLIC/CHAD
UN • MINURCAT 1 obs

SUDAN
UN • UNMIS 256; 10 obs; 1 inf bn
UN • UNAMID 3,228 ; 7 obs; 4 inf bn

Senegal SEN

CFA Franc BCEAO fr		2008	2009	2010
GDP	fr	5.82tr	5.99tr	
	US$	13.0bn	13.5bn	
per capita	US$	976	985	
Growth	%	2.5	1.5	
Inflation	%	5.8	-0.9	
Def bdgt	fr	97.2bn		
	US$	217m		
US$1=fr			447	444

Population   13,711,597

Ethnic groups: Wolof 36%; Fulani 17%; Serer 17%; Toucouleur 9%; Man-dingo 9%; Diola 9% (of which 30-60% in Casamance)

Age	0–14	15–19	20–24	25–29	30–64	65 plus
Male	21%	6%	5%	4%	13%	1%
Female	20%	6%	5%	4%	14%	2%

Capabilities

ACTIVE 13,620 (Army 11,900 Navy 950 Air 770)
Paramilitary 5,000
Terms of service conscription, 2 years selective

ORGANISATIONS BY SERVICE

Army 11,900 (incl conscripts)
FORCES BY ROLE
4 Mil Zone HQ

Armd	3 bn
Inf	6 bn
Cdo/AB	1 bn
Arty	1 bn
Engr	1 bn
Presidential Guard	1 bn (horsed)
Construction	3 coy

EQUIPMENT BY TYPE
RECCE 118: 30 AML-60; 74 AML-90; 10 M-8; 4 M-20

APC 36+
APC (T) 12 M-3 half-track
APC (W) 24: 16 M-3 *Panhard*; 8 *Casspir*
ARTY 28
TOWED 12: **105mm** 6 HM-2/M-101; **155mm** ε6 Model-50
MOR 16: **81mm** 8 Brandt; **120mm** 8 Brandt
AT • MSL • MANPATS 4 *Milan*
RL **89mm** 31 LRAC
AD • GUNS • TOWED 33: **20mm** 21 M-693; **40mm** 12 L/60

Navy 950
EQUIPMENT BY TYPE
PATROL AND COASTAL COMBATANTS 9
PCO 6: 1 *Fouta* (DNK *Osprey*); 1 *Njambour* (FRA SFCN 59m); 2 *Saint Louis* (PR-48); 2 VCSM Class
PFI 1 *Senegal* II
PCI 2 *Alioune Samb*
AMPHIBIOUS • LCT 2 *Edic* 700
FACILITIES
Bases Located at Dakar and Casamance

Air Force 770
FORCES BY ROLE

MP/SAR	sqn with C-212; UH-1H
Surv	1 unit with BN-2T *Islander* (anti-smuggling patrols)
Tpt	1 sqn with B-727-200 (VIP); F-27-400M *Troopship*
Trg	sqn with *Rallye* 235 *Guerrier**; TB30 *Epsilon*
Hel	sqn with Mi-35P *Hind*; SA-318C *Alouette II*; S355F *Ecureuil*; Bell 206

EQUIPMENT BY TYPE
AIRCRAFT 1 combat capable
SURV 2 BN-2T *Islander* (govt owned, mil op)
TPT 8: 1 B-727-200 (VIP); 6 F-27-400M *Troopship*; 1 C-212
TRG 3: 1 *Rallye* 235 *Guerrier**; 2 TB30 *Epsilon*
HELICOPTERS
ATK 2 Mi-35P *Hind*
SPT 2 Mi-171 *Hip*;
UTL 6: 2 Mi-2; 2 SA-318C *Alouette II*; 1 AS355F *Ecureuil*; 12 Bell 206; 1 UH-1H

Paramilitary 5,000

Gendarmerie 5,000
APC (W) 12 VXB-170

Customs
PATROL AND COASTAL COMBATANTS 2 PCI less than 100 tonnes

DEPLOYMENT

BURUNDI
UN • BINUB 1 obs

CENTRAL AFRICAN REPUBLIC/CHAD
UN • MINURCAT 13; 1 obs

CÔTE D'IVOIRE
UN • UNOCI 327; 9 obs; 1 inf bn

COMOROS
AU • MAES 120

DEMOCRATIC REPUBLIC OF CONGO
UN • MONUC 460; 23 obs; 1 inf bn

LIBERIA
UN • UNMIL 2; 1 obs

SUDAN
UN • UNAMID 811; 13 obs; 1 inf bn

FOREIGN FORCES

France Army 575; 1 (Marine) mech inf bn; 1 recce sqn with ERC-90F *Lynx*; Navy 230: 1 LCT; 1 *Atlantique*; Air Force: 1 C-160 *Transall*; 1 AS-555 *Fennec*

Seychelles SYC

Seychelles Rupee SR		2008	2009	2010
GDP	SR	8.8bn		
	US$	930m		
per capita	US$	10,754		
Growth	%	-1.9	-8.7	
Inflation	%	37.0	33.4	
Def bdgt	SR	ε80m		
	US$	ε8.5m		
US$1=SR			9.4	10.5

Population	87,476

Age	0–14	15–19	20–24	25–29	30–64	65 plus
Male	13%	5%	5%	4%	19%	2%
Female	13%	5%	5%	5%	21%	4%

Capabilities

ACTIVE 200 (Army 200) Paramilitary 450

ORGANISATIONS BY SERVICE

Army 200
FORCES BY ROLE
Sy 1 unit
Inf 1 coy
EQUIPMENT BY TYPE†
RECCE 6 BRDM-2†
ARTY• MOR 82mm 6 M-43†
AT • RL 73mm RPG-7 *Knout*†
AD • SAM • MANPAD 10 SA-7 *Grail*†
  GUNS • TOWED 14.5mm ZPU-2†; ZPU-4†; 37mm M-1939†

Paramilitary

Coast Guard 200 (incl 80 Marines)
EQUIPMENT BY TYPE
PATROL AND COASTAL COMBATANTS 9
  PCC 2: 1 *Andromache* (ITA *Pichiotti* 42m); 1 *Topaz*
  PCI 7: 1 *Zhuk* less than 100 tonnes; 6 less than 100 tonnes
  AMPHIBIOUS • LCT 1 *Cinq Juin* (govt owned but civilian op)
FACILITIES
Base   Located at Port Victoria

National Guard 250

Air Wing 20
AIRCRAFT
  TPT 2: 1 BN-2 *Islander*; 1 Cessna 152
  UTL 1 F406 *Caravan II*

FOREIGN FORCES

United States US Africa Command: some MQ-9 *Reaper* UAV

Sierra Leone SLE

Sierra Leonean Leone L		2008	2009	2010
GDP	L	7.10tr		
	US$	2.38bn		
per capita	US$	474		
Growth	%	5.3	4.0	
Inflation	%	14.8	10.6	
Def bdgt	L	41.6bn	40.0bn	
	US$	14m	11m	
US$1=L			2,985	3.645

Population	5,132,138

Age	0–14	15–19	20–24	25–29	30–64	65 plus
Male	22%	5%	4%	4%	12%	2%
Female	23%	5%	4%	4%	13%	2%

Capabilities

ACTIVE 10,500 (Joint 10,500)

ORGANISATIONS BY SERVICE

Total Armed Forces 10,500
UK-trained national army has formed, which has an initial target strength of 13–14,000. This initial strength is set to reduce to some 10,000 over a ten-year period.
ARTY • MOR 31: 81mm ε27; 82mm 2; 120mm 2
AT • RCL 84mm *Carl Gustav*
HELICOPTERS • SPT 2 Mi-17 (Mi-8MT) *Hip H*/Mi-8 *Hip*†
AD • GUNS 7: 12.7mm 4; 14.5mm 3

Navy ε200

EQUIPMENT BY TYPE
PATROL AND COASTAL COMBATANTS 4
PCI 1 *Shanghai* III
PCR 3 (various craft gifted '06)
FACILITIES
Base   Located at Freetown

DEPLOYMENT

LEBANON
UN • UNIFIL 2

SUDAN
UN • UNMIS 3 obs
UN • UNAMID 11; 4 obs

NEPAL
UN • UNMIN 2 obs

TIMOR-LESTE
UN • UNMIT 1 obs

FOREIGN FORCES

Canada IMATT 7
Jamaica IMATT 1
Nigeria IMATT 1
United Kingdom IMATT Army: 63 (incl Trg Team, Tri-service HQ and spt)
United States IMATT 3

Somalia SOM

Somali Shilling sh		2008	2009	2010
GDP	US$			
per capita	US$			

Definitive economic data unavailable

Population	9,832,017

Age	0–14	15–19	20–24	25–29	30–64	65 plus
Male	22%	5%	4%	3%	14%	1%
Female	22%	5%	4%	4%	13%	2%

Capabilities

No national armed forces since 1991. Transitional government attempting to establish armed forces but hampered by defections, financial difficulties, UN arms embargo and institutional deficiencies. Militia forces and armed groups within the country. Somaliland and Puntland have their own militias. Hy equipment in poor repair or inoperable.

MILITARY FORCES

Transitional Federal Government

Army ε2,000 (Ethiopian trained)

SELECTED NON-STATE GROUPS

A number of groups, including those based on clan ties, operate forces within Somalia. These include the **al-Shabaab** grouping, which is assessed as having artillery systems, mines and IEDs, mortars and SALW among its inventory. The strength of the group is not known.

FOREIGN FORCES

Burundi AMISOM 2,550; 3 inf bn
Uganda AMISOM 2,550; 3 inf bn

TERRITORY WHERE THE RECOGNISED AUTHORITY (TFG) DOES NOT EXERCISE EFFECTIVE CONTROL

Data presented here represent the de facto situation. This does not imply international recognition as a sovereign state.

Somaliland
Population   3.5m

Militia unit strengths are not known. Equipment numbers are generalised assessments; most of this equipment is in poor repair or inoperable.

ORGANISATIONS BY SERVICE

Army ε15,000
FORCES BY ROLE
Armd	2bde
Mech Inf	1 bde
Inf	14 bde
Arty	2 bde
Spt	1bn

EQUIPMENT BY TYPE †
MBT 33: M47; T54/55
RECCE (T) BTR-50
RECCE (W *Panhard* AML 90; BRDM-2
APC(W) 15-20 Fiat 6614;
ARTY 69
    TOWED 122mm 12 D-30
    MOR MRL: 8-12 BM21
    45: **81mm** ; **120mm**
AT
RCL 106mm 16 M-40A1
RL 73mm RPG-7 *Knout*
AD
GUNS numerous†
TOWED 20mm; **23mm** ZU-23;

Coast Guard ε350

Ministry of the Interior
EQUIPMENT BY TYPE
PATROL AND COASTAL COMBATANTS 26
PB 7 *Dolphin* 26
PBR 19
FACILITIES
Base   Located at Berbera
Secondary regional bases at Zeylac and Mait

Puntland

Armed Forces ε5–10,000; coastguard

South Africa RSA

South African Rand R		2008	2009	2010
GDP	R	2.28tr	2.08tr	
	US$	276bn	283bn	
per capita	US$	5,666	5,767	
Growth	%	3.1	-2.2	
Inflation	%	11.8	7.2	
Def exp	R	27.7bn		
	US$	3.35bn		
Def bdgt	R	27.8bn	32.0bn	32.4bn
	US$	3.37bn	4.35bn	
US$1=R		8.26	7.36	

Population   49,052,489

Age	0–14	15–19	20–24	25–29	30–64	65 plus
Male	15%	6%	5%	4%	16%	2%
Female	15%	6%	5%	4%	18%	3%

Capabilities

ACTIVE 62,082 (Army 37,141 Navy 6,244 Air 10,653 South African Military Health Service 8,044)

CIVILIAN 12,382 (Army 6,452 Navy 2,000 Air 2,144 South African Military Health Service 1,786)

RESERVE 15,071 (Army 12,264 Navy 861 Air 831 South African Military Health Service Reserve 1,115)

ORGANISATIONS BY SERVICE

Army 37,141

FORCES BY ROLE

Formations under direct command and control of SANDF Chief of Joint Operations: 9 Joint Operational Tactical HQs, tps are provided when necessary by permanent and reserve force units from all services and SF Bde.

A new army structure is planned with 2 divisions (1 mechanised, 1 motorised) with 10 bdes (1 armd, 1 mech, 7 motorised and 1 rapid reaction). Training, Support and Land Commands with the 10 Bdes to be established (Mar 2010); Divisional HQ to be re-established (Mar 2011).

HQ	2 bde
Tk	1 bn
Armd recce	1 bn
Mech inf	2 bn
SF	1 bde (2 SF bn under strength)
Mot inf	10 bn (1 bn roles as AB, 1 as Amph)
Arty	1 bn
ADA	1 bn
Engr	1 regt

EQUIPMENT BY TYPE

MBT 167: 34 *Olifant* 1A; 133 *Olifant* 1B in store
RECCE 176: 82 *Rooikat*-76; 94 in store
AIFV 1,200: 534 *Ratel*-20 Mk III-20/ *Ratel*-60 Mk III-60/ *Ratel*-90 Mk III-90 FSV 90; 666 in store
APC (W) 810: 370 *Casspir*; 440 *Mamba*
ARTY 1,467
   SP 155mm 43: 2 G-6; 41 in store
   TOWED 147: **140mm** 75 G2 in store; **155mm** 72: 6 G-5; 66 in store
   MRL 127mm 51: 26 *Valkiri* Mk I in store (24 tube); 21 *Valkiri* Mk II MARS *Bataleur* (40 tube); 4 in store (40 tube)
   MOR 1,226: **81mm** 1,190 (incl some SP); **120mm** 36
AT • MSL • MANPATS 95: 16 ZT-3 *Swift*; 36 in store; 43 *Milan* ADT/ER
   RCL 106mm 100 M-40A1 (some SP)
   RL 92mm FT-5
AD • GUNS 76
   SP 23mm 36 *Zumlac*
   TOWED 35mm 40 GDF-002
UAV • TACTICAL up to 4 *Vulture*
RADAR • LAND ESR 220 *Kameelperd*; 2 Thales *Page*

Reserve Organisations

Regular Reserve 12,264 reservists (under strength)

Tk	3 bn
Armd Recce	2 bn
Recce	1 bn
Mech Inf	6 bn
Mot Inf	16 bn (incl 2 dual roles: 1 AB, 1 Amph
Lt Inf	3 converting to mot inf
AB	1 bn
Arty	7 regt
Engr	2 regt
AD	4 regt

Navy 6,244

FORCES BY ROLE

Navy   Fleet HQ and Naval base located at Simon's Town; Naval Office located at Pretoria; Naval stations Durban and Port Elizabeth

EQUIPMENT BY TYPE

SUBMARINES • TACTICAL • SSK 3 Type 209 with 8 533mm TT
PRINCIPAL SURFACE COMBATANTS • CORVETTES
   FSG 4 *Valour* (MEKO A200) with 2 quad (8 eff.) with MM-40 *Exocet* tactical ASSM (upgrade to Block III planned); 2 octuple VLS with *Umkhonto*-IR naval SAM, (capacity 1 *Lynx* Srs 300 *Super Lynx* ASW/ ASUW hel)
PATROL AND COASTAL COMBATANTS 26:
   PFM 2 *Warrior* (ISR *Reshef*) each with 6 *Skerpioen* tactical SSM (ISR *Gabriel*†); (2 additional vessels in reserve)
   PCI 24: 21 *Namacurra*; 3 craft less than 100 tonnes
MINE WARFARE • MINE COUNTERMEASURES 2
   MHC 2 *River* (GER *Navors*) (Limited operational roles; training and dive support); (additional vessel in reserve)

AMPHIBIOUS 6 LCU

LOGISTICS AND SUPPORT 7:

AORH 1 *Drakensberg* with 1 spt hel (capacity 4 LCU; 100 troops)

AGOS 1 (use for Antarctic survey, operated by private co. for Dept of Environment)

AGHS 1 (UK *Hecla*)

YTM 4

FACILITIES

Bases Located at Durban Salisbury Island (Naval Station); Port Elizabeth (Naval Station); Pretoria, Simon's Town

Air Force 10,653

Air Force office, Pretoria, and 4 op gps
Command & Control: 2 Airspace Control Sectors, 1 Mobile Deployment Wg
1 Air Force Command Post

FORCES BY ROLE

Multi-role 1 sqn with JAS-39C/D *Gripen* forming at Makhado

Tkr/EW/tpt 1 sqn with B-707-320

Tpt 1 (VIP) sqn with B-737 BBJ; CE-550 *Citation II*; *Falcon* 50; *Falcon* 900; 1 sqn with C-47TP (Basler *Turbo*-67) (6 maritime, 4 tpt, 1 PR/EW trg); 2 sqns with C-130B;C-130BZ *Hercules*; CN-235; CASA 212; Cessna 185; 1 tpt and trg school with Beech 200 *Super King Air*; Beech 300 *Super King Air*; Cessna 208 *Caravan I*; PC-12 *Aviocar*; 9 AF Reserve sqns with ε130 private light tpt ac

Tpt hel 4 mixed sqn with *Oryx* (AS-332B) *Super Puma*; BK-117; A109UH;
1 hel trg school with *Oryx* and A109

Hel 1 (cbt spt) sqn with CSH-1 *Rooivalk**

ASuW/SAR 4 *Super Lynx* 300 deployed on Navy *Valour* class frigates

Trg 1 (Lead-in Ftr Trg) sqn with *Hawk* Mk120; 1 basic flying trg school with PC-7 MkII *Astra*; 1 air nav school

EQUIPMENT BY TYPE

AIRCRAFT 33 combat capable

Multi-role: 9 JAS-39D *Gripen* (further 17 JAS-39C to be delivered by 2012)

LIFT 24 *Hawk* Mk120

TPT 47: 1 B-737 BBJ; 3 Beech 200 *Super King Air*; 1 Beech 300 *Super King Air*; 8 C-130B/C-130BZ *Hercules*; 11 C-47TP (Basler *Turbo*-67); 4 CASA 212 *Aviocar*; 2 CE-550 *Citation II*; 1 CN-235; 13 Cessna 185; 2 *Falcon* 50; 1 *Falcon* 900

UTL 12: 11 Cessna 208 *Caravan I*; 1 PC-12

TRG 53 PC-7 Mk II *Astra*

HELICOPTERS

ASLT 11 CSH-1 *Rooivalk**

ASuW/SAR 4 *Super Lynx* 300

SPT 39 *Oryx* (AS-332B) *Super Puma*

UTL 38: 8 BK-117; 30 A109UH

UAV *Seeker II*

MSL •**AAM** V3C *Darter*; V4 *R-Darter*; *A-Darter*; IRIS-T

Ground Defence

FORCES BY ROLE

Air some SAAF regt (*total:* 12 (security) Air sqn)

EQUIPMENT BY TYPE

2 Radar (static) located at Ellisras and Mariepskop; 2 (mobile long-range); 4 (tactical mobile)

FACILITIES

Radar air control sectors Located at Pretoria, Hoedspruit

South African Military Health Service 8,044; ε1,115 reservists (total 9,159)

A separate service within the SANDF

DEPLOYMENT

BURUNDI

AU • AUSTF • *Operation Curiculum* 417

CENTRAL AFRICAN REPUBLIC

Operation Vimbazela (bilateral support) 54

DEMOCRATIC REPUBLIC OF CONGO

UN • MONUC • *Operation Mistral* 1,205; 17 obs; 1 inf bn; 1 engr coy; 1 avn unit, (air med evacuation team, air base control det)

Operation Teutonic 17

SUDAN

UN • UNAMID • *Operation Cordite* 642; 14 obs; 1 inf bn

Sudan SDN

Sudanese Dinar d		2008	2009	2010
GDP	d	116bn	123bn	
	US$	52.7n	49.6bn	
per capita	US$	1,311	1,207	
Growth	%	6.9	4.0	
Inflation	%	14.3	11.0	
Def bdgt	d	n.a.		
	US$	n.a.		
US$1=d		2.2	2.5	

Population   41,087,825

Ethnic and religious groups: Muslim 70% mainly in North; Christian 10% mainly in South; 52% mainly in South; Arab 39% mainly in North

Age	0–14	15–19	20–24	25–29	30–64	65 plus
Male	22%	6%	5%	4%	13%	1%
Female	21%	5%	5%	4%	13%	1%

Capabilities

ACTIVE 109,300 (Army 105,000 Navy 1,300 Air 3,000) **Paramilitary 17,500**

Terms of service conscription (males 18–30) 2 years

RESERVE NIL Paramilitary 85,000

ORGANISATIONS BY SERVICE

Army 85,000; ε20,000 conscripts (total 105,000)

FORCES BY ROLE

Armd	1 div
Mech inf	1 div; 1 indep bde
Inf	6 div; 7 indep bde
Recce	1 indep bde
SF	5 coy
AB	1 div
Arty	3 indep bde
Engr	1 div
Border Guard	1 bde

EQUIPMENT BY TYPE

MBT 360: 20 M-60A3; 60 Type-59/Type-59D; 270 T-54 / T-55; 10 *Al-Bashier* (Type-85-IIM)

LT TK 115: 70 Type-62; 45 Type-63

RECCE 238: 6 AML-90; 60 BRDM-1/BRDM-2; 50–80 *Ferret*; 42 M1114 *HMMWV*; 30–50 *Saladin*

AIFV 75 BMP-1/BMP-2

APC 419

  APC (T) 66: 36 M-113; 20-30 BTR-50

  APC (W) 353: 55-80 V-150 *Commando*; 10 BTR 70; 7 BTR-80A; 50–80 BTR-152; 20 OT-62; 50 OT-64; 96 *Walid*; 10 Type-92 (reported)

ARTY 778+

  SP 20: **122mm** 10 2S1 *Carnation*; **155mm** 10 (AMX) Mk F3

  TOWED 123+ **105mm** 20 M-101; **122mm** 16+: 16 D-30; D-74; M-30; **130mm** 75 M-46/Type-59-I; 12 M-114A1

  MRL 635: **107mm** 477 Type-63; **122mm** 158: 90 BM-21; 50 *Saqr*; 18 Type-81

  MOR 81mm; **82mm**; **120mm** AM-49; M-43

AT • MSL • MANPATS 4+: 4 *Swingfire*; AT-3 9K11 *Sagger*

  RCL 106mm 40 M-40A1

  RL 73mm RPG-7 *Knout*

  GUNS 40+: 40 **76mm** ZIS-3/**100mm** M-1944; **85mm** D-44

AD • SAM • MANPAD 54 SA-7 *Grail*

  GUNS 996+

  SP 20: **20mm** 8 M-163 *Vulcan*; 12 M3 VDAA

  TOWED 976+: 740+ **14.5mm** ZPU-2/**14.5mm** ZPU-4/**37mm** Type-63/**57mm** S-60/**85mm** M-1944; **20mm** 16 M-167 *Vulcan*; **23mm** 50 ZU-23-2; **37mm** 110: 80 M-1939; 30 unserviceable; **40mm** 60

RADAR • LAND RASIT (veh, arty)

Navy 1,300

FORCES BY ROLE

Navy 1 HQ located at Port Sudan

EQUIPMENT BY TYPE

PATROL AND COASTAL COMBATANTS 15

  PBR 8: 4 *Kurmuk*; 4 *Sewart* (all less than 100 tonnes)

  PBI 7 *Ashroora*

AMPHIBIOUS 7

  LCT 2 *Sobat*

  LCVP 5

FACILITIES

Bases Located at Port Sudan, Flamingo Bay (Red Sea), Khartoum (Nile)

Air Force 3,000

The two main air bases are at Khartoum International Airport and Wadi Sayyidna north of Omdurman. The air force also has facilities at civilian airports - El Geneina, Nyala and El Fasher have been used for Darfur ops. Aircrew trg has been reported at Dezful-Ardestani air base, southern Iran.

FORCES BY ROLE

incl Air Defence

FGA   sqns with A-5 *Fantan*; MiG-29SE; MiG-29UB *Fulcrum*; F-7M (MiG-21); *Shenyang* J-6 ; Su-25 *Frogfoot*

Tpt   sqns with An-26 *Curl* (modified for bombing); *Falcon* 20/*Falcon* 50; C-130H *Hercules*; DHC-5D *Buffalo*; Y-8; An-30 *Clank*; An-74TK-200/300; *Falcon* 20 (VIP); *Falcon* 50 (VIP); Fokker 27 (VIP)

Trg   sqns with K-8 *Karakorum*,

Hel   sqns with Mi-24V *Hind E**; Mi-8/Mi-171 (assault); IAR-330 (SA-330) *Puma*

AD   5 bty with SA-2 *Guideline*

EQUIPMENT BY TYPE

AIRCRAFT 79 combat capable

  FGA 67: 15 A-5 *Fantan*; 21 MiG-29SE; 2 MiG-29UB *Fulcrum*; 3 MiG-23BN; 10 F-7 (MiG-21); 6 *Shenyang* J-6; 10 Su-25 *Frogfoot*

  TPT 25: 1 An-26 *Curl* (modified for bombing)*; 4 C-130H *Hercules*; 3 DHC-5D *Buffalo*; 2 Y-8; 1 An-30 *Clank*; 1 An-74TK-200/300; 1 *Falcon* 20 (VIP); 1 *Falcon* 50 (VIP); 1 Fokker 27 (VIP)

  TRG 12 K-8 *Karakorum**

HELICOPTERS

  ATK 23 Mi-24V *Hind E**

  SPT 21+: 20+ Mi-8/Mi-171 ; 1 IAR-330 (SA-330) *Puma* (10 non operational)

AD • SAM • TOWED: 90 SA-2 *Guideline*

Paramilitary 17,500

Popular Defence Force 17,500 (org in bn 1,000); 85,000 reservists (total 102,500)

mil wing of National Islamic Front

SELECTED NON-STATE GROUPS

Darfur

Janjaweed militia Est strength: 20,000 Major equipments include: armoured vehicles, mortars, SALW **Justice and Equality Movement** Est strength: n.k. Major equipments include: armoured vehicles, mortars, SALW

South Sudan

Sudan People's Liberation Army / Movement Est strength: n.k. Major equipments include: armoured vehicles, artillery, mortars, SALW

DEPLOYMENT

COMOROS
AU • MAES 200

FOREIGN FORCES

(all UNMIS, unless otherwise indicated)
Australia 9; 6 obs
Bangladesh 1,451; 19 obs; 1 inf bn; 1 engr coy; 1 de-mining coy; 1 MP coy; 1 fd hospital; 1 tpt coy; 1 rvn coy • UNAMID 591; 7 obs; 2 log coy
Belgium 4 obs
Benin 4 obs
Bolivia 11 obs • UNAMID 1
Brazil 2; 20 obs
Burkina Faso UNAMID 279; 6 obs; elm 1 inf bn
Burundi UNAMID 4; 7 obs
Cambodia 53; 5 obs 1 de-mining coy • UNAMID 5 obs
Canada 8 (*Op Safari*); 21 obs
China, People's Republic of 444; 12 obs; 1 engr coy; 1 tpt coy; 1 fd hospital • UNAMID 325; 1 engr coy
Croatia 5
Denmark 4; 8 obs
Ecuador 17 obs
Egypt 1,235; 20 obs; 1 inf coy; 1 engr coy; 1 med coy • UNAMID 2,420; 12 obs; 1 inf bn; 1engr coy; 1 sigs coy; 1 tpt coy
El Salvador 4 obs
Ethiopia UNAMID 1,763; 9 obs; 1 inf bn; 1 recce coy; 1 tpt coy
Fiji 6 obs
Finland 1
Gambia UNAMID 201; 1 obs; 1 inf coy
Germany 5; 26 obs • UNAMID 7
Ghana UNAMID 10; 3 obs;
Greece 1; 2 obs
Guatemala 1; 2 obs • UNAMID 2
Guinea 6 obs
India 2,600; 17 obs; 2 inf bn; 1 engr coy; 1 avn unit; 1 fd hospital
Indonesia 6 obs • UNAMID 3
Iran 2 obs
Italy UNAMID 1
Jordan 5; 10 obs • UNAMID 12; 4 obs
Kenya 726; 4 obs; 1 inf bn; 1 de-mining coy • UNAMID 84; 2 obs; 1 MP coy
Korea, Republic of 1; 6 obs • UNAMID 2
Kyrgyzstan 6 obs
Malawi UNAMID5; 6 obs
Malaysia 2; 8 obs • UNAMID 14; 2 obs
Mali 3 obs • UNAMID 7; 9 obs
Moldova 2 obs
Mongolia 2 obs
Mozambique UNAMID 7 obs
Namibia 7 obs • UNAMID 12; 5 obs
Nepal 8; 9obs • UNAMID 23; 16 obs
Netherlands 2; 12 obs • UNAMID 1
New Zealand 1; 1 obs

Nigeria 2; 9 obs • UNAMID 3,331; 8 obs; 4 inf bn
Norway 7; 14 obs
Pakistan 1,481; 14 obs; 1 inf bn; 1 engr coy; 2 avn unit; 1 tpt coy; 1 de-mining coy; 1 fd hospital • UNAMID 507; 3 obs; 1 engr coy; 1 fd hospital
Paraguay 9 obs
Peru 13 obs
Philippines 11 obs
Poland 2 obs
Romania 1; 10 obs
Russia 122; 12 obs; 1 avn unit
Rwanda 256; 10 obs; 1 inf bn • UNAMID 3,228; 7 obs; 4 inf bn
Senegal UNAMID 811; 13 obs; 1 inf bn
Sierra Leone 3 obs • UNAMID 11; 4 obs
South Africa UNAMID 642; 14 obs; 1 inf bn
Sri Lanka 6 obs
Sweden 2; 1 obs
Tanzania 11 obs • UNAMID 287; 7 obs ; elm 1 inf bn
Thailand 10 obs • UNAMID 15; 6 obs
Togo UNAMID 1 obs
Turkey 3 • UNAMID 1
Uganda 5obs • UNAMID 2 obs
Ukraine 11 obs
United Kingdom 2 • UNAMID 1
Yemen, Republic of 2; 21 obs • UNAMID 14; 12 obs
Zambia 349;14 obs; 1 inf coy •UNAMID 15; 12 obs
Zimbabwe 12 obs • UNAMID 8; 6 obs

Tanzania TZA

Tanzanian Shilling sh		2008	2009	2010
GDP	sh	24.1tr	27.9tr	
	US$	20.2bn	21.3bn	
per capita	US$	501	519	
Growth	%	7.5	5.0	
Inflation	%	10.3	10.6	
Def bdgt	sh	ε220bn		
	US$	ε183m		
US$1=sh		1,200	1,313	

Population	41,048,532

Age	0–14	15–19	20–24	25–29	30–64	65 plus
Male	22%	6%	5%	4%	11%	1%
Female	22%	6%	5%	4%	12%	1%

Capabilities

ACTIVE 27,000 (Army 23,000 Navy 1,000 Air 3,000)
Paramilitary 1,400
Terms of service incl civil duties, 2 years

RESERVE 80,000 (Joint 80,000)

ORGANISATIONS BY SERVICE

Army ε23,000

FORCES BY ROLE

Tk 1 bde

Inf 5 bde

Arty 4 bn

Mor 1 bn

AT 2 bn

ADA 2 bn

Engr 1 regt (bn)

EQUIPMENT BY TYPE†

MBT 45: 30 T-54/T-55; 15 Type-59

LT TK 55: 30 *Scorpion*; 25 Type-62

RECCE 10 BRDM-2

APC (W) 14: ε10 BTR-40/BTR-152; 4 Type-92 (reported)

ARTY 378

TOWED 170: **76mm** ε40 ZIS-3; **122mm** 100: 20 D-30; 80 Type-54-1 (M-30) *M-1938*; **130mm** 30 Type-59-I

MRL 122mm 58 BM-21

MOR 150: **82mm** 100 M-43; **120mm** 50 M-43

AT • RCL 75mm Type-52 (M-20)

RL 73mm RPG-7 *Knout*

GUNS 85mm 75 Type-56 (D-44)

Navy ε1,000

EQUIPMENT BY TYPE

PATROL AND COASTAL COMBATANTS 8

PHT 2 *Huchuan* each with 2 533mm ASTT

PFC 2 *Shanghai II* (PRC)

PCC 4: 2 VT; 2 *Ngunguri*

AMPHIBIOUS • LCU 2 *Yunnan*

FACILITIES

Bases Located at Dar es Salaam, Zanzibar, Mwanza (Lake Victoria)

Air Defence Command ε3,000;

FORCES BY ROLE

Ftr 3 sqn with J-7 (MiG-21F) *Fishbed C*; J-5 (MiG-17F) *Fresco C*; J-6 (MiG-19S) *Farmer B*; K-8 *Karakorum*

Tpt 1 sqn with Y-5 (An-2) *Colt*; DHC-5D *Buffalo*; F-28 *Fellowship*; HS-125-700; HS-748; Y-12(II)

Liaison some sqn with Cessna 310; Cessna 404 *Titan*; Cessna U-206 *Stationair*; Bell 206B *Jet Ranger II*

Trg sqn with PA-28-140 *Cherokee*; MiG-15UTI *Midget*

Hel some sqn with 4 AB-205 (Bell 205); Bell 412; SA-316

EQUIPMENT BY TYPE

Virtually no air defence assets serviceable.

AIRCRAFT 25 combat capable†

FTR 9: 6 J-7 (MiG-21F) *Fishbed C*; 3 J-5 (MiG-17F) *Fresco C*

FGA 10 J-6 (MiG-19S) *Farmer B*

TPT 26: 5 Cessna 310; 2 Cessna 404 *Titan*; 3 DHC-5D *Buffalo*; 2 F-28 *Fellowship*; 1 HS-125-700; 3 HS-748; 5 PA-28-140 *Cherokee*; 2 Y-8; 2 Y-12(II); 1 Y-5 (An-2) *Colt*

UTL 1 Cessna U-206 *Stationair*

TRG 8: 6 K-8 *Karakorum**; 2 MiG-15UTI *Midget*

HELICOPTERS

UTL 18: 4 AB-205 (Bell 205); 6 Bell 206B *Jet Ranger II*; 4 Bell 412; 4 SA-316

AD

SAM 160:

SP 20 SA-6 *Gainful*†; 20 SA-3 *Goa*†

MANPAD 120 SA-7 *Grail*†

GUNS 200

TOWED 14.5mm 40 ZPU-2/ZPU-4†; **23mm** 40 ZU-23; **37mm** 120 M-1939

Paramilitary 1,400 active

Police Field Force 1,400

18 sub-units incl Police Marine Unit

Air Wing

AIRCRAFT • UTL 1 Cessna U-206 *Stationair*

HELICOPTERS

UTL 4: 2 AB-206A (Bell 206A) *JetRanger*; 2 Bell 206L *LongRanger*

TRG 2 AB-47G (Bell 47G) Trg hel/Bell 47G2

Marine Unit 100

PATROL AND COASTAL COMBATANTS • MISC BOATS/CRAFT: some boats

Armed Forces 80,000 reservists

DEPLOYMENT

COMOROS

AU • MAES 150

CÔTE D'IVOIRE

UN • UNOCI 2; 1 obs

LEBANON

UN • UNIFIL 72; 1 MP coy

SUDAN

UN • UNMIS 11 obs

UN • UNAMID 287; 7 obs; elm 1 inf bn

Togo TGO

CFA Franc BCEAO fr		2008	2009	2010
GDP	fr	1.31tr	1.33tr	
	US$	3.0bn	3.0bn	
per capita	US$	504	498	
Growth	%	1.1	2.4	
Inflation	%	8.4	2.8	
Def bdgt	fr	ε25bn	ε30bn	
	US$	ε56m	ε67m	
US$1=fr		447	444	

Population 6,031,808

Age	0–14	15–19	20–24	25–29	30–64	65 plus
Male	21%	6%	5%	4%	12%	1%
Female	21%	6%	5%	4%	13%	2%

Capabilities

ACTIVE 8,550 (Army 8,100 Navy 200 Air 250)
Paramilitary 750
Terms of service conscription, 2 years (selective)

ORGANISATIONS BY SERVICE

Army 8,100+

FORCES BY ROLE

Inf	1 regt (some spt unit (trg), 2 armd sqn, 3 inf coy); 1 regt (1 mot inf bn, 1 mech inf bn)
Cdo/Para	1 regt (3 cdo/para coy)
Spt	1 regt (1 fd arty bty, 1 engr/log/tpt bn, 2 ADA bty)
Presidential Guard	1 regt (1 Presidential Guard bn, 1 cdo bn, 2 Presidential Guard coy)

EQUIPMENT BY TYPE
MBT 2 T-54/T-55
LT TK 9 *Scorpion*
RECCE 61: 3 AML-60; 7 AML-90; 36 EE-9 *Cascavel*; 3 M-20; 4 M-3A1; 6 M-8; 2 VBL
AIFV 20 BMP-2
APC (W) 30 UR-416
ARTY 30
    SP 122mm 6
    TOWED 105mm 4 HM-2
    MOR 82mm 20 M-43
AT • RCL 22: **75mm** 12 Type-52 (M-20)/Type-56; **82mm** 10 Type-65 (B-10)
    GUNS 57mm 5 ZIS-2
AD • GUNS • TOWED 43 **14.5mm** 38 ZPU-4; **37mm** 5 M-1939

Navy ε200 (incl Marine Infantry unit)

EQUIPMENT BY TYPE
PATROL AND COASTAL COMBATANTS • PFC 2 *Kara* (FRA *Esterel*)
FACILITIES
Base   Located at Lomé

Air Force 250

FORCES BY ROLE

FGA	sqn with EMB-326G; *Alpha Jet**
Tpt	sqn with B-707 (VIP); Beech 58 *Baron*; Reims Cessna 337 (Cessna 337) *Skymaster*; DHC-5D *Buffalo*; F-28-1000 (VIP); Do-27
Trg	sqn with TB-30 *Epsilon**
Hel	sqn with AS-332 *Super Puma*; SA-330 *Puma*; SA-315 *Lama*; SA-319 *Alouette III*

EQUIPMENT BY TYPE†
AIRCRAFT 10 combat capable
    FGA 4 EMB-326G
    TPT 8: 1 B-707 (VIP); 2 Beech 58 *Baron*; 2 DHC-5D *Buffalo*; 1 F-28-1000 (VIP); 2 Reims Cessna 337 *Skymaster*
    TRG 7: 3 *Alpha Jet**; 1 Do-27; 3 TB-30 *Epsilon**

HELICOPTERS
    SPT 2: 1 AS-332 *Super Puma*; 1 SA-330 *Puma* (both in storage)
    UTL 3: 2 SA-315 *Lama*; 1 SA-319 *Alouette III*

Paramilitary 750

Gendarmerie 750
Ministry of Interior
FORCES BY ROLE
2 reg sections
Paramilitary   1 (mob) sqn
FACILITIES
School 1

DEPLOYMENT

CENTRAL AFRICAN REPUBLIC/CHAD
UN • MINURCAT 457; 1 HQ coy; elm 1 inf coy

CÔTE D'IVOIRE
UN • UNOCI 313; 7 obs; 1 inf bn

LIBERIA
UN • UNMIL 1; 2 obs

SUDAN
UN • UNAMID 1 obs

Uganda UGA

Ugandan Shilling Ush		2008	2009	2010
GDP	Ush	28.3tr		
	US$	16.5bn		
per capita	US$	525		
Growth	%	9.0	7.0	
Inflation	%	7.3	14.2	
Def exp	Ush	476bn		
	US$	277m		
Def bdgt	Ush	406bn	464bn	
	US$	236m	243m	
US$1=Ush		1,720	1,910	

Population   32,369,558

Age	0–14	15–19	20–24	25–29	30–64	65 plus
Male	25%	6%	5%	4%	10%	1%
Female	25%	6%	5%	4%	10%	1%

Capabilities

ACTIVE 45,000 (Ugandan People's Defence Force 45,000) **Paramilitary 1,800**

ORGANISATIONS BY SERVICE

Ugandan People's Defence Force ε40,000-45,000

FORCES BY ROLE

Army 5 div (*each:* up to 5 army bde)

Armd 1 bde

Arty 1 bde

EQUIPMENT BY TYPE†

MBT 162 T-54/T-55 ; 10 T-72

LT TK ε20 PT-76

RECCE 46: 40 *Eland*; 6 *Ferret*

AIFV 31 BMP-2

APC (W) 79: 15 BTR-60; 20 *Buffel*; 40 *Mamba*; 4 OT-64

ARTY 312+

  SP 155mm 3 ATMOS 2000

  TOWED 243+: **76mm** ZIS-3; **122mm** M-30; **130mm** 221; **155mm** 4 G-5; 18 M-839

  MRL 6+: **107mm** (12-tube); **122mm 6+:** BM-21; 6 RM-70

  MOR 60+ : **81mm** L16; **82mm** M-43; **120mm** 60 *Soltam*

AD • SAM • MANPAD 200+: 200 SA-7 *Grail*; SA-16 *Gimlet*

  GUNS • TOWED 20+: **14.5mm** ZPU-1/ZPU-2/ZPU-4; **37mm** 20 M-1939

Air Wing

FORCES BY ROLE

FGA   sqn with MiG-23 *Flogger*; MiG-21 *Fishbed*

Tpt   sqn with Y-12

Tpt Hel sqn with Mi-172 (VIP); Mi-17 (Mi-8MT) *Hip H*; Bell 206 *Jet Ranger*; Bell 412 *Twin Huey*

Trg   sqn with L-39 *Albatros*†*; SF-260* (non-operational)

Hel   sqn with Mi-24 *Hind*

EQUIPMENT BY TYPE

AIRCRAFT 16 combat capable

  FTR 12: 5 MiG-23 *Flogger*; 7 MiG-21 *Fishbed*

  TPT 2 Y-12

  TRG 4: 3 L-39 *Albatros*†*; 1 SF-260* (non-operational)

HELICOPTERS

  ATK 6: 1 Mi-24 *Hind*; 5 non-operational

  SPT 5: 1 Mi-172 (VIP); 3 Mi-17 (Mi-8MT) *Hip H*; 1 non-operational

  UTL 5: 3 Bell 206 *Jet Ranger*; 2 Bell 412 *Twin Huey*

Paramilitary ε1,800 active

Border Defence Unit ε600
Equipped with small arms only

Police Air Wing ε800
HELICOPTERS • UTL 1 Bell 206 *JetRanger*

Marines ε400
PATROL AND COASTAL COMBATANTS 8 PCR less than 100 tonnes

Local Militia Forces Amuka Group ε3,000; ε7,000 (reported under trg) (total 10,000)

SELECTED NON-STATE GROUPS

Lord's Resistance Army Est strength: 1,500 Major equipments include: mines and IEDs, SALW • **Allied Democratic Front** Est strength: 200 Major equipments include: SALW

DEPLOYMENT

CÔTE D'IVOIRE
UN • ONUCI 2; 3 obs

SOMALIA
AU • AMISOM 2,550; 3 inf bn

SUDAN
UN • UNMIS 5 obs

UN • UNAMID 2 obs

Zambia ZMB

Zambian Kwacha K		2008	2009	2010
GDP	K	55.4tr	59.5tr	
	US$	14.8bn	12.8bn	
per capita	US$	1,268	1,078	
Growth	%	5.8	4.5	
Inflation	%	12.4	14.0	
Def bdgt	K	981bn	1,068bn	
	US$	261m	229m	
US$1=K		3,745	4,660	

Population	11,862,740

Age	0–14	15–19	20–24	25–29	30–64	65 plus
Male	23%	6%	5%	4%	10%	1%
Female	23%	6%	5%	4%	11%	1%

Capabilities

ACTIVE 15,100 (Army 13,500 Air 1,600) **Paramilitary 1,400**

RESERVE 3,000 (Army 3,000)

ORGANISATIONS BY SERVICE

Army 13,500

FORCES BY ROLE

Army 3 bde HQ

Armd 1 regt (1 tk bn, 1 armd recce bn)

Inf   6 bn

Arty 1 regt (1 MRL bn, 2 fd arty bn)

Engr 1 regt

EQUIPMENT BY TYPE

Some equipment†

MBT 30: 20 Type-59; 10 T-55

LT TK 30 PT-76

RECCE 70 BRDM-1/BRDM-2 (ε30 serviceable)

APC (W)33: 20 BTR-70; 13 BTR-60

ARTY 182

  TOWED 61: **105mm** 18 Model 56 pack howitzer; **122mm** 25 D-30; **130mm** 18 M-46

  MRL 122mm 30 BM-21 (ε12 serviceable)

  MOR 91: **81mm** 55; **82mm** 24; **120mm** 12

AT • MSL • MANPATS AT-3 9K11 *Sagger*
RCL 12+: **57mm** 12 M-18; **75mm** M-20; **84mm** *Carl Gustav*
RL **73mm** RPG-7 *Knout*
AD • SAM • MANPAD SA-7 *Grail*
GUNS • TOWED 136: **20mm** 50 M-55 (triple); **37mm** 40 M-1939; **57mm** ε30 S-60; **85mm** 16 M-1939 *KS-12*

Reserve 3,000

Inf   3 bn

Air Force 1,600

FORCES BY ROLE

FGA   1 sqn with F-6 (MiG-19); 1 sqn with MiG-21MF/ MiG-21U; *Fishbed J*†

Tpt   1 sqn with An-26 *Curl*; DHC-5D *Buffalo*; Y-12(II)/(IV); MA60

VIP   1 fleet with HS-748; Yak-40 *Codling*

Liaison sqn with 5 Do-28

Trg   sqns with FT-6*; K-8*; SF-260TP; MFI-17

Hel   1 sqn with Mi-8 *Hip*; some (Liaison) sqn with Bell 47G; UH-1H *Iroquois*/AB-205 (Bell 205)

AD   3 bty with SA-3 *Goa*;

EQUIPMENT BY TYPE
Very low serviceability.
AIRCRAFT 28 combat capable
FGA 16: 8 F-6 (MiG-19); 8 MiG-21MF *Fishbed J*
TPT 27: 4 An-26 *Curl*; 4 DHC-5D *Buffalo*; 5 Do-28; 1 HS-748; 4 Y-12(II); 5 Y-12(IV); 2 Yak-40 *Codling*; 2 MA60
TRG 17+: 8 K-8*; 2 MiG-21U *Mongol A**; 5 SF-260TP; 2 FT-6*; some MFI-17
HELICOPTERS
SPT 4 Mi-17 *Hip*
UTL 13: 10 UH-1H *Iroquois*/AB-205 (Bell 205); 3 Bell 212
TRG 5 Bell 47G
AD • SAM SA-3 *Goa*
MSL • ASM AT-3 *Sagger*

Paramilitary 1,400

Police Mobile Unit 700
Police 1 bn (4 Police coy)

Police Paramilitary Unit 700
Paramilitary 1 bn (3 Paramilitary coy)

DEPLOYMENT

CÔTE D'IVOIRE
UN • UNOCI 2 obs

DEMOCRATIC REPUBLIC OF CONGO
UN • MONUC 23 obs

LIBERIA
UN • UNMIL 3 obs

NEPAL
UN • UNMIN 1 obs

SUDAN
UN • UNMIS 349; 14 obs; 1 inf coy
UN • UNAMID 15; 12 obs

Zimbabwe ZWE

Zimbabwe Dollar Z$		2008	2009	2010
GDP	Z$	n.a.	n.a.	
	US$	ε1.3bn	ε1.5bn	
per capita	US$	115	132	
Growth	%	-14.1	3.7	
Inflation	%	156	9.0	
Def bdgt	Z$	n.a.	2.82bn	
	US$	n.a.	n.a.	
US$1=Z$		n.a.	n.a.	

Population   11,392,629

Age	0–14	15–19	20–24	25–29	30–64	65 plus
Male	19%	7%	6%	5%	11%	2%
Female	19%	7%	6%	4%	12%	2%

Capabilities

ACTIVE 29,000 (Army 25,000 Air 4,000) **Paramilitary 21,800**

ORGANISATIONS BY SERVICE

Army ε25,000
FORCES BY ROLE

Armd	1 sqn
Mech	1 bde HQ
Mech Inf	1 bn
Inf	5 bde HQ; 15 bn
Cdo	1 bn
Para	1 bn
Arty	1 bde
Fd arty	1 regt
Engr	2 regt
Gd	3 bn
Presidential Guard	1 gp
AD	1 regt

EQUIPMENT BY TYPE
MBT 40: 30 Type-59 mostly non-operational; 10 Type-69 mostly non-operational
RECCE 100: 20 *Eland*; 15 *Ferret*†; 80 EE-9 *Cascavel* (90mm)
APC 85
  APC (T) 30: 8 Type-63; 22 VTT-323
  APC (W) 55 TPK 4.20 VSC *ACMAT*
ARTY 242
  TOWED 122mm 20: 4 D-30; 16 Type-60 (D-74)
  MRL 76: **107mm** 16 Type-63; **122mm** 60 RM-70 *Dana*
  MOR 146: **81mm/82mm** ε140; **120mm** 6 M-43
AD • SAM • MANPAD 30 SA-7 *Grail*†

GUNS • TOWED 116: **14.5mm** 36 ZPU-1/ZPU-2/ZPU-4; **23mm** 45 ZU-23; **37mm** 35 M-1939

Air Force 4,000

Flying hours   100 hrs/year

FORCES BY ROLE

Ftr	1 sqn with F-7N (F-7M) *Airguard*†; F-7II (J-7II) *Fishbed*†; FT-7 (JJ-7) *Mongol A*†
FGA	1 sqn with Hawker *Hunter*; 1 sqn with K-8
RECCE/Trg/ Liaison	1 sqn with SF-260M; SF-260TP*; SF-260W *Warrior**
RECCE/COIN	1 sqn with Cessna 337 *Skymaster**
Tpt	1 sqn with BN-2 *Islander*; CASA 212-200 *Aviocar* (VIP); IL-76 *Candid*
Hel	1 sqn with Mi-35 *Hind**; Mi-35P *Hind* (armed/liaison); SA-319 *Alouette III*; AS-532UL *Cougar* (VIP); 1 trg sqn with Bell 412 *Twin Huey*, SA-319 *Alouette III*
AD	1 sqn with 37mm; 57mm

EQUIPMENT BY TYPE
AIRCRAFT 46 combat capable
  FTR 10: 4 F-7N (F-7M) *Airguard*†; 3 F-7II (J-7II) *Fishbed*†
  FGA 12; 12 Hawker *Hunter* FGA* in store
  TPT 38: 5 BN-2 *Islander*; 10 C-47 *Skytrain* in store; 8 CASA 212-200 *Aviocar* (VIP); 14 Cessna 337 *Skymaster*; 1 IL-76 *Candid*
  TRG 32: 2 FT-7 (JJ-7) *Mongol A*†*; 12 K-8*; 5 SF-260M; 5 SF-260TP*; 5 SF-260W *Warrior**; 5 SF-260F

HELICOPTERS
  ATK 6: 4 Mi-35 *Hind**; 2 Mi-35P *Hind* (armed/liaison)
  UTL 2 AS-532UL *Cougar* (VIP);
  TRG 10: 8 Bell 412 *Twin Huey*; 2 SA-319 *Alouette III**;
AD • GUNS 100mm (not deployed); **37mm** (not deployed); **57mm** (not deployed)

FACILITIES

School 1 with 100mm Guns (not deployed); 37mm Guns (not deployed); 57mm Guns (not deployed) (AD)

Paramilitary 21,800

Zimbabwe Republic Police Force 19,500

incl Air Wg

Police Support Unit 2,300

DEPLOYMENT

CÔTE D'IVOIRE
UN • UNOCI 1 obs

LIBERIA
UN • UNMIL 2 obs

NEPAL
UN • UNMIN 2 obs

SUDAN
UN • UNMIS 12 obs
UN • UNAMID 8; 6 obs

Table 28 **Selected arms procurements and deliveries, sub-Saharan Africa**

Designation	Type	Quantity	Contract Value	Supplier Country	Prime Contractor	Order Date	First Delivery Due	Notes
Chad (CHA)								
Su-25 *Frogfoot*	FGA	6	–	UKR	Sukhoi	2007	2008	Ex-UKR stock. Delivery status unclear
Kenya (KEN)								
Nyayo-class	PFM	2	–	Dom/ITA	Fincantieri	2008	2010	Refit, incl removal of SSM capability. KNS *Nyayo* and KNS *Umoja*
F-5E *Tiger*-2	Ftr	15	US$23.2m	JOR	–	2008	2008	Ex-JOR stock. Delivery status unclear
Namibia (NAM)								
Grajaú-class	PCC	4	–	BRZ	INACE	2004	2009	First vessel, *Brendan Simbwaye*, delivered January 2009
Chetak, Cheetah	Utl hel	3	US$10m	IND	Hindustan Aero-nautics	2009		2 *Chetak*, 1 *Cheetah*
Nigeria (NGA)								
38m Fast Patrol Craft	PFM	2	n.k.	MYS	Nautica Nova Ship-building & Engine-ering	2007		Unverified deliveries reported during 2009
F-7NI	Ftr	12	See notes	PRC	–	2005	2006	Combined cost with 3 FT–7NI is US$251m. Subject to delays
FT-7NI	Trg ac	3	See notes	PRC	–	2005	2006	Combined cost with 12 F–7NI is US$251m. Subject to delays
G222	Tpt ac Upgrade	6	US$74.5m	ITA	Alenia	2005	2005	Upgrade. Incl refurbishment, trg and log spt for 5 G222. Nga also to receive a fmr ITA air force G222.
ATR 42 MP *Surveyor*	MP / SAR	2	US$73m	ITA	Alenia	2007	2009	Delivery status unclear
South Africa (RSA)								
AMV 8x8	IFV	264	ZAR8.8bn (US$1.2bn)	FIN/Dom	Patria/ Denel	2007	–	5 variants to be produced: comd, mor, msl, section, and fire spt vehicles
JAS 39 C/D *Gripen*	FGA	26	US$1.47bn	SWE	SAAB	2000	2008	17 C single seat variant and 9 D twin seat variant. Final delivery due 2012. 5 JAS-39D delivered by end-08
A-*Darter*	AAM	–		Int'l	Denel	2007	–	As of 2009, AAM undergoing flight trials and delayed by budget problems. Intended to arm *Gripen*
A-400M	Tpt ac	8	US$516m	Int'l	Airbus	2005	2010	In development. Official unit cost US$80m. First deliveries delayed
Zimbabwe (Zw)								
FC-1 *Xiaolong*	FGA	12		PRC		2004	–	Delivery status unclear

Chapter Seven
South and Central Asia

SOUTH ASIA

India

The 26–28 November 2008 terrorist attack in Mumbai jolted the Indian security establishment and raised tensions sharply with Pakistan. A total of 163 people (including 22 foreign nationals) were killed by ten terrorists. While nine of the terrorists also died, one of them, Ajmal Amir Kasab, a Pakistani national belonging to the Lashkar-e-Tayiba (LeT) terrorist organisation, was captured by Indian security forces and was put on trial in Mumbai in April 2009. India initially blamed 'elements in Pakistan' for the attack; Indian Prime Minister Manmohan Singh stated in January 2009 that the attack had the 'support of some official agencies in Pakistan'. Subsequently, a senior Indian official accused Pakistan's Inter-Services Intelligence (ISI) of complicity in the Mumbai attack. Neither country mobilised its military forces, though both put them on alert, and there was speculation that India might strike LeT targets. Pakistan belatedly admitted that Kasab was a Pakistani national and the attacks were partly planned in Pakistan, but denied accusations of official involvement in the attacks.

Security restructuring
Due largely to the Mumbai attacks, India's 2009/10 defence budget (excluding pensions), passed in July, was increased by a third to Rs1,417bn (US$32 billion). Of this, US$8.5bn was allocated for the acquisition of major armaments, though the total sum seemed likely to reach US$50bn over the next five or six years. India has been spending additional funds on the modernisation and expansion of its seven paramilitary forces, including establishing 38 new battalions (about 39,000 security personnel) in the Central Reserve Police Force (CRPF) and on the acquisition of arms and equipment for its police forces, while fast-tracking arms and equipment for its commandos and special forces. The navy has set up a new specialised force, the Sagar Prahari Bal, to protect naval assets and bases, comprising 1,000 personnel and 80 fast interception craft. The force is currently undergoing training.

A major overhaul of India's coastal and maritime security was set in motion following the revelation that the Mumbai terrorists had reached the city by sea. On 28 February, Defence Minister A.K. Antony announced that the navy was to be designated the main authority responsible for maritime security, both coastal and offshore, in close coordination with the coastguard, the state marine police and other central/state government and port authorities. Meanwhile, the coastguard is to be responsible for overall coordination between central and state agencies in all matters relating to coastal security, with the director general coastguard to be designated the commander of a newly constituted coastal command. Four joint operation centres were established in May–September 2009 to improve navy–coastguard coordination, with existing naval commanders-in-chief designated commanders-in-chief of coastal defence.

The coastguard and marine police are also being strengthened and expanded and a coastal security network created. A new coastguard regional headquarters was established at Gandhinagar in Gujarat in September 2009 to enhance surveillance of the coastal state. (A new squadron with Dornier maritime-surveillance aircraft was activated at Porbandar in Gujarat in June 2009.) Nine new coastguard stations were to be set up and integrated with coastal police stations, of which 64 have been newly established, along with 25 new checkpoints out of a planned 97. Nationally, the coastguard was to acquire additional ships, aircraft and helicopters, as well as a revamped intelligence structure, while a chain of 46 radars was also being established on the coast and island territories, to include sensors to identify vessels near the coast. But the precise roles and functions of the navy commanders-in-chief, designated as commanders-in-chief of coastal defence, remain unclear in relation to the coastguard chief, designated Commander, Coastal Command. It also remains to be seen how effective navy and coastguard coordination with state administrative and police forces will be in a coastal command, if and when it is established.

Service developments
India sees a modernised and capable **navy** as supporting its realignment of strategic focus to fit its

widening economic and diplomatic interests beyond South Asia. In August 2009 the navy updated its maritime doctrine for the first time in nearly six years. In his foreword, then Chief of Naval Staff Admiral Sureesh Mehta wrote that, 'as the largest democracy and an emerging major economy, India's role as a responsible player on the global stage, towards promoting peace, stability and development, has been recognised in the international arena'. The document focuses on the spectrum of conflict, India's maritime environment and interests, and the application of maritime power. The latter chapter incorporates new constabulary missions for the navy, including counter-terrorism and anti-piracy operations. For the first time, it is stated that India's maritime forces could be deployed on specific counter-terrorism missions 'both independently and as cooperative endeavours with friendly foreign naval and coast guard forces'.

The key strategic challenge, and priority for the navy, is the Chinese People's Liberation Army Navy. Days before retiring in August 2009, Mehta stated that India neither had the military capability nor the intention 'to match China force for force', and advocated the use of maritime domain awareness and network-centric operations along with 'a reliable stand-off deterrent' as means of coping with China's rise. India's new maritime doctrine categorises India's secondary maritime areas of interest as including, for the first time, 'the South China Sea, other areas of the west Pacific Ocean and friendly littoral countries located therein', and the deliberately vaguely worded 'other areas of national interest based on considerations of diaspora and overseas investments'. These represent key indicators of Indian naval trends or aspirations.

In July, the navy launched the first locally built *Arihant* nuclear-powered submarine. Its weapons fit has yet to be announced, and commissioning is expected in 2012. In 2010, the navy is expected to acquire its first *Akula*-class nuclear-powered submarine on lease from Russia. The former Russian carrier *Admiral Gorshkov*, due for commissioning in 2012 or 2013, is to augment the navy's single current *Viraat*-class carrier, and the first of two locally built carriers is to be commissioned the following year. India was also acquiring technologically sophisticated missile-armed 'stealth' warships and augmenting its maritime-surveillance capabilities (see Defence Economics, p. 349 and the essay on p. 473).

Enhancing the security of small island states in the Indian Ocean against terrorism and piracy is also an emerging concern. In August 2009, India boosted defence cooperation with the Maldives by agreeing to set up a network of 26 radars across the Maldives atolls to be networked to the Indian coastal radar system, along with the establishment of an air station to conduct surveillance flights and coordinate naval patrols in the Maldives Exclusive Economic Zone. The Indian navy regularly carries out coordinated anti-piracy patrols off the Seychelles coast and since mid October 2008 has deployed a warship to the Gulf of Aden for maritime-security operations.

Following the reopening of the Daulat Beg Oldi and Fuk Che airfields in Ladakh, close to the 4,000km Line of Actual Control, the de facto border between India and China, India's **air force** also plans to turn the Neoma advanced landing ground in Ladakh into a runway proper. The new Indian air force chief, Air Chief Marshal P.V. Naik, publicly complained that his fighter-aircraft strength, a third of China's, was inadequate and needed to be increased.

The **army** continues its long-standing counter-terrorism and counter-insurgency operations in Indian-administered Kashmir, where there are signs of increasing infiltration across the Line of Control, as well as in the insurgency-affected northeastern provinces of Assam, Nagaland and Manipur. Despite pressure from the local administration in Kashmir, Antony ruled out repealing the Armed Forces (Special Powers) Act, which provides the armed forces with extraordinary powers of arrest and detention, in Kashmir or parts of the northeast.

There is uncertainty over how best to deal with continued violence by the Maoist Naxalites, who reportedly operate in nearly a third of the country's districts. While the prime minister called them the gravest internal security threat, he also sought a nuanced political and developmental strategy to tackle the violence. The government was ready to hold a dialogue with the Naxalites provided they give up their arms, a condition they rejected, and the order banning the Communist Party of India (Maoist) as a terror organisation was renewed on 22 June. Meanwhile, the air force was refused permission to use force against the Naxalites in self-defence during surveillance and search-and-rescue operations, while a new anti-Naxalite force, the Commando Battalion for Resolute Action (CoBRA), was also established under the command and control of the central reserve police force. In October the central government announced a new anti-Naxalite plan that included deployment of over 40,000 central police personnel in affected provinces.

Pakistan

Democratically elected President Asif Ali Zardari (co-chair of the Pakistan People's Party) completed his first year in office in September 2009. But Zardari's popularity had declined due to growing economic and security problems and weak leadership. General Ashfaq Kayani, who replaced Pervez Musharraf as Chief of Army Staff in November 2007, continued to play a dominant but discreet role in the affairs of the country amid widening policy differences with Zardari. Following the army's moves to scotch the transfer of the ISI to civilian control in July 2008, and ensure the restoration of Supreme Court Chief Justice Iftikhar Muhammad Chaudhry in March 2009, in mid October it expressed concerns over the Zardari-supported US Enhanced Partnership with Pakistan Act of 2009 (the Kerry–Lugar Act). The act's conditions on ensuring civilian control of the army and counter-terrorism were perceived, not only by the army but also by influential sections of the public and the opposition parties, as intrusive and an infringement of Pakistani sovereignty.

War against the Taliban

The spread of Islamist militancy and terrorism from the Federally Administered Tribal Areas (FATA) bordering Afghanistan to the adjoining areas of the North-West Frontier Province (NWFP) and to Pakistan's heartland of South Punjab poses a growing challenge. Washington expressed concern over the rise of attacks in Afghanistan by Afghan Taliban fighters, attributed largely to their use of Pakistan's tribal areas as a sanctuary from which to launch incursions, while the banned Tehrik-e-Taliban (TTP or Pakistan Taliban) poses a growing threat to Pakistan's own national security.

Although Pakistan had deployed 120,000 Army and Frontier Corps troops to the border regions they were, until recently, unable to effectively counter the Afghan and Pakistan Taliban militants. The beleaguered provincial government of NWFP signed an agreement on 16 February 2009 with Sufi Mohammed, a pro-Taliban leader of the outlawed Tehrik-e-Nifaz-e-Shariat-e-Mohammadi militant group, allowing the imposition of sharia law in the Swat Valley and Malakand Division (which comprises a third of the NWFP), in return for a ceasefire by the TTP. But the Taliban militants refused to disarm and in April expanded their control over parts of Buner, adjacent to Swat, only some 100km northwest of Islamabad.

Under pressure from the US, Islamabad reversed its policy. On 28 April Pakistani troops began a major military offensive with air support against the TTP in Malakand Division, beginning with Lower Dir District and then Buner and Swat. On 1 July security forces captured the town of Shah Dheri, the last Taliban stronghold in the Swat Valley. Some 1,600 TTP and other militants were reportedly killed in this two-month operation, which also led to an estimated 2 million civilians leaving their homes. Sufi Mohammed and his two sons were arrested on 26 July in Peshawar, but no TTP leaders were killed or captured.

The army announced in early June that it was shifting its offensive against the Pakistan Taliban and al-Qaeda to the South Waziristan region of FATA, dominated by the Mehsud tribe and TTP leader Baitullah Mehsud. The army deployed around 30,000 soldiers, some withdrawn from its eastern sector in Kashmir, along with the Frontier Corps, while the number of Taliban militants was variously estimated at 10,000–20,000, including al-Qaeda-linked Uzbek and Arab fighters.

In early August, Baitullah Mehsud was killed by a US drone attack; the TTP then appointed as leader Hakimullah Mehsud, Baitullah's spokesman and TTP commander for the Khyber, Orakzai and Kurram Agencies of South Waziristan. Following fixed- and rotary-wing air-strikes, an army ground offensive began on 17 October. By early November, the security forces had captured Hakimullah Mehsud's hometown of Kotkai as well as Sherwangi, and nearly 500 militants were reported killed. As in the Swat Valley, the operations caused large numbers of civilians to flee their homes.

It remains to be seen how successful the security forces' operations will be in South Waziristan, amidst stiff resistance from the Pakistan Taliban, and what impact these operations will have on morale. Previous offensives and peace deals in South Waziristan have had limited impact. The ongoing South Waziristan operations were expected to be far more difficult and protracted than those in Swat, due to difficult terrain and the onset of winter. Meanwhile, the army ruled out launching military operations against Taliban fighters in North Waziristan, dominated by the Wazir tribes, by pledging to honour the 17 February 2008 peace accord signed with tribal leaders.

A number of terrorist attacks, the majority by the TTP, were carried out in retaliation for the ongoing military operations in Swat and South Waziristan.

The Sri Lankan cricket team was attacked in Lahore on 3 March and, in the deadliest attack in more than two years, 120 people were killed by a car bomb in a crowded women's market in Peshawar on 28 October. On 2 November there was a suicide attack on a busy commercial area close to the Pakistan Army's General Headquarters (GHQ) in Rawalpindi, and three days later leading anti-Taliban cleric Sarfraz Ahmed Naeemi was assassinated in Lahore.

The TTP has increasingly targeted Pakistan's national-security establishment. On 19 November 2008, the former head of the army's elite Special Service Group was assassinated. On 27 May 2009, a suicide bomb explosion killed 27 near the regional headquarters of the ISI in Lahore. Nine militants stormed GHQ in Rawalpindi on 10 October, killing 22 people including a brigadier and briefly holding 56 hostages. On 22 and 27 October and 6 November, three serving Brigadiers were targeted by militants (one was killed); on 23 October there was a suicide bombing near the Pakistan Aeronautical Complex (PAC) at Kamra; and on 13 November multiple car bombs targeted the regional headquarters of the ISI in Peshawar.

On 26 October Pakistani Interior Minister Rehman Malik accused India of funding Taliban militants in the tribal areas bordering Afghanistan in an attempt to destabilise Pakistan, an allegation rejected by the Indian prime minister. On 2 November, Pakistan's information minister also alleged that the security forces had seized Indian-made arms, ammunition, literature and medical equipment from the recently captured Taliban stronghold of Sherwangi in South Waziristan. Pakistan continued to allege Indian involvement in the uprising in Baluchistan (also denied by India) and recently offered to provide evidence of such activities at an appropriate time. At the same time, a number of terror attacks by the 'Punjab Taliban' have taken place in that province, posing a growing risk to the security of Pakistan's heartland.

Sri Lanka

The 26-year Sri Lankan civil war ended on 19 May 2009 with the defeat of the separatist Liberation Tigers of Tamil Eelam (LTTE or Tamil Tigers) and the death of LTTE chief Velupillai Prabhakaran (see *Strategic Survey 2009*, pp. 320–22). On 2 January 2009, government forces took control of the northern town of Kilinochchi, the LTTE's administrative headquarters, pushing the Tigers into coastal areas. A week

later, the military captured Elephant Pass and on 14 January captured the Chundikulam area, gaining control of the entire Jaffna Peninsula. After government forces secured the northern port of Mullaitivu on 25 January, LTTE fighters were confined to a small zone bordered by a lagoon and the sea in Mullaitivu District. Colombo rejected international demands for a ceasefire to allow aid agencies to reach Tamil civilians trapped within the 5km-long 'safety zone' declared by the military. On 18 May, the 25,000 troops involved in the operation took control over the last remaining Tamil Tiger stronghold and 10,000 militants reportedly surrendered.

According to official casualty figures, 6,261 security-forces personnel were killed between July 2006 and May 2009, and 29,551 wounded. Some 22,000 LTTE militants were killed. An estimated 80,000–100,000 people were killed since the conflict began in 1983, and at the end of the conflict some 300,000 Tamil civilians were displaced from their homes. This number had declined to 135,000 by mid November 2009, with the government pledging to resettle a majority of internally displaced people (IDPs) by 31 January 2010. The IDPs are kept in camps guarded by security forces and there has been international concern over humanitarian and sanitary conditions in the camps. In October 2009, the US administration filed a report to Congress on incidents during the January–May offensive that 'may constitute' war crimes by both the Sri Lankan armed forces and the LTTE. Colombo denied all allegations of war crimes and rejected calls for an international investigation.

The Sri Lankan armed forces are currently being expanded and reorganised. The army wishes to recruit 20,000–50,000 more troops to maintain and administer areas liberated from the LTTE, having already nearly doubled in size to 200,000 personnel in the last few years. This will put further pressure on defence spending, which saw a 24% rise in 2009/10 to $1.74bn, accounting for 17% of total government spending.

The Chief of Defence Staff (CDS) Act was formalised in June, with General Sarath Fonseka, the army chief and military architect of the war against the LTTE, appointed CDS. Although the CDS chairs meetings of the three service chiefs and is responsible for coordination among the services, he does not have operational control of the services and, controversially, can only act or advise the government with the consent of the defence secretary, currently Gotabaya Rajapaksa, the president's brother. General

Fonseka resigned as CDS on 12 November. A new post of national security adviser to the president was also created, with naval chief Vice Admiral Vasantha Karannagoda appointed to the post.

Bangladesh

Soon after taking office on 6 January 2009, Bangladeshi Prime Minister Sheikh Hasina was faced with a mutiny within the paramilitary border-guard force, the Bangladesh Rifles (BDR). In a 20-hour siege on 25 and 26 February, BDR soldiers killed 74 people, including their chief and 56 officers on secondment from the army. The mutiny spread from BDR headquarters in Dhaka to 11 other paramilitary camps, including those in Chittagong, Sylhet and Rajshahi. It was finally brought to a negotiated end, with an angry army threatening to storm BDR headquarters. Hasina initially promised amnesty to mutineers who surrendered, but subsequently changed her position and pledged severe punishment for those responsible for the killings. Official reports found no evidence of links between the mutineers and extremist groups, instead blaming years of pent-up anger among BDR troops over pay scales, status and facilities.

The BDR was renamed the Border Guard Bangladesh (BGB), with changes in the laws governing the force, while improved pay structures and changes in promotion rules began to be introduced. The BGB counter-intelligence unit was also being overhauled. A number of the 3,700 BDR soldiers and 30 civilians arrested were expected to face trial on charges of murder, looting and rebellion.

CENTRAL ASIA

Defence and security planning in Central Asia continued to be dominated by concerns relating to Afghanistan, ranging from soft security issues such as drug and weapons smuggling to the prospect of a future withdrawal by Western military forces. This dominance has manifested itself in recent multilateral and bilateral initiatives, principally driven by Moscow and focused on strengthening specific local military capabilities, while advancing limited cooperation with NATO on issues such as supply routes in support of the International Security Assistance Force (ISAF) in Afghanistan. Russia and the Central Asian states have opened their territories and airspace for the transit of both lethal and non-lethal supplies. In May, Russian Foreign Minister Sergei

Lavrov confirmed that NATO military supplies had already passed through Russian territory, and that this was likely to continue. However, the emphasis has been on non-lethal supplies transiting through the northern distribution network (NDN), which includes an air corridor through the South Caucasus, as an alternative to the Pakistan route which had come under increasing attack from the Taliban.

This apparent cooperative dynamic, however, masked divergent views in the region on the nature of the threat posed by Islamist militancy. Although regional security threats are defined by the Shanghai Cooperation Organisation (SCO) and Collective Security Treaty Organisation (CSTO) as stemming from drug trafficking, terrorism, extremism and separatism, there has been renewed interest in enhancing hard security measures and strengthening the Russian military footprint in the region. The absence of any reference to a terrorist threat in Russia's new National Security Strategy in May 2009 underscores the disparity in threat perception. Russian President Dmitry Medvedev, in the aftermath of the Russia–Georgia war in August 2008, has pushed strongly for the creation of permanent readiness reaction forces under the CSTO. First mooted during an informal CSTO meeting in December 2008 held in Borovoye, Kazakhstan (which Uzbekistan did not attend, principally due to its decision to withdraw from the Eurasian Economic Community), the plan to form a new collective force evolved through meetings in February and June 2009. The Collective Operational Reaction Forces (CORF) agreement was signed on 14 June by all members apart from Belarus and Uzbekistan. While the resolution of minor differences over the issue between Minsk and Moscow paved the way for Belarusian participation in the new force, Tashkent has remained opposed on principle.

Uzbekistan's objections, partly reflecting the fact that its armed forces remain the most combat capable in the region, have been mainly political and legal. Tashkent argued that any regional emergency or security crisis can be adequately dealt with by deploying national forces, and it questioned the need to involve a collective force. Moreover, fearing the militarisation of the region, the Uzbek government has been sceptical about the merits of CORF. Its legal objections have been based on the CSTO charter, which states that consensus is required among the members of the organisation before embarking on such a significant policy step. Uzbek legislation also prohibits the deployment of its armed forces abroad. The lack of parliamentary ratification of the CORF agreement by members raised issues of protocol surrounding the first exercise, *Interaction 2009*, conducted by the new force in Belarus and Kazakhstan in September and October. Similar arguments were proffered by the Uzbeks against another Russian initiative announced in July 2009, the opening of an additional Russian military base in southern Kyrgyzstan. The memorandum of understanding between Moscow and Bishkek envisaged establishing a base in Osh under the CSTO, with negotiations ongoing as of late November 2009. Following Uzbek opposition to the planned base, and disclosure that Moscow had made no effort to consult Tashkent on the issue, Russian diplomats actively attempted to secure Uzbek support retroactively.

CORF was hurriedly formed, based on the nucleus of the existing Collective Rapid Reaction Forces, and enhanced from battalion-sized contributions to a new structure centred on the Russian 98th Airborne Division and 31st Air-Assault Brigade. Kazakhstan agreed to provide a brigade drawn from its airmobile forces based in Kapchagai, while Kyrgyzstan and Tajikistan were to contribute supporting battalions. The emerging structure was therefore Russian dominated, and given reported widespread corruption in Kazakhstan's airmobile forces and their ageing and obsolete equipment inventory, it is likely that Astana's participation in CORF would demand significant levels of assistance from the Russian armed forces.

The rapprochement between the US and Uzbekistan culminated in August 2009 with Uzbek Defence Minister Kabul Berdiyev and US CENTCOM commander General David Petraeus signing a bilateral agreement on a programme of military educational exchanges and training. Indeed, Washington's defence relations with Tashkent have become more sophisticated, accompanied by efforts to downplay US military cooperation and assistance to Uzbekistan. The Uzbek government agreed indirectly to grant access to Navoi airport for the transit of supplies to Afghanistan by leasing the facility to South Korea, which in turn subcontracted to the US.

Kyrgyzstan skilfully exploited its concerns about the US base at Manas to extract a significant increase in rent for the facility. Kyrgyz President Kurmanbek Bakiyev first announced his intention to close the base in February 2009 at the CSTO summit in Moscow, only to agree a last-minute deal with Washington prior to his re-election in late July 2009. Officially, the Manas base is now designated a 'transit centre', and its future appears secure so long as the NDN receives continued support from Moscow. Russia has also provided air-defence systems deployed in southern Kyrgyzstan, and developed the railway infrastructure around the sensitive naval testing facility on Lake Issyk Kul it leases from Bishkek.

Tajikistan also engaged in 'base politics', notably in relation to reported attempts to extract rent from Moscow for the 201st Division's base in Dushanbe. The Tajik government also failed to reach agreement with Moscow on exclusive Russian use of the Ayni airfield, which was being upgraded by India. A Russian–Tajik counter-terrorist exercise held in southern Tajikistan in September 2009 was justified by both sides on the basis that the Taliban might cross the Tajik border and seek to destabilise the country or the wider region. Tajik defence-cooperation programmes with NATO and its members have focused on border security and demining, while its border service continued to receive support from Russian border-guard advisers. Despite high-level visits to the region by senior officials from CENTCOM, NATO officials and contacts at bilateral level between Alliance members and the country, defence cooperation has become more cautious and sensitive to the concerns of Moscow. While the Barack Obama administration has pursued a more cooperative approach to dealing with Russia through the CSTO and at a bilateral level, Moscow has been asserting greater influence. Broadly ambivalent to Alliance assistance to the regional militaries that might build local defence capabilities, Moscow has liaised closely with its CSTO partners on issues where it perceives its interests to be at stake.

Kazakhstan has continued to diversify its foreign military cooperation, including intensifying defence relations with Belarus and India and exchanging defence attachés with Iran, though in the latter case Astana is wary of damaging relations with Israel. The underlying cause of this diversification is the need to modernise and repair the Kazakh air force's ageing aircraft fleet; Belarusian aircraft-repair plants are currently undertaking such work. The large quantities of Russian-made weapons and equipment in the Indian military's inventory have stimulated considerable interest among Kazakh defence officials. Despite these growing ties, however, Kazakhstan's armed forces remain heavily reliant on cooperation with Russia. In March 2009, for example, a contract was signed with Moscow to procure up to ten further

S-300 air-defence batteries, beyond those already protecting Astana and Almaty; some of these are planned for deployment in protection of energy infrastructure against unspecified threats. Western assistance has concentrated on enhancing peace-support operations capabilities, Caspian security, language training and developing professional NCOs, though the latter effort suffered after the decision to increase the number of conscripts. Kazakhstan's Defence Institute for Foreign Languages, formed in 2005, has seen a haemorrhaging of trained linguists and has reportedly suffered from internal corruption, undermining its value.

In June 2009, a scandal relating to efforts to procure *Nayza*, *Aybat* and *Semser* artillery systems from Israel for the airmobile forces precipitated the sacking of Defence Minister Daniyal Akhmetov; he was replaced by Adilbek Zhaksybekov, the former Kazakh ambassador to Moscow. Kazakhstan's peace-keeping brigade (KAZBRIG), which has received considerable assistance and training from the US, UK and NATO, is the country's most capable formation, and as such can present a misleading impression of the overall effectiveness of its military. The annual US, UK and Kazakh military exercise *Steppe Eagle* in September 2009 provided another opportunity to pressure Astana to agree to operationally deploy elements of KAZBRIG to Afghanistan. Although the decision has not been taken at a political level in Astana, the structure has achieved a level of, albeit not full, interoperability with NATO. The options facing the Kazakh government, if it decided to send troops to support ISAF, appeared limited to medical or command elements, or to a company conducting force-protection duties, stopping short of combat operations.

Table 29 **Insurgent groups in Afghanistan and Pakistan**

Organisation/group	Aims and remarks
TALIBAN AND AFFILIATES	
Afghan Taliban	Regain power in Kabul; foreign withdrawal from AFG. Estimated strength 10–20,000; led by Mullah Omar and Quetta Shura. Presence predominantly in S. and E. AFG provinces. In main utilise low-level insurgent tactics but have undertaken conventional engagement of int'l military forces in lightly protected outlying areas. Funding through opium trade and donors (AQ included)
Haqqani Network	Fight coalition forces in AFG as part of Afghan Taliban. Regain control of traditional bases in Khost, Paktia and Paktika. Led by Sirajuddin Haqqani. Based mainly in N. Waziristan, PAK
Hizb-e Islami Gulbuddin (HIG)	Officially seeks foreign withdrawal from AFG; establish Islamic fundamentalist state. Two factions, Gulbuddin Hekmatyar's Hizb-e Islami in Nuristan and Khalis faction, part of the AFG Taliban. Affiliates of Hizb-e Islami political faction (established 2005 and not officially associated with Hekmatyar), have won seats in the National Assembly and are active in the Wolesi Jirga in Kabul
OTHER INSURGENT GROUPS	
Pakistan-based Baluch Liberation Army (BLA)/Baluch People's Liberation Front (BPLF)/Popular Front for Armed Resistance/ Baluch Students Organisation	Independence for former Baluchistan encompassing S.W. PAK, IRN Sistan province and S.W. AFG. Liberation of Baluch land; establishment of sovereign Baluch government. Interim demands are greater regional autonomy and fairer distribution of Baluchi natural resources (gas/oil)
Harkat-ul-Jihad-i-Islami (HuJI)/Harkat ul-Mujahideen (HuM)/ Harkat ul-Ansar (HuA)/ Jaish-e-Mohammed (JeM)	Pro-Pakistan Islamic groups; seek Kashmir's accession to PAK. Main area of operation is Pakistan-administered Kashmir, though recent focus on AFG. HuA resulted from the amalgamation of HuJI and HuM. Majority of HuM's capability now resides under JeM. Leader Maulana Masood Azhar. Support and fundraising networks throughout EU
Lashkar-e-Tayiba (LeT)/Jama'at ud Dawa (JuD)/Army of the Righteous	Islamic fundamentalist group. Established 1989 following the move of Mujahadeen from AFG to fight in Pakistan-administered Kashmir. JuD is LeT's charitable and social arm. Led by Zakiur Rehman Lakhwi (arrested following Mumbai attacks in 2008). Hafiz Saeed leader of JuD; has been under house arrest
Lashkar-e-Islam (Army of Islam)	Khyber-based. Led by Mangal Bagh. Increasingly active in PAK. Allegedly seeks Islamic state in PAK. Does not align with AQ elements within Khyber. Allegedly maintains secure road link through Khyber Pass used to re-supply ISAF

Table 29 **Insurgent groups in Afghanistan and Pakistan**

Organisation/group	Aims and remarks
Lashkar-e-Omar (LeO)/ al-Qanoon	Extremist Islamist ideology. Conglomerate of Harkat-ul-Jihad-i-Islami (HuJI), Lashkar-e-Jhangvi (LeJ) and Jaish-e-Mohammed (JeM) members. Initially designed to undertake terrorist attacks against US citizens in PAK. Led by Qari Abdul Hai (chief of LeJ Supreme Council)
Tehrik-e-Nafiz-e-Shariat-e-Mohammadi/ Movement for the Enforcement of Islamic Laws/Black Turbans	Imposition of sharia in PAK. Former leader Maulana Sufi Mohammed, who tried to negotiate a peace settlement between Islamabad and TTP over sharia in Swat Valley, handed leadership to son-in-law Maulana Fazalullah. Links with Jamaat-i-Islami, TTP Swat and the Afghan Taliban
Sipah-e-Sahaba (SSP)/ Lashkar-e-Jhangvi (LeJ)	Sunni state in PAK; restoration of caliphate. Primarily targets Shia; opposes US–Pakistan cooperation; announced jihad against US in 2001. Led by Qari Zafar. Based in S. Punjab and Karachi. Logisitic and training support to TTP; links with Harkat ul-Mujahideen (HuM) and Jaish-e-Mohammed (JeM). Involved in two assassination attempts on Musharraf, Marriot Hotel bombing and attack on Sri Lanka cricket team
AL-QAEDA AND AFFILIATES	
Al-Qaeda (AQ) in Afghanistan and Pakistan	Create Islamic state in AFG and PAK; jihad against the 'near enemy' (perceived puppet states supported by West); create Islamic state worldwide; jihad against the 'far enemy' (West, specifically the US); eject Western forces from the area. De facto alliance with the Taliban. Rallying point for int'l Islamic fundamentalist insurgent and terrorist organisations. Islamic Movement of Uzbekistan believed to be key affiliate group. UAV strikes have resulted in attrition of operational command structures in PAK
Islamic Movement of Uzbekistan (IMU)/ Islamic Movement of Turkestan (IMT)	Creation of a fundamentalist Islamic state in Uzb and Central Asia. Coalition of Islamic militants from Uzb, other Central Asian states and PRC. Several thousand fighters aligned to and fight for AQ. Predominantly based in S. Waziristan, PAK. Leader Tahir Yuldashev killed by a US UAV strike in August 2009
Islamic Jihad Union/ Islamic Jihad Group	Splinter group from IMU. Based in Waziristan, PAK. Aims incl. jihad in Central Asia and wider region; establishment of Islamic state; actively supports Taliban and AQ in AFG. Leaders Tahir Yuldashev and Najmiddin Jalolov killed in US UAV strikes
East Turkestan Liberation Organisation (ETLO)	Establish separate Eastern Turkestan state for Uighurs in Xingiang Province NW PRC
East Turkestan Islamic Movement (ETIM)	Establish independent Islamic regime; separation of Xinjiang from PRC. US assert ETIM Uighur detainees in AFG confirm financial and insurgent links to AQ. Leader Hasan Mahsum killed by Pakistani troops in 2003
Tehrik-e-Taliban (TTP)/ Pakistani-Taliban	Umbrella group for Pakistan Taliban factions. Several thousand fighters based throughout PAK FATA. Seek sharia law in PAK. Increasingly anti-Shia and anti-Western. Led by Hakimullah Meshud after Baitullah Mehsud killed by US UAV strike August 2009. Close links with AQ, Lashkar-e-Islam, Lashkar-e-Jhangvi and Tehrik-e-Nifaz-e-Shariat-e-Mohammadi
Punjab Taliban	Sees Islamabad fighting for US against PAK population. Removal of Western forces from AFG. Longer-term aim likely to be the extension of sharia law within PAK, in line with TTP objectives. Has been increase in number of Punjabi recruits to the Taliban. Three principal groups constitute the Punjab Taliban: Lashkar-e-Jhangvi (LeJ), Sipah-e-Sahaba Pakistan (SSP) and Jaish-e-Mohammed (JeM). All reportedly trained by PAK and originally viewed as Kashmir-focused. The movement of Punjabis to the relative safety of S. Waziristan increased after 2001, when Musharraf proscribed main militant Islamic groups

AFGHANISTAN

International concern grew in 2009 over the situation in Afghanistan, with rising violence, inadequate governance and security, and growing international uncertainty over the objectives for the Afghanistan mission all raising doubts. In December, President Obama announced a further 30,000 troops would deploy in 2010. The strategy has 'the protection of the Afghan population' as its core objective with the accelerated training of Afghan national security forces as its key mission. It also aims to enable a phased drawdown of US forces from 2011.

Ongoing civil war: echoes of recent past

When international forces intervened in Afghanistan in 2001, there was a civil war between the Taliban and the Northern Alliance, ongoing since the Saur Revolution of April 1978 that toppled the administration of Mohammed Daoud Khan. The new government, formed by the communist People's Democratic Party (PDP), led to a growing rebellion in large part in reaction to attempts to modernise state structures and the economy, moves seen by many as contrary to Afghan traditions. The subsequent Soviet invasion in support of the Kabul government added an ideological dimension to the rebellion; the Soviet strategy challenged Islam in Afghanistan, which added to the traditional Afghan dislike of foreign involvement in their affairs. Many of today's Afghan leaders, such as President Hamid Karzai, were among the leaders of the insurgents in the 1980s. The mujahadeen, which led the rebellion, received vital financial and technical support from Western countries, with the US seeing the conflict as an opportunity to fight a proxy war against the USSR. The critical deployment of US *Stinger* surface-to-air missiles helped turn the tide of war in favour of the Afghan resistance, particularly when the mujahadeen began to use them against Soviet attack helicopters. (Today's Taliban were formed to fight as part of the mujahadeen).

In 1986, following a significant increase in Soviet troop numbers, President Mikhail Gorbachev announced at the 27th Congress of the Communist Party that he would withdraw forces after two years if progress had not been made. This statement on an exit strategy energised the insurgency. The eventual withdrawal of Soviet forces in 1989 left the mujahadeen to continue its insurgency against the communist government in Kabul. The regime finally fell in 1992, and the mujahadeen governed until it was ousted in 1996 by the Taliban movement, which had rebelled against mujahadeen corruption and abuse of the population. A new civil war began between the Taliban and the Northern Alliance, dominated by former mujahadeen.

By the time the US-led *Operation Enduring Freedom* began in October 2001 in reaction to the 11 September terrorist attacks in the US, the Taliban was coming under increasing pressure. A conventional campaign by the Northern Alliance, supported by a small number of US and allied special-forces troops and overwhelming US airpower, overthrew the Taliban, which withdrew to safe havens on both sides of the Afghanistan–Pakistan border, or Durand Line. From these bases they built an insurgency that has grown in strength and influence. The international community failed to capitalise on the initial military success of *Operation Enduring Freedom* and to recognise the true scale involved in rebuilding a state destroyed by decades of conflict. A vacuum in governance, particularly in the Pashtun areas of southern Afghanistan, allowed the Taliban and its allies to return in increasing numbers and to steadily re-establish varying degrees of influence over communities. Taliban influence has subsequently spread to some areas in the north and west of the country that had, until recently, been relatively free of violence.

With international counter-insurgency operations now in their eighth year, the spreading insurgency poses domestic political problems as well as military challenges for countries contributing troops to ISAF. German forces deployed in Regional Command (North) under strictly imposed caveats, for example, are being increasingly drawn into combat, leading then Foreign Minister Frank-Walter Steinmeier to suggest during the September 2009 German election campaign that German troops might withdraw by 2013 and hand the Faizabad base over to the Afghan National Army (ANA) in 2011. Other countries may be forced to review their continuing commitment to operations, while the US continues to press for more troops.

New impetus and direction

During the 2008 US presidential campaign, Barack Obama emphasised the importance of Afghanistan, and immediately after he took office on 22 January 2009 he announced the 'Af–Pak strategy' which explicitly recognised the need to address the problems of Pakistan and Afghanistan jointly. The announcement included an affirmation of the need to increase the effort against al-Qaeda and was followed by the announcement of a troop 'surge' in Afghanistan to put more pressure on the Taliban and to ensure security for the run-up to the Afghan presidential elections on 20 August. On 4 April, at the NATO summit in Strasbourg–Kehl, European NATO member states backed the US commitment by pledging an additional 5,000 troops. The initial US surge involved 17,000 troops in a deployment to the south and east, with an additional 4,000 to speed up training of the ANA. Such training is seen as a priority, as coalition countries seek to hand over more military and security tasks to the Afghan National Security Forces (ANSF), including the Afghan National Police (ANP) and border guards.

Obama's appointment of political and military leaders whom he deemed would bring faster results in Afghanistan gave impetus to the new strategy. Among the new appointees was Lieutenant-General Stanley McChrystal, who replaced General David McKiernan as ISAF commander in May 2009. The appointment of an experienced special-forces officer was seen as an attempt to increase the tempo of counter-insurgency operations. In a review of counter-insurgency strategy following the election period and a summer characterised by increasing violence and high casualties among ISAF and ANSF personnel, McChrystal called for 40,000 more US and NATO troops to be deployed to Afghanistan. Obama's announcement will bring the total US commitment to around 100,000 troops. At the same time, the UK announced it could send an extra 500 troops to boost its total deployment to 9,500, with 500 being re-deployed from Kabul to Helmand.

The UK made its extra troop allocation subject to a number of conditions, among them that all troop-contributing countries should bear a fair share of the military commitment and that ANSF capacity-building should be accelerated. The intention was that ANA strength should increase from about 80,000 to 134,000 by the end of 2010, the force being infantry-centric, with Kandaks in the south and east having four companies instead of three (thus concentrating on building capacity in areas where there are most problems). However, the US wanted a further increase to around 260,000. The Kabul Military Training Center was set up in 2009 to accelerate training of Afghan national security forces. It is intended that the centre have the capacity to train 5,000 personnel monthly by March 2010. At the same time, the strength of the ANP was to increase to 80,000 by 2011 and the Afghan National Border Police (ANBP) was to increase from 12,000 to 18,000. The ANBP continues to be trained under Combined Security Transition Command-Afghanistan (CSTC-A). In addition to the state security forces, Public Protection Forces (PPF) were being formed at local level, in 200-person detachments. The initial phase called for 8,000 personnel to be trained by July 2009 in 40 districts (out of 365). US troops started this training in Wardak, a province with a large Taliban presence close to Kabul and considered a priority for the programme. However, there has been concern that the creation of the PPF may detract from efforts to create a proper national police force. But the critical problem remains that of retention of trained personnel; in a bid to assist this process, pay for Afghan security forces has been increased.

Insurgency

The Taliban-led insurgency now affects many areas of the country and there has been a broadening in the scope of its operations. While the insurgents have lost virtually every military engagement, they expanded their areas of influence from 30 to 160 of Afghanistan's 364 districts between 2003 and the end of 2008, and attacks increased by 60% between October 2008 and April 2009. A mixture of tactics was geared to address the operating conditions in different parts of the country. In areas with a heavy international military presence the Taliban resorted to improvised explosive devices (IEDs), a tactic employed to great effect against ISAF operations during the election period. In July alone there were an estimated 828 IED attacks, almost double the number in July 2008. There were also occasional full-scale assaults on coalition positions, mostly in the southeastern provinces, similar to the 17 August 2008 attack against US Forward Operating Base Salerno in Khost province. An attack on a US base in Nuristan by some 300 insurgents on 4 October 2009 resulted in the deaths of eight US and two ANA soldiers.

Suicide attacks, particularly against government targets in urban areas, have become a key insurgent tactic. On 11 February 2009 19 people were killed in a multiple attack involving a suicide bomber and gunmen against government institutions in Kabul, including the Ministries of Education and Justice and the Department of Prisons. The attack was seen as a direct assault on state judicial and legal authorities. On 15 August 2009, a suicide bomber killed seven near ISAF headquarters, and on 8 October 2009 a

Map 3 **Afghanistan**

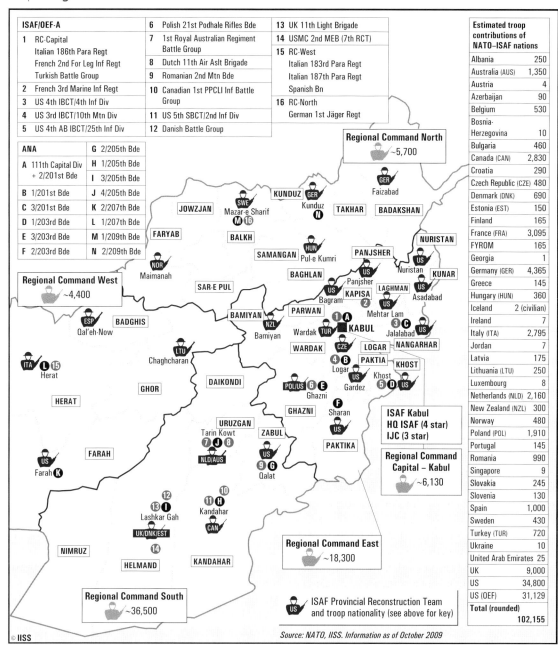

ISAF/OEF-A		

1 RC-Capital
    Italian 186th Para Regt
    French 2nd For Leg Inf Regt
    Turkish Battle Group
	6 Polish 21st Podhale Rifles Bde	13 UK 11th Light Brigade

	7 1st Royal Australian Regiment Battle Group	14 USMC 2nd MEB (7th RCT)
	8 Dutch 11th Air Aslt Brigade	15 RC-West Italian 183rd Para Regt
2 French 3rd Marine Inf Regt	9 Romanian 2nd Mtn Bde	Italian 187th Para Regt
3 US 4th IBCT/4th Inf Div	10 Canadian 1st PPCLI Inf Battle Group	Spanish Bn
4 US 3rd IBCT/10th Mtn Div		16 RC-North
5 US 4th AB IBCT/25th Inf Div	11 US 5th SBCT/2nd Inf Div	German 1st Jäger Regt
	12 Danish Battle Group	

ANA		
A 111th Capital Div + 2/201st Bde	G 2/205th Bde	
	H 1/205th Bde	
B 1/201st Bde	I 3/205th Bde	
C 3/201st Bde	J 4/205th Bde	
D 1/203rd Bde	K 2/207th Bde	
E 3/203rd Bde	L 1/207th Bde	
F 2/203rd Bde	M 1/209th Bde	
	N 2/209th Bde	

Regional Command North ~5,700

Regional Command West ~4,400

Regional Command Capital – Kabul ~6,130

ISAF Kabul HQ ISAF (4 star) IJC (3 star)

Regional Command East ~18,300

Regional Command South ~36,500

ISAF Provincial Reconstruction Team and troop nationality (see above for key)

Estimated troop contributions of NATO–ISAF nations	
Albania	250
Australia (AUS)	1,350
Austria	4
Azerbaijan	90
Belgium	530
Bosnia-Herzegovina	10
Bulgaria	460
Canada (CAN)	2,830
Croatia	290
Czech Republic (CZE)	480
Denmark (DNK)	690
Estonia (EST)	150
Finland	165
France (FRA)	3,095
FYROM	165
Georgia	1
Germany (GER)	4,365
Greece	145
Hungary (HUN)	360
Iceland	2 (civilian)
Ireland	7
Italy (ITA)	2,795
Jordan	7
Latvia	175
Lithuania (LTU)	250
Luxembourg	8
Netherlands (NLD)	2,160
New Zealand (NZL)	300
Norway	480
Poland (POL)	1,910
Portugal	145
Romania	990
Singapore	9
Slovakia	245
Slovenia	130
Spain	1,000
Sweden	430
Turkey (TUR)	720
Ukraine	10
United Arab Emirates	25
UK	9,000
US	34,800
US (OEF)	31,129
Total (rounded)	**102,155**

Source: NATO, IISS. Information as of October 2009

© IISS

South and Central Asia

suicide car bomber carried out an attack opposite the Indian embassy, which is a continued target. India is a strong ally of the Afghan government and is seen as a direct threat to the Taliban and its allies.

Attacks on ISAF supply routes and facilities in Pakistan resulted in new arrangements with Russia and neighbouring Central Asian states to open routes through less hostile territory. On 6 February 2009, an agreement was reached with Russia for the 'Northern Route', a rail connection running from the Baltic Sea via Russia to Central Asia to carry non-lethal military consignments. On 6 July Russia extended the agreement to allow air and land transit of lethal military supplies to NATO and US forces in Afghanistan. Meanwhile, on 3 April Uzbekistan agreed to the use of Navoi air base by US aircraft; Tajikistan also agreed to the movement of supplies through either Kulyab or Dushanbe air bases for onward movement to Afghanistan by road. In June 2009, after months of uncertainty over the use of the Manas air base in Kyrgyzstan, Bishkek agreed to its continuing use for international operations in Afghanistan as an air transit and logistics base, with security being handed over to the Kyrgyz authorities. Under the agreement the US will increase its annual payment for the base from US$17.4m to US$60m and will spend US$66m on improving airport facilities. An additional US$51m has been given to Kyrgyzstan in economic aid and for counter-terrorist and counter-narcotics training programmes.

Counter-insurgency

General McChrystal's counter-insurgency strategy changed the emphasis and direction of the campaign. He put the protection of the Afghan people at the centre of the strategy, focusing on reduction of the high rate of civilian casualties caused by international and government forces, particularly through excessive use of airpower. In June 2009, following a spate of civilian casualties and an incident which involved the possible use of white-phosphorous munitions (see IISS *Strategic Survey 2009*, pp. 309–10), McChrystal briefed the US Senate Armed Services Committee on his intention to reduce civilian casualties by limiting the use of airpower and tightening rules of engagement. Although civilian casualty rates dropped significantly following the introduction of the new rules, there was a setback when, on 4 September, up to 90 people were killed in an air-strike which aimed to destroy two fuel tankers stolen by the Taliban. McChrystal's decisive action in removing the officers who took the decision to launch the strike indicated his unwillingness to compromise on the policy. To improve command of the operation a new three-star headquarters was formed under Lieutenant-General David Rodriguez the 'Independent Joint Command', that has taken direct command of the two-star Regional Command headquarters. The effect of this has been to bring more direction to military operations; a weakness in the strategy remains in the way that Provincial Reconstruction Teams (PRTs), the civil component to the strategy, are under national command, outside McChrystal's direct control. Another aspect of the new strategy was to find a way to deal with insurgents through re-integration into wider Afghan society. Retired British Lieutenant-General Graeme Lamb, who had been involved in similar initiatives in Iraq, was brought in to advise McChrystal on possible approaches. While these initiatives were at the time of writing at an early stage, the prospects for re-integration in Afghanistan are complicated by the fallout of the previous 31 years of civil war. One factor complicating any chance at meaningful negotiation was that many former PDP members were now in government, while many of their former Western-backed opponents were fighting with the Taliban.

Operational tempo

In a series of operations that concluded on 27 November 2008, ISAF and ANA troops were deployed to prevent Taliban and other groups escaping into safe havens on and across the Durand Line inside Pakistan. In Afghanistan's Kandahar province, Operations *Mutafiq Tander 6, Janubi Tapu 1* and *Joosh Karay* were conducted simultaneously by Canadian and ANA forces to pressure the Taliban. In Panjwayi district, a Canadian battlegroup was deployed to prevent insurgents escaping while British forces, deployed on *Operation Janubi Tapu*, conducted an airmobile operation to further limit the movement of insurgents. Meanwhile, in Helmand province, *Operation Joosh Karay* was launched in the eastern region of Maiwand. During these operations, 600kg of explosives, a quantity of 107mm rockets and 500kg of hashish were found. A senior Taliban leader, Mullah Asad, was killed on 19 November in the Garmsir district of Helmand province. His death followed that of another Taliban leader in the southern provinces, Mullah Mashar, three weeks earlier. The attempt by international forces to target key Taliban commanders may have had some impact, but there is some redundancy in Taliban command structures that allows personnel to be replaced with what seems to be relative ease.

The US surge in the first six months of 2009 aimed, firstly, to cope with an expected upsurge in violence during the summer election campaign and, secondly, to address one of the military shortcomings of the counter-insurgency campaign: an inability to hold territory once it had been cleared of insurgents. The increase in ANA numbers is an important component of this effort as ISAF seeks to hand over more military tasks to Afghan units.

The period leading up to the 20 August presidential elections was the most violent since 2001. August was the bloodiest month ever for international forces in Afghanistan – the US lost 77 service personnel and the UK lost 45. Altogether, the international forces lost 175 in a one-month period. An increase in oper-

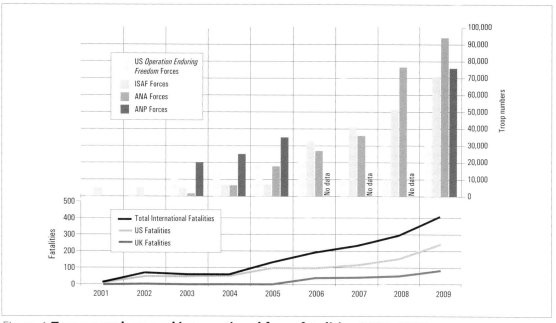

Figure 1 **Troop numbers and international force fatalities 2001–2009**

ational tempo by ISAF and Afghan forces was met with well-prepared and sustained resistance by insurgents. International forces sought to regain territory in southern and eastern provinces which had been under Taliban influence for some time and which contained large numbers of Pashtuns, whose participation in the elections was vital for a valid ballot. A British-led operation, *Panther's Claw,* took place in Helmand province between 19 June and 20 July with the aim of clearing Taliban forces from territory that would be of importance during the election and then holding it beyond polling day to enable reconstruction and development. Subsidiary aims included the destruction of heroin production and storage facilities. After intense fighting and 37 UK fatalities (with 150 wounded, mostly from insurgent IED attacks), enough ground was secured for about 13 polling stations to be opened. However, only a small number of the 80,000 people entitled to vote in the area registered for the elections. Meanwhile, July 2009 saw 4,000 US Marines and 650 Afghan soldiers and police launch *Operation Khanjar* in central Helmand, again in an effort to secure the local population from the threat of Taliban and other insurgent intimidation and violence. 500 US Marines and ANA similarly conducted *Operation Eastern Resolve II* to secure the ground for elections in eastern provinces as well as parts of Helmand. The town of Naw Zad, lost to the insurgency in 2005, was recaptured.

All the operations in the southern and eastern provinces aimed to interdict insurgent lines of communication across the Durand Line into Pakistan. The practice of locating small, isolated bases near the frontier in an attempt to control insurgent movement was called into question by attacks on the bases, and McChrystal subsequently withdrew the most isolated ones.

Counter-narcotics strategy

The insurgency continued to benefit from the proceeds of the opium and heroin trade. In May 2009, Admiral Mike Mullen, chairman of the US Joint Chiefs of Staff, said the international community was losing the battle against the production of illicit drugs in Afghanistan. But by October there was growing recognition that the illicit trade in drugs was not the Taliban's only, nor even necessarily main, source of income. Donations from some organisations within the Muslim world were cited by the CIA as possibly providing more financial support to the insurgency than drugs. Other forms of racketeering were also considered significant. But the illicit drugs trade was considered crucial not just because it helped fund the insurgency, but because of its place in Afghanistan's socio-economic structure.

In October 2008, ISAF's mandate was extended to include a counter-narcotics mission for the first time. The new mission was limited to the 'targeting of facil-

South and Central Asia

ities and facilitators' involved in the trade, rather than farmers growing opium who, it was hoped, would benefit from the diversion of funds that would have been used for eradication into the purchase of alternative crops.

Some European countries providing troops to ISAF were reluctant to accept the new mission, fearing an element of 'mission creep' and the possible alienation of sections of the population. Germany, Poland, Italy and Spain declined to participate. A statement by then NATO Supreme Allied Commander Europe General John Craddock that it was 'no longer necessary to produce intelligence or other evidence that each particular drug trafficker or narcotics facility in Afghanistan meets the criteria of being a military objective' was rejected by several European military and political leaders, some of whom continued to regard the counter-narcotics mission as a police task and question its legality. The then commander of ISAF General McKiernan, also questioned the way the new mission was set out, saying that the directive added a 'new category' to US rules of engagement and 'seriously undermined the commitment ISAF has made ... to restrain our use of force and avoid civilian casualties'. Despite this opposition, then NATO Secretary-General Jaap de Hoop Scheffer said in February 2009 that a number of 'buffers and filters' had been established to maintain the legality of counter-narcotics operations. He did, however, allow countries that disagreed with the policy to ignore it. He said that 'if nations at a certain stage think that they would rather not participate, they will not be forced to participate'.

The border and Pakistan

In November 2008 a joint operation, *Lionheart,* was carried out by some 5,000 US troops operating in conjunction with Afghan forces and Pakistani troops across the Durand Line. In 2009 the issue of insurgent re-supply and movement across the border gained new salience, with Pakistani forces fighting an intense counter-insurgency campaign against the Tehrik-e-Taliban Pakistan (TTP or Pakistan Taliban) in the Swat Valley and Buner in the North-West Frontier Province (NWFP). Their success in retaking these areas from the TTP was followed by further operations to recapture militant strongholds in the Federally Administered Tribal Areas (FATA), particularly in North Waziristan. The success or failure of Pakistani operations in these areas was expected to have a substantial impact on activities by groups acting with the Afghan Taliban, who continued to conduct operations from Pakistan (see Table 29).

The future

International military forces in Afghanistan are in a new and uncertain phase of the eight-year campaign. The success or failure of Pakistan's counter-insurgency efforts against its own radical groups, including the Tehrik-e-Taliban and emerging Punjab Taliban, is a crucial part of the future course of the insurgency in Afghanistan. Achievement of some sustained success through the McChrystal strategy (which has now received the boost of a pledged increase of 30,000 US troops) will be crucial to maintaining US Congressional support, and thus funding for the overall effort. But some countries contributing troops to ISAF may be wearying of the mission, while the increasing complexity of the political landscape in Afghanistan after the flawed election process (marred by allegations of corruption) left critical uncertainty over what sort of government the international community is now supporting. The elections also deepened the divide within Afghanistan between those who want a modern twenty-first-century state and those who wish to adhere to a more traditional model of governance.

SOUTH ASIA – DEFENCE ECONOMICS

After five years in which the economy grew by an average of 8.75% annually, growth in **India** fell to 7.3% in 2008 and is forecast to fall to 5.4% in 2009. Propelled by the fall in economic activity, the government introduced a sizeable fiscal stimulus that – together with existing subsidies on oil, fertiliser and food – resulted in a budget deficit of 9.9% of GDP. Both the Asian Development Bank and the IMF have warned that India's large and persistent budget imbalance threatens fiscal sustainability, and they have urged the authorities to consider a new, stronger budgetary framework when the existing Fiscal Responsibility and Budget Management Act (FRBMA) expires in 2010. Under the FRBMA, established in 2004, the government undertook to reduce the budget deficit by 0.4% a year with the intention of executing a balanced current budget by 2008. Although the deficit had fallen to 0.7% of GDP in 2007, it had risen to 4% of GDP in 2008.

Despite the tight fiscal background, the financial priority given to the military in recent years is clear: between 2000 and 2009 the defence budget will have increased by 50% in real terms. Not surprisingly following the 2008 Mumbai attacks, the 2009 state budget included a 21% increase in defence spending, up from Rs1.37tr (US$28.4bn) in 2008 to Rs1.66tr (US$35.9bn). Furthermore, the immediate impact of the late November attacks can be seen in revised budget figures for 2008, which included a 32% increase in spending by the army over its original allocation. The Indian government has often hinted that

it would like defence spending to reach 3% of GDP, but despite the dramatic increases of recent years the budget still only measures 2.1% of national output. In the short to medium term, it is highly probable that the Mumbai attacks will result in the reallocation of some resources away from the long-term modernisation plan – with its focus on the replacement of obsolete legacy equipment – towards equipment needed by National Security Guards units, such as dedicated transport aircraft and helicopters, night-vision devices and so on. The armed forces have drawn up a long list of such priority equipment, particularly targeted towards their special forces and coastal-protection forces, which they would like to see fast-tracked.

The under-spending and procurement malpractice that has plagued the Ministry of Defence (MoD) for a generation remains chronic: between 2002 and 2008 a combination of bureaucratic delay, inefficiency and corruption in the procurement process saw the MoD forced to return some Rs225bn (US$5.5bn) of procurement funds to the Treasury. Defence Minister A.K. Antony said that getting enough money in the budget was not a problem, noting that his 'pockets [were] full', but he lamented the lack of 'timely and judicious utilisation of money allocated'. The problem of corruption was highlighted with the arrest in May 2009 of five members of the state-owned Ordnance Factory Board by the Central Bureau of Investigation. Seven different defence companies have been blacklisted while they are investigated for possibly corrupt procurement practices, and the government has been forced to suspend US$279m in contracts, most notably with

Table 30 **South and Central Asia Regional Defence Expenditure** as % of GDP

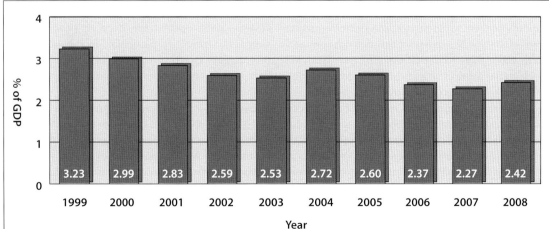

Israeli Military Industries. This will further delay equipment programmes.

The Comptroller and Auditor General's (CAG) office published a report in July 2009 criticising several recent procurement programmes. In particular, it condemned the purchase of defective laser-guided munitions and the acquisition of 40 advanced light helicopters with an operational ceiling of only 5,000 metres instead of the required 6,500m. Further criticism is guaranteed when the CAG finally publishes its report into India's acquisition of the ex-Soviet *Admiral Gorshkov* aircraft carrier. Initial estimates suggested that a Russian refit of the vessel would cost around US$750m. However, with the delivery now pushed back from 2008 to 2012, and the price having risen above US$2bn, the CAG has already suggested that the Indian Navy will be acquiring 'a second-hand ship with a limited lifespan' and will be 'paying more that it would have paid for a new ship'.

The MoD's procurement woes are compounded by the country's embryonic defence-industrial base. It has been a longstanding goal that India should be capable of producing at least 70% of its own military equipment. However, at a seminar in January 2009 Defence Minister Antony said his country was still a long way from becoming a major producer of military platforms. India's defence companies were only supplying around 30% of the armed forces' hardware, he said, describing the situation as 'highly undesirable'. India has only had a private defence sector since 2001 and, despite reforms, the move towards self-reliance appears halting. In recent years, three measures have been introduced to kick-start the process: a provision that allows overseas defence companies to invest up to 26% in domestic defence companies; the publication of Defence Procurement Procedures (DPP), which favour indigenous research and development programmes; and the introduction of an offsets policy stipulating that defence contracts worth more than Rs3bn (US$69.7m) must provide offsets to the value of 30% of the deal. However, Bell Helicopters has called these requirements 'restrictive and narrow', citing them as a factor in its decision to withdraw from the US$600m Reconnaissance and Surveillance Helicopter competition in December 2008. The latest initiative designed to boost domestic defence-industrial activity is incorporated in a new DPP category called 'Buy and Make (Indian)' under which request for proposals (RfPs) can now be issued directly to Indian companies that have the 'requisite financial and technical capabilities to absorb tech-

nology', an update of the previous policy by which RfPs could only be issued to foreign vendors who were then required to transfer technology to Indian companies in order to facilitate licensed production (see p. 473).

Given the slow progress in getting the domestic defence industry up to speed, India remains largely dependent on importing its major weapons systems. In this regard, it continues to build particularly on its relationships with Russia and Israel. Despite the friction that has arisen over the *Gorshkov* acquisition, India has signed several recent deals with Russian manufacturers allowing domestic companies to build Russian equipment under licence; the most notable of these is for the construction of hundreds of T-90S tanks and dozens of Su-30MKI fighter aircraft. In December 2008, India's Hindustan Aeronautics Limited (HAL) announced it had signed a deal with Russia's United Aircraft Corporation (UAC) to jointly develop a fifth-generation fighter aircraft, with a view to completing the project by 2015. That same month, there was further proof that the relationship remained intact, when India signed a deal to buy 80 Russian-built Mi-17 medium-lift helicopters. During 2009, the air force also outlined an ambitious Indo–Russian programme to develop a military transport plane with a 20-tonne cargo capacity. Costs of the proposed US$600m programme are to be equally shared between India's HAL and Russia's UAC. The two countries are expected to further solidify their defence cooperation by renewing the Indo-Russian Inter-Governmental Commission on Military Technical Co-operation for a further ten years during Prime Minister Singh's visit to Moscow in December 2009.

However, the delays and cost overruns that have dogged India's procurement of certain Russian systems have opened the door to new weapons suppliers. Israel in particular has benefited. In recent years Israeli companies have supplied India with a wide range of military equipment, including *Phalcon* airborne warning and control (AWAC) aircraft, *Barak* missiles, unmanned aerial vehicles (UAVs) and *Tavor* rifles. Several further deals were agreed during 2009, triggered in part by the Mumbai attacks. The navy, for example, was quick to acquire five aerostat-programmable radars from Israeli Aerospace Industries (IAI) to plug gaps in its coastal-security system. In April India successfully launched its first all-weather imaging satellite, built by IAI, to help monitor its porous borders

Table 31 **Indian Defence Budget by Function, 2006–2009**

Current Rsbn Personnel, Operations and Maintenance	2007 outturn	2008 budget	2008 outturn	2009 budget
MoD	17.7	23.7	23.9	31.7
Defence Pensions	152.4	155.6	202.3	217.9
Army	342.1	362.7	481.9	585.5
Navy	70.9	74.2	80.3	83.2
Air Force	103.5	108.5	122.0	143.2
Defence Service – R&D	32.0	33.9	38.4	47.5
Defence Ordnance factories	70.0	73.9	89.7	105.8
Recoveries and Receipts	-70.6	-77.4	-76.5	-97.5
Sub-total	718.0	755.1	962.0	1117.3
Procurement and Construction				
Tri-Service R&D	27.0	30.9	30.9	37.2
Army	114.3	130.8	111.1	177.6
Navy	86.2	117.2	89.3	109.6
Air Force	142.0	191.1	169.3	199.4
Other	7.5	10.0	9.4	24.4
Sub-total	377.0	480.0	410.0	548.2
Total Defence Budget	**1,095.0**	**1,235.1**	**1,372.0**	**1,665.5**

with Bangladesh, China and Pakistan. The latest major deal between the two countries is a US$1.4bn contract for the development and procurement of a medium-range surface-to-air missile system, based on IAI's *Barak* long-range naval air-defence system. Under the contract, IAI will work with India's Defence Research and Development Organisation (DRDO) to develop an air-defence system capable of detecting and destroying hostile aircraft, cruise missiles and surface-to-surface rockets at a range of 70–80km.

Since they signed a defence-cooperation agreement in 2005, India and the United States have been forging closer defence-manufacturing ties. These have seen India purchase former LPD USS *Trenton*, six *Sea King* helicopters and six C-130J transport aircraft. In early 2009, however, these contracts were dwarfed by a US$2.1bn deal under which India will purchase eight Boeing P-8I *Poseidon* multi-mission maritime-reconnaissance aircraft (MRAs) from Boeing. Indian officials said that the aircraft had become a priority after ten of the terrorists involved in the Mumbai attacks were able to travel undetected to the city aboard a hijacked trawler. Following a July 2009 final agreement relating to the End User Verification Agreement, necessary under US law to ensure compliance with military technology-transfer requirements, the first of the *Poseidon* aircraft, which will have an anti-submarine warfare capability, will be delivered in 2013.

As usual, the Indian Army, which accounts for more than 80% of the country's active personnel, received the largest share of the 2009 budget: Rs762bn (US$16.4bn), up 28% from the previous year. However, with a significant amount of this post-Mumbai increase earmarked for equipment needed by the special forces and National Security Guards, extra pressure will be put on existing modernisation programmes, several of which are already well behind schedule.

For example, the army's main-battle-tank development and modernisation plan remains mired in delay and bureaucratic inefficiencies. The MoD had been hoping to phase out its ageing T-55 tanks and replace them with upgraded T-72s and newly built T-90s. However, upgrades to the fleet of T-72s, to provide a night-fighting capability, are running around four years late and 1,000 domestically built T-90s have also been delayed because of technology-transfer disagreements with Russia. The domestically designed and produced *Arjun* main battle tank has also lurched from crisis to crisis, with the Indian parliament suggesting in 2007 that the DRDO should seek foreign assistance to overcome ongoing problems with the vehicle. The programme was launched more than 30 years ago and costs have increased dramatically since. Only about 45 of an initial 124 units have been delivered; at least 15 have been returned with defects to the Combat Vehicles Research and Development Establishment.

Efforts by the Army Aviation Corps to replace obsolete assets, such as *Chetak* and *Cheetah* helicopters, were postponed after the MoD scrapped the acquisition of 197 Eurocopter *Fennec* light observation helicopters, despite four years of trials and evaluations. The MoD claimed there had been irregularities in the selection process. In July 2008, a new RfP was issued to at least four overseas manufacturers, stipulating that the successful bid would entail an offset requirement of 50% and the transfer of 'maintenance-related technology' to HAL. Bell Helicopters quickly withdrew from the tender process, saying the terms of the RfP did not provide sufficient scope for a competitive commercial bid.

The army's ambitious Field Artillery Rationalisation Plan – under which it intends to acquire a mixture of 3,600 towed, wheeled and tracked guns – is already ten years overdue. During early 2008, the MoD issued tenders for the procurement of 140 ultra-light, 155mm howitzers and 180 wheeled guns. By August it had withdrawn both tenders, saying there had been an 'inadequate' response from overseas vendors – although observers suggested this was likely the result of bureaucratic delay and unrealistic requirements. By June 2009 it appeared that the only remaining bidder for the ultra-light programme was Singapore Technologies Engineering (ST Engineering), which was offering its *Pegasus* gun. However, ST Engineering was one of the seven companies under the spotlight in the Central Bureau of Investigation's corruption probe in mid 2009, so the potential deal had to be suspended.

In light of India's growing dependence on gas, oil and other commodities from all parts of the globe, the Indian Navy has begun a comprehensive programme to acquire power-projection platforms, ranging from aircraft carriers to landing platform dock ships. Over the next decade, the navy plans to field a fleet of 140–145 vessels (including two nuclear-powered submarines). Half of these will be designated ocean-going, the remainder assigned to coastal duties. The fleet will be built around two carrier battle groups: the first based on the much delayed *Gorshkov* and the second based on an indigenously designed, 37,500-tonne 'air defence vessel' (ADV), construction of which began in 2005. By 2022, the fleet is scheduled to have grown to 160 vessels, equipped with around 350 fixed-wing and rotary aircraft.

However, the acquisition of the *Gorshkov* is not the only naval programme holding up the navy's ambitious modernisation plans. The ADV is at least two years late and several other projects have fallen well behind schedule, not least due to the inefficiency of domestic shipyards. Around 39 out of an order book of 44 vessels are being constructed by Indian contractors. In July 2009, the MoD acknowledged that the domestic construction of six French-designed *Scorpene* submarines was running at least two years behind schedule because of difficulties with the 'absorption of technologies'. This raised questions about a potential follow-on order of another six *Scorpene* vessels. The navy's lack of submarines was highlighted in a report by the CAG, which warned that India faces the prospect of operating with less than half its current fleet by 2012, when two-thirds of its submarines are due for retirement. The report said prolonged refit schedules meant the submarine fleet had been operating at as little as 48% capacity between 2002 and 2006. It added that serious problems with inertial navigation systems and new sonar equipment meant several vessels were operating at sub-optimal levels.

There were more encouraging developments with the navy's plan to acquire two nuclear-powered submarines, as India finally agreed the lease of an *Akula II*-class vessel from Russia. The arrangement, initiated in 2004, was thrown into some doubt when the vessel in question, the *Nerpa*, was involved in an accident in late 2008 in which 20 sailors and technicians died through the release of freon gas. Although the sale of nuclear-powered attack submarines (SSNs) is forbidden by international treaty, leases are permitted if a vessel does not have missiles with a greater than 300km range. India is thought to have leased the submarine for ten years at a cost of around US$700m. The confirmation that the lease would go ahead was followed in July 2009 by the launch of India's indigenously built nuclear submarine, three decades after the programme was initiated. The 6,000-tonne Advanced Technology Vessel (ATV) is reportedly based on an original Russian design, and Russian involvement in designing the ship and miniaturising its reactor has long been an open secret. However, military officials have suggested that it might be at least two years before the vessel is commissioned, and that ultimately it may be retained only as a technology-demonstrator rather than as an operational strategic asset. The hulls of two further ATV submarines have already been completed and these ships are expected to be ready by 2017.

The biggest naval procurement agreed during 2009 was for seven new stealth frigates. The US$9.2bn project is a follow-up to the *Shivalik*-class programme, and work on the new ships will be shared between local firms Mazagoan Dockyards Ltd (MDL) and Garden Reach Shipbuilders and Engineers (GRSE). The original cost of each ship had been in the region of US$800m. However, to enable them to build the ships using modular construction technology, both the MDL and GRSE shipyards will require considerable modernisation, including large, covered workshops with sliding roofs and 300-tonne, 138m-span cranes. As a result, the cost of each ship will rise to around US$1.3bn. Despite the insistence by the Defence Acquisition Council that the ships be constructed locally, both shipyards will in fact require significant assistance from an overseas shipbuilder.

Following the deal for eight Boeing P-8I *Poseidon* multi-mission MRAs, the Indian Navy has turned its attention to further boosting its maritime-domain awareness and has dispatched a supporting request for information (RfI) for a new fleet of medium-range MRAs to several countries. The RfI anticipates the outright purchase of six aircraft with a range of four to five hours and 500 nautical miles. There will be an option for a further six units. It is thought that the coastguard will procure six similar aircraft through a separate programme.

The 2009 budget allocated Rs342bn (US$7.3bn) to the air force, including Rs199bn (US$4.2bn) in procurement funds, as the service continues to invest in assets to fulfil its long-term plan of becoming a 'continental rather than limited sub-continental force' able to confront challenges such as conventional and nuclear warfare, safeguard energy security, deploy on domestic counter-insurgency operations and undertake disaster-relief management at home and abroad.

With one eye firmly on developments in China and Pakistan, the air force's short-term priority is to prevent the continued decline of its combat squadrons. These have fallen to 30 from the sanctioned 39 in recent years, and will fall further with the imminent retirement of large numbers of MiG-21, MiG-23 and MiG-27 aircraft. With Pakistan taking delivery of American F-16s, and Chinese J-10 and J-17 aircraft, air-force chiefs have warned that India risks losing its long-held conventional edge over its neighbour. Several major programmes are under way to avoid this, including both the upgrade of existing platforms and the procurement of new aircraft.

The major programme yet to be decided is for at least 126 medium multirole combat aircraft (MMRCA). Trials began in late 2009 of six competing aircraft: Boeing's F/A-18E/F *Super Hornet*, Saab's JAS-39 *Gripen*, the Eurofighter *Typhoon*, Dassault's *Rafale*, Lockheed Martin's F-16 and Russia's MiG-35. The aircraft faced a range of tests in the tropical heat of Bangalore, the western Rajasthan desert and the mountainous Jammu and Kashmir region – all areas where the MMRCA will be deployed. It was hoped that a contract could be signed by 2012–14, but negotiations about offsets and technology-transfer agreements, plus India's dismal procurement record, suggest this may be optimistic. Given the likely delays to the MMRCA programme, the air force has asked HAL to step up production of the Su-30MKI aircraft it is building under licence from Russia. Instead of 14 planes a year, the air force wanted 23 produced annually. In October 2009, it ordered another 50 units, bringing the total order so far to 280 aircraft. The slow pace of deliveries has delayed plans to deploy them to the Chinese Assam border until 2010. The purchase of new aircraft will be augmented by the upgrade of all existing platforms over the next ten years, including all MiG-29s, *Jaguars*, and *Mirage*-2000s. Particular attention will be paid to upgrading avionics and weapons-delivery systems.

A tender process started in 2008 for 22 attack and 15 heavy-lift helicopters was cancelled when the competing companies withdrew, complaining that onerous offset requirements made the projects commercially unviable. In 2009, the air force issued new RfPs to overseas vendors for the helicopters' urgent procurement. The modified attack helicopter RfP has reduced the offset obligation to the standard 30% of the contract value, and has permitted an acquisition under the US Foreign Military Sales process to enable Bell and Boeing to take part in the competition. The RfP for heavy-lift helicopters has been sent to Boeing for the *Chinook* CH-47, Sikorsky for the Ch-35 *Sea Stallion* and Mil/Kazan for the Mi-26.

Given recent natural disasters in **Bangladesh** and the broad range of threats the country faces – from piracy to increasing competition for offshore resources – the newly elected government announced an ambitious procurement plan and boosted the 2009 defence budget by 30%. Under the proposed programme, all three services will benefit. However, in the near term the army will benefit the most, as it is scheduled to receive new main battle tanks, guided missiles, surface-to-air missiles, self-propelled artillery, rifles, night-vision equipment and communication systems.

Once the army has been re-equipped, the focus will switch to the navy. It has been promised three new frigates, three maritime-patrol aircraft, four helicopters, 12 patrol craft, two utility landing craft, one hydrographic ship, one salvage vessel and four missile-armed, fast-attack craft. By 2019, it will also receive a submarine. New naval bases are to be constructed, along with a submarine base, and the force will be increased by 4,000 personnel. In the meantime, the navy's existing frigates will be modernised with new anti-ship missiles.

The air force, which currently gets only 16% of the annual defence budget, will see its budget increase by 10% a year over the next ten years. The first phase of the modernisation programme will include upgrades to the existing fleet of F-7 fighters and Russian helicopters. By 2021 the plan is to have replaced these platforms with new aircraft and to have also procured new jet trainers and an airborne early warning and control (AWAC) capability.

However, Bangladeshi governments of all persuasions have a history of promoting grandiose schemes for their armed forces, which fail to materialise in anything like the original scale. It should be noted that even with this year's budget increase, spending will only reach US$1.2bn annually. This appears insufficient for the proposed modernisation programmes.

In late 2008, **Pakistan** was forced to turn to the International Monetary Fund (IMF) for a three-year, US$10bn loan to avoid defaulting on its current-account payments. The Pakistan media initially suggested that, in return for the loan, the IMF would stipulate a cut of some 30% in the country's defence budget. However, publication of the 2009–10 state budget revealed that rather than falling, defence spending would increase by 15% to PKR342bn (US$4.11bn). Indeed, with tensions between Pakistan and India rising after the 2008 Mumbai terror attacks, the Pakistani government cut its non-development expenditures by 20% to ensure the military had sufficient funds to respond to any threat. As previously noted in the *Military Balance*, the official defence budget in Pakistan does not include all military-related expenditure; it omits items such as military pensions, benefits for retired and serving personnel, military aid from Gulf states, space and nuclear programmes, and income generated by the armed forces' diverse business interests. Furthermore, because of its special relationship with China, Pakistan is able to purchase Chinese-produced weapons at favourable prices. It has also been the recipient of significant amounts of US military aid. All of this indicates that the level of actual defence spending is substantially higher than the official budget suggests.

Since 2001, Pakistan has received more than US$11bn in military aid from the US, thanks largely to the government's ongoing support in counter-terrorism. Pakistani soldiers have complained, however, that this money has only been sufficient to cover the army's increased operational costs and that very little has been made available for capability improvements in basic areas such as night-vision equipment. The US Government Accountability Office itself has also called for better oversight of how any future aid money is spent in Pakistan, highlighting that the US government has never received documentation from Pakistan on a 'large number of reimbursement claims'. Upon assuming office, President Barack Obama said the US would not give the Pakistani army 'a blank cheque' and that funds must be targeted towards those 'tools, training and support that Pakistan needs to root out the terrorists'. To that end, General David Petraeus announced in April that the US would introduce a new funding mechanism called the Pakistani Counter-Insurgency Capability Fund (PCCF). The fund will provide a total of US$2.8bn specifically to the military over the next five years. This is in addition to US$7.5bn that the US will donate to civilian projects in Pakistan during the same period.

Ever mindful of the arms embargo placed on it by the US in the 1990s, Pakistan continues to diversify its foreign weapons suppliers, as well as attempting to improve its own indigenous defence-industrial capabilities. Pakistan and China have already cooperated on several defence-manufacturing projects, including F-22P frigates and the *Al-Khalid* main battle tank. The two countries announced in March 2009 that serial production of the joint JF-17 fighter aircraft would begin with an order of 42 aircraft built by Pakistan Aeronautical Complex (PAC). The air force intends the JF-17 to become the backbone of its fleet and plans to acquire up to 250 of the aircraft by 2015. However, given the dire state of Pakistan's public finances, it seems likely that China has agreed to a long-term credit facility, or some other arrangement, for the programme to have been given the go-ahead. A joint marketing organisation has also been created between the two countries to promote sales of the JF-17 aircraft as an ideal choice for countries that are 'mindful of their finances' but wish to replace their existing second-generation aircraft. The air force is also planning to acquire up to 36 of the more advanced J-10 fighter aircraft from China. Again, if the acquisition is to go ahead, some form of financing from China appears inevitable.

There was a demonstration of Pakistan's growing indigenous defence-industrial capability in 2009, when Pakistan Aeronautical Complex formally launched plans to start producing parts for the Italian-designed *Falco* UAV, which is already in service with the Pakistan Air Force.

In August, Pakistan took delivery of the first of four air-to-air refuelling training aircraft leased from Ukraine. By 2010 the Pakistan Air Force plans to have four *Ilyushin* Il-78 aircraft operating over its border area. Other force-multiplying programmes in development include the purchase of four *Erieye*-equipped AEW&C aircraft from Sweden's Saab and four unspecified AEW&C platforms from China that are scheduled for delivery by 2012.

Although the Pakistan Navy only receives a small part of the official defence budget, it is moving ahead with major equipment programmes. The government has also provided funds to modernise Karachi Shipyard & Engineering Works (KSEW), to strengthen the country's naval and commercial shipbuilding capabilities. KSEW will construct four Chinese-designed, F-22P frigates; the first was delivered in July 2009 and the other three should have entered service by 2013. Beijing has also agreed to supply Z9-C helicopters to equip the ships. The navy's main outstanding requirement remains a replacement for its legacy *Hashmat*-class submarines. It had appeared almost certain that the navy would choose German HDW's Type 214 design for its next-generation submarine. However, no contract has yet been announced and a French offer of further *Agosta* vessels is also reportedly being considered. Pakistan already operates three *Agosta* 90B vessels, the last of which was commissioned in 2008.

Afghanistan AFG

New Afghan Afghani Afs		2008	2009	2010
GDP	US$	11.9bn	14.8bn	
per capita	US$	444	534	
Growth	%	3.4	15.7	
Inflation	%	26.8	-9.3	
Def exp[a]	US$	180m		
US$1=Afs		50	47	

[a] Domestic budget only

Population   28,395,716

Ethnic groups: Pashtun 38%; Tajik 25%; Hazara 19%; Uzbek 12%; Aimaq 4%; Baluchi 0.5%

Age	0–14	15–19	20–24	25–29	30–64	65 plus
Male	23%	5%	5%	4%	13%	1%
Female	22%	5%	4%	4%	13%	1%

Capabilities

ACTIVE 93,800 (Army 90,800 Air 3,000)

The Afghan government aims to boost control by developing the national army and police forces. The ANA (HQ Kabul) currently comprises some 90,800 troops. Org and strength of the ANA is detailed below. The NATO-led ISAF has over 71,000 troops in theatre with some 31,000 US troops remaining on OEF duties. ISAF established the Kabul Military Training Center in 2009; it is intended that the centre have the capacity to train 5,000 monthly by March 2010.

ORGANISATIONS BY SERVICE

Afghan National Army 90,800

The ANA is expanding rapidly but suffers from high wastage and poor retention. The development of ANA units is measured in terms of Capability Milestones (CM) 1-4. For the purpose of *The Military Balance* only units that have reached CM1-3 status are listed.

FORCES BY ROLE

5 regional comd

Inf   1 corps (201st) with (1 inf bde (1st CM1) with (2 inf bn; 1 cbt spt bn; 1 spt bn); 1 inf bde (2nd) (CM3) with (4 inf bn; 1 cbt spt bn; 1 spt bn); 1 corps (203rd) with (3 inf bde (1st, 2nd CM1 3rd CM2), (each: 3 inf bn; 1 cbt spt bn); 1 corps (205th) with (1 inf bde (1st CM1) with (3 inf bn; 1 cbt spt bn; 1 spt bn); 1 inf bde (2nd CM1) with (2 inf bn; 1 cbt spt bn); 1 inf bde (3rd CM1) with (4 inf bn); 1 inf bde (4th CM3) with (1 inf bn; 1 cbt spt bn); 1 corps (207th) with (1 inf bde (1st CM2) with (3 inf bn; 1 cbt spt bn; 1 spt bn); 1 inf bde (2nd CM3) with (2 inf bn; 1 spt bn); 1 corps (209th) with (1 inf bde (1st CM1) with (3 inf bn; 1 cbt spt bn); 1 inf bde (2nd CM3) with (3 inf bn; 1 spt bn); 1 div (111th Capital CM3) with (2 inf bde HQ; 1 sy bde (CM1) with (2 inf bn)

Reaction   1 mech bde (part of 201st Corps) (CM1) with (1
Force   inf bn; 1 mech inf bn; 1 armd bn; 1 cbt spt bn; 1 spt bn)

Cdo   1 bde (CM3) with (1bn); 5 indep cdo bn (CM1) (one per corps)

EQUIPMENT BY TYPE

MBT T-62; T-55
RECCE BRDM-1/BRDM-2
AIFV BMP-1/BMP-2
APC (T) 173 M-113A2
APC (W) BTR-40/BTR-60/BTR-70/BTR-80
ARTY
  TOWED 76mm M-1938; ZIS-3 M-1942; **122mm** D-30; M-30 M-1938; BM 21; **130mm** M-46; **140mm** BM 14; **152mm** D-1; **220 mm** BM1 *Oragan*
  MRL 122mm BM-21; **140mm** BM-14; **220mm** 9P140 *Uragan*
  MOR 82mm M-37; **107mm**; **120mm** M-43
AT • MSL • MANPATS *Milan*; AT4 9K111 *Spigot*
  RCL 73mm SPG9; **82mm** B-10
  GUNS 85mm D-48
AD • SAM
  SP SA-13 *Gopher*
  MANPAD SA-7 *Grail*
  GUNS
  SP ZSU-23-4
  TOWED 12.7mm; **14.5mm**; **23mm** ZU-23; **37mm** M-139; **57mm** S-60; **85mm** M-1939 *KS-12*; **100mm** KS-19
MSL • SSM FROG-7; SS-1 *Scud*

Afghan National Army Air Corps (ANAAC) 3,000

3 bases - Kabul North is primary ANAAC airfield with Presidential Flt and bulk of tpt and hel assets. Kandahar with 6 tpt ac, 6 Mi-17 and 2 Mi-24. Shindand with 2 tpt ac and 4 Mi-17.

EQUIPMENT BY TYPE

TPT 13: 2 An-26; 7 An-32B; 4 C-27 (16 more on order); (18 Alenia G222 on order)
HELICOPTERS
  ATK 9 Mi-35
  SPT 24 Mi-17
  TRG 2 L-39

Afghan National Police

Under control of Interior Ministry. To be 80,000

Border Police

Under control of Interior Ministry. To be 18,000

SELECTED NON-STATE GROUPS

See p. 341.

FOREIGN FORCES

All under ISAF comd unless otherwise specified. ISAF HQ resembles a static HQ with contributing NATO countries filling identified posts.
Albania 250; 1 inf coy; 1 inf pl

Australia 1,350; 1 inf BG with (1 mot inf coy; 1 armd recce sqn); 1 cdo BG (elm 2 cdo bn); elm 1 arty regt; 1 hel gp with 2 CH-47D; 1 UAV det with *Scaneagle*; 25 *Bushmaster IMV LFV*; 3 C-130J *Hercules* • UNAMA 1 obs

Austria 4

Azerbaijan 90

Bangladesh UNAMA 1 obs

Belgium 530; 6 F-16 (reinforce Dutch F-16s)

Bosnia – Herzegovina 10

Bulgaria 460; 1 mech inf coy

Canada (*Op Athena*) 2,830; 1 lt inf BG with (3 lt inf coy; 1 armd sqn; 1 armd recce sqn; 1 arty bty; 1 UAV flt; 1 cbt engr sqn); 1 MP coy; 20 *Leopard* C2 MBT; some LAV III *Kodiak*; some LAV-25 *Coyote*; 6 M-777; 6 CH-147 *Chinook*; 8 CH-146 *Griffon*; CU-170 *Heron* • *Operation Enduring Freedom - Afghanistan* (*Op Archer*) 12 • UNAMA (*Op Accius*) 2 obs

Croatia 290

Czech Republic 480; 19 IVECO DV LMV *Panther* • *Operation Enduring Freedom - Afghanistan* up to 100 • UNAMA 1 obs

Denmark 690; 1 mech inf BG with (2 mech inf coy; 1 tk pl; 1 hel det) • UNAMA 1 obs

Estonia 150; 1 mech inf coy with 14 XA-180 *Sisu*; 1 mor det with 3 81mm

Finland 165

France (*Operation Pamir*) 3,095; 1 bde HQ; 1 (Marine) inf BG; 1 (Foreign Legion) inf BG; 6 *Mirage* 2000D/SEM; 1 cbt hel bn with (3 AS-665 Tiger; 2 AS-532 *Cougar*; 3 EC-725; 3 *Gazelle*) • *Operation Enduring Freedom - Afghanistan* (*Op Epidote*) 35

Georgia 1

Germany 4,365; 1 bde HQ; 1 air mob inf regt Army: 100 APV-2 *Dingo II* APC (W); some CH-53G *Stallion* spt hel Air Force: 6 *Tornado* ECR SEAD ac; C-160 *Transall* tpt ac • UNAMA 1 obs

Greece 145; 1 engr coy; 1 C-130 *Hercules* tpt ac

Hungary 360; 1 lt inf coy;

Ireland 7

Italy 2,795; 1 AB bde HQ; 3 para regt; some *Dardo* AIFV; 6 A-129 *Mangusta*; 3 CH-47; 2 RQ-1 *Predator* Air Force: 2 C-27J at Herat; some C-130

Jordan 7

Korea, Republic of UNAMA 1 obs

Latvia 175

Lithuania 250

Luxembourg 8

Macedonia, Former Yugoslav Republic of 165

Netherlands 2,160; Army: 1 air aslt bde HQ; 1 armd inf BG; 40 *Bushmaster* IMV LFV; some YPR-675; 3 Pzh SP; 12 *Fennek*; some *Sperwer* UAV Air Force: 4-8 F-16 *Fighting Falcon*; 6 AH-64D *Apache*; 5 AS-532U2 *Cougar*; some C-130

New Zealand 300 (PRT Bamiyan) • UNAMA 1 obs

Norway 480; 1 mech inf coy; 1 spt coy • UNAMA 2 obs

Paraguay UNAMA 1 obs

Poland 1,910; 1 mtn inf bde HQ; 1 mtn inf BG; 1 air cav bde HQ with (elm 2 hel bn); 35 *Rosomak* AIFV; 68 IFV; 6 Mi-24; 4 Mi-17

Portugal 145 • UNAMA 1 obs

Romania 990; 1 mtn inf bde HQ; 1 inf bn; some TAB-77; some TAB-79; some Piranha IIIC • *Op Enduring Freedom-Afghanistan* 37 • UNAMA 1 obs

Singapore 9

Slovakia 245

Slovenia 130

Spain 1,000; 1 inf bn

Sweden 430 • UNAMA 1 obs

Turkey 720; 1 inf bn

Ukraine 10

United Arab Emirates 25

United Kingdom 9,000; **Army:** 1 div HQ (6th); 1 lt inf bde HQ (11th) with (5 lt inf bn; 1 armd recce regt; 1 fd arty regt; 1 engr regt); 1 GMLRS tp; 1 UAV bty; 1 EOD tp; 1 spt bn; 1 theatre log spt gp; 1 medical bn; 29 *Warrior*; 130 *Mastiff*; 12 L-118; 4 GMLRS; 8 AH-64D *Apache*; 5 *Lynx*; some *Hermes* 450; some *Predator* B; some *Desert Hawk* **Navy:** 55 *Viking*; 6 *Sea King* HC MK 4 **Air Force:** 8 *Tornado* GR4; 4 C-130 *Hercules*; 8 CH-47 *Chinook*; 6 HC Mk3 *Merlin*; 4 *Shadow R1* (Beechcraft *King Air 350*) • UNAMA 1 obs

United States 34,800; **Army:** 1 AB div HQ; 1 mech inf SBCT; 2 lt inf IBCT; 1 AB IBCT; 2 cbt avn bde **Marines:** 1 MEB with (1 RCT) • *Operation Enduring Freedom – Afghanistan* 31,129 **Army:** 1 AB IBCT (trg role); 1 ARNG lt inf IBCT (trg role); some AH-64 *Apache*; some OH-58 *Kiowa*; some CH-47 *Chinook*; some Stryker; some M-ATV; 3,200 MRAP; some M119; some M198 **Navy;** some EA-6B *Prowler* **Air Force:** some F-15E *Strike Eagle*; some A-10 *Thunderbolt II*; some EC-130H *Compass Call*; some C-130 *Hercules*; some HH-60 *Pave Hawk*; some MQ-1 *Predator*; some MQ-9 *Reaper* (Equipment includes both and OEF-A forces) **USMC:** some MV-22B *Osprey*; some AV-8B *Harrier*; some AH-1W *Cobra*; some CH-53 *Sea Stallion*; some UH-1N *Iroquois*; some RQ-7B *Shadow*

Uruguay UNAMA 1 obs

Bangladesh BGD

Bangladeshi Taka Tk		2008	2009	2010
GDP	Tk	5.45tr	6.14tr	
	US$	79.4bn	89.1bn	
per capita	US$	515	571	
Growth	%	6.0	5.4	
Inflation	%	7.7	5.3	
Def exp	Tk	81.9bn		
	US$	1.19bn		
Def bdgt	Tk	64.0bn	83.8bn	
	US$	934m	1.21bn	
US$1=Tk		68.6	69.0	

Population 156,050,883

Religious groups: Muslim 90%; Hindu 9%; Buddhist 1%

Age	0–14	15–19	20–24	25–29	30–64	65 plus
Male	17%	6%	6%	4%	16%	2%
Female	16%	6%	6%	4%	15%	2%

Capabilities

ACTIVE 157,053 (Army 126,153 Navy 16,900 Air 14,000) **Paramilitary 63,900**

ORGANISATIONS BY SERVICE

Army 126,153

FORCES BY ROLE

Armd   1 bde (1 armd regt); 6 regt
Inf   7 div HQ; 17 bde (*total*: 68 inf bn)
Cdo   1 bn
Arty   20 regt
Engr   1 bde
Sigs   1 bde
Avn   1 regt (2 sqn)
AD   1 bde

EQUIPMENT BY TYPE

MBT 232: 58 Type-69; 174 Type-59
LT TK 8 Type-62
APC 226
  APC (T) 134 MT-LB
  APC (W) 92: 75 BTR-80; 17 *Otocar*
ARTY 815+
  TOWED 343+: **105mm** 170: 56 Model 56A1; 114 Model 56/L 10A1 pack howitzer; **122mm** 111: 57 Type-54/54-1 (M-30), 54 T96 (D-30), **130mm** 62 Type-59-1 (M-46)
  MOR 472: **81mm** 11 M-29A1; **82mm** 366 Type-53/87/M-31 (M-1937); **120mm** 95 MO-120-AM-50 M67/UBM 52
AT • RCL 106mm 238 M-40A1
AIRCRAFT • TPT 6: 5 Cessna 152; 1 Piper *Cheyenne*
AD • SAM • MANPAD QW-2; 20 HN-5A (being replaced by QW-2)
  GUNS • TOWED 164: **37mm** 132 Type 65/74 **57mm** 34 Type 59 (S-60)

Navy 16,900

FORCES BY ROLE

Navy   1 HQ located at Dhaka

EQUIPMENT BY TYPE

PRINCIPAL SURFACE COMBATANTS • FRIGATES 5
  FFG 2:
  1 *Osman* (PRC *Jianghu* I) with 2 twin (4 eff.) each with HY-2 (CSS-N-2) *Silkworm* tactical SSM, 2 RBU 1200 (10 eff.), 4 100mm gun
  1 *Khalid Bin Walid* (ROK *Modified Ulsan*) with 4 Otomat Mk 2 tactical SSM, 1 76mm gun, 4 40mm gun
  FF 3:
  2 *Abu Bakr*† (UK *Leopard*) each with 2 115mm twin gun (4 eff.)
  1 *Umar Farooq*† training (UK *Salisbury*) with 3 *Squid*, 1 115mm twin gun (4 eff.)
PATROL AND COASTAL COMBATANTS 39
  PFM 9:
  5 *Durbar* less than 100 tonnes (PRC *Hegu*) each with 2 single with 2 SY-1 tactical SSM

4 *Durdarsha* (PRC *Huangfeng*) each with 4 single each with 1 HY-2 (CSS-N-2) *Silkworm* tactical SSM
  PCT 4 *Huchuan* less than 100 tonnes (PRC) each with 2 single 533mm TT each with 2 YU 1 Type 53 HWT
  PCO 8:
  1 *Nirbhoy* (PRC *Hainan*) with 4 RBU 1200 (20 eff.)
  1 *Madhumati* (*Sea Dragon*) with 1 76mm and 1 40mm gun
  6 *Kapatakhaya* (UK *Island* class)
  PFC 8: 4 *Shaheed Daulat*; 4 *Titas* (ROK *Sea Dolphin*)
  PCC 6: 2 *Karnaphuli*; 2 *Meghna* (fishery protection); 1 *Ruposhi Bangla*; 1 *Salam*
  PCI 4: 2 *Akshay*; 1 *Bakat*; 1 *Bishkali*
MINE WARFARE • MINE COUNTERMEASURES 5
  MSI 4 *Shapla* (UK *River*)
  MSO 1 *Sagar*
AMPHIBIOUS • CRAFT 10: 2 LCU†; 3 LCVP†; 1 LSL
  LCM 4 *Yuchin*
LOGISTICS AND SUPPORT 10
  AOR 2 (coastal)
  AR 1†
  AG 1
  ATF 1†
  AGHS 1 *Agradoot*
  TRG 1 *Shaheed Ruhul Amin*
  YTM 3

FACILITIES

Bases   Located at Chittagong, Dhaka, Kaptai, Khulna, Mangla

Air Force 14,000

Three major bases - Bashar AB (consists of Dhaka-Tejgaon and Dhaka-Kurmitola); Matiur Rahman AB (Jessore) and Zahurul Haque AB (Chittagong). Kurmitola is the main fast jet fighter/FGA base. Tejgaon houses two helicopter squadrons. Jessore houses the transport squadrons, the Air Force Academy and the Flying Training Wing. Bogra houses the flying instructors' school; Chittagong has a combat training/light attack squadron plus a helicopter squadron.
Flying hours   17,000+ flying hrs/year

FORCES BY ROLE

FGA   2 sqn with F-7MB, F-7BG (recce capable), FT-7BG, FT-7B *Airguard*; A-5C (Q-5III) *Fantan*; 1 OCU with L-39ZA *Albatros*; FT-6 (MiG-19UTI) *Farmer*
Ftr   1 sqn with MiG-29B/MiG-29UB *Fulcrum*
Tpt   1 sqn with An-32 *Club*; 1 sqn with C-130B *Hercules*
Hel   5 sqn with Mi-17/MI-171/MI-17MI-IV *Hip*; Bell 206L *LongRanger-4*; Bell 212 *Huey*
Trg   1 trg school with PT-6 (CJ-6) basic trg; T-37B *Tweet* (jet conversion trg); Bell 206L *LongRanger-4* (hel trg)

EQUIPMENT BY TYPE†

AIRCRAFT 75+ combat capable
  FGA 59+: 31 F-7MB/F-7BG (recce capable)/FT-7BG/FT-7B *Airguard*; 18 A-5C (Q-5III) *Fantan*; 10 FT-6 (MiG-19UTI) *Farmer*
  FTR 8: 6 MiG-29 *Fulcrum*; 2 MiG-29UB *Fulcrum*
  TPT 7: 3 An-32 *Club* †; 4 C-130B *Hercules*

TRG 30: 8 L-39ZA *Albatros**; 10 PT-6 (CJ-6); 12 T-37B *Tweet*

HELICOPTERS
SPT 17 Mi-17/MI-171/MI-17MI-IV *Hip*
UTL 13: 2 Bell 206 *Longranger*; 11 Bell 212
MSL • AAM AA-2 *Atoll*

Paramilitary 63,900

Ansars 20,000+
Security Guards

Armed Police 5,000
Rapid action force (forming)

Border Guard Bangladesh 38,000
Border Guard
Paramilitary 41 bn

Coast Guard 900
PATROL AND COASTAL COMBATANTS 10
PFC 2 *Shaheed Daulat*
PCI 1 *Bishkali*
PCR 5 *Pabna*
PB 2 *Meghna*

DEPLOYMENTS

AFGHANISTAN
UN • UNAMA 1 obs

BURUNDI
UN • BINUB 1 obs

CENTRAL AFRICAN REPUBLIC/CHAD
UN • MINURCAT 5; 2 obs

CÔTE D'IVOIRE
UN • UNOCI 2,082; 15 obs; 2 inf bn; 1 engr coy; 1 sig coy; 1 fd hospital

DEMOCRATIC REPUBLIC OF CONGO
UN • MONUC 1,520; 26 obs; 1 mech inf bn; 2 avn unit

LIBERIA
UN • UNMIL 2,340; 11 obs; 2 inf bn; 2 engr coy; 1 sigs pl; 2 log coy; 1 MP unit

SUDAN
UN • UNAMID 591; 7 obs; 2 log coy
UN • UNMIS 1,451; 19 obs; 1 inf bn; 1 engr coy; 1 de-mining coy; 1 tpt coy; 1 rvn coy; 1 MP coy; 1 fd hospital

TIMOR-LESTE
UN • UNMIT 4 obs

WESTERN SAHARA
UN • MINURSO 8 obs

India IND

Indian Rupee Rs		2008	2009	2010
GDP	Rs	53.2tr	60.33tr	
	US$	1,223bn	1,300bn	
per capita	US$	1,073	1,124	
Growth	%	7.3	5.4	
Inflation	%	8.3	8.7	
Def exp	Rs	1,372bn		
	US$	31.54bn		
Def bdgt	Rs	1,235bn	1,665bn	
	US$	28.39bn	35.88bn	
US$1=Rs		43.5	46.4	

Population   1,156,897,766

Religious groups: Hindu 80%; Muslim 14%; Christian 2%; Sikh 2%

Age	0–14	15–19	20–24	25–29	30–64	65 plus
Male	16%	5%	5%	5%	18%	2%
Female	15%	5%	4%	4%	18%	2%

Capabilities

ACTIVE 1,325,000 (Army 1,129,900, Navy 58,350 Air 127,200, Coast Guard 9,550) Paramilitary 1,300,586

RESERVE 1,155,000 (Army 960,000 Navy 55,000 Air 140,000) Paramilitary 987,821
Army first line reserves (300,000) within 5 years of full time service, further 500,000 have commitment to the age of 50.

ORGANISATIONS BY SERVICE

Strategic Forces Command
India's Nuclear Command Authority (NCA) controls the nation's nuclear weapons. The NCA comprises a Political Council and an Executive Council. The Political Council, chaired by the Prime Minister, is the only body that can authorise nuclear weapons use; the Executive Council, chaired by the National Security Advisor to the Prime Minister, provides inputs for decision making by the NCA and executes directives given by the Political Council. Strategic Forces Command (SFC) is a tri-service command established in 2003. The Commander-in-Chief of SFC, a senior three-star military officer, manages and administers all Strategic Forces through separate Army and Air Force chains of command, with the army responsible for all nuclear-capable land-based ballistic missiles and the air force responsible for all nuclear-capable fixed-wing aircraft (the navy is not yet nuclear-capable). The navy is also establishing its own chain of comd, following the launch of INS *Arihant* in July 2009. The C-in-C SFC reports directly to the Chairman, Chiefs of Staff Committee.

South and Central Asia

FORCES BY ROLE

Msl 2 Gps with SS-150/SS-250 *Prithvi*
   1 Gp with *Agni* I
   1 Gp with *Agni*-II

EQUIPMENT BY TYPE
MSL • STRATEGIC

IRBM 80–100 *Agni* I; 20–25 *Agni*-II; *Agni*-III (successfully tested)

SRBM 60 msl produced 1993–1999. Up to 20 SS-150 *Prithvi* I/SS-250 *Prithvi* II msl produced each year; SS-350 *Dhanush* (naval testbed)

Some Indian Air Force assets (such as *Mirage* 2000H or Su-30MKI) could be tasked with a strategic role

Army 1,129,900,

FORCES BY ROLE

6 Regional Comd HQ (Northern, Western, Central, Southern, Eastern, South Western), 1 Training Comd (ARTRAC), 13 corps HQ (3 (1st 2nd 21st) strike corps, 10 (3th, 4th, 9th–11th, 12th (Desert), 14th–16th, 33rd), 'holding' corps

Armd	3 div (*each*: 2–3 armd bde ,1 SP arty bde (1 medium regt, 1 SP arty regt)); 8 indep bde; 13 regt each with 55 T-55; 35 regt each with 55 T-72M1; 5 regt each with 55 T-90S; 14 regt each with 55 *Vijayanta*
Mech Inf	4 RAPID div (*each*: 2 mech inf, 1 armd bde); 2 indep bde (25 bn in total)
Inf	18 div (*each*: 1 arty bde, 2–5 inf bde); 6 indep bde; (319 bn in total)
Mtn Inf	10 div (*each*: 3–4 mtn inf bde, 3-4 arty regt); 2 indep bde
SF	5-7 bn
AB	1 para bde , 5 bn
Arty	2 div (*each*: 2 arty bde (*each*: 3 med arty, 1 composite regt (1 SATA/MRL regt))
Med Arty	63 regt (bn)
SP Med Arty	1 regt (bn)
Fd Arty	118 regt
SP Fd Arty	3 regt (bn)
MRL	4 regt (bn)
Mor	15 regt
SSM	2 (*Prithvi*) regt; 1 (*Agni*) regt; 2-3 PJ-10 (*BrahMos*) regt
Engr	4 bde
Hel	14 sqn
AD	6 bde; 5 'flak' regt with 320 ZU-23-2 (some SP); 30 'flak' regt with 1,920 L40/70 (*each*: 4 AD bty); 35+ regt
SAM	12 regt; 2 gp (*each*: 2–5 SAM bty)

EQUIPMENT BY TYPE

MBT 4,047+ (ε1,133 in reserve): 320+ T-90S (to replace *Vijayanta* and T-55); ε54 *Arjun* (non operational, 79 more in construction); 1,950 T-72M1 1,008 *Vijayanta* (modified) 715 T-55 (modifications similar to *Vijayanta*); ε67 in reserve
RECCE 110 BRDM-2 each with AT-4 *Spigot*/AT-5 *Spandrel*; *Ferret* (used for internal security duties along with some indigenously built armd cars)

AIFV 1,455+: 350+ BMP-1; 980 *Sarath* (BMP-2); 125 BMP-2K
APC 317+
   APC (W) 317+: ε160 *Casspir*; 157+ OT-62/OT-64; 14 *Yukthirath* MPV (of 327 order)
ARTY 11,258+
   SP 20+: **130mm** 20 M-46 *Catapult*; **152mm** 2S19 *Farm*
   TOWED up to 4510+: **105mm** up to 1,350+: 600+ IFG Mk1/Mk2/Mk3 (being replaced); up to 700 LFG; 50 M-56; **122mm** 550 D-30; **130mm** 2,200: 1,200 M-46; 500 (in process of upgrading to 155mm); 500 in reserve in store; **155mm** 410 FH-77B
   MRL 208: **122mm** ε150 BM-21/LRAR; **214mm** 30 *Pinaka* (non operational) **; 300mm** 28 9A52 *Smerch*
   MOR 6,520+
      SP 120mm E1
      TOWED 6520+: **81mm** 5,000+ E1; **120mm** ε1,500 AM-50/E1; **160mm** 20 M-58 *Tampella*
AT • MSL
   SP AT-4 9K111 *Spigot*; AT-5 9K113 *Spandrel*
   MANPATS AT-3 9K11 *Sagger* (being phased out); AT-4 9K111 *Spigot*; AT-5 9K113 *Spandrel*; *Milan* 2
   RCL 84mm *Carl Gustav* ; **106mm** 3,000+ M-40A1 (10 per inf bn)
HELICOPTERS
   ASLT 12 *Lancer*
   UTL 210: 120 HAL *Cheetah* (SA-315B) *Lama*; 60 HAL *Chetak* (SA-316B) *Alouette III*; 30 *Dhruv* (ALH)
UAV 14 *Nishant*
   RECCE • TACTICAL *Searcher*
AD • SAM 3,500+
      SP 880+: 180 SA-6 *Gainful*; 50+ SA-8B; 400 SA-9 *Gaskin*; 250 SA-13 *Gopher*;
      MANPAD 2,620+: 620 SA-7 *Grail* (being phased out); 2,000+ SA-16 *Gimlet*
   GUNS 2,395+
      SP 155+: **23mm** 75 ZSU-23-4; ZU-23-2 (truck mounted); **30mm** 20-80 2S6 *Tunguska*
      TOWED 2,240+: **20mm** Oerlikon (reported); **23mm** 320 ZU-23-2; **40mm** 1,920 L40/70
UAV 26: 12 *Searcher* I and II; 14 *Nishant*
RADAR • LAND 12+: 12 AN/TPQ-37 *Firefinder*; BSR Mk.2; *Cymbeline*; EL/M-2140; M-113 A1GE *Green Archer* (mor); MUFAR; *Stentor*
AMPHIBIOUS 2 LCVP
MSL • SSM 8–10 PJ-10 *BrahMos*; 70–90 *Agni* I; 15–20 *Agni* II; *Agni* III; up to 20 SS-150 *Prithvi* I/SS-250 *Prithvi* II msl produced each year

Reserve Organisations

Reserves 300,000 reservists (1st line reserve within 5 years full time service); 500,000 reservists (commitment until age of 50) (total 800,000)

Territorial Army 160,000 reservists (only 40,000 regular establishment)

Army	6 Ecological bn; 37 Non-departmental units (raised from government ministries)
Inf	25 bn
AD	20 'flak' regt with 1,280 L40/60

Navy 58,350 (incl 7,000 Naval Avn and 1,200 Marines)

FORCES BY ROLE
Navy Fleet HQ New Delhi; Commands located at Mumbai (Bombay), Vishakhapatnam and Kochi (Cochin)

EQUIPMENT BY TYPE
SUBMARINES • TACTICAL 16
SSN 1 *Chakra* (RUS *Nerpa*) each with 4 single 533mm TT each with SS-N-27 SLCM, 4 single 650mm TT each with T-65 HWT); (RUS lease agreement - under trials; not at full OC)
SSK 16:
  2 *Vela* (FSU *Foxtrot*) each with 10 single 533mm TT (6 forward, 4 aft)
  4 *Shishumar* (GER T-209/1500) each with 1 single 533mm TT
  4 *Sindhughosh* (FSU *Kilo*) each with 6 single 533mm TT (1 undergoing phased refit of SS-N-27)
  6 *Sindhughosh* (FSU *Kilo*) with 6 single 533mm TT each with SS-N-27 *Club-S* tactical SSM
PRINCIPAL SURFACE COMBATANTS 45
  AIRCRAFT CARRIERS • CV 1 *Viraat* (UK *Hermes*) (capacity 30 Sea Harrier FRS MK51 (*Sea Harrier FRS MKI*) FGA ac; 7 Ka-27 *Helix* ASW hel/*Sea King* MK42B ASW hel)
  DESTROYERS • DDG 8:
  3 *Delhi* each with 4 quad (16 eff.) each with SS-N-25 *Switchblade* tactical SSM, 2 single with 24 SA-N-7 SAM, 5 x1 533mm ASTT, 1 100mm gun, (capacity either 2 Sea King MK42A ASW hel or 2 ALH utl hel)
  5 *Rajput* (FSU *Kashin*) each with 2 twin (4eff.) PJ-10 BrahMos ASCM (one ship fitted; phased upgrades planned for rest of class), 2 Twin (4 eff.) each with SS-N-2C *Styx* tactical SSM, 2 (4 eff.) each with 16 SA-N-1 *Goa* SAM, 5x1 533mm ASTT, 2 RBU 6000 *Smerch 2* (24 eff.), 1 76mm gun, (capacity either 1 Ka-25 *Hormone*/KA-28 hel)
  FRIGATES 12
    FFG 11:
    3 *Brahmaputra* each with 4 quad (16 eff.) each with SS-N-25 *Switchblade* tactical SSM, 20 SA-N-4 *Gecko* SAM, 2 triple 324mm ASTT (6 eff.), 1 76mm gun, (capacity either 2 HAL *Chetak* (SA-316B) *Alouette III* SA-316 utl/*Sea King* MK42 ASW hel or 2 *Sea King* MK42 ASW hel) (2nd of class awaiting full weapons fit)
    3 *Godavari* each with 2 triple 324mm ASTT (6 eff.), 4 single each with SS-N-2D *Styx* tactical SSM, 1 twin (2 eff.) with 20 SA-N-4 *Gecko* SAM, (capacity either 2 Sea King MK42 ASW hel or 2 HAL *Chetak* (SA-316B) *Alouette III* SA-316 utl/*Sea King* MK42 ASW hel)
    3 *Talwar I* each with SS-N-27 *Club* tactical SSM, 6 single with SA-N-7 *Gadfly* SAM, 2 533mm ASTT (4 eff.), 2 RBU 6000 *Smerch 2* (24 eff.), 2 CADS-N-1 *Kashtan* CIWS (4 eff.), 1 100mm gun, (capacity either 1 KA-31 *Helix B* AEW hel/KA-28 ASW hel or 1 ALH utl hel)
    2 *Shivalik* each with SS-N-27 *Club* tactical SSM, 6 single with SA-N-7 *Gadfly* SAM, 1 76mm gun, (capacity 1 *Sea King Mk42-B* ASW hel) (3rd vessel expected ISD '10)

FF 1 *Krishna* (UK *Leander*) trg role
CORVETTES 24
  FSG 20:
    4 *Khukri* each with 1 76mm gun, 2 twin (4 eff.) each with SS-N-2C *Styx* tactical SSM, 1 hel landing platform (For ALH/*Chetak*)
    4 *Kora* each with 4 (16 eff.) each with SS-N-25 *Switchblade* tactical SSM, 1 quad (4 eff.) with SA-N-5 *Grail* SAM, 1 76mm gun, 1 hel landing platform (For ALH/*Chetak*)
    5 *Veer* (FSU *Tarantul*) each with 4 single each with SS-N-2D *Styx* tactical SSM, 2 quad (8 eff.) (quad manual aiming) each with SA-N-5 *Grail* SAM, 1 76mm gun
    5 *Vibhuti* (mod *Veer*) each with 4 quad (16 eff.) with 16 SS-N-25 *Switchblade* tactical SSM, 1 quad (4 eff.) (quad manual aiming) with SA-N-5 *Grail* SAM, 1 76mm gun
    2 *Vibhuti* (advanced version) each with 4 quad (16 eff.) each with 16 SS-N-25 *Switchblade* tactical SSM, 1 quad (4 eff.) (manual aiming) with SA-N-5 *Grail* SAM, 1 76mm gun
  FS 4:
    4 *Abhay* (FSU *Pauk* II) each with 1 quad (4 eff.) (quad manual aiming) with SA-N-5 *Grail* SAM, 2 x1 533mm ASTT (twin), 2 RBU 1200 (10 eff.), 1 76mm gun
PATROL AND COASTAL COMBATANTS 28
  PSOH 6 *Sukanya* (capacity 1 HAL *Chetak*)
  PCC 15: 6 *Trinkat* SDB MK 5; 5 SDB MK 3; 4 *Car Nicobar* (additional vessels in build)
  PFI 7 *Super Dvora* less than 100 tonnes
MINE WARFARE • MINE COUNTERMEASURES 10
  MSO 10 *Pondicherry* (FSU *Natya*)
AMPHIBIOUS 17
  PRINCIPAL AMPHIBIOUS VESSELS • LPD 1
  Jalashwa (US *Austin* class) (capacity up to 6 med spt hel; either 9 LCM or 4 LCM and 2 LCAC; 4 LCVP; 930 troops)
  LS 10
    LSM 5 *Kumbhir* (FSU *Polnocny* C) (capacity 5 MBT or 5 APC; 160 troops)
    LST 5:
    2 *Magar* (capacity 15 MBT or 8 APC or 10 trucks; 500 troops)
    3 *Magar* mod (capacity 11 MBT or 8 APC or 10 trucks; 500 troops)
  CRAFT • LCU 6 *Vasco de Gama* MK2/3 LC (capacity 2 APC; 120 troops)
LOGISTICS AND SUPPORT 47
  AORH 3: 1 *Aditya* (mod *Deepak*); 1 *Deepak*; 1 *Jyoti*
  AOL 6
  ASR 1
  AWT 2
  AGOR 1 *Sagardhwani*
  AGHS 8 *Sandhayak*
  AGS 1 *Makar*
  ATF 1
  TPT 3 *Nicobar*
  TRG 3: 1 *Tir*; 2 **AXS**
  TRV 1

YDT 3
YTL/YTM 14

FACILITIES

Bases   Located at Mumbai (Bombay), Karwar
                 (under construction), Calcutta,
                 Vishakhapatnam, Port Blair (Andaman Is),
                 Kochi (Cochin)

Naval airbase   Located at Arakonam, Goa

Naval Aviation 7,000

Flying   125 hrs/year on T-60 trg ac; 125-150 hrs/year
hours   on *Sea Harrier* FRS MK51 (*Sea Harrier* FRS
            MKI) FGA ac

FORCES BY ROLE

Air   1 HQ located at Arakonam

FGA   1 sqn with *Sea Harrier* FRS MK51 (*Sea Harrier*
        FRS MKI); T-60*

ASW   5 sqn with Ka-31 *Helix B*; Ka-25 *Hormone*; 18
        Ka-28 (Ka-27PL) *Helix A*; *Sea King* MK42A/*Sea
        King* MK42B; HAL *Chetak* (SA-316B) *Alouette III*

MR   2 sqn with Il-38 *May*; Tu-142M *Bear F*; Do-228-
        101; BN-2 *Islander*

SAR   1 sqn with *Sea King* MK42C; HAL *Chetak* (SA-
        316B) *Alouette III* (several in SAR role)

Tpt   1 sqn with HAL-784M (HS-748M); 1 sqn with
        UH-3H *Sea King* (spt/utl role)

Comms   1 sqn with Do-228

Trg   2 sqn with HJT-16 MKI *Kiran*; HJT-16 MKII
        Kiran II; HPT-32 *Deepak*

UAV   1 sqn with *Searcher* MkII, 4 *Heron*

EQUIPMENT BY TYPE

AIRCRAFT 23 combat capable
  FGA 11 *Sea Harrier* FRS MK51 (*Sea Harrier* FRS MKI)
  ASW 4 Tu-142M *Bear F**
  MP 20: 14 Do-228-101; 6 Il-38 *May**
  TPT 37: 17 BN-2 *Islander*; 10 Do-228; 10 HAL-784M
  (HS-748M)
  TRG 22: 6 HJT-16 MKII; 6 HJT-16 MKII *Kiran II*; 8
  HPT-32 *Deepak*; 2 T-60*
HELICOPTERS
  ASW 54: 7 Ka-25 *Hormone*; 12 Ka-28 (Ka-27PL) *Helix
  A*; 21 *Sea King* MK42A ASW; 14 *Sea King* MK42B ASW/
  ASUW*
  AEW 9 KA-31 *Helix B*
  SAR 5 *Sea King* MK42C
  UTL 49+: 4 *Dhruv* ALH 2; 6 HAL *Chetak* (SA-316B)
  Alouette III; some (several in SAR role); 23 SA-319
  Alouette III; up to 6 UH-3H *Sea King*
UAV 12: 8 *Searcher* MK II; 4 *Heron*
MSL
  ASM *Sea Eagle*; KH-35/*Sea Skua* (*Bear* and *May* a/c now
  cleared to fire *Sea Eagle* and Kh-35)
  ASCM PJ-10 *BrahMos*
  AAM R-550 *Magic* 2/R-550 *Magic* tactical AAM

Marines ε1,200 (Additional 1,000 for SPB duties)

Amph   1 bde
Cdo   1 (marine) force

As a consequence of the Mumbai attacks, the Sagar
Prahari Bal (SPB) was established to protect critical
maritime infrastructure. The estimated force strength is
1,000 pers with 80 PBF

Western Command

Navy 1 HQ located at Mumbai (Bombay)

Southern Command

Navy 1 HQ located at Kochi (Cochin)

Eastern Command

Navy 1 HQ located at Vishakhapatnam

Andaman and Nicobar Command (joint command)

Navy 1 HQ located at Port Blair (Andaman Is)

Air Force 127,200

5 regional air comds: Western (New Delhi), South-Western
(Gandhinagar), Eastern (Shillong), Central (Allahabad),
Southern (Trivandrum)
Maintenance Cmd (Nagpur), Trg Comd (Bangalore)

Flying hours   180 hrs/year

FORCES BY ROLE

Ftr   3 sqn with MiG-29B *Fulcrum*; 3 sqn with MiG-
            21FL *Fishbed*

FGA   6 sqn with Su-30 MKI *Flanker*; 3 sqn with
            M-2000H (M-2000E) *Mirage*/ (secondary ECM
            role); 8 sqn with MiG-21bis/Bison; 4 sqn with
            MiG-21M/MF *Fishbed*); 4 sqn with *Jaguar* S(I); 6
            sqn with MiG-27ML *Flogger*

Maritime   1 sqn with *Jaguar* S(I) with *Sea Eagle* tactical
attack   ASM

AEW/   1 sqn with IL-76 TD *Phalcon*
AWACS

Recce   1 sqn with Gulfstream IV

Tpt   2 sqn with Il-76 *Candid*; 7 sqn with An-32 *Cline*;
            4 sqns and units with HS-748; 2 sqn with Do-
            228; 1 sqn with BBJ B-737, EMB-145BJ; 1 flt with
            EMB-135BJ

Tkr   1 sqn with Il-78 *Midas*

Atk hel   2 sqn with Mi-24/Mi-35 *Hind*

Hel   9 sqn with Mi-8 *Hip*; 6 sqn with Mi-17 *Hip* H/
            Mi-17 IV; 1 sqn with Mi-26 *Halo*); 2 sqn with
            ALH *Dhruv*; 3 sqn with HAL *Cheetah* (SA-315B)
            Lama; 5 sqn *with* HAL *Chetak* (SA-316B)

Trg   trg units with HJT-16 *Kiran*; HPT-32 *Deepak*;
            MiG-21; MiG-21bis; MiG-21M/MF; MiG-21FL;
            MiG-27ML*; MiG-23BN*; *Jaguar* IS/2 –IM; *Hawk*
            Mk 132 AJT; Chetak; An-32; Dornier Do-228

UAV   5 sqn with *Searcher* MkII

SAM   25 sqn with S-123M *Pechora* (SA-3) *Goa*; 6 sqn
            with OSA-AK (SA-8B *Gecko*); 10 flt with SA-18
            Gimlet

EQUIPMENT BY TYPE

AIRCRAFT 632 combat capable
  FTR 96: 48 MiG-29B *Fulcrum*; 48 MiG-21FL
  FGA 536: 98 Su-30 MKI *Flanker*; 36 M-2000H (M-2000E)

Mirage/M-2000TH (M-2000ED) *Mirage* (secondary ECM role); 88 MiG-27ML *Flogger J2*; 90 *Jaguar* S International (incl 16 maritime attack with *Sea Eagle* tactical ASM); 152 MiG-21bis *Fishbed L & N* (125 being upgraded to MiG-21bis-93); 16 MiG-21MF/PFMA *Fishbed*; 56 MiG-21M
AEW&C: 1 IL-76 TD *Phalcon* (2 more to follow by 2010)
RECCE 3 Gulfstream IV SRA-4
TKR 6 Il-78 *Midas*
TPT 213: 24 Il-76 *Candid*; 112 An-32 *Cline*; 6 B-707; 4 B-737; 20 BAe-748; 40 Do-228; 4 EMB-135BJ; 3 BBJ
TRG 271: 25 *Hawk* Mk 132AJT; 120 HJT-16 MKI; 56 HJT-16 MK11 *Kiran II*; 70 HPT-32 *Deepak*
HELICOPTERS
  ATK 20 Mi-25 *Hind D*/Mi-35 *Hind*
  SPT 178: 4 Mi-26 *Halo* (hy tpt); 102 Mi-8; 72 Mi-17 (Mi-8MT) *Hip H*
  UTL 128: 20 *Dhruv* ALH (150 on order); 60 HAL *Cheetah* (SA-315B) *Lama* SA-315; 48 HAL *Chetak* (SA-316B) *Alouette III*
UAV: some *Searcher* MK II
AD • SAM S-125 (SA-3B) *Goa*
  SP SA-8B
  MANPAD SA-16 *Gimlet*
MSL • TACTICAL • ASM AM-39 *Exocet*; AS-11; AS-11B (ATGW); AS-12 *Kegler*; AS-17 *Krypton*; AS-30; AS-7 *Kerry*; *Sea Eagle*
  ARM AS-11; AS-11B (ATGW); AS-12 *Kegler*; AS-17 *Krypton*
  AAM AA-10 *Alamo*; AA-11 *Archer*; AA-12 *Adder*; AA-7 *Apex*; AA-8 *Aphid*; R-550 *Magic*; Super 530D

Coast Guard 9,550

Control of the Coast Guard is exercised through the Director General under the Ministry of Defence (HQ Delhi). The CG is organised into 11 districts with three regional Command Head Quarters at Mumbai, Chennai, Port Blair; in addition there are two principal air stations at Daman and Chennai with additional air stations at Mumbai, Goa, Kochi, Kolkata and Port Blair for maritime surveillance with a total of 9 Air Squadrons.

EQUIPMENT BY TYPE
PATROL AND COASTAL COMBATANTS 70+
  PSOH 14: 2 *Sankalp* (Additional vessels in build); 4 *Samar*; 8 *Vikram*
  PCO 8: 7 *Sarojini-Naid*; 1 *Rani Abbakka* (ISD expected '10; additional vessels in build)
  PCC 23: 7 *Jija Bai* mod 1; 8 *Priyadarshini*; 6 *Tara Bai*; 2 *Rajkiran*
  PBC 14
  PBI 5+
  ACV 6 *Griffon 8000*
AIRCRAFT • TPT 24 Do-228
HELICOPTERS • UTL • SA-316 17 HAL *Chetak* (SA-316B) *Alouette III*

Paramilitary 1,300,586

Rashtriya Rifles 65,000

Ministry of Defence
Paramilitary 65 bn (in 15 sector HQ)

Assam Rifles 63,883

Ministry of Home Affairs. Security within north-eastern states, mainly army-officered; better trained than BSF

FORCES BY ROLE
Equipped to roughly same standard as an army inf bn
Paramilitary 7 HQ; 42 bn each with 6 81mm mor

EQUIPMENT BY TYPE
ARTY • MOR 81mm 240

Border Security Force 208,422

Ministry of Home Affairs.

FORCES BY ROLE
Paramilitary 157+ bn each with 6 81mm

EQUIPMENT BY TYPE
Small arms, lt arty, some anti-tank weapons
ARTY • MOR 81mm 942+
AIRCRAFT • TPT (air spt)

Central Industrial Security Force 94,347 (lightly armed security guards only)

Ministry of Home Affairs. Guards public-sector locations

Central Reserve Police Force 229,699

Ministry of Home Affairs. Internal security duties, only lightly armed, deployable throughout the country
Paramilitary 2 Mahila (female) bn; 125 bn; 13 rapid action force bn

Defence Security Corps 31,000

Provides security at Defence Ministry sites

Indo–Tibetan Border Police 36,324

Ministry of Home Affairs. Tibetan border security
SF/guerrilla warfare and high-altitude warfare specialists; 30 bn

National Security Guards 7,357

Anti-terrorism contingency deployment force, comprising elements of the armed forces, CRPF and Border Security Force

Railway Protection Forces 70,000

Sashastra Seema Bal 31,554

Guards Indo-Nepal/Bhutan borders

Special Frontier Force 10,000

Mainly ethnic Tibetans

Special Protection Group 3,000

Protection of VVIP

State Armed Police 450,000

For duty primarily in home state only, but can be moved to other states. Some bn with GPMG and army standard infantry weapons and equipment
Paramilitary 24 (India Reserve Police (cdo-trained)) bn

Reserve Organisations

Civil Defence 500,000 reservists
Fully train in 225 categorised towns in 32 states. Some units for NBC defence

Home Guard 487,821 reservists (515,000 authorised str)
In all states except Arunachal Pradesh and Kerala; men on reserve lists, no trg. Not armed in peacetime. Used for civil defence, rescue and fire-fighting provision in wartime; 6 bn (created to protect tea plantations in Assam)

SELECTED NON-STATE GROUPS

CPI-Maoist (Naxalites) Est strength: 6,500 Major equipments include: mines and IEDs, SALW

DEPLOYMENT

AFGHANISTAN
400 ε2 cdo coy (Protection for road construction project)

ARABIAN GULF AND INDIAN OCEAN
Maritime Security Operations 1 FFG

CÔTE D'IVOIRE
UN • UNOCI 8 obs

DEMOCRATIC REPUBLIC OF CONGO
UN • MONUC 4,249; 52 obs; 3 mech inf bn; 1 inf bn; 2 avn unit; 1 atk hel unit; 1 fd hospital

LEBANON
UN • UNIFIL 898; 1 inf bn; 1 fd hospital

SUDAN
UN • UNMIS 2,600; 17 obs; 2 inf bn; 1 engr coy; 1 avn unit; 1 fd hospital

SYRIA/ISRAEL
UN • UNDOF 195; elm 1 log bn

TAJIKISTAN
IAF Forward Op Base, Farkhar

TIMOR-LESTE
UN • UNMIT 1 obs

FOREIGN FORCES

Total numbers for UNMOGIP mission in India and Pakistan
Chile 2 obs
Croatia 9 obs
Denmark 1 obs
Finland 5 obs
Italy 7 obs
Korea, Republic of 9 obs
Philippines 3 obs
Sweden 5 obs
Uruguay 2 obs

Kazakhstan KAZ

Kazakhstani Tenge t		2008	2009	2010
GDP	t	16.4tr	15.1tr	
	US$	138bn	101bn	
per capita	US$	8,899	6,550	
Growth	%	3.2	-2.0	
Inflation	%	17.2	7.5	
Def bdgt	t	193bn	ε200bn	
	US$	1.61bn	ε1.33bn	
FMA (US)	US$	1.3m	1.5m	2.5m
US$1=t		120	150	

Population   15,399,437

Ethnic groups: Kazakh 51%; Russian 32%; Ukrainian 5%; German 2%; Tatar 2%; Uzbek 2%

Age	0–14	15–19	20–24	25–29	30–64	65 plus
Male	12%	6%	5%	4%	19%	3%
Female	12%	5%	5%	4%	21%	6%

Capabilities

ACTIVE 49,000 (Army 30,000 Navy 3,000 Air 12,000 MoD 4,000) **Paramilitary 31,500**
Terms of service 24 months

ORGANISATIONS BY SERVICE

Army 30,000

4 regional comd: Astana, East, West and Southern.

FORCES BY ROLE

Mech Inf	10 bde (1 Bde Astana Region, 4 Bde East Region, 5 bde South Region)
Air Aslt	4 bde
Arty	7 bde
MRL	2 (102nd, 402nd) bde with total of 180 BM 27 9P140 *Uragan*
AT	2 bde
SSM	1 bde
Coastal Def	1 (West Region) bde
Cbt Engr	3 bde
SSM	1 bde
Peacekeeping	1 (KAZBRIG) bde

EQUIPMENT BY TYPE
MBT 980 T-72
RECCE 280: 140 BRDM; 140 BRM
AIFV 1,520: 730 BMP-1; 700 BMP-2; 90 BTR-80A
APC 370
  APC (T) 180 MT-LB
  APC (W) 190 BTR-70/BTR-80
ARTY 1,460
  SP 240: **122mm** 120 2S1 *Carnation*; **152mm** 120 2S3
  TOWED 670: **122mm** 400 D-30; **152mm** 270: 180 2A36; 90 2A65

GUN/MOR 120mm 25 2S9 *Anona*
MRL 380: **122mm** 200: 150 BM-21 *Grad*, 50 in store;
220mm 180 9P140 *Uragan*
MOR 120mm 145 2B11/M-120
AT • MSL • MANPATS AT-4 9K111 *Spigot*; AT-5 9K113
Spandrel; AT-6 9K115 *Spiral*
RL 73mm RPG-7 *Knout*
GUNS 100mm 68 MT-12/T-12
MSL • SSM 12 SS-21 *Tochka* (*Scarab*)

FACILITIES
Training centre   1

Navy 3,000
PATROL AND COASTAL COMBATANTS
PCI 14: 4 *Almaty*; 1 *Dauntless*; 5 *Guardian*; 2 *Zhuk*; 2 *Turk*
(AB25)

Air Force 12,000 (incl Air Defence)
1 air force div, 164 cbt ac, 14 atk hel

Flying hours   100 hrs/year

FORCES BY ROLE

Comd   regt with Tu-134 *Crusty*; Tu-154 *Careless*

Ftr   1 regt with MiG-29UB *Fulcrum*; 1 regt with MiG-
31 *Foxhound*; MiG-25 *Foxbat*

FGA   1 regt with Su-24 *Fencer*; 1 regt with Su-25
Frogfoot; 1 regt with Su-27 *Flanker*

Recce   1 regt with Su-24 *Fencer**

Atk hel   some regt with Mi-24V

Trg   some regt with L-39 *Albatros*; Yak-18 *Max*

Hel   some regt with Mi-171V5, Mi-8 *Hip*, UH-1H

SAM   some regt with 100 SA-2 *Guideline*/SA-3 *Goa*;
SA-10 *Grumble* (quad); SA-4 *Ganef*/SA-5 *Gammon*;
SA-6 *Gainful* (60 eff.)

EQUIPMENT BY TYPE
AIRCRAFT 162 combat capable
FTR 97: 42 MiG-31/MiG-31BM *Foxhound*; 39 MiG-29/UB
Fulcrum; 16 MiG-25 *Foxbat*
FGA 65: 14 Su-25 *Frogfoot*; 14 Su-24 *Fencer*; 12* Su-24
(recce); 25 Su-27 *Flanker*
TPT 3: 2 Tu-134 *Crusty*; 1 Tu-154 *Careless*
TRG 16: 12 L-39 *Albatros*; 4 Yak-18 *Max*
HELICOPTERS
ATK 40+ Mi-24V (first 9 upgraded)
SPT 76: 20 Mi-171V5; 50 Mi-8 *Hip*; 6 UH-1H
AD • SAM 147+
SP 47+: 20 SA-6 *Gainful*; 27+ SA-4 *Ganef* /SA-5 *Gammon*
static; SA-10 *Grumble* (quad)
TOWED 100 SA-2 *Guideline*; SA-3 *Goa*
MSL
ASM AS-10 *Karen*; AS-11 *Kilter*; AS-7 *Kerry*; AS-9 *Kyle*
ARM AS-11 *Kilter*
AAM AA-6 *Acrid*; AA-7 *Apex*; AA-8 *Aphid*; AA-12 (on
MiG-31BM)

Paramilitary 31,500

Government Guard 500

Internal Security Troops ε20,000
Ministry of Interior

Presidential Guard 2,000

State Border Protection Forces ε9,000
Ministry of Interior.
HEL • SPT 1 Mi-171

DEPLOYMENT

ARMENIA/AZERBAIJAN
OSCE • Minsk Conference 1

Kyrgyzstan KGZ

Kyrgyzstani Som s		2008	2009	2010
GDP	s	185bn		
	US$	5.1bn		
per capita	US$	946		
Growth	%	7.5	1.5	
Inflation	%	24.5	8.0	
Def bdgt	s	1.7bn	ε1.9bn	
	US$	46m	ε43m	
FMA (US)	US$	0.8m	0.9m	2.9m
US$1=s		36.5	43.7	

Population   5,431,747

Ethnic groups: Kyrgyz 56%; Russian 17%; Uzbek 13%; Ukrainian 3%

Age	0–14	15–19	20–24	25–29	30–64	65 plus
Male	16%	6%	5%	4%	15%	3%
Female	15%	6%	5%	4%	17%	4%

Capabilities

ACTIVE 10,900 (Army 8,500 Air 2,400) **Paramilitary 9,500**
Terms of service 18 months

ORGANISATIONS BY SERVICE

Army 8,500
FORCES BY ROLE
MR   2 bde; 1(mtn) bde
SF   1 bde
Arty   1 bde
AD   1 bde

EQUIPMENT BY TYPE
MBT 150 T-72
RECCE 30 BRDM-2
AIFV 320: 230 BMP-1; 90 BMP-2
APC (W) 35: 25 BTR-70; 10 BTR-80
ARTY 246
SP **122mm** 18 2S1 *Carnation*
TOWED 141: **100mm** 18 M-1944; **122mm** 107: 72 D-30;
35 M-30 *M-1938*; **152mm** 16 D-1

GUN/MOR 120mm 12 2S9 *Anona*
MRL 21: 122mm 15 BM-21; 220mm 6 9P140 *Uragan*
MOR 120mm 54: 6 2S12; 48 M-120
AT • MSL • MANPATS 26+: 26 AT-3 9K11 *Sagger*; AT-4 9K111 *Spigot*; AT-5 9K113 *Spandrel*
RCL 73mm SPG-9
RL 73mm RPG-7 *Knout*
GUNS 100mm 18 MT-12/T-12
AD • SAM • MANPAD SA-7 *Grail*
GUNS 48
SP 23mm 24 ZSU-23-4
TOWED 57mm 24 S-60

Air Force 2,400

FORCES BY ROLE

Tac   1 regt with L-39 *Albatros* ; 1 (comp avn) regt with MiG-21 *Fishbed*; An-12 *Cub*; An-26 *Curl*

Ftr   1 regt with L-39 *Albatros*

Hel   1 regt with Mi-24 *Hind*; Mi-8 *Hip*

SAM   some regt with SA-3 *Goa*; SA-4 *Ganef*; SA-2 *Guideline*

EQUIPMENT BY TYPE

AIRCRAFT 52 combat capable
FTR 72: 48 MiG-21 *Fishbed*; 24 in store
TPT 4: 2 An-12 *Cub*; 2 An-26 *Curl*
TRG 28: 4 L-39 *Albatros**; 24 in store
HELICOPTERS
ATK 9 Mi-24 *Hind*
SPT 23 Mi-8 *Hip*
AD • SAM
SP SA-4 *Ganef*
TOWED SA-2 *Guideline*; SA-3 *Goa*

Paramilitary 9,500

Border Guards 5,000 (KGZ conscripts, RUS officers)

Interior Troops 3,500

National Guard 1,000

DEPLOYMENT

BOSNIA-HERZEGOVINA

OSCE • Bosnia and Herzegovina 1

LIBERIA

UN • UNMIL 2 obs

SUDAN

UN • UNMIS 6 obs

FOREIGN FORCES

France Air Force: 1 C-135FR tkr ac
Russia Military Air Forces: 20+ Mi-8 *Hip* spt hel/Su-24 *Fencer* FGA ac/Su-25 *Frogfoot* FGA ac/Su-27 *Flanker* ftr ac; ε500

Nepal NPL

Nepalese Rupee NR		2008	2009	2010
GDP	NR	352bn	369bn	
	US$	5.1bn	5.0bn	
per capita	US$	179	174	
Growth	%	4.7	4.0	
Inflation	%	7.7	13.2	
Def bdgt	NR	12.3bn	15.5bn	
	US$	175m	209m	
US$1=NR		69.7	74.2	

Population   28,563,377

Religious groups: Hindu 90%; Buddhist 5%; Muslim 3%

Age	0–14	15–19	20–24	25–29	30–64	65 plus
Male	20%	6%	5%	4%	14%	2%
Female	19%	5%	5%	4%	14%	2%

Capabilities

ACTIVE 95,753 (Army 95,753) Paramilitary 62,000
Nepal is attempting to integrate the 23,500-strong (Maoist) People's Liberation Army (PLA) into the Nepalese national army. This process has been delayed.

ORGANISATIONS BY SERVICE

Army 95,753

FORCES BY ROLE

Comd   6 inf div HQ; 1 (valley) comd
Inf   16 bde (*total*: 63 Inf bn); 32 indep coy
SF   1 bde (1 AB, 1 mech inf, 1 indep SF bn)
Ranger   1 bn
Arty   1 HQ (4 arty regt,)
AD   1 HQ (2 AD regt, 4 indep AD coy)
Engr   1 HQ (5 engr bn)

EQUIPMENT BY TYPE

RECCE 40 *Ferret*
APC (W) 40 *Casspir*
ARTY 109+
TOWED 39: 75mm 6 pack; 94mm 5 3.7in (mtn trg); 105mm 28: 8 L-118 Lt Gun; 14 Pack Howitzer (6 non-operational)
MOR 70+: 81mm; 120mm 70 M-43 (est 12 op)
AD • GUNS • TOWED 32+: 14.5mm 30 Type-56 (ZPU-4); 37mm (PRC); 40mm 2 L/60

Air Wing 320

AIRCRAFT • TPT 5: 1 BAe-748; 2 M-28 *Skytruck*; 2 BN2T *Islander*
HELICOPTERS
SPT 6: 1 SA 330J *Super Puma*; 2 AS-350 *Ecureuil* B2/B3; 3 Mi-17 1V & V5
UTL 6: 1 ALH *Dhruv*; 2 *Lancer* (SA 316); 1 HAL SA-315B *Cheetah*; 2 SA-316B *Alouette III*

Paramilitary 62,000

Armed Police Force 15,000

Ministry of Home Affairs

Police Force 47,000

SELECTED NON-STATE GROUPS

People's Liberation Army armed component of former Maoist rebel group, awaiting integration into Nepalese army under terms of the Comprehensive Peace Agreement. Presently located in cantonments under UN supervision. Est strength: n.k. Major equipments include: SALW **Young Communist League** Est strength: n.k. Major equipments include: n.k.

DEPLOYMENT

CENTRAL AFRICAN REPUBLIC/CHAD
UN • MINURCAT 302; 1 obs; 1 inf bn; 1 MP pl

CÔTE D'IVOIRE
UN • UNOCI 1; 3 obs

DEMOCRATIC REPUBLIC OF CONGO
UN • MONUC 1,030; 24 obs; 1 mech inf bn; 1 engr coy

HAITI
UN • MINUSTAH 1,076; 2 inf bn

IRAQ
UN • UNAMI 2 obs

LEBANON
UN • UNIFIL 868; 1 mech inf bn

LIBERIA
UN • UNMIL 18; 2 obs; 1 MP unit

MIDDLE EAST
UN • UNTSO 3 obs

SUDAN
UN • UNAMID 8; 9 obs
UN • UNMIS 23; 16 obs

TIMOR-LESTE
UN • UNMIT 1 obs

FOREIGN FORCES

(all opcon UNMIN unless stated)
Austria 2 obs
Brazil 6 obs
Egypt 5 obs
Guatemala 1 obs
Indonesia 5 obs
Japan 6 obs
Jordan 4 obs
Malaysia 7 obs
Nigeria 5 obs
Paraguay 6 obs
Romania 7 obs
Sierra Leone 2 obs
South Africa 1 obs
Sweden 2 obs
Switzerland 3 obs
United Kingdom Army 280 (Gurkha trg org)
Uruguay 3 obs
Zambia 1 obs
Zimbabwe 2 obs

Pakistan PAK

Pakistani Rupee Rs		2008	2009	2010
GDP	Rs	10.5tr	13.1tr	
	US$	149n	157bn	
per capita	US$	866	902	
Growth	%	2.0	2.0	
Inflation	%	12.0	20.8	
Def exp	Rs	311bn		
	US$	4.42bn		
Def bdgt	Rs	296bn	342bn	
	US$	4.20bn	4.11bn	
FMA (US)	US$	297m	300m	298m
US$1=Rs		70.4	83.2	

Population   174,578,558
Religious groups: Hindu less than 3%

Age	0–14	15–19	20–24	25–29	30–64	65 plus
Male	20%	6%	5%	4%	14%	2%
Female	19%	5%	5%	4%	14%	2%

Capabilities

ACTIVE 617,000 (Army 550,000 Navy 22,000 Air 45,000) Paramilitary 304,000

ORGANISATIONS BY SERVICE

Strategic Forces

The National Command Authority (NCA) formulates nuclear policy and is the key decision-making body for the employment and development of strategic systems. The NCA has two committees: the Employment Control Committee and the Development Control Committee. The Strategic Plans Division (SPD) acts as the secretariat, and among other duties formulates nuclear policy, strategy and doctrine and strategic and operational plans for deployment and employment. While operational control rests with the NCA, Army and Air Force strategic forces are responsible for technical aspects, training and administrative control of the services' nuclear assets.

Army Strategic Forces Command commands all land based strategic nuclear forces.
12,000-15,000 personnel
MSL • TACTICAL • SSM 190: 105 *Hatf*-1; *Abdali/Hatf*-2; 50 *Hatf*-3 (PRC M-11); up to 10 *Shaheen*-1/*Hatf*-4; up to 25 *Hatf*-5/*Ghauri*; *Ghauri* II

Some Pakistan Air Force assets (such as *Mirage* or F-16) could be tasked with a strategic role

Army 550,000
FORCES BY ROLE
Army   9 corps HQ
Armd   2 div; 7 (indep) bde

Mech   1 (indep) bde

Inf   1 (area) comd; 18 div; 6 bde

SF   1 gp (3 SF bn)

Arty   9 (corps) bde; 5 bde

Engr   7 bde

Avn   1 (VIP) sqn; 5 (composite) sqn

Hel   10 sqn

AD   1 comd (3 AD gp (*total:* 8 AD bde))

EQUIPMENT BY TYPE

MBT 2,461+: 45 MBT 2000 *Al-Khalid*; 320 T-80UD; 51 T-54/T-55; 1,100 Type-59; 400 Type-69; 275+ Type-85; 270 M-48A5 in store

APC 1,266

APC (T) 1,100 M-113

APC (W) 166: 120 BTR-70/BTR-80; 46 UR-416

ARTY 4,291+

SP 260: **155mm** 200 M-109/M-109A2; **203mm** 60 M-110A2/M-110

TOWED 1,629: **105mm** 329: 216 M-101; 113 M-56; **122mm** 570: 80 D-30 (PRC); 490 Type-54 *M-1938*; **130mm** 410 Type-59-I; **155mm** 292: 144 M-114; 148 M-198; **203mm** 28 M-115

MRL 122mm 52 *Azar* (Type-83)

MOR 2,350+: **81mm**; **120mm** AM-50; M-61

AT

MSL 10,500+

SP M-901 TOW

MANPATS 10,500 HJ-8/TOW

RCL 3,700: **75mm** Type-52; **106mm** M-40A1

RL 73mm RPG-7 *Knout*; **89mm** M-20

GUNS 85mm 200 Type-56 (D-44)

AIRCRAFT

RECCE 30 Cessna O-1E *Bird Dog*

TPT 4: 1 Cessna 421; 3 Y-12(II)

UTL 90 SAAB 91 *Safrai* (50 obs; 40 liaison)

HELICOPTERS

ATK 26: 25 AH-1F *Cobra* (TOW); 1 Mi-24 *Hind*

SPT 54: 31 SA-330 *Puma*; 10 Mi-8; 13 Mi-17 (Mi-8MT) *Hip H*

UTL 81: 26 Bell-412; 5 AB-205A-1 (Bell 205A-1); 13 Bell 206B *JetRanger II*; 12 SA-315B *Lama*; 20 SA-319 *Alouette III*; 5 UH-1H *Iroquois*

TRG 22: 12 Bell 47G; 10 Hughes 300C

UAV *Bravo*; *Jasoos*; *Vector*

AD

SAM • MANPAD 2,990+: 2,500 Mk1/Mk2; 60 FIM-92A *Stinger*; HN-5A; 230 *Mistral*; 200 RBS-70

GUNS • TOWED 1,900: **14.5mm** 981; **35mm** 215 GDF-002/GDF-005; **37mm** 310 Type-55 (M-1939)/Type-65; **40mm** 50 L/60; **57mm** 144 Type-59 (S-60); **85mm** 200 Type-72 (M-1939) KS-12

RADAR • LAND AN/TPQ-36 *Firefinder* (arty, mor); RASIT (veh, arty)

MSL • TACTICAL • SSM 166: 95 *Hatf*-1; *Abdali/Hatf*-2; 50 *Hatf*-3 (PRC M-11); 6 *Shaheen*-1/*Hatf*-4; up to 20 *Hatf*-5/*Ghauri*; *Ghauri* II

Navy 22,000 (incl ε1,400 Marines and ε2,000 Maritime Security Agency (see Paramilitary))

EQUIPMENT BY TYPE

SUBMARINES • TACTICAL 8

SSK 5:

2 *Hashmat* (FRA *Agosta 70*) each with 4 x1 533mm ASTT with 20 F17P HWT/UGM- 84 *Harpoon* tactical USGW

3 *Khalid* (FRA *Agosta 90B* – 1 AIP) each with 4 x1 533mm ASTT with 20 F17 MOD 2 HWT; 4 SM-39 *Exocet* tactical USGW

SSI 3 MG110 (SF delivery)

PRINCIPAL SURFACE COMBATANTS • FRIGATES 7

FFG 7:

4 *Tariq* (UK *Amazon*) each with 2 Mk-141 *Harpoon* twin each with RGM-84D *Harpoon* tactical SSM, 2 single each with TP 45 LWT, 1 114mm gun, (capacity 1 *Lynx* utl hel)

2 *Tariq* each with 1 sextuple (6 eff.) with LY-60 (Aspide) SAM, 2 triple 324mm ASTT (6 eff.) each with Mk 46 LWT, 1 114mm gun, (capacity 1 *Lynx* utl hel)

1 *Sword* (PRC *Type 054*) with 2 quad (8 eff.) each with YJ-83 SSM, 1 octuple (8 eff.) with HQ-7 SAM, 2 triple 324mm ASTT (6 eff.) with Mk 46 LWT, 1 76mm gun, (capacity 1 Z-9C *Haitun*); (2 additional vessels in build, ISD's expected mid/late 2010)

PATROL AND COASTAL COMBATANTS 8

PFM 4:

2 *Jalalat* II each with 2 twin (4 eff.) each with C-802 (CSS-N-8) *Saccade* tactical SSM

2 *Zarrar* (MRTP-33)(weapons fit not known)

PCC 2: 1 *Larkana*; 1 *Rajshahi*

PBF 2 *Kaan* 15

MINE WARFARE • MINE COUNTERMEASURES • MHC 3 *Munsif* (FRA *Eridan*)

LOGISTICS AND SUPPORT 10

AORH 2:

1 *Fuqing* (capacity 1 SA-319 *Alouette III* utl hel)

1 *Moawin* (capacity 1 *Sea King* MK45 ASW hel)

AOT 3: 1 *Attock*; 2 *Gwadar*

AGS 1 *Behr Paima*

YTM 4

FACILITIES

Bases Located at Ormara, Gwadar, Karachi

Marines ε1,400

Cdo 1 gp

Naval Aviation

AIRCRAFT 12 ac combat capable

MP 12: 3 *Atlantic* (also ASW)*; 5 F-27-200 MPA*; 4 P-3C *Orion** (additional 6 ac on order)

HELICOPTERS

ASW 6: 5 *Sea King* MK45 ASW hel; 1 Z-9C *Haitun* (additional ac on order)

UTL 4 SA-319B *Alouette III* (additonal ac on order)

MSL • ASM AM-39 *Exocet*

Air Force 45,000

FORCES BY ROLE

3 regional comds: Northern (Peshawar) Central (Sargodha) Southern (Masroor). The Composite Air Tpt Wg, Combat

Cadres School and PAF Academy are Direct Reporting Units.

Ftr	2 sqn with *Mirage* IIIEP/OD; 1 sqn with F-16A *Fighting Falcon;* F-16B *Fighting Falcon;* 5 sqn with F-7PG *Skybolt;* 2 sqn with F-7PG (F-7MG) *Airguard;* F-16 C/D
FGA	1 sqn with *Mirage* IIIEP each with AM-39 *Exocet* tactical ASM; 2 sqn with A-5C (Q-5III) *Fantan;* 2 sqn with *Mirage* 5PA3 (A5uW); 5PA2/5PA *Mirage;* FC-1/JF-17 *Thunder* undergoing test and evaluation
ELINT/ECM	1 sqn with Da-20 *Falcon*
Recce	1 sqn with *Mirage* IIIRP (*Mirage* IIIR)*
SAR	6 sqn with SA-316 *Alouette III;* 1 sqn with Mi-171 (SAR/liaison)
Tpt	sqns with An-26 *Curl;* B-707; Beech 200 *Super King Air;* C-130B/C-130E *Hercules;* CN-235; F-27-200 *Friendship* (1 with navy); Falcon 20; L-100 *Hercules;* Y-12; Beech F-33 *Bonanza*
Trg	sqns with FT-5 (MiG-17U); FT-6 (MiG-19UTI); K-8; FT-7 (JJ-7)*; MFI-17B *Mushshak; Mirage* 5DPA/5DPA2; *Mirage* IIIB*; *Mirage* IIIOD*; T-37C *Tweet*
SAM	1 bty with 6 CSA-1 (SA-2) *Guideline;* SA-16 *Gimlet;* 6 bty each with 24 *Crotale*

EQUIPMENT BY TYPE
AIRCRAFT 383 combat capable
    FTR 233: 8 FC-1/JF-17 *Thunder* (150+ on order); 50 *Mirage* III EP; 54 F-7PG (F-7MG) *Airguard;* 75 F-7P *Skybolt;* 46 F-16A/F-16B *Fighting Falcon* (all to be given Mid-Life Update); 1 F-16D Block 52 (12 more F-16C/5 F-16D on order)
    FGA 104: 41 A-5C (Q-5III) *Fantan;* 10 *Mirage* 5PA3 (ASuW), 40 *Mirage* 5PA /*Mirage* 5PA2; 13 *Mirage* IIIEP each with AM-39 *Exocet* tactical ASM
    RECCE 15 *Mirage* IIIRP (*Mirage* IIIR)*
    EW • ELINT 2 Da-20 *Falcon*
    TPT 25: 1 An-26 *Curl;* 3 B-707; 1 Beech 200 *Super King Air;* 11 C-130B *Hercules*/C-130E *Hercules;* 4 CN-235; 2 F-27-200 *Friendship* (1 with navy); 1 *Falcon* 20; 1 L-100 *Hercules;* 1 Y-12; 1 Beech F-33 *Bonanza*
    TRG 183: 25 FT-5 (MiG-17U) *Fresco;* 15 FT-6 (MiG-19UTI) *Farmer;* 12 K-8; 19 FT-7 (JJ-7)*; 80 MFI-17B *Mushshak;* 3 *Mirage* 5DPA/*Mirage* 5DPA2*; 2 *Mirage* IIIB* (trg); 7 *Mirage* IIIOD (*Mirage* IIID)*; 20 T-37C *Tweet*
HELICOPTERS 19: 4 Mi-171; 15 SA-316 *Alouette III*
AD • SAM 150+
    TOWED 150: 6 CSA-1 (SA-2) *Guideline;* 144 *Crotale*
    MANPAD SA-16 *Gimlet*
RADAR • LAND 51+: 6 AR-1 (AD radar low level); some *Condor* (AD radar high level); some FPS-89/100 (AD radar high level)
    MPDR 45 MPDR/MPDR 60 MPDR 90 (AD radar low level)
    TPS-43G Type 514 some (AD radar high level)
MSL ASM: SD-10/PL-12 BVRAAM; AGM-65 *Maverick;* AM-39 *Exocet*
    AAM AIM-9L *Sidewinder*/AIM-9P *Sidewinder;* R-Darter, Super 530

FACILITIES

Radar air control sectors	4
Radar control and reporting station	7

Paramilitary up to 304,000 active

Coast Guard
PATROL AND COASTAL COMBATANTS 28
PB 1
PBF 4
MISC BOATS/CRAFT 23

Frontier Corps up to 65,000 (reported)
Ministry of Interior
FORCES BY ROLE
Armd recce   1 indep sqn
Paramilitary   11 regt (*total:* 40 paramilitary bn)
EQUIPMENT BY TYPE
APC (W) 45 UR-416

Maritime Security Agency ε2,000
PRINCIPAL SURFACE COMBATANTS •
DESTROYERS • DD 1 *Nazim* (US *Gearing,* no ASROC)
PATROL AND COASTAL COMBATANTS 11:
    PCO 4 *Barkat*
    PCC 3: 2 *Subqat* (PRC *Shanghai*); 1 *Sadaqat* (ex-PRC *Huangfen*)
    PB 4 (various)

National Guard 185,000
Incl *Janbaz* Force; *Mujahid* Force; National Cadet Corps; Women Guards

Northern Light Infantry ε12,000
Paramilitary   3 bn

Pakistan Rangers up to 40,000
Ministry of Interior

SELECTED NON-STATE GROUPS
See p. 341.

DEPLOYMENT

ARABIAN GULF AND INDIAN OCEAN
Maritime Security Operations 1 DDG; 1 FFG

BURUNDI
UN • BINUB 1 obs

CENTRAL AFRICAN REPUBLIC/CHAD
UN • MINURCAT 5

CÔTE D'IVOIRE
UN • UNOCI 1,137; 12 obs; 1 inf bn; 1 engr coy; 1 tpt coy

DEMOCRATIC REPUBLIC OF CONGO
UN • MONUC 3,589; 51 obs; 4 mech inf bn; 1 inf bn

LIBERIA
UN • UNMIL 3,072; 9 obs; 1 mech inf bn; 2 inf bn; 3 engr coy; 1 fd hospital

SUDAN

UN • UNAMID 507; 3 obs; 1 engr coy; 1 fd hospital

UN • UNMIS 1,481; 14 obs; 1inf bn; 1 engr coy; 2 avn unit; 1 tpt coy; 1 de-mining coy; 1 fd hospital

TIMOR LESTE

UN • UNMIT 4 obs

WESTERN SAHARA

UN • MINURSO 11 obs

FOREIGN FORCES

Unless specified, figures represent total numbers for UNMOGIP mission in India and Pakistan

Chile 2 obs

Croatia 9 obs

Denmark 1 obs

Finland 5 obs

Italy 7 obs

Korea, Republic of 9 obs

Philippines 3 obs

Sweden 5 obs

United Kingdom some (fwd mounting base) air elm located at Karachi

Uruguay 2 obs

Sri Lanka LKA

Sri Lankan Rupee Rs		2008	2009	2010
GDP	Rs	4.66tr	5.04tr	
	US$	43.2bn	44.3bn	
per capita	US$	2,043	2,076	
Growth	%	6.1	3.0	
Inflation	%	22.6	4.6	
Def exp	Rs	193bn		
	US$	1.79bn		
Def bdgt	Rs	166bn	180bn	
	US$	1.54bn	1.57bn	
US$1=Rs		108	114	

Population	21,324,791

Age	0–14	15–19	20–24	25–29	30–64	65 plus
Male	13%	4%	5%	4%	20%	3%
Female	12%	4%	5%	4%	22%	4%

Capabilities

ACTIVE 160,900 (Army 117,900 Navy 15,000 Air 28,000) Paramilitary 62,200

RESERVE 5,500 (Army 1,100 Navy 2,400 Air Force 2,000) Paramilitary 30,400

ORGANISATIONS BY SERVICE

Army 78,000; 39,900 active reservists (recalled) (total 117,900)

FORCES BY ROLE

9 Div HQ

Armd	3 regt
Armd Recce	3 regt (bn)
Air Mob	1 bde
Inf	33 bde
SF	1 indep bde
Cdo	1 bde
Fd Arty	1 light regt; 2 (med) regt
Fd Engr	3 regt

EQUIPMENT BY TYPE

MBT 62 T-55AM2/T-55A

RECCE 15 *Saladin*

AIFV 62: 13 BMP-1; 49 BMP-2

APC 217

    APC (T) 35 Type-85

    APC (W) 182: 31 *Buffel*; 21 FV603 *Saracen*; 105 *Unicorn*; 25 BTR-80/BTR-80A

ARTY 460

    TOWED 154: **122mm** 74; **130mm** 40 Type-59-I; **152mm** 40 Type-66 (D-20)

    MRL 122mm 22 RM-70 *Dana*

    MOR 784: **81mm** 520; **82mm** 209; **120mm** 55 M-43

AT • RCL 40: **105mm** ε10 M-65; **106mm** ε30 M-40

    GUNS 85mm 8 Type-56 (D-44)

UAV 1 *Seeker*

AD • GUNS • TOWED 27: **40mm** 24 L/40; **94mm** 3 (3.7in)

RADAR • LAND 2 AN/TPQ-36 *Firefinder* (arty)

Navy 15,000 (incl 2,400 recalled reservists)

FORCES BY ROLE

Navy 1 (HQ and Western comd) located at Colombo

EQUIPMENT BY TYPE

PATROL AND COASTAL COMBATANTS 130

    PSOH 2: 1 *Reliance*; 1 *Sayurala* (IND *Vigraha*)

    PSO 1 *Jayesagara*

    PFM 2 *Nandimithra* (ISR *Sa'ar* 4) each with 3 single each with 1 GII *Gabriel II* tactical SSM, 1 76mm gun

    PCC 11: 3 *Abeetha* (PRC mod *Shanghai*); 2 *Prathapa* (PRC mod *Haizhui*); 3 *Ranajaya* (PRC *Haizhui*); 1 *Ranarisi* (PRC *Shanghai* II); 2 *Weeraya* (PRC *Shanghai*)

    PBF 56: 28 *Colombo*; 3 *Dvora*; 3 *Killer* (ROK); 6 *Shaldag*; 5 *Trinity Marine*; 8 *Super Dvora* (Mk1/MkII); 3 *Simonneau* (all vessels less than 100 tonnes)

    PBR 51

    PB 7

AMPHIBIOUS

    LSM 1 *Yuhai* (capacity 2 tanks; 250 troops)

    CRAFT 8

        LCU 2 *Yunnan*

        LCM 2

        LCP 3 *Hansaya*

        ACV 1 M 10 (capacity 56 troops)

LOGISTICS AND SUPPORT 2: 1 TPT; 1 SPT/TRG

FACILITIES

Bases   Located at Trincomalee (Main base and Eastern Comd), Kankesanthurai (Northern Comd), Galle (Southern Comd), Medawachiya (North Central Comd) and Colombo (HQ and Western Comd)

Air Force 28,000 (incl SLAF Regt)

FORCES BY ROLE

Ftr   1 sqn with Chengdu F-7BS/GS, FT-7;

FGA   1 sqn with MiG-27M *Flogger J2*, MiG-23UB *Flogger C*; 1 sqn with *Kfir* C-2/C-7/TC-2; 1 sqn with K-8 *Karakoram*

Tpt   1 sqn with An-32B *Cline*; C-130K *Hercules*; Cessna 421C *Golden Eagle*; 1 (light) sqn with Beech B200 HISAR, Y-12 II

UAV   2 air surv sqns with IAI *Searcher* II, EMIT *Blue Horizon*-2

Atk hel   1 atk sqn with Mi-24P, Mi-24V, Mi-35P *Hind*

Trg   1 fg trg wg with NAMC PT-6, Cessna 150L

Hel   1 sqn with with Mi-17, Mi-17-IV, Mi-17I; 1 sqn with Bell 206A/206B (incl basic trg), Bell 212; 1 (VIP) sqn with Bell206A/206B *JetRanger*, Bell 412/412EP *Twin Huey*; Mi-17

SLAF Regiment   12,000

EQUIPMENT BY TYPE

AIRCRAFT 22 combat capable

  FTR 3 F-7BS/GS

  FGA 13: 7 *Kfir* C-2; 2 *Kfir* C-7; 4 MiG-27M *Flogger J2*

  TPT 13: 7 An-32B *Cline*; 2 C-130K *Hercules*; 1 Cessna 421C *Golden Eagle*; 3 Y-12 II

  TRG 26: 1 FT-7* (JJ-7); 3 K-8 *Karakoram*; 2 *Kfir* TC-2*; 1 MiG-23UB *Flogger* C (conversion trg)*; 7 PT-6 (CJ-6); 5 Cessna 150L

HELICOPTERS

  ATK 13: 1 Mi-24V *Hind E*; 12 Mi-35P *Hind*

  SPT 6: 3 Mi-17 (Mi-8MT) *Hip H*; 3 in store

  UTL 21: 5 Bell 206 *JetRanger*; 10 Bell 212; 6 Bell 412 *Twin Huey* (VIP)

UAV 3

  RECCE 3+: 2 Searcher II; some Blue-Horizon-2

Paramilitary ε88,600

Home Guard 13,000

National Guard ε15,000

Police Force 30,200; 1,000 (women); 30,400 reservists (total 61,600)

Ministry of Defence

Special Task Force 3,000

Anti-guerrilla unit

SELECTED NON-STATE GROUPS

The **Liberation Tigers of Tamil Eelam (LTTE)** were militarily defeated by government forces in May 2009. While major equipments will have largely been destroyed, some LTTE cadres are reported to have sought refuge among civilians temporarily residing in IDP camps.

DEPLOYMENT

DEMOCRATIC REPUBLIC OF CONGO

UN • MONUC 2 obs

HAITI

UN • MINUSTAH 959; 1 inf bn

SUDAN

UN • UNMIS 6 obs

WESTERN SAHARA

UN • MINURSO 3 obs

Tajikistan TJK

Tajikistani Somoni Tr		2008	2009	2010
GDP	Tr	15.7bn		
	US$	4.6bn		
per capita	US$	635		
Growth	%	7.9	2.0	
Inflation	%	20.4	8.0	
Def bdgt	Tr	273m	300m	
	US$	79m	80m	
US$1=Tr		3.44	3.72	

Population   7,349,145

Ethnic groups: Tajik 67%; Uzbek 25%; Russian 2%; Tatar 2%

Age	0–14	15–19	20–24	25–29	30–64	65 plus
Male	19%	6%	5%	4%	13%	2%
Female	19%	6%	5%	4%	14%	3%

Capabilities

ACTIVE 8,800 (Army 7,300, Air Force/Air Defence 1,500) **Paramilitary 7,500**
Terms of service 24 months

ORGANISATIONS BY SERVICE

Army 7,300

FORCES BY ROLE

MR   3 bde with 1 trg centre

Air Aslt   1 bde

Arty   1 bde

SAM   1 regt

EQUIPMENT BY TYPE

MBT 37: 30 T-72; 7 T-62

AIFV 23: 8 BMP-1; 15 BMP-2

APC (W) 23 BTR-60/BTR-70/BTR-80

ARTY 23

  TOWED 122mm 10 D-30

  MRL 122mm 3 BM-21

  MOR 120mm 10

AD • SAM 20+

  TOWED 20 SA-2 *Guideline*; SA-3 *Goa*

  MANPAD FIM-92A *Stinger* (reported); SA-7 *Grail*

Air Force/Air Defence 1,500

FORCES BY ROLE

Tpt sqn with Tu-134A *Crusty*

Hel sqn with Mi-24 *Hind*; Mi-17TM *Hip H*/Mi-8 *Hip*

EQUIPMENT BY TYPE
AIRCRAFT • TPT 1 Tu-134A *Crusty*
HELICOPTERS
  ATK 4 Mi-24 *Hind*
  SPT 12 Mi-17TM *Hip H*/Mi-8 *Hip*

Paramilitary 7,500

Interior Troops 3,800

National Guard 1,200

Emergencies Ministry 2,500

Border Guards

DEPLOYMENT

BOSNIA-HERZEGOVINA
OSCE • Bosnia and Herzegovina 1

MOLDOVA
OSCE • Moldova 1

FOREIGN FORCES

France Air Force: 160; 1 C-130 *Hercules*; 2 C-160 *Transall*
India Air Force: 1 Fwd Op Base located at Farkhar
Russia Army: 120 MBT; 350 ACV; 190 Arty/mor/MRL; 3 MR bde (subord to Volga-Ural MD); 5,500; Military Air Forces: 5 Su-25 *Frogfoot* FGA ac, 4 Mi-8 *Hip* spt hel

Turkmenistan TKM

Turkmen Manat TMM		2008	2009	2010
GDP	TMM	168tr	21.9bn	
	US$	12.2bn	11.8bn	
per capita	US$	2,448	1,546	
Growth	%	10.5	4.0	
Inflation	%	14.5	0.4	
Def bdgt	TMM	ε1.2tr		
	US$	84m		
USD1=TMM		14,267	2.9	

Population   4,884,887

Ethnic groups: Turkmen 77%; Uzbek 9%; Russian 7%; Kazak 2%

Age	0–14	15–19	20–24	25–29	30–64	65 plus
Male	18%	6%	5%	4%	15%	2%
Female	17%	6%	5%	4%	16%	3%

Capabilities

ACTIVE 22,000 (Army 18,500 Navy 500 Air 3,000)
Terms of service 24 months

ORGANISATIONS BY SERVICE

Army 18,500
FORCES BY ROLE
5 Mil Districts
MR   3 div; 2 bde; 1 div (trg)
Air Aslt 1 indep bn

Arty	1 bde
MRL	1 regt
AT	1 regt
Engr	1 regt
SAM	2 bde
Msl	1 (Scud) bde

EQUIPMENT BY TYPE †
MBT 680: 10 T-90S; 670 T-72
RECCE 170 BRDM/BRDM-2
AIFV 942: 930 BMP-1/BMP-2; 12 BRM
APC (W) 829 BTR-60/BTR-70/BTR-80
ARTY 564
  SP 56: **122mm** 40 2S1 *Carnation;* **152mm** 16 2S3
  TOWED 269: **122mm** 180 D-30; **152mm** 89: 17 D-1; 72 D-20
  GUN/MOR 120mm 17 2S9 *Anona*
  MRL 131: **122mm** 65: 9 9P138; 56 BM-21; **220mm** 60 9P140 *Uragan*
  300mm 6 BM 9A52 *Smerch*
  MOR 97: **82mm** 31; **120mm** 66 PM-38
AT
  MSL • MANPATS 100 AT-3 9K11 *Sagger*; AT-4 9K111 *Spigot*; AT-5 9K113 *Spandrel*; AT-6 9K115 *Spiral*
  RL 73mm RPG-7 *Knout*
  GUNS 100mm 72 MT-12/T-12
AD • SAM 53+
  SP 53: 40 SA-8 *Gecko*; 13 SA-13 *Gopher*
  MANPAD SA-7 *Grail*
  GUNS 70
    SP 23mm 48 ZSU-23-4
    TOWED 57mm 22 S-60
MSL • SSM 10 SS-1 *Scud*

Navy 500
Intention to form a combined navy/coast guard and currently has a minor base at Turkmenbashy. Caspian Sea Flotilla (see Russia) is operating as a joint RUS, KAZ, TKM flotilla under RUS comd based at Astrakhan.

EQUIPMENT BY TYPE
PATROL AND COASTAL COMBATANTS 10
PB 6: 1 *Point* class; 5 *Grif-T*
PBI 4 *Kalkan*

FACILITIES
Minor base   Located at Turkmenbashy

Air Force 3,000
incl Air Defence

FORCES BY ROLE
Ftr /	2 sqn with MiG-29 *Fulcrum*; Su-17 *Fitter*; MiG-
FGA	29U *Fulcrum*; Su-25MK
Tpt /Utl	1 sqn with An-26 *Curl*; Mi-24 *Hind*; Mi-8 *Hip*
Trg	1 unit with Su-7B; L-39 *Albatros*
SAM	sqns with 50 SA-2 *Guideline*/SA-3 *Goa*/SA-5 *Gammon*

EQUIPMENT BY TYPE
AIRCRAFT 94 combat capable
  FTR 22 MiG-29 *Fulcrum*
  FGA 67: 65 Su-17 *Fitter*; 2 Su-25MK (+41 more being refurbished)
  TPT 1 An-26 *Curl*
  TRG 7: 2 L-39 *Albatros*; 2 MiG-29U *Fulcrum**; 3 Su-7B*

HELICOPTERS
ATK 10 Mi-24 *Hind*
SPT 8 Mi-8 *Hip*
AD • SAM 50 SA-2 *Guideline* towed/SA-3 *Goa*/SA-5 *Gammon* static

Uzbekistan UZB

Uzbekistani Som s		2008	2009	2010
GDP	s	36.4tr	41.0tr	
	US$	27.2bn	27.4bn	
per capita	US$	996	991	
Growth	%	9.0	7.0	
Inflation	%	12.7	12.5	
Def bdgt	s	n.a.		
	US$	n.a.		
US$1=s		1,336	1,500	

Population 27,606,007

Ethnic groups: Uzbek 73%; Russian 6%; Tajik 5%; Kazakh 4%; Karakalpak 2%; Tatar 2%; Korean <1%; Ukrainian <1%

Age	0–14	15–19	20–24	25–29	30–64	65 plus
Male	17%	6%	5%	4%	15%	2%
Female	16%	6%	5%	4%	16%	3%

Capabilities

ACTIVE 67,000 (Army 50,000 Air 17,000)
Paramilitary 20,000
Terms of service conscription 12 months

ORGANISATIONS BY SERVICE

Army 50,000

FORCES BY ROLE
4 Mil Districts; 2 op comd; 1 Tashkent Comd
Tk	1 bde
MR	11 bde
Mtn Inf	1 (lt) bde
Air Aslt	3 bde
AB	1 bde
SF	1 bde
Arty	6 bde
MRL	1 bde

EQUIPMENT BY TYPE
MBT 340: 70 T-72; 100 T-64; 170 T-62
RECCE 19: 13 BRDM-2; 6 BRM
AIFV 399: 120 BMD-1; 9 BMD-2; 270 BMP-2
APC 309
  APC (T) 50 BTR-D
  APC (W) 259: 24 BTR-60; 25 BTR-70; 210 BTR-80
ARTY 487+
  SP 83+: **122mm** 18 2S1 *Carnation*; **152mm** 17+: 17 2S3; 2S5 (reported); **203mm** 48 2S7
  TOWED 200: **122mm** 60 D-30; **152mm** 140 2A36
  GUN/MOR 120mm 54 2S9 *Anona*
  MRL 108: **122mm** 60: 24 9P138; 36 BM-21; **220mm** 48 9P140 *Uragan*

MOR 120mm 42: 5 2B11; 19 2S12; 18 PM-120
AT • MSL • MANPATS AT-3 9K11 *Sagger*; AT-4 9K111 *Spigot*
GUNS 100mm 36 MT-12/T-12

Air Force 17,000

FORCES BY ROLE
7 fixed wg and hel regts.
FGA/Bbr	1 regt with Su-24 *Fencer*; Su-24MP *Fencer F* (recce); 1 regt with Su-25 *Frogfoot*/Su-25BM *Frogfoot*; Su-17MZ (Su-17M) *Fitter C*/Su-17UMZ (Su-17UM-3) *Fitter G*
Ftr	1 regt with MiG-29 *Fulcrum*/MiG-29UB *Fulcrum*; Su-27 *Flanker*/Su-27UB *Flanker C*
ELINT/Tpt	1 regt with An-12 *Cub*/An-12PP *Cub*; An-26 *Curl*/An-26RKR *Curl*
Tpt	sqns with An-24 *Coke*; Tu-134 *Crusty*
Trg	sqns with L-39 *Albatros*
Hel	1 regt with Mi-24 *Hind* (attack); Mi-26 *Halo* (tpt); Mi-8 *Hip* (aslt/tpt); 1 regt with Mi-6AYa *Hook* (comd post); Mi-6 *Hook* (tpt)

EQUIPMENT BY TYPE
AIRCRAFT 135 combat capable
  FTR 55: 30 MiG-29 *Fulcrum* MiG-29UB *Fulcrum*; 25 Su-27 *Flanker* Su-27UB *Flanker C*
  FGA 69: 20 Su-25 *Frogfoot* Su-25BM *Frogfoot*; 23 Su-24 *Fencer*; 26 Su-17MZ (Su-17M) *Fitter C*/Su-17UMZ (Su-17UM-3)
  RECCE/EW 11 Su-24MP *Fencer F**
  ELINT/Tpt 39: 26 An-12 *Cub* Tpt/An-12PP *Cub*; 13 An-26 *Curl* Tpt/An-26RKR *Curl* ELINT EW
  TPT 2: 1 An-24 *Coke*; 1 Tu-134 *Crusty*
  TRG 14: 5 L-39 *Albatros*; 9 in store
HELICOPTERS
  ATK 29 Mi-24 *Hind*
  COMD 2 Mi-6AYa *Hook*
  SPT 79: 1 Mi-26 *Halo* (tpt); 26 Mi-6 *Hook* (tpt); 52 Mi-8 *Hip* (aslt/tpt)
AD • SAM 45
  TOWED SA-2 *Guideline*; SA-3 *Goa*
  STATIC SA-5 *Gammon* static
MSL
  ASM AS-10 *Karen*; AS-11 *Kilter*; AS-12 *Kegler*; AS-7 *Kerry*; AS-9 *Kyle*
  ARM: AS-11 *Kilter*; AS-12 *Kegler*
  AAM AA-10 *Alamo*; AA-11 *Archer*; AA-8 *Aphid*

Paramilitary up to 20,000

Internal Security Troops up to 19,000
Ministry of Interior

National Guard 1,000
Ministry of Defence

DEPLOYMENT

SERBIA
OSCE • Kosovo 2

FOREIGN FORCES

Germany 163; some C-160 *Transall*

Table 32 **Selected arms procurements and deliveries, South and Central Asia**

Designation	Type	Quantity	Contract Value	Supplier Country	Prime Contractor	Order Date	First Delivery Due	Notes
Afghanistan (AFG)								
G222	Tac tpt ac	18	US$257m	ITA	Alenia Aero-nautica	2008	2009	ITA stock ordered by US. Refurbished and modernised by Alenia Aeronautica. First delivered July 2009
Mi-24	Hel	6		CZE		2007	2008	Ex-CZE stock. Modernised at NATO expense. Delivery status unclear
India (IND)								
Prithvi II	SRBM	54	INR12.13bn	Dom	Bharat Dynamics	2006	–	For air force
Sagarika K-15	SLBM	–	–	Dom	Bharat Dynamics	1991	–	In development. First test reported successful; est 700km range with 1 ton payload
Nirbhay	Cruise msl	–	–	Dom	DRDO	–	–	In development. First flight test due 2009. Designed for air, land and sea platforms. Est 1,000km range. First tests due late 2009
Agni III	IRBM	–	–	Dom	DRDO	–	2010	In development. Designed to carry 200-250 KT warhead with a range of 3,000km.
Agni IV	IRBM	–	–	Dom	DRDO	–	2012	In development. Est 5,000km range
Arjun	MBT	124	See notes	Dom	ICVRDE	2000	2009	Development costs per vehicle est INR3bn. Low-rate production began 2004. Deliveries ongoing
T-90S Bhishma	MBT	347	US$1.23bn	Dom/RUS	Avadi Heavy Vehicles	2007	–	First ten delivered June 2009
BrahMos Block II (Land Attack)	Cruise msl	10 lnchr	INR83.52bn (US$1.64bn)	RUS/Dom	Brahmos Aerospace	2006	2009	10 lnchr entered test regime; 2 accepted March 2009
Medium -range SAM	SAM/AD	18 units	US$1.4bn	ISR	IAI	2009	2016	For air-force. Development and procurement contract for a medium range version of the Barak long-range naval AD system
Advanced Technology Vessel (ATV)	SSBN	5	–	Dom	DRDO	–	–	SLBM devt programme. INS Arihant launched July 2009; 2 yr of sea trials expected
Akula-class (Type 971)	SSN	1	approx US$700m	RUS	Rosoboron-export	2004	2009	10 year lease from RUS. Nerpa in RUS service, to be renamed INS Chakra. Delivery expected end-2009
Scorpene	SSK	6	US$3.5bn	FRA/Dom	DCNS	2005	2012	First delivery had been due 2012, with one per year thereafter, reports now suggest a delay of one year. Option for a further 6 SSK. Delivery delayed
Sindhughosh-class	SSK Upgrade	10	–	RUS	ORDTB/ Rosoboron-export	2002	–	Upgrade incl mod to accept Klub-S 3M-14E msl. Delayed due to problems with msl system
3M14E Klub-S (SS-N-27 Sizzler)	SLCM	28	INR8.44bn (US$182m)	RUS	Novator	2006	–	For a number of Sindhughosh- class SSK. Delivery status unclear
Kiev-class Admiral Gorshkov	CV	1	US$2.7-3bn	RUS	Rosoboron-export	1999	2008	Incl 16 MiG 29 K. To be renamed INS Vikramaditya. Expected to be commissioned 2012
Project 71/ Indigenous Aircraft Carrier	CV	1	US$730m	Dom	Cochin Shipyard	2001	2012	To be named Vikant. Formerly known as Air Defence Ship (ADS). Second vessel of class anticipated

Table 32 **Selected arms procurements and deliveries, South and Central Asia**

Designation	Type	Quantity	Contract Value	Supplier Country	Prime Contractor	Order Date	First Delivery Due	Notes
Project 15A (*Kolkata* -class)	DDG	3	US$1.75bn	Dom	Mazagon Dockyard	2000	2013	First of class launched 2006, second launched in 2009. First delivery delayed, expected for 2013.
Advanced Talwar	FFG	3	US$1.5bn	RUS	Yantar shipyard	2006	2011	Option exercised 2006. Expected to be commissioned from 2012
Project 17 *Shivalik*- class	FFG	3	INR69bn	Dom	Mazagon Dockyard	1999	2009	Lead vessel commissioned late 2009. INS *Sahyadri* and INS *Satpura* due for delivery by 2010
Project 17A- *Shivalik*	FFG	7	INR450bn (US$9.24 bn)	Dom	Mazagon Dockyard/ GRSE	2009	2014	Follow up to Project 17. Requires shipyard upgrade
Nicobar-class	PCF	10	INR500m (US$10.m) per unit	Dom	GRSE	_	2009	INS *Car Nicobar* and INS *Chetlat* commissioned Feb 2009. INS *Cinque* and INS *Cheriyam* launched Jul 2008, final commissioning due 2011
High-speed interceptor boats		15	INR2.8bn (US$54.2m)	Dom	Bharati	2009		For coast guard
BrahMos PJ-10	ASCM	_	US$2bn	RUS/Dom	Brahmos Aerospace	2006	2010	Built jointly with RUS. For army, navy and air force. Air and submarine launch versions undergoing testing
SU-30 MKI	FGA	140	See notes	Dom/RUS	Hindustan Aeronautics Ltd/ Rosoboron-export	2000	_	Delivered in kit form and completed in IND under licence. Part of a 1996 US$8.5bn deal for 238 SU-30. Deliveries ongoing. Final delivery due 2015
SU-30 MKI	FGA	40	US$1.6bn	RUS	Rosoboron-export	2007	2008	First 4 delivered early 2008. Order of additional 50 acs likely
Tejas	Ftr	20	INR20bn US$445m	Dom	HAL	2005	2011	Limited series production. To be delivered in initial op config. Option for a further 20 in full op config. Plans for 140
Hawk Mk132 Advanced Jet Trainer	Trg ac	66	US$1.45bn	UK/Dom	BAE/HAL	2004	2007	24 in fly-away condition and 42 built under licence. Final delivery due 2011
C-130J *Hercules*	Tpt ac	6	INR40bn (US$1.02bn)	US	Lockheed Martin	2007	2012	For special forces ops. SF config with AN/AAR-47 msl approach warning sys and radar-warning receivers
P-8i	MPA	8	US$2.1bn	US	Boeing	2008	2013	To replace current *Ilyushin* Il-38 and *Tupolev* Tu-142M. Deliveries due 2013–15
EMB-145	AEW&C	3	US$210m	BRZ	Embraer	2008	2011	Part of a INR18bn (US$400m) AEW&C project
Dhruv	Hel	245	_	Dom	HAL	2004	2004	159 *Dhruvs* and 76 *Dhruv*-WSI. Deliveries ongoing
Mi-17 *Hip*-H	Hel	80	INR58.41bn (US$1.2bn)	RUS	Rosoboron-export	2008	2010	To be weaponised and replace current Mi-8 fleet. Final delivery due 2014
KA-31	AEW Hel	5	US$20m	RUS	Rosoboron-export	2009	_	For navy
Mistral (ATAM)	AAM	Undis-closed	Undisclosed	Dom	MBDA	2006	–	For new combat version of *Dhruv* hel. No and value undisclosed. Basic fit for *Dhruv* to be 4 ATAM in 2 launchers. To be deployed 2009

Table 32 **Selected arms procurements and deliveries, South and Central Asia**

Designation	Type	Quantity	Contract Value	Supplier Country	Prime Contractor	Order Date	First Delivery Due	Notes
Kazakhstan (KAZ)								
S-300	AD	40	–	RUS	Rosoboron-export	2009	2009	To equip each of up to 10 bn with four missile launchers and support systems. Delivery status unclear
MiG-31	Ftr Upgrade	20	US$60m	RUS	Rosoboron-export	2007	2007	Upgrade to MiG-31BM configuration. 10 to be modernised in 2007, 10 in 2008. Delivery status unclear
Pakistan (PAK)								
Hatf 8 (Raad)	ALCM	–	–	Dom	–	–	–	In development. Successfully test fired.
Spada 2000	AD system	10	€415m	ITA	MBDA	2007	2009	Final delivery due 2013
F-22P/Sword-class	FF	4	See notes	PRC/Dom	Hudong-Zhonghua Shipyard	2005	2009	Improved version of Jiangwei II FF. 4th ship to be built indigenously at Karachi. Deal worth est US$750m incl 6 Z-9EC hels. First vessel ISD Oct 2009. Final delivery due 2013
Oliver Hazard Perry-class	FF	1	US$65m	US	–	2008	2010	To be refurbished for US$65m
SM-2 Block II AURS	Msl	10		US	Raytheon	2006	–	With 10Mk 631
F-16C/D Block 50/52	Ftr	18	US$1.4bn	US	Lockheed Martin	2008	2010	12 single-seat C-model Block 52 ac and 6 two-seat D-model ac. Option for a further 18 dropped
F-16 Block 15	FGA Upgrade	42	US$75m	TUR	TAI	2009	2014	Upgrade to Block 40 standard. Will begin Oct 2010. Remainder to be upgraded in PAK
JF-17 (FC-1)	Ftr	up to 250	–	Dom/ PRC	PAC	2006	2008	8 of a batch of 16 delivered by mid 2008. Two PRC produced versions delivered Feb 2007. Contract signed for 42 production ac in early 2009
F-10 (Jian-10)	Ftr	36	Est US$1.5bn	PRC	CAC	2006	2014	In development
P-3C Orion	MPA	8	US$970m	US	–	2004	2007	Ex-US stock. First delivered Jan 2007. Final delivery due 2011. One for spares
2000 Erieye	AEW&C	5	SEK8.3bn (US$1.05bn)	SWE	SAAB	2006	2009	Order reduced from 6. Delivery status unclear
K-8	Trg ac	27	–	PRC	JHA	2005	2008	Final delivery due 2011
Zhi-9EC	ASW Hel	6	–	PRC	Harbin	2007	2009	Anti-submarine warfare hels. Part of F-22P deal. Delivery status unclear
Bravo+	UAV	–	–	Dom	Air Weapons Complex	2008	2009	For recce and info gathering missions. Delivery status unclear
Falco	UAV	25	–	ITA	Selex Galileo	2006	2009	For MALE recce and surv missions. Delivery status unclear
AIM-120 AMRAAM	AAM	500	See notes	US	Raytheon	2007	2008	US$284m inc. 200 Sidewinder AAM. Final delivery due 2011
AIM-9M Sidewinder	AAM	200	See notes	US	Raytheon	2007	–	US$284m inc 500 AMRAAM

Chapter Eight
East Asia and Australasia

CHINA

China's armed forces showcased the progress of their accelerating modernisation drive at the 60th anniversary celebrations of their air force and navy, and of the People's Republic itself. Through a series of carefully scripted parades and large-scale exercises, the People's Liberation Army (PLA) sent notice that it was generating a comprehensive set of state-of-the-art capabilities that would enable the projection of its military power onto the global stage.

At the 1 October parade in Beijing, the air force, navy and Second Artillery (China's strategic missile forces) were given increased prominence, which signalled a shift away from the previous ground-force-oriented, continental mindset. Prominently featured weapons included the latest variants of the DF-21C medium-range ballistic missile, the DF-31A intercontinental ballistic missile, the DH-10 (CJ-10) land-attack cruise missile, the J-10 fighter, the H-6U air-refuelling tanker, and electronic-warfare platforms such as the KJ-2000 Airborne Warning and Control aircraft. Most of these systems are the locally designed products of a more modern and capable Chinese defence industry that is enjoying surging domestic demand.

A key theme of these military displays, also underlined in the latest defence White Paper published at the end of 2008, was the growing confidence of the PLA. While little new information was disclosed, the White Paper pointed out that China has reached a 'historic turning point' and that it was playing a major role in the international security order.

Although the units that took part in the National Day parade were mostly drawn from elite formations, recapitalisation of the wider front-line inventory has been gathering pace in recent years. According to estimates from the US Department of Defense (DoD), 25% of Chinese naval surface forces in 2008 could be categorised as modern (defined as multi-mission platforms with significant capabilities in at least two warfare areas) compared with 7% in 2004; 46% of the submarine fleet in 2008 was modern (capable of firing anti-ship cruise missiles) in contrast to less than 10% in 2004; and 20% of the air force had modern fourth-generation combat aircraft in 2008, double the ratio

in 2004. China's ground forces, by comparison, have lagged far behind, with the DoD estimating that only 200 main battle tanks (MBTs) out of a DoD-reported inventory of 6,700 were modern third-generation Type-98 and -99 models; more emphasis has been placed on the acquisition of armoured infantry vehicles and the building up of special forces. While older generations of 1960s- and 1970s-era MBTs are being phased out, later models are undergoing limited upgrading.

In April, the PLA Navy (PLAN) held a fleet review in Qingdao for its 60th anniversary celebrations, displaying some of its latest warships and submarines, such as the Type-052C *Luyang* II-class DDG, Type-051C *Luzhou*-class DDG and Type-054A *Jiangkai*-class frigates. The Chinese surface force is currently estimated by the DoD to have around 75 major surface combatants. Additionally, there are approximately 45 coastal missile-patrol craft and 50 medium and heavy amphibious-lift vessels, which have been increasing in size in recent years. The submarine fleet is also undergoing rapid expansion, with five types of nuclear and conventional submarines under procurement, including the *Jin*-class SSBN, *Shang*-class SSN, and Improved *Song*, *Yuan* and Russian *Kilo* SS. Moreover, growing official public discussion of the acquisition of an aircraft-carrier force appears to be paving the way for a programme go-ahead in the near future. Senior Chinese navy officials have said that the local shipbuilding industry is actively conducting research into aircraft-carrier construction and could be ready to build a vessel by the end of this decade; refurbishment of the former Ukrainian aircraft carrier *Varyag* is also a much-discussed option.

Personnel and training

With the PLA inventory becoming increasingly high-tech, greater attention is being paid to the personnel that will have to operate these systems. Military authorities, aware that staff will have to be well-trained professionals, are reforming the personnel system. An important priority is the overhaul of the non-commissioned officer (NCO) corps, with new entrants requiring at least high-school diplomas, and more effort is being made to retain senior personnel with improved pay and benefits. The size of the NCO force will be modestly expanded to 900,000 slots in both the PLA and paramilitary People's Armed Police.

The PLA's training regime is being overhauled to make it more modern and robust, and more tailored to changing missions. A new PLA-wide training and evaluation programme was initiated at the beginning of 2009 that emphasises joint operations and the conduct of a more diverse range of duties beyond training for traditional war-fighting contingencies. Entrenched compartmentalisation among the service arms has hindered the PLA's efforts to fashion a truly integrated force, and this concerted effort to promote joint training is intended to break this logjam.

The *Stride 2009* series of large-scale, inter-theatre exercises held between August and September 2009 exemplified the revamped training system and offered a more realistic appraisal of the PLA's combat readiness than the anniversary parades. *Stride 2009* involved the first-ever long-distance deployment of four army divisions of more than 50,000 troops and 60,000 pieces of heavy equipment drawn from the Shenyang, Lanzhou, Jinan and Guangzhou Military Regions to different parts of the country. The air force and ground forces reportedly worked closely together through joint command and operational mechanisms, especially in airlifting large numbers of troops and equipment over several thousand kilometres and coordinating air-strikes to support ground attacks. One problem is that the PLA rarely trains with foreign counterparts, the only exception being limited exercises with Russia once every two years.

New security challenges

Since 2008, preparing for 'diversified missions' has become an operational and training priority. This term is used by the PLA to refer to expanded non-traditional security responsibilities such as helping to safeguard the country's increasingly global economic and energy interests, adopting more proactive anti-terrorist and anti-separatist strategies, and participating in long-range multilateral anti-piracy escort duties. It also includes non-military missions such as domestic and international disaster and humanitarian relief, and dealing with infectious diseases. Since 2004, China's President and Central Military Commission Chairman Hu Jintao has championed the idea that the PLA should undertake an ever-expanding portfolio of new missions under the official moniker of the 'historic missions of the PLA in

the new period of the new century'. However, this policy initiative did not gain operational traction until a series of natural disasters struck China in 2008, including a massive earthquake in Sichuan. The PLA was caught unprepared and lacked the expertise and capabilities to respond effectively to these challenges (see *The Military Balance 2009*, p. 363).

The PLA has also been drafting detailed rules of engagement on the conduct of anti-terrorist military operations within and outside China. This will draw upon lessons learnt from the PLA's participation in *Peace Mission 2009*, the third joint military exercise conducted with Russia under the framework of the Shanghai Cooperation Organisation (SCO). PLA Chief of General Staff General Chen Bingde said during the exercises that China would consider deploying troops for counter-terrorist operations in Central Asia, under the SCO, if asked to do so. With serious ethnic unrest in Xinjiang in northwest China in the summer of 2009, domestic security issues have risen the top of the Chinese leadership's priorities.

The PLAN has also taken on an important new task though its participation in multinational anti-piracy operations off the coast of Somalia. This is the first time that the PLAN has conducted such operations in its 60-year history. A three-ship task force has been deployed on rotation in the Indian Ocean since the end of 2008 and Chinese navy chiefs say they are prepared to carry out this duty for an extended period. Although the Somali escort mission was an unexpected opportunity, this type of long-distance and long-endurance deployment fits squarely into the PLAN's new strategic focus to protect Chinese interests beyond its traditional territorial boundaries, with new priorities to include 'maritime rights and development interests'. This alludes to the PLAN's role in supporting China's efforts to gain secure global access to energy, commodity and export markets.

The challenge for PLAN chiefs is to meet these new mission requirements while also developing the training and infrastructure necessary for missions of sustained duration and, at the same time, continuing to strengthen naval capabilities to secure territorial waters and build up an effective anti-access capacity towards the US. Strategic rivalry between the US and Chinese navies has been quietly intensifying in the past few years and was highlighted by a confrontation between a US naval survey ship, the USNS *Impeccable*, and Chinese government and fishing vessels off Hainan Island in March 2009. China accused the US ship of intruding into its exclusive economic waters,

Map 4 China: military regions and major formations

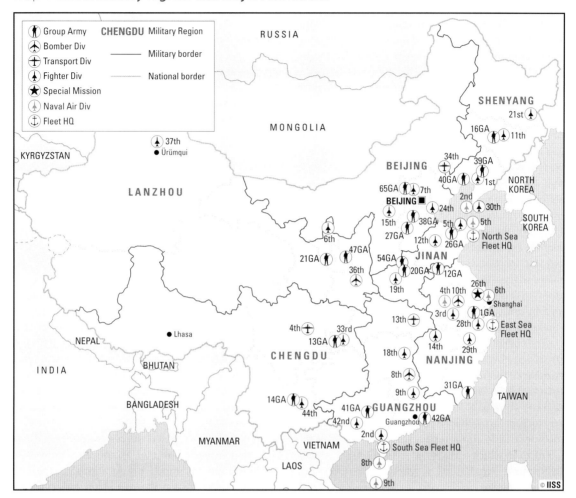

while the US countered that it was operating in international waters. Sino–Indian border tensions also rose in summer 2009 over Indian troop deployments in Arunachal Pradesh, Indian claims of Chinese violations along the Line of Actual Control, and alarmist media reporting over these tensions in India.

The reduction in political and military tensions between mainland China and Taiwan is a key factor in allowing this shift to new non-traditional security threats and missions. The 2008 election of Kuomintang leader Ma Ying-jeou has led to a relative softening in the PLA's rhetoric regarding the threat situation in the Taiwan Strait. China's 2008 defence White Paper judged that 'the attempts of the separatist forces for "Taiwan independence" to seek "de jure Taiwan independence" have been thwarted, and the situation across the Taiwan Straits has taken a significantly positive turn'.

But while the PLA's public statements have become more tempered, initial hopes that this political thaw might lead to a structural lowering of military tensions with a peace agreement, and the removal of some of the estimated 1,500 Chinese ballistic missiles targeted against Taiwan or other types of confidence-building measures have yet to materialise. Given the volatility of Taiwanese domestic politics, the PLA's missile build-up is unlikely to be halted or reversed in the short to medium term despite the improved dynamics in cross-strait relations.

TAIWAN

In early 2009, the Ma administration offered its strategic vision of Taiwan's defence posture over the next four years with the release of the island's first-ever Quadrennial Defence Review. The new guidelines advocated a defensively oriented posture that placed a premium on conflict prevention with mainland China through confidence-building initiatives, while strengthening deterrence capabilities and overhauling the island's armed forces to create a leaner and more professional fighting force. This contrasts with the strategy pursued under the previous government of Chen Shui-bian.

A key goal of the new strategy is to reduce the size of the armed forces by around 20% over 5 years to just over 210,000 and to replace compulsory military service with an all-volunteer force. Analysts argue that the present one-year conscription system is a serious constraint to the armed forces' combat capabilities because of constant turnover of personnel. However, the switch to a professional structure will require significant increases in personnel outlays to pay for increased salaries and benefits. Some estimates suggest that this could increase personnel costs from 39% of the current annual defence budget to 45% by 2014, which would squeeze already severely constrained procurement budgets.

The viability of a number of big-budget acquisition projects is now in doubt as defence spending is being curtailed. (The 2010 defence budget is being trimmed by around 6% to US$9.5 billion as the government seeks to cut a ballooning deficit and divert funds to pay for repairs resultant from natural disasters.) These include a US$6.4bn arms package approved by the US in 2008, which includes 30 AH-64D *Apache* attack helicopters, *Patriot* PAC-3 systems and UGM-84L *Harpoon* missiles.

Taiwan has also placed orders for 12 P-3C *Orion* maritime-patrol aircraft, is in advanced negotiations for 60 UH-60M *Black Hawk* utility helicopters, and continues to lobby for the F-16C/D fighter aircraft that the US has refused so far to sell. The reduced budget may also delay plans to carry out mid-life upgrades on the ageing front-line arsenal of F-16A/B fighters, *Ching-kuo* Indigenous Defence Fighters, and *La Fayette*-class frigates.

The missions – and credibility – of the Taiwanese armed forces came under domestic political criticism in August 2009 in the aftermath of Typhoon Morakot, which devastated parts of the island and killed more than 500 people. The military was heavily criticised for an ineffective response, especially its inability to reach affected areas. Following the debacle, Ma announced that 'in the future, the armed forces will have disaster prevention and rescue as their main job'. This could see funding diverted from combat programmes to beef up logistics and transport capabilities as the army tries to improve reaction times; it is also likely that training will become more diverse, encompassing disaster-relief activities.

KOREAN PENINSULA

North Korea's long- and short-range missile and nuclear tests in spring and summer 2009, its rejection of the Six-Party Talks, and other provocative actions again focused attention on the volatile Korean Peninsula. Pyongyang's motives for carrying out these actions despite strong warnings from the international community were unclear, though a plausible explanation was the need to show strength in the face of external and internal vulnerabilities highlighted by the stroke suffered by paramount leader Kim Jong Il in August 2008. Further emphasis was placed on the militarisation of the economy and society at the expense of economic reforms. After Kim reappeared in public in late spring 2009, this more bellicose strategy was toned down and Pyongyang sought to tentatively re-engage with the international community. However, Pyongyang has ruled out returning to Six-Party negotiations over the future of its nuclear-weapons development and has insisted that it should be recognised as a nuclear-weapons state.

South Korea's armed forces were placed on high alert in early summer as concerns grew that the North might launch provocations to spark a military clash between the two sides, especially in contested waters in the Yellow Sea. Despite heightened tensions, military chiefs were unable to win major increases in defence allocations in the face of a severe economic downturn (see Defence Economics, p. 387). The 2010 defence budget led to reductions in a number of acquisition programmes, including mine-sweeping helicopters and XK-2 main battle tanks, and a scaling back of efforts to indigenously develop a military satellite-communications system, the next-generation KF-X local fighter and the KAH attack helicopter. Core programmes designed to defend against North Korean missile attacks such as the acquisition of *Aegis* destroyers, missile interceptors and early-warning radars will not be affected. US and South Korean officials have reiterated that the 2012 timetable for the transfer of operational wartime command from Washington to Seoul is also on schedule and unaffected by budgetary or inter-Korean problems.

JAPAN

Japan's defence policy in 2009 faced another challenging year on both the domestic and international fronts. The country contended domestically with continuing political gridlock between the governing Liberal Democratic Party of Japan (LDP) and main opposition Democratic Party of Japan (DPJ); internationally with North Korea's ballistic-missile and nuclear tests in April and May; and also with the need to maintain alliance confidence with the incoming Obama administration. In the first half of 2009, Japan's defence establishment did manage to maintain and augment planning for key Japan Self-Defense Force (JSDF) capabilities and overseas commitments, and began to lay the groundwork for the release of the revised National Defense Program Guidelines (NDPG) at the end of the year. However, the DPJ's decisive victory in the 30 August elections raised as yet unanswered questions about the long-term direction of Japan's security policy.

Under Taro Aso's LDP administration, Japan was able to maintain its commitments to the US and international community in relation to operations in Afghanistan, and to actually increase deployments of the JSDF in the Indian Ocean and beyond. In December 2008, Aso used the LDP's 'super-majority' in the Lower House of the National Diet to override the DPJ's Upper House opposition to the renewal of the Replenishment Support Special Measures Law (RSSML), enabling a one-year extension of the Maritime Self-Defense Force's (MSDF) refuelling mission in the Indian Ocean (see *The Military Balance 2009*, p. 366). In March, Aso succeeded – again in the face of DPJ opposition – in dispatching the MSDF to participate in Combined Task Force 150 in the Gulf of Aden. In June, the National Diet passed a new Anti-Piracy Law which expanded the role of the MSDF to protect not only Japanese-related but all international shipping from piracy. Japan deployed two destroyers and two P-3Cs, as well as 50 airborne troops, from the Ground Self-Defense Force (GSDF) Central Readiness Group rapid-reaction force, to operate out of Djibouti. The deployment provided further important experience for the JSDF in joint operations and multinational coalitions.

Meanwhile, Japan developed a response to North Korea's missile and nuclear tests. Amid much domestic media reporting, Tokyo deployed its Ballistic Missile Defense (BMD) system for the first time to attempt to intercept the *Taepo-dong*-2 missile in case it, or any associated debris, strayed off course and threatened Japanese territory. The Air Self-Defense Force (ASDF) deployed two PAC-3 batteries to northern Honshu and two more to the Ministry of Defense (MoD) compound in central Tokyo, while the MSDF sent two BMD-capable *Aegis* destroyers to the Sea of Japan and one *Aegis* destroyer to the Pacific Ocean. In addition, the US deployed five BMD-capable *Aegis* cruisers around Japan. Although no debris fell on Japan, Tokyo regarded the test as a provocation and demonstration of Pyongyang's growing missile capabilities. Japan similarly interpreted North Korea's second nuclear test the following month as a demonstration of its growing mastery of nuclear technologies, and of its advancement towards combining these with ballistic technologies to create a credible nuclear system. Japan's immediate diplomatic response was to join the US and South Korea in condemning the tests at the UN and to maintain its unilateral sanctions on North Korea. The LDP also attempted in mid 2009 to pass a new law in the National Diet to enable the MSDF and Japan Coast Guard to inspect North Korean ships in international waters for WMD, an attempt which, although supported by the DPJ in principle, failed because of insufficient time in the Diet's schedule to pass the law before the impending general elections.

Japan's concerns over North Korea were further compounded by anxieties over the strength of the US–Japan alliance relationship. US Secretary of State Hillary Clinton visited Japan in her first overseas visit in February. This initially reassured Japanese policymakers of the Obama administration's pro-Japan credentials, but alliance confidence was subsequently eroded by Japanese suspicions that the US had failed to provide full early-warning satellite information to Japan in the run-up to the North Korean missile and nuclear tests; by Washington's decision not to prolong production of the F-22 (thereby denying it to Japan as a candidate for its new F-X fighter); and by the slow pace of progress in the realignment of US bases in Japan. (The two sides did sign an agreement in February covering Japan's financial burden for the relocation of bases from Okinawa to Guam.)

These insecurities over North Korea, the US–Japan alliance and, in the longer term, China, have been manifested in planning for new military capabilities, which could be developed in a more autonomous fashion. The MoD announced in its budget request for 2010 an expansion of PAC-3 interceptor units in order to significantly broaden coverage of the system and Japan's defensive deterrence. In addition, Japan has hinted at new interest in offensive deterrence versus North Korea, with open discussion of the need to reinforce coordination with the US on retaliatory measures against the North, but also of Japan's exercise of its own options to strike against North Korean missile bases with future capabilities such as *Tomahawk* missiles. The Prime Minister's Office, MoD and LDP released reports in 2009 indicating that Japan should expand its early-warning satellite capabilities in order to reduce dependence on the US.

Japan's procurement plans are clearly influenced by Chinese systems. The MoD, in its budget requests, has focused on upgrades to the ASDF's F-15Js to counter China's expanded air-defence and cruise-missile capabilities; new anti-submarine and helicopter-carrier capabilities in the shape of the *Hyuga*-class DDH (the first of which was commissioned in March); and boosting the ability of the GSDF, MSDF and ASDF to conduct joint operations to defend outlying Japanese islands from invasion.

But the formation of Prime Minister Yukio Hatoyama's DPJ government in September 2009 has thrown Japan's security-policy planning into doubt, especially with the government's stated intent to pursue a more 'equal' alliance with the US and a more 'Asia-centred' diplomatic policy. The DPJ has argued that the MSDF's refuelling mission in the Indian Ocean is unconstitutional and that it will cease with the expiry of the RSSML at the start of 2010. However, the DPJ may look to maintain the MSDF anti-piracy mission as a visible manifestation of Japan's contribution to international security. Japan–US relations also look to be troubled by the DPJ's determination to review the Status of Forces Agreement (SOFA) and bilateral agreements on the funding and realignment of US bases in Japan. The DPJ appears reluctant to increase or even maintain current levels of defence spending, and may move to reduce funding for BMD programmes and further delay the introduction of the F-X. Nevertheless, the DPJ's shared concerns about North Korea's nuclear programme and China's growing military power will likely oblige the DPJ to avoid jeopardising US–Japan alliance relations and to continue much of the defence-procurement programme of the LDP.

SOUTHEAST ASIA AND AUSTRALASIA

In the face of pervasive strategic uncertainty stemming from sensitive relations among Southeast Asian neighbours as well as China's growing power, and against a backdrop of regional security institutions that remain of limited effectiveness as confidence-building mechanisms (see *Strategic Survey 2009*, pp. 64–73), states in Southeast Asia and Australasia have persisted with efforts to enhance national military capabilities. This is despite the impact of straitened economic conditions on defence budgets. In Southeast Asia, **Singapore**'s heavy long-term investment in defence and close collaboration between the armed forces, local defence science and R&D agencies, and the defence industry (notably in the form of the government-linked Singapore Technologies Engineering and its subsidiaries), is supporting the evolution of the so-called '3G SAF' (Third Generation Singapore Armed Forces). In doctrinal terms, the 3G SAF is based on the IKC2 (Integrated Knowledge-based Command and Control) concept, effectively Singapore's own version of the Revolution in Military Affairs. Key to the 3G SAF is the networking of sensors and firepower across all military branches. The Army Technology Symposium in August 2009 showcased the Advanced Combat Man System, an array of portable sensors, computers and communications equipment intended to 'seamlessly' integrate command headquarters with troops on the ground; several months earlier, a contract to supply the system to the army had been awarded to Singapore Technologies Electronics. Other new army equipment displayed at the symposium and at the biennial Army Open House in September included the Battlefield Management System, which networks platforms such as the newly deployed *Terrex* ICV (developed jointly by Singapore Technologies Engineering and an Irish company, Timoney Technology) and the upgraded ex-Bundeswehr *Leopard* 2A4 MBTs, which entered service in 2008. The first *Leopard* unit, 48 Singapore Armoured Regiment, was scheduled to attain full operational capability in late 2009, following its participation in *Exercise Matilda* in Australia's Northern Territory alongside an Australian Army M1 *Abrams* regiment during September.

The Singapore Armed Forces' primary role remains national defence through the deterrence of potential adversaries in the immediate region. But a widening threat spectrum has led to 'operations other than war' figuring increasingly prominently in planning, training and deployments. Naval elements participate in the Maritime Security Task Force alongside the Police Coast Guard, Customs, the Immigration and Checkpoint Authority and other agencies, with the aim of protecting Singapore's maritime approaches from piracy, terrorism, illegal immigration and other low-intensity challenges. The army's largely reservist 2nd People's Defence Force Command (2 PDF) provides the Island Defence Headquarters, which includes a full-time infantry battalion trained for a 'protection of installations' role and the SAF's CBRE (Chemical, Biological, Radiological and Explosive) Group. In June 2009, more than 60 CBRE Group personnel travelled to China's Guangzhou Province to participate in the SAF's first joint exercise with the PLA, following a bilateral agreement on military cooperation in 2008. While trained for the conventional military defence of the island, 2 PDF is additionally tasked with cooperating closely with the police and other civil agencies in the event of terrorist or other non-military threats. The main wartime role of the SAF's special forces remains strategic operations in enemy territory, but they also have an important peacetime role: in July 2009, the annual *Operation Northstar* counter-terrorism exercise saw troops from the newly formed Special Operations Task Force (SOTF), which brings together the SAF's active and reservist parachute-trained Commando regiments, Special Operations Force and Naval Diving Unit in a single formation, mount a raid on a hotel on Sentosa Island using helicopters and fast boats to free 'hostages' seized in a scenario derived from the 2008 Mumbai attack. Supporting Singapore's participation in the US-led Proliferation Security Initiative will be among the SOTF's roles.

Though its operational experience remains limited, the SAF has increasingly deployed units abroad. In February 2009, it announced that it would send a landing-ship tank (LST) with 200 personnel and two *Super Puma* helicopters to Combined Task Force 151 in the Gulf of Aden to protect international shipping. The LST returned to Singapore in July, but a Singapore naval officer will command CTF-151 from January–March 2010. In June, the defence ministry revealed that later in the year a Singapore artillery-locating radar unit would deploy to Uruzgan province in central Afghanistan for 9–12 months. The role would be to help protect ISAF troops from Taliban rocket attacks. In addition, Singapore's air force is expected to deploy KC-135 and UAV assets in support of Afghan operations. Meanwhile, overseas training remains as important as ever to Singapore,

where domestic exercise areas and airspace are extremely limited. At the IISS *Shangri-la Dialogue* in June 2009, Singapore's Defence Ministry signed an agreement with Australia extending the SAF's use of the Shoalwater Bay Training Area in Queensland – site for the large-scale annual unilateral combined-arms manoeuvres – *Exercise Wallaby* until 2019. The same event saw Singapore also reach an agreement on defence cooperation with New Zealand. Before the end of 2009, a new agreement with the US on air-force training is expected to allow not just the continuing long-term deployment of a squadron of F-16C fighters to Luke Air Force Base in Arizona, but also the use of leased USAF F-16s at an Air National Guard base in Ohio. According to the US Defense Security Cooperation Agency's notification to Congress in September 2009 regarding the proposed arrangement, it would not only boost Singapore's capability to defend itself but also 'ensure interoperability with US forces for coalition operations. Singapore is a firm supporter of US overseas contingency operations.' The implication that Singapore might contribute to future coalition air operations, despite not being a formal US ally, was clear.

Perhaps at least partly in reaction to Singapore's impressive military developments, **Malaysia's** defence establishment now emphasises the importance of exploiting information and communications technology to enhance its armed forces' effectiveness. Interviewed in September 2009, soon after becoming Malaysia's first chief of defence forces not drawn from the army, air force General Tan Sri Azizan Ariffin highlighted the three main features of the '4-D MAF' (Fourth Dimension Malaysian Armed Forces) plan, which is supposed to guide the development of Malaysian military capabilities to 2020 and beyond: joint force integration and operations; information superiority; and multi-dimensional operations including information warfare. In consequence, there is particular emphasis on developing Malaysian armed forces' C^4ISR capabilities, and on embracing network-centred operations. However, funding shortfalls have delayed implementation of the 4-D MAF plan, with significant budget allocations only likely under the 10th Malaysia Plan (10 MP) from 2011–15.

While the 'Army Two Ten Plus Ten' development plan emphasises increased readiness, enhanced mobility and new surveillance, electronic-warfare and communications capabilities, the army has been undergoing important structural changes, most importantly the conversion of the 3rd Division from

384 THE MILITARY BALANCE 2010

an infantry into a combined-arms formation, now that PT-91M MBTs are coming into service. But the operational readiness of the new formation and its units seems doubtful: in March 2009, army commander General Tan Sri Muhammad Ismail Jamaluddin candidly admitted that there was no combat ammunition for the tanks' 125mm main guns and that their battle-management system (BMS) was not fitted to other vehicles in their brigade. The general claimed, 'We don't have enough bandwidth capability in the country yet to support an overall BMS for the army'. Longer-term plans call for converting a second division to a combined-arms role. In the meantime, budget cuts have stymied procurement: in March 2009, plans for acquiring new 8×8 AFVs, self-propelled artillery and MANPADS were postponed in light of funding shortages. Nevertheless, the army was due to take delivery in September 2009 of a second regiment of *Astros* II multiple-rocket launchers, to be based in Kedah near the Thai border, financed by a supplementary funding bill in March. Malaysia's new defence minister, Datuk Dr Ahmad Zahid Hamidi, who took over the portfolio in April 2009, spoke of the need to review Malaysia's defence doctrine, which dated from 1993. In the short term, his main initiative was to announce the '600K TA' plan to substantially expand the Territorial Army (TA) to an eventual strength of 600,000 troops, including personnel transferred from paramilitary organisations such as RELA (the People's Volunteer Corps), to be organised in 300-strong units in every one of Malaysia's more than 200 parliamentary constituencies. Plans to convert some existing full-time TA units into two brigade-strength Border Management Regiments (one each for the frontiers with Indonesia and Thailand) are proceeding.

Malaysia's most important international military deployment is to the West Sector of UNIFIL in Lebanon, where the army increased the size of its deployment to battalion strength in mid 2009. Following serviceability problems with the battalion's *Sibmas* wheeled IFVs and *Condor* APCs, in October 2009 army chief Jamaluddin announced plans to lease at least a squadron of more modern APCs to meet the urgent operational requirement in Lebanon. Having initially deployed three naval vessels to the Gulf of Aden in September 2008 on anti-piracy duties, in June 2009 the Royal Malaysian Navy commissioned and deployed a modified commercial container vessel specifically equipped for the low-intensity patrol role. Closer to home, the 'Ambalat block' off the coast of Borneo was an important focus of activity for the navy. This maritime area is believed to have massive oil and natural-gas potential, and a bilateral dispute with Indonesia reignited in mid 2009. Indonesian legislators accused the Malaysian navy and maritime enforcement agency of 'violating Indonesia's maritime boundary' 19 times during May and June; in late May, there was a stand-off between Indonesian and Malaysian patrol vessels. Soon afterwards, Malaysian Defence Minister Hamidi felt it necessary to say that there would be 'no war' between the two countries despite rising tensions over the Ambalat block. Indonesian Defence Minister Juwono Sudarsono said both sides had agreed to reduce their naval deployments in the disputed area in order to rein in bilateral tensions. Nevertheless, in July the TNI (Indonesian armed forces) announced that it was staging a large tri-service exercise near the border between Indonesia's East Kalimantan province and Malaysia's Sabah state. In August, Indonesia still had seven vessels deployed in the Ambalat block to prevent Malaysian 'incursions'. Meanwhile, during the same month, the Malaysian armed forces held the fourth 2009 exercise in the *Angkasa Samudera* (Ocean Air) series, aimed at developing navy and air force joint-operations capabilities in a 'real combat situation' and including a cyber-warfare dimension.

While the Ambalat dispute illustrates the maritime challenges facing **Indonesia**, the reorientation of the TNI, away from a traditional emphasis on counter-insurgency towards expanded naval and air capabilities to defend the country's maritime interests, remains an incremental and long-term process. The army, which was politically powerful from the time of the independence struggle during the 1940s until the downfall of Suharto's military-backed dictatorship in 1998, remains the dominant service. In September 2009, army chief General Agustadi Sasongko Purnomo rejected the much-vaunted idea that the army should dismantle its territorial structure, under which army units are widely dispersed throughout the nation, even to the extent of NCOs being stationed in many villages. General Agustadi claimed that the existing structure was a vital component of the TNI's 'total defence' doctrine, which required such deployments for intelligence-gathering purposes. But while the TNI's structure still needs radical changes in order to defend Indonesia effectively against contemporary threats, large-scale investment is required in new equipment. In June 2009, following four crashes of military-transport aircraft and helicopters within two months, including that of a C-130 which claimed more than 100 lives, President Susilo Bambang Yudhoyono requested an audit of TNI equipment serviceability. In September, TNI commander General Djoko Santoso revealed that the audit showed that only 62% of army vehicles, 31% of military aircraft and 17% of naval vessels were serviceable. In the meantime, though, a wave of sympathy from the public and legislators had allowed the TNI to secure a 21% budget increase in August, with the aim that the substantial funding boost should be directed towards improving equipment maintenance and servicing. However, while some equipment can be repaired, other items may need to be discarded, and the TNI is widely expected to prioritise the procurement of replacement C-130s.

In several Southeast Asian states, the armed forces have remained heavily committed to counter-insurgency operations, though not to the exclusion of efforts to improve external defence capabilities. In southern **Thailand**, the insurgency by ethnic Malay Muslim militants continued unabated, and insurgent activity increased again during 2009, with drive-by shootings and bombings using IEDs remaining common. (Violence had declined during 2008 because of a surge in Thai military deployments that led to the arrest and surrender of insurgent leaders, coupled with a decline in popular support for the insurgents.) Despite a continuing daily concern with low-intensity operations in the south, including efforts to implement a 'hearts-and-minds' strategy, the Thai armed forces continue to use their procurement funds to improve the country's capacity for external defence, including establishment of a third cavalry (armour) division over the next decade in the country's northeast. Concern over the need to deter regional threats has risen in the wake of border clashes with Myanmar in 2001–02, and with Cambodia in 2008–09. After confrontations with Cambodian forces in July and October 2008, there was a fresh clash in April 2009 which resulted in the deaths of three Thai and two Cambodian troops.

In the **Philippines**, the armed forces have continued their campaign against the New People's Army, reducing the Maoist rebels' strength through a combination of military action and a social-integration programme. The Armed Forces of the Philippines (AFP) have also continued operations against the Abu Sayyaf Group (ASG). Though these operations weakened the ASG considerably during 2008, the group's kidnapping of three officials from the International Committee of the Red Cross in January

2009 provoked major offensives by the AFP over the following six months on Basilan and Jolo, including deployment of more than 300 Special Action Force troops at one stage. Following a dramatic resurgence of conflict with the Moro Islamic Front during 2008 after the breakdown of peace talks, President Gloria Macapagal Arroyo ordered a new ceasefire by the AFP in July 2009 as the separatist group agreed to resume negotiations. There is now a realistic prospect of internal security operations becoming relatively less important for the AFP in future, and in the face of growing threats to the Philippines' perceived maritime interests (including in the Spratly Islands), there is growing interest in Manila in resuscitating the country's naval and air capabilities. The Philippine Navy plans to improve its infrastructure on the features in the Spratly Islands that it occupies, including extending the runway on Pag-asa (Nanshan) Island. According to naval chief Admiral Ferdinand Golez there are also long-term plans for 30 more coastal- and island-monitoring stations under the inter-agency 'Coast Watch Philippines' (CWP) project to improve surveillance of Filipino waters. CWP will be modelled on the existing Coast Watch South scheme, which enables the Philippine Navy, with US and Australian support, to monitor all surface movements in the sea area bounded by the Philippines, Indonesia and Malaysia. Meanwhile, the Philippine Air Force has revealed plans to re-acquire combat aircraft by 2012–13, having decommissioned its last F-5A fighters in 2005.

In **Myanmar**, the army has maintained its offensive against the main ethnic-minority rebel group continuing its military struggle, the Karen National Union, and its armed wing, the Karen National Liberation Army. Simultaneously, as a result of a government policy of trying to force non-government groups to reduce their armed strength and accept integration into its own forces ahead of the national elections planned for 2010, tensions have grown between the State Peace and Development Council (SPDC) regime and various ethnic-minority groups with which it had previously entered into ceasefire arrangements. Meanwhile, the SPDC has apparently become increasingly concerned over the possibility of external intervention aimed at forcing regime change, as well as the need to defend Myanmar's maritime claims against neighbouring states' encroachment. The appearance of sizeable US and other Western naval forces off Myanmar's coast following Cyclone Nargis in May 2008, and a naval stand-off with Bangladesh in November 2008 over conflicting sea boundaries, reinforced the SPDC's sense of weakness and spurred its efforts to enhance its external defence capabilities. While there is no credible evidence to support allegations by exiles and some foreign analysts that Myanmar is developing nuclear weapons (see *Preventing Nuclear Dangers in Southeast Asia and Australasia*, IISS Strategic Dossier, 2009, pp. 101–18), it is apparently trying to modernise its air-defence and naval forces to the extent that its resources, international contacts and defence-industrial capacities allow. Ultimately, though, in the event of an invasion the regime would almost certainly be forced quickly to fall back on a strategy of mass mobilisation and guerrilla warfare.

Australia and New Zealand continue to watch political and military developments in Asia closely. In May 2009, **Australia** released its first defence White Paper since 2000. *Defending Australia in the Asia Pacific Century: Force 2030* was written amidst a widespread perception in Australian analytical and policy circles that the distribution of power in the Asia-Pacific and Indian Ocean regions is in flux, and it outlines plans for significant improvements in Australian defence capabilities over the next two decades. In its chapter on Australia's strategic outlook to 2030, the White Paper says tensions between major powers in the region are likely to increase, that miscalculation between them is possible and that there is even some chance of 'growing confrontation'. If China fails to explain its military modernisation more carefully, regional states are likely to question the 'long-term strategic purpose of its force development'. Closer to home, the White Paper stresses that while Indonesia has made remarkable gains over the past decade, it could be a 'source of threat' if it became weak and fragmented, while an 'authoritarian or overtly nationalistic regime' in Jakarta could create 'strategic risks'. The paper also says that the Indian Ocean will assume much greater strategic significance over the next two decades.

The Australian White Paper argues that defending Australia against direct armed attack remains the country's 'basic strategic interest'. But Australia does have wider strategic interests, most importantly 'the security, stability and cohesion' of the immediate neighbourhood. The paper claims that the government has factored into future military-capability planning the heightened defence posture that Australia would almost certainly need in the event of instability in Indonesia. The White Paper also discusses Australia's enduring strategic interest in the stability of the broader Asia-Pacific region. To this end, Canberra is attempting to bolster the regional security architecture through its proposal for a pan-regional Asia-Pacific community aimed at strengthening political, economic and security cooperation. Nevertheless, the White Paper is clear that the United States' alliances and security partnerships, including with Australia, remain crucial to regional stability. Australia will continue to support the US in maintaining global security where their interests 'align'. This assessment of Australia's strategic interests means that some commentators' efforts to frame the debate as a choice between 'defence of Australia' and an expeditionary approach are misleading. The White Paper implies that elements of both approaches are needed, explaining that while defence policy will still be based on the 'principle of self-reliance in the direct defence of Australia', the country needs 'the capacity to do more when required'.

According to the White Paper, Australia will need to project power and demonstrate strategic presence beyond its 'primary operational environment'. The Australian Defence Force (ADF) will need to prepare for offensive operations 'as far from Australia as possible' using 'strike capabilities, including combat aircraft, long-range missiles and special forces'. The ADF will further need to be ready to contribute, potentially substantially, to supporting Southeast Asian security partners and to operations as part of US-led coalitions, while simultaneously defending Australia itself. While the government under Prime Minister Kevin Rudd has decided that ADF deployment on land operations against heavily armed foes in the Middle East, Central and South Asia or Africa should not be seen as a primary potential task (thus constraining any expectation that Australia could become involved in major combat operations in Iraq or Afghanistan, let alone potential new theatres such as Pakistan or Somalia), the White Paper emphasises the importance for national strategic interests of the present deployment of special forces and other troops in Afghanistan.

The maritime strategy that defence planners see as necessary to defend Australia's homeland and Australian interests requires 'forces that can operate with decisive effect throughout the northern maritime and littoral approaches'. To this end, the ADF of 2030 will be significantly strengthened in key areas, notably undersea warfare and anti-submarine warfare, maritime surface warfare including air defence, air superiority, strategic strike, special forces, intelligence,

Australia's *Force 2030*: Key capability improvements

- Doubling the navy's submarines from the present six *Collins*-class vessels to 12 larger and more capable boats
- Land-attack cruise missiles to arm new submarines, surface vessels and combat aircraft
- Eight new frigates, larger and better equipped than the present *Anzac* class
- New class of around 20 offshore combatant vessels of up to 2,000 tonnes
- Large strategic sealift ship of 10–15,000 tonnes to enhance amphibious capability
- New long-range maritime-patrol aircraft
- High-altitude, long-endurance unmanned aerial vehicles
- New armoured fighting vehicles
- CH-47F transport helicopters
- Improvements in ISR capabilities, including an intelligence-collection satellite
- Establishment of a cyber-security operations centre

surveillance and reconnaissance, and cyber warfare. The White Paper spells out significant new equipment procurements intended to bolster these capabilities.

The White Paper represents a bold, public attempt to set out defence plans for many years ahead. Importantly, it also promises that the exercise will be repeated every five years to allow for adjustments in light of changes in Australia's strategic circumstances. However, the White Paper has provoked criticism, with some Australian commentators pointing to what they see as the weakness of the arguments over the emerging and supposedly more threatening strategic circumstances on which the future force structure is based. Critics have also claimed that this force structure does not reflect a sufficiently decisive reassessment of Australian defence needs. Analysts and opposition politicians alike have seized on the document's lack of detail regarding how the force structure will be developed – and financed. The White Paper claims that its objectives are fully funded, with 3% annual real growth in defence spending guaranteed until 2017–18 and 2.2% real growth thereafter. However, critics say that the government's commitment to developing new military capabilities will depend on favourable economic conditions.

With the election of a government in **New Zealand** led by the conservative National Party in November 2008 came the prospect of a re-evaluation of the country's defence outlook and capabilities. Though

the new prime minister, John Key, quickly damped down suggestions that his government might revive the air force's fast-jet operations (perhaps by taking its MB339C advanced trainers out of storage), in April 2009 the government announced the first comprehensive defence review since the 1997 Defence White Paper. The review will culminate in a new White Paper, to be published in the first half of 2010.

EAST ASIA AND AUSTRALASIA – DEFENCE ECONOMICS

The impact of the global recession on East and Southeast Asia has been mixed. The newly industrialised Asian (NIA) economies (Hong Kong, Korea, Singapore and Taiwan) will experience a significant drop in GDP of 5.6% in 2009; in Singapore the economy may contract by more than 10%. The ASEAN-5 (Indonesia, Malaysia, the Philippines, Thailand and Vietnam) will probably fare much better, with growth potentially unchanged from the previous year. Both the NIA and ASEAN economies have been hit particularly hard by the drop in global trade. However, because most ASEAN countries are less exposed to the durable-goods sector, the sector most negatively affected by the recession, this has provided some insulation from the most damaging consequences of the global downturn. Japan, on the other hand, suffering from both a huge collapse in demand and financial contagion from the rest of the world, saw its economy contract by more than 6%. Economic difficulties have had an impact on some countries' immediate defence plans; South Korea, for example, has had to scale back aspects of its 2020 reform programme. But the drivers behind the region's military-modernisation efforts are unchanged, so any delay to long-term plans caused by current budgetary constraints are likely to prove temporary.

South Korea is undertaking a major overhaul of its military posture, as the United States reduces its presence on the peninsula and Seoul prepares to assume greater responsibility for its own defence. Nevertheless, the government announced that it needed to adjust its long-term military spending in light of its deteriorating finances. Under the Defense Reform 2020 programme drawn up in 2005, the defence budget had originally been scheduled to increase by a fixed amount each year until 2020, and would amount to SKW621tr (US$563bn) during that period. Of that total, new equipment acquisition (under Force Improvement programmes) would account for SKW230tr (US$208bn). However, in summer 2009 it emerged that the total budget would fall by at least 3.5% and that certain procurement programmes would be affected.

In setting out its priorities, the revised plan acknowledged that developments in North Korea required the speedier delivery of certain weapons systems, such as artillery, cruise missiles and torpedoes, which would come at the expense of longer-term programmes. It also recommended a smaller cut in troop numbers, down to 517,000 instead of the originally planned 500,000.

The revised 2020 plan includes delays to several naval and air-force platforms, including KSS-III submarines and air-to-air refuelling aircraft, as well as a 50% cut in the proposed number of XK-2 main battle tanks, down to just 300. Also in the pipeline is a major rethink of the future KF-X programme, aimed at developing a new fifth-generation stealth fighter aircraft. In July 2009, the Defense Acquisition Program Administration (DAPA) suggested that, rather than build a fighter with superior stealth fighting attributes, a cheaper option may be necessary and that the programme might be downgraded to create a multi-role jet on a par with an F-16 Block 50 aircraft. It had been hoped that the KF-X programme would be entirely indigenous. However, President Lee Myung-bak is thought to be more interested in a thorough cost–benefit analysis, which in practice would leave the door open to some level of participation with a foreign manufacturer.

It had seemed that North Korea's continuing military activities and the ongoing modernisation of China's armed forces would reverse the seven-year decline in **Japan's** defence budget. The ruling Liberal Democratic Party (LDP) had appeared to view defence spending as an emerging priority when it implemented the Honebutu initiative, whereby the Prime Minister's Office is able to exert influence in the development of budgets and arrange priorities. The Honebutu initiative for the first time named North Korea as a possible threat and stressed the need to deal 'appropriately' with Pyongyang's missile threat. Before the country's general elections, the ruling LDP defence-policymaking panel had also requested that 2010's new five-year National Defense Program Guidelines (NDPG) include multi-year budgets for sea-launched cruise missiles and a domestic early-warning satellite system, so that Japan would not be reliant on the US. The Ministry of Defence (MoD) requested an additional US$2bn for the lower tier of its two-tier ballistic-missile shield. However, after the August 2009 elections, the victorious Democratic Party of Japan (DPJ) indicated it will more inclined to further reduce, rather than increase, the country's military budget. It promised instead to increase spending on social-welfare and tuition-aid programmes.

After 16 months of preparation, **Australia** released its new Defence White Paper on 2 May 2009. Entitled *Defending Australia in the Asia Pacific Century: Force 2030*, the document sets out the strategic framework to be adopted by Australia's armed forces over the coming two decades in order for them to achieve 'the defence of Australia, the security and stability of the regional security environment and a rules-based global order'. In pursuit of that goal, the White Paper highlighted specific capability improvements needed to make the Australian Defence Force a 'more potent force', including undersea and anti-submarine warfare, surface naval warfare, air superiority, strategic strike, special forces, intelligence, surveillance and reconnaissance, and cyber defence.

All three services are intended to grow, particularly the navy, which will double its submarine fleet to 12, acquire eight new frigates with anti-submarine warfare (ASW) capabilities, two Landing Helicopter Dock ships and at least 24 naval-combat helicopters. The future air force will be built on a fleet of 100 joint strike fighters, eight maritime-patrol aircraft (MPAs) and several high-altitude, long-range unmanned aerial vehicles (UAVs). Although no new major acquisitions are envisaged for the army, the document confirms previously announced equipment programmes, including the acquisition of seven *Chinook* helicopters and 7,000 support vehicles. It also outlines a project to deliver a combat vehicle system that will 'greatly improve fire power, protection and mobility'.

To achieve these ambitious long-term procurement goals the White Paper included a new funding model with three specific elements:

- a 3% real growth in the defence budget to 2017, followed by 2.2% real annual growth from 2018 to 2030;
- a 2.5% fixed indexation to the defence budget from 2009 to 2030; and
- a strategic reform programme that will release A$20bn of savings for redirection to priority areas.

The government claimed these measures would ensure a 'fully costed' and 'affordable' business plan for the 21-year period of the White Paper, but the trajectory of actual funding was thrown into doubt only ten days later when the 2009/10 defence budget was announced and actually included cuts to near-term defence spending. In particular, the benefits of the new indexation regime were deferred for four years; A$2bn (US$1.8bn) of existing spending was removed from the next four years' budgets and deferred into the future; and A$1bn (US$910m) in 2015 and A$500m (US$450m) in 2016 were also deferred. So despite the initiatives outlined in the White Paper, some A$8.8bn (US$8bn) has been 'lost' from the near-term budget plan. This prompted the Australian Strategic Policy Institute to suggest that defence spending may be viewed as something of a budget-balancing item, pointing out that the schedule of cuts and deferrals coincides with the government's principle economic goal of returning to a budget surplus in 2015.

Central to the long-term funding plan laid out in the White Paper is the initiative to deliver more than A$20bn (US$18bn) in gross savings over the next decade. Indeed, the government is relying on realisation of these measures to provide two-thirds of its proposed A$30bn (US$27bn) increase in defence funding in the next ten years; the remaining A$10bn (US$9bn) will come from the new indexation regime. Broadly speaking, these 'new' funds will be allocated as follows: A$6bn (US$5.4bn) for major capital equipment; A$10bn (US$9bn) for personnel and operating costs associated with new equipment; A$6bn (US$5.4bn) for estate, information technology and so on; and A$8bn (US$7.2bn) for other budget provisions related to mediation. Defence Minister Joel Fitzgibbon acknowledged that the failure of previous initiatives to save money would make some people sceptical about the reform plan's chances of success, but he stressed that the goals of the broader *Force 2030* programme could only be realised if savings are achieved. To date, however, only sketchy details have emerged about how the MoD will go about saving what is in effect 7% of the present annual defence budget. With personnel and deployments on the increase, savings clearly will not be possible in these areas. Thus, it appears that the bulk of the savings are to be generated through the more prudent purchasing of goods and services provided by the private sector. Details so far published show that savings are expected to be made as follows: efficiencies in payroll, finance and human-resource management A$1.4bn (US$1.2bn), 'smart' non-equipment procurement A$4.4bn (US$4bn), standardised IT A$1.9bn (US$1.7bn), better inventory management A$700m (US$635m), 'smart' maintenance of equipment A$4.4bn (US$4bn) and workforces reform A$1.9bn (US$1.7bn).

Whatever the eventual evolution of long-term defence spending, the 2009/10 budget reached a historic high of A$26.6bn (US$24.1bn), a real-terms increase of 16% over the previous year. There were several one-off factors contributing to this: A$1.7bn (US$1.5bn) of additional spending for overseas deployments (A$1.4bn in Afghanistan, A$214m for East Timor and A$60m for Iraq); the provision of an additional A$1.5bn (US$1.3bn) to compensate for the depreciation of the Australian dollar; A$1bn (US$910m) of capital investment that had been deferred out of last year's budget; plus the impact

Table 33 **East Asia and Australasia Regional Defence Expenditure** as % of GDP

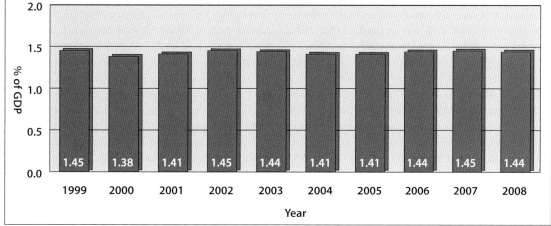

Year	1999	2000	2001	2002	2003	2004	2005	2006	2007	2008
% of GDP	1.45	1.38	1.41	1.45	1.44	1.41	1.41	1.44	1.45	1.44

East Asia and Australasia

of the 3% annual increase in base spending that was introduced in the 2000 White Paper. In the absence of such one-off provisions, future budgets will show more modest year-on-year growth over the next four years.

Of all the Southeast Asian countries, **Thailand** has been hit particularly hard by the global recession. The country was already suffering from an investment slump because of the political turmoil triggered in 2006, and when its export markets contracted because of the global economic crisis, the country was deprived of its main engine of growth. As a result, the economy is expected to contract by at least 3% in 2009, while the government will record a budget deficit of more than 4% of GDP. Against this background, the ambitious two-stage military-modernisation programme outlined in 2008 is already in difficulty. The original plan, drawn up to both combat internal unrest and replace the armed forces' most obsolete equipment, had outlined a significant financial commitment of some THB300bn (US$9.2bn) over a ten-year period. The most high-profile purchase announced had been the plan to procure 12 JAS-39 *Gripen* fighter aircraft and two *Erieye* airborne early-warning and control (AWAC) aircraft from Saab of Sweden, to be delivered in two tranches. However, in June 2009 the Thai cabinet announced that it had postponed the purchase of the final six aircraft and one *Erieye* platform by at least two years because of growing economic pressure. Other programmes that have apparently suffered because of budgetary constraints include the army's plans to acquire armoured personnel carriers as well as the air force's purchase of four search-and-rescue helicopters. Instead of making any progress with these major acquisitions, the government was reduced to allocating a sum of just THB10bn (US$307m) for the purchase of several 2.5-tonne trucks, three 41-metre coastal-patrol craft and the upgrade of six S-70 *Seahawk* helicopters to include an ASW capability.

Following the conclusion of controversial talks between Taipei and Washington in 2008 that saw **Taiwan** finally agree to buy part of a comprehensive weapons range from the US, little progress was made in resolving the outstanding items, particularly Taiwan's desire to procure extra F-16 aircraft. The original package offered by the George W. Bush administration in 2001 had included eight submarines, new maritime-patrol aircraft and several *Patriot* PAC-3 air-defence systems. However, after seven years of domestic political wrangling, Taiwan

settled for a smaller and cheaper deal that included 12 second-hand P-3C *Orion* MPAs, three PAC-3 systems and funds that only cover an 'evaluation study' of the proposed submarine programme. Purchase of the P-3Cs is accompanied by a significant offset requirement of 70% of the contract value (equivalent to nearly US$500m). This is a much higher level than the 40% threshold usually sought by Taiwan's Industrial Co-operation Programme office, and illustrates the island's growing commitment to becoming more self-reliant in the defence sector. In this regard, members of the Washington-based Taiwan Defense Working Group have called on Taiwan to abandon its proposed purchase of diesel-electric submarines and instead allocate the money towards producing more domestic weapons systems, albeit with US assistance.

Despite improved cross-straits relations following the election of Taiwan's President Ma Ying-jeou, hopes that Taiwan's air force would get the go-ahead for its plans to acquire 66 F-16C/D aircraft appear to have receded. The country's first-ever Quadrennial Defence Review (QDR) published in March 2009 acknowledged that the chance of procuring the F-16s was slim but said the Ministry of National Defence would continue to push the US while laying the groundwork for the procurement of a next-generation fighter aircraft. Suggestions that candidates would include the Eurofighter *Typhoon* and F-22 and F-35 planes look unrealistic. However, in July 2009 the US Senate Armed Services Committee passed a bill calling for a presidential report on the status of Taiwan's air force to be included in the National Defense Authorisation Act. This report could help chances for the F-16 sale, should it conclude that China enjoys significant air superiority over Taiwan. The QDR also stated that Taiwan would continue to develop its indigenous *Hsiung Feng* IIE surface-to-surface cruise missile, despite sharp criticism from Washington, and included plans to downsize the military to an estimated force of 210,500 professional service personnel by 2014. In the short term, however, the cost of completing this latter initiative will wipe out any potential savings that may accrue from the reduction in personnel.

Unlike some other countries in the region, **Indonesia** entered the global slowdown with strong economic fundamentals, brought about through sound macroeconomic policy implementation, prudent debt management and a sound financial sector. In its 2009 Article IV Consultation, the

International Monetary Fund (IMF) remarked on the resilience of the Indonesian economy and noted that, barring another round of global risk aversion, the outlook remained positive. Growth of 4.5% has been forecast for 2010. In this environment, the government was able to fully fund the 2009 defence budget of IDR33.6tr (US$3.5bn) – even if this was IDR2.4tr (US$250m) less than the Ministry of National Defence had originally requested. It was even able to allocate an additional IDR500bn (US$52m) to cover extra running costs. Following his victory in the July 2009 elections, Indonesian President Susilo Bambang Yudhoyono promised that the military would enjoy substantially higher budgets in coming years in order to establish a 'minimum essential force'. He proposed an increase of 21% in the 2010 defence budget and suggested that in coming years the budget would rise in line with the country's economic growth towards a target level of IDR100tr (US$10.5bn). As noted in previous editions of the *Military Balance*, the official defence budget in Indonesia is unlikely to capture the true extent of total defence-related expenditure, as it fails to include pensions and benefits for retired military personnel, overseas procurement (which is often financed through barter arrangements) or the revenue generated by the military's considerable business interests. That said, under legislation outlined in 2004, the military's business interests are due to be transferred to the state in 2009, and this may well have been a factor in the significant jump in the official budget over the past two years.

Despite a growing military budget, the Indonesian armed forces do not receive sufficient funds to purchase all the equipment they need, and are therefore forced to rely on some creative financing arrangements to procure big-ticket weapons systems, particularly from overseas. In September 2007, during a state visit to Indonesia by then Russian President Vladimir Putin, the Russian government agreed to provide Jakarta with a US$1bn line of credit with which to purchase Russian military equipment. Items thought to be part of the deal included 17 Mi-17 multi-role helicopters, six Mi-35 attack helicopters, 20 BMP-3 infantry combat vehicles and two *Kilo*-class submarines. However, with the Russian state arms-export intermediary, Rosoboronexport, struggling to find capital in the wake of the global credit crunch, the terms of the deal and the likelihood of its completion have become less certain. The arrangement probably will proceed, even if the commercial terms finally agreed are unfavourable to Russia. Because Moscow

is unwilling to relinquish its strategic partnership with Indonesia, particularly in light of growing military–technical ties between Jakarta and the US and China. However, the episode highlights one of the difficulties that Indonesia will continue to face in its modernisation drive.

The country's four state-owned defence companies have urged the government to support their effort to supply more domestic military equipment to the Indonesian armed forces. At present, around 80% of procurement funds are spent with foreign suppliers forcing domestic defence companies to operate in the commercial sector, leading to widespread inefficiencies. Indeed, in 2008 the government was forced to lend US$750m to the four major companies, as high oil prices and rising inflation threatened to put them out of business. Afterwards, the four companies made policy suggestions that they believed would encourage growth and stability in the sector, and would help to avert similar problems in the future. These included a greater level of budget certainty, supportive tax regulations, guidance on issues such as diversification, and help in boosting military exports.

Following years of double-digit GDP growth, **China** succumbed to the global economic slowdown. Weak external demand, particularly from the US, weighed on exports, and growth eased to 9% in 2008 and was forecast to fall to 8.5% in 2009. In response, the government was quick to introduce decisive monetary and fiscal policies to offset the drag from declining world demand and falling private investment. Low levels of public debt resulting from years of fiscal discipline allowed the introduction of several major infrastructure projects, including efforts to rebuild the Sichuan region following the devastating earthquake in 2008. The IMF supported these measures and even urged the Chinese authorities to implement additional short-term stimulus measures should they be required. Early indications, however, suggest that further measures are unlikely to be needed as the existing initiatives are having some success. Consumption indicators are relatively strong, the decline in industrial production appears to have bottomed out, and labour markets seem to be absorbing those workers laid off from export industries.

The weaker economic environment has not yet had any direct impact on the level of Chinese military spending or the ongoing modernisation of the People's Liberation Army (PLA). Although the current Five Year Economic Programme (2006–11) made no

Table 34 **China – Estimated Total Military-Related Funding 2008**

	A	B	C
	RMB bn	US$bn at market exchange rates	US$bn incl. PPP estimates[a]
Official PLA budget (Including local militia funding)	417	60.1	83.5[b]
Foreign weapons purchase (2001–2008 average)	13.9	2.0	2.0
Defence Industry Subsidies	See text (p. 392)		
R&D	46.1	6.6	6.64
Government funded science and technology	34.5	4.9	4.97
People's Armed Police			
Central funding	50.2	7.2	12.9
Local funding	16.1	2.3	4.1
Total	577.8	83.1	114.1
% of GDP	1.88		

Sources: *China Statistical Yearbook 2009* and 'Conventional Arms Transfers to Developing Nations 2001–2008', Congressional Research Service.
[a]Where appropriate.
[b]Arms Includes PPP estimate.

specific mention of defence spending, emphasising instead demographic developments, the environment and rural development, funds allocated to the PLA continue to grow at a significant pace. The official 2009 state budget included yet another hefty increase in defence spending, up 15% from the previous year to RMB480bn (US$70.3bn at market exchange rates). As pointed out in the essay 'Calculating China's Defence Expenditure' in *The Military Balance 2006* (pp. 249–53), the official defence budget, although the best indicator of the overall trend in military spending, does not reflect the true level of resources devoted to the PLA.

According to the 2008 White Paper on China's National Defence published by the Chinese authorities, the official defence budget is broadly distributed in three equal shares: personnel, operations and equipment. However, it is widely believed that the official budget takes no account of other military-related expenditures, including weapons purchased from overseas or research and development (R&D) funding. In addition, attempts to calculate China's true military burden should include funds allocated to the People's Armed Police (PAP). For many years analysts suggested that calculations of Chinese military spending should include reference to substantial government subsidies provided to the state's loss-making defence enterprises. While China's defence companies operated at a significant loss and required considerable financial support from central government during the 1990s and the early part of this century, in 2003 the Chinese defence sector moved into profit and is now one of the most profitable sectors of the Chinese economy. Furthermore,

the nature of the state's role in the sector is changing rapidly as Chinese defence companies now raise investment funds in capital markets through bond issues, stock-market listings and private investment. Meanwhile, changes in the procurement system mean the state is finally paying closer to the market rate for weapons systems. As such, the level of state subsidies to the defence industry is now unlikely to be significant and is no longer taken into account by *The Military Balance*.

Table 34 includes estimates for additional military-related elements. Column A includes figures for the 2008 official budget plus estimates of foreign-weapons purchases, R&D and new product expenditure, and outlays on the PAP. These figures are all in local currency and when combined suggest that total military-related spending amounted to RMB577.8bn (US$83.1bn), about 1.4 times greater than the official budget figure. However, in attempting to determine the level of total Chinese defence expenditure, there is also the problem of exchange rates to consider. In 2008, for example, when converted at the average market exchange rate for the year, China's GDP measured US$4.4 trillion. However, the World Bank calculated that using PPP rates China's 2008 GDP was the equivalent of US$7.9 trillion. (In the case of countries at different stages of economic development it is conventional to use Purchasing Power Parity (PPP) to help compare macroeconomic data.)

In consideration of these variables, Table 34 includes data using two alternative methodologies for calculating Chinese military spending. Column B uses the data from column A and converts it to US dollars using the market exchange rate for 2008. In column C, data are converted into US dollars using a combination of both market exchange and PPP rates. Not surprisingly, this methodology dramatically boosts the apparent size of Chinese military spending and partly explains the wide range of spending estimates often referred to in the media.

In the 1990s, the difference between the official budget and true military spending in China was considerable. In those days China's armed forces received significant additional funds from their own business activities, and China's defence industry received massive government subsidies. During the past decade, however, as the official budget has risen by more than 10% per year, the likely gap between the official budget and true spending has narrowed considerably. Whatever the true extent of China's military-related spending – and the Chinese govern-

ment continues to insist that no spending exists outside of the official budget – the continued fine-tuning of differing methodologies to determine a definitive figure, particularly one expressed in US dollars, is becoming a less revealing exercise than in the past.

Note: The use of PPP rates is a valid tool when comparing macroeconomic data, such as GDP, between countries at different stages of development. However, no specific PPP rate exists for the military sector, and its use for this purpose should be treated with caution. Furthermore, there is no definitive guide as to which elements of military spending should be calculated using the limited PPP rates available. The figures presented here are only intended to illustrate a range of possible outcomes depending on which input variables are used.

Australia AUS

Australian Dollar A$		2008	2009	2010
GDP	A$	1.18tr	1.23tr	
	US$	992bn	1,119bn	
per capita	US$	47,242	52,632	
Growth	%	2.5	0.7	
Inflation	%	4.4	1.9	
Def exp[a]	A$	26.4bn	30.3bn	
	US$	22.21bn	27.6bn	
Def bdgt	A$	23.2bn	26.4bn	27.0bn
	US$	19.6bn	24.2bn	
US$1=A$		1.19	1.10	

[a] Including military pensions

Population   21,262,641

Age	0–14	15–19	20–24	25–29	30–64	65 plus
Male	10%	4%	3%	3%	24%	6%
Female	10%	3%	3%	3%	23%	7%

Capabilities

ACTIVE 54,747 (Army 27,461 Navy 13,230 Air 14,056)

RESERVE 19,915 (Army 15,315 Navy 2,000 Air 2,600)

The High Readiness Reserve of 2,800 army and 1,400 air force personnel is intended to strengthen the Australian Defence Force (ADF) with members trained to the same skill levels as the Regular Force. Integrated units are formed from a mix of reserve and regular personnel. All ADF operations are now controlled by Headquarters Joint Operations Command (HQJOC).

ORGANISATIONS BY SERVICE

Army 27,461

The army intends (under its Adaptive Army initiative) to reorganise into a structure consisting of Army HQ and three functional commands: HQ 1 Div; Special Operations Command and Forces Command.

Land Command

FORCES BY ROLE

1 Land HQ, 1 Deployable Joint Force HQ, 1 Logistic Support Force HQ

Mech	1 bde HQ (1st) (1 armd regt, 1 recce regt, 2 (5th, 7th.) mech inf bn 1 med arty regt, 1 cbt engr regt, 1 cbt spt regt, 1 cbt service spt bn)
Lt Inf	1 bde HQ (3rd) 3 inf bn, 1 IMV sqn (provides 2 coy lift), 1 fd arty regt, 1 cbt engr regt, 1 cbt spt regt, 1 cbt service spt bn)
Mot Inf	1 bde HQ (7th) (1 recce regt, 2 mot inf bn, (incl 1 lt inf bn (8/9th) op by 2010), 1 fd arty regt, 1 cbt engr regt, 1 cbt spt regt, 1 cbt service spt bn)

Surv	3 (regional force) integrated units
EW	1 (7th) regt
Int	1 bn
Avn	1 bde HQ (16th) (1 avn regt (6th) (1 Special Ops sqn, 1 (FW) surv sqn), 1 avn regt (1st) (2 recce hel sqn), 1 avn regt (5th) (2 tpt hel sqn, 1 spt hel sqn))
STA	1 (20th) regt (1 STA bty, 1 UAV bty, 1 CSS bty)
CSS	1 bde HQ (17th) (3 log bn, 3 health bn (integrated))
AD	1 regt (16th) (integrated)
Engr	2 construction sqn, 1 Topo sqn

Special Operations Command

FORCES BY ROLE

1 Special Operations HQ. 1 SF trg centre located at Singleton.

SF	1 SAS regt
Cdo	2 bn (1st, 2nd) (2nd formerly 4th RAR)
Incident Response	1 regt
Sigs	3 sqn (incl 1 reserve)
CSS	1 Sqn

EQUIPMENT BY TYPE

MBT 149: 59 M1-A1 *Abrams*; 90 *Leopard 1* A3 in store (decommissioned awaiting disposal)

AIFV (W) 257 ASLAV-25 (all variants)

APC APC (T) 774: 647 M-113A1 (350 to be upgraded to AS3), 119 in store; 8 M-113AS4 (Test)

LFV 697 *Bushmaster* IMV

ARTY 566

  TOWED 270: **105mm** 234: 109 L-118 Light Gun; **155mm** 36 M-198

  MOR 81mm 296

AT • MSL • MANPATS *Javelin*

  RCL 651: **84mm** 577 *Carl Gustav*; **106mm** 74 M-40A1

AMPHIBIOUS 21: 15 LCM-8 (capacity either 1 MBT or 200 troops); 6 LCM-2000 (not yet operational)

AIRCRAFT • TPT 3 Beech 350 B300 (on lease)

HELICOPTERS 22 attack helicopters

  ATK 22 AS-665 *Tiger* (all delivered by end 2010)

  SPT 44: 6 CH-47D *Chinook*; 34 S-70 A-9 (S-70A) *Black Hawk*; 4 MRH-90 TTH (NH-90) (ongoing delivery of 40)

  UTL 66: 41 Bell 206B-1 *Kiowa* (being replaced by *Tiger*); 20 UH-1H *Iroquois* in store (decommissioned)

UAV 18

AD • SAM 48

  MANPAD 30 RBS-70

RADAR • LAND 21: 7 AN/TPQ-36 *Firefinder* (arty, mor); 14 RASIT (veh, arty)

Training Command 3,160

Reserve Organisations

Land Command 17,200 reservists

FORCES BY ROLE

Comd	6 bde HQ

Inf	6 bde HQ (4/5/8/9/11/13) each with (1 -2 inf bn, 1 recce unit, CS, CSS units)
Engr	2 construction regt

Navy 13,230

EQUIPMENT BY TYPE

SUBMARINES • TACTICAL • SSK 6 *Collins* each with UGM-84C *Harpoon* tactical USGW, 6 single 533mm TT each with Mk48 *Sea Arrow* ADCAP HWT

PRINCIPAL SURFACE COMBATANTS • FRIGATES 12
  FFG 4 *Adelaide* (Mod) with 1 Mk 13 GMLS with RGM-84C *Harpoon* SSM, SM-2 MR naval SAM, 1 8 cell Mk 41 VLS (32 eff.) with up to 32 RIM-162 Evolved *Sea Sparrow* naval SAM, 2 Mk32 triple 324mm ASTT with MU90 LWT, 1 76mm gun, (capacity 2 S-70B *Seahawk* ASW hel)
  FF 8 *Anzac* (GER MEKO 200) each with 2 Mk 141 *Harpoon* quad (8 eff.) each with RGM-84C *Harpoon* tactical SSM, 1 8 cell Mk 41 VLS (32 eff.) each with up to 32 RIM-162 *Evolved Sea Sparrow* naval SAM, 2 triple 324mm ASTT with MU 90 LWT, 1 127mm, (capacity 1 SH-2G *Super Seasprite* ASW hel), (capability upgrades in progress)

PATROL AND COASTAL COMBATANTS • PCO 14 *Armidale* each with 1 25mm gun

MINE WARFARE • MINE COUNTERMEASURES 11
  MHC 6 *Huon*
  MSC 2 *Bandicoot* (reserve status)
  MSD 3

AMPHIBIOUS
  PRINCIPAL AMPHIBIOUS SHIPS • LPH 2:
    2 *Kanimbla* (capacity either 4 UH-60 *Black Hawk* utl hel or 3 *Sea King* MK-50A utl hel; 2 LCM; 21 MBT; 450 troops)
  LS • LST 1 *Tobruk* (capacity 2 *Sea King* MK-50A utl hel; 2 LCM; 2 LCVP; 40 APC and 18 MBT; 500 troops)
  LANDING CRAFT 6:
    LCH 6 *Balikpapan* (capacity 3 MBT or 13 APC)

LOGISTICS AND SUPPORT 23
  AORH 2: 1 *Success*; 1 *Sirius*
  AOL 4 *Warrigal*
  AE 3 *Wattle*
  ASR 3
  AGHS (SVY) 2 *Leeuwin*
  AGS 4 *Paluma*
  TRG 2: 1 **AXL**; 1 **AXS**
  TRV 3

Naval Aviation 990

FORCES BY ROLE

ASW	1 sqn
ASuW	1 sqn
Trg/Spt	1 sqn

EQUIPMENT BY TYPE

HELICOPTERS 40
ASW 16 S-70B-2 *Seahawk*
MAR SPT 8: 6 *Sea King* MK50A; 2 MRH-90 (NH-90) (additional ac on order)
SPT/TRG 16: 13 AS-350BA *Ecureuil*; 3 Agusta A109E

FACILITIES

Bases Located at Sydney (NSW), Darwin (NT), Cairns (QLD), Garden Island (WA), Jervis Bay (NSW), Nowra (NSW), Flinders(SA).

Fleet Command

Navy 1 HQ located at Stirling

Naval Systems Comd

Navy 1 HQ located at Canberra

Air Force 14,056

Flying hours   175 hrs/year on F/A-18 *Hornet* FGA; 200 hrs/year on F-111 *Aardvark* bbr ac

FORCES BY ROLE

Air Comd coordinates air force operations. HQ Air Comd is responsible for developing and delivering the capability to command and control air operations. The air commander controls the activities of six subordinate Force Element Groups – Air Cbt, Air Lift, Aerospace Ops Support, Combat Support, Surveillance and Response, Air Force Training.

Air cbt	1 gp (135 ac and 2,000 personnel) with (1 recce/strike wg (2 FGA/recce sqn with F-111C *Aardvark*; RF-111 *Aardvark* (photo recce); (F/A-18F *Super Hornet* to replace F-111 from 2010); (1 ftr/tac wg (1 OCU, 3 ftr sqn with F/A-18A *Hornet*/F/A-18B *Hornet*), 2 LIFT sqn with *Hawk* MK127)); 1 fwd air cbt dev unit with PC-9/A(F)
Surv/ Response	1 gp with (1 wg (2 sqn, 1 OCU) with AP-3C *Orion*; 1 sqn with Boeing 737-700 *'Wedgetail'* AEW&C (being delivered); 1 control and reporting wg with 4 tactical AD radars; 1 radar surv unit with *Jindalee* Operational Radar Network correlation centre at Edinburgh (S. Australia), 2 *Jindalee* radar sensors at Laverton (W.Australia) and Longreach (N. Queensland); 1 *Jindalee* facility at Alice Springs; 2 AD Command & Control Centres at Williamtown (NSW) and Tindal (NT))
SAR	S-76 (civil contract) at 4 air bases
Airlift	1 gp (2 wg): 1 tkr/tpt sqn with KC-30B MRTT (being delivered); 1 special purpose/VIP tpt sqn with B-737 BBJ; CL-604 *Challenger*, 1 sqn with C-17; 1 medium tac tpt sqn with C-130H *Hercules*/C-130J *Hercules*)
Trg	Air trg wg manages: Basic Flying Training School (Tamworth) PC-9/A; No 2 Flying Training School (Pearce) PC-9/A; Combat Survival and Training School (Townsville); Central Flying School and Roulettes Aerobatic Team (East Sale); School of Aviation Warfare (East Sale); School of Air Traffic Control (East Sale); and No 32 Squadron with 8 Beech 300 *Super King Air* (navigation trg) (East Sale). Flt trg sch with 58 PC-9/A
Cbt spt	2 cbt spt wgs; 1 Expeditionary cbt spt wg; 1 airfield def wg (3 sqn); 1 Health Services Wg

Reserve Training Wing 13 Sqn (Darwin); 21 Sqn (Williams); 22 Sqn (Richmond); 23 Sqn (Amberley); 24 Sqn (Edinburgh); 25 Sqn (Perth); 26 Sqn (Williamtown); 27 Sqn (Townsville); 28 Sqn (Canberra); 29 Sqn (Hobart).

EQUIPMENT BY TYPE

AIRCRAFT 109 combat capable
BBR 15: 15 F-111C *Aardvark*; (24 F/A-18F *Super Hornet* from 2010)
RECCE 4 RF-111C *Aardvark**
FGA 71: 55 F/A-18A *Hornet*; 16 F/A-18B *Hornet*
LIFT 33 *Hawk* Mk127
MP 19 AP-3C *Orion**
AWACS 6 B-737 *Wedgetail* (being delivered)
TPT 33: 4 C-17 *Globemaster*; (5 KC-30B MRTT being delivered); 2 B-737 BBJ (VIP); 12 C-130H *Hercules*; 12 C-130J *Hercules*; 3 CL-604 *Challenger* (VIP)
TRG 70: 62 PC-9/A (incl 4 PC-9/A(F) for tgt marking); 8 Beech 300 *Super King Air* (navigation trg);
HELICOPTERS • UTL 5–7 S-76 (civil contract)
RADAR • AD RADAR 8
OTH-B *Jindalee* 4
Tactical 4
MSL • TACTICAL •
ASM AGM-84A *Harpoon*; AGM-142E *Raptor*; AGM-158 JASSM (on order)
AAM AIM-120 AMRAAM; AIM-9M *Sidewinder*; AIM-132 ASRAAM: AIM-7M *Sparrow*;
BOMBS
Conventional Mk 82 500lb GP; Mk 84 2,000lb GP; BLU-109/B 2,000lb penetrator
Laser-guided *Paveway* II/IV
INS/GPS guided JDAM (on order)

Paramilitary

Border Protection Command

Border Protection Command (BPC), has assumed responsibility for operational coordination and control of both civil and military maritime enforcement activities within Australia's Exclusive Economic Zone (EEZ). The BPC is staffed by military and civilian officials from Defence, Customs, the Australian Fisheries Management Authority (AFMA) and the Australian Quarantine Inspection Service (AQIS).
PATROL AND COASTAL COMBATANTS 10:
PSOH 1 *Triton*
PSO 1
PCC 8 *Bay*
AIRCRAFT
MP/Surv 14: 6 BN-2B *Islander*; 5 DHC-8 *Dash 8*; 3 F406 *Caravan II*
SAR 1 AC50 *Shrike*
HELICOPTERS • UTL 1 Bell 206L *LongRanger*; 1 Bell 214

DEPLOYMENT

AFGHANISTAN

NATO • ISAF 1,350; 1 inf BG with (1 mot inf coy; 1 armd recce sqn); 1 cdo BG with (elm 2 cdo bn); elms 1 arty regt; 1 hel gp with 2 CH-47D; 1 UAV det with *Scaneagle*; 25 *Bushmaster* IMV
UN • UNAMA 1 obs

ARABIAN GULF AND INDIAN OCEAN

Maritime Security Operations 1 FF; 1 AP-3C *Orion*

EGYPT

MFO (*Operation Mazurka*) 25

IRAQ

Army 80; 1 sy det
UN • UNAMI 2 obs

MALAYSIA

Army 115; 1 inf coy (on 3-month rotational tours)
Air force 13; 1 AP-3C *Orion* crew

MIDDLE EAST

UN • UNTSO 11 obs;
Air Force 313; 1 tpt det with 3 C-130 *Hercules*; 1 MP det with 2 AP-3C *Orion*

PAPUA NEW GUINEA

Army 38; 1 trg unit

SOLOMON ISLANDS

RAMSI (*Operation Anode*) 80; 1 inf pl; 4 OH-58 *Kiowa*; 2 S-70 *Black Hawk*; 2 *Armidale* PCO; 2 DHC-4 *Caribou*

SUDAN

UN • UNMIS 9; 6 obs

TIMOR LESTE

ISF (*Operation Astute*) 650 1 inf bn HQ; 2 inf coy; 1 AD bty; elm 1 cbt engr regt; 1 hel det with 4 S-70 *Black Hawk*; 3 C-130
UN • UNMIT 3 obs

FOREIGN FORCES

New Zealand Army: 9 (air navigation) trg
Singapore Air Force 230: 1 school located at Pearce with PC-21 trg ac; 1 op trg sqn located at Oakey with 12 AS-332 *Super Puma* Spt/AS-532 *Cougar* utl
United States US Pacific Command: Army 29; Navy 21; USAF 63; USMC 25; 1 SEWS located at Pine Gap; 1 comms facility located at NW Cape; 1 SIGINT stn located at Pine Gap

Brunei BRN

Brunei Dollar B$		2008	2009
GDP	B$	20.4bn	
	US$	14.5bn	
per capita	US$	37,937	
Growth	%	-1.5	0.2
Inflation	%	2.7	1.2
Def bdgt	B$	508m	ε550
	US$	360m	ε395m
US$1=B$		1.41	1.39

Population 388,190

Ethnic groups: Malay, Kedayan, Tutong, Belait, Bisaya, Dusun, Murut 66.3%; Chinese 11.2%; Iban, Dayak, Kelabit 6%; Other 11.8%

Age	0–14	15–19	20–24	25–29	30–64	65 plus
Male	15%	5%	4%	5%	22%	1%
Female	14%	4%	4%	4%	19%	2%

Capabilities

ACTIVE 7,000 (Army 4,900 Navy 1,000 Air 1,100)
Paramilitary 2,250

RESERVE 700 (Army 700)

ORGANISATIONS BY SERVICE

Army 4,900

FORCES BY ROLE
Inf 3 bn
Spt 1 bn (1 armd recce sqn, 1 engr sqn)
Reserves 1 bn

EQUIPMENT BY TYPE
LT TK 20 Scorpion (16 to be upgraded)
APC (W) 39 VAB
ARTY • MOR 81mm 24
AT • RL 67mm Armbrust

Navy 1,000

FORCES BY ROLE
SF 1 sqn

EQUIPMENT BY TYPE
PATROL AND COASTAL COMBATANTS 16+
PFM 3 Waspada each with 2 MM-38 Exocet tactical SSM
PFI 3 Perwira
PBI 3 Bendahara
PBR 7 (various)
AMPHIBIOUS • CRAFT 4 LCU

Air Force 1,100

FORCES BY ROLE
MP 1 sqn with 1 CN-235M
Trg 1 sqn with 4 PC-7 Turbo Trainer; 2 SF-260W Warrior; 2 Bell 206B Jet Ranger II
Hel 1 sqn with 5 Bo-105 (armed, 81mm rockets); 1 sqn with 4 S-70A Black Hawk; 1 S-70C Black Hawk (VIP); 10 Bell 212; 1 Bell 214 (SAR)

AD 2 sqn with 12 Rapier each with Blindfire; 16 Mistral

EQUIPMENT BY TYPE
AIRCRAFT
MP 1 CN-235M
TRG 6: 4 PC-7 Turbo Trainer; 2 SF-260W Warrior
HELICOPTERS
SPT 5: 4 S-70A Black Hawk; 1 S-70C Black Hawk (VIP)
UTL 18: 5 Bo-105 (armed, 81mm rockets); 2 Bell 206B Jet Ranger II; 10 Bell 212; 1 Bell 214 (SAR)
AD • SAM 28: 12 Rapier each with Blindfire; 16 Mistral

Paramilitary ε2,250

Gurkha Reserve Unit 400-500
2 bn

Royal Brunei Police 1,750
PATROL AND COASTAL COMBATANTS
PCI 7 less than 100 tonnes

DEPLOYMENT

LEBANON
UN • UNIFIL 7

PHILIPPINES
Army: 30 (awaiting potential IMT reactivation)

FOREIGN FORCES

Singapore Army: 1 trg camp with infanty units on rotation Air Force; trg school; 1 hel det with Super Puma
United Kingdom Army: 550; 1 Gurkha bn; 1 trg unit; 1 hel flt with 3 hel

Cambodia CAM

Cambodian Riel r		2008	2009	2010
GDP	r	44.9tr	42.6tr	
	US$	11.1bn	10.2bn	
per capita	US$	778	706	
Growth	%	6.7	-2.7	
Inflation	%	25.0	-0.6	
Def bdgt	r	1.03tr	929bn	1.41tr
	US$	254m	222m	
US$1=r		4,054	4,167	

Population 14,494,293

Ethnic groups: Khmer 90%; Vietnamese 5%; Chinese 1%

Age	0–14	15–19	20–24	25–29	30–64	65 plus
Male	18%	7%	6%	3%	14%	1%
Female	18%	6%	5%	3%	16%	2%

Capabilities

ACTIVE 124,300 (Army 75,000 Navy 2,800 Air 1,500 Provincial Forces 45,000) Paramilitary 67,000

East Asia and Australasia

Terms of service conscription authorised but not implemented since 1993

ORGANISATIONS BY SERVICE

Army ε75,000

FORCES BY ROLE

6 Military Regions (incl 1 special zone for capital)

Armd	3 bn
Recce	some indep bn
Inf	22 div (established str 3,500; actual str uner 1,500); 3 indep bde; 9 indep regt
AB/SF	1 regt
Arty	some bn
Protection	1 bde (4 bn)
Engr construction	1 regt
Fd engr	3 regt
AD	some bn

EQUIPMENT BY TYPE

MBT 150+: 50 Type-59; 100+ T-54/T-55
LT TK 20+: Type-62; 20 Type-63
RECCE BRDM-2
AIFV 70 BMP-1
APC 190+
  APC (T) M-113
  APC (W) 190: 160 BTR-60/BTR-152; 30 OT-64
ARTY 428+
  TOWED 400+ **76mm** ZIS-3 *M-1942*/**122mm** D-30 /**122mm** M-30 *M-1938* /**130mm** Type-59-I
  MRL 28+: **107mm** Type-63; **122mm** 8 BM-21; **132mm** BM-13-16 (BM-13); **140mm** 20 BM-14-16 (BM-14)
  MOR 82mm M-37; **120mm** M-43; **160mm** M-160
AT • RCL 82mm B-10; **107mm** B-11
AD • GUNS • TOWED 14.5mm ZPU-1/ZPU-2/ZPU-4; **37mm** M-1939; **57mm** S-60

Navy ε2,800 (incl. 1,500 Naval Infantry)

EQUIPMENT BY TYPE
PATROL AND COASTAL COMBATANTS 11
  PFC 2 *Stenka*
  PCR 2 *Kaoh Chhlam*
  PB 7: 4 (PRC 46m); 3 (PRC 20m)
FACILITIES
Bases Located at Phnom Penh (river), Ream (maritime)

Naval Infantry 1,500

Inf	7 bn
Arty	1 bn

Air Force 1,500

FORCES BY ROLE

Ftr	1 sqn with 14 MiG-21bis *Fishbed L & N†*; 5 MiG-21UM *Mongol B†* (up to 9 to be upgraded by IAI: 2 returned but status unclear)
Recce/trg	some sqn with 5 P-92 *Echo* (pilot trg/recce); 5 L-39 *Albatros** (lead-in trg)
Tpt	1 (VIP (reporting to Council of Ministers)) sqn with 2 An-24RV *Coke*; 1 AS-350 *Ecureuil*; 1 AS-365 *Dauphin 2*; 1 sqn with 1 BN-2 *Islander*; 1 Cessna 421; 2 Y-12
Hel	1 sqn with 1 Mi-8P *Hip K* (VIP); 2 Mi-26 *Halo*; 13 Mi-17 (Mi-8MT) *Hip H*/Mi-8 *Hip*

EQUIPMENT BY TYPE
AIRCRAFT 24 combat capable
  FTR 14 MiG-21bis *Fishbed L & N†*
  TPT 6: 2 An-24RV *Coke*; 1 BN-2 *Islander*; 1 Cessna 421; 2 Y-12
  UTL 5 P-92 *Echo* (pilot trg/recce)
  TRG 10: 5 L-39 *Albatros** (lead-in trg); 5 MiG-21UM *Mongol B**†
HELICOPTERS • SPT 18: 1 AS-350 *Ecureuil*; 2 Mi-26 *Halo*; 13 MI-17 (Mi-8MT) *Hip H*/Mi-8 *Hip*; 1 Mi-8P *Hip* (VIP); 1 AS-365 *Dauphin 2*

Provincial Forces 45,000+

Reports of at least 1 inf regt per province, with varying numbers of inf bn with lt wpn

Paramilitary

Police 67,000 (including gendarmerie)

DEPLOYMENT

SUDAN
UN • UNMIS 53; 5 obs; 1 de-mining coy
UN • UNAMID 5 obs

China, People's Republic of PRC

Chinese Yuan Renminbi Y		2008	2009	2010
GDP	Y	30.68tr	33.22tr	
	US$	4.42tr	4.86tr	
per capita	US$	3,324	3,634	
Growth	%	9.0	8.5	
Inflation	%	5.9	-0.1	
Def exp[a]	US$	See text page 391		
Def bdgt[b]	Y	417bn	480bn	
	US$	60.1bn	70.3bn	
US$1=Y		6.94	6.83	

[a] PPP estimate including extra-budgetary military expenditure
[b] Official defence budget at market exchange rates

Population 1,338,612,968

Ethnic groups: Tibetan, Uighur and other non-Han 8%

Age	0–14	15–19	20–24	25–29	30–64	65 plus
Male	11%	5%	4%	4%	24%	4%
Female	10%	5%	4%	4%	23%	4%

Capabilities

ACTIVE 2,285,000 (Army 1,600,000 Navy 255,000
Air 300,000-330,000 Strategic Missile Forces 100,000)
Paramilitary 660,000

Terms of service selective conscription; all services 2 years

RESERVE ε510,000

Overall organisation: Army leadership is exercised by the
four general headquarters/departments. A military region
exercises direct leadership over the Army units under it.
The Army has 18 combined corps, which are mobile combat
troops. Each of the Navy, Air Force and Second Artillery
Force have a leading body consisting of the headquarters,
political department, logistics department and armaments
department. These direct the military, political, logistical
and equipment work of their respective troops, and take
part in the command of joint operations.

ORGANISATIONS BY SERVICE

Strategic Missile Forces (100,000+)

Offensive

The Second Artillery Force organises and commands
its own troops to launch nuclear counterattacks with
strategic missiles and to conduct operations with
conventional missiles. It comprises missile and training
bases, and relevant support troops

Org as 27 launch bdes subordinate to 6 army-level msl
bases; org varies by msl type; one testing and one trg
base

MSL • STRATEGIC 442

    ICBM 66: ε12 DF-31 (CSS-9) (1 bde); ε24 DF31A (CSS-
9 Mod 2) (2 bde); ε10 DF-4 (CSS-3) (1 bde); 20 DF-5A
(CSS-4 Mod 2) (3 bdes)

    IRBM 118: ε80 DF-21 (CSS-5) (5 bde); ε36 DF21C (CSS-
5 Mod 3) (2 bde); ε2 DF-3A (CSS-2 Mod) (1 bde)

    SRBM 204
        108 DF-11A/M-11A (CSS-7 Mod 2) (4 bde); 96 DF-
15/M-9 (CSS-6) (6 bde)

    LACM ε54 CJ-10 (DH-10); (2 bde)

Navy

SUBMARINES • STRATEGIC • SSBN 3:
    1 *Xia* equiped with 12 JL-1 (CSS-N-3) strategic SLBM
    2 *Jin* equiped with up to 12 JL-2 (CSS-NX-4) strategic
SLBM (full operational status unknown; 3rd and 4th
vessels in build)

Defensive

RADAR • STRATEGIC: some phased array radar; some
detection and tracking radars (covering Central Asia and
Shanxi (northern border)) located at Xinjiang

People's Liberation Army ε800,000; ε800,000
conscript (reductions continue) (total
1,600,000)

Ground forces are organised into eight service arms
(branches)—infantry, armour, artillery, air defence, aviation,

engineering, chemical defence and communications—as
well as other specialised units, including electronic countermeasures (ECM), reconnaissance and mapping. 7 military
region comds are sub-divided into 28 Military Districts.
18 Group Armies, org varies, normally with 2–3 mech/
mot inf div/bde, 1 armd div/bde, 1 arty div/bde, 1 SAM/
AAA or AAA bde (reorg to bde structure still in progress).
Five Regions have rapid reaction units (RRU). The PLA
Air Force has 3 RRU airborne divisions and the Navy two
marine bde. 31st, 38th, 39th, 42nd and 54th GA have received
air regiments that have in the past been MR or MD assets.

North East–Shenyang MR ε250,000

3 Group Army (16, 39, 40) (Heilongjiang, Jilin, Liaoning
MD): 1 GA (16) (1 armd div, 2 mot inf div, 2 mot inf
bde, 2 arty bde, 1 AD bde, 1 engr regt); 1 GA (39) (1
armd div, 2 mech inf div, 1 mech inf bde, 1 arty bde, 1
AD bde, 1 avn regt); 1 GA (40) (1 armd bde, 1 mech inf
bde, 1 mot inf bde, 1 arty bde, 1 AD bde, 1 engr regt); 1
mot inf bde; 1 EW regt; 1 spec ops unit.

North–Beijing MR ε300,000

3 Group Army (27, 38, 65) (Beijing, Tianjin Garrison,
Inner Mongolia, Hebei, Shanxi MD): 1 GA (27) (1 armd
bde, 3 mech inf bde, 1 mot inf bde, 1 arty bde, 1 AD bde,
1 engr regt); 1 GA (38) (1 armd div, 2 mech inf div, 1
arty bde, 1 AD bde, 1 engr regt, 1 avn regt); 1 GA (65)
(1 armd div, 1 mot inf div, 1 mot inf bde, 1 arty bde, 1
AD bde, 1 engr regt, 1 avn regt); 2 (Beijing) sy div; 1
(OPFOR) armd bde; 1 mot inf bde; 1 spec ops unit; 1
AAA bde.

West–Lanzhou MR ε220,000

2 Group Army (21, 47) (Ningxia, Shaanxi, Gansu, Qing-
hai, Xinjiang, South Xinjiang MD): 1 GA (21) (1 armd
div, 1 mot inf div (RRU), 1 arty bde, 1 AD bde, 1 engr
regt); 1 GA (47) (1 armd bde, 1 mech inf bde, 2 mtn mot
inf bde, 1 arty bde, 1 AD bde, 1 engr regt); Xinjiang (1
mtn mech div, 3 mtn mot div, 1 arty bde, 1 AD bde, 2
indep mech inf regt, 1 engr regt, 1 avn regt); 1 EW regt,
1 spec ops unit.

East–Nanjing MR ε250,000

3 Group Army (1, 12, 31) (Shanghai Garrison, Jiangsu,
Zhejiang, Fujian, Jiangxi, Anhui MD): 1 GA (1) (1 armd
bde, 1 amph div, 1 arty div, 1 mot inf bde , 1 AD bde, 1
engr regt, 1 avn regt); 1 GA (12) (1 armd div, 3 mot inf
bde (1 RRU), 1 arty bde, 1 AD bde, 1 engr regt); 1 GA
(31) (2 mot div (1 RRU) , 1 amph armd bde , 1 mot inf
bde, 1 arty bde, 1 AD bde, 1 avn regt); 1 SSM bde; 1 spec
ops unit.

Centre–Jinan MR ε190,000

3 Group Army (20, 26, 54) (Shandong, Henan MD): 1 GA
(1 mech inf bde, 1 mot inf bde, 1 arty bde, 1 AD bde, 1
engr regt); 1 GA (26) (1 armd div, 3 mot inf bde, 1 arty
bde, 1 AD bde, 1 avn regt); 1 GA (54) (1 armd div, 1
mech inf div (RRU), 1 mot inf div (RRU), 1 arty bde,
1 AD bde, 1 avn regt); 1 EW regt, 1 spec ops unit, 2
pontoon br regt.

South–Guangzhou MR ε180,000

2 Group Army (41, 42) (Hubei, Hunan, Guangdong, Guangxi, Hainan MD): 1 GA (41) (1 mech inf div(RRU), 1 mot inf div, 1 armd bde, 1 arty bde, 1 AD bde, 1 engr regt); 1 GA (42) (1 mot inf div, 1 amph asslt div (RRU), 1 arty div, 1 armd bde, 1 AD bde, 1 avn regt); 1 EW regt, 1 mot inf bde, 1 SAM bde; 1 pontoon br bde, 1 (composite) mot inf bde (Composed of units drawn from across the PLA and deployed to Hong Kong on a rotational basis); 1 SSM bde; 1 spec ops unit

South-West–Chengdu MR ε180,000

2 Group Army (13,14) (Chongqing Garrison, Sichuan, Guizhou, Yunnan, Tibet MD): 1 GA(13) (1 mtn mech inf div (RRU), 1 mot inf div, 1 armd bde, 1 arty bde, 1 AD bde, 1 avn regt, 1 engr regt); 1 GA (14) (1 jungle mot inf, 1 mot inf div, 1 armd bde, 1 arty bde, 1 AD bde); 2 indep mtn inf bde; 1 EW regt, 1 spec ops unit.

FORCES BY ROLE

Comd	7 mil regions (MR)
Armd	8 div, 8 bde, 1 (OPFOR) bde
Mech Inf	6 inf div, 7 mech inf bde, 2 indep regt
Mot Inf	11 mot inf div, 17 mot inf bde
Mtn Inf	2 (mech) inf div, 3 (mot) inf div, 4 (mot) bde
AB	1 (manned by AF) corps with (3 AB div (35,000)
Amph	2 amph aslt div, 1 armd bde
Jungle Inf	1 (mot) div
Spec Ops	7 units
Arty	2 arty div, 16 arty bde
SSM	2 indep bde; 9 (coastal defence) regt
AD	21 bde, 1 indep regt
Engr	13 engr regt, 1 indep bde, 1 pontoon br bde, 2 pontoon br regt
EW	5 regt
Sigs	50 regt
Avn	1 bde; 9 avn regt, 2 (indep) regt (trg)
Security	2 (Guard) div

EQUIPMENT BY TYPE

MBT 6,550+: 4,000+ Type-59-II/Type-59-I; 300 Type-79; 500 Type-88A/Type-88B; 1,500 Type-96; ε250 Type-98A/99
LT TK 1,000: 400 Type-62-I (in store); 400 Type-63A; ε200 Type-05 AAAV *ZTD-05*
AIFV 1,140: 600 Type-86A WZ-501; 300+ Type-04 *ZBD-04*; ε200 Type-05 AAAV ZBD-05; 40 Type-03 ZBD-03
APC 3,300+
    APC (T) 2,500: 2,000 Type-63-II/Type-63-I/Type-63A/Type-63C; 200 Type-77-II; 300 Type-89-I
    APC (W) 800+: 600+ Type-92; 100 WZ-523; 100 Type-09 *ZBL-09*
ARTY 17,700+
    SP 1,280+: **122mm** 700+: ε200 Type-70-I; ε500 Type-89; some Type-07 PLZ-07 **152mm** ε500 Type-83; **155mm** ε80 Type-05 PLZ-05
    TOWED 14,000: 13,850 **100mm** Type-59 (M-1944)/**122mm** Type-54-1 (M-30) *M-1938*/Type-83/Type-60 (D-74)/Type-96 (D-30); **130mm** Type-59 (M-46)/Type-59-I/**152mm**

Type-54 (D-1)/Type-66 (D-20); **155mm** 150 Type 88 WAC-21
GUN/MOR 150: **120mm** 150: 100 2S23 *NONA-SVK*; up to 50 PLL-05
MRL 2,400+
    SP **122mm** Type-81/Type-82/Type-89; **130mm** Type 63/Type-70/Type 82; **300mm** Type-03 *PHL-03*; **400mm** WS-2/WS-2D
    TOWED **107mm** Type-81
MOR
    TOWED **81mm** Type-W87; **82mm** Type-53 (M-37)/Type-67 /Type-82; **100mm** Type-71 (reported); **120mm** Type-55 (incl SP); **160mm** Type-56 (M-160)
AT • MSL 7,200
    SP 24 HJ-9 *Red Arrow 9*
    MANPATS 7,176 HJ-73A/HJ-73B/HJ-73C/HJ-8A/HJ-8C/HJ-8E
    RCL **75mm** Type-56; **82mm** Type-65 (B-10)/Type-78; **105mm** Type-75; **120mm** Type-98
    RL **62mm** Type-70-1
    GUNS 260+: **100mm** Type-73 (T-12)/Type-86; ε160 Type-02 *PTL02* **120mm** 100+ Type-89 SP
HELICOPTERS
    ATK 126 100 Z-9 WA; 26 Z-9W
    SAR 7 SA-321 *Super Frelon*
    SPT 278: 53 AS-350 *Ecureuil*; 57 Mi-171; 9 Mi-171V; 42 Mi-171V5; 12 Mi-17V7; 8 Mi-172; 3 Mi-6 *Hook*; 18 S-70C2 (S-70C) *Black Hawk*; 22 Mi-17 (Mi-8MT) *Hip H*; 50 Mi-8T *Hip*; 4 Mi-26 *Halo*
    UTL 88+: 80 Z-9/9B (AS-365 *Dauphin 2*) 8 SA-316 *Alouette III*; Z-10
UAV ASN-15 (hand-launched); ASN-104; ASN-105; ASN-206; W-50; WZ-5; D-4 NPU (Xian NPU); WZ-6 *BZK-006*; BZK-005;
AD • SAM 290+:
    SP 290: 200 HQ-7A; 60 SA-15 *Gauntlet* (*Tor*-M1); 30 HQ-6D *Red Leader*
    MANPAD HN-5A/HN-5B *Hong Nu*; FN-6/QW-1/QW-2
    GUNS 7,700+
SP **25mm** Type-95; **37mm** Type-88; **57mm** Type-80
TOWED **23mm** Type-80 (ZU-23-2); **25mm** Type-85; **35mm** Type-90 (GDF-002); **37mm** Type-55 (M-1939)/Type-65/Type-74; **57mm** Type-59 (S-60); **85mm** Type-56 (M-1939) KS-12; **100mm** Type-59 (KS-19)
RADAR • LAND *Cheetah*; RASIT; Type-378
MSL • SSM HY-1 (CSS-N-1) *Silkworm*; HY-2 (CSS-C-3) *Seersucker*; HY-4 (CSS-C-7) *Sadsack* ; YJ-62C (C-602C)

Reserves

Inf	18 div; 3 bde; 3 regt
Arty	3 div; 6 bde
Engr	10 regt
AT	1 bde
AD	17 div; 6 bde; 6 regt
Logistic	8 bde
Sigs	10 regt
Chemical	8 Regt

Navy ε215,000; 40,000 conscript (total 255,000)

The PLA Navy organises and commands maritime operations conducted independently by its troops or in support of maritime operations. The PLA Navy is organised into five service arms: submarine, surface, naval aviation, coastal defence and marine corps, as well as other specialised units. There are three fleets, the Beihai Fleet (North Sea), Donghai Fleet (East Sea) and Nanhai Fleet (South Sea).

SUBMARINES 65

STRATEGIC • SSBN 3:

1 *Xia* equiped with 12 JL-1 (CSS-N-3) strategic SLBM

2 *Jin* equiped with up to 12 JL-2 (CSS-NX-4) strategic SLBM (full operational status unkown; 3rd and 4th vessels in build)

TACTICAL 62

SSN 6:

4 *Han* (Type 091) each with YJ-82 SSM, 6 single 533mm TT

2 *Shang* (Type 093), 6 single 533mm TT (full operational status unknown, 3rd vessel in build)

SSG 1 mod *Romeo* (Type SSG) with 6 YJ-1 (CSS-N-4) *Sardine* SSM, 8 single 533mm TT (test platform)

SSK 54:

12 *Kilo* each with SS-N-27 *Club* ASCM; 6 single 533mm TT with up to 18 *Test-71/96 HWT*

19 *Ming* (Imp, type ES5E) each with 8 single 533mm TT

8 *Romeo†* (Type ES3B) each with 8 533mm TT

13 *Song* each with YJ-82 (CSS-N-8) *Saccade* ASCM, 6 single 533mm TT

2 *Yuan* each with 6 533mm TT (undergoing sea trials, expected ISD 2010)

SS 1 *Golf* (SLBM trials)

PRINCIPAL SURFACE COMBATANTS 80

DESTROYERS • DDG 28:

4 *Hangzhou* (RF *Sovremenny*) each with 2 quad (8 eff.) each with SS-N-22 *Sunburn* SSM, 2 SA-N-7 *Grizzly* SAM, 2 twin 533mm ASTT (4 eff.), 2 RBU 1000 *Smerch* 3, 2 twin 130mm (4 eff.), (capacity either 1 Z-9C (AS-565SA) *Panther* ASW/ASUW hel or 1 Ka-28 *Helix* A ASW hel)

2 *Luzhou* each with 2 quad (8 eff.) YJ-83 (C-803) SSM; SA-N-20 *Grumble* SAM

2 *Luyang* each with 4 quad (16 eff.) each with YJ-83 SSM, 2 x24 (48 eff.) each with 48 SA-N-7 *Grizzly* SAM, 2 triple 324mm TT (6 eff.) each with Yu-7 LWT, 1 100mm, (capacity 1 Ka-28 *Helix* A ASW hel)

2 *Luyang II* each with 2 quad (8 eff.) each with YJ-62 SSM, 8 sextuple VLS (48 eff.) with total of 48 HHQ-9 SP SAM, 2 triple 324mm TT (6 eff.) each with Yu-7 LWT, 1 100mm, (capacity 2 Ka-28 *Helix* A ASW hel)

10 *Luda* Type-051 each with 2 triple 324mm ASTT (6 eff.), 2 FQF 2500 (24 eff.), 2 twin 130mm (4 eff.)

3 *Luda* mod Type-051DT each with 2 quad (8 eff.) each with YJ-1 (CSS-N-4) *Sardine* SSM, 1 octuple (8 eff.) with HQ-7 *Crotale* SAM, 2 FQF 2500 (24 eff.), 2 twin 130mm (4 eff.), mines (capability)

1 *Luda* II each with 2 triple 324mm ASTT (6 eff.), 2 triple (6 eff.) each with HY-2 (CSS-N-2) *Silkworm* SSM, 1 twin 130mm (2 eff.), (mine-laying capability), (capacity 2 Z-9C (AS-565SA) *Panther* ASW/ASUW hel)

1 *Luda* III with 2 triple (6 eff.) each with HY-2 (CSS-N-2) *Silkworm* SSM / YJ-1 (CSS-N-4) *Sardine* SSM, 4 twin (8 eff.) each with 2 YJ-1 (CSS-N-4) *Sardine* SSM, 2 triple 324mm ASTT (6 eff.), 2 twin 130mm (4 eff.)

1 *Luhai* with 4 quad (16 eff.) each with YJ-83 SSM, 1 octuple (8 eff.) with 8 HQ-7 SAM, 2 triple 324mm ASTT (6 eff.) each with Yu-7 LWT, 1 twin 100mm (2 eff.), (capacity either 2 Z-9C (AS-565SA) *Panther* ASW/ASUW hel or 2 Ka-28 *Helix* A ASW hel)

2 *Luhu* (Type 052A) each with 4 quad (16 eff.) each with YJ-83 SSM, 1 octuple (8 eff.) with HQ-7 SAM, 2 triple 324mm ASTT (6 eff.) each with Yu-7 LWT, 2 FQF 2500 (24 eff.), 1 twin 100mm (2 eff.), (capacity 2 Z-9C (AS-565SA) *Panther* ASW/ASUW hel)

FRIGATES • FFG 52:

11 *Jianghu* Type I each with 2 triple (6 eff.) each with 1 SY-1 (CSS-N-1) *Scrubbrush* SSM, 4 RBU 1200 (20 eff.), 2 100mm

9 *Jianghu* Type II each with 1 triple (3 eff.) with SY-1 (CSS-N-1) *Scrubbrush* SSM, 2 RBU 1200 (10 eff.), 1 twin 100mm (2 eff.), (capacity 1 Z-9C (AS-565SA) *Panther* ASW/ASUW hel)

3 *Jianghu* Type III each with 8 YJ-1 (CSS-N-4) *Sardine* SSM, 4 RBU 1200 (20 eff.), 2 twin 100mm (4 eff.)

1 *Jianghu* Type IV with 1 triple (3 eff.) with 1 SY-1 (CSS-N-1) *Scrubbrush* SSM, 4 RBU 1200 (20 eff.), 1 100mm, 1 Z-9C (AS-565SA) *Panther* ASW/ASUW hel

6 *Jianghu* Type V each with 1 triple (3 eff.) with SY-1 (CSS-N-1) *Scrubbrush* SSM, 2 RBU 1200 (10 eff.), 1 twin 100mm (2 eff.), (capacity 1 Z-9C (AS-565SA) *Panther* ASW/ASUW hel)

4 *Jiangwei* I each with 2 triple (6 eff.) each with 1 YJ-8 SSM, 1 sextuple (6 eff.) with 1 HQ-61 (CSA-N-2) SAM, 2 RBU 1200 (10 eff.), 1 twin 100mm (2 eff.), (capacity 2 Z-9C (AS-565SA) *Panther* ASW/ASUW hel)

10 *Jiangwei* II each with 2 quad (8 eff.) each with YJ-83 SSM, 1 octuple (8 eff.) with 1 HQ-7 SAM, 2 RBU 1200 (10 eff.), 2 100mm, (capacity 2 Z-9C (AS-565SA) *Panther* ASW/ASUW hel)

2 *Jiangkai* each with 2 quad (8 eff.) each with YJ-83 SSM, 1 octuple (8 eff.) with 1 HQ-7 SAM, 2 triple 324mm TT (6 eff.) each with Yu-7 LWT, 2 RBU 1200 (10 eff.), 1 100mm, (capacity either 1 Ka-28 *Helix* A ASW hel or 1 Z-9C (AS-565SA) *Panther* ASW/ASUW hel)

6 *Jiangkai* II each with 2 quad (8 eff.) each with YJ-83 SSM, 1 VLS (32 eff.) with HQ-16 SAM (reported), 2 triple 324mm TT (6 eff.) each with Yu-7 LWT, 2 RBU 1200 (10 eff.), 1 76mm gun, (capacity either 1 Ka-28 *Helix* A ASW hel or 1 Z-9C (AS-565SA) *Panther* ASW/ASUW hel)

PATROL AND COASTAL COMBATANTS 253

PFM 83:

16 *Houxin* each with 4 YJ-1 (CSS-N-4) *Sardine* SSM

7 *Houjian* each with 6 YJ-1 (CSS-N-4) *Sardine* SSM

60+ *Houbei* each with 4 YJ-82 (CSS-N-8) *Saccade* SSM

PFC 93 *Hainan* each with ε4 RBU 1200 (20 eff.)

PCC 27:

2 *Haijui* each with 4 RBU 1200 (20 eff.)

25 *Haiqing* each with 2 type-87 (12 eff.)

PCI 50: 15 *Haizui* less than 100 tonnes; 35 *Shanghai II* less than 100 tonnes
MINE WARFARE 69
  MINE COUNTERMEASURES 68
    MCMV 4 *Wochi*
    MSO 14 T-43
    MSC 4 *Wosao*
    MSD • **MSD INSHORE** 46: 4 *Futi*-class (Type 312); 42 in reserve
  MINELAYERS • **ML** 1 *Wolei*
AMPHIBIOUS
  PRINCIPAL AMPHIBIOUS VESSELS • **LPD** 1 *Yuzhao* (Type 071), (capacity 4 ACV plus supporting vehicles; 500 – 800 troops; 2 hel)
  LS 83
    LSM 56:
      1 *Yudao*
      1 *Yudeng* (capacity 6 tanks; 180 troops)
      13 *Yuhai* (capacity 2 tanks; 250 troops)
      31 *Yuliang* (capacity 5 tanks; 250 troops)
      10 *Yunshu* (capacity 6 tanks)
    LST 27:
      7 *Yukan* (capacity 10 tanks; 200 troops)
      10 *Yuting* (capacity 10 tanks; 250 troops; 2 hel)
      10 *Yuting* II (capacity 4 LCVP; 10 tanks; 250 troops)
  LC 160
    LCU 130:
      10 *Yubei* (capacity 10 tanks or 150 troops)
      120 *Yunnan*
    LCM 20 *Yuchin*
    ACV 10 **UCAC**
LOGISTICS AND SUPPORT 205
  AORH 5: 2 *Fuqing*; 2 *Fuchi*; 1 *Nanyun*
  AOT 50: 7 *Danlin*; 20 *Fulin*; 2 *Shengli*; 3 *Jinyou*; 18 *Fuzhou*
  AO L 5 *Guangzhou*
  AS 8: 1 *Dazhi*; 5 *Dalang*; 2 *Dazhou*
  ASR 1 *Dajiang* with 2 SA-321 *Super Frelon*
  ARS 2: 1 *Dadong*; 1 *Dadao*
  AG 6: 4 *Qiongsha* (capacity 400 troops); 2 *Qiongsha* (hospital conversion)
  AK 23: 2 *Yantai*; 2 *Dayun*; 6 *Danlin*; 7 *Dandao*; 6 *Hongqi*
  AWT 18: 10 *Leizhou*; 8 *Fuzhou*
  AGOR 5: 1 *Dahua*; 2 *Kan*; 1 *Bin Hai*; 1 *Shuguang*
  AGI 1 *Dadie*
  AGM 5 (space and missile tracking)
  AGS 6: 5 *Yenlai*; 1 *Ganzhu*
  AGB 4: 1 *Yanbing*; 3 *Yanha*
  ABU 7 *Yannan*
  ATF 51: 4 *Tuzhong*; 10 *Hujiu*; 1 *Daozha*; 17 *Gromovoy*; 19 *Roslavl*
  AH 1 *Daishan*
  TRG 2: 1 *Shichang*; 1 *Daxin*
  YDG 5 *Yen Pai*

Naval Aviation 26,000

FORCES BY ROLE

Bbr	2 regt with H-6D/H6M, 1 regt with H-6D/H-5
Ftr	1 regt with SU-30MK2, 1 regt with J-7E, 2 regt J-8I/J-8F, 1 regt with 24 J-7II
FGA	3 regt with JH-7A, 1 regt with JH-7A/Q-5C
ELINT/ Recce	1 regt with SH-5, 1 regt with Y-8J/Y-8JB
Tpt	2 regt with Y-8/Y-7
Trg	1 regt with HY-7/K-8; 1 regt with HY-7/ HJ-5; 1 regt with CJ-6; 1 regt with JJ-6/JJ-7

AIRCRAFT 290 combat capable
  BBR 50: 20 H-5,F-5,F-5B (Il-28) *Beagle* (torpedo-carrying lt bbr - mostly retired); 30 H-6D
  FTR 84: 48 J-8I/J-8F/J-8B/J-8D *Finback*; 36 J-7 (MiG-21F) *Fishbed C* (being retired)
  FGA 138: 84 JH-7; 30 Q-5 *Fantan*; 24 Su-30Mk2 *Flanker*; (J-6 has been retired)
  ASW 4 PS-5 (SH-5)
  RECCE 13: 7 HZ-5 (Il-28R) *Beagle*; 6 Y-8J/Y-8JB *Cub/ High New 2*
  MP 4 Y-8X
  TKR 3 HY-6
  TPT 66: 4 Y-8 (An-12BP) *Cub A*; 50 Y-5 (An-2) *Colt*; 4 Y-7 (An-24) *Coke*; 6 Y-7H (An-26) *Curl*; 2 Yak-42
  TRG 122: 14 JJ-6 (MiG-19UTI) *Farmer**; 4 JJ-7 *Mongol A**; 38 PT-6 (CJ-6); 21 HY-7; 12 K-8; 33 HJ-5
HELICOPTERS
  ASW/ASuW 25 Z-9C (AS-565SA) *Panther*
  SAR 40: 15 SA-321; 20 Z-8/Z-8A (SA-321Ja) *Super Frelon*; 2 Z-8S (SAR), 3 Z-8JH;
  ASW 13 Ka-28 (Ka-27PL) *Helix A* (6 additional ac on order)
  SPT 8 Mi-8 *Hip*
MSL • **TACTICAL** • **ASM** YJ-61 (CAS-1 (improved)) *Kraken*; YJ-8K (CSS-N-4) *Sardine*; YJ-83 (CSSC-8) *Saccade*
BOMBS
  Conventional: Type-200-4/Type-200A
  Laser-Guided: LS-500J;
  TV-Guided: KAB-500KR; KAB-1500KR

Marines ε10,000

FORCES BY ROLE

Marine inf 2 bde (*each*: 1 inf bn, 1 msl (AT/AD) bn, 3 mech inf bn, 1 amph recce coy, 1 arty bn, 2 tk bn; 1 comms bn, 1 eng bn); 1 spec ops unit

EQUIPMENT BY TYPE

LT TK 100+ Type-63/63A; ε60 Type-05 AAAV *ZTD-05*
  APC (T) 180+ Type-63C/Type-77 II/Type-86; ε200 Type-05 AAAV *ZBD-05*
ARTY • **TOWED 122mm** Type-83
  MRL 107mm Type-63
AT • **MSL** • **MANPATS** HJ-73; HJ-8; Type-98 *Queen Bee*
AD • **SAM** • **MANPAD** HN-5 *Hong Nu/Red Cherry*

North Sea Fleet

Coastal defence from DPRK border (Yalu River) to south of Lianyungang (approx 35°10′N); equates to Shenyang, Beijing and Jinan MR, and to seaward; 9 coastal defence districts

FORCES BY ROLE

Navy 1 HQ located at Qingdao

FACILITIES

Support bases Located at Lushun

East Sea Fleet

Coastal defence from south of Lianyungang to Dongshan (approx 35°10′N to 23°30′N); equates to Nanjing Military Region, and to seaward; 7 coastal defence districts

FORCES BY ROLE

Navy 1 HQ located at Dongqian Lake (Ninsbo)

FACILITIES

Bases Located at Fujian, Zhousnan, Dongqian Lake (Ninsbo)

South Sea Fleet

Coastal defence from Dongshan (approx 23°30′N) to VNM border; equates to Guangzhou MR, and to seaward (including Paracel and Spratly Islands)

FORCES BY ROLE

Navy 1 comd HQ located at Guangzhou

FACILITIES

Bases Located at Yulin, Guangzhou, Zuanjiang

Air Force 300,000-330,000

The PLA Air Force (PLAAF) is organised into four service branches: aviation, SAM, AAA and airborne. It also has comms, radar, ECM, chemical defence, tech recce and other specialised units. The PLAAF organises and commands air and AD operations throughout China, as well as airborne operations. The PLAAF organises its command through seven military region air forces (MRAF) – Shenyang, Beijing, Lanzhou, Jinan, Nanjing, Guangzhou and Chengdu – and 13 div-level command posts. Within a MRAF are aviation divisions, ground-to-air missile divisions (brigades and regiments), anti-aircraft artillery brigades (regiments), radar brigades (regiments) and other support troops.

29 air div (incl up to 4 regt, each with 10–15 ac, 1 maint unit, some tpt and trg ac) are distributed between the military regions as follows:

Headquarters Air Force

1 air division (34th, VIP Tpt) with Il-76MD, Tu-154M, B-747, CRJ200, Y8, Y7, An-30; 100th; 101st; 102nd Regt; Air Force Flight Test Regiment

Northeast – Shenyang MRAF

1 air div (1st ftr) with (1 ftr regt with J-11/J-11B; 1 FGA regt with J-10; 1 ftr regt with J-8A); 1 air div (11th atk) with (2 FGA regt with Q-5D); 1 air div (21st ftr) with (1 ftr regt with J-8H; 1 ftr regt with J-7; 1 ftr regt with J-8B); 1 air div (30th ftr) with (1 ftr regt with J-8A/E; 1 ftr regt with J-8F; 1 ftr regt with J-7E); 1 indep recce regt with JZ-8; 3 trg schools with An-30/CJ-6/H-5/HJ-5/JJ-5/K-8/Y-7; 1 (mixed) AD bde; 1 SAM bde

North – Beijing MRAF

1 air div (7th ftr) with (1 ftr regt with J-11; 1 ftr regt with J-7B); 1 air div (15th ftr/atk) with (1 ftr regt with J-7C; 1 FGA regt with Q-5; 1 ftr regt J-7D); 1 air div (24th ftr) with (1 FGA regt with J-10; 1 ftr regt with J-8; 1 ftr regt with J-8A); 1 Flight Test Centre with Su-30, Su-27/J-11, J-8C, J-10, J-7E, JJ-7 (on rotation); 1 trg base with J-7B, JJ-7; 2 trg schools with CJ-6/JJ-5/K-8; 3 SAM div; 1 (mixed) AD div

West – Lanzhou MRAF

1 air div (6th ftr) with (1 ftr regt with J-11; 1 ftr regt with J-7E; 1 ftr regt with J-7); 1 air div (36th bbr) with (1 surv regt with Y8I I-1; 1 bbr regt with I I-6E; 1 bbr regt with H-6A); 1 air div (37th ftr) with (1 ftr regt with J-8H; 1 ftr regt with J-7E; 1 ftr regt with J-7G); 2 trg schools with CJ-6, JJ-5; PLAAF Msl Testing Regt with JJ-6, J-7B; 1 (mixed) AD div; 1 SAM bde; 4 indep SAM regt

Centre – Jinan MRAF

1 air div (5th atk) with (1 FGA regt with Q-5E; 1 FGA regt with JH-7A); 1 air div (12th ftr) with (2 ftr regt with J-8B; 1 ftr regt with J-7G); 1 air div (19th ftr) with (1 ftr regt with Su-27SK; 1 ftr regt with J-11; 1 ftr regt with J-7E); 1 indep recce regt with JZ-6; 4 SAM bn

East – Nanjing MRAF

1 air div (3rd ftr) with (1 FGA regt with J-10; 1 ftr regt with J-7E; 1 FGA regt with Su-30MKK); 1 air div (10th bbr) with (2 bbr regt with H-6E; 1 ECM regt with Y-8D); 1 air div (14th ftr) with (1 ftr regt with J-11A; 1 ftr regt with J-7H); 1 air div (26th Special Mission) with (1 AEW/AWCAS regt with KJ-2000/KJ-200; 1 CSAR regt with M-171/Z-8; 1 recce regt with JZ-8F); 1 air div (28th atk) with (1 FGA regt with JH-7A; 2 FGA regt with Q-5D); 1 air div (29th ftr) with (1 FGA regt with Su-30MKK; 1 ftr regt with J-7C; 1 ftr regt with J-8B/D); 1 indep recce regt with JZ-6; 1 trg school with K-8, JJ-5, CJ-6; 3 SAM bde; 1 ADA bde; 2 indep SAM regts

South – Guangzhou MRAF

1 air div (2nd ftr) with (1 ftr regt with J-7B; 1 FGA regt with J-10; 1 ftr regt with Su-27SK); 1 air div (8th bbr/tkr) with (1 bbr regt with H-6E; 1 tkr regt with H-6U); 1 air div (9th ftr) with (1 ftr regt with J-8B; 1 ftr regt with J-8D; 1 ftr regt with J-7B); 1 air div (13th airlift) with (2 tpt regt with IL-76MD; 1 tpt regt with Y-7/Y-8); 1 air div (18th ftr) with (1 ftr regt with J-7B; 1 FGA regt with Su-30MKK); 1 air div (42nd ftr) with (1 ftr regt with J-7B; 1 ftr regt with J-7H); 1 indep recce regt with JZ-6; 4 SAM Bde, 1 ADA bde, 1 indep ADA regt

Southwest – Chengdu MRAF

1 air div (4th airlift) with Y-7/Mi-17; 1 air div (33rd ftr) with (1 ftr regt with J-7E; 1 ftr regt with J-7B; 1 ftr regt with J-11); 1 air div (44th ftr) with (2 ftr regt with J-7B; 1 FGA regt with J-10); 1 trg school with H-5, HJ-5, CJ-6; 1 (mixed) AD bde; 3 indep SAM regt

Flying hours Ftr, ground attack and bbr pilots average 100-150 hrs/yr. Tpt pilots average 200+ per year. Each regt has two quotas to meet during the year – a total number of hours, and the percentage of flight time dedicated to tactics trg.

FORCES BY ROLE

Bbr 4 regt with H-6E/H-6F/H-6H (of which some with YJ-63 cruise missile); 1 (nuclear ready) regt with H-6 (Tu-16) *Badger*

Ftr	2 regt with J-7 *Fishbed*; 8 regt with J-7B *Fishbed*; 2 regt with J-7H *Fishbed*;2 regt with J-7C *Fishbed*; 1 regt with J-7D *Fishbed*; 6 regt with J-7E *Fishbed*; 2 regt with J-7G *Fishbed*; 1 regt with J-8 *Finback*; 2 regt with J-8A *Finback*; 1 regt with J-8A/J-8E *Finback*; 4 regt with J-8B *Finback*; 1 regt with J-8B/J-8D *Finback*; 1 regt with J-8D *Finback*; 2 regt with J-8H *Finback*; 1 regt with J-8F *Finback*; 8 regt with J-11 (Su-27SK)/J-11B *Flanker*
FGA	3 regt with Su-30MKK *Flanker*; 5 regt with Q-5/Q-5D/Q-5E *Fantan*; 5 regt with J-10; 3 regt with JH-7/7A
Recce	3 regt with JZ-6 (MiG-19R); 1 regt with JZ-8 *Finback*;1 regt with JZ-8F *Finback*
ECM	1 regt with Y-8D
AEW/ AWACS	1 regt with KJ-2000/KJ-200
Surv	1 regt with Y-8H1
Tpt	2 regt with Il-76MD *Candid B* (to support 15th and 16th Airborne armies); 1 regt with Y-7(An-26), Y-8; 1 regt with Y-7
Tkr	1 regt with H-6U
VIP	3 regt with Il-76MD, Tu-154M, B-737-200, Y-8, An-30
ADA	1 bde located in Centre; 1 bde located in East; 1 bde located in North-East
Trg	1 regt with 12 H-6H; some regt with CJ-6/-6A/-6B); H-5; HJ-5; Y-7; JL-8 (K-8); JJ-5; JJ-6; JJ-7
Hel	1 regt with Mi-171, Z-8 (SA-321). Some regts with AS-332 *Super Puma* (VIP); Mi-8 *Hip*; Z-9 (AS-365N) *Dauphin 2*; Bell 214
AD	3 SAM div; 2 mixed AD div; 9 SAM bde; 2 mixed AD bde; 2 ADA bde; 9 indep SAM regt; 1 indep ADA regt; 4 indep SAM bn

EQUIPMENT BY TYPE
AIRCRAFT 1,617 combat capable
  BBR up to 82 H-6/H-6E/H-6F/H-6H
  FTR 1,100+: 48 J-7 *Fishbed*; 192 J-7B *Fishbed*; 48 J-7H *Fishbed*; 48 J-7C *Fishbed*; 24 J-7D *Fishbed*; 144 J-7E *Fishbed*; 48 J-7G *Fishbed*; 24 J-8 *Finback*; 60 J-8A *Finback*; 108 J-8B *Finback*; 36 J-8D *Finback*; 12 J-8E *Finback*; 24 J-8F *Finback*; 48 J-8H *Finback*; 120+ J-10; 116 J-11 (Su-27SK) *Flanker*;
  FGA 283: 73 Su-30MKK *Flanker*; 18+ J-11B *Flanker*; 72 JH-7/JH-7A; 120 Q-5/Q-5D/Q-5E *Fantan*
  RECCE 120: 72 JZ-6 (MiG-19R)*; 24 JZ-8 *Finback**; 24 JZ-8F *Finback**
  AEW 8+: 4 KJ-2000; 4 KJ-200
  EW 10 Y-8D
  TKR 18: 10 H-6U; 8 IL-78M on order
  TPT 296: 15 B-737-200 (VIP); 5 CL-601 *Challenger*; 2 Il-18 *Coot*; 18 Il-76MD *Candid B* (30 on order); 17 Tu-154M *Careless*; some Y-8; 20 Y-11; 8 Y-12; 170 Y-5 (An-2) *Colt*; 41 Y-7 (An-24) *Coke*/Y-7H (An-26) *Curl*
  SURV 3 Y-8H1
  TRG 522: 400 CJ-6/-6A/-6B; 50 JJ-7; 40 JL-8 (K-8); 32 Su-27UBK *Flanker**
HELICOPTERS
  SAR: Some Z-8 (SA-321)

  SPT 56+: some Mi-171; 6 AS-332 *Super Puma* (VIP); 50 Mi-8 *Hip*
  UTL 24: 20 Z-9 (AS-365N) *Dauphin 2*; 4 Bell 214
UAV CH-1 *Chang Hong*; *Chang Kong 1*; BQM-34 *Firebee*; *Harpy*
AD
  SAM 600+
    SP 300+: 24 HD-6D; 60+ HQ-7; 32 HQ-9; 24 HQ-12 (KS-1A); 32 S-300PMU (SA-10B)/64 S-300PMU1 (SA-10C) *Grumble*/64 S-300PMU2 (SA-10C) *Grumble*;
    TOWED 300+ HQ-2 (SA-2) *Guideline* Towed/HQ-2A/HQ-2B(A)
  GUNS 16,000 **100mm/85mm**
MSL • TACTICAL 4,500+
  ASM AS-14 *Kedge*; AS-17 *Krypton*; AS-18 *Kazoo*; YJ-63; YJ-88; YJ-91 (X-31 II)
  AAM AA-12 *Adder*; P-27 (AA-10) *Alamo*; P37 (AA-11) *Archer*; PL-12; PL-2B; PL-5B/C; PL-8; PL-8A

Paramilitary ε660,000 active

People's Armed Police ε660,000

Internal Security Forces ε400,000

Security	14 (mobile) div; 22 (mobile) indep regt; some (firefighting & garrison) units

Border Defence Force ε260,000

Border Guard	30 div HQ; 110 (border) regt; 20 (marine) regt

DEPLOYMENT

ARABIAN GULF AND INDIAN OCEAN
Maritime Security Operations 2 FFG; 1 AORH

CÔTE D'IVOIRE
UN • UNOCI 7 obs

DEMOCRATIC REPUBLIC OF CONGO
UN • MONUC 218; 15 obs; 1 engr coy; 1 fd hospital

LEBANON
UN • UNIFIL 344; 1 engr coy; 1 fd hospital

LIBERIA
UN • UNMIL 566; 4 obs; 1 engr coy; 1 tpt coy; 1 fd hospital

MIDDLE EAST
UN • UNTSO 4 obs

SUDAN
UN • UNAMID 325; 1 engr coy
UN • UNMIS 444; 12 obs; 1 engr coy; 1 tpt coy; 1 fd hospital

TIMOR-LESTE
UN • UNMIT 2 obs

WESTERN SAHARA
UN • MINURSO 12 obs

Fiji FJI

Fijian Dollar F$		2008	2009	2010
GDP	F$	4.9bn	5.2bn	
	US$	3.1bn	2.7bn	
per capita	US$	3,308	2,897	
Growth	%	0.2	-2.5	
Inflation	%	7.8	5.0	
Def bdgt	F$	ε90m	ε100m	
	US$	ε56m	ε52m	
US$1=F$		1.59	1.90	

Population   944,720

Ethnic groups: Fijian 51%; Indian 44%; European/Others 5%

Age	0–14	15–19	20–24	25–29	30–64	65 plus
Male	16%	5%	5%	4%	18%	2%
Female	15%	5%	5%	4%	18%	2%

Capabilities

ACTIVE 3,500 (Army 3,200 Navy 300)

RESERVE ε6,000
(to age 45)

ORGANISATIONS BY SERVICE

Army 3,200 (incl 300 recalled reserves)
FORCES BY ROLE
Inf   7 bn (incl 4 cadre)
Spec Ops   1 coy
Arty   1 bty
Engr   1 bn
EQUIPMENT BY TYPE
ARTY 16
    TOWED 85mm 4 25-pdr (ceremonial)
    MOR 81mm 12
HELICOPTERS
    SPT 1 AS-355 Ecureuil
    UTL 1 AS-365 Dauphin 2

Navy 300
EQUIPMENT BY TYPE
PATROL AND COASTAL COMBATANTS 7
    PCC 3 Kula
    PCI 4: 2 Levuka; 2 Vai
LOGISTICS AND SUPPORT 1
    TRG 1 Cagi Donu (Presidential Yacht)
FACILITIES
Bases Located at Viti (trg), Walu Bay

DEPLOYMENT

EGYPT
MFO 338; 1 inf bn

IRAQ
UN • UNAMI 221; 3 sy unit

SUDAN
UN • UNMIS 6 obs

TIMOR LESTE
UN • UNMIT 2 obs

Indonesia IDN

Indonesian Rupiah Rp		2008	2009	2010
GDP	Rp	4,954tr	5,289tr	
	US$	511bn	559bn	
per capita	US$	2,151	2,328	
Growth	%	6.1	4.0	
Inflation	%	9.8	5.0	
Def exp[a]	US$	5.10bn		
Def bdgt	Rp	32.8tr	33.6tr	40.6tr
	US$	3.4bn	3.5bn	
FMA (US)	US$	12.8m	15.7m	20.0m
US$1=Rp		9,699	9,455	

[a] including extra-budgetary funding estimate

Population   240,271,522

Ethnic groups: Javanese 45%; Sundanese 14%; Madurese 8%; Malay 8%; Chinese 3%; other 22%

Age	0–14	15–19	20–24	25–29	30–64	65 plus
Male	15%	5%	5%	5%	19%	2%
Female	14%	4%	5%	5%	19%	3%

Capabilities

ACTIVE 302,000 (Army 233,000 Navy 45,000 Air 24,000) **Paramilitary 280,000**
Terms of service 2 years selective conscription authorised

RESERVE 400,000
Army cadre units; numerical str n.k., obligation to age 45 for officers

ORGANISATIONS BY SERVICE

Army ε233,000

11 Mil Area Command (KODAM) 150,000
Provincial (KOREM) and District (KODIM) Comd
Cav   8 bn
Inf   2 bde (6 bn); 60 bn
AB   5 bn
Fd Arty   10 bn
Engr   7 bn
Avn   1 composite sqn
Hel   1 sqn
AD   7 bn

Special Forces Command (KOPASSUS) ε5,000

SF 3 gp (*total:* 2 cdo/para unit, 1 counter-terrorist unit (Unit 81), 1 trg unit, 1 (int) SF unit)

Strategic Reserve Command (KOSTRAD) 40,000

Comd	2 div HQ
Armd	2 bn
Inf	4 bde (9 bn)
AB	2 bde; 1(3rd) indep bde
Fd Arty	2 regt (6 bn)
AD	1 regt (2 bn)
Engr	2 bn

EQUIPMENT BY TYPE

LT TK 350: 275 AMX-13 (to be upgraded); 15 PT-76; 60 *Scorpion* 90

RECCE 142: 55 *Ferret* (13 upgraded); 69 *Saladin* (16 upgraded); 18 VBL

AIFV 11 BMP-2

APC 356

APC (T) 115: 75 AMX-VCI; 40 FV4333 *Stormer*

APC (W) 241: 80 BTR-40; 34 BTR-50PK; 22 *Commando Ranger*; 45 FV603 *Saracen* (14 upgraded); 60 LAV-150 *Commando*

ARTY 1,010

TOWED 135: **105mm** 130: 120 M-101; 10 M-56; **155mm** 5 FH-2000

MOR 875: **81mm** 800; **120mm** 75 Brandt

AT • RCL 135: **106mm** 45 M-40A1; **90mm** 90 M-67

RL 89mm 700 LRAC

AIRCRAFT • TPT 11: 3 DHC-5 *Buffalo*; 6 NC-212 (CASA 212) *Aviocar*; 2 Rockwell *Turbo Commander* 680

HELICOPTERS

ATK 6 Mi-35P *Hind*

SPT 16 Mi-17 *Hip*

UTL 37: 8 Bell 205A; 12 NB-412 (Bell 412) *Twin Huey*; 17 NBo-105 (Bo-105)

TRG 12 Hughes 300C

AD • SAM 68: 51 *Rapier*; 17 RBS-70

GUNS • TOWED 413: **20mm** 121 Rh 202; **40mm** 36 L/70; **57mm** 256 S-60

Navy ε45,000 (including Marines and Aviation)

Fleet Command

FORCES BY ROLE

Navy	Two fleets: East (Surabaya), West (Jakarta). Planned: 1 HQ (Surabaya): 3 commands: Riau (West); Papua (East); Makassar (Central)
Forward Operating Bases	1 Kupang (West Timor); 1 Tahuna (North Sulawesi)

EQUIPMENT BY TYPE

SUBMARINES • TACTICAL • SSK 2 *Cakra*† each with 8 single 533mm TT with 14 SUT HWT

PRINCIPAL SURFACE COMBATANTS 30

FRIGATES 7

FFG 7

6 *Ahmad Yani* each with 2 Mk 141 *Harpoon* quad (8 eff.) each with RGM-84A *Harpoon* tactical SSM, 2 SIMBAD twin manual each with *Mistral* SAM, 2 triple 324mm ASTT (6 eff.) each with Mk 46 LWT, 1 76mm gun, (capacity either 1 HAS-1 *Wasp* ASW hel or 1 NBo-105 (Bo-105) utl hel)

1 *Hajar Dewantara* (trg) with 2 twin (4 eff.) each with MM-38 *Exocet* tactical SSM, 2 single 533mm ASTT each with SUT HWT, (capacity 1 NBo-105 (Bo-105) utl hel)

CORVETTES • FS 23:

16 *Kapitan Patimura*† each with 4 x1 400mm ASTT, Twin each with SA-N-5 *Grail* SAM, 2 RBU 6000 *Smerch* 2 (24 eff.), 1 57mm gun

3 *Fatahillah* each with 2 twin (4 eff.) each with MM-38 *Exocet* tactical SSM, 2 B515 *ILAS-3*/triple 324mm ASTT (2-6 eff.) (not on *Nala*) with 12 A244/Mk 46, 1 2 tube *Bofors* 375mm (2 eff.), 1 120mm gun

4 *Sigma* each with 2 *Tetral* quad (8eff.) *Mistral* SAM, each with 4 MM-40 *Exocet* Block II tactical SSM, 2 triple 324mm ASTT (6 eff.), 1 76mm gun

PATROL AND COASTAL COMBATANTS 41

PFM 4 *Mandau* each with 4 MM-38 *Exocet* tactical SSM

PCT 4 *Singa* each with 2 single 533mm TT (capability upgrade programme in progress)

PCO 8: 4 *Kakap*; 4 *Todak*

PCC 21:

13 *Kobra* KAL-35 each with 2 20mm gun

8 *Sibarau*

PC 4

MINE WARFARE • MINE COUNTERMEASURES 11

MCC 2 *Pulau Rengat*

MSC 9 *Palau Rote*†

AMPHIBIOUS

PRINCIPAL AMPHIBIOUS VESSELS • LPD 3: 1 *Dr Soeharso* (Ex-*Tanjung Dalpele*; capacity 2 LCU/LCVP; 13 tanks; 500 troops); 2 *Makassar* (capacity 2 LCU/LCVP; 13 tanks; 500 troops); (2 additional vessels in build)

LS • LST 26: 1 *Teluk Amboina* (capacity 16 tanks; 200 troops); 12 *Teluk Gilimanuk*; 7 *Teluk Langsa* (capacity 16 tanks; 200 troops); 6 *Teluk Semangka* (capacity 17 tanks; 200 troops)

CRAFT 54 LCU

LOGISTICS AND SUPPORT 27

AGF 1 *Multatuli*

AORLH 1 *Arun* (UK *Rover*)

AOT 3: 2 *Khobi*; 1 *Sorong*

AKSL 6

AGOR 6: 4 *Baruna Jaya*; 1 *Jalanidhi*; 1 *Burujulasad*

AGHS 1

ATF 2

TRG • AXS 2

YTM 3

TPT 2 *Tanjung Nusanive* (troop transport)

Naval Aviation ε1,000

AIRCRAFT

MP 24: 2 CASA 235 MPA; 16 GAF N-22B *Searchmaster B*; 6 GAF N-22SL *Searchmaster L*

TPT 23: 3 CN-235M; 2 DHC-5 *Buffalo*; 4 CASA 212-200 *Aviocar*; 4 PA-34 *Seneca*; 4 Rockwell *Commander* 100†; 6 PA-38 *Tomahawk*

HELICOPTERS
ASW 9 HAS-1 *Wasp*†

SPT 15: 8 PZL Mi-2 *Hoplite* AS-332; 4 Mi-17 (additional ac on order); 3 NAS-322L *Super Puma*

UTL 13: 3 EC-120B *Colibri* (+6 on order); 4 NB-412 (Bell 412) *Twin Huey**; 6 NBo-105 (Bo-105)

Marines ε20,000

FORCES BY ROLE
SF   1 bn

Marine 1ˢᵗ marine corps gp (total: 3 marine bn) based Surabaya; 1 indep marine corp gp (total: 3 bn) based Jakarta; 1 marine bde (total: 3 bn) based Teluk, Rata and Sumatra

Cbt spt 1 regt (arty, AD)

EQUIPMENT BY TYPE
LT TK 55 PT-76†

RECCE 21 BRDM

AIFV 34: 24 AMX-10P; 10 AMX-10 PAC 90

APC (W) 100 BTR-50P

ARTY 62+

    TOWED 50+: **105mm** 22 LG1 MK II; **122mm** 28 M-38 *M-1938*

    MRL 140mm 12 BM-14

    MOR 81mm

AD • GUNS 150: **40mm** 5 L/60 / L/70; **57mm** S-60

Air Force 24,000

2 operational comd (East and West) plus trg comd. Only 45% of ac op

FORCES BY ROLE
Ftr   1 sqn with F-5E *Tiger II*; F-5F *Tiger II*

Ftr/FGA 1 sqn with Su-30 MKI *Flanker* (multi-role); Su-27SK *Flanker* (AD); 1 sqn with F-16A/ F-16B *Fighting Falcon*; 1 sqn with A-4E *Skyhawk*; TA-4H *Skyhawk*; TA-4J *Skyhawk*; 2 sqn with *Hawk* MK109; *Hawk* MK209

FAC   1 flt with OV-10F *Bronco** (mostly non-operational)

MR   1 sqn with B-737-200

Tpt/Tkr 5 sqn with B-707; C-130B *Hercules*; KC-130B *Hercules*; C-130H *Hercules*; C-130H-30 *Hercules*; NC-212 (CASA 212) *Aviocar*; CN-235-110; Cessna 401; Cessna 402; F-27-400M *Troopship*; F-28-1000; F-28-3000; L-100-30; SC.7 3M *Skyvan* (survey); Cessna 207 *Stationair*

Trg   3 sqn with Cessna 172; AS-202 *Bravo*; *Hawk* MK53*; KT-1B; SF-260M/SF-260W *Warrior*; T-34C *Turbo Mentor*; T-41D *Mescalero*

Hel   3 sqn with S-58T; NAS-332L (AS-332L) *Super Puma* (VIP/CSAR); NAS-330 (SA-330) *Puma* (NAS-330SM VIP); EC-120B *Colibri*

EQUIPMENT BY TYPE
AIRCRAFT 96 combat capable

FTR 25: 3 Su-27SK *Flanker* (AD); 7 F-16A *Fighting Falcon*; 3 F-16B *Fighting Falcon*; 8 F-5E *Tiger II*; 4 F-5F *Tiger II*

FGA 49: 3 Su-30 MKI *Flanker*; 11 A-4E *Skyhawk*; 7 *Hawk* MK109; 28 *Hawk* MK209

FAC 12 OV-10F *Bronco** (mostly non-operational)

TKR 2 KC-130B *Hercules*

TPT 61: 1 B-707; 3 B-737-200; 8 C-130B *Hercules*; 4 C-130H *Hercules*; 6 C-130H-30 *Hercules*; 2 L-100-30; 10 CN-235-110; 5 Cessna 401; 2 Cessna 402; 6 F-27-400M *Troopship*; 1 F-28-1000; 2 F-28-3000; 10 NC-212 (CASA 212) *Aviocar*; 1 SC.7 3M *Skyvan* (survey)

UTL 6: 2 Cessna 172; 4 Cessna 207 *Stationair*

TRG 101: 39 AS-202 *Bravo*; 7 *Hawk* MK53*; 7 KT-1B; 19 SF-260M/SF-260W *Warrior*; 20 T-34C *Turbo Mentor*; 6 T-41D *Mescalero*; 1 TA-4H *Skyhawk**; 2 TA-4J *Skyhawk**

HELICOPTERS
SAR 10 S-58T

SPT 16: 5 NAS-332L (AS-332L) *Super Puma* (VIP/CSAR); 11 NAS-330 (SA-330) *Puma* (1 NAS-330SM VIP)

UTL 12 EC-120B *Colibri*

MSL • TACTICAL
ASM AGM-65G *Maverick*

AAM AIM-9P *Sidewinder*

Special Forces (Paskhasau)

Special Ops 3 (PASKHASAU) wg (*total*: 6 special ops sqn); 4 indep coy

Paramilitary ε280,000 active

Naval Auxiliary Service
PATROL AND COASTAL COMBATANTS 71

    PCC 65 *Kal Kangean*

    PCI 6 *Carpentaria*

Customs
PATROL AND COASTAL COMBATANTS • PCI 55

Marine Police
PATROL AND COASTAL COMBATANTS 85

    PSOH 2 *Bisma*

    PCC 14 *Bango*

    PC 37

    PBI 32

Police ε280,000 (including 14,000 police 'mobile bde' (BRIMOB) org in 56 coy, incl CT unit (Gegana))
APC (W) 34 *Tactica*

AIRCRAFT • TPT 5: 2 Beech 18; 2 NC-212 (CASA 212) *Aviocar*; 1 Rockwell *Turbo Commander* 680

HELICOPTERS • UTL 22: 3 Bell 206 *Jet Ranger*; 19 NBO-105 (BO-105)

KPLP (Coast and Seaward Defence Command)
Responsible to Military Sea Communications Agency

PATROL AND COASTAL COMBATANTS 11

    PSO 2 *Arda Dedali*

PCC 9: 4 *Golok* (SAR); 5 *Kujang*
LOGISTICS AND SUPPORT • ABU 1 *Jadayat*

Reserve Organisations

Kamra People's Security ε40,000 (report for 3 weeks' basic training each year; part time police auxiliary)

SELECTED NON-STATE GROUPS

Organisasi Papua Merdeka Est strength: 150 Major equipments include: SALW • **Jemaah Islamiah** Est strength: 550 Major equipments include: mines and IEDs, SALW

DEPLOYMENT

DEMOCRATIC REPUBLIC OF CONGO
UN • MONUC 174; 16 obs; 1 engr coy

LEBANON
UN • UNIFIL 1,248; 1 inf bn; 1 FS

LIBERIA
UN • UNMIL 2 obs

NEPAL
UN • UNMIN 5 obs

SUDAN
UN • UNAMID 3
UN • UNMIS 6 obs

Japan JPN

Japanese Yen ¥		2008	2009	2010
GDP	¥	507tr	474tr	
	US$	4.92tr	5.30tr	
per capita	US$	38,699	41,723	
Growth	%	-0.7	-5.4	
Inflation	%	1.4	-1.4	
Def bdgt	¥	4.74tr	4.70tr	
	US$	46.0bn	52.6bn	
US$1=¥		103	89	

Population   127,078,000
Ethnic groups: Korean <1%

Age	0–14	15–19	20–24	25–29	30–64	65 plus
Male	7%	3%	3%	3%	24%	8%
Female	7%	3%	3%	3%	24%	10%

Capabilities

ACTIVE 230,300 (Ground Self-Defense Force 138,400; Maritime Self- Defense Force 42,400; Air 34,760; Central Staff 2,200) **Paramilitary 12,250**

RESERVE 41,800 (Navy 900; Air 700; General Reserve Army (GSDF) 33,800; Ready Reserve Army (GSDF) 6,200)

ORGANISATIONS BY SERVICE

Space Defence
4 recce satellites (2 radar, 2 optical)

Ground Self-Defense Force 138,400
FORCES BY ROLE
5 Army HQ (regional comds)

Composite	1 bde
Armd Inf	8 div, 5 bde
Armd	1 div
Spec Ops	1 unit
AB	1 bde
Arty	1 bde; 2 unit
Engr	4 bde; 1 unit
Hel	1 bde
Trg	2 bde; 2 regt
AD	2 bde; 4 gp

EQUIPMENT BY TYPE
MBT 880: 560 Type-74; 320 Type-90
RECCE 100 Type-87
AIFV 70 Type-89
APC 780
  APC (T) 310 Type-73
  APC (W) 470: 220 Type-82; 250 Type-96
ARTY 1,880
  SP 210: **155mm** 130: 80 Type-75; 50 Type-99; **203mm** 80 M-110A2
  TOWED 155mm 420 FH-70
  MRL 227mm 100 MLRS
  MOR 1,150
    SP 120mm 20
    TOWED 1,130: **81mm** 670; **107mm** 50; **120mm** 410
AT
  MSL • MANPATS 630: 190 Type-79 *Jyu-MAT*; 440 Type-87 *Chu-MAT*
  RCL 2,740: **SP 106mm** 30 Type-60; **84mm** 2,710 *Carl Gustav*
  RL 230 **89mm**
AIRCRAFT
  UTL 10 LR-1 (MU-2) / LR-2 (Beech 350) *Super King Air*
HELICOPTERS
  ATK 200: 10 AH-64D *Apache*; 70 AH-1S *Cobra* ; 100 OH-1; 20 OH-60 (MD-500);
  SPT 53: 3 EC-225LP (VIP); 50 CH-47J (CH-47D) *Chinook*/ CH-47JA *Chinook*
  UTL 170: 140 UH-1J (UH-1H) *Iroquois*; 30 UH-60JA (UH-60L) *Black Hawk*
AD • SAM 740
  SP 170: 60 Type-81 *Tan-SAM*; 110 Type-93 *Kin-SAM*
  TOWED 190: 180 MTM-23B *I-HAWK*; 10 Type-03 *Chu-Sam*
  MANPAD 380: 50 FIM-92A *Stinger*; 330 Type-91 *Kin-SAM*
  GUNS 60
    SP 35mm 50 Type-87 SP
    TOWED 35mm 10 (twin)
MSL • SSM • COASTAL 100 Type-88

Maritime Self-Defense Force 42,400

FORCES BY ROLE

Surface units organised into 4 Escort Flotillas with a mix of 7–8 warships each. Bases at Yokosuka, Kure, Sasebo, Maizuru, Ominato. SSK organised into 2 Flotillas with bases at Kure and Yokosuka. Remaining units assigned to 5 regional districts.

EQUIPMENT BY TYPE

SUBMARINES • TACTICAL • SSK 16:

4 *Harushio* each with 6 single 533mm TT each with T-89 HWT/UGM-84C *Harpoon* tactical USGW

11 *Oyashio* each with 6 single 533mm TT each with T-89 HWT/UGM-84C *Harpoon* tactical USGW

1 *Soryu* (AIP fitted) each with 6 single 533mm TT each with T-89 HWT/UGM-84C *Harpoon* tactical USGW (additional vessels in build)

PRINCIPAL SURFACE COMBATANTS 52

DESTROYERS 44

DDG 40:

6 *Asagiri* each with 2 triple 324mm ASTT (6 eff.) each with Mk 46 LWT, 1 Mk 112 octuple (8 eff.) with tactical ASROC, 2 Mk 141 *Harpoon* quad (8 eff.) each with RGM-84C *Harpoon* tactical SSM, 1 Mk 29 *Sea Sparrow* octuple with 16 *Sea Sparrow* SAM, 1 76mm gun, (capacity 1 SH-60J/K *Seahawk* ASW hel)

2 *Atago* (*Aegis* Base Line 7) each with 2 quad SSM launchers (8 eff.) with tactical SSM-1B, 1 MK 41 VLS (64 eff.) with SM-2 MR SAM, tactical ASROC, 1 MK 41 VLS (32 eff.) with SM-2 MR SAM, 2 triple 324mm ASTT (6 eff.) each with MK 46 LWT, 1 127mm gun, (capacity 1 SH-60J *Seahawk* ASW hel)

2 *Hatakaze* each with 2 Mk 141 *Harpoon* quad (8 eff.) each with RGM-84C *Harpoon* tactical SSM, 1 Mk 13 GMLS with 40 SM-1 MR SAM, 2 triple 324mm ASTT (6 eff.), 2 127mm gun, 1 hel landing platform

11 *Hatsuyuki* each with 1 Mk 112 octuple (8 eff.) with tactical ASROC, 2 Mk 141 *Harpoon* quad (8 eff.) each with RGM-84C *Harpoon* tactical SSM, 1+ Mk 29 *Sea Sparrow* octuple with 16 RIM-7F/M *Sea Sparrow* SAM, 2 triple ASTT (6 eff.) each with Mk 46 LWT, 1 76mm gun, (capacity 1 SH-60J/K *Seahawk* ASW hel)

4 *Kongou* (with hel deck) *Aegis* Baseline 4/5 each with 2 Mk 141 *Harpoon* quad (8 eff.) each with RGM-84C *Harpoon* tactical SSM, 1 29 cell Mk 41 VLS (29 eff.) with SM-2 MR SAM, tactical ASROC, 1 61 cell Mk 41 VLS (61 eff.) with SM-2 MR SAM, tactical ASROC, 2 triple 324mm ASTT (6 eff.), 1 127mm gun

9 *Murasame* each with 2 quad (8 eff.) each with tactical SSM-1B, 1 16 cells Mk 41 VLS with up to 16 tactical ASROC, 1 16 cell Mk 48 VLS with RIM-7M *Sea Sparrow* SAM, 2 triple 324mm TT (6 eff.) each with Mk 46 LWT, 2 76mm gun, (capacity 1 SH-60J/K *Seahawk* ASW hel)

1 *Tachikaze* each with 1 Mk 13 GMLS with 8-16 RGM-84C *Harpoon* tactical SSM, 32 SM-1 MR SAM, 1 Mk 112 octuple (8 eff.) with up to 16 tactical ASROC, 1 2 triple 324mm ASTT (6 eff.) each with Mk 46 LWT, 127mm gun

5 *Takanami* (improved *Murasame*) each with 2 quad SSM launchers (8 eff.) each with tactical SSM-1B, 1 32 cell Mk 41 VLS (32 eff.) with tactical ASROC/RIM-7M/ESSM *Sea Sparrow* SAM, 2 triple 324mm TT (6 eff.) each with Mk 46 LWT, 1 *Otobreda* 127mm gun, (capacity 1 SH-60J/K *Seahawk* ASW hel)

DD 4:

1 *Hyuga* with 1 Mk 41 VLS (16 cells) with up to 16 tactical ASROC/RIM-162/ESSM *Sea Sparrow*, 2 triple 324mm TT (6 eff.) each with Mk46 LWT, 2 20mm CIWS gun, (normal ac capacity 3 SH-60J/K *Seahawk* ASW hel; plus additional ac embarkation up to 7 SH-60J/K *Seahawk* or 7 MCH-101) (additional vessel in build)

1 *Haruna* each with 1 Mk 112 octuple (8 eff.) with tactical ASROC, 1 Mk 29 *Sea Sparrow* octuple with RIM-7F/M *Sea Sparrow* SAM, 2 triple ASTT (6 eff.) each with Mk 46 LWT, 2 127mm gun, (capacity 3 SH-60J/K *Seahawk* ASW hel)

2 *Shirane* each with 1 Mk 112 octuple (8 eff.) with tactical ASROC, 1+ Mk 29 *Sea Sparrow* octuple with 24+ RIM-162A *Sea Sparrow* SAM, 2 triple ASTT (6 eff.) each with Mk 46 LWT, 2 127mm gun, (capacity 3 SH-60J/K *Seahawk* ASW hel)

FRIGATES • FFG 8:

6 *Abukuma* each with 2 Mk 141 *Harpoon* quad (8 eff.) each with RGM-84C *Harpoon* tactical SSM, 1 Mk 112 octuple (8 eff.) with tactical ASROC, 2 triple ASTT (6 eff.) each with Mk 46 LWT, 1 76mm gun

2 *Yubari* each with 2 Mk 141 *Harpoon* quad (8 eff.) each with RGM-84C *Harpoon* tactical SSM, 2 triple ASTT (6 eff.), 1 Type 71/ 4 tube Mitsubishi 375mm Bofors (4 eff.), 1 76mm gun

PATROL AND COASTAL COMBATANTS 7

PFM 6 *Hayabusa* each with 4 tactical SSM-1B, 1 76mm gun

PHM 1 *Ichi-Go* each with 4 tactical SSM-1B

MINE WARFARE • MINE COUNTERMEASURES 32

MCM SPT 4:

2 *Nijma*

2 *Uraga* each with 1 hel landing platform (for MH-53E)

MSO 3 *Yaeyama*

MSC 25: 2 *Hatsushima*; 12 *Sugashima*; 9 *Uwajima*; 2 *Hirashima*

AMPHIBIOUS

LS • LST 5:

3 *Osumi* each with 1 hel landing platform (for 2 x CH-47) (capacity 10 Type-90 MBTs; 2 LCAC(L) ACV; 330 troops)

2 *Yura* (capacity 70 troops)

LANDING CRAFT 20

LCU 2 *Yusotei*

LCM 12

ACV 6 **LCAC(L)** (capacity either 1 MBT or 60 troops)

LOGISTICS AND SUPPORT 76:

AOE 5: 2 *Mashuu*; 3 *Towada*

AS 1 *Chiyoda* (submarine rescue facilities)

ASR 1 *Chihaya*

ARC 1 *Muroto*

AG 2: 1 *Kurihama*; 1 *Asuka* (wpn trials)

AGOS 2 *Hibiki*

AGS 4: 2 *Futami*; 1 *Suma*; 1 *Nichinan*

AGB 1 *Shirase*
ATF 22
TRG 6: 1 *Kashima*; 1 *Shimayuki*; 2 *Yamagiri* TV35 with 2 triple ASTT (6 eff.) each with Mk 46 LWT, 1 Mk 112 octuple (8 eff.) with tactical ASROC, 1 Type 71/ 4 tube Mitsubishi 375mm Bofors (4 eff.), 4 76mm gun; 1 *Tenryu* (trg spt ship); 1 *Kurobe* (trg spt ship)
SPT 5 *Hiuchi*
YDT 6
YTM 20

FACILITIES
Bases   Located at Kure, Sasebo, Yokosuka, Maizuru, Ominato

Naval Aviation ε9,800

FORCES BY ROLE
7 Air Groups
ASuW/ 7 sqn (shipboard / trg) with SH-60J/K *Seahawk*;
ASW
MR   6 sqn(1 trg) with P-3C *Orion*
EW   1 sqn with EP-3 *Orion; OP-3C*
MCM   1 sqn with MH-53E *Sea Dragon*
SAR   2 sqn with UH-60J *Black Hawk*; 1 sqn with *Shin Meiwa* US-1A
Tpt   1 sqn with YS-11M; LC-90
Trg   1 sqn with OH-6D (MD-500MD); OH-6DA (MD-500ME); 3 sqn with T-5; TC-90; YS-11T

EQUIPMENT BY TYPE
AIRCRAFT 80 combat capable
  MP 80 P-3C *Orion**
  SAR 7: 4 *Shin Meiwa* US-1A; 3 *Shin Meiwa* US-2
  TPT 9: 4 YS-11M; 5 LC-90
  TRG 63: 33 T-5; 24 TC-90; 6 YS-11T
HELICOPTERS 91 combat capable
  ASW 91: 62 SH-60J *Seahawk*; 29 *SH-60K*
  MCM 9 MH-53E *Sea Dragon*
  SAR 18 UH-60J *Black Hawk*
  SPT 3: 2 MCH-101; 1 CH-101 (additional ac being delivered)
  UTL 4: 3 S-61A *Black Hawk*; 1 USH-60K
  TRG 8: 3 OH-6D (MD-500MD); 5 OH-6DA (MD-500ME)

Air Self-Defense Force 43,760

Flying hours   150 hrs/year

FORCES BY ROLE
7 cbt wings
Ftr   7 sqn with F-15J *Eagle*; 2 sqn with F-4EJ (F-4E) *Phantom II*; 3 sqn with Mitsubishi F-2
Recce   1 sqn with RF-4EJ (RF-4E) *Phantom II**
EW   2 sqn with Kawasaki EC-1; YS-11E
AEW   2 sqn with E-2C *Hawkeye*; E-767 (AWACS)
SAR   1 wg with U-125A *Peace Krypton*; LR-1 (MU-2); UH-60J *Black Hawk*; KV-107 (Boeing Vertol 107)
Tkr   1 sqn with KC-767J

Tpt   3 sqn with C-1; C-130H *Hercules*; YS-11; 1 sqn with B-747-400 (VIP); 4 (hy-lift) flt with CH-47 *Chinook*
Liaison some sqn with U-4; Kawasaki T-4
CAL   1 sqn with U-125-800 *Peace Krypton*; YS-11
Test   1 wg with F-15 *Eagle*; Kawasaki T-4
Trg   F-15 *Eagle** aggressor sqn; 5 trg schools with T-7 (basic), Mitsubishi F-2B and Kawasaki T-4 (advanced); Beech T-400

EQUIPMENT BY TYPE
AIRCRAFT 260 combat capable
  FTR 250: 160 F-15 *Eagle*; 50 Mitsubishi F-2; 40 F-4EJ (F-4E) *Phantom II*
  RECCE 10 RF-4J (RF-4E) *Phantom II**
  EW 11: 1 Kawasaki EC-1; 10 YS-11E
  AEW 14: 10 E-2C *Hawkeye*; 4 E-767 (AWACS)
  SAR 20 U-125A *Peace Krypton*
  TPT 30: 20 C-1; 10 C-130H *Hercules*
  TKR 4 KC-767J
  UTL 10 U-4
  TRG 240: 170 T-4; 20 Mitsubishi F-2B; 40 T-7; 10 T-400
HELICOPTERS
  SAR 42: 40 UH-60J *Black Hawk*; 2 KV-107 (Boeing Vertol 107)
  SPT 10 CH-47 *Chinook*

Air Defence

FORCES BY ROLE
ac control and warning
AD   4 wg; 28 radar sites; 1 (Air Base Defence) gp with Type-81 *Tan-SAM*; FIM-92A *Stinger*; Type-91 *Kin-SAM*; M-167 *Vulcan*
SAM   6 gp, comprising 24 SAM bty each with 5 launchers MIM-104 *Patriot*) 16+ bty of PAC-3 (incl 4 bty for trg)

EQUIPMENT BY TYPE
AD • SAM 208+
  SP Type-81 *Tan-SAM*
  TOWED 208+: 192+ MIM-104 *Patriot*; 16+ PAC-3
  MANPAD FIM-92A *Stinger*; Type-91 *Kei-SAM*
  GUNS • TOWED 20mm M-167 *Vulcan*
MSL
  ASM ASM-1Type-80; ASM-2 Type-93;
  AAM AAM-4 (Type-99); AIM-7 *Sparrow*; AIM-9 *Sidewinder*; Type-90 (AAM-3)

FACILITIES
Radar stn   28 (ac control and warning)

Paramilitary 12,250

Coast Guard
Ministry of Transport, no cbt role
PATROL AND COASTAL COMBATANTS 348
  PSOH 24: 1 *Izu*; 1 *Kojima* (trg); 2 *Mizuho*; 1 *Shikishima*; 10 *Soya*; 1 *Miura*; 1 *Nojima*; 7 *Ojika*
  PSO 60: 22 *Shiretoko*; 3 *Aso*; 14 *Teshio*; 2 *Takatori*; 15 *Bihoro*; 4 *Amani*
  PCO 3 *Tokara*
  PFC 27 *PS-Type*

PCC 60 *PC-Type*
PCI 174: 170 *CL-Type*; 4 *FM-Type*
LOGISTICS AND SUPPORT 74: 4 ABU; 13 AGHS; 54 small tenders; 3 Trg
AIRCRAFT
MP 2 *Falcon 900*
SAR 2 SAAB 340B
TPT 17: 10 LR-2 (Beech 350) *Super King Air*; 5 Beech 200T; 2 *Gulfstream V* (MP)
UTL 6: 1 Cessna U-206G *Stationair*; 5 YS-11A
HELICOPTERS
SPT 4 AS-332 *Super Puma*
UTL 40: 4 Bell 206B *JetRanger II*; 26 Bell 212; 8 Bell 412 *Twin Huey*; 3 S-76C

DEPLOYMENT

ARABIAN GULF AND INDIAN OCEAN
Maritime Security Operations 3 DDG; 1 AOE

MIDDLE EAST
UN • UNDOF 31; elm 1 log bn

NEPAL
UN • UNMIN 6 obs

SUDAN
UN • UNMIS 2

FOREIGN FORCES

United States US Pacific Command: **Army** 2,548; 1 HQ (9th Theater Army Area Command) located at Zama **Navy** 3,708; 1 CVN; 2 CG; 8 DDG; 1 LCC; 2 MCM; 1 LHD; 2 LSD; 1 base located at Sasebo; 1 base located at Yokosuka **USAF**: 12,758; 1 HQ (5th Air Force) located at Okinawa–Kadena AB; 1 ftr wg located at Okinawa–Kadena AB (2 ftr sqn with total of 18 F-16 *Fighting Falcon* located at Misawa AB); 1 ftr wg located at Okinawa–Kadena AB (1 SAR sqn with 8 HH-60G *Pave Hawk*, 1 AEW sqn with 2 E-3B *Sentry*, 2 ftr sqn with total of 24 F-15C *Eagle*/F-15D *Eagle*); 1 airlift wg located at Yokota AB with 10 C-130E *Hercules*; 2 C-21J; 1 special ops gp located at Okinawa–Kadena AB **USMC** 14,378; 1 Marine div (3rd); 1 ftr sqn with 12 F/A-18D *Hornet*; 1 tkr sqn with 12 KC-130J *Hercules*; 2 spt hel sqn with 12 CH-46E *Sea Knight*; 1 spt hel sqn with 12 MV-22B *Osprey*; 3 spt hel sqn with 10 CH-53E *Sea Stallion*

Korea, Democratic People's Republic of DPRK

North Korean Won		2008	2009	2010
GDP	US$	n.a.		
per capita	US$	n.a.		
Def bdgt	won	n.a.		
	US$	n.a.		

US$1=won

definitive economic data not available

Population   22,665,345

Age	0–14	15–19	20–24	25–29	30–64	65 plus
Male	12%	4%	4%	3%	22%	3%
Female	12%	4%	4%	3%	23%	5%

Capabilities

ACTIVE 1,106,000 (Army 950,000 Navy 46,000 Air 110,000) **Paramilitary 189,000**
Terms of service Army 5–12 years Navy 5–10 years Air Force 3–4 years, followed by compulsory part-time service to age 40. Thereafter service in the Worker/Peasant Red Guard to age 60.

RESERVE 4,700,000 (Army 600,000, Armed Forces 4,035,000 Navy 65,000), **Paramilitary 3,500,000**
Reservists are assigned to units (see also Paramilitary)

ORGANISATIONS BY SERVICE

Army ε950,000

FORCES BY ROLE

Army	corps tps: 14 arty bde (incl 122mm, 152mm, SP, MRL); 1 (FROG) SSM regt; 1 *Scud* SSM bde, 6 hy arty bde (incl MRL)
Armd	1 corps; 15 bde
Mech	4 corps
Inf	12 corps; 27 div; 14 bde
Arty	2 corps; 21 bde
MRL	9 bde
Capital Defence	1 corps

Special Purpose Forces Command 88,000

Army	6 sniper bde
Recce	17 bn
Amph	2 sniper bde
SF	8 Bureau of Reconnaissance bn
Lt inf	9 bde
AB	2 sniper bde; 3 bde; 1 bn

Reserves 600,000

Inf 40 div; 18 bde

EQUIPMENT BY TYPE

MBT 3,500+ T-34/T-54/T-55/T-62/Type-59

LT TK 560+: 560 PT-76; M-1985

APC 2,500+

APC (T) Type-531 (Type-63); VTT-323

APC (W) 2,500 BTR-40/BTR-50/BTR-60/ BTR-80A/BTR-152

ARTY 17,900+

SP 4,400: **122mm** M-1977/M-1981/M-1985/M-1991; **130mm** M-1975/M-1981/M-1991; **152mm** M-1974/M-1977; **170mm** M-1978/M-1989

TOWED 3,500: **122mm** D-30/D-74/M-1931/37; **130mm** M-46; **152mm** M-1937/M-1938/M-1943

GUN/MOR 120mm (reported)

MRL 2,500: **107mm** Type-63; **122mm** BM-11/M-1977 (BM-21)/M-1985/M-1992/M-1993; **240mm** M-1985/M-1989/M-1991

MOR 7,500: **82mm** M-37; **120mm** M-43; **160mm** M-43

AT • MSL

SP AT-3 9K11 *Sagger*

MANPATS AT-1 *Snapper*; AT-4 9K111 *Spigot*; AT-5 9K113 *Spandrel*

RCL 82mm 1,700 B-10

AD • SAM • MANPAD ε10,000+ SA-16 *Gimlet*/SA-7 *Grail*

GUNS 11,000

SP 14.5mm M-1984; **23mm** M-1992; **37mm** M-1992; **57mm** M-1985

TOWED 11,000: **14.5mm** ZPU-1/ZPU-2/ZPU-4; **23mm** ZU-23; **37mm** M-1939; **57mm** S-60; **85mm** M-1939 *KS-12*; **100mm** KS-19

MSL • SSM 64+: 24 FROG-3/FROG-5/FROG-7; ε10 *No-dong* (ε90+ msl); 30+ *Scud*-B/*Scud*-C (ε200+ msl)

Navy ε46,000

FORCES BY ROLE

Navy 2 (Fleet) HQ located at Tasa-ri; 1 HQ located at Nampo; 1 HQ located at Toejo Dong

EQUIPMENT BY TYPE

SUBMARINES • TACTICAL 63

SSK 22 PRC Type-031/FSU *Romeo*† each with 8 single 533mm TT with 14 SAET-60 HWT

SSC 21 *Sang-O*† each with 2 single 533mm TT each with Russian 53–65 ASW

SSI 20†

PRINCIPAL SURFACE COMBATANTS 8

FRIGATES • FF 3:

2 *Najin* each with 2 single each with 1 SS-N-2 tactical SSM, 2 RBU 1200 (10 eff.), 2 100mm sun

1 *Soho* with 4 single each with 1 SS-N-2 tactical SSM, 2 RBU 1200 (10 eff.), 1 100mm gun, 1 hel landing platform (for med hel)

CORVETTES • FS 5:

4 *Sariwon* each with 1 85mm gun

1 *Tral* each with 1 85mm gun

PATROL AND COASTAL COMBATANTS 329+

PTG 16:

6 *Sohung*

10 *Soju* each with 4 single each with 1 SS-N-2 tactical SSM

PFM 18:

4 *Huangfen* each with 4 single each with 1 SS-N-2 tactical SSM

6 *Komar* each with 2 single each with 1 SS-N-2 tactical SSM

8 *Osa* II each with 2 single each with 1 SS-N-2 tactical SSM

PHT 100: 60 *Ku Song*; 40 *Sin Hung*

PFC 19:

6 *Hainan* each with 4 RBU 1200 (20 eff.)

13 *Taechong* each with 2 RBU 1200 (10 eff.)

PFI 12 *Shanghai* II

PC 6 *Chong-Ju* each with 2 RBU 1200 (10 eff.), 1 85mm gun

PCI 158 (less than 100 tons); 12 FSU SO-1, 54 *Chong-Jin*, 59 *Chaho*, 33 *Sinpo*

MINE WARFARE • MINE COUNTERMEASURES 24: 19 *Yukto* I; 5 *Yukto* II

AMPHIBIOUS

LSM 10 *Hantae* (capacity 3 tanks; 350 troops)

CRAFT 244:

LCPL 96 *Nampo* (capacity 35 troops)

LCM 18

LCVP 130 (capacity 50 troops)

LOGISTICS AND SUPPORT 23:

AS 8 (converted cargo ships); **ASR** 1 Kowan; **AGI** 14 (converted fishing vessels)

FACILITIES

Bases Located at Tasa-ri, Koampo, Chodo-ri, Sagon-ni, Pipa Got, Nampo (West Coast); Puam-Dong, Toejo Dong, Chaho Nodongjagu, Mayang-do, Mugye-po, Najin, Songjon-pardo, Changjon, Munchon (East Coast)

Coastal Defence

FORCES BY ROLE

SSM 2 regt (*Silkworm* tactical SSM in 6 sites, and probably some mobile launchers)

EQUIPMENT BY TYPE

ARTY • TOWED 122mm M-1931/37; **152mm** M-1937

COASTAL 130mm M-1992; SM-4-1

Air Force 110,000

4 air divs. 1st, 2nd and 3rd Air Divs (cbt) responsible for N, E and S air defence sectors respectively. 8th Air Div (trg) responsible for NE sector. 33 regts (11 ftr/fga, 2 bbr, 7 hel, 7 pt, 6 trg) plus 3 indep air bns (recce/EW, test and evaluation, naval spt). The AF controls the national airline. Approx 70 full time/contingency air bases.

Flying hours   20 hrs/year on ac

FORCES BY ROLE

Bbr   3 (lt) regt with H-5 (Il-28) *Beagle*

Ftr/FGA   1 regt with MiG-29 *Fulcrum*; 1 regt with Su-7 *Fitter*; 6 regt with J-5 (MiG-17F) *Fresco C*; 5 regt with J-7 (MiG-21F) *Fishbed C*; 4 regt with J-6 (MiG-19S) *Farmer B*; 1 regt with MiG-23 *Flogger* ML/P; 1 regt with Su-25 *Frogfoot*; 1 regt with F-7B *Airguard*

Tpt regts with An-2 *Colt* to infiltrate 2 air force sniper brigades deep into ROK rear areas (possibly grounded); An-24 *Coke*; Il-18 *Coot*; Il-62M *Classic*; Tu-134 *Crusty*; Tu-154 *Careless*

Aslt hel regt with Mi-24 *Hind*

Trg regts with MiG-21 *Fishbed*; FT-2 (MiG-15UTI) *Midget*; CJ-6 (Yak-18)

Hel some regt with Z-5 (Mi-4) *Hound*; Mi-17 (Mi-8MT) *Hip H*/Mi-8 *Hip*; PZL Mi-2 *Hoplite*; Hughes 500D (Tpt)

SAM 19 bde with SA-3 *Goa*; SA-2 *Guideline*; SA-5 *Gammon*; SA-14 *Gremlin*/SA-16 *Gimlet*/SA-7 *Grail* (Possible Western systems, reverse-engineered *Stinger*)

EQUIPMENT BY TYPE
AIRCRAFT 620 combat capable
BBR 80 H-5 (Il-28) *Beagle*†
FTR 388: ε35 MiG-29A/S *Fulcrum*; 46 MiG-23ML *Flogger*; 10 MiG-23P *Flogger*; 30 MiG-21bis *Fishbed*†; 120 J-7 (MiG-21F) *Fishbed C*†; 107 J-5 (MiG-17F) *Fresco C*; 40 F-7B *Airguard*
FGA 152: 34 Su-25 *Frogfoot*; 18 Su-7 *Fitter*; 100 J-6 (MiG-19S) *Farmer B*;
TPT 215: 6 An-24 *Coke*; 2 Il-18 *Coot*; 2 Il-62M *Classic*; 2 Tu-134 *Crusty*; 4 Tu-154 *Careless*; 1 Tu-204-300; ε200 Y-5 (An-2) *Colt*
TRG 217: 180 CJ-6 (Yak-18); 35 FT-2 (MiG-15UTI) *Midget*
HELICOPTERS
ATK 20 Mi-24 *Hind*
SPT 202: 48 Z-5 (Mi-4) *Hound*; 15 Mi-17 (Mi-8MT) *Hip H*/Mi-8 *Hip*; 139 PZL Mi-2 *Hoplite*
UTL 80 Hughes 500D (Tpt)
UAV *Shmel*
AD • SAM 3400+
TOWED 312+: 179+ SA-2 *Guideline*; 133 SA-3 *Goa*
STATIC/SHELTER 38 SA-5 *Gammon*
MANPAD 3,050+ SA-7 *Grail*/SA-14 *Gremlin*/SA-16 *Gimlet* (Possible Western systems, reverse-engineered *Stinger*)
MSL • AAM AA-10 *Alamo*; AA-11 *Archer*; AA-2 *Atoll*; AA-7 *Apex*; AA-8 *Aphid*; PL-5; PL-7

Paramilitary 189,000 active

Security Troops 189,000 (incl border guards, public safety personnel)
Ministry of Public Security

Worker/Peasant Red Guard 3,500,000+ reservists
Org on a provincial/town/village basis; comd structure is bde–bn–coy–pl; small arms with some mor and AD guns (but many units unarmed)

Korea, Republic of ROK

South Korean Won		2008	2009	2010
GDP	won	1,023tr	1,027tr	
	US$	928bn	882bn	
per capita	US$	19,188	18,188	
Growth	%	2.2	-1.0	
Inflation	%	4.7	2.5	
Def bdgt	won	26.6tr	28.6tr	29.6tr
	US$	24.18bn	24.51bn.	
US$1=won		1,100	1,164	

Population 48,508,972

Age	0–14	15–19	20–24	25–29	30–64	65 plus
Male	10%	3%	4%	4%	25%	4%
Female	9%	3%	4%	4%	25%	5%

Capabilities

ACTIVE 687,000 (Army 560,000 Navy 68,000 Air 64,000) Paramilitary 4,500
Terms of service conscription: Army, Navy and Air Force 26 months

RESERVE 4,500,000

Reserve obligation of three days per year. First Combat Forces (Mobilisation Reserve Forces) or Regional Combat Forces (Homeland Defence Forces) to age 33

Paramilitary 3,500,000
Being re-organised

ORGANISATIONS BY SERVICE

Army 420,000; 140,000 conscript (total 560,000)
FORCES BY ROLE
Command 3 fd army, 1 special warfare, 1 capital defence, 1 army avn; 8 corps

Armd 4 indep bde

Mech Inf 5 div (*each:* 3 mech inf bde with (3 tk bn, 1 recce bn, 1 fd arty bde, 1 engr bn))

Inf 17 div (*each:* 1 arty regt (4 arty bn), 1 recce bn, 1 engr bn, 1 tk bn, 3 inf regt); 2 indep bde

SF 7 bde

Air aslt 1 bde

Counter-Infiltration 3 bde

SSM 3 bn

ADA 3 bde

SAM 2 (*Nike Hercules*) bn (10 sites); 3 (I *HAWK*) bn (24 sites)

EQUIPMENT BY TYPE
MBT 2,750: 1,420 *K/K1A1*; 80 T-80U; 400 M-47 (in store); 597 M-48A5; 253 M-48
AIFV 40 BMP-3;

APC 2,780
  APC (T) 2,560: 1,700 KIFV; 420 M-113; 140 M-577; 300 Bv 206
  APC (W) 220; 20 BTR-80; 200 KM-900/-901 (Fiat 6614)
ARTY 10,774+
  SP 1,089+: **155mm** 1076: ε36 K-9 *Thunder*; 1,040 M-109A2; **175mm** M-107; **203mm** 13 M-110
  TOWED 3,500+: **105mm** 1,700 M-101/KH-178; **155mm** 1,800+ KH-179/M-114/M-115
  MRL 185: **130mm** 156 *Kooryong*; **227mm** 29 MLRS (all ATACMS capable)
  MOR 6,000: **81mm** KM-29 (M-29); **107mm** M-30
AT • MSL • MANPATS AT-7 9K115 *Saxhorn*; TOW-2A
  RCL **57mm**; **75mm**; **90mm** M-67; **106mm** M-40A2
  RL **67mm** PZF 44 *Panzerfaust*
  GUNS 58
    SP **90mm** 50 M-36
    TOWED **76mm** 8 M-18 *Hellcat* (AT gun)
HELICOPTERS
  ATK 60 AH-1F *Cobra*/AH-1J *Cobra*
  SPEC OP 6MH-47E (MH-47E) *Chinook*
  SPT 21: 3 AS-332L *Super Puma*; 18 CH-47D *Chinook*
  UTL 337: 12 Bo-105; 130 Hughes 500D; 45 MD-500; 20 UH-1H *Iroquois*; 130 UH-60P *Black Hawk*
AD • SAM 1,138+
  SP *Chun Ma Pegasus*
  TOWED 158 I-*HAWK* MIM-23B; 48 *Patriot* being delivered
  STATIC 200 MIM-14 *Nike Hercules*
  MANPAD 780+: 60 FIM-43 *Redeye*; ε200 FIM-92A *Stinger*; 350 *Javelin*; 170 *Mistral*; SA-16 *Gimlet*
  GUNS 330+
    SP 170: **20mm** ε150 KIFV *Vulcan* SPAAG; **30mm** 20 BIHO *Flying Tiger*
    TOWED 160: **20mm** 60 M-167 *Vulcan*; **35mm** 20 GDF-003; **40mm** 80 L/60/L/70; M1
RADAR • LAND AN/TPQ-36 *Firefinder* (arty, mor); AN/TPQ-37 *Firefinder* (arty); RASIT (veh, arty)
MSL • SSM 12 NHK-I/-II *Hyonmu*

Reserves

FORCES BY ROLE

Comd   1 army HQ
Inf   24 div

Navy 24,000; ε19,000 conscript (total 68,000; incl marines)

FORCES BY ROLE

Naval HQ (CNOROK) located at Gyeryongdae, with an Operational Cmd HQ (CINCROKFLT) located Jinhae with 3 Separate Fleet Elements; 1st Fleet Donghae (East Sea – Sea of Japan); 2nd Fleet Pyeongtaek (West Sea – Yellow Sea); 3rd Fleet Busan (South Sea – Korea Strait); additional 3 Flotillas (incl SF, mine warfare, amphibious and spt elements) and 1 Naval Air Wing (3 gp plus Spt gp)

EQUIPMENT BY TYPE
SUBMARINES • TACTICAL 13
  SSK 11:
    9 *Chang Bogo* each with 8 single 533mm TT each with SUT HWT

    2 *Son Won-ill* (AIP fitted) each with 8 single 533mm TT each with SUT HWT (additional vessels in build)
  SSI 2 KSS-1 *Dolgorae* each with 2 single 406mm TT
PRINCIPAL SURFACE COMBATANTS 47
  DESTROYERS • DDG 10:
    1 *Sejong* KDX-3 each with 2 Mk 41 VLS quad (8 eff.) each with RGM-84 *Harpoon* tactical SSM, 2 32/64 cell Mk 41 VLS with *Sea Sparrow* SAM and ESSM, 1 127mm gun, (capacity *Super Lynx* utl hel); (Additional 2 of class in build)
    3 *Gwanggaeto Daewang* KDX-1 each with 2 Mk 41 VLS quad (8 eff.) each with RGM-84 *Harpoon* tactical SSM, 1 16 cell Mk 48 VLS with *Sea Sparrow* SAM, 1 127mm gun, (capacity 1 *Super Lynx* utl hel)
    6 *Chungmugong Yi Sun-Jhin* KDX-2 each with 2 Mk 141 VLS quad (8 eff.) each with 8 RGM-84C *Harpoon* tactical SSM, 2 Mk 41 VLS-32 cells each with SM-2 MR SAM, 1 127mm gun (capacity 1 *Super Lynx* utl hel)
  FRIGATES • FFG 9:
    9 *Ulsan* each with 2 Mk 141 VLS quad (8 eff.) each with RGM-84C *Harpoon* tactical SSM, 2 triple ASTT (6 eff.) each with Mk 46 LWT, 2 76mm gun
  CORVETTES • FS 28:
    4 *Dong Hae* each with 2 triple ASTT (6 eff.) each with Mk 46 LWT
    24 *Po Hang* each with 2 MM-38 *Exocet* tactical SSM (fitted on some vessels), 2 triple ASTT (6 eff.) each with Mk 46 LWT
PATROL AND COASTAL COMBATANTS ε76
  PFM 1 *Yoon Young Ha* each with *Hae Song* (*Sea Star*) tactical SSM (reported) 1 76mm gun (additional vessels in build)
  PFI 75 *Sea Dolphin*
MINE WARFARE 10
  MINE COUNTERMEASURES 9
    MHC 6 *Kan Kyeong*
    MSC 3 *Yang Yang*
  MINELAYERS • ML 1 *Won San*
AMPHIBIOUS
PRINCIPAL AMPHIBIOUS SHIPS • LPD 1 *Dodko* (capacity 2 LCVP; 10 tanks; 700 troops)
  LS 11
    LST 8: 4 *Alligator* (capacity 20 tanks; 300 troops); 4 *Un Bong* (capacity 16 tanks; 200 troops)
    ACV 3 *Tsaplya* (capacity 1 MBT; 130 troops)
  CRAFT 36: 6 LCT; 20 LCVP; 10 LCM
LOGISTICS AND SUPPORT 24
  AORH 3 *Chun Jee*
  ARS 1
  AG 1 *Sunjin* (trials spt)
  ATS 2
  AGOR 17 (civil manned, funded by the Min. of Transport)
FACILITIES
Bases Located at Pusan, Mukho, Cheju, Pohang, Mokpo, Jinhae (Fleet HQ and 3rd Fleet), Donghae (1st Fleet), Pyongtaek (2nd Fleet)

Naval Aviation

AIRCRAFT 8 combat capable
  MP ASW 8 P-3C *Orion**

UTL 5 F406 *Caravan II*
HELICOPTERS
  ASW 24: 11 *Lynx* MK99; 13 *Lynx* MK99-A
  UTL 5 IAR-316 (SA-316) *Alouette III*

Marines 25,000

FORCES BY ROLE

Spt   some unit

Marine 2 div; 1 bde

EQUIPMENT BY TYPE

MBT 60 M-47
AAV 102: 42 AAV-7A1; 60 LVTP-7
ARTY TOWED: **105mm**; **155mm**
LNCHR: some single (truck mounted) each with RGM-84A *Harpoon* tactical SSM

Air Force 64,000

FORCES BY ROLE

4 Cmds (Ops, Southern Combat Logs, Trg), Tac Airlift Wg and Composite Wg are all responsible to ROK Air Force HQ.

FGA/Ftr   1 wg with F-15K; 2 wg with KF-16C *Fighting Falcon*; KF-16D *Fighting Falcon* F-4E *Phantom II*; 3 wg with F-5E *Tiger II*; F-5F *Tiger II*

FAC   1 wg with KO-1

ELINT   (SIGINT) sqn with *Hawk*er 800XP

Recce/   1 gp with *Hawk*er 800RA; RF-4C *Phantom II**;
TAC   RF-5A *Tiger II**; *Harpy*; *Searcher*

SAR   1 sqn with Bell 212; UH-1H *Iroquois*

CCT/FAC 1 wg with equipping with A-50 *Golden Eagle*

Tpt   some wg with B-737-300 (VIP); BAe-748 (VIP); C-130H *Hercules*; CN-235-220/CN-235M; AS-332 *Super Puma*; CH-47 *Chinook*; KA-32 *Helix C* (SAR); S-92A *Superhawk* (VIP); UH-60 *Black Hawk* (Spec Ops)

Trg   some schools/sqn with F-5B *Freedom Fighter**; *Hawk* MK67; KT-1; T-38 *Talon*; T-50; Il-103

EQUIPMENT BY TYPE

AIRCRAFT 490 combat capable
  FTR/FGA 467: 39 F-15K *Eagle* (20 more on order 2010–2012); 20 F-5B *Freedom Fighter**; 142 F-5E *Tiger II*; 32 F-5F *Tiger II*; 118 KF-16C *Fighting Falcon*; 46 KF-16D *Fighting Falcon*; 70 F-4E *Phantom II*; (some F-4D *Phantom II* in store)
  RECCE 47: 4 Hawker 800RA; 20 KO-1; 18 RF-4C *Phantom II**; 5 RF-5A *Tiger II**
  EW • ELINT 4 Hawker 800SIG
  TPT 33: 1 B-737-300 (VIP); 2 BAe-748 (VIP); 10 C-130H *Hercules*; 20 CN-235-220/CN-235M
  TRG 150: 17 *Hawk* MK67; 83 KT-1; 10 T-38 *Talon* (being returned to the USAF); 15 Il-103; 25 A-50/T-50
HELICOPTERS
  SPT 8: 2 AS-332 *Super Puma*; 6 CH-47 *Chinook*
  UTL 48: 5 Bell 212/412; 7 KA-32 *Helix C* (SAR); 5 UH-1H *Iroquois*; 3 S-92A *Superhawk* (VIP); 28 UH-60 *Black Hawk*
  UAV 100+: some *Night Intruder*
  RECCE • TAC 103: 100 *Harpy*; 3 *Searcher*

MSL • TACTICAL
  ASM AGM-130; AGM-142 *Popeye*
  AGM AGM-65A *Maverick*; AGM-84 *Harpoon*; AGM-84-H SLAM-ER
  ARM AGM-88 *HARM*
  AAM AIM-120B *AMRAAM*/AIM-120C5 *AMRAAM*; AIM-7 *Sparrow*; AIM-9 *Sidewinder*

Paramilitary ε4,500 active

Civilian Defence Corps 3,500,000 reservists (to age 50)

Maritime Police ε4,500

PATROL AND COASTAL COMBATANTS 87+:
  PSO 6: 1 *Sumjinkang*; 3 *Mazinger*; 1 *Han Kang*; 1 *Sambongho*
  PCO 12: 6 *Sea Dragon/Whale*; 6 *430 Ton*
  PCC 31: 4 *Bukhansan*; 5 Hyundai Type; 22 *Sea Wolf/Shark*
  PCI ε20
  PBI 18 *Seagull*
LOGISTICS AND SUPPORT • ARS 10
HELICOPTERS • UTL 9 Hughes 500

DEPLOYMENT

AFGHANISTAN
UN • UNAMA 1 obs

ARABIAN GULF AND INDIAN OCEAN
Maritime Security Operations; 1 DDG

CÔTE D'IVOIRE
UN • UNOCI 2 obs

INDIA/PAKISTAN
UN • UNMOGIP 9 obs

LEBANON
UN • UNIFIL 367; 1 inf bn

LIBERIA
UN • UNMIL 1; 1 obs

NEPAL
UN • UNMIN 4 obs

SUDAN
UN • UNMIS 1; 6 obs
UN • UNAMID 2

WESTERN SAHARA
UN • MINURSO 2

FOREIGN FORCES

Sweden NNSC: 5 obs

Switzerland NNSC: 5 officers

United States US Pacific Command: **Army** 17,130; 1 HQ (8th Army) located at Seoul; 1 div HQ (2nd Inf) located at Tongduchon; 1 armd HBCT; 1 cbt avn bde; 1 arty (fires) bde; 1 AD bde with MIM 104 *Patriot*/FIM-92A *Avenger*; some M-1 *Abrams* MBT; some M-2/M-3 *Bradley* AIFV; some M-109 SP arty; some MLRS; some AH-64 *Apache*; some CH-47 *Chinook*; some UH-60 *Black Hawk* **Navy** 254;

USAF 7,857; 1 HQ (7th Air Force) located at Osan AB; 1 ftr wg located at Kunsan AB (1 ftr sqn with 20 F-16C *Fighting Falcon*/F-16D *Fighting Falcon*); 1 ftr wg located at Kunsan AB (1 ftr sqn with 20 F-16C *Fighting Falcon*/F-16D *Fighting Falcon*, 1 ftr sqn with 24 A-10 *Thunderbolt II*/OA-10 *Thunderbolt II* (12 of each type) located at Osan AB) **USMC** 133

Laos LAO

New Lao Kip		2008	2009	2010
GDP	kip	46.2tr		
	US$	5.3bn		
per capita	US$	792		
Growth	%	7.5	4.6	
Inflation	%	7.6	0.2	
Def bdgt	kip	ε150bn		
	US$	ε17m		
US$1=kip		8,744	8,477	

Population   6,834,345

Ethnic groups: Lao 55%; Khmou 11%; Hmong 8%

Age	0–14	15–19	20–24	25–29	30–64	65 plus
Male	21%	6%	5%	4%	13%	1%
Female	21%	5%	5%	4%	14%	2%

Capabilities

ACTIVE 29,100 (Army 25,600 Air 3,500) **Paramilitary 100,000**

Terms of service 18 month minimum conscription

ORGANISATIONS BY SERVICE

Army 25,600

FORCES BY ROLE
4 Mil Regions

Armd	1 bn
Inf	5 div; 7 indep regt; 65 indep coy
Arty	5 bn
ADA	9 bn
Engr	1 regt
Avn	1 (liaison) lt flt
Engr construction	2 regt

EQUIPMENT BY TYPE
MBT 25: 15 T-54/T-55; 10 T-34/85
LT TK 10 PT-76
APC (W) 50: 30 BTR-40/BTR-60; 20 BTR-152
ARTY 62+
   TOWED 62: **105mm** 20 M-101; **122mm** 20 D-30/M-30 M-1938; **130mm** 10 M-46; **155mm** 12 M-114
   MOR 81mm; 82mm; 107mm M-1938/M-2A1; **120mm** M-43
AT • RCL 57mm M-18/A1; **75mm** M-20; **106mm** M-40; **107mm** B-11

RL 73mm RPG-7 *Knout*
AD • SAM • MANPAD SA-7 *Grail*
  GUNS
   SP 23mm ZSU-23-4
   TOWED 14.5mm ZPU-1/ZPU-4; **23mm** ZU-23; **37mm** M-1939; **57mm** S-60

Army Marine Section ε600
PATROL AND COASTAL COMBATANTS 52+
PBR 40 **PCR** 12 less than 100 tonnes
AMPHIBIOUS LCM 4

Air Force 3,500
FORCES BY ROLE

FGA 2 sqn with up to 22 MiG-21bis *Fishbed L & N*†; up to 2 MiG-21UM *Mongol B*†

Tpt 1 sqn with 4 An-2 *Colt*; 5 Y-7 (An-24) *Coke*; 3 An-26 *Curl*; 1 An-74 *Coaler*; 1 Y-12; 1 Yak-40 *Codling* (VIP)

Trg sqn with 8 Yak-18 *Max*

Hel 1 sqn with 3 SA-360 *Dauphin*; 1 KA-32T *Helix C* (5 more on order); 1 Mi-26 *Halo*; 1 Mi-6 *Hook*; 9 Mi-8 *Hip*; 12 Mi-17 (Mi-8MT) *Hip H*

EQUIPMENT BY TYPE
AIRCRAFT 22† combat capable
  FTR up to 22 MiG-21bis *Fishbed L & N*†
  TPT 15: 4 An-2 *Colt*; 3 An-26 *Curl*; 1 An-74 *Coaler*; 1 Y-12; 5 Y-7 (An-24) *Coke*; 1 Yak-40 *Codling* (VIP)
  TRG up to 10: 2 MiG-21UM *Mongol B*†; 8 Yak-18 *Max*
HELICOPTERS
  SAR 3 SA-360 *Dauphin*
  SPT 24: 1 KA-32T *Helix C* (5 more on order); 1 Mi-26 *Halo*; 1 Mi-6 *Hook*; 9 Mi-8; 12 Mi-17 (Mi-8MT) *Hip H*
MSL • AAM AA-2 *Atoll*†

Paramilitary

Militia Self-Defence Forces 100,000+
Village 'home guard' or local defence

Malaysia MYS

Malaysian Ringgit RM		2008	2009	2010
GDP	RM	740bn		
	US$	222bn		
per capita	US$	8,792		
Growth	%	4.6	-3.6	
Inflation	%	5.4	-0.1	
Def bdgt	RM	13.92bn	13.66bn	
	US$	4.18bn	4.03bn	
US$1=RM		3.33	3.39	

Population   25,715,819

Ethnic groups: Malay and other indigenous (Bunipatre) 64%; Chinese 27%; Indian 9%

Age	0–14	15–19	20–24	25–29	30–64	65 plus
Male	17%	5%	5%	4%	18%	2%
Female	16%	5%	4%	4%	18%	3%

Capabilities

ACTIVE 109,000 (Army 80,000 Navy 14,000 Air 15,000) Paramilitary 24,600

RESERVE 51,600 (Army 50,000, Navy 1,000 Air Force 600) Paramilitary 244,700

ORGANISATIONS BY SERVICE

Army 80,000 (to be 60–70,000)
FORCES BY ROLE
2 mil regions, 1 HQ fd comd, 4 area comd (div)

Armd	5 regt
Mech Inf	1 bde (3 mech bn)
Inf	9 bde (36 bn)
SF	1 bde (3 SF bn)
AB	1 bde (10th) (Rapid Deployment Force) (1 lt tk sqn, 1 light arty regt, 3 AB bn)
Med Arty	2 regt
Fd Arty	7 regt
MRL	1 regt
ADA	3 regt
Engr	5 regt
Avn	1 hel sqn
Arty Loc	1 regt

EQUIPMENT BY TYPE
MBT 48 PT-91M *Twardy*
LT TK 26 *Scorpion*
RECCE 314: 140 AML-60/AML-90; 92 *Ferret* (60 mod); 82 SIBMAS
AIFV 44: 31 ACV300 *Adnan (Bushmaster)*; 13 ACV300 *Adnan* AGL
APC 835
   APC (T) 333: 120 ACV300 *Adnan*, 77 variants; 25 FV4333 *Stormer*; 98 K-200A, 13 variants
   APC (W) 502: 452 *Condor* (incl variants); 50 LAV-150 *Commando*
ARTY 436
   TOWED 164: **105mm** 130 Model 56 pack howitzer; **155mm** 34: 12 FH-70; 22 G-5
   MRL 18 *ASTROS II* (equipped with 127mm SS-30)
   MOR 254: **81mm SP** 14: 4 K281A1; 10 ACV-300; **120mm** 8 ACV-S
   81mm: 232
AT MSL
   SP 8 ACV300 *Baktar Shikan*;
   MANPATS 60+: 18 AT-7 9K115 *Saxhorn*; 24 *Eryx*; 18 *Baktar Shihan* (HJ-8); METIS-M; C90-CRRB
   RCL 260: **84mm** 236 *Carl Gustav*; **106mm** 24 M-40
   RL 73mm 584 RPG-7 *Knout*
AMPHIBIOUS • LCA 165 *Damen* Assault Craft 540 (capacity 10 troops)
HELICOPTERS • UTL 20: 9 SA-316B *Alouette III*; 11 A109
AD SAM 15 *Jernas (Rapier 2000)*
   MANPAD 48+: 48 *Starburst*; *Anza*; SA-18 *Grouse (Igla)*
   GUNS • TOWED 60: **35mm** 24 GDF-005; **40mm** 36 L40/70

Reserves

Territorial Army
Some paramilitary forces to be incorporated into a re-organised territorial organisation.
5 highway sy bn
Border Security 2 bde (being created from existing Territorial units)
Inf   16 regt

Navy 14,000
FORCES BY ROLE
1 Naval HQ located at Lumut with 3 additional Regional Commands (Reg Cmd); Reg Cmd 1 Kuantan – East Coast; Reg Cmd 2 Kota Kinabalu – Borneo; Reg Cmd 3 Langkawi – West Coast
EQUIPMENT BY TYPE
SUBMARINES • TACTICAL • SSK 2 *Tunku Abdul Rahman* (Scorpene) each with 6 single 533mm TT for WASS *Black Shark* LWT (2nd vessel expected ISD 2010)
PRINCIPAL SURFACE COMBATANTS 12
   FRIGATES 2:
   FFG 2 *Lekiu* each with 2 B515 *ILAS-3* triple 324mm each with *Sting Ray* LWT, 2 quad (8 eff.) each with MM-40 *Exocet* tactical SSM, 1 *Sea Wolf* VLS with 16 *Sea Wolf* SAM, (capacity 1 *Super Lynx* ASW/ASUW hel)
   CORVETTES 10
      FSG 8:
      4 *Laksamana* each with 1 quad (4 eff.) with 12 *Aspide* SAM, 2 B515 *ILAS-3* triple 324mm each with A244 LWT, 3 twin (6 eff.) each with Mk 2 *Otomat* SSM, 1 76mm gun
      4 *Kedah* (MEKO) each fitted for MM-40 *Exocet* tactical SSM; each fitted for RAM CIWS and 1 76mm gun (Further 2 of class in build)
      FS 2 *Kasturi* each with 2 twin (4 eff.) each with MM-38 *Exocet* tactical SSM, 1 Mle 54 *Creusot-Loire* 375mm Bofors (6 eff.), 1 100mm gun, 1 hel landing platform
PATROL AND COASTAL COMBATANTS 14
   PFM 8:
   4 *Handalan* (*Spica*-M) each with 2 twin (4 eff.) each with MM-38 *Exocet* tactical SSM, 1 57mm gun
   4 *Perdana* (*Combattante* II) each with 2 single each with MM-38 *Exocet* tactical SSM, 1 57mm gun
   PFC 6 *Jerong* (Lurssen 45)
MINE WARFARE • MINE COUNTERMEASURES
MCO 4 *Mahamiru*
AMPHIBIOUS
   CRAFT 115 **LCM/LCU**
LOGISTICS AND SUPPORT 9
   AOR 2; **AOL** 4; **AGS** 2; **TRG •AXS** 1
FACILITIES
Bases   Located at Tanjung Pengelih, Semporna, Langkawi (under construction), Lumut, Labuan, Kuantan, Sepanggar Bay (under construction)

Naval Aviation 160
HELICOPTERS
   ASW/ASUW 6 *Lynx* Srs300 *Super Lynx*
   UTL 6 AS-555 *Fennec*

MSL
  ASM *Sea Skua*

Special Forces

| Mne cdo | 1 unit |

Air Force 15,000

1 Air Op HQ, 2 Air Div, 1 trg and Log Cmd, 1 Intergrated
Area Def Systems HQ

Flying hours   60 hrs/year

FORCES BY ROLE

Ftr   1 sqn with MiG-29N/MiG-29NUB *Fulcrum* (to
            be withdrawn from service)

FGA   1 sqn with F/A-18D *Hornet*; 1 sqn with Su-
            30MKM; 2 sqn with *Hawk* MK108; *Hawk*
            MK208

FGA/Recce   1 sqn with F-5E *Tiger II*/F-5F *Tiger II*; RF-5E
            Tigereye

MR   1 sqn with Beech 200T

SF   1 Air Force Commando unit (airfield defence/
            SAR)

Tpt   2 sqn with KC-130H *Hercules* (tkr); C-130H
            Hercules; C-130H-30 *Hercules*; Cessna 402B (2
            modified for aerial survey); 1 (VIP) sqn with
            B-737-700 BBJ; 1 Airbus A319CT; BD700 *Global
            Express*; F-28 *Fellowship*; *Falcon* 900; S-61N;
            S-70A *Black Hawk*; A-109; 1 sqn with CN-235

Trg   1 trg school with MB-339A/C; MD3-160; PC-7/
            PC-7 MK II *Turbo Trainer*; SA-316 *Alouette III*

Hel   4 (tpt/SAR) sqn with S-61A-4 *Nuri*; S-61N;
            S-70A *Black Hawk*

SAM   1 sqn with *Starburst*

EQUIPMENT BY TYPE

AIRCRAFT 74 combat capable
  FTR 29: 13 F-5E *Tiger II*/F-5F *Tiger II*; 16 MiG-29N *Fulcrum*
  (to be withdrawn from service during 2010)
  FGA 28: 8 F/A-18D *Hornet*; 12 Su-30MKM (6 more on
  order); 8 *Hawk* MK108
  RECCE 2 RF-5E *Tigereye*
  MP 4 Beech 200T
  TKR 2 KC-130H *Hercules*
  TPT 32: 1 Airbus A319CT; 1 B-737-700 BBJ; 1 BD700
  Global Express; 4 C-130H *Hercules*; 8 C-130H-30 *Hercules*; 6
  CN-235 (incl 2 VIP); 9 Cessna 402B (2 modified for aerial
  survey); 1 F-28 *Fellowship*; 1 *Falcon* 900
  TRG 101: 15 *Hawk* MK208*; 8 MB-339AB; 8 MB-339C; 20
  MD3-160; 2 MiG-29NUB *Fulcrum**; 30 PC-7/18 PC-7 MK
  II *Turbo Trainer*
HELICOPTERS
  ASW 20 S-61A-4 *Nuri*
  SPT 8: 4 S-61N; 4 S-70A *Black Hawk*
  UTL 9: 1 A-109; 8 SA-316 *Alouette III*
UAV • RECCE • TAC 3 *Eagle* 150; *Aludra*
AD • SAM •MANPAD *Starburst*
MSL
  ASM AGM-65 *Maverick*; AGM-84D *Harpoon*
  AAM AA-10 *Alamo*; AA-11 *Archer*; AIM-7 *Sparrow*; AIM-
  9 *Sidewinder*

Paramilitary ε24,600

Police-General Ops Force 18,000
FORCES BY ROLE
Police   5 bde HQ; 2 (Aboriginal) bn; 19 bn;
          4 indep coy
Spec Ops 1 bn
EQUIPMENT BY TYPE
RECCE ε100 S52 *Shorland*
APC (W) 170: 140 AT105 *Saxon*; ε30 SB-301

Malaysian Maritime Enforcement Agency (MMEA) ε4,500

1 MMEA HQ Putrajaya with designated control for
the Malaysian Maritime Zone, which is divided into
5 Maritime Regions (Northern Peninsula; Southern
Peninsula; Eastern Peninsula; Sarawak; Sabah) and sub-
divided into a further 18 Maritime Districts. Supported
by one provisional MMEA Air Unit.

EQUIPMENT BY TYPE
PATROL AND COASTAL COMBATANTS 51+:
  PSO 2 *Musytari* each with 1 100mm gun, 1 hel landing
  platform
  PCC 19: 15 *Sipadan* (ex-*Kris*); 4 *Sabah*
  PC 5 *Ramunia*
  PBF 14 *Gagah*
  PB 10
  TRG 1
HELICOPTERS
  MP/SAR 3 *Dauphin* AS-365

Marine Police 2,100
EQUIPMENT BY TYPE
PATROL AND COASTAL COMBATANTS 150
  PFI 30: 9 *Imp* PX; 15 *Lang Hitam*; 6 *Sangitan*
  PBI 120
LOGISTICS AND SUPPORT 8: 2 **AT**; 6 Tpt
FACILITIES
Bases Located at Kuala Kemaman, Penang, Tampoi,
       Sandakan

Police Air Unit
AIRCRAFT
  TPT 7 PC-6 *Turbo-Porter*
  UTL 10: 4 Cessna 206; 6 Cessna 208 *Caravan I*
HELICOPTERS
  SPT 2 AS-355F *Ecureuil II*
  UTL 1 Bell 206L *LongRanger*

Area Security Units (R) 3,500
(Auxillary General Ops Force)
Paramilitary 89 unit

Border Scouts (R) 1,200
in Sabah, Sarawak

People's Volunteer Corps 240,000 reservists (some 17,500 armed)
RELA

Customs Service
PATROL AND COASTAL COMBATANTS 44
  PFI 8: 2 *Combatboat* 90H; 6 *Perak*
  MISC BOATS/CRAFT 36 craft

DEPLOYMENT

DEMOCRATIC REPUBLIC OF CONGO
UN • MONUC 17 obs

LEBANON
UN • UNIFIL 742; 1 inf bn

LIBERIA
UN • UNMIL 6 obs

NEPAL
UN • UNMIN 7 obs

SUDAN
UN • UNMIS 2; 8 obs
UN • UNAMID 14; 2 obs

TIMOR LESTE
UN • UNMIT 2 obs

WESTERN SAHARA
UN • MINURSO 20; 12 obs; 1 fd hospital

FOREIGN FORCES

Australia Air Force: 13 with 1 AP-3C *Orion* crew; Army: 115; 1 inf coy (on 3-month rotational tours)

Mongolia MNG

Mongolian Tugrik t		2008	2009	2010
GDP	t	5.5tr		
	US$	4.7bn		
per capita	US$	1,556		
Growth	%	9.0	0.5	
Inflation	%	26.8	8.5	
Def bdgt	t	ε60bn		
	US$	ε51m		
FMA (US)	US$	1.0m	1.0m	7.0m
US$1=t		1,165	1,451	

Population   3,041,142

Ethnic groups: Khalka 80%; Kazakh 6%

Age	0–14	15–19	20–24	25–29	30–64	65 plus
Male	15%	6%	5%	5%	17%	2%
Female	14%	6%	5%	5%	18%	2%

Capabilities

ACTIVE 10,000 (Army 8,900 Air 800 Construction Troops 300) **Paramilitary 7,200**
Terms of service conscription: males 18–25 years, 1 year

RESERVE 137,000 (Army 137,000)

ORGANISATIONS BY SERVICE

Army 5,600; 3,300 conscript (total 8,900)
FORCES BY ROLE
MRR 6 (under strength) regt
Lt Inf 1 bn (rapid deployment – 2nd bn to form)
AB   1 bn
Arty   1 regt

EQUIPMENT BY TYPE
MBT 370 T-54/T-55
RECCE 120 BRDM-2
AIFV 310 BMP-1
APC (W) 150 BTR-60
ARTY 570
  TOWED ε300: **122mm** D-30/M-30 *M-1938*; **130mm** M-46; **152mm** ML-20 *M-1937*
  MRL 122mm 130 BM-21
  MOR 140: **120mm**; **160mm**; **82mm**
AT • **GUNS** 200: **85mm** D-44 /D-48; **100mm** M-1944 /MT-12

Air Forces 800
FORCES BY ROLE
Tpt   1 sqn with A-310-300; An-2 *Colt*; An-26 *Curl*; B-737
Hel   1 sqn with Mi-24 *Hind**; Mi-8 *Hip*; Mi-171 (SAR)
AD   2 regt with 150 S-60/ZPU-4/ZU-23

EQUIPMENT BY TYPE
AIRCRAFT • **TPT** 9: 1 A-310-300; 6 An-2 *Colt*; 1 An-26 *Curl*; 1 B-737
HELICOPTERS
  ATK 11 Mi-24 *Hind*
  SPT 13: 11 Mi-8 *Hip*; 2 Mi-171
AD • **GUNS** • **TOWED** 150: **14.5mm** ZPU-4; **23mm** ZU-23; **57mm** S-60

Paramilitary 7,200 active

Border Guard 1,300; 4,700 conscript (total 6,000)

Internal Security Troops 400; 800 conscript (total 1,200)
Gd 4 unit

Construction Troops 300

DEPLOYMENT

CENTRAL AFRICAN REPUBLIC/CHAD
UN • MINURCAT 1

DEMOCRATIC REPUBLIC OF CONGO
UN • MONUC 2 obs

LIBERIA
UN • UNMIL 250; 1 inf coy

SUDAN

UN • UNMIS 2 obs

WESTERN SAHARA

UN • MINURSO 4 obs

Myanmar MMR

Myanmar Kyat K		2008	2009	2010
GDP		26.85tr	29.22tr	
	US$a	22.6bn	26.7bn	
per capita	US$a	473	555	
Growth	%	4.0	4.3	
Inflation	%	22.5	6.9	
Def bdgt	K	n.a.		
	US$	n.a.		
US$1=K		5.38	6.42	

a PPP estimate

Population   48,137,741

Ethnic groups: Burmese 68%; Shan 9%; Karen 7%; Rakhine 4%; Chinese 3+%; Other Chin, Kachin, Kayan, Lahu, Mon, Palaung, Pao, Wa, 9%

Age	0–14	15–19	20–24	25–29	30–64	65 plus
Male	13%	5%	5%	5%	18%	2%
Female	13%	5%	5%	5%	19%	3%

Capabilities

ACTIVE 406,000 (Army 375,000 Navy 16,000 Air 15,000) Paramilitary 107,250

ORGANISATIONS BY SERVICE

Army ε375,000

FORCES BY ROLE

12 regional comd, 4 regional op comd, 14 military op comd, 34 tactical op comd (TDC)

Armd   10 bn

Inf   100 bn; 337 bn (regional comd)

Lt Inf   10 div

Arty   7 bn; 37 indep coy

AD   7 bn

EQUIPMENT BY TYPE

MBT 150: 50 T-72; 100 Type-69-II

LT TK 105 Type-63 (ε60 serviceable)

RECCE 115: 45 Ferret; 40 Humber Pig; 30 Mazda

APC 325

APC (T) 305: 250 Type-85; 55 Type-90

APC (W) 20 Hino

ARTY 238+

TOWED 128+: 105mm 96 M-101; 122mm; 130mm 16 M-46; 140mm; 155mm 16 Soltam

MRL 30+: 107mm 30 Type-63; 122mm BM-21 (reported)

MOR 80+: 82mmType-53 (M-37); 120mm 80+: 80 Soltam; Type-53 (M-1943)

AT

RCL 1,000+: 106mm M-40A1; 84mm ε1,000 Carl Gustav

RL 73mm RPG-7 Knout

GUNS 60: 57mm 6-pdr; 76.2mm 17-pdr

AD • SAM • MANPAD HN-5 Hong Nu/Red Cherry (reported); SA-16 Gimlet

GUNS 46

SP 57mm 12 Type-80

TOWED 34: 37mm 24 Type-74; 40mm 10 M-1

Navy ε16,000

Naval Forces experienced considerable damage during Tropical Cyclone Nargis in 2008 with up to 30 vessels destroyed.

EQUIPMENT BY TYPE

PRINCIPAL SURFACE COMBATANTS 3:

CORVETTES FS 3 Anawrahta each with 1 76mm gun

PATROL AND COASTAL COMBATANTS 50:

PFM 6 Houxin each with 2 twin (4 eff.) each with 4 C-801 (CSS-N-4) Sardine tactical SSM

PTG 9 Myanmar each with 2 twin (4 eff.) each with 4 C-801 (CSS-N-4) Sardine tactical SSM

PCO 2 Indaw

PCC 9 Hainan

PFI 3 PB-90

PCI 9: 6 PGM 401; 3 Swift

PCR 12: 2 Nawarat; 9 Y-301; 1 Imp Y-301

AMPHIBIOUS • CRAFT 18: 8 LCU 10 LCM

LOGISTICS AND SUPPORT 10

AOT 1; AK 1; AKSL 5; AGS 2; ABU 1

FACILITIES

Bases Located at Bassein, Mergui, Moulmein, Seikyi, Rangoon (Monkey Point), Sittwe

Naval Infantry 800

Navy 1 bn

Air Force ε15,000

FORCES BY ROLE

Ftr	3 sqn with MiG-29B Fulcrum; F-7 (MiG-21F) Fishbed C; FT-7 (JJ-7) Mongol A*; MiG-29UB Fulcrum*
FGA	2 sqn with A-5M (Q-5II) Fantan
CCT	2 sqn with G-4 Super Galeb*; PC-7 Turbo Trainer*; PC-9*
Tpt	1 sqn with An-12 Cub; F-27 Friendship; FH-227; PC-6A Turbo Porter/PC-6B Turbo Porter
Trg/liaison	sqn with Ce-550 Citation II; Cessna 180 Skywagon; K-8
Hel	4 sqn with PZL W-3 Sokol; Mi-17 (Mi-8MT) Hip H*; PZL Mi-2 Hoplite*; Bell 205; Bell 206 Jet Ranger; SA-316 Alouette III

EQUIPMENT BY TYPE

AIRCRAFT 125 combat capable

FTR 58: 8 MiG-29B Fulcrum; 50 F-7 (MiG-21F) Fishbed C

FGA 22 A-5M (Q-5II) *Fantan*

TPT 15: 2 An-12 *Cub*; 1 Ce-550 *Citation II*; 3 F-27 *Friendship*; 4 FH-227; 5 PC-6A *Turbo Porter*/PC-6B *Turbo Porter*

UTL 4 Cessna 180 *Skywagon*

TRG 57: 10 FT-7 (JJ-7) *Mongol A**; 12 G-4 *Super Galeb**; 12 K-8; 2 MiG-29UB *Fulcrum**; 12 PC-7 *Turbo Trainer**; 9 PC-9*

HELICOPTERS

SPT 39: 10 PZL W-3 *Sokol*; 11 Mi-17 (Mi-8MT) *Hip H**; 18 PZL Mi-2 *Hoplite**

UTL 27: 12 Bell 205; 6 Bell 206 *Jet Ranger*; 9 SA-316 *Alouette III*

Paramilitary 107,250

People's Police Force 72,000

People's Militia 35,000

People's Pearl and Fishery Ministry ε250

PATROL AND COASTAL COMBATANTS 12

PCC 3 *Indaw*

PCI 9: 6 *Carpentaria*; 3 *Swift*

SELECTED NON-STATE GROUPS

Karen National Liberation Army Est strength: 3,000 Major equipments include: mines and IEDs, SALW • **Kachin Independence Army** Army Est strength: n.k. Major equipments include: mines and IEDs, SALW • **Democratic Karen Buddhist Army (government aligned)** Army Est strength: n.k. Major equipments include: mines and IEDs, SALW • **Shan State Army (South)** Army Est strength: n.k. Major equipments include: SALW • **United Wa State Army** Army Est strength: n.k. Major equipments include: mines and IEDs, mortars, SALW

New Zealand NZL

New Zealand Dollar NZ$		2008	2009	2010
GDP	NZ$	179bn	180bn	
	US$	126bn	132bn	
per capita	US$	30,204	31,412	
Growth	%	0.2	-2.2	
Inflation	%	4.0	1.9	
Def exp	NZ$	2.49bn		
	US$	1.75bn		
Def bdgt	NZ$	2.62bn	2.82bn	
	US$	1.85bn	2.07bn	
US$1=NZ$		1.42	1.36	

Population 4,213,418

Ethnic groups: NZ European 58%; Maori 15%; Other European 13%; Other Polynesian 5% ; Chinese 2%; Indian 1%; Other 6%

Age	0–14	15–19	20–24	25–29	30–64	65 plus
Male	11%	4%	3%	3%	22%	6%
Female	10%	3%	3%	4%	23%	7%

Capabilities

ACTIVE 9,702(Army 5,003 Navy 2,104 Air 2,595)

RESERVE 2,249 (Army 1,709 Navy 342 Air Force 198)

ORGANISATIONS BY SERVICE

Army 5,003

FORCES BY ROLE

Comd	2 Gp HQ
Recce	1 sqn
Mech Inf	2 bn (1 being converted)
SF	1 gp
Arty	1 regt (2 fd arty bty, 1 AD tp)
Engr	1 regt under strength

EQUIPMENT BY TYPE

AIFV 102 NZLAV-25

LFAV 188 *Pinzgauer*

ARTY 74

  TOWED 105mm 24 L-118 Light Gun

  MOR 81mm 50

AT • MSL 24 *Javelin*

  RCL 84mm 42 *Carl Gustav*

AD • SAM • MANPAD 12 *Mistral*

Reserves

Territorial Force 1,709 reservists

Responsible for providing trained individuals for incrementing deployed forces

Trg 6 (Territorial Force Regional) regt

Navy 2,104

FORCES BY ROLE

Navy 1 (Fleet) HQ and 1 Naval Base located at Auckland

EQUIPMENT BY TYPE

PRINCIPAL SURFACE COMBATANTS

FRIGATES

  FF 2 *Anzac* each with 1 octuple Mk41 *Sea Sparrow* (8 eff.) with RIM-7M *Sea Sparrow* SAM, 2 triple 324mm TT (6 eff.), 1 MK 15 *Phalanx* CIWS guns, 1 127mm gun, with 1 SH-2G (NZ) *Super Seasprite* ASW hel,

PATROL AND COASTAL COMBATANTS 6:

  PSO 2 *Otago* † (capacity 1 SH-2G *Super Seasprite*) (subject to contractual dispute in arbitration)

  PCO 4 *Rotoiti*

LOGISTICS AND SUPPORT 5

  MRV 1 *Canterbury* (capacity 4 NH90 tpt hel; 1 SH-2G *Super Seasprite* ASW hel; 2 LCM; 16 NZLAV; 14 NZLOV; 20 trucks; 250 troops)

  AO 1 *Endeavour*

  AGHS (SVY) 1 *Resolution*

  YDT/spt 1 *Manawanui*

FACILITIES

Base Located at Auckland

East Asia and Australasia

Air Force 2,595

3 air bases – Whenuapai, Ohakea and Woodbourne

Flying hours   190

FORCES BY ROLE

MR   1 sqn with 6 P-3K *Orion* (being progressively upgraded)

Tpt   1 sqn with 2 B-757-200 (upgraded); 5 C-130H *Hercules* (being progressively upgraded)

Hel   1 sqn with 14 UH-1H *Iroquois* (to be replaced by 8 NH90 in 2010/11)

ASuW/1 sqn RNZAF/RNZN sqn with 5 SH-2G(NZ) *Super*
ASW   *Seasprite*

Trg   Fg Trg Wg with 13 Airtrainer CT-4E (leased); 5 Beech 200 *King Air* (leased, to be replaced); 5 Bell 47G trg hel (to be replaced by 5 twin-turbine A109 trg/light utl aircraft 2010/11)

EQUIPMENT BY TYPE

AIRCRAFT 6 combat capable

MP 6 P-3K *Orion**

TPT 7: 2 B-757-200 (upgraded); 5 C-130H *Hercules* (being upgraded)

TRG 13 CT-4E (leased); 5 Beech 200 *King Air* (leased, to be replaced)

HELICOPTERS

UTL 14 UH-1H *Iroquois* (to be replaced by 8 NH90 in 2010/11)

ASW 5 SH-2G(NZ)

TRG 5 Bell 47G (to be replaced by 5 twin-turbine A109 T/ LUH aircraft 2010/11))

MSL • ASM AGM-65B *Maverick*/AGM-65G *Maverick*

DEPLOYMENT

AFGHANISTAN

NATO • ISAF 300

UN • UNAMA 1 obs

EGYPT

MFO 26 1 trg unit; 1 tpt unit

IRAQ

UN • UNAMI 1 obs

LEBANON

UN • UNIFIL 1

MIDDLE EAST

UN • UNTSO 7 obs

SOLOMON ISLANDS

RAMSI 44; 1 inf pl

SUDAN

UN • UNMIS 1; 1 obs

TIMOR LESTE

ISF *(Operation Astute)* 155; 1 inf coy

UN • UNMIT 1 obs

Papua New Guinea PNG

Papua New Guinea Kina K		2008	2009	2010
GDP	K	16.9bn		
	US$	6.3bn		
per capita	US$	1,076		
Growth	%	7.0	3.9	
Inflation	%	10.7	8.2	
Def bdgt	K	95m	133m	
	US$	35m	50m	
US$1=K		2.70	2.64	

Population   5,940,775

Age	0–14	15–19	20–24	25–29	30–64	65 plus
Male	19%	5%	5%	5%	16%	2%
Female	19%	5%	4%	4%	15%	2%

Capabilities

ACTIVE 3,100 (Army 2,500 Air 200 Maritime Element 400)

ORGANISATIONS BY SERVICE

Army ε2,500

FORCES BY ROLE

Inf   2 bn

Engr   1 bn

EQUIPMENT BY TYPE

ARTY • MOR 3+: 81mm; 120mm 3

Maritime Element ε400

FORCES BY ROLE

Navy   1 HQ located at Port Moresby

Maritime   some sqn located at Lombrun (Manus Island) with Patrol and Coastal Combatants

EQUIPMENT BY TYPE

PATROL AND COASTAL COMBATANTS 4:

PCC 4 *Pacific*

AMPHIBIOUS 2:

LSM 2 *Salamaua*

CRAFT 6: 4 (civil manned); 2

FACILITIES

Bases   Located at Alotau (forward), Kieta (forward), Lombrun (Manus Island), Port Moresby

Air Force 200

FORCES BY ROLE

Tpt   1 sqn with 1 CASA 212 *Aviocar*; 2 CN-235; 3 IAI-201 *Arava*

Hel   sqn with 4 UH-1H *Iroquois*†

EQUIPMENT BY TYPE

AIRCRAFT • TPT 6: 1 CASA 212 *Aviocar*; 2 CN-235; 3 IAI-201 *Arava*

HELICOPTERS • UTL 4 UH-1H *Iroquois*†

FOREIGN FORCES

Australia Army 38; 1 trg unit

Philippines PHL

Philippine Peso P		2008	2009	2010
GDP	P	7.49tr	7.63tr	
	US$	168bn	164bn	
per capita	US$	1,758	1,680	
Growth	%	3.8	1.0	
Inflation	%	9.3	2.8	
Def bdgt	P	63.3bn	54.2bn	57.7bn
	US$	1.42bn	1.16bn	
FMA (US)	US$	27.7m	30.0m	15.6m
US$1=P		44.4	46.4	

Population   97,976,603

Age	0–14	15–19	20–24	25–29	30–64	65 plus
Male	18%	5%	5%	4%	16%	2%
Female	17%	5%	5%	4%	16%	2%

Capabilities

ACTIVE 120,000 (Army 80,000 Navy 24,000 Air 16,000) Paramilitary 40,500

RESERVE 131,000 (Army 100,000 Navy 15,000 Air 16,000) Paramilitary 40,000 (to age 49)

ORGANISATIONS BY SERVICE

Army 80,000

FORCES BY ROLE
5 Area Unified Comd (joint service), 1 National Capital Region Comd

Armd	1 lt armd div with (5 lt armd bn; 2 lt armd coy; 3 mech inf bn; 1 armd cav tp; 1 avn bn; 1 cbt engr coy
Spec Ops	1 comd (1 Scout Ranger regt, 1 SF regt, 1 lt reaction bn
Lt Inf	10 div (*each:* 1 arty bn, 3 inf bde)
Arty	1 regt HQ
Engr	5 bde
Presidential Guard	1 gp

EQUIPMENT BY TYPE
LT TK 65 *Scorpion*
AIFV 85 YPR-765
APC 520
   APC (T) 100 M-113
   APC (W) 420: 150 Sinba; 100 LAV-150 *Commando*; 150 *Simba*; 20 V-200 *Chaimite*
ARTY 282+
   TOWED 242: **105mm** 230 M-101/M-102/M-26/M-56; **155mm** 12 M-114/M-68

MOR 40+: **81mm** M-29; **107mm** 40 M-30
AT • RCL 75mm M-20; **90mm** M-67; **106mm** M-40A1
AIRCRAFT
   TPT 3: 1 Beech 80 *Queen Air*; 1 Cessna 170; 1 P-206A
   UTL 1 Cessna 172
UAV *Blue Horizon*

Navy ε24,000

EQUIPMENT BY TYPE
PRINCIPAL SURFACE COMBATANTS • FRIGATES
   FF 1 *Rajah Humabon* with 3 76mm gun
PATROL AND COASTAL COMBATANTS 62
   PCO 13:
      3 *Emilio Jacinto* each with 1 76mm gun
      8 *Miguel Malvar* each with 1 76mm gun
      2 *Rizal* each with 3 Twin ASTT (6 eff.)†, 2 76mm guns
   PFC 1 *Cyclone*
   PCC 14: 3 *Aguinaldo*; 3 *Kagitingan*; 8 *Thomas Batilo*
   PCI 34: 22 *Jose Andrada*; 10 *Conrodo Yap*; 2 *Point*
AMPHIBIOUS
   LS • LST 7:
      2 *Bacolod City* (*Besson*-class) each with 1 hel landing platform (capacity 32 tanks; 150 troops)
      5 *Zamboanga del Sur* (capacity 16 tanks; 200 troops)
   CRAFT 39: 3 **LCU**; 6 **LCVP**; 30 **LCM**
LOGISTICS AND SUPPORT 6: **AOL** 1; **AR** 1; **AK** 1; **AWT** 2; **TPT** 1

FACILITIES
Bases Located at Sangley Point/Cavite, Zamboanga, Cebu

Naval Aviation
AIRCRAFT • TPT 6
   4 BN-2A *Defender*
   2 Cessna 177 *Cardinal*
HELICOPTERS • UTL 5 Bo-105

Marines ε7,500

FORCES BY ROLE
Marine 2 bde (*total:* 6 marine bn)

EQUIPMENT BY TYPE
APC (W) 24 LAV-300
AAV 85: 30 LVTP-5; 55 LVTP-7
ARTY 150+
   TOWED 105mm 150 M-101
   MOR 107mm M-30

Air Force ε16,000

FORCES BY ROLE
PAF HQ, 5 Cmds (AD, tac ops, air ed and trg, air log and spt, air res)

Ftr	1 sqn with Augusta S-211*
RECCE	1 Rockwell *Turbo Commander* 690A
MP	1 sqn with F-27 MK 200MPA; GAF N-22SL *Nomad*
SAR/Comms	4 sqn with AB-412SP *Griffon*; UH-1M *Iroquois*

East Asia and Australasia

Tpt	1 sqn with C-130B *Hercules*; C-130H *Hercules*; C-130K *Hercules*; 1 sqn with Cessna 210 *Centurion*; GAF N-22B *Nomad*; 1 sqn with F-27-200 *Friendship*
FAC	1 sqn with OV-10 *Bronco**
Trg	1 sqn with SF-260TP; 1 sqn with T-41D *Mescalero*; 1 sqn with R172 *Hawk* XP
Hel	4 sqn with UH-1H *Iroquois*; 1 (VIP) sqn with S-70 A-5 (S-70A) *Black Hawk*; SA-330L *Puma*; Bell 412EP *Twin Huey*/Bell 412SP *Twin Huey*; 2 sqn with AUH-76; MD-520MG

EQUIPMENT BY TYPE
30 combat capable
AIRCRAFT
FAC 15 OV-10 *Bronco*
MP 1 F-27 MK 200MPA
TPT 17: 2 C-130B *Hercules* (6 in store); 2 C-130H *Hercules*; 4 C-130K *Hercules*; 1 F-27-200 *Friendship*; 1 L-100-20 in store; 1 Rockwell *Turbo Commander* 690A
UTL 4: 2 Cessna 210 *Centurion*; 1 GAF N-22B; 1 GAF N-22SL *Nomad*;
TRG 44: 15 Augusta S-211*; 6 R172 *Hawk* XP; 12 SF-260TP; 11 T-41D *Mescalero*; 18 SF-260F* being delivered by end 2010
HELICOPTERS
ASLT 25: 5 AUH-76; 20 MD-520MG
SPT 2: 1 S-70 A-5 (S-70A) *Black Hawk*; 1 SA-330L *Puma*
UTL 79: 6 AB-412SP *Griffon*; 6 Bell 412EP *Twin Huey*/Bell 412SP *Twin Huey*; 40 UH-1H *Iroquois*; 27 UH-1M *Iroquois*
UAV 2 *Blue Horizon* II
MSL • **AAM** AIM-9B *Sidewinder*

Paramilitary

Philippine National Police 40,500
Deptartment of Interior and Local Government
FORCES BY ROLE
Regional   15 comd
Provincial 73 comd
Aux   62,000
EQUIPMENT BY TYPE
PATROL AND COASTAL COMBATANTS • **PCI** 14 Rodman
AIRCRAFT
TPT 2 BN-2 *Islander*
TRG 3 Lancair 320

Coast Guard
PATROL AND COASTAL COMBATANTS 51
PCO 5: 4 *San Juan*; 1 *Balsam*
PCC 6: 4 *Ilocosnorte*; 2 *Tirad*
PCI 19: 4 *Agusan*; 3 *De Haviland*; 12 *Swift*
PBR 11
PB 10
HELICOPTERS 3 SAR

Citizen Armed Force Geographical Units 50,000 reservists
CAFGU

Militia 56 bn (part-time units which can be called up for extended periods)

SELECTED NON-STATE GROUPS
Moro Islamic Liberation Front Est strength: 11,000 Major equipments include: mines and IEDs, mortars, SALW • **New People's Army** Est strength: 6,000 Major equipments include: mines and IEDs, SALW • **Abu Sayyaf Group** Est strength: 300; Major equipments include: mines and IEDs, mortars, SALW • **Jemaah Islamiah** Est strength: 550 Major equipments include: mines and IEDs, SALW

DEPLOYMENT
CÔTE D'IVOIRE
UN • UNOCI 3; 4 obs
HAITI
UN • MINUSTAH 157; 1 HQ coy
INDIA/PAKISTAN
UN • UNMOGIP 3 obs
LEBANON
UN • UNDOF 12
LIBERIA
UN • UNMIL 136; 2 obs; 1 inf coy
SUDAN
UN • UNMIS 11 obs
TIMOR LESTE
UN • UNMIT 3 obs

FOREIGN FORCES
Brunei 30
Libya 6
United States US Pacific Command: Army 14; Navy 5; USAF 10; USMC 82

Singapore SGP

Singapore Dollar S$		2008	2009	2010
GDP	S$	257bn	236bn	
	US$	182bn	170bn	
per capita	US$	39,554	36,454	
Growth	%	1.1	-3.3	
Inflation	%	6.5		
Def bdgt	S$	10.80bn	11.45bn	
	US$	7.66bn	8.23bn	
US$1=S$		1.41	1.39	

Population   4,657,542
Ethnic groups: Chinese 76%; Malay 15%; Indian 6%

Age	0–14	15–19	20–24	25–29	30–64	65 plus
Male	8%	3%	3%	4%	27%	3%
Female	8%	3%	3%	4%	29%	4%

Capabilities

ACTIVE 72,500 (Army 50,000 Navy 9,000 Air 13,500)
Paramilitary 93,800

Terms of service conscription 24 months

RESERVE 312,500 (Army 300,000 Navy 5,000 Air 7,500) **Paramilitary 44,000**

Annual trg to age of 40 for army other ranks, 50 for officers

ORGANISATIONS BY SERVICE

Army 15,000; 35,000 conscripts (total 50,000)

FORCES BY ROLE

Combined Arms 3 div (mixed active/reserve formations) (*each*: 2 inf bde (*each*: 3 inf bn), 1 armd bde, 1 recce bn, 1 AD bn, 1 engr bn, 2 arty bn)

Rapid Reaction 1 div (mixed active/reserve formations) (1 amph bde (3 amph bn), 1 air mob bde, 1 inf bde)

Recce/Lt Armd 4 bn
Inf 8 bn
Cdo 1 bn
Arty 4 bn
Engr 4 bn
MI 1 bn

Reserves

9 inf bde incl in mixed active/inactive reserve formations listed above; 1 op reserve div with additional inf bde; People's Defence Force Comd (homeland defence) with inf bn 12

Mech Inf 6 bn
Recce/Lt Armd ε6 bn
Inf ε56 bn
Cdo ε1 bn
Arty ε12 bn
Engr ε8 bn

EQUIPMENT BY TYPE

MBT 196: 96 *Leopard* 2A4; 80–100 *Tempest* (*Centurion*) (being replaced)
LT TK ε350 AMX-13 SM1
RECCE 22 AMX-10 PAC 90
AIFV 272+: 22 AMX-10P; 250 IFV-25; M-113A1/M-113A2 (some with 40mm AGL, some with 25mm gun);
APC 1,280+
  APC (T) 1,000+: 250 IFV-40/50; 750+ M-113A1/M-113A2; ATTC *Bronco*
  APC (W) 280: 250 LAV-150 *Commando*/V-200 *Commando*; 30 V-100 *Commando*
ARTY 335
  SP 155mm 18: ε18 SSPH-1 *Primus*
  TOWED 125: **105mm** 37 LG1 (in store); **155mm** 70: 18 FH-2000; ε18 *Pegasus*; 52 FH-88;
  MOR 192+
    SP 90+ **81mm**; **120mm** 90: 40 on *Bronco*; 50 on M-113
    TOWED 160mm 12 M-58 *Tampella*

AT • **MSL** • **MANPATS** 30+ *Milan/Spike MR*
  RCL 290: **84mm** ε200 *Carl Gustav*; **106mm** 90 M-40A1
  RL 67mm *Armbrust*; **89mm** M-20
AD • **SAM** 75+
  SP *Mistral*; RBS-70; SA-18 *Grouse (Igla)* (on V-200/M-113)
  MANPAD *Mistral*/RBS-70/SA-18 *Grouse (Igla)*
  GUNS 30
  SP 20mm GAI-C01
  TOWED 20mm GAI-C01
UAV *Skylark*
RADAR • **LAND** AN/TPQ-36 *Firefinder*; AN/TPQ-37 *Firefinder* (arty, mor)

FACILITIES

Training camp 3 located in Taiwan (Republic of China) incl inf and arty, 1 located in Thailand, 1 located in Brunei

Navy 3,000; 1,000 conscript; ε5,000 active reservists (total 9,000)

EQUIPMENT BY TYPE

SUBMARINES • **TACTICAL** • **SSK** 4:
  4 *Challenger* each with 4 single 533mm TT
  2 *Archer* (SWE *Västergötland* class) (AIP fitted) each with 6 single 533mm TT for *WASS Black Shark* LWT (Undergoing sea trials expected ISD '10 '11 respectively)
PRINCIPAL SURFACE COMBATANTS 12:
  FRIGATES • **FFGHM** 6 *Formidable* each with 8 RGM-84 *Harpoon* SSM, 4 octuple (32 eff.) VLS with *Aster15* SAM, 1 76mm gun, (capacity for 1 S-70B *Sea Hawk*)
  CORVETTES • **FSG** 6 *Victory* each with 2+ Mk 140 *Harpoon* quad (8 eff.) each with 1 RGM-84C *Harpoon* tactical SSM, 2 octuple (16 eff.) each with 1 *Barak* SAM, 2 triple ASTT (6 eff.), 1 76mm gun
PATROL AND COASTAL COMBATANTS 23:
  PCO 11 *Fearless* each with 2 *Sadral* sextuple each with *Mistral* SAM, 1 76mm gun
  PBI 12
MINE WARFARE • **MINE COUNTERMEASURES**
  MHC 4 *Bedok*
AMPHIBIOUS
  LS • **LST** 4 *Endurance* each with 2 twin (4 eff.) each with *Mistral* SAM, 1 76mm gun with hel deck (capacity 2 hel; 4 LCVP; 18 MBT; 350 troops)
  LANDING CRAFT 34 LCU
LOGISTICS AND SUPPORT 2
  AS 1 *Kendrick*
  Trg 1

FACILITIES

Bases Located at Changi, Tuas (Jurong)

Air Force 13,500 (incl 3,000 conscript)

5 Cmds: Air Defence and Operations Comd (includes Air Operations Control Group, Air Defence Group, and Air Surveillance and Control Group); Unmanned Aerial Vehicle (UAV) Comd; Participation Comd (includes Helicopter Group and Tactical Air Support Group: coordinates airlift, close air support and maritime air surveillance, and also raises, trains and sustains RSAF

helicopters, divisional ground-based air-defence systems and tactical support elements); Air Combat Comd (includes Fighter Group and Transport Group); Air Power Generation Comd (controls air base support units including Field Defence Sqns).

FORCES BY ROLE

FGA/Recce   3 sqn with F-16C/F-16D *Fighting Falcon* (some used for recce with pods). Also F-16D+ with conformal fuel tanks for long-range strike; 2 sqn with F-5S *Tiger II*; F-5T *Tiger II*; 1 recce sqn with RF-5

Recce/tkr/   1 sqn with KC-130B *Hercules* (trk/tpt); KC-
tpt   130H *Hercules*; C-130H *Hercules* (2 ELINT); 1 sqn with F-50 (5 *Maritime Enforcer*, 4 tpt)

AEW   1 sqn with E-2C *Hawkeye*

Tkr   1 sqn with KC-135R *Stratotanker*

Trg   1 sqn with F-16C/D at Luke AFB, AZ; AH-64D *Apache* located at Marana, (AZ), US; CH-47D *Chinook* located at Grand Prairie, (TX), US; F-15 trg taking place at Mountain Home (ID), US on F-15E and F-15SG; 1 sqn with A-4SU *Super Skyhawk*; TA-4SU *Super Skyhawk*; 1 sqn with PC-21

Hel   1 sqn with AH-64D *Apache*; 1 sqn with CH-47SD *Super D Chinook*; 2 sqn with AS-332M *Super Puma* (incl 5 SAR); AS-532UL *Cougar*; Trg: EC-120B *Colibri* (leased)

UAV   2 sqn with *Searcher* MkII; 1 sqn with *Hermes* 450. Staffed by personnel from all three services

EQUIPMENT BY TYPE

AIRCRAFT 104 combat capable
   FGA 99: 2 F-15SG (22 more to be delivered by 2012); 60 F-16C *Fighting Falcon*/F-16D *Fighting Falcon* (incl reserves); 28 F-5S *Tiger II*; 9 F-5T *Tiger II*
   MP 5 F-50 *Maritime Enforcer**
   AEW 4 E-2C *Hawkeye*
   TKR 9: 4 KC-130B *Hercules* (trk/tpt); 1 KC-130H *Hercules*; 4 KC-135R *Stratotanker*
   TPT 9: 5 C-130H *Hercules* (2 *ELINT*); 4 F-50
   TRG 41: 27 S-211; PC-21; 10 TA-4SU; 4 A-4SU
HELICOPTERS
   ATK 12 AH-64D *Apache*
   SPT 40: 18 AS-332M *Super Puma* (incl 5 SAR); 10 CH-47SD *Super D Chinook*; 12 AS-532UL *Cougar*
   TRG 12: EC-120B *Colibri* (leased); 6+ CH-47D *Chinook*
UAV some *Hermes* 450; 40 *Searcher* MK II
MSL • TACTICAL
   ASM: AGM-45 *Shrike*; *Hellfire*; AGM-65B/G *Maverick*; AGM-84 *Harpoon*; AM-39 *Exocet*
   AAM AIM-120C *AMRAAM* in store (US); AIM-7P *Sparrow*; AIM-9N *Sidewinder*/AIM-9P *Sidewinder*

Air Defence Group

FORCES BY ROLE
4 (field def) sqn

Air Defence Bde

FORCES BY ROLE
Air   Some bde (*total*: 1 AD sqn with Oerlikon, 1 AD sqn with 18+ MIM-23 *HAWK*, 1 AD sqn with *Rapier-Blindfire*)

Air Force Systems Bde
Air   bde (*total*: 1 AD sqn with radar (mobile), 1 AD sqn with LORADS)

Divisional Air Def Arty Bde
Attached to army divs

FORCES BY ROLE
AD   Bde (*total*: 1 AD bn with 36 *Mistral*, 1 AD bn with SA-18 *Grouse (Igla)*, 3 AD bn with RBS-70)

EQUIPMENT BY TYPE
AD • SAM 36+
   TOWED *Mistral*; RBS-70
   MANPAD SA-18 *Grouse (Igla)*

Paramilitary 93,800 active

Civil Defence Force 81,800 incl. 1,600 regulars, 3,200 conscripts, 23,000 reservists; 54,000+ volunteers; 1 construction bde (2,500 conscripts)

Singapore Police Force (including Coast Guard) 8,500; 3,500 conscript; 21,000 reservists (total 33,000)

EQUIPMENT BY TYPE
PATROL AND COASTAL COMBATANTS 101+
   PCI 12 *Swift*
   PBF 32
   PBC 2 *Manta Ray*
   PB 55: 11 *Shark*; 44 (various)

Singapore Gurkha Contingent (under police) 1,800

6 coy

DEPLOYMENT

AFGHANISTAN
NATO • ISAF 9

AUSTRALIA
Air force 2 trg schools: 1 with 12 AS-332 *Super Puma* Spt/AS-532 *Cougar* utl hel (flying trg) located at Oakey; 1 with 27 S-211 trg ac (flying trg) located at Pearce

BRUNEI
Army 1 trg camp with infantry units on rotation
Air force; 1 hel det with AS-332 *Super Puma*

FRANCE
Air force 200: 1 trg sqn with 4 A-4SU *Super Skyhawk* FGA ac; 10 TA-4SU *Super Skyhawk* trg ac

TAIWAN (REPUBLIC OF CHINA)
Army 3 trg camp (incl inf and arty)

THAILAND
Army 1 trg camp (arty, cbt engr)

TIMOR LESTE
UN • UNMIT 2 obs

UNITED STATES
Air force trg units at Luke AFB (AZ) with F-16 C/D; Mountain Home AFB (ID) with F-15E (F-15 SG from 2009); AH-64D *Apache* hel at Marana (AZ); 6+ CH-47D *Chinook* hel at Grand Prairie (TX)

FOREIGN FORCES

United States US Pacific Command: Army 8; Navy 83; USAF 13; USMC 18; 1 USN support facility located at Changi naval base; 1 USAF log spt sqn located at Paya Lebar air base

Taiwan (Republic of China) ROC

New Taiwan Dollar NT$		2008	2009	2010
GDP	NT$	12.3tr	11.2tr	
	US$	380bn	349bn	
per capita	US$	16,599	15,172	
Growth	%	0.1	4.1	
Inflation	%	4.1		
Def bdgt	NT$	341bn	315bn	
	US$	10.49bn	9.78bn	
US$1=NT$		32.5	32.2	

Population 22,974,347

Ethnic groups: Taiwanese 84%; mainland Chinese 14%

Age	0–14	15–19	20–24	25–29	30–64	65 plus
Male	10%	4%	4%	4%	24%	5%
Female	9%	3%	4%	4%	23%	5%

Capabilities

ACTIVE 290,000 (Army 200,000 Navy 45,000 Air 45,000) **Paramilitary 17,000**
Terms of service 12 months

RESERVE 1,657,000 (Army 1,500,000 Navy 67,000 Air Force 90,000)
Army reservists have some obligation to age 30

ORGANISATIONS BY SERVICE

Army ε200,000 (incl MP)
FORCES BY ROLE

Comd	4 defence HQ
Army	3 corps
Armd	5 bde
Armd Inf	1 bde
Inf	28 bde
Avn/SF	1 comd (1 spec war bde, 3 avn bde)
Mot Inf	3 bde
SSM	1 coastal def bn

Missile Command
AD 1 AD msl comd (2 AD / SAM gp (*total:* 6 SAM bn with total of 100 MIM-23 *HAWK*; with up to 6 PAC-3 *Patriot* (systems); up to 6 Tien Kung I *Sky Bow* / Tien Kung II *Sky Bow*))

Reserves
Lt Inf 7 div

EQUIPMENT BY TYPE
MBT 926+: 376 M-60A3; 100 M-48A5; 450+ M-48H *Brave Tiger*
LT TK 905: 230 M-24 *Chaffee* (90mm gun); 675 M-41/Type-64
AIFV 225 CM-25 (M-113 with 20–30mm cannon)
APC 950
  APC (T) 650 M-113
  APC (W) 300 LAV-150 *Commando*
ARTY 1,815+
  SP 405: **105mm** 100 M-108; **155mm** 245: 225 M-109A2/M-109A5; 20 T-69 ; **203mm** 60 M-110
  TOWED 1,060+: **105mm** 650 T-64 (M-101); **155mm** 340+: 90 M-59; 250 T-65 (M-114); M-44; **203mm** 70 M-115
  COASTAL 127mm ε50 US Mk 32 (reported)
  MRL 300+: **117mm** *Kung Feng* VI; **126mm** *Kung Feng* III/*Kung Feng* IV; RT 2000 *Thunder* (KF towed and SP)
  MOR
    SP 81mm M-29
    TOWED 81mm M-29; **107mm**
AT MSL 1,060: **SP** TOW
    MANPATS 60 *Javelin*; TOW
  RCL 500+: **90mm** M-67; **106mm** 500+: 500 M-40A1; Type-51
HELICOPTERS
  ATK 101: 62 AH-1W *Cobra*; 39 OH-58D *Warrior*
  SPT 9 CH-47SD *Super D Chinook*
  UTL 80 UH-1H *Iroquois*
  TRG 30 TH-67 *Creek*
UAV *Mastiff* III
AD • **SAM** up to 678+
    SP 76: 74 FIM-92A *Avenger*; 2 M-48 *Chaparral*
    TOWED up to 137: 25 MIM-104 *Patriot*; 100 MIM-23 *HAWK*; up to 6 PAC-3 *Patriot* (systems); up to 6 *Tien Kung* I *Sky Bow*/Tien Kung II *Sky Bow*
    MANPAD 465+ FIM-92A *Stinger*
  GUNS 400
    SP 40mm M-42
    TOWED 40mm L/70
MSL • **SSM** *Ching Feng*

Navy 45,000

FORCES BY ROLE

Navy 3 district; 1 (ASW) HQ located at Hualein; 1 Fleet HQ located at Tsoying; 1 New East Coast Fleet

EQUIPMENT BY TYPE

SUBMARINES • TACTICAL • SSK 4:

2 *Hai Lung* each with 6+ single 533mm TT each with 20+ SUT HWT

2 *Hai Shih* (trg only) each with 4 Single 533mm TT (aft) each with SUT HWT, 6 (fwd) each with SUT HWT

PRINCIPAL SURFACE COMBATANTS 26

DESTROYERS • DDG 4 *Keelung* (ex US *Kidd*) with 1 quad with 4 RGM-84L *Harpoon* SSM, 2 Mk 112 octuple with 16 ASROC, 2 twin MK 26 (4 eff) eqpt with 37 SM-2 MR naval SAM, 2 127mm guns, (capacity 2 med hel)

FRIGATES • FFG 22:

8 *Cheng Kung* each with 2 quad (8 eff.) each with *Hsiung Feng* tactical SSM, 1 Mk 13 GMLS with 40+ SM-1 MR SAM, 2 triple ASTT (6 eff.) each with Mk 46 LWT, 1 76mm gun, (capacity 2 S-70C *Defender* ASW hel)

8 *Chin Yang* each with 1 Mk 112 octuple with ASROC/RGM-84C *Harpoon* SSM, 2 Twin 324mm ASTT (4 eff.) each with Mk 46 LWT, 1 127mm gun, (capacity 1 MD-500 utl hel)

6 *Kang Ding* each with 2 quad (8 eff.) each with *Hsiung Feng* tactical SSM, 1 quad (4 eff.) with *Sea Chaparral* SAM, 2 triple 324mm ASTT (6 eff.) each with Mk 46 LWT, 1 76mm gun, (capacity 1 S-70C *Defender* ASW hel)

PATROL AND COASTAL COMBATANTS 73

PTG 4 *Kwang Hua* each with 2 twin with *Hsiung Feng II* tactical SSM (additional vessels in build)

PFM 61:

47 *Hai Ou* each with 2 single each with 2 *Hsiung Feng* tactical SSM

12 *Jinn Chiang* each with 1 quad (4 eff.) with 4 *Hsiung Feng* tactical SSM

2 *Lung Chiang* each with 4 single each with 4 *Hsiung Feng* tactical SSM

PFC 8 *Ning Hai*

MINE WARFARE • MINE COUNTERMEASURES 12

MSC 8: 4 *Yung Chuan*; 4 *Yung Feng*

MSO 4 *Aggressive* (Ex US)

COMMAND SHIPS • LCC 1 *Kao Hsiung*

AMPHIBIOUS

PRINCIPAL AMPHIBIOUS SHIPS • LSD 2:

1 *Shiu Hai* (capacity either 2 LCU or 18 LCM; 360 troops) with 1 hel landing platform

1 *Chung Cheng* (capacity 3 LCU or 18 LCM)

LS 17

LSM 4 *Mei Lo*

LST 13: 11 *Chung Hai* (capacity 16 tanks; 200 troops); 2 *Newport* (capacity 3 LCVP, 400 troops)

LANDING CRAFT 290: 20 LCU; 100 **LCVP**; 170 **LCM**

LOGISTICS AND SUPPORT 11:

AOE 1 *WuYi* with 1 hel landing platform

ARS 6

AK 2 *Wu Kang* with 1 hel landing platform (troop tpt

capacity 1,400 troops)

AGOR 1 *Ta Kuan*

AGS 1

FACILITIES

Bases Located at Makung (Pescadores), Keelung, Tsoying, Hualein, Suo

Marines 15,000

FORCES BY ROLE

Marine 3 bde

Spt   some amph elm

EQUIPMENT BY TYPE

AAV 204: 54 AAV-7A1; 150 LVTP-5A1

ARTY • TOWED 105mm; 155mm

AT • RCL 106mm

Naval Aviation

FORCES BY ROLE

ASW   3 sqn with 20 S-70C *Defender**

MR   2 sqn with 24 S-2E *Tracker*; 8 S-2G *Tracker*

EQUIPMENT BY TYPE

AIRCRAFT 32 combat capable

ASW 32: 24 S-2E *Tracker**; 8 S-2G *Tracker**

HELICOPTERS • ASW 20 S-70C *Defender**

Air Force 55,000

Flying hours   180 hrs/year

Four Cmds: Air Cbt Comd (Air Tac Ctrl Wg; Comms & Avn Ctrl Wg; Weather Wg); Log Comd (1st Log Depot (Pingtung); 2nd Log Depot (Taichung); 3rd Log Depot (Kangshan); Air Defence & Security Comd; Education, Trg & Doctrine Devt Comd

Tactical Fighter Wings

1st (443rd) Tactical Fighter Wing (TFW)(Tainan) incl 3 Tac Ftr Gp (TFG) (1st, 3rd, 9th) with F-CK-1A/B

2nd (499th) TFW (Hsinchu) incl 2 TFG (41st, 42nd) with *Mirage* 2000-5Di/Ei; 1 Trg Gp (48th) with *Mirage* 2000-5Di/Ei

3rd (427th) TFW (Ching Chuan Kang) incl 2 TFG (7th, 28th) with F-CK-1A/B

4th (455th) TFW (Chiayi) incl 3 TFG (21st, 22nd, 23rd) with F-16A/B; 1 Air Rescue Gp with S-70C

5th (401st) TFW (Hualien) incl 3 TFG (17th, 26th, 27th) with F-16A/B; 1 Tac Recce Sqn (12th) with RF-16A

7th (737th) TFW (Taitung) with 1 TFG (7th) incl 3 ftr sqn (44th, 45th, 46th (Aggressor)) with F-5E/F

Composite Wing

439th Composite Wg (Pingtung) with 10th Tac Airlift Gp incl 2 airlift sqn (101st, 102nd) with C-130H; 1 EW Gp (20th); 1 EW Sqn (2nd) with E-2T/E-2T *Hawkeye* 2000; 1 EW Sqn (6th) with C-130HE

Airbase Commands

Sungshan Air Base Comd incl Spec Tpt Sqn with Beech 1900C, Fokker 50; Presidential Flt Sect with Boeing 737,

Fokker 50 • Makung Air Base Command incl 1 Det with F-CK-1A/B

Air Force Academy
incl Basic Trg Gp with T-34C; Ftr Trg Gp with AT-3; Airlift Trg Gp with Beech 1900C 2

FORCES BY ROLE

Ftr   3 sqn with *Mirage* 2000-5EI (M-2000-5E)/*Mirage* 2000-5DI (M-2000-5D)

FGA   6 sqn with F-16A/F-16B *Fighting Falcon*; 1 sqn with AT-3 *Tzu-Chung*; 3 sqn with F-5E/F-5F *Tiger II*; 5 sqn with F-CK-1A/B *Ching Kuo*

Recce   1 sqn with RF-16A *Fighting Falcon*

EW   1 sqn with C-130HE *Tien Gian*

AEW   1 sqn with E-2T (E-2) *Hawkeye*

SAR   1 sqn with S-70C *Black Hawk*

Tpt   2 sqn with C-130H *Hercules* (1 EW); 1 (VIP) sqn with B-727-100; B-737-800; Beech 1900; Fokker 50

Trg   Trg school with T-34C *Turbo Mentor*; AT-3A/AT-3B *Tzu-chung*

Hel   sqn with CH-47 *Chinook*; S-70 *Black Hawk*; S-62A (VIP)

EQUIPMENT BY TYPE
AIRCRAFT 477 combat capable
  FTR 291: 88 F-5E *Tiger II*/F-5F *Tiger II* (some in store); 146 F-16A/F-16B *Fighting Falcon*; 10 *Mirage* 2000-5DI (M-2000-5D); 47 *Mirage* 2000-5EI (M-2000-5E)
  FGA 150: 128 *Ching Kuo*; 22 *Tzu-Chung AT-3*
  RECCE 8 RF-5E *Tigereye*
  EW 2 C-130HE *Tien Gian*
  AEW 6 E-2T (E-2) *Hawkeye*
  TPT 39: 4 B-727-100; 1 B-737-800; 10 Beech 1900; 19 C-130H *Hercules* (1 EW); 2 CC-47 (C-47) *Skytrain*; 3 Fokker 50
  TRG 78: 36 AT-3A *Tzu-Chung*/AT-3B *Tzu-Chung**; 42 T-34C *Turbo Mentor*
HELICOPTERS
  SPT 34: 3 CH-47 *Chinook*; 14 S-70; 17 S-70C *Black Hawk*
  UTL 1 S-62A (VIP)
MSL • TACTICAL
  ASM AGM-65A *Maverick*; AGM-84 *Harpoon*
  ARM *Sky Sword* IIA
  AAM AIM-120C *AMRAAM*; AIM-4D *Falcon*; AIM-9J *Sidewinder*/AIM-9P *Sidewinder*; MICA; R-550 *Magic 2*; *Shafrir*; *Sky Sword* I/II

Paramilitary 17,000

Coast Guard 17,000
New service formed with the merging of agencies from the ministry of finance, customs and marine police.
PATROL AND COASTAL COMBATANTS 50
  PSO 16: 2 *Ho Hsing*; 2 *Taipei*; 2 *Mou Hsing*; 1 *Yun Hsing*; 3 *Dao Hsing*; 4 *Shun Hu*; 2 *Kinmen*

PCO 1 *Shun Hsing*
PCC 20: 4 *Hai Cheng*; 4 *Hai Ying*; 12 (various)
PBF 13 (various)

FOREIGN FORCES
Singapore Army: 3 trg camp (incl inf and arty)

Thailand THA

Thai Baht b		2008	2009	2010
GDP	b	9.10tr	8.63tr	
	US$	273bn	259bn	
per capita	US$	4,168	3,927	
Growth	%	2.6	-3.5	
Inflation	%	5.7	-1.2	
Def bdgt	b	143bn	169bn	151bn
	US$	4.29bn	5.13bn	
US$1=b		33.3	33.3	

Population   65,998,436
Ethnic and religious groups: Thai 75%; Chinese 14%; Muslim 4%

Age	0–14	15–19	20–24	25–29	30–64	65 plus
Male	11%	4%	4%	5%	22%	4%
Female	11%	4%	4%	4%	23%	4%

Capabilities

ACTIVE 305,860 (Army 190,000 Navy 69,860 Air 46,000) **Paramilitary 113,700**
Terms of service 2 years

RESERVE 200,000 Paramilitary 45,000

ORGANISATIONS BY SERVICE

Army 120,000; ε70,000 conscript (total 190,000)
4 Regional Army HQ, 2 Corps HQ
FORCES BY ROLE
Armd Air Cav	1 regt (3 air mob coy)
Rapid Reaction	1 force (1 bn per region forming)
Cav	2 div; 1 indep regt
Recce	4 coy
Mech Inf	2 div
Armd Inf	3 div
Inf	8 indep bn
SF	2 div
Lt Inf	1 div
Arty	1 div
ADA	1 div (6 ADA bn)
Engr	1 div
Hel	some flt
Economic development	4 div

EQUIPMENT BY TYPE

MBT 333: 53 M-60A1; 125 M-60A3; 50 Type-69 (trg) in store; 105 M-48A5

LT TK 515: 255 M-41; 104 *Scorpion*; 50 in store; 106 *Stingray*

RECCE 32+: 32 S52 Mk 3; M1114 *HMMWV*

APC 950

  APC (T) 790: 340 M-113A1/M-113A3; 450 Type-85

  APC (W) 160: 18 *Condor*; 142 LAV-150 *Commando*

ARTY 2,473+

  SP 155mm 20 M-109A2

  TOWED 553: **105mm** 353: 24 LG1 MK II; 285 M-101/-Mod; 12 M-102; 32 M-618A2; **130mm** 15 Type-59-I; **155mm** 185: 42 GHN-45 A1; 50 M-114; 61 M-198; 32 M-71

  MRL 130mm Type-85 (reported)

  MOR 1,900

    SP 33: **81mm** 21 M-125A3; **120mm** 12 M-1064A3

    TOWED 1,867: **81mm**; **107mm** M-106A1

AT • MSL 318+

  SP 18+ M-901A5 (TOW)

  MANPATS 300 M47 *Dragon*

  RCL 180: **75mm** 30 M-20; **106mm** 150 M-40

  RL 66mm M-72 *LAW*

AIRCRAFT

  RECCE 40 Cessna O-1A *Bird Dog*

  TPT 10: 2 Beech 1900C; 2 Beech 200 *Super King Air*; 2 CASA 212 *Aviocar*; 2 *Jetstream* 41; 2 Short 330UTT

  UTL 10 U-17B

  TRG 33: 18 MX-7-235 *Star Rocket*; 15 T-41B *Mescalero*

HELICOPTERS

  ATK 5 AH-1F *Cobra*

  SPT 6 CH-47D *Chinook*

  UTL 159: 65 AB-212 (Bell 212)/Bell 206 *JetRanger*/Bell 214/Bell 412 *Twin Huey*; 92 UH-1H *Iroquois*; 2 UH-60L *Black Hawk*

  TRG 42 Hughes 300C

UAV • RECCE • TACTICAL *Searcher*

AD • SAM

  STATIC *Aspide*

  MANPAD FIM-43 *Redeye*; HN-5A

  GUNS 202+

    SP 54: **20mm** 24 M-163 *Vulcan*; **40mm** 30 M-1/M-42 SP

    TOWED 148+: **20mm** 24 M-167 *Vulcan*; **37mm** 52 Type-74; **40mm** 48 L/70; **57mm** 24+: ε6 Type-59 (S-60); 18+ non-operational

RADAR • LAND AN/TPQ-36 *Firefinder* (arty, mor); RASIT (veh, arty)

Reserves

Inf 4 div HQ

Navy 44,011 (incl Naval Aviation, Marines, Coastal Defence); 25,849 conscript (total 69,860)

FORCES BY ROLE

Air wing 1 div

Navy 1 (Fleet) HQ located at Sattahip; Mekong River Operating Unit HQ located at Nakhon Phanom

EQUIPMENT BY TYPE

PRINCIPAL SURFACE COMBATANTS 20

  AIRCRAFT CARRIERS • CVH 1:

    1 *Chakri Naruebet* (capacity 9 AV-8A *Harrier*† FGA ac; 6 S-70B *Seahawk* ASW hel)

  FRIGATES 10

    FFG 8:

      2 *Chao Phraya* each with 4 twin (8 eff.) each with CSS-N-4 *Sardine* tactical SSM, 2 (4 eff.) non-operational each with HQ-61 (CSA-N-2) SAM non-operational, 2 RBU 1200 (10 eff.), 2 twin 100mm gun (4 eff.), 2 twin 37mm gun (4 eff.), 1 hel landing platform

      2 *Kraburi* each with 4 (8 eff.) each with CSS-N-4 *Sardine* tactical SSM, 2 twin (4 eff.) with HQ-61 (CSA-N-2) SAM, 2 RBU 1200 (10 eff.), 1 twin 100mm gun (2 eff.), 2 twin 37mm gun (4 eff.), (capacity 1 AB-212 (Bell 212) utl hel)

      2 *Naresuan* each with 2 Mk 141 *Harpoon* quad (8 eff.) each with RGM-84A *Harpoon* tactical SSM, 1 8 cell Mk 41 VLS with RIM-7M *Sea Sparrow* SAM, 2 triple 324mm TT (6 eff.), 1 127mm gun, (1 *Lynx* SRS 300 *Super Lynx* ASW/ASUW hel)

      2 *Phuttha Yotfa Chulalok* (leased from US) each with 1 Mk 112 octuple with RGM-84C *Harpoon* tactical SSM, tactical ASROC, 2 Twin ASTT (4 eff.) with 22 Mk 46 LWT, 1 127mm gun, (capacity 1 AB-212 (Bell 212) utl hel)

    FF 2:

      1 *Makut Rajakumarn* with 2 triple ASTT (6 eff.), 2 114mm gun

      1 *Pin Klao* (trg) with 6 single 324mm ASTT, 3 76mm gun

  CORVETTES 9

    FSG 2 *Rattanakosin* each with 2 Mk 140 *Harpoon* quad (8 eff.) each with RGM-84A *Harpoon* tactical SSM, 1 *Albatros* octuple with *Aspide* SAM, 2 triple ASTT (6 eff.), 1 76mm gun

    FS 7:

      3 *Khamronsin* each with 2 triple ASTT (6 eff.), 1 76mm gun

      2 *Tapi* each with 6 single 324mm ASTT each with Mk 46 LWT, 1 76mm gun

      2 *Pattani* each with 1 76mm gun

PATROL AND COASTAL COMBATANTS 90

  PFM 6:

    3 *Prabparapak* each with 2 single each with 1 GI *Gabriel I* tactical SSM, 1 triple (3 eff.) with GI *Gabriel I* tactical SSM, 1 40mm gun, 1 57mm gun

    3 *Ratcharit* each with 2 twin (4 eff.) each with MM-38 *Exocet* tactical SSM, 1 76mm gun

  PSO 3 *Hua Hin* each with 2 20mm gun, 1 76mm gun

  PFC 3 *Chon Buri* each with 2 76mm gun

  PC 6 *Sattahip* each with 1 40mm gun, 1 76mm gun

  PCC 3 each with 1 40mm gun, 1 76mm gun

  PCI 47: 9 *Swift*; 10 T-11; 13 T-213; 3 T-81; 9 T-91; 3 T-991

  PCR 6

  PBR 16

MINE WARFARE • MINE COUNTERMEASURES 19
  MCC 2 *Bang Rachan*
  MCM SPT 1 *Thalang*
  MCMV 2 *Lat Ya*
  MS ε12
  MSC 2 *Bangkeo*
AMPHIBIOUS
  LS 8: 2
    LST 6:
      4 *Chang* each with 6 40mm gun (capacity 16 tanks; 200 troops)
      2 *Sichang* training each with 2 40mm gun, 1 hel landing platform (capacity 14 tanks; 300 troops)
  LANDING CRAFT • LCU 13: 3 *Man Nok*; 6 *Mataphun* (capacity either 3–4 MBT or 250 troops); 4 *Thong Kaeo*
LOGISTICS AND SUPPORT 15
  AORH 1 *Similan* (1 hel)
  AOR 1 *Chula*
  AOL 5: 4 *Prong*; 1 *Samui*
  AWT 1
  AGOR 1
  AGS 1
  ABU 1
  TRG 1
  YPT 1
  YTM 2

FACILITIES

Bases   Located at Bangkok, Sattahip, Songkhla, Phang Nga, Nakhon Phanom

Naval Aviation 1,200

AIRCRAFT 21 combat capable
  FGA 7 AV-8A *Harrier*†
  RECCE 9 *Sentry* 02-337
  MP 12: 6 Do-228-212*; 3 F-27 MK 200MPA*; 3 P-3T (P-3A) *Orion**
  TPT 2 F-27-400M *Troopship*
  UTL 8: 2 CL-215-III; 5 GAF N-24A *Search Master*; 1 UP-3T (UP-3A) *Orion*
  TRG 16: 14 TA-7; 4 TA-7C *Corsair II*; 2 TAV-8A *Harrier*†*

HELICOPTERS
  8 atk hel
  ASW 6 S-70B *Seahawk*
  ASW/ASuW 2 *Lynx* SRS 300 *Super Lynx*
  UTL 15: 4 AB-212 (Bell 212); 5 AB-214ST; 4 S-76B; 2 *Super Lynx*
MSL • TACTICAL • ASM: AGM-84 *Harpoon*

Marines 23,000

FORCES BY ROLE

Recce   1 bn
Amph Aslt 1 bn
Inf   2 regt (6 bn)
Arty   1 regt (1 ADA bn, 3 fd arty bn)
Marine   1 div HQ

EQUIPMENT BY TYPE
APC (W) 24 LAV-150 *Commando*
AAV 33 LVTP-7

ARTY • TOWED 48: **105mm** 36 (reported); **155mm** 12 GC-45
AT • MSL 24+
  TOWED 24 HMMWV TOW
  MANPATS M47 *Dragon*; TOW
AD • GUNS 12.7mm 14

Air Force ε46,000

4 air divs, one flying trg school

Flying hours   100 hrs/year

FORCES BY ROLE

FTR/ FGA   3 sqn with F-16A *Fighting Falcon*; F-16B *Fighting Falcon*; 2 sqn with L-39ZA/MP *Albatros*; 4 sqn (1 aggressor) with F-5E *Tiger II*/F-5F *Tiger II*, F-5B

Recce/   1 sqn with IAI-201 *Arava*, Learjet 35A
ELINT

Tpt   1 sqn with Basler *Turbo-67*; GAF N-22B *Nomad*; 1 sqn with BAe-748; G-222; 1 sqn with C-130H *Hercules*; C-130H-30 *Hercules*

VIP   1 (Royal Flight) sqn with A-310-324; Airbus A319CJ; B-737-200; BAe-748; B737-400; Beech 200 *Super King Air*; SA-226AT *Merlin IV/IVA*; AS-532A2 *Cougar MKII*; AS-332L *Super Puma*; Bell 412 *Twin Huey*

Utl   1 sqn with AU-23A *Peacemaker**, 1 sqn with L-39EA*, 1 with *Alpha Jet**

Liaison   1 sqn with Beech 65 *Queen Air*; Beech E90 *King Air*; Rockwell *Commander* 500; Cessna 150; T-41D *Mescalero*

Survey   1 sqn with SA-226AT *Merlin IV/IVA*; GAF N-22B *Nomad*

Trg   Trg school with CT-4B/E *Airtrainer*; PC-9; Bell 206B *JetRanger II*

Hel   1 sqn with UH-1H *Iroquois*; 1 sqn with Bell 212

EQUIPMENT BY TYPE

AIRCRAFT 165 combat capable
  FTR/FGA 87: 35 F-5E *Tiger II*/F-5F *Tiger II* (32 being upgraded), 2 F-5B (to be replaced by 4 JAS-39C/2 JAS-39D *Gripen* from 2011); 41 F-16A *Fighting Falcon*; 9 F-16B *Fighting Falcon*
  TPT 57: 1 A-310-324; 1 A-319CJ; 1 B-737-200; 2 B737-400; 6 BAe-748; 9 Basler *Turbo-67*; 2 Beech 200 *Super King Air*; 2 Beech 65 *Queen Air*; 1 Beech E90 *King Air*; 7 C-130H *Hercules*; 5 C-130H-30 *Hercules*; 3 G-222; 3 IAI-201 *Arava*; 2 *Learjet* 35A; 3 Rockwell *Commander* 500; 9 SA-226AT *Merlin IV/IVA*
  UTL 40: 22 AU-23A *Peacemaker**; 18 GAF N-22B *Nomad*
  TRG 123: 10 *Alpha Jet**; 29 CT-4B/E *Airtrainer*; 3 Cessna 150; 46 L-39ZA/MP *Albatros**; 23 PC-9; 12 T-41D *Mescalero*

HELICOPTERS
  SPT 19: 3 AS-332L *Super Puma*; 3 AS-532A2 *Cougar MKII*; 13 Bell 212
  UTL 28: 6 Bell 206B *JetRanger II*; 2 Bell 412 *Twin Huey*; 20 UH-1H *Iroquois*

East Asia and Australasia

MSL
    AAM AIM-120 *AMRAAM*; AIM-9B *Sidewinder*/AIM-9J *Sidewinder*; *Python* III
    ASM: AGM-65 *Maverick*

Paramilitary ε113,700 active

Border Patrol Police 41,000

Marine Police 2,200
PATROL AND COASTAL COMBATANTS 135
    PSO 3: 1 *Srinakrin*; 2 *Hameln*
    PCC 4: 2 *Chasanyabadee*; 1 *Yokohama*; 1 *Sriyanont*
    PCI 13: 6 *Ital* Thai Marine; 1 *Burespadoog kit*; 3 *Cutlass*; 3 *Technautic* 810-812 series
    PBR 85
    PB 30

National Security Volunteer Corps 45,000 – Reserves

Police Aviation 500
AIRCRAFT
    TPT 16: 2 CN-235; 1 Fokker 50; 8 PC-6 *Turbo-Porter*; 3 SC.7 3M *Skyvan*; 2 Short 330UTT
    UTL 6 AU-23A *Peacemaker*
HELICOPTERS • UTL 67: 20 AB-212 (Bell 212); 27 Bell 205A; 14 Bell 206 *Jet Ranger*; 6 Bell 412 *Twin Huey*

Provincial Police 50,000 (incl est. 500 Special Action Force)

Thahan Phran (Hunter Soldiers) ε20,000
Volunteer irregular force
Paramilitary   13 regt (*each:* 107 Paramilitary coy)

DEPLOYMENT

SUDAN
UN • UNAMID 15; 6 obs
UN • UNMIS 10 obs

Timor Leste TLS

Timorian Escudo TPE	2008	2009	2010

Population	1,040,880		

Age	0–14	15–19	20–24	25–29	30–64	65 plus
Male	19%	6%	5%	3%	16%	1%
Female	18%	6%	5%	3%	16%	2%

Capabilities

ACTIVE 1,332 (Army 1,250 Naval Element 82)

ORGANISATIONS BY SERVICE

Army 1,250

Training began in Jan 2001 with the aim of deploying 1,500 full-time personnel and 1,500 reservists. Authorities are engaged in developing security structures with international assistance.
Inf 2 bn

Naval Element 82
    PATROL AND COASTAL COMBATANTS
    PB 2 *Albatros*

FOREIGN FORCES
Australia ISF *(Operation Astute)* 650; 1 bn HQ; 2 inf coy; 1 AD bty; elm 1 cbt engr regt; 1 hel det with 5 S-70A-9 (S-70A) *Black Hawk*; 4 OH-58 *Kiowa* obs hel; 3 C-130; • UNMIT 3 obs
Bangladesh UNMIT 4 obs
Brazil UNMIT 4 obs
China, People's Republic of UNMIT 2 obs
Fiji UNMIT 2 obs
India UNMIT 1 obs
Malaysia UNMIT 2 obs
Nepal UNMIT 1 obs
New Zealand ISF *(Operation Astute)* 155; 1 inf coy • UNMIT 1 obs
Pakistan UNMIT 4 obs
Philippines UNMIT 3 obs
Portugal UNMIT 3 obs
Sierra Leone UNMIT 1 obs
Singapore UNMIT 2 obs

Vietnam VNM

Vietnamese Dong d		2008	2009	2010
GDP	d	1,487tr	1,677tr	
	US$	91bn	94bn	
per capita	US$	1,042	1,061	
Growth	%	6.3	4.6	
Inflation	%	23.1	7.0	
Def bdgt	d	47.3tr	ε50.0tr	
	US$	2.90bn	ε2.80bn	
US$1=d		16,300	17,844	

Population	88,576,758	

Ethnic groups: Chinese 3%

Age	0–14	15–19	20–24	25–29	30–64	65 plus
Male	14%	6%	5%	5%	17%	2%
Female	13%	5%	5%	4%	19%	3%

Capabilities

ACTIVE 455,000 (Army 412,000 Navy 13,000 Air 30,000) **Paramilitary 40,000**
Terms of service 2 years Army and Air Defence, 3 years Air Force and Navy, specialists 3 years, some ethnic minorities 2 years

RESERVES 5,000,000

ORGANISATIONS BY SERVICE

Army ε412,000

9 Mil Regions (incl capital), 14 Corps HQ

FORCES BY ROLE

Armd	10 bde
Mech inf	3 div
Inf	58 div (div strength varies from 5,000 to 12,500); 15 indep regt
SF	1 bde (1 AB bde, 1 demolition engr regt)
Fd arty	10+ bde
Engr	8 div; 20 indep bde
Economic construction	10–16 div

EQUIPMENT BY TYPE

MBT 1,315: 70 T-62; 350 Type-59; 850 T-54/T-55; 45 T-34
LT TK 620: 300 PT-76; 320 Type-62/Type-63
RECCE 100 BRDM-1/BRDM-2
AIFV 300 BMP-1/BMP-2
APC 1,380
  APC (T) 280: 200 M-113 (to be upgraded); 80 Type-63
  APC (W) 1,100 BTR-40/BTR-50/BTR-60/BTR-152
ARTY 3,040+
  SP 30+: **152mm** 30 2S3; **175mm** M-107
  TOWED 2,300 **100mm** M-1944; **105mm** M-101/M-102; **122mm** D-30/Type-54 (M-30) *M-1938*/Type-60 (D-74); **130mm** M-46; **152mm** D-20; **155mm** M-114
  GUN/MOR 120mm 2S9 *Anona* (reported)
  MRL 710+: **107mm** 360 Type-63; **122mm** 350 BM-21; **140mm** BM-14
  MOR 82mm; **120mm** M-43; **160mm** M-43
AT • MSL • MANPATS AT-3 9K11 *Sagger*
  RCL 75mm Type-56; **82mm** Type-65 (B-10); **87mm** Type-51
  GUNS
    SP 100mm Su-100; **122mm** Su-122
    TOWED 100mm T-12 (arty)
AD • SAM • MANPAD SA-7 *Grail*/SA-16 *Gimlet*/SA-18 *Grouse (Igla)*
  GUNS 12,000
    SP 23mm ZSU-23-4
    TOWED 14.5mm/30mm/37mm/57mm/85mm/100mm
MSL • SSM *Scud*-B/*Scud*-C (reported)

Navy ε13,000

FORCES BY ROLE

Navy 1 HQ located at Haiphong

EQUIPMENT BY TYPE

SUBMARINES • TACTICAL • SSI 2 DPRK *Yugo*†
PRINCIPAL SURFACE COMBATANTS 11
  FRIGATES • FF 5:
    3 FSU *Petya* II each with 2 x5 406mm ASTT (10 eff.), 4 RBU 6000 *Smerch* 2 (48 eff.), 4 76mm gun
    2 FSU *Petya* III each with 1 triple 533mm ASTT (3 eff.), 4 RBU 2500 *Smerch* 1 (64 eff.), 4 76mm gun

  CORVETTES • FSG 6:
    4 FSU *Tarantul* each with 2 twin (4 eff.) each with SS-N-2D *Styx* tactical SSM
    2 BPS-500 with 2 quad (8 eff.) each with SS-N-25 *Switchblade* tactical SSM non-operational, SA-N-5 *Grail* SAM (manually operated)
PATROL AND COASTAL COMBATANTS 38
  PFM 10:
    8 *Osa* II each with 4 single each with 1 SS-N-2 tactical SSM
    2 *Svetlyak* (Further 2 on order)
  PFT 3 FSU *Shershen*† each with 4 single 533mm TT
  PHT 5:
    2 *Turya*†
    3 *Turya*† each with 4 single 533mm TT
  PCI 16: 2 FSU *Poluchat*; 4 FSU SO-1; 10 *Zhuk*†
  PBR 4 *Stolkraft*
MINE WARFARE • MINE COUNTERMEASURES 14
  MCMV 5 K-8
  MSC 7: 4 *Sonya*; 1 *Vanya*; 2 *Yurka*
  MSI 2 *Yevgenya*
AMPHIBIOUS
  LS 6
    LSM 3:
      1 *Polnochny* A† (capacity 6 MBT; 180 troops)
      2 *Polnochny* B† (capacity 6 MBT; 180 troops)
    LST 3 US LST-510-511 (capacity 16 tanks; 200 troops)
  LANDING CRAFT 23: 5 LCU; 18 LCM
LOGISTICS AND SUPPORT 20:
  AKSL 17; **AWT** 1; **AGS** 1; **AT** 1
SPT 2 (floating dock)

Naval Infantry ε27,000

FACILITIES

Bases Located at Hanoi, Ho Chi Minh City, Da Nang, Cam Ranh Bay, Ha Tou, Haiphong, Can Tho

Air Force 30,000

3 air divs (each with 3 regts), a tpt bde

FORCES BY ROLE

Ftr	7 regt with MiG-21bis *Fishbed L*
FGA	2 regt with Su-30MKK *Flanker*; Su-27SK/Su-27UBK *Flanker*; Su-22M-3/Su-22M-4 *Fitter* (some recce designated)
ASW SAR	1 regt (The PAF also maintains VNM naval air arm) with Ka-25 *Hormone*; Ka-28 (Ka-27PL) *Helix A*; KA-32 *Helix C*; PZLW-3 *Sokol*
MR	1 regt with Be-12 *Mail*
Tpt	3 regt with An-2 *Colt*; An-26 *Curl*; Yak-40 *Codling* (VIP); Mi-6 *Hook*; MI-17 (Mi-8MT) *Hip H*/Mi-8 *Hip*; UH-1H
Atk hel	1 regt with Mi-24 *Hind*
Trg	Trg regt with L-39 *Albatros*; MiG-21UM *Mongol B**; BT-6 (Yak-18) *Max*
AD/ SAM	4 bde with 100mm; 130mm; 37mm; 57mm; 85mm; some (People's Regional) force (total: ε1,000 AD unit, 6 radar bde with 100 radar stn)

EQUIPMENT BY TYPE
AIRCRAFT 219 combat capable
  FTR 140 MiG-21bis *Fishbed L & N*
  FGA 64: 4 Su-30MKK *Flanker*; 7 Su-27SK *Flanker*; 53 Su-22M-3/M-4 *Fitter* (some recce dedicated)
  ASW 4 Be-12 *Mail*
  TPT 28: 12 An-2 *Colt*; 12 An-26 *Curl*; 4 Yak-40 *Codling* (VIP)
  TRG 43: 10 BT-6 (Yak-18) *Max*; 18 L-39 *Albatros*; 10 MiG-21UM *Mongol B**; 5 Su-27UBK *Flanker**
HELICOPTERS
  ATK 26 Mi-24 *Hind*
  ASW 13: 3 Ka-25 *Hormone**; 10 Ka-28* (Ka-27PL) *Helix A*
  SPT 48: 2 KA-32 *Helix C*; 4 Mi-6 *Hook*; 30 MI-17 (Mi-8MT) *Hip H*/Mi-8 *Hip* Spt; 12 UH-1H *Iroquois*
  SAR 4 PZL W-3 *Sokol*
AD • SAM
  SP SA-6 *Gainful*
  TOWED SA-2 *Guideline*; SA-3 *Goa*
  MANPAD SA-7 *Grail*; SA-16 *Gimlet*

GUNS 37mm; 57mm; 85mm; 100mm; 130mm
MSL
  ASM AS-14 *Kedge*; AS-17 *Krypton*; AS-18 *Kazoo*; AS-9 *Kyle*
  AAM AA-10 *Alamo*; AA-12 *Adder*; AA-2 *Atoll*; AA-8 *Aphid*
FACILITIES

SAM site	66 with SA-16 *Gimlet* MANPAD/SA-2 *Guideline* Towed/SA-3 *Goa*/SA-6 *Gainful* SP/SA-7 *Grail* MANPAD

Paramilitary 40,000 active

Border Defence Corps ε40,000

Local Forces ε5,000,000 reservists
Incl People's Self-Defence Force (urban units), People's Militia (rural units); comprises of static and mobile cbt units, log spt and village protection pl; some arty, mor and AD guns; acts as reserve.

Table 35 **Selected arms procurements and deliveries, East Asia and Australasia**

Designation	Type	Quantity	Contract Value	Supplier Country	Prime Contractor	Order Date	First Delivery Due	Notes
Australia (AUS)								
RIM-162 ESSM	SAM	–	See notes	US	Raytheon	2007	2010	Part of US$223m NATO *Sea Sparrow* Consortium contract for collective purchase of 294 ESSM. Final delivery due Feb 2010
M113 A1	APC	350	AUD590m	Dom	BAE	2002	2010	Upgrade to AS3/AS4 (S) standard. Deliveries ongoing
Bushmaster	LACV	146	AUD99m (US$82m)	Dom	Thales Australia	2007	–	Extension of 2002 contract for 300. 5 variants. Final delivery Mar 2009
Bushmaster	LACV	293	–	Dom	Thales Australia	2008	–	Deliveries ongoing
F100 *Hobart*-class	DD	3	US$8bn	ESP/Dom	AWD Alliance	2007	2014	Aka *Air Warfare Destroyer* (AWD). 2nd to be delivered 2016, 3rd 2017. Option on 4th All to be fitted with *Aegis*
Anzac	FFG Upgrade	–	AD260m	Dom	CEA Technologies	2005	2009	Upgrade: CEA-FAR Anti-Ship Missile Defence. Completion due 2012
Canberra-class	LHD	2	AUD3.1bn (US$2.8bn)	Dom/ESP	Navantia	2007	2012	To replace HMAS *Tobruk* and 1 *Kanimbla*-class amph tpt. To be named *Canberra* and *Adelaide*
F/A-18F Block II *Super Hornet*	FGA	24	AUD6bn (US$4.6bn)	US	Boeing	2007	2010	To replace current F111. Advanced targeting forward-looking infrared (ATFLIR) pods for 18 F/A-18F. First delivered July 2009. 12 to be in *Growler* configuration. Final delivery 2011
A330-200 (MRTT)	Tkr/tpt	5	AUD1.5bn (US$1.4 bn)	Int'l	EADS	2004	2010	(KC-30B). IOC of first ac mid-2010
B-737 *Wedgetail*	AEW&C	6	AUD3.6bn (US$3.4bn)	US	Boeing	2000	2006	Increased from 4 to 6 in 2004. Delivery originally due 2006 but integration problems mean first 2 due early 2010 and final 4 late 2010
A109 *Power*	Trg hel	3	–	ITA	Agusta-Westland	2007	–	For navy
NH90	Tpt hel	46	AUD2bn (US$1.47bn)	Int'l / Dom	NH Industries	2005 2006	2007	Replacement programme. 6 for navy 40 for army. Aus variant of NH90. First 4 built in Europe; remainder in Aus. Option for a further 26. Deliveries ongoing
CH-47F *Chinook*	Spt hel	7	AUS$1bn (US$780m)	US	Boeing	2016	2018	Incl 4 spare engines, miniguns and comms eqpt
China, People's Republic of (PRC)								
DF-41/ CSS-X-10	ICBM	–	–	Dom	–	1985	–	DF-41 – range 12,000km. Programme possibly either halted or terminated in 2002. May have been restarted with new performance requirement
JL-2/CSS-NX-5	SLBM	–	–	Dom	–	1985	2009	In development; range 8,000km. Reportedly to equip new Type 094 SSBN. ISD unknown
4x4 *Tigr*	LACV	100	–	RUS	Military Industrial Company	2008	2009	Delivery status unclear

Table 35 **Selected arms procurements and deliveries, East Asia and Australasia**

Designation	Type	Quantity	Contract Value	Supplier Country	Prime Contractor	Order Date	First Delivery Due	Notes
Type 094	SSBN	4	_	Dom	_	1985	2008	Construction reportedly began 1999. First of class launched 2004. Currently undergoing sea-trials. Full commissioning status unknown
Zubr Class Hovercraft	LCAC	4	US$315m	Dom/UKR	PLAN/Morye Shipyard	2009	_	For PLAN. Talks about procuring up to 10 *Zubr* ended without agreement.
IL-76TD	Tpt ac	30	See notes	RUS	Rosoboron-export	2005	–	Combined cost with order for 8 IL-78M tkr reported to be €850-1.5bn (US$1-1.8bn). Reports suggest contract currently frozen
IL-78 *Midas*	Tkr ac	8	See notes	RUS	Rosoboron-export	2005	–	Combined cost with order for 30 IL-76TD reported to be €850-1.5bn (US$1-1.8bn). Reports suggest contract currently frozen
Be-103	Ac	6	_	RUS	_	2007	–	Amphibious ac
EC-120 *Colibri*	Hel	–	_	Dom	_	1990	2005	With Pak (150 units). Delivery status unclear
Ka-28 ASW	AS hel	9	_	RUS	Kumertau Aviation Production Enterprise	_	2009	For navy. First delivered Oct 2009
Indonesia (IDN)								
Satellite	Sat	1	_	PRC	_	2009	_	Remote-sensing sat, to monitor IDN seas
QianWei-3 man-portable surface-to-air missile (SAM) units	SAM	3	_	PRC	CPMIEC	2009	_	
BMP-3F	AIFV	17-20	US$40m	RUS	Rosoboron-export	2008	2010	Petroleum supply offset; funding unconfirmed. To replace PT-76
Panser 6x6	APC	40	INR480bn (US$40m)	Dom	PT Pindad	_	2010	Order reduced from 150 in Feb 2009.
LVTP7	AAV	–	_	ROK	_	2008	_	Ex-ROK stock. Number undisclosed, but believed to be dozens. Delivery status uncertain
Kilo - class	SSK	2	See notes	RUS	Rosoboron-export	2006	–	Part of US$1bn deal incl Mi-17, Mi-35, BMP-3F and ASSM. Petroleum supply offset; funding unconfirmed and contract not finalised
Makassar class	LPD	4	US$150m	Dom/ROK	PT Pal/ Dae Sun	2003	2008	KRI *Makassar* commissioned 04/07, KRI *Surabaya* launched 05/07, 3rd vessel 08/08, 4th vessel 2009. 2 vessels delivered
ASM package	ASSM	2	See notes	RUS	_	2006	–	Part of US$1bn deal incl Su-27/30, Mi-17, Mi-35, BMP-3F, 2 SSK. Petroleum supply offset; funding unconfirmed
Su-27SKM	FGA	3	See notes	RUS	Rosoboron-export	2007	2008	US$335m incl 3 Su-30. Final delivery due 2009
CN-235	Tpt ac	2	Value undisclosed	Dom	PT Dirgantara	2008	_	
NAS-332 *Super Puma*	Hel	12	_	Dom	PT Dirgantara	1998	2004	Delays due to funding problems. Contract reduced from 16 to 12 in 2008

Table 35 **Selected arms procurements and deliveries, East Asia and Australasia**

Designation	Type	Quantity	Contract Value	Supplier Country	Prime Contractor	Order Date	First Delivery Due	Notes
Japan (JPN)								
Theatre Missile Defence System	BMD	–	–	Dom/US	–	1997	–	Joint development with US from 1998. Programme ongoing and incl SM-3 and PAC-3 systems
Hyuga-class	DDGH	2	Y200bn	Dom	IHI Marine United	2001	2008	2nd vessel due for commissioning 2011
19DD	DDGH	4	Y84.8 bn (US$700m)	Dom	Mitsubishi Heavy Industries	2007	2011	To replace the oldest 5 *Hatsuyuki*-class. First 19DD laid down July 2009. Commissioning due 2011
Standard Missile 3 (SM-3)	SAM	9	US$458m	US	Raytheon	2006	–	Part of *Aegis* BMD System for *Kongou*-class DDGH
Hirashima-class	MCMV	3	–	Dom	Universal SB	2004	2009	Fourth vessel expected. Final delivery (*JS Takashima*) due March 2010
Souryu-class	SSK	4	–	Dom	Kawasaki/ Mitsubishi	2004	2009	Second batch may be ordered. 2nd vessel (*Unryu*) due to commission March 2010
KC-767J	Tpt/tkr	4	–	US	Boeing	2003	2008	Final ac delivered in 2009
AH-64D *Apache*	Hel	13	–	Dom	Boeing	2001	2006	Up to 6 in *Longbow* config. 10 delivered by early 2008. Deliveries ongoing
EH-101 *Merlin* (MCH101)	Hel	14	–	UK	Agusta-Westland/ KHI	2003	2006	For JMSDF to replace MH-53E and S-61 hel under MCH-X programme. Deliveries ongoing
Korea, Republic of (ROK)								
(Multi-function Surface to Air Missile) M-SAM	SAM	–	–	Dom	–	1998	2009	In development. To replace current army *Hawk* SAMs. Due to enter service by 2010
XK2	MBT	600	KWR3.9trn (US$2.6bn)	Dom	Hyundai Rotem	2007	–	–
K-21 NIFV	IFV	500 (est)	US$3.5 m per unit	Dom	Doosan Infracore	2008	2009	Delivery status unclear
Sejong Daewang-class KDX-3	DDGH	3	–	Dom	DSME	2002	2008	3 additional vessels may be ordered. First vessel (*Sejong Daewang*) commissioned Dec 2008. Final delivery 2012
Ulsan - 1 class FFX	FFGH	6	KRW1.7bn (US$1.8bn)	Dom	Hyundai Heavy Industries	2006	2015	To replace current *Isan*-class FFG. ISD by 2015. Up to 15 vessels may be built
Unknown Class	PCO	5	KRW150bn (US$120m)	Dom	Hyandai Heavy Industries	2009	–	For Coast Guard. Due to be completed by 2012
Haeseong (Sea Star - ASM/SSM-700K)	ASCM	100	KRW270m (US$294m)	Dom	–	2006	2010	–
KSS-II (Type 214)	SSK	3	KRW1.27tn (US$1.4bn)	GER/Dom	Hyundai Heavy Industries	2000	2007	Third vessel (*An Jung-geun*) due to be commissioned November 2009

Table 35 **Selected arms procurements and deliveries, East Asia and Australasia**

Designation	Type	Quantity	Contract Value	Supplier Country	Prime Contractor	Order Date	First Delivery Due	Notes
KSS-II (Type 214)	SSK	1	US$500m est	Dom	DSME	2008	2014	First vessel of a second batch of 6 KSS-II (with AIP) for which funding has been cleared, but orders for remaining 5 are pending
KSS-III	SSK	3	–	Dom	–	2006	2015	Construction due to start 2012. Further 3 or 6 SSK to follow in a second phase. To replace Chang Bogo-class (Type 209) KSS-I SSK
SM-2 Block IIIA/ SM-2 Block IIIB/ SM-2 IIB	SAM	84	US$170m	US	Raytheon	2009	–	For KDX-2 and KDX-3 destroyers. Acquired through Foreign Military Sales Program. Pending US Congressional approval
F-15K Eagle	FGA	20/21	US$2.2bn (KRW2.3trn)	US	Boeing	2008	2010	Exercised option of earlier 2002 contract. Final delivery due 2012
AW139	MPA	2	–	UK	Agusta-Westland	2008	2009	For Coast Guard for maritime patrol and SAR missions. Delivery status unclear
CN-235-110	MPA	4	INR1trn (US$91m)	IDN	PT Dirgantara	2008	2010	Final delivery due 2011
737-700 AEW&C (E-737)	AEW&C	4	US$1.7bn	US	Boeing	2006	2011	E-X programme. Delivery likely to be delayed due to integration problems
T-50 / TA-50 Golden Eagle	Trg ac	50	Approx US$1bn	Dom	KAI	2006	–	–
AIM-9X Sidewinder	AAM	102	US$31m	US	Raytheon	2008	–	Contract value inc 26 containers
Malaysia (MYS)								
ACV-300 Adnan	APC	48	US$136m	Dom	DEFTECH	2008	–	–
Vehiculo de Alta Movilidad Tactica (VAMATAC) 4 x 4 tactical vehicles	ACV	85	MYR60 million (US$19.1m)	ESP/Dom	Urovesa	2008	–	Incl 24 Metis-M ATGW carriers and 25 Igla MANPAD system self-launching unit carriers
Astros II	MRL	18	–	BRZ	Avibras	2007	2009	Final system delivered in 2009
Kedah-Class MEKO A100-class	FFG	6	–	GER/Dom	Boustead Naval Shipyard	2008	–	Second batch. To be built under licence in MYS. Building to commence 2010. Final ship launched July 2009
Scorpene	SSK	2	MYR 3.7bn (US$974m)	ESP	DCNS and Navantia	2002	2008	Tunku Abdul Rahman handed over Jan 2009. Tun Razak launched Oct 2008, commissioning due 2010
A-400M	Tpt ac	4	MYR907m (US$246m)	Int	EADS	2006	2013	In development. Official unit cost US$80m. First deliveries delayed
MB-339 CM	Trg ac	8	€88m (US$112.8m)	ITA	Alenia Aermacchi	2006	2009	Final delivery due 2010
Mi-8 Hip	Hel	10	–	RUS	Rosoboron-export	2003	2005	Deliveries ongoing. Delivery status uncertain
ALUDRA	UAV	–	MYR5m (US$1.4m)	Dom	UST Consortium	2007	–	In development. For army and navy

Table 35 **Selected arms procurements and deliveries, East Asia and Australasia**

Designation	Type	Quantity	Contract Value	Supplier Country	Prime Contractor	Order Date	First Delivery Due	Notes
New Zealand (NZL)								
C-130H *Hercules*	Tpt ac SLEP	5	NZ$226m	CAN	L-3 Spar	2004	2010	SLEP. Life-extension programme. Final delivery due 2010
C-130H *Hercules*	Tpt ac Upgrade	5	NZ$21.2m (US$15.6m)	US	L-3 Spar	2007	2007	Upgrade programme in addition to 2004 SLEP. EW Self-protection systems (EWSPS). Final delivery due 2011
P-3K *Orion*	MPA Upgrade	6	–	US	L-3 Spar	2005	2010	Mission systems, comms and nav equipment
NH-90	Hel	8	NZ$771m (US$477m)	FRA	NH Industries	2006	2010	Final delivery by 2013
A-109	Hel	5	NZ$139m (US$109m)	Int'l	Agusta-Westland	2008	2011	Likely to replace Bell 47G-3B *Sioux*
Philippines (PHL)								
SF-260F/PAF	Trg ac	18	US$13.8m	It	Alenia Aermacchi	2008	2010	Final delivery due 2012
Singapore (SGP)								
Bedok-class	MCMV SLEP	4	–	FRA/SGP	Thales	2009	–	Incl upgraded sonar and C2
Submarine spt and rescue ship (SSRV)	SSAN	1	SGD400m (US$261.8m)	Dom/UK	ST Marine	2007	2009	To replace MV *Kendrick* and MV *Avatar*. Launched Nov 2008 and named *Swift Rescue*. ISD 2009
F-15SG *Eagle*	FGA	12	–	US	Boeing	2005	2008	SGP trg sqn based at Mtn Home AB (US). First batch to be del in 2009. Deliveries ongoing
F-15SG *Eagle*	FGA	12	–	US	Boeing	2007	2010	8 were option in original 2005 contract. Incl 28 GBU-10 and 56 GBU-12 PGM, several thousand cartridges and practice bombs
C-130 *Hercules*	Tpt ac Upgrade	10	–	US	Rockwell Collins	2007	–	Avionics upgrade. To be completed in 7 years
G550 CAEW	AEW	4	–	ISR	IAI	2007	2008	To replace E-2C *Hawkeye* AEW ac. Final delivery due 2011
G550	Trg ac	1	US$73m		ST Aerospace	2008	–	Part of a 20 year trg contract
S-70 B *Seahawk*	Hel	6	–	US	Sikorsky	2005	2008	To operate with *Formidable*-class FFG. Final delivery due 2010
AIM-120 AMRAAM	AAM	100	–	US	Raytheon	2006	2008	–
Taiwan (Republic of China) (ROC)								
Patriot PAC-3	AD	Up to 6	US$6bn	US	Raytheon	2009	–	FMS purchase of at least 4 additional OFUs. 3 existing being upgraded PAC-2 - PAC-3
Patriot PAC-3 upgrade kits	AD	–	US$154m	US	Raytheon	2009	–	Upgrade from config 2 to config 3
Jinn Chiang	PFM	24	–	Dom	–	1992	2010	Final delivery due 2010
AGM-84L *Harpoon* Block II	ASM	60	US$89m	US	Boeing	2007	2009	For F-16. Delivery status unclear
Hsiung Feng IIE	ASM	–	–	Dom	–	2005	–	In development

Table 35 **Selected arms procurements and deliveries, East Asia and Australasia**

Designation	Type	Quantity	Contract Value	Supplier Country	Prime Contractor	Order Date	First Delivery Due	Notes
E2C *Hawkeye*	AEW Upgrade	6	US$154m	US	Northrop Grumman	2009	_	Upgrade from Group II config to *Hawkeye* 2000 (H2K) export config. To be completed by 2013
Thailand (THA)								
TSP-77 long-range air surv	Radar	1	_	US	Lockheed	2007	2009	Part of a multi-phase national AD system. Delivery status unclear
BTR-3E1 8x8	APC	96	THB4bn (US$134m)	UKR	ADCOM	2007	–	Amphibious APC. To be completed in 2-3 years. Order on hold since Oct 2007
WMZ 551	APC	97	US$51.3m	PRC	NORINCO	2005	–	Delivery date unknown
Type 25T *Naresuan*	FF Upgrade	2	€5m (US$7m)	FRA	_	2007	–	Hel landing system upgrade
141 m landing platform dock	LPD	1	THB5bn (US$144m)	SGP	ST Marine	2008	2012	Contract value incl two 23 m landing craft mechanised and two 13 m landing craft vehicle and personnel
JAS 39C/D *Gripen*	FGA	6	See notes	SWE	SAAB	2008	2010	SEK2bn (US$308m) incl two 340 *Erieye*. Four JAS 39D, two JAS 39C. To replace F-5B/E *Tiger* II ac. Final delivery due 2017
C-130H *Hercules*	Tpt ac	12	THB1bn	Dom / US	Rockwell Collins	2007	–	Phase 1: avionics upgrade. Phase 2: Comms, Nav, Surv/Air Traffic Management (CNS/ATM). Delivery status unclear
340 *Erieye*	AEW	2	See notes	SWE	SAAB	2007	2011	SEK2bn (US$308m) inc 6 JAS 39 *Gripen*. Final delivery by 2017
Vietnam (VNM)								
VNREDSat-1	Sat	1	US$100m	Dom	_	2009	2012	
T-72	MBT	150	See notes	POL	Profus	2005	2005	Part of US$150m POL spt contract to supply ac, electronics and equipment. Delivery status unclear
Gepard	FFG	2	US$300m	RUS	Rosoboron-export	2005	2010	Construction began 2007
Su-30MK2	FGA	12	US$500m	RUS	Rosoboron-export	2010	_	Procurement contract does not include weaponry
PZL M-28B *Bryza*-1R/ *Skytruck*	MPA/tpt	10	_	POL	Profus	2005	2005	Part of POL spt contract. 1 ac in service. Plans for up to 12 ac. Owned by Coast Guard but operated by Air Force. Deliveries ongoing

Chapter Nine

Country comparisons – commitments, force levels and economics

Table 36 **UN Deployments 2009–2010**

Latin America and Caribbean

Location	HAITI
Operation	UN Stabilisation Mission in Haiti (MINUSTAH)
Original Mandate:	Resolution 1542 (30 Apr 2004)
Mandate Renewed:	Resolution 1892 (13 Oct 2009)
Renewed Until:	15 Oct 2010
Mission:	Support the political process, help to strengthen state institutions and support the work of both the Haitian National Police and the National Commission on Disarmament, Dismantlement and Reintegration.

Country	Forces by role	Troops
Brazil	1 inf bn, 1 engr coy	1,282
Uruguay	2 inf bn, 1 avn unit	1,146
Nepal	2 inf bn	1,076
Sri Lanka	1 inf bn	959
Jordan	2 inf bn	727
Argentina	1 inf bn, 1 avn unit, 1 fd hospital	560
Chile	1 inf bn, 1 avn unit, elms 1 engr coy	500
Bolivia	1 mech inf coy	208
Peru	1 inf coy	207
Philippines	1 HQ coy	157
Guatemala	1 MP coy	118
Ecuador	elm 1 engr coy	67
Paraguay		31
Canada		5
United States		4
Croatia		2
France		2
TOTAL (excluding police)		7,051

Non-NATO Europe

Location	CYPRUS
Operation	UN Peacekeeping Force in Cyprus (UNFICYP)
Original Mandate:	Resolution 186 (4 Mar 1964)
Mandate Renewed:	Resolution 1873 (29 May 2009)
Renewed Until:	15 Dec 2009
Mission:	Prevent a recurrence of conflict between Greek Cypriot and Turkish/Turkish Cypriot forces; help to maintain law and order.

Country	Forces by role	Troops
Argentina	2 inf coy, 1 avn unit	294
UK	1 inf coy	257
Slovakia	elm 1 inf coy, 1 engr pl	196
Hungary	elm 1 inf coy	84
Austria		4
Croatia		4
Peru		2
Canada		1
TOTAL (excluding police)		842

Location	SERBIA
Operation	UN Mission in Kosovo (UNMIK)
Original Mandate:	Resolution 1244 (10 Jun 1999)
Renewed Until	Cancelled by the Security Council
Mission:	UNMIK has scaled down and transitioned from an executive role to providing support for local institutions.

Country	Military Observers
Romania	2
Denmark	1
Norway	1
Poland	1
Russia	1
Spain	1
Turkey	1
Ukraine	1
TOTAL (excluding police)	9

Middle East and North Africa

Location	IRAQ
Operation	UN Mission Assistance Mission in Iraq (UNAMI)
Original Mandate	Resolution 1500 (14 Aug 2003)
Mandate Renewed	Resolution 1883 (7 Aug 2009)
Renewed Until	7 Aug 2010
Mission	Support ongoing political process, help humanitarian assitance to refugees and displaced persons, and promote human rights.

Location	Forces by role	Troops	Mil Obs
Fiji	3 sy units	221	
Australia			2
Denmark			2
Jordan			2
Nepal			2
United States			2
New Zealand			1
UK			1
		221	12
TOTAL (excluding police)			233

Location	ISRAEL, SYRIA AND LEBANON
Operation	UN Truce Supervision Organisation (UNTSO)
Original Mandate	Resolution 50 (29 May 1948)
Mandate Renewed	Resolution 339 (23 Oct 1973)
Renewed Until	Cancelled by the Security Council
Mission	UNTSO's tasks include providing a channel for communication between hostile powers; it can provide the nucleus for establishing other peacekeeping operations at short notice.

Country	Military Observers
Finland	15
Ireland	12
Netherlands	12
Australia	11
Denmark	11
Norway	11
Switzerland	10
Italy	8
Austria	7
Canada	7
New Zealand	7
Sweden	7
Argentina	6
Russia	5
Chile	4

Table 36 **UN Deployments 2009–2010**

Location	ISRAEL, SYRIA AND LEBANON (continued)	
China, People's Republic of		4
Nepal		3
Belgium		2
France		2
Slovakia		2
Slovenia		2
United States		2
Estonia		1
TOTAL (excluding police)		151

Location	LEBANON	
Operation	UNIFIL	
Original Mandate	Resolutions 425 and 426 (19 Mar 2008)	
Mandate Renewed	Resolution 1884 (27 Aug 2009)	
Renewed Until	31 Aug 2010	
Mission	Assist the Lebanese government in securing its borders and establishing a de-militarised zone in Southern Lebanon; help ensure access for humanitarian aid.	
Country	Forces by role	Troops
Italy	3 inf bn, 1 avn unit, 1 MP coy, 1 FF	2,576
France	1 armd inf bn, 1 armd sqn, 1 engr coy	1,585
Indonesia	1 inf bn, 1 FS	1,248
Spain	1 inf bn, 1 avn coy	1,045
India	1 inf bn, 1 fd hospital	898
Ghana	1 inf bn	874
Nepal	1 mech inf bn	868
Malaysia	1 inf bn	742
Poland	1 inf coy, 1 log bn	461
Germany	2 PC, 1 Spt	459
Korea, Republic of	1 inf bn	367
Turkey	1 engr coy, 2 PB	366
China, People's Republic of	1 engr coy, 1 fd hospital	344
Belgium	1 engr coy	229
Portugal	1 engr coy	146
Tanzania	1 MP coy	72
El Salvador	1 inf pl	52
Greece	1 PB	45
Slovenia		14
Ireland		8
Brunei		7
Hungary		4
Luxembourg		3
Qatar		3
Cyprus		2
Guatemala		2
Sierra Leone		2
Croatia		1
FYROM		1
New Zealand		1
TOTAL (excluding police)		12,425

Location	SYRIAN GOLAN HEIGHTS	
Operation	UN Disengagement Observer Force (UNDOF)	
Original Mandate	Resolution 350 (31 May 1974)	
Mandate Renewed	Resolution 1875 (23 June 2009)	
Renewed Until	31 Dec 2009	
Mission	Supervise the implementation of the disengagement of forces agreement signed by Israel and Syria after the war of October 1973.	
Country	Forces by role	Troops
Austria	1 inf bn	378
Poland	1 inf bn	333
India	elm 1 log bn	195
Croatia	1 inf coy	94
Japan	elm 1 log bn	31
Philippines		12
Canada		2
TOTAL		1,045

Location	WESTERN SAHARA		
Operation	UN Mission for the Referendum in the Western Sahara (MINURSO)		
Original Mandate	Resolution 690 (29 Apr 1991)		
Mandate Renewed	Resolution 1871 (30 Apr 2009)		
Renewed Until	30 Apr 2010		
Mission	Ensuring compliance with the ceasefire agreed between Morocco and POLISARIO whilst efforts continue to establish a longer term solution to the situation in Western Sahara.		
Country	Forces by role	Troops	Mil Obs
Malaysia	1 fd hospital	20	12
Egypt			21
Ghana			17
Russia			15
France			13
China, People's Republic of			12
Honduras			12
Pakistan			11
Brazil			10
Yemen			10
Nigeria			9
Bangladesh			8
Croatia			7
Hungary			7
Paraguay			5
Italy			4
Mongolia			4
Argentina			3
El Salvador			3
Guinea			3
Ireland			3
Sri Lanka			3
Uruguay			3
Austria			2
Djibouti			2
Jordan			2
Korea, Republic of			2
Greece			1
Poland			1
		20	205
TOTAL (excluding police)			225

Table 36 UN Deployments 2009–2010

Sub-Saharan Africa

Location	BURUNDI
Operation	UN Integrated Office in Burundi (BINUB)
Original Mandate	Resolution 1719 (25 Oct 2006)
Mandate Renewed	Resolution 1858 (22 Dec 2008)
Renewed Until	31 Dec 2009
Mission	Support government in peace consolidation and governance, disarmament and security sector reform, and promotion of human rights.

Country	Military Observers
Bangladesh	1
Niger	1
Pakistan	1
Senegal	1
Switzerland	1
TOTAL (excluding police)	5

Location	CENTRAL AFRICAN REPUBLIC AND CHAD
Operation	UN Mission in the Central African Republic and Chad (MINURCAT)
Original Mandate	Resolution 1778 (25 Sep 2007)
Mandate Renewed	Resolution 1861 (14 Jan 2009)
Renewed Until	15 Mar 2010
Mission	Trains and supports Chadian Police; liaises with security forces in Chad and the CAR, as well as the UNHCR, to provide security for local civilians. Also monitoring human rights and the rule of law.

Country	Forces by role	Troops	Mil Obs
Togo	1 HQ coy, elm 1 inf coy	457	
Ireland	elm 1 inf bn	427	
Poland	elm 1 inf bn	311	
France	elm 1 inf coy, 1 engr coy, 1 log bn, elm 1 tpt coy	308	
Nepal	1 inf bn, 1 MP pl	302	1
Ghana	1 mech inf bn	219	1
Norway	1 med coy	177	
Austria	elm 1 tpt coy	131	
Russia	1 avn bn	117	
Finland	elm 1 inf bn	74	
Albania	1 HQ coy	63	
Croatia		17	
Nigeria		15	2
Senegal		13	1
Ethiopia		13	
Bangladesh		5	2
Malawi		5	
Pakistan		5	
Kenya		4	
Namibia		4	
Tunisia		3	1
Egypt		1	2
Brazil			3
United States		2	
Yemen			2
Democratic Republic of Congo		1	
Mongolia		1	
Gabon			1
Rwanda			1
		2,675	17
TOTAL (excluding police)		2,692	

Location	CÔTE D'IVOIRE
Operation	UN Operation in Côte d'Ivoire (UNOCI)
Original Mandate	Resolution 1528 (27 Feb 2004)
Mandate Renewed	Resolution 1880 (30 Jul 2009)
Renewed Until	31 Jul 2010
Mission	Monitor ceasefire agreement and arms embargo, assist in disarming militia groups, security sector reform, protecting human rights, law and order and providing support to the Electoral Commission.

Country	Forces by role	Troops	Mil Obs
Bangladesh	2 inf bn, 1 engr coy, 1 sigs coy, 1 fd hospital	2,082	15
Pakistan	1 inf bn, 1 engr coy, 1 tpt coy	1,137	12
Jordan	1 inf bn, 1 SF coy	1,057	7
Morocco	1 inf bn	726	
Ghana	1 inf bn, 1 avn unit, 1 fd hospital	542	6
Benin	1 inf bn	428	8
Niger	1 inf bn	386	6
Senegal	1 inf bn	327	9
Togo	1 inf bn	313	7
Tunisia		4	7
France		8	2
Paraguay		2	8
Yemen		1	8
India			8
Brazil		3	4
Philippines		3	4
China, People's Republic of			7
Nigeria			7
Romania			7
Russia			7
Uganda		2	3
Guatemala			5
Nepal		1	3
Poland			4
Tanzania		2	1
Bolivia			3
El Salvador			3
Gambia			3
Guinea			3
Moldova			3
Peru			3
Serbia			3
Chad		1	1
Ecuador			2
Ethiopia			2
Ireland			2
Korea, Republic of			2
Namibia			2
Uruguay			2
Zambia			2
Egypt		1	
Zimbabwe			1
		7,026	192
TOTAL (excluding police)		7,218	

Table 36 **UN Deployments 2009–2010**

Location	DEMOCRATIC REPUBLIC OF CONGO
Operation	UN Organisation Mission in the Democratic Republic of Congo (MONUC)
Original Mandate	Resolution 1279 (30 Nov 1999)
Mandate Renewed	Resolution 1856 (22 Dec 2008)
Renewed Until	31 Dec 2009
Mission	Maintain a deterrent presence, protect civilians and UN staff; assist in destroying illegal arms and assist the Congolese government in disarming foreign and local armed forces.

Country	Forces by role	Troops	Mil Obs
India	3 mech inf bn, 1 inf bn, 2 avn unit, 1 atk hel unit, 1 fd hospital	4,249	52
Pakistan	4 mech inf bn, 1 inf bn	3,589	51
Bangladesh	1 mech inf bn, 2 avn unit	1,520	26
Uruguay	1 inf bn, 1 engr coy, 3 mne coy, 1 air spt unit	1,324	47
South Africa	1 inf bn, 1 engr coy, 1 avn unit	1,205	17
Nepal	1 mech inf bn, 1 engr coy	1,030	24
Morocco	1 mech inf bn 1 fd hospital	831	5
Benin	1 inf bn	749	10
Tunisia	1 mech inf bn	461	26
Ghana	1 mech inf bn	462	23
Senegal	1 inf bn	460	23
China, People's Republic of	1 engr coy, 1 fd hospital	218	15
Bolivia	2 inf coy	200	7
Indonesia	1 engr coy	174	16
Guatemala		150	4
Malawi	1 CSS coy	111	19
Jordan	1 fd hospital	65	24
Belgium		22	6
Russia			28
Egypt			26
Kenya			23
Zambia			23
Nigeria			22
Romania			22
Mali			19
Malaysia			17
Paraguay			17
Ukraine			13
Canada			11
Niger			11
Peru			7
Serbia		6	
UK			6
Algeria			5
Bosnia-Herzegovina			5
Cameroon			5
France			5
Yemen			5
Sweden			4
Ireland			3
Switzerland			3
Burkina Faso			2
Czech Republic			2
Denmark			2
Mongolia			2
Mozambique			2
Poland			2
Spain			2
Sri Lanka			2
Norway			1
		16,826	692
TOTAL (excluding police)			**17,518**

Location	LIBERIA
Operation	UN Mission in Liberia (UNMIL)
Original Mandate	Resolution 1509 (19 Sep 2003)
Mandate Renewed	Resolution 1885 (15 Sep 2009)
Renewed Until	30 Sep 2010
Mission	Support for peace process, humanitarian assistance, security sector reform.

Country	Forces by role	Troops	Mil Obs
Pakistan	1 mech inf bn, 2 inf bn, 3 engr coy, 1 fd hospital	3,072	9
Bangladesh	2 inf bn, 2 engr coy, 2 log coy, 1 sigs pl, 1 MP unit	2,340	11
Nigeria	1 inf bn, 3 sigs pl	1,626	13
Ethiopia	1 inf bn	872	12
Ghana	1 inf bn	707	8
China, People's Republic of	1 engr coy, 1 tpt coy, 1 fd hospital	564	2
Ukraine	2 avn unit	302	1
Mongolia	1 inf coy	250	
Philippines	1 inf coy	136	2
Jordan	1 fd hospital	119	4
Nepal	1 MP unit	18	2
United States		5	4
Malaysia			6
Egypt			5
Namibia		3	1
Peru		2	2
Russia			4
Serbia			4
Croatia		3	
Senegal		3	
Benin		1	2
Bolivia		1	2
Ecuador		1	2
Paraguay		1	2
Togo		1	2
Zambia			3
Brazil		2	
Finland		2	
Korea, Republic of		1	1
Bulgaria			2
Denmark			2
El Salvador			2
Guniea			2
Indonesia			2
Kyrgyzstan			2
Mali			2
Moldova			2
Montenegro			2
Niger			2
Poland			2
Romania			2
Zimbabwe			2
France		1	
Yemen		1	
		10,033	131
TOTAL (excluding police)			**10,164**

Table 36 **UN Deployments 2009–2010**

Location	SUDAN		
Operation	UN Mission in Sudan (UNMIS)		
Original Mandate	Resolution 1590 (24 Mar 2005)		
Mandate Renewed	Resolution 1870 (30 Apr 2009)		
Renewed Until	30 Apr 2010		
Mission	Monitor and verify the implementation of the Comprehensive Peace Agreement; provide security conditions to enable the return of refugees and the provision of humanitarian assistance.		

Country	Forces by role	Troops	Mil Obs
India	2 inf bn, 1 engr coy, 1 avn unit, 1 fd hospital	2,600	17
Pakistan	1 inf bn, 1 engr coy, 2 avn unit, 1 tpt coy, 1 demining coy, 1 fd hospital	1,481	14
Bangladesh	1 inf bn, 1 engr coy, 1 demining coy, 1 MP coy, 1 fd hospital, 1 tpt coy, 1 rvn coy	1,451	19
Egypt	1 inf coy, 1 engr coy, 1 demining coy, 1 med coy	1235	20
Kenya	1 inf bn, 1 demining coy	726	4
China, People's Republic of	1 engr coy, 1 tpt coy, 1 fd hospital	444	12
Zambia	1 inf coy	349	14
Rwanda	1 inf bn	256	10
Russia	1 avn unit	122	12
Cambodia	1 demining coy	53	5
Germany		5	26
Canada		8	21
Yemen		2	21
Brazil		2	20
Norway		7	14
Ecuador			17
Nepal		8	9
Australia		9	6
Jordan		5	10
Netherlands		2	12
Peru			13
Denmark		4	8
Zimbabwe			12
Nigeria		2	9
Romania		1	10
Bolivia			11
Philippines			11
Tanzania			11
Ukraine			11
Malaysia		2	8
Thailand			10
Paraguay			9
Korea, Republic of		1	6
Namibia			7
Fiji			6
Guinea			6
Indonesia			6
Kyrgyzstan			6
Sri Lanka			6
Croatia		5	
Uganda			5
Belgium			4
Benin			4
El Salvador			4
Turkey		3	
Sweden		2	1
Greece		1	2

Location	SUDAN (continued)		
Guatemala		1	2
Mali			3
Sierra Leone			3
Japan		2	
UK		2	
New Zealand		1	1
Iran			2
Moldova			2
Mongolia			2
Poland			2
Finland		1	
		8,793	486
TOTAL (excluding police)			**9,279**

Location	SUDAN (DARFUR REGION)		
Operation	UN-AU Mission in Darfur (UNAMID)		
Original Mandate	Resolution 1769 (31 Jul 2007)		
Mandate Renewed	Resolution 1881 (30 Jul 2009)		
Renewed Until	31 Jul 2010		
Mission	Protect the civilian population from violence, monitor implementation of ceasefire agreements, establish safe environment for provision of humanitarian assistance and economic reconstruction, promote human rights and the rule of law, monitor the situation on Sudan's borders with Chad and the CAR.		

Country	Forces by role	Troops	Mil Obs
Nigeria	4 inf bn	3,331	8
Rwanda	4 inf bn	3,228	7
Egypt	1 inf bn, 1 engr coy, 1 sigs coy, 1 tpt coy	2,420	12
Ethiopia	1 inf bn, 1 recce coy, 1 tpt coy	1,763	9
Senegal	1 inf bn	811	13
South Africa	1 inf bn	642	14
Bangladesh	2 log coy	591	7
Pakistan	1 engr coy, 1 fd hospital	507	3
China, People's Republic of	1 engr coy	325	
Tanzania	elms 1 inf bn	287	7
Burkina Faso	elms 1 inf bn	279	6
Gambia	1 inf coy	201	1
Kenya	1 MP coy	84	2
Nepal		23	16
Zambia		15	12
Yemen		14	12
Thailand		15	6
Namibia		12	5
Malaysia		14	2
Jordan		12	4
Mali		7	9
Sierra Leone		11	4
Zimbabwe		8	6
Ghana		10	3
Malawi		5	6
Burundi		4	7
Germany		7	
Mozambique			7
Cambodia			5
Indonesia		3	
Korea, Republic of		2	
Guatemala		2	
Uganda			2
Bolivia		1	

Table 36 **UN Deployments 2009–2010**

Location	SUDAN (DARFUR REGION) (continued)	
Italy		1
Netherlands		1
Turkey		1
UK		1
Togo		1
	14,638	196
TOTAL (excluding police)		**14,834**

South and Central Asia

Location	AFGHANISTAN
Operation	UN Assistance Mission in Afghanistan (UNAMA)
Original Mandate	Resolution 1401 (28 Mar 2002)
Mandate Renewed	Resolution 1868 (23 Mar 2009)
Renewed Until	23 Mar 2010
Mission	Assist Afghan government in developing good governance and the rule of law; support human rights; coordinating role for delivery of humanitarian aid.

	Military Observers
Norway	2
Australia	1
Bangladesh	1
Czech Republic	1
Denmark	1
Germany	1
Korea, Republic of	1
New Zealand	1
Paraguay	1
Portugal	1
Romania	1
Sweden	1
UK	1
Uruguay	1
TOTAL (excluding police)	**15**

Location	INDIA AND PAKISTAN
Operation	UN Military Observer Group in India and Pakistan (UNMOGIP)
Original Mandate	Resolution 47 (21 Apr 1948)
Mandate Renewed	Resolution 307 (21 Dec 1971)
Renewed Until	Cancelled by the Security Council
Mission	Monitor the ceasefire between India and Pakistan in Kashmir.

Country	Military Observers
Korea, Republic of	9
Croatia	9
Italy	7
Finland	5
Sweden	5
Philippines	3
Chile	2
Uruguay	2
Denmark	1
TOTAL	**43**

Location	NEPAL
Operation	UN Mission in Nepal (UNMIN)
Original Mandate	Resolution 1740 (23 Jan 2007)
Mandate Renewed	Resolution 1879 (23 Jul 2009)
Renewed Until	23 Jan 2010
Mission	Monitor continued compliance of the Nepalese Army and Maoist forces with the Comprehensive Peace Agreement. Assist OHCHR in monitoring human rights; assist in disposal of landmines and IEDs.

Country	Military Observers
Malaysia	7
Romania	7
Brazil	6
Japan	6
Paraguay	6
Egypt	5
Indonesia	5
Nigeria	5
Jordan	4
Korea, Republic of	4
Switzerland	3
Uruguay	3
Austria	2
Sierra Leone	2
Sweden	2
Zimbabwe	2
Guatemala	1
Zambia	1
TOTAL	**71**

East Asia and Australasia

Location	TIMOR-LESTE
Operation	UNMIT
Original Mandate	Resolution 1704 (25 Aug 2005)
Mandate Renewed	Resolution 1867 (26 Feb 2009)
Renewed Until	26 Feb 2010
Mission	Provide training and support to the Timorese National Police (PNTL) and assistance to Timorese government and institutions. Also helps in provision of economic assistance.

	Military Observers
Bangladesh	4
Brazil	4
Pakistan	4
Australia	3
Philippines	3
Portugal	3
China, People's Republic of	2
Fiji	2
Malaysia	2
Singapore	2
India	1
Nepal	1
New Zealand	1
Sierra Leone	1
TOTAL (excluding police)	**33**

Table 37 **Non-UN Deployments 2009–2010**

NATO Europe	
Location:	**MEDITERRANEAN SEA**
Operation:	*Active Endeavour*
Primary Organisation:	NATO
Mission:	Naval deployment to the eastern Mediterranean to provide deterrent presence and surveillance of maritime traffic. (Standing NATO Maritime Group 1)
Contributor:	Forces by role
Portugal	1 FFG
United States	1 FFG
Germany	1 AOT

Non-NATO Europe	
Location:	**ARMENIA AND AZERBAIJAN**
Operation:	The Personal Representative of the Chairman-in-Office on the Conflict Dealt with by the OSCE Minsk Conference
Primary Organisation:	OSCE
Mission:	Represent OSCE in issues related to Nagorno-Karabakh conflict, and assist in confidence-building and other measures contributing to the peace process.
Contributor:	Total:
Bulgaria	1
Czech Republic	1
Hungary	1
Kazakhstan	1
Poland	1
UK	1
TOTAL	**6**

Location:	**BOSNIA-HERZEGOVINA**	
Operation:	EUFOR (*Operation Althea*)	
Primary Organisation:	EU	
Mission:	Ensure compliance with the Dayton/Paris agreement; maintain security and stability within Bosnia-Herzegovina.	
Contributor:	Forces by role (where known)	Total:
Spain	1 inf bn HQ, 1 inf coy, 1 recce pl	304
Italy		300
Turkey	1 inf coy	246
Poland	1 inf coy	188
Hungary	1 inf coy	160
Germany		129
Bulgaria		119
Austria		96
Netherlands		73
Romania		56
Portugal		51
Greece		44
Ireland		43
Slovakia		32
Slovenia		25
Switzerland		25
Chile		21
Albania		13
FYROM		12
UK		9
Finland		4
France		4
Estonia		2
Lithuania		1
Luxembourg		1
TOTAL		**1,958**

Location:	**BOSNIA-HERZEGOVINA**
Operation:	OSCE Mission to Bosnia and Herzegovina
Primary Organisation:	OSCE
Mission:	Promote human rights, democracy building and regional military stabilisation.
Contributor:	Total:
United States	11
France	7
Italy	7
Ireland	5
Greece	4
Spain	4
Austria	3
Germany	3
Russia	3
Sweden	3
Canada	2
Hungary	2
Slovakia	2
Belarus	1
Belgium	1
Bulgaria	1
Croatia	1
Czech Republic	1
Finland	1
Kyrgyzstan	1
Netherlands	1
Portugal	1
Romania	1
Slovenia	1
Tajikistan	1
Turkey	1
UK	1
TOTAL:	**70**

Location:	**GEORGIA**
Operation:	EUMM
Primary Organisation:	EU
Mission:	Monitoring compliance with the Sarkozy-Medvedev six-point Agreement, following the Aug 2008 war.
Contributor	Total (Civilian):
Germany	45
France	38
Poland	27
Sweden	26
Romania	20
Italy	19
Finland	16
Bulgaria	14
Greece	12
UK	12
Spain	11
Czech Republic	9
Denmark	9
Netherlands	9
Lithuania	7
Austria	5
Ireland	5
Hungary	4
Slovakia	4
Belgium	3
Estonia	3
Latvia	2

Table 37 **Non-UN Deployments 2009–2010**

Location:	GEORGIA (continued)	
Malta		2
Slovenia		2
TOTAL		**304**

Location:	GEORGIA	
Operation:	Abkhazia and South Ossetia	
Primary Organisation:	Russia	
Mission:	Russian forces remaining in Abkhazia and South Ossetia.	
Contributor:	Forces by role (where known)	Total:
Russia	2 MR bde	3,400

Location:	MOLDOVA		
Operation:	Trans-dniester Peacekeeping Force		
Primary Organisation:	Russia/Moldova/Ukraine		
Mission:	Peacekeeping operations in the Trans-dniester region under the terms of the 1992 cease-fire agreement; aim of contributing to a negotiated settlement.		
Contributor		Obs	Troops
Russia			500
Moldova			500
Ukraine		10	
TOTAL			**1,010**

Location:	MOLDOVA	
Operation:	OSCE Mission to Moldova	
Primary Organisation:	OSCE	
Mission:	Negotiate a lasting solution to Trans-dniestrian conflict. Also deals with issues of human rights, democratisation and removal and destruction of former Russian munitions.	
Contributor:		Total:
Estonia		2
Poland		2
Bulgaria		1
Finland		1
France		1
Germany		1
Italy		1
Latvia		1
Tajikistan		1
UK		1
United States		1
TOTAL		**13**

Location:	SERBIA	
Operation:	OSCE Mission to Serbia	
Primary Organisation:	OSCE	
Mission:	Help Serbia to build democratic institutions, particularly in fields of human rights and the rule of law.	
Contributor:		Total:
Sweden		4
United States		4
Germany		3
Italy		3
Netherlands		3
Norway		3
UK		3
Bosnia-Herzegovina		2
Estonia		2
Ireland		2

Location:	SERBIA (continued)	
Moldova		2
Turkey		2
Croatia		1
France		1
Georgia		1
Greece		1
Hungary		1
Slovakia		1
Slovenia		1
Ukraine		1
TOTAL		**41**

Location:	SERBIA (KOSOVO)	
Operation:	KFOR (Joint Enterprise)	
Primary Organisation:	NATO	
Mission:	Under UNSCR 1244 (10th June 1999) KFOR is mandated to enforce law and order in Kosovo until UNMIK can assume responsibility for this task.	
Contributor:	Forces by role (where known)	Total:
Germany	1 inf bn HQ, 3 inf coy, elm 1 hel bn, elm 1 recce coy, elm 1 engr coy, 1 sigs bn, 1 CIMIC coy, elm 1 log unit, elm 1 MP coy, 1 med unit	2,486
Italy	1 mech inf BG, 1 engr unit, 1 hel unit, 1 sigs unit, 1 CSS unit	1,819
United States	1 ARNG cbt spt bde	1,475
France	1 armd inf BG, 1 Gendarmerie regt, some spt units (incl. atk hel)	1,294
Greece	1 mech inf bn	588
Turkey	1 inf bn HQ, 2 inf coy, 1 marine coy, 1 log coy, 1 Gendarmerie pl, elm 1 hel bn, elm 1 recce coy, elm 1 engr coy, elm 1 MP coy	509
Austria	1 inf bn HQ, 2 inf coy, elm 1 hel bn, elm 1 recce coy, elm 1 engr coy, elm 1 MP coy, elm 1 log unit	447
Finland	1 inf coy, 1 int/surv/recce coy, 1 log coy	405
Czech Republic	1 inf coy	393
Slovenia	1 inf bn HQ, 2 mot inf coy, 1 CSS coy	389
Portugal	1 mech inf bn (KTM)	295
Sweden	1 inf coy	245
Hungary	1 mot inf coy	243
Denmark	1 inf gp (1 scout sqn, 1 inf coy)	242
Ireland	1 mech inf coy, 1 log coy	233
Poland	elm 1 inf bn	226
Morocco	1 inf det	222
Belgium	1 mech inf coy	219
Switzerland	1 inf coy, 1 spt coy, elm 1 hel bn, elm 1 MP coy, elm 1 log unit	207
Ukraine	elm 1 inf bn	180
Romania		145
Slovakia	1 inf coy	145
Armenia		70
Bulgaria	1 engr pl	47
Lithuania		36
Estonia	1 inf pl	31
Luxembourg		23
Croatia		20
Netherlands		8
UK		8
Canada		6
Norway		6
TOTAL		**12,662**

Table 37 **Non-UN Deployments 2009–2010**

Location:	SERBIA (KOSOVO)
Operation:	OSCE Mission in Kosovo
Primary Organisation:	OSCE
Mission:	Institution and democracy building in Kosovo; promoting human rights and the rule of law.

Contributor:	Total:
Germany	16
Austria	15
France	14
Italy	14
United States	11
Spain	10
Turkey	10
Bosnia-Herzegovina	7
Croatia	7
Ireland	7
Greece	5
Portugal	5
Georgia	4
Hungary	4
Romania	4
UK	4
Azerbaijan	3
Bulgaria	3
FYROM	3
Netherlands	3
Belarus	2
Canada	2
Finland	2
Moldova	2
Poland	2
Russia	2
Sweden	2
Ukraine	2
Uzbekistan	2
Armenia	1
Lithuania	1
Malta	1
Montenegro	1
Slovenia	1
Slovakia	1
TOTAL	**173**

Middle East and North Africa

Location:	EGYPT
Operation:	MFO
Mission:	Supervising implementation of the Egyptian–Israeli peace treaty's security provisions.

Contributor:	Forces by role (where known)	Total:
United States	1 inf bn, 1 spt bn	688
Colombia	1 inf bn	354
Fiji	1 inf bn	338
Italy	1 coastal patrol unit	78
Uruguay	1 engr/tpt unit	58
Hungary	1 MP unit	38
Canada		28
New Zealand	1 trg unit, 1 tpt unit	26
Australia		25
France		18
Norway		6
TOTAL		**1,657**

Location:	IRAQ
Operation:	MNF-Iraq/ US Forces Iraq
Primary Organisation:	United States
Mission:	Help Baghdad maintain security and stability, including cooperation in operations against al-Qaeda and and other groups and remnants of the former regime.

Contributor	Forces by role (where known)	Total:
United States	1 corps HQ, 2 div HQ, 1 USMC MEF HQ, 4 HBCT, 2 SBCT, 2 IBCT, 1 armd inf bde, 1 (AAB) IBCT, 1 ARNG div HQ, 1 ARNG HBCT, 3 (LoC) ARNG IBCT	120,000

Location:	IRAQ
Operation:	NTM-I
Primary Organisation:	NATO
Mission:	Train Iraqi Security Forces

Contributor:	Total:
Italy	91
UK	15
United States	12
Denmark	10
Ukraine	9
Netherlands	7
Hungary	4
Lithuania	4
Estonia	3
Poland	3
Romania	3
Bulgaria	2
Turkey	2
TOTAL	**165**

Location:	ARABIAN GULF AND INDIAN OCEAN
Operation:	*Atalanta*
Primary Organisation:	EU
Mission:	Maritime Security Operations in the Gulf of Aden.

Contributor	Forces by role
France	3 FFH, 1 SSN, 1 *Atlantique* 2
Germany	2 FFG, 1 AP3-C *Orion*
Spain	1 FFG, 1 P-3 *Orion*
Belgium	1 FFG
Greece	1 FFG
Netherlands	1 FFG
Norway	1 FFG

Table 37 **Non-UN Deployments 2009–2010**

Location:	ARABIAN GULF AND INDIAN OCEAN
Operation:	Maritime Security Operations
Mission:	Maritime Security Operations in the Arabian Gulf, the Gulf of Oman and the Gulf of Aden (The ships listed comprise CTFs-150, 151 and 152 and third states cooperating with the above).

Contributor	Forces by role
United States	1 CG (CTF-151), 3 DDG, 1 FFG, 4 MCM, 5 PFC, 1 T-AKEH, 2 T-AO, 1 ATF, 6 (USCG) PBC
UK	3 FFG, 1 FFG (CTF-150), 4 MHO, 2 LSD, 1 AORH (CTF-150)
Japan	2 DDG, 1 DDG (CTF-150), 1 AOE (CTF-150)
China, People's Republic of	2 FFG, 1 AORH
Russia	1 DDG, 1 AOE, 1 ATF
Pakistan	1 DDG (CTF-150), 1 FFG (CTF-151)
Saudi Arabia	2 FFG
France	1 FFG (CTF-150), 1 AORH (CTF-150)
Korea, Republic of	1 DDG (CTF-151)
Germany	1 FFG (CTF-150)
India	1 FFG
Turkey	1 FFG (CTF-151)
Australia	1 FF (CTF-151)

Location:	ARABIAN GULF AND INDIAN OCEAN
Operation:	*Ocean Shield*
Primary Organisation:	NATO
Mission:	Counter-piracy operations in the Gulf of Aden. (Standing NATO Maritime Group 2)

Contributor	Forces by role
United States	1 DDG
Greece	1 FFG
Italy	1 FFG
Turkey	1 FFG
UK	1 FFG

Sub-Saharan Africa

Location:	BURUNDI
Operation:	*Curriculum*
Primary Organisation:	South Africa (Support of AU)
Mission:	Supporting the AU Special Task Force in Burundi.

Contributor	Total:
South Africa	417

Country	CENTRAL AFRICAN REPUBLIC
Operation:	*Vimbezela*
Primary Organisation:	South Africa
Mission:	Military assistance to the government of the Central African Republic.

Contributor:	Total:
South Africa	54

Country	CENTRAL AFRICAN REPUBLIC
Operation:	*Boali*
Primary Organisation:	France
Mission:	Technical and operational support to CAR armed forces.

Contributor:	Forces by role	Total:
France	1 inf coy, 1 spt det	240

Location:	CENTRAL AFRICAN REPUBLIC
Operation:	MICOPAX
Primary Organisation:	Economic Community of Central African States (ECCAS)
Mission:	Provide security, protect civilians, contribute to the national reconciliation process and facilitate political dialogue.

Contributor:	Total:
Gabon	139
Chad	121
Cameroon	120
Congo, Republic of	60
Equatorial Guinea	60
TOTAL	500

Location:	CHAD
Operation:	*Epervier*
Primary Organisation:	France
Mission:	Provide technical support and military training to the armed forces of Chad.

Contributor:	Forces by role	Total:
France	1 mech inf BG; 1 avn gp; 1 hel det	1,200

Location:	COMOROS
Operation:	MAES
Primary Organisation:	AU
Mission:	Provides security assistance to the Comoran government on the island of Anjouan.

Contributor:	Total:
Sudan	200
Tanzania	150
Senegal	120
TOTAL	470

Location:	CÔTE D'IVOIRE
Operation:	*Licorne*
Primary Organisation:	France (in support of UN)
Mission:	Assist UNOCI peacekeeping operation and provide UNOCI force commander with a QRF.

Contributor:	Forces by role	Total:
France	1 (Marine) mech inf BG, 1 hel unit, 1 Gendarme sqn	900

Location:	DEMOCRATIC REPUBLIC OF CONGO
Operation:	EUSEC RD Congo
Primary Organisation:	EU
Mission:	Advise and assist in armed forces reform.

Contributor:	Total:
Belgium	6
Italy	4
Germany	3
Netherlands	3
Austria	1
TOTAL	17

Location:	DEMOCRATIC REPUBLIC OF CONGO
Operation:	*Teutonic*
Primary Organisation:	Bilateral
Mission:	Assist reconstruction of DRC armed forces.

Contributor:	Total:
South Africa	17

Table 37 Non-UN Deployments 2009–2010

Location:	SIERRA LEONE	
Operation:	IMATT	
Mission:	Train and advise the Sierra Leone Army.	
Contributor:		Total:
UK		63
Canada		7
United States		3
Jamaica		1
Nigeria		1
TOTAL		75

Location:	SOMALIA	
Operation:	AMISOM	
Primary Organisation:	AU	
Mission:	Support the TFG's efforts to stabilise Somalia and facilitate the provision of humanitarian assistance.	
Contributor:	Forces by role (where known)	Total:
Burundi	3 inf bn	2550
Uganda	3 inf bn	2550
TOTAL		5,100

South and Central Asia

Location:	AFGHANISTAN	
Operation:	ISAF	
Primary Organisation:	NATO	
Mission:	Under UNSCR 1386 (Dec 2001), and its extension by subsequent resolutions, ISAF has a peace-enforcement mandate. Tasks include counter-insurgency and counter-narcotics operations and the provision of training and support to the Afghan National Army.	
Contributor:	Forces by role (where known)	Total:
United States	1 div HQ, 1 SBCT, 3 IBCT, 2 cbt avn bde, 1 USMC MEB with (1 RCT)	34,800
UK	1 div HQ, 1 lt inf bde HQ, 5 lt inf bn, 1 armd recce regt, 1 arty regt, 1 engr regt regt, 1 engr regt	9,000
Germany	1 bde HQ, 1 air mob inf regt	4,365
France	1 bde HQ, 1 (Marine) inf regt, 1 (Foreign Legion) inf BG	3,095
Canada	1 inf BG	2,830
Italy	1 AB bde HQ; 3 para regt	2,795
Netherlands	1 air aslt bde HQ, 1 armd inf BG	2,160
Poland	1 mtn inf bde HQ, 1 mtn inf bn, 1 air cav bde HQ with (elm 2 hel bn)	1,910
Australia	1 inf BG, 1 cdo BG	1,350
Spain	1 inf bn	1,000
Romania	1 mtn bde HQ, 1 inf bn	990
Turkey	1 inf bn	720
Denmark	1 mech inf BG	690
Belgium		530
Czech Republic		480
Norway	1 mech inf coy, 1 spt coy	480
Bulgaria		460
Sweden		430
Hungary	1 lt inf coy	360
New Zealand		300
Croatia		290
Albania	1 inf coy, 1 inf pl	250
Lithuania		250
Slovakia		245
Latvia		175

Location:	AFGHANISTAN (continued)	
Finland		165
FYROM		165
Estonia	1 mech inf coy; 1 mor det	150
Greece	1 engr coy	145
Portugal		145
Slovenia		130
Azerbaijan		90
United Arab Emirates		25
Bosnia-Herzegovina		10
Ukraine		10
Singapore		9
Luxembourg		8
Ireland		7
Jordan		7
Austria		4
Georgia		1
Iceland		2 (civilian)
TOTAL		71,026

Location:	AFGHANISTAN	
Operation:	Operation Enduring Freedom-Afghanistan (OEF-A)	
Primary Organisation:	United States Coalition	
Mission:	Combat operations against al-Qaeda, and training Afghan security forces.	
Contributor:	Forces by role (where known)	Total:
United States	1 IBCT, 1 ARNG IBCT	31,129

East Asia and Australasia

Location:	NORTH/SOUTH KOREA	
Operation:	NNSC	
Mission:	Monitor ceasefire between North and South Korea.	
Contributor:		Total:
Switzerland		5
Sweden		5
TOTAL		10

Location:	SOLOMON ISLANDS	
Operation:	RAMSI	
Primary Organisation:	Coalition of 15 Pacific nations	
Mission:	Ensure the security and stability of the Solomon Islands, and help to rebuild the Islands' government and economy.	
Contributor:	Forces by role (where known)	Total:
Australia	1 inf pl	80
New Zealand	1 inf pl	44
Tonga	1 inf pl	32
TOTAL		156

Location:	TIMOR-LESTE	
Operation:	ISF (Operation Astute)	
Primary Organisation:	International Coalition	
Mission:	Assist Timorese government in restoring peace and stability.	
Contributor:	Forces by role (where known)	Total:
Australia	1 bn HQ, 2 inf coy, 1 AD bty, elm 1 cbt engr regt, 1 hel det	650
New Zealand	1 inf coy	155
TOTAL		805

Index of contributing nations

Malta
NON-UN: EUMM
Moldova
UN: UNMIL, UNMIS, UNOCI
NON-UN: OSCE Kosovo, OSCE Serbia, Transdniester PKF
Mongolia
UN: MINURCAT, MINURSO, MONUC, UNMIL, UNMIS
Montenegro
UN: UNMIL
NON-UN: OSCE Kosovo
Morocco
UN: MONUC, UNOCI
NON-UN: KFOR
Mozambique
UN: MONUC, UNAMID
Namibia
UN: MINURCAT, UNAMID, UNMIL, UNMIS, UNOCI
Nepal
UN: MINURCAT, MINUSTAH, MONUC, UNAMI, UNAMID, UNIFII, UNMIL, UNMIS, UNOCI, UNTSO
Netherlands
UN: UNAMID, UNMIS, UNTSO
NON-UN: Atalanta, EUFOR Althea, EUMM, EUSEC RD Congo, ISAF, KFOR, NTM-I, OSCE Bosnia, OSCE Kosovo, OSCE Serbia
New Zealand
UN: UNAMA, UNAMI, UNIFIL, UNMIS, UNMIT, UNTSO
NON-UN: ISAF, ISF, MFO, RAMSI
Niger
UN: BINUB, MONUC, UNMIL, UNOCI
Nigeria
UN: MINURCAT, MINURSO, MONUC, UNAMID, UNMIL, UNMIN, UNMIS, UNOCI
NON-UN: IMATT
Norway
UN: MINURCAT, MONUC, UNAMA, UNMIK, UNMIS, UNTSO,
NON-UN: Atalanta, ISAF, KFOR, MFO, OSCE Serbia
Pakistan
UN: BINUB, MINURCAT, MINURSO, MONUC, UNAMID, UNMIL, UNMIS, UNMIT, UNOCI
NON-UN: Maritime Security Ops
Paraguay
UN: MINURSO, MINUSTAH, MONUC, UNAMA, UNMIL, UNMIN, UNMIS, UNOCI
Peru
UN: MINUSTAH, MONUC, UNFICYP, UNMIL, UNMIS, UNOCI
Philippines
UN: MINUSTAH, UNDOF, UNMIL, UNMIS, UNMIT, UNMOGIP, UNOCI
Poland
UN: MINURSO, MINURCAT, MONUC, UNOCI, UNDOF, UNIFIL, UNMIK, UNMIL, UNMIS
NON-UN: EUFOR Althea, EUMM, ISAF, KFOR,

NTM-I, OSCE Kosovo, OSCE Minsk Conf, OSCE Moldova
Portugal
UN: UNAMA, UNIFIL, UNMIT
NON-UN: Active Endeavour, EUFOR Althea, ISAF, KFOR, OSCE Bosnia, OSCE Kosovo,
Qatar
UN: UNIFIL
Romania
UN: MONUC, UNAMA, UNMIK, UNMIL, UNMIN, UNMIS, UNOCI
NON-UN: EUFOR Althea, EUMM, ISAF, KFOR, NTM-I, OSCE Bosnia, OSCE Kosovo
Russia
UN: MINURCAT, MINURSO, MONUC, UNMIK, UNMIL, UNMIS, UNOCI, UNTSO
NON-UN: Abkhazia/South Ossetia, Maritime Security Ops, OSCE Bosnia, OSCE Kosovo, Trans-dniester PKF
Rwanda
UN: MINURCAT, UNAMID, UNMIS
Saudi Arabia
NON-UN: Maritime Security Ops
Senegal
UN: BINUB, MINURCAT, MONUC, UNAMID, UNMIL, UNOCI
NON-UN: MAES
Serbia
UN: MONUC, UNMIL, UNOCI
Sierra Leone
UN: UNAMID, UNIFIL, UNMIN, UNMIS, UNMIT
Singapore
UN: UNMIT
NON-UN: ISAF
Slovakia
UN: UNFICYP, UNTSO
NON-UN: EUFOR Althea, EUMM, ISAF, KFOR, OSCE Bosnia, OSCE Kosovo, OSCE Serbia
Slovenia
UN: UNIFIL, UNTSO
NON-UN: EUFOR Althea, EUMM, ISAF, KFOR, OSCE Bosnia, OSCE Kosovo, OSCE Serbia
South Africa
UN: MONUC, UNAMID
NON-UN: Teutonic, Vimbezela
Spain
UN: MONUC, UNIFIL, UNMIK
NON-UN: Atalanta, EUFOR Althea, EUMM, ISAF, OSCE Bosnia, OSCE Kosovo
Sri Lanka
UN: MINURSO, MINUSTAH, MONUC, UNMIS
Sudan
NON-UN: MAES
Sweden
UN: MONUC, UNAMA, UNMIN, UNMIS, UNMOGIP, UNTSO
NON-UN: EUMM, KFOR, ISAF, NNSC, OSCE Bosnia, OSCE Kosovo, OSCE Serbia
Switzerland
UN: BINUB, MONUC, UNMIT, UNTSO

NON-UN: EUFOR Althea, KFOR, NNSC
Tajikistan
NON-UN: OSCE Bosnia, OSCE Moldova
Tanzania
UN: UNAMID, UNIFIL, UNMIS, UNOCI
NON-UN: MAES
Thailand
UN: UNAMID, UNMIS
Togo
UN: MINURCAT, UNAMID, UNMIL, UNOCI
Tonga
NON-UN: RAMSI
Tunisia
UN: MINURCAT, MONUC, UNOCI
Turkey
UN: UNAMID, UNIFIL, UNMIK, UNMIS
NON-UN: EUFOR Althea, KFOR, Maritime Security Ops, NTM-I, Ocean Shield, OSCE Bosnia, OSCE Kosovo, OSCE Serbia
Uganda
UN: UNAMID, UNMIS, UNOCI
NON-UN: AMISOM
Ukraine
UN: MONUC, UNMIK, UNMIL, UNMIS
NON-UN: ISAF, KFOR, NTM-I, OSCE Kosovo, OSCE Serbia, Trans-dniester PKF
United Arab Emirates
NON-UN: ISAF
United Kingdom
UN: MONUC, UNAMA, UNAMI, UNAMID, UNFICYP, UNMIS
NON-UN: EUFOR Althea, EUMM, IMATT, ISAF, KFOR, Maritime Security Ops, NTM-I, Ocean Shield, OSCE Bosnia, OSCE Kosovo, OSCE Minsk Conf, OSCE Moldova, OSCE Serbia
United States
UN: MINURCAT, MINUSTAH, UNAMI, UNMIL, UNTSO
NON-UN: Active Endeavour, IMATT, ISAF, KFOR, Maritime Security Ops, MFO, NTM-I, Ocean Shield, OEF-A, OSCE Bosnia, OSCE Kosovo, OSCE Moldova, OSCE Serbia, US Forces-Iraq
Uruguay
UN: MINURSO, MINUSTAH, MONUC, UNAMA, UNMIN, UNMOGIP, UNOCI
NON-UN: MFO
Uzbekistan
NON-UN: OSCE Kosovo
Yemen
UN: MINURCAT, MINURSO, MONUC, UNAMID, UNMIL, UNMIS, UNOCI
Zambia
UN: MONUC, UNAMID, UNMIL, UNMIN, UNMIS, UNOCI
Zimbabwe
UN: UNAMID, UNMIL, UNMIN, UNMIS, UNOCI

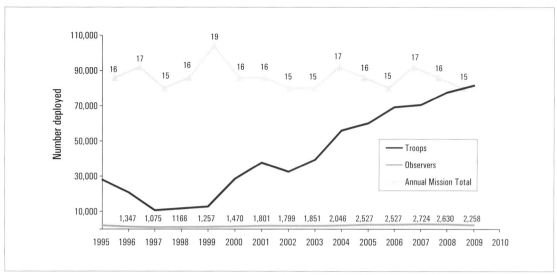

Figure 2 **UN deployment 1995–2009**

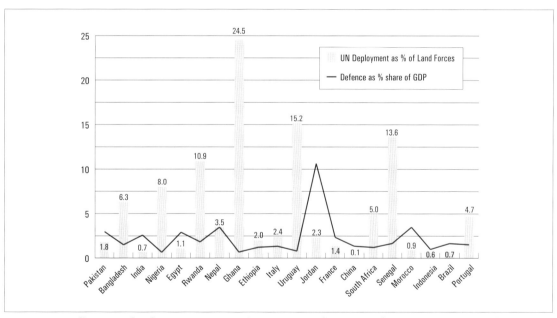

Figure 3 **Leading UN deployment countries 2009:** Defence (% of GDP) and UN land force deployment

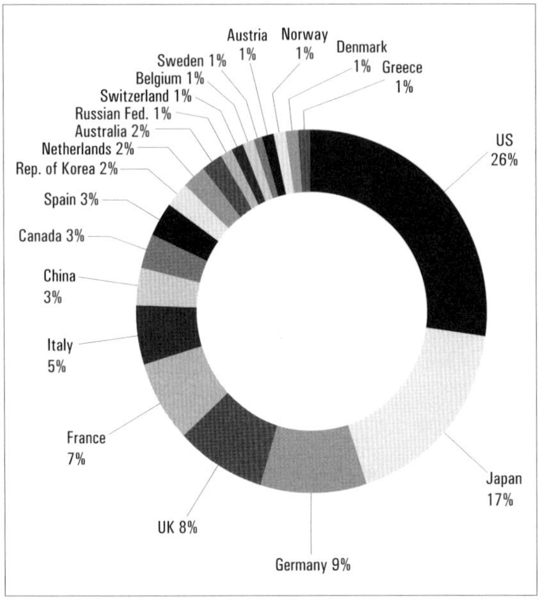

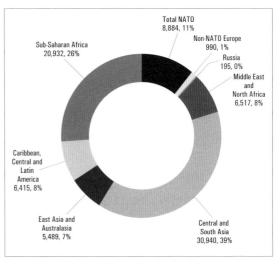

Figure 4 **Main UN budget providers for peacekeeping operations 2009**

Figure 5 **Regional share of UN deployed armed forces 2009**

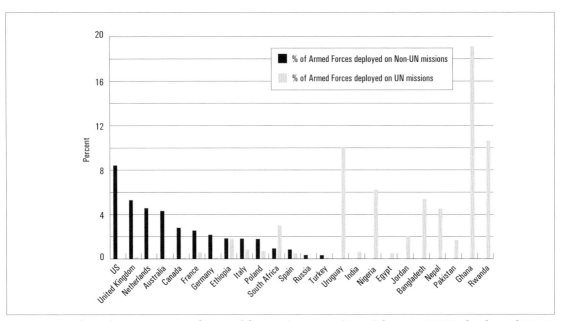

Figure 6 **Deployed percentage of armed forces in countries with over 2,000 deployed 2009**

Table 38 **Selected training activity 2009**

Date	Title	Location	Aim	Principal Participants/Remarks
North America (US and Canada)				
October 2008–24 Sept 2009	GREEN FLAG-WEST 09-1 - 09-10	US (Nellis AFB)	Series of air & ground trg ex to supplement Ex Red Flag	US; BEL; UK; GER; ITA
26 January–04 September	RED FLAG 09-2 - 09-5	US (Nellis AFB)	Tac-air ex	US; UK; AUS; ITA; UAE
27 February–07 March	MARITIME RAIDER 09	US (Fort Pickett, VA)	COIN ex for poss AFG deployment	CAN: 500 pers; US: 145 pers
20 April–07 May	UNITAS GOLD 2009	US (off Jacksonville, FL)	MSO, ASuW, AAW, amphib and SF trg ex.	US; ARG; BRZ; CAN; CHL; COL; DOM; ECU; GER; MEX; PER; URY. 25 ships, four SS, over 50 ac, 650 marines and 6,500 pers.
15–26 June	NORTHERN EDGE 2009	US (Elmendorf AFB)	Joint air-land and tac-air ex to improve C3	US: 1 CSG, 9,000 pers, 200 ac
18–24 June	ARDENT SENTRY 09	US (NORAD & Northcom)	AD and civ response ex	US Army, Navy, Air Force, ARNG
06–31 July	EMPIRE CHALLENGE 09	US (China Lake, CA)	LIVEX, Joint and coalition ISR interoperability ex	US; UK; CAN; AUS; NLD
60–28 August	NANOOK 2009	CAN (Baffin Island)	SAR; ASWEX	Joint Task Force (North): 700 pers; 1 SS; 1 FFH; 1 MCDV; MP ac; Coast Guard
04–14 September	JOINT TASK FORCE EXERCISE (JTFEX) 2009	US (East Coast)	Coalition interoperability trg incl ASWEX	US: 1 CSG; BEL 1 MH; BRZ 1 FFG; CAN 1 FFG; DNK 1 OPV; EST 1 MH; ITA 1 SS; NLD: 2 FFG, 1 MH; NOR 1 MS; UK 1 MS
14–24 September	GUNFIGHTER FLAG	US (Mountain Home AFB)	Multinational air cbt trg ex	US: F-15C (390th FS), F-15E (389th FS & 391st FS), EA-6B (137th Sqn), E-3 (963rd AAC Sqn), KC-135 (197th AR Sqn); Ca: CF-18 (409th TFS). Total: 450 pers
Latin America and Caribbean				
04–18 March	TRADEWINDS 2009	BHS	MSOEX, focus on C2	US 500 pers; UK RM detachment; BHS; BRB; BLZ; DOM; Grenada; GUY; HTI; HND; JAM; NIC; St. Kitts-Nevis; St. Lucia; St. Vincent and Grenadines; SUR; TTO
March–September	BEYONBD THE HORIZON 2009	COL; DOM; JAM; HND; SUR; TTO	Humanitarian and civic assistance ex	COL; DOM; JAM; HND; SUR; TTO; US: 350 pers each in COL, DOM, JAM; smaller gps in HND, SUR, TTO
16–29 April	FUERZAS ALIADAS HUMANITARIAS	ATG; CRI; HND; Grenada	HADR FTX and CPX	25 nations incl ATG; BHS; BDS; BZE; CRI; DOM; ELS; GUA; HND; NIC; SUR; TTO; US
31 May–14 June	SOUTHERN PARTNER	GUY; TTO; BRB; St. Lucia; Grenada; JAM; BZE	Enhance US & Central American/Caribbean interop (civ/mil)	BRB; BZE; GUY; JAM; St. Lucia; Grenada; TTO; US. Total: est 8,500 pers
28 June–12 July	TEAM WORK SOUTH 2009	CHL	MSO, ASW, AAWEX	BRZ: 1 FFG, Super Lynx; CHL: 4 FFG, 2 SSK, 4 PFM, 1 PB, 2 PCO, 1 AOR, 1 AT, P-3ACH, P-111, C-212, PC-72, SH-32; FRA: 1 FFG, Alouette III; UK: 1 DDG, Lynx; US: 3 FFG, SH-60B. Total: 3,000 pers
01 July–12 September	NEW HORIZONS GUYANA	GUY	Humanitarian and civic assistance ex	US: 650 pers (mostly ARNG, USAR med/engr units); GUY
13–31 July	SOUTHERN EXCHANGE 2009	BRZ	PKO & HADR	Marines and naval forces from US: 450 pers, incl elm II MEF, 1 LSD; ARG; CHL; BRZ; COL; PER; URY
11–22 September	FUERZAS ALIADAS PANAMAX 2009	PAN	US-led CT and MSOEX	ARG; BZE; CAN: 1 FFG; CHL: 1 FFG; COL: 1 FSG; DOM; ECU; ELS; GUA; NLD: 1 AORH; NIC; PAN; PRY; PER: 1 FFG; US: 1 FFG, 1 LPD, 1 PSOH; URY: 1 FF; FRA & MEX obs. Total: 30 ships, 4,500 pers, 12 ac
17 October–2 November	SALITRE II	CHL (Cerro Moreno AB, Diego Aracena AB)	Coalition AIREX incl SAR and CAOC trg with PKO and HADR elm	ARG; BRZ; CHL: F-16, F-5; FRA; US: 2 KC-130H, 2 KC-135, 6 F-15C
Europe and Nato				
13–27 February	NOBLE MANTA 2009	Ionian Sea	NATO ASWEX	CAN; FRA; GER: 2 FFG, 1 SSK, 2 AFH; GRC: 1 FFG, 1 SSK; ITA: 2 FFG, 1 AWT, 1 SSK; TUR: 1 FFG, 2 SSK; UK: 1 FFG, 1 SSN; US: 1 DDG
02–13 March	LOYAL MARINER 2009	ITA (off Sardinia)	MCMEX	SNMG1; SNMCMG 2; SNMCMG 3; incl pers from BEL, DNK, EST, FRA, GER, GRC, ITA, LVA, PRT, ESP, NLD, TUR, US

Table 38 **Selected training activity 2009**

Date	Title	Location	Aim	Principal Participants/Remarks
02–06 March	*BALTIC HOST 2009*	EST (Tartu)	Improve NATO interop	EST; LAT; LTU; POL; UK; US
06–17 March	*THRACIAN SPRING 2009*	BLG (Bezmer airbase)	AB ex	BLG, incl elm SF Bde; US incl elm USAF 786 Sy Forces Sqn, US Army 5th QM Coy
13–30 March	*EXERCISE EGEMEN (SOVEREIGN) 2009*	TUR (Doğanbey Exercise Area); Aegean Sea	Multinational amphib trg, CSAR, mtn ops ex	BEL; FRA 1 DDG; NLD: 2 LPD, Marines; TUR; US; UK: 1 LPD, 1 LPH, 2 FFG, 2 SSN, 1 AFSH, 1 AGSH, 1 AORH, 2 LSD, 3,000 pers (part of Taurus 09 deployment)
16–25 March	*COLD RESPONSE 2009*	NOR (Tromso and Nordland)	Joint QRF ex, incl SAR & CT trg	BEL; CZE; DNK 1 mech bn; EST; FRA: 1 inf bn; GER C-160; LVA; NLD ISTAR elm 1 mech inf coy; NOR 2,500 pers, 1 C-130J, ECR ac, F-16; POL 1 mech bn; ESP: ISTAR elm; SWE: 1 inf coy, JAS-39 ac; TUR; US; UK. Total: 7,000 pers (incl 700 SF)
23 March–3 April	*COLLECTIVE SHIELD 2009*	CZE; SVK	To prepare CZE-SVK EU Battlegroup	CZE: over 2,000 tps incl 4th Taskforce Bde; SVK over 300 tps
27 April–15 May	*FLYING RHINO 09-1*	CZE (Namest AB)	Air/land ex incl CAS and trg for Joint Tactical Air Controllers	CZE: L-39; DNK; CAN; GER; LTU; UK: Tornado GR-4, Hawk, AWACs, 1,800 pers. Total: 30 ac, AD systems
06 May–01 June	*COOPERATIVE LONGBOW – COOPERATIVE LANCER 09*	GEO (Vaziani)	NATO-led PfP CMX (CPX-LIVEX with UN-mandate PKO scenario); FTX (Cooperative Lancer)	ALB; ARM; AZE; BIH; CAN; CRO; CZE; GEO; HUN; GRC; FYROM; MDA; SRB; ESP; TUR; UAE; UK; US. 1,300 pers
11–22 May (and 05–23 Oct)	*JOINT WARRIOR 09-1; 09-2*	UK (maritime ops off NW Scotland)	Joint trg ex	AUS; BRZ: 1 FFG; CAN: 2 FFG, 1 DDH, 1 AORH, hel, ac; DNK: AG, hel; FRA: 1 MCD, 1 SSN, hel, ac; NOR: 2 sub, ac; ITA; PRT; NZL; TUR: FFG; UK: 1 CV with 10 Harrier GR9, 2 FFG, 3 MHC, 1 SSN, Tornado GR4, Typhoon, Hawk; BEL: ground forces; GER: ac; US: 2 DDG, 1 FFG, 1 AOH, hel
13–18 May	*MARE APERTO 09-1*	ITA (Med Sea off Sicily)	Multinational NAVEX incl ASW & cbt trg	CAN: 1 FFG, 1 DDG; 1 AORH; GER; GRC; ITA: 1 SSK; TUR; UK
27 May–05 June	*CONTEX/PHIBEX*	PRT	Joint interop ex	PRT; FRA: 1,400 pers, naval vessels, ac
02 June–17 June	*BALTIC EAGLE 2009*	LVA	FTX; evaluation of the Baltic Battalion	LTU; LVA; EST. 1,100 pers
08–19 June	*BALTOPS 2009*	Baltic Sea	MSOEX	EST; DNK; FIN; FRA; GER; LVA; LTU; UK; US; POL; SWE; NLD
09–19 June	*ANATOLIAN EAGLE 2009*	TUR	Multinational Air Ex	JOR; TUR 22 ac; UAE; UK; US. Total 83 ac incl NATO AWACs
12–21 June	*MARE APERTO 09-2*	ITA (Med Sea off Sicily)	Multinational NAVEX incl surv elm	FRA, GRC, ITA: 3 FFG, 1 FSM, 2 LPD, 1 AORH, 2 MHSC, 2 SSK, ac, hel; ESP, US
21–27 June	*FRUKUS 2009*	FRA (Bay of Biscay)	NAVEX to enhance cooperation incl anti-piracy trg	FRA 1 DDG; RUS 1 DDG; US 1 FFG; UK 1 DDGH
28 August–11 September	*OPEN SPIRIT 2009*	Baltic Sea	Multinational MCM/EODEX	EST; FRA; DNK; GER; LTU; POL; SWE. Total 16 ships
04–17 September	*COMBINED ENDEAVOR 2009*	BIH	Comms interoperability ex (PfP/NATO)	US, BIH 150 pers; 15 other NATO nations. Total 500-1,000 pers
07–18 September	*FLYING RHINO 09-2*	UK	Air/land ex. Incl CAS and FAC trg	UK, US F-15E
08–10 September	*WYCOMBE WARRIOR 09-2*	UK	Multinational Air Ex to enhance coop and interop	UK; BEL; FRA; GER; NOR; US
14–21 September	*BALTIC REGION TRAINING EVENT IV ALPHA-1*	EST (Tallinn)	Trg for EST FAC & tac air spt for land forces	US: F-15Es of 494 Sqn; EST (Scouts) Bn
14–25 September	*BOLD AVENGER 2009*	DNK	Multinational Air Ex	DNK; GER; NOR; SWE; BEL; NLD; GRC; POL; TUR; UK; FRA; PRT; US
21 September–03 October	*LOYAL MIDAS 2009*	Med Sea	Test C2 of NRF maritime and expeditionary elms	GER; ESP; US; FRA; GRC; ITA; PRT; TUR
22–25 September	*BALTIC REGION TRAINING EVENT IV ALPHA-2*	LTU (Radviliskis)	Train NATO Air Surveillance and Air Policing assets	US F-15Es of 494 Sqn; LTU AD btn
28 September–02 October	*SQUALO'09*	ITA	SAREX	ITA; FRA; ESP

Table 38 **Selected training activity 2009**

Date	Title	Location	Aim	Principal Participants/Remarks
Russia and Collective Security Treaty Organisation				
mid-January	*TURRUS-2009*	Mediterranean	Incl SAR and RAS trg	RUS 1 CV, 1 AT; TUR 1 FFG, 3 PFM
17–20 April	*n.k.*	TJK	SCO CT coordination ex	PRC; KAZ; KGZ; RUS; TJK; UZB
19–22 May	*n.k.*	RUS (Noginsk)	HADR	RUS; PRC; KAZ; TJK (IND, PAK, IRN, MNG to obs)
29 June–06 July	*CAUCASUS 2009*	RUS	North-Caucasus MD joint trg ex	Total over 8,500 pers, 200 tk, 450 AV, 250 arty
22–26 July	*PEACE MISSION 2009*	RUS; PRC	CT	PRC; RUS. 1,300 pers each
10 August–28 September	*LADOGA 2009*	RUS (Kola Peninsula)	Sea/land ex to test C2 reorg	RUS: Siberian MD, Northern Fleet, Baltic Fleet (60,000 pers)
25–28 August	*ZAPAD-2009 (WEST-2009)-1*	BLR	Test CSTO's new Collective Operational Reaction Forces	RF: Moscow MD, Army, Air Force, AD Forces, AB Tps, Baltic Fleet naval task forces (est 5,000 pers); BLR est 7,000 pers; KAZ: 30 pers. Total of 228 MBT, 470 IFV, 228 arty, 63 ac, est 40 hel. Obs from LVA, LIB, LTU, POL, UKR
26 August–24 October	*INTERACTION 2009-1*	RUS (Moscow); KAZ (Astana)	CSTO rapid response ex for pol/mil/environmental crises	KAZ 6,000 pers; RUS; ARM; BLR; KGZ; TJK. Total over 6,000 pers, 200 veh, 60 ac & hel
29 August–19 October	*n.k.*	RUS	Prepare CRDF for conventional mil threats	RUS; CSTO nations
September	*INTERACTION 2009-2*	BLR; KAZ (various)	FTX, AT and SF trg	RUS; KAZ; BLR; KGZ; TJK. 1,600 pers total
18–29 September	*ZAPAD-2009 (WEST-2009)-2*	BLR	AD trg esp integrated BLR/RUS AD systems	RUS: Moscow MD, Army, Air Force, AD forces, AB Tps, Baltic Fleet naval task forces (est 5,000 pers); BLR est 7,000 pers; KAZ 30 pers. Total 228 MBT, 470 IFVs, 228 tk, 234 arty, 63 ac, over 40 hel. Obs from LVA
02–15 October	*INTERACTION 2009-3*	KAZ (Matybulak)	Practice CRRF deployment in crisis situations in CSTO territory	KAZ; RUS; KGZ; TJK. Est 7,000 pers total
Middle East and North Africa				
19 Feb–17 March	*FRIENDSHIP ONE*	SAU	Enhance manouevre and logs coord	SAU; US
28 March–7 April	*EASTERN MAVERICK 2009*	QTR	Enhance bilateral cooperation; incl small unit veh trg, pilot trg and live fire ex	QTR; US, incl elm 13 MEU
16–25 April	*BLUE TOREADOR*	Arabian Sea	ASW & MSO trg	UK: 2 FFG, 1 LPH, 1 SSN, 1 AORH, 250 pers (part of Taurus 09 deployment) US: DDG
05–15 April	*PERLE DE L'OUEST 2009*	KWT	Joint force and CJTF HQ trg	FRA 1,000 pers; KWT 1,300 pers
19 April	*LION'S ROAR*	South IRQ	Ground forces FTX	IRQ (10th Army Div); US (4th HBCT, 1st Cav Div; 41st Fires Bde; elm USAF)
28 April–04 June	*AFRICAN LION 2009*	MOR (Tifnit)	Trg incl comms, C2, PKO, medical and avn ops	MOR: 650 pers, incl F-5, C-130 US: 650 pers incl USMC, KC-130
04–06 May	*EAGLE RESOLVE 2009*	QTR	Enhance mil-mil coop & prepare for various mil contingencies incl HADR	US; QTR; other GCC states
28–29 July	*REGIONAL INTERACTION, KEY TO A SAFE AND A CLEAN CASPIAN SEA*	Caspian Sea	MSOEX and MARPOL EX	IRN; RUS. Over 30 vessels, 2 hel
10–18 September	*BLUE PEACE SHIELD 2009*	Arabian Sea (off Somalia)	Anti-piracy & ship-boarding trg	RUS: 1 DDG, 1 AT; PRC: 2 FFG. 2 other ships, SF contingent
27 September	*THE GREAT PROPHET IV*	IRN	Test new missile capabilities	IRN: IRGC forces, msl incl *Shahab*-3 and *Sajjil*
10–20 October	*BRIGHT STAR 09-2*	EGY	Jonit trg ex between EGY & coalition forces. Incl naval, amph aslt, AB and C2 trg	EGY 2 LCU; GER; KWT; PAK; US: 1 LHD, 1 LPD, 1 LSD, 22 MEU, 12 ac, over 2,200 pers
21 October–5 November	*JUNIPER COBRA*	ISR (Sinai)	BMD ex to test interoperability of *Arrow* 2, PAC variants, THAAD, *Aegis* & X-band radar systems.	ISR; US: incl over 1,000 pers and 1 DDG

Table 38 **Selected training activity 2009**

Date	Title	Location	Aim	Principal Participants/Remarks
Sub–Saharan Africa				
17 January–12 February	*DASSA 2009*	BEN	Joint ex incl avn and AB trg	BEL: 600 pers; BEN: 400 pers
22–28 February	*GOLFINHO PHASE I*	ANG (Cabo Ledo, northern Bengo province)	Prep mapex for later *Golfinho* ex	SADCBRIG participants, 250 pers
14–24 April	*GOLFINHO PHASE II*	MOZ (Maputo)	Prep CPX for later ex stages	ANG: 33 pers; BWA; RSA; NAM; DRC; COG; MRT; MWI; Swaziland; ZMB; ZWE. 6,000 pers total
19–26 May	*ARG/MEU*	DJB (Camp Lemonier)	Inf trg & CSAREX	US: 13th MEU, USS Boxer ARG, 1 LCU, 1 LSD; FRA: elm French Foreign Legion
05–25 June	*SHARED ACCORD 09*	BEN	Bilateral FTX incl inf and staff officer trg	US: 400, BEN
01–29 September	*GOLFINHO PHASE III*	RSA (Lohatla and Walvis Bay)	Improve SADCBRIG capacity. Joint trg incl pol trg	SADC members incl ANG; BWA; DRC; LSO; MWI; MOZ; NAM; RSA 5,000 pers; Swaziland; TZA; ZMB; ZWE
03–26 September	*MLIMA KILIMANJARO 2009*	TZA (Arusha/ Tanga)	First EAC ex incl CT and HADR trg	TZA: RWA; BDI; KEN; UGA: 1,556 pers.
29 September–13 October	*AFRICA ENDEAVOR 2009*	GAB (Camp Baraka)	Enhance comms interoperability	BEN; BWA; BFA; BDI; CMR; CPV; CHA; DJB; ETH; GAB; GHA; GAM; KEN; LSO; MWI; MRT; MOR; NAM; NGA; RWA; Sao Tome & Principe; SEN; SLE; RSA; Swaziland; TZA; UGA; US; ZMB
16–25 October	*NATURAL FIRE 10*	UGA (Kitgum District & Entebbe)		UGA; KEN; TZA; RWA; BDI; US: 450 pers. 133 pers each from others
South and Central Asia				
26–31 January	*INDRA*	Arabian Sea	Anti-piracy, CT and counter-narcotics trg	IND; RF: 1 CGN, 5 other vessels
02–21 March	*BOLD KURUKSHETRA*	IND	Armoured forces trg	IND; SGP incl 500 tps from 4th Singapore Armoured Bde
05–14 March	*AMAN 09/PEACE 09*	North Arabian Sea	MSO ex incl AD and EOD trg	AUS; FRA; JPN; KWT; MYS; NGA; PAK; PRC DDG; TUR; UK; US
29 April–03 May	*SHOMUDRO TORONGO (SEA WAVE)*	BGD	Joint trg for UK forces incl amphib, jungle and HADR	UK: 1 LPD, 1 FFG, 1 LSD, 250 pers (part of *Taurus 09* deployment); BGD: naval units & ground troops
31 July–09 August	*REGIONAL COOPERATION 2009*	TJK	Disaster preparedness and sy coop ex; themes incl CT and crisis response	Est 240 tps from AFG; KAZ; KGZ; TJK; US; obs from TKM; UZB
05 September–n.k	*SAFFRON BANDIT 2009–10*	PAK	Air ex incl CT trg	PAK
14–29 September	*STEPPE EAGLE 2009*	KAZ (Illisky trg area)	Trg mil pers in PKO in conflict zones	KAZ, KAZBRIG (Bde HQ plus 1 inf bn); US; UK. Over 1,300 troops, 100 veh & ac
09–30 October	*AGNI WARRIOR 2009*	IND (Devlali)	Artillery trg ex	IND, incl 283 Fd Regt; SGP incl tps from 23 and 24 Bn, Singapore Artillery
12–29 October	*YUDH ABHYAS 09*	IND (Babina)	PKO-focused FTX	IND: 7th Mech Inf Bn (94th Armd Bde, 31st Armd Div); US incl 2-14 Cav Regt (2nd SBCT, 25th ID)
19–24 October	*COPE INDIA*	IND (Agra)	HADR	US: 1 C-17, 1 C-130J, 3 C-130H, 150 pers; IND: 1 IL-76, 4 AN-32, 2 Mi-17; 1 Chetak
East Asia and Australasia				
04–17 February	*COBRA GOLD*	THA	CPX, FTX, PSO & HADR	IDN 113 pers; JPN 75 pers; SGP 106 pers; THA 4,000 pers; US: 1 LHDM, 2 LSD, F-16, F/A-18, AV-8B, 7,000 pers
02–12 March	*NORTH WIND*	JPN (Camp Makomanai, Hokkaido)	FTX incl cold weather trg	JPN; US; total est 800 pers
09–20 March	*KEY RESOLVE/FOAL EAGLE*	ROK (various locations)	Key Resolve mainly a CPX; Foal Eagle mainly an FTX.	ROK: 50,000 pers; US: 26,000 pers incl 1 CSG
24 March–02 April	*SIMBEX*	Andaman Sea, South China Sea	ASWEX	IND: 2 DDG, 1 FS, 1 AOR, MPA SGP: 2 FSG, FFG, SS, FGA, MPA

Table 38 **Selected training activity 2009**

Date	Title	Location	Aim	Principal Participants/Remarks
16–30 April	*BALIKATAN 2009*	PHL (Bicol, Luzon, Zamboanga)	CT, HADR	PHL 5,200 pers. US 4,700 USN, Army, USMC. 25th in ex series.
26 April–03 May	*MALABAR 2009*	East of Okinawa	MSOEX incl ASW, AD, trg	IND: 2 DDG, 1 FSG, 1 AORH; JPN: JMSDF; US: 1 LCC, 2 DDG, 1 SSN, P-3C/SH-60 ac
04–08 May	*ARF-VDR*	PHL	FTX: ARF national capabilities in disaster relief scenario	400 participants from PHL; US; IDN; THA; MYS; MMR; LAO; VNM; SGP; AUA; BGD; CAN; PRC; IND; JPN; ROC; ROK; NZL; PAK; PNG; RUS; LKA; TLS; US
19–29 May	*BERSAMA SHIELD 09*	MYS; SGP; South China Sea	Joint interoperability trg for FPDA nations	UK: 1 FFG, 1 LPH, 1 AORH, hel; AUS: 1 AORH, 8 F/A-18, AP-3C, 1,000 pers; NZL: 1 FFH, 1 AORH; MYS; SGP. Total: 4 FF, 2 OPB, 3 AORH, est 90 ac & hel
20 May–13 August	*CARAT*	PHL; BRN; IDN	Cooperation Afloat Readiness and Training (CARAT) incl HADR trg	BRN; IDN; MYS; SGP; THA; US
07–12 June	*COMMANDO RAJAH*	BRN	Amphib & jungle trg for UK forces	UK: 1 LPD, 1 LPH, 1 FFG, 1 AORH, 3,000 pers, (part of *Taurus 09* deployment); AUS: 1 LCC; BRN, NZL, US: DDG, USMC
16–29 June	*GARUDA SHIELD 2009*	IDN	CPX, FTX, HADR ex (maintain and improve US-IDN PSO readiness)	Incl IDN; JPN; SGP; THA; US. 2009 Global Peace Operations Initiative (GPOI) capstone exercise
18–26 June	*COOPERATION 2009*	PRC	Imp CT capacities	PRC 60 pers; SGP 60 pers
06–26 July	*TALISMAN SABRE 2009*	AUS	CPX, FTX to test CTF ops in PKO and other post-conflict ops	AUS 8,000, US: 16,500, III MEF
01–20 August	*PACIFIC REACH 2009*	JPN	Assess readiness of US Army's Prepositioned Set 4 equipment	JPN, US
03–26 August	*KHAAN QUEST 2009*	MNG	PKO FTX to improve coord and interop	MNG 250; US: 150, CAM 51; ROK; IND; JPN. Over 700 pers total
11 August–11 October	*STRIDE-2009*	PRC	Test PLA log and C2 capacity and integrated joint warfare capability	PRC 50,000 pers, 60,000 veh & wpn systems, civilian assets also employed
12–19 August	*SUMAN WARRIOR 2009*	MYS (Kota Bharu)	Improve coop; part of FPDA ex series	SGP; UK; AUS; NZL; MYS 380 pers total (65 per country)
17–27 August	*ULCHI FREEODM GUARDIAN*	ROK	Computerised C2 ex to improve joint readiness	US: 10,000 pers; ROK
18–25 September	*SINGAROO*	South China Sea	Surv, AD and ASW naval trg	SGP: 1 FFG, 1 FSG, 1 SSK; AUS: 1 FSG, 1 OPB
21–22 September	*GREEN LIGHTNING*	AUS	Air ex	incl 13-hour US aerial sortie to targets in Aus. US: 3 B-52; Aus: FAC
05–23 October	*BERSAMA LIMA*	SGP & South China Sea	Comb. air, land, sea ex incl HADR trg	AUS; MYS; NZL; SGP; UK. Incl 240 pers, 19 ships, 59 ac, 1 submarine
11–13 October	*VANGUARD 2009*	PRC (Jinan Military Region)	Aim to test mil doctrine, tac reforms & inter-service joint ops in mtn areas	PRC: <10,000 pers, 58th Mech Inf Bde, 300 AFV, arty, 11 hel, AB pers, SF, tactic miss, ac;
13–23 October	*n.k.*	TLS (Dili)	Joint coop ex incl HADR, jungle, amph elms	TLS; AUS; US
27–30 October	*DEEP SABRE II*		PSI table-top and MSOEX	Approx 2,000 pers from ARG; AUS 1 PCO; BRN; FRA; CAN; GER; ITA; JPN 1 DDG, MPA; ROK; NZL 1 AT, MPA; PNG; PHL; POL; RUS; SGP 1 FFG, 2 LST, MPA; ESP; TUR; UAE; US 1 DDG, 1 AT, P-3C MPA

Table 39 International Comparisons of Defence Expenditure and Military Manpower

(Current US$ m)	Defence Expenditure US$ m			Defence Expenditure per capita US$			Defence Expenditure % of GDP			Number in Armed Forces (000)	Estimated Reservists (000)	Paramilitary (000)
	2006	2007	2008	2006	2007	2008	2006	2007	2008	2010	2010	2010
North America												
Canada	15,103	17,995	19,836	456	539	597	1.19	1.26	1.31	66	34	0
USA	617,155	625,850	696,268	2,068	2,077	2,290	4.68	4.53	4.88	1,580	865	0
Nato Europe												
Albania	141	198	254	39	55	70	1.54	1.83	1.90	14	0	0
Belgium	4,294	5,168	5,551	414	497	534	1.08	1.13	1.10	38	2	0
Bulgaria	882	1,206	1,315	119	165	181	2.84	3.03	2.62	35	303	0
Croatia	693	837	1,090	154	186	243	1.41	1.43	1.57	19	21	0
Czech Republic	2,408	2,539	3,165	235	248	310	1.68	1.48	1.46	18	0	0
Denmark	3,901	4,178	4,468	716	764	815	1.42	1.35	1.31	27	54	0
Estonia	238	388	450	179	295	344	1.44	1.86	1.94	5	25	0
France	55,474	61,838	67,185	911	1,012	1,049	2.46	2.38	2.35	353	70	0
Germany	37,956	42,589	46,943	461	517	570	1.31	1.28	1.28	251	162	0
Greece	7,286	8,215	10,141	682	767	946	2.37	2.63	2.85	157	238	4
Hungary	1,413	1,783	1,869	142	179	188	1.26	1.29	1.22	29	44	12
Iceland	46	n.a	n.a	153	n.a	n.a	0.27	n.a	n.a	0	0	0
Italy	33,289	37,770	30,934[2]	573	650	532[2]	1.79	1.79	1.34[2]	293	42	143
Latvia	318	447	542	140	198	241	1.59	1.55	1.60	6	11	0
Lithuania	353	453	547	99	127	153	1.17	1.16	1.16	9	7	15
Luxembourg	246	286	232	519	596	478	0.58	0.57	0.43	1	0	1
Netherlands	10,181	11,489	12,276	617	693	738	1.55	1.48	1.41	47	3	0
Norway	5,014	5,877	5,869	1,088	1,270	1,264	1.49	1.51	1.30	24	45	0
Poland	6,136	7,855	10,176	159	204	264	1.79	1.85	1.94	100	0	0
Portugal	3,143	3,312	3,729	296	311	349	1.62	1.48	1.53	43	211	48
Romania	2,259	2,616	3,005	101	117	135	1.84	1.57	1.53	73	45	80
Slovakia	917	1,239	1,477	169	227	271	1.62	1.52	1.55	17	0	0
Slovenia	629	741	834	313	369	415	1.69	1.64	1.53	7	4	5
Spain	14,385	16,738	19,263	356	414	476	1.17	1.16	1.20	128	319	80
Turkey	11,630	11,840	13,531	165	158	179	2.18	1.83	1.85	511	379	102
United Kingdom	59,454	68,868	60,794	981	1,133	998	2.42	2.46	2.28	175	199	0

Table 39 **International Comparisons of Defence Expenditure and Military Manpower**

(Current US$ m)	Defence Expenditure US$ m			Defence Expenditure per capita US$			Defence Expenditure % of GDP			Number in Armed Forces (000)	Estimated Reservists (000)	Paramilitary (000)
	2006	2007	2008	2006	2007	2008	2006	2007	2008	2010	2010	2010
Subtotal NATO Ex-US	277,787	316,469	325,478	482	545	556	1.77	1.75	1.65	2,446	2,216	489
Total NATO	894,942	942,319	1,021,746	1,023	1,068	1,149	3.10	2.95	3.01	4,026	3,081	489
Non-Nato Europe												
Armenia	184	296	396	62	99	133	2.87	3.13	3.32	47	0	5
Austria	2,630	3,603	3,193	321	439	389	0.82	0.97	0.77	27	195	0
Azerbaijan	658	936	1,585	82	115	194	3.13	2.96	3.23	67	300	15
Belarus	466	573	674	48	59	70	1.26	1.28	1.12	73	290	110
Bosnia	179	196	244	40	43	53	1.57	1.42	1.32	11	0	0
Cyprus	240	498	537	306	474	503	1.29	2.30	2.16	10	50	1
Finland	2,750	3,151	3,632	526	601	693	1.31	1.29	1.33	23	350	3
Georgia	339	573	1,037	73	123	224	4.38	5.60	8.13	21	0	12
Ireland	1,113	1,329	1,588	274	323	382	0.51	0.51	0.60	10	15	0
Macedonia	134	157	192	65	76	93	2.10	1.98	2.06	8	5	0
Malta	46	44	49	114	109	122	0.69	0.59	0.60	2	0	0
Moldova	13	19	22	3	4	5	0.40	0.44	0.36	6	66	2
Montenegro	53	55	71	79	80	105	2.36	2.11	2.31	3	0	10
Serbia	812	985	1,034	80	132	139	2.51	2.67	2.10	29	50	0
Sweden	6,006	6,773	6,659	666	750	736	1.53	1.49	1.39	13	200	1
Switzerland	3,473	3,526	4,110	462	467	542	0.89	0.83	0.83	22	174	0
Ukraine	1,269	1,877	1,804	27	41	39	1.19	1.32	1.00	130	1,000	85
Total	20,364	24,590	26,828	158	195	213	1.14	1.18	1.14	502	2,695	243
Russia [1]												
Russia	24,577	32,215	40,484	173	228	288	2.48	2.48	2.41	1,027	20,000	449
Middle East and North Africa												
Algeria	3,096	4,270	5,179	94	128	153	2.64	3.18	3.03	147	150	187
Bahrain	532	579	553	761	816	768	3.42	3.28	2.76	8	0	11
Egypt	4,337	4,464	4,562	55	59	59	4.01	3.36	2.90	469	479	397
Iran	8,864	8,040	9,595	136	123	146	3.98	2.81	2.84	523	350	40
Iraq	n.a.	n.a.	n.a.	n.a.	n.a.	n.a.	n.a.	n.a.	n.a.	578	0	0
Israel	11,582	11,607	14,772	1,823	1,806	2,077	8.05	7.07	7.41	177	565	8

Table 39 **International Comparisons of Defence Expenditure and Military Manpower**

(Current US$ m)	Defence Expenditure US$ m			Defence Expenditure per capita US$			Defence Expenditure % of GDP			Number in Armed Forces (000)	Estimated Reservists (000)	Paramilitary (000)
	2006	2007	2008	2006	2007	2008	2006	2007	2008	2010	2010	2010
Jordan	1,115	1,621	2,127	189	270	347	7.54	9.84	10.63	101	65	10
Kuwait	5,024	5,250	6,812	2,077	2,095	2,623	4.92	4.62	4.38	16	24	7
Lebanon	589	733	751	152	187	189	2.60	2.99	2.71	59	0	20
Libya	593	656	800	100	108	129	1.13	1.19	1.22	76	40	0
Mauritania	18	19	20	6	6	7	0.69	0.72	0.69	16	0	5
Morocco	2,161	2,409	2,977	65	79	96	3.78	3.21	3.48	196	150	50
Oman	4,076	4,376	4,671	1,314	1,366	1,410	10.99	10.39	8.53	43	0	4
Palestinian Authority	n.a.	n.a.	n.a.	n.a.	n.a.	n.a.	n.a.	n.a.	n.a.	0	0	56
Qatar	1,072	1,266	1,756	1,210	1,554	2,129	1.89	1.79	1.75	12	0	0
Saudi Arabia	29,541	35,446	38,223	1,093	1,284	1,357	8.30	9.24	8.15	234	0	16
Syria	1,330	1,376	1,941	70	67	91	4.09	3.48	3.78	325	314	108
Tunisia	502	491	534	49	48	51	1.61	1.39	1.28	36	0	12
UAE	9,482	11,253	13,733	3,643	2,532	2,972	5.58	5.67	5.09	51	0	0
Yemen	1,066	1,211	1,492	50	56	67	6.11	6.58	6.35	67	0	71
Total	**84,979**	**95,068**	**110,498**	**241**	**269**	**306**	**5.29**	**5.06**	**4.71**	**3,131**	**2,137**	**1,003**
South and Central Asia												
Afghanistan	118	153	180	4	6	7	1.53	1.58	1.51	94	0	0
Bangladesh	938	998	1,195	6	7	8	1.56	1.45	1.50	157	0	64
India	22,428	26,513	31,540	20	24	28	2.46	2.32	2.58	1,325	1,155	1,301
Kazakhstan	800	1,164	1,608	53	76	105	1.03	1.12	1.18	49	0	32
Kyrgyzstan	35	44	47	7	8	9	1.24	1.17	0.92	11	0	10
Maldives	56	37	43	156	102	111	6.07	3.52	3.40	0	0	0
Nepal	156	167	176	6	6	6	3.55	3.34	3.48	96	0	62
Pakistan	4,156	4,530	4,422	25	27	26	3.28	3.15	2.97	617	0	304
Sri Lanka	863	1,383	1,793	42	66	85	3.00	4.25	4.15	161	6	62
Tajikistan	73	78	80	10	11	11	2.60	2.13	1.74	9	0	8
Turkmenistan	91	99	84	18	21	17	0.90	0.81	0.71	22	0	0
Uzbekistan	n.a.	n.a.	n.a.	n.a	n.a	n.a	n.a	n.a	n.a	67	0	20
Total	**29,714**	**35,166**	**41,167**	**19**	**22**	**26**	**2.37**	**2.27**	**2.42**	**2,607**	**1,161**	**1,861**

Table 39 International Comparisons of Defence Expenditure and Military Manpower

(Current US$ m)	Defence Expenditure US$ m			Defence Expenditure per capita US$			Defence Expenditure % of GDP			Number in Armed Forces (000)	Estimated Reservists (000)	Paramilitary (000)
	2006	2007	2008	2006	2007	2008	2006	2007	2008	2010	2010	2010
East Asia and Australasia												
Australia	17,208	20,216	22,194	849	974	1,056	2.35	2.24	2.24	55	20	0
Brunei	324	346	360	854	895	945	2.83	2.81	2.49	7	1	2
Cambodia	123	137	255	9	10	18	1.69	1.59	2.30	124	0	67
China [1]	35,223	46,174	60,187	27	35	45	1.32	1.36	1.36	2,285	510	660
Fiji	43	50	57	47	54	61	1.61	1.78	1.84	4	6	0
Indonesia	3,645	4,320	5,108	16	18	22	1.00	1.00	1.00	302	400	280
Japan	41,144	41,039	46,044	323	322	362	0.95	0.93	0.93	230	42	12
Korea, North	n.a	n.a	n.a	n.a.	n.a.	n.a.	n.a.	n.a.	n.a.	1,106	4,700	189
Korea, South	24,645	26,588	24,182	505	551	500	2.59	2.53	2.60	687	4,500	5
Laos	13	15	17	2	2	3	0.38	0.36	0.32	29	0	100
Malaysia	3,206	3,979	4,370	131	160	173	2.15	2.13	1.97	109	52	25
Mongolia	39	43	52	14	15	17	1.22	1.04	1.10	10	137	7
Myanmar	n.a.	n.a.	n.a.	n.a.	n.a.	n.a.	n.a.	n.a.	n.a.	406	0	107
New Zealand	1,544	1,611	1,754	379	391	420	1.46	1.24	1.39	10	2	0
Papua New Guinea	31	37	35	6	6	6	0.68	0.74	0.56	3	0	0
Philippines	899	1,130	1,427	10	12	15	0.76	0.78	0.85	120	131	41
Singapore	6,321	7,007	7,662	1,407	1,539	1,663	4.55	4.22	4.20	73	313	94
Taiwan	8,232	9,015	10,495	357	389	458	2.35	2.32	2.76	290	1,657	17
Thailand	2,373	3,333	4,294	37	51	65	1.15	1.36	1.57	306	200	114
Timor-Leste	n.a.	n.a.	n.a.	n.a.	n.a.	n.a.	n.a.	n.a.	n.a.	1	0	0
Vietnam	2,054	2,159	2,907	24	25	33	3.37	3.04	3.19	455	5,000	40
Total	147,066	167,199	191,400	69	78	88	1.44	1.45	1.44	6,611	17,670	1,759
Latin America and Caribbean												
Antigua and Barbuda	6	7	7	86	80	79	0.59	0.58	0.56	0	0	0
Argentina	1,873	2,093	2,031	47	52	50	0.87	0.80	0.61	73	0	31
Bahamas, The	48	50	49	159	166	161	0.66	0.67	0.65	1	0	0
Barbados	27	28	30	95	97	106	0.82	0.80	0.79	1	0	0
Belize	n.a.	n.a.	n.a.	n.a.	n.a.	n.a.	n.a.	n.a.	n.a.	1	1	0
Bolivia	156	162	250	17	17	26	1.40	1.24	1.50	46	0	37

Table 39 International Comparisons of Defence Expenditure and Military Manpower

(Current US$ m)	Defence Expenditure US$ m			Defence Expenditure per capita US$			Defence Expenditure % of GDP			Number in Armed Forces (000)	Estimated Reservists (000)	Paramilitary (000)
	2006	2007	2008	2006	2007	2008	2006	2007	2008	2010	2010	2010
Brazil	16,206	20,559	26,254	86	106	134	1.48	1.54	1.66	328	1,340	395
Chile	4,677	5,238	5,561	290	322	338	3.19	3.19	3.28	61	40	42
Colombia	5,377	6,806	9,546	123	160	221	3.96	3.96	3.91	285	62	144
Costa Rica	123	140	156	30	34	37	0.55	0.53	0.53	0	0	10
Cuba	1,700	2,148	2,296	149	188	201	4.00	4.00	4.00	49	39	27
Dominican Republic	256	270	278	28	29	29	0.72	0.66	0.60	50	0	15
Ecuador	653	773	1,105	48	55	77	1.58	1.80	1.99	58	118	0
El Salvador	106	111	115	16	16	16	0.57	0.55	0.52	16	10	17
Guatemala	146	166	180	12	13	14	0.48	0.48	0.42	15	64	19
Guyana	17	18	67	22	23	89	1.9	1.7	5.8	1	1	2
Haiti	n.a.	n.a.	n.a.	n.a.	n.a.	n.a.	n.a.	n.a.	n.a.	0	0	0
Honduras	55	76	96	8	10	12	0.50	0.61	0.67	12	60	8
Jamaica	78	87	96	28	31	34	0.65	0.68	0.65	3	1	0
Mexico	3,229	3,982	4,346	30	37	40	0.34	0.39	0.40	268	40	37
Nicaragua	35	37	42	6	6	7	0.66	0.64	0.66	12	0	0
Panama	171	200	226	54	61	68	1.00	1.03	0.97	0	0	12
Paraguay	67	100	132	10	15	19	0.73	0.83	0.83	11	165	15
Peru	1,108	1,226	1,424	39	43	49	1.20	1.14	1.11	114	188	77
Suriname	20	26	31	44	54	65	0.98	1.16	1.33	2	0	0
Trinidad and Tobago	114	127	143	107	103	116	0.59	0.58	0.59	4	0	0
Uruguay	227	304	260	66	88	75	1.17	1.29	0.81	25	0	1
Venezuela	2,597	2,578	3,328	101	99	126	1.40	1.13	1.04	115	8	0
Total	39,073	47,310	58,048	70	84	101	1.25	1.29	1.35	1,549	2,136	887
Sub-Saharan Africa												
Angola	1,588	2,247	2,425	132	183	194	3.51	3.66	3.05	107	0	10
Benin	49	55	67	6	7	8	1.04	0.93	0.98	5	0	3
Botswana	289	317	293	176	166	150	2.57	2.57	2.19	9	0	2
Burkina Faso	72	95	112	5	7	7	1.18	1.34	1.21	11	0	0
Burundi	74	78	83	9	9	9	7.67	8.37	7.48	20	0	31
Cameroon	257	297	306	15	16	17	1.43	1.43	1.28	14	0	9

Table 39 International Comparisons of Defence Expenditure and Military Manpower

(Current US$ m)	Defence Expenditure US$ m			Defence Expenditure per capita US$			Defence Expenditure % of GDP			Number in Armed Forces (000)	Estimated Reservists (000)	Paramilitary (000)
	2006	2007	2008	2006	2007	2008	2006	2007	2008	2010	2010	2010
Cape Verde	7	8	9	17	19	21	0.62	0.55	0.51	1	0	0
Central African Republic	16	18	20	4	4	5	1.00	0.99	0.95	3	0	0
Chad	64	89	145	6	9	14	0.92	1.35	1.78	25	0	10
Congo	84	94	112	23	25	29	1.13	1.23	0.89	10	0	2
Cote d'Ivoire	266	290	336	15	15	17	1.45	1.38	1.45	17	10	2
Democratic Republic of Congo	163	166	168	3	3	3	1.88	1.71	1.49	151	0	0
Djibouti	17	18	15	36	25	22	2.21	1.98	1.46	10	0	3
Equatorial Guinea	8	8	11	14	15	18	0.08	0.07	0.06	1	0	0
Eritrea	n.a.	n.a.	n.a.	n.a.	n.a.	n.a.	n.a.	n.a.	n.a.	202	120	0
Ethiopia	345	336	366	5	4	4	2.27	1.75	1.23	138	0	0
Gabon	111	123	134	78	85	90	1.09	1.06	0.89	5	0	2
Gambia	4	8	16	2	5	9	0.70	1.23	2.17	1	0	0
Ghana	83	104	105	4	5	4	0.66	0.70	0.69	16	0	0
Guinea	36	52	51	4	5	5	1.17	1.11	1.04	12	0	7
Guinea Bissau	13	15	18	9	10	12	3.95	3.94	3.74	6	0	0
Kenya	398	681	735	11	18	19	1.75	2.47	2.14	24	0	5
Lesotho	35	40	36	17	20	17	2.37	2.38	2.13	2	0	0
Liberia	n.a.	n.a.	n.a.	n.a.	n.a.	n.a.	n.a.	n.a.	n.a.	2	0	0
Madagascar	54	82	103	3	4	5	0.98	1.12	1.09	14	0	8
Malawi	39	42	43	3	3	3	1.79	1.71	1.50	5	0	2
Mali	132	132	157	11	10	12	2.23	1.77	2.14	7	0	5
Mauritius	11	27	36	9	22	28	0.17	0.36	0.39	0	0	2
Mozambique	57	57	76	3	3	4	0.81	0.74	0.83	11	0	0
Namibia	197	239	287	96	116	137	2.47	2.70	3.25	9	0	6
Niger	38	48	58	3	3	4	1.02	1.09	1.08	5	0	5
Nigeria	768	980	1,339	6	7	9	0.53	0.59	0.66	80	0	82
Rwanda	72	62	71	7	6	7	2.52	1.82	1.83	33	0	2
Senegal	149	193	218	12	15	16	1.49	1.64	1.67	14	0	5
Seychelles	15	11	8	178	134	98	1.40	1.12	0.91	0	0	0
Sierra Leone	28	15	14	5	3	3	1.71	0.75	0.59	11	0	0

Table 39 **International Comparisons of Defence Expenditure and Military Manpower**

(Current US$ m)	Defence Expenditure US$ m			Defence Expenditure per capita US$			Defence Expenditure % of GDP			Number in Armed Forces (000)	Estimated Reservists (000)	Paramilitary (000)
	2006	2007	2008	2006	2007	2008	2006	2007	2008	2010	2010	2010
Somali Republic	n.a.	n.a.	n.a.	n.a.	n.a.	n.a.	n.a.	n.a.	n.a.	2	0	0
South Africa	3,518	3,577	3,359	80	74	69	1.37	1.26	1.22	62	15	0
Sudan	n.a.	n.a.	n.a.	n.a.	n.a.	n.a.	n.a.	n.a.	n.a.	109	0	18
Tanzania	147	162	184	4	4	5	1.04	0.99	0.91	27	80	1
Togo	34	42	56	6	7	10	1.52	1.60	1.90	9	0	1
Uganda	192	232	277	7	8	9	1.74	1.71	1.68	45	0	2
Zambia	300	200	262	27	17	22	2.81	1.72	1.77	15	3	1
Zimbabwe	156	n.a.	n.a.	13	n.a.	n.a.	2.78	0.16	n.a.	29	0	22
Total	9,888	11,242	12,113	13	14	15	1.33	1.31	1.24	1,281	228	246
Summary												
US	617,155	625,850	696,268	2,068	2,077	2,290	4.68	4.53	4.88	1,580	865	0
NATO Ex-US	277,787	316,469	325,478	482	545	556	1.77	1.75	1.65	2,446	2,216	489
Total NATO	894,942	942,319	1,021,746	1,023	1,068	1,149	3.10	2.95	3.01	4,026	3,081	489
Non-NATO Europe	20,364	24,590	26,828	158	195	213	1.14	1.18	1.14	502	2,695	243
Russia [1]	24,577	32,215	40,484	173	228	288	2.48	2.48	2.41	1,027	20,000	449
Middle East and North Africa	84,979	95,068	110,498	241	269	306	5.29	5.06	4.71	3,131	2,137	1,003
South and Central Asia	29,714	35,166	41,167	19	22	26	2.37	2.27	2.42	2,607	1,161	1,861
East Asia and Australasia	147,066	167,199	191,400	69	78	88	1.44	1.45	1.44	6,611	17,670	1,759
Latin America and Caribbean	39,073	47,310	58,048	70	84	101	1.25	1.29	1.35	1,549	2,136	887
Sub-Saharan Africa	9,888	11,242	12,113	13	14	15	1.33	1.31	1.24	1,281	228	246
Global totals	1,296,027	1,404,396	1,547,801	199	213	232	2.67	2.56	2.56	20,734	49,106	6,937

1. Official Budget only at market exchange rates.
2. New methodology adopted.

Table 40 Arms Deliveries to Developing Nations
Leading Recipients in 2008
(current US$m)

1	Saudi Arabia	1,800
2	India	1,800
3	Venezuela	1,500
4	South Korea	1,400
5	Israel	1,200
6	Egypt	1,100
7	China	1,100
8	Singapore	800
9	Iraq	800
10	Pakistan	700

Table 41 Arms Transfer Agreements with Developing Nations
Leading Recipients in 2008
(current US$m)

1	UAE	9,700
2	Saudi Arabia	8,700
3	Morocco	5,400
4	India	4,000
5	Iraq	2,000
6	Egypt	1,400
7	South Korea	1,300
8	Taiwan	1,300
9	Israel	1,000
10	Pakistan	800

Table 42 Global Arms Deliveries
Leading Suppliers in 2008
(current US$m)

1	United States	12,232
2	Russia	5,400
3	Germany	2,900
4	UK	2,000
5	China	1,400
6	France	900
7	Israel	900
8	Sweden	800
9	Netherlands	700
10	Austria	500

Table 43 Global Arms Transfer Agreements
Leading Suppliers in 2008
(current US$m)

1	United States	37,796
2	Italy	3,700
3	Russia	3,500
4	France	2,600
5	Germany	1,000
6	Netherlands	900
7	China	800
8	Sweden	600
9	Israel	500
10	Brazil	500

Table 44 Value of Global Arms Transfer Agreements and Market Share by Supplier, 2001–2008 (constant 2008US$m – % in italics)

	Total	US		Russia		France		UK		Germany		Italy		All Other European		China		Others	
2001	38,586	13,918	36.1	6,873	17.8	5,400	14.0	736	1.9	2,455	6.4	1,350	3.5	3,314	8.6	1,350	3.5	3,191	8.3
2002	34,194	15,536	45.4	6,817	19.9	718	2.1	837	2.4	1,196	3.5	478	1.4	5,502	16.1	478	1.4	2,631	7.7
2003	36,252	16,942	46.7	5,383	14.8	3,277	9.0	2,926	8.1	1,755	4.8	702	1.9	2,575	7.1	702	1.9	1,989	5.5
2004	47,052	14,384	30.6	8,394	17.8	3,289	7.0	4,764	10.1	4,537	9.6	681	1.4	6,125	13.0	1,134	2.4	3,743	8.0
2005	49,241	14,040	28.5	6,580	13.4	8,005	16.3	3,071	6.2	2,303	4.7	1,645	3.3	8,225	16.7	2,851	5.8	2,522	5.1
2006	57,176	16,898	29.6	15,500	27.1	5,905	10.3	4,323	7.6	1,476	2.6	1,265	2.2	6,116	10.7	1,476	2.6	4,218	7.4
2007	59,749	25,368	42.5	10,776	18.0	2,053	3.4	10,057	16.8	1,539	2.6	1,232	2.1	5,234	8.8	1,334	2.2	2,155	3.6
2008	55,196	37,796	68.5	3,500	6.3	2,600	4.7	200	0.4	1,000	1.8	3,700	6.7	3,200	5.8	800	1.4	2,400	4.3

Table 45 Value of Global Arms Deliveries and Market Share by Supplier, 2001–2008 (constant 2008US$m – % in italics)

	Total	US		Russia		France		UK		Germany		Italy		All Other European		China		Others	
2001	34,043	11,215	32.9	5,768	16.9	2,455	7.2	5,277	15.5	859	2.5	614	1.8	3,682	10.8	1,105	3.2	3,068	9.0
2002	34,261	11,776	34.4	4,306	12.6	1,794	5.2	5,980	17.5	1,435	4.2	718	2.1	3,588	10.5	1,076	3.1	3,588	10.5
2003	40,616	12,997	32.0	5,032	12.4	2,809	6.9	8,075	19.9	2,692	6.6	468	1.2	4,798	11.8	819	2.0	2,926	7.2
2004	39,311	13,336	33.9	6,352	16.2	6,239	15.9	3,743	9.5	2,042	5.2	227	0.6	2,722	6.9	1,021	2.6	3,630	9.2
2005	34,072	13,126	38.5	3,728	10.9	2,851	8.4	4,057	11.9	1,974	5.8	1,097	3.2	3,290	9.7	877	2.6	3,071	9.0
2006	36,748	13,129	35.7	6,643	18.1	1,582	4.3	4,745	12.9	2,952	8.0	422	1.1	3,901	10.6	1,160	3.2	2,214	6.0
2007	34,551	12,792	37.0	5,235	15.2	2,258	6.5	2,053	5.9	2,874	8.3	718	2.1	4,106	11.9	1,540	4.5	2,976	8.6
2008	31,832	12,232	38.4	5,400	17.0	900	2.8	2,000	6.3	2,900	9.1	400	1.3	4,000	12.6	1,400	4.4	2,600	8.2

US DoD Price Deflator. All data rounded to nearest $100m. Source: Richard F. Grimmett, Conventional Arms Transfers to Developing Nations 2001–2008 (Washington DC: Congressional Research Service)

Table 46 **Arms Deliveries to Middle East and North Africa, by Supplier**

(current US$m)

2001–2004	US	Russia	China	Major West European*	All other European	Others	Total
Algeria		300	100		100	100	600
Bahrain	300						300
Egypt	5,000	200	400	100	100		5,800
Iran		100	100		100	300	600
Iraq					100		100
Israel	3,500				100		3,600
Jordan	300			100	100	100	600
Kuwait	800	100	200			200	1,300
Lebanon							-
Libya		100			100	200	400
Morocco				200			200
Oman				200			200
Qatar							-
Saudi Arabia	4,300			15,900	2,400		22,600
Syria		200			100	100	400
Tunisia							-
UAE	300	300		5,700	300	100	6,700
Yemen		400	100	100	200	100	900

2004–2007	US	Russia	China	Major West European*	All other European	Others	Total
Algeria		1,400	100				1,500
Bahrain	300			100			400
Egypt	4,800	100	500		400		5,800
Iran		500	100			100	700
Iraq	900	100			200	100	1,300
Israel	5,600	100					5,700
Jordan	800	100	100		200		1,200
Kuwait	1,600						1,600
Lebanon							-
Libya		200			100		300
Morocco	100	100				100	300
Oman	700			100			800
Qatar							-
Saudi Arabia	4,400		400	6,500			11,300
Syria		1,000				400	1,400
Tunisia							-
UAE	600	200		1,100	300		2,200
Yemen		200	100		100	100	500

* Major West European includes UK, Germany, France, Italy

All data rounded to nearest $100m

Source: Richard F. Grimmett, Conventional Arms Transfers to Developing Nations 2001–2008
(Washington DC: Congressional Research Service)

Table 47 **Selected Operational Military Satellites 2010**

Country	Designations	Quantity	Orbit	Launch	Description and Remarks
Communications					
China	Fenghuo (Zhong Xing)	4	GSO	2000-2008	dual use telecom satellites for civ/mil comms
Italy	Sicral	2	GSO	2001-2009	
NATO	NATO-4	2	GSO	1993	military, diplomatic and data comms
Russia	Molniya-1	2	HEO	1997-2003	dual use telecom satellites for civ/mil comms
Russia	Geizer/Potok 11	1	GSO	2000	data relay
Russia	Globus (Raduga-1)	3	GSO	2000-2007	
Russia	Strela	9	LEO	2001-2004	replacement by Rodnik reportedly underway
Russia	Rodnik (Gonets-M)	4	GSO	2005-2008	reported to be replacing Strela
Spain	Spainsat	1	GSO	2006	secure comms
France	Syracuse 3	2	GSO	2005-2006	secure comms; to integrate with UK Skynet and ITA Sicral
UK	Skynet-4	3	GSO	1990-2001	
UK	Skynet-5	3	GSO	2007-2008	secure comms for mil and govt.
USA	DSCS-3	8	GSO	1989-2003	incl 1 in reserve
USA	Milstar-1	2	GSO	1994-1995	
USA	Milstar-2	3	GSO	2001-2003	
USA	SDS-III	6	HEO/GSO	1998-2007	relay; polar replay functions may have moved to other satellites
USA	UFO	7	GSO	1995-2003	3 with Global Broadcast Service
USA	WGS SV2 (GS-F1and F2)	2	GSO	2007-2009	first 2 of 5; will replace DSCS system
Navigation, Positioning and Timing					
China	Beidou	5	GSO	2000-2009	
Russia	Parus	9	LEO	1999-2009	also relay
Russia	Glonass	19	MEO	2003-2008	an operational constellation needs 24 satellites; additions planned
USA	Navstar GPS	32	MEO	1989-2009	also carry a Nuclear Detonation Detection System
Meteorology and Oceanography					
USA	DMSP-5	5	SSO/LEO	1995-2006	early warning
USA	GFO	1	SSO	1998	oceanography, geodesy
Intelligence, Surveillance and Reconnaissance					
China	Haiyang 1	2	LEO	2002-2007	Haiyang 2 and 3 series planned; Haiyang 2A due to be launched 2010
China	Yaogan Weixing	5	LEO	2006-2009	remote sensing; Yaogan 7 due to launch in 2009
China	Zhangguo Ziyuan (ZY-2)	2	LEO	2002-2004	recce/surv; remote sensing
China	Shi Jian-6	4	SSO	2004-2008	Pairs of 2 (A, B; C, D) reports of poss ELINT/SIGINT roles
France	Helios-1/2	2	SSO	1995-2004	optical recce; partnership with Italy and Spain
Italy	Cosmo (Skymed)	3	LEO	2007-2008	surv
Israel	Ofeq-5 and 7	2	SSO/LEO	2002-2007	recce/surv
Israel	TecSAR 1 (Polaris)	1	LEO	2008	recce
Japan	IGS-1/2/3/4	4	SSO	2003-2007	optical recce
Russia	Araks 1 and 2	2	ellipticLEO	1997-2002	recce/surv
Russia	Tselina-2	1	LEO	2002-2007	recce/surv; ELINT
Russia	US-PU	1	LEO	2006	naval recce and targeting system; ELINT
Russia	Kobolt-M	1	LEO	2009	recce/surv
Taiwan	Rocsat-2	1	SSO/LEO	2004	recce/surv

Table 47 **Selected Operational Military Satellites 2010**

Country	Designations	Quantity	Orbit	Launch	Description and Remarks
USA	Keyhole (KH-12) (Crystal/Misty)	4	SSO/LEO	1996-2005	recce/surv; high-res surv
USA	Lacrosse (Onyx)	2	SSO/LEO	2000-2005	recce/surv
USA	Mentor 1/2/3 (Orion)	3	GEO	1995-2003	ELINT
USA	Advanced Mentor (NROL-26)	1	GSO	2009	surv; SIGINT
USA	Mercury	2	GEO	1994-1996	COMINT
USA	Trumpet	5	elliptic HEO	1994-2008	SIGINT; NROL-22 and -28; reports of poss SIGINT role
USA	SBWASS	8	LEO	2001-2007	ocean and wide-area sigint; each paired with sub-satellite
India	RISAT-2	1	LEO	2009	surv
Germany	SAR-Lupe (1-5)	5	LEO	2006-2008	surv
Early Warning					
Russia	Oko	6	HEO/GSO	2001-2008	
Russia	Prognoz	2	GSO	2001-2008	
USA	DSP	4	GSO	1997-2004	an operational constellation needs 3 satellites
France	Spirale	2	elliptic	2009	future BMEWS

Chapter Ten
Reforming India's defence industries

India's vast defence-industrial infrastructure is undergoing major reform. At the same time, India is modernising and expanding its armed forces to encompass widening political and security interests beyond South Asia. To equip these forces, the country now aspires to develop and build sophisticated weapon systems, moving away from the historical pattern of foreign-origin kit assembly and licensed production. These plans are also being pursued with a view towards entering potentially lucrative export markets.

Defence industries in India currently employ over 1.4 million people and receive about 21%, or just under US$2 billion, of India's annual defence-procurement budget. But due to inefficiencies in India's public-sector defence industries (where there are often long delays and high costs in the production of largely low- to medium-technology arms and equipment), over 70% of India's arms are imported. Even as the government seeks to encourage foreign technological and financial investment in the defence sector, along with a greater role for the Indian private sector, it needs to implement bolder reforms and restructure its defence-production establishment if it is to become a major producer of high-technology and sophisticated arms and equipment.

Public-sector defence-production agencies

On independence in 1947, India had 16 ordnance factories manufacturing small arms, ammunition, mines and explosives, with a nascent capacity to service imported arms and equipment. In an attempt to maintain an independent foreign policy, the government of Prime Minister Jawaharlal Nehru aimed for national self-reliance in defence acquisition and rejected, as lacking ambition, a 1948 report by British physicist P.M.S. Blackett, which recommended that India first produce low-performance, older-technology weapons.

In the 1950s, India built several new public-sector ordnance factories, which had to maintain operational capacity during slack periods by producing goods for the civil market. An accusation following India's defeat by China in the 1962 war that India's weapons factories were producing coffee percolators instead of arms prompted an expansion of production facilities, with a new administrative department within the Defence Ministry becoming responsible for defence-production activities. By the mid 1980s, the number of ordnance factories manufacturing primarily land-based systems (such as main battle tanks (MBTs), armoured vehicles, trucks, small arms and ammunition and explosives) rose to 35; in 2009 there were 39. Two more factories are under construction; one in Nalanda, in eastern India and the other in Korwa, in northern India, although the latter has been delayed by the June 2009 suspension from trading in India of Israel Military Industries, its co-developer, following the arrest of a former Indian ordnance board chief on corruption charges.

The largest existing 'defence public-sector undertaking' grew out of the 1964 amalgamation of Hindustan Aircraft Ltd (established in 1940 by Indian industrialist Walchand Hirachand) with Aeronautics India Ltd. Hindustan Aeronautics Ltd (HAL) now has 12 divisions located in six states and is tasked with the manufacture of combat aircraft and helicopters. The products of the seven other specialised defence firms controlled by the Defence Ministry include warships, missiles, defence electronics, heavy earth-moving equipment and special metals and alloys.

India's first industrial-policy resolution, in 1948, made it clear that a major portion of industrial capacity was to be reserved for the public sector, including all arms production. When this document was revised in 1956, it placed the munitions, aircraft and shipbuilding industries in the public sector under central government control, preventing private-sector production. Even though a new defence-supplies department was set up in 1965 within the Defence Ministry, the private sector could only produce components and spare parts. By the mid 1990s, private-sector production encompassed elementary and intermediate products, components and spare parts. In April 1994, the chief of the powerful Defence Research and Development Organisation (DRDO) announced a ten-year plan for defence and the defence-industrial base, aimed at increasing the element of self-reliance in the Indian armed services from 30% to 70% of annual expenditure on defence acquisitions. By 2004, however, this had failed, with the proportion of spending remaining the same and DRDO's production record drawing some criticism.

In 2004, the government established a committee, led by Vijay Kelkar, to recommend improvements in India's defence-acquisitions system and defence production. In April 2005, the first report of the Kelkar Committee recommended a series of measures including the generation of a 15-year plan for defence acquisition and sharing armed forces' requirements with industry, as well as identifying entry points for the private sector in the acquisition process. In its second report in November 2005, the committee focused on revitalising public-sector production agencies.

Meanwhile, licensed production of major arms and equipment achieved some successes. The most noteworthy were the production of T-72MI MBTs and MiG-21 combat aircraft with Russian technology, along with the *Jaguar* combat aircraft and the *Nilgiri*-class frigates (based on the *Leander* frigate) with British technology. Though there were time and cost overruns, as well as allegations of corruption, these systems were successfully integrated into India's inventories. But the indigenous production of arms, sometimes with elements of foreign technology, has also had major failures, resulting in some cases in the armed services refusing to accept equipment. The most notable case is that of the *Arjun* MBT, which took over 37 years to develop and build; the army remains reluctant to deploy them. The *Tejas* light combat aircraft (LCA) has taken over 25 years to develop and flight-test, a delay which led to the proposed US$12bn order for 126 medium multi-role combat aircraft (MMRCA) to make up the short-fall in fast-depleting fighter squadrons. Meanwhile, the crash of the prototype 14-seater *Saras* multi-role aircraft in March 2009 and the crash of the prototype airborne surveillance platform in January 1999 served to underscore the risks inherent in the development processes for new military technologies.

Service experiences

The primary location for **army** vehicle production, the Heavy Vehicles Factory at Avadi in southern India, has successfully produced over 1,000 *Vijayanta* (ex-British) and T-72MI (ex-Russian) MBTs under license for the army since the mid 1960s. It has also built over 90 of the ill-fated *Arjun* tanks and is currently building another 20 ordered by the Defence Ministry. It is also constructing 347 recently imported T-90S tanks, the *Bhishma*, from kits supplied by the Uralvagonzavod tank plant in Russia; the first batch of ten was delivered to the army in August 2009. The army had previously inducted 310 T-90S MBTs in 2001, 124 complete and the remainder assembled at Avadi. A US$3.5bn order for the licensed production of 1,000 *Bhishma* tanks is expected and the Avadi factory plans to produce 100 annually.

The **navy** has the highest number of principal platforms built locally among the armed services. While this can partly be ascribed to the long lead times and planning involved in naval construction, also important is the growing confidence of the naval design organisation and the navy's extensive links with the three shipyards run by the Defence Ministry (led by Mazagon Dockyard Ltd in Mumbai) and Cochin Shipyard Ltd run by the Shipping Ministry. Indian shipyards are currently building vessels including the second and third *Shivalik*-class (Project 17) stealth frigates; two air-defence ships (the keel for the first was laid in February 2009 with commissioning expected in 2014); and the first of six *Scorpene* submarines produced under license with French technology. India's first nuclear-powered submarine, INS *Arihant*, was launched on 26 July 2009. But time and cost overruns persist. In July 2009, the Defence Ministry acknowledged that *Scorpene* production was running at least two years behind schedule due to difficulties with the 'absorption of technologies'. This has delayed the expected follow-on order for an additional six diesel-electric submarines. The construction of six improved Project 17A frigates, which were ordered in 2009, is also expected to be delayed due to lack of sufficient construction capacity and the modernisation that is required in Indian defence shipyards.

The **air force** is largely dependent on HAL. HAL successfully produced the MiG-21 and *Jaguar* and is currently building the *Tejas* LCA as well as assembling, under license, 42 out of 66 *Hawk* trainer aircraft. The first locally built *Hawk* was delivered to the air force in August 2008, though the project is suffering delays. HAL is also building the locally designed *Dhruv* advanced light helicopter. To boost its capacity in the area of combat aircraft, HAL is also building 140 *Sukhoi* Su-30 MKI aircraft and, in October 2009, it ordered another 50 units. In addition, there are plans for 108 of the 126 MMRCA aircraft, trials for which are currently under way, to be built in India. HAL announced a deal with Russia's United Aircraft Corporation (UAC) in December 2008 to jointly develop a fifth-generation fighter aircraft by 2015, and there were plans for another new joint venture with UAC, to manufacture a medium multi-role transport aircraft (MTA), to be registered at the end of 2009; deadlines for both are, however, likely to be extended.

Joint ventures

There has been considerable pressure on the government to permit foreign investment, and involve India's growing private sector, in defence production. This pressure has come from within government as well as from industry. In 2001, India allowed full Indian private-sector participation in defence production (subject to government licensing for the manufacture of arms and equipment) and up to 26% foreign investment in defence joint ventures. The following year, revisions to India's 1992 Defence Procurement Procedure (DPP) incorporated these changes. (A new DPP was issued in 2005, and revised in 2006 and 2008.) Interest from foreign companies, however, has been limited. From April 2000 to August 2009, total foreign direct investment (FDI) in defence was US$150m. Overseas companies remain concerned about having a minority share as well as the onus to transfer technology. The vetting process for contracting with private Indian firms is bureaucratically cumbersome; until 2008 private Indian companies engaged in defence business had to be licensed by the defence and industry ministries. Moreover, the requirement for Indian companies in joint ventures to provide 74% of the total cost was in a number of cases prohibitive.

But the fact remains that the Indian defence market is one of the largest in the world, with defence procurement projected to be some US$50bn by 2015. Several joint-venture defence agreements between foreign companies and the Indian private sector were announced in 2009, including those between:

- The UK's BAE Systems and vehicle manufacturer Mahindra & Mahindra, in January 2009, to develop land systems for the armed forces (construction started in March on a facility in Faridabad to manufacture 500 mine-resistant ambush-protected vehicles per year);
- Thales of France and Samtel Display Systems, in March 2009, for helmet-mounted sight and display systems for civil and military avionics; and

- Boeing and Tata Industries to supply components for Boeing military aircraft, including the *Super Hornet*.

Other key joint-venture proposals include: EADS and Larsen & Toubro for defence electronics; Agusta-Westland and Tata for helicopters; and BAE Systems with an Indian shipbuilding company.

To encourage greater foreign participation, Defence Minister A.K. Antony said in September 2008 that the government might consider increasing the FDI limit in defence joint ventures to 49% on a case-by-case basis. In July 2009, the Finance Ministry's annual survey of the economy went a step further urging the government to raise the FDI limit in defence industries to 49% and allow up to 100% FDI on a case-by-case basis in high-technology, strategic defence goods, services and systems that could help eliminate import dependence.

The 2008 DPP was significantly revised in November 2009 in a bid to bolster India's defence industry through a new 'Buy and Make (Indian)' category. Official 'request[s] for proposals' can now be issued directly to Indian companies that had the requisite financial and technical capabilities to absorb technology and manufacture products in India. While these were previously issued only to foreign vendors who preferred transferring engineering skills for non-critical items rather than critical technology, supply orders can now be placed with capable Indian companies, with foreign companies required to set up joint ventures to provide products through technology transfer (the indigenous content of the product has, in value terms, to be at least 50%).

Defence offsets

The 2005 DPP, revised in 2006 and 2008, made note of the concept of offsets in defence deals. This means that all foreign companies bidding for Indian defence contracts worth more than Rs3 billion (US$69.7m) are required to invest a minimum of 30% of the order in the local defence sector. Offsets can be served by FDI in infrastructure (through joint ventures) or research and development (R&D), or through purchasing Indian defence exports. Though India has not given a formal reason for such offsets, analysts believe that the policy was undertaken to boost domestic production. (For the planned multi-role fighter programme, the offset was raised to 50% of the total value of the contract by the 2006 DPP.) In the 2008 DPP, urgent acquisitions were exempt from offset obligations, while for other projects the concept of banking of offsets, valid for a maximum of two-and-a-half years, was introduced (see *The Military Balance 2009*, pp. 335–6). A dedicated body, the Defence Offsets Facilitations Agency (DOFA), headed by the joint secretary (exports), has been set up in the Defence Ministry to facilitate defence offsets. A US$300m private venture-capital fund, called the *India Rizing Fund*, was created in 2008 to support small Indian defence firms. The 2009 DPP revisions enabled foreign firms to change Indian offset partners during the contractual period in 'exceptional cases'.

There is much unease over the implementation of defence offsets. The policy has been criticised by foreign firms as inflexible. In December 2008, Bell-Helicopters called the requirements 'restrictive and narrow', and cited them as a factor in its decision to withdraw from the US$600m Reconnaissance and Surveillance Helicopter competition. The Indian armed services feel offsets will delay acquisitions, the civil bureaucracy feels they will increase the cost of weapon systems and industry fears it may not be able to absorb the required technology. There is also no provision for offset 'multipliers' or allowance for indirect non-defence offsets, at a time when there is no national offsets policy, although this is under consideration. If it is to operate effectively, moreover, the DOFA will need to be strengthened and provided with senior bureaucratic leadership at least at the level of special secretary to the government. As a result, while the amount to be invested under offset arrangements is expected to increase to US$10bn by March 2012, only US$1.5bn had been invested by foreign firms into offsets since 2006, with the major offset contract being the 2005 *Scorpene* submarine deal.

Indian private-sector companies

As a result of policies on joint ventures and defence offsets, Indian private-sector companies have become more actively engaged in defence production; they currently receive about 9%, or some US$760m, of the annual defence-procurement budget. But there is still some inequality with public-sector production agencies in terms of tax and related fiscal benefits. The largest private-sector defence company, Larsen & Toubro, plans to build a shipyard on India's west coast exclusively for defence orders. Along with two other private Indian companies, Pipavav Shipyard and ABG Shipyard, it has been shortlisted for the navy's offshore patrol vessel programme. Other influential private-sector defence players include Mahindra &

Mahindra, Tata Advanced Systems, Ashok Leyland, Godrej & Boyce and Punj Lloyd, all of whom have agreed a series of joint ventures with foreign vendors. In the first move of its kind for Indian defence firms, Dynamatic Technologies Ltd – a private Bangalore-based engineering firm producing radar components and hydraulic parts for US and Russian combat aircraft – in October 2008 paid US$16m for UK-based Oldland CNC Ltd, specialising in the manufacture of aerospace components and tooling.

Exports

Historically, there has been little scope for defence exports, given the dominance of assembled or license-produced weapons systems and the equipment demands of the Indian armed services. The Indian political leadership, moreover, has traditionally disapproved of arms exports in general, and the Foreign Ministry maintains a list of countries to which the export of Indian arms and equipment is forbidden. Defence exports are also the administrative responsibility of the joint secretary (exports), now additionally burdened with the responsibility for defence offsets. As a result, Indian defence exports were worth only US$100m in 2007.

But as India's defence-industrial base expands, arms exports are expected to increase. The *BrahMos* supersonic cruise missile is being aggressively marketed by its Indian manufacturers, BrahMos Aerospace (an India–Russia joint venture), in Southeast and East Asia and the Gulf. The multi-role *Dhruv* advanced light helicopter has been sold to Nepal, Sri Lanka, Myanmar and the Maldives. Latin America also appears to be an important market for Indian arms and equipment; 2008 saw India's first major defence-export agreement in the region with the sale of seven *Dhruv* helicopters to Ecuador's air force for an estimated US$51m. (A follow-on order is being sought, and Argentina, Paraguay and Uruguay have been identified as potential markets.) In addition, India has been trying to sell *BrahMos* to Brazil and Chile. Significantly, the first Kelkar Committee report recommended re-examining the concept of the 'negative list' for defence exports and the establishment of an Export Marketing Organisation.

Conclusion

Given the Indian armed services' demand for modern and sophisticated weapons and equipment, and the inability of the defence-industrial infrastructure to meet these requirements, India's dependence on

Table 48: **Major Current Domestic Defence Production, India**

Service	Production Agency	Production
Army	Heavy Vehicles Factory, Avadi	*Arjun* and T-90S *Bhishma* MBTs; upgrade of T-72MI (night-vision capability)
	Bharat Dynamics, Hyderabad	Ballistic missiles
Navy	Mazagon Dockyards Ltd, Mumbai	Three Kolkota (P-15A) destroyers; two *Shivalik* (P-17) stealth frigates; six *Scorpene* submarines
	Garden Reach Shipbuilders & Engineers Ltd, Kolkata	Landing ship tanks – large; fast attack craft; four P-28 corvettes
	Goa Shipyard Ltd, Mormugao	Patrol vessels; fast attack craft
	Cochin Shipyard Ltd, Cochin	Two air-defence ships (P-71)
	Ship Building Centre, Vishakapatnam	Three *Arihant* nuclear-powered submarines
Air Force	Hindustan Aeronautics Ltd	*Tejas* light combat aircraft; *Dhruv* advanced light helicopter; Sukhoi Su-30 MKI; *Hawk* light trainer; upgrading existing *Jaguar*, MiG-27M and MiG-21bis
Joint	BrahMos Aerospace, Hyderabad	*BrahMos* supersonic cruise missile

foreign acquisitions could increase from the present level of 70% in the short term. Analysts believe that this high percentage of foreign acquisitions will decline with the implementation of bold reforms and significant restructuring within India's defence-industrial establishment. This includes raising the level of FDI to 49%, providing greater clarity for defence offsets, insisting on technology transfer, modernising public-sector defence-production agencies, facilitating the establishment of private-sector defence majors and establishing a defence-export marketing organisation.

An influential government task force headed by Arun Singh (a special adviser to the foreign minister) criticised in 2001 the 'visible dysfunction' in the interface between R&D, defence producers and users. It recommended measures to overhaul the high-level planning and coordination of defence production. Controversially, it hinted at bolstering the role of defence producers in relation to DRDO in the development of major weapon systems, saying that this could start with short-term R&D on parts, compo-

nents and sub-assemblies by the production agencies, leading to these producers becoming 'nodal agencies' for the development and production of platforms. While the report stated that DRDO needed to focus more on core technologies, it also stated that the body could provide necessary expertise or guidance to the production agencies. The report also advocated the rationalisation of DRDO laboratories and the creation of a close-knit interface between specific laboratories and production agencies. In 2007–08, an independent committee of experts also recommended structural changes within the DRDO, now under way, that would make it more effective and relevant to India's military requirements. Significant reforms of India's defence industries, and the acquisition processes used by government, are currently underway in a bid to improve the armed services' arms and equipment. However, analysts note that to take full effect it is required that these reforms are implemented; they also need to be bolder, otherwise they will not serve to make India's vast defence-industrial complex fit for purpose.

PART TWO
Reference

Table 49 **Designations of Aircraft**

NOTES

1 [Square brackets] indicate the type from which a variant was derived: 'Q-5 … [MiG-19]' indicates that the design of the Q-5 was based on that of the MiG-19.
2 (Parentheses) indicate an alternative name by which an aircraft is known, sometimes in another version: 'L-188 … *Electra* (P-3 *Orion*)' shows that in another version the Lockheed Type 188 *Electra* is known as the P-3 *Orion*.
3 Names given in 'quotation marks' are NATO reporting names, e.g., 'Su-27… *"Flanker"*'.
4 For country abbreviations, see 'Index of Country/Territory Abbreviations' (p. 490/491).

Type	Name/designation	Country of origin/Maker
Fixed-wing		
A-1	AMX .... **BRZ/ITA** AMX
A-1	*Ching-Kuo* .... **ROC** AIDC
A-3	*Skywarrior* .... **US** Douglas
A-4	*Skyhawk* .... **US** MD
A-5	(Q-5) .... **PRC** SAF
A-7	*Corsair* II .... **US** LTV
A-10	*Thunderbolt* .... **US** Fairchild
A-36	*Halcón* (C-101) .... **ESP** CASA
A-37	*Dragonfly* .... **US** Cessna
A-50	*'Mainstay'* (Il-76) .... **RUS** Beriev
A300	.... **UK/FRA/GER/ESP** Airbus Int
A310	.... **UK/FRA/GER/ESP** Airbus Int
A340	.... **UK/FRA/GER/ESP** Airbus Int
AC-47	(C-47) .... **US** Douglas
AC-130	(C-130) .... **US** Lockheed
Air Beetle	.... **NGA** AIEP
Airtourer	.... **NZL** Victa
AJ-37	(J-37) .... **SWE** Saab
Alizé	(Br 1050) .... **FRA** Breguet
Alpha Jet	.... **FRA/GER** Dassault–Breguet/Dornier
AMX	.... **BRZ/ITA** Embraer/Alenia/Aermacchi
An-2	*'Colt'* .... **UKR** Antonov
An-12	*'Cub'* .... **UKR** Antonov
An-14	*'Clod'* (Pchyelka) .... **UKR** Antonov
An-22	*'Cock'* (Antei) .... **UKR** Antonov
An-24	*'Coke'* .... **UKR** Antonov
An-26	*'Curl'* .... **UKR** Antonov
An-28/M-28	*'Cash'* .... **UKR** AntonovPOL**I** PZL
An-30	*'Clank'* .... **UKR** Antonov
An-32	*'Cline'* .... **UKR** Antonov
An-72	*'Coaler-C'* .... **UKR** Antonov
An-74	*'Coaler-B'* .... **UKR** Antonov
An-124	*'Condor'* (Ruslan) .... **UKR** Antonov
Andover	[HS-748] .... **UK** BAe
Arava	.... **ISR** IAI
AS-202	*Bravo* .... **CHE** FFA
AT-3	*Tsu Chiang* .... **ROC** AIDC
AT-6	(T-6) .... **US** Beech

Type	Name/designation	Country of origin/Maker
AT-11	.... **US** Beech
AT-26	EMB-326 .... **BRZ** Embraer
AT-33	(T-33) .... **US** Lockheed
Atlantic	(*Atlantique*) .... **FRA** Dassault–Breguet
AU-23	*Peacemaker* [PC-6B] .... **US** Fairchild
AV-8	*Harrier* II .... **US/UK** MD/BAe
Aztec	PA-23 .... **US** Piper
B-1	*Lancer* .... **US** Rockwell
B-2	*Spirit* .... **US** Northrop Grumman
B-5	H-5 .... **PRC** HAF
B-6	H-6 .... **PRC** XAC
B-52	*Stratofortress* .... **US** Boeing
B-65	*Queen Air* .... **US** Beech
BAC-167	*Strikemaster* .... **UK** BAe
BAe-125	.... **UK** BAe
BAe-146	.... **UK** BAe
BAe-748	(HS-748) .... **UK** BAe
Baron	(T-42) .... **US** Beech
Basler T-67	(C-47) .... **US** Basler
Be-6	*'Madge'* .... **RUS** Beriev
Be-12	*'Mail'* (Tchaika) .... **RUS** Beriev
Beech 50	*Twin Bonanza* .... **US** Beech
Beech 95	*Travel Air* .... **US** Beech
BN-2	*Islander, Defender, Trislander* .... **UK** Britten-Norman
Boeing 707	.... **US** Boeing
Boeing 727	.... **US** Boeing
Boeing 737	.... **US** Boeing
Boeing 747	.... **US** Boeing
Boeing 757	.... **US** Boeing
Boeing 767	.... **US** Boeing
Bonanza	.... **US** Beech
Bronco	(OV-10) .... **US** Rockwell
BT-5	HJ-5 .... **PRC** HAF
Bulldog	.... **UK** BAe
C-1	.... **JPN** Kawasaki
C-2	*Greyhound* .... **US** Grumman
C-5	*Galaxy* .... **US** Lockheed
C-7	DHC-7 .... **CAN** DHC
C-9	*Nightingale* (DC-9) .... **US** MD

Type	Name/designation	Country of origin/Maker
C-12	Super King Air (Huron) ....US Beech	
C-17	Globemaster III ....US McDonnell Douglas	
C-18	[Boeing 707] ....US Boeing	
C-20	(Gulfstream III) ....US Gulfstream	
C-21	(Learjet) ....US Learjet	
C-22	(Boeing 727) ....US Boeing	
C-23	(Sherpa) ....UK Shorts	
C-26	Expediter/Merlin ....US Fairchild	
C-27	Spartan ....ITA Alenia	
C-32	[Boeing 757] ....US Boeing	
C-37A	[Gulfstream V] ....US Gulfstream	
C-38A	(Astra) ....ISR IAI	
C-42	(Neiva Regente) ....BRZ Embraer	
C-46	Commando ....US Curtis	
C-47	DC-3 (Dakota) (C-117 Skytrain) ......US Douglas	
C-54	Skymaster (DC-4) ....US Douglas	
C-91	HS-748 ....UK BAe	
C-93	HS-125 ....UK BAe	
C-95	EMB-110 ....BRZ Embraer	
C-97	EMB-121 ....BRZ Embraer	
C-101	Aviojet ....ESP CASA	
C-115	DHC-5 ....CAN De Havilland	
C-117	(C-47) ....US Douglas	
C-118	Liftmaster (DC-6) ....US Douglas	
C-123	Provider ....US Fairchild	
C-127	(Do-27) ....ESP CASA	
C-130	Hercules (L-100) ....US Lockheed	
C-131	Convair 440 ....US Convair	
C-135	[Boeing 707] ....US Boeing	
C-137	[Boeing 707] ....US Boeing	
C-140	(Jetstar) ....US Lockheed	
C-141	Starlifter ....US Lockheed	
C-160	Transall ....FRA/GER EADS	
C-212	Aviocar ....ESP CASA	
C-235	Persuader ....ESP/IDN CASA/Airtech	
C-295M		ESP CASA
Canberra		UK BAe
CAP-10		FRA Mudry
CAP-20		FRA Mudry
CAP-230		FRA Mudry
Caravelle	SE-210 ....FRA Aérospatiale	
CC-115	DHC-5 ....CAN DHC	
CC-117	(Falcon 20) ....FRA Dassault	
CC-132	(DHC-7) ....CAN DHC	
CC-137	(Boeing 707) ....US Boeing	
CC-138	(DHC-6) ....CAN DHC	
CC-144	CL-600/-601 ....CAN Canadair	
CF-5a		CAN Canadair
CF-18	F/A-18 ....US MD	
CH-2000	Sama ....JOR JAI	
Cheetah	[Mirage III] ....RSA Atlas	
Cherokee	PA-28 ....US Piper	
Cheyenne	PA-31T [Navajo] ....US Piper	
Chieftain	PA-31-350 [Navajo] ....US Piper	

Type	Name/designation	Country of origin/Maker
Ching-Kuo	A-1 ....ROC AIDC	
Citabria		US Champion
Citation	(T-47) ....US Cessna	
CJ-5	[Yak-18] ....PRC NAMC (Hongdu)	
CJ-6	[Yak-18] ....PRC NAMC (Hongdu)	
CL-215		CAN Canadair
CL-415		CAN Canadair
CL-600/604	Challenger ....CAN Canadair	
CM-170	Magister [Tzukit] ....FRA Aérospatiale	
CM-175	Zéphyr ....FRA Aérospatiale	
CN-212		ESP/IDN CASA/IPTN
CN-235		ESP/IDN CASA/IPTN
Cochise	T-42 ....US Beech	
Comanche	PA-24 ....US Piper	
Commander	Aero-/TurboCommander ....US Rockwell	
Commodore	MS-893 ....FRA Aérospatiale	
CP-3	P-3 Orion ....US Lockheed	
CP-140	Acturas (P-3 Orion) ....US Lockheed	
CT-4	Airtrainer ....NZL Victa	
CT-114	CL-41 Tutor ....CAN Canadair	
CT-133	Silver Star [T-33] ....CAN Canadair	
CT-134	Musketeer ....US Beech	
CT-156	Harvard II ....US Beech	
Dagger	(Nesher) ....ISR IAI	
Dakota		US Piper
Dakota	(C-47) ....US Douglas	
DC-3	(C-47) ....US Douglas	
DC-4	(C-54) ....US Douglas	
DC-6	(C-118) ....US Douglas	
DC-7		US Douglas
DC-8		US Douglas
DC-9		US MD
Deepak	(HPT-32) ....IND HAL	
Defender	BN-2 ....UK Britten-Norman	
DHC-3	Otter ....CAN DHC	
DHC-4	Caribou ....CAN DHC	
DHC-5	Buffalo ....CAN DHC	
DHC-6	Twin Otter, CC-138 ....CAN DHC	
DHC-7	Dash-7 (Ranger, CC-132) ....CAN DHC	
DHC-8		CAN DHC
Dimona	H-36 ....GER Hoffman	
Do-27	(C-127) ....GER Dornier	
Do-28	Skyservant ....GER Dornier	
Do-128		GER Dornier
Do-228		GER Dornier
E-2	Hawkeye ....US Grumman	
E-3	Sentry ....US Boeing	
E-4	[Boeing 747] ....US Boeing	
E-6	Mercury [Boeing 707] ....US Boeing	
E-26	T-35A (Tamiz) ....CHL Enaer	
EA-3	[A-3] ....US Douglas	
EA-6	Prowler [A-6] ....US Grumman	
EC-130	[C-130] ....US Lockheed	
EC-135	[Boeing 707] ....US Boeing	

Type	Name/designation	Country of origin/Maker
EF-111	*Raven* (F-111)	**US** General Dynamics
Electra	(L-188)	**US** Lockheed
EMB-110	*Bandeirante*	**BRZ** Embraer
EMB-111	*Maritime Bandeirante*	**BRZ** Embraer
EMB-120	*Brasilia*	**BRZ** Embraer
EMB-121	*Xingu*	**BRZ** Embraer
EMB-145	(R-99A/-99B)	**BRZ** Embraer
EMB-201	*Ipanema*	**BRZ** Embraer
EMB-312	*Tucano*	**BRZ** Embraer
EMB-314	*Super Tucano*	**BRZ** Embraer
EMB-326	*Xavante* (MB-326)	**BRZ** Embraer
EMB-810	[*Seneca*]	**BRZ** Embraer
EP-3	(P-3 Orion)	**US** Lockheed
ERJ-145		**BRZ** Embraer
Etendard/Super Etendard		**FRA** Dassault
EV-1	(OV-1)	**US** Rockwell
F-1	[T-2]	**JPN** Mitsubishi
F-4	*Phantom*	**US** MD
F-5	-A/-B *Freedom Fighter* -E/-F *Tiger* II	**US** Northrop
F-6	J-6	**PRC** SAF
F-7	J-7	**PRC** CAC-GAIC
F-8	J-8	**PRC** CACC
F-10	J-10	**PRC** SAC
F-11	J-11	**PRC** SAC
F-14	*Tomcat*	**US** Grumman
F-15	*Eagle*	**US** MD
F-16	*Fighting Falcon*	**US** GD
F-18	[F/A-18], *Hornet*	**US** MD
F-21	*Kfir*	**ISR** IAI
F-22	*Raptor*	**US** Lockheed
F-27	*Friendship*	**NLD** Fokker
F-28	*Fellowship*	**NLD** Fokker
F-35	*Lightning*	**US** LM (prime)
F-35	*Draken*	**SWE** SAAB
F-50/-60		**NLD** Fokker
F-104	*Starfighter*	**US** Lockheed
F-111	EF-111	**US** GD
F-117	*Nighthawk*	**US** Lockheed
F-172	(Cessna 172)	**FRA/US** Reims-Cessna
F-406	*Caravan*	**FRA** Reims
F/A-18	*Hornet*	**US** MD
Falcon	*Mystère-Falcon*	**FRA** Dassault
FB-111	(F-111)	**US** GD
FBC-1	*Feibao* [JH-7]	**PRC** CAC-GAIC
FC-1/JF-17	(*Sabre 2, Super-7*)	**PRC/RUS/PAK** CAC/MAPO/Pak
FH-227	(F-27)	**US** Fairchild-Hiller
Firefly	(T-67M)	**UK** Slingsby
Flamingo	MBB-233	**GER** MBB
FT-5	JJ-5	**PRC** CAF
FT-6	JJ-6	**PRC** SAF
FT-7	JJ-7	**PRC** GAIC
FTB-337	[Cessna 337]	**US** Cessna
G-91		**ITA** Aeritalia
G-115E	*Tutor*	**GER** Grob

Type	Name/designation	Country of origin/Maker
G-222		**ITA** Alenia
Galaxy	C-5	**US** Lockheed
Galeb		**FRY** SOKO
Genet	SF-260W	**ITA** SIAI
GU-25	(*Falcon 20*)	**FRA** Dassault
Guerrier	R-235	**FRA** Socata
Gulfstream		**US** Gulfstream Aviation
Gumhuria	(*Bücker* 181)	**EGY** Heliopolis
H-5	[Il-28]	**PRC** HAF
H-6	[Tu-16]	**PRC** XAC
H-36	*Dimona*	**GER** Hoffman
Halcón	[C-101]	**ESP** CASA
Harrier	(AV-8)	**UK** BAe
Hawk		**UK** BAe
Hawker 800XP	(BAe-125)	**US** Raytheon
HC-130	(C-130)	**US** Lockheed
HF-24	*Marut*	**IND** HAL
HFB-320	*Hansajet*	**GER** Hamburger FB
HJ-5	(H-5)	**PRC** HAF
HJT-16	*Kiran*	**IND** HAL
HPT-32	*Deepak*	**IND** HAL
HS-125	(*Dominie*)	**UK** BAe
HS-748	[*Andover*]	**UK** BAe
HT-2		**IND** HAL
HU-16	*Albatross*	**US** Grumman
HU-25	(*Falcon* 20)	**FRA** Dassault
Hunter		**UK** BAe
HZ-5	(H-5)	**PRC** HAF
IA-50	*Guaraní*	**ARG** FMA
IA-58	*Pucará*	**ARG** FMA
IA-63	*Pampa*	**ARG** FMA
IAI-201/-202	*Arava*	**ISR** IAI
IAI-1124	*Westwind, Seascan*	**ISR** IAI
IAI-1125	*Astra*	**ISR** IAI
Iak-52	(Yak-52)	**ROM** Aerostar
IAR-28		**ROM** IAR
IAR-93	*Orao*	**FRY/ROM** SOKO/IAR
IAR-99	*Soim*	**ROM** IAR
Il-14	'Crate'	**RUS** Ilyushin
Il-18	'Coot'	**RUS** Ilyushin
Il-20	'Coot-A' (Il-18)	**RUS** Ilyushin
Il-22	'Coot-B' (Il-18)	**RUS** Ilyushin
Il-28	'Beagle'	**RUS** Ilyushin
Il-38	'May'	**RUS** Ilyushin
Il-62	'Classic'	**RUS** Ilyushin
Il-76	'Candid' (tpt), 'Mainstay' (AEW)	**RUS** Ilyushin
Il-78	'Midas' (tkr)	**RUS** Ilyushin
Il-82	'Candid'	**RUS** Ilyushin
Il-86	'Camber'	**RUS** Ilyushin
Il-87	'Maxdome'	**RUS** Ilyushin
Impala	[MB-326]	**RSA** Atlas
Islander	BN-2	**UK** Britten-Norman
J-5	[MiG-17F]	**PRC** SAF
J-6	[MiG-19]	**PRC** SAF

Type	Name/designation	Country of origin/Maker
J-7	[MiG-21] ....**PRC** CAC/GAIC
J-8	*Finback* ....**PRC** SAC
J-10	[IAI *Lavi*] ....**PRC** SAC
J-11	[Su-27] ....**PRC** SAC
J-32	*Lansen* ....**SWE** SAAB
J-35	*Draken* ....**SWE** SAAB
J-37	*Viggen* ....**SWE** SAAB
JA-37	(J-37) ....**SWE** SAAB
Jaguar	....**FRA/UK** SEPECAT
JAS-39	*Gripen* ....**SWE** SAAB
Jastreb	....**FRY** SOKO
Jetstream	....**UK** BAe
JH-7	[FBC-1] ....**PRC** XAC
JJ-5	[J-5] ....**PRC** CAF
JJ-6	[J-6] ....**PRC** SAF
JJ-7	[J-7] ....**PRC** GAIC
JZ-6	(J-6) ....**PRC** SAF
JZ-8	(J-8) ....**PRC** SAC
K-8	....**PRC/PAK/EGY** Hongdu/E
KA-3	[A-3] ....**US** Douglas
KA-6	[A-6] ....**US** Grumman
KT-1B	....**ROK** KAI
KC-10	*Extender* [DC-10] ....**US** MD
KC-130	[C-130] ....**US** Lockheed
KC-135	[Boeing 707] ....**US** Boeing
KE-3A	[Boeing 707] ....**US** Boeing
KF-16	(F-16) ....**US** GD
Kfir	....**ISR** IAI
King Air	....**US** Beech
Kiran	HJT-16 ....**IND** HAL
KJ200	(Y-8) ....**PRC** SAC
KJ2000	(Il-76) ....**PRC** XAC
Kraguj	....**FRY** SOKO
KT-1	....**ROK** KAI
L-4	*Cub* ....**US** Piper
L-18	*Super Cub* ....**US** Piper
L-19	O-1 ....**US** Cessna
L-21	*Super Cub* ....**US** Piper
L-29	*Delfin* ....**CZE** Aero
L-39	*Albatros* ....**CZE** Aero
L-59	*Albatros* ....**CZE** Aero
L-70	*Vinka* ....**FIN** Valmet
L-90	*Redigo* ....**FIN** Valmet
L-100	C-130 (civil version) ....**US** Lockheed
L-188	*Electra* (P-3 *Orion*) ....**US** Lockheed
L-410	*Turbolet* ....**CZE** LET
L-1011	*Tristar* ....**US** Lockheed
Learjet	(C-21) ....**US** Gates
LR-1	(MU-2) ....**JPN** Mitsubishi
M-28	*Skytruck/Bryza* ....**POL** MIELEC
Magister	CM-170 ....**FRA** Aérospatiale
Marut	HF-24 ....**IND** HAL
Mashshaq	MFI-17 ....**PAK/SWE** PAC/SAAB
Matador	(AV-8) ....**US/UK** MD/Bae

Type	Name/designation	Country of origin/Maker
Maule	M-7/MXT-7 ....**US** Maule
MB-326	....**ITA** Aermacchi
MB-339	(*Veltro*) ....**ITA** Aermacchi
MBB-233	*Flamingo* ....**GER** MBB
MC-130	(C-130) ....**US** Lockheed
Mercurius	(HS-125) ....**UK** BAe
Merlin	....**US** Fairchild
Mescalero	T-41 ....**US** Cessna
Metro	....**US** Fairchild
MFI-17	*Supporter* (T-17) ....**SWE** SAAB
MiG-15	'Midget' trg ....**RUS** MiG
MiG-17	'Fresco' ....**RUS** MiG
MiG-19	'Farmer' ....**RUS** MiG
MiG-21	'Fishbed' ....**RUS** MiG
MiG-23	'Flogger' ....**RUS** MiG
MiG-25	'Foxbat' ....**RUS** MiG
MiG-27	'Flogger D' ....**RUS** MiG
MiG-29	'Fulcrum' ....**RUS** MiG
MiG-31	'Foxhound' ....**RUS** MiG
MiG-35	'Fulcrum' ....**RUS** MiG
Mirage	....**FRA** Dassault
Missionmaster	N-22 ....**AUS** GAF
Mohawk	OV-1 ....**US** Lockheed
MS-760	*Paris* ....**FRA** Aérospatiale
MS-893	*Commodore* ....**FRA** Aérospatiale
MU-2	LR-1 ....**JPN** Mitsubishi
Musketeer	*Beech* 24 ....**US** Beech
Mystère-Falcon	...........................**FRA** Dassault
N-22	*Floatmaster, Missionmaster* ....**AUS** GAF
N-24	*Searchmaster* B/L ....**AUS** GAF
N-262	*Frégate* ....**FRA** Aérospatiale
N-2501	*Noratlas* ....**FRA** Aérospatiale
Navajo	PA-31 ....**US** Piper
NC-212	C-212 ....**ESP/IDN** CASA/Nurtanio
NC-235	C-235 ....**ESP/IDN** CASA/Nurtanio
Nesher	[*Mirage* III] ....**ISR** IAI
NF-5	(F-5) ....**US** Northrop
Nightingale	(C-9) ....**US** MD
Nimrod	[*Comet*] ....**UK** BAe
Nomad	....**AUS** GAF
O-1	*Bird Dog* ....**US** Cessna
O-2	(Cessna 337 *Skymaster*) ....**US** Cessna
OA-4	(A-4) ....**US** MD
OA-37	*Dragonfly* ....**US** Cessna
Orao	IAR-93 ....**FRY/ROM** SOKO/IAR
Ouragan	....**FRA** Dassault
OV-1	*Mohawk* ....**US** Rockwell
OV-10	*Bronco* ....**US** Rockwell
P-3	*Orion* [L-188 *Electra*] ....**US** Lockheed
P-92	....**ITA** Teenam
P-95	EMB-110 ....**BRZ** Embraer
P-166	....**ITA** Piaggio
P-180	*Avanti* ....**ITA** Piaggio
PA-18	*Super Cub* ....**US** Piper

Type	Name/designation	Country of origin/Maker
PA-23	*Aztec*	**US** Piper
PA-28	*Cherokee*	**US** Piper
PA-31	*Navajo*	**US** Piper
PA-32	*Cherokee Six*	**US** Piper
PA-34	*Seneca*	**US** Piper
PA-36	*Pawnee Brave*	**US** Piper
PA-38	*Tomahawk*	**US** Piper
PA-42	*Cheyenne III*	**US** Piper
PBY-5	*Catalina*	**US** Consolidated
PC-6	*Porter*	**CHE** Pilatus
PC-6A/B	*Turbo Porter*	**CHE** Pilatus
PC-7	*Turbo Trainer*	**CHE** Pilatus
PC-9		**CHE** Pilatus
PC-12		**CHE** Pilatus
PD-808		**ITA** Piaggio
Pillán	T-35	**CHL** Enaer
PL-1	*Chien Shou*	**ROC** AIDC
PLZ M-28	[An-28]	**POL** PZL
Porter	PC-6	**CHE** Pilatus
PS-5	[SH-5]	**PRC** HAMC
PZL M-28	M-28 [An-28]	**POL** PZL
PZL-104	*Wilga*	**POL** PZL
PZL-130	*Orlik*	**POL** PZL
Q-5	A-5 *'Fantan'* [MiG-19]	**PRC** NAMC (Hongdu)
Queen Air	(U-8)	**US** Beech
PD-808		**ITA** Piaggio
Rafale		**FRA** Dassault
R-160		**FRA** Socata
R-235	*Guerrier*	**FRA** Socata
RC-21	(C-21, *Learjet*)	**US** Learjet
RC-26	(C-26)	**US** Fairchild
RC-47	(C-47)	**US** Douglas
RC-95	(EMB-110)	**BRZ** Embraer
RC-135	[Boeing 707]	**US** Boeing
RF-4	(F-4)	**US** MD
RF-5	(F-5)	**US** Northrop
RF-35	(F-35)	**SWE** SAAB
RF-104	(F-104)	**US** Lockheed
RG-8A		**US** Schweizer
RT-26	(EMB-326)	**BRZ** Embraer
RT-33	(T-33)	**US** Lockheed
RU-21	(*King Air*)	**US** Beech
RV-1	(OV-1)	**US** Rockwell
S-2	*Tracker*	**US** Grumman
S-208		**ITA** SIAI
S-211		**ITA** SIAI
SA 2-37A		**US** Schweizer
Saab 340H		**SWE**we SAAB
Sabreliner	(CT-39)	**US** Rockwell
Safari	MFI-15	**SWE** SAAB
Safir	SAAB-91 (SK-50)	**SWE** SAAB
SB7L-360	(*Seeker*)	**AUS/JOR** KADDB/Seabird
SC-7	*Skyvan*	**UK** Short
SE-210	*Caravelle*	**FRA** Aérospatiale

Type	Name/designation	Country of origin/Maker
Sea Harrier	(*Harrier*)	**UK** BAe
Seascan	IAI-1124	**ISR** IAI
Searchmaster	N-24 B/L	**AUS** GAF
Seneca	PA-34 (EMB-810)	**US** Piper
Sentinel	(*Global Express*)	**CAN** Bombardier
Sentry	(O-2)	**US** Summit
SF-37	(J-37)	**SWE** SAAB
SF-260	(SF-260W *Warrior*)	**ITA** SIAI
SH-5	PS-5	**PRC** HAMC
SH-37	(J-37)	**SWE** SAAB
Sherpa	Short 330, C-23	**UK** Short
Short 330	(*Sherpa*)	**UK** Short
Sierra 200	(*Musketeer*)	**US** Beech
SK-35	(J-35)	**SWE** SAAB
SK-37	(J-37)	**SWE** SAAB
SK-60	(SAAB-105)	**SWE** SAAB
SK-61	(*Bulldog*)	**UK** BAe
Skyvan		**UK** Short
SM-90		**RUS** Technoavia
SM-1019		**ITA** SIAI
SP-2H	*Neptune*	**US** Lockheed
SR-71	*Blackbird*	**US** Lockheed
Su-7	*'Fitter-A'*	**RUS** Sukhoi
Su-15	*'Flagon'*	**RUS** Sukhoi
Su-17/-20/-22	*'Fitter-B'* - *'-K'*	**RUS** Sukhoi
Su-24	*'Fencer'*	**RUS** Sukhoi
Su-25	*'Frogfoot'*	**RUS** Sukhoi
Su-27	*'Flanker'*	**RUS** Sukhoi
Su-29		**RUS** Sukhoi
Su-30	*'Flanker'*	**RUS** Sukhoi
Su-33	(Su-27K) *'Flanker-D'*	**RUS** Sukhoi
Su-34	(Su-27IB) *'Flanker-C2'*	**RUS** Sukhoi
Su-35	(Su-27) *'Flanker'*	**RUS** Sukhoi
Su-39	(Su-25T) *'Frogfoot'*	**RUS** Sukhoi
Super		**FRA** Dassault
Shrike Aerocommander		**US** Rockwell
Super Galeb		**FRY** SOKO
T-1		**JPN** Fuji
T-1A	*Jayhawk*	**US** Beech
T-2	*Buckeye*	**US** Rockwell
T-2		**JPN** Mitsubishi
T-3		**JPN** Fuji
T-6	*Texan* II	**US** Beech
T-17	(*Supporter*, MFI-17)	**SWE** SAAB
T-23	*Uirapurú*	**BRZ** Aerotec
T-25	*Neiva Universal*	**BRZ** Embraer
T-26	EMB-326	**BRZ** Embraer
T-27	*Tucano*	**BRZ** Embraer
T-28	*Trojan*	**US** North American
T-33	*Shooting Star*	**US** Lockheed
T-34	*Mentor*	**US** Beech
T-35	*Pillán* [PA-28]	**CHL** Enaer
T-36	(C-101)	**ESP** CASA
T-37	(A-37)	**US** Cessna

Type	Name/designation	Country of origin/Maker
T-38	*Talon*	**US** Northrop
T-39	*(Sabreliner)*	**US** Rockwell
T-41	*Mescalero (Cessna 172)*	**US** Cessna
T-42	*Cochise (Baron)*	**US** Beech
T-43	*(Boeing 737)*	**US** Boeing
T-44	*(King Air)*	**US** Beech
T-47	*(Citation)*	**US** Cessna
T-67M	*(Firefly)*	**UK** Slingsby
T-400	*(T-1A)*	**US** Beech
TB-20	*Trinidad*	**FRA** Aérospatiale
TB-21	*Trinidad*	**FRA** Socata
TB-30	*Epsilon*	**FRA** Aérospatiale
TB-200	*Tobago*	**FRA** Socata
TBM-700		**FRA** Socata
TC-45	*(C-45, trg)*	**US** Beech
TCH-1	*Chung Hsing*	**ROC** AIDC
TL-1	*(KM-2)*	**JPN** Fuji
Tornado		**UK/GER/ITA** Panavia
TR-1	*[U-2]*	**US** Lockheed
Travel Air	*Beech 95*	**US** Beech
Trident		**UK** BAe
Trislander	BN-2	**UK** Britten-Norman
Tristar	L-1011	**US** Lockheed
TS-8	*Bies*	**POL** PZL
TS-11	*Iskra*	**POL** PZL
Tu-16	*'Badger'*	**RUS** Tupolev
Tu-22	*'Blinder'*	**RUS** Tupolev
Tu-22M	*'Backfire'*	**RUS** Tupolev
Tu-95	*'Bear'*	**RUS** Tupolev
Tu-126	*'Moss'*	**RUS** Tupolev
Tu-134	*'Crusty'*	**RUS** Tupolev
Tu-142	*'Bear* F'	**RUS** Tupolev
Tu-154	*'Careless'*	**RUS** Tupolev
Tu-160	*'Blackjack'*	**RUS** Tupolev
Tucano	*(EMB-312/314)*	**BRZ** Embraer
Turbo Porter	PC-6A/B	**CHE** Pilatus
Twin Bonanza	*Beech 50*	**US** Beech
Twin Otter	DHC-6	**CAN** DHC
Typhoon		**GER,ITA,ESP,UK** Eurofighter
Tzukit	*[CM-170]*	**ISR** IAI
U-2		**US** Lockheed
U-3	*(Cessna 310)*	**US** Cessna
U-4	*Gulfstream* IV	**US** Gulfstream
U-7	*(L-18)*	**US** Piper
U-8	*(Twin Bonanza/Queen Air)*	**US** Beech
U-9	*(EMB-121)*	**BRZ** Embraer
U-10	*Super Courier*	**US** Helio
U-17	*(Cessna 180, 185)*	**US** Cessna
U-21	*(King Air)*	**US** Beech
U-36	*(Learjet)*	**US** Learjet
U-42	*(C-42)*	**BRZ** Embraer
U-93	*(HS-125)*	**UK** BAe
U-125	*BAe 125-800*	**UK** BAe
U-206G	*Stationair*	**US** Cessna

Type	Name/designation	Country of origin/Maker
UC-12	*(King Air)*	**US** Beech
UP-2J	*(P-2J)*	**US** Lockheed
US-1		**JPN** Shin Meiwa
US-2A	*(S-2A, tpt)*	**US** Grumman
US-3	*(S-3, tpt)*	**US** Lockheed
UTVA-66		**FRY** UTVA
UTVA-75		**FRY** UTVA
UV-18	*(DHC-6)*	**CAN** DHC
V-400	*Fantrainer 400*	**GER** VFW
V-600	*Fantrainer 600*	**GER** VFW
Vampire	DH-100	**CAN** DHC
VC-4	*Gulfstream* I	**US** Gulfstream
VC-10		**UK** BAe
VC-11	*Gulfstream* II	**US** Gulfstream
VC-25	*[Boeing 747]*	**US** Boeing
VC-91	*(HS-748)*	**UK** BAe
VC-93	*(HS-125)*	**UK** BAe
VC-97	*(EMB-120)*	**BRZ** Embraer
VC-130	*(C-130)*	**US** Lockheed
VFW-614		**GER** VFW
Vinka	L-70	**FIN** Valmet
VU-9	*(EMB-121)*	**BRZ** Embraer
VU-93	*(HS-125)*	**UK** BAe
WC-130	*[C-130]*	**US** Lockheed
WC-135	*[Boeing 707]*	**US** Boeing
Westwind	IAI-1124	**ISR** IAI
Winjeel	CA-25	**AUS** Boeing
Xavante	EMB-326	**BRZ** Embraer
Xingu	EMB-121	**BRZ** Embraer
Y-5	*[An-2]*	**PRC** Hua Bei
Y-7	*[An-24/-26]*	**PRC** XAC
Y-8	*[An-12]*	**PRC** STAF
Y-12	*Turbo/Twin Panda*	**PRC** HAMC
Yak-11	*'Moose'*	**RUS** Yakovlev
Yak-18	*'Max'*	**RUS** Yakovlev
Yak-28	*'Firebar' ('Brewer')*	**RUS** Yakovlev
Yak-38	*'Forger'*	**RUS** Yakovlev
Yak-40	*'Codling'*	**RUS** Yakovlev
Yak-42	*'Clobber'*	**RUS** Yakovlev
Yak-52	*(IAK 52)*	**ROM** Aerostar
Yak-55		**RUS** Yakovlev
YS-11		**JPN** Nihon
Z-142/143		**CZE** Zlin
Z-226		**CZE** Zlin
Z-242		**CZE** Zlin
Z-326		**CZE** Zlin
Z-526		**CZE** Zlin
Zéphyr	CM-175	**FRA** Aérospatiale

Tilt-Rotor Wing
V-22/MV-22/CV-22 *Osprey* .... **US** Bell/Boeing

Helicopters
A-109 *Hirundo* .... **ITA** Agusta

Type	Name/designation	Country of origin/Maker
A-129	*Mangusta* ....**ITA** Agusta
AB-	(Bell 204/205/206/212/214, etc.) .**ITA /US** Agusta/Bell
AH-1	*Cobra/Sea Cobra* ....**US** Bell
AH-2	*Rooivalk* ....**RSA** Denel
AH-6	(Hughes 500/530) ....**US** MD
AH-64	*Apache* ....**US** Hughes
ALH	*Adv Light Hel* ....**IND** HAL
Alouette II	SA-318, SE-3130 ....**FRA** Aérospatiale
Alouette III	SA-316, SA-319 ....**FRA** Aérospatiale
AS-61	(SH-3) ....**US/ITA** Sikorsky/Agusta
AS-313 – AS-365/-366	(ex-SA-313 – SA-365/-366) **FRA** Aérospatiale
AS-332	*Super Puma* ....**FRA** Aérospatiale
AS-350	*Ecureuil* ....**FRA** Aérospatiale
AS-355	*Ecureuil* II ....**FRA** Aérospatiale
AS-365	*Dauphin* ....**FRA** Aérospatiale
AS-532	*Cougar* ....**FRA** Eurocopter
AS-550/555	*Fennec* ....**FRA** Aérospatiale
AS-565	*Panther* ....**FRA** Eurocopter
ASH-3	(*Sea King*) ....**ITA/US** Agusta/Sikorsky
AUH-76	(S-76) ....**US** Sikorsky
Bell 47	(*Sioux*) ....**US** Bell
Bell 205	....**US** Bell
Bell 206	....**US** Bell
Bell 212	....**US** Bell
Bell 214	....**US** Bell
Bell 222	....**US** Bell
Bell 406	*Kiowa* ....**US** Bell
Bell 407	....**CAN** Bell
Bell 412	....**US** Bell
Bo-105	(NBo-105) ....**GER** MBB
CH-3	(SH-3) ....**US** Sikorsky
CH-34	*Choctaw* ....**US** Sikorsky
CH-46	*Sea Knight* ....**US** Boeing-Vertol
CH-47	*Chinook* ....**US** Boeing-Vertol
CH-53	*Stallion* (*Sea Stallion*) ....**US** Sikorsky
CH-54	*Tarhe* ....**US** Sikorsky
CH-113	(CH-46) ....**US** Boeing-Vertol
CH-124	SH-3 (*Sea King*) ....**US** Sikorsky
CH-136	*Kiowa* ....**CAN** Bell
CH-139	Bell 206 ....**US** Bell
CH-146	Bell 412 ....**CAN** Bell
CH-147	CH-47 ....**US** Boeing-Vertol
CH-149	*Cormorant* (*Merlin*) ....**UK/ITA** Westland/Agusta
Cheetah	[SA-315] ....**IND** HAL
Chetak	[SA-319] ....**IND** HAL
Commando	(SH-3) ....**UK/US** Westland/Sikorsky
Dhruv	....**IND** HAL
EC-120B	*Colibri* ....**FRA/GER** Eurocopter
EH-60	(UH-60) ....**US** Sikorsky
EH-101	*Merlin* ....**UK/ITA** Westland/Agusta
F-28F	....**US** Enstrom
FH-1100	(OH-5) ....**US** Fairchild-Hiller
Gazela	(SA-342) ....**FRA/FRY** Aérospatiale/SOKO
Gazelle	SA-341/-342 ....**FRA** Aérospatiale

Type	Name/designation	Country of origin/Maker
H-34	(S-58) ....**US** Sikorsky
H-76	S-76 ....**US** Sikorsky
HA-15	Bo-105 ....**GER** MBB
HB-315	*Gavião* (SA-315) .....**BRZ/FRA** Helibras Aérospatiale
HB-350	*Esquilo* (AS-350) .....**BRZ/FRA** Helibras Aérospatiale
HD-16	SA-319 ....**FRA** Aérospatiale
HH-3	(SH-3) ....**US** Sikorsky
HH-34	(CH-34) ....**US** Sikorsky
HH-53	(CH-53) ....**US** Sikorsky
HH-65	(AS-365) ....**FRA** Eurocopter
Hkp-2	*Alouette* II/SE-3130 ....**FRA** Aérospatiale
Hkp-3	AB-204 ....**ITA/US** Agusta/Bell
Hkp-4	KV-107 ....**JPN/US** Kawasaki/Vertol
Hkp-5	Hughes 300 ....**US** MD
Hkp-6	AB-206 ....**ITA/US** Agusta/Bell
Hkp-9	Bo-105 ....**GER** MBB
Hkp-10	AS-332 ....**FRA** Aérospatiale
HR-12	OH-58 ....**US** Bell
HSS-1	(S-58) ....**US** Sikorsky
HSS-2	(SH-3) ....**US** Sikorsky
HT-17	CH-47 ....**US** Boeing-Vertol
HT-21	AS-332 ....**FRA** Aérospatiale
HU-1	(UH-1) ....**JPN/US** Fuji/Bell
HU-8	UH-1B ....**US** Bell
HU-10	UH-1H ....**US** Bell
HU-18	AB-212 ....**ITA/US** Agusta/Bell
Hughes 300	....**US** MD
Hughes 500/520	*Defender* ....**US** MD
IAR-316/-330	(SA-316/-330) ....**ROM/FRA** IAR/Aérospatiale
Ka-25	'Hormone' ....**RUS** Kamov
Ka-27/-28	'Helix-A' ....**RUS** Kamov
Ka-29	'Helix-B' ....**RUS** Kamov
Ka-32	'Helix-C' ....**RUS** Kamov
Ka-50	*Hokum* ....**RUS** Kamov
KH-4	(Bell 47) ....**JPN/US** Kawasaki/ Bell
KH-300	(Hughes 269) ....**JPN /US** Kawasaki/MD
KH-500	(Hughes 369) ....**JPN /US** Kawasaki/MD
Kiowa	OH-58 ....**US** Bell
KV-107	[CH-46] ....**JPN /US** Kawasaki/Vertol
Lynx	....**UK** Westland
MD-500/530	*Defender* ....**US** McDonnell Douglas
Merlin	EH-101 ....**UK/ITA** Westland/Agusta
MH-6	(AH-6) ....**US** MD
MH-53	(CH-53) ....**US** Sikorsky
Mi-2	'Hoplite' ....**RUS** Mil
Mi-4	'Hound' ....**RUS** Mil
Mi-6	'Hook' ....**RUS** Mil
Mi-8	'Hip' ....**RUS** Mil
Mi-14	'Haze' ....**RUS** Mil
Mi-17	'Hip-H' ....**RUS** Mil
Mi-24, -25, -35	'Hind' ....**RUS** Mil
Mi-26	'Halo' ....**RUS** Mil
Mi-28	'Havoc' ....**RUS** Mil
NAS-330	(SA-330) ....**IDN/FRA** Nurtanio/Aérospatiale

Type	Name/designation	Country of origin/Maker
NAS-332	AS-332 .... **IDN/FRA** Nurtanio/Aérospatiale
NB-412	Bell 412 ....**IDN/US** Nurtanio/Bell
NBo-105	Bo-105 ....**IDN/GER** Nurtanio/MBB
NH-300	(Hughes 300) ....**ITA/US** Nardi/MD
OH-6	*Cayuse* (Hughes 369) ....**US** MD
OH-13	(Bell 47G) ....**US** Bell
OH-23	*Raven* ....**US** Hiller
OH-58	*Kiowa* (Bell 206) ....**US** Bell
OH-58D	(Bell 406) ....**US** Bell
Oryx	(SA-330) ....**FRA** Aérospatiale
PAH-1	(Bo-105) .... **GER** MBB
Partizan	(*Gazela*, armed) ....**FRA/FRY** Aérospatiale/SOKO
RH-53	(CH-53) ....**US** Sikorsky
S-58	(*Wessex*) ....**US** Sikorsky
S-61	SH-3 ....**US** Sikorsky
S-65	CH-53 ....**US** Sikorsky
S-70	UH-60 ....**US** Sikorsky
S-76	....**US** Sikorsky
S-80	CH-53 ....**US** Sikorsky
SA-313	*Alouette* II ....**FRA** Aérospatiale
SA-315	*Lama* [*Alouette* II] ....**FRA** Aérospatiale
SA-316	*Alouette* III (SA-319) ....**FRA** Aérospatiale
SA-318	*Alouette* II (SE-3130) ......**FRA** Aérospatiale
SA-319	*Alouette* III (SA-316) ....**FRA** Aérospatiale
SA-321	*Super Frelon* ....**FRA** Aérospatiale
SA-330	*Puma* ....**FRA** Aérospatiale
SA-341/-342	*Gazelle* ....**FRA** Aérospatiale
SA-360	*Dauphin* ....**FRA** Aérospatiale
SA-365/-366	*Dauphin* II (SA-360) ....**FRA** Aérospatiale
Scout	(*Wasp*) .... **UK** Westland
SE-316	(SA-316) ....**FRA** Aérospatiale

Type	Name/designation	Country of origin/Maker
SE-3130	(SA-318) ....**FRA** Aérospatiale
Sea King	[SH-3] .... **UK** Westland
SH-2	*Sea Sprite* ....**US** Kaman
SH-3	(*Sea King*) ....**US** Sikorsky
SH-34	(S-58) ....**US** Sikorsky
SH-57	Bell 206 ....**US** Bell
SH-60	*Sea Hawk* (UH-60) ....**US** Sikorsky
Sokol	W3 ....**POL** PZL
TH-50	*Esquilo* (AS-550) ....**FRA** Aérospatiale
TH-55	Hughes 269 ....**US** MD
TH-57	*Sea Ranger* (Bell 206) ....**US** Bell
TH-67	*Creek* (Bell 206B-3) ....**CAN** Bell
Tiger	AS-665 ....**FRA** Eurocopter
UH-1	*Iroquois* (Bell 204/205/212) ....**US** Bell
UH-12	(OH-23) ....**US** Hiller
UH-13	(Bell 47J) ....**US** Bell
UH-19	(S-55) ....**Ca** Bell
UH-34T	(S-58T) ....**US** Sikorsky
UH-46	(CH-46) .... **US** Boeing/Vertol
UH-60	*Black Hawk* (SH-60) ....**US** Sikorsky
UH-72	*Lakota* ....**US** EADS
VH-4	(Bell 206) ....**US** Bell
VH-60	(S-70) ....**US** Sikorsky
W-3	*Sokol* ....**POL** PZL
Wasp	(*Scout*) .... **UK** Westland
Wessex	(S-58) ....**US/UK** Sikorsky/Westland
Z-5	[Mi-4] ....**PRC** HAF
Z-6	[Z-5] ....**PRC** CHAF
Z-8	[AS-321] ....**PRC** CHAF
Z-9	[AS-365] ....**PRC** HAMC
Z-11	[AS-352] ....**PRC** CHAF

Table 50 **List of Abbreviations for Data Sections**

– part of unit is detached/less than

* combat capable

″ unit with overstated title/ship class nickname

+unit reinforced/more than

<under 100 tonnes

† serviceability in doubt

ε estimated

AAA anti-aircraft artillery

AAB Advisory and Assistance Brigade

AAM air-to-air missile

AAV amphibious assault vehicle

AB airborne

ABM anti-ballistic missile

ABU sea-going buoy tender

ac aircraft

ACCS Air Command and Control System

ACM advanced cruise missile

ACP airborne command post

ACV air cushion vehicle / armoured combat vehicle

AD air defence

ADA air defence artillery

adj adjusted

AE auxiliary, ammunition carrier

AEW airborne early warning

AF Air Force

AFB Air Force Base / Station

AFS logistics ship

AG misc auxiliary

AGB icebreaker

AGF command ship

AGHS hydrographic survey vessel

AGI intelligence collection vessel

AGL automatic grenade launcher

AGM air-to-ground missile

AGOR oceanographic research vessel

AGOS oceanographic surveillance vessel

AGS survey ship

AH hospital ship

AIFV armoured infantry fighting vehicle

AIP air independent propulsion

AK cargo ship

aka also known as

AKR fast sealift ship / cargo ship

AKSL stores ship (light)

ALARM air-launched anti-radiation missile

ALCM air-launched cruise missile

amph amphibious/amphibian

AMRAAM advanced medium-range air-to-air missile

AO tanker with RAS capability

AOE auxiliary fuel and ammunition, RAS capability

AORH tanker with hel capacity

AORL replenishment oiler light

AORLH oiler light with hel deck

AOT tanker

AP armour-piercing/anti-personnel

APC armoured personnel carrier

AR/C repair ship/cable

ARG amphibious ready group

ARL airborne reconnaissance low

ARM anti-radiation missile

armd armoured

ARS salvage ship

ARSV armoured reconnaissance/ surveillance vehicle

arty artillery

ARV armoured recovery vehicle

AS anti-submarine

ASaC airborne surveillance and control

ASCM anti-ship cruise missile

aslt assault

ASM air-to-surface missile

ASR submarine rescue craft

ASROC anti-submarine rocket

ASSM anti-surface-ship missile

ASTOR airborne stand-off radar

ASTROS II artillery saturation rocket System

ASTT anti-submarine torpedo tube

ASW anti-submarine warfare

ASuW anti-surface warfare

AT tug / anti-tank

ATBM anti-tactical ballistic missile

ATF tug, ocean going

ATGW anti-tank guided weapon

ATK attack

ATP advanced targeting pod

ATTACMS army tactical missile system

ATTC all terrain tracked carrier

AV armoured vehicle

AVB aviation logistic ship

avn aviation

AWACS/AEW&C airborne warning and control system

AWT water tanker

AXL training craft

AXS training craft, sail

BA budget authority (US)

Bbr bomber

BCT brigade combat team

bde brigade

bdgt budget

BfSB battlefield surveillance brigade

BG battle group

BMD ballistic missile defence

BMEWS ballistic missile early warning system

bn battalion/billion

BSB brigade support battalion

BSTB brigade special troops battalion

bty battery

C2 command and control

CAB combat aviation brigade

CALCM conventional air-launched cruise missile

CAS close air support

casevac casualty evacuation

CASM conventionally armed stand-off missile

cav cavalry

cbt combat

CBU cluster bomb unit

CBRNE chemical, biological, radiological, nuclear, explosive

CCS command and control systems

cdo commando

CET combat engineer tractor

CFE Conventional Armed Forces in Europe

C/G/GN/L cruiser/guided missile/guided missile, nuclear powered/light

cgo cargo (freight) aircraft

CIMIC civil-military cooperation

CIS Command Information Systems

CIWS close-in weapons system

CLOS command-to-line-of-sight

COIN counter insurgency

comb combined/combination

comd command

COMINT communications intelligence

comms communications

CPV crew protected vehicle

CPX command post exercise

CS combat support

CSAR combat search and rescue

CSG carrier strike group

C-RAM counter rocket, artillery and mortar

CT counter terrorism

CTOL conventional take off and landing

CV/H/N/S aircraft carrier/helicopter/ nuclear powered/VSTOL

CVBG carrier battlegroup

CW chemical warfare/weapons

DD/G/GH destroyer/guided missile/with helicopter

DDS dry dock shelter

def defence

demob demobilised

det detachment

DISTEX disaster training exercise

div division

dom domestic

DSCS defense satellite communications system

ECCAS Economic Community of Central Africa States

ECM electronic counter measures

ECR electronic combat and reconnaissance

EELV evolved expendable launch vehicle

ELINT electronic intelligence

elm element/s

engr engineer

EOD explosive ordnance disposal

eqpt equipment

ESG expeditionary strike group

ESM electronic support measures

est estimate(d)

ETS engineer tank systems

EW electronic warfare

EWSP electronic warfare self protection

excl excludes/excluding

exp expenditure

FAC forward air control

FF/G/H/L frigate/guided missile/ helicopter/light

FGA fighter ground attack

FLIR forward looking infra-red

flt flight

FMA Foreign Military Assistance

FMTV family of medium transport vehicles

FROG free rocket over ground

FS/G corvette/guided missile

FSSG force service support group

FSTA future strategic tanker aircraft

Ftr fighter

FTX field training exercise

FW fixed-wing

FY fiscal year

GA group army

GBAD ground-based air defences

GBU guided bomb unit

gd guard

GDP gross domestic product

GEODSS ground-based electro-optical deep space surveillance system

GMLS guided missile launch sytem

GMLRS guided multiple-launch rocket system

GNP gross national product

gp group

GPS global positioning system

GW guided weapon

HADR humanitarian assistance and disaster relief

HARM high-speed anti-radiation missile

HBCT heavy brigade combat team

hel helicopter

HIMARS high-mobility artillery rocket system

HMMWV high-mobility multi-purpose wheeled vehicle

HMTV high-mobility tactical vehicle

HOT high-subsonic optically teleguided

how howitzer

HQ headquarters

HSV high speed vessel

HUMINT human intelligence

HVM high-velocity missile

HWT heavyweight torpedo

hy heavy

IBCT infantry brigade combat team

IBU inshore boat unit

ICBM inter-continental ballistic missile

IFV infantry fighting vehicle

IMET international military education and training

IMINT imagery intelligence

imp improved

IMV infantry mobility vehicle

incl includes/including

indep independent

inf infantry

INS inertial navigation system

IR incident response

IRBM intermediate-range ballistic missile

IRLS infra-red line scan

ISD in-service date

ISR intelligence, surveillance and reconnaissance

ISTAR intelligence, surveillance, target acquisition and reconnaissance

JDAM joint direct attack munition

JSF Joint Strike Fighter

JSTARS joint surveillance target attack radar system

LACV light armoured combat vehicle

LAM land-attack missile

LAMPS light airborne multi-purpose system

LANTIRN low-altitude navigation and targeting infra-red system night

LAV light armoured vehicle

LAW light anti-tank weapon

LC/A/AC/D/H/M/PA/PL/T/U/VP landing craft / assault / air cushion / dock / heavy / medium / personnel air cushion / personnel light / tank / utility / vehicles and personnel

LCC amphibious command ship

LCS littoral combat ship

LFV light forces vehicles

LGB laser-guided bomb

LHA landing ship assault

LHD amphibious assault ship

LIFT lead-in ftr trainer

LKA amphibious cargo ship

lnchr launcher

log logistic

LORADS long range radar display system

LP/D/H landing platform / dock / helicopter

LPV lifespan patrol vessel

LRAR long range artillery rocket

LRSA long-range strike/attack

LS/D/L/LH/M landing ship / dock / logistic / logistic helicopter / medium

LST landing ship tank

Lt light

LWT lightweight torpedo

MAMBA mobile artillery monitoring battlefield radar

MANPAD man portable air-defence

MANPAT man portable anti-tank

MARDIV marine division

MAW marine aviation wing

MBT main battle tank

MCC mine countermeasure coastal

MCD mine countermeasure diving support

MCDV maritime coastal defence vessel

MCI mine countermeasure inshore

MCLOS manual CLOS

MCM mine countermeasures

MCMV mine countermeasures vessel

MCO mine countermeasures ocean

MD military district

MEADS medium extended air defence system

MEB marine expeditionary brigade

mech mechanised

med medium

MEF marine expeditionary force

MEU marine expeditionary unit

MFO multinational force and observers

MGA machine gun artillery

MH/C/D/I/O mine hunter / coastal / drone / inshore /ocean

MI military intelligence

mil military

MIRV multiple independently targetable re-entry vehicle

MIUW mobile inshore undersea warfare

mk mark (model number)

ML minelayer

MLRS multiple-launch rocket system

MLU mid-life update

MLV medium launch vehicle

mne marine

mob mobilisation/mobile

mod modified/modification

mor mortar

mot motorised/motor

MP maritime patrol

MPA maritime patrol aircraft

MPS marine prepositioning squadron

MR maritime reconnaissance / motor rifle

MRAP mine-resistant ambush-protected

MRAAM medium-range air-to-air missile

MRBM medium-range ballistic missile

MRL multiple rocket launcher

MRTT multi-role tanker transport

MS/A/C/D/I/O/R mine sweeper / auxiliary / coastal / drone / inshore / ocean /

msl missile

MSTAR manportable surveillance and target acquisition radar

Mtn mountain

NAEW NATO Airborne Early Warning & Control Force

n.a. not applicable

n.k. not known

NBC nuclear biological chemical

NCO non-commissioned officer
NLACM naval land attack cruise missile
nm nautical mile
nuc nuclear
O & M operations and maintenance
OBS observation/observer
OCU operational conversion unit
op/ops operational/operations
OPFOR opposition training force
OPV off-shore patrol vessel
org organised/organisation
OSV oceanographic survey vessel
OTH/-B over-the-horizon/backscatter (radar)
OTHR/T over-the-horizon radar/targeting
PAAMS principal anti-air missile system
PAC *Patriot* advanced capability
para paratroop/parachute
pax passenger/passenger transport aircraft
PB/C/I/O/R patrol boat / coastal / inshore / offshore / riverine
PC/C/I/M/O/OH/R/T/F patrol craft / coastal / inshore / with SSM / offshore / offshore with helicopter / riverine / torpedo / fast
PDMS point defence missile system
pdr pounder
pers personnel
PF/C/I/M/OH/T fast patrol craft / coastal / inshore / with SSM / offshore with helicopter/ torpedo
PGM precision guided munitions
PHM patrol hydrofoil with SSM
PHT patrol hydrofoil with torpedo
PKO peacekeeping operations
PPP purchasing-power parity
PR photo-reconnaissance
prepo pre-positioned
PSO/H offshore patrol vessel over 60 metres / with helicopter
PTG guided missile patrol craft
PTRL/SURV patrol / surveillance
PVO anti-aircraft defence (Russia)
qd quadrillion
R&D research and development
RAM rolling airframe missile
RAS replenishment at sea
RCL ramped craft logistic
RCWS remote controlled weapon station
RCT regimental combat team
recce reconnaissance

RF response force
regt regiment
RIB rigid inflatable boat
RL rocket launcher
ro-ro roll-on, roll-off
RPV remotely piloted vehicle
RRC/F rapid-reaction corps/force
RRC rapid raiding craft
RSTA reconnaissance, surveillance and target acquisition
RV re-entry vehicle
RY royal yacht
SACLOS semi-automatic CLOS
SAM surface-to-air missile
SAR search and rescue
sat satellite
SBCT Stryker brigade combat team
SDV swimmer delivery vehicles
SEAD suppression of enemy air defence
SEWS satellite early warning station
SF special forces
SHORAD short range air defence
SIGINT signals intelligence
SLAM stand-off land-attack missile
SLBM submarine launched ballistic missile
SLCM submarine launched cruise missile
SLEP service life extension programme
SMASHEX submarine search, escape and rescue exercise
SMAW shoulder-launched multi-purpose assault weapon
SOC special operations capable
SP self propelled
Spec Op special operations
SPAAGM Self-propelled anti-aircraft gun and missile system
spt support
sqn squadron
SRAM short-range attack missile
SRBM short-range ballistic missile
SS diesel submarine
SSAN submersible auxiliary support vessel
SSBN ballistic-missile submarine nuclear-fuelled
SSC diesel submarine coastal
SSG attack submarine diesel, non-ballistic missile launchers
SSGN SSN with dedicated non-ballistic missile launchers
SSI diesel submarine inshore
SSK patrol submarine with ASW capability

SSM surface-to-surface missile
SSN attack submarine nuclear powered
START Strategic Arms Reduction Talks/ Treaty
StF stabilisation force
STO(V)L short take-off and (vertical) landing
str strength
SUGW surface-to-underwater GW
SURV surveillance
SUT surface and underwater target
sy security
t tonnes
tac tactical
TASM tactical air-to-surface missile
temp temporary
THAAD theatre high altitude area defence
tk tank
tkr tanker
TLAM tactical land-attack missile
TLE treaty-limited equipment (CFE)
TMD theatre missile defence
torp torpedo
TOW tube launched optically wire guided
tpt transport
tr trillion
trg training
TriAD triple AD
TRV torpedo recovery vehicle
TT torpedo tube
UAV unmanned aerial vehicle
UCAV unmanned combat aerial vehicle
URG under-way replenishment group
USGW underwater to surface guided weapon
utl utility
UUV unmanned undersea vehicle
V(/S)TOL vertical(/short) take-off and landing
veh vehicle
VLS vertical launch system
VSHORAD very short range air defence
VSRAD very short range air defence
wg wing
WLIC Inland construction tenders
WMD weapon(s) of mass destruction
WTGB Icebreaker tugs
YDG degaussing
YDT diving tender
YTL light harbour tug
YTM medium harbour tug

Index of Countries and Territories

Index of Country/Territory Abbreviations

AFG..Afghanistan	**GAM**..Gambia	**NOR**...Norway
ALB...Albania	**GEO**...Georgia	**NPL**...Nepal
ALG..Algeria	**GER**...Germany	**NZL**.................................New Zealand
ANG..Angola	**GF**..French Guiana	**OMN**...Oman
ARG...Argentina	**GHA**..Ghana	**PAL**.........Palestinian Autonomous Areas
ARM...Armenia	**GIB**...Gibraltar	of Gaza and Jericho
ATG.......................Antigua and Barbuda	**GNB**.......................................Guinea Bissau	**PAN**...Panama
AUS...Australia	**GRC**..Greece	**PAK**...Pakistan
AUT..Austria	**GRL**..Greenland	**PER**..Peru
AZE...Azerbaijan	**GUA**...Guatemala	**PHL**...Philippines
BDI...Burundi	**GUI**...Guinea	**POL**..Poland
BEL..Belgium	**GUY**..Guyana	**PNG**...........................Papua New Guinea
BEN..Benin	**HND**..Honduras	**PRC**.................China, People's Republic of
BFA......................................Burkina Faso	**HTI**...Haiti	**PRT**...Portugal
BGD......................................Bangladesh	**HUN**...Hungary	**PRY**...Paraguay
BHR..Bahrain	**ISL**...Iceland	**PYF**.............................French Polynesia
BHS..Bahamas	**ISR**..Israel	**QTR**...Qatar
BIH.........................Bosnia–Herzegovina	**IDN**...Indonesia	**ROC**.................Taiwan (Republic of China)
BIOT................British Indian Ocean Territory	**IND**..India	**ROK**...............................Korea, Republic of
BLG...Bulgaria	**IRL**...Ireland	**ROM**..Romania
BLR..Belarus	**IRN**...Iran	**RSA**.......................................South Africa
BLZ...Belize	**IRQ**...Iraq	**RUS**..Russia
BOL..Bolivia	**ITA**...Italy	**RWA**...Rwanda
BRB...Barbados	**JAM**...Jamaica	**SAU**.....................................Saudi Arabia
BRN...Brunei	**JOR**...Jordan	**SDN**...Sudan
BRZ..Brazil	**JPN**...Japan	**SEN**..Senegal
BWA...Botswana	**KAZ**..Kazakhstan	**SGP**...Singapore
CAM...Cambodia	**KEN**...Kenya	**SLB**.................................Solomon Islands
CAN..Canada	**KGZ**.......................................Kyrgyzstan	**SLE**.......................................Sierra Leone
CAR.......................Central African Republic	**KWT**...Kuwait	**SLV**...El Salvador
CHA..Chad	**LAO**..Laos	**SOM**.............................Somali Republic
CHE.......................................Switzerland	**LBN**...Lebanon	**SRB**...Serbia
CHL..Chile	**LBR**..Liberia	**STP**.................São Tomé and Principe
CIV.......................................Côte d'Ivoire	**LBY**...Libya	**SUR**...Suriname
CMR...Cameroon	**LKA**...Sri Lanka	**SVK**..Slovakia
COG...Congo	**LSO**..Lesotho	**SVN**..Slovenia
COL..Colombia	**LTU**...Lithuania	**SWE**..Sweden
CPV.......................................Cape Verde	**LUX**.......................................Luxembourg	**SYC**...Seychelles
CRI...Costa Rica	**LVA**..Latvia	**SYR**..Syria
CRO...Croatia	**MDA**...Moldova	**TGO**..Togo
CUB..Cuba	**MDG**......................................Madagascar	**THA**..Thailand
CYP...Cyprus	**MEX**..Mexico	**TJK**..Tajikistan
CZE...............................Czech Republic	**MHL**.................................Marshall Islands	**TLS**...Timor Leste
DJB...Djibouti	**MLI**...Mali	**TTO**..................Trinidad and Tobago
DNK...Denmark	**MLT**...Malta	**TKM**..................................Turkmenistan
DOM.............................Dominican Republic	**MMR**...Myanmar	**TUN**...Tunisia
DPRK. Korea, Democratic People's Republic of	**MNE**.......................................Montenegro	**TUR**...Turkey
DRC...............Democratic Republic of Congo	**MNG**..Mongolia	**TZA**..Tanzania
ECU..Ecuador	**MOR**...Morocco	**UAE**.......................United Arab Emirates
EGY...Egypt	**MOZ**.......................................Mozambique	**UGA**..Uganda
ERI...Eritrea	**MRT**.......................................Mauritania	**UK**.......................................United Kingdom
ESP..Spain	**MUS**...Mauritius	**UKR**...Ukraine
EST..Estonia	**MWI**...Malawi	**URY**...Uruguay
ETH...Ethiopia	**MYS**...Malaysia	**US**.......................................United States
FIN..Finland	**NAM**..Namibia	**UZB**...Uzbekistan
FLK....................................Falkland Islands	**NCL**.....................................New Caledonia	**VEN**...Venezuela
FJI...Fiji	**NER**...Niger	**VNM**...Vietnam
FRA...France	**NGA**...Nigeria	**YEM**...Yemen
FYROM Macedonia, Former Yugoslav Republic	**NIC**...Nicaragua	**ZMB**..Zambia
GAB..Gabon	**NLD**......................................Netherlands	**ZWE**...Zimbabwe

Reference